for Claire Dillon
with many thanks

F. C. N.

# THE
# LEGAL ASPECT
# OF MONEY

*With special reference to*
*Comparative Private and Public*
*International Law*

BY

F. A. MANN, C.B.E., F.B.A.

LL.D. (LOND.), DR. JUR. (BERLIN), HON. DR. JUR. (KIEL)
*Member of the Institut de Droit International*
*Honorary Member of the American Society of International Law*
*Honorary Professor of Law in the University of Bonn*
*Solicitor of the Supreme Court*
*London*

FOURTH EDITION

CLARENDON PRESS · OXFORD
1982

Oxford University Press, Walton Street, Oxford OX2 6DP
London Glasgow New York Toronto
Delhi Bombay Calcutta Madras Karachi
Kuala Lumpur Singapore Hong Kong Tokyo
Nairobi Dar es Salaam Cape Town
Melbourne Auckland
and associate companies in
Beirut Berlin Ibadan Mexico City

Published in the United States by
Oxford University Press, New York

FIRST EDITION 1938
SECOND EDITION 1953
THIRD EDITION 1971
FOURTH EDITION 1982

British Library Cataloguing in Publication Data
Mann, F. A.
    The legal aspect of money. — 4th ed.
    1. Finance — Law and legislation
    I. Title
    341.7'5        K4430
    ISBN 0-19-825367-2

Typeset by Anne Joshua Associates, Oxford
Printed in Great Britain by
Billings & Sons, Ltd.,
Guildford, London, Oxford, and Worcester

# PREFACE TO THE FOURTH EDITION

Studeamus ergo nec desidiae nostrae praetendamus alienam. Sunt qui audiant, sunt qui legant, nos modo dignum aliquid auribus dignum chartis elaboremus.—Pliny iv.16.

So let us pursue our studies rather than make the idleness of others the pretext for our own. There are always those who listen and those who read. It is for us to labour towards what is worth being heard or printed.

SINCE the publication of the third edition in 1971 radical changes have transformed the law of money: inflation which resulted in a depreciation of the pound's internal purchasing power by more than 70 per cent between the beginning of 1971 and 1981 and rendered it necessary to reorganize and enlarge the first part of this book; the increase of comparative material, largely due to the universal existence of inflation,—during the ten years mentioned the purchasing power of the U.S. dollar fell by more than 50 per cent and that of the Deutsche Mark by about 65 per cent; the failure of monetary economists to agree on the causes of or a remedy for our economic ills or even to describe the problems in terms of acceptable simplicity such as is required by Sir Winston Churchill's wise and prescient words which served as the motto to the Preface to the third edition; the collapse of the International Monetary Fund's par value system in 1971, the consequent floating of currencies, including sterling, and the absence of an effective international monetary system; the demonetization of gold, the commercial price of which at times increased about twenty times; the creation of the European Monetary System; the emergence of basket clauses such as the ECU and the Special Drawing Right (though, in another sense, the former is being used as a unit of account and the latter also has the different function of providing intergovernmental credit facilities); the vast expansion of 'Eurocurrencies'; the much delayed lifting of exchange control in Britain thirty-five years after the end of the war,—since it was effected by a general consent rather than abrogation of the legislation, it seemed advisable to retain Chapter XIII, particularly since it still appears to be the only available attempt at a rational and systematic analysis of the Act; the sensational decision of the House of Lords in *Miliangos* v. *George Frank (Textiles) Ltd.*, [1976] A.C. 443, provoked by an equally sensational, but in the Preface of 1970 hoped for, step taken by Lord Denning's Court of Appeal in

*Schorsch Meier G.m.b.H.* v. *Hennin,* [1975] Q.B. 416, and the total change, long advocated in this book, which it caused to the whole of English law on foreign money obligations. I am conscious of the good fortune that permitted me to make a fourth edition available, which, while leaving unchanged the general character, purpose, and scope of the book as described in the earlier Prefaces, attempts to take care of these and other developments and states the law as at 1 May 1981.

I have to thank many foreign friends who were kind enough to send me interesting material which otherwise I would probably have overlooked—even so the comparative surveys do not claim to be complete or unerring; the book by Professor Lopez-Santa Maria on *Le Droit des obligations et des contrats et l'inflation monetaire: Chili et droits hispano-americains* (Paris, 1980) became available while the manuscript was in the hands of the printer and could be taken into account only in exceptional cases. I also have to thank Miss Claire Dillon, B.A. (Oxon.), who prepared the Tables of Cases and the Index and helped in correcting proofs.

Once again this Preface is being written on the day on which forty-eight years ago I married. But she to whom veiled tribute was thus paid and intended to be repeated today, died almost a year ago. Let this book be a means of remembering and honouring 'uxorem singularis exempli'.

F. A. M.

*London*
*12 October 1981*

# PREFACE TO THE THIRD EDITION

There is no sphere of human thought in which it is easier for a man to show superficial cleverness and the appearances of superior wisdom than in discussing questions of currency and exchange.

Sir Winston Churchill, *Hansard*, vol. 468, col. 160 (28 September 1949).

ATHOUGH the prefaces to the previous editions have been reprinted and, in essence, the present edition which states the law as at 1 October 1970 leaves the character of this book unchanged, it may be as well, probably for the last time, to explain its purpose and scope.

It is a book about money. This is a conception which means many different things to different readers. If a lawyer decides to shut out certain subjects, his decision is not necessarily wrong merely because others may expect them to be included. The law of bank or postal Giro accounts or the law relating to Treasury Bills or the Bank Rate or credit or financial transactions between international persons—these are only some of the many matters which a book on money could legitimately discuss. The present one does not do so, because a line had to be drawn somewhere and there seemed to be strong arguments for drawing it at the point which leaves intact such distinct, or at least distinguishable, branches of the law as, for instance, banking and finance, negotiable instruments, or the status and function of the Central Government and the Bank of England within the framework of the country's financial organization.

This is a book about the law of money. It is not a book about economics, finance, sociology, political science, or history. To the lawyer economic life and its incidents are facts which, if and in so far as they are material to the elaboration or application of legal rules, depend on evidence. Just as a book on the sale of goods does not usually discuss, for instance, the causes of variations in demand and supply or the practices adopted by various trades, so a book on the law of money should not, and the present work does not, venture outside the boundaries of the strictly legal approach. Thus the origin, growth, and function of that misnamed and by no means novel phenomenon, the Euro-currency market, or problems of the supply of money or the management of exchange rates cannot be explained or even described within the covers of this book. Similarly the law has to accept the remarkable fact that, while man has conquered the moon, he has signally failed to conquer the problem of the value of money, its stability and its relationship with full employment, credit, and economic growth. A lawyer will refrain from entering unfamiliar territory, for he is much too conscious of the wisdom of that great man's words which form the motto to this Preface and which, alas, have remained largely unheeded.

This is a book on the English law of money. There is no law of money that is common to the nations of the world. But money is a universal institution. Hence the comparative method has peculiar value. It discloses where English law has adopted the right or the wrong road. The lesson, however, is useless if practical conclusions are not drawn from it. Chapter X dealing with the effect of legal proceedings upon foreign money obligations, is the foremost example of a field which English law has stubbornly refused to plough afresh in accordance with foreign experience and objectively ascertainable principles of logic and justice. This country's failure even to consider the European Convention on Foreign Money Liabilities, printed in Appendix IV, is explained, though not neces- sarily excused, by the majority Report of the (unfortunately defunct) Standing Committee on the Reform of Private International Law (Cmnd. 1648). Now Lord Denning has, perhaps somewhat sur- prisingly, decried the present state of the English law,—compare his speech in *Re United Railways of Havana and Regla Warehouses Ltd*, [1961] A.C. 1007, at pp. 1067, 1068, with the pronouncement heading Chapter X. Perhaps the Master of the Rolls's voice will succeed where, for more than thirty years, others have failed.

The fact that this book is devoted to English law imposes some limits upon the use of foreign material, for not all of it is of potential interest to the English lawyer. Such is the test that was applied throughout; it accounts for most omissions of foreign sources, which have occurred, although, no doubt, some of these have been overlooked inadvertently.

On the other hand the concern with English law does not by any means exclude, but, on the contrary, demands the consideration of such rules of public international law as bind Britain. The develop- ment in this branch of the law has been so rapid and far-reaching that the fourth Part of the book has probably been more thoroughly changed than any other, though all parts have been fully revised and brought up to date and many have been rewritten. In that connection the course of lectures on *Money in Public International Law* given at the Hague Academy of International Law (Recueil 96 (1959 i) 1) has, with the kind permission of the Academy's

Curatorium, to some extent been incorporated into the present work.

A German translation of the second edition appeared in 1960. A German translation of the present edition is planned.

F. A. M.

*London*
*12 October 1970*

# PREFACE TO THE SECOND EDITION

SINCE the first edition of this book appeared in October 1938 the legal aspect of money has undergone radical changes. In preparing the second edition it thus became necessary, while retaining the broad character of the work, to write what to a large extent can only be presented as a new book.

Those changes arise from four causes, viz. the establishment of the International Monetary Fund by the Articles of Agreement, concluded by forty-four nations in July 1944 at Bretton Woods and at present binding upon fifty-four nations; the introduction of exchange control in this country and the extension of exchange control over the greater part of the world; the depreciation of money during and after the Second World War which in some countries led to the ruin of the existing, and the creation of new, currency systems and which in this country provoked devaluation in September 1949; and the very considerable amount of new, or old but newly discovered, material. Many important decisions rendered both in this country and abroad had to be considered. The literature on the subject was greatly enriched by Professor Nussbaum's book on *Money in the Law*, of which two editions appeared in 1939 and 1950 respectively, and by discussions in almost all modern textbooks on Private International Law, particularly in the sixth edition of Dicey's *Conflict of Laws* to which more than forty pages dealing with foreign currency obligations were contributed by Professor Kahn-Freund.

The present edition of this book contains eight new chapters. Chapter VII takes the place of the inadequate discussion on pp. 197–200 of the former edition and incorporates portions of an article published in the *Law Quarterly Review* of 1952. Chapters XI to XIV constitute an elaboration of problems of exchange control and of the rate of exchange, which was necessitated by the events referred to above; the substance of Chapter XIII was published during the current year in the *International and Comparative Law Quarterly*, while Chapter XIV is in many respects founded upon a paper published in 1944 in the *Modern Law Review*. Finally, Chapters XV to XVII are new, though they almost repeat what appeared in the *British Year Book of International Law* for 1949. The author is indebted to the editors of these four publications for their permission to make use of this material. The rest of the book has been extensively revised and although in some places it was possible to shorten the discussion, the book exceeds the size of the first edition by more than half.

F. A. M.

*London*
*12 October 1953*

# PREFACE TO THE FIRST EDITION

'Although the civil law is not of itself authority in an English Court it affords great assitance in investigating the principles on which the law is grounded.'—Blackburn J. in *Taylor* v. *Caldwell* (1863), 3 B. & S. 826.

IN general words, the object of this work is to treat the legal aspects of money in a systematic and comprehensive manner. There were, however, so many obstacles on the way to this goal which the author was unable to overcome in their entirety, that he must ask for the reader's indulgence. In support of this plea for leniency a few observations may perhaps be offered.

The first cause of the difficulties lies in the fact that there does not seem to exist any English (or American[1]) work dealing with the subject as defined above. The century from the end of the Bank Restriction period to the outbreak of the Great War in 1914, which witnessed so rich a development in the field of law, was marked by an unheard-of stability of economic and, consequently, of monetary conditions. It is, therefore, not surprising that lawyers were led to regard money, not as a problem of paramount importance, but as an established fact. This security was not shaken until the great and sometimes even chaotic disturbances of the monetary systems with which every country has been visited since 1914,[2] and which deeply imprinted themselves on the economic situation and the law not only of foreign countries but also of this country. Though it was never doubted that, whatever happened, the pound sterling remained the same in character and (internal) value, business men and courts were confronted with many intricate questions which originated from the depreciation or collapse of foreign currencies or from the changes in the international value of the pound. Thus, many important decisions of the English courts came into being, and yet it is probably no exaggeration to say that, in so far as the fundamental legal problems of money are concerned, the observations of Sir John Davis on the *Case de Mixt Moneys*[3] still were the only English source of information, and that in respect of many questions of

[1] The book by Bakewell, *Past and Present Facts about Money in the United States* (New York, 1936), is only of very limited value.

[2] A survey is given by Griziotti, 'L'Évolution monétaire dans le monde depuis la guerre de 1914', *Rec.* 1934 (48), pp. 1 sqq.

[3] (1604) Davis's Rep. (Ireland) 18.

detail there was no guidance at all in the otherwise rich treasures of the common law. There is obviously a gap to be filled, but, in view of the lack of preliminary studies on the one hand, and the immense number of problems and foreign material on the other, this gap is so great that it could not be attempted to give more than a first introduction on the lines of a general survey of and a guide to an inaccessible, though theoretically fascinating and practically vital, part of the law.

The choice of problems suitable for and requiring discussion has been restricted to three groups. In the first place, all those questions have been included which, for the sake of systematical elucidation, had to be answered; for it is believed that the subject demands particular care in putting and arranging the questions, in drawing clear distinctions and demarcations, and in working a way through the labyrinth of material. Secondly, all those questions have been dealt with which have been raised or answered in the cases decided by English courts; it is hoped that all, or at least all important, cases have been considered, but as some have been hunted up which hitherto have escaped the attention due to them, the suspicion is justified that there are many more either hidden in the reports or known but treated under the head of other than purely monetary problems. Thirdly, only those problems have been treated which had been, or might reasonably be expected to be, of practical importance from the point of view of English (municipal or private international) law; mere theory and speculation have in general been eliminated, though in the first part it was necessary to give a certain amount of space to theory; the question of which problems might become important for the law of this country is naturally a difficult one, but in such connections judgment has been based on the experiences of foreign countries.

Within these limits the legal aspects of money will be discussed from a purely legal point of view. Though economic theory will not be disregarded, it is no disparagement of it to say that its usefulness for legal research is not very great. Anglo-American monetary science has undoubtedly neglected the problem which from the point of view of the law is the vital one, namely nominalism and its various phenomena. In this respect it has therefore been necessary to have resort to the research of continental economists. Nevertheless, the lawyer's gratitude is due to those economists who have dealt with the economic and, more particularly, the monetary history of Great Britain, to which the law will have to attribute considerable importance. Mr. Feavearyear's short but excellent book on *The Pound Sterling* (1931) is of particular assistance.

Though this book is devoted to the discussion of English law, an extensive space has been conceded to comparative research. The usual argument that comparative studies are necessary and useful because they place a wealth of experience at our disposal, and show what is right and what is wrong with us, is fortified by many circumstances. When Sir John Davis wrote more than 300 years ago, he largely drew on continental scholars, and if his observations have been accepted by the common law, as in the absence of other material they seem to have been, it follows that the sources of the English law of money are to a great extent of foreign origin. This may perhaps also be regarded as a justification for the fact that it is a lawyer originally trained under a foreign legal system who now ventures to revive the study of the law of money. Furthermore, the developments since 1914 have given rise to an abundance of foreign decisions and legal literature to which international value may justly be ascribed. In France, Italy, and Germany three important works have been published by Mater, Ascarelli, and Nussbaum respectively. The writer is particularly indebted to Professor Nussbaum,[4] who by his indispensable treatise as well as by many other publications dealing with various monetary problems paved the way for further research to a greater extent than any one of his contemporaries. Finally, it appears that in many foreign laws monetary problems have not been regulated by legislative measures, but left to be moulded and solved by judge-made law. This is a further reason why a comparison with English law is interesting.

The foreign material is so vast that the selection presented to the English reader is bound to be incomplete. Paramount importance has been attributed to the decisions of Supreme Courts; decisions of courts of first and second instance have generally been disregarded, because it is believed that decisions of such courts are very often unsuitable for comparative research, as their authority, under no circumstances binding, is especially assailable, and as the picture they convey can, therefore, too easily become misleading. Legal literature will be referred to rather eclectically, though a much greater quantity of books and articles have been consulted. All available decisions of the Supreme Court of the United States which

[4] Formerly Professor at Berlin University, now visiting Professor at Columbia University in New York. Professor Nussbaum has announced that he is engaged in preparing a comprehensive study of the legal aspects of monetary theory and practice which, prepared under the auspices of the Columbia Council for Research in the Social Sciences, will 'primarily rest on Anglo-American law and will consider as well important developments which have occurred since the publication of the German volume'. See the article in 35 (1937) *Mich. L.R.* 865, which constitutes the first chapter of the forthcoming volume.

'are always considered with great respect in the courts of this country'[5] and many decisions of American State Courts have been used. Otherwise, comparative research has chiefly been directed to French and German law. The method of dealing with comparative material will vary. Sometimes it will be used as a mere illustration; in other connections it will be referred to as a persuasive, or at least supporting, authority; in a third group of cases it will serve as a contrast to elucidate a rule of English law or to test its soundness.

Within these limits and on these foundations an attempt has been made to investigate the legal aspects of money, the subject being divided into two distinct parts the difference between which needs emphasis: the first part deals almost exclusively with English money in English municipal law, and comparative material is used for the single purpose of showing the position of a given domestic currency within the frame of the given domestic law. Where questions connected with a currency other than the domestic one are considered in the first part, this is due to the necessity of elaborating certain connections between both. But otherwise, all questions relating to foreign currency, i.e. to the position of a currency within the ambit of a municipal or private international law of a country other than that to which the currency belongs (e.g. American money in England, German currency in France), have been reserved for the second part. It is the present writer's experience and conviction that this separation between domestic and foreign money obligations is absolutely essential for a clear exposition of the subject although it cannot be carried through without exceptions, and although it may sometimes cause inconvience or overlapping. There is in each case not only a difference of problems, but there are also many differences of approach to the problems, which make it impossible to apply to the one case, without qualification, considerations operative in, or decisions relating to, the other.

The final revisions of the manuscript were completed on 29 July 1938; decisions and literature which appeared after that date could not be taken into consideration.

F. A. M.

*London*
*12 October 1938*

---

[5] *Beresford* v. *Royal Insurance Co.*, [1937] 2 All E.R. 243 (C.A.), at p. 252 B per Lord Wright.

# CONTENTS

## PART I

### THE LEGAL PROBLEMS OF MONEY IN GENERAL

commodity (p. 184). III. Foreign money debts as contracts to pay money or as contracts to deliver a commodity (p. 190). IV. Euro-currency (p. 193). V. The legality of foreign money obligations (p. 196). VI. Money of account and money of payment (p. 199). VII. Foreign currency clauses: (1) '£100 payable in dollars at the rate of exchange of $3 to £1' (p. 201); '£100 payable at the rate of exchange of $3 to £1' (p. 201); (2) '£100, £1 = $3' (p. 202). VIII. Option of currency, option of place (p. 207). IX. A survey of the two preceding sections (p. 213). X. The place of payment: (1) its meaning in comparative law (p. 214); (2) its meaning in private international law (p. 214); (3) the law of the place of performance and its effect in private international law (p. 215)

## VIII.   THE DETERMINATION OF THE MONEY OF ACCOUNT: INITIAL UNCERTAINTY                                          220

I. The problem stated (p. 220). II. The determination of the money of account in case of fixed indebtedness: (1) the rules of municipal law (p. 223); (2) the problem of private international law; the *Adelaide* and the *Auckland Corporation* cases in particular (p. 233). III. The determination of the money of account in case of unforeseen liability: (1) the rules of municipal law in general and in particular cases (p. 242): (*a*) indication in the contract (p. 242); (*b*) restitution of value (p. 244); (*c*) conversion into the injured party's domestic currency (p. 245); (*d*) agency (p. 249); (2) the rule of private international law (p. 250)

## IX.   THE DETERMINATION OF THE MONEY OF ACCOUNT (*continuation*): S U B S E Q U E N T  U N C E R T A I N T Y          252

I. The problem stated (p. 252). II. The effect of the curtailment of the monetary system upon the money of account: (1) municipal law (p. 254); (2) private international law (p. 256). III. The extinction of the money of account: (1) by the substitution of one monetary system for another (p. 262); (2) by the dissolution of a unitary currency system into separate systems (p. 263); (*a*) municipal law (p. 263); (*b*) private international law (p. 265)

## X.   THE NOMINALISTIC PRINCIPLE, ITS SCOPE, INCIDENTS, AND EFFECTS                                               266

I. The province of the law of currency (p. 266). II. The private international law governing revalorization (p. 275). III. The rules of municipal law relating to compensation in respect of depreciation of foreign money obligations (p. 282): (1) the quantum of simple debts (p. 282); (2) damages for non-payment (p. 286); (3) determination of the amount of unliquidated damages (p. 288); (4) frustration (p. 289); (5) equitable remedies (p. 289). IV. Protective clauses; gold clauses in particular (p. 290). The law governing (1) the existence of a gold clause (p. 292);

to revalorize (p. 469); (4) exchange control (p. 471). II. Monetary sovereignty and the international character of legal disputes (p. 472). III. Monetary legislation as confiscation (p. 473). IV. Monetary legislation in disregard of fair and equitable treatment of aliens (p. 475)

compensation (p. 535). III. Nominalism as applicable to treaties: (1) the principle (p. 539); (2) revalorization as a possible remedy (p. 541); (3) damages for delayed payment (p. 543); (4) the calculation of damages (p. 546). IV. Protective clauses: (1) the existence of a gold clause (p. 550); (2) the effect of the abrogation of gold clauses (p. 553). V. The payment of inter-State debts: (1) where? (p. 554); (2) how? (p. 555); (3) in which currency? (p. 555); (4) at which rate of exchange? (p. 556); (5) which type of rate of exchange? (p. 557). VI. The effect of exchange control (p. 559)

# TABLE OF STATUTES

# TABLE OF ENGLISH CASES

# TABLE OF SCOTTISH AND
# COMMONWEALTH CASES

# TABLE OF CASES
# DECIDED IN THE
# UNITED STATES OF AMERICA

# TABLE OF DECISIONS OF INTERNATIONAL TRIBUNALS

## E. EUROPEAN COURT OF JUSTICE

# TABLE OF SOME BOOKS REFERRED TO
# MERELY BY THE AUTHOR'S NAME

ASCARELLI, *La Moneta* (1928)
—— *Obbligazioni Pecuniarie* (1959) [referred to as 'Ascarelli']

BATIFFOL-LAGARDE, *Droit International Privé* (6th ed., 1974–1976)

CARREAU, *Souveraineté et coopération monétaire international* (1970)

CHESHIRE and NORTH, *Private International Law* (10th edition, 1979)

DELAUME, *Legal Aspects of International Lending and Economic Development Financing* (1967)

DICEY and MORRIS, *Conflict of Laws* (10th edition, 1980)

FEAVEARYEAR, *The Pound Sterling* (2nd edition by E. Victor Morgan, 1963)

FÖGEN, *Geld- und Währungsrecht* (1969)

GUTZWILLER, *Der Geltungsbereich der Währungsvorschriften* (1940)

VAN HECKE, *Problèmes juridiques des emprunts internationaux* (2nd edition, 1964)

HELFFERICH, *Money* (English translation by L. Infield, London, 1927)

HUBRECHT, *La Stabilisation du franc et la valorisation des créances* (1928)

KNAPP, *The State Theory of Money* (English abbreviated edition and translation by Lucas and Bonar, London 1924)

KRISPIS, *Money in Private International Law*, 120 (1967 i), *Recueil des Cours* 195.

MALAURIE, 'Le doirt monétaire dans les relations privées internationales', *Rec.* 160 (1978 ii) 265

MATER, *Traité juridique de la monnaie et du change* (Paris, 1925)

NEUMEYER, *International Verwaltungsrecht*, volume iii, part ii (1930)

NUSSBAUM, *Money in the Law, National and International* (2nd edition, 1950)

PIRET, *Les Variations monétaires et leurs répercussions en droit privé belge* (1935)

PLANIOL–RIPERT, *Traité pratique de droit civil français* (Paris, 1925–34)

WOLFF, 'Geld' in Ehrenbergs *Handbuch des Handelsrechts*, volume IV. i. (1917)

# SOME ABBREVIATIONS

| | |
|---|---|
| A.M.C. | American Maritime Cases |
| BFH. | *Amtliche Sammlung von Entscheidungen des Bundesfinanzhofs* (Official Reports of Decisions of the Federal Tax Court, Germany) |
| BGE. | *Entscheidungen des Bundesgerichts* (Collection of decisions of the Swiss Federal Tribunal) |
| BGHSt. | *Amtliche Sammlung von Entscheidungen des Bundesgerichtshofs in Strafsachen* (Official Reports on Criminal Law Cases of the Federal Supreme Court, Germany) |
| BGHZ. | *Amtliche Sammlung von Entscheidungen des Bundesgerichtshofs in Zivilsachen* (Official Reports on Civil Law Cases of the Federal Supreme Court, Germany) |
| B.I.J.I. | *Bulletin de l'Institut juridique internationl* |
| BVerfGE | *Amtliche Sammlung von Entscheidungen des Bundesverfassungsgerichts* |
| Cass. | Cour de cassation |
| Cass. Civ. | Cour de cassation, Chambre civile |
| Cass. Req. | Cour de cassation, Chambre des requêtes |
| Clunet | *Journal du droit international privé*, founded by Clunet |
| C.M.L.R. | Common Market Law Reports |
| D. | *Recueil périodique de jurisprudence de Dalloz* |
| D.H. | *Recueil hebdomadaire de jurisprudence de Dalloz* |
| Gaz. Pal. | *Gazette du Palais* |
| IPRspr. | *Deutsche Rechtsprechung auf dem Gebiete des internationalen Privatrechts* (Collection of German decisions relating to Conflict of Laws) |
| JW. | *Juristische Wochenschrift* |
| NJW. | *Neue Juristische Wochenscrift* |
| RabelsZ. | *Zeitschrift für ausländisches und internationales Privatrecht*, edited by Rabel and others |
| Rec. | *Recueil des Cours de l'Académie de droit international* (La Haye) |

| | |
|---|---|
| *Rép. dr. int.* | *Répertoire du droit international*, founded by Darras, edited by Lapradelle and Niboyet (1929-34) |
| *Rev. dr. banc.* | *Revue du droit bancaire*, edited by Mater |
| *Rev. Crit.* | *Revue Critique de Droit International Privé* |
| *RGSt.* | *Amtliche Sammlung von Entscheidungen des Reichsgerichts in Strafsachen* (Official Reports on Criminal Law Cases of the German Supreme Court) |
| *RGZ.* | *Amtliche Sammlung von Entscheidungen des Reichsgerichts in Zivilsachen* (Official Reports on Civil Law Cases of the German Supreme Court) |
| *ROHG.* | *Amtliche Sammlung von Entscheidungen des Reichsoberhandelsgerichts* (Official Reports of the former German Supreme Commercial Court) |
| *RzW.* | *Rechtsprechung zum Wiedergutmachungsrecht* |
| *S.* | *Recueil de jurisprudence de Sirey* |
| *WM.* | *Wertpapiermitteilungen* |

# PART I

# THE LEGAL PROBLEMS
# OF MONEY IN
# GENERAL

# I

# The Conception of Money

I. Importance of a definition. II. Law and economics of money. III. Requirements of money in law: (1) chattel personal; (2) creature of the law: (a) the prerogative over money; (b) the aspects of the State theory of money; (c) the 'societary' theory of money; (3) denomination; (4) universal medium of exchange. IV. The intrinsic nature of money.

## I

THE troublesome question, What is money? has so constantly engaged the minds of economists that a lawyer might hesitate to join in the attempt to solve it. Yet the true answer must, if possible, be determined. For 'money answereth all things'.[1] It is a fundamental notion not only of the economic life of mankind but also of all departments of law. In fact, a great deal of a lawyer's daily work centres around the term 'money' itself and the many transactions or institutions based on that term, such as debt, damages, value, payment, price, capital, interest, tax, pecuniary legacy. Money is a term so frequently used and of such importance that one is apt to overlook its inherent difficulties, and to forget that the multitude of its functions has led to a multitude of meanings.

Thus it is an essential requisite of a contract of sale of goods that the goods be agreed to be transferred 'to the buyer for a money consideration, called the price'.[2] If there is no money consideration the contract constitutes a barter, which in many respects differs from a contract of a sale of goods.[3] It is an essential requisite of a bill of exchange that it require the drawee to pay a sum certain 'in money',[4] and therefore an instrument requiring payment of something other than 'money' is not a negotiable instrument. On the other hand, though we speak of an action for money had and received, an equivalent of or a security for money can form the subject matter of such an action provided that 'the parties have treated it as money or a sufficient time has elapsed so as to raise an

---

[1] Ecclesiastes 10:19. See also Grotius, *De Jure Belli ac Pacis*, ii. 12. 17.
[2] s. 2 (1), Sale of Goods Act, 1979.
[3] Chalmers, *Sale of Goods Act* (17th ed., 1975), p. 7; Benjamin, Sale of Goods, (1974) Nos. 27–30.
[4] Bills of Exchange Act, 1882, s. 3 (1).

inference that it has been converted into money by the defendant'.[5] Or for the purposes of the equitable doctrine of tracing 'money' means something much wider than sovereigns in a bag; the doctrine applies to all assets capable of being identified in or disentangled from a mixed fund.[6] Again, although under the Theft Act, 1968, stolen 'goods' (which term is expressly stated to include money) may be ordered to be restored to the owner,[7] it is an open question whether money passed and accepted bona fide from hand to hand as currency is 'money' for the purpose of an order for restitution.[8] The term 'money' carries a much wider meaning when it is used in a will. Here it has no fixed meaning which the courts must adopt as being the 'legal' as opposed to the 'popular' meaning; the duty of the court is to ascertain without prejudice as between various usual meanings which is the correct interpretation of the particular document, so that the word may include the whole personal, perhaps even the real estate.[9] A final example is supplied by the Truck Acts, 1831 and 1887, which provide that all wages in contracts of hiring of workmen shall be payable 'in current coin of the realm', which term comprises bank notes.[10] Except where the Payment of Wages Act, 1960 as amended by s. 125 (3) of the Employment Protection Act 1975, applies, what is meant thereby is 'actual payment in coin. Payment in account will not do. Payment in goods will not do. Nothing is to discharge the wages debt except actual payment in current coin.'[11] It thus becomes evident that the meaning of the term

---

[5] *MacLachlan* v. *Evans* (1827), 1 Y. & J. 380, 385 *per* Hullock B.; see *Pickard* v. *Bankes* (1810), 13 East 20; and *Spratt* v. *Hobhouse* (1827), 4 Bing. 173, where Best C.J. said at p. 179 that everything may be treated as money in an action for money had and received 'that may be readily turned into money.'

[6] *Re Diplock*, [1948] Ch. 465, 517 sqq. *per* Lord Greene M.R. with a discussion at p. 521 of the meaning of 'money'. The decision was affirmed sub nomine *Ministry of Health* v. *Simpson*, [1951] A.C. 251, but the opinion delivered by Lord Simonds does not deal with the point.

[7] ss. 28, 34 (2) (b).

[8] Under s. 100 of the Larceny Act, 1861, replaced by s. 45 (1) of the Larceny Act, 1916, the answer was in the negative: *Moss* v. *Hancock*, [1899] 2 Q.B. 111. It would be satisfactory if the new Act permitted the same conclusion to be reached. See *In re Kirkham*, [1952] N.Z.L.R. 75.

[9] *Perrin* v. *Morgan*, [1943] A.C. 399; and see *In re Taylor*, [1923] 1 Ch. 99 (C.A.); *In re Collings*, [1933] Ch. 920. In *re Stonham*, [1963] 1 All E.R. 377 Wilberforce J. (as he then was) held that the terms 'cash', 'ready money', and 'money' in a will usually comprise money on deposit account. In *re Barnes' Will Trusts*, [1972] 1 W.L.R. 587 Goulding J. held that 'money' included a share account with a building society and certain government bonds.

[10] This follows from the Currency and Bank Notes Act, 1954, s. 1 (2).

[11] Language of Bowen L.J. in *Hewlett* v. *Allen*, [1892] 2 Q.B. 662, 666, approved of in *Williams* v. *North's Navigation Collieries (1889) Ltd.*, [1906] A.C. 136, 142, *per* Lord Davey; *Penman* v. *The Fife Coal Co.*, [1936] A.C. 45, at p. 53, *per* Lord Macmillan, at p. 61, *per* Lord Wright.

'money' varies, and consequently it is necessary in each individual context to examine its meaning. No hard-and-fast rule exists.

But it would be wrong to be satisfied with this result. Whatever the meaning of money may be in an individual case, clearly the word has an ordinary general meaning which requires definition not only for the sake of theoretical classification, but also for practical purposes.

It should be made clear at the outset that a distinction must be drawn between money in its concrete form and the abstract conception of money. It is with respect to the former that we ask: What are the characteristics in virtue of which a thing is called money? It is with regard to the latter that we inquire: What is the intrinsic nature of the phenomenon described by the word 'money'?

## II

In answering these two questions economic theory is unlikely to assist the lawyer to any appreciable extent. Lawyers, it is true, accept that, among all the functions of money which economists have analysed, the basic function is that of serving as a universal medium of exchange,[12] and will take this into account when defining money in the legal sense.[13] Yet such problems as monetary policy, the management and supply, the quantity and soundness of money are no concern of the lawyer. He will benefit more from the economist's view that postal giro accounts, bank accounts, treasury bills, perhaps even bankers' drafts, bills of exchange and cheques are characterized as money, for in the presence of a special context such 'bank money' (*monnaie scripturale, Buchgeld*), let it be emphasized, may well be treated by the law as money. As a rule, however, the economist's view that everything is money that functions as money is unacceptable to lawyers. Bank accounts, for instance, are debts, not money, and deposit accounts are not even debts payable on demand. Similarly, bills of exchange are not money; on the contrary, they require the drawee to pay 'a sum certain in money'.[14] Debts are contracted in

---

[12] This now seems to be generally accepted: see, for instance, Lord Crowther, *An Outline of Money* (1940), p. 35; L. von Mises, *The Theory of Money and Credit* (1934), pp. 34 sqq.; Kemmerer, *Principles of Money* (1935), p. 10. For a fundamental discussion see Menger, *Grundsätze der Volkswirtschaftslehre* (2nd ed., 1923), pp. 251 sqq., 259 sqq., 278 sqq. On Menger see Hayek, Introduction to the reprint of the first edition (1871), in No. 17 of the Series of Reprints of Scarce Tracts in Economic and Political Science, London, 1934. Modern economic literature rarely deals with this question or, indeed, with any question material to the lawyer. See, however, Newlyn and Bootle, *Theory of Money*, (3rd ed., 1978) pp. 1, 2.

[13] Below, p. 8.                         [14] Above, p. 3, n. 4.

terms of money, not in terms of bank accounts or bills. In the absence of the creditor's consent, express or implied, debts cannot be discharged otherwise than by the payment of what the law considers as money, namely legal tender.[15] Nor can the important consequences of tender[16] be achieved except by the offer of lawful money. Money is not the same as credit. Nor is the law of money identical with the law of credit.[17] Nor does the fact that 'bank money' largely functions as money prove that in law it necessarily and invariably is money.

Seeing that everywhere in the world the vast majority of transactions is completed by the transfer of some kind of 'bank money', that complications arise only in an infinitesimal number of cases, and that payment of large sums by way of legal tender is so impracticable as to appear absurd, most modern economists,[18] all commercial men and some lawyers[19] cavil at the alleged narrowness of the legal approach. Yet the positive law of money leaves no alternative, for in principle means of payment other than bank notes and coins may freely be rejected by a creditor to whom they are tendered.[20] Much of the discussion, accordingly, would seem to be of little practical impact, for it turns on a few words of qualification. On the one hand lawyers readily admit that in the eyes of economists

[15] The conclusion is inherent in the very notion of legal tender and is beyond doubt: see, for instance, Chitty, *Contracts* (24th ed., 1977) i, section 1325, and below p. 40.

[16] See below p. 71.

[17] The very opposite has been suggested in Germany by Duden, *Der Gestaltwandel des Geldes und seine rechtlichen Folgen* (1968), p. 22 and *passim*. Also RabelsZ. 1973, 783. Meichsner, *Osterreichisches Bank-Archiv*, 1980, 114 largely follows him, but also shows how sterile much of the discussion is to a lawyer. Against him Hahn *Festschrift für Konrad Zweigert* (1981) 625. It is certain, for instance, that as a matter of English law the 'right to receive foreign currency in respect of any credit or balance at a bank' would not have been treated as 'foreign currency' in the absence of an express provision in s. 1 (3) (*a*) of the Exchange Control Act 1947. Silard, p. 1 puts forward the following 'general concept of Money': it is 'an accounting unit that is (1) standardized by those dealing with it as a matter of convenience and in the light of evolving needs; (2) may be transferred within the framework of national or international institutional and legal structures and established practices; and (3) whose transfer permits the ready, that is, unconditional, effective, and speedy, conversion of direct or indirect claims to real resources into the unit.' Whatever else may be said about such a definition, it is certain that lawyers will not find it helpful.

[18] Thus Lord Crowther (above, p. 5, n. 12), p. 36 describes as money 'anything that is generally acceptable as a means of exchange', or Sir Dennis Robertson, *Money*, p. 2, defines as money anything that is 'widely' acceptable. For a representative German view in the same sense see Schmölders, *Geldpolitik* (1962), p. 11.

[19] Mainly in Germany: Spiros Simitis, *Archiv für die civilistische Praxis* 159 (1961), p. 432 with further references, or Staudinger (Weber), *Recht der Schuldverhältnisse*, Note 9 before § 244 (1967), among others. German judicial practice and the prevailing academic opinion so far support the traditional approach.

[20] See below p. 40. There is, accordingly, no room in a book on the law of money for a discussion of such problems as bank accounts, deposits and deposit certificates or negotiable instruments. All these and similar matters are traditionally treated in separate books.

bank money is unconditionally to be regarded as money.[21] On the other hand economists should recognize that to almost all lawyers bank money, as a rule, is money only with the creditor's express or implied consent and that, while lawyers are very ready to imply consent, they cannot dispense with this requirement, not only on account of statutory provisions, but also for the protection of the creditor, that is to say, for reasons with which economists are not concerned.

## III

Purely legal definitions of money *in concreto* used to include characteristics exclusively relating to coinage. Thus regard was had to weight, fineness, and impression.[22] But although even modern economists and jurists[23] have gone so far as to exclude things of valueless material, such as bank notes, from the notion of money, such a view is today certainly irreconcilable with the facts of commerical life.[24] It follows that incidents relating to substance can no longer be included in the notion of money. Blackstone,[25] on the

---

[21] German scholars have in recent years suggested that money should no longer be considered as a chattel subject to the law of property and protected by proprietary remedies, but as something comprising bank money. On these endeavours see Kaser, *Archiv für die civilistische Praxis* 143 (1937), 1, and on the history in Roman law, *Tijdschrift voor Rechtsgeschiedenis* xxix (1961), 169; Spiros Simitis, above p. 6, n. 19; Hefermehl, *Kommentar zum Handelsgesetzbuch* (4th ed., 1965) vol. iii, p. 1639; Westermann, *Sachenrecht* (5th ed., 1973), pp. 135-8, whose concise and clear discussion shows clearly that in the last resort the German difficulties derive from the absence of the possibility of following money, which exists in English law (see below, pp. 10, 11). In support of the same tendencies see in particular Duden (above, p. 6, n. 17) and Fögen pp. 14, 15, who treats only current bank accounts as money. Against such views M. Wolff-Raiser, *Sachenrecht* (10th ed., 1957), p. 233; Reinhardt, *Festschrift für Gustav Böhmer* (1954), pp. 60, 84, 94, and many others.

[22] *Case de Mixt Moneys* (1604), Davis, 18, 19; Comyns, *Dig.*, tit. 'Money', B. 1; Viner, *Abr.*, tit. 'Money', xv. 420; Blackstone, i. 277.

[23] For references see Nussbaum, p. 72, or Wolff, *Geld*, p. 566, n. 7. The view has found favour in France: see Mater, Nos. 65 to 71. It was put forward, e.g. by Immanual Kant, *Metaphysik der Sitten* (1797), § 31 (I).

[24] Already in *Wright v. Reed* (1790), 3 T.R. 554, it was held that bank notes are money within the Annuity Act, 17 Geo. III, ch. 26; and Lord Kenyon said: 'Bank notes are considered as money to many purposes', and Buller J. added: 'In a case on the other side of the hall, the Lord Chancellor once suggested a doubt whether these notes were money; but here we have always been inclined to consider them as such, though the question has never yet been directly determined.' But in *R. v. Hill* (1811), Russ & Ry. 191, it was held that bank notes were not 'money goods wares &c.' within the statute 30 Geo. II. ch. 24 (relating to the crime of obtaining by false pretences). See also *Klauber v. Biggerstaff* (1879), 47 Wis. 551, 3 N.W. 357; *Woodruff v. State of Mississippi* (1895), 162 U.S. 292, at p. 300 *per* Chief Justice Fuller.

[25] i. 276.

other hand, has said that 'money is the medium of commerce . . . is a universal medium, or common standard, by comparison with which the value of all merchandize may be ascertained, or it is a sign which represents the respective values of all commodities'. It has already been observed that such descriptions of the economic functions of money are, from the point of view of the law, insufficient, though not unimportant. In his book on *Money, Trade and Industry*[26] Mr. F. A. Walker stated that money is 'that which passes freely from hand to hand throughout the community in final discharge of debts and full payment for commodities, being accepted equally without reference to the character or credit of the person who offers it and without the intention of the person who receives it to consume it or apply it to any other use than in turn to tender it to others in discharge of debts or payment for commodities'. Had this definition not been approved by Darling J. in *Moss* v. *Hancock*.[27] it would hardly be necessary to say that, though perfectly correct from the viewpoint of economics, it does not explain money in the legal sense.

It is suggested that, in law, the quality of money is to be attributed to all chattels which, issued by the authority of the law and denominated with reference to a unit of account, are meant to serve as universal means of exchange in the State of issue. These characteristics will be explained separately.

1. Although at times money was not expressed by any corporeal symbols but was represented by accounts with a bank, which, for the purpose of effecting payments, were credited or debited[28] (bank money), yet from primitive periods until the present day men have been accustomed to connect the idea of money with definite symbols, whether these were animals, commodities, quantities of metal,[29] or coins and bank notes, as we today find them in all civilized countries. Money is a chattel personal.[30]

---

[26] London, 1882.

[27] [1899] 2 Q.B. 111, 116. The *German* Supreme Court repeatedly defined money as 'a medium of payment which, being certified as a bearer of value by the State or its authorized agent, is designated for public circulation regardless of its being a legal tender': 11 July 1924, *RGStr.* 58, 255, 256; 14 June 1937, *JW.* 1937, 2381.

[28] The chief examples are the Bank of Amsterdam, founded in 1609 and described by Adam Smith (*Wealth of Nations*, Book IV, ch. iii, before part ii), and the Hamburg Mark Banco from 1770 to 1873, about which see Nussbaum, pp. 232 sqq., or Wolff, p. 578, where further references will be found. On Banco currency generally see Sombart, *Moderner Kapitalismus*, i (1) 424 (1924).

[29] About early or modern, but unusual, forms of money see A. R. Burns, *Money and Monetary Policy in Early Times* (London, 1927); Paul Einzig, *Primitive Money* (2nd ed., 1966); W. Gerloff, *Die Entstehung des Geldes* (3rd ed., 1947); Mater, s. 2; Menger, *Grundsätze der Volkswirtschaftslehre* (2nd ed., 1923), pp. 251 sqq.

[30] But money is not a 'personal chattel' within the meaning of the Administration of Estates Act, 1925: s. 55 (x).

From the point of view of the rights which can be exercised over them, both coins and bank notes are chattels in possession, but bank notes are also choses in action, because (as, for instance, in this country) they express, or (as in other countries) they imply[31] the 'promise to pay the Bearer on Demand the sum of . . . '; in other words, bank notes are promissory notes within the meaning of s. 83 of the Bills of Exchange Act, 1882.[32] But it must not be overlooked that a bank note 'is not an ordinary commerical contract to pay money. It is in one sense a promissory note in terms, but no one can describe it simply as a promissory note. It is part of the currency of the country.[33]

As regards money as a chattel the general rule, 'nemo potest dare quod non habet', was apparently never applied to coins, which always passed by delivery and which could not be specifically recovered from a person who honestly and for valuable consideration had obtained possession.[34] The reason for this is not that the loser cannot know his money again, or in other words, that money has no earmark; 'for if his guineas or shilling had some private marks on

---

[31] See *Banco de Portugal* v. *Waterlow & Sons*, [1932] A.C. 452, 487 *per* Lord Atkin; but see German Supreme Court 20 May 1926, *RGZ.* 114, 27; 20 June 1929, *JW.* 1929, 3491. Cf. below, pp. 39, 40. It has been suggested that, since the termination of the Bank's duty to pay gold, the promise 'to pay' is meaningless; see, for instance, the minority in the Canadian case referred to below p. 12, n. 52 or Fögen, pp. 17, 23, 24. But the bearer is entitled to a new note in case of accidental alteration or demonetization, and it is difficult to see why this should not be a payment in discharge of the promise. In Britain, in particular, s. 1 (3) of the Currency and Bank Notes Act, 1954 makes it clear that bank notes 'shall be payable' at the Bank of England, although for many years they have not been payable in gold.

[32] S.C. and Chalmers, *Bills of Exchange* (13th ed., 1964), p. 274. Section 3 of the Currency and Bank Notes Act 1954 defines bank notes as 'notes of the Bank of England payable to bearer on demand'.

[33] *Suffel* v. *Bank of England* (1882), 9 Q.B.D. 555, at p. 563 *per* Jessel M.R. at p. 567 *per* Brett L.J.; also *The Guardians of the Poor of the Lichfield Union* v. *Greene* (1857), 26 L.J. Ex. 140 *per* Bramwell B.

[34] *Higgs* v. *Holiday*, Cro. Eliz. 746; *Millar* v. *Race* (1758), 1 Burr. 452; *Wookey* v. *Poole* (1820), 4 B. & Ald. 1. This rule, it is submitted also applies where coins lawfully made by the Mint, but stolen from it come into the hands of a *bona fide* holder, for they are valid money (cf. Coinage Act 1971, s. 2). This seems to be different in the United States of America: *United States* v. *Barnard*, 72 F. Supp. 531 (1947) where a District Court in Tennessee held that a gold coin of the United States which had been stolen from the Mint 'was not at any time money or currency, but was a chattel or an article of virtu' and that, therefore, a purchaser in good faith and for consideration could not maintain title against the original owner. The law becomes more difficult if coins are made at the Mint (or notes are printed at the Bank of England) without lawful authority and then put into circulation, possibly only as collectors' items. It is submitted that a bona fide holder for value should be protected, because the coins (or notes) are to him indistinguishable from those put lawfully into circulation. But can the wrongdoer be punished for counterfeiting and uttering false money? An affirmative answer was given by the Federal Supreme Court of Germany: 27 Sept. 1977, *JZ* 1977, 807. It is believed that English courts would have more difficulty in treating such money as counterfeit.

them by which he could prove they had been his, he could not get them back from a bona-fide holder. The true reason of this rule is that by the use of money the interchange of all other properties is most readily accomplished. To fit it for its purpose the stamp denotes its value and possession alone must decide to whom it belongs';[35] or in the words of Lord Mansfield,[36] 'the true reason is upon account of the currency of it'.[37] When bank notes came before the courts, this reasoning, and the rules based thereon, were applied to them. Lord Mansfield[38] rejected the comparison of bank notes 'to what they do not resemble and what they ought not to be compared to, viz. to goods, or to securities or documents for debts. Now they are not goods, not securities, nor documents for debts, nor are so esteemed, but are treated as money, as cash'. In 1820 it came to be said[39] 'that the representation of money which is made transferable by delivery only, must be subject to the same rules as the money which it represents'. Thus both coins and bank notes came to be united under the heading of 'negotiable chattels', i.e. if they 'were received in good faith and for valuable consideration, the transferee got property though the transferor had none'.[40] As Lord Haldane L.C. summarized the development:[41]

in most cases money cannot be followed. When sovereigns or bank notes are paid over as currency, so far as the payer is concerned, they cease *ipso facto* to be the subject of specific title as chattels. If a sovereign or bank note be offered in payment, it is, under ordinary circumstances, no part of the duty of the person receiving it to inquire into title. The reason of this is that chattels of such kind form part of what the law recognizes as currency and treats as passing from hand to hand in point, not merely of possession, but of property.

Where, however, money was capable of being recovered specifically,[42] i.e. from a holder who obtained it mala fide or without valuable

---

[35] *Wookey* v. *Poole* (1820), 4 B. & Ald. 1, 7 *per* Best J.

[36] *Millar* v. *Race* (1758), 1 Burr. 452, 457.

[37] According to Stair, *Institutions of the Law of Scotland* (1st ed., 1681) ii. 1. 34, Scottish law may have been different in that marking was, but notice was not, material: 'in fungibles . . . possession is generally esteemed to constitute property, which is most evident in current money, which, if it be not sealed, and during its remaining unsealed, is otherwise undiscernible, it doth so far become the property of the possessor that it passeth to all singular successors without any question of the knowledge, fraud or other fault of the author; without which commerce could not be secured, if money, which is the common mean of it, did not pass currently without all question, whose it had been, or how it ceased to be his.'

[38] *Ubi supra*; see Smith, *Leading Cases*, i. 532 sqq.

[39] *Wookey* v. *Poole* (1820), 4 B. & Ald. 1, 6 *per* Best J.

[40] *Banque Belge* v. *Hambrouck*, [1921] 1 K.B. 321, 329 *per* Scrutton L.J.

[41] *Sinclair* v. *Brougham*, [1914] A.C. 398, 418.

[42] An action for trover or detinue or, as it is now called, for wrongful interference with goods (see the Torts (Interference with Goods) Act 1977) does not lie for money at

consideration,[43] the common law granted an extension of the remedy by allowing recovery also of the produce of money, provided its identity could be ascertained.[44] However, it stopped short of the point where the relationship of creditor and debtor superseded the right *in rem*[45] and where, therefore, money was not identifiable. It was at this stage that the equitable doctrine of tracing money intervened[46] and the modern law is that money can be followed *in rem* against a holder who is mala fide or a volunteer, if it can be identified in or disentangled from a mixed fund.[47] Hence the old doctrine that 'money has no earmark' is today of little practical significance.

Bank notes as choses in action or promissory notes are subject to the Bills of Exchange Act, 1882, though the provisions relating to bills apply only 'with the necessary modifications'.[48] Thus, on the one hand, s. 84, according to which a promissory note is inchoate and incomplete until delivery, applies to bank notes, so that a piece of paper lost by or stolen from the bank of issue before delivery is not a bank note.[49] Yet it seems likely that the holder in due course of a Bank of England note which is genuine, but has been unlawfully and surreptitiously put in circulation is protected.[50] Further, it

large, such as a sum of money, but only for specific coins or notes, so that, in practice, the plaintiff must be able to identify them: *Banks v. Wheston* (1596), Cro. Eliz. 457; *Orton v. Butler* (1822), 5 B. & Ald. 652. The proprietary remedies of the owner are similarly limited in Germany and in France (Cass. Civ. 17 July 1929, D.H. 1929, 540; Cass. Req. 25 Nov. 1929, D.H. 1930, 3).

[43] *Clarke v. Shee* (1774), 1 Cowp. 197. In so far as bank notes are concerned, the Bills of Exchange Act, 1882, makes it clear that value and good faith are presumed (ss. 30, 90), so that the holder is not required to prove more than possession which is prima facie evidence of property. This corresponds with the common law (*King v. Milson* (1809), 2 Camp. 7; *Solomons v. Bank of England* (1810), 13 East 136). In the same sense *Wyer v. The Dorchester and Milton Bank* (1853), 11 Cush. (65 Mass.) 51.

[44] *Golightly v. Reynolds*, Lofft. 88; *Taylor v. Plumer* (1815), 3 M. & S. 562.

[45] See, for example, the explanation by Lord Haldane in *Sinclair v. Brougham*, [1914] A.C. 398, 419. For a useful discussion of the law summarised in the text see Goff and Jones, *Law of Restitution* (2nd ed., 1978) 50 sqq.

[46] *Re Hallett's Estate* (1880), 13 Ch. D. 696 overruling *Re West of England and South Wales District Bank, ex parte Dale* (1879), 11 Ch. D. 772 where Fry J. discussed the earlier cases.

[47] The principal authorities are *Sinclair v. Brougham, ubi supra; Banque Belge v. Hambrouck*, [1921] 1 K.B. 321; *Re Diplock*, [1948] Ch. 465, 517 sqq., affirmed on other grounds sub nomine *Ministry of Health v. Simpson*, [1951] A.C. 251.

[48] See s. 89.

[49] *Banco de Portugal v. Waterlow & Sons*, [1932] A.C. 452, 490 *per* Lord Atkin. Cf. *Baxendale v. Bennet* (1878), 3 Q.B.D. 525.

[50] See ss. 20, 21 and such authorities as *Smith v. Prosser*, [1907] 2 K.B. 735. Cf. in particular, *Cooke v. United States* (1875), 91 U.S. 389. *Banco de Portugal v. Waterlow & Sons*, [1932] A.C. 452 gave an affirmative answer to the question whether in the particular circumstances the bank was entitled to honour the spurious notes. The case did not deal with the question whether as against the innocent holder the bank was bound to do so. As regards the German law on the problem see Mann, *Juristenzeitung* 1970, 212, 409, and the literature there referred to. See above, p. 9, n. 34.

follows from ss. 69, 89 (2) that the owner who loses a bank note is, upon giving security, entitled to have a new one issued to him,[51] but a bank note destroyed by fire has to be replaced unconditionally.[52] S. 24, according to which, in the absence of estoppel,[53] a forged bill is inoperative, applies to bank notes. On the other hand, the well-established principle that, where a bill or note is given by way of payment, the payment may be absolute or conditional, the strong presumption being in favour of conditional payment,[54] does not apply to Bank of England notes; their delivery amounted to absolute payment even when gold coins were in circulation.[55] Again, a bill of exchange may not,[56] but a bank note may be reissued after payment in due course.[57] And while in case of an accidental alteration of a bill or a bank note the holder is entitled to payment, if he can prove the contract by the mutilated document or oral evidence,[58] the case of a deliberate alteration would appear to require a differentiation. If the alteration is immaterial or latent, the holder of a bill may be

[51] In this sense *Gillet* v. *Bank of England*. 6 (1889-1890) T.L.R. 9. The section which seems to confer a discretion applies only if the bank note is lost in the sense of its whereabouts being unknown and does not deal with destruction; see the Canadian case referred to in the following note. The section, it is submitted, requires clear identification of the instrument. See *Mayor* v. *Johnson* (1813), 3 Camp. 324: the owner of half a note cannot obtain payment without production of the other half, but Lord Ellenborough seemed to think that, if the owner had lost both halves, payment upon indemnity could be demanded. On the American law on this point see Nussbaum, p. 82.

[52] This was decided by the Court of Appeal of Ontario in *Bank of Canada* v. *Bank of Montreal*, (1972) 30 D.L.R. (3d) 24, 1972 3 O.R.881, and the decision was affirmed by a four to four decision of the Supreme Court of Canada: (1977) 76 D.L.R. (3d) 385, commented upon in detail by Mann, Canadian Business L.J. 2 (1978) 471. The decision is likely to command approval by English courts. Other legal systems do not necessarily distinguish between loss and destruction. On American law see Nussbaum p. 82. In France the owner is not entitled to the replacement of a destroyed bank note: Cass. Civ. 8 July 1867, D. 1867, 1. 289. As to Germany see s. 14 (3) of the *Gesetz über die Deutsche Bandesbank* of 26 July 1957, and comments by Gramlich, *RIW/AWD* 1981, 203.

[53] Cf. the decision of the Supreme Court of the United States in *Bank of the United States* v. *Bank of the State of Georgia*, 10 Wheat. (23 U.S.) 333 (1825): while a payment in forged bank notes is in general bad, this does not apply to a payment made bona fide to the bank of its own notes which are received as cash and afterwards discovered to be forged.

[54] See Chitty, *On Contracts* (24th ed., 1977) paragraph 1314.

[55] *Currie* v. *Misa* (1875), L.R. 10 Eq. 153, 164 *per* Lush J. who, however, does not attribute such effect to country bank notes. But on this point see *The Guardians of the Poor of the Lichfield Union* v. *Greene* (1857), 26 L.J. Ex. 140. In *Cross* v. *London & Provincial Trust Ltd.*, [1938] 1 K.B. 792, 803, MacKinnon L.J. even said that, though 'Bank of England notes, if subjected to the unusual treatment of being read, will be found to be promises by a third party to pay', they are 'the best form of payment in the world'.

[56] See ss. 59, 37.

[57] Stamp Act, 1891, s. 30; see Chalmers, *Bills of Exchange* (13th ed., 1964), p. 274. Pending reissue a bank note retains the character of money within the meaning of an indictment of larceny: *R.* v. *West* (1856), Dears & Bell 109; cf. *R.* v. *Ranson* (1812), 2 Leach 1090.

[58] *Hong Kong & Shanghai Bank* v. *Lo Lee Shi*, [1928] A.C. 181 where Lord Buckmaster said (p. 182) that the notes issued by the appellant bank, 'are not legal currency, but owing to the high credit of the appellants, they are used as if they were.'

protected by s. 64. But Bank of England notes have been held to be altogether excluded from the operation of s. 64;[59] they are subject to the common law rule according to which any material alteration[60] is a complete defence, even against a holder in due course to whom the alteration is not apparent. Finally, although in the conflict of laws the transfer of both bills[61] and bank notes (as well as coins) is governed by the *lex rei sitae*, the rules relating to the determination of the *situs* are not uniform. In the case of bills the debt represented by the paper may sometimes have to be treated as situate at the place where the debtor has bound himself to pay; indeed, it has been held that bills, drawn in India and payable in London, which at the time of the holder's death were on board a ship on the high seas, where assets situate in England and therefore subject to English death duty, because 'they represent, but do not constitute the asset'.[62] But this reasoning cannot apply to modern bank notes. They are situate where they are actually found rather than where they can be enforced.

2. Only those chattels are money to which such character has been attributed by law, i.e. by or with the authority of the State. This is the State or Chartalist theory of money which in modern times has come to be connected with the name of G. F. Knapp, to whose principal work[63] it has given the title.

[59] *Leeds & County Bank Ltd.* v. *Walker* (1883), 11 Q.B.D. 84. The reasoning of Denman J. (at p. 90) is perhaps not altogether convincing. That bank notes are in many respects different from ordinary promissory notes, that they do not require endorsement and are legal tender, is certain, but hardly apt to prove the inapplicability of s. 64. A note of doubt may be inferred from Lord Buckmaster's opinion in the case referred to in the preceding note.

[60] The alteration of the number is material: *Suffel* v. *Bank of England* (1882), 9 Q.B.D. 555.      [61] Dicey and Morris, p. 856, with references.

[62] *Pratt* v. *Attorney-General* (1874), L.R. 9 Ex. 140. In *Popham* v. *Lady Aylesbury* (1748), Amb. 69, Lord Hardwicke held that bank notes passed under the provision of a will disposing of a house 'with all that should be in it at his death', the reason being that bank notes are ready money, not bonds or securities, which are only evidence of money due. In *Stuart* v. *Bute* (1813), 11 Ves. 657, 662, however, Lord Eldon queried the decision and seemed inclined to hold that bank notes as well as securities were evidence of title to things out of the house, not to things in it. See also *Southcot* v. *Watson* (1745), 3 Atk. 228, 232, where bank notes were held to be cash, not securities within the meaning of a will.

[63] *Staatliche Theorie des Geldes*, 4th ed., 1923; English (abbreviated) edition and translation sub nomine *State Theory of Money* by Lucas and Bonar, London, 1924. On Knapp's work see Ellis, *German Monetary Theory 1905-1933* (Harvard University Press, (1934), It attracted a great deal of discussion among economists, partly exuberant praise, partly the most adverse criticism; see, on the one hand, Max Weber, 'Wirtschaft und Gesellschaft' in *Grundriss der Sozialökonomik*, iii (1), 2nd ed., 1925, at pp. 40, 105, 109, and, on the other hand, L. v. Mises, *The Theory of Money and Credit* (London, 1934), pp. 415 sqq.; in view of the universal acceptance of nominalism and the great influence of the Austinian jurisprudence it is less than fair to say of Knapp's theory that it 'is typical of the tendency in German thought to make the State the centre of everything' (B. M. Anderson, *The*

(a) The State theory of money is the necessary consequence of the sovereign power or the monopoly over currency[64] which over a long period of history the State has succeeded in assuming[65] and which modern constitutional law almost invariably establishes.[66] To permit the circulation of money that is not created or at least authorized by the State would be tantamount to a denial of the State's monetary prerogative.[67] In fact the Uniform Commercial Code (1958) which applies almost everywhere in the United States of American expressly defines money by the test of sanction of government: money is 'a medium of exchange authorized or adopted' by government 'as a part of its currency'.[68]

*Value of Money* (1926), p. 433). Among jurists for whom Knapp's theory was less revolutionary its essence was readily accepted, although they were emphatic that it should not be regarded as a legal work: see M. Wolff, *Geld*, pp. 566, 568, 571, and *Internationales Privatrecht* (3rd ed., 1954), p. 158, n. 9. Knapp's theories are further discussed below, pp. 44, 85 sqq. See also Keynes, *Treatise of Money* (1930), i. 4: 'Today all civilised money is, beyond the possibility of dispute, chartalist'; Gréciano, *Du rôle de l'Etat en matière monétaire*, Paris, 1896; Gerber, *Geld und Staat*, 1926; Nolde, *Rec*. 27 (1929), 243, 249, sqq.

[64] It is hardly necessary to mention that this comprises not only the right to issue, or authorize the issue of, money, but also numerous other incidents of the regulation of money. Thus it extends to the introduction of exchange control, the abrogation of gold clauses, the decision to revalorize or not to revalorize debts and so forth. Accordingly, customary international law recognizes the sovereignty of the State in these matters: see below, p. 465.

[65] Nussbaum, p. 32, with further references. The historical development is connected with the problem of the *valor impositus* or *extrinsecus*, i.e. nominalism; see below, pp. 86 sqq. According to Dareste de la Chavanne, *Histoire de l'Administration en France*, ii (1848), 145, the French King's monopoly was established only by Charles VIII (1483–98).

[66] Written Constitutions usually contain express powers. The Constitution of the United States grants to Congress the power 'to coin money, regulate the value thereof, and of foreign coin' (Art. I. s. 8, par. 5). It was never doubted that 'to determine what shall be lawful money and a legal tender is in its nature, and of necessity a governmental power. It is in all countries exercised by the governments': *Hepburn* v. *Griswold* (1869), 75 U.S. 603, 615, 616 *per* Chief Justice Chase; *Knox* v. *Lee* and *Parker* v. *Davies* (1870), 79 U.S. 457, 549, 552 *per* Mr. Justice Strong; *Juilliard* v. *Greenman* (1883), 110 U.S. 421, 447 *per* Mr. Justice Gray, who quoted *Emperor of Austria* v. *Day* (below, p. 17, n. 81). But until *Knox* v. *Lee* and *Parker* v. *Davies* upheld the validity of the Legal Tender Acts on broad principles, it was denied that the power to import the quality of legal tender of greenbacks could be derived from the coinage power or from any other power expressly given in the Constitution of the United States. Another problem of delimiting the monetary monopoly of the federal state occurred in the Federal Republic of Germany. The Federal Constitutional Court held (20 July 1954, *BVerfG*. 4, 60) that an enactment by a *Land*, which, 'in its economic result', allows revalorization of executed obligations in order to adjust the effects of currency reform, forms part of the currency and monetary system and therefore falls within the exclusive jurisdiction of the Federal government.

[67] Even if treaties had anything to say about the money circulating in a State, this would not affect the validity of the State theory of money, for the treaty only applies by virtue of the State's decision. There is, therefore, no force in the suggestion by Aufricht ('The Fund Agreement and the Legal Theory of Money', *Österreichische Zeitschrift für Öffentliches Recht* 1959, 26, at p. 75) that a realistic theory of money must 'include both international and domestic law'. Customary international law contains no pertinent rule.

[68] Section 1–201 (24), and see the comment on section 3–107. The important fact stated in the text is ignored by far too many scholars who discuss the conception of money.

It cannot be open to doubt that in this country that prerogative exists and, accordingly, the State theory of money rules. The right of coinage has for many centuries been recognized as part of the Crown's prerogative,[69] and Blackstone[70] went even so far as to say that 'the coining of money is in all states the act of the sovereign power'. Although for the most part these rights of the Crown have now been put on a statutory basis, the principle is not affected.[71]

With regard to bank notes the development of the law was different, for their history is connected with that of bills of exchange and banking. Bank notes in the modern sense were not always distinguishable from other negotiable instruments. When goldsmiths and bankers began to issue notes,[72] nobody thought of the necessity or desirability of authorization or restriction by the government. The position is well described by Sir Albert Feavearyear, whose words deserve quotation:[73]

It will be remembered that in the first half of the eighteenth century the customers of the London banks made use to about an equal extent of the notes of those banks and of drafts upon cash accounts kept with them. Between these two documents at the outset there was really very little difference. The notes were issued in favour of the person who deposited the money, were generally for large, and often for broken, amounts, were frequently made out, not to 'bearer', but to 'order', and in the latter case passed current by endorsement like a cheque. . . . It is not surprising therefore to find that the early writers upon paper currency drew no distinction between the various forms in which they found it. They grouped them all together as 'paper credit', and held that, all of them drove out and took the place of metallic money. There was no important difference between the note signed by Francis Child, the banker, which said: 'I promise to pay Mr. John Smith or order, on demand, the sum of £186 14s. 2d.', and the draft signed by John Smith and addressed to Francis Child which said: 'Pay to Robert Brown or order the sum of £186 14s. 2d.' No one regarded the former as in any way more entitled to be considered money than the latter. Davenant, Hume, and Sir James Steuart all spoke of notes, bills, drafts, bank

---

[69] *Case de mixt Moneys* (1604), Davis, 18, 19; Viner, *Abr.*, tit. 'Money', xv. 420; Comyns, *Dig.*, tit. 'Money', B. 1. *Dixon* v. *Willows*, 3 Salkeld 238, dealt with guineas made in respect to the value of £1. 1s. 4d. set upon broadpieces by proclamation; it was said that 'though there is no Act of Parliament or Order of State for these guineas as they are now taken, yet being coined at the Mint and having the King's insignia on them, they are lawful money and current at the value they were coined and uttered at the Mint'. As to the judicial notice of the value of guineas see also Holt C.J. in *Pope* v. *St. Leiger* (1694), 5 Mod. 1, at p. 7. On the history of the prerogative in England and the United States see S. P. Breckenridge, *Legal Tender* (Chicago, 1903), and Holdsworth, *History of English Law*, x. 407. On the general history of coinage and its implications see the great work by A. Luschin von Ebengreuth, *Allgemeine Münzkunde und Geldgeschichte des Mittelalters und der Neueren Zeit* (2nd ed., 1926).

[70] i. 277.

[71] Halsbury (Hailsham) viii. sections 1018, 1022; see especially Coinage Act, 1971, s. 3.

[72] Feavearyear, pp. 107 sq. *et passim.*  [73] p. 258.

credits, and even securities, as though they were a part of the circulating money of the country. Adam Smith gave most of his attention to notes, which by that time had become by far the most important form of credit currency, but his well-known account of the bank money of Amsterdam makes it clear that he regarded that equally as money; and indeed he says: 'There are several sorts of paper money; but the circulating notes of banks and bankers are the species which is best known and which seems best adapted for this purpose.'

When in 1694 the Bank of England was created,[74] it was not a bank of issue in the modern sense. The statute did 'not confer any exclusive privilege whatever on the Bank . . . and the Statute is silent as to the intention of the legislature whether the Bank should be a bank of circulation and issue or merely a bank of deposit'.[75] Nevertheless, immediately after its incorporation, the Bank began to act as a bank of circulation and issue, 'probably to a very considerable extent',[76] and, in addition, various country banks continued to issue notes without government control.

The serious problems thus raised were not appreciated before the second quarter of the nineteenth century, when they became the chief topic of discussion between the Currency and Banking Schools. The former school aimed at using the terms money and currency for notes and coins only, at separating the creation of money from its distribution, and at 'putting the business of note issue under direct Government control, as was the business of issuing coin'.[77] These views were adopted by the Bank Charter Act, 1844,[78] by which the modern position was established and which made it clear that the privilege of issuing notes constituting money in England and Wales was exclusive to the Bank of England, whose notes had been made legal tender by the Bank of England Act, 1833,[79] and are now legal tender under the Currency and Bank Notes Act, 1954.[80]

In view of the fact that in the 1840s innumerable notes issued by various banks circulated in England and that the radical changes effected by the Act of 1844 were not made without serious struggles and controversies, it is somewhat astonishing to find that less than twenty years later it could be said 'that the right of issuing notes for payment of money, as part of the circulating medium, in Hungary, seems to follow from the *jus cudendae monetae* belonging to the

---

[74] 5 & 6 W. and M., ch. 20.

[75] *Bank of England* v. *Anderson* (1837), 3 Bing. N.C. 590, 652 *per* Tindal C.J.; see Feavearyear, p. 126.        [76] Ibid.

[77] Feavearyear, p. 264.        [78] 7 & 8 Vict., ch. 32.

[79] s. 6; but in Scotland and Northern Ireland the limited rights to issue bank notes under 8 & 9 Vict., chs. 37 and 38 are still in force.

[80] s. 1, subsection 2: in England and Wales generally and in Scotland and Northern Ireland in respect of notes of less than £5.

supreme power in every State',[81] and that there was 'no reason to doubt that the prerogative right reaches to the issue of paper money'.[82] If these words were meant to apply not only to Hungary, but also to this country, they were perhaps somewhat premature, but they do show how easily the State theory of money, the correctness of which cannot now be denied, was accepted in England.[83]

(b) The State theory of money has a twofold aspect.

In the first place it means that circulating media of exchange in law constitute money only if they are created by or with the authority of the State or such other supreme authority as may temporarily or *de facto* exercise the sovereign power of the State. It follows that, for example, promissory notes of £10 each,[84] made payable to bearer on demand, which a large industrial concern in England may issue, do not in law possess the attributes and privileges of bank notes or money, though they may circulate in a large area and be treated by the community as if they were money. Or when an English statute speaks of 'gold coin', it refers, in the absence of a special definition or context, to coins issued by the competent authority in England as a means of exchange and excludes privately produced replicas of such coins.[85] On the other hand, when during the Franco-German War of 1870-1 certain French towns, while being besieged, issued what was called *'monnaie obsidionale'*, or when, during and after the First World War, German towns, chambers of commerce or industrial undertakings issued 'emergency money' (*Notgeld*), the circulating media were in law money and their forger, as certain French police courts[86] and the German Supreme Court[87] held, was liable to be punished for counterfeiting of currency; in the case of the latter tribunal this meant no departure from its repeatedly expressed view[88] that money only exists by authority

---

[81] *Emperor of Austria* v. *Day* (1861), 3 De G. F. & J. 217, 234 *per* Lord Campbell. Though this case includes many useful dicta, the decision cannot, it is submitted, be supported: Mann, *Transactions of the Grotius Society*, 40 (1955), 25, at p. 37, or *Studies in Institutional Law* (1973), p. 505.        [82] S.C. p. 251 *per* Turner L.J.

[83] Recent and most impressive applications are to be found in *Adelaide Electric Supply Co. Ltd.* v. *Prudential Assurance Co. Ltd.*, [1934] A.C. 122 and *Bonython* v. *Commonwealth of Australia*, [1951] A.C. 201.

[84] Promissory notes under £5 may not be issued: Bank Notes Act, 1826, s. 3; Bank Notes (No. 2) Act, 1928, s. 1. On the private issue of token coins during the Bank Restriction Period and during the nineteenth century in general, see Falkner, 16 (1901), *Political Science Quarterly*, 303.

[85] *Freed* v. *Director of Public Prosecutions*, [1969] 2 Q.B. 115, which relates to the Exchange Control Act, 1947, and also denies that such coins are 'gold bullion' within the meaning of that Act.        [86] Mater, p. 57, who rejects these decisions.

[87] 14 June 1937, *JW.* 1937, 2381, with reference to older, partly different decisions.

[88] 28 Nov. 1923, *RGZ.* 107, 78: Reichsbank notes were not legal tender in the former German Protectorate of South-West Africa; 25 Sept. 1919, *RGZ*, 96, 262: 'Money

of the State, for its decision was plainly put on the ground that the
State had tolerated and even sanctioned the issue of such money.
Further, if in the course of a civil war rebels assume power within
a certain district and, by irresistible force, impose a currency upon
the ·inhabitants, this is lawful money: although the insurgents do
not form a recognized government, they exercise *de facto* supremacy
in all matters of government which make obedience to their authority
in civil and local matters not only a necessity but a duty.[89] Similarly,
notes issued and made legal tender by a belligerent occupant in the
course of an international war are money, because they are imposed
by that power which *de facto*, though temporaily, exercises supreme
authority and is responsible for public order and administration;[90]
accordingly, loans made in military currency are loans, they do not
constitute a barter transaction,[91] and a sum of money expressed and
payable in the lawful currency of the occupied State may be discharged by the payment of so many military currency notes as,
under the belligerent occupant's legal tender legislation, express the
nominal value of the debt.[92]

The second consequence of the State theory of money is that in
law money cannot lose its character except by virtue of formal
demonetization.[93] History supplies ample material relating to periods

is measurement of value and means of payment by authority of the State only.' See the
definitions, p. 8, n. 27, above.

[89] This is the effect of a long line of decisions of the Supreme Court of the United
States: *Thorington* v. *Smith* (1869), 75 U.S. 1; *Hanauer* v. *Woodruff* (1872), 82 U.S. 439;
*Effinger* v. *Kenney* (1885), 115 U.S. 566; *New Orleans Waterworks* v. *Louisiana Sugar Co.*
(1888), 125 U.S. 18; *Baldy* v. *Hunter* (1898), 171 U.S. 388; *Houston & Texas C.R. Co.* v.
*Texas* (1900), 177 U.S. 66. But see *Thomas* v. *Richmond* (1871), 79 U.S. 453. In the same
sense an opinion given by Sir John Harding, Queen's Advocate, printed by Sir Arnold McNair
in *British Year Book of International Law*, 1949, 26. In *Lindsay, Gracie & Co.* v. *Russian
Bank for Foreign Trade* (1918), 34 T.L.R. 443 Bailhache J. seems to have held that so long
as the Soviet Government was unrecognized notes issued by it could not be treated as
Russian currency. The authority in England of the United States practice is further impaired
by the unconvincing reasoning of the majority in *Madzimbamuto* v. *Lardner-Burke*, [1969]
A.C. 645, pp. 727 sqq. and see *In re James*, [1977] Ch. 41.

[90] Oppenheim (−Lauterpacht), *International Law*, ii (7th ed., 1952), pp. 433 sqq.

[91] *Contra* the practice of the Courts of Burma (on which see Maung, 30 (1948), *Journal
of Comparative Legislation*, 3rd series, 11, 13 sqq): *Ko Maung Tin* v. *U Gon Man*, A.D. 1947,
Case No. 104; *U Hoke Wan* v. *Maung Ba San*, ibid. Case No. 105, and in particular the
decision of the Supreme Court in *Dooply* v. *Chan Taik*, International L.R. 1952, 619, and
*Taik* v. *Ariff*, A.D. 1948 Case No. 191.

[92] Supreme Court of the Philippine Republic in *Haw Pia* v. *China Banking Corporation*,
*The Lawyer's Journal* (Manila), 13 (1948), 173 (a majority decision of seven to three),
followed in *Madlambayon* v. *Aquine*, International L.R. 1955, 994, and *Aboitiz & Co.* v.
*Price*, 99 F. Supp. 602 (District Court, Utah, 1951), both with a very elaborate discussion.
Again it seems that a different view is being taken by the courts in Burma, at least where
payment is made to a person other than the creditor himself: *Dawsons Bank Ltd.* v. *Ko Sin
Sein*, 36 (1968), International L.R. 497.

[93] Cf., generally, *Marrache* v. *Ashton*, [1943] A.C. 311, at p. 318 *per* Lord Macmillan. The

during which, as a result of debasement, in accordance with Gresham's law bad money drove out of circulation good money,[94] so that valuable, but undervalued coins were withheld, or during which even 'good' money lost its purchasing power. But such events did not render it impossible to make use of the coins or notes at their nominal value, and therefore it cannot be said that they lost their monetary character.[95] Thus a gold sovereign, though its market value now is about £65 and has been even higher, is still money and therefore capable of being taken as such in execution according to its nominal value[96] and of

statement in the text only applies, of course, to the money issued by a currently existing State and excludes currency of States long since extinct such as gold coins issued by the Kingdom of Hawaii which ceased to exist in 1898: U.S. v. Gertz, 249 F. 2d 662 (1957).

[94] It was H. D. MacLeod, A Dictionary of Political Economy (1863), pp. 17, 18, 450 who first attributed the discovery and the formulation of the law to Sir Thomas Gresham. However, although it is now universally known as Gresham's law (see, for instance, H. Laurent, La Loi de Gresham au Moyen Age (Brussels, 1933)), there is no evidence to the effect that Gresham was aware of it, and it is astonishing how it came about that MacLeod's erroneous impression came to be accepted as fact all the world over. The fact is that the law was known already to Aristophanes (for a translation of his verses see J. L. Laughlin, Money, Credit and Prices (Chicago, 1931, p. 51), as MacLeod, l.c., himself recognizes, and was first formulated by Copernicus in his Monete Cutendo Ratio (1526): 'quanto hic magis erratum est vetere meliore remanente viliorem novam introducendoque non solum infecit antiquam sed, ut ita dicam, expugnavit' (it is a greater error to introduce, while the old good money remains in circulation, bad new money which not only debases, but also, so to speak, wipes out the old). For Copernicus' text see e.g. Wolowski, Traictie de la première invention des Monnoies de Nicole Oresme et Traité de la Monnoie de Copernic (Paris, 1864). On MacLeod's self-confessed 'invention' see De Roover, Gresham on Foreign Exchange (1949), p. 91.

[95] In such circumstances, however, the valuable money, being quoted at a premium will usually be treated as a commodity: see below, p. 24. The summary of Turkish law which Lord Thankerton gave in Ottoman Bank v. Menni, [1939] 4 All E.R. 9, 13 and according to which Turkish gold pounds had ceased to be money and became a mere commodity, probably does not intend to assert a different principle. Where a State purports to nullify all currency situate outside its territory, a confiscation occurs: below p. 474.

[96] This view is supported by Denning L.J. in Treseder-Griffin v. Co-operative Insurance Society, [1956] 2 Q.B. 127, at p. 146 and by the practice of American courts during the greenback period (1861-79), when gold dollars were at a premium. One gold dollar was always regarded as one dollar. Thus it was said by Chief Justice Waite in Thompson v. Butler (1877), 5 Otto (95 U.S.), 694, 696 that 'a coin dollar is worth no more for the purpose of tender in payment of an ordinary debt than a dollar'. Or if the creditor of a mere dollar debt of $5,000 had obtained $5,000 gold through the realization of a security given to him, the debtor could not recover the amount of the premium: Standwood v. Flagg (1867), 98 Mass. 124; Start v. Coffin (1870), 105 Mass. 328; Hancock v. Franklin Insurance Co. (1873), 114 Mass. 155. In Frothingham v. Morse (1864), 45 N.H. 545 the plaintiff had deposited $50 in gold coin as bail. He was held to be entitled to the return of $50 in currency only. Nussbaum's view that such circumstances prove the 'societary' doctrine of money (below, p. 20) is therefore unjustified. As gold sovereigns are still legal tender, it is submitted that if my debtor pays a debt of £1 by delivering a gold sovereign which has been stolen, I am not exposed to any claim by the real owner. But if an English firm delivers a gold sovereign, by way of Christmas bonus, to each of its employees, the latter are likely to be liable to income tax in respect of an emolument of, say, £80 rather than £1. Browne-Wilkinson J. was therefore fully justified in deciding in Jenkins v. Horn (Inspector of Taxes), (1979) 2 All E.R. 1141 that if a workman is entitled to wages of £40 a week and is paid one gold sovereign he is liable to tax on £40, not, as he contended, on £1. If the wage had been

being counterfeited as currency.[97] And while a yearly rent of 3s. payable under a lease for a term of 1,000 years from February 1607 may be of little 'value', it still has money value so that the owner cannot enlarge his term into a fee simple under s. 153, Law of Property Act, 1925.[98]

Similarly, Canada's Maple Leaf[99] has a commercial value of about £250, yet having been issued in pursuance of a Proclamation of the Governor General of 8 November 1979 it is legal tender for C$ 50.[100]

(c) The State theory of money is opposed by those who believe that it is the usage of commercial life or the confidence of the people that at any rate in situations of crisis or emergency, have the power to make things money, 'that in the phenomenon of money the attitude of society, as distinguished from State, is paramount'.[101] This so-called 'societary theory of money', propounded by mainly economists,[102]

agreed at £1 and the workman was paid one gold sovereign he would have been liable to tax on £1 only. It is not certain whether the distinction would be accepted by Browne-Wilkinson J. who fastened upon the sovereigns being 'perquisites or profits'. This was so in the case before him. In the case put above it would not be so.

[97] That the gold sovereign continues to be money in the sense of the criminal law relating to the counterfeiting of currency was decided by the supreme tribunals of *Italy* (31 Oct. 1957, *Giurisprudenza Italiana*, 1958, ii. 81, also International L.R. 1957, 48; 19 Dec. 1957, *Giustizia Penale*, 1958, ii. 780; 21 Feb. 1959, *Giurisprudenze Italiana*, 1960, ii. 57), *France* (17 Feb. 1959, *Bull. Cass. Crim.*, 1959, 218), *Germany* (27 Jan. 1959, *BGSt.* 12, 344, also *NJW*. 1959, 947; 7 July 1964, *BGSt.* 19, 357, also *NJW*. 1964, 1629, accepting almost verbally the German version of the above text) and *Tangier* (27 Oct. 1956, S. 1956, 159). In relation to the Convention of 20 Apr. 1929 (on which see below, p. 485) the opposite view was taken by the *Swiss* Federal Tribunal (16 July 1952, *BGE*. 78 i. 225; similarly, in regard to Saudi Arabian gold coin, 2 Nov. 1956, *BGE*. 82 iv. 198); this decision rested on inadequate expert evidence and a somewhat perfunctory certificate by the Bank of England to the effect 'that the sovereign retains its legal tender status', and is rightly critized by Nussbaum, *American Journal of Comparative Law*, 3 (1954), 360 sqq., 371. 372. Pre-1914 German gold coins were held not to be currency within the meaning of German restitution legislation, because they were not actually current: Supreme Restitution Court Herford, 30 May 1961, *RzW*. 1961, 491. Against this view, in relation to gold dollars, Supreme Restitution Court Berlin, 16 Dec. 1966, *RzW*. 1967, 257. Similarly Court of Appeal Hamm, 5 Nov. 1962, Betriebsberater 1963, 67, which, on inadequate grounds, is supported by Fögen, pp. 25, 27, 28.

[98] *Re Smith & Stott* (1885), 29 Ch.D. 1009 n. But a yearly rent of one silver penny payable under a lease for a term of 500 years from Michaelmas 1646 has no money value, because a silver penny, though it may have value (e.g. as a curiosity), is no longer money: *Re Chapman & Hobbs* (1885), 29 Ch.D. 1007.

[99] See below p. 24. The South African Krugerrand has a different character. The Mint and Coinage Act No. 78 of 1964 indirectly describes it as legal tender. But the amount in respect of which it may be tendered in payment is not specified. Not being related to a specific Rand value the Krugerrand cannot in law have the quality of legal tender. It is a commodity and, therefore, for instance, should be liable to V.A.T.

[100] This clearly follows from ss. 3, 4, and 7 of the Canadian Currency and Exchange Act.

[101] Nussbaum, p. 8.

[102] See W. Gerloff, *Geld und Gesellschaft* (1952).

but also by some jurists,[103] would be tenable in law only if it could explain the relevance of crises for the legal definition of money, if it were reconcilable with the undeniable monopoly of the modern State over currency, and if it could point to a single case where money in the legal sense was created or lost its character by the will of the community against or without the will of the supreme *de jure* or *de facto* authority.[104]

3. Only those chattels issued by or on behalf of the State are money which are denominated with reference to a distinct unit of account.

The early jurists were agreed that denomination is a necessary ingredient of coins,[105] while naturally they omitted to deal with bank notes. Thus Blackstone said[106] that denomination is 'the value for which the coin is to pass current'. There can be no objection to this definition, if it is understood that the 'value of money', in so far as it is not restricted to the mere denomination as such, but comprises the problem of nominalism or valorism, is not an ingredient of money itself but of monetary obligations, their subject-matter and their extent; denomination or value of money in the sense of discharging power will therefore be dealt with in another connection.[107]

---

[103] Nussbaum, pp. 5–10, who mentions some adherents to the same school of thought. See in particular Savigny, *Obligationenrecht*, p. 408 or Reinhardt, *Festschrift für Gustav Böhmer* (1954), 60, at p. 68. The theory has attracted few lawyers outside Germany and is by no means widely followed there: see Staudinger-Weber, *Kommentar zum BGB*, note 5 before § 244 (1967), but against him Staudinger-Werner, ibid., § 291, note 8.

[104] This is what the 'societary' theory of money has to prove. It is not proved by pointing to cases in which privately issued media of exchange in fact circulated, but their recognition as money for legal purposes was never put to the test. Nor does it assist to rely on examples taken from a period when the modern monetary systems had not yet come into existence and when, in particular, the legal character of the bank note was not yet clarified. Nussbaum's reliance on the fate of Confederate notes is misplaced, because, as was shown above, p. 18, n. 89, their monetary character was expressly explained by *Thorington* v. *Smith* (1869), 75 U.S. 1 on the ground that 'to the extent of actual supremacy, however unlawfully gained, in all matters of government within its military lines the power of the insurgent government cannot be questioned'. And the assertion that in *Emperor of Austria* v. *Day* (1861), 3 De G. F. & J. 217 the 'societary theory' was recognized by Lord Campbell's observation that Hungarian notes 'were *de facto* legal tender because of their common circulation' (Nussbaum, p. 8, n. 17) is equally untenable. This follows from Lord Campbell's reasoning (p. 234) that 'as *de facto* they are legal tender according to the law administered in Hungary, we can hardly inquire in an English Court of Justice whether this is a stretch of prerogative'.

[105] See p. 15, n. 69.

[106] i. 278.

[107] Below, p. 84. This view is not unquestioned. Nussbaum, for example, defines money as a 'thing which, irrespective of its composition, is by common usage given and received as a fraction, integer or multiple of an ideal unit' (p. 13). But the orthodox and correct view connects the problem of nominalism not with money but with monetary obligations and their extent (see, for example, the valuable remarks of Breit in Düringer-Hachenburg, *Kommentar zum Handelsgestzbuch*, iv. 743). Nevertheless, in so far as Nussbaum emphasizes

While denomination with reference to a specific unit of account is necessary to confer upon a chattel the quality of money (so that bullion, though it may be 'monetary gold',[108] can never be money), not everything that is so denominated is money. Treasury bills, for example, are expressed in terms of a unit of account, but they represent merely claims to money, their reference to the unit of account is only indirect. A Bank of England note, on the other hand, is nothing but the corporeal form, the embodiment of the unit of account, its fraction or multiple. In this sense there is force in Humphreys J.'s dictum that it cannot be said 'that the possession of a pound note is evidence that you have got anything at all'.[109] You have in fact a pound, you do not have a claim to a pound.

The definition of the unit of account (pound, dollar, franc) is supplied by the various monetary systems and will have to be discussed elsewhere.[110] Here it must suffice to say that a chattel cannot in law be regarded as money if it represents anything else than the mere embodiment of a unit of account, its fraction or multiple.

4. Chattels which have been created by law and which are denominated by reference to a unit of account are money if they are meant to serve as universal media of exchange in the State of issue.

It has already been observed[111] that of the many functions of money that of being the medium of exchange is the fundamental one. In this connection lawyers cannot but accept what economic theory has elaborated, and they are compelled to do so because it is impossible to describe money *in concreto* without reference to its cardinal function. As has been mentioned above,[112] this experience has led lawyers even to accept definitions of money which merely refer to that economic function.

Because money is the medium of exchange, it is not an object of exchange or, in other words, it is not a commodity. 'Economic goods and money thus appear as opposite concrete phenomena.'[113] As Nussbaum points out,[114] this antithesis does not mean that

---

the importance of a reference to a distinct unit of account, he should be followed. The chief distinction between Nussbaum's and the present writer's definition of money is that Nussbaum adopts the 'societary' theory of money and includes the value of money in the notion of money.

[108] For a reference to 'monetary gold' see the material referred to below, p. 29, n. 3.

[109] *Hill v. R.*, [1945] K.B. 329, at pp. 334, 335. In another sense, of course, a Bank of England note is evidence; the owner is e.g. entitled as against the Bank of England to have a new one issued to him.

[110] See below, pp. 42 sqq.                [111] Above, p. 5.                [112] p. 8.

[113] Helfferich, p. 2. In the same sense Hawtrey, *Currency and Credit* (1950), p. 44; L. v. Mises, *Theory of Money and Credit* (1934), pp. 79 sqq.; Nogaro, *La Monnaie* (Paris, 1935), pp. 385 sqq., 389. For the classical economists, notably John Stuart Mill, money was nothing but a commodity.                [114] p. 22.

money is exempt from the economic rules relating to supply and demand; on the other hand, it does not follow from such submission to economic rules of general validity that money has no distinct qualities in the eyes of the law, but is simply a commodity. Mater's conclusion[115] that money is a commodity ('la monnaie est une marchandise') is due to a misunderstanding of this situation.

But the quality of serving universally as a medium of exchange within a given economic area and in a given national system is an essential requirement of money. This is one of the reasons why bills of exchange, cheques, bank bills, stamps, postal orders, chips such as are widely used in Monte Carlo, coupons, gold bars, treasury bills, and so forth are excluded from the legal notion of money.[116] In times of crisis, it is true, one or another of such objects has been assimilated to money. Thus at the beginning of the First World War, postal orders were made legal tender by s. 1 (6) of the Currency and Bank Notes Act, 1914;[117] in Nazi Germany, within the meaning of foreign exchange restrictions, unused stamps were money and therefore prohibited from being sent abroad without permission, 'if they fulfil the functions of money, i.e. are being used to effect payments'.[118] Even in less extraordinary circumstances or connections such things are sometimes put on the same level with[119] or used as or instead of money. Nevertheless, as a rule, they are not money, because they are accepted as media of exchange only by a small circle or only occasionally. Further, it is in accordance with principle that the expression 'goods, wares and merchandise' or 'goods and chattels', where they occur in penal statutes, do not generally include money.[120] But there may be exceptions to this rule. Thus by virtue

---

[115] pp. 17–47. Mater's reasoning, chiefly based on certain remarks made by economists and in the French Parliament from 1789 to 1807, is unsatisfactory and without following in modern France. See, e.g., Carbonnier, *Droit Civil* II (5th ed., 1967) p. 25.

[116] See Wolff, p. 565. That even 'certified cheques' are not money suitable for payment into court was decided in Germany: Königsberg Court of Appeal, 22 Dec. 1930, *JW.* 1931, 3148.  [117] Repealed by Currency and Bank Notes Act, 1928, s. 13.

[118] Runderlass, Nr. 157/36, Reichssteuerblatt, 1936, 1071.

[119] See, for example, Forgery Act, 1913, s. 18 (1).

[120] Note to *John Howard's* case (1751), Foster's c.c. 77; *R.* v. *Leigh* (1764), 1 Leach 52; *R.* v. *Guy* (1782), 1 Leach 241. See *R.* v. *Hill*, p. 7, n. 24 above. According to *Buckingham* v. *Securitas Properties Ltd.*, (1980) 1 W.L.R. 380 the expression 'goods' in s. 7 (1) (*e*) of the Capital Allowances Act 1968, does not include currency filled into wage packets. But under ss. 4 (1) and 34 (2) (*b*) of the Theft Act, 1968, the terms 'property' as well as 'goods' include money. Under the common law nothing could be taken in execution that could not be sold; it was held, therefore, that money could not be taken (*Knight* v. *Criddle* (1807), 9 East 48); nor was it possible to take bank notes, for 'though they are assignable over, they remain in some measure choses in action' (*Francis* v. *Nash* (1734), Hard. 53). This state of affairs was remedied by s. 12 of the Judgments Act, 1838; see *Wood* v. *Wood* (1843), 4 Q.B. 397. On money as 'goods, wares and merchandise' in American law see Professor Corbin, *On Contracts* (1950), s. 479.

of s. 34 (2) (*b*) of the Theft Act 1968 the term 'goods' includes
money and *R*. v. *Dickinson*[121] dealt with the question whether gold
sovereigns were 'goods' within the meaning of the Defence of the
Realm Regulations, 30 E, 48 & 58, prohibiting an attempt to melt
down or use otherwise than as currency any current coin and giving
power to order forfeiture of such 'goods'. As it was found that 'it
was intended to put these sovereigns into a crucible and melt them
down',[122] it was held that they were goods.

On the other hand, often in an individual transaction things
which generally are and remain money are in fact used as commodities rather than as media of exchange. Money in a bag, being
sold per weight,[123] or a coin, being purchased as a curiosity,[124]
cannot be described as money for the purposes of the respective
transaction.[125] Money is in these cases not intended to be a medium
of exchange.

The authorities referred to were ignored and the wrong test was
applied by the European Court of Justice in *R*. v. *Thompson*.[126]
The question was whether (i) Krugerrands which the Advocate-
General M. Henri Mayras wrongly described as being 'in principle
legal tender in South Africa',[127] (ii) silver alloy coins such as pre-
1947 English coins of sixpence, one shilling and two shillings which
are still legal tender in the United Kingdom, and (iii) silver alloy
coins such as half-crowns which ceased to be legal tender, but are

---

[121] [1920] 3 K.B. 553; see also *R*. v. *Goswani*, [1968] 2 W.L.R. 1163.

[122] At p. 555 *per* Bray J.

[123] Cf. *Taylor* v. *Plumer* (1815), 3 M. & S. 562, and the remarks of Bankes L.J. in
*Banque Belge* v. *Hambrouck*, [1921] 1 K.B. 321, 326.

[124] *Moss* v. *Hancock*, [1899] 2 Q.B. 111. See also *Morris* v. *Ritchie* (1934), N.Z.L.R.
196, a decision which rests on the distinction between gold coins as commodities rather
than currency: 'The giving of 30*s*. in exchange for a gold sovereign is a purchase of that
sovereign. It is taken by the purchaser not as a current coin of the realm, but as a piece of
gold.' See above, p. 19.

[125] In the case of *Gay's Gold* (1872), 13 Wall. 358, the Supreme Court of the United
States held gold coins in a package to be 'goods wares and merchandize' within the meaning
of a certain statute. The New York courts also held that in certain circumstances gold coins
were the subject-matter of a sale requiring the application of the Statute of Frauds: *Peabody*
v. *Speyers* (1874), 56 N.Y. 230; *Fowler* v. *New York Gold Exchange Bank* (1867), 67 N.Y.
138 at p. 146. But during the inflation it was held in Germany that, if the plaintiff's servant
stole his master's German gold coins and sold them to the defendant at a much higher price
than their nominal value, the latter was not liable to return them to the plaintiff, because
the gold coins were regarded as money: Dresden Court of Appeal, 19 Jan. 1922, *Bankarchiv*,
xxii. 241. The decision is criticized by Breit in Düringer–Hachenburg, *Kommentar zum
Handelsgestzbuch*, iv. 1000 and Nussbaum, 35 (1937) *Mich. L.R.* 865, 905, and must surely
be wrong, because in the particular context the gold coins were not issued as money but as
commodities. A better view was taken by the German Supreme Finance Court, which held
that a turnover tax was payable where gold coins were sold as a commodity: 31 Jan. 1922,
*Entscheidungen des Reichsfinanzhofs*, 8, 100.

[126] (1980), All E.R. 102. See also below p. 64.

[127] p. 51. They are not legal tender: above p. 20.

not allowed to be melted down,[128] were 'goods' within the meaning of Art. 30 of the Treaty of Rome. As to (i) the Court held that on money markets these coins 'are treated as being equivalent to currency',—a factually very doubtful and unproven statement; they were therefore held to be the object of 'a monetary transfer' outside Art. 30. The same applied to (ii), but in regard to (iii) it was said that they could not 'be regarded as means of payment' and therefore were goods the trade in which according to Art. 30 was in general unrestricted, but the exportation of which could be prohibited under Art. 36 on account of 'the need to protect the right to mint coinage which is traditionally regarded as involving the fundamental interests of the State.'[129] The Court ought to have asked whether in the context of the particular transaction the coins were used as objects of commerce or currency. All of them were clearly used as goods. In any event the Court should have answered the oddly formulated questions of the Court of Appeal (Criminal Division) in England by directing it to decide upon the application of Art. 30 in the light of the question whether *in casu* the coins were dealt with by way of trade or by way of payment. In so far as point (i) relating to Krugerrands is concerned the same facts had to be considered by the Court of Appeal in *Allgemeine Gold & Silberscheideanstalt* v. *Commissioners of Customs & Excise,*[130] when they became clearer. The plaintiffs as owners claimed the Krugerrands which the defendants in *R. v. Thompson* had purported to purchase from them for £80 a piece, but in fact obtained by fraud and then smuggled into England, so that the Customs authorities claimed to be entitled to forfeit the coins under s. 52 of the Customs and Excise Act 1952. Their right to do so depended on the Krugerrands being 'goods'. In the circumstances the smugglers clearly obtained and handled them as metal at a market value of £80 rather than as currency at a sterling value of about 60p per rand. The Court of Appeal was for this reason fully entitled to treat the coins as subject to forfeiture, irrespective of the historical interpretation of the word 'goods' in customs legislation and irrespective of the unsatisfactory decision of the European Court of Justice.[131]

---

[128] Coinage Act 1971, s. 10.

[129] p. 71. On this basis a decision on the Art. 30 could have been dispensed with.

[130] (1980), Q.B. 390.

[131] In *R. v. Behm*, the Quebec Court of Appeal correctly held Canadian silver coins to be 'goods', the Chief Justice making the clear distinction between coins as instruments of exchange and coins as 'the substance of which money is constituted': 12 (1970) D.L.R. (3d) 260. For a case in which money was 'goods' within the meaning of an insurance policy see *Prudential Staff Union* v. *Hall*, [1947] K.B. 685.

## IV

The foregoing considerations are concerned with the question, in what circumstances may circulating objects rightly be described as money? They have, however, nothing to do with a different problem; what is money in an abstract sense, what is its essence, its intrinsic attribute, its inherent quality?

The answer given by economic theory is that money is 'wealth power', is 'purchasing power in terms of wealth in general'.[132] This conception deserves to be, and has been, approved of by the law.

As far as can be ascertained, the first lawyer to express it was Savigny:[133]

In the first place money appears in the function of a mere instrument for measuring the value of individual parts of wealth. As regards this function, money stands on the same basis as other instruments of measurement. . . . But money also appears in a second and higher function, viz. it embraces the value itself which is measured by it, and thus it represents the value of all other items of wealth. Therefore ownership over money gives the same power which assets measured thereby are able to give, and money thus appears to be an abstract means to dissolve all property into mere quantities. Therefore money gives its owner a general wealth power, applicable to all objects of free intercourse, and in its second function it appears as an independent bearer of such power, placed at the side of, and equivalent to, and equally efficient as all particular objects of wealth. Such wealth power, characterizing money, has, moreover, the attribute of being independent of individual abilities and necessities, and consequently of having equal usefulness for all and under all circumstances.

The idea that, according to its intrinsic nature, money is abstract purchasing power, though not unopposed, has been widely accepted by German jurists,[134] and it has also been expressed by Lord Macmillan when he said[135] that money[136] is 'purchasing power in terms of commodities', Indeed, it is a useful guide for appreciating one of the

---

[132] R. G. Hawtrey, *Encyclopædia Britannica*, 14th ed. xv. 693. It is needless to say that this view is not undisputed.        [133] *Obligationenrecht*, i. 405.

[134] Wolff, *Geld*, p. 569; Düringer–Hachenburg–Breit, iv, pp. 742 sqq. See also G. Simmel, *Die Philosophie des Geldes*, (3rd ed., 1920), pp. 87 sqq., where he also discusses the reciprocity and relativity as a feature of the essence of money, the conclusion being that (p. 98) money is 'die entschiedenste Sichtbarkeit, die deutlichste Wirklichkeit der Formel des allgemeinen Seins, nach der die Dinge ihren Sinn *aneinander* finden und die Gegenseitigkeit der Verhältnisse, in denen sie schweben, ihr Sein und Sosein ausmacht' (the most decisive image, the clearest reality of the formula of all being, according to which things acquire their meaning by their relation to each other and the reciprocity of the surroundings in which they find themselves signifies their existence and quality). An English translation of Simmel's work, *The Philosophy of Money*, by Bottomore and Frisby appeared only in 1978. The above sentence is based on, but slightly different from, the translation at pp. 128, 129 of that work.

[135] *Banco de Portugal* v. *Waterlow & Sons*, [1932] A.C. 452, 508.

[136] Lord Macmillan spoke of issued notes, but his remark applied to money in general.

essential features of the memorable case of *Banco de Portugal* v. *Waterlow & Sons Limited*,[137] the principal facts of which were as follows: The defendants were employed by the plaintiffs, the Portuguese bank of issue, to print a series of bank notes, known as Vasco da Gama 500 escudo notes, and they develivered 600,000 of these to the plaintiffs, who put them into circulation. Subsequently, an ingenious criminal managed to obtain from the defendants 580,000 notes of the same type, printed from the original plates and indistinguishable from the first set. A great part of these notes was put into circulation in Portugal, but when the plaintiffs discovered the circulation of these unauthorized notes, they withdrew the whole of the issue of Vasco da Gama notes and undertook to exchange them for other notes. When the plaintiffs brought an action against the defendants in the English courts, many difficult questions connected with the measure of damages and banking law fell to be decided. But one of the most important problems was whether the plaintiffs were entitled to damages on the basis of the face value of the genuine notes issued by them in exchange for unauthorized notes, or whether the damages suffered by them consisted only of the cost of printing notes to replace the genuine notes with which they had parted. The latter view commended itself to Scrutton L.J. in the Court of Appeal and to Lords Warrington and Russell of Killowen in the House of Lords, while the former view was accepted by a majority both in the Court of Appeal (Greer and Slesser L.JJ.) and in the House of Lords (Lords Sankey, Atkin, and Macmillan). In this connection it is of special interest to note that Lord Atkin as well as Lord Macmillan made it clear that, having regard to their note-issuing power, the plaintiffs, when issuing the new notes, were parting with and putting into circulation a portion of their wealth, or in other words, were parting with money.[138] Thus Lord Macmillan said:[139]

In my opinion this argument (that the Bank had only sacrificed some stationery) is fallacious. It overlooks the cardinal fact that a note when issued by the Bank of Portugal becomes by the mere fact of its issue legal tender for the sum which it bears on its face. The issued note represents so much purchasing power in terms of commodities. It can be used by the holder of it to purchase at current prices any commodity in the market, including gold and securities. It can equally be used by the Bank to purchase commodities, including gold and securities, or to discharge debts due by it. It must be accepted by the Bank in discharge of debts due to it.

[137] [1932] A.C. 452; on this case see Sir Cecil Kisch, *The Portuguese Bank Note Case* (London, 1932); R. G. Hawtrey, 52 (1932) *Economic Journal*, 391; M. T. Hollond, 5 (1932) *Cambridge L.J.* 91 (all of them from the point of view of economics).

[138] Lord Atkin, pp. 487 sqq.; Lord Macmillan, pp. 507 sqq.　　　[139] p. 508.

Or to quote Lord Atkin:[140]

I therefore find the position to be that the Bank by issuing its note like the trader issues its promise to pay a fixed sum: issues a bit of its credit to that amount; like the trader, it is bound to pay the face value in currency; like the trader it is liable on default to judgment for the face value exigible out of its assets; and like the trader, if it is compelled by the wrong of another to incur that liability, its damages are measured by the liability it has incurred.

These words also permit the general conclusion that according to its intrinsic nature money represents purchasing power.[141]

---

[140] p. 489.

[141] Nussbaum's criticism of the decision of the House of Lords (pp. 84 sqq.) is mainly based on the fact that in normal circumstances a bank of issue cannot create the conditions of issue by its own action, but discounts commercial paper offered to it. The author concludes that the only loss suffered by the bank was the discounting profit and the cost of printing new notes. But the loss suffered by the bank was measured by the increase of its liabilities resulting from the necessity for issuing new notes in replacement of the discredited Vasco da Gama notes. In other words, the bank paid both the genuine and the spurious notes. The decision was, therefore, clearly correct.

# II

# The Monetary System,
## its Organization and Incidents

I. Introduction. II. Sterling within the international legal order: (1) the gold standard before 1931; (2) the gold parity standard of Bretton Woods; (3) the international monetary system since 1978. III Sterling within the British legal order. IV. Types of currency: (1) convertible and inconvertible currency; (2) legal tender. V. The unit of account and its definition. VI. Changes in the monetary system. VII. Monetary systems with common characteristics: identity and diversity. VIII. Changes in the value of the unit of account. IX. Eurocurrency.

## I

CHIEFLY in the course of the nineteenth century almost all States enacted legislation with a view to organizing their respective currencies. This led to the creation of monetary systems as they are familiar to the modern world. It does not fall within the scope of a discussion of the legal problems of money to describe in detail the numerous matters which are included in the organization of a monetary system; methods of issuing money, forms or symbols of money, the composition of coins, standards of fineness, limits of error, remedy allowances — these are some of the elements of a monetary system which the legislator has to take care of and which economists have often described.[1] The system usually comprises a central bank enjoying peculiar privileges and functions[2] and the creation of monetary reserves, including gold (though it cannot any longer be described as 'monetary gold'[3]), but, again, these are aspects which tend to fall

---

[1] Mainly in the older literature: see, for instance, the exhaustive discussion by Helfferich, *Money*, pp. 352 sqq. On the modern monetary system and its framework, see Otto Veit, *Grundriss der Währungspolitik* (3rd ed., 1969), a comprehensive and valuable work which, it seems, has no counterpart in the English language. The international system, in particular, is lucidly discussed by a Swiss author, Franz E. Aschinger, *Das Währungssystem des Westens* (1971) and *Das Neue Währungssystem* (1978).

[2] Much material is collected by Aufricht, *Central Banking Legislation*, vol. i (1961), vol. ii (1967). It was analysed by Aufricht, *Comparative Survey of Central Banking Law* (1965). See also M. H. de Kock, *Central Banking* (4th ed., 1974); Oswald Hahn, *Die Währungsbanken der Welt*, vol. i (1968).

[3] This term was used in the Final Act of the Paris Conference on Reparations signed in Jan. 1946 (Cmd. 7173), and was later defined as 'all gold which at the time of its looting or wrongful removal was carried as part of the claimant country's monetary reserve'': see *Dollfus Mieg & Cie* v. *Bank of England*, [1949] 1 Ch. 369, at p. 374. The question in what circumstances 'monetary gold' could be said to 'belong' to a particular country was decided

within the scope of constitutional rather than monetary law. What has to be dealt with here and may give rise to problems confronting the practising lawyer is the legislation regulating the international and national order applicable to sterling and its value as well as the identity of the unit of account which is the basic feature of every monetary system. These and certain incidental matters to which it is now necessary to turn will have to be viewed against the background of the historical development without which they cannot be understood and which may throw light on future, as yet unforeseeable events, for the present state of an almost complete lack of legal obligation is unlikely to continue for ever.

## II

1. The gold standard, in its historically older function of the regulator or stabilizer of the (international) value of money in general and sterling in particular, originated in England in the eighteenth century, when, on the basis of a Proclamation of 1717 fixing the price of a guinea at 21 shillings, 'it came to be recognized that gold had definitely supplanted silver as the standard upon the basis of a guinea weighing 129.4 gr. at 21s. 0d. or at a Mint price of £3. 17s. 10½d. per standard ounce'.[4] By 1819 this figure of £3. 17s. 10½d. an ounce had come 'to be regarded as a magic price for gold from which we ought never to stray and to which, if we do, we must always return';[5] and when Peel's Act[6] put an end to the Bank Restriction period under which the country had laboured since the events of 1797,[7] this was effected by providing[8] that as from 1 May 1823[9] all restrictions upon cash payments were to cease and that the Bank was to pay its notes at par, i.e. at £3. 17s. 10½d. This, then, was the gold specie standard in the classical sense of the term: it put the Bank of England under a statutory obligation to pay for all its notes in specie.[10] In England it continued until 1914

by Professor Sauser-Hall 'in an economic, functional sense': *Case of Gold Looted by Germany from Rome*, International L.R. 1953, 441. Even on this footing it is difficult to follow how the gold in issue in *Dollfus Mieg & Cie* v. *Bank of England*, [1952] A.C. 582 could ever be treated as monetary gold; see Mann, *Rec.* 96 (1959, i) 14–17. On the question of definition see the preceding note and also the decision of the Italian-Dutch Conciliation Commission (with Professor Paul Guggenheim as President) of 17 Aug. 1963, Annuaire Suisse de Droit International, 1963, 135, 148 sqq., also Int. L.R. 44,448 and *Rep.* Int. Arbitral Awards XVI, 301.                                     [4] Feavearyear, p. 154.
    [5] Ibid., pp. 148, 149.                                           [6] 59 Geo. III, ch. 49.
    [7] 37 Geo. III, chs. 28, 32, 40.                        [8] See s. IV.
    [9] By 1 & 2 Geo. IV, ch. 26, the date was fixed as from 1 May, 1821.
    [10] s. 6 of the Bank of England Act, 1833, repealed by s. 4 of the Currency and Bank Notes Act, 1954.

when it ceased to exist *de facto*.[11] When the monetary disturbances caused by the First World War were sought to be eliminated by legislation,[12] it was the gold bullion standard which was adopted by the provision[13] that only the Bank should be entitled to bring gold to the Mint and have it coined and that, so long as this provision was in force, the Bank should be required to sell gold bars of about 400 ounces of fine gold to any purchaser who tendered £3. 17s. 10½d. an ounce. The Gold Standard (Amendment) Act, 1931, relieved the Bank of its duty to sell gold for the notes issued by it and thus led to the abandonment of the gold standard.[14] For a time this country lived under a monetary system that lacked any connecting link with gold for the purpose of valuing the pound. Its value was maintained by the operations of the Exchange Equalization Fund.[15]

2. After the end of the Second World War the British monetary system rested upon this country's membership of the International Monetary Fund.[16] Under Art. IV, Section 1 of the Articles of Agreement concluded at Bretton Woods the 'par value' of the currency of each member shall be expressed in terms of gold as a common denominator or in terms of the United States dollar of the weight and fineness in effect on 1 July 1944.[17] On 18 December 1946 the par value of sterling was fixed at 3.58134 grams of fine gold or 4.03 U.S. dollars per pound sterling, but as from 18 September 1949 it

---

[11] The Currency and Bank Notes Act, 1914, permitted the issue of currency notes of £1 and 10s. without imposing any quantitative limitations or any duty to keep a reserve. The notes were legal tender and *de jure* convertible, but gold disappeared from circulation.

[12] Gold Standard Act, 1925.          [13] s. 1.          [14] s. 1.

[15] Created by ss. 24 and 25 of the Finance Act, 1932 (as amended by s. 1. of the Currency (Defence) Act, 1939), but see now the Exchange Equalisation Act 1979.

[16] Cmd. 6546. The Articles of Agreement were ratified, yet they were not incorporated into the law of the United Kingdom, by the Bretton Woods Agreement Act, 1945. This is one of the many cases in which Britain is, or believes herself to be, able to give effect to international obligations by mere executive action. The system set up at Bretton Woods and very shortly summarized in the text has often been described, mainly be economists, but also by a few lawyers. As a result of the Second Amendment to which reference is made below pp. 34, 507, 515 most of the enormous literature is obsolete. Reference should, however, be made to J. Keith Horsefield, *The International Monetary Fund 1945-1965*, three volumes of which the second ('Analysis') is the most important one; Margaret G. de Vries, *The International Monetary Fund 1966-1971*, two volumes; Carreau, *Le Fonds Monétaire International* (1970) and *Le Système Monétaire International* (1972); Carreau, Juillard et Flory, *Droit International Economique* (2nd ed., 1980) pp. 99 sqq.; Fawcett, *British Year Book of International Law 1964*, 32; Hexner, 'The New Gold Standard', *Weltwirtschaftliches Archiv*, 1960, 1; *Das Verfassungs und Rechtssystem des Internationalen Währungsfonds* (1960); Petersmann, *Zeitschrift für ausländisches öffentliches Recht und Völkerrecht*, 34 (1974) 452, and *WiR* 1974, 119; Shuster, *The Public International Law of Money* (1973) pp. 116 sqq. In addition there are the writings of Sir Joseph Gold on most aspects of the Fund — five books, more than twenty pamphlets (all published by the Fund) and innumerable articles in periodicals. Many of these publications are referred to in the latest pamphlet, *The Rule of Law in the International Monetary Fund* (1980).

[17] This was 0.888671 grams per dollar: see below, p. 33, n. 24.

was reduced to 2.48828 grams of fine gold (or 2·80 U.S. dollars), and a little more than eighteen years later, on 18 November 1967, it was further reduced to 2·13281 grams (or 2·40 dollars).[18]

The par value determined the price of gold sold and bought[19] as well as the rates for exchange transactions among member States. Moreover, the members were under a duty (which the United Kingdom discharged by the administration of the Exchange Control Act, 1947) to permit within their territories foreign exchange dealings only within narrow limits based on parity.[20] A member 'shall not propose a change in the par value of its currency except to correct a fundamental disequilibrium'. A change in excess of 10 per cent of the original par value required the Fund's authority; it could not be withheld if the proposed change arose from a fundamental disequilibrium.[21]

[18] See *Schedule of Par Values*, up to 1971 published yearly by the International Monetary Fund, Washington D.C.

[19] Art. IV, Section 2: 'The Fund shall prescribe a margin above and below par value for transactions in gold by members, and no member shall buy gold at a price above par value plus the prescribed margin or sell gold at a price below par value minus the prescribed margin.' The interpretation of this provision was open to much doubt. Did par values apply to all 'transactions in gold' taking place within the territories of members, as in the case of exchange dealings under Section 3, or only to transactions to which members were parties? The wording and the practice of the Fund supported the latter construction, but the general duty under Section 4 (a) of promoting exchange stability may on occasions have required a different result. Or were members at liberty to sell gold at a premium to, or buy gold at a discount from, non-members? The Fund seemed to think that such transactions were permitted, though they may have been undesirable. Yet Section 2 might be read as prohibiting them. On the question of interpretation see Zehetner, *AWD* 1973, 666.

[20] Art. IV, s. 3: 'The maximum and the minimum rates for exchange transactions between the currencies of members taking place within their territories shall not differ from parity (i) in the case of spot exchange transactions, by more than one per cent.; and (ii) in the case of other exchange transactions by more than the Fund considers reasonable.' Canada in the 1950s and later other states allowed their respective currencies (the par values of which remained unchanged) to 'float', i.e. to have variable rates outside the limits prescribed by Art. IV, s. 3. It is impossible to reconcile such a practice with the mandatory terms of Art. IV, s. 3. Neither the Fund nor its Managing Director had the power to 'approve' it except by the process of amendment of the Articles of Agreement. The fact that such practices occurred and had to be tolerated by the Fund should be an instructive warning to lawyers: the necessarily limited power of the law in the field of international economics should not be disguised by seemingly rigid rules. As late as 1976 Sir Joseph Gold said correctly that floating constituted a breach of the treaty and an illegality and that the Fund was unable to 'give it validity': *The Record* of the Association of the Bar of the city of New York 1976, 230. The suggestion that acquiescence *contra legem* could have a legitimating effect is irreconcilable with generally acceptable principles, but has frequently been made: Tomuschat, *Die Aufwertung der Deutschen Mark* (1970) 11; Petersmann, *WiR* 1974, 119, 140, 152; Hahn, 'Völkerrecht und internationale Zusammenarbeit', *Kiel Symposium*, (1976) 219 with further references, but against him most of the speakers at pp. 243 sqq.

[21] Art. IV, Section 5. The conception of 'fundamental disequilibrium' is so elusive and so often involves a subjective or value judgment that it is difficult to expect the Fund to withhold approval. It does not seem to have done so at any time since the Articles of Agreement came into force on 27 Dec. 1945. Although it is impossible to suggest that

This, therefore, was a type of gold standard which has aptly been described as a gold parity standard,[22] for, although bank notes were inconvertible, a large part of the Bank of England's purchases and sales of gold was subject to a fixed price. Accordingly, the value of sterling (or any other currency with a par value) was no less tied to gold than was, for example, the French franc of 1928 which was 'constitué par 65·5 milligrammes d'or au titre de 0·900 de fin',[23] or than was the United States dollar the weight of which was fixed at $15\frac{5}{21}$ grains of gold 9/10 fine or at $35 per ounce.[24] That the gold or par value of sterling could in certain circumstances be changed affected the firmness of the tie rather than its existence in principle. It could certainly be less freely changed than in earlier days.[25]

What, then, was in law the significance of the fact that the pound had a par value of 2·13281 grams, which Britain was not at liberty to change at discretion? The pound could not be said to mean 2·13281 grams of gold. On the other hand, the system of Bretton Woods involved more than a mere programme or the enunciation of a policy. Rather it defined the price which, subject to marginal variations, the Bank of England must pay or receive if it agreed to buy gold from, or sell gold to, other members of the Fund , and on which all foreign exchange transactions must be based. It was the existence of a treaty obligation to maintain the par value that in law was the essential ingredient of the gold parity standard.[26]

Bretton Woods left the members' monetary sovereignty intact, it is as well to realize that its system was in some respects not wholly effective in practice.

[22] Lord Crowther (above, p. 5, n. 12), p. 280.

[23] Art 2 of the Statute of 25 June 1928.

[24] Proclamation of 31 Jan. 1934 (No. 2072, 48 *Statutes at Large*, 1730).

[25] Hawtrey, *Currency and Credit* (4th ed., 1950), pp. 148, 211, 431, seems to see in Bretton Woods a gold exchange standard, while Lord Keynes denied that Bretton Woods involved any type of gold standard, because 'the use of gold merely as a common denominator by means of which the relative values of national currencies—these being free to change —are expressed, is obviously, quite another matter': *Parliamentary Debates, House of Lords*, 23 May 1944, vol. cxxxi, col. 845. But the duty to effect transactions in gold and foreign exchange at fixed prices based on gold is commonly regarded as a feature of the gold standard. Charles Rist, *Histoire des Doctrines relatives au Crédit et à la Monnaie* (2nd ed., 1951), p. 498, describes Lord Keynes's argument as 'plus spécieux que convainquant'. Harrod, *Money* (1969) p. 68, Keynes' biographer, correctly says that members of the International Monetary Fund 'were on the gold standard', but does not mention the statement referred to above.

[26] It was suggested that a modification of par value, though unauthorised in cases in which approval is required, 'is not considered as a failure to fulfil an obligation under the Fund Agreement': see Report of the Monetary Law Committee of the International Law Association for the 53rd Conference at Buenos Aires, 1968 (Report, p. 657) and Sir Joseph Gold who speaks of a serious departure from the treaty as opposed to a breach: American Journal of International Law 1971, 120. Although earlier he thought that 'a member cannot validly change the par value for its currency without consulting the Fund' (*The International Monetary Fund and Private Business Transactions* (1965) p. 4), his later view is accepted by Meyer and Stadtmüller, *Zeitschrift für Handelsrecht* 138 (1972)

3. The original Bretton Woods system broke down, when on 15 August 1971 President Nixon abolished the convertibility of dollar into gold.[27] During the following years the terms of the system set up in Bretton Woods were necessarily and universally disregarded.[28] In particular, all currencies, including sterling, 'floated', that is to say, failed to observe the parities conforming to the Articles of Agreement or, indeed, any fixed parities. The details of the development and the palliatives devised to minimize the disaster that had occurred are lucidly described by Kerr J. in *Lively & Co.* v. *City of Munich*,[29] where it was held that, irrespective of the formal position, in a commercial sense by 1 December 1973 no par value system was 'in force'.

Eventually, as a result of the Second Amendment of the Articles of Agreement[30] which entered into effect on 1 April 1978 the International Monetary Fund became primarily a credit institution or a bank in that it retained the function to provide or procure international credit or 'liquidity' for the benefit of member States by transactions under Art. V and by the use of Special Drawing Rights under Articles XVI to XXV of the Articles of Agreement. The Fund's powers and tasks as a monetary institution, on the other

31, 35 who, however, describe it as 'extraordinarily paradoxical'. Similarly Petersmann, WiR 1974, 119, 128. In truth an unauthorised change, had it ever occurred, would have been a clear breach of treaty: Mann, 'The Binding Character of the Gold Parity Standard', in *Jus Privatum Gentium (Festschrift für Max Rheinstein)* (1969), i. 483. Sir Joseph's special pleading was unacceptable.

[27] This is likely to have involved a breach of the Bretton Woods treaty: Jackson, *American Journal of International Law*, 1972, 110; Zehetner, *Die Suspendierung der Goldkonvertibilität des Dollars* (Vienna, 1973).

[28] On 18 December 1971 by the so-called Smithsonian Agreement the International Monetary Fund set up a temporary régime of 'practices that members may wish to follow in present circumstances'. For the text see *Selected Decisions of the International Monetary Fund* (Eighth Issue, 1978) pp. 14–21. These practices which provided for so-called central rates were, of course, *contra* or at least *extra legem*. Cf. the decision of the European Court of Justice in *Fratelli Zerbone* v. *Amministrazione delle Finanze*, European Court Reports 1978, 99, a singularly difficult decision which even in the light of illuminating submissions by the Advocate General Warner is almost incomprehensible. It is, however, clear that the Court refused to regard the Smithsonian Agreement as 'international rules' within the meaning of Regulation 974/71 (*Official Journal* 1, 106). Such character was rightly attributed only to the Articles of Agreement themselves. For further comment on the decision see below, p. 61.

[29] (1976) 1 W.L.R. 1004.

[30] Cmnd. 7331. On the Second Amendment see, in particular, Edwards, *American Journal of International Law* 1976, 722; Joseph Gold, *The Second Amendment and the Fund's Articles of Agreement* (Pamphlet No. 25, 1978); *The Conversion and Exchange of Currency under the Second Amendment* (Pamphlet No. 23, 1978); Albrecht Weber, 'Die Zweite Satzungsreform des Internationalen Währungsfonds und das Völkerrecht', *International Law and Economic Order (Essays in honour of F. A. Mann)*, (1977) p. 807. Focsaneanu, Clunet 1978, 805; Hahn, in *Völkerrecht und internationale wirtschaftliche Zusammenarbeit*, ed. by Kewenig, (Berlin 1978), p. 215.

hand, are now hardly more than nominal in character and effect, however wordily and grandiosely they may have been expressed in the amended Art. IV. The par value system is abolished and cannot be reintroduced except, in a modified form, by an eighty-five per cent majority of the total voting power. Gold has suffered 'demone-tisation' to such an extent that exchange arrangements which a member State may wish to apply may include any 'denominator, other than gold, selected by the member'.[31] Instead 'each member undertakes to collaborate with the Fund and other members to assure orderly exchange arrangements and to promote a stable system of exchange rates'.[32] Moreover, the Fund has the right of 'surveillance' over exchange arrangements, i.e. it 'shall oversee the international monetary system in order to ensure its effective opera-tion and shall oversee the compliance of each member with its obligations' of collaboration.[33] It is to be hoped that the protagonists of the Fund will refrain from overstraining the legal efficacy of such phrases, for if, as was to be expected,[34] even the strict terms of the original Bretton Woods system were unable to protect it against an economic crisis, verbiage will to an even lesser degree achieve the performance of duties by an unwilling or disabled member State.

If, therefore, the International Monetary Fund does not now provide or require a fixed, though by no means unchangeable, standard to which sterling is linked[35] the international value of sterling depends partly on market forces, that is to say on demand and supply or, in the last resort, on the confidence of investors, and partly on the operations of Britain's monetary authorities who, by the purchase and sale of currency, intervene to influence prices. In the absence of any legally binding relationship the price of sterling, like that of the majority of currencies, is in fact measured by or linked or pegged to the dollar of the United States of America. In order to accomplish this the authorities dispose of the Exchange Equalisation Account[36] the first, though not the only, purpose of which is 'checking undue fluctuations in the exchange value of

---

[31] Art. IV Section 2 (b).

[32] Art. IV Section 1.

[33] Art. IV Section 3. The actual text of the Section as well of that referred to in the preceding note is much longer and in the words of Edwards (above n. 30) p. 733 reads 'more like a press communiqué than a formal statement of legal obligations'.

[34] Cf. Mann, 'Money in Public International Law', Rec. 96 (1959 i) 21, 22.

[35] It is remarkable that already at this early stage the Fund is advocating the Special Drawing Right (SDR) as being placed 'on a course to becoming the general standard of international value': Silard, IMF Survey 1979, 159 and Proceedings of the American Society of International Law 1979, 15. It is, however, unlikely that SDRs can be described or will be acceptable as 'a general standard of international value'. For the reasons see below, pp. 159, 505.          [36] Exchange Equalisation Account Act 1979.

sterling'.[37] The funds in the Account, it is interesting to note, may be invested not only in 'securities and assets in currency of any country' and special drawing rights, but also 'in the purchase of gold'[38] the official price of which on 14 August 1971 was $35 per ounce and the commercial price of which was then about $125 and is in May 1981 about $475 per ounce.

### III

The second function of the gold standard was to regulate and limit the volume of money by the requirement of the note issue being backed by a quantity of gold held in reserve as security. The gold standard in this sense has also disappeared[39] and is, therefore, again of historical interest only.

The requirement of a gold reserve formed another of the principal points of debate between the Currency and the Banking Schools of the 1830s. The former believed that the amount of issued notes should always be identical with the amount of gold held by the issuing bank. The latter held that the note issue did not have to be regulated, but regulated itself.[40] The Bank Charter Act, 1844, established a compromise by providing that the newly created Issue Department of the Bank should limit the amount of circulating notes to the value of the bullion and coin held by it and £14 million backed by securities.[41] This is the birth of the 'fiduciary issue' which is independent of gold.[42] The Bank can now issue notes up to the amount of its gold and, in addition, of the fiduciary note issue[43] which in 1954 was £1,575 million and has since been successively increased, so that in the middle of 1981 it stood at no less than £10,700 million. It is secured by the Bank's duty to 'appropriate to and hold in' the Issue Department securities of an amount sufficient to cover it.[44] The Bretton Woods Agreement

---

[37] s. 1 (3) (a).                                                                                          [38] s. 3.

[39] The Government's function in issuing notes is now 'simply the passive one of ensuring that sufficient notes are available for the practical convenience of the public': Radcliffe Report (Cmnd. 827, August 1959), paragraph 348. This must not be understood to mean that the printing press can safely by allowed to operate freely.

[40] For a detailed description see, for example, Feavearyear, pp. 261 sqq.

[41] s. II. An increase was possible under s. V.

[42] The type of limitation described in the text originated in England. Another more usual method required a minimum proportion of gold reserves varying between 30 and 40 per cent. For a comparative survey of the enactments in force in 1932 see Kisch and Elkin, *Central Banks* (London, 1932), pp. 82 sqq. In the United States the reserve was 25 per cent. (Reserve Ratio Act, 1945, s. 1 (a), 59 *Statutes at Large*, 237) until 1968, when reserve requirements were abolished altogether: *International Legal Materials*, vii (1968), 402.

[43] Currency and Bank Notes Act, 1954, s. 2.

[44] The expression 'securities' is defined by s. 25 (7) of the Finance Act, 1932, as amended

contains no provision for the limitation or the security of the member States' bank notes.[45]

The question whether provisions for the tangible cover of the fiduciary issue, where they exist, afford any protection to the individual holders of notes, must be answered in the negative. A different idea, it is true, has sometimes been expressed, though not necessarily as a legal proposition. Napoleon and his Ministers used to refer to the 'gage' underlying bank notes;[46] in the United States the Gold Standard Act, 1900, provided[47] that the reserves 'shall be used for the redemption of the notes and certificates for which they are respectively pledged and shall be used for no other purpose, the same being held as trust funds'; British legislation, speaking of securities appropriated to and held in the Issue Department, alludes to a similar conception. Yet these formulations merely address administrative directions and prohibitions to the monetary authorities without conferring any rights upon the holder. This was made clear with regard to Imperial Russia by the decision in the remarkable case of *Marshall* v. *Grinbaum*.[48] The Russian currency reform of 1897 included a decree providing that notes must be secured by gold to the extent of 50 per cent of a total issue not exceeding 600 million roubles and that notes issued in excess of such limit must be secured by gold 'rouble for rouble'. A holder of notes (which under Russian law were legal tender and exchangeable at the State Bank for equivalent amounts in gold) claimed a charge upon gold belonging to the State Bank, but held by the defendant. Peterson J., rejecting the existence of a charge, said of the Russian decrees that[49] their

aim was to maintain the value of the notes by making them exchangeable for gold, and, in order to make this right of exchange effective, the Minister of Finance, as custodian of the State Bank, was prohibited from issuing notes without keeping the gold reserve up to the prescribed amount. Where the ukase speaks of the notes being 'secured by gold' or of the issue of notes 'against a gold security' or of 'the amount of gold securing the notes', it does not contemplate the creation of a charge or mortgage in favour of the holders of credit notes;

---

by the Exchange Equalisation Act 1979, and comprises, of course, government paper. There is therefore every justification for the remark that 'Peel's Act is nothing but a memory' (Charles Rist, *History of Monetary and Credit Theory* (London, 1940), p. 227) and 'since 1939 the gold reserve has played no part in the regulation of the note-issue which has become purely fiduciary' (R. S. Sayers, *Modern Banking* (Oxford, 1951), p. 105).

[45] But under Art. I the Fund must be guided by its purposes which include the promotion of exchange stability, the maintenance of orderly exchange arrangements and the avoidance of competitive exchange depreciation, and the adjustment of a disequilibrium.

[46] Mater, pp. 77–81.

[47] s. 4 (31 *Statutes at Large*, 45).

[48] (1921), 37 T.L.R. 913.

[49] p. 915.

it is merely making regulations for the issue of notes with the object of insuring that any holder who brings a note to the State Bank may receive the nominal amount of the note in gold.

Although or perhaps because the fiduciary issue is no longer backed by gold, the government retains complete control over it. Yet 'the government's function in issuing notes is simply the passive one of ensuring that sufficient notes are available for the practical convenience of the public'.[50] But the government does not in Britain directly control bank deposits or in other words what economists, looking to functional characteristics, regard as the creation or supply of money in the sense of transferable purchasing power only about eight per cent of which is traditionally represented by the fiduciary issue.[51] The government, it is true, determines fiscal policies or taxation as well as the size of the deposits owned by it and arising from the sale of government securities such as bonds or treasury bills issued to finance the public sector's expenditure. But such influence as it has or attempts to use is said to rest primarily on the manipulation of interest rates which are 'the centre-piece of monetary mechanism'[52] and on such additional measures as special deposits or limitations of credit facilities, which may be voluntarily arranged between the authorities and financial institutions and are, therefore, outside the scope of legal regulation and analysis.[53, 54]

## IV

Since sterling is no longer backed by any physical assets such as gold, it is obvious that the notes issued by the Bank of England are 'inconvertible'; yet British bank notes (as well as coins, including gold coins) are equally obviously legal tender.

1. Convertibility was a feature of those currency systems in which the standard money consisted of metal, generally gold, and in which any paper money that was also in circulation could always be exchanged for the standard money.[55] It is the function of such con-

---

[50] Above, n. 38.                    [51] R. F. Harrod, *Money* (1969) p. 36.

[52] Paragraph 397 of the Radcliffe Report.

[53] The matters touched upon in the text have been discussed at length by a vast number of economists. Most of their writings make difficult reading for a lawyer and do not much help him in discharging his function. For useful surveys see R. F. Harrod, *Money* (1969); Andrew Crockett, *Money* (1973) and *International Money* (1977); Newlyn and Bootle, *Theory of Money* (3rd ed., 1978).

[54] The Green Paper 'Monetary Control' published in March 1980 (Cmnd. 7858) considers a possible 'monetary base control system' of which more may be heard in the future.

[55] The term 'convertibility' may also be used to indicate the possibility of turning domestic into foreign currency. The absence or limitation of such possibility is a feature of exchange control. Convertibility in this sense, therefore, will be referred to below, p. 519.

vertibility to keep the paper money at its nominal value; for 'as long as this redeemability is not a dead letter, but an actuality, the value of the paper currency issued by the State, or of the bank notes issued by private individuals, cannot materially deviate from their nominal value expressed in terms of metallic currency. The value of the paper tokens is thus, indirectly, closely connected with the value of a specified quantity of metal which forms the basis of the existing currency system.'[56]

Convertibility, being so closely connected with the existence or non-existence of a metallic (especially a gold) standard,[57] has not existed in Britain for half a century. It had been an essential feature of the Bank of England Act, 1833,[58] but it was modified by the Gold Standard Act, 1925,[59] which exempted the Bank of England from liability to redeem its notes with gold coin and merely placed it under the obligation to sell gold bullion at a fixed price, and, moreover, granted to the Bank of England the exclusive right of obtaining coined gold from the Mint. It was this limited convertibility which was abolished by the Gold Standard (Amendment) Act, 1931.

Inconvertibility exonerates the bank of issue from paying its notes in gold and puts it merely under the obligation to pay them in currency, i.e. in its own notes, it being irrelevant whether an individual note was issued before or after the introduction of inconvertibility,[60] or whether it is held and situate inside or outside the country.[61] Therefore the promise 'to pay' which bank notes express

[56] Helfferich, p. 65; see also Gregory, *The Gold Standard and its Future*, 2nd ed. (London, 1932), pp. 1 sqq.

[57] See above, p. 30.

[58] 3 & 4 Will. IV, ch. 98.

[59] 15 & 16 Geo. V, ch. 29, s. 1.

[60] In Germany there existed at one time a considerable body of holders of old mark notes who, stirred up by demagogues, claimed that their notes, issued before the war legislation suspending convertibility, ought to be paid in gold. In two long judgments the Supreme Court disposed of this absurd contention: 20 May 1926, *RGZ*. 114, 27; 20 June 1929, *JW*. 1929, 3491.

[61] The law of the country to which the bank of issue is subject governs the obligations arising out of bank notes: *Marshall* v. *Grinbaum* (1921), 37 T.L.R. 913, 915 with regard to Russian bank notes; in the same sense with regard to German bank notes Italian Supreme Court, 28 Feb. 1939, A.D. 1938–40, No. 56 and *B.I.J.I.* 41 (1940), No. 11029 (affirming Court of Appeal Milan, 18 Feb. 1938, *B.I.J.I.* 40 (1939), 171 or Clunet, 1939, 171) and Dutch Supreme Court, *B.I.J.I.* 41 (1940), No. 10948. Yet it is sometimes maintained that the introduction of inconvertibility does not affect the position of foreign holders; but this doctrine is fallacious, as the alleged principle that monetary laws have no extraterritorial effect does not exist (see below, p. 267, n. 4). Where, however, the inability to redeem bank notes in gold is due to exchange restrictions rather than the introduction of inconvertibility —this was the position, e.g. in Germany, where the full convertibility established by s. 31 of the Bank Act of 30 August 1924 and by the decree of 17 Apr. 1930, *Reichsgesetzblatt*, 1930, ii. 691, was not interfered with until 1940—the courts of some countries will be

or imply[62] is of little significance after the introduction of inconvertibility. Nevertheless, inconvertibility does not make bank notes mere tokens of money, depriving them of their character as negotiable instruments.[63]

2. Legal tender is such money[64] in the legal sense as the legislator has so defined in the statutes organizing the monetary system. Chattels which are legal tender have, therefore, necessarily the quality of money, but, logically, the converse is not true,—not all money is necessarily legal tender.

The question what money is to be considered legal tender is usually answered by the statutes organizing the monetary system. As regards bank notes, although for a considerable time they had come to be treated as money,[65] the courts hesitated to decide that they also were legal tender. Since the Restriction Bill, 1797,[66] had been content to provide that bank notes should be 'deemed payments in cash, if made and accepted as such', it was possible to decide[67] that bank notes, in the absence of such agreement, were not legal tender. The

more readily disposed to enforce a claim for payment in gold: see below, pp. 401 sqq. On a bank of issue's right to sovereign immunity see Mann, *British Year Book of International Law* 1979, p. 60, n. 2 with fuller references and Gramlich, *RabelsZ.* 1981, 545.

[62] Above p. 9. The suggestion there made is described by Fögen, p. 17, as an error. He overlooks the passage in the text.

[63] Cf. *Banco de Portugal* v. *Waterlow & Sons* [1932] A.C. 452; also the German decisions quoted above, p. 39, n. 60, and p. 9, no. 31, and Breit in Düringer-Hachenburg, *Kommentar zum Handelsgesetzbuch*, iv. 746. Nussbaum, pp. 79, 80, is wrong in saying that after inconvertibility 'the debtor has disappeared' and the Bank's promise to 'pay' can only be explained in psychological terms. There remain many occasions when the Bank must 'pay', e.g. in case of an accidental alteration or when a particular issue is demonetized.

[64] In 1923 a Virginia court said in *Vick* v. *Howard*, 136 Va. 101, 109, that 'the authorities . . . clearly recognize the distinction between money which is, and money which is not, legal tender. In other words, all legal tender is money, but not all money is legal tender.' The latter part of this statement, on which the formulation in the text is based, is theoretically sound, as was recognized by Lord Campbell in *Emperor of Austria* v. *Day* (1861), 3 De G. F. & J. 217, 234: 'But they might pass as money without being legal tender.' But as far as this country is concerned the statement is of no practical importance, as (with the exception of foreign money which is money, but not legal tender, below, p. 186) at the present time no money circulates in England which is not legal tender. The position was different when there existed country bank notes. In Scotland and Northern Ireland, however, Bank of England notes for £5 or more would appear to be money, though they are not legal tender there (see p. 41 below). The first part of the above statement that all legal tender is money is justified, though it is opposed by Nussbaum, p. 55. Nussbaum's reasoning is based on historical examples which are of no actual significance and on cases which we preferred to solve by the admission that under certain circumstances money-things may lose the character of money and acquire that of a commodity: see above, pp. 19, 23, 24.

[65] See above pp. 7, 9, 11.                                   [66] 37 Geo. III, ch. 45.

[67] *Grigby* v. *Oakes* (1801), 2 Bos. & Pul. 527; see already *Lockyer* v. *Jones* (1796), Peake's N.P.C. 240 per Lord Kenyon. As to agreement to accept bank notes see *Brown* v. *Saul*, 4 Esp. 267. That country bank notes were good tender in case of agreement only was

position was remedied in 1811 and 1812,[68] and, after a short return to coins only,[69] it was provided[70] that notes of the Bank of England were legal tender for all sums above £5 'so long as the Bank of England shall continue to pay on demand their said notes in legal coin'. The present position results from the Currency and Bank Notes Act, 1954:[71] all Bank of England notes are now legal tender in England and Wales for the payment of any amount, but Bank of England notes of less than £5 only are legal tender in Scotland or Northern Ireland.

The legal tender quality of coins is defined by s. 2 of the Coinage Act 1971. Very significantly it provides that gold coins are legal tender for the payment of any amount,[72] while coins of denominations of more than 10 new pence are legal tender for payment of amounts not exceeding £10, coins of smaller denomination are legal tender for payment of amounts not exceeding £5 and coins of bronze for amounts not exceeding 20 new pence.[73]

Since in modern times legal tender is everywhere inconvertible (or irredeemable) in the sense discussed above, it constitutes what has been called forced[74] issue or compulsory tender or fiat money (*cours forcé, Zwangskurs*).

The effect of bank notes and coins having the quality of legal tender is that the creditor to whom the appropriate amount thereof is proffered and who refuses acceptance runs the risk of being

laid down in *Lockyer* v. *Jones* (1796), Peake's N.P.C. 239; *Tiley* v. *Courtier* (1817) not reported but referred to and approved of in *Polyglass* v. *Oliver* (1813), 2 Cr. & J. 15; see also above, p. 12, n. 55.

[68] 51 Geo. III, ch. 127; 52 Geo. III, ch. 50, extended by 53 Geo. III, ch. 5 and 54 Geo. III, ch. 52 until the resumption of cash payments.

[69] Lord Liverpool's Act, 56 Geo. III, ch. 68, s. 11.

[70] Bank of England Act, 1833, s. 6.          [71] s. 1, subsection 2.          [72] See above p. 19.

[73] s. 6 of the Coinage Act 1870 was already repealed by the Decimal Currency Act 1969. It read as follows: 'Every contract, sale, payment, bill, note, instrument and security for money, and every transaction, dealing, matter and thing whatever relating to money, or involving the payment of or the liability to pay any money, which is made, executed or entered into, done or had, shall be made, executed, or entered into, done and had according to the coins which are current and legal tender in pursuance of this Act, and not otherwise, unless the same be made, executed, entered into, done or had according to the currency of some British possession or some foreign state'. Similar provisions were and perhaps are in force in many countries of the Commonwealth, also in s. 14 of the South African Mint and Coinage Act 1964. The meaning of the section was doubtful: see Lord Tomlin in *Adelaide Electric Supply Co.* v. *Prudential Assurance Co.*, [1934] A.C. 122, 142 and Harman J. in *Treseder–Griffin* v. *Co-operative Insurance Society*, [1956] 2 Q.B. 127, at p. 142. It is submitted (and was explained at some length in earlier editions) that s. 6 was intended to ensure that no payment should be promised or made in a coin which had been called in by proclamation and was therefore not 'current and legal tender in pursuance of this Act'. It is unlikely that the point is now of any practical importance anywhere.

[74] This is the expression used by the translator of Helfferich, p. 65; as to the meaning of *cours forcé* see Nussbaum p. 56.

prejudiced in certain respects.[75] In this sense, therefore, it is, unless a different intention appears, incumbent on the creditor to accept legal tender in discharge of the debt (*cours légal, Annahmezwang*).


## V

After this brief survey of the more important aspects of a monetary system in general and the British monetary system in particular, it becomes necessary to consider more closely the unit of account[76] such as the pound sterling,[77] the dollar[78] or the franc,[79] that constitutes the basic feature of every monetary system.

'In all cases which occur in practice we deal with money in specific sums, in specific quantities, and not simply with money *per se*. Money, like all quantitive conceptions, such as length, weight, bulk, can only be expressed by a multiple or a fraction of a fixed unit. In our systems of linear measures a specific length, such as the metre or yard, functions as a unit in which all lengths can be expressed, just as in our system of weights a specific weight quantity, such as the gram, is the unit or standard by which all quantities are measured. In the same way money requires a specific quantity to serve as the unit in terms of which all sums of money can be expressed.'[80]

One of the principal legal questions is whether (to adopt a venerable adage occurring in the history of money) the unit of account is not only *mensura*, but also *mensuratum*, whether, in other words, the unit is merely a measure or is itself measured by something else, whether the currency system is independent of any other system of measurement or there exists a connecting link or tie between its unit and another substance, and whether in the latter event the organization of the monetary system produces consequences in the sphere of private law.

The problem what is to be understood by the unit of account, e.g. the pound or, as it is now statutorily described, the pound sterling,[81] presents itself in its most serious form when the currency system is in

---

[75] For details see below pp. 71, 72.

[76] The expression has become familiar to lawyers since Lord Sterndale M.R. used it in *Re Chesterman's Trusts*, [1923] 2 Ch. 466, at p. 477. The Australian Currency Act, 1963 speaks of 'the monetary unit or unit of currency': s. 8 (1).

[77] The standard work probably still is Sir Albert Feavearyear, *The Pound Sterling* (2nd ed. by E. Victor Morgan, 1963), though the discussion of the post-war system needs much elaboration.

[78] Arthur Nussbaum, *A History of the Dollar* (1958). The work by Milton Friedman and A. J. Schwartz, *A Monetary History of the United States 1867–1907* (1963), is written entirely from the point of view of the economist.

[79] René Sédillot, *Le Franc, Histoire d'une Monnaie* (Paris, 1953).

[80] Helfferich, p. 364.          [81] Decimal Currency Act, 1967, s. 1 (1).

no way based on metal but merely on inconvertible paper, or in other words on the credit of the bank of issue.

When paper money is convertible or when coins form the only currency or perhaps even when, as in the pre-1971 days, the pound had a par value of 2. 13281 grams of fine gold, it is not unreasonable to ask the question: Is the pound to be defined as a certain quantity of metal, or as something else? For many centuries an answer in the former sense was a matter of course. During the early period of monetary history, when money was given and taken by weight rather than tale, when the names nowadays employed to designate a unit of account originated and in terms described a certain weight ('pound', 'livre', 'peso',[82] 'mark'), no other conception was possible. Even after money had come to be accepted by tale,[83] the pound continued to be identified with the quantity of metal which the word denoted. But the rise of the bank note and the monetary experience of the eighteenth century (such as John Law's experiments, the Assignats, and in particular the Bank Restriction period) brought the fundamental issue to the forefront. In England the traditional idea remained dominant and in the nineteenth century it came to be generally held that the pound was nothing but a definite quantity of gold. This was in effect the conclusion reached by the famous Report of the Bullion Committee (1810), and it was the principle underlying the legislation of 1819[84] and 1844.[85]

The conflict of opinion which underlay those great debates continues to be illuminating. In 1811 Canning ridiculed Lord Castlereagh's definition of the pound as 'a sense of value in reference to currency as compared with commodities',[86] and 'the inventors and champions of "abstract currency"', those 'who after exhausting in vain every attempt to find an earthly substitute for the legal and ancient standard of our money, have divested the pound sterling of all the properties of matter and pursued it under the name of the "ideal unit" into the regions of nonentity and nonsense'.[87] In 1819 the conception of a pound which could not be defined otherwise than by the admission that it was 'difficult to explain it, but every gentleman in England knows it',[88] was similarly ridiculed by Peel, who gave

---

[82] See *St. Pierre* v. *South American Stores (Gath & Chaves) Ltd.*, [1937] 3 All E.R. 349, at p. 357 *per* MacKinnon L.J.

[83] According to Feavearyear, p. 7, this occurred as early as the ninth century.

[84] 59 Geo. III, ch. 49; Feavearyear, pp. 220 sqq.

[85] Bank Charter Act, 7 & 8 Vict., ch. 32.

[86] 8 May 1811, Hansard, xix. 1087.      [87] p. 1089.

[88] This was said in evidence before the Committee of 1819 by a London accountant, Mr. Thomas Smith, and quoted by Peel (see following note). Feavearyear, p. 1, suggests that 'Mr. Smith had at the back of his mind the germ of a truer notion of the nature of the pound than that of Peel'.

expression to the almost general view when he said in the House of Commons:[89] 'Every sound writer on the subject came to the conclusion that a certain weight of gold bullion, with an impression on it, denoting it to be of that certain weight, and of a certain fineness, constituted the only true, intelligible, and adequate standard of value.' Finally, in 1844 it was again Peel who said:[90]

If 'a pound' is a mere visionary abstraction, a something which does not exist either in law or in practice, in that case one class of measures relating to paper currency may be adopted; but if the word 'pound', the common denomination of value, signifies something more than a mere fiction, if a 'pound' means a quantity of the precious metals of certain weight and certain fineness, if that be the definition of the 'pound', in that case another class of measures relating to paper currency will be requisite. . . . According to practice, according to law, according to ancient monetary policy of this country that which is implied by the word 'pound' is a certain definite quantity of gold with a mark upon it to determine its weight and fineness and the engagement to pay a pound means nothing, and can mean nothing else than, the promise to pay to the holder when he demands it, that definite quantity of gold.

The *metallistic* doctrine expressed by these words has undoubtedly become discredited, and, indeed, in view of the experience after 1931, when the paper pound existed and proved workable, its unsoundness cannot be denied[91] and even when under the Bretton Woods system there was a par value based on gold, this was a measure rather than a synonym of the currency unit.

However evident this may be, it is more difficult to give a positive answer to the question how the unit of account is to be defined. Here, again, it was Knapp who offered a solution of very many cases by his *historical* definition. Knapp held[92] that the unit of account could be defined historically only, and that it received its meaning by nothing but by its 'recurrent linking' to the previous currency. According to Knapp, such linking is effected by the rate of conversion which the State establishes for the payment of debts denominated with reference to the old standard. Thus the present

[89] 24 May 1819, Hansard, xl. 675 sqq., 679, 680. Professor Pollard in a letter to *The Times*, 20 Jan. 1937, suggests 'that historically a pound is 240 penny-weights of silver', which thesis provoked further letters to the Editor from Lord Desborough and Sir Joseph Chitty in *The Times* of 23 Jan. 1937. It seems indeed plausible that, as Nebolsine, 42 (1933) *Yale L.J.* 1050, 1060, asserts, to the framers of the American Constitution 'money was nothing more than so many pieces of precious metal of certified weight and fineness'.

[90] 6 May 1844, Hansard, Ser. 3, lxxiv. 723.

[91] See below, p. 271, where the cases relating to foreign currency are dealt with. It is probably the contrast discussed in the text which Lord Wright had in mind when he said that 'in law the credit theory of money must supplant the commodity theory' ('Gold Clauses' in *Legal Essays and Addresses* (1938), 149).

[92] *State Theory of Money*, p. 21.

Deutsche Mark[93] equals one reichsmark which is not to be defined as 1/2790 kilogram fine gold,[94] but as 1 billion (old) marks, the mark itself being equivalent to $\frac{1}{3}$ thaler.[95] The equation therefore is: 1 Deutsche Mark = 1 reichsmark = 1,000,000 million marks = $\frac{1}{3}$ thaler. This view, it is true, has been criticized as being somewhat one-sided. It has been rightly pointed out[96] that a recurrent link does not exist where the rate of conversion varies according to the time at which the monetary obligation arose,[97] and that a rate of conversion could just as well refer to the rate of exchange of some foreign currency.[98] Nevertheless, experience shows that in most, if not all, modern cases, a unit of account can in fact be linked by a rate of conversion to an antecedent unit, and Knapp's doctrine can therefore be adopted as a useful working principle. As Martin Wolff said,[99] in a negative sense it was Knapp's merit not to have defined the unit

[93] See below, pp. 101, 102.

[94] S. 3, Coinage Act of 30 Aug. 1924, provided that out of 1 kg. fine gold there should be coined $139\frac{1}{2}$ pieces of 20 reichsmarks in gold or 279 pieces of 10 reichsmarks in gold; s. 1, Coinage Act, proclaimed that Germany adopted the gold standard. These provisions only meant that the German unit of account had a fixed relation with gold, but they did not mean that 1 reichsmark was equal to 1/1390 kg. of gold, nor did they merely indicate a policy or a programme (Nussbaum, *Geld*, p. 52; 35 (1937) *Mich. L.R.* 865, 875; above p. 33, and see also Breit in Düringer–Hachenburg, *Kommentar zum Handelsgesetzbuch*, iv. 748; Gadow in Staub, *Kommentar zum Handelsgesetzbuch*, iii. 271). Yet the Supreme Court said that 'he who owes one Reichsmark, owes 1/1395 pound fine gold, and he who is entitled to claim 1395 Reichsmark, is satisfied by the receipt of one pound fine gold': 28 Nov. 1930, *RGZ*. 130, 367, 371. This was clearly an *obiter dictum*, but it is nevertheless surprising, because the theory there enunciated is obviously wrong and irreconcilable with the actual practice of the court. The question might be more doubtful in other countries where the programmatic character of such provisions is less clearly indicated by the wording of the respective provisions; thus a French Act of 25 June 1928 provided that the franc was 'constituted by 65·5 milligrams of gold 9/10 fine'. Even in such cases it would be wrong to equiparate the unit of account to a certain quantity of gold; see above, p. 33, n. 23.

[95] See the rates of conversion in Art. 14, Coinage Act, 1873. A most interesting example of conversion is supplied by a decision of the German Supreme Court (25 Feb. 1931, *RGZ*. 141, 1). In Germany a monetary system in the modern sense did not exist before the Coinage Act of 1873, passed after the creation of the Reich in 1871. Up to that time Germany had comprised numerous sovereign States and, consequently, an extraordinary monetary confusion existed, which is well exemplified in that decision. The case, which is too long and complicated to be of interest to non-German readers, dealt with the conversion into reichsmarks of a debt of 'Reichsthaler Gold' incurred in 1854 by the then Grand Duke of Oldenburg.                    [96] Nussbaum, *Geld*, p. 48.

[97] This happened in France when in 1795 the silver franc replaced the paper currency of the Revolution and when so-called 'tableaux de dépréciation' were introduced (see Mater, pp. 153 sqq.; *Rev. dr. bancaire*, ii. 172; iii. 74); for further examples see Nusshaum, p. 122. Similarly Russia: see *Buerger* v. *New York Life Assurance Co.* (1927), 43 T.L.R. 601, 605 *per* Scrutton L.J.; *Perry* v. *Equitable Life Assurance Society* (1929), 45 T.L.R. 468, 473, 474 *per* Branson J.; Freund, *Das Zivilrecht Sowjetrusslands*, pp. 179 sqq.; Bloch, *Ostrecht*, 1927, 249 sqq.; Maklezow–Timaschew–Alexejew–Sawalski, *Das Recht Sowjetrusslands*, pp. 224 sqq.

[98] Wolff, pp. 571-3.                    [99] p. 573, n. 26.

of account according to the standard metal of the currency system, and positively, we are indebted to him for having explained a unit of account by connecting it with the unit of other systems. That Knapp explains the unit by connecting it with the antecedent unit only may be too narrow, but so long as no better definition can be found, his principle, if it is not regarded as an inflexible one, cannot be abandoned.[100]

In England, however, the doctrine of the recurrent link does not assist in defining the pound, because the history of the English pound is a continuous one.[101] Although English private international law has frequently recognized the doctrine,[102] although it explains the pound in Scotland,[103] although in regard to Ireland Parliament gave effect to it,[104] and although it is accepted by recent legislation

[100] Similarly, Wolff, p. 571, though the above qualifications should not be overlooked. Their practical importance is, however, not very great.

[101] Feavearyear, p. 2: 'The pound sterling as a unit of account came into existence in Anglo-Saxon times. There has been no break in the sequence of contracts in which pounds, shillings, and pence have been the consideration from those times to the present day.' The continuing identity of the pound is not affected by the introduction of decimal coinage by the Decimal Currency Acts, 1967 and 1969, these introduce new pence, but leave the pound intact.

[102] Below, p. 271, n. 13.

[103] The Scottish pound was equal in value to the English pound until about 1355. From then onwards through the centuries it depreciated in value until in 1600 it was only a twelfth part of the English pound and it remained at that point until the Union of the kingdoms (see Pinkerton, *Essays on Medals*, ii (1808), 124). By Art. XVI of the Treaty of Union of 1707 it was provided 'that, from and after the Union, the coin shall be of the same standard and value throughout the United Kingdom, as now in England, and a mint shall be continued in Scotland under the same rules as the mint in England. . . .' The Scottish coin and the Scottish pound as a unit of account thus disappeared. Although there was no statutory rate of conversion, in fact conversion took place at the rate which had been in force for more than 100 years, viz. at the rate of £12 Scots to £1 sterling or £1 Scots for 1s. 8d. sterling; this rate was so firmly established that shortly before the Union, in the year 1704, the Bank of Scotland had made an issue of notes of £12 Scots which was being treated as the first issue in Scotland of £1 sterling notes: Graham, *The One Pound Note* (1886), p. 14; A. W. Kerr, *History of Banking in Scotland* (1926), p. 23. However, it is remarkable that as a unit of measurement the £ Scots still exists today at the old rate of £1 Scots for 1s. 8d. sterling (see the answer given by the Chancellor of the Exchequer on 24 June 1952, Hansard, dii. 162). According to the law of Scotland a verbal legacy will be sustained to the amount of £100 Scots or £8. 6s. 8d. sterling (*Encyclopædia of the Laws of Scotland*, xv. 624) and in the case of loans not exceeding £100 Scots parol evidence is competent (ibid. ix. 308). The valuation of land for the purpose of tax legislation was until 1958 largely based on the 'valued rent' expressed in terms of Scottish pounds: see, e.g., Income Tax Act, 1952, First Schedule, Part III, repealed by the Tribunals and Enquiries Act, 1958, s. 15. On the history of the Scottish Land Tax see *Encyclopædia of the Laws of Scotland*, ix. 1 sqq., or Innes, *Scotch Legal Antiquities*, pp. 190, 274. (The author is indebted to Mr. C. A. Malcolm of the Signet Library, Edinburgh, to Lord Mitchison, Q.C., and Professor Sir Thomas Smith of Edinburgh University for references to Scottish law and lore shortly summarized in this note.)

[104] The statute 6 Geo. IV, ch. 79 (1825), provided 'for the assimilation of the currency and monies of account throughout the United Kingdom of Great Britain and Ireland'. English money was quoted at a premium of $\frac{1}{12}$ over Irish money, and s. 2 provided that

in South Africa,[105] Australia,[106] and other countries[107] which abandoned the pound sterling currency, the conception of the English pound remains elusive. Today there can be very little doubt that Mr. Thomas Smith and his fellow victims of Canning's and Peel's scorn have remained victorious. The idea of the abstract pound, the ideal unit, the sense of value, is more appropriate to modern conditions than any other explanation. Lawyers are thus driven to extra-legal, especially sociological, explanations which, though correct and interesting in themselves, are not very helpful for legal purposes. There remains nothing but to consider a unit of account, such as the pound sterling, simply as a name[108] for something which cannot be precisely defined,[109] and to be satisfied with Nussbaum's attractive exposition:[110]

Thus the value of the monetary unit becomes more or less disconnected from reality, or at least from its physical substratum. Nevertheless, in the consciousness of the social community its significance is sufficiently distinctive. To take a modern example, even between March 6, 1933, when the United States went off the gold standard, and 31 January 1934, when a new gold parity of the dollar was fixed by the President, there was at any given moment a neat idea of what a 'dollar' meant. The existence of a monetary unit apparently is a phenomenon of social psychology which can be traced historically for each unit, yet it is impossible to decompose analytically the concept of the unit into simpler logical elements. The American dollar can be traced back, through many

every sum of Irish money shall in future be paid in British money 'less by 1/13th part than the amount of such sum expressed according to the currency of Ireland'.

[105] By the Decimal Coinage Act, 1959, which, curiously enough, dealt only with coins, South Africa introduced, on 14 Feb. 1961, the rand currency at the rate of £SA 1 = 2 rand.

[106] By the Currency Act, 1963, Australia introduced, on 14 Feb. 1966, the dollar 'as the monetary unit or unit of currency of Australia' at the rate of £A 1 = 2 dollars: s.8 and see ss. 10 and 11.

[107] The examples abound. Perhaps it is sufficient to refer to the Currency Act, 1965, of the Bahama Islands. By virtue of s. 5 (2) 'the unit of currency in the Bahama Islands shall be the Bahama dollar', and by ss. 5 (4) and 6 'one Bahamian dollar shall be equivalent to seven shillings sterling'; the Currency (Amendment) Act, 1967, reduced this to 8/2sh, but it is very difficult to understand the ratio behind this statute: in the light of the completed conversion of 1965 there would seem to have been no room for it.

[108] That the unit of account is simply a name has very often been said: see, e.g., Wolff, p. 571, Austrian Supreme Court, 26 Nov. 1935, RabelsZ. 9 (1935), 891, 897, or Karl Olivecrona, The Problems of Monetary Unit (1957), pp. 119, 120, who speaks of 'the nothingness of the monetary unit'. The problem is only this, whether in law the meaning of that name can be further elucidated by relating it to another conception.

[109] The Decimal Currency Act, 1967, contains no definition of the pound sterling, but merely establishes 'the denominations of money in the currency of the United Kingdom', which since 15 Feb. 1971 are 'the pound sterling and the new penny': s.1 (1). The Act describes this (e.g. in s. 2 subsection 1 and in the marginal notes) as 'the new currency'. But the currency is not new or different from the former pound. The unit of account has remained the same. Only its subdivision into shillings and pence has been replaced by the 'new penny' which is one-hundredth part of a pound sterling.

[110] pp. 13, 14.

vicissitudes, to the Spanish 'milled dollar', or peso, the value of which was in 1792 adopted by Congress as the basis of the American monetary system. Again, the Spanish peso may eventually be traced back to a weight unit. There exists an uninterrupted chain of value notions concomitant to the use of the peso-dollar terms. But the dollar concept existing at any given time is as little susceptible of definition as, say, the concept of 'blue'. No more can be said than that 'dollar' is the name for a value which, at any definite moment, is understood in the same sense throughout the community, and since goods and services are evaluated in terms of the dollar, that unit is a standard or measure of value.

## VI

The unit of account which, in a perhaps not quite satisfactory but generally sufficient manner, has thus been defined, not as a mere name nor as a certain quantity of metal but as an abstract measure of the relation of a given currency standard to its predecessor, is the one essential characteristic of a monetary system.

Accordingly the identity of a monetary system is not affected by measures or events which touch merely the value or the purchasing power of money, whether they result from the transition from a silver to a gold standard, or from a gold to a paper standard, or from the introduction of new coins or new notes, from the diminution or increase of the weight of coins or the international value of the currency (devaluation, revaluation), from the introduction or abolition of legal or compulsory tender power, from the expansion or restriction of credit and circulating money (inflation,[111] deflation), or from similar measures. Thus it cannot be doubted that, when England went off the gold standard in 1931 by relieving the Bank of England of the obligation to sell gold bullion against notes,[112] or when in 1933 the United States of America declared gold clauses to be irreconcilable with public policy and enacted that every obligation should be discharged upon payment, dollar for dollar, in any coin or currency which at the time of payment is legal tender,[113] or when in 1949 and 1967 sterling was devalued by reducing its par value from 3·58134 grams to 2·48828 grams and again to 2·13281 grams of fine gold,[114] or when in 1971, the 'new decimal currency'

[111] See, e.g., Watkins, 'Economic Aspects of Inflation', 33 (1934) *Mich. L.R.* 153; Willis and Chapman, *The Economics of Inflation* (New York, 1935); Harwood–Ferguson, *Inflation* (Cambridge, U.S.A., 1935); Bresciani–Turroni, *The Economics of Inflation, A Study of Currency Depreciation in Post-War Germany* (London, 1937); Nussbaum, 'The Meaning of Inflation', 53 (1943) *Political Science Quarterly*, 86; Einzig, *Inflation* (1952); H. Scherf, Art. 'Inflation' in *Handwörterbuch der Wirtschaftswissenschaft* (1976).

[112] Gold Standard (Amendment) Act, 1931.

[113] Joint Resolution of Congress, 5 June 1933.          [114] Above, pp. 31, 32.

came into force in the United Kingdom[115]—in all these and similar cases recorded in monetary history the unit of account remained untouched, because there was no rate of conversion linking the 'new' currency with the 'old', and therefore the identity of the monetary system remained unchanged, however seriously the national and international value of the money may have been reduced.[116]

Alterations of a currency are of an extrinsic nature if they do not, or do not only, affect the value of the money but strike at the identity of the unit of account and, thereby, of the monetary system itself. Generally speaking, such alterations are due to two causes, either to territorial or political changes[117] or to a complete collapse of the monetary system.[118]

A decision of the German Supreme Court[119] affords interesting illustration of the view that only alterations in the constitution of the unit of account as evidenced by a rate of conversion affect the identity of a monetary system, and that other modifications of a monetary system relate merely to the value of money, unless they have consequences so disastrous as to amount to a destruction and thus to an alteration of the system. On 21 May 1931 the plaintiff bank discounted with the defendants, the German Reichsbank, a bill of exchange for 100,000 Mexican gold pesos, payable on 15 August 1931. On 27 July 1931 a new Monetary Law came into force in Mexico by which the currency was moved off the gold standard. It was provided that, though the unit of account was the peso of 75 centigrams fine gold, the token money consisted of notes, silver, and bronze only, that any payment of Mexican money had to be effected by tendering silver or bronze coins at the nominal value, and that this also applied to debts previously incurred. In view of this law, the acceptor of the bill paid at maturity the nominal amount of 100,000 Mexican gold pesos in silver coins. The defendants therefore received an amount less by 74,013·45 reichsmarks than

[115] Above, p. 47, n. 109.

[116] That the identity of the pound sterling was not affected when England went off the gold standard in 1931 was recognized by the German Supreme Court (21 June 1933, RGZ. 141, 212, 214) and by the Czechoslovakian Supreme Court, RabelsZ. 1934, 484. But the abolition of the gold clause by the United States in 1933 was regarded as an alteration of the currency system by the Austrian Supreme Court, 26 Nov. 1935, RabelsZ. 1935, 891, 895.

[117] Numerous new currency systems came into existence as a result of the two world wars. Some examples are referred to below, pp. 250 sqq.

[118] Thus the fact that the German currency collapsed in 1922–3 meant that the mark of 1923 essentially differed from that of 1913 (see German Supreme Court, 13 Oct. 1933, RGZ. 142, 23, 30, 31), and for the same reason it should be held that the collapsed Russian currency essentially differed from the antecedent and subsequent currency. As to Russia see the references above, p. 45, n. 97.

[119] 13 Oct. 1933, RGZ. 142, 23.

they would have received had the bill been paid before the law of 27 July 1931. They debited the plaintiff's account accordingly, relying, *inter alia*, on a clause in their agreement with them which read as follows: 'If bills of exchange or cheques are not paid in the currency with reference to which they are denominated, the Reichsbank reserves the right to recover subsequently any eventual balances arising from the variation of the rates of exchange.' Applying German law, the Supreme Court held that this clause was inapplicable, because the currency in which the bill was paid did not differ from that by which it was denominated. The court took the view

that the various reasons which combine to produce the international value of a currency system cannot be distinguished, and that, on the other hand, the question whether a currency has collapsed, does not depend on an examination of the circumstances which have led to a different valuation. The valuation of a monetary system can at the most indicate that an alteration of the currency has perhaps occurred. For the decision whether such an alteration in fact exists, the Court of Appeal was right in holding it to be necessary to go down to the basis of the individual monetary system, and this basis is the ideal unit on which the system is founded (Nussbaum, *Das Geld*, p. 44), or 'the value represented by the unit which is the basis of the system' (Helfferich, *Geld*, p. 413).[120] An alteration of the currency only exists, if its basis is altered, whether this is due to the legislator consciously building up a new monetary system on a new unit of account, or to the events of economic life completely destroying that legal basis in disregard of the law.

It follows from the State theory of money that, generally, extrinsic alterations of currency can only be effected by legislative measures. As regards the question under what circumstances intrinsic alterations may destroy the identity of the currency, a hard-and-fast rule cannot be laid down. With respect to depreciation of money, the working principle will probably have to be adopted that a 'collapse',[121] a 'catastrophical depreciation'[122] is required, or that the money must have become 'worthless'[122] or 'fantastically depreciated'[123] or, as was said in an American case,[124] so depreciated as to 'shock the conscience and produce an exclamation'.

---

[120] English ed., p. 353.

[121] Expression of Sankey J. (as he then was) in *Ivor An Christensen* v. *Furness Withy & Co.* (1922), 12 Ll. L.R. 288.

[122] On such circumstances the German Supreme Court founded its revalorization doctrines: see below, pp. 104, 105, and see *Franklin* v. *Westminster Bank Ltd.*, below, p. 562, at p. 565 *per* Lord Hanworth M.R.

[123] *Franklin* v. *Westminster Bank Ltd.*, below p. 562, *per* MacKinnon J.

[124] *Seymour* v. *Delancy* (1824), 3 Cowen (N.Y.) 445.

## VII

The unit of account, being the essential characteristic of a monetary system, not only serves to distinguish it from its predecessors and successors, but also identifies it in relation to other monetary systems. In most cases this is obvious; the idea that in law the modern pound sterling and the modern dollar have anything in common cannot occur, whatever their historical connection may be. Difficulties may arise, however, if the denomination of the currency circulating in two or more countries is the same (English or Turkish pounds; French, Belgian, Swiss francs, and so on). Even on this hypothesis there will normally be no problem, but sometimes it may be doubtful whether the countries concerned have one single common monetary system or separate monetary systems. And the problem may be aggravated by the fact that a country may choose to refrain from organizing its own monetary system, but incorporates into it the currency of another monetary system, which thus becomes an exogenous element, an originally alien but adopted part[125] of the monetary constitution. In pursuing the task of definition it must be remembered, therefore, that legal identity is not proved by similarity or uniformity or even by factual identity.

It is submitted that a unit of account and, consequently, a monetary system peculiar to a given country exists, if the currency rests upon the country's own and independently exercisable law-making powers. The mere power to issue limited amounts of money (such as is today to some extent possessed by the Royal Bank of Scotland) or even unlimited amounts is insufficient. On the other hand, an explicit exercise of the law-making power over currency, a deliberate organization of monetary matters with a view to moulding them into a complete system, is not required; monetary sovereignty is the cardinal feature and indicates an independent monetary system, although, as has been pointed out, a foreign currency has, perhaps by mere implication, been adopted. For this reason the importance of a rate of exchange should not be over-emphasized; the presence of a rate of exchange may be strong and perhaps even conclusive evidence of the existence of an independent monetary system, but its absence does not prove the non-existence of such a system. It is the State theory of money[126] that reappears in this connection: it is the State that creates not only money in the legal sense but also the unit of account with reference to which such money is denominated.

---

[125] See Nussbaum, pp. 116, 117, 131, 132, and below, p. 142, n. 27.
[126] See above, p. 13.

The question whether or not a distinct monetary system existed came up for judicial decision in two connections.

One of the most recent[127] examples of an international currency standard was the Latin Monetary Union of 1865 between France, Belgium, Italy, Greece, and Switzerland.[128] These countries formed a convention 'pour ce qui regarde le titre, le poids, le diamètre et le cours de leurs espèces monnayées d'or et d'argent'. The moneys were legal tender as against the Treasury of each country, but not as between nationals of different countries. Moreover, legislation was by no means uniform, and no provisions were made relating to the control of the exactness of coinage, the tolerated deficiency, the issue of inconvertible paper money, and so on; all these questions were left to the individual States. It seemed clear, therefore, that in each country there existed an independent monetary system,[129] and this was the result reached by the courts in certain cases connected with bonds issued by a Belgian company during the years 1903 to 1913, at a denomination of '500 francs' each. After the First World War some of the bonds fell due for repayment and the company proposed to effect it by paying in respect of each bond 500 francs of the then Belgian currency. One of the creditors brought an action in the English courts in the case of *Hopkins* v. *Compagnie Internationale des Wagons-Lits*,[130] where in support of the contention that the bond secured the repayment of 500 gold francs it was said 'that a number of countries had agreed upon the standard of the gold franc by various Treaties from 1865 onwards, and that it must have been in the contemplation of the parties when the bargain which is contained in the bond was made that there should be repayment in that which he (counsel for the plaintiff) has from time to time lapsed into calling the international franc, but which he says he does not really mean to call the international franc'. In view of this hesitation with which, in the English courts, the theory of the international franc was put forward, Swift J. had no difficulty in disposing of it by saying that the international franc was nothing but 'a standard which the different countries have agreed upon between themselves

[127] Another example is the Vienna Coinage Treaty of 1857 between the members of the Customs Union and Austria or the Scandinavian Union formed in 1873–5. On the subject see generally Neumeyer, pp. 227 sqq.; Nussbaum, pp. 502 sqq.; Werner Stark, 'Währungsverträge', in *Festschrift für Oskar Engländer* (1936), 263.

[128] For references see Oppenheim, *International Law*, i (7th ed. by Lauterpacht, 1948), p. 887, and, in particular, H. P. Willis, *A History of the Latin Monetary Union* (Chicago, 1901), who at pp. 271 sqq. prints the English text of the Treaties; Janssen, *Les Conventions Monétaires* (Paris, 1911); Helfferich, pp. 438 sqq.; Mater, No. 159; Nolde, 'La Monnaie en droit international public', *Rec.* 27 (1929), 243 sqq., 364 sqq.

[129] In this sense, e.g. Helfferich, pp. 140, 353.

[130] Below, p. 560.

which their franc shall attain, and on condition that it attains that standard it shall be freely interchangeable between the treasuries of the various high contracting parties'. In a case between different parties, the same question fell to be decided by the French Cour de Cassation,[131] which arrived at the result reached in England and Germany.[132]

The problems are not essentially different when one comes to consider the relationship between the monetary systems of the former colonial powers and their possessions overseas. Was the franc of the Congo the same as that of Belgium?[133] Did the Netherlands and her Indonesian territories share the guilder currency?[134] Did France and her African territories have the same 'franc' currency?[135] It is in the British Commonwealth of nations that the question whether, where, and up to what point of the historical development,

---

[131] Cass. Civ. 21 Dec. 1932, S. 1932, 1. 390, and Clunet, 1933, 1201; in the same sense Berlin Court of Appeal, 25 Sept. 1928, *JW*. 1929, 446, and certain Belgian courts: Piret, p. 255; and see Hof of Amsterdam, 11 Dec. 1929, *Weekblad*, No. 12121 (1930).

[132] Though the question which currency was meant when during the existence of the Latin Monetary Union the word 'franc' was used without a reference to a distinct country must be decided by the general principles relating to the determination of the money on account (below, Ch. VIII), the use of the word 'franc gold' can more readily be construed as referring to the gold content on which the franc was based throughout the countries which were members of the Union. Thus in 1901 the then Austrian Lloyd Triestino issued a loan of '18.000.000 kroners equal to 18.900.000 francs gold equal to 15.300.000 German marks', the coupons providing for payment of interest of 42 kroners or 42 francs gold or 34 German marks. When the holder exercised the franc option the Supreme Courts of Austria and Italy held that the company had to pay so many Austrian schillings or Italian lire as were equal to the gold content of the franc of the Latin Monetary Union, i.e. 32·25806 grammes 900/1,000 fine for 100 fr.: Austrian Supreme Court, 1 June 1937, *B.I.J.I.* 37 (1937), 245 affirming Vienna Commercial Court, 4 Dec. 1936, *B.I.J.I.* 36 (1937), 286; Italian Corte di Cassazione, 4 Aug. 1936, *Foro Italiano*, 1936, 1937, and German translation in *B.I.J.I.* 36 (1937), 307.

[133] An arbitral award of 16 April 1964, Revue de la Banque, 1965, 186, after a full discussion, concludes that 'le franc belge et le franc congolais ne peuvent donc être considérés comme constituant une seule et même monnaie de compte'. In the same sense Prud. Brussels, 15 Oct. 1962, Journal des Tribunaux, 1963, 758.

[134] The Dutch courts seem to have taken the view that the Netherlands Indies guilder was a separate currency, independent of the Dutch guilder, and that, accordingly, sums expressed in terms of Netherlands Indies guilders were, upon the creation of the sovereign State of Indonesia, converted into Indonesian currency: Hoge Raad, 14 Jan. 1955, International L.R. 1957, 73; Court of Appeal of Amsterdam, 5 Dec. 1951, International L.R. 1953, 81; 14 Jan. and 11 Feb. 1954, Nederlands Tijdschrift voor Internationaal Recht, 1954, 433, 434. For a different view see the decision of the Hoge Raad, 19 Feb. 1954, International L.R. 1954, 63 in a case in which the lower courts had regarded the Netherlands Indies guilder 'as merely a local variant' of the Dutch guilder. On the problem discussed in the text see, in particular, the study of Van Eck, *Juridische Aspecten van Geld met Name in het Vroegere Nederlands-Indie* (Deventer, 1970).

[135] Michel Leduc, *Les Institutions Monétaires Africaines* (Paris, 1965). See Bloch—Lainé, *La Zone Franc* (Paris, 1956); Geneviève Burdeau, 'Le statut juridique des Francs C.F.A.', in *International Law and Economic Order (Festschrift für F. A. Mann)* p. 657; Dominique Carreau, 'Les zones monétaires en droit international', ibid., p. 673.

there existed what one may call an Inter-Empire pound, a pound sterling common to and identical in the United Kingdom and British possessions overseas, caused particular difficulties. It is in many respects unexplored and an up-to-date history of British colonial currency and its somewhat haphazard course still remains to be written.[136] At present it is mainly the evolution of the Australian monetary system which the courts in England have been called upon to investigate.[137]

By s. 51 (xii) of the Commonwealth of Australia Act, 1900, Australia was given power to make laws with regard to currency, coinage, and legal tender. Under the Australian Coinage Act, 1909, 'Australian coins' were issued on the basis of a standard of weight and fineness identical with that laid down by the Coinage Act, 1870, and made legal tender side by side with 'British coins' (ss. 2, 4, and 5). By the Australian Notes Act, 1910, the Governor-General was given power to authorize the issue of 'Australian notes' (s. 5) which were declared to be 'a legal tender throughout the Commonwealth and throughout all territories under the control of the Commonwealth' and to be 'payable in gold coin at the Commonwealth Treasury at the seat of Government' (s. 6). As a result of the outbreak of the First World War gold coins disappeared from circulation and notes issued under the Act of 1910 were the only legal tender.[138] In these circumstances it is suggested that the Australian pound and, consequently, the independent monetary system of Australia came into being in 1900 when the Commonwealth acquired law-making power over currency,[139] and that the English pound continued in Australia as an exogenous but adopted Australian currency until British coins[140]

---

[136] The earlier development is described by Chalmers, *A History of Currency in the British Colonies* (1893). See also the informative articles by Shannon on the 'Colonial Sterling Exchange Standard' in *International Monetary Fund Staff Papers*, i (1951), 334 and ii (1952), 318, with many further references; Ida Greaves, *Colonial Monetary Conditions* (1953), and Fawcett, *The British Commonwealth in International Law* (1963), 176, 299. As to Israel see R. D. Ottensoser, *The Palestine Pound and the Israel Pound* (Geneva, 1955).

[137] It was, however, held in South Africa that in 1912 the pound was the same in England, Southern Rhodesia, and the Union (*Joffe v. African Life Assurance Society*, South African L.R. (Transvaal Division) 1933, 189), but that in Jan. 1931 the English and South African pound were distinct (*Aktiebolaget Tratalja v. Evelyn Haddon & Co. Ltd.*, South African L.R. (Cape Provincial Division) 1933, 156).

[138] The Commonwealth Bank Acts, 1920 and 1929, largely re-enacted the machinery, but do not affect the substance of the position.

[139] At that time, it is true, the Colonial Laws Validity Act, 1865, and the principle of *Ex parte Marais*, [1902] A.C. 51 continued to be applicable to Australia and ceased to have effect only by virtue of the Statute of Westminster, 1931. But in actual practice the constitutional position was such as to justify the suggestion in the text.

[140] Bank of England notes or currency notes issued under the Currency and Bank Notes Act, 1914, never were legal tender in Australia.

were wholly superseded after the outbreak of war in 1914. This view, however, is in conflict with decisions of both the House of Lords and the Privy Council, which in turn differ from each other.

In *Adelaide Electric Supply Co. v. Prudential Assurance Co.*[141] the shareholders of the appellant company, which was incorporated under the laws of England and whose business was conducted from Australia, in 1921 passed a resolution to the effect that all dividends should be declared at meetings to be held in Australasia and should be paid in and from Adelaide or elsewhere in Australasia. The respondents claimed that holders of certain preference shares of £1 each were entitled to be paid their dividends in sterling in English legal tender for the full nominal amount thereof, and not subject to deductions for Australian exchange. Reversing the Order of Farwell J. and of the Court of Appeal, and overruling the latter's decision in *Broken Hill Proprietary Co. v. Latham*,[142] the House of Lords held that the company had discharged its obligations by paying in Australian currency that which was in Australia legal tender for the nominal amount of the dividend warrants.[143] The decision was unanimous, but the options delivered show great variance so far as concerns the problem whether at the material times the Australian pound was different from the English pound. Lord Atkin thought[144] that 'at the present day the English pound and the Australian pound are not the same', but that 'at the material times (which presumably included the period from 1921 to 1932 when the writ was issued) the pound English and Australian was the same'. Lords Warrington[145] and Russell of Kilowen[146] held that—apparently at the time of the decision—the pound was one and the same in both countries. Lord Tomlin[147] expressed the same view with reference to the year 1921, and only Lord Wright arrived at the opposite conclusion. It is thus necessary to choose between his view on the one hand and the opinion expressed by the majority of the House on the other hand.[148]

---

[141] [1934] A.C. 122, 155. That the English and Australian currency are different is also the view of Mann J. of the Supreme Court of Victoria: *In re Tillam Boehme & Tickle Pty. Ltd.* (1932), Vict. L.R. 146, 148. See also the High Court of Australia in *McDonald & Co. v. Wells* (1931), 45 C.L.R. 506.

[142] [1933] Ch. 373; the question whether there exists in Australia a distinct unit of account was answered in the negative by Maugham J. at p. 391, but in the affirmative by Lawrence and Romer L.JJ. at pp. 401, 407. As in the *Adelaide* case the opinions delivered by the learned Lords differed on this point (see the text), these observations in the *Broken Hill* case still require consideration, though the actual judgments of Lawrence and Romer L.JJ. are overruled.

[143] This part of the case and the case of *Auckland Corporation v. Alliance Assurance Co. Ltd.*, [1937] A.C. 587 will be considered below, pp. 234 sqq.

[144] p. 135.    [145] p. 138.    [146] p. 148.    [147] p. 143.

[148] Whichever of these opinions is preferred, the Privy Council was justified in holding

The pith of Lord Tomlin's opinion lies in his conclusion based upon consideration of the Australian legislation, that[149]

there has never in fact been either in the United Kingdom or Australia so far as I am aware any statute or Order in Council or other act in the law having the force of statute *expressly* separating the money of account of the United Kingdom from the money of account of Australia or creating a distinct Australian unit. The Commonwealth of Australia created in 1900, was given full powers to make laws with respect to currency coinage and legal tender. It has in fact never affected *expressly* to alter the money of account or to set up a distinct Australian money of acount. ... I ask myself, if there has been a change in the money of account, when did it take place and what caused it and I find no answer.

Lord Wright, on the other hand, did not deny the identity of the unit of account; nevertheless, after tracing the history of the Australian pound and the development of the exchange rates, he regarded the two systems as distinct on the ground[150] that 'this difference is inherent in the difference of the law-making authority at either place, as well as in the different commerical conditions prevailing'. On a later occasion[151] Lord Wright explained, however, that only 'during the war [from 1914 to 1918], according to my opinion, the two currency systems fell apart'.

Lord Wright's emphasis upon the significance of the law-making power became the foundation of the opinion of the Privy Council which Lord Simonds delivered in *Bonython* v. *Commonwealth of Australia*.[152] In 1895 the Government of Queensland issued debentures in pursuance of the authority conferred upon it by the local legislature. The debentures entitled the holder to receive in 1945 payment of 'pounds sterling' in Brisbane, Sydney, Melbourne,

that neither of them could in any way affect the meaning of the word 'pound' in the Australian Assessment and Taxing Acts, neither of them being inconsistent with the view 'that for the purpose of assessing an Australian taxpayer to income tax under the Australian revenue legislation, it is necessary that his assessable income should be expressed in terms of Australian currency': *Payne* v. *The Deputy Federal Commissioner of Taxation*, [1936] A.C. 497, 509. In the case of *Auckland Corporation* v. *Alliance Assurance Co.*, [1937] A.C. 587, the Privy Council also refrained from expressing an opinion on the point; a few remarks in Lord Wright's judgment, e.g. on the one hand his reference to the pound as the unit of account common to England and New Zealand or, on the other hand, his reference to the 'New Zealand currency' and 'the sterling currency in England', do not conclusively point in either direction. See also *De Bueger* v. *Ballantyne & Co. Ltd.*, [1938] A.C. 452 (P.C.).

[149] pp. 143, 145; italics supplied. Lords Warrington and Russell did not discuss the point at length.

[150] p. 155; similarly, Romer L.J. in *Broken Hill Proprietary Co.* v. *Latham*, [1933] Ch. 373, 407 relied on the fact 'that Australia had in 1920 its own currency system and every such system must be based on a standard unit of value'.

[151] 'Gold Clauses' in *Legal Essays and Addresses* (1939), 147 sqq., 152.

[152] [1950] A.C. 201.

or London at his option. The claim was for payment of English sterling in London. The defence was that holders were entitled only to Australian currency. It thus became necessary to decide the preliminary question whether in 1895 there existed a distinct Australian pound. Although it is not all easy to follow Lord Simonds's reasoning in all its details,[153] it is clear that he saw 'the vital distinction between the two monetary systems [of England and Queensland] in that they depend on different law-making powers',[154] that 'that which was lawful money in the self-governing Colony of Queensland in 1895 was lawful money by virtue of the law of Queensland' and rested 'on the inherent law-making power of the Queensland legislature'.[155]

While Lord Simonds's principle deserves respectful approval,[156] it must be said that it is inconsistent with the views of the majority of the House of Lords in the *Adelaide* case,[157] and that its application to the circumstances in which Queensland found herself in 1895 is open to grave doubt.

In the *Adelaide* case Lord Tomlin did not merely base his conclusion on a factual appreciation of legislative developments in Australia.[158] He established and applied a legal test, viz. the 'express' exercise of the law-making power for the purpose of setting up an Australian money of account distinct from the English. To him neither the mere existence of a law-making power over currency nor its implied exercise by the incorporation of the English pound as an exogenous element nor the conversion of English sterling debts into Australian pound debts impliedly permitted by the Australian Notes Act, 1910, was sufficient. In *Bonython*'s case a monetary system was held to be characterized by the existence of the mere currency-making power. In the result it may be necessary to conclude somewhat puristically that *Bonython*'s case established a principle which ought to be of universal validity, but is in fact limited to the law of

---

[153] For a fuller discussion see Mann, 'On the Meaning of the "Pound" in Contracts', 68 (1952) *L.Q.R.* 195. [154] p. 218.

[155] p. 217. Both Lord Tomlin and Lord Simonds, therefore, proceeded on the footing of the State theory of money, though they differed in its interpretation. In the paper referred to above, n. 153, it was indicated (at p. 198, n. 12) that Nussbaum, p. 132, had charged this writer with inconsistency in that, notwithstanding his adherence to the State theory of money, he preferred the opinion of Lord Wright (and Lord Simonds) to that of Lord Tomlin. On reconsideration it appears that Nussbaum did not intend to make that charge, so that there was no room for the attempt to reject it.

[156] Accordingly most of the remaining pound currencies which form part of the sterling area are likely to be distinct from the English pound, even if there is parity of value, as, for instance, in the case of the Eire pound.

[157] [1934] A.C. 220.

[158] As, in order to draw a distinction, Lord Simonds suggested in *Bonython*'s case at p. 220.

Australia, while in England the unsatisfactory rule followed by the majority of the House of Lords in the *Adelaide* case at present may continue to prevail.[159]

However this may be, in the former case the Privy Council would appear to have misapplied its own principle. Even if in 1895 Queensland had any law-making power over her currency, it was not an independent power, owned by and peculiar to herself, because she had no right to adopt or continue a monetary system other than that of England and, therefore, lacked the power of creating her own system had she so desired; such independence, however, is an essential requirement of sovereignty in monetary matters. The restrictions imposed upon Queensland in 1895 are derived from the fact that according to the obvious meaning and purpose of the Colonial Laws Validity Act, 1865, the right of the Imperial legislature to legislate for a colony were preserved even where a legislature had been given;[160] that the specific provisions of the Coinage Act, 1870, enabled the Queen at any time to apply the English monetary system to Queensland had this been necessary or desirable,[161] and that Queensland legislation purporting to introduce a monetary system wholly divorced from the English system might well have been repugnant to the Colonial Branch Mint Act, 1866, and the Coinage Act, 1870, and, therefore, void under the Colonial Laws Validity Act, 1865.[162] In short, the sovereignty of Queensland in 1895 was certainly not greater than that of Southern Rhodesia in 1964, when the latter had none.[163]

## VIII

The value of a unit of account such as sterling may, as has been shown,[164] be established by means of governmental acts, in particular

---

[159] In *National Bank of Australasia* v. *Scottish Union and National Insurance Ltd.*, [1952] A.C. 493, on which see Morris, 2 *I.C.L.Q.* (1953), 300, Lord Cohen seemed to think that the views of the majority in the *Adelaide* case on the non-existence of an Australian monetary system were merely 'some *obiter dicta* of certain of their Lordships' (p. 512). With the greatest respect, such a suggestion is untenable: Mann, 69 (1953) *L.Q.R.* 18. The decisions of the Privy Council in this field are likely to result from judicial policies.

[160] *Ex parte Marais*, [1902] A.C. 51.      [161] ss. 11 (9), 19, and 20.

[162] For details see the paper referred to above, p. 57, n. 153, and Morris, above, n. 159. The author understands from Mr. R. Else-Mitchell, one of the Counsel for the respondent Commonwealth of Australia, that the point discussed in the text was fully argued before the Privy Council, although this does not appear from the Board's advice. It has also been pointed out to the author that the Queensland statute 56 Vict. No. 37 (1897) which, according to n. 28 of his earlier paper, he could not identify, does in fact exist. It provided for the issue of Treasury notes 'for one pound sterling or five pounds sterling each' (s. 2); they were 'everywhere within Queensland good legal tender of money' (s. 3).

[163] *Madzimbamuto* v. *Lardner-Burke*, [1969] A.C. 645.      [164] Above pp. 36 sqq.

legislation or treaty arrangements, or by market forces and may have varying significance for international and domestic purposes.

The unit of account may be fixed or 'pegged' by reference to another standard of value which in the past was normally gold used either directly or, under the former par value system of Bretton Woods, indirectly, but may also be another currency system's unit of account such as the dollar. If the relation so established is formally changed by governmental action one speaks of a devaluation or a revaluation,[165] depending on whether the unit of account concerned is depreciated or appreciated in value. So long as the standard of reference retains its value and so long as the monetary authorities, voluntarily or as a matter of duty, abide by it, a currency which is 'pegged' cannot depreciate or appreciate in value, i.e. its international purchasing power cannot fall or increase.

On the other hand the currency may be 'floating'. In this case its value is determined by the interplay of supply and demand which may be, but is not necessarily, controlled by the monetary authorities and their policies of supporting or depreciating it, i.e. by buying or selling their own currency for foreign currency or gold or other assets. A currency which is 'floating' cannot be devalued or revalued in the strict sense of the term, because its international value depends, not on governmental action, but on market forces (in the creation of which the government or the monetary authorities may or may not participate). The currency may, therefore, 'float' downwards or upwards i.e. it may have a lesser or higher international value, it may depreciate or appreciate.

These values relate to international relationships and thus influence what is known as the rate of exchange, i.e. the price of a foreign currency in terms of a country's own currency. They do not necessarily affect the unit of account's domestic purchasing power; when, for instance, on 23 June 1972 sterling was allowed to 'float', its internal value or purchasing power was not immediately changed. It became less only when imports became more expensive and other developments resulted in reducing its domestic purchasing power. Yet it seems that there is no necessary or direct connection between

---

[165] Nussbaum, p. 171 whose definition is generally accepted. Cf. Hahn, 'Fragen der Auf- und Abwertung', in *Berichte der Deutschen Gesellschaft für Völkerrecht* 20 (1979) 1. In *Federal Maritime Commission v. Australian/U.S. Atlantic and Gulf Conference,* 337 F. Supp. 1032 (1972) it was held (on 4 Feb. 1972) 'that the United States dollar has not been officially devalued, an action which can only be effected by Congress which has not acted.' The report does not make it clear whether and to what extent the court was made aware of the fact that on 15 August 1971 the President, acting alone, had abrogated the convertibility of the dollar into gold. But it is possible that this did not bring about a devaluation in the technical sense.

the domestic and the international value of the unit of account: in 1979 and 1980 the annual rate of inflation in Britain was almost twelve and more than fifteen per cent respectively, but sterling's international value rose or was at least stable in terms of both the dollar and the Swiss franc.

Where a unit of account is devalued or depreciates, the rate of exchange with other currencies is modified, but none of these other currencies can be said to be revalued or to appreciate. Conversely, where a unit of account is revalued or appreciates in relation to other currencies, none of the latter is devalued or depreciates. Their value in terms of the particular unit of account affected by the change differs, but their value *inter se*, their value in terms of gold or other commodities or their domestic value remains the same. The difference, in other words, is relative rather than absolute.

This is one of the principal lessons taught by the *Young Loan Case* (*Belgium and others* v. *the Federal Republic of Germany*), which was decided by an international Arbitral Tribunal in 1980.[166] The relevant clause, introduced by the London Agreement on German External Debts of 1953, provided that in the event of the rates of exchange of any of the nine currencies of issue altering after 1 August 1952 by more than five per cent the amounts due were to be recalculated 'on the basis of the least depreciated currency' ('auf der Grundlage der Währung mit der geringsten Abwertung', 'sur la base de la devise la moins dépréciée'). When the Deutsche Mark was revalued in 1961 and 1969, the creditor governments demanded an adjustment on the ground that, while the German text used the technical word 'Abwertung' (or devaluation), the English and French texts referred to depreciation, i.e. mere reduction in value, and that, therefore, the most appreciated currency, viz. the DM, was 'the least depreciated currency'. The majority of the Arbitral Tribunal rejected this contention, primarily because under the Bretton Woods system which was in force in 1953 there could be no depreciation beyond the permitted 'spread' of two per cent, which was not a (formal) devaluation and that, therefore, the English and French texts, when speaking of depreciation, were to be construed as meaning what the German text described as 'Abwertung', i.e. devaluation.[167] Moreover, even if this had not been so, the revaluation of one currency does not, as has been pointed out, involve the depreciation of another: the latter remains unchanged, although the rate of exchange between it and the former changes, so that in a strictly relative sense it becomes less valuable.

[166] Int. L.R. 59, 494.    [167] See, in particular, paragraphs 19 and 24, at pp. 531, 533.

It should, however, be made clear that the terms 'devaluation' and 'depreciation' are frequently used interchangeably, although in many cases the latter is a consequence rather than the equivalent of the former. Accordingly in each case a question of construction arises and its solution may not be easy. It will frequently be an important guide to remember that the fate of one unit of account does not directly affect any other unit of account: it is merely the relative value of one currency in terms of other currencies that changes, but the latter currencies do not change.[168]

## IX

The enormous expansion of the so-called Euro-currency market— it is said to involve more than 600 billions of U.S. dollars[169]—makes it appropriate to devote a few words to it in the present context, even if it is only for the negative purpose of emphasizing that Euro-currency is not a currency and that in law it lacks any novel or special features except that it is at present, though by no means necessarily or permanently, to some extent outside the control of local or, indeed, any monetary authorities.[170]

[168] Whether a particular enactment refers to revaluation or to devaluation or to both and whether in fact a revaluation or a devaluation occurs should not normally cause any difficulty. Both questions, however, arose in the unhappily phrased decision of the European Court of Justice in *Fratelli Zerbone* v. *Amministrazione delle Finanze*, European Court Reports 1978, 99 on which see also p. 34, n. 28. As regards the second of the above questions, Art. 1 (1) of Reg. 974/71 provides for the payment of monetary compensation amounts in respect of imports if 'a Member State allows the exchange rate of its currency to fluctuate by a margin wider than the one permitted by international rules.' Although the word 'fluctuate' seems to cover movements both upwards and downwards, it was generally accepted that only revaluations were contemplated' (see in particular pp. 120, 121). This was said to follow from the preamble and the texts in the other official languages, but may well involve a strained interpretation which should not serve as a precedent. As regards the first question, the Court held that the par value of the Italian lira had been established at 625 lire to 1 U.S. dollar, that in December 1971 Italy adopted 'a new exchange rate (called the "central rate") for its currency, namely the rate of Lit.581.50 per dollar' and that therefore Italy had accepted a rate of exchange higher than the par value including its margin of fluctuation of one per cent (p. 113). Accordingly, there had been a revaluation and the monetary compensation amounts for imports could, in principle, be demanded. Sir Joseph Gold, *Staff Papers of the I.M.F.* 27 (1980) 622, has, however, raised grave doubts as to whether the Court correctly assessed the facts and whether, in particular, it compared like with like. It seems that in truth the par value of the lira was in December 1971 reduced by one per cent to Lit.631.343 per U.S. dollar of 1944; that under the Smithsonian Agreement the current dollar was depreciated by 7.89 per cent; and that, consequently, the current lira appreciated by 7.48 per cent against the current dollar independently of the international rule, i.e. the Articles of Agreement of the I.M.F., which the Court regarded as alone relevant: see above p. 32, n. 20; p. 33, n. 26.

[169] The figure given by Andrew Crockett, *International Money* (1977) 168 was only 300 billion.

[170] For further legal discussions of the subject see Dach, *American Journal of Comparative Law*, 13 (1964) 30; Hahn, *Das Währungsrecht der Euro-Devisen* (1973).

There has for many decades been nothing unusual in, say, an English bank maintaining a dollar account in London for an English resident. Nor was there anything unusual in the heydays of sterling for banks or others in Continental centres to owe sterling to resident creditors. In such cases the debtor, that is to say usually the bank, sees to it that it is covered by corresponding credits which ultimately and perhaps indirectly are and must be held with banks in the home country of the currency in question. In law Euro-currency is not different: the term describes credits with and therefore debts due from banks, which are not expressed or to be paid in terms of the currency of the country in which the bank carries on business. Euro-dollars held by a bank in London, Euro-sterling held by a Swiss bank are examples. They are dollar or sterling debts which in accordance with the parties' intention are usually to be discharged by bank transfers of dollars or sterling rather than in cash.

While in law Euro-currency is clearly defined, but without special characteristics, the origin of the market is due to many and fascinating reasons of an economic and financial nature which economists have often described,[171] but which are unlikely to be legally relevant.

The existence of so large a market of funds in Euro-currency has led to the floatation of equally large and numerous Euro-currency, mainly Euro-dollar, loans in the form of bearer bonds issued by institutions and enterprises all over the world. Their placement is a no less interesting chapter of financial analysis which, again, is outside the scope of this work.[172] Suffice it to say that a substantial portion of such bonds is ultimately held in places and in circumstances of which the beneficial owner's home country is, and is intended to be, unaware.[173]

---

[171] One of the earliest books is Einzig, *The Euro-Dollar System*, 6th ed. by Brian Scott Quinn (1977). For a more recent discussion see Crockett l.c. pp. 167–82 and the literature referred to at p. 183. There is also an enormous foreign literature.

[172] Horn, *Das Recht des internationalen Anleihen* (1972); *Les Euro-Obligations*, edited by Fouchard and Kahn (Paris, 1972); E. Natermann, *Der Eurodollarmarkt in rechtlicher Sicht* (Baden–Baden, 1977); Jacquemont, *L'émission des emprunts euro-obligations* (Paris, 1976); Blaise, Fouchard, and Kahn, *Les Euro-Crédits* (Paris, 1981), a volume publishing numerous contributions to a Conference held at Dijon in October 1980.

[173] Further on Euro-currency below pp. 193 sqq.

# III

# Monetary Obligations:
# Types and Payment

I. Types of monetary obligations: (1) debts; (2) unliquidated claims. II. The payment of monetary obligations: (1) payment as a consensual act or a fact; (2) payment or tender of money; (3) the place of payment; (4) the time of payment; (5) the completion of payment.

## I

IT has already been observed[1] that it is one of the most important, though not the basic, functions of money to serve as a general medium of payment. In fact, in innumerable cases money not only functions as the contemplated or immediate means of fulfilling obligations, whether compulsorily imposed or voluntarily contracted, but may also be described as a 'medium of final compulsory liquidation or as a medium of final tender'.[2] The latter observation has particular force in this country, where the fundamental principle of the law of damages that the injured party is entitled to *restitutio in integrum*[3] cannot be taken in the literal sense of denoting *naturalis resitutio*,[4] but in the sense of the Roman maxim, 'omnis condemnatio est pecuniaria'. Thus, in the last resort, money becomes capable[5] of discharging all obligations; it is the subsidiary means of performance. Consequently it is possible to arrive at the comprehensive notion of monetary obligations the various aspects of which, divested of all procedural attire, are to be considered.

1. Monetary obligations primarily exist where the debtor is bound to pay a fixed, certain, specific, or liquidated sum of money.

While the certainty of the amount distinguishes this group from the following group of monetary obligations, it is the fact that a sum of *money* is owned which is the distinctive feature in respect of other

---

[1] Above, p. 5.    [2] Helfferich, p. 309.

[3] Halsbury (Hailsham), xii, para. 1129.

[4] As it is on principle proclaimed by the German Civil Code, s. 249; see Kahn–Freund, 50 (1934) *L.Q.R.* 512, and Dawson–Cooper, 33 (1935) *Mich. L. R.* 854, 876.

[5] The fact that in certain cases a party may be able to obtain an order for specific performance does not encroach upon the capacity referred to in the text. Cf. Carbonnier, *Droit Civil* (6th ed., 1969), ii. 16 who speaks of the absolute fungibility of money 'qui la rend apte, au moins par le jeu des dommages-intérêts, à remplacer toutes choses dans les paiements'.

obligations. If a debtor is bound to deliver a specific coin or note, e.g. the Bank of England note No. 1000 or the sovereign now lying in the left drawer of my writing-desk, this is not a money obligation, because the debtor does not owe a sum of money, but an individual object, which, in the circumstances, though being capable of having the character of money, has become a commodity.[6] Furthermore, if the parties envisage delivery of a specific quantity of a specific kind of money, e.g. 100 pieces of 20 French francs each or 100 pennies of Queen Victoria's impression, this likewise is not a monetary obligation, but an ordinary contract to transfer unascertained goods,[7] because here again the subject-matter of the contract is not a sum of money. The import of this distinction becomes clear if it is supposed that, in the above cases, the delivery of the promised objects had become impossible. In the first case the general rules relating to impossibility of performance would undoubtedly apply if the individual things promised to be delivered had perished;[8] in the second case, if the whole class had ceased to exist,[9] the same result would follow.[10]

Monetary obligations of the group now under discussion exist in three cases only. The usual type is to pay a sum of money pure and simple, e.g. £100 sterling. Secondly, the parties may agree that a certain sum of money should be paid in a certain manner, e.g. by delivery of two bronzes or of (unascertained) coins or notes of an ascertained type (£1,000 by delivery of Bank of England notes of £5 each; £5 by delivery of ten pieces of 50 new pence; £1,000 by

---

[6] See *Moss* v. *Hancock*, [1899] 2 Q.B. 111, and above, p. 24.

[7] Cf. s. 16, Sale of Goods Act, 1979 and the unconvincing decision of the European Court of Justice in *R.* v. *Thompson*, above p. 24. That contracts for the delivery of a specific quantity of coin or, still less, contracts for the delivery of a specified quantity of gold bullion are not money obligations should not be open to doubt. In *Holyoke Water Power Co.* v. *American Writing Co.* (1936), 300 U.S. 324 the Supreme Court of the United States, however, held that a lessee's promise to pay 'a quantity of gold which shall be equal to $1500 of the gold coin of the United States of the standard weight and fineness or the equivalent of this commodity in U.S. currency' fell within the ambit of the Joint Resolution of Congress of 5 June 1933 relating to 'obligations payable in money of the United States'. The decision establishes the distinction between an intention to use gold bullion for the purpose of stabilizing the value of the dollar and an intention to obtain gold for uses in manufacture, arts, or the like (without relation to money). The Joint Resolution applies in the former, but does not apply in the latter case. In the same sense *Emery Bird Thayer Dry Goods Co.* v. *Williams* 107 F. (2d) 965 (1939), which supersedes the earlier decision 98 F. (2d) 166 (1938). See also Arts. 1896, 1897 French Civil Code and Nussbaum, p. 231.

[8] Cf s. 6, Sale of Goods Act, 1979.

[9] The maxim 'genus numquam perit' (on which see Chalmers, *Sale of Goods* (15th ed., 1967), p. 35) is certainly not meant to apply to such a case.

[10] A third case which may appear to be, but is not a monetary obligation arises where, according to the express or implied terms of the contract, the creditor is entitled, not to payment, but to a credit at a bank or similar institution. This may be so in the so-called Euro-currency market on which see above p. 61 and below p. 193.

current account credit).[11] This is a genuine money obligation, because the contract, though determining the method of payment, provides for the payment of a sum of money.[12] Lastly the parties may agree that the debtor shall pay so many pounds sterling as two specific bronzes shall be valued at by Sotheby's, or as shall correspond to the value of a specific quantity of commodities at a certain date. This is a contract for 'converting bronzes into sterling',[13] it is a contract for an unascertained but ascertainable sum of money, and it therefore creates a money obligation.[14]

Again, the result can be tested by looking at the effects of impossibility. In the first case mentioned above there will be no supervening impossibility, because the theory of the 'recurrent link'[15] will practically always provide for converting the promised sum of money of the extinct currency into the corresponding sum of money of the

[11] In the United States of America there exists at present a distinction between payment of dollars in Clearing House Funds and in Federal Funds—a distinction which may involve differences of marketability and, therefore, of value.

[12] Its most important type used to be the gold coin clause, see below, p. 147. That the gold coin clause does not affect the money character of the obligation has been made clear by Lawrence L.J. in *Feist* v. *Société Intercommunale d'Électricité Belge*, [1933] Ch. 684, 702 and by Hilbery J. in *British & French Trust Corporation* v. *The New Brunswick Rly. Co.*, [1936] 1 All E.R. 13, whose remarks on this point remain valid notwithstanding the decision of the House of Lords in the same case [1939] A.C. 1. The same view has always been taken by the German Supreme Court: 22 Jan. 1902, *RGZ.* 50, 145, 148; 16 Jan. 1924, *RGZ.* 107, 401; 3 Dec. 1924, *JW.* 1925, 1183; see also Nussbaum, *Rec.* 43 (1933), 559, 563. But in the United States it was at one time thought that 'a contract to pay a certain sum in gold and silver coin is in legal effect a contract to deliver a certain weight of gold and silver of a certain fineness to be ascertained by count', see, e.g. *Bronson* v. *Rhodes* (1868), 7. Wall. (74 U.S.) 229, and *Butler* v. *Horwitz* (1868), 7 Wall. (74 U.S.) 258. This commodity theory, on which see more fully Nebolsine, 42 (1933) *Yale L.J.* 1050, 1063 sqq., was definitely rejected by the Supreme Court in *Nortz* v. *United States*, 294 U.S. 317, 326, 327 (1934) and in *Norman* v. *Baltimore & Ohio Rly. Co.*, ibid., at p. 302 *per* Chief Justice Hughes delivering the opinion of the majority of the court. In the United States it has also been held that the gold coin clause does not affect the negotiable character of an instrument: *Chrysler* v. *Renois* (1870), 43 N.Y. 209 and other cases referred to by Nussbaum, pp. 251, 252. If a note for $50,000 'in gold dust at $16 per oz.' (cf. the facts in *McDonald* v. *Belcher*, [1904] A.C. 429) provides for payment otherwise than in money, then Byles, *On Bills* (24th ed., 1979), p. 19, is correct in saying that it is not a promissory note. But it may have to be construed as stipulating for a sum of money measured by the value of 3,125 oz. of gold dust and may be valid under the decision of the Privy Council mention below, n. 14.

[13] *Latter* v. *Colwill*, [1937] 1 All E.R. 442, 451 *per* Scott L.J. The promise to pay in sterling the f.o.b. cost of goods shipped from New York (see below, p. 534) is similar in character. So is the promise 'to pay such sum of sterling as corresponds to $100' (see below, p. 200, n. 82).

[14] This type of contract frequently occurred in the shape of a gold value clause, see below, p. 147. That the gold value clause involves a monetary obligation, is obvious, but in *Syndic in Bankruptcy of Khoury* v. *Khayat*, [1943] A.C. 507 the Privy Council assumed without discussion that notwithstanding the gold value clause there existed a debt of a 'sum certain' within the meaning of the Bills of Exchange Act 1882. See note in 59 (1943) *L.Q.R.* 303 and below, p. 147, n. 60.

[15] Above, pp. 44 sqq.

existing currency. In the second case it may happen that the thing by the delivery of which the obligation is to be fulfilled, perishes, but this would leave the promise to pay a fixed sum of money unaffected.[16] In the third case difficulties cannot arise, unless the *tertium comparationis* is a specific thing, which it will very rarely be. These reflections lead to a conclusion which is fundamental to the law of money: it can never be impossible to perform monetary obligations. They are, in Nussbaum's phrase,[17] indestructible. Neither circumstances peculiar to the debtor, such as his poverty,[18] nor circumstances arising from developments in the monetary system, such as the emergence of a new currency or the elimination of protective clauses or the introduction of exchange control, ever relieve the debtor of his duty to pay.[19]

[16] Where the gold coin clause is invalid, there therefore remains the obligation to pay the nominal amount in paper: *Greene* v. *Uniacke*, 46 F. (2d) 916, 919 (C.C.A. 5th, 1931), cert. den., 283 U.S. 847 (1931) and other American cases referred to by Nussbaum, p. 297. English law is likely to be to the same effect: see *Feist*'s case, [1933] Ch. 684 (C.A.); *Treseder–Griffin* v. *Co-operative Insurance Society* [1956] 2 Q.B. 127; Dicey and Morris, p. 996. In *Germany* s. 245 of the Civil Code provides that if a monetary obligation is payable in a certain kind of money which at the time of payment is no longer in circulation, payment must be made in the same manner as if the kind of money had not been fixed. As to this provision see Supreme Court, 11 Jan. 1922, *RGZ.* 103, 384, 388; 1 Mar. 1924, *RGZ.* 107, 370; 24 May 1924, *RGZ.* 108, 166, 181 and see Breit in Düringer–Hachenburg, *Kommentar zum Handelsgesetzbuch*, iv. 760.

[17] p. 144. Of course, specific legislation may involve impossibility.

[18] See, in particular, Williston, *On Contracts*, s. 1932.

[19] For these reasons the fact that payment is impossible at the agreed place of payment should not in law be treated as a ground of discharge. This suggestion is opposed to the decision in *Ralli* v. *Compañia Naviera Sota y Aznar*, [1920] 2 K.B. 287 (C.A.), a case in which, it is submitted, insufficient weight was attached to the monetary character of the obligation. A contract which was subject to English law (at p. 290 *per* Lord Sterndale M.R., at p. 293 *per* Warrington L.J.) provided for a certain payment in Barcelona where, however, by the date of payment a Spanish statute had made it illegal both to pay and to receive the money. The action for the recovery of the deficiency was dismissed. Scrutton L.J. (at p. 304) stated the reasons in these words: 'Where a contract requires an act to be done in a foreign country, it is in the absence of very special circumstances an implied term of the continuing validity of such a provision that the act to be done in the foreign country shall not be illegal by the law of that state.' But as the stipulation of a place of payment in connection with monetary obligations is of relatively minor importance, it may safely be assumed that, if supervening illegality under the *lex loci solutionis* was within the contemplation of the parties at all, they would have made London the place of payment rather than release the debtor from a debt freely contracted. Scrutton L.J. (at p. 301) said: ' "I will do it provided I can legally do so" seems to me infinitely preferable to and more likely than "I will do it though it is illegal".' But would the debtor not have said: 'I will do it there provided I can legally do so, but if I cannot legally do it there, I will do it here'? Under German law such shifting of the place of payment would have been the solution: Supreme Court, 5 Dec. 1922, *JW.* 1924, 1357, No. 3; 19 Sept. 1923, *RGZ.* 107, 121; Supreme Court of the British Zone, 10 Mar. 1949, *NJW.* 1949, 465. See, on the other hand, a most remarkable French case: Cass. Civ., 1 Dec. 1954, Rev. Crit. 1957, 43. Russians agreed in 1918 in Russia upon a repayment of a loan of 16,500 roubles by the payment of £600 in London. The borrower, having become resident in France, failed to pay. The lender, resident in London, sued for payment of French

Another feature of these genuine money obligations is that the breach of the promise to pay a given sum does not involve an essential alteration of the structure of the obligation. It was at one time thought and even in the year 1922 said by Atkin L.J. (as he then was) that 'no doubt, technically, the action for debt is for the debt and for nominal damages for breach of the promise, expressed or implied, to pay on the due date. To satisfy the plaintiff's right of action once vested there must be an accord and satisfaction.'[20] However, as the same learned Lord Justice continued and the Court of Appeal held,[21] 'nominal damages in respect of the non-payment of a debt are a fond thing vainly invented, "a mere peg on which to hang costs" *per* Maule J. in *Beaumont* v. *Greathead.*[22] If a man being owed £50 receives from his debtor after the due date £50, what other inference can be drawn than that the debt is discharged?' This view appears to be eminently reasonable and is supported by the recently affirmed rule that it is possible to make and enforce by ordinary methods of execution an order for the specific performance of monetary obligations.[23] Today it cannot be doubted that even after action brought a debt which is overdue can be paid and discharged, there being no room for the idea of nominal damages nor any need for accord and satisfaction. Nevertheless if the failure to pay constitutes a fundamental breach or a repudiation of the contract (as it does where, for instance, three agreed instalments remain unpaid) and the creditor accepts it the debtor's primary

francs in France. The Cour d'Aix dismissed the action, because 'il était impossible . . . de considérer comme équivalent un paiement de livres à Londres et un paiement de francs en France et prononcer condamnation à ce dernier mode de paiement, alors que la convention n'avait envisagé que le premier'. The Cour de Cassation refused to interfere with what it treated as a mere question of fact. It has been suggested that the effect of *Ralli's* case is not to destroy the contract or to invoke the doctrine of frustration, but that it is merely a defence to an action on that portion of the contract providing for payment at the stipulated place of payment: *Cantiere Navale Triestina* v. *Russian Soviet Naphtha Export Agency*, [1925] 2 K.B. 172, 208 *per* Atkin L.J. Illegality at the place of payment might also be treated as a ground for suspension rather than discharge. (On suspension see *Andrew Millar & Co.* v. *Taylor & Co.*, [1916] 1 K.B. 402 (C.A.), especially at p. 411 *per* Swinfen Eady L.J.) Neither of these solutions is adequate in case of monetary obligations. Cf. *Graumann* v. *Treitel*, [1940] 2 All E.R. 188 on which see below, p. 449. The above remarks, of course, do not apply where performance of the monetary obligation as a whole becomes illegal. They are limited to the case in which, under the proper law, payment is legal, but payment at the agreed place is impossible on account of (local) illegality. On this distinction and on the effect of *Ralli's* case in the conflict of laws see the literature referred to below, p. 216, n. 150.

[20] *Société des Hôtels Le Touquet* v. *Cummings*, [1922] 1 K.B. 451, at pp. 463, 464.

[21] In the same case Bankes and Scrutton L.JJ. agreed in the result, though there are slight variations in the reasons given.

[22] (1846), 2 C.B. 494, 499, 500. See, however, Lord Russell of Killowen in *New Brunswick Railway Co.* v. *British and French Trust Corporation*, [1939] A.C. 1, at p. 29.

[23] *Beswick* v. *Beswick*, [1968] A.C. 58; see, in particular, at p. 81 *per* Lord Hodson.

obligation to pay is converted by operation of law into a secondary obligation to pay damages, though this may be no more than 'a revived obligation to pay' the debt.[24] In this case, therefore, the idea of damages reappears with the result that consequential losses may become recoverable,[25] and even in the case of liquidated sums tender may not be possible.[26]

2. Where a contractual promise to perform otherwise than by the payment of money, or where a non-contractual duty is broken, a sum of money becomes payable and the resulting obligation is therefore a monetary one.

The monetary character of the obligation is in no way impaired by the fact that, even if special damage is claimed, nothing but 'damages', i.e. an unascertained and unliquidated sum of money, is due, the special damage being 'only an item in a general claim for damages for a wrong done'.[27] It is true that this means that the debtor, though bound to pay, cannot be said to be indebted to the creditor until the amount of the compensation is agreed or ascertained by the court; consequently, though in respect of liquidated sums tender in payment is permitted and required, this is not so in respect of unliquidated sums,[28] and, moreover, rules relating to debts, as, for example, those allowing a judgment creditor to attach 'debts' of the judgment debtor in garnishee proceedings,[29] cannot be applied to cases involving the payment of unliquidated sums of money.[30] But these distinctions between debt and damages should not overshadow the fact that in both cases sums of money are to be paid, that in both cases alike the court has power to award interest for the whole or any part of the period between the date when the cause of action arose and the date of judgment,[31] that in any event,

---

[24] *Lep Air Services* v. *Rolloswin Ltd.*, [1973] A.C. 331. See, in particular, at p. 351 *per* Lord Diplock.

[25] Cf. dicta in *Trans Trust S.P.R.L.* v. *Danubian Trading Co.*, [1952] 2 Q.B. 297, though the case itself relates to the failure to provide a letter of credit rather than a mere failure to pay.

[26] *New Brunswick Railway Co.* v. *British and French Trust Corporation*, [1939] A.C. 1, at p. 29 *per* Lord Russell of Killowen. *Sed quaere.*

[27] *The Volturno*, [1921] 2 A.C. 544, 553, *per* Lord Sumner.

[28] *Dearle* v. *Barrett* (1834), 2 Ad. & El. 821; *Davys* v. *Richardson* (1888), 21 Q.B. 202 (C.A.).

[29] Rules of the Supreme Court, O.49, r. 1. Numerous cases dealing with the meaning of debt are collected in *Annual Practice*, 1980, Order 49/1/9.

[30] Nor is an unquantified claim for (unliquidated) damages 'a sum due', it is only a chose in action: *In re Collbran*, [1956] Ch. 250.

[31] Law Reform (Miscellaneous Provisions) Act, 1934, s. 3. Nevertheless it seems that in England it has not been the practice to award interest on unliquidated damages as from the date of wrong or the institution of proceedings, though in making his award the Judge may add an amount equal to the interest; this remarkable position was changed in respect of damages for personal injuries exceeding £200 by s. 22 of the Administration of Justice

the meaning of the word 'debt' depends on the context[32] and that there is therefore justification for uniting both under the heading of monetary obligations.

This is made clearer by the fact that the determination of the amounts due, though eventually reserved for the judgment of the court, is not quite discretionary. When the courts are called upon to assess damages they are guided by the principle that, in order to compensate the plaintiff for the loss suffered by him, a *value* must be put on the loss, and, as will be shown,[33] such value is measured by looking at the position existing at the material date. This fundamental principle of English law makes it possible to arrive at the somewhat closer definition that the monetary obligation created by the liability to pay damages involves the payment of that sum of money which, subject to the court's assessment, represents the value of the loss.

Monetary obligations thus appear to be obligations the subject-matter of which is the payment of a sum of money whether it is fixed at the outset or subsequently. Their principal characteristics are that in the absence of specific legislation their payment cannot ever become impossible and that they are capable of carrying interest.

To contrast liquidated and unliquidated sums is perhaps a little unusual. As a rule a distinction is made between debts and unliquidated sums. The terminology here adopted is deliberate. On the one hand the term 'liquidated sums' is intended to make it clear that it

---

Act, 1969, which, in principle, renders the award of damages mandatory. On the application of the rule see *Cookson* v. *Knowles*, [1979] A.C. 556 and *Pickett* v. *British Rail Engineering Ltd.*, [1980] A.C. 136. As to *Scotland* see *Macrae* v. *Reid*, 1961, Scots L.T. 96; *Killah* v. *Aberdeen & District Milk Marketing Board*, ibid., p. 232. In the *United States of America* interest on damages is regulated by State legislation; thus in Pennsylvania interest is payable from the date of the verdict, in Louisiana from the date of judicial demand: *New Amsterdam Casualty Co.* v. *Soileau*, 162 F. 2d 767 (1948, Court of Appeals, 5th Circuit). In *France* it is clearly established 'la créance indemnitaire . . . n'existe qu'à dater du jugement ou de l'arrêt qui la consacre' and that interest, therefore, does not begin to run before such date: Cass. Civ. 5 Nov. 1936, D.H. 1936, 585 and many other decisions. The point is open to much doubt in public international law; see, for instance, *Case of Norwegian Shipowners* (International Arbitral Awards I, 307, 341). *Royal Holland Lloyd* v. *United States* (*American Journal of International Law*, 1932, 399), *Senser's Claim* (Int. L.R. 1953, 240), *Lauritzen* v. *Government of Chile* (Int. L.R. 1956, 708), or on the other hand, *The Wimbledon* (Series A No. 1, p. 32), or the *Lighthouse Arbitration* (Int. L.R. 1956, 675), to mention only a few of the relevant cases. In *Germany* it is now clear that damages carry interest, usually from the institution of proceedings: Federal Supreme Court, 5 Jan. 1965, *NJW*. 1965, 531; 15 Jan. 1965, *NJW*. 1965, 1374 (1376). The rule is the same in *Switzerland*: Federal Tribunal, 13 Dec. 1955, *BGE*. 81 II 512, at p. 519; Oftinger, *Schweizerisches Haftpflichtrecht*, I (1958), 153 with further references.

[32] *Marren* v. *Ingles*, [1979] 1 W.L.R. 1145, at p. 1147 (C.A.), see also p. 1143 *per* Slade J. with reference to earlier cases.

[33] Below, pp. 115 sqq.

comprises not only debts in the classical sense,[34] but also such executory obligations of a monetary character as the price of goods not yet delivered. On the other hand the term should be understood as including special damages. Although these may be no more than an 'item' in a total claim for unliquidated damages,[35] from the point of view of monetary law there is no reason why sums which are so plainly liquidated should not be treated as such.

II

The distinction between liquidated and unliquidated sums of money plays a certain role when one comes to consider the conception of payment and its implications, that is to say, the question what it is that brings about the discharge by payment of a monetary obligation as well as how, where and when the money is to be, or may be treated as having been, paid.

1. On the Continent it is a much discussed problem whether performance of an obligation in general and payment of a monetary obligation in particular presupposes a consensual act, some understanding in the nature of a contract, or is simply a fact, albeit qualified by some such word as purposive. The debate goes back to the Romans and notwithstanding a clear and, indeed, impressive formulation by Gaius[36] continues to this day.[37] It has very little practical significance and is unlikely to be instructive for the English lawyer.

In this country it is well established that a claim for unliquidated sums cannot be discharged by mere payment, but by accord and satisfaction only,[38] 'The accord is the agreement by which the obligation is discharged. The satisfaction is the consideration which makes the agreement operative.'[39] In such circumstances, therefore, a contract in the strict sense of the term is required. As regards claims for liquidated sums, in the event of bank notes or coins being paid to the creditor the transfer of title obviously presupposes

---

[34] *Webb* v. *Stanton*, (1882–3) 11 Q.B.D. 518.          [35] Above p. 68, n. 27.

[36] *Inst.* 3.91 '. . . quia is qui solvendi animo dat magis distrahere vult negotium quam contrahere.'

[37] As to *France* see the monograph by Nicole Catala, *La nature juridique du payement* (Paris, 1961) or the survey by Marti et Raynaud, *Droit Civil*, Vol. II, paragraph 553. Among the enormous *German* literature see one of the earliest works by Gruchot, *Die Lehre von der Zahlung der Geldschuld* (1871), but also all modern books such as Larenz, *Lehrbuch des Schuldrechts* I (12th ed., 1979) 194 sqq. or Staudinger-Kaduk, *Kommentar zum Bürgerlichen Gesetzbuch* (10/11th ed., 1974), notes 11 sqq. before section 362 and the literature there referred to.

[38] Above p. 68, n. 28.

[39] *British Russian Gazette and Trade Outlook Ltd.* v. *Associated Newspapers Ltd.*, (1933) 2 K.B. 616, 643 *per* Scrutton L.J.

an agreement. The unilateral determination by the debtor of the purpose of the payment seems to suffice where he owes more than one debt[40] or in such contexts as the effect of the unrequested payment by a third party,[41] which, so it appears, discharges the debtor only if the third party intended to discharge the debt and the debtor adopts the payment. No modern English judge is likely to doubt that the debtor is discharged if the third party pays for his account and he does not object. Similarly, where the debtor pays the due amount to the creditor's agent who knows that payment is being made in discharge of a debt due to his principal and the latter keeps the money without objection the debt is effectively paid.[42] The agent's knowledge of the purpose is material, because if the intention had been to pay or accept the money, not *solvendi causa*, but, say, *donandi causa* there would have been no discharge. So it seems that, while no agreement is required to make an effective payment, the purpose of the payment must be communicated to the creditor.

2. No creditor is under any legal duty to accept any payment and no debtor can force any payment of any kind upon his creditor without the latter's consent express or implied, precedent or subsequent. Even if the parties agreed upon payment being made at a certain time in a certain manner an unwilling creditor cannot be compelled to accept it.[43] All the debtor can do is to tender it, i.e. to make an unconditional offer to pay in the agreed manner, and thus, in the event of non-acceptance, to bring about a situation which continental legal systems describe as the creditor's *mora*.[44] If the tender is in law a proper one (and if the debtor continues ready and willing to pay as agreed) any action brought against him, including any claim for interest,[45] will be dismissed with costs,

[40] The English rule according to which the debtor has the first right to appropriate payment (Halsbury (Hailsham), ix, section 505) seems to conform to universal practice. In *Germany*, for instance, it has frequently been decided that in order to bring about the discharge of a particular debt it must (and may) be defined by the debtor or must at least be definable: Federal Supreme Court, 7 Nov. 1965, *BGHZ.* 44, 179; 2 Dec. 1968, *BGHZ.* 51, 157; 14 July 1972, *NJW.* 1972, 1750. As to the *United States of America* see Williston (below n. 46), Vol. 15, section 1795.

[41] See Birks and Beatson, 92 (1976) L.Q.R. 188.

[42] *Société des Hôtels Le Touquet Paris–Plage* v. *Cummings*, (1922) 1 K.B. 451, particularly at p. 456 *per* Bankes L.J.

[43] In *France*, however, by virtue of a law of 12 August 1870 bank notes must in principle be accepted by the creditor and failure to accept 'monnaies nationales selon la valeur pour laquelle elles ont cours' is punishable by an administrative fine: Code Pénal Art. 30, Règlements d'administration publique R.30 No. 11. Similarly in *Italy*: see Art. 693 of the Penal Code and Ascarelli, p. 177

[44] Art. 1257 Code Civil; sections 293 sqq. German Civil Code.

[45] *Rourke* v. *Robinson*, [1911] 1 Ch. 480. But the debtor remains liable to pay interest if after tender he continues to make use of the money: *Barratt* v. *Gough–Thomas*, (1951) 2 All E.R. 48.

provided immediately after service of proceedings the money is paid into court.[46]

In English law,[47] therefore, the question of law to be answered is not how payment is to be made—it may be made by any method agreed between the parties or acceptable to the creditor. Anything so agreed and accepted constitutes a payment, provided the creditor is put in a position freely to dispose of the money or other asset.[48] The correct question is how an effective tender is to be made. The answer is that, in principle, it is to be made by proffering to the creditor the amount due in legal tender. This rule may be described as enjoying universal recognition[49] and is certainly firmly established in England. There exists a long line of decisions of the Court of Appeal which have expressed it in the clearest terms and occasionally in remarkable circumstances.[50] At the end of last century a Court of Appeal consisting of Lindley M.R., Chitty and Vaughan Williams L.JJ. held in regard to a sum of £463, then a substantial amount, that it had to be proffered in legal tender, that a solicitor had no authority to accept another solicitor's cheque instead and that such a cheque did not constitute a valid tender.[51] A year later the Court of Appeal held that an auctioneer was entitled to insist upon a deposit being paid 'in cash', i.e. in legal tender rather than by cheque,[52] and this was still accepted as the 'strictly' applicable rule in 1974.[53] The rule is, however, not only capable of being, but in fact is almost invariably, waived and the courts are[54]

---

[46] O.22 r.1 of the Rules of Supreme Court. There is also American authority for the proposition that the creditor's refusal of a proper tender involves the fulfilment of a condition precedent, the discharge of a surety, and the termination of the right to the enforcement of securities: Corbin, *On Contracts*, section 1233 (vol. 5A, 1964) or Williston (-Jaeger), *On Contracts* (3rd ed., 1972) vol. 15, section 1817.

[47] On payment and tender generally see Chitty, *On Contracts*, sections 1286–99 and 1322–34 respectively. It is doubtful whether the duplication is the result of a correct legal analysis, but the approach in many foreign countries is similar.

[48] *Seligman Bros.* v. *Brown Shipley & Co.*, (1916), 32 T.L.R. 349. In the same sense *China Mutual Trading Co. Ltd.* v. *Banque Belge Pour l'Etranger*, Hong Kong L.R. 1954, 144, 152: 'payment by a debtor into a blocked account without the consent of the creditor cannot be a good discharge of a debt.'

[49] *United States of America*: Williston (above no. 46), vol. 15, section 1810. *Germany*: see, for instance, Staudinger (-Kaduk), *Kommentar zum Bürgerlichen Gesetzbuch* (10/11th ed., 1974), notes 37 sqq. before s. 362, where it is expressly stated that, while bank money functions as money, payment by bank money does not, in the absence of the creditor's consent, discharge the debt. *France*: Carbonnier, *Droit Civil* (5th ed., 1967), vol. ii, p. 755. *Italy*: Corte di Cassazione, 3 July 1980, Giur. ital. 1981, I, 1, 95.

[50] See Chitty, l.c. section 1326 and the cases there referred to.

[51] *Blumberg* v. *Life Interests and Reversionary Securities Corporation*, [1897] 1 Ch. 171, affirmed [1898] 1 Ch. 27.          [52] *Johnston* v. *Boyes*, [1899] 2 Ch. 73.

[53] *Pollway Ltd.* v. *Abdullah*, (1974) 1 W.L.R. 493, at p. 494 *per* Roskill L.J., dealing with a sum of £555.

[54] See, generally, Dach, 'Payment in Cashless Societies', in *International Law and Economic Order* (*Essays in honour of F. A. Mann*) (Munich, 1977), p. 707.

and may be expected to become more and more astute[55] in finding waiver. Where large amounts are involved (and as a result of inflation they are becoming increasingly larger) payment by legal tender is frequently unthinkable and in many contexts cannot possibly be within the contemplation of the parties, so that a robust process of construction ought to displace the legal principle in most cases.[56] This does not mean that it would be safe to assume that a cheque would or should be held to be equivalent to legal tender—no creditor can be expected to take the risk of the cheque being stopped or dishonoured. But it does mean that if, for instance, the debtor offered a Banker's draft and the creditor insisted on legal tender the court should treat the latter's attitude as vexatious and, following an impressive opinion of Mr. Justice Holmes given in 1927 on behalf of the Supreme Court of the United States of America[57] uphold the tender. It also means that if a contract provides for payment 'in cash' to the credit of an account at a named bank, payment by bank transfer or cheque may be sufficient, for 'there is no real difference between a payment in dollar bills and a payment by payment orders which in the banking world are generally regarded and accepted as cash'.[58]

In most cases, however, the creditor will be very ready to accept any reasonable form of payment tendered to him, even if it does not strictly conform to the parties' agreement. In general creditors, particularly in the United Kingdom and the United States, will

[55] One of the most familiar methods is the rule that if the creditor's objection to the tender is founded, not upon its form, but upon some other ground such as the amount of the tender, the objection to the form is considered waived: Chitty, section 1326.

[56] In the light of the facts of the case referred to in n. 53, Roskill L.J. justifiably treated 'cash' as synonymous with legal tender. But in *The Brimnes*, (1973) 1 W.L.R. 386, at p. 400, Brandon J. (as he then was) equally correctly said that 'cash must be interpreted against the background of modern commercial practice' and 'cannot mean only payment in dollar bills or other legal tender of the United States'. Rather the conception indicates 'any commercially recognized method of transferring funds the result of which is to give the transferee the unconditional right to the immediate use of the funds transferred.' This definition was approved by Edmund David L.J. (as he then was) in the same case [1975] Q.B. 929, at p. 948 and by Cairns L.J. at p. 968, and also in *Mardorf Peach & Co. Ltd.* v. *Attica Sea Carrier Corporation of Liberia*, [1976] Q.B. 835 at pp. 849-53 by Lawton L.J. and at p. 854 by Bridge L.J. whose observations on this point remain valid, although the decision was reversed in the House of Lords, [1977] A.C. 850. For a good example of the courts' attitude see *Farquerson* v. *Pearl Assurance*, (1937) 3 All E.R. 124.

[57] *Simmons* v. *Swan*, (1927) 275 U.S. 113, where the creditor had rejected an instrument in the nature of a bankers draft. Mr. Justice Holmes said: 'If without previous notice he insisted upon currency that was strictly legal tender instead of what usually passes as money we think that at least the plaintiff was entitled to a reasonable opportunity to get legal tender notes, and as it was too late to get them that day might have tendered them on the next.'

[58] *Mardorf Peach & Co. Ltd.* v. *Attica Sea Carrier Corporation of Liberia*, [1977] A.C. 850, at pp. 879, 880 *per* Lord Salmon. See also Lawton L.J. above n. 56.

accept cheques, though in both these countries[59] as well as else-where[60] cheques constitute payment only on condition of the cheque being honoured, but if this happens, the date of payment is the date of the giving of the cheque. But if the creditor has authorized the debtor to pay by cheque and send it through the post and if the cheque is lost the creditor is said to have run the risk and been paid.[61] Moreover most creditors are likely to accept payment by transfer to the credit of their bank or postal giro account. It should be sound law, and in Germany it has been held,[62] that where the account is identified on the creditor's note-paper, invoices or in other (possibly published) documents he has invited or at least permitted his debtor to discharge liabilities by payment to the named account. No English decision treating such indications as a waiver of payment by legal tender seems to have been rendered, but the result is supported by commonsense and should readily be inferred from the parties' course of dealing or other circumstances pointing to their reasonable intentions.

On the other hand it must be strongly emphasized that the validity of any payment or tender otherwise than by legal tender does depend on the creditor's consent. Far-reaching reforms[63] the details

---

[59] Halsbury (Hailsham), vol. 9, paragraphs 500, 501; *Corpus Juris Secundum*, vol. 70, *sub verbo* Payment, paragraphs 23 and 24. And see the remarkable decision of the Appellate Division of *South Africa* in *Eriksen Motors (Wellcom) Ltd.* v. *Protea Motors, Warrenton and others*, 1973 (3) South African L.R. 685, at p. 693.

[60] *France*: Dalloz, *Nouveau Répertoire, sub verbo* Payment, No. 33, or Vasseur et Marin, *Le Chèque* (1969) No. 162, both with references to numerous decisions. *Germany*: see, generally, Staudinger (-Kaduk), *Kommentar zum Bürgerlichen Gesetzbuch* (10/11th ed., 1974) notes 47 and 50 before section 362, and in particular Federal Supreme Court, 7 Oct. 1965, BGHZ. 44, 179.

[61] This was so decided by the Court of Appeal in *Norman* v. *Ricketts*, (1886) 3 T.L.R. 182, though the effect of the decision was limited by another Court of Appeal in *Pennington* v. *Crossley*, (1897) 77 L.T. 43 according to which an established course of dealing involving the dispatch of cheques through the post does not constitute sufficient authority so as to burden the creditor with the loss of the cheque. Both decisions merit reconsideration, although they were followed in *Thairwall* v. *The Great Northern Railway Co.*, [1910] 2 K.B. 509. Payment by cheque is a conditional payment. It becomes unconditional only upon payment of the cheque. A debtor who, even by a course of dealing, is authorized to pay by cheque and to send it through the post, does not have authority to make the mere dispatch of the cheque an unconditional payment. There would be no unconditional payment even if the cheque had been handed to the creditor himself. The wholly artificial conception that the Post Office is his agent is therefore irrelevant. It is true that in the cases decided by the Court of Appeal the cheques were paid to the thief. But the condition upon which the creditor accepts the cheque is that it is paid when presented by him or with his authority.

[62] Federal Supreme Court, 13 May 1953, NJW. 1953, 897.

[63] Such as were enacted in *France* by a law of 22 Oct. 1940 as amended which imposes upon merchants the (apparently absolute) duty, enforced by a fine equal to five per cent of the sum improperly paid, to discharge many types of debts in excess of 1500 francs by crossed cheques or bank transfers. The debts comprise rent, salaries, and the price of goods,

of which are difficult to visualize would be necessary if, for instance, creditors were to be compelled without their consent to accept in unconditional discharge such 'money' other than legal tender as the debtor may determine, or to be satisfied with some form of conditional discharge such as a cheque. Nor is it certain whether actual, though unauthorized, payment by means of a transfer to the creditor's bank account would always be acceptable or even fair to him: such a transfer may prejudice him in the event of the bank's failure shortly after the transfer or of overdraft facilities becoming reduced as a result of the credit entry. If without authority the debtor pays the creditor's bank which he happens to know and if, before the creditor is informed or can object, the bank fails it is difficult to see why the creditor should be saddled with the loss, deprived of the benefit of any guarantee or other security and unable to rely on his statutory right to be paid in legal tender. Judicial practice abroad such as can be found seems to be in line with these submissions in that payment by 'bank money' does not discharge the debt except with the creditor's consent.[64] The opinion of the great majority of textbook writers is to the same effect;[65] even if some of them purport to attribute the quality of money to 'bank money' they in fact change their position, when they continue to admit that discharge by way of the transfer of such money presupposes the creditor's consent.[66] Academic criticism, where it is consistent and thus is prepared to dispense with such consent,[67] is in truth unrealistic, though it is made in the name of realism or for the sake of a definition of money which includes 'bank money'. Bank

work, services, cattle, and immovables. The law has a fiscal character and payment unlawfully made in bank notes is valid. For a detailed survey see Dalloz, *Nouveau Répertoire, sub verbo* Payement No. 30.

[64] No decision dealing with the point could be found except the important German decision referred to above, p. 74, n. 62.

[65] The German material seems to be more extensive than anywhere else: see the great *Commentaries* by Staudinger (-Kaduk) above p. 74, n. 60; Soergel (-Reimer Schmidt), 10th ed., 1967) notes 5 and 6 before s. 362 and s. 362 note 4; Alff in *RGRKommentar* II (1976) s. 244, note 2 and Weber ibid. s. 362, note 21; Heinrichs in *Münchener Kommentar*, s. 362, notes 15–17, but see von Maydell ibid. s. 244, note 7; Erman (-Sirp, 6th ed., 1975) s. 244, note 6, but see H.P. Westermann, s. 362, note 8 who, however, requires notification of the bank account and thus again reverts to the idea of consent; Canaris, *Bankvertragsrecht* (1975) notes 150 and 237 sqq.; Esser-Schmidt, *Schuldrecht* (5th ed., 1975) p. 187; Fikentscher, *Schuldrecht* (6th ed., 1976) p. 166; Larenz, *Schuldrecht* I (12th ed., 1979) pp. 138, 141, who says that in view of its function as universal means of exchange bank money is money, yet strongly emphasizes the requirement of the creditor's consent.

[66] This applies, for instance, to von Maydell, H.P. Westermann and Larenz referred to in the preceding note.

[67] Above, p. 6, nn. 17, 19. Rodière et Rives-Lange, *Droit Bancaire* (1973), s. 160 whose discussion is based on Rives-Lange, *Mélanges Henry Cabrillac*, p. 405, seem to dispense with consent and to treat 'l'écriture en compte', the entry in the bank account, as money, as 'le symbole qui la représente'.

money may in general practice be accepted by creditors as a means of payment, but it does not follow that in law they are necessarily bound to accept it as such. In short, as has been stated above,[68] with the creditor's consent bank money functions as money, but this does not mean that in law it is money and that, therefore, consent can be dispensed with.

3. The place of payment[69] is very often fixed by the parties, either expressly or impliedly. But in the absence of such determination the general rule in this country[70] as well as the United States,[71] Switzerland,[72] Holland,[73] Italy,[74] Greece,[75] and Hungary[76] is that the place of payment is the place where the creditor resides or carries on business at the time of the contract.[77] In these countries the debtor must seek his creditor. In France,[78] Belgium,[79] and Germany[80] it is the place where the debtor resides or carries on business: debts

---

[68] pp. 5 to 7.

[69] See, generally, Ernst von Caemmerer, 'Zahlungsort' in *International Law and Economic Order* (*Essays in honour of F.A. Mann*) (Munich, 1977), p. 3. Between 1966 and 1969 a Committee of Experts of which the writer as British representative was Chairman prepared a Draft European Convention on the Place of Payment of Money Liabilities. It was subsequently considered by a Sub-Committee of the European Committee on Legal Co-operation and opened for signature, but did not come into effect. See Mezger, Clunet, 1967, 548; Klingsporn, *Wertpapiermitteilungen*, 1972, 1262. According to Art. 59 of the Uniform Laws on International Sales Act 1967, the buyer shall pay the price at the seller's place of business.

[70] Halsbury (Hailsham), ix, section 490 and the cases there referred to, in particular *Rein* v. *Stein*, [1892] 1 Q.B. 753, at p. 758 *per* Kay L.J., or *Drexel* v. *Drexel*, [1916] 1 Ch. 251 or *Bremer Oeltransport G.m.b.H.* v. *Drewry*, [1933] 1 K.B. 753, at p. 765 *per* Slesser L.J. A creditor under an English judgment, though residing abroad, has only a right to be paid in England: *In re A Debtor*, [1912] 1 K.B. 53. Conversely, an award ordering payment abroad is not to the same effect as a judgment to pay a sum of money here: *Dalmia Cement* v. *National Bank of Pakistan*, (1975) Q.B. 9, where Kerr J. said *obiter* (p. 24) that an action claiming payment abroad was an action for damages. In *Pick* v. *Manufacturerers' Life Insurance Co.* (1958), 2 L1. L.R. 93, Diplock J. (as he then was), perhaps a little surprisingly, held that where payment is to be made to a foreign creditor 'in bankers' drafts on London, England, for pounds sterling', the place of payment was London, where the drafts are paid, rather than the place where they are to be delivered to the creditor. Dicey and Morris, p. 198, suggest that the choice of currency may have an influence on the identity of the place of payment; the authorities relied upon do not support this proposition which requires great caution, and in many cases may be contrary to modern practices and attitudes.

[71] *Corpus Juris Secundum*, 70, 217 (title Payment, s. 6).

[72] Art. 74, Obligationenrecht. See, generally, Küng, *Zahlung und Zahlungsort im Internationalen Privatrecht* (Fribourg, 1970).

[73] Art. 1429, Wetboek (provided that the residence of the creditor at the time of payment is the same as that at the time of the contract).

[74] Art. 1182 of the Civil Code.          [75] Art. 321.

[76] Art. 324, Commercial Code.

[77] This is so at any rate in those cases in which after the date of the contract the creditor moves abroad: *The Eider*, [1893] P. 119, at p. 131 *per* Lord Esher.

[78] Art. 1247, Code Civil.          [79] Art. 1247 Code Civil.

[80] s. 269, Civil Code. But see below, p. 214.

are 'quérables' rather than 'portables'; and in France it was held long ago that payment has to be made at the place where the debtor resides at the time of payment as opposed to the time of the conclusion of the contract.[81] Although there is no direct English authority on the point, it is suggested that in English law the place of payment[82] is the place where, according to the express or implied terms of the contract, payment ought to be made, not the place where payment is actually made.[83] Moreover, in English law the conception 'place of payment' connotes the place at which the creditor is entitled actually to receive the money due to him, not the place from which the money is to be dispatched to him or at which any other step preparatory to payment must be taken.[84]

The function of the place of payment (like that of the place of performance in general) may vary in different legal systems as well as in different contexts. In England, it is believed, the character and purpose of the place of payment is determined by the contract, its express or implied terms and its rationale.[85] Thus the place of payment may be the place at which the debtor is both entitled and bound or merely entitled to pay—payment at such places may be 'permissible'.[86] It may be the only or the optional, the 'primary',[87] but non-exclusive, the principal or the subsidiary place of payment. It may be the unalterably fixed place or one that in certain circumstances may be intended to change. The mere fact that the contract specifies a place of payment does not necessarily or conclusively mean that there cannot be another one. It may be specified so as to be binding upon both parties or for the benefit of one of them, so as to allow such party to make or require payment elsewhere. These questions are of particular significance in relation to the liability of a company at its head office for debts contracted by a branch in another country where they are stated to be payable. There is much support for the view that if the law at the head office governs the contract and if, therefore, the law of the place of payment cannot encroach upon the existence, nature or extent of the obligation the company cannot eschew liability by referring the creditor to the place of payment, where payment may be

---

[81] Cass. Civ., 9 July 1895, D. 1896, 1.349.

[82] On a possible change of the place of payment, see above, p. 66, n. 19.

[83] Since the repeal of s. 72(4) of the Bills of Exchange Act, 1882 there does not seem to be any material in England that would have a bearing on the point.

[84] But see below, p. 214.

[85] The subject is, unfortunately, wholly unexplored and the suggestions made in the text can only be tentative.

[86] See *Rossano* v. *Manufacturers Life Insurance Co.*, [1963] 2 Q.B. 352 *per* McNair J.

[87] See *Pick* v. *Manufacturers Life Insurance Co.*, (1958) 2 L1.L.R. 93 *per* Diplock J.

impossible.[88] On the other hand it must never be forgotten that, in the words of Kerr J. (as he then was), 'to compel a Pakistani bank to pay a large sum in England is certainly not the same, and in my view also not to the same effect, as compelling it to pay such sum in India. The consequences to the bank of these two obligations may be entirely different, and the obligation itself is certainly different.'[89]

4. The time at which payment should be made (or rather tendered) depends on the terms of the contract and may be a matter of construction. The only general rule is[90] that time is not of the essence of the contract, unless the express terms or the nature of the contract require a contrary conclusion or the debtor's delay becomes a fundamental breach.[91]

Where time is of the essence (and the mere indication of a specific date for payment does not normally achieve it), exact compliance is required and the courts are slow in finding waiver of the term. Thus if a contract provides for 'punctual' payment at a certain date which falls on a Sunday payment on Monday is too late.[92] Or where payment has to be made 'on demand' the debtor has to have it ready at a convenient place where he can get it within a reasonable time without having to make time-consuming arrangements.[93]

5. The time at which payment is in fact made (or rather tendered) cannot in many cases give rise to any doubt. Where bank notes are offered or where a bank account is credited[94] the time is readily ascertainable; in the latter case, in the absence of any mistake on the payor's or the bank's part, payment is made when, in the case of 'in-house' payments, the bank decides to credit the account and acts on that decision or, in the case of 'out-house' payments, the account is credited, notice to the creditor not being required in either case.[95] If the creditor accepts a cheque and this is paid, the

---

[88] See, in particular, below p. 415. In this connection, too, *Ralli's* case (above p. 66) causes great difficulty. Probably the court understood the facts found in the case stated so as to exclude a place of payment elsewhere than at Barcelona.

[89] *Dalmia Cement* v. *National Bank of Pakistan*, (1974) 3 W.L.R. 138, at p. 152.

[90] s. 41, Law of Property Act 1925, and see s. 10(1) of the Sale of Goods Act 1979.

[91] For details see Chitty, sections 1270, 1271, 1296.

[92] *Mardorf Peach & Co. Ltd.* v. *Attica Sea Carrier Corporation of Liberia*, [1977] A.C. 850.                                          [93] *Cripps* v. *Wickenden*, (1973) 1 W.L.R. 944, 955.

[94] Where an account should be credited on January 22 and it is credited on such date, but the credit is marked 'value 26', payment has not been made on January 22, still less has there been payment 'in cash' on January 22. This would seem to be obvious, but is in any case implied in the decision of the House of Lords, below, n. 97.

[95] *The Brimnes*, [1975] Q.B. 929, at p. 949 *per* Edmund Davies L.J. (as he then was), and see *Momm* v. *Barclays Bank International Ltd.*, [1977] Q.B. 791. In *Germany* it has also been held that, in the event of the creditor having consented, a credit to the bank account discharges the debt even in the absence of any notification to the creditor: Federal Supreme Court, 20 May 1955, *WM*. 1955, 1473.

payment is made on the date of the delivery of the cheque.[96] If on 22 January the creditor's bank account is credited so that the credit is complete, irrevocable and unconditional, but if by way of an 'inter-banking direction' the debtor's bank caused the account of the creditor's bank to be credited 'value 26 January' so that, when withdrawing the money on 22 January, the creditor would have to pay four days' interest, payment is not duly affected on the latter day.[97] When payment is made by telex transfer from one bank to another for the account of the latter's customer, according to Lloyd J. the payment is complete and has the effect of payment 'in cash' when the telex is received and tested by the receiving bank, it being unnecessary that the funds should have been credited to the customer's account or that all the paperwork within the bank should have been done.[98]

[96] *England:* see the dictum by Edmund Davies L.J. (preceding note). *United States of America: Corpus Juris Secundum*, Vol. 70, p. 233. The law is the same in *Germany*, (Federal Supreme Court, 7 Oct. 1965, *NJW.* 1966, 47), except that delivery is deemed to take place, when the letter containing cash or a cheque or a similar instrument is dispatched (Federal Supreme Court, 29 Jan. 1969, *NJW.* 1969, 875) or when, in case of a bank or postal giro transfer, the debtor's account is debited (Supreme Court, 11 Jan. 1912, *RGZ.* 78, 137; Federal Supreme Court, 5 Dec. 1963, *NJW.* 1964, 499). The point has been much discussed in *France*. See, for instance, Carbonnier (above p. 72, n. 49), p. 757. The latest decision of the Cour de Cassation, Ch.Soc. 17 May 1972, D.1973, 129 decides that payment is made when the cheque is received (subject to payment), while earlier decisions preferred the date of the 'encaissement effectif'. See the note by Professor Gavalda on the decision of 17 May 1972.

[97] *The Chicuma*, (1981) 1 All E.R. 652, with critical comment by Mann, 97 (1981) L.Q.R. 379.

[98] *The Afovos*, (1980) 2 L1.L.R. 479. *Sed quaere.* Completion of the paperwork cannot possibly be required to effect payment. But so long as the account has not been credited the recipient would seem to be unable to dispose of the money and the debtor may even be able to countermand his instructions.

# IV

# Monetary Obligations:
# The Extent of Liquidated Sums
# (Nominalism)

I. The foundation of nominalism. II. The historical development of nominalism (1) abroad;
(2) in England. III. The general nature and scope of nominalism: (1) public policy; (2)
judicial notice; (3) nominalism in statutes; (4) nominalism in the field of taxation; (5) the
case of the collapse of a currency. IV. The effect of nominalism in specific contexts: (1)
debts; (2) damages for default in payment; (3) depreciation as justification for discharge
of a contract; (4) specific performance.

I

THE debtor of a monetary obligation, as has been shown, is under a
duty to pay money, i.e. chattels which, among other peculiarities,
incorporate a reference to a distinct unit of account.[1] The latter
is not a quantity of metal, but an abstract unit of measurement
which in this country cannot even be defined by the historical
method.[2] It has, therefore, been said with justification that 'a debt
is not incurred in terms of currency, but in terms of units of
accounts'[3] or that 'contracts are expressed in terms of the unit of
account, but the unit of account is only a denomination connoting
the appropriate currency'.[4]

But how many such units of account, how much money is the
debtor bound to pay? It is this question of the value of money or

---

[1] Above, p. 21.

[2] Above, pp. 46 sqq.

[3] *Adelaide Electric Supply Co.* v. *Prudential Assurance Co.*, [1934] A.C. 122, 148 *per*
Lord Russell of Killowen.

[4] *Auckland Corporation* v. *Alliance Assurance Co.*, [1937] A.C. 587, 605 (P.C.) *per*
Lord Wright. In the same sense Maugham J. (as he then was) in *Broken Hill Proprietary Co.*
v. *Latham*, [1933] Ch. 373, 391, whose statement was approved of by Lord Wright in
*Adelaide Electric Supply Co.* v. *Prudential Assurance Co.*, [1934] A.C. 122, 160, and Romer
L.J. in the same case (C.A.) at pp. 407, 408, who very clearly explains that a pound is not
a coin and that a contract to pay pounds is 'a contract to pay so many standard units of
value by tendering coins or notes or other legal tender for the amount'; these remarks
are still valid, though the judgment was overruled by *Adelaide Electric Supply Co.* v.
*Prudential Assurance Co.*, [1934] A.C. 122. See also *In re Chesterman's Trusts*, [1902]
2 Ch. 260, and *Ottoman Bank* v. *Chakarian* (No. 2), [1938] A.C. 269, at p. 271.

the extent of monetary obligations which has not yet been dealt with[5] and which must now be answered.

The so-called *intrinsic* value of money, i.e. its substance or parity in terms of gold, cannot have any direct or indirect bearing on this question. As the unit of account, e.g. the pound sterling, is not identical with a quantity of metal, the obligation to pay pounds cannot be equiparated to an obligation to deliver a certain weight of metal. For the same reason it is impossible to hold that the extent of an obligation to pay pounds is determined by the rate of exchange of the standard metal, e.g. gold: the creditor of a sum of £3. 17s. 10½d. who in 1930 could obtain one ounce of standard gold cannot now claim £230 because this sum, approximately, is now required to buy the same quantity of gold. It was Savigny[6] who propounded a rate-of-exchange theory which in effect is not very different from metallism in the narrower meaning of the word. This theory presupposes that all currency systems are necessarily founded on the adoption of a certain precious metal as a standard metal. It is clear that this primary prerequisite of the theory does not exist, and, as it does not appear at present to have any adherents, it is unnecessary to review it in further detail.[7] In short, the idea of the intrinsic value of money was born in a bygone age when the bank note had not acquired its modern status and function and when only metallic money circulated which was liable to be debased by the Prince or pared by the clipper so that there existed 'one class which would give money only by tale and another which would take it only by weight'.[8]

Moreover, the extent of monetary obligations is independent of any *functional* or exchange value of money, i.e. its purchasing power. Modern economic science concentrates on the discussion of the value of money as determined by its exchange value; the quantity theory and Professor Irving Fisher's attempt to adjust by means of indices the unit of account to its fluctuating purchasing power[9] are

---

[5] That legal tender legislation (see above, pp. 40 sqq.) does not in itself or necessarily determine the quantum of the money to be paid is rightly emphasized by Eckstein, *Geldschuld und Geldwert* (Berlin, 1932), pp. 10 sqq., and Dawson-Cooper, 33 (1935) *Mich. L.R.* 852, 904 sqq. See also below, pp. 161 sqq. Legal tender legislation frequently provides that bank notes have to be accepted according to their nominal value. Such a provision has no bearing upon the question how many bank notes have to be tendered.

[6] *Obligationenrecht* (1851), 432 sqq., 454 sqq.

[7] For further criticism see Nussbaum, p. 218; Savigny's theory was expressly rejected by the Roumanian-German Mixed Arbitral Tribunal, *Rec.* VII. 738.

[8] Macaulay, *History of England*, ch. xxi, where the reader will find a vivid account of the alarming state of the English currency which had resulted from a long period of clipping and by the year 1695 called for urgent reform.

[9] *Stabilizing the Dollar* (1920); *The Purchasing Power of Money* (1931).

some of the outstanding topics of discussion among economists.[10] The functional value of money is in the minds of those legal writers who, under the influence of monetary troubles, have advanced a legal theory of *valorism*. The most remarkable attempt in this direction was made by Eckstein, who, in common with other representatives of that school of thought,[11] largely relies on the alleged intention of the parties to secure 'economic value',[12] and who, excluding certain well-defined cases only, develops a system of valorization which is to apply wherever money loses its 'relative stability of value'.[13] Monetary law, however, cannot pay any attention to the functional value of money or accept any valoristic theory based on it.[14] This is so for two reasons which need explanation. In the first place the law has to reject firmly any idea of permitting adjustments on account of changes in the price of goods, for such a risk must be borne by, and is everwhere clearly imposed on, the parties. Consequently a change of the price level could in law be material only if it were possible to attribute it to other than strictly commerical developments such as scarcity or abundance of goods. In fact for many decades it was believed by economists[15] that the exchange value of money or the price level may be determined by two different, distinguishable causes. These were thought to be either endogenous, i.e. moving from monetary developments such

[10] All economists who write on money discuss this question. The reader is referred to L. v. Mises, *Theory of Money and Credit* (London, 1934), or to Steiner, *Money and Banking* (1933), or to Hawtrey, *Currency and Credit* (1950), or to Neisser, *Der Tauschwert des Geldes* (1928). The quantity theory of money has now many different facets which do not seem to be of much help to lawyers. See, e.g. Andrew Crockett, *Money* (1973), pp. 48–65. The lawyer who cannot rely on highly specialized literature may find it helpful to refer to the article on 'Money' by Milton Friedmann, *Encyclopaedia Britannica* xii (1974), 349 or on 'Inflation and Deflation' by Professor A.J. Brown, ibid. ix (1974), 564, both with many further references.

[11] *Geldschuld und Geldwert* (Berlin, 1932), and see Hubrecht, *La Stabilisation du franc* (Paris, 1928), who mention and discuss other attempts in the same direction at pp. 131 and 203 sqq. respectively. Without adequate justification of its legal basis and effects valorism has more recently been advocated in numerous publications by E. Hirschberg: *Nominalistic Principle* (1971); *The Impact of Inflation and Devaluation on Private Legal Obligations* (1976); *Israel L.R.* 8 (1973), 530; *New England L.R.* 9 (1974), 403 and elsewhere.

[12] pp. 27–48.

[13] p. 51.

[14] It must, however, be admitted that Eckstein's criticism of the theoretical foundation of nominalism is thoughtful, interesting and partly even attractive. Thus it is indeed surprising (see Eckstein, p. 74) that nominalism should not have the character of *jus cogens* and should allow the parties to deviate from the principle by stipulating protective clauses: see below, p. 161. However, nominalism was made compulsory in certain countries such as Poland by Art. 6 of the decree of 27 July 1949 (*The Legislation of Poland* (Warsaw), ii (1949), 197).

[15] Menger, *Handwörterbuch der Staatswissenschaften*, 3rd ed., iv, 588 to 593. The terminology referred to in the text does not seem to have been accepted in this country.

as the expansion of credit or the increased use of the printing press and thus determining the so-called intrinsic exchange value of money, or exogenous, that is to say, controlled by the outer exchange value of money or the price of goods as influenced by market forces. If such a distinction were accepted by modern economists and capable of diagnosis the lawyer could conceivably, though somewhat hazardously, allow endogenous changes of substantial size to lead to an adjustment of monetary obligations on the ground that they are so far removed from anything contemplated by the parties that an intention to increase or reduce the nominal amount payable by the debtor may be implied. Economists, however, began to reject the distinction and its practicability in the early part of the century with the result that by a famous decision of 1925 the Assembled Chambers of the German Supreme Court refused to adopt a discredited theory.[16] Today no trace of it is left. Economists do not even mention it. They seem to define inflation indiscriminately as a sustained or as a persistent and general rise in prices[17] or as 'the increase (especially one that is considered excessive) of money supply, money incomes or the price level,— phenomena that often but by no means always go together'.[18] And when economists try to identify the cause of inflation, they speak of cost-push and demand-pull inflation depending on whether inflation is the consequence of the upward push of costs or the upward pull of demand on prices. In short, economic theory does not supply to the lawyer reliable means of identifying such causes of changes in the value of money in general and of inflation in particular as could be considered relevant for legal purposes. The second reason which precludes a lawyer from allowing the extent of monetary obligations to be determined by the functional value of money lies in the fact that economists cannot or at any rate do not furnish to the lawyer appropriate methods for measuring changes of monetary values. The indices which are available are not, from a legal point of view, free from arbitrariness and pitfalls.[19] They measure baskets of goods and services which *in casu* are liable to be wholly inapposite. The problem arises only in connection with long-term contracts, and they are usually of a special kind. To

---

[16] See below, p. 104, n. 116.

[17] See, e.g., Professor Harry G. Johnson, 'A survey of theories of Inflation', in *Essays in Monetary Theory* (1967), p. 104.  [18] A.J. Brown, above n. 10.

[19] See, e.g., Johnson, l.c. p. 105. During and after the great German inflation the German Supreme Court repeatedly and rightly drew attention to the dangers inherent in the selection of the appropriate index: *RGZ*. 108, 379, at pp. 381, 382; 109, 158, at p. 163. See Mügel, *Das Gesamte Aufwertungsrecht* (5th ed., 1927), p. 196. In the same sense Fögen, pp. 42, 43, 148, 149 or Schmölders, *Geldpolitik* (1962), p. 84.

measure and adjust a ground rent agreed in 1914 according to the cost-of-living index of 1981 would seem to be inadequate, because the value of land is in general independent of the cost of the goods which make up that index. Similar considerations apply in the case of long-term charterparties. Or who would suggest that the present value of a painting by Picasso which was agreed to be sold twenty years ago could be measured by any of the available indices? It thus appears that the intrinsic exchange value of money which might legally be relevant cannot be distinguished from the exogenous value of money which is undoubtedly irrelevant[20] and that, moreover, changes in value cannot be measured with a sufficient degree of congruity. It will appear later that for these and other reasons the law has fully adopted the results to which the preceding discussion leads. There is no legal rule which allows the revision of monetary obligations in consequence of changes of monetary values. But there are some legal rules which relate to the determination of prices and the influence of price changes. These rules equally apply where it is obvious that it is not the price which increases or falls but money which depreciates or appreciates, these being different aspects of the same phenomenon. It is submitted that any other solution is unworkable.[21]

The extent of monetary obligations cannot be determined otherwise than by the adoption of *nominalism*. The nominalistic principle means that a monetary obligation involves the payment of so many chattels, being legal tender at the time of payment, as, if added together according to the nominal value indicated thereon, produce a sum equal to the amount of the debt.[22] In other words, the obligation to pay £10 is discharged if the creditor receives what at the time of performance are £10, regardless of both their intrinsic and their functional value. It follows that a monetary obligation has no other 'value' than that which it expresses. Nominalism in this sense is a legal principle, but is empirically derived from a generalization of the normal factual situation.[23] In the vast majority of cases the possibility of changes in monetary value does not enter the parties'

---

[20] In the same sense Germany's Federal Finance Court, 14 May 1974, *BFHE*. 112, 546, at p. 557 or *NJW*. 1974, 2330.

[21] See the exceedingly interesting decisions of the German Supreme Court of 31 Mar. 1925, *RGZ*. 110, 371; 28 Nov. 1930, *RGZ*. 130, 308, the former of which is referred to below, p. 104. As to the part played by the conception of the functional value of money in the law of usury during the German inflation, see Supreme Court, 19 Dec. 1922, *RGStr*. 57, 35 with note by Alsberg in *JW*. 1922, 381; 6 May 1924, *JW*. 1924, 1607.

[22] See Martin Wolff's formulation in *Das Geld*, p. 637 and *Private International Law*, s. 449.

[23] This sentence (in its German version taken from the translation of the second edition

minds, though they may have a definite idea of the exchange value, or purchasing power, of the stipulated amount of money. If they have regard to that possibility, they may safeguard themselves by protective clauses; if they fail to do so, although they anticipate disarrangements of monetary value, they must be taken to have accepted the risks involved.[24] The law does not allow the implication of terms which either do not exist at all or to which the parties failed to give adequate expression. This negative statement, put into positive language, results in the rule that, in the absence of special clauses, parties must be understood to contract (or Parliament must be understood to legislate) with reference to the nominal value of the money concerned as expressed by whatever is legal tender at the time of payment. Nominalism thus finds its justification in the legally relevant intention.[25]

## II

Nominalism in the above sense, together with the view of money as a creature of the law and the 'recurrent link' principle, involving the rejection of the metallistic doctrine, forms part of the State

of this book) was accepted by Germany's Federal Finance Court, 14 May 1974, *BFHE.* 112, 546, 556 or *NJW.* 1976, 2330.

[24] This is particularly so where the risk emanates from the action of a third party, viz. the State, which has the sole power over currency. In this sense, therefore, monetary obligations are the foremost example of contracts which, in the words of Chief Justice Hughes, 'have a congenital infirmity': *Norman* v. *Baltimore and Ohio Railroad Co.* (1934), 294 U.S. 240, at pp. 307, 308.

[25] In the same sense Ascarelli, pp. 161, 178; Dicey and Morris, p. 992 and many others. The view that the nominalistic principle is based on the intention of the parties is supported, e.g. by Mr. Justice Strong of the Supreme Court of the United States (see p. 89, n. 47 below), whose opinion may today be described as the *locus classicus* of nominalism, and by the Swiss Federal Tribunal: 'Les fluctuations des changes constituent donc un des aléas du contrat' (26 Mar. 1931, *BGE.* 57, ii. 370). An early decision of the Supreme Court of the United States affords a good example of the transitory stage when a general rule had not yet been deduced from the intention of the parties. *Searight* v. *Calbraith* (1796), 4 U.S. 325, concerned an action on a bill of exchange for '150,000 livres tournois' payable in Paris. Since the bill was issued, assignats were introduced in France, acceptance of which the plaintiff refused. Mr. Justice Peters said: 'The decision depends entirely on the intention of the parties of which the jury must judge. If a specie payment was meant, a tender in the assignats was unavailing. But if the current money of France was in view, the tender in assignats was lawfully made.' Those writers who favour valorism, particularly Eckstein, l.c., pp. 28 sqq., also invoke the intention of the parties, but their method of implying imaginary terms into a contract is arbitrary. The leading Belgian textbook (Henri De Page, *Traité Elémentaire de Droit Civil Belge*, vol. ii (Brussels, 1967), p. 465) describes nominalism as 'une fiction juridique, et l'une des plus douloureuses qui soit'. But those who appreciate that nominalism derives from the intention of the parties and is capable of being displaced by them will reject the idea of a fiction. Fögen, p. 138, derives nominalism from a general principle of law which, however, is merely an abstraction from presumed intentions. Enrico Quadri, *Principio Nominalistico e Disciplina dei Rapporti Monetari*

theory of money as revived by Knapp.[26] But the nominalistic principle, although it received fresh force from Knapp's theoretical investigations and his striking formulations, goes back to ancient times; in fact, as throughout the economic history of mankind there is evidence of continuous variations in the value of money and especially of its depreciation,[27] it is not surprising to find that the principle of nominalism is almost as old as the problem of money value. Its history is of such importance and interest that it must be outlined.[28]

1. The nominalistic principle is usually said to have been laid down first by Aristotle in his *Nichomachean Ethics*, where he said:[29] 'Money has been introduced by convention as a kind of substitute for a need or demand, and this is why we call it νόμισμα, because its value is derived not from nature (φύσις) but from law (νόμος) and can be altered or abolished at will'.[30] In Rome,[31] though various

(Siena, 1978) also speaks of a 'principio giuridico' (p. 165), while according to B. von Maydell, *Geldschuld und Geldwert* (Munich, 1974) the extent of monetary obligations depends on the function which money performs in relation to various types of monetary obligations (pp. 97, 107). See also the same author in *Münchener Kommentar* (1979) s. 244, note 13. For an investigation of the reasons of economics and legal policy which in principle support nominalism see Reuter, *ZHR*. 137 (1974) 482.

[26] See above, pp. 13, 44, 51; on Knapp's nominalism see also Palyi, *Der Streit um die staatliche Theorie des Geldes* (1922); Wagemann, *Allgemeine Geldlehre* (1923).

[27] Feavearyear, p. 333.

[28] On the history of nominalism in general see Stampe, *Die geschichtliche Entwicklung des Geldnominalismus* (Berlin, 1927); Sulkowski, *Rec.* 29 (1929), 1. sqq., 5 sqq., and the literature there referred to; Ascarelli, pp. 100 sqq.; *La Moneta*, pp. 3–42; Endemann, *Studien in der romanisch-kanonistischen Wirtschafts- und Rechtslehre bis gegen Ende des 17. Jahrhunderts* (Berlin, 1883), ii. 170 sqq.; Connard, *Histoire des doctrines monétaires* (2 vols, 1935; 1936); Despaux, *Les Dévaluations monétaires dans l'histoire* (Paris, 1936); Monroe, *Monetary Theory before Adam Smith* (1923); Angelo Segrè, *Some Traits of Monetary Inflations in Antiquity and the Middle Ages*, Seminar I (1943), 20; Hubrecht, 'Quelques observations sur l'évolution des doctrines concernant les paiements monétaires du 12ᵉ au 18ᵉ siècle': Aequitas und Bona Fides, *Festgabe für August Simonius* (Basle, 1955), 133; M. Grice-Hutchinson, *The School of Salamanca* (Readings in Spanish Monetary Theory 1544-1605) (Oxford, 1952); W. Weber, *Geld und Zins in der Spanischen Spätscholastik* (1962). The numerous publications on the history of money in general usually contain very little material on the history of the legal aspects of money; this applies, e.g. to Angelo Segrè, *Metrologia e Circolazione Monetaria degli Antichi* (Bologna, 1928) or Fritz M. Heichelheim, *Wirtschaftsgeschichte des Altertums vom Paläolithikum bis zur Völkerwanderung der Germanen, Slaven und Araber* (1938), where, however, many references will be found at pp. 1061 sqq., 1198 sqq. or (in English) *An Ancient Economic History* (Leiden, 1958-70).

[29] Book 5, ch. 5, translation by F. H. Peters, 15th ed. (London, 1893), p. 156.

[30] It has been suggested that in the context νόμος does not mean law, but convention or usage: Gemaehling, *Les Grands Économistes* (1925), p. 7, quoted by Hubrecht, *La Stabilisation du franc et la valorisation des créances* (1928), p. 7. See Eric Roll, *A History of Economic Thought* (1973), pp. 33, 34 who quotes A. Gray, *The Development of Economic Doctrine*, p. 27.

[31] Mommsen, *Geschichte des römischen Münzwesens* (Berlin, 1860); Savigny, *Obligationenrecht*, i. 469 sqq.; Hartmann, *Begriff des Geldes*, pp. 111 sqq.; Knies, *Das*

depreciations of money took place,[32] the nominalistic principle does not appear to have been established quite firmly, the texts relating to the subject being inconclusive. The principal authorities are somewhat ambiguous dicta of Papinianus[33] and Paulus,[34] but as both contrast substance and quantity, and as the term 'quantity' is not quite unequivocal, a reliable conclusion cannot be drawn. Indeed, when the books of Justinian were studied by the school of glossators, the old texts came to be interpreted in the sense which Accursius (1182–1260) in his great gloss summarized by the words: 'tantum valet unus nummus quantum argenti tantundem in massa.'[35] The post-glossators, relying on their predecessors' ideas, developed the distinction between *bonitas intrinseca* and *bonitas extrinseca*, and it was the former, i.e. the metallic value of money, which they held to be the subject-matter of monetary obligations.[36] While the views expressed by the canonists generally tended in the same direction,[37] a decisive reaction set in after the publication in 1546 of Carolus Molinaeus's (Dumoulin's) *Tractatus contractuum et usurarum*. In this work, interpreting Paulus's decision by the words, 'Quantitas, id est valor impositus', the author laid the

---

*Geld*, 2nd ed., pp. 401 sqq.; Appleton, *La Monnaie romaine et la loi des XII tables*; Hubrecht, pp. 17–31. On the story of L. Veratius, told by Gellius, 20. I. 13, and the *actio de iniuriis aestimandis* see F. Schulz, *Classical Roman Law* (Oxford, 1951). p. 594.

[32] By way of example it may be mentioned that the pure silver content of the denarius was about 4.55 grammes around 200 B.C., but only 3.41 grammes at the time of Nero (54–68 A.D.) or that the price of a pound of gold, which was about 1,000 denarii at the time of Augustus, was no less than 3.3 million denarii by 419 A.D. See H. Wiesebach, 'Geldentwertung' in *Handwörterbuch der Deutschen Rechtsgeschichte* i (1971), 1456.

[33] D. 46, 3, *de solut.* 94. 1: '. . . sive in pecunia non corpora quis cogitet sed quantitatem.'

[34] D. 18. 1, *de contrah, emptione*, 1 pr.: '. . . eaque materia forma publica percussa usum dominiumque non tam ex substantia praebet quam ex quantitate', and in particular the famous passage, D. 46, 3, *de solut.*, 99, which dominates the discussion: 'creditorem non esse cogendum in aliam formam nummos accipere si ex ea re damnum aliquid passurus sit.' See on this passage, in addition to those mentioned in n. 31, E. Otto, *Thesaurus*, iii. 1256; D. F. C. Glück, *Pandekten*, xii (1809), 64 sqq.; Vangerow, *Lehrbuch der Pandekten*, 7th ed., iii. 28 sqq.

[35] See Hubrecht, pp. 31 sqq., quoting Bridrey, *Nicole Oresme* (Paris, 1908). Oresme, who died in 1382, is the author of the first French work on money, *De origine, natura, jure et mutationibus monetarum*. On Oresme's works see also Laurent, *Revue d'histoire économique et sociale*, 21 (1933), 13. According to the Jewish law of the Middle Ages changes in the metallic content of the coin, if they exceeded 20 per cent, apparently called for a corresponding change of the amount due from a borrower: see S. W. Baron, *Essays on Maimonides* (ed. by S. W. Baron, New York 1941), pp. 128 sqq., 197, 198. For the rest Maimonides (born 1135) seems to have expressed nominalistic views; in particular changes in the 'outer exchange value' were considered irrelevant. On the latter point, see also Simcha Ejges, *Das Geld im Talmud* (Giessen, 1930), pp. 52–4.

[36] Endemann, l.c., pp. 217 sqq.; Stampe, *Das Zahlkraftrecht der Postglossatorenzeit* (1928); Hubrecht, pp. 33 sqq.; Täuber, *Geld und Kredit im Mittelalter* (1933).

[37] Hubrecht, pp. 37–52.

foundations of the nominalistic principle as now understood. Dumoulin's ideas,[38] being so agreeable to the princes whose financial interests demanded a theoretical basis for their practice of debasing coins, were readily accepted in France,[39] where a decree of 1551 compelled the parties to contract by tale (sous, livres, deniers), not by weight (metal). From that moment the courts, too, adopted the nominalistic principle, which, in Germany also seems to have gained a complete victory in the course of the seventeenth century.[40] When we come to the eighteenth century, Pothier repeatedly affirms the principle and declares: 'Notre jurisprudence est fondée sur ce principe que dans la monnaie on ne considère pas les corps et pièces de monnaie, mais seulement la valeur que le prince y a attachée. . . . Il suit de ce principe que ce ne sont point les pièces de monnaie, mais la valeur qu'elles signifient qui fait la matière du prêt ainsi que des autres contracts.'[41] Under the influence of the physiocrats and their theory of the 'monnaie marchandise', a second reaction occurred during the French Revolution,[42] but the Code Civil of 1803 declares in Art. 1895:[43]

[38] See Täuber, *Molinaeus' Geldschuldlehre* (1928); Stampe, *Zur Entstehung des Nominalismus* (1932).

[39] For literature on the position in early France see Mater, p. 112; Dareste de la Chavanne, *Histoire de l'Administration en France*, ii (1848), 145 sqq.; Stampe, *Das Zahlkraftrecht in den Königsgesetzen Frankreichs von 1306-1547* (1930). A case decided in 1349 is described by Hubrecht, *Revue d'histoire du droit*, 16 (1937), 252. For the development in the second half of the sixteenth and early seventeenth centuries see the interesting article by Émile Szlechter, 'La monnaie en France au XVI<sup>e</sup> siècle', *Revue historique de droit français et étranger*, 1951, 500; 1952, 80. The operative words of the decree of 1551 were as follows: '. . . toutes personnes . . . seront tenu d'oresenavant de faire leurs contrats . . . et à sols et à livres seulement sans user de parolles d'escus ou autres especes d'or ou d'argent comme il a esté fait par cy devant'.

[40] This is denied by Stampe, *Das deutsche Schuldtilgungsrecht des 17. Jahrhunderts* (1925), according to whom the practice rested on the *bonitas intrinseca tempore contractus*, not on the *valor impositus tempore solutionis*. The former is expressly laid down, for instance, by the Frankfurt Reformatio of 1578, Second Part. title xxiv, paragraph vi. Pufendorf, Book V, chapter I. 16 in fact tends in this direction; see also Book V, chapter VII. 6. For an interesting survey of the state of the law see Johann Ludwig Schmidt, *In was für Münzsorten ist eine Geldschuld abzutragen?* (Jena, 1763), in particular sections 179 sqq. Even in 1793 Goethe rendered an opinion in the course of which he said that it was obvious 'that money is money, not on account of the stamp, but as a result of the intrinsic value': *Goethes Amtliche Schriften* (Weimar, 1968), II, 379. According to Gruchot, *Die Lehre von der Zahlung der Geldschuld* (1871), pp. 101-8, the older German statutes such as Saxony (1572), Frankfurt (1611), Hamburg (1603), Prussia (1685), allowed the value *tempore contractus* to prevail, and the principle of nominalism was recognised only by the statutes of the eighteenth and nineteenth centuries. On the history of Austrian law, see H. Charmatz, *Festschrift für Oskar Engländer* (1936), 75.

[41] *Traité du prêt de consommation*, v. 55; *du contrat de vente*, iii. 173; *du contrat de constitution de rente*, iii. 473 (édition Bugnet).

[42] For details see Mater, pp. 137 sqq., and Hubrecht, pp. 68-81.

[43] On the history of this provision see Hubrecht, pp. 86-93. It found its way into the Codes of Belgium, Holland (Art. 1973), Italy (Art. 1277), Spain (Art. 312), Portugal (Art.

L'obligation qui résulte d'un prêt en argent, n'est toujours que de la somme numérique énoncée au contrat. S'il y a eu augmentation ou diminution d'espèces avant l'époque du payement, le débiteur doit rendre la somme numérique prêtée, et ne doit rendre que cette somme dans les espèces ayant cours au moment du payment.

Although the rule is laid down with regard to loans only, it is generally recognized that it is of universal application, and the rule 'le franc égale le franc' is firmly established. Thus it is said by Planiol–Ripert.[44] 'Le débiteur doit fournir la somme due d'après la valeur nominale des monnaies au jour du paiement et non d'après la valeur qu'avaient les monnaies au jour où l'obligation a été contractée. . . . La loi a formulé cette règle à propos du prêt d'argent, en des termes qui ne laissent pas place à aucune discussion.' Although from time to time attempts have been made to replace nominalism by metallistic or valoristic doctrines,[45] it cannot be doubted that nominalism, which is 'a basic principle regulating the prevailing monetary order and economic policy',[46] universally predominates.[47]

727), Argentine (Art. 619), Mexico (Art. 2389) and until 1974 Chile (Art. 2199). The substance of the provision has also been adopted in Egypt by Art. 577 of the Code Mixte; the Court of Appeal of the Mixed Tribunal in a decision of 19 May 1927, Clunet, 1928, 765 (re Marquis de la Celle), expressed the view that Art. 1895 of the French Civil Code and Art. 577 of the Code Mixte concern 'uniquement les variations des espèces métalliques', excluding any variations in the value of paper money. This view seems to have remained isolated and has since been abandoned: 9 Mar. 1929, Gazette des Tribunaux mixtes, xx. 108, No. 115.

[44] Traité pratique du droit civil français, vii (1931), No. 1159. See in the same sense Aubry et Rau, p. 235, n. 11, with further references, the judgment of the Belgian Cour de Cassation (9 Mar. 1933), Clunet, 1933, 731, and of the Italian Corte di Cassazione (30 May 1927), Giurisprudenza Italiana, 1927, 1016; also Cour de Montpellier, 15 Nov. 1944, Rev. Crit. 1948, 88.

[45] See above, pp. 181 sqq. As to Switzerland generally see Müller and Barth, Zeitschrift für schweizerisches Recht, 43 (1924), 95a sqq., 175a sqq.; Henggeler and Guisan, ibid. 56 (1937), 158a sqq., 260a sqq.; von Büren, Schweizerisches Obligationenrecht (Allgemeiner Teil, 1964), pp. 35, 36; von Tuhr-Peter, Allgemeiner Teil des Schweizerischen Obligationenrechts (3rd ed., 1974), I, 62 with numerous references. It appears that the control of nominalism is well established.

[46] Germany's Federal Constitutional Court, 19 Dec. 1978, BVerfGE 50, 57, at p. 92 where similar remarks by Germany's other supreme tribunals are referred to. The Berlin Court of Appeal (25 Oct. 1927, JW. 1929, 446, 448) said that without nominalism 'capitalism is economically inconceivable', but it is doubtful whether widespread indexation practised in certain countries has not disproved this statement.

[47] On the Continent its existence is secured, and while with regard to individual questions reference is made to the discussion below, pp. 102 sqq., it is worth mentioning that the German Supreme Court was called upon to reject an argument to the effect that under a rule of public international law loans must be repaid according to the intrinsic gold value which the money had when the loans were given; see below, p. 468. It was wholly exceptional and surely untenable that in a single decision the Austrian Supreme Court held that a defendant who in 1914 received a loan of 80 Marks in gold coins, but without a gold clause, was liable to repay gold coins: 6 Nov. 1923, SZ v, No. 253. In the United States the modern law has repeatedly been stated, the chief authority being the interesting dictum of Mr. Justice Strong in Knox v. Lee and Parker v. Davies (1870), 12

2. The investigations of continental scholars have made themselves felt in this country. It appears to have already been recognized in the Middle Ages that the King had not only the prerogative right of issuing coin,[48] but also of determining the denomination or value at which the coin was to pass current.[49] Consequently, the King could debase or enhance the value, and this power was repeatedly made use of.[50, 51] The whole problem was very fully and learnedly discussed in Sir John Davies's report of the famous *Case de Mixt Moneys*,[52] which is still the leading authority[53] and in which the

Wall. (79 U.S.) 457, at p. 548: 'it was not a duty to pay gold or silver or the kind of money recognized by law at the time when the contract was made, nor was it a duty to pay money of equal intrinsic value in the market . . . The expectation of the creditor and the anticipation of the debtor may have been that the contract would be discharged by the payment of coined money, but neither the expectation of one party nor the anticipation of the other constitutes the obligation of the contract. There is a well recognized distinction between the expectation of the parties to a contract and the duty imposed by it. Were it not so, the expectation of results would always be equivalent to a binding engagement that they should follow. But the obligation of a contract to pay money is to pay that which the law shall recognize as money when the payment is to be made. If there is anything settled by decision, it is this, and we do not understand it to be controverted. Davis 28; *Barrington* v. *Potter*, Dyer 81*b*; *Faw* v. *Marsteller* 2 Cranch. 29. . . . Every contract for the payment of money, simply, is necessarily subject to the constitutional power of the government over the currency, whatever that power may be, and *the obligation of the parties is therefore assumed with reference to that power*.' See also *Juillard* v. *Greenman* (1883), 110 U.S. 421, at p. 449 *per* Mr. Justice Gray delivering the opinion of the Court; *Effinger* v. *Kenney* (1885), 115 U.S. 566, at p. 575 *per* Mr. Justice Field; *Woodruff* v. *State of Mississippi* (1895), 162 U.S. 292, at p. 302 *per* Chief Justice Fuller; *Ling Su Fan* v. *United States* (1910), 218 U.S. 302, where it was said 'that public law gives to such coinage a value which does not attach as a mere consequence of intrinsic value. They bear, therefore, the impress of sovereign power which fixes value and authorizes their use in exchange', and where it was concluded that this power involves that of prohibiting exportation of money. Finally, in *Deutsche Bank* v. *Humphreys* (1926), U.S. 517, 519, Mr. Justice Holmes said: 'obviously in fact a dollar or a mark may have different values at different times but to the law that establishes it, it is always the same'. As to the *Philippines* see Supreme Court in *Mayers* v. *Smith Bell*, 10 Phil. 319.

   [48] See above, p. 15.

   [49] Y.B. 21 Edw. II, f. 60*b*; 9 Edw. IV, f. 49*a*; Dyer, 81*b*–83*a*; Blackstone, i. 278; see also Breckinridge, *Legal Tender, A Study in English and American Monetary History* (1903).

   [50] Feavearyear, pp. 9, 14, 17, 30, 34 sqq., 46 sqq.

   [51] It was, however, somewhat doubtful whether the King could debase or enhance the value below or above the sterling value which Blackstone, l.c. defines by the words: 'when a given weight of gold or silver is of a given fineness, it is then of the true standard and called sterling metal. . . . And of this metal all the coin of the kingdom must be made by the Statute 25 Edw. 3 ch. 13.' Blackstone gave a negative answer to the question, while Sir Matthew Hale (1 Hale P.C. 194) answered it in the affirmative. See Halsbury (Hailsham), viii, No. 1018, n. 2. See also Vansittart's observations in the House of Commons, 13 May 1811, Hansard, p. 38.

   [52] *Gilbert* v. *Brett* (1604), Davies 18; 2 State Trials 114.

   [53] Story, s. 313; Wallace, *Reporters*, p. 235; the case was of great importance in the judgment of the Supreme Court of the United States in the notable case of *Knox* v. *Lee* and *Parker* v. *Davies* (1870), 12 Wall. (79 U.S.) 457, at p. 548 *per* Mr. Justice Strong, at p. 565 *per* Mr. Justice Bradley.

results of the Year Book period as well as the ideas developed on the Continent from Aristotle onwards were exhaustively referred to. Gilbert of London had sold goods to Brett of Drogheda for '£100 sterling current and lawful money of England' to be paid in Dublin. Before the sum became due, Queen Elizabeth, by proclamation, recalled the existing currency of Ireland and issued a new debased coinage (called mixed money) which was declared to be 'le loyall and currant money de cest realme de Ireland'. Every creditor was bound to accept it, a refusal to accept it 'solong le denominatio ou valuatio' being punishable. Tender was made in the debased coin, and the question which the Privy Council of Ireland asked the Chief Judges to decide was whether or not it was a good tender. The reporter first dealt with the necessity of having a certain standard of money in every commonwealth and with the King's right to make money, to determine its substance and form and also its value. He goes on to state[54] that

le doubt prima facie fuit, come cest mixt money serra dit sterling. Et pur le cleering de cest doubt, fuit dit que en chescun coine ou piece de money est bonitas intrinseca et bonitas extrinseca. Intrinseca consistit in pretiositate materiae et pondere, viz. finenesse and weight. Extrinseca bonitas consistit in valuatione seu denominatione, and in forma seu charactere. Budelius de re nummaria lib. 1 cap. 7. Et cest bonitas extrinseca, que cest auxy dit aestimatio sive valor imposititius est formalis and essentialis bonitas monetae; and cest forme dat nomen and esse a le money: car sans tiel forme le plus precious and pure metall que poet estre nest pas money. Et pur ceo Molinaeus libro de mutatione monetae dit, non materia naturalis corporis monae, sed valor imposititius est forma et substantia monetae, quae non est corpur physicum sed artificiale, come Aristotle dit Ethicorum lib. 5.

Thus the result was reached that the mixed money, having the impression and inscription of the Queen of England and being proclaimed for current and lawful money within the kingdom of Ireland, ought to be taken and accepted for sterling money. The reporter then turns to the constitutional question whether the mixed money circulating in Ireland could be said to be current and lawful money 'of England' within the meaning of the contract. After having given an affirmative answer, he proceeds to examine the importance of the fact that, at the time when the contract was made, better money was in circulation. This was, however, considered to be irrelevant. 'Car le temps est future', that is to say, if the said Brett shall pay or cause to be paid one hundred pounds sterling current money. 'Et pur ceo tiel money serra pay que serra

[54] p. 24.

currant a tiel future temps, issint que le temps del payment, and
nemy le temps de contract, serra respect.'[55] The case is thus a clear
authority for the nominalistic principle that the obligation to pay
£100 sterling is to pay what the law denominates as £100 sterling
at the time of the payment.

This principle, which by the seventeenth century was clearly
established, also in Scotland,[56] has never been departed from.[57] To a
considerable extent this is to be attributed to the remarkably patriotic
spirit which the British people displayed in periods of crisis.

[55] p. 27; he relied on the Year Book cases referred to above, p. 90, n. 49.

[56] Stair, *Institutions of the Law of Scotland* (1st ed., 1681), i. 11. 5, refers to Scottish
legislation of the fifteenth century according to which the Scottish custom was 'to have
the repayment of the same intrinsic value'. He continues, however, that 'that was well
altered by posterior custom, allowing the current coin for the time by the extrinsic value
to be sufficient, in all redemptions, much more in personal contracts; which is more convenient, seeing money is regarded as the token of exchange, and as a fungible, not as a
body'. Stair's contemporary, Sir George Mackenzie (quoted here from *Works*, vol. i (1716),
part 2, p. 193) is to the same effect except that he relies on legislation of the fifteenth
century in support of the rule that redemption, and indeed every repayment, is to be
made 'according to the rate money gives at the time when the redemption was used and
not according to the rate it gave at the time when the wadset was granted'. The principle
of nominalism was clearly accepted by *Hamilton* v. *Corbet* (1731), M. 10142.

[57] *Deering* v. *Parker* (1760), 4 Dallas, p. xxiii, was a very special case which should
be mentioned as a matter of historical interest. It arose from an appeal from New Hampshire heard before a Committee of the Privy Council in 1760. The defendant Parker had
given a bond to the appellant Deering, payable in 1735, for the payment of £2,460 'in good
public bills of the province of Massachusetts Bay or current lawful money of New England'.
In 1752 the defendant tendered a large sum in the bills of credit then current in New
Hampshire. The Chancery Court of New Hampshire gave judgment for a balance of
£354. 6s. 9d. in bills of credit of New Hampshire, 'being the nominal sum due at the time
of tender deducting the sums paid and endorsed. So that the Court went upon the principle
that the plaintiff should take the bills as tendered and that the debtor was not bound
to make good their depreciation nor to pay in silver or real money.' On appeal the appellant
insisted that he had not received what he contracted for, namely either bills of Massachusetts
Bay, which had been called in and sunk before the tender, or silver money agreeable to
Queen Anne's proclamation, which he insisted was the true meaning of the words 'current
lawful money of New England'. The respondent contended that this clause referred to the
bills of credit of any of the New England colonies. The court accepted the appellant's
construction that the words 'current lawful money of New England' did not mean bills
of credit of any colony. Lord Mansfield, being a member of the Board, said that he was
at a loss to determine the quantum of the debt. He quoted information given to him by
a Mr. J., 'a New England gentleman who had practised the law', from which it appeared
that the 'more general method was to take the value of the bills when they should have
been paid by contract'. The Board as a whole, 'instead of taking the price of silver at the
time of the contract and the time set for payment (which was about 27 sh. per ounce)
fixed it at 37 sh. per ounce and computed the debt, accordingly'. The case undoubtedly
seems to imply the recognition of metallistic views, but as it does not appear to have been
reported in any of the English reports, and as it has never been relied upon in this country,
it cannot be said to have even a persuasive authority. The dictum in *Pilkington* v. *Commissioners for Claims* (1821), 2 Knapp 7 at p. 18, if put at its highest, merely indicates
that to Sir William Grant's mind the authority and correctness of the decision in *Gilbert*
v. *Brett* was not so firmly established that a consideration of differing views expressed by
Vinnius could at once be dispensed with.

In 1811 the Bullion Committee in their Report, 'one of the most important documents in English currency history',[58] had arrived at the conclusion that the rise in prices was due to an over-issue of Bank of England notes, as a result of which the value of the notes had depreciated. On 6 May 1811 Horner introduced his resolution in the House of Commons supporting the Report and affirming the depreciation of money.[59] But although by 1811 gold had risen from the parity of £3. 17s. 6d. to £4. 19s. 6d. per ounce and the value in sterling of most foreign currencies and commodities had gone up by approximately 20 per cent,[60] the resolutions were lost with heavy majorities. On 13 May 1811 Vansittart introduced resolutions which rejected the Bullion Report and one of which contained the memorable words 'that the promissory notes of the said Company [the Bank of England] have hitherto been, and are at this time, held in public estimation to be equivalent to the legal coin of the realm and generally accepted as such in all pecuniary transactions to which such coin is lawfully applicable',[61] and these resolutions were carried. But shortly afterwards Lord King announced that in view of the depreciation of money he would no longer accept from his tenants bank notes at their face value in payment of rents, but calculate the rents on a gold basis. His proposals provoked great excitement and were strongly resented. His opponents 'held to the time-honoured principle that a man who contracted to receive a pound, must take whatever was by general consent called a pound when payment was made. This was the principle which had been followed for a thousand years in spite of all the many changes of form and value, some of them very rapid, which the pound had undergone.'[62] The House of Commons at once passed Lord Stanhope's Act[63] by which for all practical purposes bank notes were made legal tender[64] and which provided that no one should pay or receive more for guineas or less for bank notes than their face value.[65] The Vansittart Resolution and the promptness with which Lord King's proposals were defeated[66] should be seen together with the lack of success

---

[58] Feaveryear, p. 195.                    [59] Hansard, 6 May 1811, p. 831.

[60] Feaveryear, p. 194 and the table, p. 230.

[61] Hansard, 13 May 1811, p. 70.

[62] Feaveryear, p. 206; see also Lord King's pamphlet *Thoughts on the Effects of the Bank Restriction* (2nd ed., London, 1804).

[63] 51 Geo. III, ch. 127; it became law on 24 July 1811.

[64] See above, p. 41.                              [65] See below, p. 168.

[66] The events of 1811 are shortly but lucidly described by Feaveryear, pp. 195 sqq., but the debates in Parliament on the Horner and Vansittart Resolutions and on Lord Stanhope's Act make such exceedingly interesting reading that they should be looked up in Hansard. It is certain that the opponents of the Bulletin Report were, consciously or

of all attempts to remedy the serious effects of deflation that followed on the restoration of the gold standard in 1821.[67]

Similarly, 110 years later, the abandonment of the gold standard in 1931 was accepted so quietly and readily and entailed so insignificant a 'flight from sterling' that the monetary discipline implied in the principle of *Gilbert* v. *Brett* may be said to have survived well into the present century. Indeed, it was at that very moment that for the first time since 1604 nominalism was judicially reaffirmed by Scrutton L.J.:[68]

I take it that if a tort had been committed in England before England went off the gold standard, the plaintiff could not say: 'We insist, after England has gone off the gold standard and the pound has depreciated in international purchasing power, on being paid the value of the gold standard pound at the time of the commission of the tort.' *A pound in England is a pound whatever its international value.*

It was only after the Second World War that things changed, though perhaps only temporarily. The legal principle, it is true, continued to be supported by high judicial authority. Thus Viscount Simonds[69] said that 'the obligation to pay will be satisfied by payment of whatever currency is by the law of Queensland valid tender for the discharge of the nominal amount of the debt'. Lord Denning made a particularly clear and emphatic statement:[70]

A man who stipulates for a pound must take a pound when payment is made, whatever the pound is worth at that time. Sterling is the constant unit of value by which in the eye of the law everything else is measured. Prices of commodities may go up or down, other currencies may go up and down, but sterling remains the same.

unconsciously, under a delusion, as became clear in 1819 (see Feavearyear, pp. 219 sqq.), but this does not affect the importance of their attitude. See also Charles Rist, 'Le cours forcé en Angleterre (1797–1821)', *Revue d'histoire économique et sociale*, 23 (1937), 5.

[67] See Feavearyear, pp. 224–6. It was at this stage that there appeared in England what is probably the first proposal for something in the nature of an index currency: Joseph Lowe, *The Present State of England* (1822), who terminates a discussion of the injurious effect of fluctuation in the value of money with the suggestion (p. 279) that 'a table exhibiting from year to year the power of money in purchase would give to annuitants and other contracting parties the means of maintaining an agreement, not in its letter only, but in its spirit; of conferring on a specified sum a uniformity and permanency of value by changing the numerical amount in proportion to the change in its power to purchase'. The table at p. 95 of the Appendix is, from the point of view of modern statistics, naïve, but constitutes a remarkable appreciation of a continuing problem.

[68] *The Baarn* (No. 1), [1933] P. 251, 265.

[69] *Bonython* v. *Commonwealth of Australia*, [1951] A.C. 201, 222.

[70] *Treseder-Griffin* v. *Co-operative Insurance Society*, [1956] 2 Q.B. 127, at p. 144. In the same sense *Re United Railways of Havana*, [1961] A.C. 1007, 1069, 1070. Lord Denning's strong adherence to nominalism was also expressed in the case mentioned below, p. 125, n. 58. But see now *Staffordshire Health Authority* v. *South Staffordshire*

Yet in more recent years economic events, as will appear,[71] forced on occasions a slightly different tone upon the judiciary. The events of 1931 were followed eighteen years later by the devaluation of 1949 and, after a further period of eighteen years, by the fresh devaluation of 1967. Since 1972 sterling has been floating. For forty years a system of exchange control tried to substitute the force of law for an attitude of mind. During the same period inflation led to a marked reduction of sterling's internal purchasing power by some 95 per cent. since 1914, by more than 90 per cent. cent 1931, by around 90 per cent. since 1945, by some 70 per cent. since 1970. The following table[72] shows the decline in the purchasing power of the pound since 1914 by indicating the number of (new) pence which in any one year a person then spending 100 (new) pence would have paid in 1914 for the same goods:

| 1914 | 100p | 1936 | 67 | 1958 | 29 |
|------|------|------|-----|------|-----|
| 1915 | 80 | 1937 | 64 | 1959 | 29 |
| 1916 | 68 | 1938 | 64 | 1960 | 29 |
| 1917 | 56 | 1939 | 63 | 1961 | 27 |
| 1918 | 49 | 1940 | 54 | 1962 | 27 |
| 1919 | 46 | 1941 | 50 | 1963 | 26 |
| 1920 | 40 | 1942 | 49 | 1964 | 25 |
| 1921 | 44 | 1943 | 50 | 1965 | 24 |
| 1922 | 54 | 1944 | 49 | 1966 | 23 |
| 1923 | 56 | 1945 | 49 | 1967 | 23 |
| 1924 | 57 | 1946 | 49 | 1968 | 22 |
| 1925 | 56 | 1947 | 48 | 1969 | 21 |
| 1926 | 58 | 1948 | 45 | 1970 | 19 |
| 1927 | 59 | 1949 | 44 | 1971 | 18 |
| 1928 | 60 | 1950 | 43 | 1972 | 16 |
| 1929 | 60 | 1951 | 39 | 1973 | 15 |
| 1930 | 63 | 1952 | 36 | 1974 | 13 |
| 1931 | 67 | 1953 | 35 | 1975 | 10 |
| 1932 | 69 | 1954 | 34 | 1976 | 9 |
| 1933 | 71 | 1955 | 33 | 1977 | 8 |
| 1934 | 70 | 1956 | 31 | 1978 | 7 |
| 1935 | 69 | 1957 | 30 | 1979 | 6 |
|      |      |      |    | 1980 | 5 |

Or the long-term index of prices of consumer goods and services (January 1974 = 100) as published by the Central Statistical Office looks as follows:

*Waterworks*, [1978] 1 W.L.R. 1387, at pp. 1397, 1398: 'The time has come when we may have to revise our views'.

[71] Below, p. 351.

[72] The calculations which were made by the Bank of England are based on the Retail Price Index (1974 = 100) as published by the Department of Employment. To calculate the purchasing power of the pound in year A compared with year B the method is £1 × index in year B/ index in year A.

| | | | | | | | | | |
|---|---|---|---|---|---|---|---|---|---|
| 1914 | 11.1 | 1927 | 18.7 | 1946 | 29.4 | 1959 | 49.1 | 1972 | 85.7 |
| 1915 | 13.7 | 1928 | 18.5 | 1947 | 31.4 | 1960 | 49.6 | 1973 | 93.5 |
| 1916 | 16.2 | 1929 | 18.2 | 1948 | 33.8 | 1961 | 51.0 | 1974 | 108.5 |
| 1917 | 19.6 | 1930 | 17.6 | 1949 | 34.6 | 1962 | 53.0 | 1975 | 134.8 |
| 1918 | 22.6 | 1931 | 16.4 | 1950 | 35.6 | 1963 | 54.0 | 1976 | 157.1 |
| 1919 | 23.9 | 1932 | 16.0 | 1951 | 38.8 | 1964 | 55.8 | 1977 | 182.0 |
| 1920 | 27.7 | 1933 | 15.6 | 1952 | 41.2 | 1965 | 58.4 | 1978 | 197.1 |
| 1921 | 25.1 | 1934 | 15.7 | 1953 | 41.9 | 1966 | 60.7 | 1979 | 223.5 |
| 1922 | 20.4 | 1935 | 15.9 | 1954 | 42.6 | 1967 | 62.3 | 1980 | 263.7 |
| 1923 | 19.4 | 1936 | 16.4 | 1955 | 44.1 | 1968 | 65.2 | | |
| 1924 | 19.5 | 1937 | 17.2 | 1956 | 46.0 | 1969 | 68.7 | | |
| 1925 | 19.6 | 1938 | 17.4 | 1957 | 47.5 | 1970 | 73.1 | | |
| 1926 | 19.1 | | | 1958 | 48.8 | 1971 | 80.0 | | |

As a result of the developments indicated by these tables[73] large sections of the British people have become conscious of its progressive impoverishment and of the 'age of inflation' in which it lives and the continuation of which many observers have come to accept as a matter of probability. Yet, as will appear presently, English law is likely to abide by the broad principle of nominalism, though in the one or other specific direction a qualification of the rule 'a pound is a pound' may have to be made.

### III

It has been shown in an earlier section that in English law nominalism results from the presumed (or generalized) intention of the parties or the legislator.[74] It is this foundation that determines the nature and scope of the principle.

1. Nominalism is not, in England, derived from the law of money. It is not the product of public law, although here as elsewhere it is open to the legislator to give it statutory force.[75] Nor is it

---

[73] Tables indicating the development of foreign countries do not seem to be available in a comparable form. The decline of the purchasing power of the dollar appears from the following publication by the US Labor Department (1967 = 100 cents):

| | | | | | |
|---|---|---|---|---|---|
| 1940 | $2.381 | 1968 | .960 | 1974 | .677 |
| 1950 | 1.387 | 1969 | .939 | 1975 | .620 |
| 1955 | 1.247 | 1970 | .906 | 1976 | .587 |
| 1960 | 1.127 | 1971 | .878 | 1977 | .551 |
| 1965 | 1.035 | 1972 | .840 | 1978 | .493 |
| 1967 | 1.000 | 1973 | .744 | 1979 | .461 |
| | | | | 1980 | .404 |

[74] Above, pp. 84, 85.

[75] Such legislation would not involve the taking of property: *Knox* v. *Lee* and *Parker* v. *Davies*, 12 Wall. 457 (1870), at pp. 551, 552 *per* Mr. Justice Strong; similarly the German Supreme Court, 1 Mar. 1924, *RGZ.* 107, 370; 4 Nov. 1925, *RGZ.* 111, 320; 20 May 1926, *RGZ.* 114, 27. Nor could other monetary measures such as the prohibition to export money (*Ling Su Fan* v. *United States*, 218 U.S. 302 (1910), at p. 310 *per* Mr. Justice Lurton) or the abrogation of gold clause (*Norman* v. *Baltimore & Ohio Railroad Company*, 294 U.S. 240 (1934) at p. 306 *per* Chief Justice Hughes) ever have that character.

*jus cogens* or a matter of public policy. Hence its effects may normally be avoided by the parties' contractual arrangements.[76]

2. As nominalism is not a principle of public policy, a judge is entitled and bound to notice the fact that monetary values change. Though the case is an extreme one, this follows from the decision of the Exchequer Chamber in *Bryant* v. *Foot*[77] which concerned a claim to a marriage fee of 13*s.* made by the Rector of the parish of Horton. It had been proved to have been paid since 1808, but the court refused to draw the inference that the right existed since time immemorial, because, in view of the difference in the value of money in 1189 and 1868 of which the court took judicial cognizance, it was impossible that 13*s.* on every marriage could have been paid in 1189, so that the claim to these fees by prescription failed.

3. In the absence of statutory provisions nominalism cannot assert itself except within the realm of liquidated sums, whether they are payable by virtue of contracts, unilateral acts such as declarations of trust or wills, or statutory terms.

In the last-mentioned case nominalism means that if a statute prescribes a penalty, fine or fee, a maximum or minimum value or indeed any fixed sum, it is such sum, neither more or less, that must be paid or plied. In England[78] the statutory revision of fixed sums has har ily kept pace with the depreciation of money. Already in 1707 Bishop William Fleetwood[79] noted the complaint

That the Laws have not sufficient Regard to the different Price of Things, when they condemn People to death, for stealing Things to the value of twelve Pence; for tho' that is according to Law, yet that Law was made when twelve

---

[76] Below, p. 166. In *Treseder–Griffin* v. *Co-operative Insurance Society*, [1956] 2 Q.B. 127, 145, 163, Denning L.J. inclined towards the opposite view, but Harman J. expressed himself in the sense of the text.

[77] (1868), L.R. 3 Q.B. 497; see also *Attorney-General* v. *Lade* (1746), Park 57; *Lawrence* v. *Hitch* (1868), L.R. 3 Q.B. 521. *In re Lepton's Charity*, [1972] Ch. 277 related to a will made in 1715 which bequeathed the rents and profits of an estate as to £3 to the Protestant dissenting minister at Pudsey and 'the overplus of the profits', at the time about £2, to the poor of Pudsey. It was held that by 1967 'the original purposes . . . ceased to . . . provide a suitable and effective method of using the property, regard being had to the spirit of the gift'. A scheme under s. 13 of the Charities Act 1960 raised the £3 to £100, so that the poor of Pudsey received the balance of about £800.

[78] The famous Art. 1341 of the French Civil Code which requires a contract involving more than a certain amount to be proved by writing, provides a useful illustration of French experience. In 1804 that amount was 150 francs. In 1928 it was changed to 500 francs, in 1948 to 5,000 francs and, as a result of the introduction in 1960 of the 'hectofranc' (an expression used by Carbonnier, *Droit Civil*, 6th ed., 1969, p. 17), it is now 50 francs which in 1976 corresponded to about 15 francs of 1804: see Noirel in the collective work, *Influence de la dépréciation monétaire sur la vie juridique* (Paris, 1961), p. 85. The necessity for written proof thus acquired a very different scope and function that the legislator of 1804 envisaged. Since 1980 the figure is fixed at 5000 francs (or about £450).

[79] *Chronicum Preciosum*, p. 137 of the posthumous edition of 1745.

Pence would have purchased as much as you must now-a-days give 20, 30, nay 40s. for.

But nominalism does not permit the use of the interpretative process to override the words or figures of the statute. Bishop Fleetwood himself, it is true, argued in favour of the opposite result. He posed the question[80] whether the Statutes of an Oxford College, which had been enacted between 1440 and 1460 and required a Fellow to vacate his fellowship in the event of his inheriting an estate or a pension of £5 per annum operated according to their tenor. He answered in the negative:[81]

I can see no Cause, why 28 or 30 l. per An. should now be accounted a greater Estate, than V l. was heretofore, betwixt 1440 and 1460.

And[82]

therefore, I think, I have very sufficient Reason (not to determine, but) to conjecture, that 5 l. 260 Years ago, was equivalent to 28 l. or 30 l. now. And consequently, that he who has an Estate of Inheritance or a perpetual Pension, of that Value, now-a-days, may as honestly hold a Fellowship with it, as he, who lived 260 Years ago, might have held it, with 99s. per Ann.

The result was derived from the view[83]

That the Founder intended the same Ease and Favour to Those who should live in his College 260 Years after his Decease, as to those who lived in his own Time. . . . I only say, the Founder intended I might keep such an Estate, as would suffice to procure the same Bread, Drink, Meat, Cloth, Books etc. as the other might have procured for V Pounds, 260 Years ago.

This doctrine, however, has not prevailed. It would create wholly unacceptable uncertainty, for, quite apart from rules of statutory interpretation, the practical difficulties inherent in the process of comparison cannot readily be overcome.[84]

4. It is in the field of taxation that nominalism has at present a remarkably unjust effect. The problem extends to numerous and divers aspects of taxation.[85] Thus on the footing that the pur-

---

[80] The book was devoted to its solution. The book contains details of tables of the price of corn and other commodities during the preceding 600 years, and in the Appendix an historical account of coins.     [81] p. 137.

[82] p. 138.     [83] p. 9.

[84] Although statistical methods are now much more refined than those employed in Chaper IV of Bishop Fleetwood's book of 1707.

[85] e.g. balancing charges or stock valuations. See generally, the interesting contribution by Dach, 'Tax Aspects of Inflation', *American Journal of Comparative Law*, 1960, 657. As to France, see Decocq, pp. 257 sqq. of the collective work referred to above, p. 97, n. 78. For an economist's analysis see Peter Gurtner, *Inflation, Nominalwertprinzip und Einkommensteuerrecht* (1980).

chasing power of 6/7s. in 1948 had by 1968 been reduced to 3/6s., a widow who in 1948 had £10,000 must twenty years later have £21,666 in order to preserve her capital's intrinsic worth: yet, if she succeeded in achieving this, her death in 1969 resulted not only in a possible liability for capital gains tax,[86] but also in an increase of the rate of estate duty from nil to about 14 per cent or about £3,150. Since then the legislator frequently intervened, particularly in 1979 and 1980, to afford a measure of relief. The problem as a whole has, however, by no means been eliminated.

The attempt to treat an apparent capital gain as mere compensation for the depreciation of the original investment failed in the United States,[87] and, more recently, in England;[88] accordingly, for purposes of the capital gains tax, preservation of wealth is treated as gain, while loss of wealth is treated as preservation.

The most determined attempt at defeating nominalism in the field of taxation was made in Germany where there developed not only an enormous academic literature, but also the Federal Constitutional Court spoke on two occasions. In a first line of cases the taxpayer alleged that interest at $3\frac{1}{2}$ per cent on a savings bank account did not constitute income except in so far as it exceeded the average annual rate of monetary depreciation of about $2\frac{1}{2}$ per cent. By an unusually elaborate, yet highly interesting decision the Federal Finance Court rejected the contention[89] and the Federal Constitutional Court held the decision to be consistent with constitutional requirements.[90] The Federal Finance Court reached the same result in respect of the years 1969 to 1971[91] and 1973 and 1974.[92] The last-mentioned decision led to a fresh review by the Federal

---

[86] This followed from the unique provision of s. 24 of the Finance Act, 1965, according to which death was deemed to be a disposal of all the deceased's assets.

[87] *Bates* v. *United States*, 108 F. 2d 407 (1939), cert. den. 309 U.S. 666 (1940).

[88] *Secretan* v. *Hart* (*Inspector of Taxes*), [1969] 3 All. E.R. 1196, where Buckley J. put his decision on narrow grounds of statutory interpretation, though he was very much alive to the injustice complained of by the taxpayer. The Chancellor of the Exchequer stated on 15 Apr. 1965 that he did 'not propose any allowance for changes in the value of money': Hansard (Commons), vol. 710, col. 264.

[89] 27 July 1967, BFH. 89, 422. For similar cases see 10 Nov. 1967, BFH. 90, 396; 1 Dec. 1967, BFH. 91, 261; 12 June 1968, BStBl. 1968, ii. 653. On these cases see, e.g. Beisse, *Wertpapiermitteilungen*, Sonderbeilage No. 1, 1969. The argument of the taxpayer was unsound in law and contrary to the realities of economic and political life everywhere. One marvels at the thoroughness with which the Court examined it. A very interesting opinion on the extent of the depreciation since 1950 and on future developments, which the Court obtained from the German Federal Bank, is published in *Monatsberichte der Deutschen Bundesbank*, March 1967.

[90] 21 Jan. 1969, HFR. 1969, 347 or Betrieb 1969, 1819.

[91] 14 May 1974, BFHE. 112, 546, or NJW. 1974, 2330; BFHE. 112, 567 or NJW. 1974. 2331.

[92] 30 April 1975, BFHE. 115, 510; 1 June 1976, BFHE. 119, 75.

Constitutional Court.[93] It received submissions not only from the Federal Government and the Federal Bank, but also from numerous organizations and in the result rejected the contentions that the constitutional prohibition of discrimination or arbitrariness required the indexation of taxes or that nominalism had the effect of confiscation; the wealth of material considered and of arguments examined by the court is impressive.[94] The Austrian Constitutional Court reached the same result and stated in terms that even if on account of inflation income tax had in a commercial sense to be paid out of capital this did not constitute confiscation.[95]

5. Nominalism primarily applies to fluctuations in the value of money, which are slow, gradual, moderate, and 'creeping'. There is no certainty how English law would react in the unlikely event of the pound sterling depreciating in so violent, sudden, extreme, and 'galloping' a manner as to lead to a collapse of the monetary system. Experience proves that in such a contingency nominalism cannot, in practice, be maintained and that the legislator or, failing him, the judge must afford relief.

There is no lack of reliable comparative material dealing with the general aspects of failures of currencies such as have occurred in the course of history[96] and in recent times,[97] especially in Central and Eastern Europe.[98] It is therefore

---

[93] 19 Dec. 1978, *BVerfGE* 50, 57.

[94] It is interesting to observe (p. 83) that the decision was reached against the background of a rise of the German cost of living index as follows:

| 1970 | 3.4% | 1975 | 6% | 1980 | 5.5% |
|------|------|------|------|------|------|
| 1971 | 5.3% | 1976 | 4.5% | | |
| 1972 | 5.5% | 1977 | 3.9% | | |
| 1973 | 6.9% | 1978 | 2.3% | | |
| 1974 | 7% | 1979 | 5.4% | | |

The decision has provoked much further academic discussion; see, for instance, Kröger *JZ* 1979, 631 with numerous references. The constitutional problem is likely to be kept alive in Germany, particularly because numerous writers of authority have discussed it: see, for instance, Benda, *NJW*. 1967, 849; Bettermann, *ZRP*. 1974, 13; Kaiser, *Festschrift für E.R. Huber* (1973) 242; Reichert-Facilides *JZ* 1969, 617; Rüfner, *DVBl* 1970, 881. On the effect of inflation on taxation under *Italian* constitutional law see Corte Costituzionale, 8 Nov. 1979, *Bollettino tributario* 1979, 1842.

[95] 17 March 1976, *EuGRZ*. 1976, 384.

[96] Sobernheim, 'Die Geldentwertung als Gesetzgebungsproblem des Privatrechts', *Gruchots Beiträge*, lxvi. 260 sqq., 265–316. As regards the effect of inflation in the Southern States after the outbreak of the American Civil War in 1861, Professor Dawson and Mr. Cooper published an illuminating article in 33 (1935) *Mich. L.R. 706*. As to the French experiences from 1709 to 1800 see Mater, *Rev. dr. banc.* 1924, 72, 168, 266, 267.

[97] Harmening, 'Aufwertung', *Rechtsvergleichendes Handwörterbuch*, ii. 282; Krohn, 'Das Aufwertungsrecht des Auslands', *Niemeyer's Zeitschrift für internationales Recht*, xxxviii (1928), 1 sqq.; Wahle, *Das Valorisationsproblem in Mittel- und Osteuropa* (Vienna, 1924); Nussbaum, *Geld*, pp. 130–8, and *Bilanz der Aufwertungstheorie* (1929); Guisan, *La Dépréciation monétaire* (Lausanne, 1934), pp. 180 sqq.; Sulkowski, *Rec.* 29 (1929), 1–29. As to recent *Austrian* law see the excellent monograph by G. Ertl, *Inflation,*

not proposed to enter into a detailed discussion of the methods adopted in these circumstances and of the results reached in each individual country. However, an exception must be made in regard to Germany. Over the comparatively short period of twenty-five years or so Germany has twice experienced monetary disasters of great violence. These, it is true, were surpassed by the events, for instance, in Hungary, where on 1 August 1946 the pengö currency was replaced by the forint currency at the rate of $4 \times 100^{29}$ pengös for 1 forint,[99] or in Greece, where in November 1944 the new drachma was substituted for the old drachma at the rate of 'only' 1 new drachma for 50,000 million old drachmas, but where at the same time all old debts were completely wiped out by statute.[100] But the German experience has led to such contributions to monetary practice and thought that it is impossible to ignore the light it throws on the nominalistic idea.

In November 1923 the inflationary development of the mark reached a point where the pound sterling, whose parity was about 20 marks, had a value of approximately 20 billions of marks. Suppose 10,000 German marks were borrowed by a German in Germany in 1914 and invested in securities or real property which more or less retained their intrinsic value; should the borrower be allowed to discharge his debt by paying 10,000 marks in 1923, when the cost of a stamp was 1,000 million of marks, or in 1924, when owing to the introduction of the reichsmark currency and the recurrent link of 1,000,000,000,000 marks = 1 reichsmark, the amount to be tendered would be an inconceivable fraction of the new unit of account? Evidently it was impossible to abide by nominalism in all its rigidity, and legislative and judicial measures, encroaching upon the nominalistic principle and allowing partial or total revalorization,

*Privatrecht und Wertsicherung* (Vienna, 1980). As to *Argentina* see Buenos Aires Court of Appeal, 9 Nov. 1975, Clunet 1980, 690 with note by Lisbonne. As to *Chile* and other South American countries see the book by Lopez-Santa Maria (1980). As to *Brasil* see Bertram Huber, *Inflationsgolgen, ihre Behandlung im brasilianischen und deutschen Recht* (Frankfurt, 1979); Wald, *RabelsZ* 1971, 268; Lipkau, in *Inflationsbewältigung im Zivil-und Arbeitsrecht* (Frankfurt, 1976, p. 11. As to *Finland* see Suviranta, ibid., p. 49. As to *Italy* see Enrico Quadri, *Questioni Giuridiche sull' Inflazione* (1981) and the earlier work mentioned above n. 25.

[98] On China see S. H. Chou, *The Chinese Inflation 1937-1949* (New York, 1963).

[99] A French translation of the decrees of 26 and 28 July 1946 was published in *Bulletin de législation comparée*, 1946, 689. The *17th Annual Report of the Bank for International Settlements for the year 1946-7* (p. 28) rightly says that the figure mentioned in the text, which includes 29 noughts and is sometimes expressed as 400,000 quadrillion pengös (*21st Report for 1950-1*, p. 135), was 'hitherto confined to astronomic calculations'. See B. Nogaro, *A Short Treatise on Money and Monetary Systems* (London, 1949), 118 sqq., 200, 201.

[100] It is difficult to visualize this consequence in practice. On the legal position, see Massouridès, 'Les prestations dues en monnaie dévaluée, *Revue hellénique de droit international*, ii (1950), 20; Fragistas, 'Der Rechtsmissbrauch nach dem griechischen Zivilgesetzbuch', *Festschrift für Martin Wolff* (1952), pp. 63 sqq. and, generally, Delivanis and Cleveland, *Greek Monetary Developments 1939-1948* (Indiana University, Bloomington, Indiana). On 9 April 1953 the new drachma was again devalued by 50 per cent. The Roumanian inflation was milder: in 1947 20,000 old lei became 1 new leu and in 1951 the new leu was again converted at rates varying between 20 to 1 and 400 to 1 (*18th Annual Report of the Bank for International Settlements for 1947-8*, pp. 36, 37, and *22nd Report for 1951-2*, p. 127).

became inevitable.[101] Again, between 1945 and 1948 the reichsmark became depreciated[102] to such an extent as to compel the Occupation Authorities in the Western Zones[103] to introduce, on 20 June 1948, the Deutsche Mark on the footing of a recurrent link of 1 Deutsche Mark = 1 reichsmark,[104] though most debts were converted at the rate of 1 Deutsche Mark = 10 reichsmark.[105]

## IV

It is against the background of nominalism so defined that it is now possible to turn to the consideration of some individual questions.

1. Although in modern times most countries have passed through periods of fluctuating value of money, the nominalistic principle was, in general, adhered to in so far as *simple debts* are concerned.

This is particularly so in *France*[106] and *Italy*[107] where the depreciation of money

---

[101] For an appreciation of the German inflation 1919–23, its development and legal results see Nussbaum, pp. 199–204, 206–15; Dawson, 33 (1934) *Mich. L.R.* 171; Fischer, 'The German Revalorization Act 1925', 10 (1928) *Journal of Comparative Legislation*, 94; Kahn, 'Depreciation of Currency under German Law', 14 (1932) *Journal of Comparative Legislation*, 66. For a recent German appreciation of the judicial practice of revalorization see Renger, *Festschrift für Gerhard Müller* (1970), 275. The following discussion will consider the German revalorization practice in particular, but will disregard legislative measures taken in Germany or in any other countries since, from the point of view of monetary theory in general, they are less interesting.

[102] The cause was not so much the superabundance of the supply of money as an excess of unutilizable over utilizable money due to the fact that goods were scarce, and both the supply and the price of most goods were subject to stringent controls which precluded an adaptation of the price to the extent of the demand. For a helpful description see, for example, Duden, *Beiträge zum Deutschen Recht* (ed. by Ernst Wolff, 1950), i. pp. 309 sqq.

[103] The leading German commentaries are by Harmening–Duden, *Die Währungsgestze* (1949), with Supplement. On the history of the German currency reform of 1948, see H. Moller, *Zur Vorgeschichte der Deutschen Mark* (Basle, 1961); Colm, Dodge, and Goldschmidt, 'A Plan for Liquidation of War Finance and the Financial Rehabilitation of Germany', *Zeitschrift für die gesamte Staatswissenschaft*, 111 (1955), 204. From a legal point of view there is no justification for the claim by H. P. Jones, *Governing Post-War Germany* (ed. by E. H. Litchfield, Ithaka, New York, 1953), p. 423, that the German currency legislation of 1948 'represented the utmost in monetary sophistication'.

[104] This point, now accepted by the Federal Supreme Court (14 July 1952, BGHZ. 7, 134 at p. 140), is in no way invalidated by the fact that the amount of all *debts* except those specified by s. 18 of the Conversion Law was scaled down at the rate of 10 to 1. It is of particular importance where the debt is not governed by German law: Mann, 'Die Behandlung von Reichsmarkverbindlichkeiten bei ausländischem Schuldstatut', *Festschrift für Fritz Schulz* (Weimar, 1951), ii. 298.

[105] Sections 16, 18 of the Conversion Law. The Federal Supreme Court accepted that the Conversion Law left no room for the application of German conceptions of equity (s. 242) or the adjustment of debts on an equitable basis: 14 Jan. 1955. BGHZ. 16, 153, at p. 158; 17 Dec. 1958, BGHZ. 29, 107, at p. 112.

[106] See the impressive discussion by Carbonnier, *Droit Civil*, ii (1969), s. 6, or Mazeaud, *Leçons de droit civil*, ii (3rd ed., 1966), s. 869. See, in particular, Cass. Req., 25 June 1934, D.H. 1934, 427. The problem is frequently discussed under the head of the *imprévision*

was serious: in France, for instance, one had to spend in 1963 27,420 frs. for what in 1910 cost 100 frs., in 1938 756 frs. and in 1945 3,300 frs.[108] Special legislation, it is true, dealt with annuities[109] and rents,[110] but otherwise the principle, enshrined in Art. 1895, that a reduction of the purchasing power of the domestic currency could not impose a duty upon the debtor to make additional payments, remained in full force. Nor was the correctness of this view questioned in the *United States of America* either after 1871, when the Legal Tender Acts were held valid by the Supreme Court,[111] or since.[112]

doctrine on which see the authors just referred to in ss. 150 and 734 sqq., or Planiol-Ripert, vi, No. 395, or Aubry & Rau, pp. 484 sqq. The doctrine was categorically rejected by the Cour de Cassation (6 Mar. 1876, S. 1876, 1. 161) in connection with an attempt to increase an amount of 15 centimes promised in 1560 and 1567 to 60 centimes. The court said that 'dans aucun cas il n'appartient aux tribunaux, quelque équitable que puisse leur paraître leur décision, de prendre en considération le temps et les circonstances pour modifier les conventions des parties et substituer des clauses nouveiles à celles qui ont été librement acceptées par les contractants'. The French Conseil d'Etat took a more liberal view (see Planiol-Ripert, vi, No. 392), but it seems to be agreed that the *imprévision* doctrine can only be invoked in case of alterations of the price level, not in case of a depreciation of money (see Planiol-Ripert, vi, No. 397 (3)). As to *Belgium* see Piret, pp. 10-21, 30 sqq. and judgments of the Cour de Cassation of 26 Feb. 1931, 3 Mar. 1933, and 9 Mar. 1933, on p. 33, n. 1; certain legislative measures are dealt with on pp. 22-8.

[107] Ascarelli, p. 330. Nominalism is enshrined in Art. 1277 of the Codice civile. A statute of 1973 amended Art. 429 (3) of the Code of Civil Procedure so as to provide that an employee who has a claim against his employer is entitled not only to interest, but also to compensation for any loss suffered as a result of the depreciation of money. The provision was held valid by the Constitutional Court, 14 Jan. 1977, *Giurisprudenza Constituzionale*, 1977, I. 47.

[108] See the tables printed by J.-P. Doucet, *L'Indexation* (1965), p. 26.

[109] The original French law of the 25 Mar. 1949 relating to contractual annuities has frequently been modified. Further legislation of 24 May 1951 relates to annuities by way of damages in general and of 27 Dec. 1974 relates to annuities for damages resulting from motorcar accidents; Art. 208 paragraph 2 of the Code Civil provides for indexation of maintenance payments and Articles 273, 276, and 294 of the Code Civil as amended on 11 July 1975 deal with payments to divorced spouses. As to *Italy* see Ascarelli, p. 333, n. 2. In *Austria*, where the courts rejected a general revalorization practice for simple debts, special rules were developed for maintenance agreements, annuities, pensions in lieu of damages, and similar contractual arrangements: Stanzl in Klang's *Commentaries*, iv (1968), pp. 720-3, and see, e.g., Supreme Court, 17 Oct. 1963, SZ. xxxvi (1963), No. 132, referring to a long line of decisions since SZ. iv, No. 65; v, Nos. 232 and 252. In *Switzerland* judicial orders for payment of maintenance to children, divorced wives etc. now normally provide for indexation: Federal Tribunal *BGE*. 98 II 257; Court of Appeal Zurich, 19 May 1972, ZR. 1971 No. 71; 25 July 1974, ZR. 1974 No. 22; 13 May 1975, ZR. 1974 No. 62 with further references. This is, of course, unnecessary where, as is usual, such orders may be varied whenever circumstances change.

[110] In France rents of commercial buildings may be revised at the end of every period of three years: Art. 26 of the decree of 30 Sept. 1953. Art. 812 of the Code Rural renders it compulsory to fix agricultural rents by reference to the annual price of agricultural products.

[111] Dawson and Cooper, 33 (1935), *Mich. L.R.* 852, 860 sqq.; see especially *Dooley* v. *Smith* (1871), 13 Wall. (80 U.S.) 604; *Bigler* v. *Waller* (1871), 14 Wall. (81 U.S.) 297.

[112] A different view, unsupported by authority, appears in Corbin, *On Contracts* (1962), s. 1360, where the learned author suggests an 'adjustment', 'if the facts show that the promisee is left suffering heavy economic loss, while the promisor reaps a correspondingly

Notwithstanding heavy inflation in *Israel* nominalism remained, at any rate up to 1977, in full force.[113] Nor is there any doubt that *Germany* has followed the same practice. It is true that, as a result of the complete collapse[114] of the currency after the First World War, Germany, like, to a lesser extent, some other countries, developed a practice of *revalorization* of liquidated debts. By s. 242 of the German Civil Code the debtor has to effect the performance of his obligation according to the requirements of 'equity' and ordinary usage. The whole of the circumstances, including the financial position of both parties, were to be reviewed in order to translate a sum of marks into reichsmarks. It was, therefore, necessary and possible to investigate whether and to what extent the creditor would have been able to protect the money from the effects of inflation, and to consider the 'impoverishment factor', i.e. the general reduction of the national wealth,[115] but it is of particular interest to note that the reduction of the purchasing power of the reichsmark as compared with that of the mark could not lead to an increase in the rate of revalorization.[116] In less

great profit'. It is not always clear whether the author's remarks apply to both domestic and foreign money.

[113] Yadin in *International Law and Economic Order* (*Essays in honour of F.A. Mann*) (Munich, 1977), p. 847.

[114] At a certain period the requirement of a catastrophic depreciation was less and less strictly enforced. A decision of the Supreme Court (2 Apr. 1935, *RGZ.* 147, 286, 290) seems to allow revalorization in case of a depreciation by only 13 per cent.

[115] See the definition of the Supreme Court in the decision of 10 Jan. 1933, *JW.* 1933, 2449, and see, for example, Mügel, *Das Gesamte Aufwertungsrecht* (1927), p. 146. It must be borne in mind that 'revalorization' is only possible in case of liquidated sums. As to other monetary obligations see below, p. 115. In two cases English Courts had to apply German revalorization rules: *In re Schnapper*, [1936] 1 All E.R. 322; *Kornatzki* v. *Oppenheimer*, [1937] 4 All E.R. 133. The former of these cases concerned the revalorization of a legacy. As to the rules of revalorization applicable in case of a legacy see, e.g., German Supreme Court, 15 Dec. 1927, *JW.* 1928, 885; 14 Oct. 1929, *JW.* 1929, 3488; 13 June 1929, *JW.* 1930, 995, and on the statutory portion (*Pflichtteil*) see Federal Tribunal, 24 Jan. 1952, *BGHZ.* 5, 12, 18 and 14 July 1952, *BGHZ.* 7, 134. On claims for money paid to the defendant's use, Federal Tribunal, 27 Feb. 1952, *BGHZ.* 5, 197. As to revalorization generally see *Kommentar von Reichsgerichtsräten*, 9th ed. i (1939), 461–79 and, on the monetary principles involved, Jastrow, *Die Prinzipienfragen in den Aufwertungsdebatten* (1937). The Supreme Court had the opportunity of deciding that neither the collapse of the currency nor the practice of revalorization constituted a taking of property: 1 Mar. 1924. *RGZ.* 107, 370; 4 Nov. 1925, *RGZ.* 111, 320; 20 May 1926, *RGZ.* 114, 27. Nor does the absence of revalorization amount to a taking of property: see the decision of the Supreme Court of the Philippines, below, p. 469, n. 27. On the question whether in constitutional law changes of parity, rates of exchange etc. amout to the taking of property see Wolfgang Sammler, *Eigentum und Währungsparität* (Berlin, 1975).

[116] Supreme Court, 21 Nov. 1927, *JW.* 1928, 962; 16 June 1930, *RGZ.* 129, 208; 28 Nov. 1930, *RGZ.* 130, 368, 375. Compare the above discussion of the importance of the functional value of money: pp. 81 sqq. The problem was dealt with in an exceedingly interesting decision of the Assembled Civil Chambers of the Supreme Court: 31 Mar. 1925, *RGZ.* 110, 371. The 6th Chamber of the Supreme Court had taken the view that, at least as regards transactions between wholesale dealers, a revalorization was confined to such an amount as would compensate the plaintiff in respect of the depreciation of the 'inner exchange value' of the mark (on this conception see above, p. 83) and should not include compensation in respect of changes in the outer exchange value of the mark; it was also said that the best method of measuring variations of the inner exchange value

exceptional circumstances, however, German courts have resisted any departure from nominalism.[117] Thus in the 1930s the rise in the value of money due to deflation did not enable a debtor to reduce the pension payable to former employees; accordingly the attempt at devalorization failed.[118, 119] Similarly, in recent years, when the purchasing power of money depreciated by something like $2\frac{1}{2}$ per cent per annum, the corresponding adjustment of pensions was initially again rejected;[120] this was the more remarkable, as in the case of social security benefits the law specifically provides for the adaptation of payments to the cost-of-living index.[121] When, however, the rise of prices between 1955 and 1972 reached 40 per cent, the Federal Labour Court held an

was on the basis of the rate of exchange between the mark and one of the stable currencies, e.g. pound or dollar, and that revalorization could not exceed the amount of reichsmarks calculated by translating the originally stipulated sum of marks into dollars at the rate of exchange of the day when the contract was made, and by reconverting that amount of dollars into reichsmarks. This theory, however, did not succeed. It was laid down that the guiding principle was exclusively to be found in s. 242 of the German Civil Code requiring consideration of all the circumstances of the case, and that any other theory would be unable to do justice. In the latter connection the decisive argument was that during the inflation the price level in Germany was extremely low, and that, therefore, the method proposed by the 6th Chamber would have the effect that the revalorized prices would be far below the price level prevailing after the introduction of the reichsmark. That the decision in principle rejected the distinction between the inner and the outer exchange value of money has already been mentioned above, p. 83. See also Supreme Court, 30 May 1929, *RGZ*. 125, 3: at the height of the inflation the plaintiff agreed to let a house at a rental expressed in U.S.A. dollars; the fact that after the stabilization and the introduction of the reichsmark the purchasing power of the dollar in Germany was considerably reduced did not entitle the plaintiff to demand an increase of the rental.

[117] See, generally, Reichert–Facilides, *Juristenzeitung*, 1969, 617.

[118] 10 Aug. 1932, *JW*. 1932, 3219; 21 Jan. 1933, *JW*. 1933, 1276; 24 May 1933, *JW*. 1933, 1677. See on the subject Hamburger, *Deflation und Rechtsordnung* (Mannheim, 1933); Oertmann, *JW*. 1933, 1297. The position was slightly different in case of agreements to pay alimony; Supreme Court, 6 May 1934, *JW*. 1934, 2609; 24 Sept. and 10 Oct. 1934, *JW*. 1934, 3195.

[119] Similarly, the Supreme Court of the State of Iowa rejected a plea of a defendant in a foreclosure action that, as monetary deflation and the ensuing rise in the value of money had reduced the value of the mortgaged land, a mortgaged debt of $20,000 should be scaled down to $10,000: *Federal Land Bank of Omata* v. *Wilmarth* (1934), 252 N.W. 507.

[120] Federal Labour Court, 30 Nov. 1955, *NJW*. 1956, 485; 12 Mar. 1965, *NJW*. 1965, 1681, both making it clear that the result might be different if payment of the nominal sum 'no longer constitutes such performance as the contractual purpose requires'. In the same sense Federal Supreme Court, 11 Jan. 1968, *WM*. 1968, 473. For a refusal to adjust arrears of a civil servant's salary, see Federal Administrative Court, 7 June 1962, *NJW*. 1962, 1882. Alimony and similar payments are subject to different rules: Federal Supreme Court, 19 June 1962, *NJW*. 1962, 2147.

[121] The basic, extraordinarily complicated legislation was enacted in 1957. Since then the figures were revised annually. State insurance payments in respect of accidents are subject to adjustment in the event of a change of the average wage or salary: s. 579 of the Reich Insurance Act (RVO). The problem of the adjustment of pensions payable to retired people and dependents attracted much attention in *Switzerland*. The Government discussed it frequently (*Bundesblatt*, 1961, i. 235; 1963, ii. 517, 555; 1966, i. 1035; 1968, i. 633). It invariably rejected the idea of an automatic adjustment according to the cost-of-living index. By a statute of 4 Oct. 1968 it is provided that a review should take place either every third year or in the event of a rise of the index by not less than 8 per cent, whichever

adjustment in the case of pensions payable to an employee to be necessary[122] and the Federal Supreme Court agreed in regard to pensions payable to a former managing director.[123] These cases included a strong element of support payments towards living expenses and have, therefore, something in common with alimony and maintenance payments which in the event of a change of circumstances are always subject to review.[124] The purpose of support facilitated a decision conforming to the changing needs of the supported person. Where this feature is missing, nominalism continues to prevail. Thus, where at the beginning of the century fixed sums were agreed as consideration for the right to mine potash, the demand for an increase, made sixty years later, failed on the striking ground that the law did not know an 'implied index clause' to take care of the reduction of the purchasing power of money.[125] And although in the course of fifteen years the cost of living index rose by more than 50 per cent and rents of residential property by about 130 per cent, the Federal Supreme Court in 1974 and again in 1976 rejected claims to a proportionate increase of payments due under a security in the nature of a ground rent granted in 1954 and 1957 respectively.[126, 127] But in 1980 it appeared that a ground rent agreed in 1959 for sixty years at DM 15 had by 1975, when the cost-of-living index had risen by 222 per cent, decreased in value by almost 69 per cent; the Supreme Court, somewhat ominously, gave way, held 'the bearable limits' to have been exceeded and allowed 'revalorization' by 548 per cent to DM 84.[128]

is the earlier date. In *Britain* there is power under the Social Security Act 1975 to review and change contributions and increase benefits (sections 120 and 124).

[122] 30 March 1973, *NJW*. 1973, 959. Soon afterwards the legislator intervened by a statute of 19 Dec. 1974 (*Official Gazette* 1974 I 3610) section 16 of which provides that every three years the employer is bound to examine and make a fair decision upon an adjustment of pensions, taking into account the due interest of the pensioner and the economic condition of the employer. On the application of this law see Federal Labour Court, 17 Jan. 1980, *NJW*. 1980, 1181.

[123] 28 May 1973, *BGHZ*. 61, 31. In the case before the court the price rise between 1951 and 1971 was 53.6 per cent. For a similar case see Federal Supreme Court, 23 May 1977, *NJW*. 1977, 1536. On these cases see critical observations by Mann, *NJW*. 1974, 1299. The *Austrian* Supreme Court has so far rejected similar tendencies: 25 Jan. 1955, *Juristische Blätter* 1955, 311.

[124] In the case of judgments s. 323 of the Code of Civil Procedure applies. S. 1612a of the German Civil Code, introduced in 1976, provides that annuities payable to minors, whether under a court order, an agreement or a covenant, may be brought into line with economic circumstances as directed by adjustment orders made from time to time by the Federal Government; an order 28 September 1979 permits an increase by 11 per cent.

[125] Federal Supreme Court, 14 Oct. 1959, *NJW*. 1959, 2203; 21 Dec. 1960, *NJW*. 1961, 499; 2 Nov. 1965, *NJW*. 1966, 105, on which see Flume, *Das Rechtsgeschäft* (3rd ed., 1979), p. 519. It is significant that the Court thought that the result might be different if the value of the potash increased; but see p. 105, n. 120, above.

[126] 29 March 1974, *NJW*. 1974, 1186; 1 Oct. 1975, *NJW*. 1976, 142; 23 Jan. 1976, *NJW*. 1977, 846. See also Court of Appeal Dusseldorf, 2 March 1972, *NJW*. 1972, 1137. But see Federal Supreme Court, 23 Sept. 1958, *Betrieb* 1958, 1325.

[127] It is noteworthy that in the face of devastating inflation Japan whose law is German in origin has refused to adopt any measure of statutory or judicial revalorization: Igarashi and Rieke, 42 (1967) *Washington L.R.* 445, at p. 454.

[128] 23 May 1980, *BGHZ*. 77, 188 or *NJW*. 1980, 2241; see also another decision of the same date, *BGHZ*. 77, 194 or *NJW*. 1980, 2243. The decision is for many reasons

In *England* the unimpaired control of nominalism has never been doubted.[129] English law lacks all equipment that, in the case of liquidated sums, could lead to a revision or adjustment of the substance of the obligation. Interpretative devices such as have been resorted to abroad are not available.[130] Even the implication of terms could not permit the court to make a new contract for the parties. Relief against changes in monetary value can only be granted by the adoption of protective clauses or by the legislator. Whether he will intervene is a matter of speculation![131] If the trend which has clouded the last few decades[132] continues some relief in the case of certain long-term obligations such as leases or annuities will become unavoidable. An annual rent of £100 agreed in 1914 for a lease of 99 years, a by no means unusual case, should in 1980 be almost £2,000 to provide the landlord with the same purchasing power or in other words, has depreciated by more than 95 per cent. A pension of £100 a month agreed in 1955 is in terms of purchasing power in 1980 only about a seventh of its original value. On the other hand if the pension had been agreed in 1965, i.e. at a time people had become conscious of inflation, justice does not demand or even permit any intervention.

A case in which English courts may find it easier to afford relief is that of a legacy which is intended to equal an identifiable proportion of the estate or of property. Thus if by a will made in 1955, when his house had a value of £20,000, a testator gives to his son the option to buy the house for £10,000 and the death occurs in 1980, when its market value is £100,000, it may be

---

remarkable. Thus it differs from that of 23 Jan. 1976 (above n. 126) which had considered a reduction in value of 75 per cent as insufficient to allow any adjustment. Moreover the decision rejects the cost of living as the sole measure of adjustment, for it 'does not indicate whether and how the standard of living has changed.' This is said to be measured by the improvement of incomes. The incomes of workmen are said to have risen by 875 per cent, so that the Court allows an increase of 222 plus 875 or 1097 per cent which divided by 2 produces 548 per cent. It is difficult to understand how the cost of living and incomes increased by such totally different percentages and why the average of these two figures is the appropriate indicator of the measure of adjustment which a court should allow. It may be that these are questions for an economist rather than a lawyer who can only express his astonishment. See, on the other hand, Federal Supreme Court, 27 March 1981, NJW 1981, 1668.

[129] Certain exceptions relating to legacies, dower or the reversal of a judgment are suggested in *Gilbert* v. *Brett* (1604), Davies's Rep. (Ireland) 18, 27, 28; State Trials, ii. 130, and are mentioned in *Pilkington* v. *Commissioners for Claims on France* (1821), 2 Knapp, P.C. 7, at p. 20. They have no place in the modern law.

[130] They would be inconsistent with such cases as *British Movietonews Ltd.* v. *London and District Cinemas Ltd.*, [1952] A.C. 166.

[131] He did intervene, for instance, by the Pensions (Increase) Act 1971 and by the Social Security Pensions Act 1975, s. 21.

[132] See the table above p. 95.

possible to find an intention to bequeath an option to purchase at one half of the market value.[133]

2. The second question is whether a creditor who is not paid by his debtor at the due date[134] is entitled to claim damages in respect of the depreciation of money since the date of maturity. Is the mere reduction in the purchasing power of money an item of damage which, notwithstanding the principle of nominalism, the law recognizes as recoverable? Or is it at least possible to recover loss suffered by reason of the fact proved by the creditor that, had there been no default, he could and would have bought some property (or foreign currency) more cheaply than at the time of payment?

In *Germany* and *Austria*, it seems, such a claim may in appropriate circumstances succeed. During the great inflation 1920-3 such damages were freely allowed, the Austrian Supreme Court holding that the burden of proving actual loss was on the creditor,[135] while according to German decisions there was a rebuttable presumption in favour of the creditor.[136] In case of a creeping inflation the German courts will probably take the view that the German creditor of German currency is not precluded from claiming damages in respect of the depreciation of the German currency after maturity, though he must strictly prove his damage, but that the non-German creditor whose domestic currency remained stable may invoke the presumption that he would have avoided any loss by converting the German currency into his own.[137, 138] In

---

[133] This is what the German Supreme Court decided in circumstances which admittedly were more extreme: 21 Feb. 1924, *RGZ*. 108, 83.

[134] It is necessary to emphasize strongly that this section deals only with the case of a debt in the strict sense. Where the cause of action is a claim for damages, there are certain countries where different considerations apply, though England is perhaps not one of them. See below p. 24.

[135] Supreme Court, 8 Mar. 1923, *SZ*. v, no. 53 (Plenary Advisory Opinion); Stanzl in Klang's *Kommentar zum Allgemeinen Bürgerlichen Gesetzbuch* (2nd ed., 1968), iv. 722, 723; Wolff, ibid. vi (1951), 179.

[136] See, generally, Staudinger (Werner), *Kommentar zum Bürgerlichen Gesetzbuch*, s. 286, notes 9-11. There was no essential difference between a non-German and a German creditor of marks, although the presumption mentioned in the text was stronger in case of a non-German creditor and weaker in case of a German creditor. As to the former case see Supreme Court, 25 Sept. 1919, *RGZ*. 96, 262; 20 Feb. 1920, *RGZ*. 98, 264; 16 Mar. 1920, *JW*. 1920, 704; 22 Apr. 1923, *RGZ*. 107, 212; 22 Oct. 1926, *JW*. 1927, 980. As to the latter case see Supreme Court, 29 Sept. 1926, *JW*. 1928, 2841 with further references. After the currency reform of 1948 it was held that the party who is in default cannot take advantage of the more advantageous rate of conversion introduced by the Conversion Law or that a debtor may claim damages from a defaulting party for loss of opportunity to pay in depreciated reichsmarks: Federal Supreme Court, 28 Nov. 1950, *NJW*. 1951, 109; 28 Feb. 1951, *NJW*. 1951, 399; cf. Duden, *Deutsche Rechtszeitschrift*, 1947, 287. See, e.g., Larenz, *Lehrbuch des Schuldrechts* i (11th ed., 1976), p. 392.

[137] This is the result arrived at in *Switzerland* (Federal Tribunal, 31 Oct. 1950, *BGE*. 76, ii. 371) and in *Czechoslovakia*, where the Supreme Court held that a Prague debtor is liable to compensate his German creditor in respect of the devaluation of the Czechoslovakian

the last resort, therefore, the result will depend on the facts rather than legal principle.[139] Until recently[140] this also was the law in *Italy* where the new Code rejects the *French* rule limiting damages for non-payment to interest.[141] At the end of 1978 in a case which had been pending since 1963 and involved a loss of the lira's purchasing power by considerably more than 100 per cent the third Chamber of the Corte di Cassazione seemed to initiate a practice to the effect that the damage flowing from the debtor's *mora* and recoverable according to Art. 1224 of the Codice Civile was without further evidence presumed to include the monetary depreciation occurring during the period of default and measured by the cost-of-living index.[142] But a few months later the United Chambers of the Corte di Cassazione disapproved what was regarded as an inadmissible deviation from nominalism (Art. 1277 Codice Civile) and reestablished the rule that in case of default the creditor was entitled to the actual loss suffered as a result of his inability to deal with the money in the manner in which presumably he would have used it. At the same time it was emphasized that the judge was entitled freely to assess the evidence, to make use of general experience and of presumptions derived from the creditor's personal conditions and his quality as *homo oeconomicus*. This meant that traders might have to be treated differently from other groups such as savers who would merely have obtained interest or consumers who would have spent the money and as a rule, therefore, could only be compensated by increments based on the cost-of-living index.[143] Accordingly, while adhering to traditional principles of law, the United Chambers alleviated the burden of proof.

In *England* damages for actual loss suffered through the depreciation of sterling have, in the absence of an agreement between the parties,[144] never been awarded, but it is submitted that, on proof of appropriate facts, a claim to such damages should be recognized. It is not precluded by the rule[145] that in case of the non-payment

kroner effected after maturity, but before payment of the debt (10 Dec. 1936, *Zeitschrift für osteuropäisches Recht*, 4 (1937), 54).

[138] Similarly, the German creditor of non-German currency will be entitled to damages if the German currency remained stable, but the non-German currency depreciated, so that, when paid, it did not produce the amount of German currency the creditor would have received had payment been made punctually.

[139] On the German law (with references to Italian law) see Grunsky, 'Verzugsschaden und Geldentwertung' in *Gedächtnisschrift für Rudolf Bruns* (1980), p. 19.

[140] See Ascarelli, pp. 556–7 and the most recent decision of the Corte di Cassazione, 21 July 1975, No. 2881, *Giur. Ital.* 1976, I. 1, 1562.

[141] Art. 1153 as altered by the law of 11 July 1975: damages resulting from delay in payment consist only of interest at the statutory rate which is fixed from year to year. This is without prejudice to special rules applicable to traders and in case of guarantees. Damage which has been caused by the debtor's bad faith and is independent of the delay may also be recovered.

[142] 30 Nov. 1978, *Giur. Ital.* 1979, I. i, 972 with note by Enrico Quadri.

[143] 4 July 1979, no. 3776, *Foro Italiano* 1979, I. 1668; 25 Oct. 1979, No. 5572, *Giur. Ital.* 1980, I. 1, 452. In a fundamental decision of 8 Jan. 1975 the Supreme Court of *Chile* allowed damages for loss of monetary value in addition to interest: Lopez-Santa Maria, p. 149.

[144] Such as existed in *Aruna Mills Ltd.* v. *Dhanrajmal Gobindram*, [1968] 2 W.L.R. 101.

[145] *Fletcher* v. *Tayleur* (1855), 17 C.B. 21, 20 *per* Willes J.; *Prehn* v. *Royal Bank of*

of a debt the measure of damages is the interest of the money only,[146] for it does not apply where substantial damages are reasonably within the contemplation of the parties.[147] Nor are substantial damages necessarily too remote to be recoverable; this is again a question of fact[148] and remoteness cannot be regarded as a univerally valid defence. Nor is it right that as a matter of law a change in the rate of exchange is too remote to give rise to a claim to damages;[149] no such legal principle exists or can exist, for remoteness, as has just been stated, raises an issue of fact.[150] It is quite true that in *The Teh Hu*[151] a majority of the Court of Appeal held that a salvage award of a sum of sterling in favour of Japanese salvors could not be increased to take care of the devaluation in 1967.[152] But the point

---

*Liverpool* (1870), L.R. 5 Ex. 92, 100 *per* Piggot B. The rule is the same in the United States (Williston s. 1410), but it was severely and justifiably criticized by Jessel M.R. in *Wallis* v. *Smith* (1882), 21 Ch. D.243, 275.

[146] It should, however, be emphasized that interest is awarded to compensate for the deprivation of the use of the money due until payment, not to preserve the real value of the sum due or afford protection against inflation: *Pickett* v. *British Rail Engineering Ltd.*, [1980] A.C. 136. Where interest is awarded, the plaintiff should be paid at the rate at which he actually had to borrow, even if this was abroad and in a different currency: *Helmsing Schiffahrts G.m.b.H.* v. *Malta Docks Corporation*, (1977) 2 Ll. L.R. 444.

[147] *Trans Trust S.P.R.L.* v. *Danubian Trading Co.*, [1952] 2 Q.B. 297. And see *Ozalid Group (Export) Ltd.* v. *African Continental Bank Ltd.*, (1979) 2 Ll. L.R. 231, where without much discussion Donaldson J. (as he then was) awarded to the plaintiff £140 for bank charges and £40 for solicitors' costs incurred before the date of the writ. It is possible that in this respect the decision is unprecedented.

[148] *Mehmet Dogan Bey* v. *Abdeni & Co. Ltd.*, [1951] 2 K.B. 405. In so far as the arbitrator attached weight to ministerial protestations prior to 18 Sept. 1949, his reasoning is not convincing, for neither at that time nor prior to 18 Nov. 1967 did they, among reasonable people, in fact make sufficient or, indeed, any impact so as to affect foreseeability. Could Ministers be expected to proclaim the likelihood of devaluation? Nor is the reasoning of McNair J. convincing, for he seemed to think that foreseeability must include the precise chain of events.

[149] A submission to this effect was made by Mr. Megaw (as he then was) in the case referred to in the preceding note.

[150] The observations of Scrutton L.J. in *Di Ferdinando* v. *Simon Smits & Co.*, [1920] 3 K.B. 409, 419 arose in a case in which there was no evidence that the damage was reasonably foreseeable. They were not intended to lay down a legal principle of universal application. In the *United States of America* it is suggested by Professor Corbin, *Law of Contracts* V (1964), s. 1005, p. 52 that damages for breach of contract 'will not be increased by proof that they have depreciated in purchasing power since the date of the contract or since the date of the breach by nonpayment'. The learned author does not deal with the proof of special facts. According to Williston, *Law of Contracts* (3rd ed. by Jaeger, 1968), vol. ii, p. 605, 'in an action by a creditor against his debtor for the nonpayment of the debt no other damages are ever allowed'.

[151] [1970] P. 106. The reason why the case is material in the present context is that the majority (Salmon and Karminski L.JJ.) treated the obligation which arose upon the termination of the salvage services as a sterling obligation. It is now clear (see below p. 247) that the salvors were entitled to an award in foreign currency.

[152] In the court below Brandon J. stated in some detail that this was a supervening and unforeseeable and, therefore, in law an irrelevant event: [1970] P. 106, at p. 115. But on this question see below, p. 286.

under discussion does not seem to have been put forward. Nor does any other case discuss it. Yet in a country such as Britain where for a number of years inflation has been the talk of the day and the government and other official sources made forecasts of the annual rate of inflation it is difficult to see why a creditor should not be compensated if he can prove loss resulting from his inability, caused by the debtor's default, to make a cheaper purchase.

3. The question whether a change of monetary value and its effects can operate as a discharge of the contract depends in *England* on the scope of the general doctrine of frustration as developed since *Taylor* v. *Caldwell*.[153] On the one hand, a rise of prices such as that caused by the outbreak of a war does not bring the contract to an end,[154] nor does an unexpected turn of events if it merely makes performance more onerous.[155] Thus an English seller cannot treat his contract with an English buyer as discharged merely by reason of the fact that the goods he sold have to be imported from the United States and, in consequence of the devaluation of sterling, are more expensive. On the other hand there is no reason to assume that a serious and sudden depreciation of monetary value, causing a disruption of the intended equivalence between performances on either side, can never be regarded as a supervening change of circumstances within the above-stated principle. In fact Viscount Simon has expressly stated that, while an unexpected turn of events such as 'a wholly abnormal rise or fall in prices, a sudden depreciation of currency, an unexpected obstacle to execution, or the like' does not in itself affect the bargain, the true construction of the contract may show that the parties never agreed to be bound in a fundamentally different situation and that, accordingly, 'the contract ceases to bind at that point'.[156] Lord Denning M.R. invoked this dictum, when he held[157] that an agreement made in 1929 to supply 'at all times hereafter' water at 7d, now 2.9 pence per 1,000 gallon could be terminated by six months' notice in 1979, when the ordinary rate was 55 pence per 1.000 gallons. Viscount Simon's

---

[153] (1863), 3 B. & S. 826.

[154] *Tennants (Lancashire) Ltd.* v. *Wilson & Co. Ltd.*, [1917] A.C. 495; *Bolckow Vaughan & Co.* v. *Compañia Minera de Sierra Minera* (1916), 33 T.L.R. 111 (C.A.); *Greenway Bros. Ltd.* v. *Jones & Co.* (1916), 32 T.L.R. 184. Cf. *Blythe & Co.* v. *Richards Turpin & Co.* (1916), 114 L.T. 752. In *Universal Corporation* v. *Five Ways Property Ltd.*, (1978) 3 All E.R. 1131, Walton J. said 'quite emphatically the doctrine of frustration cannot be brought into play merely because the purchaser finds, for whatever reason, he has not got the money to complete the purchase'.

[155] *Davis Contractors Ltd.* v. *Fareham Urban District Council*, [1956] A.C. 696.

[156] *British Movietonews Ltd.* v. *London Cinemas*, [1952] A.C. 166, at p. 185.

[157] *Staffordshire Area Health Authority* v. *South Staffordshire Waterworks Co.*, (1978) 1 W.L.R. 1387.

dictum, however, seems to require a sudden depreciation and is intended to exemplify the doctrine of frustration which leads to automatic termination. Would it not be preferable to imply a term to the effect that in the event of the price becoming disproportionately low as a result of inflation (or the rise in the price of the commodity in question) the contract could be terminated on reasonable notice? Such a term[158] may well be within the contemplation of reasonable parties to a long-term contract.[159]

In other countries, too, the question is bound up with the general doctrine of frustration the application of which in connection with unforeseen depreciation of money is sometimes difficult to determine. In the *United States* there is no judicial decision covering the point, and the influence of the frustration doctrine cannot be put higher than in this country.[160] In *France* there is considerable conflict of opinion regarding the existence and scope of the 'imprévision' doctrine,[161] but outside the field of administrative law the attitude of the courts is quite uncompromising. Thus it continues to be the law that[162] 'si, en principe, le débiteur ne répond pas de la force majeure, cette règle n'est pas applicable lorsque l'empêchement invoqué a eu seulement pour effet de rendre plus difficile ou plus onéreuse l'exécution des obligations'; and that 'le juge ne saurait faire état des hausses de prix, même homologuées, pour soustraire l'un des contractants à l'accomplissement des engagements clairs et précis qu'il a librement assumés'.

In *Germany*, it is true, the extraordinary depreciation of the mark between 1920 and 1923 forced upon the courts a general 'clausula rebus sic stantibus' doctrine,[163] but in times of relative monetary stability, where there occurs no more than a creeping inflation, a rise of prices or a depreciation of the German currency does not constitute a ground of relief from contractual obligations.[164]

---

[158] Cf. Art. 1467 of the Italian Civil Code.

[159] It would also avoid the unconvincing interpretation of the words 'at all times hereafter', which were supposed to have meant 'at all times during the subsistence of this agreement', with the result that notice could have been given at any time and in any circumstances. What better word of permanency could have been employed than 'at all times hereafter'? In *Attorney-General* v. *Prince Ernest Augustus of Hanover*, [1957] A.C. 436 it was held that 'all' meant all.

[160] The clearest case is *Columbus Railway, Power & Light Co.* v. *City of Columbus*, 249 U.S. 399 (1919), where Mr. Justice Day said at p. 414 on behalf of the Court: 'But equity does not relieve from hard bargains simply because they are such.'

[161] See, for example, Planiol-Ripert, vi, Nos. 391 sqq. The doctrine of 'lésion' does not apply in the field of commercial contracts. It applies only to certain types of contract, particularly contracts for the sale of land (Art. 1674 of the Code Civil); see, generally, Mazeaud, *Leçons de Droit Civil* (3rd ed., 1966), ii. 164 sqq.

[162] Cass. Com. 18 Jan. 1950, D. 1950, 227. See Cas. Civ. 17 Nov. 1925, D.H. 1926, 35; 5 Dec. 1927, D.H. 1928, 84.

[163] *RGZ*. 106, 7 and 11; 107, 19; Warneyer's *Rechtsprechung*, 1925, No. 82, 122. As to *Switzerland* see Henggeler and Guisan, *Zeitschrift für schweizerisches Recht*, 56 (1937), 238a, 314a. In *Israel* a rise of prices caused by inflation is not an event constituting frustration: Yadin (above p. 104, n. 113), p. 857.

[164] Staudinger (Werner), s. 275 note 8 with references, now Loewisch in 12th ed. (1979)

In Anglo-Saxon countries equity, in special circumstances, provides the remedy of setting aside a contract. Thus in an action brought in August 1947 by a purchaser of land to have a sale made in September 1945 set aside on the ground of the vendor's failure to disclose material facts the Supreme Court of Missouri[165] took 'judicial notice of the fact that between the date of the transaction and the institution of the suit the purchasing power of the dollar declined steadily and materially and has ever since continued to do so'; as the sum to be refunded by the plaintiff would represent 'only a fraction of the value as of the time of the sale', cancellation was refused.

4. In view of the inherent connection between the two remedies, it is not surprising to observe that the reluctance of the courts to allow rescission made itself felt when they came to consider the equitable remedy of *specific performance.*

In the early eighteenth century, it is true, Lord Macclesfield refused to order specific performance in a case which arose out of the effects of the change in money value brought about by the collapse of the South Sea Bubble, the reason being that 'a Court of Equity ought to take notice under what a general delusion the nation was at the time when this contract was made . . . when there was thought to be more money in the nation than there really was, which induced people to put imaginary values on estates'.[166] But the case is now distinctly out of favour and cannot be regarded as an authority.[167] The leading principle as stated by Lord Eldon,[168] that the inadequacy must be such 'as shocks the conscience and amounts in itself to conclusive and decisive evidence of fraud', involves the further proposition that the question of inadequacy of consideration must be examined from the point of view of the time when the contract was made,[169] and it is therefore doubtful whether the doctrine is available even in case of a complete collapse of a currency.

In the *United States* the position is not substantially different. The leading case is *Willard* v. *Taylor,*[170] the facts of which were as follows. In 1854 the plaintiff took a ten years' lease of certain real property coupled with an option

---

s. 6 and see the decisions of the Federal Supreme Court of 1 Oct. 1975, *NJW.* 1976, 142; 8 Feb. 1978, Betrieb 1978, 1267; see also 29 Sept. 1969, Betrieb 1969, 2029.

[165] *Curotto* v. *Hammack*, 241 S.W. 2d. 897, 26 A.L.R. 2d 1302 (1951). In *Chile* the Supreme Court decided in 1975 that where a contract is rescinded and money becomes repayable the amount is to be adjusted to take care of inflation: Lopez-Santa Maria, p. 175.

[166] *Savile* v. *Savile* (1721), 1 P. Wms. 745.      [167] Fry, *Specific Performance*, s. 448.

[168] *Coles* v. *Trecothick* (1804), 9 Ves. 246.

[169] Fry, l.c.; on the hardship as a ground for refusing specific performance see *Hangkam Kwington Woo* v. *Liu Lan Fong*, [1951] A.C. 707, 722.      [170] (1869) 8 Wall. (75 U.S.) 557.

to purchase the property before the end of the lease for $22,500, $2,000 of which were to be paid at the exercise of the option. Shortly before the expiration of the lease in 1864, when, owing to the issue of greenbacks, the premium on gold was more than 50 per cent, the plaintiff exercised the option and sent the defendant a cheque for $2,000 payable in notes, and subsequently he tendered the amount in notes, but the defendant refused to accept them. The plaintiff applied for specific performance, which was granted on the condition that he paid the purchase price in gold or silver coin and executed a mortgage as security therefor. Mr. Justice Field, delivering the opinion of the court, said that they perceived no reason which should preclude the plaintiff from claiming a specific performance of the contract,[171] but as regards the compensation granted by the conditions attached, he said[172] that 'it strikes one at once as inequitable to compel a transfer of the property for notes, worth when tendered in the market only a little more than one half of the stipulated price. Such a substitution of notes for coin could not have been in the possible expectation of the parties. Nor is it reasonable to suppose, if it had been, that the covenant would ever have been inserted in the lease without some provision against the substitution.' But although the case is now 'probably the leading American case on the subject of specific performance in general',[173] it cannot be, and has never been, understood as allowing a general price revision in case of monetary fluctuations, and as regards this very question, there are many reasons for which its authority is somewhat doubtful.[174, 175]

---

[171] At p. 573.                                                                [172] At p. 574.

[173] Dawson and Cooper, 33 (1935) *Mich. L.R.* 852, 867.

[174] See the detailed arguments of Dawson and Cooper, l.c., pp. 865–76, and the decision quoted, p. 105, n. 119, above, and *Sinclair Refining Co.* v. *Miller*, 106 F. Supp. 881 (1952).

[175] During the period preceeding the currency reform of 1948 it was held in *Western Germany* that pending the expected reform the promisor could withhold performance or that a right of repurchase could not be exercised or that in other respects equity required an attitutde adapted to the extraordinary depreciation of money: Federal Supreme Court, 28 Feb. 1951, *NJW.* 1951, 399. The Supreme Court of *Israel* held that inflation between the agreed date for completion and judgment did not preclude an order for specific performance; Israel L.R. 11 (1976) 124. But the result may be different if the discrepancy is very great: see the cases discussed by Yadin (above p. 104, n. 113) p. 848. The law seems to be fluid, as appears from the most recent decision in *Ritberg* v. *Nisim* summarized by Goldstein and Cohen, 16 (1981) *Israel L.R.* 110.

# V

# Monetary Obligations: Unliquidated Amounts

I. Introduction. II. Damages: (1) a comparative survey; (2) damages in English law (*a*) for breach of contract; (*b*) for tort; (*c*) where there is mitigation. III. Compensation for expropriation. IV. Sharing a fund.

## I

NOMINALISM, as has been shown, on account of its origin and nature, has developed and operates in relation to liquidated sums, whether they stem from the parties' agreement, from a unilateral statement of intention such as a will or from statute. Consequently the question whether and to what extent nominalism operates outside the realm of fixed sums does not arise. The extent of unliquidated amounts depends upon the principles applicable to the relationship in issue rather than the law of money: it is the law of damages, breach of trust, unjustified enrichment, agency, and so forth that must decide upon the relevance and impact of variations of monetary value. In all these cases the claims are unliquidated and require assessment by means of a valuation in terms of money. Their extent or, to put it differently, the result of the valuation depends upon the time with reference to which the process of valuation is carried out.[1] Value, as opposed to a sum which is fixed and constant in character, implies variability and, therefore, a reference to a time element. Thus, if money depreciates and the decisive date is that of judgment or payment, the creditor is protected in that he receives a higher amount than in the case of the opposite solution which would prefer the value at the date when the claim arose or the action was brought, and which would involve a quasi-nominalistic approach. Which of the various possible dates should prevail is decided, not by the law of money, but by the legal rules developed in the respective contexts, or, possibly, by the law of procedure. It is true that in case of such a liability (sometimes described as *Wertschuld, dette*

[1] See the definition given by the Federal Supreme Court of Germany (23 Oct. 1958, *BGHZ.* 28, 259, at p. 265): while these claims 'contemplate the payment of money, their extent is determined by a relation to non-monetary elements such as the price of goods at a given moment or the value of a thing (*BGHZ.* 7, 137; 9, 60)'.

*de valeur*[2] or *debito di valore*) nominalistic ideas or tendencies have occasionally made themselves felt: thus in choosing the time judges have been guided by the idea that their decision should be such that monetary depreciation would be concealed. Since, however, nominalism is not a principle of public policy, such inclinations should be and usually have been resisted. On the other hand, where the date is prescribed by statute, the judge must give effect to the monetary consequences and leave it to the legislator to change them,[3] as the French legislator did in a spectacular fashion in 1960.[4]

## II

The principal problem concerns the extent of claims for the payment of *damages* or, in other words, the date with reference to which the loss has to be assessed, whether the liability arises from breach of contract or tort. In either case it is necessary to answer the distinct question of how the victim is to be treated if, voluntarily or in discharge of a duty to mitigate the loss, he has spent money and whether in such circumstances further damage resulting from delayed payment has to be made good.[5] After a comparative survey each of these matters will be discussed separately from the point of view of English law.

1. In *Germany* the broad principle of *restitutio in integrum* (s. 249 of the Civil Code) is understood to require that, in the absence of specific statutory provisions and so long as the damage is not quantified, the decision of the court must be based on a valuation as at the time of judgment, this being the only method which reasonably ensures that the plaintiff will receive the amount necessary to make good the damage.[6] The principle does not exclude the

---

[2] See, generally, Georges L. Pierre-François, *La notion de dette de valeur en droit civil* (Paris, 1975).

[3] It is possible that, when discussing numerous examples, Ascarelli, pp. 484 sqq., does not always adhere to this rule.

[4] He altered Articles 548, 549, 554, 555, 587, 660, 661 of the Code Civil so as to provide for valuations as at the date of payment.

[5] These questions, of course, only occur where the damage has to be made good by the payment of a capital sum. Where, as for instance in Germany or France, the wrongdoer in personal injury cases may or must be ordered to pay an annual sum, this is usually subject to review in the event of a change of circumstances or may be indexed, as is now possible in France: the practice of the lower courts was finally sanctioned by Cass. Chambre Mixte, 6 Nov. 1974, J.C.P. 1975, II. 17978 with note by Savatier. As a result of this decision a statutory regime for the indexation of annual payments in case of motorcar accidents was introduced by law No. 74–1118 of 27 Dec. 1974.

[6] Supreme Court, 6 Oct. 1933, *RGZ*. 142, 8, at p. 11; Federal Supreme Court, 12 Jan. 1951, *BGHZ*. 1, 52; see generally, Staudinger (Medicus), s. 249 note 238. In *Switzerland* damages are also assessed as at the date of judgment: Oftinger, *Schweizerisches Haftpflichtrecht* (1958), i. 153, 197; von Büren, *Schweizerisches Obligationenrecht*

possibility of taking into account the fact that at the time when the claim arose, or subsequently between that time and the judgment, the value was higher than at the time of judgment; in such a case the plaintiff must, however, prove that he would have benefited from such higher value, e.g. by selling the goods which the defendant failed to deliver.[7] On the other hand, if the value since the time of breach or wrong has increased and is higher at the time of judgment, the principle of *restitutio in integrum* demands that the plaintiff be awarded so much as at the time of judgment will enable him to make good his loss. These rules are primarily designed for a valuation of a loss suffered through damage to goods, but it is obvious that there is no difficulty in adapting them to cases where the change of value is attributable not to changes in the value of the thing, the subject-matter of the breach or wrong, but to monetary factors, or, in other words, where the fluctuations moving from the side of money affect not the damage but the measurement of value on the basis of which the damage is calculated. Therefore fluctuations of monetary value and their effect on prices are easily taken into account, and during the monetary crises of 1920 to 1923 and 1945 to 1948 there was neither a need for nor a possibility of any revalorization, but general rules of German law made a *transvalorization* (*Umwertung*) practice readily available.[8] Transvalorization consists in measuring the loss at the time of assessment, in monetary terms then prevailing rather than in adapting a sum of money to them; therefore the individual circumstances of the parties or the 'impoverishment factor' cannot on principle be taken into account. Thus if through the defendant's wrongful act damage is caused to the plaintiff's horse, 'the defendant must compensate the plaintiff in respect of that value which, in view of the reduction of the purchasing power of the mark which set in after the wrong was done corresponds to the valuation of money at the time of judgment. For only by this method does the plaintiff

(Allgemeiner Teil, 1964), pp. 45-7; von Tuhr-Peter, *Allgemeiner Teil des Schweizerischen Obligationenrechts* (3rd ed., 1979), I, 123 who add that if the victim has made good the damage he can only claim the sum paid by him. For a detailed review of the practice in cases of tort see Szöllösy, *Zeitschrift des bernischen Juristenvereins* 112 (1976), 20.

[7] Supreme Court, l.c.; and 25 Oct. 1934, *RGZ.* 145, 296, 299.

[8] See Supreme Court, 10 Jan. 1933, *JW.* 1933, 2449. Some cases of transvalorization are mentioned there. They are collected by Mügel, *Das Gesamte Aufwertungsrecht* (1927), pp. 146 sqq., or in *Kommentar von Reichsgerichtsräten*, 9th ed. i (1939), 476 sqq. It should be observed that the 'impoverishment factor' was not always disregarded: see Supreme Court, 15 June 1927, *RGZ.* 117, 252. After the currency reform of 1948 it was again held that 'transvalorization' rather than conversion had to take place in case of claims for damages (Supreme Court for the British Zone, 27 May 1949, *NJW.* 1949, 624; 25 Nov. 1949, *NJW.* 1950, 261, No. 1; 2 Dec. 1949, *NJW.* 1950, 261, No. 2; 15 Feb. 1950, *NJW.* 1950, 464; 22 Sept. 1950, *NJW.* 1951, 112; Federal Tribunal, 11 Jan. 1951, *NJW.* 1951, 189; 6 Nov. 1951, *BGHZ.* 3, 321, 327; *contra* Court of Appeals (U.S.A. Court) Nürnberg, 17 May 1950, *NJW.* 1950, 908 with note by Mann, *NJW.* 1951, 156). But claims for unjustified enrichment which after 1923 the Supreme Court 'transvalorized' (11 Oct. 1927, *RGZ.* 118, 185, with references; Belgian–German Mixed Arbitral Tribunal iii. 291; Roumanian–German Mixed Arbitral Tribunal vii. 738) were after 1948 'converted': Supreme Court for the British Zone, 21 July 1948, *NJW.* 1947-8, 688; 30 Sept. 1948, *NJW.* 1949, 64; 7 Oct. 1948, *NJW.* 1949, 62; Federal Tribunal, 14 June 1952, *BGHZ.* 6, 277; 3 Oct. 1952, *BGHZ.* 7, 252. For a fundamental discussion of the German practice see *BGHZ.* 7, 134 at p. 137.

receive the value of the horse at the time when the wrong was done and the due compensation for his damage, as he could not at the present time buy the same horse at the former nominal sum of depreciated paper marks. . . .'[9]

In a number of cases, however, German law provides that the plaintiff is entitled to recover the value of goods as it existed at a certain moment, e.g. in the case of claims against a railway company for damage to goods where their value must be ascertained as at the date when they were delivered to the railway company. The amount so ascertained was, after the currency reforms, revalorized or converted rather than transvalorized.[10] In other words, the statutory rule was observed. Similarly, no variation, by transvalorization or otherwise, can take place in those cases in which the damage has in fact been quantified, for instance, by the victim of the tortious act replacing or repairing the goods destroyed or damaged by the wrongdoer:[11] the plaintiff is not entitled to more than the sum fixed by such quantification, he is not entitled to transvalorization. Hence he should not (and, except in special circumstances, is not bound to)[12] spend his own money to make good the damage.

It is worthy of notice that in *Austria*, where revalorization of liquidated sums was, as a rule, not granted either by the legislator or the courts, there was never any doubt that damages were to be assessed as at the date of judgement[13] and were, therefore, subject to 'transvalorization'.[14] This rule applied both during the great inflation in the 1920s and in periods of less violent depreciation. Where the law provides for assessment, and the damage thus becomes quantified, at an earlier date, a fundamental decision of the Supreme Court in 1924[15] laid down the rule that the amount had to be increased so as to take the depreciation of money into account: 'This is not revalorization in the technical sense . . . but the necessary consequence of the measurement of value function of money . . . no statute lays it down that an altered measure should remain the basis of measurement without having regard to the alteration. . . .' It is, however, doubtful whether in periods of creeping inflation the decision of 1924 would be followed.[16]

In *France* it is now firmly established that both contractual and non-contractual damages are to be assessed on the basis of the value of the loss at the date of judgment,[17] except that where the victim has used his own resources

---

[9] Supreme Court, 6 May 1924, *JW.* 1924, 1358.

[10] Federal Supreme Court, 12 Jan. 1951, *BGHZ.* 1, 52.

[11] Federal Supreme Court, 11 Jan. 1951, *BGHZ.* 1, 34, at p. 40; 27 Sept. 1951, *BGHZ.* 3, 162, at p. 178.

[12] Supreme Court, 25 Oct. 1911, *JW.* 1912, 31, and see Palandt-Heinrichs, § 254 note 3 (b) (ee). The duty to spend money does not arise except where in a given case it is reasonable to do so to minimize the damage (s. 254 Civil Code).

[13] See, e.g., Supreme Court, 4 Apr. 1923, *SZ.* v, no. 72.

[14] See Wolff in Klang's *Commentaries*, vi (1951), p. 170 with numerous references to decisions. Gschnitzer, *Schuldrecht* (1963), p. 160, and Ertl (above p. 100, n. 97), p. 164. For a recent decision see Supreme Court, 11 Sept. 1975, *Juristische Blätter* 1976, 315.

[15] 18 June 1924, *SZ.* vi, No. 226, also *JW.* 1925, 1326, and see Mügel, *JW.* 1931, 636.

[16] Particularly because the decision of 1924 attracted much criticism. See Stanzl in Klang's *Commentaries*, iv, p. 723.

[17] See, generally, Mazeaud et Juglart, *Leçons de droit civil* ii (5th ed., 1973), s. 625, or

to make good the damage (which he is under no duty to do)[18] he can only recover the sum spent by him.[19] After much hesitation the rule was finally laid down in 1942 for non-contractual damages[20] on the ground that 'la victime a droit à la réparation totale du dommage qu'elle a subi' and that 'il s'ensuit que l'indemnité nécessaire pour compenser le préjudice doit être calculée sur la valeur du dommage au jour du jugement ou de l'arrêt'. As regards contractual damages the same rule was finally established in 1954.[21] In the latter case the adherents of the opposite view relied, in particular, on the provision that, in principle, the debtor is only liable for foreseeable damage,[22] but it does not apply 'aux variations résultant des fluctuations des prix, qui ne modifient que le quantum du gain manqué',[23] or, as it has been put by learned authors,[24] there is only one loss which, ex hypothesi, is foreseeable, and the depreciation of money is not a second, unforeseeable loss, but affects merely the valuation of the single loss which the wrongdoer must make good in its entirety. It is even open to the Court of Appeal 'de prendre en considération le montant réel du préjudice qui reste à réparer à l'époque où elle statue'; if, therefore, the value of money has depreciated since the decision of the court of first instance, 'le préjudice ne peut être couvert que par l'allocation des dommages-intérêts plus élevés'.[25]

In *Belgium* the modern law is very similar.[26] It stems from a decision of the Cour de Cassation of 1931. This established that the claim to damages is 'une dette de valeur' and, therefore, its amount is fixed, not by Art. 1895 which applies the nominalistic principle to 'dettes de sommes', but by the rule 'que le dommage soit "réparé", en d'autres termes que la valeur due soit reconstituée intégralement; qu'alors seulement l'indemnité sera juste et répondra

---

Carbonnier, *Droit Civil* ii (1969), ss. 8, 10, 160, 195, or Dalloz, *Encyclopédie de droit civil*, sub titulo *Dommages-Intérêts*, ss. 75 sqq. For a particularly illuminating survey see Mazeaud et Chabas, *Responsibilité Civile* (6th ed., 1978), III, sections 2420 sqq. or, much more shortly, Weill et Terré, *Droit Civil* (3rd ed., 1980), sections 435 and 787. In *Israel* the same rule is equally firmly established: Yadin, 13 (1978), *Israel L.R.* 111 and Tedeschi ibid., p. 10; Yadin (above p. 104, n. 113), p. 854. Yoran, *Israel L.R.* 1979, 515; 1980, 106; Gilad, ibid. 1980, 79.

[18] Cass. Civ. 10 May 1950, D. 1950, 465, among other decisions, particularly Cass. Civ. 2 Aug. 1950, Bull. Cass. Civ. 1950, i. 144.

[19] For references see Mazeaud, l.c., or Dalloz, s. 79, who points out that in such a case the victim 'a "cristallisé" son droit à réparation en une créance de somme d'argent d'un montant invariable'. The leading case is Cass. Civ. 24 March 1953, D. 1953, 354.

[20] Cass. Req. 24 Mar. 1942, D.A. 1942, 118 and since then numerous other decisions, particularly Cass. Civ. 10 May 1950, D. 1950, 465.

[21] Cass. Com. 16 Feb. 1954, D. 1954, 534 and many earlier and later cases, particularly Cass. Civ. 24 Jan. 1955, D. & S. 1956, 12.

[22] Art. 1150 Code Civil.

[23] Cass. Com. 1 June 1959, J.C.P. 1959, ii. 11206 with note by Hémard. Accordingly the rule also applies to damages for loss of profits: Cass. Civ. 27 Jan. 1964, J.C.P. 1964, II, 13636.

[24] Mazeaud, l.c., and see the article at p. 596.

[25] Cass. Civ. 19 Nov. 1953, D. 1954, 361.

[26] For an excellent survey see Roger O. Dalcq, *Traité de la responsabilité civil* ii (Brussels, 1962), Nos. 4041–4137. Numerous references to Belgian judicial practice are given by Mazeaud et Chabas, above p. 118, n. 17.

à ce qu'exige la loi'. This can only be achieved by calculating the amount due so that at the date of judgment it makes good the loss suffered by the victim.[27] The principle which extends to cases of breach of contract[28] is most impressively illustrated by a case in which the plaintiff claimed damages for the deprivation of perishable goods in 1942. The fact that the goods would have had to be sold in 1943 at the latest did not disentitle the plaintiff to the very much higher sum awarded in 1950, which 'n'est pas un enrichissement pour la victime, celle-ci ne recevant que l'équivalent de la chose dont elle a été dépouillée'. The alleged enrichment is nothing but 'la conséquence du retard mis par l'auteur responsable à exécuter son obligation de réparation'.[29] It even seems that in Belgium, as opposed to France, the principle applies where the victim, at his own expense, has carried out repairs or obtained replacement.[30] This, so the Cour de Cassation decides,[31] 'n'a pas pour efet d'opérer novation, de faire entrer la dette de réparation dans la catégorie des dettes de sommes numériques, arrêtées d'avance, et d'imposer ainsi, au créancier des dommages et intérêts, dus en raison d'un délit ou d'un quasi-délit, le risque de la diminution d'espèces, en étendant, en dehors de son champ d'application, la disposition de l'article 1895 du Code civil'.

The law of *Italy* seems to be very similar to French and Belgian law[32] except in one remarkable respect. In 1978 the United Civil Chambers of the Corte de Cassazione laid down the rule that where the victim of a wrongful act has at his own expense made good or reduced the damage the wrongdoer's duty of paying compensation does not lose its character of a 'debito di valore' and therefore the amount spent is susceptible of revalorization in relation to the loss of the purchasing power of money.[33]

In view of its experience during the greenback period 1861–79, when gold coin and treasury notes were both legal tender and, at one point, the premium on the former was more than 100 per cent in terms of the latter, the law of the *United States of America* was confronted much earlier than other legal systems with the problem of whether, to what extent and how, in assessing damages, the real purchasing power of notes could be taken into account.[34] But the

---

[27] 26 Feb. 1931, Pasicrisie 1931, i. 94. For a more recent statement of the principle see Cass., 24 Jan. 1966, Pasicrisie 1966, i. 658: 'le juge, pour fixer l'indemnité appelée à réparer le dommage causé par l'acte illicite, doit se placer au jour de sa décision'. In the case of an appeal the Court of Appeal may be both bound and entitled to 'apprécier le préjudice au moment où il statue': Dalcq, l.c., Nos. 4136, 4137 with references. It should be pointed out that the judgment-date is chosen, because it is the moment 'théoriquement le plus proche de la réparation': Dalcq, l.c., No. 4049.

[28] That is clearly established already since the decision of the Cour de Cassation, 28 May 1931, Pasicrisie 1931, i. 180.

[29] Cass., 8 May 1952, Pasicrisie 1952, i. 570.

[30] As to the question in what circumstances such an obligation exists, see Dalcq, l.c., Nos. 3436, 4130.

[31] Above, n. 27. On the problem see Dalcq, l.c., Nos. 4070, 4071, 4125.

[32] Ascarelli, pp. 514 sqq.

[33] 9 Jan. 1978, no. 57, *Foro Italiano* 1978, I. 336 with note by Amatucci.

[34] For a most interesting and illuminating discussion see Dawson and Cooper, 33 (1935) *Mich. L.R.* 852. The problem became pressing after *Bronson* v. *Rodes* (1868), 7 Wall.

developments of a century ago, though of great historical interest, do not seem
at the present time to have much influence on judicial practice. Up to recent
times, it is true, the starting principle was often said to be that damages are
assessed as at the date of wrong,[35] and this, indeed, continues to be firmly
established in case of breach of contract.[36] Yet on closer analysis recent practice
appears to have introduced many qualifications into the rule, so that the
Restatement (Second) would seem to be correct in stating[37] that 'any event
occurring prior to the trial that increases the harmful consequences of the
defendant's tortious conduct . . . increases the damages recoverable to the same
extent, whether the event has occurred before suit is brought or after suit.'
In cases of personal injury it is now clear that a verdict based on the value of
the dollar at the date of the verdict rather than that of the injury will not
be set aside either on the ground of excessiveness or on the ground of an
erroneous application of the law.[38] On the contrary, as was said, for instance, in

(74 U.S.) 229, had given judicial recognition to the depreciation of legal tender notes.
See, for example, the Californian case of *Spencer* v. *Prindle* (1865), 28 Cal. 276, where the
jury was charged on the strength of the evidence that the value of the services the subject-
matter of the claim was $1,000 in notes or $500 in coin. On the defendant's appeal this
instruction was approved, because for measuring the value of services the question was
'not whether a dollar in greenbacks is worth more or less than a dollar in gold, but what
are the goods or services worth'.

[35] See, e.g., *Kunianly* v. *Overmyer Warehouse Co.*, 406 F. 2d 818, 822 (1968).

[36] See Williston, *Law of Contracts* (3rd ed. 1968, by Jaeger), vol. ii, s. 1384 and the
recent case of *Rodriguez & Co. Inc.* v. *Moore McCormack Lines Inc.*, 32 N.Y. 2d 428, 299
N.E. 2d 243 (1973). The general principle that damages for non-delivery of goods must
be measured with reference to the time when they should have been delivered has recently
been reaffirmed by the Supreme Court in *Ansaldo San Giorgio* v. *Rheinstrom Bros.* (1934),
294 U.S. 494. For further references see n. 6 ibid. and *Effinger* v. *Kenney* (1885), 115
U.S. 566, at p. 575 *per* Mr. Justice Field, and see *Hopkins* v. *Lee* (1821), 6 Wheat. 109;
*Preston* v. *Prather* (1891), 137 U.S. 604. It should, however, be noted that the doctrines of
highest replacement value or of highest intermediate value which, as will be mentioned
in the text, have been developed in regard to damages for conversion, are frequently applied
to damages for failure to deliver goods: T. McCormick, *Law of Damages* (1935), p. 197.

[37] (1979), § 910 comment b.

[38] In *Hurst* v. *Chicago B.Q.R. Co.* (1920), 280 Mo. 566, 219 S.W. 566, the Supreme
Court of Missouri said: 'The value of money lies not in what it is, but in what it will buy.
It follows that if $10,000 was a fair compensation in value for such injuries (loss of leg)
as are here involved 10 years ago, when money was dear and its purchasing power was
great, a larger sum will now be required when money is cheap and its purchasing power
is small.' Therefore $15,000 were not held to be excessive. The court cited numerous
authorities and emphasized that 'ordinary variations' should not give rise to any increase
or reduction. 'But when radical, material, and apparently permanent changes in social
and economic conditions confront mankind, courts must take cognisance of them.' In the
same sense *Talbert* v. *Chicago R.I. & P. Ry. Co.*, 15 S.W. 2d 762 (1929) (Supreme Court
of Missouri). In *Halloran* v. *New England Tel. & Tel. Co.* (1920), 95 Vt. 273, 115 A. 143,
it was held that in an action for personal injuries the jury could be instructed that they
might consider the impaired purchasing power of the dollar in assessing damages. As to
this case, see the comments in 35 (1922) *Harv. L.R.* 616. For more recent cases see the
Note on Fluctuating Dollars and Tort Damage Verdicts, 48 (1948) *Col. L.R.* 264 and, in
particular, *Calihan* v. *Yellow Cab Co. of San Diego* (1932), 13 P. (2d) 931; *Petty* v. *Kansas
City Public Services Co.* (1945), 191 S.W. (2d) 653; *Butler* v. *Allen* (1946), 167 P. (2d)
488; *O'Brien* v. *Chicago and North Western Rly. Co.* (1946), 68 N.E. (2d) 638; *Eichten*
v. *Central Minnesota Cooperative Power Association of Redwood County* (1947), 28 N.W.

California,[39] in approval of a charge to a jury to award damages 'based upon the present value of the dollar—that is, its value at the time of the verdict', 'it is plain common sense and simple honesty for a court or jury in appraising the damages suffered by reason of any tortious act of defendant to compute the amount of damages according to the current value of the dollar'. The question whether future inflation may be taken into account in awarding damages is, in the words of Friendly C.J.,[40] 'in a state of uncertainty and flux'; it seems that the First, Third, and Fifth Circuit Courts of Appeal at present treat future inflation as too speculative to permit consideration,[41] while the Second, Ninth, and Tenth Circuits tend to allow this element of damages if expert evidence by trained economists supports it[42] and the Sixth and Eighth Circuits do not require expert evidence, but allow the jury to apply its common-sense.[43] No case seems to have pronounced upon the question whether the date of the verdict also prevails in cases in which the victim has made good or minimized the whole or part of the damage. As regards injury to property, in particular conversion, American cases have invariably arisen from the fluctuating value of the property, such as stock exchange securities, but there is every reason to believe that the rule so developed is capable of, and is in fact, being applied to changes in the value of money, which, as submitted earlier,[44] are indistinguishable.[45] In 1889, the Supreme Court of the United States relying heavily on the law of England (where, it will appear,[46] the law is today far from settled), enunciated the rule that the victim, at any rate if the defendant had

---

(2d) 862 and, in particular, *New Amsterdam Casualty Co.* v. *Soileau*, 167 F. 2d 767 (1948, Court of Appeals, 5th Circuit); and *Willard* v. *Hudson*, 378 P. 2d 966 (1963), a decision of the Supreme Court of Oregon with a long list of earlier authorities.

[39] *Gist* v. *French*, 288 P. 2d 1003, at p. 1020 (1955) (Californian District Court of Appeal).

[40] *Feldman* v. *Allegheny Airlines Inc.*, 524 F. 2d 384 (1975).

[41] *Williams* v. *United States*, 435 F. 2d 804 (1970); *Magill* v. *Westinghouse Electric Corporation*, 464 F. 2d 294 (1972); *Hoffman* v. *Sterling Drug Inc.*, 485 F. 2d 726 (1974); *Huddell* v. *Levin*, 537 F. 2d 726 (1974); *Johnson* v. *Penrod Drilling Co.*, 510 F. 2d 234 (1975),—a most important decision rendered by the Fifth Circuit by a majority of 12 to 3. But see *Higginbotham* v. *Mobil Oil Co.*, 545 F. 2d 422 (1977).

[42] *Feldman* v. *Allegheny Airlines Inc.*, 524 F. 2d 384 (1975); *United States* v. *English*, 521 F. 2d (1975); *Burlington Northern Inc.* v. *Boxberger*, 529 F. 2d 284 (1975); *Sauers* v. *Alaska Barge*, 600 F. 2d 238 (1979); *Steckler* v. *United States*, 549 F. 2d 1372. The most recent decision of the Second Circuit which is likely to become leading is *Doca* v. *Marina Mercante Nicaraguense*, 634 F. 2d 30 (1980).

[43] *Bach* v. *Penn Central Transportation Co.*, 502 F. 2d 1117 (1974); *Johnson* v. *Serra*, 521 F. 2d 1289 (1975); *Riba* v. *Jasper Blackburn Corporation*, 516 F. 2d 840 (1975); *Hysell* v. *Iowa Public Service Co.*, 559 F. 2d 468 (1977). In the same sense the Supreme Courts of Wisconsin and Oregon in *Dabareiser* v. *Weisflog*, 253 Wis. 23, 33 N.W. 2d 220 (1948) and *Willard* v. *Hudson*, 378 P. 2d 966 (1973) respectively. See on the American law the helpful notes by an anonymous writer at 63 (1977) Virginia L.R. 105, and by McQueen, 62 (1976) Cornell L.R. 803.

[44] Above, p. 82.

[45] See, in particular, T. McCormick, *Law of Damages* (1935), pp. 190 sqq., one of the very few American authors who has dealt with the point under the heading 'Fluctuations in the Value of Money' and who makes it clear that, whether prices have risen or the value of money has fallen, the same 'legal devices' apply.

[46] Below, p. 127.

sold shares, was entitled to 'the highest intermediate value reached . . . between the time of the wrongful act complained of and a reasonable time thereafter to be allowed to the party injured to place himself in the position he would have been in had not his rights been violated'.[47] In other jurisdictions the rule is said to be the highest market value between the time of conversion and the time of judgment, provided the plaintiff brings his action within a reasonable time.[48] In any event there is ample machinery to enable the courts to have regard to the value at a time later than that of the conversion or destruction 'where that is necessary to give just compensation'.[49, 50]

2. The law of *England*, in so far as it relates to damages, has in recent years changed so as to produce a new, yet clearly-drawn picture. In 1976 Lord Wilberforce still spoke of the fact 'that as a general rule in English law damages for tort or for breach of contract are assessed as at the date of the breach'.[51] Already on that occasion he continued, however, as follows: 'It is for the courts, or for arbitrators, to work out a solution in each case best adapted to giving the injured plaintiff that amount in damages which will most fairly compensate him for the wrong which he has suffered'.[52] Today very little of the former 'general rule' would seem to be left. Instead the guiding principle of restoration[53] has been moved into the forefront so as to underline the courts' present tendency of achieving the result which in a given case most efficaciously complies with the demands of justice.

(*a*) As regards damages for breach of contract, it was again Lord Wilberforce who, with the concurrence of Lord Salmon, Lord

[47] *Galigher* v. *Jones*, 129 U.S. 193, at p. 200 (1889).

[48] For a survey and lists of authorities see, among others, McCormick, l.c., pp. 183-97, or F. Harper and F. James, *The Law of Torts* (1956), i, p. 192, or Williston (above, p. 121, n. 36). The law in regard to damage to land seems to be different: McCormick, l.c., pp. 480 sqq.

[49] Restatement, *Torts* (1939), section 927. The Restatement 2nd (1979) is much less clear. See generally Harper and James, *The Law of Torts*, ii (1956), s. 25. 11.

[50] Where repairs are effected, the owner is entitled to recover their cost, but if they enhance the pre-tort value the increase must be deducted: *Freeport Sulphur Co.* v. *S.S. Hermosa*, 526 F. 2d 300 (1977), with a very important concurring judgment by Wisdom J.

[51] *Miliangos* v. *Frank (Textiles) Ltd.*, [1976] A.C. 443, at p. 468. Cf. Halsbury (-Hailsham), *Laws of England* (4th ed., 1975), xii, section 1134: 'While assessment would normally be as at the date of the breach of duty, notice can be taken at the trial of subsequent realities which reduce the limits of speculation'. The strict adherence to the principle that 'damages must be assessed according to the general rule as at the time of the wrong' caused Lord Finlay to dissent from the judgment of the majority of the Permanent Court of International Justice at The Hague in the case concerning the factory at *Chorzow*: Judgment No. 13, Collection of Judgments, Series A, 1928-30, pp. 71 sqq.

[52] Strictly the *dicta* cited in the text were *obiter*, but they occurred in a context which previously had been dominated by pronouncements on the general law of damages and, therefore, have much relevance to the continuing validity of the latter.

[53] As laid down by Parke B. in *Robinson* v. *Harman*, (1848) 1 Exch. 850, 855.

Fraser of Tullybelton, Lord Keith of Kinkel and Lord Scarman, said in 1979:[54]

> The general principle for the assessment of damages is compensatory, i.e. the innocent party is to be placed, so far as money can do so, in the same position as if the contract had been performed. Where the contract is one of sale, this principle normally leads to assessment of damages as at the date of breach,— a principle recognised and embodied in s. 51 of the Sale of Goods Act 1893. But this is not an absolute rule: if to follow it would give rise to injustice the court has power to fix such other date as may be appropriate in the circumstances.

There have for a long time been cases in the books in which, in awarding damages for breach of contract, courts have had regard to circumstances, such as changes of value, occurring after the date of breach.[55] Even where prima facie the value at the date of breach may have to be accepted as a starting point but at such date the victim cannot be expected to go into the market, a subsequent rise in value is likely to be treated as a consequential loss,[56] for this is what normally the compensatory character of the award requires. At least since the 1950s inflation has been and is a foreseeable and almost invariably foreseen event. Apparent rises in value must and can be taken into account to afford full compensation to the injured party. In other words in most cases justice requires the court to assess damages as at the date of judgment. Thus where the seller repudiates his obligation to deliver a specially built machine and at the date of breach it costs twice and at the date of judgment three times the agreed price, the damages, it is submitted, should be so assessed as to enable the buyer to buy the machine at the date of judgment: he should receive the price payable on that day less the originally agreed sum. Similar result should in principle prevail where there is at the date of breach an available market and where the circumstances are such that the buyer cannot be expected to mitigate by going into the market.

In *Philips* v. *Ward*[57] the Court of Appeal held that a surveyor who

---

[54] *Johnson* v. *Agnew*, (1979), 2 W.L.R. 487, at p. 499; and see *Radford* v. *De Froberville*, (1977), 1 W.L.R. 1262.

[55] See, for example, *Harrison* v. *Harrison* (1824), 1 C. & P. 412; *Owen* v. *Routh & Ogle* (1854), 14 C.B. 327; *Elliot* v. *Hughes* (1863), 3 F. & F. 387. But the date of the breach of contract was said to be controlling in such cases as *Rice* v. *Baxendale* (1861), 7 H. & N. 96; *O'Hanlan* v. *Great Western Railway Co.*, 6 B. & S. 484, 491 *per* Blackburn J.; *Ströms Bruks Aktie Bolag* v. *Hutchison*, [1905] A.C. 515; *The Arpad*, [1934] P. 189.

[56] McGregor, *On Damages* (14th ed., 1980), sections 224, 225, 591, 837, 841-3, 976-8.

[57] (1956), 1 W.L.R. 471. If the repairs had been carried out by the plaintiff in 1952 he would not have been entitled to any betterment value which they would have created, so that probably the result would not have been different.

in 1952 broke his contract by rendering an inaccurate report on the state of a house purchased by the plaintiff was liable, not for the cost of repairs amounting to £7,000 in 1952, but for the difference between the price paid (£25,000) and the value of the house without the repairs (£21,000) in 1952. Denning L.J. (as he then was) said that a fall after 1952 in the value of money 'does not in law affect the figure, for the simple reason that sterling is taken to be constant in value'.[58] It is open to doubt whether the case which rests on earlier, now overruled decisions[59] and is inconsistent with Lord Denning's more recent views[60] is still authoritative; in 1980 the Court of Appeal answered in the negative.[61] Moreover it has now been held by the House of Lords that where in breach of his contract an architect fails to discover a defect of a building the owner is entitled to the cost of reinstatement at or at a reasonable time after the discovery of the defect.[62] In order fully to compensate the owner the court, it is submitted, should have awarded at least the difference between the value of the house in 1956 in the condition in which it would then have been had the report been correct and the value in 1956 which the house then actually had without the necessary work having been done.

(b) The present practice is much more firmly established in regard to damages for tort.

For a long time a certain type of case was governed by a dictum by Lord Wrenbury[63] according to which, if the plaintiff has been damaged by the defendant tortiously depriving him on 1 January of three cows at the value of £150,

> It would be *nihil ad rem* to say that in July similar cows would have cost in the market £300. The defendant is not bound to supply the plaintiff with cows. . . . The defendant is liable to pay damages, that is to say, money to some amount for the loss of the cows: the only question is, how much? The answer is, such sum as represents the market value at the date of the tort of the goods of which the plaintiff was tortiously deprived.

The case in which this passage occurs is now in fact, though not in

---

[58] At p. 474. But we know that under the impact of economic events Lord Denning has abandoned this view which in the strict formulation used by him was probably always open to criticism.

[59] They were *Di Ferdinando* v. *Simon Smits & Co. Ltd.*, (1920), 3 K.B. 409 and *The Volturno*, [1921] 2 A.C. 544.

[60] Above p. 95.

[61] *Dodd Properties (Kent) Ltd.* v. *Canterbury City Council*, (1980), 1 W.L.R. 433, a tort case.

[62] *East Ham Corporation* v. *Bernard Sunley & Sons Ltd.*, [1966] A.C. 406, on which see Duncan Wallace, 96 (1980) L.Q.R. 101, who also refers to a New Zealand case. See below p. 133.      [63] *The Volturno*, [1921] 2 A.C. 544, at p. 563.

form, overruled,[64] but in any event the dictum, it is submitted, cannot be supported. The wrongdoer's duty is, not to 'supply the plaintiff with cows' on 1 July, but to pay 'damages for having on 1 January deprived him of cows'. Therefore the wrongdoer has to put the plaintiff in the position on 1 July (or the date of judgment) in which he can procure the three cows. If on 1 July they were worth £300, this sum should be awarded to the owner, because it represents his loss. It is in fact the sum which, as will appear, the court would now award if the cows had been converted rather than killed. If, on the other hand, in July the value of the cows is £75, the owner who is awarded such sum should be considered adequately compensated and £150 would be excessive; this would be different only if at some time between January and July the value had exceeded £75 and the owner proves that he would have had the benefit of such higher price, for instance by effecting a sale.[65] Any complaint by the owner that, had he been paid £150 in January, he could have invested his money so as to have six cows in July is irrelevant, because the law compensates for three, not for six cows, nor for delayed payment which has not caused a loss. The owner's right to *restitutio in integrum* in the sense of receiving such sum as enables him to obtain three cows in July (or whenever judgment is given), should be considered lost only if he should in fact have replaced the cows before that date,[66] though he may not normally be bound to do so.[67] Moreover, the suggestion that the rise in prices (or the depreciation of money) between January and July is not foreseeable and, therefore, too remote rests on facts which in the light of the experience of recent years are unlikely to be proved correct. In any event it is answered by French scholars, when they epitomize French judicial practice by the striking phrase that the law requires 'la prévisibilité portant sur la nature et l'étendue du dommage, non sur son expression monétaire'.[68]

In a rational legal system the abandonment of Lord Wrenbury's theory is required also for this reason that, as has been pointed out, the case of the destruction of cows should not be decided differently from that of conversion. In an action for conversion, where the defendant has the goods in his possession and could, but refuses to, hand them over, the value of the goods claimed,

---

[64] *The Despina R.*, [1979] A.C. 685.

[65] English law is, however, likely to be to the opposite effect: see McGregor, section 1049; and see the American law referred to above p. 122.

[66] As to *France* see Cass. Crim. 6 June 1946, D. 1947, 234; as to *Germany* see Staudinger (Werner) s. 249, note. 27.

[67] See below, p. 131.

[68] Carbonnier, *Droit Civil*, ii (1967), p. 541 among others.

but not returned, has to be assessed as at the date of judgment or verdict,[69] and it seems that this rule is in course of being extended to claims of a cognate type.[70] It is true that the decision of the Court of Appeal on which these submissions rest was rendered in a case involving an action for detinue,[71] and such an action was abolished in 1977.[72] But this does not provide justification for disregarding that decision[73] or the statement in all the authorities that damages for detinue and conversion should be assessed on the same basis. On the other hand there exists a long line of *dicta* of the highest authority in shipping cases to the effect that damage to or loss of property is to be assessed with reference to the value as at the date (and place) of wrong.[74] It is perhaps not altogether certain whether in any of these cases the difference (if any) in value as at the date of wrong and the date of judgment was in issue. It does not seem unlikely, however, that if this issue should arise in the changed economic conditions of the present time the courts will come down in favour of the value at the date of judgment, for it alone can lead to the restoration of the plaintiff's financial position which would exist had there been no tort.

Finally, as regards damages for personal injuries, 'there is today universal acceptance of the sensible and realistic rule that trial courts must look at the position at the time of their judgment and

---

[69] *Sachs* v. *Miklos*, [1948] 2 K.B. 23; *Munro* v. *Willmott*, [1949] 1 K.B. 295. The qualification introduced by the former case is merely an application of the rule according to which the plaintiff is under a duty to mitigate the damage.

[70] *Joseph D. Ltd.* v. *Ralph Wood & Co. Ltd.* (1951), W.N. 224. In a remarkable decision the Supreme Court of *Israel* held that a defendant who is contractually bound, but fails to return particular goods lent to him is liable to pay by way of damages their market value at the date of the judgment of the court of first instance: *Kor Gavish Refrigerating Co. Ltd.* v. *Baruch Pettigrew, Jerusalem Post*, 23 Aug. 1956.

[71] *Rosenthal* v. *Alderton & Sons Ltd.*, [1946] K.B. 374. At the time this decision caused difficulty: see *Beaman* v. *A.R.T.S. Ltd.*, (1948), 2 All E.R. 89, 93 (reversed on other grounds at [1949] 1 K.B. 550) *per* Denning J., as he then was, and *Strand Electric and Engineering Co. Ltd.* v. *Brisford Entertainments Ltd.*, [1952] 2 Q.B. 246, 255 *per* Denning L.J. But most of the authorities which caused these doubts are now discredited. In *Canada* it was held in 1975 that the value at the date of conversion was decisive: *Canadian Laboratory Supplies Ltd.* v. *Engelhard Industries of Canada Ltd.*, 68 D.L.R. (3d) 65 (High Court of Ontario).

[72] Torts (Interference with Goods) Act 1977, section 2.

[73] As Winfield and Jolowicz, *Torts* (11th ed. by Rogers, 1979) do on p. 449, where it is (quite wrongly) stated that 'it now seems to be generally accepted that the value should be assessed at the date of conversion, and this is in accord with the principle that damage should be assessed at the date of the wrong'. No such principle exists. See also McGregor, *Damages*, section 1050 and Salmond, *Law of Torts* (17th ed., 1977, by Hunter), pp. 564, 565.

[74] The principal cases are *The Columbus* (1849), 3 Wm. Rob. 158; *The Harmonides*, [1903] P. 1; *The Philadelphia*, [1917] P. 101; *Liesbosch Dredger* v. *S.S. Edison*, [1933] A.C. 463, 464 *per* Lord Wright. And see, for instance, Winfield and Jolowicz, l.c., p. 621.

take account of any changes of circumstances which may have taken place since the injury was inflicted'.[75]

This means in the first place that a judge is, for the purpose of assessing damage, entitled to have regard to such monetary depreciation as occurred prior to the damage or, in the words of Barwick C.J. in the High Court of Australia,[76] to 'accrued depreciation'. It follows that where a conventional scale has been adopted, as, for instance, for the loss of expectation of life or, in Scotland, for *solatium*, an award is not excessive for the sole reason that it takes such depreciation into account and therefore exceeds the conventional sum. If this was £200 in 1941,[77] when the value of the pound was $2\frac{1}{2}$ times what it is in 1967, then an award of £500 in the latter year is not excessive.[78] As Lord Normand said,[79] 'permanent changes in the value of money must be considered in making awards for *solatium*'.

Secondly, the principle means that 'in considering damages occasioned by a wrongful act all those facts which have actually happened down to the date of the trial must be taken into account'.[80] If, by the time of the trial, 'what was uncertainty has been turned into certainty',[81] it is the judge's duty to have regard to accomplished facts rather than to prophecies, to calculate rather than to guess. This rule which has been applied in numerous contexts,[82] undoubtedly

---

[75] McGregor, *Damages*, section 1144.

[76] *O'Brian* v. *McKean*, Australian Argus L.R. (1969), 65, at p. 67; in *South Africa* it also seems to be firmly established that the decrease in the value of money is an element which, in awarding damages or comparing awards may be taken into account: see the decision of the Appellate Division in *Norton* v. *Ginsberg*, 1953 (4) *South African L.R.* 537, and see in the same sense *May* v. *Parity Insurance Co. Ltd.*, 1967 (1) *South African L.R.* 644; *Lutzkie* v. *South African Railways and Harbours*, 1974 (4) *South African L.R.* 396; *Burger* v. *Union National South British Insurance Co.*, 1975 (4) *South African L.R.* 72; *Matross* v. *Minister of Police*, 1978 (4) *South African L.R.* 78. See also the Rhodesian Appellate Division in *Stephenson* v. *General Accident Fire & Life Assurance Corporation*, 1974 (4) *South African L.R.* 503.

[77] *Benham* v. *Gambling*, [1941] A.C. 157.

[78] *Naylor* v. *Yorkshire Electricity Board*, [1968] A.C. 529, particularly at p. 538 *per* Viscount Dilhorne. Similarly in South Africa: *Norton* v. *Ginsberg*, 1953 (4) *South African L.R.* 537. In 1973 the Court of Appeal increased the conventional sum to £750: *McCann* v. *Shepherd*, [1973] 1 W.L.R. 540. And see McGregor, section 1231. By June 1979 the figure was £1,250: *Gammell* v. *Wilson*, (1980), 2 All E.R. 557.

[79] *Glasgow Corporation* v. *Kelley* (1951), 1 T.L.R. 345, at p. 347 (H.L.). In the same sense already *Sands* v. *Devan* (1945), S.C. 380 and, in England, *Hart* v. *Griffiths-Jones*, [1948] 2 All E.R. 729. See also Dixon J. in *Pamment* v. *Pawelski* (1949), C.L.R. 406, at p. 411.

[80] *Carslogie Steamship Co. Ltd.* v. *Royal Norwegian Government*, [1952] A.C. 292, at p. 300 *per* Viscount Jowitt, at p. 307 *per* Lord Normand.

[81] Hodson J. (as he then was) in *Bishop* v. *Cunard White Star Ltd.*, [1950] P. 240, at p. 259 (pension awarded to a widow eight years after the accident causing her husband's death).

[82] *Bwllfa and Merthyrdare Steam Collieries (1891) Ltd.* v. *Pontypridd Waterworks Co.*,

means that if by the time of the trial the earnings of the deceased victim of an accident would have risen as a result of promotion or shortage of labour the judge will take the increase into account. He will also do so where the rise in earnings results from a depreciation of money.[83]

In 1970 Lord Diplock recognized that 'during the last twenty years sterling has been subject to continuous inflation. Its purchasing power has fallen at an average rate of 3 per cent to $3\frac{1}{2}$ per cent per annum and the increase in wage rates has more than kept pace with the fall in the value of money.' Accordingly, 'damages will be paid in currency which has the value of sterling at the date of the judgment', but 'money should be treated as retaining its value at the date of judgment'. It follows that the judge has to ignore speculations about future monetary developments and it must be left to the victim to take care of subsequent inflation 'by prudent investment in buying a home, in growth stocks or in the short-term high-interest bearing securities'.[84] After some hesitation this rule was affirmed by the House of Lords in 1979.[85] It is in line with a fundamental decision of the High Court of Australia, in the course of which Barwick C.J. stated the principle applicable to the case of personal injuries that 'the date of verdict is, in my opinion, the proper date as at which to make the assessment' and that, therefore, the assessment will 'in general be made in relation to the purchasing power of the currency at the date of the assessment of the damages';[86] no allowance for future changes in the value of the currency will be made in so far as it affects the future earning capacity, but future increases in the cost of goods and services (such as medical treatment, nursing etc.) may be recovered on 'solid proof', but should in general be ignored, since the evidence is likely to be too speculative. On the other hand Lord Diplock's approach was rejected by the Supreme Court of Canada as having

---

[1903] A.C. 426; *The Kingsway*, [1918] P. 344, at p. 362 *per* Scrutton L.J.; *Williamson v. John I. Thorneycroft & Co. Ltd.*, [1940] 2 K.B. 658; *Re Bradberry*, [1943] Ch. 35; *Curwen* v. *James*, [1963] 1 W.L.R. 748; *Simpson* v. *Jones*, [1968] 2 All E.R. 929; *Jobling v. Associated Dairies Ltd.*, (1981) 3 W.L.R. 155 (H.L.).

[83] *The Swynfleet* (1948), 81 Ll. L.R. 116 and many later cases. The point is not open to doubt.

[84] *Mallet* v. *McMonagle*, [1970] A.C. 166, at p. 175; see already *Fletcher* v. *Autocar & Transporters Ltd.*, [1968] 2 Q.B. 322, at p. 348 *per* Diplock L.J. (as he then was). In the same sense *Taylor* v. *O'Connor*, [1971] A.C. 115.

[85] *Lim Poh Choo* v. *Camden and Islington Area Health Authority*, [1980] A.C. 174, at p. 193, leaving room for a different decision in exceptional cases (which, however, are difficult to visualize and should be extremely rare).

[86] *O'Brien* v. *McKean*, (1968), 118 C.L.R. 540. The law of New Zealand seems to be different: *Attorney-General* v. *Green*, (1967) N.Z. L.R. 888.

'an air of irreality' or as 'starting with an unrealistic base'.[87] The Supreme Court held that 7 per cent was the discount or capitalization rate 'to be used in calculating the present value of the awards for future care and loss of earnings'. This rate was the average of the present investment rate in Canada of $10\frac{1}{2}$ per cent and the forecast long term rate of inflation of $3\frac{1}{2}$ per cent.

Thirdly, where damage is done, not to a person, but to a building or a chattel and reinstatement or repairs are possible and reasonable, the victim is entitled to the cost, not at the date of the wrong, but at the earliest date, when in all the circumstances the victim could reasonably be expected to undertake them; this may be at the date of the trial or even at a later date.[88]

In conclusion it is submitted that as a general rule one may expect judges to be inclined towards the assessment of compensation as at the date of judgment, seeing that in a similar context the House of Lords has disapproved the use of 'an out-of-date valuation' and stated that 'the word "compensation" would be a mockery if what was paid was something that did not compensate'.[89] In a period of inflation assessment of damages as at the date of judgment invariably leads to higher awards than would have been awarded on the basis of the date of wrong. But there is no trace of a public policy to the effect 'that inflation must be contained and the victim of the tortfeasor should help to contain it by a progressive reduction in the real value of the compensation awarded'.[90] Inflation neither can nor should be fought by means of inflicting harm upon the unfortunate victims of a wrongful act.

(c) There remains the question whether the victim of a breach of contract or tort is under a duty to spend money to mitigate the damage and whether, if he has done so, he is entitled to recover the money spent (with interest) or can claim compensation for the loss in purchasing power which repayment of the expenditure in depreciated currency would cause him and which he might not have suffered had he obtained judgment based on a valuation as at its date: to

[87] *Andrews* v. *Grand & Toy Alberta Ltd.*, (1978), 2 S.C.R. 229, at p. 254 or 83 D.L.R. (3d) 452; *Arnold* v. *Teno*, (1978), 2 S.C.R. 287, at p. 327 or 83 D.L.R. (3d) 609. Two other cases in the same sense are *Thornton* v. *Board of School Trustees*, ibid. pp. 267 and 480 respectively and *Keizer* v. *Hanna and Buch*, ibid. at pp. 342 and 444 respectively. On these cases see Rea, Can. Bar R. 111 (1980), 280. Similarly the Federal Supreme Court of *Germany* requires future monetary developments to be taken into account: 8 Jan. 1981, BGHZ 79, 187.

[88] *Dodd Properties (Kent) Ltd.* v. *Canterbury City Council*, (1980), 1 W.L.R. 433, see above, p. 125.

[89] *West Midland Baptist (Trust) Association* v. *Birmingham Corporation*, [1970] A.C. 874, at p. 904 *per* Lord Morris of Borth-y-Gest, on which see below, p. 133.

[90] *Walker* v. *John McLean & Sons Ltd.*, (1979) 1 W.L.R. 760, at p. 766 *per* Cumming-Bruce L.J.

return to Lord Wrenbury's example, as a result of the defendant's negligence three cows are destroyed in 1975, when they have a market value of £150 and the owner buys three cows in replacement at that price. At the date of the judgment in 1980 the market value of three similar cows is £300. Is the owner entitled to £150 or to more?[91]

Contrary to the law of a number of foreign countries[92] in England the victim, while he 'need not risk his money too far',[93] is required to incur expense if in all the circumstances it is reasonable to do so, but 'a plaintiff who is under a duty to mitigate is not obliged, in order to reduce the damages, to do that which he cannot afford to do.'[94] In judging reasonableness the court should ask itself whether the victim who incurs expense runs the risk of being burdened with the effect of future inflation and whether this is reasonable.

Since, as would seem to be the case, the damage is, in the words of Hodson J. (as he then was),[95] 'crystallized' by the expenditure, the amount is fixed and, like all liquidated sums, subject to the principle of nominalism, so that the plaintiff can claim the amount actually spent, but not more.[96] It may be that in certain cases the plaintiff who has spent money in mitigation may claim losses resulting from inflation as consequential damages or as damage flowing from the delay in payment.[97] These are uncertainties with which the victim cannot always be expected to be burdened. Much will depend on the size of the expenditure, on his and the defendant's means, the likelihood and speed of recovery and similar facts. No firm rule of universal application should be allowed to come into existence.

## III

Where property is expropriated in the public interest and just compensation becomes payable, the problems are very similar to those just discussed in connection with unliquidated damages. Usually the date with reference to which the value is to be assessed and the compensation to be calculated is determined by statute, but between the material date, such as the date of the notice to

---

[91] See, generally, Feldman and Libling, 95 (1979), L.Q.R. 270; Waddams, Oxford Journal of Legal Studies i (1981) 134.

[92] Above pp. 118-20 sqq. on the law of Germany, France, Belgium and Italy.

[93] McGregor, l.c., section 233.

[94] *Dodd Properties (Kent) Ltd.* v. *Canterbury City Council*, [1980] 1 W.L.R. 433, *per* Megaw L.J.          [95] *Bishop* v. *Cunard White Star Lines Ltd.*, [1950] P. 240, 246.

[96] *Dodd Properties (Kent) Ltd.* v. *Canterbury City Council*, [1980] 1 W.L.R. 433, *per* Donaldson L.J.          [97] See above pp. 109, 110.

treat or of the order for expropriation, and the actual payment of compensation, there frequently occurs a long time-lag, so that the effects of monetary depreciation may be substantial. Should they be borne by the owner?

An affirmative answer was in fact given in *Italy*[98] on the interesting ground that the amount due has the character, not of damages, but of a price for property compulsorily acquired.[99] *German* practice is more complicated. While after the events of both 1923 and 1948 a practice of transvalorization was developed and, accordingly, compensation was assessed with reference to the value at the date of judgment,[100] it seems that in more normal times the amount duly ascertained with reference to the relevant date was absolutely binding; thus it was held in 1930 that if at the date of the decree of expropriation real property had a certain value in terms of reichsmarks this amount could not be increased by reason of the fact that at the time of payment the value of the reichsmark was reduced.[101] More recent practice would seem to indicate that, although the quality of the property must be ascertained with reference to the date fixed by statute, the value of such property will, in periods of fluctuating values, be assessed as at a date nearest to actual payment, which usually is the date of the final judicial decision, provided that the owner was not responsible for the delay by commencing unjustified proceedings.[102] In *Austria*, on the other hand, the Supreme Court laid down the rule that compensation is to be assessed with reference to the value at the date of the decree of expropriation. Only in the event of extraordinarily large and rapid depreciation resulting in depriving money of its function as a constant measure of value is it permitted to 'transvalorize' and assess compensation as at the date of the judicial decision.[103]

In *France* the legislator intervened in 1962 by providing that the value of expropriated property, assessed with reference to certain defined dates, should be revised in accordance with variations in building costs as ascertained by the National Institute of Statistics between such dates and the judgment fixing the compensation.[104] In *Belgium* it was the full Cour de Cassation which in 1979 broke with a firmly established rule[105] and held in a case in which between

---

[98] Ascarelli, p. 536.

[99] On the history and implication of this idea see (1959) *L.Q.R.* 196, 204–6.

[100] Supreme Court, 15 Jan. 1924, *RGZ.* 107, 228, 13 Dec. 1924, *JW.* 1925, 348; 20 Feb. 1925, *JW.* 1925, 1105; 5 May 1925, *JW.* 1926, 2364; 11 Jan. 1927, *JW.* 1927, 986, 988; 29 Mar. 1927, *RGZ.* 116, 324. For the period after the currency reform of 1948, see Federal Supreme Court (Great Senate in Civil Matters), 16 Nov. 1953, *BGHZ.* 11, 156.

[101] Supreme Court, 28 Nov. 1930, *RGZ.* 130, 368.

[102] Federal Supreme Court, 23 Sept. 1957, *BGHZ.* 25, 226; 25 Sept. 1958, *BGHZ.* 28, 164; 22 Jan. 1959, *BGHZ.* 29, 217; 4 Oct. 1962, *BGHZ.* 38, 104; 21 June 1965, *BGHZ.* 44, 52; 18 May 1972, *NJW.* 1972, 1317; 24 March 1977, *NJW.* 1977, 1535.

[103] 20 Dec. 1977, Juristische Blätter 1978, 541, following 29 Nov. 1973, ibid. 1974, 202.

[104] Ordinance of 24 July 1962, D. 1962, 243. Cf. Cass. Civ., 3 May 1954, D. 1954, 568. For recent illustrations see Cass., 7 Jan. 1963, Bull. 1963, i, No. 15; 18 Mar. 1963, ibid., No. 168.

[105] For a recent decision see Cass., 21 Oct. 1966, *Journal des Tribunaux* 1967, 241. The rule as well as the exception is most clearly stated by Cass., 14 Feb. 1929, Clunet 1931,

the taking in 1965 and the payment of compensation in 1974 there had been a great change in the value of real estate that the value of the property had to be assessed as at the date of the judicial assessment: 'ainsi le juge ne prend pas en considération un préjudice postérieur à l'expropriation, mais se borne à fixer, au jour de sa décision, la juste indemnité due à l'exproprié'.[106] Notwithstanding the constitutional requirement of just compensation for expropriated property, the law of the *United States of America*, on the whole, seems to maintain the rule that no effect should be accorded to changes in the purchasing power of money occurring after the date of taking.[107] Although the material is very limited and no case seems to have discussed the problem in depth, the conclusion derives strong support from a decision of the Court of Appeals, Second Circuit,[108] which disapproved the trial judge's invitation to the jury 'to take into consideration in this case the purchasing power of money as it is today', and reversed on the ground that 'the fair market value of the property must be found as of the date of taking'. More recently the Supreme Court, relying on *United States* v. *Miller,*[109] has indicated that, while property taken by governmental action has to be valued as at the date of taking, in condemnation the taking usually occurs in the course of the proceedings and, therefore, current values are likely to govern;[110] but when taking occurs by physical invasion and the landowner sues for compensation, it is the invasion which constitutes the taking.[111]

In *England* it was thought for more than a hundred years that the value at the date of the notice to treat was decisive, but in 1969 the House of Lords held[112] that where the owner is entitled to the cost of reinstatement the assessment has to be made with reference to the date when reinstatement becomes reasonably possible; the House also indicated that where the owner is entitled to compensation for the value of the land the relevant date is the date of assessment or, if it is earlier, the date when possession is taken. Although the last-mentioned part of the new rule is open to much doubt,[113] the decision constitutes a landmark in the development of monetary law in England.

---

1195 or S. 1929, 4. 12 or *Rev. dr. banc.* 1929, 196. Similarly, Cass., 15 Jan. 1965, *Journal des Tribunaux*, 8 May 1965. See Piret, pp. 164, 169.

[106] 20 Sept. 1979, *Pasicrisie Belge* 1980 I 69 with most interesting submissions of Procureur-Général Dumon. For the interesting development of judicial practice in *Chile* and *Argentina*: see Lopez-Santa Maria, pp. 45, 53.

[107] The most informative survey is to be found in Mr. G. B. Crook's 'Annotation' in 92 American L.R. 2d 772 who arrives at the conclusion reproduced in the text.

[108] *United States* v. *158·76 Acres of Land*, 298 F. 2d 559 (1962), also 92 American L.R. 2d 766.        [109] 317 U.S. 369, at p. 374 (1942).

[110] *United States* v. *Clarke*, 63 L.Ed. 2d 373 (decided 18 March 1980).

[111] *United States* v. *Dow*, 357 U.S. 17 (1958). Perhaps the Supreme Court would apply the same rule in case of the tortious interference with property.

[112] *West Midland Baptist (Trust) Association* v. *Birmingham Corporation*, [1970] A.C. 874 on which see Mann, 85 (1969) *L.Q.R.* 516.

[113] See the article referred to in the preceding note.

## IV

There are many contexts in which the law requires property to be valued for the purpose of calculating a share in a fund. The most familiar example, perhaps, is the beneficiary who is under a duty to bring advances into hotchpot.[114] If property other than money given to or settled upon a child is valued as at the date of the gift or settlement, as in *France*,[115] and the *United States of America*,[116] the law in effect disregards a subsequent rise of values or decrease of the purchasing power of money, and is, therefore, nominalistic in character; this may greatly prejudice beneficiaries who do not have to account for advances. If, on the other hand, the valuation is made with reference to the date of death (or a later date such as distribution), as in *England*[117] or in *Italy*,[118] changes in value will be taken care of and equality between the beneficiaries will, in substance, be achieved. In the absence of express provisions the question whether the law contemplates the one or other solution is likely to be one of construction and to be decided in the light of the principle of equality which, as far as possible, should be paramount.

Yet there are cases in which injustice seems to be unavoidable: where a sum of money has to be brought into hotchpot, it must, it is submitted, in accordance with the rule of nominalism, be taken at the stated figure, for it expresses its own value and cannot be the subject-matter of a valuation.[119] Hence a son who in the year 1940 was given by his father a sum of £5,000 and bought a house now worth £150,000, has to account, on the father's death in 1980, for £5,000, while a daughter who at the same time in 1940 was given a house worth £5,000 will have to account for its value in 1980, viz. £150,000. If the result is unjust, this is in the present

---

[114] See, generally, J. B. Villela, *Contribuição à teoria do valor dos bens na colação hereditaria* (1964), and the review by Sanntleben, *RabelsZ*. 1968, 587.

[115] Articles 860 and 868 of the Code Civil.

[116] Page, *On Wills* (1962), vi. 318; T. Atkinson, *On Wills* (2nd ed., 1953), p. 724.

[117] As to intestacy see s. 47 (1) (iii) of the Administration of Estates Act, 1925, now Sched. 1 to the Intestates' Estates Act 1952. As to testate succession see *Re Hillas-Drake*, [1944] Ch. 235.

[118] Art. 747 on which see Ascarelli, p. 498.

[119] Although according to the provision referred to in note 117 above '. . . *any money* or property . . . shall be brought into account at a valuation . . .'. it cannot be so construed as to require (or permit) a valuation of money. It is submitted that even where a sum of foreign money was given, it is to be valued in terms of sterling as at the date of the gift rather than the date of death. Cf. the telling formulation by the Belgian Cour de Cassation, 15 Dec. 1966, *Journal des Tribunaux*, 1967, 150, 152: 'lorsque . . . l'apport consiste en deniers numériquement déterminés, il n'y a point lieu à évaluation, la créance de reprise ayant pour l'objet, même en cas de variation monétaire, la somme fixée à son montant nominal.'

context no less unavoidable than elsewhere,[120] though it is possible (and to be hoped) that the law relating to the administration of estates rather than monetary law will find a way of affording relief.

It seems to be only in *Austria* that the courts felt able to reach a different result: thus money paid by a father to his daughter in 1912 and in 1920 had in the year 1928 to be brought into account at 'its intrinsic value' calculated on the basis of the price of gold.[121] Or property (other than money) which according to the statutory rule is to be valued as at the date of the gift is to be brought into account at a figure which, in view of the principle of non-discrimination between children, will be 'revalorized'; in effect, therefore, notwithstanding the statutory rule, the property will be valued as at the date of death.[122] In the *Federal Republic of Germany* the courts do not seem to have gone quite so far yet. Where, for instance, assets other than money have to be brought into hotchpot, the statutory provision[123] according to which the value is to be assessed as at the date of the gift has in effect been set aside. Recent judicial practice calculates the value of the gift in terms of the value at the time of death by using the cost of living index: if a gift made in 1958 has to be valued in terms of 1968 the courts require the value in 1958 of, say, DM 12.000 to be multiplied by the cost-of-living index of 1968 (which is assumed to be 120) and the resulting sum to be divided by the cost-of-living index in 1958 (which is assumed to be 90), so that the gift has a 1968 value of DM 16.000.[124] This practice is open to considerable doubt, not only on account of its inconsistency with the statutory rule, but also because it makes no distinction between genuine increases in value resulting from a scarcity of goods, changes of taste or similar circumstances and the depreciation of money. The practice does not yet seem to have been extended to money, but if it were so extended it would gravely offend against the principle of nominalism.[125]

---

[120] See above, pp. 97, 98.        [121] Supreme Court, 13 Nov. 1928, *SZ*. x, No. 261.
[122] Supreme Court, 24 Nov. 1966, *SZ*. xxxix, no. 198. In the same sense already Supreme Court, 23 Nov. 1955, *Juristische Blätter* 1956, 339; 25 April 1956, ibid., 1956, 403. See generally Egon Weiss in *Klang's Commentaries* (2nd ed., 1952), iii, 951, 952.
[123] Section 2055 subsection 2 of the Civil Code.
[124] 14 Nov. 1973, *BGHZ*. 61, 385; 4 July 1975, *BGHZ*. 65, 75.
[125] In a different, but related context the *Austrian* Supreme Court repeatedly held that, where a co-owner or a beneficial owner is entitled to require the sale of a property the court may refuse an order if the request is unreasonable on the ground that the proceeds of sale would be exposed to the collapse of the currency (as opposed to a mere creeping inflation): 19 Dec. 1972, *Juristische Blätter* 1973, 466; 9 Jan. 1974, ibid., 1974, 421; 6 Nov. 1974, ibid., 1975, 481.

# VI

# Methods of Excluding the Effects of Nominalism

I. Methods of protection in general. II. The gold clause: (1) its existence as a result of (*a*) an express, (*b*) an implied agreement; (2) gold coin or gold value clause? (3) the operation of a gold clause: (*a*) absence of a definition; (*b*) uncertainty as to the price of gold; (*c*) local differences in the price. III. Index clauses. IV. The unit-of-account clause. V. Validity of protective clauses under (1) nominalism; (2) ordinary legal tender legislation; (3) compulsory tender legislation; (4) public policy; (5) special legislation. VI. The legislative problem.

## I

THE conclusion to be drawn from the discussion in Chapter IV is that the effects of nominalism can to a very limited degree only be averted by the general principles of private law. It is therefore not surprising that contracting parties often agree upon special stipulations for the purpose of protecting themselves against fluctuations in the value of money. This is particularly so in long-term contracts, such as bonds, insurance policies, or charterparties, especially if they have an international character. In this country, it is true, such provisions are rare. Only two purely internal contracts containing such a clause have come up for judicial decision, and even in international transactions British creditors were in the past generally content to provide for payment in pounds sterling and to rely on the stability of the British currency. This spirit sometimes prompted the British Government to abstain from the insertion of protective clauses even in transactions in which other co-contracting governments, placing less confidence in their currencies, insisted on protection.[1] Consequently it is not so much the frequency of such clauses in England as the intricacy of the legal problems raised by them, which renders it necessary to scrutinize their nature and application.

[1] See Art 262, Treaty of Versailles: 'Any monetary obligation due by Germany arising out of the present Treaty and expressed in terms of gold marks shall be payable at the option of the creditor in pounds sterling payable in London; gold dollars of the United States payable in New York; gold francs payable in Paris; or gold lire payable in Rome.' See also Art. 214, Treaty of St. Germain; Art. 197, Treaty of Trianon; Art. 146, Treaty of Neuilly.

If parties wish to provide for protection against monetary fluctuations, they have several methods at their disposal.

In the first place they may introduce clauses which lack any monetary character and are therefore outside the scope of this study. The most obvious example is a contract of barter, that is to say, a provision contemplating performance by the delivery of a quantity of commodities such as gold or wheat.[2] Or the parties may agree upon a clause which in defined circumstances permits a variation of the contractual terms, in particular the monetary obligations arising from the contract. Thus in a long-term contract hardship, adaptation, revision or 'escalation'[3] clauses may provide for the fresh assessment or the periodical revision of the price of goods or of the quantity of goods to be delivered or of rent or hire to be paid; great care will have to be taken in drafting the precise conditions in which such rights come into existence as well as the methods by which these are to be determined in case of disagreement, for in many legal systems such clauses may be unenforceable by judicial or arbitration proceedings, unless very specific powers are conferred upon the adjudicator. However this may be, no general rules, certainly no general rules of monetary law can be laid down in regard to the interpretation, effect and enforcement of such and similar clauses,—they belong to the law of contract rather than the law of money.

In the strictly monetary field parties may agree upon the consideration to be paid in, or related to, a foreign currency in which they have greater confidence than in that of their own country. Thus they may create a foreign currency obligation, whether in its simple form or in conjunction with an option of currency, or they may add a foreign currency clause to the promise to pay domestic currency. These are matters which will be discussed in the second part of this book.[4]

Finally it is open to the parties to agree upon the payment of a sum of money of domestic currency and link it to something which may be expected to retain its 'value' in terms of money. Even if one

---

[2] It is interesting to remember that extreme depreciation of the value of money during the third century AD led Diocletian to issue a decree fixing maximum prices which in turn produced an extensive system of barter as a monetary system within the Roman Empire: Schönbauer, *The Journal of Juristic Papyrology* (Warsaw, 1956), ix, 15, at pp. 53 sqq. or Dulckeit-Schwarz, *Römische Rechtsgeschichte* (4th ed., 1966), p. 226 with further references.

[3] For an example see the decision of Ackner J. (as he then was) in *Finland Steamship Co. Ltd.* v. *United Baltic Corporation Ltd.*, (1980) 2 Lloyd's Rep. 287, who may be the author of the expression.

[4] Below p. 201 on foreign currency clauses and pp. 266 sqq. on foreign currency debts.

disregards for the present foreign currency the nature of this 'something' may vary greatly.[5]

So long as there existed a gold standard in any of its various emanations,[6] that is to say, until 15 August 1971, gold was the most stable standard of value and dominated the world of money. Since gold was 'demonetized' in the 1970s no fixed and stable standard of value exists. It is very necessary to emphasize and ponder this fact of singular starkness. Gold has become a commodity which, as against the fixed price of US $35 per oz, which it enjoyed from 1934 to 1971 or 1972, has at present a price of almost US $700 or almost £300 per oz. Although it is possible to take the price of gold as a standard or measure, just as it is possible to refer to other, perhaps less volatile commodities such as silver, copper or wheat, no sensible person will do so. Yet, although gold clauses are at present a matter of history, they continue to be entitled to the lawyer's attention. The law of protective clauses has largely developed within the framework of the gold clause, so that its teachings may be relevant to other types of clauses which are in or may come into existence. Moreover many contractual obligations still exist which include, directly or indirectly, gold clauses requiring analysis and explanation. Finally it is possible that a gold standard may be revived and a gold clause may become possible again. For these reasons the rich legal material which it produced cannot be suppressed in this book.

In domestic transactions the most widely applied protective clause is the index clause (*échelle mobile*) linked to price or other indices. Its primary object is to afford protection against the (internal) depreciation of the domestic currency's purchasing power as a result of inflation.[7]

In international transactions[8] where the external value of a currency

---

[5] In 1980 the Sunshine Mining Company of Texas, USA issued silver certificates the principal amount of each certificate being the greater of $1,000 or the price of a stated quantity of troy ounces of silver bullion. This is a new development which may have to be watched.          [6] See above pp. 30 sqq.

[7] In the United States of America, particularly in Florida, so-called 'shared appreciation mortgages' (Sam mortgages) have recently become fashionable: the mortgagee accepts a moderate rate of interest, but shares the profit made by the owner in the event of a sale. In Mexico a government-owned development bank since 1977 has issued 'petrobonos', i.e. bonds which are backed by a specific number of barrels of crude oil.

[8] See, generally, Sulkowski, Rec. 29 (1929 i), 77 sqq.; Planiol-Ripert, vii, Nos. 1166 sqq.; Hubrecht, pp. 341 sqq.; Piret, p. 227; Reports of the Monetary Law Committee of the International Law Association for the 56th Conference (New Dehli, 1974), 73; 57th Conference (Madrid, 1976), 165; 58th Conference (Manila, 1978), 339; 59th Conference (Zagreb, 1980); Hahn, *Festschrift für Johannes Bärmann* (1975), 395; *German Yearbook of International Law* 22 (1979), 53 or *Liber Amicorum Adolf F. Schnitzer* (1979), 197; Sacerdoti, *Comunicazioni e Studi* (Milan, 1978), xv, 195; Silard, *Law & Policy in International Business* 5 (1973), 398 and (in French) Clunet 1972, 213 as well as the books

in terms of another currency is usually the parties' main preoccupation protective clauses based on one of the units of account such as have developed in recent years[9] are available for adoption. Although they are not yet, and are perhaps unlikely to become, popular with the general body of investors,[10] they cannot be ignored. There is much to be said for treating them as a special type of foreign currency clauses, but the classification is without legal interest or significance and it is proposed, therefore, to deal with them in the present chapter.

Accordingly this chapter will discuss the gold clause as a largely obsolete, though perhaps revivable, and in any case legally instructive phenomenon (below section II), the index clause as a practical, albeit far from widely used, method of protecting the value of domestic obligations (below section III), and the unit-of-account clause as a by no means popular or effective, yet not entirely unattractive method of international protection (below section IV).[11]

It should, however, be clearly understood that the purpose of any protective clause invariably is to protect the creditor against a reduction in the value of the currency to which the clause is attached. In domestic contracts the need for such protection usually, though not necessarily[12] arises from (internal) inflation. In international contracts the reduction in value occurs as a result of a change in the rate of exchange. Where the protected currency is devalued, there cannot be any doubt about the effectiveness of the protective clause. In case of the protected currency being allowed to 'float' downwards and thus to depreciate, it is likely to be equally plain that the clause becomes operative. When another currency is revalued

---

by P.C. Gutzwiller, *Vertragliche Abreden zur Sicherung des Geldwerts* (1972); E. Quadri, *Le Clausole Monetarie* (1981), and Franz Zehetner, *Geldwertklauseln im grenzüberschreitenden Wirtschaftsverkehr* (1976); see also Zehetner, 'Konstruktionsprobleme kombinierter Währungsklauseln', in *Kredit und Kapital* xi (1978), 213 and the Report by the Secretary-General on Clauses protecting parties against the effects of currency fluctuations, U.N. Document A/Cn. 9/164 (20 March 1979). [9] See p. 159.

[10] The reasons are mentioned below p. 508.

[11] It is likely to be a general rule that, whatever method of protection is adopted, the clause must be certain and free from vagueness. The *Austrian* Supreme Court repeatedly had occasion to emphasize this requirement: see Ertl, *Inflation, Privatrecht und Wertsicherung* (Vienna 1980), p. 124. Thus the Supreme Court held that the clause 'the intrinsic value shall always remain the same' is invalid: 10 Nov. 1966, *Juristische Blätter* 1967, 430; 15 Oct. 1953, ibid. 1954, 285. It is not an index clause. As a gold clause it would be prohibited. 'Purchasing power as such cannot be measure of value, because the purchasing power of money does not uniformly change in respect of all goods, so that such performance as is measured by changes of the purchasing power cannot be objectively ascertained.' See, however, Supreme Court, 29 April 1971, *Juristische Blätter* 1971, 471.

[12] If an English importer sells for sterling to an English manufacturer a machine which he has to buy in the United States of America and for which he has to pay dollars he may require protection against the fall of value of sterling in terms of the dollar.

or appreciates, i.e. floats upwards, the protected currency remains stable in terms of gold and of all other currencies save one in relation to which its value is reduced or depreciates. The protective clause does not in these circumstances operate, for it affords no safeguard against the indirect and relative decrease in value of a currency which has remained stable. The result is likely to be different only when the clause is so framed as to protect, not against the depreciation of the protected currency, but against any disturbance of an intended pattern of uniformity and equivalence with the appreciated currency and possibly others.[13]

## II

1. The gold clause[14] owed its existence to an agreement between the parties, which may be express or implied.

(a) Wherever the word 'gold' is attached to a monetary obligation,[15] a gold clause of some type exists.

While a gold standard of any kind was in force, it was, however, sometimes said that the reference to 'gold' was no more than a 'statutory synonym' for the currency in question, i.e. a description of the statutory quality of a currency based on a gold standard, and that therefore its character was descriptive rather than contractual. Such a view was originally[16] but was not more recently[17] held in *Chile* of even so elaborate a clause as the promise to pay '. . . pesos of 183·057 millionths of a gramme of fine gold'. Similarly, the *Austrian* Supreme Court held[18] that the clause 'effectiv in Goldwährung des Deutschen Reiches' had no greater import than that payment must be made according to German currency laws. In *Belgium* the clause 'au cours de l'or' was held to be a mere 'clause de style' and therefore disregarded.[19] In *Sweden*,[20] though not in *Norway*,[21] the words 'in

---

[13] In this sense the *Young Loan Case*, Int. L.R. 59, 494 on which see above, p. 60. See in particular paragraph 24 of the majority opinion.

[14] The literature on the gold clause is immense. For numerous references see Nussbaum, p. 223; see also Wortley, *British Year Book of International Law*, 1936, 112, and Lord Wright, *Legal Essays and Addresses* (1939), 147. The problem of the gold clause has by now become largely clarified. Much of the disproportionately voluminous literature is obsolete.

[15] Sometimes it is doubtful whether the world 'gold', occurring in the contractual documents, but not attached to the monetary obligation itself, imports a gold clause. This is a problem of implication, on which see below, p. 141.

[16] *St. Pierre v. South American Stores Ltd.*, [1937] 1 All E.R. 206, affirmed by the Court of Appeal, [1937] 3 All E.R. 349.

[17] Supreme Court of Chile, 1 Jan. 1938, *B.I.J.I.* 39 (1938), 349.

[18] 12 Mar. 1930, *JW.* 1930, 2480.     [19] Cass. 19 June 1930, *Rev. dr. banc.* 1931, 266.

[20] Supreme Court, 10 June 1938, *B.I.J.I.* 39 (1938), 108 (bonds of the City of Stockholm) where the court, however, also relied on other circumstances negativing a gold clause.

Gold' were held not to involve a gold clause on the ground that they merely referred to the provisions of the relevant monetary laws at the time of the contract. The same result was reached in a case decided by the Supreme Court of *Czechoslovakia*.[22] Although it is possible that national habits or legislative developments in a particular country may deprive the reference to 'gold' of its contractual character,[23] such cases must be very rare, for they are inconsistent with the principle which the Permanent Court of International Justice has formulated.[24]

One argument against the efficacy of the provision for gold payments is that it is simply a clause of 'style' or a routine form of expression. This, in substance, would eliminate the word gold from the bonds. The contract of the parties cannot be treated in such a manner. When the Brazilian Government promised to pay 'gold francs', the reference to a well-known standard of value cannot be considered as inserted merely for literary effect or as a routine expression without significance. The Court is called upon to construe the promise, not to ignore it.

These words are fully in accord with English principles of construction and should be followed in Britain.[25]

(*b*) The question whether a gold clause may be implied into a contract which contains no express reference to gold, requires the utmost care so as not to give an affirmative answer in defiance of the nominalistic principle. It must be emphasized again that, if there exists a mere promise to pay a certain sum of money of a certain currency, payment must be made in whatever is the money of that

---

[21] Supreme Court, 2 May 1962, *Norsk Retstidende*, 1962, 369. This important judgment has unfortunately not been reported elsewhere, but is referred to here on the basis of a French translation available to the author and of the excellent summary by Judge Bahr, *American Journal of Comparative Law*, 12 (1963), 1, at p. 7, and by Hambro, Clunet, 1965, 613 who, contrary to the statement p. 616, n. 6, in fact does not publish the French text.

[22] 17 Mar. 1927, Ostrecht, 1928, 1208.

[23] Cf. Greek–Bulgarian Mixed Arbitral Tribunal, *Rec.* vi. 321: 'leva-or' was not a real gold clause in Bulgaria.

[24] Case of Brazilian Loans, Collection of Judgments, Series A, No. 21 (1928–30), pp. 115, 116.

[25] They were not observed by McNair J. in *Campos* v. *Kentucky & Indiana Terminal Railway Co.*, [1962] 2 Ll. L.R. 459, a decision which in many respects is unsatisfactory: Mann, 12 (1963) *I.C.L.Q.* 1005. The same result had, on equally unsatisfactory grounds, previously been reached in the United States of America: *Lemaire* v. *Kentucky & Indiana Terminal Railroad Co.*, (1957) 242 F. 2d 884. The decision of the majority of the Court of Appeal in *Treseder-Griffin* v. *Co-operative Insurance Society Ltd.*, [1956] 2 Q.B. 127 also had the effect (described in Harman J.'s powerful dissenting judgment as a 'counsel of despair') of disregarding some of the express terms of a written contract. The absence of words defining the weight and fineness of gold has no bearing upon the question of the existence of a gold clause. It raises the problem of interpreting an existing gold clause.

currency system at the time of maturity,[26] and it does not matter that at the time when the contract was made that currency was understood to be of a specific 'value' or on the gold standard. Thus the bare promise to pay francs ('francs sans épithète') did not imply the promise to pay gold francs, and it follows that the protection given by a special clause, whether it is a gold or any other clause, cannot come into existence save by agreement between the parties. 'La stipulation d'un paiement international à effectuer en francs-or ne peut résulter que de la convention des parties'.[27] On the other hand, it is not necessary that such a clause be expressed; it suffices if it can be inferred. But as Mr. Justice Strong has so pointedly remarked, 'the implication must be found in the language of the contract. It is not to be gathered from the presumed or real expectation of the parties.'[28]

The circumstances in which it is permissible to imply terms vary from country to country, but it can be stated broadly that the proposed implication can occur only rarely, requires clear words, and must be supported by the contractual documents or by necessary inference from the whole of the material facts.

---

[26] Above, p. 84.

[27] Cass. Civ. 23 Jan. 1924, Clunet, 1925, 169 (3ᵉ espèce); Cass. Civ. 21 Dec. 1932, Clunet, 1933, 1201 and S. 1932, 1. 390; Cass. Req. 6 Dec. 1933, Clunet, 1934, 946 and D.H. 1934, 34; Cass. Civ. 24 Jan. 1934 (2ᵉ espèce), D.P. 1934, 1. 78; 14 Feb. 1934, ibid. Cass. Req. 5 Nov. 1934, S. 1935, 1. 34; cf. Cass. Civ. 23 Jan. 1924, S. 1925, 1. 257. In view of the international character of the franc and its importance in certain Eastern countries, it is not surprising to find that at one time a different solution was reached in *Egypt*. Thus the Court of Appeal of the Mixed Tribunal in Alexandria held that the Suez Canal Company had to pay their bonds, denominated in 'francs', at the gold value, the reason being that the franc referred to was 'ni le franc dit française, ni le franc dit égyptien, mais que ce franc était plus exactement le franc tout court, le franc universel d'un étalon monétaire commun à plusieurs pays, ayant une valeur fixe et déterminée en Égypte où le louis d'or avait alors cours légal en vertu des dispositions législatives de 1834' (4 June 1925, Clunet, 1925, 1080; cf. also Paris Court of Appeal, 25 Feb. 1924, Clunet, 1924, 688). But a more recent judgment of the Court of Appeal departed from these decisions and held that the 'franc' was not 'une monnaie internationale', but that it was legal tender in Egypt at the tariff fixed in 1834, 'non pas comme une monnaie étrangère, mais comme une monnaie nationalisée ou adoptée: see the three judgments of 18 Feb. 1936 in *Gazette des Tribunaux Mixtes* xxvi. 147, No. 127 (*re* Crédit Foncier Égyptien and Land Bank of Egypt); one of them also in Clunet, 1936, 1004, and D. 1936, 2, 78. It is somewhat surprising that the argument was revived in the *French* Crédit Foncier Égyptien case: Trib. Civ. de la Seine, 31 May 1933, and Cour de Paris, 3 April 1936, D. 1936, 2, 88. See also Cour de Cassation of *Syria*, 20 June 1928, S. 1929, 4. 1, where it was said that 'le mot franc signifie non pas la monnaie ayant cours libératoire dans tel ou tel pays, mais un certain poids d'or relié par un rapport fixe avec le poids de métal fin contenu dans la livre turque'. It is an entirely different matter that, when the Codex Juris Canonici speaks of francs or lire, it contemplates the quantity of gold of the Latin Monetary Union, i.e. 1,000 francs or lire being equal to 10/31 kilograms of gold: in this sense Hoyer, *Festschrift für Oskar Engländer* (1936), 101.

[28] *State of Maryland* v. *Baltimore & Ohio Railroad Co.* (1874), 89 U.S. 105, at p. 111; see also *Ottoman Bank* v. *Chakarian (No. 2)*, [1938] A.C. 260, at p. 272.

As regards the former, the absence of any reference to gold anywhere in the contractual documents will, in this country, make it almost impossible to imply a gold clause: a gold clause must be 'expressed in clear language'.[29] While it seems that in some countries the phrase 'en espèces sonnantes' or 'in klingender Münze' was held to be a gold clause,[30] the French Cour de Cassation refused to read a gold clause into the promise to repay 'en bonnes espèces ayant cours de monnaie impériale allemande'.[31] Moreover, a debtor's promise to pay *foreign* currency, even if the parties regarded it as equal to gold, cannot be treated as a promise to pay domestic currency at its gold value; the promise to pay $420 was not the same as a promise to pay £100 in gold.[32]

If, then, some reference to gold is usually necessary, the question arises what reference to gold is sufficient. It has been held by the House of Lords that a gold clause contained in the body of a bond is not rendered non-existent by the fact that the description on the face of the bond omits the reference to gold.[33] Conversely, it would seem that if a bond provides merely for payment of francs in Paris, Brussels, or Toronto, a gold clause cannot be inferred from the description '5% Gold Bond' appearing in the heading.[34] The House of Lords has also decided that, where bonds headed 'First Mortgage Gold Bonds' contained an express gold clause, but the coupons attached to them did not, a gold clause would not be read into the latter.[35] On the other hand, there is strong persuasive authority for

---

[29] *New Brunswick Railway Co.* v. *British and French Trust Corporation*, [1939] A.C. 1, at pp. 18, 19 *per* Lord Maugham.

[30] Cf. Greek–Bulgarian Mixed Arbitral Tribunal, *Rec.* vi. 321. The Court of Appeal at Liège held that the clause 'en monnaie suisse de 1930' was a gold clause: 10 Feb. 1939, *B.I.J.I.* 40 (1939), 283.

[31] Cass. Civ. 11 Jan. 1926, Clunet, 1926, 441.

[32] See German Supreme Court, 20 April 1940, *RGZ*. 163, 324; 28 May 1937, *RGZ*. 155, 133 with references to earlier decisions.

[33] *Feist* v. *Société Intercommunale Belge d'Électricité*, [1934] A.C. 161, at p. 168 *per* Lord Russell.

[34] *Derwa* v. *Rio de Janeiro Tramway Light & Power Co.*, [1928] 4 D.L.R. 542, 553, 554 (Ontario Supreme Court, Rose J.). In the case of bonds issued by the Haitian Government in 1910 which were denominated in francs, but in the heading described as gold bonds and secured by revenues payable in gold, the Government of the United States refused a French request to intervene at Port au Prince with a view to obtaining payment in gold francs: *Foreign Relations of the United States*, 1923, ii. 415. The point ought to have been decided judicially.

[35] *New Brunswick Railway Co.* v. *British and French Trust Corporation*, [1939] A.C. 1. This decision should not be generalized, for much depends on the wording and it is odd that the amount upon which interest is calculated should differ from the amount repayable to the lender. The result in England is, for instance, likely to be different, if the bonds provide for the payment of interest in gold, but the interest coupons do not: Case of Brazilian Loans, Collection of Judgments of the Permanent Court of International Justice,

the proposition that if a gold clause is attached to the interest payments it extends to the capital.[36] If the contract provides for payment in one of several currencies at the option of the creditor (option of currency) and a gold clause is attached to one currency only, it does not extend to the other currencies.[37] The question whether a gold clause exists, if bonds do not but the prospectus does contain it, is likely to be answered in the negative by English courts,[38] but the opposite view was taken by the Permanent Court of International Justice[39] and in France.[40] In the latter country it has even been held that if bonds refer to the published minutes of the shareholders' meeting authorizing an issue 'produisant intérêt de 5% en or', interest as well as capital is payable in gold.[41] But the mere fact that bonds are secured by gold or by assets valued in gold, does not even in France import a gold clause into the bonds.[42, 43]

---

Series A, No. 21 (1928–30), p. 110. In Germany it was held that a gold clause applicable to the capital extended to interest: Supreme Court, 11 April 1931, DJZ 1931, 1021.

[36] Case of Brazilian Loans (see preceding note), p. 114, referring to the opposite view as an 'anomaly'; Swiss Federal Tribunal, 11 Feb. 1931, *BGE*. 57, ii. 69 and Clunet, 1931, 510, at p. 518 (Société d'Héraclée), describing it as 'une anomalie et une absurdité'; Cass. Civ. 24 Jan. 1934, D.P. 1934, l. 73 (Compagnie du Chemin de fer de São Paulo à Rio Grande). Cf., however, the decision of McNair J. (above, p. 141, n. 25) where the bond, though not the coupon, referred to 'interest . . . in like gold coin' and where, notwithstanding the word 'like' and the prominent description 'gold bond', no gold clause was held to be attached to the principal sum.

[37] *International Trustee for the Protection of Bondholders A.G.* v. *The King*, [1936] 3 All E.R. 407 (C.A.), at pp. 430, 431 *per* Lord Wright. Similarly the judgment of the Norwegian Supreme Court, 2 May 1962, on which see above p. 141, n. 21. For a different view see Swiss Federal Tribunal, 11 Feb. 1931, *BGE*. 57, ii. 69 and Clunet, 1931, 510 (Société d'Héraclée); Cass. Civ. 7 July 1931, Clunet, 1932, 403, and S. 1932, 1. 255, and Cass. Req. 25 July 1933, S. 1933, 1. 350 (both Société d'Héraclée). See also Dutch Hoge Raad, 28 April. 1939, S. 1939, 4. 20 (Messageries Maritimes) and German Supreme Court, 12 Nov. 1934, *JW*. 1935, 189 and 5 Oct. 1936, *RGZ*. 152, 213.

[38] A document such as a prospectus should be inadmissible, particularly in the case of negotiable instruments. See, however, *International Trustee for the Protection of Bondholders A.G.* v. *The King*, [1937] A.C. 500; and the comments by Mann, *British Year Book of International Law*, 1959, 42.      [39] Case of Brazilian Loans, l.c., p. 113.

[40] Cass. Civ. 9 July 1930, Clunet, 1931, 124 (Société du Port de Rosario); but see Cass. Civ. 14 Feb. 1934, S. 1934, 1. 297 and D.P. 1934, 1. 73, 78 (Banque hypothécaire franco-argentine). See also German Supreme Court, 12 Nov. 1934, *JW*. 1935, 189; 7 Feb. 1938, *JW*. 1938, 1109. On the problem, in general, see Delaume, p. 280.

[41] Cass. Civ. 24 Jan. 1934 (1ᵉ espèce), D.P. 1934, 1. 73, with note by Trotabas (Compagnie du Chemin de fer de São Paulo à Rio Grande); but see the decision of the same day relating to the same bonds which, illustrating the very restricted power of the French Cour de Cassation, was to a different effect, because the minutes of the shareholders' meeting were not relied upon before the Court of Appeal: ibid. at p. 78 (2ᵉ espèce).

[42] Cass. Civ. 24 Jan. 1934 (2ᵉ espèce) D.P. 1934, 1. 78; 5 Nov. 1934, Clunet, 1936, 177; see also German Supreme Court, 7 Feb. 1938, *JW*. 1938, 1109.

[43] Cf. *Sturge & Co.* v. *Excess Insurance Co.*, [1938] 4 All E.R. 424, where Branson J. held that an insurance against the failure of the issuer to redeem a bond of $1,000 at par by the payment of $1,000 does not extend to payment in gold provided for in the bond.

The cases in which a gold clause can be inferred from the circumstances, must, as has been pointed out, be exceptional; in particular, the conduct of the parties is material only in so far as it permits the inference that at the date of the contract or as a result of a variation of the contract a gold clause was agreed.[44] It was on the footing of highly peculiar facts that the Privy Council held that, when interest had over a period of years been paid on a gold basis, a gold clause might be read into the loan itself.[45] In another case, *Ottoman Bank of Nicosia* v. *Dascalopoulos*,[46] the Privy Council also adopted rather liberal canons of constructions.

In 1905 the plaintiff became a member of the pensionable staff of a Turkish bank and in 1923 was transferred to its Cyprus branch, the appellant company. His salary, on which his pension was based, was a sum in Turkish pounds. Before 1915 the Turkish pound was a coin of specified gold content, but in 1915 paper money was issued in Turkey. Until the end of 1931, when the plaintiff retired, his salary was paid in Cyprus at the rate of 100 Cyprus pounds per 110 Turkish pounds. That rate was adopted when both England and Turkey were on the gold standard. But subsequently the Cyprus currency was moved off the gold standard and depreciated in terms of gold. The plaintiff contended that he was entitled to a pension payable in Turkish gold pounds translated into Cyprus currency at the rate of exchange of the day; while the bank contended primarily that he was entitled to a sum of Turkish pounds pure and simple, or, alternatively, that he was entitled to a sum of Turkish pounds payable in Cyprus pounds at the fixed rate of £cp. 100 to £tq. 110. The Privy Council decided in the plaintiff's favour, though there was nowhere an express reference to gold pounds. Lord Blanesburgh, delivering the opinion of the Board, said that the parties, when they referred to Turkish pounds, intended to indicate gold pounds[47] and that this intention was made clear by their conduct, inasmuch as the salary was never paid in Turkish paper pounds, but always on a gold basis,[48] and as in the bank's salary book the plaintiff's net salary of £tq.46·75 was equiparated to a sum of £cp.42 10s., which in the opinion of the Board could only refer to 'the Cyprus equivalent for a Turkish gold pound and for nothing else'.[49]

In the later case of *Ottoman Bank* v. *Chakarian* (No. 2),[50] however, in which the facts were almost identical, the Privy Council arrived at the opposite result.

The plaintiff-respondent retired from active service in 1931, when he became

---

[44] *Ottoman Bank of Nicosia* v. *Chakarian (No. 2)*, [1938] A.C. 260, at p. 272 *per* Lord Wright.
[45] *Apostolic Throne of St. Jacob* v. *Said*, [1940] 1 All E.R. 54.
[46] [1934] A.C. 354.
[47] p. 357.                    [48] p. 362.                    [49] p. 360.
[50] [1938] A.C. 260; and see *Sforza* v. *Ottoman*, ibid. at p. 282; *Ottoman Bank* v. *Meuni* [1939] 4 All E.R. 9 (P.C.).

entitled to a pension of 48 per cent of the basic salary of £tq.30 a month, received on 31 December 1930, i.e. £tq.14·40 a month. The defendants-respondents declared that they were bound and prepared to pay that sum in accordance with the terms of a letter written to the plaintiff when he was transferred to Cyprus, namely, 'on the basis of the system customary in that island', which was to pay the salary at the rate of £tq.110 to £cp.100. On 31 December 1930 the actual rate of exchange was £tq.900 to £cp.100,[51] so that whereas under the terms of the letter the plaintiff was entitled to a salary of about £cp.27$\frac{1}{3}$, the rate of exchange would have given him only about £cp.3$\frac{1}{3}$. But in view of the depreciation of British and, consequently, of Cyprus sterling in September 1931 the plaintiff demanded payment on the basis of a gold value clause, namely, of a fluctuating sum of money sufficient to purchase the quantity of gold bullion which would have been represented by the sum of Turkish pounds on a gold basis. This claim failed. Lord Wright, delivering the judgment of the Board, started from the fact that the contract, which was governed by Turkish law, contained no express stipulation of a gold clause. He emphasized that a contract providing for a sum of money pure and simple was subject to the nominalistic principle,[52] as opposed to any metallistic theory, and that this principle would be blurred 'if it were now to be held that the gold clause is unnecessary because it is to be implied in every contract which was made at a time when the country was on gold and when payments were normally made on a gold basis'.[53] The evidence of the experts on Turkish law showed that by Turkish law a contract made, say, in 1912, subject to Turkish law, to pay £tq.20 a month would not be construed by that law as a contract to pay twenty pieces of gold, even though gold was the normal form of the then legal tender, but as a contract to pay £tq.20 in whatever might be legal tender in Turkey according to Turkish law at the material time.[54] Lord Wright proceeded to state that a gold clause might have been inserted subsequently by the conduct of the parties if this had been so clear and unambiguous as to 'raise the inference that the parties have agreed to modify their contract'.[55] He could find no such facts and was of opinion that the practice to pay the basic salary at the rate of 110:100 'had the effect of making up to some extent the depreciation of the Turkish currency. It did not, however, put the payment of the

---

[51] At p. 278.        [52] As explained above, pp. 76 sqq.        [53] At p. 272.
[54] p. 270. Lord Wright reviewed the relevant provisions of Turkish law. They are also referred to in *Dascalopoulos's* case at pp. 361, 362, and in *Kricorian* v. *Ottoman Bank* (1932), 48 T.L.R. 247. It is, however, very remarkable that Turkey is perhaps the only country in the world where the existence of the nominalistic principle is by no means secure; moreover, the effect of the Turkish legislation of 1915 authorizing the issue of paper money, particularly on payments to be made outside Turkey, is not at all free from doubt. See Cour de Cassation at Constantinople, 24 June 1921, discussed by Ténékidès Clunet, 1922, 71 sqq.; 24 July 1924, Clunet, 1925, 492, with note by Salem, and Supreme Court of Syria, 30 Dec. 1931, A.D. 1931-2, Case No. 151. The result reached in *Dascalopoulos's* case was also arrived at by the Court of Appeal of the Mixed Tribunal at Alexandria, 18 June 1934, *Gazette des Tribunaux Mixtes*, xxiv. 349, No. 412 (*Hanna* v. *Ottoman Bank*), whose judgment was followed by Trib. Comm. Alexandria, 15 Apr. 1935, *Gazette des Tribunaux Mixtes*, xxv. 320, No. 361 (*Nacouz* v. *Ottoman Bank*), but rejected by Trib. Comm. Cairo, 13 Apr. 1935, ibid. xxv. 326, No. 362 (*Mazas* v. *Ottoman Bank*).
[55] At p. 272.

Turkish salary when converted into Cyprus currency on a gold basis.'[56] Finally, he distinguished *Dascalopoulos*'s case on the paramount ground that there the Board had no evidence before them on Turkish law.

The decision in the later case deserves approval. In both cases the actions were misconceived. There was nothing in the nature of a gold clause. But there existed a promise to pay Turkish pounds coupled with a foreign currency clause '110 Turkish pounds being equal to 100 Cyprus pounds'. It will appear later[57] that in such circumstances the only problem could be whether that clause afforded an absolute or a relative measure of value. There was no justification for the view that the basic sum of Turkish pounds was meant to be a sum of gold pounds; it would have been another matter if the plaintiffs had contended that the *Cyprus* pound referred to in the clause was the gold pound.[58]

2. Where a gold or other commodity clause has either expressly or impliedly been incorporated into a contract, the question very often arises whether the stipulated amount is to be paid by the delivery of that to which the clause refers (gold coin, quantity of rye, and so forth) or whether the amount, being uncertain and variable, is to be paid in whatever is money at the time of payment, but in so much of such money as corresponds to the then existing value of the thing mentioned in the clause.[59, 60] In other words, the

---

[56] At p. 276.  [57] Below, pp. 203 sqq.

[58] Lord Wright said at p. 278 that 'it was, in the strict sense, merely accidental that the English pound was on gold in December 1930'. *Sed quaere*. This was certainly not the point of view prevailing in foreign countries: see the German decisions discussed below, p. 000. Neither of the cases discussed is now likely to carry much weight on a point of English law.

[59] A third method of construction was adopted in the United States: If the debtor undertakes to pay, say, $1,000 'in paper hangings at the regular trade price' the American courts held that the contract provided for an alternative promise, namely, either to pay $1,000 or to deliver paper hangings, and that the option was stipulated for the benefit of the debtor who, unless he chose to deliver the commodity, was bound to pay not the stipulated sum of money, but the value of the paper hangings: see, for example, *Meseroe* v. *Ammidon* (1872), 109 Mass. 415, and recently *Moore* v. *Clines* (1933), 247 Ky. 605, 57 S.W. (2d) 509, where, however, on the particular facts of the case, a different construction was arrived at. From the point of view of English law it seems far-fetched to read into such a contract an alternative promise. It would seem preferable to regard the clause as a monetary obligation to which a modality clause is added: to deliver so many paper hangings as at the regular trade price prevailing at the date of performance have a value of $1,000.

[60] The essence of a gold value clause has been very well described as 'a measuring rod or measure of liability' (*International Trustee for the Protection of Bondholders A.G.* v. *The King*, [1936] 3 All E.R. 407 (C.A.), 419 *per* Lord Wright) or as 'a measuring point or yardstick' (*New Brunswick Railway Co.* v. *British and French Trust Corporation*, [1939] A.C. 1, and p. 30 *per* Lord Wright). In view of the nature of the gold value clause it is not easy to contend that it involves the promise to pay a 'sum certain' within the meaning of the Bills of Exchange Act, 1882. Yet this was the result reached by *Syndic in Bankruptcy* v. *Khayat*, [1943] A.C. 507. The decision cannot be regarded as conclusive, because the

question arises whether the clause fixes the instrument or mode of payment (*modality clause*) or the substance or amount of the debt (*value clause*).

In periods of stability this distinction, though theoretically important, may be without great practical interest, because it does not matter to either party whether the creditor is entitled to £10 in gold (or to a quantity of rye), or is entitled to a sum of money in notes with which he can buy the gold (or rye). The distinction, however, becomes important when monetary disturbances occur; for experience shows that in such circumstances modern States often resort to the remedy of permitting monetary obligations to be discharged by the payment of notes according to their nominal value.[61] If the clause defines the instrument of payment, the creditor is only entitled to receive so many notes as correspond to the nominal amount of the debt;[62] if, on the other hand, it determines the substance of the obligation, i.e. the amount, the creditor is entitled to receive so much in addition to the nominal amount of the debt as corresponds to the increased value of the *tertium comparationis* referred to in the clause. This distinction between modality and value clauses is recognized in all countries, particularly since it was accepted by the Permanent Court of International Justice at The Hague.[63]

In some cases it clearly follows from the wording of the clause that it has the character of a value clause. This is obviously so if the parties refer to the price of commodities, not to the commodities themselves. Even in the absence of an express stipulation of 'value' it is now clear law in most countries and, particularly, in England that any gold clause almost invariably imports a gold value clause.[64]

---

Board did not investigate the point and reached its decision without the benefit of an argument on behalf of the respondent (see Mann, 59 (1943) *L.Q.R.* 303). The result, however, is probably satisfactory. It is in conformity with the law of the United States: *Chrysler* v. *Renois* (1870), 43 N.Y. 209 and Nussbaum, l.c., p. 252, n. 26. Cf. the decision of the German Supreme Court, 12 Aug. 1925, *RGZ.* 111, 280. See above, p. 65, n. 12, on the gold coin clause in negotiable instruments.

[61] See above, p. 65, n. 11.                          [62] But see p. 66, n. 16.

[63] Case of Serbian Loans, Collection of Judgments, Series A, No. 14 (1928–30), pp. 32. 41.

[64] It should never have been open to doubt that certain statutory provisions made in consequence of international Conventions, but now superseded envisaged a value clause. Thus in regard to the carriage of goods by sea Art. IX of the Schedule to the Carriage of Goods by Sea Act 1924 provided that sterling sums 'mentioned in these Rules are to be taken at gold value'. Gold value was also contemplated when, in the field of international carriage by air, the fixed limits of the carrier's liability were 'deemed to refer to the French franc consisting of $65\frac{1}{2}$ milligrams gold of millesimal fineness 900' (Art. 22 (5) of the Convention scheduled to the Carriage by Air Act, 1932 and of the Convention scheduled to the Carriage by Air Act, 1961; the latter refers to a 'currency unit' rather than 'French

The lead was given by the Permanent Court of International Justice when, with reference to the promise to pay 'gold francs' *simpliciter*, it said that 'the treatment of the gold clause as indicating a mere modality of payment without reference to a gold standard of value, would be, not to construe, but to destroy it'.[65] Under the influence of this decision it was held in *England* that not only the elaborate clause '£100 in sterling in gold coin of the United Kingdom of or equal to the standard of weight and fineness existing on September 1, 1928',[66] but also the slightly less elaborate clause '£100 sterling gold coin of Great Britain of the present standard of weight and fineness'[67] and even the mere words '2,000 gold Turkish pounds',[68] expressed a gold value clause. And although the last-mentioned case probably will not at present be followed by many judges of first instance,[69] it makes sound sense and is in line with the letter and spirit of three decisions of the House of Lords[70] and many decisions of foreign courts of high persuasive authority.[71] In particular, in the present context, the absence of words specifying the weight and fineness of gold should be immaterial.[72] Moreover even if words of

---

francs', but the difference in wording was without substantial effect). Similarly, as regards the international carriage of passengers and goods by rail (Art. 57 (1) of the Conventions of 1961, Cmnd. 2811 and 2810) and by road (Art. 23 (3) of the Convention scheduled to the Carriage of Goods by Road Act, 1965) the amounts of francs limiting the carrier's liability were 'deemed to relate to the gold franc weighing $\frac{10}{31}$ of a gramme and being of a millesimal fineness 900'. And where the owner of a sea-going ship limited his liability in accordance with the Merchant Shipping legislation, the amount was determined by the value of the franc which was deemed to be a unit of $65\frac{1}{2}$ milligrams of gold of the usual fineness: see the Convention concluded in Brussels in 1957 (Cmnd. 353) and adopted by the Merchant Shipping (Liability of Shipowners & Others) Act, 1958. The sterling equivalent of the francs mentioned in the Convention was fixed by S.I. 1958 No. 1287 and after devaluation by S.I. 1967 No. 1725. Similar references to the 'franc' as a currency unit consisting of $65\frac{1}{2}$ milligrams of gold occurred in Art. 11 of the Rome Convention of 1952 on Damage caused by Foreign Aircraft to Third Parties on the Surface (Cmd. 8886) or in Art. 6 of the Brussels Convention of 1961 relating to Carriage of Passengers by Sea (*Rev. Crit.* 1965, 589); neither of them were signed or ratified by the United Kingdom.

[65] Case of Serbian Loans, p. 32. The case related to 'francs-or'.

[66] *Feist v. Société Intercommunale Belge d'Électricité*, [1934] A.C. 161.

[67] *The King v. International Trustee for the Protection of Bondholders A.G.*, [1937] A.C. 500, at p. 556 *per* Lord Russell, at p. 562 *per* Lord Maugham, at p. 573 *per* Lord Roche: *New Brunswick Railway Co.* v. *British and French Trust Corporation*, [1939] A.C. 1, at p. 18 *per* Lord Maugham, at p. 26 *per* Lord Russell, at p. 39 *per* Lord Romer.

[68] *Syndic in Bankruptcy v. Khayat*, [1943] A.C. 507. Strictly speaking this case which Nussbaum, p. 253, somewhat surprisingly, describes as 'unique in the vast body of gold decisions' is only an authority of the law of Palestine.

[69] This is due to the three recent cases referred to above, p. 141, n. 25. On the last-mentioned case see below, p. 152, n. 88.

[70] Above, nn. 66, 67.

[71] Above, p. 141, and below, pp. 150, 151.

[72] The absence of words of specification was fastened upon by McNair J. in *Campos*'s case and by Morris L.J. (as he then was) at pp. 152, 153 of *Treseder-Griffin*'s case, both referred to above, p. 140, n. 25. In the latter case the clause required the payment of

specification are described as a definition the existence of a protective clause should probably not be denied.[73] In sum, it still seems possible and proper to submit that any reference in an English contract to payment in 'gold' prima facie constitutes a gold value clause.[74]

The at one time usual *American* clause 'in gold coin of the United States of America of or equal to the standard of weight and fineness existing on . . .' was held to be a value clause by the Supreme Court of the United States[75] whose interpretation was uniformly accepted in other countries.[76] In *France*[77] and *Switzerland*,[78] it appears, the

£1,900 'in gold sterling or Bank of England notes to the equivalent value in gold sterling', and thus included a clear emphasis on 'value'. The gap raises a mere problem of construction. Can it be filled? If so, there exists a gold value clause. If not, the clause, whether a gold coin or a gold value clause, is void for uncertainty. See Dicey and Morris, p. 995, and below, p. 152.

[73] In *Judah* v. *Delaware Trust Co.*, 378 A. 2d 624 (1977) the Supreme Court of Delaware was concerned with debentures expressed in terms of 'Chinese silver dollar' which was 'defined as a unit of currency containing' a certain quantity of silver. It was held (p. 633) that these words in fact amounted to a definition only and did not have the character of a protective clause. A similar result had previously been arrived at by the Californian District Court of Appeal in *Sternberg* v. *West Coast Life Insurance Co.*, 16 Cal. Rep. 546 (1961), where a life insurance policy issued in 1925 at Shanghai provided for payment in San Francisco of '5,000 Taels, Shanghai Sycee' payable in 'Taels, Shanghai Sycee currency of the present weight and fineness'. This was held to be, not a 'commodity contract for silver', but a monetary obligation. The court probably meant to say that the clause was not a protective one. *Sed quaere.* In both cases the courts seem to have applied Delaware and/or Californian law. If there was a silver clause its abolition by Chinese law would have had to be disregarded: below, p. 291. If there was no silver clause the obligations undoubtedly became valueless: below p. 270.

[74] In the same sense foreign writers such as Ascarelli, p. 250; Van Hecke, p. 155; Rabel, *Conflict of Laws*, iii (1950), 21. Older English decisions such as *Modiano Bros.* v. *Bailey & Sons* (1933), 47 Ll. L.R. 134 ('freight collect on basis of pound sterling equals 4·86 U.S. gold dollars') are now of doubtful authority. The principle that a (gold) coin clause imples a value clause seems to have been established in Scotland in the seventeenth century. Sir George Mackenzie (quoted here from *Works* I (1716), Part 2, p. 193) speaks of the case 'if the money . . . be talied', i.e. of what we would now call a coin clause: 'it may be paid in as much of the present coin as will answer to that kind of money, being of the same value as the gold and silver specified in the reversion, conform to the common law, which the Lords interpret to be payment according to the price and value that the said talied money was worth at the time of granting the obligation, Mar. 3, 1623'.

[75] *Norman* v. *Baltimore & Ohio Railway Co.* (1934), 294 U.S. 240, at p. 302 *per* Chief Justice Hughes; *Perry* v. *United States* (1934), 294 U.S. 330, at p. 348 *per* Chief Justice Hughes, at p. 338 *per* Mr. Justice Stone, at p. 336 *per* Mr. Justice McReynolds.

[76] *England: The King* v. *International Trustee for the Protection of Bondholders A.G.*, [1936] 3 All E.R. 407 (C.A.); though on appeal the decision was reversed ([1937] A.C. 500), the *ratio decidendi* being that the contract was governed by American law under which the clause was illegal, the construction of the Court of Appeal was *obiter* approved of by Lords Atkin, Russell, and Roche (pp. 555, 556, 573). *Austria:* Supreme Court, 26 Nov. 1935, *RabelsZ.* 1935, 891, 892. *Germany:* Supreme Court, 24 April 1936, *B.I.J.I.* 35 (1936), 124, and Plesch, *The Gold Clause*, ii. 25; 28 May 1936, *RabelsZ.* 1936, 385, and Plesch, l.c., p. 30, confirming Berlin Court of Appeal, *B.I.J.I.* 33 (1935), 78, and Plesch, l.c. i. 99. *Holland:* Hoge Raad, 13 May 1936, Plesch, *The Gold Clause*, ii. 8.

[77] Cass. Civ. 23 Jan. 1924, Clunet, 1924, 685, and Clunet, 1925, 166, 168 (three judgments); Cass. Civ. 9 July 1930, S. 1931, 1. 124 (Société du Port de Rosario); 7 July 1931,

mere fact that the word 'gold' is used in such connections as francs-or, piastres-or, and so on, renders the clause a value clause. The law of *Norway*,[79] *Finland*,[80] *Denmark*,[81] and *Austria*[82] seems to be similar. Although the practice of some countries is different,[83] it is submitted, with respect, that Lord Russell of Killowen was justified in summarizing the broad picture as follows:[84]

> The gold clauses have, however, come under the review of judicial tribunals in many countries and the 'Feist construction' has prevailed in that they are generally regarded merely as clauses to protect one of the contracting parties against a depreciation of the currency. It would I think be regrettable if a uniformity in this respect did not prevail, and that a different construction should be applied, except in cases where the 'Feist construction' is expressly excluded.

3. The operation of gold and other protective clauses frequently raises problems caused by bad draftsmanship or by unforeseen and unforeseeable developments which in this field are by no means rare.

(*a*) The parties may fail to define the *tertium comparationis*, particularly the weight and fineness of gold, with sufficient precision. The problem of construction which thus arises cannot be answered except in the light of the facts of each case. But if in 1911 'gold bonds' are issued under English law and provide for the payment in England of £100 in 1961 with interest 'in like gold coin', then the

S. 1932, 1. 255 (Société d'Héraclée); 21 Dec. 1932, S. 1932, 1. 390, and Clunet, 1933, 1201 (Chemin de der de Rosario); cf. 14 Jan. 1931, S. 1931, 1. 125, and Clunet, 1931, 126 (Ville de Tokio); Conseil d'État, 28 Nov. 1958, Clunet, 1960, 442, 444. It is probably no exaggeration to say that in France every gold clause is a gold value clause.

[78] Federal Tribunal, 11 Feb. 1931, Clunet, 1931, 510 (Société d'Héraclée).

[79] Supreme Court, 2 May 1962, referred to above, p. 141, n. 21.

[80] Supreme Court, 18 Jan. 1933, *RabelsZ*. 1933, 467 ('in Finnish Goldmark of the weight and fineness fixed by the Coinage Act').

[81] Supreme Court, 21 June, 1933, *RabelsZ*. 1933, 960 ('all payments to be made in gold'), though the decision contains a warning against generalization.

[82] In a very interesting decision the Supreme Court held that an old clause 'guilders of Austrian currency in silver' was a silver value clause and thus survived many monetary changes: 17 Dec. 1930, *Bankarchiv* 30 (1931), 247.

[83] The most restrictive interpretation was adopted by the *German* Supreme Court when dealing with such clauses as 'Goldmark', 'in Gold deutscher Reichswährung', 'in Gold', and so forth, at any rate in so far as they were agreed before the great inflation of 1922–3. These clauses were always held to be gold coin clauses (Supreme Court, 30 Apr. 1932, *RGZ*. 136, 169, 172 with numerous references to previous decisions). Having treated these clauses as gold coin clauses, the court refused to transform them into value clauses. The same attitude has been taken by the *Belgian* courts: see, for example, 27 Apr. 1933, Clunet 1933, 739; Piret, pp. 246–8. On the other hand, it seems that in *Switzerland* a gold coin clause imports a gold value: Guhl, *Das schweizerische Obligationenrecht* (3rd ed., 1944), p. 72, and above, n. 78.

[84] *The King* v. *International Trustee for the Protection of Bondholders A.G.*, [1937] A.C. 500, 556.

gold clause, whether limited to interest or extending to capital[85] and whether a gold coin or a gold value clause,[86] cannot reasonably have contemplated any standard other than the classical standard laid down in the Coinage Act, 1870.[87] If a lease granted in 1930 provides for a rent of £1,900 payable 'either in gold sterling or Bank of England notes to the equivalent value in gold sterling', the like standard must, by necessary implication, have been in the parties' minds. If the same lease was granted in 1938, when this country was off the gold standard, the answer is much more doubtful, but it is submitted that it is not unreasonable to impute to the parties the intention to take as a standard 270 ounces of gold, i.e. the quantity which £1,900 would at that time buy.[88] Again, if in 1968 an English debtor promised 'gold pounds', it may be asked what the gold pound was at a time when gold coins were not in circulation and a large part of the population was unaware of the gold parity standard to which this country was committed. The answer is that the gold pound is the pound sterling of par value as declared to the International Monetary Fund.[89] Finally if in 1980, when gold was demonetized and as a commodity had reached prices of almost US $800 or about £450 per oz., the surrounding circumstances may possibly establish that parties who agree upon 'gold pounds' contemplate gold as a commodity, but this will not often appear likely, so that it may be easier to impute the intention to contract in terms of the classical gold pound as defined in the Coinage Act 1870.

The clearest method of expressing a gold value clause is pointed out by the Order made by the House of Lords in *Feist*'s case,[90] and should, wherever possible, be adopted. It is, however, a remarkable fact that, although the lack of definition has led to serious

---

[85] The latter alternative is likely to be correct: above, p. 144, n. 36.

[86] The latter alternative is likely to be correct: above, p. 149, n. 72.

[87] This, it is believed, was the solution which should have been reached in *Campos* v. *Kentucky & Indiana Railroad Co.* (1962), 2 Ll.L.R. 459 and in *Lemaire* v. *Kentucky & Indiana Railroad Co.*, 242 F. 2d 884 (1957), on which see Mann, 12 (1963) *I.C,L.Q.* 1005.

[88] This, it is believed, was one of the real problems in *Treseder-Griffin* v. *Co-operative Insurance Society*, [1956] 2 Q.B. 127. Lord Goddard in the court of first instance and Harman J. in the Court of Appeal expressed different views. The solution mentioned in the text was proposed by Mann (1957), 73 *L.Q.R.* 181. If the Court of Appeal had held that the point mentioned in the text permitted no certain solution and that the clause was therefore invalid, it would have been easier to acquiesce in the decision.

[89] See above, p. 31.

[90] [1934] A.C. 161: 'to pay £100 in gold coin of the United Kingdom or in so much current legal tender of the United Kingdom that every pound comprised in the nominal amount of such payment represents the price in London in sterling (calculated at the due date of payment) of 123·27447 grains of gold of the standard of fineness specified in the First Schedule to the Coinage Act, 1870'.

difficulties, particularly in connection with the term 'gold franc'[91] and in Germany,[92] even modern documents of a formal character, such as treaties,[93] seem to disregard the lessons taught by past experience.

In any case it should be clear that the standard of value at the time of the contract will have to be given effect. The Permanent Court of International Justice has laid it down[94] that the standard must 'manifestly' be taken as of the time of the contract: 'the engagement would be meaningless, if it referred to an unknown standard of a future day'.[95]

If the preceding considerations are borne in mind it is difficult to understand the doubts which arose in connection with Art. IX of the Rules attached to the Carriage of Goods by Sea Act, 1924, which, without defining the time, provided that the monetary units mentioned in the Rules 'are to be taken to be gold value'; this applied, for instance, to Art. IV of the same Rules which limited liability to £100 per package or unit.[96] It would appear that at least

---

[91] When contained in a document issued before 1914, these words have the meaning assigned to them by the Permanent Court of International Justice, Case of Serbian Loans, p. 33: it was the franc of the Latin Monetary Union, as defined by national laws, and thus had an 'international character' and 'constituted a well-known standard of value to which reference could appropriately be made in loan contracts when it was desired to establish a sound and stable basis for repayment'. See also Swiss Federal Tribunal in the case of the Société d'Héraclée (above, p. 151, n. 78). On the alleged international character of the 'franc' (*sans épithète*) see above, pp. 52 and 142, and Clunet, 1946-9, 134-41.

[92] German law on this point was almost absurdly complicated. During and after the inflation of 1922-3 several types of 'Goldmark' came into existence and were dealt with in numerous enactments relating to mortgages, bills of exchange, balance sheets, and so forth. The details are conveniently collected in the decision of the Bavarian Supreme Court, 7 Mar. 1929, *JW.* 1929, 3022. In connection with mortgages 'Goldmark' meant a 'Fine Gold Mark' of the price in reichsmarks of 1/2790 kilogram of gold fine (cf. Court of Appeal Berlin, 6 Sept. 1924, *JW.* 1924, 2047). In connection with bills the term meant 10/42 U.S.A. dollars (cf. Supreme Court, 12 Aug. 1925, *RGZ.* 111, 280; 13 Aug. 1935, *JW.* 1935, 3304). In ordinary debts it is said to have meant the 'Fine Gold Mark' mentioned above: see Nussbaum, *Vertraglicher Schutz gegen Schwankungen des Geldwerts* (1928), p. 40. A further difficulty arose from the fact that the London price of gold controlled the German practice and, being based on ounces and sterling, had to be translated into German weights and currency; on these matters see the decree of 10 Oct. 1931 (*RGBl.* 1931, i. 569) and Nussbaum, p. 256; *Vertraglicher Schutz gegen Schwankungen des Geldwerts*, pp. 41 sqq. In view of the developments referred to below, pp. 169 to 171, these matters are now of historical interest only.

[93] See below, p. 551.

[94] *Case of Brazilian Loans*, pp. 116, 117.

[95] The promise, fully spelled out, reads: 'to pay such sum of sterling as at the date of payment represents the value of the quantity of gold referred to at the time of the contract'. If the promise reads: 'to pay such sum of sterling as corresponds to $100', slightly different considerations apply. The amount of sterling payable by the debtor depends on the dollar rate of exchange at the date of payment. See below, pp. 199, 200.

[96] Making use of the power given by the second sentence of Art. IX of the Brussels Convention (League of Nations Treaty Series, vol. cxx (1931), 155) the United States of

up to 1945, Art. IX was widely ignored in this country[97] in that claims were 'customarily settled on the basis of a maximum liability of £100 without regard to the gold value', but in 1950, when the value of £100 gold was almost £300, a 'gentleman's's agreement' was made between the representative British shipping and insurance organizations, whereby the limit imposed by Art. IX was interpreted as '£200 sterling lawful money',[98] and this remained in force, although the value of £100 gold rose very considerably before the law was altered. It cannot be readily appreciated why the City of London found the Act of 1924 so mysterious.[99] In any event if and in so far as the Agreement of 1950 purported to limit the shipowner's liability to a greater extent than that permitted by the Hague Rules, it was invalid.[100] The point is now, however, obsolete[101] and nothing but an odd experience remains to be recorded.

(b) Another difficulty is liable to arise from the unforeseen absence or plurality of a price for gold at the relevant time, particularly the time for payment.

The latter state of affairs occurred between 17 March 1968 and 15 August 1971, when there existed a 'two-tier' market for gold, i.e. a market for gold as a commodity and a market for monetary gold based on the convertibility of the U.S. dollar at the price of $35 per oz. Numerous treaties relating to international transport by land, sea, and air provided for sums limited by the value of the 'gold franc' as defined. Where the municipal legislator had failed to translate such sums into national currency, it was left to the courts to find the appropriate rate of conversion. No English decision was rendered, but in the Netherlands the Hoge Raad decided (rightly, it is believed) that with reference to the 2 May 1969 the official rate of gold should be applied; the *ratio decidendi* was that the price of the commodity was changing from day to day and place to place

---

America has fixed the figure at $500 without a gold clause in the Carriage of Goods by Sea Act, 1936.

[97] *The Times*, 29 June 1945, p. 9.

[98] Scrutton, *On Charterparties* (17th ed., 1964), p. 432. The text of the Gold Clause Agreement of the British Maritime Association of 1 Aug. 1950 is printed at p. 503.

[99] The Convention from which it stems cannot have contemplated any other gold value of sterling than that fixed by the Coinage Act, 1870, and still treated as 'classical' in 1923, when the Rules were drafted. It seems to have been understood in this sense in foreign countries: Court of Appeal Aix-en-Provence, 11 Jan. 1955, Droit Maritime Français 1956, 272; High Court at Dacca in *Mackinnon Mackenzie & Co.* v. *Dada Ltd.*, All-Pakistan Legal Decisions 10 (iv) (1958), 101. The Convention provides, incidentally, a strong argument against McNair J.'s view (above, p. 149, n. 72) that in the absence of words defining weight and fineness there does not exists a gold (value) clause.

[100] See Art. III, Rule 8 of the Hague Rules. Colinvaux, *Carriage by Sea* in *British Shipping Laws 3*, vol. ii, p. 1663, seemed to take a similar view.

[101] See below, p. 160.

and that therefore the object of achieving certainty and uniformity could only be fulfilled by the application of the rate for monetary gold.[102]

The problem became much more difficult, when, in consequence of the demonetization of gold caused by the United States of America on 15 August 1971 rendering foreign official holdings of dollars inconvertible into gold, there existed only a market for gold as a commodity and the par value system created in Bretton Woods collapsed. Where the municipal legislator had failed to intervene and the treaty provision contemplating 'gold francs' had to be applied,[103] the gap had to be filled by a process of construction, which, it is suggested, involved the assessment of the 'official' value of gold according to the practice of the central bank in the country of the place of payment. This would appear to be in line with the approach of the Court of Appeal at Hamburg[104] and may not be very different from the view adopted in England in January 1977 by the Department of Trade.[105] But the Court of Appeal at Trieste[106] resorted to the market price of gold.

The specific problem[107] was solved, when it became the practice to

[102] 14 April 1972, *NJ.* 1972, 728, also in English, *Rivista di diritto internazionale privato e processuale* 1973, 936 or (in Italian) *Il diritto marittimo* 1974, 193 or (in French) *Uniform Law Review* 1974, 292. On the other hand the value of gold as a commodity was taken as a basis by the Court of Appeal in Athens, 10 Jan. 1974, as reported by Larsen, Georgetown L.J. 63 (1975), 817, at p. 824, and by the Tribunal of Genoa, 6 Sept. 1978 (*Il diritto marittimo* 1979, 91) and the Tribunal of Milan, 25 Oct. 1976, *Il diritto marittimo* 1978, 83 with note by Treves; the latter decision relates to a loss on 14 Aug. 1971.

[103] In the present context it is only the municipal law and its application that is relevant. The effect of developments in the monetary field upon treaties is not material to the present discussion and is of purely academic interest. Some authors have discussed the question whether such doctrines as frustration or the *clausula rebus sic stantibus* may be applicable to the treaties, but this is open to grave doubt.

[104] 2 July 1974, *Versicherungsrecht* 1974, 993, also *European Transport Law* 9 (1974), 701 and *Uniform Law Review* 1975, 240. The decision applied the 'central rate' established and for a time practised extralegally under the so called Smithsonian Agreement of 18 Dec. 1971 to cope with the quagmire which had arisen in international monetary affairs.

[105] The Carriage by Air (Sterling Equivalents) Order 1977, S.I. 1977 No. 1 (which is no longer in force) specified the sterling amounts for the purpose of Article 22 in the First Schedule to the Carriage by Air Act 1961. It is understood that the calculation was made on the basis of Art. xxi (2) of the Articles of Agreement of the International Monetary Fund in its second version: 'The unit of value of special drawing rights shall be equivalent to 0.888671 gram of fine gold' (i.e. the gold content of the dollar before 1972). Although this provision had, of course, nothing to do with the Carriage of Air Conventions or statutes or gold value, it was said to be 'the only available basis'.

[106] 3 March 1978, *Il diritto marittimo* 1979, 215. In the same sense the Tribunale of Milan, 19 Nov. 1979, *Rivista di diritto internazionale privato e processuale* 1980, 271.

[107] It led to an enormous literature. See, among others, Asser, *Journal of Maritime Law and Commerce*, 5 (1974) 654; Gold, *Floating Currencies, Gold and SDRs*, IMF Pamphlets Nos. 19 and 22 (1976, 1977); Heller, 7 (1973) *Journal of World Trade Law* 126 and 6 (1974) *Journal of Maritime Law and Commerce* 73; Jeanprêtre, *Schweizerische Juristenzeitung* 1969, 185; Larsen, above n. 102; Treves, *Il Diritto Marittimo* 1974, 12;

adopt the SDR as an international unit of account,[108] and does not now merit prolonged discussion, yet the experience from 1968 until about 1977 should be noted as an instructive precedent.

(c) Finally, the spatial operation of protective clauses requires a word of explanation. The gold clause, in particular, usually omits to indicate the place with reference to which the money value of the defined quantity of gold is to be ascertained. Even before the Second World War the price of gold varied to some extent from place to place, but in view of the pre-eminent position which London occupied as a market for gold, the price of gold in London was often, and perhaps normally, regarded by the parties as decisive.[109] In the present world the fluctuations are much wider; moreover, there exists no market which controls the price of gold everywhere. One will have to choose between the price of gold at the place of performance and the price of gold at the place which controls it in terms of the particular currency that is *in obligatione*. Thus, if a merchant in Cairo promises to pay 'French gold francs' in Bombay, the choice lies between the valuation prevailing at the market in Bombay or in Paris. The decision will depend on the construction of each particular contract, but the price at the expressly agreed place of performance is likely to have been intended. It would, however, not be in harmony with public policy to have regard to a 'black market', i.e. a market, for instance, established or tolerated in defiance of the duties imposed by exchange restrictions.[110]

### III

While gold clauses used to be the most popular method of securing the creditor against the effects of nominalism, recent tendencies suggest that, at any rate within the realm of domestic relationships, index clauses are acquiring practical importance to an increasing extent.[111]

In this country a clause of such type was statutorily imposed

---

*Italian Yearbook of International Law* 1 (1975), 132; *Rivista si diritto internazionale privato e processuale* 1976, 16. And see below p. 553, n. 100. See also Monetary Law Committee, Madrid Conference (1976) of the International Law Association, p. 165.

[108] Below, p. 159.

[109] This was certainly so in Germany; see p. 153, n. 92 above.

[110] See the Supreme Court of Israel in *Marrache* v. *Masri*: Gorney, *International Laywers Convention in Israel* (Jerusalem, 1959), pp. 309, 310.

[111] See, generally, *Indexation of Fixed Interest Securities*, published by the OECD in 1973, which contains interesting material on Finland, Germany and Switzerland and a complete bibliography. It should also be noted that on 10 May 1975 the influential Advisory Council to Germany's Federal Ministry of Economics recommended in a lengthy Opinion to permit in principle the indexation of monetary claims.

in 1575 by an 'Act for the maintenance of the Colleges in the Universities, and of Winchester and Eaton':[112] 'for the better maintenance of learning and the better relief of scholars' it required leases made by the Colleges to reserve a third of the rent in corn, 'that is to say in good wheat after 6/8 the quarter or under and good malt at 5 sh the quarter or under', and in default thereof 'to pay . . . after the rate of the best wheat and malt in the market of Cambridge'. This may have been an isolated, though remarkable example, but a more general and more elaborate scheme was put forward in 1887, when Alfred Marshall suggested that contracts should be made optionally in terms of currency or in terms of a standard unit of purchasing power called 'the unit'.[113] Since then index clauses, frequently described as cost-of-living or sliding scale clauses, have for many years been widely used in collective agreements,[114] and in March 1981 the British Government issued to 'eligible holders' £1 billion of 2 per cent index-linked Treasury Stock, 1996: the value of the principal on repayment will be related to the movement, during the life of the Stock, of the United Kingdom General Index of Retail Prices; interest payments will similarly be multiplied by the Index ratio applicable to the month in which the payment falls due. This has also occurred in the *United States of America*[115] where such clauses are by no means confined to the field of industrial relations.[116] In *France* they have become a regular feature of long-term credit arrangements, while in *Finland* they were until 1968 an ingredient of the normal operation of the monetary

---

[112] 18 Eliz. 1. c. 6. Leases which failed to include the prescribed term were declared to be void.

[113] Remedies for Fluctuations of General Prices, *Contemporary Review* li. (1887), 355. Marshall clearly saw the need for and the attraction of contracting in terms of the unit, but he failed to see the dangers. Yet his article still makes fascinating reading.

[114] They are now out of fashion. See *Productivity, Prices and Incomes Policy in 1968 and 1969* (Cmnd. 3590), paragraph 41: 'Cost of living sliding scales are of diminishing importance in industry'; or *Pay and Conditions in the Building Industry 1968* (Cmnd. 3837), paragraph 6: 'it was agreed in 1965 to abandon the practice'. As to the earlier practice see *Industrial Relations Handbook* (published for the Ministry of Labour and National Service by H.M. Stationery Office, 1944), pp. 184 sqq. and *passim*; Milne-Bailey, *Trade Union Documents* (1929), p. 263, where the text of the clause applicable to the building industry is printed; *British Trade Unionism* (published by PEP. Political and Economic Planning, 1949), pp. 75, 76. On the 'selling price sliding scale' used in the Iron and Steel Industry see I. G. Sharp, *Industrial Conciliation and Arbitration in Great Britain* (1950), pp. 58 sqq. As to Australia see the facts in *Australian Workers Union v. Commonwealth Railways Commissioners* (1933), 49 C.L.R. 589.

[115] Nussbaum, p. 303.

[116] In fact at least since 1952 variable annuities have become popular: 19 (1965) *Rutgers L.R.* 345 (note). There exists also a widespread practice of fuel cost or other escalator clauses in Public Utility Rate Schedules: Trigg, *University of Pennsylvania L.R.* 106 (1958), 964.

system.[117] 'Index loans' are at present not usual in the principal financial centres of the world; in *Sweden*, however, a Committee under the chairmanship of Per Eckerberg reported in 1965 by no means unfavourably upon the need or the feasibility of index loans.[118]

The great attraction of index clauses lies in the fact that only in a very few countries, particularly in *France, Germany,* and *Finland*, has their legality been restricted by the legislator.[119] Moreover they are designed readily to take care of internal changes in the purchasing power of money, which are, it will be remembered, not necessarily in line with the external valuation of the currency in terms of gold; within the realm of domestic transactions, therefore, they are more likely than gold clauses to serve the creditor's purpose.

In practice the adoption of an index clause presupposes the existence and identification of a suitable index or scale, but if this is defined a carefully drawn index clause[120] will not give rise to much difficulty in operation. In fact problems of construction have rarely come up for judicial decision.[121] The effect to be attributed to the disappearance or a change of the index chosen by the parties, or of its constitution, will have to be viewed in the context of the agreement; if the parties have failed to make provision for such an event it should be open to the court to imply an intention to adopt such successor index as corresponds most closely to the discontinued index.[122] Where the clause is so framed as to allow for 'tolerance', i.e. to render a minimum variation immaterial, complicated calculations may be necessary, but there will hardly be a legal problem.

---

[117] Between the end of the Second World War and 1968, national wages and pensions were tied to an index. Index clauses were attached to bonds, insurance policies and, since 1955, bank deposits. See *The Index Clause System in Finnish Money and Capital Markets,* published by the Bank of Finland, Oct. 1964. The whole system disappeared in 1968. See below, p. 169, n. 181.

[118] *Index Loans* (Stockholm, 1965), a summary published by the Swedish Ministry of Finance.                                                            [119] See below, p. 169.

[120] For a useful precedent see *Encyclopaedia of Forms and Precedents* (4th ed., 1965), 11, 302 (rent varying with index of retail prices). A loan stock with a cost of living clause was issued in 1965; *The Times Book of New Issues of Public Companies*, vol. 137 (1965), p. 30.

[121] The only case in the English language seems to be *Stanwell Park Hotel Co. Ltd.* v. *Leslie* (1952), 85 Commonwealth L.R. 189. An interesting point was decided by the Austrian Supreme Court, 1 Mar. 1961, *Entscheidungen des Österreichischen Obersten Gerichtshofs in Zivilsachen*, xxxiv, No. 31: in the absence of an express provision to the contrary, it must be assumed that the parties intended to take as a standard the level of the index at the time of the contract rather than completion.

[122] The question has frequently arisen in France where it has been held to be within the scope of the sovereign appreciation of the facts by the lower court to find the index 'la plus apte' to take the place of the discontinued one: see, e.g., Cass. Civ., 15 Feb. 1972, D. 1973, 417; 6 March 1974, D. 1974, 249.

## IV

Mainly in international transactions the place of the gold clause, rendered nugatory by the demonetization of gold, has to a certain extent been taken over by unit-of-account clauses of various types.[123] Their common feature is that they are based on the idea of a 'basket': the unit is derived from averaging the values of the constituent currencies. Most of them are derived from some official methods of accounting, but some are privately devised. Such legal problems as are liable to arise relate to the construction of frequently complicated clauses. No court has so far had to consider them.

For about twenty years beginning in the early 1950s it was in particular Belgium's Kredietbank which sponsored the 'European Unit of Account' (EUA) for a substantial number of issues.[124] Other banks preferred the 'European Composite Unit' (Eurco). In more recent years the Special Drawing Right (SDR) of the International Monetary Fund[125] and the European Currency Unit (Ecu)[126] provide the advantage that they are not only based on officially recognized formulae, but also have a value in terms of currency which can readily be ascertained by referring to daily newspapers such as the *Financial Times*. On the other hand from the point of view of the private investor these units of account have certain disadvantages which have meant that only few issues denominated in SDRs and apparently none denominated in terms of Ecu have taken place. The Ecu is not only too young and uncertain an institution, but also does not include dollars or any currency other than that of members of the European Economic Community. And the SDR is under the control of the International Monetary Fund which is widely believed to be subject to political influence so as to permit or tolerate possibly unwelcome changes in composition. In fact in the eyes of many the SDR was discredited by the change which occurred on 1 July 1978, when the Saudi Arabian riyal and the Iranian rial were substituted for the Danish krone and the South African rand. Since 1 January 1981, however, the SDR comprises only the U.S. dollar,

---

[123] In addition to the literature referred to above p. 138, n. 8, see Coussement, 'Le régime des unités de compte et leur utilisation dans les contrats', *Revue de la Banque*, Cahier 4 (1979), 42; Ballegooisin, *Units of Account in Eurobonds*, 22 (1975) Netherlands Int. L.R. 51; Treves, 'Les clauses monétaires dans les émissions d'euro-obligations', *Riv. dir. int. pr. proc.* 1971, 775.

[124] In their original form which was based on the former European Payments Union they gave rise to the question whether they involved a gold clause. The answer was probably in the affirmative, for the extent of the obligation was measured by gold. See note in 71 (1962), *Yale L.J.* 1294. The existence of a gold clause was denied by the author of the scheme, Fernand Colin (e.g. in *Formation of a European Capital Market*, p. 25), by Blondeel, 64 (1964), *Col. L.R.* 995, 1005 and Delaume, pp. 271 sqq.

[125] Below p. 507.                           [126] Below p. 504.

the French franc, the Deutsche Mark, the Japanese yen and the pound sterling. Although important and relatively stable currencies are omitted from the basket and although the Fund may at any time determine to change it, it may well be that the present composition will inspire greater confidence. Those who agree upon an SDR clause without further words of definition must be clear that they are contracting in terms of a unit such as it exists from time to time.

These clauses like all 'basket' clauses do not guarantee the absolute maintenance of values; they merely provide such relative stability as the averaging permits, the depreciation of one (or more than one) of the constituent currencies reducing the value of the total. Since there are governments and governmental institutions which dispose of or owe sums expressed in SDRs, a liability or an asset similarly denominated may be attractive to them.[127] Yet, while the absolute amount of capital raised by the issue of bonds carrying unit-of-account clauses has been substantial, it seems to constitute only a fraction of the total.[128] On the other hand those private investors who are not prepared to trust a single currency without a protective clause will have to accept that in the absence of an absolutely stable standard of value the unit-of-account clause is at present probably the least ineffective, though far from ideal method of maintaining value.

As a result of a number of international Conferences, particularly those concerned with transport by sea and air,[129] the SDR has largely been substituted for gold francs as a measure for valuing or limiting liability.[130] In so far as the law of England is concerned

---

[127] For an example see the Republic of Finland's $8\frac{3}{4}$ per cent SDR Notes of 1979, due in 1984.

[128] Sacredoti (above p. 138, n. 8) quotes at p. 204 *Financial Market Trends* of February 1978, according to which the fraction was 6.7 per cent in 1974, 6.9 per cent in 1975, 0.5 per cent in 1976 and 0.2 per cent in 1977.

[129] The development which is now only of historical interest has been described in great detail by Sir Joseph Gold, *Floating Currencies, Gold and SDRs*, IMF Pamphlets No. 19, pp. 40 sqq.; No. 22, pp. 24 sqq.; No. 26, pp. 19 sqq., also by Bristow, 1978, *Lloyd's Maritime and Commercial L.Q.* 31; Costable, 1979, *Lloyd's Maritime and Commercial L.Q.* 326; Klingsporn, *Wertpapiermittielungen* 1978, 918; Treves, *Annuaire Français de Droit International Public* 1974, 755, and *Riv. dir. int. pr. proc.* 1976, 16. On the Montreal Conference, in particular, see Treves, 'International Law and Economic Order', *Festschrift für F.A. Mann*, 1977, p. 795.

[130] Under Art. 23 (3) of the Convention for the International Carriage of Goods by Road scheduled to the Carriage of Goods by Road Act 1965 compensation shall not 'exceed 25 francs per kilogram of gross weight'. 'Francs' means the gold franc weighing $\frac{10}{31}$ of a gramme and being of millesimal fineness of 100. Similarly the Convention scheduled to the Carriage of Passengers by Road Act 1974 limits liability by fixed amounts of 'francs' which, according to Art. 19 shall be the gold franc weighing $\frac{10}{31}$ of a gramme and being of millesimal fineness of 900.' These provisions do not seem to have been changed nor has the amount been translated into sterling.

the amounts so arrived at have been converted into sterling by Orders embodied in Statutory Instruments.[131] They are liable to differ from the figures adopted in other countries and apply only if in the case in point English law governs.[132]

## V

The next question is whether and how far agreements made for the purpose of averting the consequences of nominalism and discussed in the preceding sections are valid in law. This problem[133] must be treated under four different headings.

1. It seems to be generally recognized that the *nominalistic principle as such,* apart from any legal tender or special legislation, does not invalidate gold or similar clauses.[134] This is so even in France and some other countries where nominalism has been put on a statutory basis.[135] The question whether the rule of Art. 1895 Code Civil has the character of *jus cogens* or of *jus dispositivum* was long in dispute, but is now firmly settled in the latter sense,[136] and gold and similar clauses were in normal circumstances held to be

---

[131] The Order in Council at present in force is the Merchant Shipping (Sterling Equivalents) (Various Enactments) (No. 2) Order 1980, S.I. 1980 No. 1872 relating to the Merchant Shipping (Liability of Shipowners and Others) Act 1958; Carriage of Goods by Sea Act 1971; Merchant Shipping (Oil Polution) Act 1971; Merchant Shipping Act 1974 and the Unfair Contract Terms Act 1977. In future these will be replaced by Orders made under the Merchant Shipping Act 1979. See, in addition, the Carriage by Air and Road Act 1979 which also substitutes SDR for gold francs. So long as it is not in force the Carriage by Air (Sterling Equivalents) (No. 2) Order 1980, S.I. 1980 No. 1873 applies. The Orders do not define the SDR value of a gold franc. The International Conventions preceding the Orders fix the number of units of account and invariably declare them to be the SDRs 'as defined by the International Monetary Fund', but the relation between the number of units of account and gold is nowhere disclosed. The Department of Trade, however, kindly informed the writer that the rate used was 0.888671 grammes of fine gold per SDR. This was the definition of an SDR in Art. XXI of the I.M.F. Articles of Agreement in the version which was in force before 1 April 1978. After such date the rate had no realistic basis. New Conventions are likely to adopt the SDR as the unit of account. See e.g. Art. 31 of the proposed U.N. Convention on International Multimodal Transport of Goods of 24 May 1980, *Int. L.M.* 1980, 938.

[132] Cf. Mann, 95 (1979), *L.Q.R.* 348.

[133] For comparative surveys see Guisan, *La Dépréciation monétaire* (1934), pp. 155 sqq.; Reiss, *Portée internationale des lois interdisant la clause-or* (1936), pp. 11-90.

[134] If an English authority is wanted, it is supplied by *Feist*'s case ([1934] A.C. 161) which, though it does not solve all problems relating to the question of validity and though it does not expressly discuss the question of validity at all, by giving judgment for the plaintiffs implies the validity of the gold value clause.

[135] See above, p. 88.

[136] In this sense the fundamental decision Cass. Civ., 27 June 1957, D. 1957, 649 and numerous subsequent cases, in particular 4 Dec. 1962, Clunet, 1963, 750 ('texte non impératif') or 26 Nov. 1963, Bull. 1963, i. No. 516. In the same sense *Belgian* Cour de Cassation, 12 May 1932, Pas. 1932, i. 167; 1 Mar. 1945, Pas. 1945, i. 128.

valid.[137] The fact that nominalism does not have the character of mandatory law is certainly at first sight surprising, and has therefore been used as an argument against the soundness of the nominalist principle.[138] But the explanation is that nominalism is not founded on public policy, but on the supposed intention of the parties.[139]

2. Nor are protective clauses irreconcilable with classical *legal tender legislation* providing for convertible money. In so far as (gold) value clauses and foreign currency clauses are concerned, this proposition is not doubted.[140] It was, however, at some times and in some countries a serious problem whether to promise to pay in one kind of money only to the exclusion of others (gold coin clause) was valid, and if not, how the validity of the contract in general was affected thereby. While in Germany, for instance, the validity of the gold coin clause used to be firmly established,[141] the problem was much discussed in France.[142] In this country, too, the question was an open one. The difficulties arose from s. 6 of the Coinage Act, 1870, and s. 2 of the Exchange Control Act, 1947. As the former was repealed by the Decimal Currency Act, 1969, and the latter is not now operative, it is unnecessary to pursue the point.[143]

3. The question whether the issue of *inconvertible paper money,* i.e. the introduction of fiat money or compulsory tender,[144] renders gold and similar clauses invalid has repeatedly caused great difficulties in various countries.

Before the decisions of the Supreme Court of the United States in *Bronson* v. *Rodes*[145] and *Butler* v. *Horwitz*[146] enforcing the gold clause by way of judgments for gold and silver coins, its invalidity

---

[137] Planiol-Ripert, ii, No. 424; vii, Nos. 1167, 1169.

[138] See Eckstein, *Geldschuld und Geldwert*, pp. 60-74.

[139] Above, pp. 84, 85.

[140] See the concluding remarks of Lord Russell in *Feist* v. *Société Intercommunale Belge d'Électricité*, [1934] A.C. 161, 174.

[141] It even does not matter that gold coins are not in circulation, because it follows from s. 245, Civil Code (above, p. 66, n. 16), that so long as this situation persists, obligations are to be fulfilled by the tender of paper money at the nominal rate.

[142] See Mater, p. 178, n. 8, with further references; but see also Planiol-Ripert, who regard the gold coin clause as invalid (vii, No. 1167) and apparently adopt the same attitude with regard to gold value clauses (vii, No. 1170), though commodity and sliding scale clauses, unless they refer to gold, are regarded as valid (vii, Nos. 1174, 1175). According to Lyon–Caen et Renault, *Traité de droit commercial* (1925), iv, No. 762, gold coin clauses are valid.

[143] It was fully dealt with in previous editions of this work and arose from observations made in the Court of Appeal in *Feist* v. *Société Intercommunale Belge d'Électricité*, [1934] A.C. 181. [1933] Ch. 684, 687-93; see also the Australian case of *Jolley* v. *Mainka* (1933), 49 C.L.R. 242 and the inconclusive observations in *Treseder–Griffin* v. *Co-operative Insurance Society*, [1956] 2 Q.B. 127, at p. 148 *per* Denning L.J., at p. 156 *per* Morris L.J.

[144] On these terms see above, p. 41.

[145] (1868) 7 Wall. (74 U.S.) 229.      [146] Ibid. 258.

was in fact asserted by an imposing number of American State courts, which regarded the gold clause as invalidated by implication, inasmuch as the legislation of Congress had made the inconvertible greenbacks legal tender.[147] The contrary decisions of the Supreme Court were at the time 'a real innovation'.[148]

Shortly after these decisions upholding the gold clause the French Cour de Cassation, falling into line with the arguments of the American State courts, inaugurated[149] and continued for a little more than eighty years a practice to the effect that a *cours forcé* introduced in France in August 1870, and then again in August 1914, invalidated all gold (coin or value) and other protective clauses referring to gold or foreign exchange, the reasons being that the monetary laws in question were 'd'ordre public' and that consequently 'le créancier ne peut légalement se refuser à recevoir en paiement un papier de crédit auquel la loi a attribué une valeur obligatoirement équivalent à celle des espèces métalliques'.[150] The very wide meaning thus given to the 'force libératoire de la monnaie-papier', it is true, did not apply when the clause was attached to a 'paiement international', 'l'ordre public, exclusivement fondé sur un intérêt national, n'étant intéressé au cours forcé qu'en ce qui concerne les paiements en France par les Français'.[151] On the other hand, the principle

---

[147] See the references in Dawson, 'Gold Clause Decisions', 33 (1935) *Mich. L.R.* 647, 674, n. 54; Sedgwick, *On Damages*, 9th ed. (1912), i, s. 270.    [148] Dawson, l.c., p. 675.

[149] See, however, Szlechter (quoted above, p. 88, n. 39), who shows that the decree of 1551 introducing the *cours forcé* did not apply to the transactions of foreign merchants and left protective clauses largely intact.

[150] Cass. Civ. 11 Feb. 1873, S. 1873, l. 97. See on this question the discussion and the material collected by Mater, *Rev. dr. banc.* 1923, 193, 289; Planiol–Ripert–Esmein, vii, Nos. 1165 sqq.; Degand, *Rép. dr. int.* iii (1929), 'Change', Nos. 33 sqq.; André–Prudhomme, Clunet, 1931, 5, or the more recent survey by Mazeaud, *Leçons de Droit Civil* (3rd ed., 1966), ii, sections 872 sqq.

[151] Cass. Req. 7 June 1920, S. 1920, l. 193 (Compagnie d'Assurance La New York *v.* Deschamps). On the meaning of the term 'paiement international' there exists an extensive line of later decisions collected and discussed by the authors mentioned in the preceding note. An excellent survey is also given by Mestre, *Quelques Aspects juridiques des paiements internationaux* (Cahiers de droit étranger, No. 5, 1934), pp. 9–38. It seems to be *communis opinio* in France that the best definition of a 'paiement international' is that given by the Attorney-General Paul Matter in his argument in the case resulting in the decision of the Cour de Cassation of 17 May 1927, D. 1928, 1. 25 (Pélissier du Besset), when he said that 'il faut que le contrat produise, comme un mouvement de flux et de reflux au-dessus des frontières, des conséquences réciproques dans un pays et dans un autre'. This definition underlies Art. 6 of the Statute of 1 Oct. 1936 repealed by Art. 1 of the Statute of 18 Feb. 1937 ('impliquant double transfert de fonds de pays à pays'). At a later stage the Cour de Cassation seems to prefer the following formula: 'le caractère international d'une opération ne dépend pas du lieu stipulé pour son règlement, mais de sa nature et des divers éléments qui entrent en ligne de compte, quel que soit le domicile des contractants, pour imprimer aux mouvements de fonds qu'elle comporte un caractère dépassant le cadre de l'économie interne' (Cass. Civ. 14 Feb. 1934, D.P. 1934, l. 78, *re* Banque hypothécaire franco-argentine). The principle that in case of 'paiements internationaux' gold and similar clauses

extended to all protective clauses[152] such as foreign currency liabilities or currency clauses[153] or 'clauses d'échelle mobile' which link the amount due with the price of commodities or an index, though in the case of the latter clauses another remarkable distinction for a time reared its head: they were valid if the parties had an 'intention économique' and, accordingly, aimed at protection against fluctuations of prices or other economic changes, but they were struck down as illegal if the parties had an 'intention monétaire', i.e. contemplated protection against the depreciation of money;[154] while in this respect all the circumstances had to be taken into consideration, the reciprocity of the arrangements (or its absence) and the connection of the yardstick with the nature and purpose of the contract were treated as particularly indicative. In 1957, however, in a case of a loan of francs granted by a corn merchant to farmers and repayable by amounts based on the price of wheat, most, if not the whole, of this judge-made edifice, created by many hundreds of reported cases, was swept away by a truly revolutionary decision of the Cour de Cassation: rediscovering the limits of the judicial function and remitting the problem to the legislator,[155] it denied the existence of any *ordre public* that could render clauses 'd'échelle mobile' invalid.[156] Thus one can now read that 'l'ordre public n'exige

are valid was put on a statutory basis by the Acts of 25 June 1928 and 18 Feb. 1937 (printed, e.g., Clunet, 1928, 1161 or D.P. 1937, 4. 65).

[152] There was at no time any doubt about the validity of commodity clauses in the strict sense such as a tenant's promise to supply by way of rent 'deux quintaux de blé par hectare': Cass. Req. 18 Feb. and 18 Mar. 1929, S. 1930, 1. 1.

[153] See below, p. 196.

[154] Some of the more important decisions are Cass. Req. 1 Aug. 1929, S. 1930, 1. 97; Cass. Civ. 2 Aug. 1948, S. 1949, 1. 188; 26 Oct. 1948, S. 1949, 1. 89; 28 Feb. 1949, S. 1949, 1. 179; 15 Nov. 1950, S. 1951, 1. 131; 12 Mar. 1952, D. 1952, 337; Cass. Civ. 3 Nov. 1953, S. 1954, 1. 17. The clause is invalid, if the parties 'ont eu en vue non un changement des circonstances économiques, mais uniquement une variation du pouvoir d'achat de la monnaie française': Cass. Civ. 24 July 1939, G.d.T. 3 Feb. 1940; 22 Nov. 1951, Gaz. Pal. 1951, 2. 395 on which see a note at 65 (1952) Harv. L.R. 1459. The distinction is not made less tenuous by the formula adopted in the last mentioned decision which invalidates clauses of the type in question, which 'dans l'intention des parties sont conclus en vue de faire échec aux dispositions de la loi sur le cour forcé'. Cass. Civ. 15 Nov. 1950, S. 1951, 1. 131, held that a 'clause d'échelle mobile' is invalid, if a minimum sum, payable in any event, is fixed and if, therefore, 'en excluant la réciprocité la clause litigieuse n'avait d'autre but que de prémunir le bailleur contre la dépréciation possible de la monnaie'. The literature is enormous. Apart from the usual textbooks see Doucet, *L'Indexation* (1965). For the earlier period see, for instance, Hubert, *Revue Trimestrielle de Droit Civil* 1947, 1, or Rist, *L'Échelle mobile* (1954), or Vasseur, 4 (1955) *I.C.L.Q.* 315; 20 (1955) *Tulane L.R.* 75. Ligeropoulos, *Revue hellénique de droit international* 8 (1955), 20, 22 reports that the French practice had a counterpart in Greece where by virtue of legislation gold and index clauses are invalid, but where it was decided in 1953 that a protective clause based on the price of commodities is valid if the parties had reasonable economic motives, and did not aim at protection against the depreciation of money.        [155] Below, p. 169.

[156] Cass. Civ. 27 June 1957, D. 1957, 649 with note by Ripert, also *RabelsZ.* 1959,

pas, dans le prêt d'argent, une protection des emprunteurs contre la libre acceptation du risque d'une majoration de la somme à rembourser, destinée à conserver à celle-ci le pouvoir d'achat de la somme prêtée apréciée par rapport au coût d'une denrée, dès lors qu'ils peuvent assumer des risques de même importance dans d'autre contrats'. Nor were such clauses a danger to the stability of monetary values, 'l'influence desdites clauses à cet égard apparaissant en l'état trop incertaine pour légitimer une nullité, portant une atteinte grave à la sécurité de l'épargne et du crédit'. Nor could the nullity of protective clauses be derived from current monetary laws, 'celles-ci ne pouvant impliquer l'invariabilité du pouvoir d'achat de la monnaie'. In view of such reasoning it is not surprising that since 1957 gold value clauses[157] as well as foreign currency liabilities[158] have been held to be valid even where there was no question of an international payment.[159] These French developments which at no time had a counterpart in any other country.[160, 161] teach a great

534. See also Cass. Civ. 18 Mar. 1958, D. 1958, 653, also *RabelsZ.* 1959, 536. For a clear summary (in German) see Mezger, ibid. p. 437.

[157] Cass. Civ. 4 Dec. 1962, Clunet, 1963, 751 with note by Goldman, 26 Nov. 1963, Sem. Jur. 1964, 13652, or Bull. 1963, i. No. 516.

[158] Cass. Civ. 10 May 1966, Clunet, 1967, 90 with note by Goldman; see 17 Jan. 1961, Bull. Cass. Civ. 1961, i. 32. See below, p. 000, n. 65.

[159] The state of the law seems to be somewhat fluid, since there are, surprisingly, at least two decisions which render the international character of the payment the ratio decidendi: Cass. Com. 27 Apr. 1964, Clunet, 1964, 819 with note by Dayant; Cass. Civ. 4 May 1964, Rev. Crit. 1965, 348 with not eby Eck. About the problem Eck, *Rev. Crit.* 1964, 441; Malaurie, Clunet, 1966, 571.

[160] In particular the Belgian Cour de Cassation held that, while the gold coin was invalid (27 Apr. 1933, Clunet, 1933, 739), the gold value clause was valid: 12 May 1932, Pas. 1932, i. 167. So is the index clause: Cass. 1 Dec. 1966 Rev. Crit. *Jurisprudence Belge*, 1968, 419. See De Vos, *Le Problème des conflits de lois* (Brussels, 1946), ii. 669 and Poullet, *Manuel de droit international privé belge* (3rd ed., 1947), p. 525. The French practice applied wherever the French monetary system was in control, e.g. in the Saar Territory: Court of Appeal Sarrebruck, 21 July 1949, Clunet, 1952, 354, and in Monaco: Cour de Monaco, 22 Apr. 1939, Clunet, 1939, 772. The French distinction between 'paiement international' and 'paiement national' was rejected in Egypt: Mixed Appeal Court, 31 Mar. 1938, B.I.J.I. 39 (1938), 352. There is no point in collecting material to prove a negative. For a general survey see, for instance, Van Hecke, pp. 158, 159, and, as regards index clauses, Vasseur, 'L'indexation à l'étranger', *Revue économique*, 1955, 275. Toulemon, *Rev. Trim. de Droit Commercial*, 1963, 443. It should, however, be noted that as regards the law of *Switzerland* Herzfeld, *Festgabe zum Schweizerischen Juristentag 1963* (Basel, 1963), 77, suggests the invalidity of index clauses on the ground of public policy; but, as he admits, his view is not generally accepted. On the other hand, the Supreme Court of *Israel* held that protective clauses are not contrary to public policy, as experts were not agreed that they had inflationary effect so as to prejudice the economy as a whole: *Rosenbaum v. Asher, Selected Judgments of the Supreme Court of Israel*, vol. ii (1954–8), 10; similarly *Becher v. Biderman, Jerusalem Post*, 30 June 1963.

[161] Something akin to the French conception of the 'paiement international' is envisaged by the London Agreement on German External Debts, which provides for a special rate of conversion for such debts expressed in German currency 'as had a specific foreign character': Cmnd. 626 (Art. VI (2), Annex IV and Annex VII). The numerous decisions

lesson and for this reason alone they should not be allowed to sink into oblivion. As will appear, the law at present prevailing in France is laid down by parliamentary rather than judicial legislation.

In view of the decision of the House of Lords in *Feist* v. *Société Intercommunale Belge d'Électricité*[162] it cannot be doubted that in English law (gold) value clauses are not affected by the issue of inconvertible paper money initiated by the Gold Standard (Amendment) Act, 1931. Commenting on the decision of the House of Lords in *Feist's* case, Professor Gutteridge,[163] it is true, pointed out that the clause had been upheld 'notwithstanding the provisions of the Currency and Bank Notes Act, 1928'. There is, however, nothing in this Act that expressly or by necessary implication can be said to invalidate a gold or other protective clause.

4. In the course of the comment just referred to Professor Gutteridge also said that the decision 'is silent on the question whether such clauses are contrary to public policy or not, but it is significant that this issue was not raised either by counsel for the defendants or by the Court'. But although the decision is silent on the point, silence in this case is affirmation, because the gold value clause was in fact enforced. Moreover in 1952, in a domestic Australian case, the High Court of Australia held[164] that in the case of an index clause there was no question concerning the medium or form of currency to be used in paying the debt. 'Whatever the liability of the purchaser may be ascertained to be, that liability is to be discharged in whatever the law regards as legal tender when payment is made by as many units of currency as amount to the sum so ascertained.' In particular,

There is no principle of law preventing parties adopting a fixed figure as the primary monetary expression of a liability and then proceeding to effect a substantive variation of the liability by providing that more or less money must be actually paid according as index numbers evidence a variation of price levels. That is only a method of measuring the actual liability contracted for.

Nonetheless in 1956 Denning L.J. (as he then was) denied, or at any rate was 'not altogether sure', that in a purely domestic English contract a gold clause was lawful: he strongly inclined to the view that as a matter of public policy gold clauses should not be allowed to render sterling 'a discredited currency unable to look its enemy

---

are collected by Staudinger–Weber, vol. ii, Part 1a, at p. 1007. Add Federal Supreme Court, 30 Jan. 1967, IPRspr. 1966–7, No. 214. See the fundamental decision of the Mixed Arbitral Commission, 7 Nov. 1956, *Int. L.R.* 1958, i. 326. The French distinction has, in effect, partly been adopted by the German legislator: below, p. 197, n. 67.

[162] [1934] A.C. 161.       [163] 51 (1935), *L.Q.R.* 115.

[164] *Stanwell Park Hotel Co. Ltd.* v. *Leslie*, [1952] 85 C.L.R. 189, at pp. 200, 201.

inflation in the face'.[165] It is submitted that such a view would be without statutory basis and contrary to the practice of the House of Lords in gold clause cases, that English municipal law knows no distinction between national and international contracts and that in the English legal system it is not for the Judiciary to proclaim a political policy which Parliament has refrained from carrying into effect.[166]

It is, therefore, satisfactory to note that in *Multiservice Bookbinding Ltd.* v. *Marden*[167] Browne-Wilkinson J. rejected the submission that 'an index-linked money obligation is contrary to public policy'. In that case an English mortgage included the clause that 'moneys hereby secured shall be increased or decreased proportionately . . . if the rate of exchange between the Swiss franc and the pound sterling shall vary by more than 3 per cent from the rate of 12.07 francs to £1.' While the clause was somewhat untypical, the learned Judge's general and unqualified statement is to be welcomed.

He held at the same time that, while a mortgage could be unenforceable if its terms were unfair and unconscionable, the mere addition of an index clause did not have this effect. As the learned Judge pointed out, it would have been difficult to decide otherwise, seeing that index-linked Savings Bonds have been issued by the Government and the Pensions (Increase) Act, 1971, also provides for indexation.[168, 169]

5. There thus remains only one possibility of invalidating gold and other clauses, and that is special and express *legislation*. Indeed, this method has been resorted to whenever it was desired in this country to ensure the strictest observation of the nominalistic principle, and its absence is further proof, if such be needed, of the validity of gold clauses under present conditions.

It is interesting to note that as early as 1352 the statute 25 Edw.

---

[165] *Treseder–Griffin* v. *Co-operative Insurance Society*, [1956] 2 Q.B. 127, at p. 145.

[166] This is a summary of the principal criticism expressed by Goodhart, 72 (1956), *L.Q.R.* 311; Mann, 73 (1957), *L.Q.R.* 181; Unger, 20 (1957), *Mod.L.R.* 260; Yale, 1956, *C.L.J.* 169; Hirschberg, *Israel L.R.* 1970, 155. Cf. Chitty, *On Contracts* (24th ed., 1977), section 1312.

[168] Section 2, and see the Pensions (Increase) Act, 1974. See also Finance Act 1971, s. 32 and Finance Act 1980; s. 24 about the 'Indexation of income tax thresholds and allowances.'                                                    [167] [1979] Ch. 84.

[169] In *Aztec Properties Inc.* v. *Union Planters National Bank of Memphis*, 530 S.W. 2d 756 (1975), the Supreme Court of Tennessee (where usury laws are in force) held that 'indexed principal' constituted usurious interest, though the decision is possibly limited 'to the principal of a debt evidenced by a promissory note'. At the same time the court emphasized that there was 'no impropriety' in measuring future rentals, wages or salaries by a consumer price index, such indexing being 'a current and very legitimate concept in modern business transactions.' Usury as a ground of invalidity was rejected by the Supreme Court of *Chile*: Lopez-Santa Maria, pp. 45, 67.

III, ch. 12, prohibited the making of any profit on exchanging coined gold for coined silver or coined silver for coined gold, and this provision was re-enacted by the Statute 5 & 6 Edw. VI, ch. 19, which provided

that if any person or persons after the 1st April next shall exchange any coined gold, coined silver or money, giving receiving or paying any more in value benefit profit or advantage for it than the same is or shall be declared by the King's Majesty his proclamation to be current for, within this his Realm and other dominions.

the money was forfeited and the wrongdoer was liable to imprisonment. It was this Act which, during the Bank Restriction period, prevented people from quoting openly two prices for commodities, one for payment in guineas and the other for payment in paper, but the practice existed in secret and it was also usual to buy guineas for paper at more than face value.[170] Two obscure men were prosecuted, but after the case had given rise to considerable public excitement,[171] the accused were acquitted.[172] The effect of this decision was, however, promptly remedied by Parliament,[173] and by Lord Liverpool's Act of 1816[174] it was provided (s. 13)

that from and after the passing of this Act no person shall by any means device, shift or contrivance whatsoever receive or pay for any gold coin lawfully current within the United Kingdom of Great Britain and Ireland any more or less in value, benefit, profit, or advantage than the true lawful value which such gold coin does or shall by its denomination import.

This provision as well as the earlier enactments have long ago been repealed.[175] Although as a result of monetary disturbances many countries felt compelled to invalidate gold and similar clauses by legislative measures,[176] no such steps were taken in this country,

---

[170] Feavearyear, pp. 200, 207.

[171] Lord King published a pamphlet on it, and see the debates in the House of Commons on 5 Apr. and 9 July 1811 in Hansard, xix. 723 and xx. 881 sqq.

[172] De Yonge's case (1811), 14 East 403; Feavearyear, p. 207, suggests that the reason was that there had been no paper money in the reign of Edward VI. But this is not mentioned by the reporter.

[173] 51 Geo. III, ch. 127 (24 July 1811); see 52 Geo. III, ch. 50.

[174] 56 Geo. III, ch. 68.

[175] By 2 & 3 Will. IV, ch. 34, s. 1; Coinage Act, 1870, s. 20; and by Statute Law Revision Act, 1873.

[176] Nussbaum, p. 280, n. 5, collected a great number of enactments, particularly in Australia, Austria, Belgium, Brazil, Canada, Chile, Colombia, Costa Rica, Cuba, Denmark, Ecuador, Egypt, Germany, Greece, Guatemala, Honduras, Hungary, Italy, Luxemburg, Mexico, Netherlands, Paraguay, Poland, Salvador, South Africa, Sweden, Turkey, United States of America. For a useful survey of the law in thirteen countries in the 1950s see the material collected by Norway in the Case of Certain Norwegian Loans (France v. Norway) in the International Court of Justice: Pleadings, i. 491 sqq.

and in the course of the last few years the demonetization of, and the freedom of dealings in, gold, accompanied by increasing inflation, produced much more liberal tendencies in many parts of the world. In particular, by an Act of 28 October 1977,[177] the United States of America repealed the notorious Joint Resolution of Congress of 5 June 1933 in respect of future obligations and thus brought to an end a period during which the condemnation of gold and similar clauses seemed to be almost an article of faith in the United States.[178]

The scope of abrogating legislation varies considerably. Some statutes are limited to certain types of contract.[179] Others are limited to gold clauses or even to such gold clauses as are attached to debts expressed in domestic currency.[180] The *Finnish* legislation of 1968 is directed against index clauses only.[181] On the other hand, the *French* legislation of 1958-9 applies to most types of protective clauses, but also exempts a large class of transactions.[182]

[177] Public Law 95-147, section 3 (c).

[178] For the text of the Joint Resolution see e.g. Nussbaum, p. 282. The suggestion that the law of 31 Dec. 1974 which had lifted the prohibition of dealings in gold had impliedly repealed the Joint Resolution was rejected by the Sixth Circuit Court of Appeals in *The Equitable Life Assurance* v. *Grosvenor*, 582 F. 2d 1279 (1978), affirming without opinion 426 F. Supp. 2d 67 (1976), and by the Eighth Circuit Court of Appeals in *Southern Capital Corporation* v. *Southern Pacific Co.*, 568 F. 2d 590 (1978), as well as in New York in *Feldman* v. *Great Northern Railway*, 428 F. Supp. 979 (1977) and in California in *Henderson* v. *Mann Theaters Corporation*, 135 Cal. Rep. 266 (1977).

[179] See, for example, Belgium (law of 11 Apr. 1935, Piret, pp. 264 sqq.) or the Netherlands (law of 14 May 1937, RabelsZ. 1937, 275). In Switzerland Art. 14 of a decree of 11 Sept. 1931 precludes insurance companies from agreeing to perform contracts of insurance on the basis of a protective clause.

[180] The American Joint Resolution applied to all obligations requiring payment of dollars 'in gold or a particular kind of coin or currency', but did not affect index clauses: Dach, 12 (1945), *George Washington L.R.* 328.Yet, somewhat surprisingly, in *Aztec Properties Inc.* v. *Union Planters National Bank of Memphis*, 530 S.W. 2d 756 (1975), the Supeme Court of Tennessee held that, subject to the mysterious qualifications mentioned above, p. 167, n. 169, the Joint Resolution applied to index clauses. The law of *Brazil* prohibits gold and foreign currency clauses, but, at any rate in most cases, seems to allow index clauses: Wald, RabelsZ. 1971, 268, at p. 278; Lipkau in Kötz-Reichert-Facilides, *Inflationsbewältigung im Zivil- und Arbeitsrecht* (Frankfurt, 1976), p. 11. The same publication includes a helpful general survey by Spiros Simitis on mastering inflation: p. 49. On South America generally see Lopez-Santa Maria, pp. 59 sqq.

[181] Economic Special Powers Act, 1968; Suviranta, p. 41 of the German publication referred to in the preceding note.

[182] The effect of the decree of 30 Dec. 1958 as amended by the decree of 4 Feb. 1959 and supplemented by statutes of 1970 and 1977 is very uncertain and has given rise to many decisions and much discussion. See, for example, Doucet, *L'Indexation* (1965); de la Marnierre, *Revue Trimistrielle de Droit Civil* 1977, 54; Tendler, D. Chron. 1977, 245 or such general works as Marty & Raymaud, *Droit Civil* II (1962), pp. 613 sqq.; Weill et Terré, *Droit Civil*, II (3rd ed., 1980), sections 1004 sqq.; or Mazeaud, *Leçons de Droit Civil* (3rd ed., 1966), s. 879. In contracts made after 1958 all clauses determining the amount due by reference to the level of prices or salaries or the price of goods, products or services are prohibited if there is no direct relation with the subject matter of

In *Germany* the Occupation Authorities of England, France, and the United States of America probably succeeded in abrogating all protective clauses agreed before 21 June 1948;[183] moreover their legislation was no doubt intended by a most comprehensive and sweeping provision to prohibit protective clauses agreed after such date without the permission of the Federal Bank,[184] but judicial practice restricted the prohibition in so remarkable a manner as to create many opportunities of avoidance.[185]

the contract or the business of one of the parties. Clauses agreed before the end of 1958 (if valid under the law then prevailing) cease to have effect beyond the level then reached if they directly or indirectly concern reciprocal obligations involving successive performances.

[183] The first step had been taken by the decree of 16 Nov. 1940 (*Reichsgesetzblatt*, i. 1521) in conjunction with s. 14 (s) of the Reichsbank Law of 15 June 1939 (*Reichsgesetzblatt*, i. 1015) which provided, in effect, that Goldmark debts were performable by the payment of reichsmark at the rate of one Goldmark to one reichsmark. The next stage was reached by Art. II of *Allied Military Law*, No. 51, as amended on 1 July 1947, *Military Government Gazette*, p. 567 which the German courts confined to extremely narrow limits; see p. 129, note 1 of the second edition of this work and the literature referred to below. Thirdly, the Conversion Law of 1948 abrogated all protective clauses (Federal Supreme Court 24 Mar. 1960, *WM*. 1960, 940; 4 Dec. 1963, *Wertpapiermitteilungen*, 1964, 248) except in so far as they did not relate to fixed sums, but provided for the payment of a sum to be determined by a defined process (e.g. an amount corresponding to the proceeds of sale of certain machinery): Federal Supreme Court 7 May 1951, *NJW*. 1951, 841, and (in the same case) 14 July 1952, *BGHZ*. 7, 143. For a useful survey of the legal development in Germany from 1914 to 1953 see von Caemmerer, *Deutsche Landesreferate zum IV. Internationalen Kongress für Rechtsvergleichung in Paris 1954* (ed. by E. Wolff, 1955), p. 84.

[184] S. 3 of the Currency Law of 1948 requires permission for the contracting of 'money debts the Deutsche Mark amount of which is to be fixed in terms of the exchange rate for some other currency or by the price or quantity of fine gold or other goods or performances'. The provision does not create an illegality, but suspends the effectiveness of the contract pending the grant or refusal of a licence; this was correctly decided by the Austrian Supreme Court (28 Oct. 1969, *Zeitschrift für Rechtsvergleichung* 1971, 32) and is likely to mean that even in the eyes of a German court a clause violating s. 3 is valid if the contract is governed by a non-German law. As a result of progressive inflation s. 3 is being criticized by many: see, for instance, von Arnim, *Zeitschrift für Rechtspolitik* 1980, 201 with numerous references, but against him the Federal Minister of Finance, ibid. p. 325. It may well be that the retention of the provision will one day be held unconstitutional. It was, of course, introduced into German law by the American occupation authorities at a time when the abrogation of the gold clause was a policy of faith in the United States of such strength that it succeeded in compelling Germany's foreign creditors to waive by the Agreement on German External Debts of 27 February 1953 (Cmnd. 626) gold clauses attached to debts of German debtors irrespective of the proper law to which they were subject.

[185] In particular the Federal Supreme Court held that the Deutsche Mark amount is not 'fixed' and that, therefore, s. 3 is inapplicable if, for instance, (1) the rent is fixed but subject to equitable adjustment in the event of a change of the cost of living (4 June 1962, *NJW*. 1962, 1393; 25 Jan. 1967, *NJW*. 1967, 830; and 12 Jan. 1968, *NJW*. 1969, 91) or if (2) the amount due is to be brought into line with the future price or rate payable in comparable circumstances such as the salary of civil servants or the rent or similar premises (17 Sept. 1954, *BGHZ*. 14, 306; 27 June 1973, *NJW*. 1973, 1498; 17 Dec. 1973, *NJW*. 1974, 273; 26 Nov. 1975, *NJW*. 1976, 422; 23 Feb. 1979, *NJW*. 1979, 1545) or if

As regards the territorial scope of such statutes its definition often raises difficult questions of construction (not of private international law). As a general rule it may be a workable suggestion that they do not affect protective clauses attached to promises to pay another money than that of the legislating State. This rule has been repeatedly applied,[186] especially in connection with the interpretation of the American Joint Resolution of Congress of 5 June 1933.[187] But otherwise no hard-and-fast rule can be laid down, and as regards the Joint Resolution, various attempts to exclude its application were bound to fail, because its wording left no doubt that it applied irrespective of whether creditor or debtor was a national of or residing or domiciled in the United States,[188] or whether the place of payment or collection was or was not situate within the United States.[189, 190]

(3) the promisee's own costs rise and the amount payable to him is to rise correspondingly, as where the price of electricity rises with the price of coal (21 Oct. 1958, *Betriebsberater* 1958, 1220; 4 July 1979, *WM.* 1979, 1097) or if (4) the consideration exclusively or alternatively consists of the delivery of goods, as in the case in which the borrower undertakes to repay the loan or to deliver a quantity of wheat or pay the price of the latter (12 Feb. 1953, *BGHZ.* 9, 56, 63; 9 July 1956, *NJW.* 1957, 342; 8 Feb. 1961, *Betriebsberater* 1961, 586). For full details see the usual Commentaries on s. 244 of the Civil Code or Dürkes, *Wertsicherungsklauseln* (8th ed., 1972). The most remarkable aspect of the practice of the Federal Supreme Court is that if on account of the refusal of permission a clause is invalid it is the duty of the court to imply a clause as having been agreed which would be valid even in the absence of permission: 30 Oct. 1974, *BGHZ.* 63, 132; 6 Dec. 1978, *NJW.* 1979, 2250. The circumstances in which the Federal Bank will grant a permission are explained in a Directive of 1978, *NJW.* 1978, 2381.

[186] See, for example, Supreme Court of Romania, 29 Sept. 1925, *Zeitschrift für Ostecht*, 1925, 600.

[187] But see the cases below, p. 197, n. 68. The wording of the Resolution made it quite clear that only dollar obligations are caught.

[188] *Compañia de Inversiones* v. *Industrial Mortgage Bank of Finland* (1935), 269 N.Y. 22, 198 N.E. 617, cert. den. (1936), 297 U.S. 705; Swedish Supreme Court, 30 Jan. 1937, *British Year Book of International Law*, 1937, 215, 217, and *B.I.J.I.* 36 (1937), 327; German Supreme Court 28 May 1936, *JW.* 1936, 2058, 2060, and Plesch, *The Gold Clause*, ii. 30; Cologne Court of Appeal, 13 Sept. 1935, *JW.* 1936, 203; Düsseldorf Court of Appeal, 29 June 1934, *IPRspr.* 1934, 200, 301; Brussels Court of Appeal, 4 Feb. 1936, S. 1937, 4. 1, with note by Mestre.

[189] See German Supreme Court, 28 May 1936, *ubi supra*. This point which is more doubtful, is also discussed by Rabel, *RabelsZ.* 10 (1936), 492, 507.

[190] Problems of the character discussed in the text arise in connection with numerous statutes other than those relating to the abrogation of gold clauses. Thus it was held that the American legislation restricting dealings in gold was valid also against foreign owners of gold: *Übersee Finanz Corporation A.-G.* v. *Rosen*, 83 F. (2d) 225 (C.C.A. 2d. 1936) and *B.I.J.I.* 35 (1936), 314, cert. den. (1936), 298 U.S. 679; the Privy Council held that the Victorian Financial Emergency Acts, reducing the amount of interest payable, did not affect debentures governed by New Zealand law and charging land situate in New Zealand, though the place of payment was in Victoria: *Mount Albert Borough Council* v. *Australian Temperance and General Mutual Life Assurance Society Ltd.*, [1938] A.C. 224. The extraterritorial effects of such a statute must be considered under the head of three entirely different questions. First, as a matter of the conflict of laws, is the foreign law applicable? If so, the next question is whether and to what extent it attributes to

Finally, doubts sometimes arise as to the effect in point of time, which is to be attributed to abrogating legislation. Are protective clauses prohibited for the future only? Or are they invalidated whenever made? If so, does such invalidity extend to clauses which at the date of the legislation are already repudiated? The answers depend on the terms of the particular statute and general rules cannot be laid down.[191] It has been suggested[192] that the abrogation of gold clauses with retrospective effect 'might well expose the debtors . . . to immediate actions for money had and received'; but even if there existed any legal foundation for such actions, they could not lead to an indirect enforcement of the gold clause, but in accordance with the nominalistic principle would merely secure to the creditor the repayment of the sum of money paid by him, i.e. give him what he is entitled to under the contract from which the gold clause has been deleted.

VI

The problem of legislative policy, to which protective clauses give rise, has been appreciated for many centuries,[193] but is still neglected[194] and certainly unsolved.

itself any such effects; if it claims to have extraterritorial effects, the third question arises whether the private international law of the forum refuses to recognize them. (On this point see below, pp. 301 sqq.) The Privy Council in the above-mentioned case arrived at the correct conclusion on the basis of the Victorian legislation, though the point should have been settled by the mere fact that Victorian law was not applicable. But in the decision of the German Supreme Court of 28 May 1936 (see above, n. 188) the problem was treated as a question of German private international law, not as a question relating to the construction of the American legislation under discussion. On the general problem see Mann, 'Statutes and the Conflict of Laws', *British Year Book of International Law* 46 (1972–1973), 117.

[191] Questions of this type arose in connection with the Canadian Gold Clauses Act 1937 in *New Brunswick Rly. Co. v. British & French Trust Corporation*, [1939] A.C. 1. Probably the *ratio decidendi* is to be found in the view expressed by Lord Thankerton (p. 26), Lord Russell (p. 29), and Lord Wright (p. 34) that the Canadian Statute did not have retrospective effect; in none of these opinions, however, is it made quite clear whether the decisive element was the fact that before 1937 the bonds had been repudiated, or the fact that before 1937 there had been a (wrong) judgment in the court of first instance. The opinions delivered by Lord Maugham (pp. 22 sqq.) and by Lord Romer pp. 44 sqq.) proceed on somewhat different lines which cannot be described as altogether attractive and have provoked severe criticism by Nussbaum, p. 437. The construction put by the House of Lords on the Statute of 1937 was so surprisingly narrow that the Canadian Parliament passed the Gold Clause Act, 1938, which largely nullified the effect of the decision of the House of Lords. Nussbaum (l.c., n. 23) speaks of a 'little piece of intra-empire legal warfare'. The Canadian Acts are published also in *B.I.J.I.* 32 (1937), 109 and 41 (1939), 84.

[192] *New Brunswick Rly. Co. v. British and French Trust Corporation*, [1939] A.C. 1, at p. 24 *per* Lord Maugham L.C.

[193] Endemann, *Studien in der romanisch-kanonistischen Rechtslehre* (1883), ii. 220.

[194] It was discussed at length by the 40th Conference of German Lawyers in 1953:

So long as monetary stability prevails these clauses are unnecessary. In the event of monetary disturbances, however, they are, if widely used, liable to become intolerable, for they may create pronounced social disparity.[195] Moreover, although economists are far from unanimous on the point and lawyers will therefore refrain from forming an independent view,[196] there exists much support for the suggestion that index clauses in particular are liable to promote inflationary tendencies.[197] Consequently, a country in which such

*Verhandlungen des 40. Deutschen Juristentags*, vol. i, 5 (Opinion by Duden) and ii. D. 8 (Reports by von Caemmerer and Mann).

[195] This was emphasized by Chief Justice Hughes, when on behalf of the Court, he said in *Norman v. Baltimore & Ohio Railroad Co.*, (1934), 294 U.S. 240, at pp. 315, 316 with reference to the constitutional validity of the Joint Resolution of 1933: 'It requires no acute analysis or profound economic inquiry to disclose the dislocation of the domestic economy which would be caused by such a disparity of conditions in which, it is insisted, those debtors under gold clauses should be required to pay $1·69 in currency, while respectively receiving their taxes, rates, charges and prices on the basis of $1 of that currency.'

[196] The disagreement between economists about the effect of indexing was one of the reasons which led Browne-Wilkinson J. in *Multiservice Bookbinding Ltd. v. Mardon*, [1979] Ch. 84, at p. 104 to refuse to hold index clauses contrary to public policy. Similarly the German Federal Constitutional Court, 19 Dec. 1978, *BVerfGE* 50, 57, at pp. 101, 102 held the effect of index clauses on inflation to be a 'multilayered problem' which involves both advantages and disadvantages and is not suitable for judicial decision. On the other hand, the German Federal Administrative Court, 3 Oct. 1972, *NJW*. 1973, 529 at p. 531 declared that the increasing use of index clauses served to reinforce lack of confidence and instability and 'thus to accelerate inflationary tendencies'.

[197] The tentative conclusion stated in the text has much support which, in the absence of a comprehensive discussion of the problem by economists, must be referred to in some detail. *England*: In 1958 the Council of Prices, Productivity, and Incomes reported (First Report, paragraph 98) that sliding scale clauses were not 'a satisfactory alternative to the policy of arresting inflation' and that their 'most important result is likely to be that the upward movement of prices would cease to be slow. The final result might well be a situation so disastrous that a remedy would have to be sought at all costs.' In 1963 the Radcliffe Committee reported (Cmnd. 827, paragraph 573) on the proposal of index bonds. Such a plan 'would spread to other interest payments, and it would not be easy to restrain extension to a wide range of other payments hitherto fixed in money. Such an extension . . . would inevitably tend to accelerate the inflation.' It would be 'an expedient which would too plainly be a confession of failure to maintain a reasonable degree of stability in the value of money'. In 1980 The Wilson Committee *To Review the Functioning of Financial Institutions* (Cmnd. 7937) expressed views much more favourable to indexation in the capital markets: paragraphs 821-71. *United States of America*: the most important publication probably is *Monetary Policy and the Management of the Public Debt* (Washington D.C. 1952, U.S. Government Printing Office, No. 92245), which deals with the issue of index bonds. The Secretary to the Treasury (pp. 142 sqq.), the Council of Economic Advisers (p. 888) and the majority of the economists who were consulted (pp. 1097 sqq.) rejected the proposal, mainly on the ground that 'it would reduce the inherent resistance of the economic system to inflation'. *France*: The most important contributions are M. Vasseur, 'Le droit des clauses monétaires et les enseignements de l'économie politique', *Revue Trimestrielle de Droit Civil*, 1953, 430; and Hamel and others, 'La pratique de l'indexation', *Revue économique*, 1955, 161-321. See Planiol–Ripert, vii, No. 1185: 'L'échelle mobile peut devenir une charge écrasante pour le débiteur. Mais surtout son emploi généralisé et sans limites, quant à l'amplitude de ses effets, représenterait un

clauses are frequent will abolish them at the very moment when they are meant to prove their worth. As a distinguished economist has put it, such clauses 'are either superfluous or prejudicial or invalid'.[198] The idea that they should not be abrogated and that abrogation would *a priori* be obnoxious is 'narrow-minded and utterly unsound';[199] an idea in the opposite sense is a more serious proposition and would have much more to commend it. Indeed, there can be no doubt that it was only because protective clauses were (and are) rare in this country that Parliament could, since 1931, afford not to interfere with them; that such was and is the position in Switzerland is a matter of record.[200]

Yet it is a curious fact that no legislator, however wide he tried to cast his net, has ever succeeded in eliminating protective clauses altogether. In the United States of America index clauses[201] as well as promises to pay foreign currency[202] remained valid, and the same applied to promises to deliver commodities other than gold,[203] to make the illegality of gold clauses an article of faith (as was being done in the United States), yet to permit, for example, the index clause, does not disclose consistency of thought. In post-war Germany, it is true, the Western Allies have abolished index clauses along with gold and similar clauses,[204] but contracts for the delivery of commodities or many other types of clauses have remained valid.[205] It must be recognized that no legislator can eliminate barter. If he makes it too difficult for the parties to secure for a monetary

---

dangereux facteur d'inflation.' *Belgium*: see the illuminating discussion in the *Bulletin of the Banque Nationale de Belgique*, Vol. 50 (i), No. 5 (May 1975). *Germany*: An important opinion of the Academic Advisers to the Federal Ministry of Economics (*Gutachten des Wissenschaftlichen Beirats beim Bundeswirtschaftsministerium*, vol. 5, p. 19, published at Göttingen, 1961) concludes that 'the automatism of the index, proposed as protection against the effect of inflation, means that inflationary tendencies are generalized and accelerated'. In the same sense Otto Veit, *Grundriss der Währungspolitik* (3rd ed., 1969), 164 sqq.; Hahn, below, n. 198; but see also Lubasch, *Die volkswirtschaftlichen Wirkungen von Geldwertsicherungsklauseln* (Berlin, 1964). For a particular guarded discussion see Ottmar Issing, *Indexklauseln und Inflation* (Tübingen, 1973), particularly pp. 39 sqq. Much further material is mentioned by Bernd von Maydell, *Geldschuld und Geldwert*, p. 389. *Sweden*: the Report referred to above, p. 158, n. 118, seems to be alone in concluding that index bonds would not endanger a stable monetary value (pp. 35, 92). *Hungary*: Nogaro, *A Short Treatise on Money and Monetary Systems* (London, 1949, pp. 118, 121, 200, attributes much of the Hungarian inflation to the widespread use of sliding wage scales.

[198] L. Albert Hahn, *Zeitschrift für das Gesamte Kreditwesen*, 10 (1957) 501. See Gadolin, ibid., p. 373 on Finland.

[199] Wolff, *Private International Law* (2nd ed., 1950), p. 469.

[200] *Schweizerische National Bank*, 1907–57 (Zürich, 1957), p. 166; Bachmann, *Zeitschrift für schweizerisches Recht*, 56 (1937), 472a, 473a.

[201] Above, p. 169, n. 180.                    [202] Below, p. 197, n. 68

[203] Dealings in gold became illegal by virtue of the Gold Reserve Act of 30 Jan. 1934.

[204] Above, p. 170, n. 183 and n. 184.            [205] Above, p. 170, n. 185.

obligation such protection as may be required, he will merely drive them into barter transactions of a somewhat old-fashioned type. In the case of agricultural rents or mortgages a solution on these lines will be readily found, but even in other cases a skilful draftsman will often succeed by adopting revision, adaptation or hardship clauses.

In these circumstances the question arises whether, accepting the hopelessness of his task and the fortuitous character of his measures, the legislator should refrain altogether from attempting to abolish protective clauses. The question should not be put, and certainly cannot be answered, dogmatically. Much will depend on the circumstances prevailing in the country concerned. The danger of inflation, inherent in the maintenance of protective clauses, and the danger of creating too pronounced a distinction between classes of creditors may be too pressing to be ignored. On the other hand it must be realized that inflationary tendencies cannot be resisted by legal weapons in general or the abolition of protective clauses in particular, and that, to encourage savings and investments, it is justifiable and necessary to create, and not at the crucial moment to disappoint, a sense of security and confidence. But in no event should the creditor's disillusionment be increased by arbitrarily limiting the abolition to particular types of protective clauses.

For these reasons it is submitted that the legislator should arrive at a deliberate decision about protective clauses of all types in times of economic stability and that he should abide by that decision in times of crisis; in no case should the judiciary assume, on this point, the functions of the legislature.[206] That decision, it is further suggested, will not necessarily have to be uniform, but may have to differentiate both between various types of protective clauses and between various types of transactions, and should be secured by appropriate constitutional guarantees. Nothing would be more discreditable or contrary to public policy than for a legislator to allow protective clauses, if only by implication, thus to create the impression that they afford effective protection, yet in a critical situation to abrogate them almost automatically and perhaps haphazardly.

---

[206] As was formerly done in France, see above, p. 163.

# PART II

# FOREIGN MONEY
# OBLIGATIONS

# INTRODUCTION

# Foreign Currency and its General Relations with Municipal and Private International Law

## I

THE first part of this book is devoted to the legal position of a domestic currency within the sphere of its own domestic law (e.g. English money in England under English law). The second part, on which we are now entering, deals with the position of a currency other than that of the given country, within the sphere of such country's private international and municipal law (e.g. French currency in England). But the case of a sum of English money payable under an obligation governed by a foreign law (e.g. pounds sterling under a French contract) is nowhere treated in the present work. This has been found unnecessary, since in respect of the purely monetary problems raised by such a case no difficulty will arise in adapting to it the rules which have already been and which will in the following part be evolved in connection with the other combinations just mentioned.

## II

There is probably no branch of the law where the intrinsic connection between private international law and municipal law is more apparent and more difficult than that relating to foreign currency.[1]

Wherever foreign currency comes into play, three legal systems may have to be considered: the law of the obligation or the proper law or the *lex causae*;[2] the law of the currency, i.e. the law of the country whose currency is stipulated to be payable; and the *lex fori*, i.e. English law.

---

[1] There are in monetary law many examples of confusion between these distinct branches of the law. Such confusion also underlies large parts of Arts. 426–42 of Frankenstein's *Projet d'un Code Européen de droit international privé* (Bibliotheca Visseriana, 1950).

[2] These terms are here and throughout used in their widest sense, covering all cases where a foreign money obligation arises, whether it be under a contract, will, tort, etc., and denoting that law which in the respective case applies, whether it be the proper law of the contract, the law of the testator's domicil, the law governing the tort, and so forth.

The necessity for having regard to these three legal systems is most evident where under a foreign obligation there arises the duty to pay a sum of foreign money, whether it be the money of the country whose law governs the obligation, or of a third country: e.g. where under a contract governed by French law the debtor is obliged to pay French francs or Chilean pesos. Here it falls to English private international law to ascertain the proper law of the obligation and the law of the currency, and to decide how far the former applies and which questions are to be answered by the latter. The province of the law of the obligation and of the law of the currency thus having been determined by the rules of English private international law, all further questions are to be answered by the respective municipal laws, a comparative survey of which, in so far as monetary problems are concerned, will be found in the first part.

But the three systems mentioned above must also be considered in the other case where a conflict of laws of a more limited nature is involved. If an obligation governed by English law results in a duty to pay a sum of foreign money (e.g. a business man in London makes a loan of U.S.$100 to a Liverpool merchant), it is clear that foreign law, namely U.S. federal law, cannot have any influence except for the fact that U.S.A. dollars are payable. Though the law of the obligation and the forum is English, the law of the currency may have to be considered. The question might be raised whether the necessity for having regard to American law is due to the fact that federal law is referred to as the 'proper law' in respect of the particular questions connected with currency, or to the fact that the law of the United States is merely incorporated pro tanto into an obligation entirely governed by English law (*materiellrechtliche Verweisung*).[3] A dictum of Warrington L.J. in *Re Chesterman's Trusts*[4] must probably be understood in the latter sense. The case related to the conversion into sterling of a sum of German money payable under trust instruments governed by English[5] law. Dealing with the method of applying German law in such circumstances, Warrington L.J. (as he then was) said[6] that 'the nature of that [German] currency must necessarily be regulated by German law which thus becomes for this purpose a part of the "proper law" of the contract—to use the term

---

[3] See Dicey and Morris, p. 758. The same view is held by Kegel in *Soergel's Commentaries*, note 620 preceding Art. 7.

[4] [1923] 2 Ch. 466.

[5] At pp. 481, 482 *per* Warrington L.J., at p. 486 *per* Younger L.J.

[6] At p. 483. Similarly the Swiss Federal Tribunal said: 'If the parties express a debt in foreign currency, it must prima facie be assumed that in that respect they refer to the law of the currency of the respective country as *lex contractus*' (3 June 1925, *BGE*, 51 ii. 303, also *JW*. 1925, 1818, and Clunet, 1926, 1118). See, generally, Vischer, *Internationales Vertragsrecht* (1962), p. 215.

adopted by Professor Dicey'. It would, however, appear that, apart perhaps from questions relating to the method of interpreting statutory provisions, the distinction between reference to and incorporation of a foreign law, however important it may be in other connections, is of no practical significance for currency problems, and, notwithstanding its academic interest, will therefore not be further pursued.

The *lex fori*, the third legal system to be considered, will prove to be of less general relevance. It will have to be taken into account under the head of English public policy and in connection with the effects of the institution of legal proceedings. But rules of public policy are not often involved in currency problems. Moreover, it is proposed to eliminate procedural aspects from the discussion of the substantive law of money and to consider the law of procedure, now fortunately much reduced in scope, in one comprehensive chapter only.[7] Therefore English law in the capacity of *lex fori*, as distinct from applicable municipal law, will not require much attention.

A more systematic treatment of the subject would have required the division of the second part of this book into two separate sections, the first dealing with foreign money obligations under a given municipal law (dollars under English law, pounds sterling under French law), the second being devoted to the problems of private international law. But in view of a number of circumstances, especially the fact that this separation between two distinct groups of problems has hitherto not been observed in English case law, its adoption has not been found practicable.

### III

Unless problems of a purely monetary character are involved, the general principles of English private international law will not form one of the subjects treated in this book. We shall speak of the law governing the interpretation of a contract or a will, the discharge of a promise to pay, or of a legacy, and so forth, but as a rule a detailed discussion of the law applicable in the one or the other case will be regarded as outside the scope of this treatise. It is only in a few connections that certain general questions of the conflict of laws will unavoidably require more extensive discussion.

### IV

The arrangement of the second part of this book becomes clear if the following hypothetical case is considered. Suppose a San Francisco

---

[7] Below, pp. 336 sqq.

merchant and a Montreal merchant meet in Vancouver, where they enter into a contract under which the Canadian undertakes to pay 100 dollars in London. The subject-matter of this obligation being dollars, it first becomes necessary to review the general aspects of a foreign money obligation in English law (Chapter VII). The next step of the inquiry is to ascertain the money which is promised, i.e. whether Canadian or American dollars are the subject-matter of the obligation (Chapters VIII and IX). Thereafter the quantum of the debt, which in case of an intervening fluctuation of value may be doubtful, must be determined (Chapter X). When the extent of the debt is thus ascertained the question arises whether the debtor must tender dollars or pounds in order to discharge his debt at the stipulated place of payment (Chapter XI). If he fails to keep his promise and the creditor is compelled to institute legal proceedings in this country, it becomes necessary, finally, to assess the influence, if any, of the institution of legal proceedings upon foreign money obligations (Chapter XII).

Though it will appear that many further matters will have to be dealt with in addition to those directly raised by this hypothetical case, the above affords a rough indication of the head under which they will fall.

# VII

# The General Position of Foreign Money and Foreign Money Obligations in English Law

I. Definition of foreign money. II. Foreign money as money or commodity. III. Foreign money debts, as contracts to pay money or as contracts to deliver a commodity. IV. Euro-currency. V. The legality of foreign money obligations. VI. Money of account and money of payment. VII. Foreign currency clauses: (1) '£100 payable in dollars at the rate of exchange of $3 to £1'; '£100 payable at the rate of exchange of $3 to £1'; (2) '£100, £1 = $3'. VIII. Option of currency, option of place. IX. A survey of the two preceding sections. X. The place of payment: (1) its meaning in comparative law; (2) its meaning in private international law; (3) the law of the place of performance and its effect in private international law.

'No suspense can be more harassing than the vagaries of foreign exchanges.'
Lord Sumner in *Larrinaga & Co. Ltd.* v. *Société Franco-Américaine de Medulla* (1923), 129 L.T. 65 (H.L.), at p. 72.

# I

THE question what money is to be regarded as foreign money cannot be so easily answered as might be supposed. It appears to be thought by some that foreign money is such money as belongs to a currency system of a country other than that whose law governs the obligation. Another author[1] considers that money is foreign money if it is owed as a result of private agreement as opposed to public law. A view more widely held is that such money is foreign as is different from the currency of the place of payment,[2] and this solution has been accepted by Article 41 of the Uniform Law on Bills and Notes, 1930, and by Article 36 of the Uniform Law on Cheques, 1931, which laws, in pursuance of the Convention made under the auspices of the League of Nations, have been put into force in a number of countries.[3] The usual and most acceptable understanding, however, is that foreign money is such money as is not the currency of the United

---

[1] Mayer, *Die Valutaschuld nach deutschem Recht* (1934), p. 1.
[2] Béquignon, *La Dette de monnaie étrangère* (1925), p. 5; cf. Falconbridge, *The Law of Banks and Banking* (1956), p. 486.
[3] The text of the Articles will be found below, p. 308, n. 9 and p. 229, n. 37.

Kingdom[4] and, in the absence of any other indicative material, this definition is probably the only one entitled to universal authority in this country.[5]

On the basis of this view the further question arises whether English money can in England under any circumstances be regarded as foreign money. Having regard to what is believed to be the general trend of ideas prevailing in this country the answer, which can only be put forward with considerable diffidence, is that probably English money is never foreign money. If a Dutch debtor promised to pay his Swiss creditors pounds sterling in Vienna, this would probably not be regarded in England as a foreign currency transaction; if an Englishman exchanged francs against pounds sterling in Calais, English courts would not classify the transaction as a sale of English, but as a purchase of French money, the purchase price being expressed in English currency, although at Calais the transaction was certainly regarded as a sale of English money; and if an Englishman exchanged pounds sterling against French francs in Amsterdam, this would be a purchase of French francs, while in Amsterdam, where the contract was made, it would be regarded as barter.

If this is the view taken by English law, it differs from that of the German Supreme Court, which once decided that German money could be *bought* as foreign exchange, e.g. if francs were given for marks by a German in Luxemburg, the *ratio decidendi* apparently being that the marks were regarded as foreign exchange at the place where the contract was made.[6]

## II

The mere fact that something has been found to be the money of a particular State in the sense discussed above,[7] neither necessitates nor permits the conclusion that such foreign money has the character of money in other countries too. On the contrary the problem

---

[4] Similarly Guisan, *Zeitschrift für schweizerisches Recht*, 56 (1937), 279a, and Van Hecke, p. 165, regard that money as foreign which is not that of the country of the forum. For a special meaning of the words 'foreign currency' see s. 1 (3) (a) of the Exchange Control Act, 1947.

[5] The constitutional structure of a particular State may be such that what appears to be the distinct currency of a particular territory is in truth not a foreign but a domestic currency. Thus it was held in Australia that a judgment of the Supreme Court of Papua New Guinea which was expressed in the local currency of Kinas could be registered in Australia, for the Kina was 'a form of Australian currency'. This was, of course, five years before Papua New Guinea became a sovereign State. See *R.* v. *White and Newman* (1975), A.L.J.R. 351 and *T. A. Fuld Pty. Ltd.* v. *Chief Collector of Taxes* (1975), 2 N.S.W.L.R. 101.

[6] 3 Jan. 1925, *JW*. 1925, 1986.                                                [7] pp. 21 sqq.

whether foreign money is money or a commodity[8] is everywhere a subject of discussion.

This problem does not admit of a rigid solution. In the same way as the meaning of money may vary, and as a chattel which usually is money may sometimes be a commodity,[9] so the question whether foreign money is to be treated as a commodity or money depends on the circumstances of the case, on the import of the words of a statute or an agreement, or on the legal nature of the individual transaction. Foreign money may be money, but it is not always money. Commodity is not a legal, but an economic concept; a commodity is that which is an object of commercial intercourse. But the conception of a commodity has a relative character; it cannot be attributed to any particular thing as such. Thus foreign money is dealt in and quoted on the foreign exchange market, and is there a commodity. On the other hand, foreign money very often serves the same functions as domestic money; it serves as a medium of exchange and is used for the purpose of the other functions fulfilled by the domestic currency which have been described as secondary functions.[10] This view that no hard-and-fast rule exists and that foreign money is a commodity where it is, or is referred to as, an object of commercial intercourse, and that it is money where it serves monetary functions,[11] makes it necessary to examine each individual case and to refrain from overrating the importance of statements made or conclusion arrived at in the one or the other connection.[12,13]

[8] The comparative material and the arguments on each side are collected and discussed by Neumeyer, pp. 128 sqq. The commodity theory is widely accepted in France: see, for example, Planiol–Ripert, vii, No. 1172; Mater, No. 162 (for whom this is, however, a consequence of his view that even domestic money is a commodity, see above, p. 23); in the United States of America foreign money has in innumerable cases been described as a commodity, mostly as an argument for the view that in case of legal proceedings instituted to recover a sum of foreign money the conversion into dollars must be effected at the rate of exchange at the date of breach. But there are also cases where the commodity theory was rejected: see, for example, *Matter of Lendle* (1929), 250 N.Y. Supp. 502, 166 N.E. 182. On foreign money as 'goods, wares, and merchandise' see Corbin, *On Contracts* (1950), s. 480.

[9] See above, p. 24.                                    [10] Above, p. 5.

[11] This is the view which of late has begun to prevail in Germany. It is accepted by M. Wolff, *Ehrenbergs Handbuch*, iv (1), p. 634; Neumeyer, l.c.; Mayer, p. 5; Geiler in Düringer–Hachenburg, i. 163; and also by Nussbaum, *Geld*, p. 42, although he also says that prima facie foreign money is a commodity. The present problem is in no way influenced by the State theory of money which does not concern the question whether the legal system of one State treats the money created by another State as money or as a commodity; in this sense Mayer, l.c., pp. 7 sqq., whose reasoning has been adopted in the text. But see Gerber, *Geld und Staat* (1926), pp. 83 sqq., and German Supreme Court, 25 Sept. 1919, *RGZ.* 96, 262, 265, where the State theory is used as an argument for regarding foreign money as a commodity. As to further German decisions see below, n. 12 and p. 192, n. 47.

[12] Thus it was held in France that foreign money, namely Russian roubles, was covered by a statute prohibiting the importation of foreign 'goods': Paris Court of Appeal, 30 May 1921, S. 1921, 2. 89 where the court said 'que l'expression marchandises embrasse toutes les choses qui se vendent et s'achètent, et que les billets de banque et les billets d'État de

[See p. 186 for n. 12 cont. and n. 13]

Where these principles lead to foreign money being regarded as money, the conclusion is in no way affected by the established rule that foreign money is not legal tender, for·not all money is legal tender, but all legal tender is money.[14] Legal tender is such money as is 'current coin of the realm'. This does not mean more than that foreign money cannot be tendered in discharge of a debt to pay pounds sterling, but it does not touch the question of the manner of discharging in England a debt expressed in foreign money.[15]

Nor is the monetary character of foreign money impaired by the fact that foreign money is said to be not necessarily negotiable in England. This is a consequence, not of foreign money being treated as a commodity, but of the rule that in order to be negotiable here a foreign instrument, whether it is foreign money or anything else, must be negotiable under *English* law or custom.[16] It was in support of this principle that in the case of *Picker* v. *London & County Banking Co.*,[16] where the negotiability of Prussian State Bonds was negatived, Bowen L.J. said:[17]

> Then is evidence that an instrument or piece of money forms part of the mercantile currency of another country any evidence that it forms part of the mercantile currency in this country? Such a proposition is obviously absurd, for if it were true, there could be no such thing as a national currency. For the same reason, as it appears to me, that a German dollar is not the same thing as its equivalent in English money for this purpose, and that the barbarous tokens of some savage tribe, such as cowries, are not part of the English currency, evidence that the instrument would pass in Prussia as a negotiable instrument does not shew that it is a negotiable instrument here.

These observations which were in substance approved of by Lindley L.J. in *Williams* v. *Colonial Bank*,[18] are neither meant nor able to prove more than that foreign money is not current in England and therefore is not necessarily a negotiable instrument. But the fact that, as regards negotiability, foreign money is not on the same level as

provenance étrangère ont bien ce caractère, puisqu'ils font ou ont fait l'objet de transactions commerciales suivies'. The same result was reached by the German Reichswirtschaftsgericht (19 Mar. 1921, *JW.* 1921, 650; 2 Dec. 1922, *JW.* 1924, 726), but the Supreme Court decided in the opposite sense (14 July 1921, *JW.* 1922, 168; 12 Aug. 1921, *JW.* 1921, 1459). See also German Supreme Court, 19 Feb. 1924, *JW.* 1926, 2847: during the inflation the plaintiff pledged with the defendant a 10-dollar note as security for a mark debt. The court applied the rules relating to pledge of movables rather than money.

[13] On the question whether notes which, under a system of exchange control, cannot be exported or imported, continue to be 'money' capable of discharging a debt abroad, see below, p. 422.

[14] Above, p. 40, n. 62.      [15] As to this question see below, pp. 312 sqq.

[16] *Picker* v. *London & County Banking Co.* (1887), 18 Q.B. 515; see Dicey and Morris, Rule 145.

[17] At p. 520; similarly Fry L.J. at p. 520.

[18] (1888), 38 Ch.D. 388, 404; affirmed [1890] 15 A.C. 267.

English money,[19] does not render it permissible to conclude that this is so in other respects too.

While the fact that foreign money is generally not legal tender and perhaps not negotiable, therefore, does not support the commodity theory, many instances can be adduced where foreign money has been treated as money. As regards the payment of stamp duties, s. 122, Stamp Act, 1891, expressly provides 'that the expression "money" includes all sums expressed in British or in any foreign or colonial currency'. For the purpose of criminal liability in cases of imitation of currency foreign money has also expressly been put on an equal footing with English money.[20] The case of *Harington* v. *MacMorris*[21] concerned an action brought under the old system of pleading to recover a sum of money which had been lent in India in pagodas. It was held that 'upon an allegation of a loan of lawful money of Great Britain, it is no variance that the loan is proved to have been of foreign coins, as pagodas', Gibbs J. adding[22] that 'as to the foreign money, the doctrine contended for has been exploded these 30 years'. The case of *Ehrensperger* v. *Anderson*[23] dealt with an action for money had and received brought to recover the proceeds of a sale received in rupees. The objection that the proceeds were not received in money was overruled. Baron Parke,[24] relying on *Harington* v. *MacMorris*,[25] held that

the real meaning of such a count is that the defendant is indebted for money of such a value or amount in English money. However the objection appears to have been listened to, perhaps more than it ought to have been, in a subsequent

---

[19] The soundness of the rule that prima facie foreign money is not negotiable here, and that therefore the bona-fide purchaser from a thief does not acquire a good title, is open to much doubt. The words of Bowen L.J. quoted above were only *obiter dicta* and do not necessarily bar the way to the better solution which prevailed in New York: *Brown* v. *Perera*, 182 App. Div. 922, 176 N.Y. Supp. 215 (Supreme Court of New York, App. Div., 1st Dept. 1918). In the final analysis negotiability means no more than that the instrument is capable of being transferred, not by assignment, but by endorsement or delivery. Has anyone ever heard of a bank note being transferred otherwise than by delivery? That foreign money is regarded as 'money' within the meaning of the provisions relating to the bona-fide acquisition of stolen money is well recognized in Germany (Breit in Düringer-Hachenburg, *Kommentar zum Handelsgesetzbuch*, iv. 1000 or Enneccerus-Nipperdey, *Lehrbuch des bürgerlichen Rechts*, i (1), s. 123, i. 3. c.) and in France (Lyon-Caen et Renault, *Traité de droit commercial* (1925), iv. No. 764).

[20] S. 18 (1), Forgery Act, 1913; s. 1 (1) and (2), Counterfeit Currency (Convention) Act, 1935 (by the Schedule of this Act foreign money is equiparated to British money for the purpose of the Coinage Offences Act, 1861); s. 2, Revenue Act, 1889; s. 12 (5) (a), Criminal Law Act 1967. The international practice of punishing the falsification of foreign money is old. See the interesting decision of the U.S.A. Supreme Court in *United States* v. *Arjona* (1887), 120 U.S. 479 and below, p. 484. In *Australia* it was held that the words 'currency, coinage and legal tender' in Australian currency legislation includes foreign money: *Watson* v. *Lee* (1979), 26 Australian L.R. 461, 481, 482.

[21] (1813) 5 Taunt 228.          [22] At p. 230.          [23] (1848) 3 Exch. 148.
[24] At p. 155.                                             [25] See above, n. 21.

case of *McLachlan* v. *Evans*,[26] but the Court of Exchequer held that an action for money had and received for English money would not lie, unless there had been a reasonable time after the receipt of the foreign money to convert it into English. Possibly that case cannot be received as very satisfactory; at all events, we do not decide this case against the plaintiff on this ground.

These words would suggest that for the purpose of an action for money had and received foreign money is always to be regarded as money.[27]

The most recent case on the subject is *Rhokana Corporation Limited* v. *Inland Revenue Commissioners*.[28] According to the terms of a trust deed, interest due in respect of debentures issued by the appellant company was payable in London in pounds sterling, or in New York in U.S.A. dollars at the fixed rate of exchange of $4.86 to the pound, or in Amsterdam in Dutch florins at the fixed rate of exchange of 12.11 Dutch florins to the pound. On 31 December 1931 the company duly posted warrants to registered holders which set out the amounts payable in sterling after deduction of income tax and, with regard to the net sterling amount, also contained the options as to currency and place of payment, the specific rates for conversion into dollars or guilders being added. The company deducted income tax at the rate of 5s. in the £ upon the sterling amount of interest. Certain warrants were cashed in New York in dollars at the fixed rate of exchange, the rate of exchange ruling on 31 December 1931 being only $3.39 to the £, and the revenue authorities therefore contended that a larger sum should have been deducted by the company for British income tax, such sum being arrived at by converting the total amount of interest paid into dollars at $4.86 to the £, deducting income tax in dollars at the rate of 5s. to the £, and reconverting the balance into sterling at the rate of $3.39 to the £. The decision *inter alia* depended on the question whether the facts of the case involved a 'payment of any interest of money' within the meaning of Income Tax Act, 1918, All Schedules Rules, r. 21, now s. 53 of the Income and Corporation Tax Act, 1970. Lawrence J. held[29] that foreign money was a commodity, not interest of money within rule 21. The decision was reversed in the Court of Appeal. Lord Wright, who read the judgment of the Court, did not enter into a discussion whether foreign money is or is not a commodity, but preferred to rest the decision on the ground[30] that in the Income Tax Act 'foreign money is clearly included, or, at least, is clearly not excluded', and that

---

[26] 1 Y. & J. 380.       [27] See also above, p. 4, n. 5.       [28] [1938] A.C. 380.
[29] [1936] 2 All E.R. 678; see p. 192, n. 45, below.       [30] [1937] 1 K.B. 788, 807, 808.

the truth is that the words 'payment of interest of money, annuity, or other annual payment charged with tax under Schedule D', read in connection with the machinery for 'deduction' provided for it in r. 21, are, in the context of the Income Tax Act, wide enough to cover not merely transactions effected in what is legal tender in the United Kingdom but also everything which is in a commercial sense a 'payment' upon the making of which the statutory 'deduction' can be made.

The House of Lords, however, restored the order of Lawrence J.[31] Lord Atkin's *ratio decidendi* was that 'for income tax purposes the company pay the interest in sterling and perform their obligation to the revenue by deducting the correct amount in sterling'. Lord Thankerton concurred and added that the time when the warrant is drawn is the period of distribution with reference to which tax is to be deducted. Lord Maugham also relied on the fact that payment and deduction are concurrent, and that, as interest is paid at the date of posting the warrant, the deduction ought to be made then. Lord Russell delivered a dissenting opinion, while Lord Macmillan agreed with the majority. The reasoning of the law lords is based on highly technical grounds and on machinery provisions of the Finance Acts and is therefore of small interest for the present purposes. It is, however, remarkable that Lord Atkin found it difficult to apply the terms of rule 21 to a payment and deduction of tax in a foreign currency; he did not see 'how one can deduct income tax, which is a tax in sterling, from dollars' and he, therefore, 'should have found great difficulty in supporting this assessment had the obligation been a direct obligation confined to payment in dollars'. In the result, though these are *obiter dicta*, it would appear to be rather doubtful whether, so far as concerns the payment of income tax, it does not sometimes make a material difference whether the income arises in terms of sterling or foreign money.

Although in the majority of these cases foreign money was clearly treated as money,[32] and although there does not appear any case where the decision was based on the ground that foreign money necessarily was a commodity, it would be rash to generalize. Thus the Court of Appeal has held, rightly, that for purposes of income tax profits arising from the sale of dollars were to be regarded as a trading profit and taxable accordingly.[33] The only conclusion which

---

[31] [1938] A.C. 380.
[32] See, however, *Marrache* v. *Ashton*, [1943] A.C. 311, 317, where Lord Macmillan said that since Spanish bank notes were not currency in Gibraltar, 'they must be regarded in Gibraltar as commodities'.
[33] *Landes Brothers* v. *Simpson* (1934), T.C. 62; *Imperial Tobacco Co. Ltd.* v. *Kelly*, [1943] 2 All E.R. 119. But a different view was taken in *McKinlay* v. *H. T. Jenkins & Sons*

can be drawn with safety is that the working principle stated above must be adhered to: foreign money is money where it functions as such; it is a commodity where it is an object of commercial intercourse. In the vast majority of circumstances, however, the former will be the case and Brandon J. (as he then was) cannot be criticized for stating categorically:[33a] the term 'money' includes 'money in foreign currency as well as in sterling'. And where the words 'money' on the one hand and 'goods', 'commodity', 'merchandise' on the other hand appear in a statute, it is a matter of interpretation whether foreign money is included in the former or the latter phrase.


# III

This principle will also provide a basis for answering the question whether the obligation to pay a sum expressed in foreign money is a monetary obligation or a contract to provide a commodity.

Here the same differentiation is called for. Where the payment of a sum of foreign money is promised, a monetary obligation exists, because the foreign money functions as money, the legal character of the obligation being inherently identical with that of an obligation to pay a sum of domestic money.[34] Only where foreign money is the object of commercial intercourse it will, according to the nature of the transaction, be regarded as a commodity.

Although this distinction between the obligation to pay a sum of foreign money and the obligation to deliver foreign money is not unquestioned,[35] both practical requirements and the legal aspects of individual cases support it.[36]

If a Londoner exchanges a pound sterling note against 10 French francs at Cook's in London, or if he requests his banker to convert a sum of pounds sterling into 1,000 U.S.A. dollars or to pay dollars

---

(1926), 10 T.C. 372 and *Davies* v. *The Shell Company of China* (1951), 32 T.C. 133; see Anonymous, 'Taxation of Foreign Currency Transactions', 61 (1952) *Yale L.J.* 1181. Foreign currency (as opposed to sterling is a chargeable asset for capital gains tax,—one may gain or lose by owning and selling it.

[33a] *The Halcyon the Great* (1975), 1 W.L.R. 515, 520.

[34] Above, pp. 63, 69. Cf. s. 38 (1) of the Finance Act, 1957, speaking of property other than 'a sum of money in sterling or any other currency'.

[35] It is accepted by Rabel, *Conflict of Laws*, iii (1950), 26, and Graveson, *Lectures in the Conflict of Laws and International Contracts* (Ann Arbor, Michigan, 1951), p. 113. According to Nussbaum, pp. 318, 340, foreign money is normally a commodity, but a foreign currency debt is a monetary obligation.

[36] In addition to the following cases attention must be drawn to the fact that the principle of nominalism applies to obligations to pay foreign money (below, pp. 267 sqq.), which rule presupposes the monetary character of such an obligation.

to his American creditor,[37] nobody will hesitate to draw the inference that this customer buys francs and dollars as a commodity and that the delivery of the foreign money is the subject-matter of a sale.[38] The 'money market' which exists in financial centres rests on the fact that the participants, usually bankers, discount or finance houses, 'buy' or 'sell' large sums of foreign money from each other, although in most cases they buy or sell credits at a bank.

But if the banker grants his customer a loan of 100 U.S.A. dollars, this is not a bailment, but a contract of loan of money differing from bailment in that the actual money lent is not to be redelivered by the borrower, but an equivalent sum is to be repaid. If it were not so, the general rule that, in the absence of an express or implied agreement, interest is payable according to banker's usage[39] could not apply, as interest is payable on money obligations only. Again, if a London firm enters into a contract with a Liverpool firm by which the latter undertakes to deliver a quantity of timber for a certain amount of Swedish kroners, this is not a barter, but a sale of goods, and the kroners are 'a money consideration called the price';[40] it is, indeed, a truism that 'the word "sell" as generally used in the English law of sale of goods includes selling for a price in foreign currency'.[41] Nor does it matter whether the foreign money is payable here or abroad, whether the creditor is a resident or a non-resident, or whether the money is due under an English or a foreign contract. The legal nature of the transaction is always to be tested by the question: does the currency function as money, that is to say, as a medium of exchange, or is it the object of commercial intercourse?

The results in these examples and, in particular, the suggestion

[37] In the U.S.A. it was repeatedly held that if the defendant has sold foreign money against dollars and undertakes to deliver it at a certain place abroad, his failure to do so makes him liable to repay the dollars received, not the value of the foreign money promised: *Chemical National Bank* v. *Equitable Trust Co.* (1922), 201 App. Div. 485, 194 N.Y. Supp. 177; *Safian* v. *Irwing National Bank* (1922), 202 App. Div. 459, 196 N.Y. Supp. 141, aff'd (1923) 142 N.E. 264; *Buckman* v. *American Express Co.* (1928), 262 Mass. 299, 159 N.E. 629; *American Union Bank* v. *Swiss Bank Corp.*, 40 F. (2d) 446 (C.C.A., 2d, 1930). See below, p. 288.

[38] Though not necessarily within the meaning of the Sale of Goods Act, 1979, since s. 61 (1) defines 'goods' as 'all chattels personal other than things in action and money'. In the instant case the foreign money may not be 'money' within the meaning of that section; but if bank notes were sold, they are 'things in action'. An example of a case where foreign money was the object of commercial intercourse and therefore a commodity is to be found *In re British American Continental Bank Ltd., Goldzieher & Penso's Claim*, [1922] 2 Ch. 575; *Lisser & Rosenkranz's Claim*, [1923] 1 Ch. 276. In the latter case Warrington L.J. said at p. 586: 'The subjects of these contracts for sale and purchase were sums of foreign currency.' The point may be important, if foreign money is bought and the seller delivers false notes; see Nussbaum, p. 320, and, on the relevant German law, Supreme Court, 8 Sept. 1922, JW. 1923, 176; 28 May 1924, RGZ. 108, 279.

[39] Halsbury (Hailsham), iii. 161.                [40] Sale of Goods Act, 1979, s. 2 (1).

[41] *The Halcyon the Great* (1975), 1 W.L.R. 515, at p. 519 *per* Brandon J.

that a contract for the payment of foreign money is a monetary obligation or a debt should, it is submitted, always have been obvious. Such a conclusion, however, is now firmly supported by the effect of, and the philosophy underlying, the decision of the House of Lords in *Miliangos* v. *George Frank (Textiles) Ltd.*,[42] where it was held that in the case of a foreign money obligation English courts were entitled and bound to give judgment in terms of the foreign currency contracted for. There were, it is true, earlier statements[43] and, indeed, decisions[44] pointing in the same direction. On the other hand it had often been said 'that a contract to pay in a foreign currency is a contract to provide a commodity'[45] and unfortunate conclusions were drawn from a theory which stemmed from what Lord Wilberforce described as 'the inevitable contract to supply a foreign cow'[46] and was always wholly unrealistic. They could not at any time be supported in logic or commonsense and do not now require discussion. It follows, in particular, that in most contexts the promise to pay foreign currency constitutes a debt.[47] This was in fact so held by

[42] [1976] A.C. 443. The case will be fully discussed below, p. 347.

[43] See, in particular, a most striking dictum by Lord Radcliffe *In re United Railways of Havana and Regla Warehouses Ltd.*, [1961] A.C. 1007, at p. 1059, and see Lord Denning at p. 1069.

[44] *Syndic in Bankruptcy* v. *Khayat*, [1943] A.C. 507. See also *Cohn* v. *Boulken* (1920), 36 T.L.R. 767. As has been pointed out (above, p. 149), the authority of the Privy Council decision as a precedent is perhaps not unassailable, and it is not enhanced by the fact that the Board does not seem to have been referred to many of the relevant cases. That the promise to pay foreign currency is a promise to pay 'in money' within the meaning of s. 83 of the Bills of Exchange Act 1882 is so obvious a point that it is not often made expressly. But see Halsbury (Simonds), iii. 151, Cowen, *Law of Negotiable Investments in South Africa* (4th ed., 1966), p. 77, and Falconbridge, *The Law of Banks and Banking* (1956), p. 486. The decision of the Privy Council clearly also applies to inland bills. There can be no doubt that the law on the Continent is in conformity with the decision of the Privy Council. The same now applies to the United States of America (where, according to Nussbaum, p. 346, the position used to be unsettled): Uniform Commercial Code, s. 3-107.

[45] *In re British American Continental Bank Ltd. Crédit Général Liégeois' Claim*, [1922] 2 Ch. 589, 595 *per* P. O. Lawrence J.; *Rhokana Corporation Ltd.* v. *Inland Revenue Commissioners*, [1936] 2 All E.R. 678, 681 *per* Lawrence J., affirmed on other grounds by the House of Lords, [1938] A.C. 380. And see *Manners* v. *Pearson*, [1898] 1 Ch. 581, 592 *per* Vaughan Williams L.J.; *Lloyd Royal Belge* v. *Louis Dreyfus & Co.* (1927), 27 Ll. L.R. 288, 294 *per* Romer J.; *The Baarn (No. 1)*, [1933] P. 251, 272 *per* Romer L.J.; *Pyrmont Ltd.* v. *Schott*, [1939] A.C. 145, at p. 156 *per* Lord Porter; *Marrache* v. *Ashton*, [1943] A.C. 311, 317, 318 *per* Lord Macmillan; see also *The Volturno*, [1921] 2 A.C. 544, 562, 563 *per* Lord Wrenbury.

[46] *Miliangos'* case (above, n. 42) at p. 468.

[47] The view that the obligation to pay a sum of foreign money is a monetary obligation is almost generally recognized on the Continent, but it has been most consistently upheld in Germany where interest is payable on outstanding debts even if their subject-matter is a sum of foreign money and where it is undoubted that a bill of exchange does not lose its character if it provides for payment in a foreign currency. The following case is of particular interest (*JW.* 1921, 22). In December 1914 the defendant owed the plaintiff a sum of 56,000 odd Dutch florins. As the defendant did not pay, the plaintiff brought an action for 104,000 odd marks, i.e. the equivalent of the amount of Dutch money at the rate of ex-

Atkinson J. in 1940,[48] by Jenkins J. (as he then was) in 1949[49] and finally by the Court of Appeal in 1980, when, overruling a decision of Hill J. in *Richardson* v. *Richardson*,[50] it decided that a bank keeping a dollar account for a judgment debtor was 'indebted' to him so as to permit a garnishee order to be made.[51]

## IV

The distinctions outlined in the preceding section are peculiarly marked in the case of Euro-currency dealings (other than Euro-sterling which for present purposes may be disregarded). It will be remembered[52] that these relate, for instance, to Eurodollars, i.e. dollars deposited with banks outside the United States.

The banks, institutions or multinational companies which hold such deposits, frequently of enormous size, and which deal in them

change of the day. He obtained judgment, but when the mark amount was paid, the mark had depreciated and he could not obtain the promised amount of Dutch florins in exchange for the sum recovered. He therefore brought a further action claiming 56,000 florins less the marks which he had received. The defendant contended that foreign money was a commodity the value of which the plaintiff had received by the first judgment so that the principle of *res judicata* stopped the plaintiff from recovering again. The plaintiff replied that he was entitled to payment of a sum of money, not delivery of a commodity, and that therefore his claim did not involve a repetition, but an extension of his claim which had hitherto only partly been pursued, and this was upheld by the Supreme Court on these grounds: 'Undoubtedly foreign coins may in individual transactions assume the character of and be dealt in as commodities. As a matter of principle, however, they are not only in their own country but also for the purpose of international transactions, i.e. in foreign countries, means of payment, just as much as the coins of the domestic currency. The fact that there they do not always have the same value and the same purchasing power as in their country, but that they may be affected by fluctuations in the rate of exchange, does not deprive them of their character as means of payment. If the appellant were right, the exchange of goods against foreign money would not be a sale, but a barter. Such a view would, however, be irreconcilable with that of the trade, especially the international trade. The vendor who stipulates for payment in foreign money, does not regard himself as a creditor of goods, but of money, and he is indeed justified in doing so. . . . The plaintiff, too, does not claim goods, but payment of his debt in the stipulated currency.' It is submitted that this reasoning is unanswerable.

[48] *Graumann* v. *Treitel* (1940), 2 All E.R. 188: the promise to pay a sum of reichsmarks in Berlin was a debt and, consequently, there was no point in the defence that, payment in Berlin being illegal, the debtor's failure to pay had not caused the creditor any damage.

[49] *Re Rickett, ex parte Insecticide Activated Products Ltd.* v. *Official Receiver* (1949), 1 All E.R. 737: a creditor to whom a sum of French francs is due has a 'debt' and is accordingly entitled to vote at a creditors' meeting in bankruptcy proceedings.

[50] [1927] P. 228, 234.

[51] *Choice Investments Ltd.* v. *Jeromnimon and Midland Bank Ltd.*, [1981] Q.B. 149. The cases mentioned in nn. 48 and 49 were not cited. That the dollars were held on a deposit account rather than a current account was clearly irrelevant: s. 38 of the Administration of Justice Act 1956. It could not be doubted that the dollars were 'a sum' within the meaning of that provision.

[52] Above, pp. 61 sqq.

are said to buy and sell money such as dollars. In law it is likely, however, that they deal in credits, so that a bank which has a large amount of dollars standing to the credit of its account with another (European) bank probably does not and cannot expect it to be 'paid' or discharged otherwise than through the medium of a credit to an account with another bank. In the case of dollars it seems to be the rule (and therefore possibly a term of the contract) that such credit should be effected through the Clearing House Interbank Payments System (Chips) in New York.[53] Accordingly, the creditor will probably be entitled, not to payment, but to specific performance by way of a credit, which can only be effected in New York, so that the obligation is not a monetary one. The remedy, therefore, is discretionary and the enforcement different from execution for a debt. Since the obligation is not a monetary one, discharge may become impossible. And in bankruptcy proceedings the creditor would have to prove the just value rather than a debt. In view of the enormous sums involved it could often be a national disaster if the creditor bank were entitled to payment, for in the last resort this might mean the sale of a vast amount of dollars and the purchase of an equally large sum of sterling so as to upset the exchange rates.[54] In short, as economists have said, the Eurodollar market is a mere account market rather than a money market.[55]

No judicial decision has as yet discussed the legal aspects of the Eurocurrency market as it has developed during the last two or three decades and in the absence of detailed evidence on the facts the above suggestions must be tentative, but an English case, though arising in an entirely different context, seems to support the suggested approach. Although since the nineteenth century it was 'Euro-sterling' which in fact rather than by name was a familiar feature of

[53] Marcia Stigum, *The Money Market* (1978), pp. 100, 434; see, generally, Einzig, *The Euro-Dollar System* (2nd ed., 1965). In the same sense Ronald I. McKinnon, *The Euro-currency Market* (Princeton, 1977), p. 13 who speaks of the 'mirror-shuffling of dollar claims (usually demand deposits) among American correspondent banks' and says that the 'proximate means of payment within the Eurocurrency system is "M 1" in the form of American demand deposits, while the ultimate means of payment among the American correspondents is federal funds'. He adds that Eurosterling or Euroguilder transactions work in an analogous fashion.

[54] The problem is touched upon by Dach, *American Journal of Comparative Law*, 1964, 38 (written before the introduction of Chips) and Hahn, *Das Wahrungsrecht der Euro-Devisen* (1973), pp. 37, 38. See also Eberhard Natermann, *Der Eurodollarmarkt in rechtlicher Sicht* (1977), a study of little value. Freymond, *Rec.* 131 (1970, iii), 1, 44 sqq. suggests (p. 46) that if Eurodollars are held by creditors other than banks the money of payment may be the currency of the country where the bank carries on business. This surely is contrary to the parties' intentions and the nature of the transactions.

[55] A theory on the above lines was first put forward by the writer in the course of a lecture given in Berne in April 1980 and subsequently published in *Annuaire Suisse de Droit International*, 1980, 93.

international commerce, the case, curiously enough, relates to what today one would call 'Eurolire'. The London branch of the Banca Commerciale Italiana had current and deposit accounts in lire. Customers had no right to draw cheques on such accounts or to obtain payment in sterling or currency notes to the debit thereof. Their only right was to request the branch to draw a lire draft payable in Italy or make a telegraphic or mail transfer to an account in Italy. When the branch was wound up under the Trading with the Enemy Act, 1939, the question arose whether in such circumstances the customer was a 'creditor' who had a 'debt' due from the branch. Simonds J. (as he then was) answered in the negative.[56] Although the learned judge did not so put it, the ultimate reason, it is believed, was that, as in the case of modern Euro-currency accounts, the customer was entitled, not to payment, but only to a credit to his or his nominee's account in Italy.

Nothing said in the preceding paragraphs is intended to suggest that dollars deposited with a bank in a non-dollar country are necessarily Euro-dollars or that there cannot be in Europe ordinary bank accounts denominated in dollars and constituting a debt of the bank in the usual sense. An English company which carries on a substantial business in markets which normally employ the dollar currency may entertain a dollar account with an English bank, which is not a Euro-dollar account. The distinction appears from the method used in operating the account. If it is an ordinary current account showing payments of varying amounts in and out and usually made by cheque or in a similar manner appropriate to any ordinary bank account, whether denominated in sterling or foreign currency, then the characteristics of the Euro-dollar market are missing. These are that large sums, almost invariably in round figures, are dealt with as part of the international money market by way of transfers from one bank account to another through the medium (in the case of dollars) of Chips.[57]

Nor is anything said in the preceding paragraphs intended to suggest that bonds issued or credits granted in terms of dollars (or any other currency) change their legal characteristics by reason of the fact that they are called Euro-bonds or Euro-credits because they are made by banks to the debit of accounts which may (or may not) be Euro-currency accounts. This is a matter without any relevance to the legal nature of the bond or credit, which in every respect is a foreign currency debt in the established sense of the term.

---

[56] *In re Banca Commerciale Italiana* (1942), 2 All E.R. 208.          [57] See above, p. 194.

## V

The question whether and how far parties are at liberty to provide in their contract for the payment of a sum of foreign money calls for a few observations only.

The nominalistic principle, concerning the quantum of the obligation, obviously does not affect the question whether a foreign currency may be promised to be paid. Nor is a stipulation to pay in foreign money in any way irreconcilable with ordinary legal tender legislation.[58] This was always so even in France[59] and certainly in this country.[60]

In France, however, such stipulations were at one time held to be invalid under a system of *cours forcé*. This point of view, falling in line with the unique French doctrine which we have already had occasion to notice,[61] was put by the Cour de Cassation in the leading judgment as follows:[62]

ce texte a pour objet de garantir à ces billets, dans la circulation monétaire intérieure, leur pleine valeur de monnaie équivalente à l'or et de frapper d'une nullité d'ordre public toute stipulation obligeant le débiteur résidant en France ou en Algérie à s'acquitter en France ou en Algérie soit en or, soit en une monnaie autre que celle ayant cours forcé dans le pays; d'où il suit qu'en condamnant les consorts Pélissier du Besset résidant en France, à payer en monnaie anglaise à Londres ou à Alger, au choix de l'Algiers Land and Warehouse Company Limited, les termes de loyer qui leur étaient réclamés, l'arrêt attaqué a violé le texte ci-dessus visé . . .

Here again, only one exception was allowed, namely in case of a 'paiement international'.[63] But there is room for the clear impression that

---

[58] Above, pp. 38 sqq.

[59] Cass. Req. 18 Nov. 1895, S. 1899, 1. 270; Degand, *Rép. droit int.* iii (1929), art. 'Change', No. 28.

[60] A curious dictum in the opposite sense by Romer L.J. in *Société Intercommunale Belge d'Electricité* v. *Feist*, [1933] Ch. 684, 710 rested on a misreading of s. 6 of the Coinage Act, 1870, but, since this was repealed in 1969, may now be ignored.

[61] Above, p. 163.

[62] 17 May 1927, S. 1927, 1. 289. See also Cass. Req. 31 Dec. 1928, S. 1930, 1. 41; 27 Mar. 1929, S. 1929, 1. 174; 27 Mar. 1930, Clunet, 1930, 395; Cass. Civ. 10 Mar. 1942, *Rev. Crit.* 1946, 96; Planiol–Ripert, vii, No. 1172; Degand, *Rép. dr. int.* iii (1929), art. 'Change', No. 41 bis.

[63] Planiol–Ripert, vii, No. 1179; Degand, l.c., Nos. 89 sqq. The courts did not uphold a foreign money obligation except in regard to a 'paiement international', and this required 'opérations se traduisant par un double mouvement de marchandises ou de valeurs de la France vers un pays étranger et de celui-ci vers la France': Cass Civ. 4 Nov. 1958, Clunet, 1960, 440; 7 July 1959, Clunet, 1960, 818; 12 Jan. 1960, *Rev. Crit.* 1960, 573 with note by Anselme-Rabinovitch; 27 Apr. 1964, Clunet, 1964, 819 with note by Dayant; 4 May 1964, *Rev. Crit.* 1965, 348; 3 May 1965, *Rev. Crit.* 1966, 696.

this doctrine which has remained an isolated one[64] has been superseded by legislative developments.[65]

The only method of invalidating stipulations providing for payment in a foreign currency is express legislation. Statutes relating to
foreign exchange restrictions frequently prohibit parties from incur-
ring liabilities expressed in a foreign currency, and sometimes even
provide for a compulsory conversion of foreign money obligations
into domestic currency.[66] But although the stipulation of a foreign
money obligation and the stipulation of a gold or similar clause aim-
ing at protection against fluctuations of the domestic currency are
often due to the same motives,[67] the invalidity of the latter does not
necessarily involve the invalidity of the former stipulation. It depends
on the interpretation of the individual enactment whether the abolition of the gold clause involves the invalidity of a promise to pay
foreign money.[68]

[64] It has not been adopted in Belgium: Cass. 30 May 1929, S. 1930, 4. 22 and Clunet,
1931, 1192 (and see De Page, *Traité Élémentaire de Droit Civil Belge*, iii (1967), s. 459) nor
in Italy or Greece; see Clunet, 1921, 999; 1926, 1087, 1089, but is followed in Monaco:
Cour de Monaco, 22 Apr. 1939, Clunet, 1939, 773.

[65] The decree of 1957 as amended (see above, pp. 164, 169) certainly covers domestic
transactions. Whether international transactions are valid to a greater extent than the decree
would seem to permit is open to doubt; in any case the payment is subject to exchange control legislation, but this is an entirely different point. See Eck, *Travaux de Comité Français
de Droit International Privé 1969-1971*, 85 and Malaurie, ibid. 1975, 22; also the purely
domestic cases Cass. Civ. 3 May 1965, *Rev. Crit.* 1966, 696; Cass. Civ. 10 May 1966, Clunet,
1967, 90; Cass. Civ. 4 Feb. 1969 and Cass. Com. 30 April 1969, Clunet 1970, 74 with note
Malaurie.

[66] This was, for example, done in Greece, where a Statute of 26 Apr. 1932 provides for
the conversion of all foreign currency obligations into drachmas: see Ténékidès, Clunet,
1933, 555; Ligeropoulos, *Revue Hellénique de Droit International*, viii (1955), 20, and the
decisions in Clunet, 1936, 684 sqq., 1019 sqq. Foreign currency obligations are prohibited
in Poland: Art. 1 of the decree of 27 July 1949 (*The Legislation of Poland* (Warsaw), ii
(1949)), 197.

[67] In Germany the first sentence of s. 3 of the Currency Law of 1948 (referred to above,
p. 170, n. 184) originally prohibited contracts providing for the payment of foreign currency except with the permission of the Federal Bank. By virtue of s. 49 (2) of the Aussen-
wirtschaftsgesetz of 1961 this provision does not apply to transactions between residents
and non-residents. Presumably it is equally inapplicable in the case of two non-residents
contracting under German law. In other words, the prohibition is now limited to contracts
between residents. According to Fögen, p. 150, in such event the prohibition is applicable
irrespective of whether or no the contract is subject to German law. This is open to much
doubt. Cf. Mann, 133 (1970), ZHR, 399, 400.

[68] In the United States of America the question whether the Joint Resolution of Congress of 5 June 1933 providing that 'every obligation . . . shall be discharged upon payment,
dollar for dollar, of any coin or currency which at the time of payment is legal tender for
public and private debts' involved the invalidity of promises to pay foreign money was at no
time raised, but would clearly have to be answered in the negative. If, by way of options of
currency, such promises are added to the promise to pay gold dollars, the result ought to
be the same. This follows not only from a correct analysis of the legal character of such
alternative promises (on which see below, p. 207) but also from the absurdity of the idea
that a creditor should be penalized for having been granted the additional security of a gold
dollar clause. The courts at first decided in this sense; see, in particular, *Anglo-Continentale*

While it thus appears that, in the absence of special legislation, parties are free to enter into contracts providing for payment in foreign money, it must be pointed out that in particular connections the use of domestic currency is very often required. In the United States of America it was enacted in 1792 that 'the money of account of the United States shall be expressed in dollars or units, dimes or tenths, cents or hundredths, and mills or thousandths . . . and all proceedings in the courts shall be kept and had in conformity to this regulation'.[69] Similarly the Canadian Currency and Exchange Act 1970[70] provides that 'all public accounts throughout Canada shall be kept in the currency of Canada, and any statement as to money or money value, in any indictment or legal proceeding, shall be stated in such currency'. In other countries the use of the domestic currency is prescribed in a less general way. Thus it is sometimes provided that entries in the land register,[71] notarial acts,[72] shares and capital of a limited company,[73] balance sheets,[74] must be expressed in the

---

*Treuhand A.G.* v. *St. Louis Southwestern R.R. Co.*, 81 F. (2d) 11 (C.C.A. 2d, 1936), also in *B.I.J.I.* 35 (1936), 141 and Plesch, l.c., p. 1, cert. den. 298 U.S. 655. Later, however, by a majority of five to four, the Supreme Court took the opposite view: *Guaranty Trust Co.* v. *Henwood* (1939), 307 U.S. 247 and *Bethlehem Steel Co.* v. *Zürich General Accident & Liability Insurance Co.* (1939), 307 U.S. 265. These decisions are justifiably criticized by Nussbaum, p. 435; see also Nussbaum, 84 (1935) *Pennsylvania L.R.* 569 and Rabel, *Conflict of Laws*, iii (1950), 45. These decisions, however, did not apply where the option of currency did not include the promise to pay gold dollars. They applied still less where there was no promise to pay dollars: *English Transcontinental Ltd.* v. *Public Tramway, Light & Power Co.*, 61 N.Y. Supp. 2d 356 (1946).

[69] Revised Statutes, s. 3563, U.S.C.A. s. 371; Act of 2 Apr. 1792, ch. 16, s. 20, 1 Statutes at Large, p. 250.

[70] S. 11.

[71] *Germany*: Grundbuchordnung, s. 28; *Switzerland*: ss. 783, 794, Zivilgesetzbuch; *France*: Planiol-Ripert, xii, No. 740; in *Victoria*, Australia, it was held that a mortgage securing a sum of U.S. dollars could not be registered in the land registry on the ground that in Australia the dollar was a commodity: *Bando Trading Co. Ltd.* v. *Registrar of Titles* (1975), V.R. 353. The reason given is far from convincing: see above, p. 184. There does not seem to be any reason why in England a mortgage securing a sum of foreign currency should not be registered by the Land Registry.

[72] *Belgium*: Art. 3 of the Statute of 10 Dec. 1885, on which see Piret, No. 22. *France*: Art. 5 of the Statute of 4 July 1837; Art. 17 of the Statute of 16 Mar. 1803, on which see Hubrecht, p. 288; Béquignon, pp. 92 sqq.

[73] *Germany*: ss. 7, 8, Companies Act of 6 Sept. 1965; also in *Austria, Sweden, Argentine* and elsewhere: see Hallstein, *Die Aktiengesetze der Gegenwart*, pp. 83, 86. In England the Board of Trade in fact allows the capital of a company to be expressed in foreign currency, although Lord Wright said in *Adelaide Electric Supply Co.* v. *Prudential Assurance Co.*, [1934] A.C. 122, 150: 'As the appellant company was registered in England, it is clear that its capital must be fixed in British sterling.' Also *France*: Escarra, *Traité de Droit Commercial*, ii (1951) 96.

[74] *Germany*: s. 40, Commercial Code (this applies even where the books are kept in a foreign currency: Supreme Finance Court, 30 Mar. 1927, *JW.* 1927, 2325). In the *Adelaide* case Lord Wright added to the words quoted in the preceding note that 'similarly, all the returns and accounts required by the Companies Act must have been rendered and kept according to the same currency'.

domestic currency, but it is remarkable that there does not seem to exist any such statutory provision in this country.

## VI

Wherever an obligation is validly expressed in a foreign currency, it becomes necessary to have regard to a distinction of fundamental importance, viz. that between the *money of account*[75] and the *money of payment*.[76] Its source is that fertile contrast between the substance of the obligation and the mode of performance which is generally recognized in connection with protective (especially gold) clauses,[77] and another aspect of which will here again provide a useful guiding principle.[78]

The money of account is that currency in which an obligation is expressed, while the money of payment is the currency with which the obligation is to be discharged. Or in the vivid words of Lord Denning M.R.:[79] 'The money of account is the currency in which an obligation is measured. It tells the debtor how much he has to pay. The money of payment is the currency in which the obligation is to be discharged. It tells the debtor by which means he has to pay.'

If foreign money is the subject-matter of an obligation, the proper method of discharging it will prima facie be by paying to the creditor that foreign money which has been promised. In other words, the money of account will also be the money of payment. But this is not always and everywhere so.

If goods are bought for '1,000 U.S.A. dollars, payable in pounds sterling', it is obvious that while foreign money is the money of

[75] Expression of Lord Tomlin in *Adelaide Electric Supply Co.* v. *Prudential Assurance Co.*, [1934] A.C. 122, 146.

[76] The distinction is now accepted by the House of Lords: *Woodhouse A.C. Israel Cocoa Ltd.* v. *Nigerian Produce Marketing Co. Ltd.*, [1972] A.C. 741. For a particularly clear explanation of the distinction see Lord Denning M.R. in the Court of Appeal: [1972] 2 Q.B. 23, at p. 54.

[77] Above, pp. 147 sqq.

[78] In connection with foreign money obligations the distinction between 'monnaie de compte' or 'monnaie de contrat' and 'monnaie de paiement' has with particular force been evolved in *France*, where it has repeatedly been recognized by the Cour de Cassation; see, for example, Cass. Civ. 14 Jan. 1931 (Ville de Tokio), Clunet, 1931, 126 with the speech of the Attorney-General Paul Matter; Cass. Civ. 5 June 1934 (Est Lumière), Clunet, 1935, 90; Planiol–Ripert, vii, Nos. 1190, 1191, 1193. Cass. Civ. 21 July 1936, Clunet, 1937, 299 (Papeteries Bergès) speaks of 'monnaie de base'. See also Hubert's note to Cass. Req. 25 Jan. 1928, S. 1928, 1. 161. In the same sense Van Hecke, p. 166. In *Germany* it is also usual to differentiate between 'Schuldwährung' and 'Zahlungswährung': Nussbaum, *Geld*, p. 187; Mayer, *Valutaschuld*, p. 78; but see Neumeyer, p. 182. The distinction is also recognized in *Switzerland*: Federal Tribunal, 23 May 1928, Clunet, 1929, 497 (Crédit Foncier Franco-Canadien).

[79] In the Court of Appeal in the case referred to above, n. 76: [1971] 2 Q.B. 23, at p. 54.

account and thus determines the measure of value or the scale of payment, the mode of payment is by handing to the creditor pounds sterling.[80] This may be so even in the absence of an express provision requiring or allowing the debtor to effect the actual payment in pounds sterling.[81]

Conversely, although pounds sterling are the money of account, foreign money may be the instrument of payment: '£100 payable in U.S.A. dollars' or '£100 payable in U.S.A. dollars at the fixed rate of $3 per £1'.[82] In this case the obligation, though referring to the domestic currency as money of account, is really a foreign money obligation in disguise.[83]

It follows that two questions must be distinguished: the first concerns the determination of the money of account, i.e. of the subject-matter of the obligation or, to use the Latin phrase, of that money which is *in obligatione* (below, Chapters VIII and IX); secondly, it is necessary to ascertain the money of payment, i.e. the proper mode or instrument of payment or that money which is *in solutione* (below, Chapter XI). If this distinction is not strictly adhered to, it may easily happen that a wrong decision is arrived at in an individual case. It may suffice to point out that according to the rules of private international law each question may be governed by a different law,[84] and that the quantum of the obligation is determined by the money of account, not by the money of payment. Thus a contract made in Geneva in 1936 (when 5 French francs were equal to 1 Swiss

[80] *In B.P. Exploration Co. (Libya) Ltd.* v. *Hunt* (1979), 1 W.L.R. 783, at pp. 840, 841. Robert Goff J. suggested that in such a case, i.e. where the contract distinguishes between the money of account and the money of payment, on the date of maturity 'the indebtedness crystallises and so fails to be converted from the currency of account to the currency of payment' with the result that in the event of delayed payment 'the parties will be taking the risk of fluctuation in the currency of payment' rather than the money of account. It is submitted that this approach cannot be supported. Since *Miliangos*'s case (on which see below, p. 347) the idea of a foreign money obligation 'crystallising' and changing its character has fortunately disappeared from English law. Nor does a sterling debt change its character as a result of default in payment: above, p. 67. Until payment the debt remains what it is and remains expressed in the money of account. The money of payment merely indicates the method of discharge and is without influence upon what is *in obligatione*.

[81] Below, pp. 314 sqq.

[82] This case is obviously different from the clause 'to pay such sum of sterling as corresponds to $100', on which see above, p. 65, n. 13, and p. 153, n. 95.

[83] See below, p. 201, n. 86. The distinction developed in the text also arises when a loan is made in the one currency, but is stated to be repayable in another currency. Thus in *Boissevain* v. *Weil*, [1950] A.C. 327 the borrower of 320,000 French francs undertook to repay £2,000, so that the money of account was expressed in pounds sterling and French francs were the money of payment. For a similar set of facts see the decision of the Supreme Court of Missouri in *Re De Gheest's Estate*, 243 S.W. (2d) 83 (1951). It depends on the intention of the parties whether in such cases the true nature of the transaction is not the sale of French francs for a price expressed in sterling.

[84] See below, pp. 233 sqq., 320 sqq.

franc) may provide for the payment of 1,000 'francs' in Paris in 1952 (when the rate of exchange was about 100 : 1); the decision of the question whether at maturity the creditor is entitled to 1,000 or to 100,000 French francs depends on a clear differentiation between the stipulated money of account, which determines the quantum of the debt, and the money of payment, which is merely the instrument of payment.

## VII

The distinction between the money of account and the money of payment will also afford a useful guide to the solution of the problems raised by foreign currency clauses. The forms of such clauses vary so much that it is difficult to find a way through the maze of factual material and judicial decisions. Moreover, the meaning of such clauses may greatly differ in individual cases, and it is therefore impossible to lay down rules of universal application. It must suffice to state the governing considerations with special emphasis on the distinction between the various types of clauses.[85]

1. It has already been explained in the preceding section that the simple promise to pay £100 (domestic money obligation) or to pay 100 U.S.A. dollars (foreign money obligation) may become more complicated by a separation of money of account and money of payment. If the promise reads 'to pay £100 payable in dollars' or 'to pay $100 in pounds sterling' the money of account, determining the quantum of the debt, and the money of the payment, determining the mode of payment, are different; the creditor is entitled to be paid in dollars or pounds only, but the amount depends on the value of the stipulated money of account.

This uncertainty as to the amount eventually payable is avoided if the parties not only differentiate between money of account and money of payment, but also stipulate a rate of exchange on the basis of which the former is to be converted into the latter: '£100 payable in dollars, at the rate of exchange of $3 to £1' or '$300 payable in pounds sterling at the rate of exchange of £1 to $3'. In these cases it is clear that it is in fact an amount of $300 or, in the second instance, of £100 which is exclusively payable, and there exists therefore either a foreign money or a domestic money obligation in disguise.[86]

---

[85] It is clear that in the case of a conflict of laws the construction of such clauses depends on the proper law of the obligation. A remarkably elaborate currency clause found its way into the Young Loan which Germany issued in 1930 (for its text see Hudson, *International Legislation*, v. 575); probably it was subject to public international law: *British Year Book of International Law*, 1944, 17–22.

[86] See above, pp. 199, 200. That under such circumstances there exists a foreign money

Such clauses are usually due to the parties' lack of confidence in the stability of the money of account. If the creditor is entitled to a sum of sterling payable in dollars,[87] whether it be at the actual rate of exchange at the date of payment or at a fixed rate of exchange, and if therefore there exists a circuitously expressed foreign money obligation, it confers all the advantages and imposes all the disadvantages of such obligations: the creditor will be protected in the event of a depreciation of sterling, but takes the risk of a depreciation of the dollar. This, no doubt, is in conformity with the parties' intentions.

2. The legal position is less clear if the promise does not contain the words 'in dollars', but simply reads '£100 at the rate of exchange of $3 to £1' or '£100, £1 being equal to $3', or £100, £1 = $3', or '£100 = $300'.[88] There are two distinct questions to which such clauses give rise.

The first is whether the words 'in dollars' can be read into the clause. If so, the clause is of the same type as that discussed in the preceding section, and imports the same consequences. As a general rule one should be reluctant to treat the clauses at present under consideration as merely disguising a foreign money obligation; for the parties have in no way expressed their intention to make dollars both the money of account and the money of payment and thus, in effect, to contract exclusively in terms of dollars.[89] While, in accordance

obligation was repeatedly decided by the *German* Supreme Court in connection with mark loans stated to be repayable in Swiss francs or Dutch guilders at a fixed rate: 27 June 1923, *JW.* 1924, 173; 25 May 1927, *JW.* 1927, 1829; 2 Feb. 1928, *JW.* 1928, 1385; 4 July 1929, *JW.* 1929, 2709. The Supreme Court even held that a mark loan which was stated to be repayable at the rate of 123 Swiss francs per 100 marks, but which was not stated to be repayable *in* Swiss francs, was an obligation to pay Swiss money: 29 Nov. 1920, *JW.* 1921, 231. Though the decision has been approved, e.g. by Nussbaum, *Geld*, p. 206, and Breit in Düringer–Hachenburg, *Kommentar zum Handelsgesetzbuch*, iv. 765, it is submitted that there did not exist a foreign money obligation, but a foreign currency clause added to the promise to pay marks, and that the case belonged to the group presently to be discussed in the text. In *Bechar* v. *Biderman*, Jerusalem Post (Law Report), 30 June 1963, the Supreme Court of Israel held that a promise to repay a loan 'in dollars at the rate of $4.98 to the Palestine pound' was not invalid, but to be construed as if the words 'in dollars' did not exist and there had been a value clause promising such sum of pounds as corresponds to the agreed rate.

[87] The following discussion will disregard the converse case of a promise 'to pay $100, $3 being equal to £1'. In this case the question arises whether there exists a foreign money obligation or a domestic money obligation in disguise. Its solution depends on the same considerations as those applying to the case discussed in the text.

[88] In very exceptional circumstances it may be possible to read such a clause into a contract: thus it was held in Belgium that a clause '1,25 frs. for 1 mark' was to be read into the borrower's promise to repay a mark loan (Cass. 26 Feb. 1925, Clunet, 1926, 505 = Pasicrisie Belge, 1925, 1. 157). See also French Cass. Req. 10 Mar. 1925, Clunet, 1926, 70 (Banque Internationale de Luxembourg *c.* Ville de Sedan). But the German Supreme Court declined to read the clause '4,20 RM. being equal to $1' into a promise to pay dollars: 15 Mar. 1937, *RGZ.* 154, 187; similarly 7 Feb. 1938, *JW.* 1938, 1109.

[89] Vischer, *Internationales Vertragsrecht* (1962), p. 216, agrees.

with the general rules of construction, such an intention may sometimes have to be inferred, this will not normally be so. An example
of a case in which it could fairly be assumed that payment 'in dollars'
was within the contemplation of the parties and that, therefore, they
agreed upon a fixed sum of dollars rather than a variable sum of sterling, is provided by a decision of the Supreme Court of Pennsylvania.[90]
A bill of lading made freight payable in pounds sterling, but contained
the clause 'freight, if payable at destination (Philadelphia), to be at
the rate of exchange of $4.866'. Since payment in Philadelphia was
envisaged, the court held that the freight was payable in dollars, the
amount being ascertained by the agreed, not the current, rate of
exchange.

In the event of the words 'in dollars' not being implied, the second
question arises: what is the true meaning and effect of the clause? It
certainly does not, in the absence of a particular context, involve an
option of currency[91] or a gold clause.[92] Its function rather is to
define the quantum of the debt or to provide a measuring rod: the
debtor has to pay pounds sterling, but so many pounds sterling as
correspond to the fixed relation indicated by the clause. On this
footing the clause may mean that the debtor has to pay in sterling
the equivalent of $300. Such a construction would have the same
practical effect as if the words 'in dollars' had been added and there
had been a dollar obligation in disguise. Moreover, the stipulation of

---

[90] *Pennsylvania Railway Co.* v. *Cameron* (1924), 280 Pa. 458, 124 A. 628. For a similar
implication see *Brown* v. *Alberta & Great Waterways Rly. Co.* (1921), 59 D.L.R. 520.

[91] The clause does not in any way indicate an intention to agree upon more than one
money of account or payment; the debtor owes pounds, neither dollars nor pounds or dollars. The clause merely determines the extent of the sterling obligation. Cf. *Brown* v. *Alberta
& Great Waterways Rly. Co.* (1921), 59 D.L.R. 520, discussed below, p. 210. Where bonds
contained the clause 1,000 marks = 1,240 frs. the German Supreme Court originally held
that German holders could only claim the stipulated sums of marks: 21 Dec. 1925, *JW.*
1926, 1320. But in subsequent decisions it was held that even German holders could claim
payment in Swiss francs or their equivalent in reichsmarks: 1 July 1926, *JW.* 1926, 2675;
22 Dec. 1927, *IPRspr.* 1928, No. 66. For the reasons mentioned in the text the result
reached in the later decision is correct; but the reason propounded by Nussbaum in a note
to the previous decision and accepted by the Supreme Court that there existed an 'option
de change' can hardly meet with approval. See below, p. 209, n. 122.

[92] The clause will frequently have the same effect as a gold clause. But it is not helpful
to overlook the distinctions between both types of protective clauses; they are vital in case
the gold clause is abrogated, but the foreign currency clause remains in force. In all the
German cases discussed in the text the foreign currency clause was added to the promise
to pay 'Goldmarks', but this was accidental and does not justify Nussbaum's presentation
at pp. 259 and 382 respectively. In *Ottoman Bank* v. *Dascalopoulos*, [1934] A.C. 354,
*Ottoman Bank* v. *Chakarian* (No. 2), [1938] A.C. 260, and *Sforza* v. *Ottoman Bank*, ibid.,
p. 282, the Privy Council dealt with the plaintiff's contention that a gold clause was impliedly
added to a promise to pay a sum of Turkish pounds. It has been stated above that the actions
were misconceived; in truth, it was a foreign currency clause of the type described in the
text ('110 Turkish pounds equal to 100 Cyprus pounds') which was attached to the promise
to pay Turkish pounds. See pp. 145 sqq.

'£100' would have little significance: it would merely indicate a cumbersome method of calculating the sum of $300 which alone is *in obligatione*. This is a possible construction which would protect the creditor against a depreciation of sterling (or an appreciation of the dollar) but would expose him to the risk of the depreciation of the dollar (or the appreciation of sterling).[93]

Thirdly, the clause may have to be construed as protecting the creditor against the depreciation of sterling only without imposing upon him the risk of the depreciation of the dollar. It would mean that the creditor would receive the sterling equivalent of $300 subject to a minimum of £100. It is this view which is more likely to do justice to the real intention of the parties. The principles applicable to the construction of a gold clause should not be lost sight of in the present connection: it is essential to determine the real purpose of the clause[94] and to have in mind the rule that 'it is fundamental that the terms of a contract qualifying the promise are not to be rejected as superfluous'.[95] It would appear that in most cases the purpose of these clauses will be the same as that aimed at by gold clauses, namely, 'to protect one of the contracting parties against a depreciation of the currency'.[96] If parties add the words '£1 being equal to $3' to a promise to pay £100, this will generally be due to the fear that the pound sterling will depreciate, and, accordingly, to the wish to protect the creditor against the effects of such depreciation. This being so, the clause should probably not provide the creditor with more than £100 if, owing to a revaluation of the dollar, the rate of exchange of the dollar should become £1 to $2;[97] for if the clause was applied to such a case, not expected by the parties, it would mean that the creditor would receive more in 'real value' than he had contracted for. Nor should the clause come into operation if it is the pound sterling which appreciates to a ratio of £1 to $4; the debtor

[93] The legal position would be the same as if the promise read: 'to pay such sum of sterling as corresponds to $300'. This clause, repeatedly referred to in these pages (above, p. 65, n. 13; p. 153, n. 95; p. 200, n. 82) looks to the dollar rate at the date of payment and therefore protects the creditor against a depreciation of sterling without a minimum sum of sterling the stipulation of which would protect against a depreciation of the dollar.

[94] See *Feist* v. *Société Intercommunale Belge d'Électricité*, [1934] A.C. 161, 172 *per* Lord Russell. See also the Canadian case mentioned below, p. 210, n. 123, and the dictum on p. 210.

[95] Permanent Court of International Justice, Case of Serbian Loans, Collection of Judgments 1928–30, Judgment No. 14, p. 32, as approved of in *Feist's* case (above, n. 94).

[96] *The King* v. *International Trustee for the Protection of Bondholders A.G.*, [1937] A.C. 500, at p. 556 *per* Lord Russell.

[97] This is a very doubtful case, because the appreciation of the dollar means that sterling depreciates in terms of the dollar, although its own monetary system has not been subject to any direct action by the British authorities. Yet if the purpose was protection against the depreciation of sterling, the appreciation of the dollar does not come within the purview of the clause.

will generally be unable to satisfy the creditor by the payment of £75, since the altered rate of exchange was contrary to the expectations of the parties and to the purpose of the clause, which usually is the protection of the creditor, not of the debtor, so that the insertion of the fixed sum of £100 has the character of a minimum figure. Finally, if it is the dollar which depreciates to a rate of £1 to $4, the quantum of the debt should not be affected. Since the clause does not provide an absolute measure of value, but is intended as a protection for the creditor against a depreciation of the stipulated currency, i.e. pounds, the debtor should not be allowed to discharge his debt by a payment of less than £100. This construction was favoured in continental countries when sterling and dollar unexpectedly depreciated between 1931 and 1933. After the German inflation it became a widespread practice to secure a Reichs- or Goldmark debt by inserting the clause '1 Reichsmark (or 1 Goldmark) equal to $\frac{10}{42}$ U.S.A. dollars.' The German Supreme Court held that, in view of the German currency experiences, it was the intention of the parties and the purpose of the clause to protect the creditor against a depreciation of the sum of German money payable by the debtor, that the dollar was therefore not an absolute measure of value, and that it was the gold dollar, not the currency dollar, which was referred to when it was equiparated to a Goldmark which in fact did not exist, the result being that the debtor had to pay the fixed sum of German money as a minimum sum.[98] Similar cases arose in other countries and the same result was arrived at in Sweden,[99] and (after some hesitation) in Belgium,[100] Czechoslovakia,[101] and Israel[102] while in Italy[103] the dollar was regarded as an absolute measure of value.

It thus appears that generally the clause will only have its full effect if the pound sterling depreciates to a rate of, say, £1 to $2. This is

[98] See particularly 22 Oct. 1936, *RGZ.* 152, 166 and the numerous decisions referred to therein, one of which is translated by Plesch, *The Gold Clause*, i. 97. In addition see: 14 Dec. 1933, *IPRspr.* 1934, No. 88; 24 Sept. 1934, *JW.* 1934, 3198; 23 Oct. 1934, *IPRspr.* 1934, No. 90. The principle is best explained in *RGZ.* 146, 1 sqq., 5 (14 Dec. 1934) and *RGZ.* 148, 42 sqq., 44 (5 July 1935) = Clunet, 1936, 412. On these decisions see Ernst Wolff, *Schuldverschreibungen auf Reichs- oder Goldmark mit unechter Valutaklausel* (1935), and Stoeber, *Niemeyers Zeitschrift für internationales Recht*, 52 (1938), 240, and the material there collected.

[99] Supreme Court, *B.I.J.I.* 33 (1935), 278 (27 Apr. 1935).

[100] See Piret, pp. 256–64, with reference to the decisions. See also Dubois–Clavier Clunet, 1933, 730; some of the decisions will be found in Clunet, 1933, 722, 724, 728, and *Rev. dr. banc.* 1932, 377 and 453.

[101] Supreme Court, 22 Oct. 1937, *Zeitschrift für osteuropäisches Recht*, 4 (1938), 467, with note by Hochberger; but see the earlier decision 27 Nov. 1936, ibid., 3 (1937), 654.

[102] *Bechar* v. *Biderman*, Jerusalem Post, 30 June 1963 above n. 86.

[103] Cass., 11 Jan. 1936, *Riv. dir. com.* 34 (1936), 386, with note by Grassetti; but see in the opposite sense Milan Court of Appeal, 19 July 1934, *Foro Lomb.* 1934, 660, discussed in *RabelsZ.* 1935, 201. See, generally, Ascarelli, p. 225.

the case against which the parties must have primarily intended to protect the creditor. In the example given above the creditor should therefore be entitled to demand payment of £150. But, curiously enough, in these very circumstances English courts refused to give effect to the clause. The decision of the House of Lords in *Howard Houlder & Partner Ltd.* v. *Union Marine Insurance Co.*[104] related to a case where the plaintiffs had effected on behalf of American principals a policy of marine insurance with the defendants in respect of cargo to be conveyed from the West Indies to Canada. The cargo was valued at $108,000 and was insured for an aggregate sum of £26,025. The policy contained the clause, added at the request of the plaintiffs after the conclusion of the contract: 'Claims if any to pay at the rate of 4.15 dollars to 1 pound sterling.' A total loss having occurred and the pound sterling having depreciated, the plaintiffs claimed £2,886 in excess of £26,025 to enable them to obtain $108,000. Bailhache J. dismissed the action,[105] and his order was confirmed by a majority of the Court of Appeal (Bankes and Warrington L.JJ.), Atkin L.J. dissenting,[106] and by a unanimous House of Lords (Lords Buckmaster, Dunedin, Atkinson, Sumner, and Parmoor). The opinions delivered rest on two grounds: in the first place, it was considered that if the plaintiffs' claim was dismissed, i.e. if the clause was disregarded in connection with the claim for the principal sum of £26,025 due in respect of a total loss, the clause would nevertheless not be deprived of all meaning, since certain cases (which were unlikely to be in the forefront of the parties' minds) could be imagined in which claims for damages expressed in dollars would arise which would have to be converted into pounds sterling at the stipulated rate. Secondly, it was emphasized that 'this is a sterling policy and it appears to me impossible to give to these latter words a meaning which would produce the effect of changing the whole nature of the policy by converting it into a dollar policy'.[107] It is submitted with respect that, as in the circumstances the insertion of the clause was probably due to the intention to protect the plaintiffs' principals against a depreciation of the pound sterling, the decision is not entirely satisfactory, and one may well understand the fact that Atkin L.J. (as he then was) dissented and that the decision of the House of Lords was not followed in the United States.[108] The decision cannot, however, be regarded as laying down any general rule and may not necessarily have to be followed in future, because, since

---

[104] (1922) 10 Ll. L.R. 627.                               [105] (1920) 5 Ll. L.R. 48.
[106] (1921) 6 Ll. L.R. 551.                          [107] At p. 628 *per* Lord Atkinson.
[108] *Marine Insurance Co.* v. *J. Craig McLanahan* (1923), 290 F. 685; 1923 American Maritime Cases 754 and in *Rev. du droit maritime comparé*, 4 (1923), 269 (C.C.A., 4th), affirming 283 F. 240 (1922).

*Feist's* case was decided in 1934,[109] greater emphasis has to be placed on the purpose of the clause, and because it rested to a considerable extent on the fact that in the particular case it was possible to disregard the clause without rendering it thereby devoid of any meaning at all. Two similar cases[110] which have come before the English courts do not throw much fresh light on the problem.[111]

## VIII

A foreign money obligation may also take the form of an alternative promise ('option de change', option of currency):[112] '£100 or 240 U.S.A. dollars', '1,000 French francs or 150 U.S.A. dollars'. The promise to pay dollars in the first case and both promises in the second case are foreign money obligations of a kind which used to be found in international transactions, especially in loan agreements, where it is intended to safeguard one of the parties against fluctuations of monetary value by giving an option of choosing between two or more currencies. Such alternative promises are often coupled with

[109] [1934] A.C. 161.

[110] *Poulsen & Carr* v. *Massey* (1919), 1 Ll. L.R. 497, where a charterer of a ship had to pay a monthly hire of £4,068. 15s., there being later in the charter-party the clause: 'rate of exchange not being below 17 kroners to the £'. Bailache J. held that this clause did not affect the amounts of British money owed in respect of hire, apparently because it was held to refer to other claims under the contract. See also *Royal Commission on Wheat Supplies* v. *Bulloch Bros.* (1922), 13 Ll. L.R. 418 (C.A.): 'rate of exchange ... fixed at sh. 1/5½ to the rupee; fluctuations being at buyers' account'.

[111] Reference should be made to two interesting *French* cases: The Cour de Bordeaux, 23 Mar. 1921, Clunet, 1921, 567, dealt with a case where invoices were expressed in French francs, but contained clauses to the effect that payment was to be made in sterling at the rate of 25 frs. per £. It was contended by the plaintiffs 'que C. [defendant] doit leur remettre à Londres autant de fois une livre sterling que les factures contiennent de fois 25 frs. tandis que C. prétend qu'il lui suffit de remettre à Marsden & Hunter autant de fois 25 frs. qu'il leur devra de livres sterling, ou bien la somme correspondante de francs en livres au cours du jour'. The court gave judgment for the plaintiffs for £2,589. 3s. 4d., but it explained that if at the time of the payment the rate of exchange for pounds was less than 25 frs., the profit would have been the defendant's. The second case is a decision of Cass. Civ. 2 Nov. 1932, Clunet 1933, 1197 (Société des Music-Halls Parisiens v. Victoria Palace Ltd.). The subscriber of bonds denominated in francs was promised that his money would be repaid at the rate of 25 frs. per pound sterling. The French franc fell in terms of pound sterling, but the debtor was held liable to repay 'autant de livres sterling par obligation de 5,000 francs qu'il y a de fois 25 frs. dans 5,000 frs. c'est à dire 200 livres'. See also Cass. Civ. 5 Dec. 1927, S. 1928, 1. 138. The Court of Appeal of the Mixed Tribunal in *Egypt* had to deal with a case where a borrower had promised to repay '67401,16 Frs. soit P.T. 260,000, au cours du change de Paris'. It was held that he was bound to repay not French francs, but 'le franc, vingtième partie du louis d'or tel qu'il a été tarifé en Égypte et adopté par les Codes Mixtes, soit P.T. 3,8575, puisque c'est sur cette base que, dans l'Acte même, les francs ont été convertis en piastres': 19 May 1927, Clunet, 1928, 765 (*re* Marquis de la Celle).

[112] See, generally, Nussbaum, 'Multiple Currency and Index Clauses', 84 (1935) *Pennsylvania L.R.* 569; Seignol, *L'Option de change et l'option de place* (Paris, 1936), Van Hecke, pp. 178 sqq.

the stipulation of corresponding alternative places of payment: '£100 in London or $240 in New York or 1,350 French francs in Paris'.[113] Although it provides the creditor with a high degree of security, the option of currency is not now popular with borrowers or issuing houses, because it involves risks for the former and also technical problems for them and the paying agent.

The essential feature of such promises lies in the fact that the subject-matter of the obligation, i.e. the money of account, itself varies. The alternative promises, whether or not they are coupled with alternative places of payment, are 'entirely independent; each provides for the payment of a particular sum in a particular place in a particular way'.[114] The optional currencies are 'on the same level', and none of them is merely superadded; there is also 'only one payment, single and indivisible, which takes place, once for all, at the place and in the currency selected'.[115] It follows, for instance, that alternative promises are not interchangeable, so that each currency can only be demanded at the particular place designated for it.[116] And although at the date of the contract the alternative promises are no doubt expected to be of equal value and effect, it is inherent in their legal nature that they may become subject to divergent developments. This is so wherever legal rules encroach upon the one or the other promise rather than the contract as a whole. Thus, just as a gold clause attached to the one promise cannot be read into the other,[117] so the abrogation of the gold clause in the case of the one option does not extend to the gold clause[118] (or the foreign money obligation[119]) agreed in the case of the other option.

[113] Very often the promise reads '£100 in London or in New York at the fixed rate of exchange of $3 to £1 or in Paris at the fixed rate of 1,000 French francs to £1'. In this case there also exists an option of currency and not only an option of place, on which see below, p. 210. For the stipulation of a fixed rate of exchange has the effect that in New York or Paris the debtor owes a fixed sum of dollars or francs so that the amount payable in these places is independent of the rate of exchange for sterling current at the date of payment. There thus exist dollar or franc debts in disguise in the sense mentioned above, p. 200. The following discussion in the text shows that there exists no 'option de change' if the promise simply reads '£100 in London or in New York in dollars' or '£100 in London or in New York at the current rate of exchange'.

[114] *International Trustee for the Protection of Bondholders A.G. v. The King*, [1936] 3 All E.R. 407, 431 *per* Lord Wright.

[115] *Rhokana Corporation Ltd. v. Inland Revenue Commissioners*, [1937] 1 K.B. 788, 806 *per* Lord Wright. The House of Lords reversed the decision: [1938] A.C. 380. But the opinions delivered rest on grounds which do not affect the correctness of Lord Wright's words relating to the character of multiple currency clauses. Lords Atkin and Thankerton, it is true, spoke of the 'primary obligation' to pay in sterling (pp. 389, 391), but this remark was clearly confined to the particular question of the law of income tax with which they were concerned and which was discussed above, p. 188.

[116] In the same sense see, for example, Danish Supreme Court, 17 Dec. 1925, *JW.* 1926, 2030.                                                                [117] Above, p. 144.

[118] Below, p. 298.                                          [119] Above, p. 197, n. 68.

The alternative character of an option of currency usually relates to the stipulation of several moneys of account. But sometimes alternative moneys of payment are promised.[120] Thus it may be agreed that the debtor should pay £100 in sterling or in dollars. In such a case there is one money of account, but there are alternative moneys of payment, viz. sterling or dollar. In the absence of a clause guaranteeing a fixed rate of exchange to the creditor, such a provision will usually be inserted into the contract for the debtor's convenience only. An example is to be found in the American case of *Booth & Co.* v. *Canadian Government*[121] where a bill of lading contained the clause:

Freight for the said goods to be paid in cash at the rate of sh. 85/- per ton payable in port of delivery [New York], in British sterling or equivalent, rate of exchange to be calculated on current rate at date of steamer's arrival at loading port [New Zealand].

There was one money of account, namely sterling, but there were alternative moneys of payment, namely sterling or dollars, and it was held that the consignee had the option of paying in dollars or sterling and that the amount of sterling payable after England had gone off the gold standard need not equal in value the dollars which would have been payable had the consignee elected to pay dollars. The clause, as the Court pointed out, intended to protect the parties against a depreciation of the dollar rather than sterling.

Whether there exist independent alternative promises in the sense mentioned above is sometimes doubtful.[122] Some of the difficulties

---

[120] Such a case is *Ross T. Smyth & Co. Ltd.* v. *W. N. Lindsay Ltd.*, [1953] 2 All E.R. 1064, at pp. 1065, 1066: if the debtor has the option of paying sterling in London or gold in New York he remains liable to pay sterling in London, though it becomes illegal to pay gold in New York. In continental law this case is called a *facultas alternativa*. See German Supreme Court, 17 Mar. 1932, *RGZ.* 136, 127. While in the case of an option of currency in the usual technical sense there exist two or more moneys of account, in the case of a *facultas alternativa* there exists only one money of account, but more than one money of payment: *una res in obligatione, duae in solutione*. As regards the distinction in general, see Selb in Staudinger's *Kommentar zum bürgerlichen Gesetzbuch* (12th ed., 1979), s. 262, n. 7; Planiol–Ripert, vii, Nos. 1052, 1053. Probably the remarkable decision of the German Supreme Court of 28 Nov. 1928, *IPRspr.* 1929 No. 107, is to be explained by the distinction between option of currency and *facultas alternativa*: the promise to pay '5,000 marks = £250 = 6,250 francs' was held to involve neither an option of currency nor a protective currency clause.

[121] 63 F. (2d) or [1933] A.M.C. 399 (C.C.A. 2d. 1933).

[122] For draft clauses of options of currency see H. Guisan in *Report of the International Law Association's 50th Conference* (Brussels, 1962), pp. 554–74. The promise to pay at the rate of '£1 = $3' contains a foreign currency clause in the sense discussed above, pp. 201 sqq., but there exists no option of currency. Apart from the cases presently to be mentioned in the text see, in this sense, *Derwa* v. *Rio de Janeiro Tramway Light & Power Co.* (1928), 4 D.L.R. 542 and the decision of the German Supreme Court of 28 Nov. 1928 referred to above, n. 120. The German decisions mentioned, p. 203, n. 92, take a different

are well exemplified by two Canadian cases. In *Brown* v. *Alberta &
Great Waterways Railway Co.*[123] bonds issued by the defendant
company contained the words 'to pay the sum of $1,000 of lawful
money of Canada at the Counting House of J. P. Morgan & Co. in the
City of London, England; the principal and interest shall be payable
there at the fixed rate of exchange of $4.86⅔ for the pound sterling'.
The coupons repeated these words, although there was no amount
specified in the text of the coupons; but on the margin there was the
clause: '$25 or £5 2s. 9d.' The question arose whether the holder was
entitled to demand for each coupon 25 Canadian dollars in London
or whether the defendant company could satisfy each coupon by the
payment of £5. 2s. 9d. which at the time were less than 25 Canadian
dollars. The court rejected the idea that there was an option of currency and upheld the defendants' point of view, since otherwise the
provisions relating to the fixed rate of exchange would have been
disregarded; the court added:

> The lenders were the ones to impose the terms on borrowers. They . . . desired
> to protect themselves against any change to their detriment by providing that
> they should receive back exactly as many pounds sterling as they advanced and
> that in the meantime they should receive in their own currency exactly 5%
> interest.

In *Royal Trust Co.* v. *Oak Bay*[124] there was a promise to pay '$500
of lawful money of the Dominion of Canada or £102 14s. 10d., its
sterling equivalent, at the rate of $4.86⅔ to the one pound sterling'.
The plaintiff demanded payment of £102. 14s. 10d. which at the
time had a greater value than $500, but the court held that the
defendants' liability was confined to $500. The judgments are not
very satisfactory, but the case was a difficult one, since the addition
of a fixed rate of exchange to the promise to pay a fixed sum of sterling made it doubtful whether there was an option of currency.[125]

The mutual independence of alternative promises each of which
provides for the payment of a fixed sum of money is the feature
view and so does the Court of Appeal of the Mixed Tribunal in Egypt which held that a loan
of Egyptian pounds stated to be 'equivalent to' fixed sums of sterling, belgas, French francs,
and Swiss francs incorporated an option of currency: 31 Mar. 1938, *B.I.J.I.* 39 (1938), 352.
The question, of course, is one of construction and it is dangerous to be too dogmatic, but
as a rule an option of currency exists only if the parties intend, not merely to secure the
immutability of the value of a single monetary obligation, but also to create several independent monetary obligations. The definition of values by equiparation is not the same thing as
the creation of distinct values.

[123] (1921) 59 D.L.R. 520 (Alberta Supreme Court App. Div.).

[124] (1934) 4 D.L.R. 697 (British Columbia Supreme Court).

[125] Probably the indication of the rate of exchange had no contractual character, but
was added *informationis causa*, so that there existed a true option of currency. Similarly
Nussbaum, p. 393.

which distinguishes an option of currency from the case where it is not the promise of currency, but merely the place of payment that is alternative ('option de place', option of place): '£100 payable in London, New York, or Paris'; '£100 in London or in New York at the rate for sterling at the date of payment'.[126] While in the former case there exist alternative promises to pay fixed sums in the respective currencies, an option of place includes only one promise to pay one sum expressed in one particular currency, but dischargeable in various places; even if the creditor is entitled to be paid in local currency at each designated place, the amount of the money of payment depends on the value, as determined by the rate of exchange, of that single money of account.[127, 128]

The distinction is thus clear and simple and should be strictly adhered to. But it is comprehensible that bondholders have sometimes attempted to transform an option of place into an option of currency. Such an attempt was rejected by the Ontario Supreme Court.[129] A coupon contained the promise to pay 12.50 francs in Paris, Brussels, or Toronto as interest on bonds issued by the defendant company. The bonds were headed by the words '3.5 million pounds = 88,060,000 francs', but the court refused to construe this clause 'as a representation or promise that the holders of the French bonds (or detached

[126] But if the clause reads: '£100 in London or in New York at the fixed rate of $2.80 to the pound', there exists an option of currency (see above, p. 208, n. 113). It follows that *New Brunswick Rly. Co.* v. *British and French Trust Corporation*, [1939] A.C. 1 involved an option of place, while *The King* v. *International Trustee for the Protection of Bondholders*, [1937] A.C. 500 involved an option of currency. The decision of the Court of Appeal at Zürich in the case of the Royal Dutch loan (21 Feb. 1941), *Nouvelle Revue de droit international privé*, 1942, 451, related to bonds for $1,000 in gold payable in New York or, *inter alia*, in Zürich in Swiss francs at the rate of exchange of the day of presentment. The court held that the Joint Resolution did not apply, because it affected only dollar obligation, and this was a Swiss franc obligation. In truth there was a single money of account, i.e. dollars, and Swiss francs were merely one of the moneys of payment. Hence there existed a mere option of place.

[127] The essence of an option of place was well explained by the Permanent Court of International Justice at The Hague in the case of the Serbian Loans (Judgment No. 14, Collection of Judgments 1928-30, at p. 35) when it was said: 'The mere provision for payment in the places named at the rate of exchange on Paris cannot affect the amount due: it must in fact be construed in the light of the principal stipulation which is for payment at gold value. That provision is plainly, not for the purpose of altering the amount agreed to be paid, but for the placing of the equivalent of that amount according to banking practice at the command of the bondholder in the foreign money in the designated cities.'

[128] There is no legal difference between an option of place and an option of collection. In American legal language bonds are sometimes expressed to be 'payable' in a certain place and 'collectible' in other places. For such cases see Nussbaum, p. 388; 44 (1934) *Yale L.J.* 53; Rabel, *RabelsZ.* 10 (1936), 492, 498; Hamel, *Nouvelle Revue de droit international privé*, 1937, 499. There exists in these cases merely an option of place. Whether a bond provides for certain sums to be payable in London, New York, or Paris, or to be payable in London and collectible in New York or Paris, the legal results will normally be the same and no advantage is gained by introducing unjustifiable refinements.

[129] *Derwa* v. *Rio de Janeiro Tramway & Power Co.* (1928), 4 D.L.R. 542.

coupons) should have the option of being paid in pounds'.[130] Similar attempts were made in France, where the courts at one time took a rather liberal view, but where now the stricter tendency begins to prevail.[131, 132]

Whether there exists an option of currency or an option of place, in most cases it is the creditor's protection or convenience which the parties had in view when they stipulated the option, and it will therefore generally be the creditor's right to exercise it. This is well recognized on the Continent,[133] and cannot be different in this country. Where the creditor has to take the first step by presenting his dividend warrant or bond, the principle that prima facie the election is in the

[130] At pp. 554 sqq., 560.

[131] The starting-point of the modern development is the case concerning the bonds issued by the Banco El Hogar Argentine (Cass. Civ. 17 July 1929, Clunet, 1929, 1075) where there obviously was an 'option de change'. A remarkable extension is to be found in the next case, concerning the bonds of the Crédit Foncier Franco-Canadien: Cass Civ. 3 June 1930, Clunet, 1931, 103, with the important arguments of the Attorney-General Paul Matter: a bond expressed in francs, but payable in Paris in francs, in Geneva in francs, in London and other places at the current rate of exchange, was held to give the holder an 'option de change' in Geneva. But later decisions on very similar facts take a much stricter view: Cass. Civ. 21 Dec. 1932, Clunet, 1933, 1201 (Chemin de fer de Rosario à Puerto-Belgrano); Cass. Civ. 5 June 1934, Clunet, 1935, 90 (Est Lumière); Cass. Civ. 17 July 1935, Clunet, 1936, 880 (Brasseries Sochaux); Cass. Civ. 21 July 1936, Clunet, 1937, 299 (Papeteries Bergès); Cass. Req. 24 Feb. 1937, Gaz. Pal. 1937, 1. 860 = Clunet, 1937, 765 (Crédit Foncier Franco-Canadien); Cass. Civ. 28 Mar. 1938, Clunet, 1938, 776 (Chemin de fer de Rosario à Puerto-Belgrano). Reference should be made to Planiol–Ripert, vii, No. 1194, where it is well said: 'Mais l'option de place n'entraîne pas par elle-même option de change. Si l'instrument monétaire offert au prêteur varie dans son genre suivant le lieu de paiement, il ne varie pas quant à la valeur réelle qui lui est remise: le montant du versement demeure identique en tous lieux, son expression seule diffère.' If there does not exist an 'option de change', but merely an obligation stipulated in francs and payable in France and Switzerland, a further and different problem arises, namely, to determine whether the money of account was French or Swiss; as to this question and the decisions relating thereto see below, pp. 000 sqq. The Court of Appeal of the Mixed Tribunal in Egypt declined to regard as an 'option de change' the promise to pay francs 'payable à Paris en monnaie française, ainsi qu'en Égypte, à Londres, Bâle, Genève, Amsterdam et Bruxelles, au cours du change à vue sur Paris': 29 Dec. 1927, Clunet, 1928, 769 (re Land Bank of Egypt).

[132] For a Dutch case where the plaintiff, a Belgian subject, sold to the defendant, a Dutch subject, real estate situate in Holland for '32,500 frs. or 15,000 guilders in Dutch money', and where the court disregarded the alternative promise, see Court of Appeal at The Hague, 8 June 1931, Weekblad 12338 and Nederlandsche Jurisprudentie, 1931, 1499.

[133] This was achieved, although the codes contain prima facie rules to the effect that the debtor has the right of election: Art. 1190, French Code Civil; s. 262, German Civil Code; Art. 72, Swiss Obligationenrecht. As to France see, for example, Cass. Req. 17 July 1929, Clunet, 1929, 1075 (Banco el Hogar Argentino); Batiffol et Lagarde, No. 613; Planiol-Ripert, vii, No. 1192; Degand, Rép. dr. international, iii (1929), 'Change', Nos. 129 sqq.; X (1931), Paiement, Nos. 67, 68. As to Germany, see already Supreme Court, 19 Feb. 1887, RGZ. 19, 48 relating to one of the 'Coupons Actions', on which see below, p. 268; also 1 July 1926, JW. 1926, 2675; 14 Nov. 1929, RGZ. 126, 196; 5 Oct. 1936, RGZ. 152, 213, 218. In the 'Coupons Actions' and also in later cases the Austrian courts rejected the assertion of an 'option de change', but regarded the promises to pay non-Austrian currency as being added merely informationis causa; see Walker, Internationales Privatrecht, pp. 408 sqq.

person who has to do the first act[134] will apply without difficulties. Even where no such presentation is required, the purpose of the option will usually indicate that it is to be exercised by the creditor.[135]

## IX

The foregoing survey shows that in law there are substantial distinctions between the various types of foreign currency clauses, although all of them may be intended to serve the same commercial purpose. The clause '£100, £1 being equal to $3', as has been seen, is different not only from the clause '£100 payable in dollars at the rate of £1 to $3', but also from the clause '£100 or $300'. Again the promise to pay '£100 in sterling in London or in dollars in New York' is not the same thing as the promise to pay '£100 in London or $300 in New York'. The choice of formulation will often be fortuitous and this indubitable fact will lead to the argument that in construing these clauses regard should be had, not to their wording, but to their purpose and to the intentions of the parties. It would indeed be impossible to state categorically that the tenor of a foreign currency clause cannot in any case be overriden by the principles of construction. But it is essential to abide by the established canons of interpretation. They include the rule that interpretation presupposes ambiguity. Thus the clause '£100, £1 being equal to $3' is ambiguous in that it is uncertain whether it constitutes an absolute or a relative measure of value; in this case, therefore, effect may be given to the purpose of the clause. But where there is no ambiguity, the parties will almost invariably be unable to escape from what is clearly expressed by the words they have chosen; nor would it be desirable to confer upon them the power to do so. It follows that the draftsman will have to take great care in expressing his thoughts, and the justification for this elaborate discussion lies in the necessity for giving him guidance by an explanation of the exact meaning of the words which he so often employs inexactly.

## X

In view of the very great importance which, in connection with foreign money obligations, is to be attached to the place of payment

---

[134] See Chitty, *On Contracts* (24th ed., 1977), No. 1265, n. 21.

[135] *In Rhokana Corporation Ltd.* v. *Inland Revenue Commissioners*, [1937] 1 K.B. 788, 804 Lord Wright said: 'We think that the option is the holder's option given to him for his benefit, and is exercisable by him.' But although counsel's argument that it was the debtor's option was thus rejected, the value of the dictum is somewhat reduced by the fact that the warrant expressly gave the option to the holder.

and its law, it seems advisable to offer a few observations on its meaning and ambit in the international sphere.[136]

1. If it is desired to ascertain the equivalent, in a foreign legal system, of the place of payment in the English sense, it is necessary to ask where, in the eyes of the foreign law, the creditor is entitled to the money contractually due to him. It would be dangerous to stop short at what the foreign law calls the place of payment. It is the function, not the terminology that matters. Thus German law provides that the place of the debtor's residence at the time of the contract usually is the place of performance,[137] but the debtor must transmit money at his risk and expense to the place where the creditor resides.[138] This, therefore, is the place where, under German law, the creditor is entitled to be paid, and is the equivalent of the English conception of the place of payment.[139] It is irrelevant that German law calls it the place of destination or delivery and describes the place of the debtor's residence at the time of the contract as the place of performance.[140]

2. The place of performance or payment may be of importance in connection with a rule of private international or of municipal law.[141] If an English rule of private international law refers to the law of the place of payment, this term 'place of payment' must, in the absence of any indication by the parties, be understood in the English sense, i.e. as the place where the creditor resides. Only after the application of English private international law has led to the application of another municipal law as the governing law can that law's conception of the meaning of 'place of payment' be considered. This inherent difference between private international law and municipal law[142]

---

[136] On the meaning of the term in municipal law, see above, p. 76.

[137] Art. 269.                                                                     [138] Art. 270.

[139] It is on this ground that the remarkable case of *Bamberger* v. *Clark*, 390 F. 2d 485 (1968), in which s. 270 was not even referred to, should have been decided.

[140] The passages in the text were relied on by the Arbitral Tribunal for the Agreement on German External Debts in *Swiss Confederation* v. *German Federal Republic*, Int. L.R. 25 (1958, i.) 33, pp. 57 sqq. The question was whether by a contract which described the creditor as having 'its head office' in Switzerland 'it was expressly agreed . . . that the place of payment' was outside Germany within the meaning of the London Debt Agreement of 1952. The Tribunal, by a majority of five to four, held that (1) the meaning of the term 'place of payment' was determined, not by the proper law of the contract between the parties, but autonomously by the treaty; (2) it was the place where the creditor was entitled actually to receive the money, i.e. Switzerland; and (3) the indication of the creditor's address involved an express agreement of the place of payment. The decision on point (1) relates to a very difficult point of general importance, and may deserve support. See below, p. 000, n. 109. On point (2) the Tribunal was clearly right. On point (3) the majority's judgment is wholly unconvincing.

[141] Or a treaty under public international law: see the preceding note.

[142] See, for example, Dicey and Morris, p. 772, or M. Wolff, *Private International Law*, 2nd ed., p. 136.

may be elucidated by an example. It is a rule of English private international law that the construction of a contract is governed by the
proper law. Let us assume that the determination of the money of
account, if it is doubtful, is a matter of construction and therefore
governed by the proper law.[143] If under a contract the proper law
of which is French, a French merchant owes francs to a Geneva merchant, and if, in the absence of other indications, it is doubtful
whether French or Swiss francs were meant, English private international law refers to French law as the proper law, and it thus
becomes necessary and permissible to apply the rule of French municipal law that prima facie the money of account is that which circulates at the place of payment. It is obvious that the meaning of the
words 'place of performance', when they occur in French municipal
law duly found to be applicable, must be ascertained according to
French law, which refers to the debtor's residence. Thus it may
appear that French francs are owed. On the basis of English (private
international or municipal) law the result would have been that Swiss
francs were due.

3. It is a matter of some difficulty to determine the influence of
the law of the place of payment in English private international law.
The law of the place of performance may be the proper law of the
contract, and in the absence of other circumstances this inference
will often have to be drawn where the place of performance is intended to be in a country other than that in which the contract was
made.[144] These are rules relating to the selection of the proper law
and they are of no particular interest in connection with monetary
questions.

But there remains the question of defining the weight attached to
the law of the place of payment, if it is not identical with the proper
law of the contract. No doubt 'in English law a transaction may be
regulated in general by the law of one country although as to parts of
that transaction which are to be performed in another country the
law of that other country may be the law applicable'.[145] But in what
circumstances is it possible to apply the law of the place of payment
to a transaction the proper law of which is different?

In the first place the law of the place of performance may apply as

---

[143] See below, pp. 233 sqq.

[144] *Chatenay* v. *Brazilian Submarine Telegraph Co.*, [1891] 1 Q.B.D. 79, 82, 83 *per*
Lord Esher as understood, for example, by Lord Hanworth in *Broken Hill Proprietary Co.*
v. *Latham*, [1933] Ch. 373, 397. *Chatenay*'s case has often been misunderstood. It is submitted that the only principle expressed by the decision is the proposition stated in the
text. See Dicey and Morris, p. 771.

[145] Lord Roche in *International Trustee for the Protection of Bondholders A.G.* v. *The
King*, [1937] A.C. 500, 574.

regards the mode or method of performance. The existence of this rule in English private international law,[146] cannot be doubted. But it is not easy to define the matters falling under the head of 'mode' of performance. Though the distinction between the substance of an obligation and the mode of performance is well known in many respects,[147] the interconnection between both parts of an obligation is so great that very careful consideration is required. This is especially so when the distinction serves as a basis for a rule of private international law which involves the submission of one contract to two different legal systems. Thus Lord Wright said[148] that 'that principle (i.e. that the mode of performance is governed by the law of the place of performance), no doubt, is limited to matters which can fairly be described as being the mode or method of performance and is not to be extended so as to change the substantive or essential conditions of the contract'.

Secondly, the law of the place of performance is said to be of importance as regards the validity of the contract. It is said that a contract, whether lawful by its proper law or not, is invalid in so far as the performance is unlawful by the *lex loci solutionis*. Notwithstanding the judicial approval which this alleged rule has received, it is still possible to submit[149] with respect, but also with a measure of confidence, that it does not constitute a rule of the English conflict of laws at all.[150]

Thirdly, a dichotomy of proper law and law of the place of performance may result from the application of the dictum of Lord Wright[151] that:

. . . *prima facie*, whatever is the proper law of the contract regarded as a whole, the law of the place of performance should be applied in respect of any particular obligation which is performable in a particular country other than the country of the proper law of the contract.

This dictum is certainly too widely formulated, inasmuch as it does not restrict the application of the *lex loci solutionis* to those cases

[146] *Lloyd* v. *Guibert* (1865), L.R. 1 Q.B. 115, 126 *per* Willes J. delivering the opinion of the Court; *Jacobs* v. *Crédit Lyonnais* (1884), 12 Q.B.D. 589, 604 *per* Bowen L.J.; *Broken Hill Proprietary Co.* v. *Latham*, [1933] Ch. 373, 397 *per* Lord Hanworth; *Auckland City Council* v. *Alliance Assurance Co.*, [1937] A.C. 587, 606 *per* Lord Wright; Dicey and Morris, p. 812.

[147] Above, p. 199.

[148] *Auckland City Council* v. *Alliance Assurance Co.*, [1937] A.C. 587, 606; and see *Mount Albert Borough Council* v. *Australasian Temperance & General Mutual Life Assurance Society Limited*, [1938] A.C. 224, 241, 242, where Lord Wright also qualified his statement in *Adelaide Electric Supply Co.* v. *Prudential Assurance Co.*, [1934] A.C. 122, 151.

[149] *British Year Book of International Law*, 1937, pp. 107 sqq.

[150] See Dicey and Morris, pp. 796, 797, with further references; Wolff, p. 444, 445; Cheshire and North, pp. 227, 228.

[151] *Adelaide Electric Supply Co.* v. *Prudential Assurance Co.*, [1934] A.C. 122, 151.

where the place of performance is expressly fixed, and as it comprises 'any particular obligation', i.e. even the whole of the substance of the debt.[152] Though this wide principle cannot be accepted and though its importance is greatly restricted by a later decision of the Privy Council in which Lord Wright delivered the judgment of the Board,[153] its kernel was adopted by the Court of Appeal when, in a case involving an option of place, it submitted the 'measure of payment' to the *lex loci solutionis* rather than the proper law of the contract.[154]

Yet it cannot be said that any such principle is firmly established in English law,[155] nor has it ever been possible to find a satisfactory formulation for delimiting the 'measure of payment' from the mere method of payment (clearly governed by the *lex loci solutionis*) or from the substance of the obligation (equally clearly governed by its proper law). In these circumstances comparative law may point the way. An Italian statute which provided that bonds issued by an Italian company and containing an 'option de change' could be discharged by the payment in Italy of lire of the nominal amount with an additional sum of 25 per cent thereof was held in France not to prevent bondholders from recovering in France French francs promised in the 'option de change'.[156] In another case the Cour de

---

[152] See the paper quoted above, p. 216, n. 149.

[153] *Mount Albert Borough Council* v. *Australasian Temperance & General Mutual Life Assurance Society Ltd.*, [1938] A.C. 224, 241 *per* Lord Wright: 'Mr. O'Shea relied on certain expressions used in *Adelaide Electric Supply Co.* v. *Prudential Assurance Co.*, [1934] A.C. 122 as indicating that the House of Lords there laid down that the law of the place of performance applied for all purposes relating to performance, even to the extent of changing the substance of the obligation expressed or embodied in the contract, with the result in the present case that the amount of the interest was reduced by the effect of the Financial Emergency Acts. Their Lordships cannot accept this reading of the *Adelaide* case. The House of Lords was not concerned there with any such general questions, or with questions of the substance of the obligation, which, in general, is fixed by the proper law of the contract under which the obligation is created. The House of Lords was concerned only with performance of that obligation with regard to the particular matter of the currency in which payment was to be made. There was no question such as a reduction in the amount of the debt or liability, or other change in the contractual obligation. The House of Lords had no intention of questioning the distinction emphasized in *Jacobs* v. *Crédit Lyonnais* (12 Q.B.D. 589) between obligation and performance. . . .' This qualification of the *Adelaide* case is indeed very fortunate, though it is not quite correct that, on the basis adopted by Lord Wright in that case, a question of performance, not of substance, was involved: see below, pp. 233 sqq.

[154] *British & French Trust Corporation* v. *New Brunswick Rly. Co.*, [1937] 4 All E.R. 516, discussed below, p. 000.

[155] Against it *Montreal Trust Co.* v. *Stanrock Uranium Mines Ltd.* (1966), 53 D.L.R. (2d) 594. See Dicey and Morris, p. 749, n. 15; M. Wolff, *Private International Law*, 2nd ed., s. 437; 'E.' in *British Year Book of International Law*, 1937, pp. 218 sqq., 220; Cheshire and North, p. 247. On the matters discussed in the text, see Morris, vi (1953) Vanderbilt L.R. 505.

[156] Trib. Civ. Seine, 18 Jan. 1928, Clunet, 1928, 669 (Société Italienne de Chemins de Fer Méridionaux). The value of the judgment is impaired by the fact that it was given by default.

Paris held that a Polish company which had issued bonds with an 'option de change' for various European currencies could not rely on a Polish statute reducing the amount due to one-third of its denomination and could not prevent the bond-holder from demanding payment of the stipulated amount of Dutch guilders.[157] The point was also dealt with in an interesting decision of the German Supreme Court.[158] The Municipality of Vienna in 1902 issued bonds entitling the holder to claim 500 kroners, equal to 425 marks, equal to 525 francs, equal to 20 pounds sterling 15 shillings, equal to 251.50 Dutch florins, equal to 100 U.S.A. gold dollars. The plaintiff demanded 525 Swiss francs per bond, but the defendants relied on an Austrian statute of 1922 which had authorized them to repay the bonds in Austrian kroners at their nominal value. Although the court held that on principle the bonds, especially as regards the formation and interpretation of the contract, were subject to Austrian law, it denied any

[157] 19 Apr. 1928, Clunet, 1928 695 (Sté de Charbonnages de Sosnovice), and see the judgment in the preceding action rendered by the Cour de Paris, 25 Nov. 1926, Clunet, 1927, 700. In the course of the later judgment the court said 'qu'en émettant ses obligations sur des places étrangères et en donnant à ses créanciers la faculté de toucher leurs coupons ainsi que le capital de leurs titres en pays étranger et en monnaie étrangère la société débitrice a entendu précisément les garantir contre toute dépréciation intérieure qui surgirait ou qui serait organisée dans la monnaie du pays auquel elle appartient par sa nationalité'.

[158] 14 Nov. 1929, RGZ. 126, 196; 16 Apr. 1931, IPRspr. 1931, No. 33. See also 23 June 1927, RGZ. 118, 370; 22 Dec. 1927, IPRspr. 1928, No. 66. Against these decisions Haudek, Die Autonomie des Parteiwillens (1931), p. 69, and Nussbaum, Die Bilanz der Aufwertungstheorie (1929), p. 37. But see M. Wolff, Internationales Privatrecht, 2nd ed., 1949, p. 132, and Raape, Internationales Privatrecht, 5th ed., 1961, p. 539, who speaks of an 'option de change' in a sense importing an 'option de loi'. That the loan referred to in the text included an option of currency was not open to doubt, but was expressly affirmed by the Tripartite Claims Commission for the United States, Austria and Hungary of 1924: Crane's case, Reports of International Arbitral Awards vi. 244. A re-examination of the decisions of the Permanent Court of International Justice at The Hague in the cases of Serbian and Brazilian loans shows that these judgments have no bearing on the question dealt with in the text; for further details see below, p. 000. For other foreign material bearing on the point see below, p. 000, n. 144. Whether a prohibitory law which is contained in a foreign legal system other than the proper law but claims to be applicable to the particular transaction concerned can and ought to be enforced by the forum is a question that has often attracted the attention of Continental writers. German scholars have suggested an affirmative answer, if there exists 'a sufficiently close connection' of the transaction with the prohibitory law (Wengler, Zeitschrift für vergleichende Rechtswissenschaft, 54 (1941), 168), or if the movement of funds resulting in performance occurs wholly or in part within the country which has enacted the prohibitory law (Zweigert, RabelsZ. 14 (1942), 283); the latter formula resembles that which the French Cour de Cassation employed to define 'paiement international' (above, p. 163, n. 151). For a similar view see Neumayer, Rev. Crit. 1957, 579; 1958, 53, who takes the legislator's 'social sphere' as a test. Against these theories Vischer, Internationales Vertragsrecht (1962), 188 sqq., but see more recently Rec. 142 (1974 ii), 23, 24; Serick, RabelsZ. 1953, 646, or Van Hecke, p. 137 and others. The Federal Supreme Court (17 Dec. 1959), BGHZ. 31. 367, seems to reject them. In this country there is no indication of any departure from the control of the proper law. Nor is it possible to discover any practical necessity or theoretical justification for any such departure which would have far-reaching effects in connection with gold clauses and exchange restrictions. On the problem see Mann, Rec. 132 (1971 i), pp. 157 sqq. or Festschrift für Günther Beitzke (1979), 607.

effect to the law of 1922 and applied to the 'payment transaction' the law of the place of performance, i.e. Swiss law, at least so far as concerned subsequent encroachments by Austrian law on the extent of the obligation.

These cases afford a useful guide when an attempt is made to elucidate the correct principle applicable to monetary obligations. The possibility of applying a legal system other than the proper law depends on the intention of the parties. But the 'splitting' of the contract is so serious a step that the parties' intention to concentrate part of the transaction at the place of payment must not only be expressed, but must be expressed with a sufficient degree of intensity so as to afford to the creditor a definite measure of protection. Such conditions exist, and exist only, in the case of an option of currency. It owes its existence to the parties' desire to create obligations which, up to a point, are independent of each other,[159] and thus to provide a safeguard against developments which at the date of the contract are unforeseeable. This leads to the only suggestion which can safely be made: the effect of supervenient enactments which encroach upon the measure of payment due under such monetary obligations as embody an option of currency, should be governed by the law of the place where, in accordance with the exercise of the option, payment is to be made.[160]

---

[159] See above, p. 208.

[160] The suggestions in the text are accepted by Van Hecke, pp. 205, 206. Against them Vischer, *Internationales Vertragsrecht* (1962), p. 218. For instances of the suggested rule see below, pp. 276, n. 43, 298. Rabel, *Conflict of Laws*, iii (1950), 46 goes further than the text: 'a genuine multiple currency clause includes an implied choice of law under the condition of its exercise'. See now on the general problem Heini, *Zeitschrift für Schweizerisches Recht* 1981, 65.

# VIII

# The Determination of the
# Money of Account:
# Initial Uncertainty

I. The problem stated. II. The determination of the money of account in case of fixed indebtedness: (1) the rules of municipal law; (2) the problem of private international law; the *Adelaide* and the *Auckland Corporation* cases in particular. III. The determination of the money of account in case of unforeseen liability: (1) the rules of municipal law in general and in particular cases: (*a*) indication in the contract; (*b*) restitution of value; (*c*) conversion into the injured party's domestic currency; agency. (2) the rule of private international law.


I

La vérité consiste dans les nuances. RENAN

WHEN one approaches the problem of identifying the money of account, it is essential to differentiate between the three types of circumstances which may give rise to uncertainty. They depend on whether one has to consider the money of account of a monetary system common to the territories concerned or of monetary systems that were at all material times distinct, or of monetary systems which at the time of payment are distinct, but were originally identical.[1]

In the first case, then, uncertainty exists within the ambit of a single currency system. It is due to the fact that the circulating currency, though everywhere identical in law, has locally a different

---

[1] On the existence of independent monetary systems see above, p. 51. The first case referred to in the text is exemplified by *Adelaide Electric Supply Co. Ltd.*v. *Prudential Assurance Co. Ltd.*, [1934] A.C. 122, and *Auckland Corporation* v. *Alliance Assurance Co.*, [1937] A.C. 587. For an example of the second case see *Bonython* v. *Commonwealth of Australia*, [1951] A.C. 201. The third case has not so far arisen in England (but see below, p. 259, n. 25, but was dealt with in Australia in *Goldsbrough Mort & Co. Ltd.* v. *Hall* (1949), 78 C.L.R. 1, to which, although it relates to a fundamentally different set of circumstances, Lord Simonds referred with approval in *Bonython*'s case. In addition to the three cases mentioned in the text a fourth is conceivable: two originally distinct monetary systems are by the time of payment unified into a single system. Once the original money of account has been determined, there will be no difficulty in translating it into the new currency by means of the statutory rate of conversion (recurrent link); see below, p. 274.

commercial value—an unlikely situation, but one which, in view of a decision of the House of Lords,[2] cannot be ignored: if it is assumed that England and Scotland share a monetary system, but the pound in Edinburgh is at a discount in relation to the pound in London, it may become necessary to ascertain whether the debtor has to pay 'English' or 'Scottish' pounds. This is not a problem of the money of account, for *ex hypothesi* there exists only one single pound which in both territories is in law the same. At the most this is a problem of the money of payment: how many pounds has the debtor to pay in Edinburgh to discharge a debt expressed in pounds common to London and Edinburgh?

Secondly, uncertainty may arise from the fact that the parties have contracted in terms of the one or the other standard of currency having the same name, but belonging, respectively, to distinct monetary systems: in a contract for the sale of goods it may be doubtful whether the parties contemplated the price to be payable in Canadian or U.S.A. dollars (or even in sterling). Here the ambiguity exists *ab initio* and the lawyer is faced with the task of determining which of two or three possible but different moneys of account the parties had in mind at the time of the contract.

Thirdly, at the date of the contract there existed a single monetary system with reference to which the parties have in fact contracted, but subsequently it is split into two or more systems which, possibly, even continue to use, or adopt, identical names for their standards of currency: thus, assuming that the Palestine pound was at some time the same as the English pound,[3] i.e. that both countries shared a common monetary system, what, in a given case, would be the money of account after the independent State of Israel was created and introduced its own standard of currency, the Israeli pound? In such a case there did not, at the time of the contract, exist any (initial) difficulty, but at the time of payment the money of account in which the debt has become expressed and is to be discharged is uncertain.

The second and third case involve entirely different considerations and will be dealt with in separate chapters.

It is the purpose of the present chapter[4] to discuss primarily what has been described as the second type of uncertainty, though

[2] *Adelaide Electric Supply Co. Ltd.* v. *Prudential Assurance Co. Ltd.*, [1934] A.C. 122, where it was held that the pound was the same in Britain and Australia.

[3] In *Rivlin* v. *Wallis*, Jerusalem Post (Law Reports), 2 Feb. 1958, the Supreme Court of Israel surmised that this is a mere assumption made *arguendo*. In fact there existed no such identity.

[4] For a detailed discussion of the matters treated in this chapter see Dicey and Morris, pp. 999 sqq.

some reference will have to be made to such authorities as, strictly, relate only to the first type, and to do so with a view to two groups of problems and two methods of approach to them.

On the one hand, payments may have been agreed or ordered to be made, as in contracts or wills. In such a situation the currency whose units of account are the subject-matter of the obligation will mostly be fixed. But this is not always so and, therefore, the familiar aids of construction will have to be resorted to (section II, below). On the other hand, there are many and varied circumstances in which the amount to be paid is not, and in the nature of things cannot be, fixed by the parties, as in connection with claims for unliquidated damages or indemnities, and in which interpretation of the contract does not usually help (section III, below). The following investigation of these questions deals only with the determination of that money which constitutes the substance of the obligation, i.e. the money of account. The determination of the money of payment, i.e. the mode or instrument of payment, will be treated elsewhere.[5]

However, it is essential to remember throughout this chapter, firstly, that the question what law governs the determination of the currency owed must be strictly distinguished from the fundamentally different question of what currency is owed according to the legal system found to be applicable; in other words, a clear line of demarcation must be drawn between private international law and municipal law. In particular, it should be clearly understood that the question of determining the currency is not concluded 'by saying that the proper law . . . is the law of England, for though . . . in a contract of which the proper law is English the word "pound" prima facie means an English pound, it does not so necessarily; it is a question of construction'.[6, 7] As Lord Denning M.R. put it, 'we must apply the proper law of the contract and then, as a matter

---

[5] Below, pp. 305 sqq.

[6] In this sense *National Mutual Life Association* v. *Attorney-General for New Zealand*, [1956] A.C. 369, at p. 387; Romer L.J. in *Broken Hill Proprietary Co.* v. *Latham*, [1933] Ch. 373, 409; *Joffe* v. *African Life Assurance Society*, South African L.R. (Transvaal Division) 1933, 189; Latham C.J. in *National Bank of Australasia Ltd.* v. *Scottish Union National Insurance* (1951), 84 C.L.R. 177, 208. But see Sankey J. in *Ivor An Christensen* v. *Furness Withy & Co.* (1922), 12 Ll. L.R. 288; Lord Wright in *Westralian Farmers* v. *King Line* (1932), 43 Ll. L.R. 378, 382, and Lord Tomlin in *Adelaide Electric Supply Co.* v. *Prudential Assurance Co.*, [1934] A.C. 122, 145.

[7] Conversely, the choice of a money of accout is of little or no value in determining the proper law of the contract: Dicey and Morris, p. 763 with reference to the cases in some of which too much weight may have been attributed to the choice of currency; Swiss Federal Tribunal, 6 Dec. 1950, *Annuaire Swisse de Droit International*, 1951, 246; 24 Oct. 1950, ibid., p. 247.

of construction, decide what was the currency of account'.[8] Secondly, it must be emphasized that what matters to the parties is the identity of the money of account, for it defines the quantum of the obligation. The money of payment is not usually of equal or, indeed, any significance, for it only determines the method of paying the amount due and has no bearing on the 'value' paid or received.

## II

Turning now to those cases where the indebtedness is fixed in terms rendering the identity of the money of account doubtful, we shall first examine the municipal law and then consider what municipal law governs the question in case of a conflict of laws.

1. Doubts may arise for many reasons. It may happen that the parties have omitted to determine the currency altogether; thus goods may have been sold from England to Brazil at a reasonable price or at market price so that it is necessary to ascertain whether the parties contemplated sterling or Brazilian currency.[9] At the other end of the scale is the case in which, although the money of account is prima facie fixed, a different money of account is in fact the subject-matter of the obligation. This may be due to a subsequent agreement between the parties varying the originally stipulated money of account to another,[10] or to the fact that it

---

[8] W.J. Alan v. El Nasr Export and Import Co., [1972] 2 Q.B. 189, at p. 206. See also Donaldson J. (as he then was) in The Alexandra I, (1971), 2 Ll. L.R. 469, at p. 474.

[9] There does not seem to be any English decision dealing with such a case. The report of Russian Commercial & Industrial Bank v. British Bank of Foreign Trade (No. 1), [1921] 2 A.C. 438 does not indicate why it was uncertain whether sterling or roubles were owed. See, however, the remarkable decision of the Austrian Supreme Court, 5 Dec. 1961, Entscheidungen des Österreichischen Obersten Gerichtshofs in Zivilsachen, xxxiv (1961), No. 180: In 1938 two Austrian Jews met in Czechoslovakia, where the plaintiff lent to the defendant 34,000 kroners to enable him to finance his further emigration to either Belgium or Uruguay. The court denied the defendant's liability to repay Czechoslovakian kroners or their present value. Without having any material in support the court imputed to the parties the intention that 'repayment, in whatever currency, had to correspond to the then value of the amount lent. Accordingly the defendant . . . has to pay such sum as corresponds to the then convertible value of Czechoslovakian kroners, i.e. these must be converted, at the rate of the time of the loan, into one of those currencies which at that time could be chosen by the defendant as borrower for exchange.' Such cases which have also arisen in Germany (see below, p. 274, n. 32) would not, it is hoped, be decided in England in a similarly arbitrary manner.

[10] As to these cases see p. 225, n. 16. In the international banking practice one frequently meets agreements to the effect that in the event of a foreign currency credit not being punctually repaid the bank is entitled to convert it into a domestic currency credit. This does not mean that if a domestic currency credit is secured by a guarantee or a bill of exchange expressed in foreign currency the bank is entitled to demand domestic currency from the defaulting guarantor or acceptor. In this sense Federal Supreme Court of Germany, 29 May 1980, NJW. 1980, 2017.

appears on proper construction that there was an intention to adopt a money of account other than that stated. Thus, if a testator leaves to five of his children £12,000 each, and to two daughters 24,000 marks each, which at the time of the will were the equivalent of £12,000, he may have intended to give £12,000 to each of them.[11] Another example of a case in which what appeared as the money of account was merely a reference to some measure of value is provided by a decision of the House of Lords: where charterers of a Norwegian ship had undertaken to procure a policy against war risks 'on Norwegian terms for 2,000,000 kroners . . . towards the cost of which the owner agrees to contribute a premium at the rate of £4½ per cent', it was held that this was an agreement to provide a sterling policy,[12] the reference to kroners being merely 'to value and not to currency'.[13] It is also possible that a contract provides for two different monies of account in different parts or for different purposes.[14] The most frequent and at the same time the most difficult case of doubt, however, arises where the parties have chosen an ambiguous denomination such as 'pound' (England, Israel, Turkey, Egypt) or 'dollar' (United States of America, Canada, Australia, Hong Kong) or 'francs' (Switzerland, Belgium, France, Luxemburg).[15] It is this situation that requires particular attention.

It cannot be gainsaid that the determination of the money of account is a matter or interpretation of the contract, and is so treated in all legal systems. As in connection with all other problems of construction so it is here necessary to have regard to all the circumstances of the case and so to deduce the true intention of the parties. The nature of the transaction, the nationality, residence,

---

[11] *Oppenheimer* v. *Public Trustee*, below, p. 566, at p. 570 *per* Lord Hanworth M.R., at p. 574 *per* Lawrence L.J. For a case in which French francs were held to be the money of account, although the contract referred to Swedish kroners, see Cour de Paris, 22 Dec. 1951, *Rev. Crit.* 1953, 379. In this connection reference should be made to Cass. Civ. 14 Jan. 1931, Clunet, 1931, 126 (Ville de Tokio): the French part of a loan issued in London, Paris, and New York provided for French francs as money of account, but as the amount of the French part of the loan, namely 100,880,000 francs, was stated to be equal to £4,000,000, it was held that the money of account of the French part was in fact expressed in pounds. In 1934 the Supreme Court of Japan decided in the opposite sense, as appears from the summary of the facts by Mr. Black, acting as *amiable compositeur*, in his 'Opinion' of 1 Apr. 1960: International L.R. 29, 11. A very similar case was decided in a different sense by the Ontario Supreme Court: *Derwa* v. *Rio de Janeiro Tranway Light & Power Co.* (1928), 4 D.L.R. 542, when a loan for '3,500,000 pounds = 88,060,000 francs' was held to be denominated in francs only, because the text of the bonds and coupons merely provided for francs. See above, p. 211.

[12] *Larsen* v. *Anglo-American Oil Co. Ltd* (1924), 20 Ll. L.R. 67; cf. *Ivor An Christensen* v. *Furness Withy & Co.* (1922), 12 Ll. L.R. 288.          [13] At p. 69 *per* Lord Cave.

[14] *The Alexandra I*, (1971), 2 Ll. L.R. 469, at p. 474.

[15] As to particular meanings of the word 'francs' see p. 23, n. 132; p. 142, n. 27; p. 153, n. 91; p. 269, n. 9.

and domicile of the parties, the valuation of the respective currencies at the time when the contract was made, the place where the contract was made and where it was to be performed, all these and similar facts will have to be looked at and weighed.[16] Sometimes the contract itself supplies an indication: thus, where a certain percentage is payable, e.g. in respect of commission, it may generally be assumed that units of account of that currency are owed in which the principal sum is expressed.[17] The government of a self-governing

---

[16] In England the state of facts at the time of the contract is exclusively relevant, for according to English rules of interpretation the subsequent conduct of the parties is not a legitimate means of interpretation: *F.L. Schuler A.G.* v. *Wickenden Machine Tool Sales Ltd.*, [1974] A.C. 235. With reference to the money of account, in particular, this was made clear in *Noel* v. *Rochford* (1836), 4 Cl. & Fin. 158, 201 and by Lord Wright in *Auckland Corporation* v. *Alliance Assurance Co.*, [1937] A.C. 587, 603, where he used words which at the same time draw a clear distinction between the money of account and the money of payment: 'There are two dates which in a case of this sort may have to be considered as material dates. One is the date when the contract is made, and the other is the date at which the contract requires payment to be effected. It is at the latter date that the measure of value expressed by the word "pound" in the contract will have to be ascertained, and that will depend on the precise state of the relevant currency at the particular date. But it is as at the date of the contract that it must be decided what currency is meant by the contract as the currency or measure of value in which the contract obligation is to be discharged.' Perhaps it would have been still clearer if the term 'expressed' instead of 'discharged' had been used. In *National Bank of Australasia* v. *Scottish Union and National Insurance Co.*, [1952] A.C. 493 the Privy Council refused to attach weight to the subsequent conduct of the parties; on this point see Mann, 63 (1953) *L.Q.R.* 18, and above, pp. 145 sqq. (gold clause inferred from conduct), and cf. Hambro, *The Case Law of the International Court* (1952), p. 55. See also *Liebeskind* v. *Mexican Light & Power Co. Ltd.*, 116 F. (2d) 971 (C.C.A. 2d, 1941). The Supreme Court of *Canada* held that the capital payable on a life insurance policy in Indianapolis (U.S.A.) and expressed in 'dollars' could be paid in Canadian dollars, one of the decisive reasons being that the premiums were so paid: *Weiss* v. *State Life Insurance Co.*, Canada Law Reports (Supreme Court), 1935, 461; *Groner* v. *Lake Ontario Portland Cement Co. Ltd.* (1960), 23 D.L.R. (2d) 602. Dicey and Morris, p. 1005–6, relying on the last-mentioned case, do not state English law as clearly as may be desirable. This appears to be a legitimate process of construction. It is difficult to support the *German* Supreme Court's holding that in a life insurance policy Swiss francs had been substituted as the money of account for the originally stipulated French francs, because after the depreciation of the latter currency the premiums had been paid in Swiss francs: 9 May 1930, *IPRepr.* 1930, No. 100. The Court of Appeal at Hamburg was certainly justified in holding that, where the seller is entitled to a price in dollars but receives from the buyer and discounts a bill in French francs, no substitution of francs for dollars takes place: 5 Aug. 1958, *NJW.* 1958, 1919. Still less does such substitution take place if the seller sends to the buyer an invoice for a sum of francs and the buyer pays it; he remains liable for any balance of the dollar price. On the other hand the acceptance by the seller of a sterling letter of credit for a price expressed in Kenya shillings will change the money of account: *W.J. Alan & Co. Ltd.* v. *El Nasr Export and Import Co.*, [1972] 2 Q.B. 189.

[17] *Westralian Farmers* v. *King Line* (1932), 43 Ll. L.R. 378 (H.L.), at p. 383 *per* Lord Wright; see German Supreme Court, 7 Dec. 1921, *JW.* 1922, 711. In *Myers* v. *Union Natural Gas Co.* (1922), 53 Ontario L.R. 88, a payment of $1\frac{1}{2}$ cents for each 1,000 cubic feet of gas produced on the premises was promised. As all parties knew that the gas was produced and sold in Canada and paid for in Canada in Canadian currency, it was held that the American lessors were entitled to Canadian and not to American money.

country must be presumed in its legislation[18] as well as in its contracts[19] to refer to its own monetary system, even if the terms used by it are apt to refer to another system also; but where the Government of New Zealand undertakes to pay 'pounds' in Melbourne, the presumption founded upon the place of payment and presently to be mentioned should prevail,[20] except, oddly enough, where the payment is stated to be made 'free of exchange'.[21] Similarly a court may be presumed to give judgment in terms of its own currency.[22] Stock exchange transactions will usually have to be settled in the currency circulating at the place of the stock exchange.[23] If the transaction relates to immovables, it will often be safe to assume that the parties intended to adopt the money

[18] *Payne v. The Deputy Federal Commissioner of Taxation*, [1936] A.C. 497, the *ratio decidendi* of which, it is submitted, is the point mentioned in the text. This has been held to be so even in cases in which the local legislator, perhaps inadvertently, used the words 'pounds sterling': *Roberts* v. *Victorian Railway Commissioners* (1953), V.L.R. 383; *Jones* v. *Skelton*, 79 W.N. N.S.W. 249, affirmed by the Privy Council (1962), 1 W.L.R. 840. Nothing in these and other cases on which see Cowen, 78 (1962) *L.Q.R.* 533, should justify the conclusion that the use of the word 'sterling' is completely neutral. See p. 228, nn. 30, 31, below. It is in conformity with the principle suggested in the text that when the Merchant Shipping Act, 1894, refers in s. 503 to 'pounds' it means even in Australia English pounds, for the language is that of the Imperial legislator who intends to make provision for all British territories to which the statute extends: *The Commonwealth* v. *Asiatic Steam Navigation Co. Ltd.* (1956), 1 Ll. L.R. 658 (High Court of Australia).

[19] *Bonython* v. *Commonwealth of Australia*, [1951] A.C. 201, at p. 222 *per* Lord Simonds; see the comments in 68 (1952) *L.Q.R.* 195, 202.

[20] The conflicting presumptions fell to be considered by the Full Court of the Supreme Court of New Zealand in *National Mutual Life Association of Australasia Ltd.* v. *Attorney-General for New Zealand* (1954), N.Z.L.R. 754. In effect the majority held the latter presumption to be the stronger. This seems convincing, at any rate in the case of a single place of payment being expressly agreed and where, in addition, the contract is one of loan, for a borrower is prima facie bound to repay the same sum as that borrowed. For an exceptional case (loan of sterling held to be repayable in reichsmark) see German Supreme Court, 15 Jan. 1942, *RGZ.* 168, 240 (but, as the date indicates, the decision is in every respect suspect).

[21] On this ground the Privy Council affirmed the decision referred to in the preceding note: [1956] A.C. 369 on which see 19 (1956) *Modern L.R.* 424. The argument that if Australian pounds were *in obligatione* the words 'free of exchange' were otiose was perhaps not refuted by Lord Reid's comments upon it. Those words seem to point to the New Zealand pound being *in obligatione*. The result can be supported on the ground that the place of payment was in Australia.

[22] German Federal Supreme Court, 29 Sept. 1961, *Juristenzeitung*, 1962, 678 with note by Lüderitz. In a European case the European Court of Justice, when determining costs, will express them in the currency of the lawyer concerned: *European Ballage Corporation* v. *E.E.C. Commission*, *C.M.L.R.* 1976, I. 587.

[23] German Supreme Court, 15 Dec. 1920, *RGZ.* 101, 122; 11 July 1923, *RGZ.* 108, 191; but see 24 Oct. 1925, *RGZ.* 112, 27. If the balance due by either side is inserted in a current account based on a different currency and the parties agree to an account stated, the money of account may change. But whether this conclusion can be drawn from a mere insertion in a current account is doubtful. See notes by Nussbaum, *JW.* 1921, 891; 1922, 1721; 1924, 181.

of the country where the property is situated.[24] Lawyers and other professional men will have to be paid in the currency of the place where they practise, 'but the U.S. dollar is the currency most closely linked to oil. The dollar is the currency of the international oil industry.'[25] Where an insurance policy is taken out at the place of the company's head office and the premiums are paid in the money of that place, the policy will be taken to be denominated in that money;[26] but if the policy is taken out by a Frenchman in France with the French agency of a Swiss insurance company and the premiums are paid in French francs, the policy is payable in French francs, although there is an optional place of payment in Switzerland.[27, 28] If, on marrying a Swiss husband, a French woman contributes to the *communauté* a sum of French francs, 'l'économie de la convention' renders Swiss francs the money of account of the matrimonial régime and on dissolution of the marriage the husband has to repay the sum of Swiss francs which the wife's money produced at the time of the marriage rather than

[24] But see Story, s. 271a, and *Lansdowne* v. *Lansdowne* (1820), 2 Bli. 60, where there was, however, a clause 'lawful money of England'. See also Paris Court of Appeal, 12 Feb. 1925, Clunet, 1925, 745; Cass. Civ. 21 July 1936, Clunet, 1937, 299 (Papeteries Bergès); Cass. Civ. 21 July 1936, D.H. 1936, 473 (Papeteries de France), and particularly Cass. Civ. 19 July 1937, S. 1937, 1. 399 = Clunet, 1938, 76 (Société dos Hôtels Splendide, Royal et Europe d'Aix-les-Bains): a loan of 'francs' repayable in Geneva, Lausanne, Montreux, and Vevey at the Paris rate of exchange was secured by a mortgage on property at Aix-les-Bains and, for this reason, held to be expressed in French francs. In *Mundell* v. *Radcliffe*, 50 (1933), *South African L.J.* 402 the High Court of Southern Rhodesia held that, if rent for premises in Southern Rhodesia is payable in South Africa, it is expressed in South African rather than Rhodesian pounds. In *Ehmka* v. *Border Cities Improvement Co.* (1922), 52 Ontario L.R. 193, it was held that, although the real property, the subject-matter of the transaction, and the place of payment were in Canada, American dollars were the money of account, as both parties were resident in the U.S.A., and as they had in fact shown by their subsequent attitude that American dollars were owed.

[25] *B.P. Exploration Co. (Libya) Ltd.* v. *Hunt* (1979), 1 W.L.R. 783, at p. 843 *per* Robert Goff J., affirmed by the Court of Appeal (1981), 1 W.L.R. 232.

[26] Cass. Req. 21 Mar. 1933, Clunet, 1934, 373 (Société Suisse d'Assurance Générale).

[27] Cass. Req. 28 Nov. 1932, Clunet, 133 (La Bâloise); see also Cass. Req. 1 Mar. 1926, Clunet, 1926, 661 (Comptoir d'Escompte de Genève). On the effect of an option of place see below, p. 231, n. 48.

[28] As it is contrary to the nature of insurance contracts to involve the company in currency fluctuations or speculations, the company's domestic money will most frequently have been meant by the parties. Foreign insurance companies are often subject to certain statutes requiring them to keep reserve funds in the currency of the country where they are admitted. But this cannot have any influence on the determination of the money of account in an individual policy. As to *Germany* see Supreme Court, 6 July 1923, *RGZ*. 107, 111; 25 Mar. 1924, *JW*. 1924, 1364; 17 June 1924, *JW*. 1924, 1366; see also 31 Jan. 1936, *RGZ*. 150, 153. As to *France* see the decisions quoted above, nn. 26 and 27, and Cass. Civ. 30 June 1931, S. 1931, 1. 348, and the literature referred to in the notes to these decisions. But see Supreme Court of Canada in *Weiss* v. *State Life Assurance*, Canada Law Reports (Supreme Court), 1935, 461; as the Ontario Insurance Act requires payments due to policy holders to be made in Canadian dollars, the presumption relating to the place of payment which was in U.S.A. was rebutted.

the French francs contributed to her or their present equivalent in terms of Swiss francs.[29] Where a contract refers to 'sterling', this means[30] and probably always meant[31] that the parties contemplated English currency as the money of account. If a Kenyan seller fixed the price of 'shs 262/-' the money of account was Kenyan currency rather than sterling.[32] In Israel the use of the sign '£' denoted English currency, since local currency was invariably referred to as '£P' or '£I'.[33] As general principles cannot be laid down, each case requiring an examination of its particular facts, it would be unwise to dwell on further examples or to enter into a discussion of the vast material which is supplied by the decisions of foreign courts, especially those of France.[34] It may suffice to refer to the English decisions

[29] Cass. Civ. 18 Dec. 1951, *Rev. Crit.* 1952, 720. In the same sense Belgian Cass. 15 Dec. 1966, *Journal des Tribunaux*, 1967, 150. A less convincing decision in the opposite sense is Cass. Civ. 17 Nov. 1924, S. 1925, 1. 113 with note by Niboyet: a marriage settlement provided for a dowry of 50,000 French francs which were actually paid in piastres. On the dissolution of the marriage the husband was held liable to repay piastres rather than francs. The Project Arminjon, submitted to, but fortunately rejected by the Institut de Droit International (*Annuaire* 43 (1950), ii. 1 at p. 5 (Art. 13)) suggested that, in principle, the currency of the spouse's habitual residence should be paid.

[30] *De Bueger v. J. Ballantyne & Co. Ltd.*, [1938] A.C. 452. See s. 1, Decimal Currency Act, 1967.

[31] The statement in the text is inconsistent with *Bonython v. Commonwealth of Australia*, [1951] A.C. 201, where the Privy Council decided that it was impossible to infer from the use of the word 'sterling' in a contract made in the year 1895 in Australia and subject to Australian law that the currency of England rather than that of Australia (or Queensland) was intended. The *ratio decidendi* was that 'alike in London and Brisbane the pound was the pound sterling, and the unit of account was properly denominated by either name' (p. 216 *per* Lord Simonds). It is submitted with respect that this reasoning is not convincing and should in no event be treated as a general principle. Firstly, it is difficult to reconcile Lord Simonds' words with his conclusion (p. 219) that in 1895 England and Queensland had 'in a real sense two monetary systems'. Secondly, a question of construction is involved and it should be decided in the light of the circumstances and habits at the time of the contract (see 68 (1952) *L.Q.R.* 195, 206), though this could not be done in *Bonython*'s case which was a decision on a case stated. Thirdly, there is strong evidence that the word 'sterling' in fact had the meaning which Lord Simonds refused to attribute to it; see the statements and references in *De Bueger v. J. Ballantyne & Co., ubi supra*; or Latham C.J. in *Bonython v. Commonwealth of Australia* (1948), 75 C.L.R. 589, 603; see the reference to 'English or sterling currency' and similar language by Lord Wright in *Auckland Corporation v. Alliance Assurance Co.*, [1937] A.C. 587, 597, 603, 604, 606; Sir W. Page Wood in *Boyes v. Bedale* (1862), 1 H. & M. 798; Kay J. in *Re Andros* (1883), 24 Ch. D. 637, at p. 639. And see the *Shorter Oxford English Dictionary*, s.v. 'Sterling': 'English money as distinct from foreign money. Formerly often in contrast to currency, i.e. the depreciated pounds, shillings and pence of certain colonies, 1601.' The view that 'sterling does not mean English money is also taken by *Maudsley v. Colonial Mutual Life Assurance Society Ltd.* (1945), V.L.R. 161 and *Fisher Simmons & Rodway Ltd. v. Munesari* (1932), South African L.R., Natal Provincial Division, 77.

[32] *W. J. Alan & Co. v. El Nasr Export & Import Co.*, [1972] 2 Q.B. 189.

[33] Israel Supreme Court in *Rivlin v. Wallis*, Jerusalem Post (Law Reports), 2 Feb. 1958.

[34] It is collected by Degand, *Rép dr. int.* iii (1929), 'Change', Nos. 111 sqq.; x (1931), 'Paiement', Nos. 62 sqq. For significant examples see Cass. Req. 19 Nov. 1924, D.H. 1925, 6; Cass. Req. 15 Apr. 1926, Clunet, 1926, 970; Cass. Req. 2 Aug. 1926, Clunet, 1927,

relating to contracts, where, the proper law being or being treated as English, the courts proceeded to construe the contracts according to English canons of construction in order to ascertain the money of account.[35] It should be noted, however, that the parties' belief as to the identity of the money of account selected by them is irrelevant, if on construction it appears that they were in fact contracting in terms of another money of account the mere existence of which was unknown to them.[36]

But there still remains the question whether there is any rule of law which, in the absence of circumstances conclusively pointing to one or other direction, will provide a guide and perhaps turn the scale. In fact there exists a widely recognized principle according to which, in the absence of countervailing circumstances, there is a presumption in favour of the money of the place of payment being the money of account.[37] As regards the law of this country, the

102; Cass. Civ. 19 June 1933, Clunet, 1934, 939 (Compagnie Électrique de la Loire et du Centre). As to Belgium see Piret No. 27.

[35] *Lansdowne* v. *Lansdowne* (1820), 2 Bli. 60: Irish or English pounds; *Noel* v. *Rochford* (1836), 4 Cl. & Fin. 158: Irish or English pounds; *Young* v. *Lord Waterpark* (1842), 13 Sim. 199; Irish or English pounds; *Cope* v. *Cope* (1846), 15 Sim. 118: 'Sterling lawful money of Ireland'; *Macrae* v. *Goodman* (1846), 5 Moo. P.C.C. 315: Holland currency; *Bain* v. *Field* (1920), 5 Ll. L.R. 16 (C.A.): Canadian or American dollars; and see *Adelaide Electric Supply Co.* v. *Prudential Assurance Co.*, [1934] A.C. 122: English or Australian pounds; *Auckland Corporation* v. *Alliance Assurance Co.*, [1937] A.C. 587; English or New Zealand pounds; *De Bueger* v. *J. Ballantyne & Co. Ltd.*, [1938] A.C. 452: English or New Zealand pounds.

[36] This surprising theory underlies the decisions in *Bonython* v. *Commonwealth of Australia*, [1951] A.C. 201 as explained by Mann, 68 (1952) *L.Q.R.* 195, 203, and in *National Bank of Australasia* v. *Scottish Union and National Insurance Ltd.*, [1952] A.C. 493.

[37] *United States:* Liebeskind v. *Mexican Light & Power Co. Ltd.*, 116 F. (2d) 971 (C.C.A. 2d, 1941), at p. 974 *per* Swan C.J.; *Canada:* Simms v. *Cherenkoff* (1921), 62 D.L.R. 703 (Saskatchewan King's Bench, Maclean J.); *Weiss* v. *State Life Insurance*, Canada Law Reports (Supreme Court), 1935, 461. *South Africa:* Joffe v. *African Life Assurance Society*, South African L.R. (Transvaal Division) 1933, 189. *Brazil:* Supreme Court, 22 May 1918, Clunet, 1921, 993; Garland, *American–Brazilian Private International Law* (New York, 1959), p. 66 with references. *Victoria:* In re Tillam, Boehme & Tickle *Pty. Ltd.* (1932), Vict. L.R. 146, 149, 150: whether English or Australian pounds are to be paid is a matter of construction, but the money of the place of payment is the last resort. *Austria:* Civil Code, ss. 905, 1420; Commercial Code, s. 336. *Germany:* s. 361, Commercial Code; see Supreme Court, 27 Jan. 1928, *RGZ.* 120, 76, 81. *Hungary:* s. 324, Commercial Code. *France:* Degand, quoted above, p. 228, n. 34; Planiol-Ripert, vii (1931), No. 1188; although there appear to be many decisions of lower courts which lay down the principle, the present writer has been unable to find any Cour de Cassation decision where it is expressed without reservation. The cases quoted below, p. 232, n. 53, seem to be rather hesitating, and in the decisions quoted below, p. 231, n. 48, greater importance is attached to the currency of the place where the contract was made. *Belgium:* the money of the place of payment is favoured, but there is no established principle; see Piret, No. 27; Van Hecke, pp. 167, 168; *Switzerland:* Federal Tribunal, 23 May 1928, *BGE.* 54 ii. 257; Vischer, *Internationales Vertragsrecht* (1962), p. 219. *Egypt:* Court of Appeal of the Mixed Tribunal, 9 Mar. 1929, *Gazette des Tribunaux Mixtes*, 20, 108, No. 115. See

rule is already laid down in the case of *Gilbert* v. *Brett*;[38] while in *Taylor* v. *Booth*,[39] which concerned an action on a bill of exchange drawn in Ireland for £256. 18s. Irish currency, and payable in England, where the equivalent was £232. 4s., Best C.J. observed during the argument:[40] 'If a man draws a bill in Ireland upon England and states that it is for sterling money, it must be taken to mean sterling in that part of the United Kingdom where it is payable: common sense will tell us this.' Authority for this principle can also be found in some more recent cases.[41, 42]

The rule that in case of doubt it is the money of the place of payment that is owed by the debtor deserves approval, for, since the money of the place of payment is often the money of payment,[43] it leads to an identity of both, and thus to the avoidance of an exchange operation. Nevertheless there are other aspects of the rule which make it necessary to apply it with care. While it is well justified

---

now Art. 41 (4), Uniform Law on Bills and Notes, and Art. 36 (4), Uniform Laws on Cheques: 'If the amount of the bill of exchange (cheque) is specified in a currency having the same denomination, but a different value in the country of issue and the country of payment, reference is deemed to be made to the currency of the place of payment.' On both laws see below, p. 308, n. 9. Arminjon's Project (above, p. 228, n. 29) suggests that the currency of the place of payment should apply only in the event of such place being expressly fixed; if this is not so 'la loi sera celle du pays où les parties ont exprimé leur consentement': Art. 17. The confusion between conflict rule and substantive law is obvious.

[38] (1604) Davies's Rep. (Ireland) 18, 28.

[39] (1824) 1 C. & P. 286.

[40] At p. 287. The decision itself concerned a point of pleading and so did *Kearney* v. *King* (1819), 2 Barn. & Ald. 301, and *Sprowle* v. *Legg* (1822), 1 Barn. & Cres. 16: if, contrary to the proof, the declaration did not state that the bill was drawn in Ireland, or if the instrument promised to pay Irish money, while according to the declaration it seemed to be English money, there was held to exist a fatal variance between declaration and proof.

[41] *Adelaide Electric Supply Co.* v. *Prudential Assurance Co.*, [1934] A.C. 122; *Auckland Corporation* v. *Alliance Assurance Co.*, [1937] A.C. 587; *De Bueger* v. *J. Ballantyne & Co. Ltd.*, [1938] A.C. 452. As to these cases see below, pp. 234 sqq. In *National Mutual Life Association of Australasia Ltd.* v. *Attorney-General for New Zealand*, [1956] A.C. 369, at p. 387, Lord Reid said that 'if there is only one place of payment that is an important, but not a decisive factor'. One cannot quarrel with this formulation, though it puts the strength of the presumption perhaps a shade too low. See also *Macrae* v. *Goodman* (1846), 5 Moo. P.C.C. 315. Dicey and Morris, Rule 176 (2) and p. 1000 now prefer the inevitable, yet less than significant formula of the currency of the country with which the contract is most closely connected. This is merely descriptive of every process of construction.

[42] In *C.A. Parsons & Co. Ltd.* v. *The Electricity Trust of South Australia*, South Australia State Reports 16 (1976–1977) 93, Bray C.J., relying on the present writer (who, however, had not made the point) stated that there was also a presumption to the effect that the money of payment at the same time expresses the money of account. It is difficult to imagine such a case. It probably did not arise in the Australian case where the total price was expressed in $A. The fact that it comprised certain items expressed in pounds sterling and valued at a certain rate of exchange did not make sterling the money of account in respect of them.

[43] Below, pp. 306 sqq.

if the place of payment is fixed by the parties,[44] it involves danger in cases where the place of payment cannot be ascertained otherwise than by the application of a further presumption[45] because the doubling of presumptions as to the intention of the parties may easily falsify their real intention.[46] Moreover, the rule is of no avail where at the place of payment a currency circulates which differs from all those which the parties can be said to have had in view,[47] or where there exist two or more places of payment whose units of account bear the same name. The last-mentioned case has led to particular difficulties in the practice of both foreign[48] and British[49]

[44] It is noteworthy that the Swiss Federal Tribunal cautiously said: 'D'une façon générale on peut poser en principe que celui qui s'engage à payer dans un lieu déterminé [sic] une somme déterminée, exprimée en la monnaie ayant cours dans ce lieu, s'oblige par là même à payer ladite somme en ladite monnaie' (23 May 1928, Clunet, 1929, 497, re Crédit Foncier Franco-Canadien). But in France not even the indication of a place of payment is necessarily decisive: see the cases below, p. 232, n. 53.

[45] Above, pp. 76, 77.

[46] Neumeyer, p. 175, therefore proposed to have regard, not to the money of the place of payment, but to the money of the place of collection.

[47] e.g. a Frenchman promises a Swiss firm to pay 'francs' in London.

[48] e.g. a Belgian promises to pay 'francs' in Paris or Zürich. It was in these cases of a promise to pay 'francs' in France or Switzerland that the *French* Cour de Cassation said: 'Si en effet, à défaut de convention contraire, un paiement est présumé devoir être effectué dans la monnaie du lieu où il a été stipulé, cette présomption ne saurait avoir pour conséquence de créer au profit des créanciers une option de change en substituant une monnaie de compte à celle visée au contrat, de manière à modifier le montant des obligations incombant au débiteur' (Cass. Civ. 21 Dec. 1932, Clunet, 1933, 1201, re Chemin de fer de Rosario à Puerto-Belgrano; Cass. Req. 6 Dec. 1933, Clunet, 1934, 946, and D.H. 1934, 34, re Société Internationale des Wagons-Lits; Cass. Civ. 5 June 1934, Clunet, 1935, 90, re Est Lumière; Cass. Civ. 21 July 1936, D.H. 1936, 473, re Papeteries de France). The danger of substituting an option of currency for an option of place was also avoided by the Appellate Division of the *New York* Supreme Court in *Levy* v. *Cleveland C.C. & St. L.R.R. Co.* (210 App. Div. 422, 206 N.Y. Supp. 261, 1st Dept., 1924). The defendant railway company had in 1910 issued bonds the entire issue of which was purchased by a banking house in France. The bonds, which were expressly stated to be subject to the law of the United States, were for a sum of '500 francs' each, principal and interest being payable to bearer at a designated banking house in Paris or, at the holder's option, at designated banks in Belgium and Switzerland. The plaintiff demanded payment in Switzerland in Swiss francs, but only depreciated French francs were offered. The company succeeded, the court saying *inter alia*: 'The obligation itself according to the denomination of the bonds is to pay francs in Paris, France, and if the agreement is to be read without the options of place, construed in the same sense in which it would be accepted by the ordinary mind, this place of payment would indicate that the currency of that country would be used in the discharge of the obligation. The option to the holder to receive payment elsewhere relates entirely to the place of payment and does not mention the currency of the other countries as the means of payment. It would seem, if there were to be optional payments in the currency of other countries, that the language would have designated Swiss francs as the means of payment in Switzerland, and Belgian francs in the statement of the place of payment in Belgium.' In the course of its judgment the court referred to the decision of the Brussels Court of Appeal, 11 Mar. 1921, B.I.J.I. 6 (1922), No. 1260, and *Pasicrisie Belge*, 1921, ii. 70 (Société d'Éclairage v. Magerman), on which see Piret, No. 27. It must be observed that in all these cases difficulties only arose when the Latin Monetary Union was dissolved and greater fluctuations in the value of the various

[See p. 232 for n. 48 cont. and n. 49]

courts. Its decision will be facilitated by remembering that an option of place involves only one money of account[50] which is the same whatever the place or money of payment, and which cannot be treated as an option of currency;[51] accordingly the existence of several places of payment 'becomes a factor of little or no weight'[52] in so far as the identity of the money of account is concerned.

The remedy against such difficulties lies in a clear realization of the fact that the rule is nothing but an easily rebuttable presumption, an emergency solution, or a last resort which may be displaced by even the slightest indication in the circumstances of the case. Thus a warning against overrating the weight of the rule was repeatedly uttered by the French Cour de Cassation:[53]

en cas de doute sur la monnaie que les parties ont eue en vue lors de la convention, l'indication dans le contrat d'un lieu de paiement ne constitue à cet égard qu'une présomption de leur intention susceptible d'être combattue par toutes présomptions contraires résultant d'autres dispositions.

The determination of the money of account has sometimes caused difficulties in connection with legacies given by a will. In such cases, too, the intention of the testator must be ascertained

---

currencies occurred. (See above, pp. 52 sqq.) In very similar circumstances the Judicial Committee of the Privy Council was less fortunate in avoiding a trap; see below, pp. 239, 240.

[49] The leading authority is *Bonython* v. *Commonwealth of Australia*, [1951] A.C. 201. For the reason mentioned below, p. 241, n. 95, *Auckland Corporation* v. *Alliance Assurance Co.*, [1937] A.C. 587 is not really of assistance in connection with the matters discussed in this chapter, but will, of course, have to be considered with due care.

[50] See above, p. 211.

[51] For an illuminating statement of the law see Lord Simonds in *Bonython*'s case, *ubi supra*, at p. 219.

[52] *Bonython*'s case, *ubi supra*, at p. 221 *per* Lord Simonds. The principle of this case was followed in *National Bank of Australasia Ltd.* v. *Scottish Union and National Insurance Co. Ltd.*, [1952] A.C. 493, on which see Mann, 69 (1953) L.Q.R. 18. It was held that where stock was issued in 1897 in discharge of and substitution for debts payable in London, Sydney, and Brisbane, and the stock was registered in registers kept in these three places and could be transferred from one register to another, its 'uniform nature' was such as to necessitate the conclusion that its money of account was (a) identical everywhere, and (b) the money of Queensland. For the decision of the High Court of Australia see 84 C.L.R. 177.

[53] Cass. Req. 13 June 1928, Clunet, 1929, 112 (La Bâloise). Literally corresponding: Cass. Req. 28 Nov. 1932, Clunet, 1934, 133 (La Bâloise); Cass. Req. 21 Mar. 1933, Clunet, 1934, 373 (Société Suisse d'Assurance Générale); Cass. Civ. 17 July 1935, Clunet, 1936, 880 (Brasseries Sochaux). See also Cass. Req. 25 Jan. 1928, S. 1928, 1. 161. But the lower courts are not always so cautious. See, for example, Cour de Paris, 29 Jan. 1923, D.P. 1923, 2. 129. (*Schwab* v. *S. Montagu & Co.*): the defendants sold gold bars for the plaintiff. They realized a price of £2,423. 4s. 6d. which they converted into French francs and remitted to Paris. The plaintiff refused acceptance and sued for pounds sterling. The action was dismissed on the ground that, in view of certain letters written by the plaintiff, the place of payment was Paris.

from the circumstances of the case, but in the absence of any indication to the contrary it will generally be possible to presume that the
testator intended to refer to the money of account of the place
where the will was made, i.e. usually the place of residence.[54] It is,
however, obvious that this principle may cause the same difficulties
as the above-mentioned rule of the law of contracts.

2. As the determination of the money of account thus appears
to be a problem of interpretation, it should not admit of any doubt
that the question of private international law, namely, which law
governs the determination of the money of account, must, like all
other questions relating to interpretation, be answered by the *lex
causae* or the proper law of the obligation, whether it be the proper
law of the contract, the law of the testator's domicile,[55] or other
law. But under no circumstances, not even in case of an 'option de
change' or an express designation of a place of payment,[56] can it
be said that the law of the place of payment should apply. For the
determination of the money of account is nothing but a question
of construction; it relates to the substance of the obligation, not to
the mode of performance; it concerns the question what is owed,
not how payment is to be effected.

The principle[57] stated in the preceding paragraph is established

---

[54] *Wallis* v. *Brightwell* (1722), 2 P. Wms. 88; *Pierson* v. *Garnet* (1786), 2 Bro. C.C.
38; *Holmes* v. *Holmes* (1830), 1 Russ. & M. 660. See also *Saunders* v. *Drake* (1742), 2
Atk. 465, and *Malcolm* v. *Martin* (1790), 3 Bro. C.C. 50, although both these cases do
not rest on the principle, but on the circumstances of the case. On the principle see also
*Lansdowne* v. *Lansdowne* (1820), 2 Bli. 60, although the case itself does not relate to
a will. None of these cases supports the statements of Dicey and Morris, p. 630, or Westlake,
7th ed., p. 156, that the currency is normally that of the domicile. If the place of execution
is casual its currency will only rarely have been intended. Domicile, if different from
residence, will hardly ever provide a guide. Dicey and Morris, l.c., overlook the exception
here made to cover the case where the place of execution is fortuitous. The above suggestions
are admittedly contrary to principle, but they are in line with the realities of the case.
To adapt the example put by Dicey and Morris, if a testator domiciled in Sweden, but
for many years resident in Copenhagen makes a will there, possibly with the assistance of
a Danish lawyer, it is hard to suppose that in the event of the will including a kronor legacy
Swedish and not Danish kroner were intended.

[55] This is, however, no absolute rule, but 'merely a prima facie rule which is displaced
if the testator has manifestly contemplated and intended that his will should be construed
according to some other system of law': Cheshire and North, p. 611, and Dicey and Morris,
Rule 176, p. 999, and the cases there cited.                    [56] See above, p. 219.

[57] It has the support of Story, ss. 271, 271a, 272; though Story refers to the place where
the contract was made, he really has in mind what is now understood to be the proper law
of the contract. The Australian courts, to some extent influenced by the first edition of this
book, never seem to have had any doubt that a question of construction, governed by the
proper law of the obligation, was involved: see, for example, *Goldsbrough Mort & Co. Ltd.*
v. *Hall* (1949), 78 C.L.R. 1, at pp. 35, 36 *per* Dixon J. The principle is well recognized in
Germany: Supreme Court, 14 Nov. 1929, *RGZ.* 126, 196, and Melchior, *Grundlagen*, pp.
277 sqq., who, however, quotes some decisions which have no bearing on the point; also
in France: Planiol–Ripert, vii, No. 1189.

by the decision of the Judicial Committee of the Privy Council in *Bonython* v. *Commonwealth of Australia*.[58] In that case it had been urged with reference to an obligation to pay 'pounds sterling' in Brisbane, Sydney, Melbourne, or London, that, if payment is demanded in London, 'the English law as the *lex loci solutionis* governs the contract and determines the measure of the obligation'. Viscount Simonds rejected this contention:[59]

The mode of performance of the obligation may, and probably will, be determined by English law; the substance of the obligation must be determined by the proper law of the contract.

However self-evident that principle may appear to be, before 1951 it was by no means certain that it had a place in the law of Great Britain. Since *Bonython*'s case might be said to be a decision on Australian law only, it remains necessary to discuss the two earlier decisions of the House of Lords and the Privy Council respectively, which caused the difficulties.

In *Adelaide Electric Supply Co.* v. *Prudential Assurance Co.*[60] the shareholders of the appellant company which was incorporated under the laws of England and whose business was conducted from Australia, in 1921 passed a special resolution altering its articles to provide that all dividends, which had hitherto been declared and paid in England, should be declared at meetings to be held in Australasia and should be paid in and from Adelaide or elsewhere in Australasia. The respondents claimed that holders of certain preference shares of £1 each issued before 1921 were entitled to be paid their dividends in sterling in English legal tender for the full nominal amount thereof and not subject to deductions for Australian exchange. Reversing the order of Farwell J. and the Court of Appeal, and overruling the latter's decision in *Broken Hill Proprietary Co.* v. *Latham*,[61] the House of Lords held that the company had discharged its obligations by paying in Australian currency that which was in Australia legal tender for the nominal amount of the dividend warrants. The decision was unanimous, but the opinions delivered show great variance. The much-discussed question whether at the material times the Australian pound was different from the English pound has been treated above[62] and does not need to be discussed again.

It seems clear that the problem whether English or Australian pounds were owed was a question of construction.[63] It is equally

---

[58] [1951] A.C. 201.      [59] p. 219      [60] [1934] A.C. 122.
[61] [1933] Ch. 373.      [62] pp. 54 sqq.
[63] This was particularly emphasized by Lords Warrington and Tomlin at pp. 136, 145.

clear that the contract between the company and its shareholders was governed by English law.[64] On this basis one would expect the following line of reasoning to be taken: the contract, the construction of which is governed by English law, originally envisaged English pounds as the money of account.[65] If the English and Australian currency are held to have been different in 1921, it was a question of construction whether that resolution substituted the promise to pay Australian money for the original promise to pay English money. If the answer is in the negative, a sum of English pounds would be owed by the appellant company and the substance of the obligation would not differ from the original promise. It would then be necessary to turn to the question, perhaps governed by Australian law,[66] of which *instrument* of payment had to be employed at the substituted place of payment, viz. in Australia, in order to discharge that obligation. The answer would probably be that it must be discharged in Australia 'either in English legal tender of the amount expressed in English money of account or in Australian legal tender of such an amount expressed in the money of account of Australia as will buy in London the amount in English legal tender of the obligation expressed in the English money of account'.[67] Probably this would have been a satisfactory result. On the other hand, if in 1921, and perhaps in 1932 when the writ was issued, the English and Australian currencies were the same, it is clear that the money of account could not have been altered by the special resolution and English pounds remained *in obligatione*; in other words no problem of the determination of the money of account could arise, and the only question to be investigated related to the money of payment. This could not involve any doubt, provided the artificiality of the basic assumption is ignored and one is firmly resolved to deny legal relevance to the difference in the commercial value of the currency as between the two countries: if the Australian and English currency are identical, the company is entitled to discharge its obligations by paying whatever is a pound in Australia or England at its nominal value, which *ex hypothesi* is the same in both countries.

The decision of the House of Lords differed in method but arrived at the latter result. As regards the opinions delivered by Lords

---

[64] This is expressly made clear by Lords Warrington, Tomlin, Russell, and Wright at pp. 138, 145, 148, 156.

[65] That this was so is confirmed by Lord Wright in *Auckland Corporation* v. *Alliance Assurance Co.*, [1937] A.C. 587, 603, 604, where he said: 'Up to that time [1921] while the place of payment was in London, there could be no question that the term "pound" used in the articles of association had reference to English or sterling currency.'

[66] See below, p. 320.          [67] Lord Tomlin at p. 146.

Warrington, Tomlin, and Russell,[68] they started from the view
that both countries had a common unit of account, although there
was a 'difference in the . . . means whereby an obligation to pay so
many of such units is to be discharged'.[69] On this basis they could,
as has been shown, confine themselves to dealing with the discharge
of the obligation, because there was no difference between the
money of account and the money of payment. As regards the discharge, it was held that it could be effected by payment of what
was legal tender in Australia, and in view of the assumed identity
of money of account and money of payment it was also held that
no additional payment was required in respect of the superior value
of the English money of account. Thus Lord Warrington said:[70]

> The particular modification material in the present case was the change of
> the *locus solutionis* as regards dividends from England to Australia. The general
> rule, I think, is well settled—namely, that in such cases monetary obligations
> are effectually discharged by payment of that which is legal tender in the *locus
> solutionis* and, unless there is something in this case to take it out of the general
> rule, the question ought, in my opinion, to be decided in favour of the con-
> tention of the appellant company

Lord Tomlin said:[71]

> Now where in an English contract governed *prima facie* by English law there
> is a provision for performance in part in another country the *prima facie* pre-
> sumption is that performance is to be in accordance with the local law, and
> I see no reason why this presumption does not apply in the present case. That
> must mean, applied to the facts of this case and upon the view I have expressed
> as to the pound, that the obligation to pay is an obligation to pay a sum of
> money expressed in a money of account common to the United Kingdom
> and Australia, and that when the payment under the terms of the obligation
> has to be discharged in Australia it has to be made in what is legal tender in
> Australia for the sum expressed in that common money of account. It cannot
> mean that it is an obligation to pay a sum of money expressed in a money of
> account which is not Australian money of account and that therefore, if payable
> in Australia it must be discharged there by payment either in English legal
> tender of the amount expressed in the English money of account or in Australian

---

[68] We may disregard Lord Atkin's short opinion (pp. 134–5), because he said that
'agreeing as I do with much of his [Lord Wright's] reasoning, subject to the qualification
I am about to express, I do not propose to discuss at length the question before the House'.
He then added a few words on the topic whether there are or were two different 'pounds',
the Australian and the English, the result being that the inclined to think they were at the
present day not the same, but that at the material dates they were the same, in which
case Australian money could be tendered. In case, however, they were different at the
material dates, the learned Lord did not dissent from the construction that, as altered,
the articles provided for payment in Australian pounds.

[69] Lord Warrington at p. 138.

[70] At pp. 138–9.                                                          [71] At pp. 145–6.

legal tender of such an amount expressed in the money of account of Australia as will buy in London the amount in English legal tender of the obligation expressed in the English money of account.

And finally Lord Russell said:[72]

If this be the correct view (namely that the English and Australian currency is identical) this problem would resolve itself into a case of the company becoming indebted from time to time in amounts payable in Australia and expressed in terms of units of account common to Australia and England. The question then is, how can the company discharge that indebtedness? The answer can I think only be, in whatever currency is legal tender in the place in which the indebtedness is dischargeable.

It thus appears that the opinions of the majority are not material to the problems of the determination of the money of account, but merely relate to the money of payment in regard to which they establish a fairly obvious proposition.

It is more difficult to understand Lord Wright's opinion. Although it is unlikely today to carry much weight, it cannot, unhappily, in the present context be ignored. He started from the prima facie rule that 'whatever is the proper law of the contract regarded as a whole, the law of the place of performance should be applied in respect of any particular obligation which is performable in a particular country other than the country of the proper law of the contract'.[73] After stating his reasons for the view that the two currencies are and were different,[74] he reverted to the question[75] 'which currency is intended on the true construction of the special resolution', and in order to find an answer, he asked the further question[76]

whether the proper law of the contract (which is English, because the appellant company is an English Company) or the law of the place of the declaration and the payment of dividends which is Australia, is to govern the meaning of the word 'pound'. In my opinion the latter is the true construction. The old cases I have cited show, as I think, that in determining what currency is intended, the general rule *prima facie* applies that the law of the place of performance is to govern.

Lord Wright thus appears to leave the determination of the money of account and probably also that of the money of payment to the *lex loci solutionis*.

In the first place from his point of view, according to which the Australian currency differs from that of England, it was vital to examine the question whether the resolution of 1921 involved an alteration of the *substance* of the obligation (not of the mode of performance) by substituting a promise to pay Australian currency for the promise to pay English money. In effect Lord

---

[72] At p. 148.                                                                 [73] At p. 151.
[74] See above, p. 56, where we ventured to express approval of this part of Lord Wright's opinion.                        [75] p. 156.                        [76] Ibid.

Wright gave an affirmative answer[77] to this question, although in a later case[78] he said that there was no such alteration, and although in a still later case he stated that no question of substance but a question of performance was involved;[79] his reasoning, however, seems to relate to the money of *payment*. Secondly, although Lord Wright held Australian law to be applicable, it is doubtful whether in fact he did not proceed on the basis of English law; if so, the explanation might be that in this case, as well as in a later case which we shall have to consider[80] he did not sufficiently distinguish between the application of the law of the place of payment and the prima facie rule of English municipal law that it is the money of the place of payment which, in case of doubt, must be taken to have been intended by the parties and which may be employed as an instrument of payment.

But even assuming that Lord Wright intended to and did apply Australian law, the question remains whether it is possible to accept this view, which, though it led to the same results, is certainly at variance with that of the majority of the House.

It is not necessary to discuss again his initial principle, formulated with extreme width, that the law of the place of performance should be applied in respect of any particular obligation performable in a country other than that of the proper law.[81] It suffices to scrutinize the somewhat narrower principle 'that in determining what currency is intended, the general rule prima facie applies that the law of the place of performance is to govern'.

The paramount argument militating against this principle is that the determination of the money of account is, as Lord Wright himself recognized, a matter of construction; it relates to the substance of the obligation, not to its performance, and therefore the law of the place of performance cannot govern it,[82] however important that law may be in connection with the instrument of

---

[77] pp. 156-7.                                    [78] See above, p. 235, n. 65.

[79] *Mount Albert Borough Council* v. *Australasian Temperance & General Mutual Life Assurance Society Limited*, [1938] A.C. 224, 241. His exact words are quoted above, p. 217, n. 153. But on the basis adopted by Lord Wright in the *Adelaide* case, namely, that Australian and English pounds are not identical, primarily a question of construction, i.e. of substance, arose, and only on the basis adopted by the majority of the House of Lords, was it, as has been shown in the text, possible to treat the case as involving a question of performance. Again, in *De Bueger* v. *J. Ballantyne & Co Ltd.*, [1938] A.C. 452, 459, 460, Lord Wright said that 'it was just this difference in the "means" of discharging the obligation—that is, the actual currency—which was the essence of the case' and that 'under a contract like that in question what matters to the parties is the means—that is, the currency—in which the obligation is discharged'. *Sed quaere*. Parties do mind whether they pay or receive 100 London pounds or 100 Australian pounds, but the creditor of 100 London pounds does not mind whether he receives £100 London currency or £125 Australian currency. Finally, in his paper on 'Gold Clauses' (*Legal Essays and Addresses* (1939), 147 sqq., 153, 154) Lord Wright stated that the question before the House was what was meant by 'pounds' in the Resolution. It is suggested once more that a clear realization of the essential difference between the money of account, determining the quid, and the money of payment, determining the quomodo, solves all problems.

[80] *Auckland Corporation*'s case, below, p. 240.

[81] See above, p. 216.

[82] See *St. Pierre* v. *South American Stores Ltd.*, (No. 2) [1937] 3 All E.R. 349 (C.A.), at p. 352 C *per* Greer L.J., at p. 354 D *per* Slesser L.J.

payment to be employed in discharge of an obligation construed according to the proper law.[83]

Lord Wright's opinion also blurs the distinction between a (national) private international law and a (national) substantive law.[84] This can be shown by an example given by Lord Wright himself:[85]

> It is natural and reasonable that the money he [the debtor] should be bound to have ready should be the legal money of that place [of performance], rather than that he should have a foreign currency, or should have an amount in his home currency which is not the agreed figure, but a different figure representing an exchange operation by which the agreed figure is converted (in this case) from sterling to currency.[86] Similarly, if a Frenchman and a Belgian were to agree that francs were to be paid by the one to the other in Brussels, it would naturally be inferred in the absence of express terms that the Belgian franc was intended.

These words fortify the suggestion that Lord Wright did not really intend to state the rule of private international law which he in fact expressed, but the rule of English municipal law that the money of the place of payment prima facie is the intended money of account. But if his words are taken literally and the alleged rule of English private international law exists, the term 'place of performance', whatever theory of classification is advanced, is a notion of English law to be defined by English law, which, in the absence of special circumstances, resorts to the place of the residence of the creditor.[87] Accordingly the Frenchman who owes 'francs' to a Belgian would have to pay Belgian francs. But according to French as well as Belgian Law he would have to pay French francs, since in both these laws the currency meant by the parties prima facie is that of the place of payment,[88] which in both laws is the place of the residence of the debtor.[89] If, on the other hand, English law allowed an English judge to apply the proper law of the contract, French francs would be payable, whether the proper law were French or Belgian—a result which seems to be more appropriate.

For all these reasons it is submitted that Lord Wright's dicta cannot impair the conclusion, supported by established principles, that it is the proper law of the contract which governs the determination of the currency owed.[90]

Unfortunately, however, the difficulties raised by the *Adelaide* case are increased by the later case of *Auckland Corporation* v.

---

[83] Below, p. 321.    [84] See p. 207.    [85] p. 156.

[86] But such exchange operations are of daily occurrence and in fact unavoidable.

[87] Above, p. 76.

[88] Above, p. 229, n. 37.

[89] Above, p. 76.

[90] If, notwithstanding the many qualifications and explanations to which it was subjected in later decisions, Lord Wright's opinion retains any authoritative value, it would in truth be material only to the issue discussed in the next chapter, viz. how uncertainty as to the money account which arises during the life of a contract is to be dealt with. See p. 259, n. 25.

*Alliance Assurance Co.,*[91] where Lord Wright delivered the opinion of the Privy Council. In 1920 the City of Auckland issued debenture bonds providing for payment of a sum of 'pounds', payable in London, England, or Auckland, New Zealand, at the holder's option. On the assumption that the London option had been duly exercised, the question arose whether the holder was entitled to demand payment of the stipulated sum of English money or of the stipulated sum of New Zealand money converted into pounds sterling at the rate of exchange of the day. Lord Wright, apparently accepting the view of the New Zealand Court of Appeal that the proper law of the contract was New Zealand law, made it quite clear that the case involved a problem of construction. But he held that, apart from certain questions connected with the New Zealand Local Bodies Loan Act, 1913, which are immaterial for present purposes, the case was governed by the *Adelaide* decision,[92] the effect of which he stated twice, but in different terms. He first said[93] that in that case

it was held that in the absence of express terms to the contrary, or of matters in the contract raising an inference to the contrary, the currency of the country in which it was stipulated that payment was to be made was the currency meant.

But later he said[94] that the principle of the *Adelaide* case was that

the House of Lords held that the true meaning of the word 'pound' must be determined on the basis of a rule depending on a well known principle of the conflict of laws—namely that the mode of performance of a contract is to be governed by the law of the place of performance.

Undoubtedly, it was the former principle which, on the basis that English law was the proper law, was in fact laid down by the majority of the House of Lords in the *Adelaide* case as a principle of English municipal law. The latter principle, on the other hand, which if it exists, states a rule of English private international law, is only to be found in Lord Wright's judgment in the *Adelaide* case. Nevertheless, in the *Auckland* case both these principles enabled Lord Wright to arrive at the result that the obligation was discharged by the payment of the stipulated amount of 'pounds' of English currency.

[91] [1937] A.C. 587. We have a further example of the confusion brought about by the statement that the determination of the money of account, being a matter relating to the mode of performance, is governed by the law of the place of performance, in the Manitoba case of *Johnson* v. *Pratt*, [1934] 2 D.L.R. 802. The confusion caused by Lord Wright's statements is also reflected in the observations of Scott L.J. in *Radio Pictures Ltd.* v. *Commissioners of Inland Revenue* (1938), 22 T.C. 106, at p. 132.

[92] [1934] A.C. 122.          [93] pp. 604-5.

[94] p. 606. In *Bonython* v. *Commonwealth of Australia*, [1951] A.C. 201 at pp. 220, 221 Lord Simonds referred to this passage and distinguished the decision on grounds which seem a little tenuous. See Mann, 68 (1951) *L.Q.R.* 195, 205.

It is submitted that the decision in the *Auckland Corporation* case proceeds on the footing that, 'as in the *Adelaide* case, the pound is the common unit of account'.[95] If this is correct, then the decision is merely an application of the principles laid down in the *Adelaide* case except that it carries them one step farther: as the holder was held to be entitled to one (English) pound for one (New Zealand) pound, both being 'the same', the decision in effect substituted an option of currency not stipulated by the parties for a mere option of place, a result which, as has been shown,[96] ought to be avoided, but which, in view of the *Adelaide* case, was probably unavoidable.

The broad conclusion is that neither the *Adelaide* case nor the *Auckland Corporation* case deals with the determination of the money of account in the event of an initial uncertainty. As regards this problem, the following three principles will guide to a solution:

1. A clear distinction must be drawn between the money of acount, i.e. the substance of the obligation, and the money of payment, i.e. the instrument of payment.
2. The determination of the money of account, being a question of construction, should be governed by the proper law of the contract, not by the law of the place of payment.
3. It is a rule of English (municipal) law, and indeed of most laws, that, in the absence of circumstances indicating a different intention of the parties, the money of the place of payment is the money of account meant by the parties.

### III

We now come to one of the most obscure chapters of the law concerning foreign money, that relating to the determination of the money of account in those cases where liability is not foreseen by the parties and where therefore the money of account is not fixed.

The problems raised by these cases are of particular difficulty, not only because they have received little attention, but also because they are often interconnected or even confused with other questions which ought to be clearly distinguished. Thus, once again, the question 'which money is the money of account according to a given municipal law' must be differentiated from the question 'which law governs the determination of the money of account'.[97] Furthermore,

---

[95] [1937] A.C. 587, at p. 606, and see p. 599.    [96] Above, p. 232.
[97] The distinction is clearly drawn by Lord Wilberforce in *The Despina R*, [1979] A.C. 685, at p. 700. This great case renders it unnecessary and inappropriate to consider

a claim may have to be *assessed* in the currency of a foreign country the identity of which may be uncertain. Where, for instance, damages are claimed for injuries to a ship, it is clear that it may make a difference whether that which is converted is a sum of French francs spent by the shipowner to carry out the repairs or a sum of dollars with which he may have bought the French francs so spent. It is the money of account of the claim to damages that must first be determined.

1. Turning now to the rules of municipal law relating to the determination of the money of account in such cases, we are bound to admit at the outset that no general principle can be laid down with safety. Some authors, it is true, suggested a working rule to the effect that liability arises in the currency of that country whose law governs the obligation.[98] This cannot be right, for it is a fact of frequent occurrence that liability arises in another currency than that of the *lex causae*. Others have suggested that, as a rule, the *moneta fori*[99] or (what is usually the same thing) the currency of the defendant's residence[100] should apply. Again, it is said that, on principle, the determination of the money of account should be treated as a mere question of fact to be decided in the light of the circumstances of the case.[101] In truth, it is submitted, no single solution is possible, but it is necessary to evolve and recognize a number of different rules conforming to the legal nature of, and the demands of justice in, a variety of cases which have to be distinguished.

(*a*) In some cases where the liability arises out of a contractual relation, it may be possible to find in the contract an indication of the money by which the liability is measured. Thus the wrongful dismissal of an employee salaried in foreign money involves a liability of the employer to pay damages expressed in the foreign money in which the salary was stipulated.[102] Similarly, if royalties payable in respect of the user of a patent are expressed in a certain currency, damages payable by the licensee for the breach of the license agreement are to be calculated on the basis of the same currency.[103, 104]

---

a number of earlier cases and dicta which for many years bedevilled the subject matter of this Chapter and which may not have been formally disapproved or overruled.

[98] Pisco, *Lehrbuch des österreichischen Handelsrechts*, p. 155; Neumeyer, pp. 158 sqq. This approach was expressly rejected by the Court of Appeal at Hamburg, 30 Dec. 1953, *IPRspr.* 1952–3, No. 21.

[99] Melchior, ss. 193, 194; Vischer, *Internationales Vertragsrecht* (1962), p. 219 with references.

[100] Federal Supreme Court, 11 Feb. 1958, *IzRspr.* 1958–9, No. 111, at p. 304.

[101] Nussbaum, *Geld*, p. 245.

[102] Cf. *Ottoman Bank v. Chakarian*, [1930] A.C. 277, 284 (P.C.) as explained in *Ottoman Bank v. Dascalopoulos*, [1934] A.C. 354, 364 (P.C.).

[103] But see German Supreme Court, 4 June 1919, *RGZ*. 96, 121, where it was held that

[*See opposite page for n. 103 cont. and n. 104*]

In more general terms Lord Wilberforce stated[105] that 'if from the terms of the contract it appears that the parties have accepted a currency as the currency of account and payment in respect of all transactions arising under the contract, then it would be proper to give a judgment for damages in that currency'.

In connection with quasi-contractual claims it will frequently be possible to determine the money of account by reference to the terms of the original contract. Thus, if dollars were paid as the price of goods, a total failure of consideration will make the seller liable to repay dollars, and this is likely to be so even if sterling was paid and accepted on account or in discharge of the dollar liability.[106]

a sum of 21,000 kroner payable in respect of damages for breach of contract were only an 'item' in a claim for damages expressed in German money, so that the creditor was entitled to demand German money. Similarly the decision referred to above, n. 100.

[104] But if goods are sold for a price expressed in a certain foreign currency, damages to which either of the parties may be entitled are not necessarily measured in the same currency. In this country the principle to be mentioned in the text under (b) seems to apply, although the case of *Bain* v. *Field* (1920), 5 Ll. L.R. 16 (C.A.) presents some difficulties: goods which were lying in New York were sold f.o.b. New York at a price which Bailhache J. ((1920) 5 Ll. L.R. 26) and the Court of Appeal held to be expressed in Canadian dollars. Damages due to the seller were assessed in Canadian dollars and then converted into pounds sterling, although New York was the place where the goods were to be delivered. In *Germany* it was held that a German buyer who claims damages from his seller for the latter's failure to deliver goods sold at a price expressed in non-German currency must measure his damages in German money, unless he can show that in the course of his business he would at once have converted the goods into non-German currency: Supreme Court, 8 Apr. 1921, *RGZ*. 102, 60; 7 Dec. 1923, *JW.* 1924, 672; 27 Feb. 1924, *JW.* 1925, 1477; see also 30 June 1925, *RGZ*. 111, 183. As to the *United States of America* see *Compañia Engraw* v. *Schenley Distillers Corporation*, 181 F. (2d) 876 (C.C.A., 9th, 1950): the American buyer who had promised to pay the Argentinian seller in pesos and repudiated the contract was held liable for damages expressed in pesos (and converted into dollars). As to *France* see Cour de Paris, 26 Jan. 1929, Clunet, 1930, 380; 16 May 1952, *Rev. Crit.* 1953, 382.      [105] *The Despina R*, [1979] A.C. 685, at p. 700.

[106] Cf. s. 1 and s. 2 (3) of the Law Reform (Frustrated Contracts) Act 1943. See above, p. 191, n. 37, but also Swiss Federal Tribunal, 30 Dec. 1948, affirming Commercial Court Zürich, 9 Apr. 1948, *Blätter für Zürcherische Rechtsprechung*, 48 (1949), 209 and *Schweizerisches Jahrbuch für Internationales Recht*, 1950, 266: a Belgian bought goods of Italian origin from a Swiss for Swiss francs and paid in lire; on rescission he was entitled to the repayment of Swiss francs. Similarly, Austrian Supreme Court, 26 Mar. 1923, *SZ*. v, No. 64: the defendant was entitled to sfrs. 125 which the plaintiff paid in Austrian currency. Later it appeared that in truth the defendant was not so entitled. He repaid Austrian currency. It was held that the plaintiff could demand sfrs. 125 or the equivalent in Austrian currency at the time of payment. Von Tuhr–Peter, *Allgemeiner Teil des Schweizerischen Obligationenrechts* (3rd ed., 1979), i. 65, suggest that, if foreign money has to be refunded on account of unjustified enrichment, the claim may be expressed, not in foreign money, but in Swiss currency at the rate of exchange of the date of receipt. The Supreme Restitution Court in Berlin held that if the price for real property in Germany was agreed and in fact paid in German currency the vendor is bound to repay on rescission Germany currency, though he converted the money paid to him in foreign currency: 26 May 1955, *RzW.* 1955, 212. The same tribunal also held that if the price is agreed in German currency, but the purchaser pays dollars the vendor has to repay dollars: 8 Dec. 1955 *RzW.* 1956, 41.

Moreover, if the court has to value the benefit of services rendered under a contract which becomes frustrated it will have regard to the currency of account for measuring the contractual indebtedness as well as the currency of the expenditure incurred in making the services available.[107] If a Parisian architect becomes entitled to a *quantum meruit* for having built an Englishman's house in London, he will receive sterling, though, if the house had been built in Cannes, under English law he may have to accept francs.

(*b*) In a second group of cases an indication as to the proper money of account may be derived from the fact that, under the law applicable to the case, the defendant is under a duty to restore to the plaintiff the value of an article or interest. In such cases it may be a guiding principle that the liability is expressed in the currency of the place where, in the circumstances, the value is ascertainable and ascertained.[108] Thus it seems that under English municipal law[109] damages for non-delivery or non-acceptance of goods are measured not only by the market value[110] at, but also in the currency[111] of the place where the goods ought to have been delivered or accepted.[112] Or if through the defendant's negligence a house in

---

[107] *B.P. Exploration Co. (Libya) Ltd.* v. *Hunt* (1979), 1 W.L.R. 783, at pp. 843, 844 *per* Robert Goff J. as affirmed by the Court of Appeal, [1980] 1 W.L.R. 232.

[108] Nussbaum, *Geld*, p. 247, and Mayer, *Valutaschuld*, p. 20, adopt the formula that the claim for the restitution of value is expressed in the same currency as that in which that value is ascertained. But this formulation contains a *petitio principii* which can only be avoided if reliance is placed on the *place* with reference to which the value is ascertained.

[109] It is necessary to emphasize that this is not a rule of private international law; other municipal laws, e.g. German law (see p. 243, n. 104), have adopted different rules. The conflict must be decided by the rules of private international law to be discussed under (2) below.

[110] See, for example, *Rodocanachi* v. *Milburn* (1886), 18 Q.B.D. 67, 78 *per* Lindley L.J.; at p. 80 *per* Lopes L.J.; *Ströms Bruks Aktie Bolag* v. *Hutchinson*, [1905] A.C. 515; *The Arpad*, [1934] P. 189, especially at p. 222 *per* Maugham L.J.

[111] *Di Ferdinando* v. *Simon Smits & Co.*, [1920] 3 K.B. 409, 414 *per* Scrutton L.J.: defendants converted goods which were to be carried from England to Milan, where they were to be delivered to an Italian consignee. The damages were assessed in Italian lire. Similarly, Austrian Supreme Court, 15 May 1923, *SZ.* v, No. 127. As to the question whether the result would be different if the consignee was a French firm, see the text under (*c*). The action concerned a claim against carriers for conversion, while in *Bain* v. *Field* (1920), 5 Ll. L.R. 16 (C.A.), a claim was made against the buyers of goods and the damages were assessed in the currency in which the purchase price was held to be expressed, not in that obtaining in the place where the goods were to be delivered (see p. 243, n. 104 above). Although the words employed by Scrutton L.J. in *Di Ferdinando*'s case warrant the statement in the text, it is doubtful whether or not they must be limited to conversion cases and whether in cases of contracts of sale where the purchase price is expressed in a certain currency they are superseded by the decision in *Bain* v. *Field*, which was not discussed in *Di Ferdinando*'s case.

[112] Where German law refers to the market value (but see p. 243, no. 104) the principle is the same. But if the market value of goods in Hamburg must be restored and it appears that the goods are quoted there in pounds sterling, the liability is measured in pounds sterling: Supreme Court, 22 Nov. 1923, *RGZ.* 107, 212.

France is destroyed, the loss must be measured in French francs, because it is in France and in French money that the value of the house is ascertained. Similarly, if the English defendant has converted the luggage of an American visitor to this country, the damages will probably be measured in sterling and it is irrelevant that the American would have taken his luggage to the United States.[113, 114]

(c) In a third group of cases the claim is expressed in the currency of the place where the victim carries on business or resides and where, for this reason, financial resources are likely to be affected.[115] Frequently this means, in particular, that the plaintiff should be entitled, not to the currency actually and directly used, but to the currency ultimately employed by him for the purpose of obtaining the currency so used. In other words, as a rule a plaintiff is likely to be able to claim his own currency in the sense of the currency 'in which the loss was effectively felt or borne' by him rather than the 'expenditure currency' in the sense of the currency 'in which the expense or loss was immediately sustained.'[116]

---

[113] Under German law the American visitor would be entitled to dollars, because *restitutio in integrum* is taken to mean that damages are to be paid at the place where, had there been no wrongful act, the goods would have served the interests of the owner: Federal Tribunal, 14 Feb. 1952, *BGHZ*. 5, 138; 14 Jan. 1953, *BGHZ*. 8, 297. A similar idea seems to underlie the decision of the Swiss Federal Tribunal, 20 Jan. 1948, *BGE*. 74, ii. 81: An Italian company was the owner of goods which a Swiss shipowner undertook to carry from Rotterdam to Bale and which perished as a result of a total loss. The shipowner's liability was measured in Swiss francs, i.e. the currency circulating at Bale where he had to perform. In *Italy* v. *Federal Republic of Germany* (Decisions vii. 213) the Arbitral Commission on Property, Rights and Interests in Germany (consisting of Messrs. Wickström, Sauser-Hall, Lagergren, Schwandt, Euler, Bennett, Arndt, Marion, and Phenix) referred to 'the general principle of law and justice that the reparation due from a person liable but unable to restitute an item of property is to put the restitutee, so far as is possible, in the same position as if he had not been deprived of the property', and understood it to entitle the victim to 'that sum of money which would permit replacement by purchase at the place of dispossession'.

[114] If, for the purpose of determining the salvor's reward, the value of the salved property has to be ascertained, English courts are inclined to think in terms of sterling; but it is submitted that such value should be arrived at in terms of the currency of the place where the owners carry on business. See *The Eastern Moon* (1927), 28 Ll. L.R. 22; *The Teh Hu*, [1970] P. 106, where the value was taken by the majority of the Court of Appeal to be sterling, but should have been assessed in terms of Panamanian, Liberian or United States currency, as Lord Denning M.R.'s powerful dissent emphasizes.

[115] This is the solution which has the support of the Permanent Court of International Justice (below, p. 537) and which, in regard to tortious liability, is propagated by Art. 8 of Arminjon's Project (above, p. 228, n. 29) as well as by French writers who suggested that liability is always expressed in the money of the injured party's nationality or domicile or place of residence; this, however, was not put forward as a general principle, but as referring to tortious liability only: Béquignon, *La Dette de monnaie étrangère*, pp. 24 sqq.; Degand, *Rép. du dr. int.* iii (1929), 'Change', No. 176; Arminjon, *Précis de droit international privé* (1934), ii. 365. Similarly Nussbaum, p. 405 and see the decision of the Court of Appeal, Berlin-West, 12 Mar. 1951, *NJW*. 1951, 486: the wrongdoer has to pay

[See p. 246 for n. 115 cont. and n. 116]

In some circumstances the solution will not be in doubt. If an English seller fails to deliver and a Germany buyer, therefore, purchases the goods against him and spends German currency for the purpose, the court has to assess the damages in the currency of Germany where the buyer is resident and carries on business.[117] If a Frenchman's car is repaired in France for French francs, clearly the victim is entitled in an English court to nothing but a sum calculated by reference to the French francs spent by him.[118] Or if a Frenchman is injured or killed in the course of an accident and it becomes necessary to calculate his or his estate's loss of earnings, an English court cannot be guided by another yardstick than the amount of French francs which the victim would have earned.[119] Are damages which are entirely at large, such as damages for pain and suffering, *dommage moral* or *Schmerzensgeld*, or damages for libel also expressed in the victim's currency? In England the answer is certainly in the negative;[120] but attention should be drawn to France where, it seems, the courts have recently adopted the opposite view. A decision of the Cour de Cassation in 1954, it is true, clearly required that such types of damage 'devaient être évalués en francs français du fait que l'indemnité y correspondant devait être payée en France par un Français domicilié en France à l'occasion d'un délit commis en France'.[121] Yet a more recent decision of the Cour de Paris[122] awarded to an American a sum of dollars which undoubtedly included such damages as *pretium doloris*, on the ground that 'l'évaluation d'un dommage subi en France doit être faite en monnaie étrangère lorsque cette manière de procéder est susceptible de le réparer d'une façon plus adéquate'. And a still later decision of the Cour de Besançon[123] adds to the confusion

damages in the currency circulating at the place of the victim's ordinary residence, but compare the decision, above n. 113.

[116] *The Despina R*, [1979] A.C. 685, 696 *per* Lord Wilberforce.

[117] *Re British American Continental Bank Ltd., Lisser and Rosenkranz's Claim*, [1923] 1 Ch. 276, at p. 285 *per* P. O. Lawrence J. in the court of first instance, whose words were approved by Lord Sterndale M.R. at p. 291 and Warrington L.J. at p. 292 in the Court of Appeal.

[118] See, in particular, *The Volturno*, [1921] A.C. 544. In respect of a corresponding set of facts this solution is well established in France: Cass. Crim. 15 July 1954, Bulletin Cass. Crim. 1954, No. 260, p. 447; 8 Jan. 1959, *Rev. Crit.* 1960, 55 with note by Mezger.

[119] *The Swynfleet* (1948), 81 Ll. L.R. 16.

[120] In no case has the point even been argued.

[121] See the decision of 15 July 1954, above, n. 118. French textbooks fail to make the vital distinction, clearly indicated in the two decisions of the Cour de Cassation, between the recovery of outlays and general damages.

[122] 29 Mar. 1957, *Rev. Crit.* 1960, 55 with note by Mezger.

[123] 14 May 1959, Clunet, 1960, 778; S. 1960, 20 and D. 1959, 517 with note by Esmein. See on the problem Mazeaud et Chabas, *Responsibilité Civile* (6th ed., 1978), No. 2325.

by awarding to the Swiss victims of an accident in France partly French, partly Swiss francs for 'préjudice matériel' and 'préjudice moral'.[124]

If, to turn to more difficult cases, a Frenchman's car is repaired in Italy for Italian lire, is the victim entitled in an English court to claim damages calculated by reference to the Italian lire spent by him or to the French francs with which he obtained the Italian lire so spent?[125] In England it is now clearly established by the decision of the House of Lords in *The Despina R.* (and its companion case)[126] that as a rule the victim is entitled to French francs or whatever currency is 'the plaintiff's currency'. In that case a 'Greek' vessel owned by a Liberian company with head office in Greece and managed by managing agents in New York was involved in a collision off Shanghai. The expenses for repairs were incurred in various currencies and met by payments to the debit of a dollar account in New York. The owners were held to be entitled to repayment in terms of dollars. In the companion case French charterers, under a charter party governed by English law, claimed from the Swedish owners damages for Brazilian cruzeiros which they had to pay to the cargo receivers and which the charterers discharged by purchasing cruzeiros with French francs. They were held to be entitled to French francs, although the hire was expressed in U.S.

[124] It is very likely that as a matter of legal policy a distinction will have to be drawn between different causes of action. As to collisions on land, sea, and air the International Law Association (*Report of the 49th Conference in Hamburg*, 1960, p. 396) suggested that in principle the victim's currency should apply. At the same Conference it was accepted that infants should be entitled to maintenance in the currency of the country of habitual residence (pp. 389, 395). On the whole this solution is in line with the result which, after many years of trial and error, was ultimately reached by West German courts in respect of maintenance due from husbands or fathers in West Germany to wives or children in the Soviet zone; on this problem which reached enormous dimensions see, for instance, Soergel (Kegel), *Commentaries*, Notes 655–65 preceding Art. 7; Staudinger (Weber), vol. ii, Part 1a, pp. 1095 sqq.; or Gamillscheg and Hirschberg, sections 388 sqq. before Art 13 in Staudinger's *Commentaries* (1973). But see Austrian Supreme Court, 13 Feb. 1923, *SZ*. v, No. 30, according to which a divorced husband living in Czechoslovakia has to pay maintenance to his former wife in Austria in terms of Czechoslovakian currency. At its 50th Conference in Brussels in 1962 (*Report*, pp. 553, 554) the International Law Association considered the money of account in the case of the infringement of industrial property rights (patents, trade marks, etc.). On this topic see Rutz, *Die Schuldwährung der Ansprüche aus Immaterialgüterrechtsverletzungen* (Fribourg, 1962), who in principle favours the money of account of the *locus delicti*, but permits the victim in certain cases to claim his own currency (p. 66).

[125] In Germany there seems to be a tendency to hold that damages are always expressed in German currency: Federal Supreme Court, 10 July 1954, *BGHZ*. 14, 212, 217; 9 Feb. 1977, *IPRspr.* 1977, No. 11. The underlying idea seems to be similar to that which Lord Sumner expressed in *The Volturno* (1921), 2 A.C. 544, 553 and according to which damage suffered in foreign currency is merely an 'item' in a general claim for damages. In England this idea may be expected to have been superseded by *The Despina R*, [1979] A.C. 685, see n. 103 above.    [126] [1979] A.C. 685.

dollars and other disbursements were payable in European convertible currencies.[127]

Accordingly, if the defendant, an Englishman, causes damage to the watch of the plaintiff, another Englishman, and this can only be repaired in Switzerland for Swiss francs which the plaintiff procures for sterling, he should in England be entitled to sterling rather than Swiss francs.[128] Similarly, if an English seller fails to deliver goods to an English exporter, so that the latter has to pay damages expressed in dollars to his New York sub-buyer and purchases the dollars for sterling, the seller's liability is fixed by the amount of sterling disbursed by the buyer. Or a French buyer whose English seller has failed to deliver goods claims damages for loss of profits arising from a contract with a New York sub-buyer and providing for payment in dollars. Can the French plaintiff claim the amount of dollars he lost, or the French francs into which, it can be proved as a fact, he would in the ordinary course of business have converted the dollars? The answer should be in the latter sense.

It should, however, be emphasized that as a result of Lord Wilberforce's reasoning in *The Despina R*[129] the law is flexible, untechnical and in favour of results which stem from a broad approach and meet the justice of the case. Thus in the case of multinational companies which maintain accounts in numerous currencies it is likely to become a mere question of fact whether the loss was in the ordinary course of business incurred in 'the plaintiff's currency' or in the currency of one or some of the accounts kept by the plaintiff. Thus an English company which has its ship repaired in Holland may use partly its Dutch guilder account, partly its dollar (rather than its sterling) account—it is a matter of evidence to prove the company's 'normal operations'.[130]

---

[127] Although the House of Lords is very careful in explaining or distinguishing such cases as *The Volturno*, [1921] 2 A.C. 544, *Di Ferdinando v. Simon, Smits & Co. Ltd.*, [1920] 3 K.B. 409 or *The Canadian Transport* (1932), 43 Ll. L.R. 409, none of them can be regarded as still being good law. On the other hand *Jugoslavenska Oceanska Plovidba v. Castle Investment Co. Inc.*, [1974] Q.B. 292 and *Jean Kraut A.G. v. Albany Fabrics Ltd.*, [1977] Q.B. 182 were expressly approved.

[128] In France the opposite rule seems to prevail: Cass. Req. 3 May 1946, S. 1951, 1. 33 or *Rev. Crit.* 1952, 767; Cour de Paris, 26 Oct. 1951, *Rev. Crit.* 1953, 376.

[129] *Ubi supra.*

[130] Brandon J. as a judge of first instance in *The Despina R* (1977), 3 All E.R. 889 alluded to certain special problems arising in Admiralty law. (a) In a both-to-blame collision case *The Khedive* (1882), 7 App. Cas. 795 requires that there should be only one judgment for the difference between the amounts of the two liabilities after set-off against the ship which has the greater liability. Brandon J. suggested that the currency of the lesser liability should be converted into the currency of the greater liability, the set-off should then be effected and judgment should be given in terms of the greater liability for the excess. This

(*d*) The law of agency provides numerous, sometimes contra-dictory examples of the rule which has been suggested, though in many cases the point now under discussion was not expressly taken.

*Ottoman Bank* v. *Jebara*[131] establishes the by no means self-evident proposition that if an English bank collects a bill drawn by an English seller upon his Beirut buyer for a sum of sterling and if the bank's local agent accepts payment in piastres, as it is bound to do,[132] it is liable for the sterling amount of the bill. The decision probably rests on its special facts and the course of business between the parties. If it were understood as laying down a firm legal rule, it would follow that an agent who carries on business in England and sells his principal's goods for dollars is liable to pay over dollars rather than sterling; but it must depend on the terms of the agree-ment whether the agent was allowed or perhaps even bound to convert the dollars into sterling. If, however, the agent is paid sterling by his principal and has to repay what he received he is liable for sterling, and it does not matter that the principal spent dollars to make the original sterling payment—the duty is to repay what was received.[133]

Another case is that of an agent who is entitled to be indemnified by his principal for expenses such as the cost of a ticket to Buenos Aires bought in Paris from an Argentine air line against dollar traveller cheques. He should be entitled to the refund, not of Argentine pesos in which the price of the ticket was expressed, nor of French francs which he could have spent had this been convenient, nor of dollars actually spent by him, but of sterling with which, so it is assumed, the traveller cheques were bought.[134] Or if the master of a ship has

process involves a possibly unjust conversion for the purpose of the set-off. *The Khedive, ubi supra,* was not concerned with this particular point. Would it perhaps be more appro-priate to put a distinguishable precedent aside and give separate judgments for each ship? (*b*) The second problem arises where the defendant's liability is limited in terms of sterling. Where the plaintiff is entitled to foreign currency and his damages exceed the limit, there is indeed no alternative but to follow Brandon J.'s suggestion that judgment should be given in sterling for the amount of the limit. Where the damages are less than the limit on the basis of the rate of exchange at the date of judgment, the court should award the amount of foreign currency, subject to the proviso that by the date of payment the limit is not exceeded. (*c*) Where a limitation action is brought and a fund is created conversion into sterling will be unavoidable: see below p. 338.

[131] [1928] A.C. 269.

[132] Cf. the international practice which is referred to below, pp. 308, 315.

[133] In this sense, the German Federal Supreme Court, 30 Sept. 1968, *IPRspr.* 1968/1969 No. 175. Many years ago the German Supreme Court decided that a bank which collects a cheque or bill denominated and paid in foreign currency is, in the absence of special terms, bound to credit its customer with the foreign currency collected and is not entitled to convert it into domestic currency and credit the customer accordingly: 10 Jan. 1925, *RGZ.* 110, 47; 20 March 1927, *RGZ.* 116, 330.

[134] In Germany the agent would probably be entitled to dollars: see, in regard to a

to pay at Rotterdam a fine in Dutch guilders on account of the cargo being of a prohibited nature and if he obtains the guilders by spending sterling, the owner of the cargo should have to refund sterling rather than guilders.[135]

2. It remains to add a few words on the much-neglected question of the law which, in case of a conflict of laws, governs the identification of the money of account of damages. It seems clear that this task can be discharged by one legal system only, namely, by the proper law of the obligation.[136] Thus, if goods are sold from Germany to England, but not accepted here, the question whether the damages are measured in German or English currency fails to be decided by the proper law of the contract. If it is German, the damages are probably expressed in German currency;[137] if it is English, the rule of English municipal law applies that the damage consists of the

comparable, though by no means identical, situation the decisions of the Federal Supreme Court, 11 May 1960, *RzW*. 1969, 459; 9 May 1968, *RzW*. 1968, 406 (relating to emigration expenses refundable by the Federal Government). The opposite view had been taken by the Federal Supreme Court, 20 Jan. 1965, *RzW*. 1965, 318. It is apparently still taken in regard to the refund of expenses for reconvalescence: Federal Supreme Court, 14 Mar. 1958, *RzW*. 1958, 225.

[135] The point is dealt with in a number of German decisions. If my agent defrays expenses, I am bound to repay to him that money which he had to spend; thus if a German forwarding agent pays Belgian francs for the consignor's account, the latter must repay to him Belgian francs: German Supreme Court, 22 Oct. 1924, *RGZ*. 109, 85; similarly 24 Apr. 1924, *JW*. 1924, 1593, No. 9; 6 May 1933, *WarnRspr*. 1933, No. 112. Similarly Austrian Supreme Court, 6 Mar. 1923, *SZ*. v, No. 47, but see Supreme Court, 3 Oct. 1933, *RabelsZ*. 1933, 741. As to Belgium see Piret, No. 25. If a consignment from Hamburg to Rotterdam is declared to contain hydrochlorates and in fact contains spirits, so that the master of the ship is made liable for a fine of 5,000 Dutch florins, the consignor's liability is measured in florins, not in German marks: German Supreme Court, 27 Feb. 1924, *JW*. 1925, 1477. But see the very doubtful decision of the German Supreme Court, 27 Jan. 1928, *RGZ*. 120, 76: in 1914 the plaintiffs had accepted accommodation bills for 180,000 French francs for the defendant; they paid the bills in 1916. The Court of Appeal ordered the defendant to indemnify the plaintiffs by the payment of 180,000 French francs together with damages in respect of the depreciation of the French currency since 20 Feb. 1925, when the defendant failed to comply with the plaintiff's demand for payment. The Supreme Court, however, reversed this convincing judgment and held that the claim was expressed in reichsmarks (i.e. in the new currency replacing the mark currency and introduced only in 1924) and that the defendant was liable to compensate the plaintiffs for the value of 180,000 French francs in 1916.

[136] See, in particular, *Jean Kraut A.G.* v. *Albany Fabrics Ltd.*, [1977] Q.B. 182. Dicey and Morris, Rule 176 (3) and p. 1006 agree. See also Cheshire and North, p. 717. Frankenstein, *Internationales Privatrecht*, ii. 203, 204; Melchior, *Grundlagen*, pp. 277 sqq. The question of the law applicable to the determination of the currency in which liability is measured was not discussed in any of the cases dealt with under (1) above. But it is submitted that in all these cases the courts proceeded on the basis of English law being the law of the obligation. This especially applies to *The Volturno*, [1921] 2 A.C. 544 and *The Canadian Transport* (1932), 43 Ll. L.R. 409, which concerned damages arising out of a collision on the high seas, in which case English law is always the governing law: see the text.

[137] See p. 243, n. 104.

market value at the place of delivery and is measured in the currency of that place.[138, 139]

A particular difficulty, however, arises in tort cases. If a collision occurs on the high seas, English courts always apply English law,[140] and there is consequently no real conflict of laws involved.[141] But if the tort is committed on land, it is not easy to say which law governs the tort and, accordingly, the determination of the money of account. A recent decision of the House of Lords[142] has, unhappily, failed to produce the clarification which is so badly needed. In the circumstances it can only be suggested that the identity of the money of account should be determined by that legal system which governs the substance rather than the remedy. Accordingly, if the plaintiff in an English court is a Dutchman resident in Belgium, if his car is damaged by the English defendant in Italy, if it is repaired in France, and if under Italian law he would be entitled, not to the French francs paid to the garage, but to the Belgian francs with which he purchased the French francs so paid, he ought to obtain judgment for the Belgian francs, notwithstanding any different rule prevailing in France, Belgium or Italy. But whether the English court will arrive at such a result is open to much doubt. Probably the English court will apply such rule of English municipal law as there may be.[143]

---

[138] See p, 244, n, 111,

[139] The question has nothing to do with the measure of damages, because it does not relate to the quantification of damages in the usual sense.

[140] See, for example, Dicey and Morris, p. 974.

[141] See above, p. 250, n. 136.

[142] *Boys* v. *Chaplin*, [1970] A.C. 356.

[143] See Dicey and Morris, pp. 965 and 1000.

# IX

# The Determination of the Money of Account (*continuation*): Subsequent Uncertainty

I. The problem stated. II. The effect of the curtailment of the monetary system upon the money of account: (1) municipal law; (2) private international law. III. The extinction of the money of account (1) by the substitution of one monetary system for another; (2) by the dissolution of a unitary currency system into separate systems: (*a*) municipal law; (*b*) private international law.

## I

THE money of account, though originally clearly defined, may during the life of a legal relationship become uncertain.

This happens where a new monetary system emerges, usually as the result of changes of territorial sovereignty,[1] and it therefore becomes doubtful whether the money of account of a particular obligation remains the same or is changed into the money of account of the successor State. Thus after the cession or annexation of territories the new sovereign introduces a new currency, but money issued by the former sovereign circulates and suddenly becomes foreign money; similarly, debts or sums provided for in statutes (such as fines or dues) are expressed in terms of the former sovereign's currency. When the new currency is introduced, there will no doubt be a 'recurrent link' indicating the rate of conversion from the old into the new currency,[2] but there will also have to be a definition of what it is that is to be converted, i.e. of the scope of conversion. Consequently, in considering whether and how far the money of account of debts expressed in terms of the old standard of currency is in fact changed, two distinct questions arise: First, what are the debts the substance of which the new sovereign, under his municipal law, purports to change? Second, what are the rules of English private international law defining the extent to which that change is allowed to operate?

These questions require investigation with a view to the two principal types of changes that may occur. On the one hand, a unitary

[1] See, generally, Neumeyer, pp. 259 sqq.; Nolde, *Rec.* 27 (1929), 283 sqq.

[2] See above, p. 44, and below, p. 273.

monetary system, while continuing to exist and retaining its identity in the residual territory, may suffer a *curtailment* of its territorial ambit by part of its original territory setting up a new or joining another monetary system.[3] This happened in Australia and, probably, certain other parts of the British Commonwealth of Nations[4] which originally shared the United Kingdom's, but in course of time came to adopt their own monetary system; or the crown of the former Austro-Hungarian monarchy circulated in territories which after the First World War were ceded to Italy, Hungary, Poland, Czechoslovakia, and Yugoslavia,[5] or German currency circulated not only in the former German colonies in South-West Africa, which are now under the administration of the Union of South Africa, but also in districts which in 1920 were acquired by France, Denmark, Poland, and other countries.[6] On the other hand, an independent monetary system may become *extinct* as a result of the fact that the whole of the territory to which it used to apply passes to one or more new sovereigns none of whom continues the old standard of currency, though the names may remain the same. The monetary history of Germany provides two examples: in the former Protectorate in East Africa, the present Tanzania, the rupee currency circulated under the German administration, but the English substituted for it the East African shilling;[7] in June 1948 both the Federal Republic of Germany and what became the German Democratic Republic discontinued the reichsmark as a unit of account and introduced new currencies both called the Deutsche Mark.

---

[3] The curtailment may be apparent rather than real. This may happen in the case of an unsuccessful revolution when legally a single independent monetary system exists in the country, but the parties believe that there are two such systems, the units of account of both bearing the same name. Thus during the civil war in the United States of America the Confederate dollar came into use, though in the events which happened it never existed in law. If two persons in the territory of the Confederation contracted in terms of dollars, it became, after the termination of the civil war, a matter of construction in what sense the word 'dollar' had been used in the contract: *Thorington* v. *Smith* (1869), 75 U.S. 1, at pp. 13, 14. The problems raised by the parties' erroneous belief in the existence of distinct monetary systems no less than the problems raised by their erroneous belief in the existence of a single monetary system (above, p. 229) must be solved by interpretation.

[4] The development in other parts of the British Commonwealth of Nations has never been fully investigated: see above, p. 54.

[5] As to legislation in the countries formerly belonging to the Austro-Hungarian monarchy see Steiner, *Die Währungsgesetzgebung der Sukzessionsstaaten Österreich-Ungarns* (Vienna, 1921). The present Republic of Austria has generally been regarded as the successor of the Austro-Hungarian monarchy rather than a new state.

[6] It would, of course, be possible to speak of the extension of the territorial ambit of a particular currency (such as that of France, Denmark, and so forth), but this would be merely another method of approach to the same problem.

[7] Ordinances Nos. 43 and 44 of 1921: see *Journal of Comparative Legislation*, 9 (1922), Review of Legislation, p. 164.

## II

1. Where the territorial ambit of a monetary system is merely reduced,[8] the legislator has, theoretically, a choice between a number
of tests for delimiting the new from the old currency: the nationality,
domicile, or residence of either creditor or debtor, the place of payment,[9] the proper law of the debt, or the economic connection of a
particular transaction with the one or the other territory. Whatever
test the legislator chooses, he may make it compulsory or optional
and he may lay it down expressly or impliedly.

The legislators of the world do not seem to have decided upon a
uniform test, though they have eliminated certain tests which are
clearly impracticable (such as nationality, domicile, or proper law)
and show a preference for the residence of the debtor or the place of
payment[10] but when Algeria became independent of France on
1 July 1962 and in 1964 introduced the dinar currency, it was provided that debts 'sont réputées libellées dans la monnaie du domicile
du contrat'.[11] Usually compulsory conversion is provided for, but
according to the text of the Austrian Schilling Law of 30 November
1945 all debts which are capable of being discharged in Austria in
reichsmarks, may, after 21 December 1945 be discharged in schillings
at the rate of 1 reichsmark to 1 schilling.[12] Australian law, it is submitted, contains an example of an implied delimitation. By s. 51 (xii)
of the Commonwealth of Australia Act, 1900, Australia was given
power to make laws with regard to currency, coinage, and legal tender. By the Australian Coinage Act, 1909, 'Australian coins' were
issued on the basis of a standard of weight and fineness identical with
that laid down by the Coinage Act, 1870 (ss. 2 and 4). Both 'British
coins' and 'Australian coins' were legal tender (s. 5). By the Australian

---

[8] This section is largely based upon the paper published in 68 (1952) *L.Q.R.* 195 sqq.

[9] For its definition see above, p. 76.

[10] See, for example, the Czechoslovakian law referred to below, p. 261, n. 41. When
after the First World War certain German provinces came under Polish sovereignty, Poland
introduced the zloty currency and statutory provision was made for the conversion of mark
debts into zloty debts. German courts often held that the Polish statute itself restricted its
application to payments to be made in Poland: Supreme Court, 11 Mar. 1922, *JW.* 1923,
123; 28 Nov. 1922, *JW.* 1922, 1122; 22 Mar. 1928, *JW.* 1928, 3108; 27 June 1928, *RGZ.*
121, 337, 344; Berlin Court of Appeal, 9 Mar. 1922, *JW.* 1922, 1135. There exist numerous
*French* decisions relating to the ambit of the rate of conversion introduced in Alsace-
Lorraine: see, for example, Cass. Civ. 26 May 1930, Clunet, 1931, 169; 8 Feb. 1932, Clunet,
1932, 1015; 29 Nov. 1932, Clunet, 1933, 686; Cass. Req. 25 Oct. 1932, Clunet, 1933, 689.
It seems that the view developed in the text is shared by Van Eck, *Juridische Aspecten van
Geld met Name in het Vroegere Nederlands-Indie* (Deventer, 1970).

[11] Art. 20 of the Evian Agreement: U.N.T.S. 507, 25 where the phrase is (probably in-
correctly) translated by the words: 'place where the contract was concluded'.

[12] S. 6 (2). For the text (in a bad French translation) see *Bulletin de législation comparée*, 1946, 664.

Notes Act, 1910, the Governor-General was given power to author-ize the issue of 'Australian notes' (s. 5). These were declared to be 'a legal tender throughout the Commonwealth and throughout all territories under the control of the Commonwealth' and to be 'pay-able in gold coin at the Commonwealth Treasury at the Seat of Government' (s. 6).[13] Thus, by the Act of 1910,[14] Australia in effect provided that, within the territory specified in s. 6, Australian notes could discharge debts expressed in 'pounds' which *ex hypothesi* were English pounds. In the first place, therefore, s. 6 contained an implied rate of conversion, i.e. one Australian pound (in notes) for one English pound, and in substance brought about a substitution of Australian for English currency, for if a debt of one English pound can be discharged by the payment of one Australian pound, this is tantamount to saying that Australian currency has taken the place of English currency. However, this is so only within the Commonwealth. Australian law had to delimit the scope of its application; it could not purport to affect all 'pound' debts. Australian law decided in favour of the place of payment as a test. It does not touch debts which are payable outside the Commonwealth.

Where the legislator omits to deal with the problem of delimita-tion, the determination of the money of account becomes a question of construction. Just as in the case of an initial ambiguity we ask what currency the parties contemplated when they made their con-tract,[15] so in the case of a subsequent ambiguity we ask what cur-rency the parties would have contemplated if they had foreseen the territorial and the concomitant monetary changes.[16] All the circum-stances will have to be reviewed and weighed and to this extent it is legitimate to try to ascertain the country in which the contract has

---

[13] As a result of the outbreak of the First World War gold coins practically disappeared from circulation and notes issued under the Act of 1910 were the only legal tender. Bank of England notes of £5, which never were legal tender in Australia (see above, p. 54, n. 140), do not appear to have been of significance in practice and were not dealt with by the legis-lature.

[14] The Commonwealth Bank Act, 1920, altered the machinery of the issue of notes, but in substance ss. 60 G and 60 H re-enacted the provisions of the Act of 1910. The Common-wealth Bank Act, 1929, gave power to require the exchange of gold coins and bullion for Australian notes.

[15] Above, p. 224.

[16] This is certainly not an easy task, but it is one with which lawyers are familiar, and by no means an impossible one. It is not essentially different from that which arises when the proper law must be ascertained and about which Lord Wright has said: 'The parties may not have thought of the matter at all. Then the court has to impute an intention, or to deter-mine for the parties what is the proper law which, as just and reasonable persons, they ought or would have intended if they had thought about the question when they made the con-tract' (*Mount Albert Borough Council* v. *Australasian Temperance and General Mutual Life Assurance Society*, [1938] A.C. 224, 240).

its 'economic home' or to which it 'belongs'.[17] But, just as in the case of an initial ambiguity, it is preferable as a matter of last resort to adopt the rule that it is the currency of the place of payment that is, or rather becomes, the money of account.[18]

2. When one comes to relationships involving international aspects, it becomes necessary to turn in the first place to the case in which the legislator has laid down a compulsory rule and the courts of his own country are involved. For instance, if it is assumed that after the First World War Czechoslovakia compulsorily converted into Czechoslovakian currency all such debts as were expressed in terms of the crown of the Austro-Hungarian monarchy and payable in Czechoslovakia, all Czechoslovakian judges may have to give effect to that ruling, irrespective of the proper law of the contract, the residence of the parties, or any other factor that ordinarily might be material.

Where the statutory provisions are *jus dispositivum* or where the courts of another country are concerned, the approach must be different. In such circumstances the paramount task will be to ascertain the proper law of the contract which alone has the power to sanction and enforce a change of the money of account, i.e. of the substance of the obligation. The rule that the rate of conversion established by the *lex monetae* must be followed,[19] is of no avail, for the very question is which of two competing laws of the currency shall prevail: if in 1914 an Englishman promised the Prague agency of a Vienna bank to pay in 1934 a sum of crowns (which were, of course, Austro-Hungarian crowns), the question whether at the date of maturity the debt is converted into Austrian schillings of the then Austrian currency or into crowns of Czechoslovakia cannot be answered otherwise than by the proper law of contract.

If the proper law is the legal system of the country whose currency was originally agreed as the money of account and continues to exist after the separation (i.e. in the above example, Austria) or if the proper law is the legal system of a third country (e.g. in the above case, England), the inquiry will not usually have to be pursued, for

[17] On these tests as employed in Australia, Austria, and Czechoslovakia see below, p. 260 and p. 261, n. 41. Cf. Brussels Court of Appeal, 24 May 1933, Clunet, 1933, 169, and A.D. 1933–4, No. 41. The decision of the Supreme Court of Romania, 20 Feb. 1931, A.D. 1931–2, No. 37 related to a case in which the defendant in Cernautzi (then Austria) bought in 1914 goods from the plaintiff in Teschen (then also Austria) for Austrian crowns. Later Cernautzi became Romanian and Teschen became part of Czechoslovakia. The plaintiff demanded payment in Czechoslovakian crowns, or in Romanian lei at the rate for such crowns. The defendant sought to discharge his debt in lei equivalent to Austrian crowns at the official rate of 2 crowns to 1 leu. He succeeded, mainly on the grounds that doubts had to be resolved in favour of the debtor.

[18] See above, p. 229; on the problems discussed in the text see Dicey and Morris, p. 1006, and Nussbaum, pp. 354, 355.

[19] Below, p. 267.

neither legal system is likely to contain any rule providing for the change of the substance of monetary obligations: the Austrian crowns would become Austrian schillings, but neither Austrian law nor English law would be likely to provide for the conversion of an Austrian debt into a Czechoslovakian debt. Or if a merchant in Melbourne promises to pay 'pounds' to a merchant in Sydney (or London) at a time when a single pound is common to England and Australia and if the contract is subject to English law, the creation of an independent Australian pound is prima facie irrelevant. The original pound is in existence, though in England alone. The Australian pound could be imported into the contract only by virtue of Australian law which does not govern the contract. The law of Australia, it is true, may contain a compulsory rule providing for substitution and an Australian judge may have to give effect to it. But a non-Australian court is neither permitted nor compelled to do so. These results could be different only if, as a result of the change of sovereignty, the proper law itself changes so that the contract becomes subject to the law of the country which has introduced the new currency (i.e. in the above examples, Czechoslovakia or Australia). This occurs where at the time of the change both parties, by their residence, are subject, or later submit themselves to, the new sovereign.[20]

If, on the other hand, the proper law is the legal system of the country which has introduced the new currency, then the rules of substitution which, as has been shown, such legal system usually contains, will have to be followed everywhere.[21]

---

[20] On this principle see M. Wolff, *Private International Law*, 2nd ed. (1950) s. 407 and numerous decisions of the German Supreme Court, for example, 22 Mar. 1928, *JW.* 1928, 1447; 27 June 1928, *RGZ.* 121, 337, 344; 25 Oct. 1928, *JW.* 1928, 3108; 16 Jan. 1929, *RGZ.* 123, 130; 5 Dec. 1932, *RGZ.* 139, 76, 81. See also French Cass. Civ. 15 May 1935, Clunet, 1936, 601, and S. 1935, 1. 244: in 1914 a firm in Alsace-Lorraine had sold goods to a Paris firm under a German contract; the contract remained subject to German law, apparently even although both parties became subject to the laws of France.

[21] For the reasons developed in the text one must feel grave doubts about the interesting decision Cass. Civ. 24 Apr. 1952, *Rev. Crit.* 1952, 504 with note by Motulsky, Clunet, 1952, 1234 and S. 1952, 1. 185 with note by Batiffol, affirming Court of Appeal at Aix, 13 July 1948, *Rev. Crit.* 1949, 332 with approving note by Dehove and Batiffol; see also the latter's remarks in *Lectures on the Conflict of Laws and International Contracts* (University of Michigan Law School, 1951), pp. 77, 78. A company in Paris sold to a company in Marseilles land situate in French West Africa for frs. 5,500,000. Completion took place in French West Africa on 18 Dec. 1945. On 26 Dec. 1945 the French West African franc was established at a rate of 100 West African francs for 170 Metropolitan francs. Art. 2 of the decree exempted from conversion debts due from a resident in one 'zone' to a resident of another 'zone', but made no provision for the case in which both parties resided in the same 'zone'. It was held that the contract was localized in French West Africa and that the debt was reduced to about 3,235,000 West African francs. If the contract was subject to West African law, the sole question was whether the decree applied to a case such as this (which seems doubtful, because payment was due before the date of the decree and because Art. 2 seems to supply an *a fortiori* argument in the case of both parties residing in Metropolitan

These principles, for the clarification of which the former German Supreme Court may claim particular credit,[22] lead to peculiar difficulties in case of an option of place. Suppose that under a contract made in 1914 and subject to Austrian law 1,000 crowns are promised to be paid in 1934 in Vienna or Prague; there being no option of currency and the creditor being entitled only to one payment of Austrian crowns[23] converted into the appropriate amount of Austrian schillings, he cannot claim in Prague in 1934 1,000 Czechoslovakian crowns, but such sum of Czechoslovakian crowns as corresponds to the converted amount of Austrian schillings. But if the contract had been subject to the law of Czechoslovakia, then the Czechoslovakian rules of conversion apply: if they should affect only payments in Prague, the result would be that the creditor would receive in Prague such sums of Czechoslovakian crowns as are indicated by Czechoslovakian law, though in Vienna he would be entitled to Austrian

France). If the contract was subject to the law of Metropolitan France, there was no warrant for changing the money of account agreed by the parties. On the other hand two decisions relating to Algeria correctly recognized the substitution of dinars for francs on the ground that the contract was governed by Algerian law: Cass. Civ. 15 Feb. 1972, *Rev. Crit.* 1973 with note Batiffol; 14 Nov. 1972, Bull. Civ. 1972, I, No. 238. The former decision gives rise to doubts, because the contract was made before Algeria became independent (1 July 1962) and was, therefore, unlikely to be subject to Algerian law. The decision of the Paris Court of Appeal, 24 March 1973, *Rev. Crit.* 1976, 73 with note Malaurie is founded on reasoning which in many respects would seem to lack persuasiveness. On the problem of the franc métropolitain and the franc colonial, see Planiol–Ripert, vii, No. 119 *bis*. On the problem of the Indonesian guilder see above, p. 53, n. 134.

[22] The court held that a debt expressed in Austro-Hungarian crowns, which was contracted by a German with the Prague office of a Vienna bank and which was subject to German or Austrian law, was in the absence of a contractual or actual submission to Czechoslovakian law expressed in the old currency or in what had replaced it by Austrian law, because neither German nor Austrian law provided for conversion into Czechoslovakian crowns: 13 July 1929, *IPRspr.* 1930, No. 30; 14 Jan. 1931, *IPRspr.* 1931, No. 30; 30 April 1931, *IPRspr.* 1931, No. 31; 16 Dec. 1931, *IPRspr.* 1932, No. 113. Similarly, the court held that mark debts contracted under German law in German South-West Africa were not affected by the Debts Settlement Proclamation of 15 Dec. 1920 providing for the conversion of mark debts into pounds sterling at the rate of 20 marks to 1 pound sterling: 8 Dec. 1930, *RGZ.* 131, 41; 31 July 1936, *RGZ.* 152, 53, and A.D. 1935–7, No. 76. On the fate of rupee debts see Czechoslovakian-German Mixed Arbitral Tribunal, *Rec.* v. 551, 575 sqq.; Greek-German M.A.T., *Rec.* vii. 14; and French-German M.A.T. *Rec.* vii. 604. Where liabilities arose from relationships which, as a result of Austria's 'secession' from Germany in 1945, acquired an international character, *Austrian* courts seem to have held the liability to be expressed in the currency of the place of performance: if this was in Austria, the RM debt was converted into schillings at the rate of 1:1 (Austrian Supreme Court, 18 Jan. 1951, *SZ.* xxiv, No. 190; 16 Jan. 1952, *SZ.* xxv, No. 11; 17 Feb. 1954, *SZ.* xxvii, No. 33), but where it was in Germany, the debt remained expressed in RM and was in 1948 converted into DM (Austrian Supreme Court, 30 Apr. 1953, *SZ.* xxvi, No. 117, also Clunet, 1957, 1014). But Stanzl in Klang's *Commentaries*, iv, p. 744, suggests that the courts in the first place ascertain the proper law of the contract and if this is not Austrian, then the currency cannot have been changed from RM into schillings even though the place of performance is in Austria. This would be in line with the approach suggested in the text.

[23] On this point see above, p. 211.

crowns or, in the event of their disappearance, to such amount of schillings as is determined by the Austrian rules of conversion. Or suppose that under a contract governed by Scottish law the debtor, in 1950, promises to pay in the year 2000 the sum of £100 in London or Edinburgh. And suppose, further, that in the year 1990 Scotland introduces its own monetary system and converts into Scottish pounds such debts expressed in terms of the old common pound as are payable in Scotland. In this case the creditor is entitled to receive in the year 2000 100 Scottish pounds in Edinburgh or 100 English pounds in London. In other words, the option of place becomes an option of currency. This would be the inevitable consequence of supervening Scottish legislation. It would not be a case of the law conferring an unexpected benefit on the creditor; it would be a case of the law (of Scotland) limiting its interference with existing contractual rights.[24]

From the point of view of the above observations only qualified approval can be given to the decision of the High Court of Australia in *Goldsbrough Mort & Co. Ltd.* v. *Hall*[25] which preceded *Bonython* v. *Commonwealth of Australia*[26] and was therefore based on the assumption that the Australian monetary system became independent in 1909, but that at the time of the contract in 1895 England and Australia had a common system.

The appellant company was incorporated in Queensland to take over the business of another company which had been financed largely in England and was indebted to a substantial number of debenture-holders there. The company issued to the debenture-holders debenture stock under a trust deed providing for English trustees. There were separate registers in Melbourne and London. The trust deed, executed in 1895, was repeatedly amended. In 1939 a consolidating deed was made under which the controversy arose. The court (Rich, Dixon, and McTiernan JJ., Latham C.J., and Starke J. dissenting) held that the company had to pay English currency.

---

[24] The situation is wholly different from that which was assumed to exist in *Auckland Corporation* v. *Alliance Assurance Co.*, [1937] A.C. 587 and which is discussed above, p. 240. As has been pointed out, the decision in that case rested on the theory that at all material times England and New Zealand had the same monetary system. The text deals with the case where in part of the territory a new and independent monetary system emerges and where, therefore, the effect of the new sovereign's supervening legislation upon existing obligations falls to be considered.

[25] (1949) 78 C.L.R.I.; see also the decision of Fullagar J. in the court below: (1948) V.L.R. 145. Strictly, Lord Wright's opinion in *Adelaide Electric Supply Co.* v. *Prudential Assurance Co.*, [1934] A.C. 122, 149 sqq. ought to be discussed in the present context rather than above, pp. 237 sqq., because it is predicated upon the view that during the life of the contract an independent Australian pound came into being. It would have been inconvenient, however, to split up the discussion of the *Adelaide* case. See p. 239, n. 90.

[26] [1951] A.C. 201.

The members of the court did not approach the case in the same fashion. Latham C.J. discussed the problem of interpretation for the solution of which he rejected what one may call the subjective test:[27]

It is, I suggest, useless here to ask the question which has in some cases been made the test in the frustration cases—What would the parties have said, if they had, when they were making their contract, known what would happen?

He preferred[28] to ask the question which in *Bonython*'s case had been formulated by Rich J.,[29] viz. 'whether any and what implication as a matter of law can be made in the new situation as to the form and means of payment to the plaintiffs', or to apply the test suggested in the same case by Dixon J.:[30] 'the point must be to which of the two [moneys of account] does the obligation "belong", on which does it depend, which does it follow', or, in the language of Lord Watson,[31] what was the meaning 'which the parties, as fair and reasonable men, would presumably have agreed upon'. Investigating the facts from this point of view Latham C.J. found that Australian pounds had become substituted for English pounds.

Similarly, Rich J. applied the test he had formulated in *Bonython*'s case, but he found[32] that the 'whole setting' was English and that, therefore, English pounds were owed by the company.

Starke J. held that the English and Australian monetary systems continued to be the same, and followed the *Adelaide* case.[33] If necessary, he would have been prepared to hold that the proper law of the contract was Australian. He concluded from this finding, without investigating the point of interpretation, that Australian pounds were *in obligatione*.[34]

Dixon J. with whom McTiernan J. agreed,[35] seems to start from the question of construction and, contrary to his formula in *Bonython*'s case,[36] to approach it subjectively:[37] 'the intention to be implied must be an intention to use the pound as the money of England or as the money of Australia'. Yet, after a detailed discussion of the facts, he takes up the question of the choice of law of which in *Bonython*'s case he had said that it was 'of no moment, for in both jurisdictions the same common rule supplies the rule'.[38] He thus arrived at the 'reasonably plain deduction that the parties to the contract, embodied in the trust deed and the stock certificates, treated the legal and financial system of England as the foundation of the

---

[27] pp. 14, 15.                                    [28] p. 15.
[29] (1948) 75 C.L.R. 589, 607.                    [30] pp. 624, 625.
[31] *Dahl* v. *Nelson* (1881), 6 App. Cas. 38, 59; cf. above, p. 255, n. 16.
[32] p. 18.                                         [33] [1934] A.C. 122.
[34] p. 32.              [35] p. 46.                [36] Above, n. 30.
[37] p. 36.                          [38] (1948) 75 C.L.R. 589, 624.

transaction. It was the country with which they instinctively contrived to connect the contract most closely.'[39] The proper law being English, it followed that English pounds remained payable.

Latham C.J. and Rich J., therefore, dealt with the question of interpretation without establishing the proper law of the contract, and arrived at opposite results. Starke J., in the course of his subsidiary reasoning, discussed the proper law of the contract, but having found it to be Australian, did not investigate how Australian law solved the question. If one disregards his introductory remarks, Dixon J., as one would expect, was wholly consistent: he discussed the proper law, found it to be English and hence was relieved of the problem of construction.

It is submitted that this is the approach which commends itself.[40] In an English court the substance of an obligation governed by English law plainly cannot be changed by Australian law. If the proper law of the contract is English and if, as it seems, Australian law does not contain a compulsory rule of conversion, *cadit quaestio*, even in an Australian court. If the proper law is Australian, it becomes necessary to ascertain and apply the express or implied rules of Australian statutory law relating to conversion and only in the absence of such rules[41] does the court become concerned with construing the contract, whether it be on the basis of an objective or subjective test.

---

[39] p. 45.

[40] In the United States of America it was rightly held that a Cuban law according to which 'all obligations contracted or payable' in Cuba should be discharged in Cuban pesos 'one for one' had the effect of substituting Cuban pesos for U.S. dollars payable under an insurance policy and governed by Cuban law: *Confederation Life Association* v. *Ugalde*, 164 So. 2d 1 (1964), affirming 151 So. 2d 315 (1963); *Johansen* v. *Confederation Life Association*, 447 F. 2d 175 (1971); *Santovenia* v. *Confederation Life Insurance*, 460 F. 2d 805 (1972). The Cuban law was not contrary to *ordre public*. There was no place of payment except in Cuba. On the other hand in *Serpa* v. *Confederation Life Association*, 43 D.L.R. (3d) 324 (1974) Keith J., sitting in the Ontario High Court, held that the policy was governed by Ontario law and the Cuban legislation was inapplicable.

[41] It has been submitted above, p. 254, that such rules do exist in Australian law, but they were ignored by the court. There exists a curious precedent for this omission. After she had become independent of the Austro-Hungarian monarchy, Czechoslovakia introduced a monetary system and a statute of 10 Apr. 1919 provided that debts expressed in Austro-Hungarian crowns and payable within the territory of the Czechoslovak State should be paid in Czechoslovak crowns, one Czechoslovak crown being equal to one Austrian crown. Before the separation of the countries a railway company whose undertaking was mainly situate on Czechoslovak territory had issued bonds expressed in 'crowns'; they were stated to be payable in Vienna where the company's principal office was and remained situate. Both the Austrian and the Czechoslovakian Supreme Courts disregarded the statutory rule, but searched for what the Czechoslovakian Supreme Court described as the 'economic home' of the obligation or for what Dixon J. described as the country it 'belongs' to, found it to be in Czechoslovakia, and thus held the bonds to be payable in Czechoslovakian crowns, although the Czechoslovakian statute confined conversion to debts payable in Czechoslovakia: Czechoslovakian Supreme Court, 4 June 1925 and Austrian Supreme Court, 14 July 1926, *Zeitschrift für Ostrecht*, i (1927), 119, 142 with illuminating note by Nussbaum.

## III

1. The extinction of a currency involves no legal difficulty if a new single currency is substituted for it as a whole.

Usually this occurs when a State adopts a new monetary system, as Germany did in 1924 when she replaced the mark currency by the reichsmark currency[42] or as in more recent days Hungary did when she introduced the forint currency in the place of the pengö currency.[43] Here, according to the principle of nominalism which will have to be discussed,[44] debts expressed in the old currency are uniformly and inevitably converted into the new currency at the rate of conversion (recurrent link) laid down by the legislator.

The legal position is in no way different if an independent monetary system comes to an end as a result of the territory to which it applies passing to a new sovereign who introduces a new or his own monetary system. Again nominalism applies and, irrespective of whether or no the contract is governed by the law of the country concerned, debts become expressed in the new currency, for the old currency has ceased to exist altogether, not only locally, and therefore the *lex monetae* and its recurrent link must be universally applied. An example is supplied by the development in Tanzania[45] to which reference has been made: the substitution of the East African shilling for the rupee had the result that, wherever the rupee was the original money of account of a debt, the shilling took its place, even if the contract was governed by German or any other law.[46] Or take the case of the Palestine pound: if in 1934 the plaintiff spent £P20 and in 1959 becomes entitled to a refund, the English court should apply the rate of 1 for 1 introduced by Israel in 1948 for the conversion of Palestinian into Israeli pounds and award £I20 (or its equivalent).[47,48]

---

[42] Above, p. 101.

[43] Law of 26 July 1946; for a French translation see *Bulletin de législation comparée*, 1946, 689. Arts. 10 and 13 apply to all sums expressed in pengös, irrespective of the proper law. See above, p. 101.

[44] Below, p. 267.          [45] Above, p. 253.

[46] In the same sense Nussbaum, *Internationales Privatrecht*, p. 254; *Geld*, p. 161; Neumeyer, p. 275; Mayer, *Valutaschuld*, p. 45, n. 9. The German Supreme Court, however, held (3 June 1924, *RGZ*. 108, 303, 304) that after the territorial change the debt became expressed in marks, because the proper law of the obligation was and remained German. But this amounts to an unfortunate confusion between the law of the currency and that of the obligation and is due to a failure to distinguish the present case from that mentioned under section (2); cf. also Supreme Court, 8 Dec. 1930, *RGZ*. 131, 42, 47.

[47] This result was correctly reached by the Federal Supreme Court, 28 Oct. 1959, *RzW*. 1960, 172 with note by Mann, affirming Court of Appeal Karlsruhe, *RzW*. 1959, 399. Against the decision Ortar, *RzW*. 1960, 30 and 294; Schwarz, *RzW*. 1960, 460. On an Israeli case, *Braunde* v. *Palestine Corporation Ltd.*, which is less easy to follow, see Mann, *American Journal of Comparative Law*, 4 (1955), 241.

[48] A situation similar to that contemplated in the text also arose when the American

2. The extinction of a currency leads to much more serious and, indeed, almost insoluble complications, if it is incidental to the partition of a State and the consequent dissolution of a unitary currency system into two (or more) new, independent systems. This does not seem to have happened prior to June 1948, when both the Federal Republic of Germany and the Eastern Zone of Germany, the German Democratic Republic, introduced new currencies and, to make confusion worse confounded, each called them Deutsche Mark.[49]

In circumstances of this kind it is vital to obtain a clear picture of the nature of the problem. It is not a problem which, in the absence of statutory provisions, can be solved by the law of either of the currencies concerned, for neither has an *a priori* claim to precedence over the other. The real question is which of two distinct monetary systems defines the substance of the obligation. It is the contract alone that can supply the answer: there is no difference of principle between the case in which the parties have at the outset failed to make an unequivocal choice of the money of account, and the case in which during the life of the contract the money of account becomes uncertain, whatever the reason for such supervening uncertainty may be. It is always a matter of construction, of the implied or presumed intention of the parties; differences arise not from the nature, but from the delicacy of the task. And that delicacy will not be greater than in other cases in which an unexpected turn of events creates a gap and compels the judge to fill it.[50]

The methods of construction, however, are not everywhere identical and this makes it necessary to trace accurately the steps required to arrive at the solution.

(*a*) A judge sitting in either of the two countries which have adopted new currencies, will primarily turn to his legislator for

Civil War came to an end and the Confederate dollar currency was replaced by the U.S. dollar. No rate of conversion for debts which had been contracted in terms of Confederate currency and which were valid (above, p. 18, n. 89) was laid down by any U.S. statute. The Supreme Court held that it was a constitutional requirement to assess the value of the Confederate currency in terms of U.S. currency and that the value of the goods bought with it was immaterial: *Thorington* v. *Smith*, 75 U.S. 1 (1869); *Wilmington and Weldon R. R. Co.* v. *King*, 91 U.S. 3 (1875); *Effinger* v. *Kenney*, 115 U.S. 566 (1885). If, therefore, a cord of wood was bought for 1 Confederate dollar and this had only a value of 5 cents in terms of the U.S. dollar, the purchaser had to pay the latter sum and the value of the wood was to be disregarded.

[49] The United Kingdom did not before 1969 recognize the so-called German Democratic Republic, but regarded and perhaps still regards the Federal Republic of (Western) Germany as the legal successor of the original German State. See Mann, *International and Comparative Law Quarterly* (1967), 760. The problems discussed in the text are perhaps unlikely to arise in this country in regard to Germany except as a result of 'transmission' in the sense explained by Dicey and Morris, p. 76. Yet the situation requires discussion from the point of view of legal principle.

[50] See, for example, above, p. 260, n. 31.

guidance. The latter may have adopted any one of the traditional tests[51] and if he lays down a mandatory rule, the courts of his own country will have to apply it. But where no such *jus cogens* exists, even the domestic courts will have to follow a circuitous road: they should ascertain whether their rules of 'inter-local' law[52] or, failing them, the analogy of their rules of private international law make the contract subject to the law of the one or the other of the successor States. Having found the answer to this preliminary question, the judge should, on the basis of the legal system so ascertained, proceed to the construction of the contract and, in the last resort, apply such principle of interpretation as may determine the money of account in case of an original ambiguity.[53]

Some courts of Western Germany, it is true, have adopted a different course and held that a reichsmark debt becomes expressed in the currency of that successor country in which at the date of the introduction of the two new currencies the debtor had his ordinary residence.[54] However, from the point of view of both legal reasoning and adequacy of result this solution is unsatisfactory. It rests on the argument that the only State which by virtue of its monetary sovereignty has the power to interfere with monetary relationships is the State in which the debtor ordinarily resides; this does not do justice to the true nature of the problem as set forth above and is wrong, because changes in the *lex monetae* are universally effective, even if they are not sanctioned by the law of the debtor's residence.[55] Moreover, the suggested solution is of no avail if at the material time the debtor does not reside in either of the two countries[56] or resides in both

[51] Above, p. 254.

[52] For a leading German discussion see Soergel (Kegel), *Commentaries on the Civil Code*, vii (1970) Notes 275, 623 preceding Art. 7.

[53] See above, p. 254.

[54] Supreme Court for the British Zone, 13 Apr. 1950, *NJW.* 1950, 644, with critical note by Mann, ibid., p. 906; Federal Tribunal, 26 Jan. 1951, *BGHZ.* 1, 109, and Clunet, 1954, 916; 31 Jan. 1952, *NJW.* 1952, 871; 3 Apr. 1952, *BGHZ.* 5, 303, 309, and Clunet, 1954, 990. In a different sense, however, Federal Tribunal, 1 Feb. 1952, *BGHZ.* 5, 35, and Clunet, 1954, 982; 30 Sept. 1952, *BGHZ.* 7, 231; 30 Mar. 1955, *BGHZ.* 17, 89; 19 Sept. 1957, *MDR.* 1958, 86; Court of Appeal Berlin, 16 Aug. 1956, *NJW.* 1957, 347 and *RabelsZ.* 23 (1958), 280 with note by Stoll; see also the decision below, p. 274, n. 32. For further references see Soergel (Kegel), loc. cit., p. 568. The whole problem is discussed at length by Mann, *NJW.* 1953, 643; W. Lewald, *Festschrift für Hans Lewald* (1953), 515; Stoll, *RabelsZ.* 21 (1956), 575 and the literature collected by him.

[55] See below, pp. 267 sqq.

[56] This was the situation in a case decided by the Swedish Supreme Court: 31 May 1950, *RabelsZ.* 1957, 290. The point was also decided by the excellently reasoned decision of the Federal Supreme Court, 24 Mar. 1960, *Wertpapiermitteilungen*, 1960, 940: under a contract governed by German law and made in Berlin where both parties were resident the plaintiff lent in 1931 RM 22,000 to the defendant. In 1948 the plaintiff lived in France and the defendant in England. The court applied West German currency law, converted at the rate of 10:1 and stated that the test of ordinary residence applied only 'in so-called East–West

countries or has no ordinary residence at all or if there are joint or
several debtors residing in different countries; finally, the suggested
solution is inappropriate in case of a close economic connection of
the debt with a place which is different from that of the debtor's
residence.[57]

(b) An English judge who is faced with a problem of the type now
under discussion should in the first place ascertain the proper law of
the contract.

If he finds that a sum of reichsmarks is due under an English contract, the question whether the debt is now expressed in terms of the
currency of Western or Eastern Germany can only be answered by
construing the contract according to the established rules of English
law; the practice developed in regard to similar cases[58] will probably
provide a measure of guidance.

If the English court finds that reichsmarks are due under a German
contract, he will immediately be confronted with an entirely novel
problem of private international law which does not appear to have
been treated anywhere:[59] what is the 'German' law referred to? Before the recognition of the German Democratic Republic it was probably the law of that part of Germany which the courts of the Federal
Republic would apply.[60] Since the recognition of the German Democratic Republic it is likely to be the law of that part of Germany with
which at its inception the contract was most closely connected.

cases in which in the case of the creditor or the debtor there are points of contact with the
Soviet Zone'. An unfortunate later decision of the Federal Supreme Court, 18 Feb. 1965,
*BGHZ.* 43, 162 or *JZ.* 1965, 448 with note by Mann (on which see below, p. 274, n. 31)
overrules the 1960 case.

[57] For example, rent is due for premises in Hamburg, but at the material date the tenant
resides in Leipzig (see Raape, *Internationales Privatrecht*, 5th ed., 1961, p. 548) or the debt
was incurred in connection with a business carried on in the East by an owner who at the
material date resides in the West. In the decision of 26 Jan. 1951, referred to in n. 54, the
Federal Tribunal held that, where a loan was secured by a mortgate on property in the East,
the personal debt could become expressed in a different currency from that applicable to
the mortgage, a highly unsatisfactory solution which, in other connections, the courts
always tried to avoid: see above, p. 227, n. 24.

[58] Above, pp. 225, 260. The approach suggested in the text has been approved by
Vischer, *Internationales Vertragsrecht* (1962), p. 220.

[59] The situations discussed by Martin Wolff, *Private International Law*, 2nd ed., 1950,
ss. 406 and 407 are different.

[60] This submission is based on the reasoning developed by Mann, *International and Comparative Law Quarterly* (1967), 760, at p. 793, and on the assumption that the decision of
the House of Lords in *Carl Zeiss Stiftung* v. *Rayner & Keeler*, [1967] A.C. 853 is likely to
rest on a misinterpretation of the certificate which the Foreign Office issued in that case.

# X

# The Nominalistic Principle, its Scope, Incidents, and Effects

I. The province of the law of the currency. II. The private international law governing re-valorization. III. The rules of municipal law relating to compensation in respect of depreci-ation of foreign money obligations: (1) the quantum of simple debts; (2) damages for non-payment; (3) determination of the amount of unliquidated damages; (4) frustration; (5) equitable remedies. IV. Protective clauses; gold clauses in particular. The law governing (1) the existence of a gold clause; (2) the construction of a gold clause; (3) the validity of a gold clause; (4) the enforcement of a gold clause governed by English law; (5) attempts made to avoid the abrogation of gold clauses by the proper law: (*a*) restrictive interpreta-tion of the parties' reference to the proper law; (*b*) denial of extraterritorial effects; (*c*) con-fiscation; (*d*) incompatibility with public policy.

I

WHEN on the strength of the principles explained in the preceding chapters, the money of a certain currency system has been found to be due by the debtor, the substance of the obligation is in general clearly fixed and no further comment is required: if it, for instance, appears that the debtor owes 10,000 French francs, it will generally be easy to determine what such 10,000 French francs are. But the matter may become more difficult if between the time when the contract was made and the time when payment becomes due the monetary system with reference to which the parties contracted, or its international estimation, suffers a change. It may then become necessary to scrutinize the question what is legal tender of the cur-rency and how much of such legal tender the creditor is entitled to claim. For example, in September 1936 a British buyer of Belgian goods promises the French exporter to pay 10,000 francs in July 1937; it appears that the parties were contracting about French francs which at the time of the conclusion of the contract were equal to £130, but which, in view of the French franc's departure from the gold standard in June 1937, are worth only £80 at the date when payment is to be made, only £10 in June 1950 when the action is started and only £7 in 1967 when the action is tried. Or a loan of 10,000 marks, made by an Englishman in 1913, is to be repaid in 1925 when the mark currency is replaced by the reichsmark cur-rency, one reichsmark being equal to one billion of paper marks. In both cases the problem arises of defining what and how much it is that forms the subject-matter of the obligation.

In view of the universal recognition of the nominalistic principle in all its aspects,[1] the solution of this question cannot be open to much doubt. The units of account referred to in a monetary obligation are defined by the 'recurrent link' rule adopted by the State. Money, being a creature of the law, is regulated by the State, and more particularly, it is the State which decides which chattels are legal tender, and the (nominal) value set upon them. As each State exercises these sovereign powers over its own currency, and as there is no State which would legislate with reference to another country's currency, it must be the *law of the currency (lex monetae)* which determines whether a thing is money and what nominal value is attributed to it.[2] What 10,000 French francs consist of is exclusively defined by French law; there is no other law in the world which would explain the meaning of that denomination and which would lay down whether certain chattels are French legal tender and for what nominal amount they are so. We therefore arrive at the rule that the law of the currency determines which things are legal tender of the currency referred to, to what extent they are legal tender, and how, in case of a currency alteration, sums expressed in the former currency are to be converted into the existing one, the metallic or functional value of money always being immaterial.[3]

Although some dissentient views have been expressed,[4] the almost

[1] See above, pp. 84 sqq.

[2] It is obvious that the question whether a distinct monetary system exists must also be answered by the law of the currency which is asserted to be a distinct one: see on this question above, pp. 51 sqq.

[3] This rule applies irrespective of whether the law of the obligation is identical with or different from the law of the currency. (In the same sense Dicey and Morris, pp. 985, 986.) For even if the law of the obligation differs from that of the currency, the nature of the money of account which is the subject-matter of the obligation can be determined only by the law of the currency, and it is of no practical interest to decide whether the law of the currency applies by reference or by incorporation (see on this point above, p. 180). Theoretically it might be proper to say that, while the law of the currency decides whether, and for which nominal value, things are legal tender, the law of the obligation should govern the question whether or not the nominal value of money determines the quantum of the obligation (see Eckstein, *Geldschuld und Geldwert*, p. 104). But as all laws have adopted the nominalistic principle, such a distinction is unnecessary. This is a case where the rules of private international law can be dispensed with, as the law of the world has become uniform.

[4] The literature is collected by Neumeyer, p. 269. The criticism is mostly expressed in the formula that the *cours forcé*, i.e. compulsory legal tender legislation (see above, p. 41), has no extraterritorial effect. In so far as such a statement refers to the influence of the issue of inconvertible paper money on gold and similar clauses, it will have to be dealt with below, p. 300. But sometimes a more general statement is made which must be mentioned in this connection. Thus it is said by Wharton (Parmele), s. 518, that 'legal tender acts [are] not extraterritorial', and similar statements can often be found in *France* (see, for example, Arminjon, *Précis de droit international privé* (3rd ed., 1947), pp. 287, 288; *Précis de droit international commercial* (1948), pp. 249 sqq.; for further references see Nussbaum, pp. 56,

universal practice of the courts adheres to this rule. It is supported not only by the great majority of scholars, but also by customary international law.[5]

For the first time in modern history the problem gained prominence in Germany in connection with the famous 'Coupons Actions'. Certain Austrian railway companies had issued bonds payable either in Austrian (silver) guilders or in thalers then circulating in

351, 463 and *passim*), in *Egypt* (see, for example, Court of Appeal of the Mixed Tribunal, 19 May 1927, Clunet, 1928, 765: Le cours forcé 'n'est évidemment pas applicable en dehors des frontières de l'État français'), and in *Syria* (see Supreme Court, 30 Dec. 1931, A.D. 1931–2, No. 151, where it was held that Turkish legal tender legislation introducing paper currency applied only internally and could not affect a contract between the Municipality of Damascus and an Egyptian contractor). In post-war *Germany* the particularly unfortunate thought has been expressed that if the foreign currency law is 'public law' (as it invariably and necessarily is) it is inapplicable in Germany: Federal Supreme Court, 18 Feb. 1965, *BGHZ.* 43, 162, also *JZ.* 1965, 448 with note by Mann. For a sound view see Federal Supreme Court, 24 Mar. 1960, *WM.* 1960, 940. The meaning of such a rule would be that currency alterations are not recognized internationally. It will be shown in the text that no such rule exists and that the above formula is sterile and meaningless (in the same sense Krispis, p. 238); moreover, it has been expressly rejected by the Privy Council in *Ottoman Bank* v. *Chakarian* (No. 2), [1938] A.C. 260, 278, where Lord Wright said: 'A further point put forward by Sir William Jowitt was based on the construction of the Turkish statute which authorized the issue of currency notes and made them legal tender. These statutes were in terms limited to Turkish currency in Turkey. Sir William Jowitt has contended that outside Turkey pre-war currency law remained in effect, so that the legal tender outside Turkey remained the Turkish gold pound. Their Lordships are unable to accept this contention. The currency in any particular country must be determined by the law of that country, and that law is naturally in terms limited to defining what is legal tender in that country. But when that is fixed by the local law it determines what is the legal tender of that country for purposes of transactions in any other country, so that a foreign Court will, when such questions come before it, give effect to the proper law of legal tender so determined. There is no foundation in their Lordships' judgment for the argument that Turkish paper is only legal tender as equivalent to gold *sub modo*, that is, within the territorial limits of Turkish jurisdiction.' In *Ottoman Bank* v. *Dascalopoulos*, [1934] A.C. 354, 362, the Privy Council had regarded it as questionable whether the Turkish currency notes 'were ever made legal tender for any payment under a Turkish contract which by that contract had to be made outside of Turkey', and there indeed exist serious doubts on this question: see the references, p. 146, n. 54. For a clear rejection of the idea of the territorial character of monetary laws see *Italian* Corte di Cassazione, 28 Feb. 1939, A.D. 1938–40, No. 56 and see Van Hecke, p. 145. It is noteworthy that such monetary changes and their effects are accepted everywhere without the question being raised whether a rule of public policy does not prevent their recognition. It is possible that ideas of public policy are at the back of those writers' minds who deny extraterritorial effect to legal tender legislation and that they influenced Holt C.J. in *Du Costa* v. *Cole* see p. 270, n. 11). But these views are out of favour, and no principle of public policy is nowadays invoked in such cases. See below, p. 273.

[5] It seemed more convenient to set forth the important teachings contained in public international law below, pp. 465 sqq., but they should not be overlooked by the municipal lawyer. It should also be remembered that modern international law contains extensive qualifications of a State's monetary sovereignty. Their effect in municipal law is not free from doubt: does the principle of nominalism as explained in the text apply if, for example, a State devalues its currency in breach of its obligations under the Articles of Agreement of the International Monetary Fund? It is believed that, probably, the answer is in the affirmative: see International Law Association, *Report of the 52nd Conference* (Helsinki, 1966), pp. 534 sqq., 549.

Germany.[6] When after the establishment of the German Reich in 1871 a uniform mark currency based on gold was adopted, it was provided by German law that debts expressed in thaler were to be converted into mark debts at the rate of 1 mark to ⅓ thaler. In view of the adoption of the gold standard in Germany, silver and, in consequence, the Austrian silver currency, heavily depreciated, and the debtors denied that they were liable in the new currency based on gold. But in Germany the Supreme Courts held that, if the thaler option was exercised, the companies had to pay the bonds and the coupons in marks at the rate of conversion established by the German legal tender act, although the contracts themselves were governed by Austrian law.[7] In more recent times this view has been consistently upheld by the German Supreme Court[8] and also by the Supreme Courts of all other countries[9] as

[6] As to the question whether or not there existed an 'option de change' see above, p. 212, n. 133.

[7] Reichsoberhandelsgericht, 19 Feb. 1878, *ROHG.* 23, 205; 8 Apr. 1879, *ROHG.* 25, 41; Supreme Court, 12 Dec. 1879, *RGZ.* 1, 23; 1 March 1882, *RGZ.* 6, 126; 9 Feb. 1887, *RGZ.* 19, 48; see Hartmann, *Internationale Geldschulden* (1883); E. J. Bekker, *Couponsprozesse* (1881), and Walker, *Internationales Privatrecht*, pp. 408 sqq.

[8] There are innumerable decisions on the point and all the decisions mentioned on p. 277, n. 45; p. 285, n. 82–8 below are based on the principle. On the German law discussed in this chapter see Roth, *Berichte der Deutschen Gesellschaft für Völkerrecht*, 20 (1979), 87.

[9] *France*: Cass. Civ. 23 Jan. 1924, S. 1925, 1. 257 (3[e] espèce) (marks); Cass. Civ. 25 Feb. 1924, Clunet, 1929, 1309 (roubles); Cour de Paris, 23 May 1931, Clunet, 1932, 441 (roubles); Trib. Civ. Seine, 28 Oct. 1925 and Cour de Paris, 18 Feb. 1926, Clunet, 1927, 1061; Trib. Civ. Seine, 23 Feb. 1931, Clunet, 1931, 396, all relating to roubles, as to which see also Degand, *Rép. dr. intern.* (1929), 'Change' No. 87. Cf. also the illuminating decision Cass. Req. 4 Apr. 1938, S. 1938, 1. 188 and Clunet, 1938, 776 (Pham-Thi-Hieu *v.* Banque de l'Indochine), relating to piastres which circulated in French Indo-China and which by virtue of the adoption of the gold standard in 1930 appreciated in value: 'le prêt d'une som somme numérique de piastres contracté sous l'empire du décret du 8 juillet 1895, devait sous celui du 31 mai 1930 être remboursé par une somme numériquement égale de piastres, sans avoir égard à l'augmentation ou à la diminution de la valeur des espèces stipulées'. This decision is a good example for the often forgotten fact that nominalism does not always operate in favour of the debtor. *Belgium*: Van Hecke, p. 144. *Italy*: Cass. 23 Mar. 1925, Clunet, 1927, 496, and *Riv. diritto commerciale*, 1925, ii. 635 (roubles); 28 Feb. 1939, *Riv. diritto commerciale*, 1940, ii. 65 and *B.I.J.I.* 41 (1940), No. 11029, and see Ascarelli, s. 39. *Hungary*: Supreme Court, 28 May 1929, Clunet, 1930, 514: a loan had been given of 217,920 'couronnes timbrées yougoslaves', i.e. Austro-Hungarian kroners of the old type provisionally used in Yugoslavia and stamped there; according to a later Yugoslavian legal tender act the kroners were converted into dinars at the rate of 4 to 1. Judgment was given for 54,480 dinars. In a number of recent cases relating to obligations to pay pounds sterling or dollars, the Hungarian Supreme Court disregarded the depreciation of these currencies, but ordered payment at the gold value: see Katinsky, *RabelsZ.* 1937, 683, and the decision of the Hungarian Supreme Court of 26 Sept. 1935 in Plesch, *The Gold Clause*, ii. 43. But it seems that these decisions did not involve a departure from the nominalistic principle, but are due to a reasoning similar to that of the German decisions discussed below, p. 285. *Greece*: Aréopage, Clunet, 1931, 1238. *Egypt*: Court of Appeal of the Mixed Tribunal, 8 Apr. 1937, *Gazette des Tribunaux Mixtes*, 28 (1938), 140. *Austria*: Supreme Court, 11 Nov. 1929, *JW.* 1929, 3519 (marks), 12 Mar. 1930, Rechtsprechung, 1930, No. 234 and *JW.* 1930, 2480 (marks); 9 Oct. 1930, Rechtsprechung, 1931, 11, and Clunet, 1931, 716, and

well as other tribunals;[10] in fact, only on the basis of this view is it understandable that in connection with foreign money obligations a revalorization doctrine was developed (see below, section II), and all decisions relating to such revalorization of foreign money obligations expressly or impliedly proceed upon the principle that purely monetary changes of a foreign currency are to be recognized and accepted everywhere.

In this country, as in others, the rule is firmly established. In *Du Costa* v. *Cole*,[11] it is true, a decision was given which is founded on a different view. The case concerned an action on a bill of exchange drawn in London on 6 August for 1,000 'Mille Rees', payable in Portugal thirty days after sight. On 14 August the King of Portugal reduced the value of the 'Mille Rees' by £20 per cent. Holt C.J. did not recognize this monetary change, but held that 'the bill ought to be paid according to the ancient value, for the King of Portugal may not alter the property of a subject of England'. *Gilbert* v. *Brett*[12]

numerous other decisions; see generally Ehrenzweig, *System des österreichischen allgemeinen Privatrechts*, ii. 1 (1928), p. 26. *Switzerland*: see generally von Tuhr-Peter, *Allgemeiner Teil des schweizerischen Obligationenrechts* (3rd ed., 1979), i. 62, 63, and Vischer, *Internationales Vertragsrecht*, p. 220, also the decisions relating to marks which are quoted below, pp. 277, n. 47; 283, n. 71, and the decision *re* Crédit Foncier Franco-Canadien, 23 May 1938, *BGE*. 54 ii. 275, also Clunet, 1929, 479, 506, 507, where the Federal Tribunal says that in the absence of a gold clause 'on ne saurait entendre par francs français autre chose que la monnaie effective qui a cours en France d'après la loi française et qui est la seule que l'on puisse se procurer tant en France qu'à l'étranger'. *Czechoslovakia*: see the decisions, p. 277, n. 48. *United States: Deutsche Bank Filiale Nürnberg* v. *Humphreys* (1926), 272 U.S. 517, the essential part of which is extensively quoted below, p. 342; *Dougherty* v. *Equitable Life Assurance Society* (Court of Appeals of New York, 1934), 266 N.Y. 71, 193 N.E. 897 (roubles); *Tillman* v. *Russo-Asiatic Bank*, 51 Fed. (2d) 1023 (Circuit Court of Appeals, 2d, 1931) (roubles); *Klocklow* v. *Petrogradski*, 268 N.Y. Supp. 433 (Supreme Court of New York, App. Div., 1st Dept., 1934) (roubles). As to roubles see also *Matter of People* (1931), 255 N.Y. 428, 175 N.E. 118, a case proceeding on wrong evidence; *Parker* v. *Hoppe* (1931), 257 N.Y. 333, N.E. 550; *Richard* v. *National City Bank of New York* (1931), 231 App. Div. 559, 248 N.Y. Supp. 113. As to marks see *Matter of Illfelder* (1931), 136 Misc. 430, 240 N.Y. Supp. 413, aff'd 249 N.Y. Supp. 903, and also the surprising decision of the Court of Appeals of New York in the *Matter of Lendle* (1929), 250 N.Y. 502, 166 N.E. 182. On these two cases see more fully below, p. 284. A recent and very striking application of the principle is to be found in *Tramontana* v. *Varig Airlines*, 350 F. 2d 467 (1965) relating to cruzeiros, and in *Sternberg* v. *West Coast Life Insurance Co.*, 16 Cal. Rep. 546, 196 Cal. App. 2d 519 (1961) and *Judah* v. *Delaware Trust Co.*, 378 A. 2d 624 (1977), relating to old Chinese currency, 'Taels, Shanghai Sycee'; see on these two cases above, p. 150 and below, p. 274. As to the problem under discussion see also the awards of the Court of Arbitration of the International Chamber of Commerce, *Revue Critique de Droit International* 1934, 472 sqq.

[10] The Tripartite Claims Commission between the United States, Austria, and Hungary was confronted by the question whether a United States citizen who was entitled to be paid in Austro-Hungarian *krone* could demand payment in American currency at the pre-war rate of exchange. The answer was in the negative, for a *krone* obligation 'is unaffected either by the purchasing power of the *krone* in Austria or by the exchange value of *krone* as measured by other currencies': *Reports of International Arbitral Awards*, vi. 212, at p. 223.

[11] (1688) Skin 272.                    [12] (1604) Davies's Rep. (Ireland) 18.

was distinguished on the ground that there it was British money which by the King's authority was changed. But though Holt C.J.'s decision does not appear to have ever been expressly overruled, it cannot be doubted that it has in fact been set aside by a number of modern cases which lay down the rule that, irrespective of the proper law of the obligation, the subject-matter of a foreign money obligation is whatever the law of the currency designates as legal tender for the nominal amount of the obligation and that, accordingly, that obligation will be satisfied by payment of whatever currency is by the *lex monetae* valid tender for the discharge of the nominal amount of the debt.[13]

This principle of nominalism which has rightly been described as fundamental to the treatment of foreign money obligations[14] is illustrated by two decisions of the Privy Council both of which arose out of loans of Spanish pesetas made in Gibraltar. In *Pyrmont Ltd.* v. *Schott*[15] it was held that the borrower could not in May 1936 repay the loan otherwise than by what was legal tender in Spain and that, therefore, he could not pay in Bank of Spain notes which were not at the time legal tender in Spain, though for certain purposes they had to be accepted and in practice were accepted in ordinary transactions;[16]

---

[13] Relating to roubles: *Lindsay Gracie & Co.* v. *Russian Bank for Foreign Trade* (1918), 34 T.L.R. 443; *British Bank for Foreign Trade* v. *Russian Commercial & Industrial Bank* (No. 2) (1921), 38 T.L.R. 65; *Buerger* v. *New York Life Assurance* (1927), 43 T.L.R. 601 (C.A.); *Perry* v. *Equitable Life Assurance Society* (1929), 45 T.L.R. 468. Relating to marks: *In re Chesterman's Trusts*, [1923] 2 Ch. 466 (C.A.); *Anderson* v. *Equitable Life Assurance Society* (1926), 134 L.T. 557 (C.A.); *Franklin* v. *Westminster Bank*, below, p. 562. Relating to francs: *Hopkins* v. *Compagnie Internationale des Wagons-Lits*, below, p. 560; see also *Société des Hôtels Le Touquet* v. *Cummings*, [1922] 1 K.B. 451, 461 *per* Scrutton L.J. Relating to piastres: *Kricorian* v. *Ottoman Bank* (1932), 48 T.L.R. 247; *Ottoman Bank* v. *Chakarian* (No. 2), [1938] A.C. 260 (P.C.); *Sforza* v. *Ottoman Bank*, [1938] A.C. 282 (P.C.). Relating to pesetas: *Pyrmont Ltd.* v. *Schott*, [1939] A.C. 145; *Marrache* v. *Ashton*, [1943] A.C. 311. Relating to Queensland pounds: *Bonython* v. *Commonwealth of Australia*, [1951] A.C. 201, at p. 222. It may be that a somewhat different principle applies in case of a claim for unliquidated damages: see *Pilkington* v. *Commissioners for Claims on France* (1821), 2 Knapp P.C. 7, 20, and the comments of Scrutton L.J. in *Société des Hôtels Le Touquet* v. *Cummings*, [1922] 1 K.B. 451, 461, which will be discussed below, p. 323. Scrutton L.J.'s suggestion that the doctrine 'mobilia sequuntur personam' may apply is untenable; if that maxim existed and if it had any bearing on the point, the English creditor of German pre-war marks would not have to suffer the effects of the depreciation of the mark—a result which would be irreconcilable with the authorities above mentioned. Scrutton L.J.'s dictum, however, led to a surprising decision of the Appellate Division of the New York Supreme Court in *Orlik* v. *Wiener Bankverein* (1923), 204 App. Div. 432, 198 N.Y. Supp. 413, on which see below, p. 346.

[14] Dicey and Morris, p. 984.                                    [15] [1939] A.C. 145.

[16] p. 153. This, therefore, was a case in which the bank notes were money, but not legal tender; see on this point above, p. 40, n. 64. The case is an authority for the proposition that the *lex monetae*, where it applies, has regard to the foreign legal tender legislation *stricto sensu*, not to the monetary legislation. It must be very doubtful whether Bank of Spain notes really lacked the quality of legal tender or whether the decision of the Privy Council should not be understood in the light of the fact that Spanish monetary legislation

As Lord Porter said,[17] the form in which a payment of pesetas is to be made 'must be regulated by the municipal law of the country whose unit of account is in question, and what would or would not be a legal tender must depend upon the law on that subject in force at the time when the tender should have been made'.[18] In *Marrache* v. *Ashton*[19] it was held that a loan of pesetas made in 1931 and repayable in 1936 could in May 1939 be repaid in peseta notes, because in January 1939 they had become legal tender in Spain;[20] the borrower, in the language of Lord Macmillan,[21] 'would have specifically performed his covenants, if he had tendered to the respondents the appropriate amount of Bank of Spain notes'.

There are some particular aspects of nominalism which require emphasis.

(*a*) A mere change in the value of a foreign unit of account, however serious it may be, is irrelevant or, in other words, nominalism puts the risk of depreciation on the creditor and the risk of appreciation (or revaluation) on the debtor and neither part can be heard to complain about unexpected losses.[22] The creditor who abstains from providing for a gold or similar protective clause must suffer the loss resulting from a depreciation of the money of account and it does not matter that he has believed it to be unshakable or as good as gold;[23] thus when the United States dollar was devalued in 1972 the mere fact that from at least 1945 until the late 1960s it was universally held to be so stable a measure of value as to be almost a substitute

had not been exhaustively proved by expert evidence. The point was repeatedly considered by the courts in Tangier; they invariably attributed, in effect, legal tender quality to Bank of Spain notes: Mixed Tribunal of Tangier, 4 Mar. 1938, S. 1938, 4. 31, and see Menard, *Rev. Crit.* 1939, 294. However, before the Privy Council it was 'common ground' that the notes were not legal tender (see p. 153). This disposes of most of the altogether unjustified criticism made by Nussbaum, p. 488.

[17] p. 158.

[18] The case had really nothing to do with the existence of the system of 'guias'. This introduced confusion and an unnecessary complication. All that mattered was that Bank of Spain notes, with or without 'guias', were not legal tender: see *Marrache* v. *Ashton*, [1943] A.C. 311, at p. 317 *per* Lord Macmillan.

[19] [1943] A.C. 311.

[20] p. 313, where it is also explained that 'it was agreed' that the date of the issue of the writ was the date at which the appellant's liability was to be ascertained. This agreement was binding on the court, but was contrary to the principle then prevailing that it was the date of maturity (1936) that mattered; see below, p. 347.

[21] p. 317.

[22] See, for example, *Bonython* v. *Commonwealth of Australia*, [1951] A.C. 201 at p. 222 *per* Lord Simonds, and the other cases referred to above, p. 271, n. 13.

[23] This particular point was decided in *British Bank for Foreign Trade* v. *Russian Commercial & Industrial Bank* (No. 2) (1921), 38 T.L.R. 65; *In re Chesterman's Trust*, [1923] 2 Ch. 466; *Ottoman Bank* v. *Chakarian* (No. 2), [1938] A.C. 260 (P.C.). See also the decisions of the German Supreme Court, 15 Mar. 1937, *RGZ.* 154, 187; 28 May 1937, *RGZ.* 155, 133; 7 Feb. 1938, *JW.* 1938, 1109; 20 April 1940, *RGZ.* 163, 324.

for a gold clause, would not permit the implication of terms designed to exclude nominalism and introduce, in effect, a protective clause.[24] It is fundamental that contracting in terms of foreign currency and, indeed, in terms of any currency involves an element of speculation, and it is of the essence of nominalism which is empirically derived from the intentions of the parties[25] that neither party can complain about the outcome of a speculation which has miscarried.

(b) There is, as has already been pointed out,[26] no room whatever for avoiding the effects of nominalism by discarding the *lex monetae* on the ground that currency laws undoubtedly have the character of public law the application of which is said to be territorially restricted,[27] or for attributing a confiscatory character to the creditor's loss[28] or for invoking public policy against a debtor who relies on the depreciation of currency or a creditor who relies on its appreciation.[29] If, therefore, in 1960 the plaintiff becomes entitled to 100,000 Brazilian cruzeiros which by 1965 have, as a result of inflation in Brazil, depreciated 'by more than 600 per cent', public policy, in the United States or elsewhere, does not require or permit any deviation from the result which would be reached 'had the value of the cruzeiro in terms of the dollar remained unchanged'. On the contrary, 'an unpredictable and virtually immeasurable factor would be imported into the decision of international conflict of laws cases if the otherwise applicable law were subject to being displaced because of the recent history of the relative values of the currencies involved'.[30]

(c) Nor can there ever be any question of a payment in foreign currency becoming impossible. Monetary obligations are 'indestructible'. In the event of the extinction of a currency system the recurrent link, connecting the new with the old monetary system, will define the amount payable.[31] The recurrent link, forming part of the

---

[24] See above, pp. 84, 141.     [25] See above, p. 84.     [26] Above, p. 267.

[27] The heresy referred to in the text rests on the failure to distinguish between the enforcement and the application of foreign law where, by virtue of a conflict rule such as the *lex monetae*, it is applicable. See Mann, *Rec.* 132 (1971 i), 182.

[28] In the same sense the decision of the International Claims Commission of the U.S.A. in *Tabar's Claim*, Int. L.R. 1953, 211; Bindschedler, *Rec.* 60 (1956), 179, 224 sqq. On confiscation see also below, p. 473.

[29] This was expressly so held by the Belgian Cour de Cassation, 28 Jan. 1967, Pasicrisie 1967 I 648. It was clearly an exception that a rate of conversion established in Poland for the purpose of converting mark debts incurred before the separation of certain eastern provinces from Germany was held by German courts to be irreconcilable with German public policy on the ground that the Polish statute was directly intended to injure German subjects: Berlin Court of Appeal, 25 Feb. 1922, 28 Oct. 1922, 2 Nov. 1928, *JW.* 1922, 398; 1923, 128; 1928, 1462.

[30] *Tramontana* v. *Varig Airlines*, 350 F. 2d 467 (1965), at p. 477 (Court of Appeals, District of Columbia Circuit). This is probably the latest of a long line of English and American cases.

[31] For a clear case on this point see *Franklin* v. *Westminster Bank*, below, p. 560.

*lex monetae*, always ensures the continuing existence and identity of the monetary obligation: in June 1948, 1 reichsmark became 1 Deutsche Mark, in October 1950, 100 zloty (old) became 1 zloty (new),[32] in February 1966, £A1 became $A2. Nor should the debtor be allowed in the absence of very special circumstances to avoid payment by invoking the legal impossibility to pay at a certain place, whether it be the place of payment or the forum.[33]

(*d*) Nor does it matter whether the place of payment is within or outside the country whose *lex monetae* applies. 'The locus of payment cannot change the selected monetary media of payment.'[34] In other words nominalism operates not only irrespective of the proper law of the contract, but irrespective of the place of payment.

(*e*) Finally, what, according to the *lex monetae*, is legal tender retains its quality until demonetization,[35] irrespective of restrictions upon its use, such as prohibitions to export or import it from or into the country of issue.[36] A pound is defined by English law, wherever the question may arise for decision and wherever the pound note may be situate. It is the character of the money which is always, everywhere and necessarily subject to the law of the currency. The use that can or cannot be made of the foreign money is a different question.[37]

---

[32] This was disregarded by the decision of the Federal Supreme Court of 18 Feb. 1965 (below, p. 281, n. 65), when the court substituted a 'reasonable amount of Deutsche Mark' under German law for a debt of 26,000 zloty agreed by the parties in 1939 in Warsaw, governed by Polish law and converted by the *lex monetae* and the *lex causae* to 780 (new) zloty.

[33] This statement is unfortunately not supported by English authorities: see above, p. 66, n. 19, and below, p. 420.

[34] *Sternberg* v. *West Coast Life Insurance Co.*, 16 Cal. Rep. 546 (1961), at p. 550.

[35] See, generally, above, p. 18.

[36] This aspect of the principle is established by *Marrache* v. *Ashton*, [1943] A.C. 311 and is further discussed below, p. 422.

[37] Usually the *lex monetae* will readily be identifiable, but great difficulties may arise where a foreign monetary system comes under the control of an unrecognized State, government, or belligerent. Suppose that in Jan. 1938 under an English contract a London merchant obtained an advance of 15,000 Austrian schillings from a London bank, and suppose that this country did not grant any degree of recognition to the annexation of Austria by Germany in Mar. 1938 and the consequent replacement of the Austrian schilling by the German reichsmark at the rate of 1.50 schilling to 1 reichsmark. Did the borrower in Jan. 1939 owe 10,000 reichsmarks? And when, after the war, Austria reintroduced the schilling currency and converted reichsmark debts into schilling debts at the rate of 1 schilling for 1 reichsmark, did the borrower in Jan. 1948 owe 10,000 or 15,000 Austrian schillings? It is submitted that the lack of recognition is immaterial and that the *lex monetae* is that law which from time to time is *de facto* enforced by the supreme authority in control of the currency. Cf. the principles applicable to the definition of money, above, p. 18. It may be that the question could be solved more elegantly by interpreting what, according to earlier explanations (above, p. 84), is at the basis of nominalism, viz. the presumed intention of the parties.

## II

It has been shown that a foreign country's legal tender legislation determining the composition, denomination, and, accordingly, the nominal value of the foreign money concerned must be recognized everywhere, and that, as to such questions, the law of the currency applies; but this does not by any means imply the further rule that the disarrangement of the real or functional value of money (i.e. the increase or reduction of purchasing power) and its effect on the quantum of the obligations also comes within the ambit of the law of the currency. It has already been explained in connection with domestic money obligations that any qualification of the rigidity of the nominalistic principle cannot result from legal tender legislation, but only from the general principles of the law of obligations or from special legislation. Legal tender legislation defines money and the nominal value of money, but it is outside its range to decide whether and under what circumstances redress against its effects may be obtained. As concerns private international law, the conclusion may be drawn from this universally accepted view, that the proper law of the obligation (not the law of the currency) governs all questions relating to any qualifications of the prima facie effect of foreign legal tender legislation on the quantum of the obligation.

In principle it is clearly recognized that it is in this sense that the line of demarcation should be drawn between the province of the law of the currency and that of the law of the obligation. Whether in case of the non-payment of a debt damages may be claimed in respect of the depreciation of the foreign money concerned since the date of maturity;[38] how unliquidated damages are to be measured;[39] whether owing to a rise or fall in the purchasing power of money a contract may be rescinded;[40]—these and similar questions should be answered in accordance with the law governing the obligation.

The only question is whether the revalorization of simple debts is governed by the law of the currency or by that of the obligation. Suppose 10,000 German marks were borrowed in 1914 under a contract governed by English law; the debt falls due in 1925, when, owing to the depreciation and collapse of the German mark and the subsequent introduction of the reichsmark currency effected by the

---

[38] That the proper law applies to this question was expressly held by Scrutton L.J. in *Société des Hôtels Le Touquet* v. *Cummings*, [1922] 1 K.B. 451, 461. In the same sense Rabel, *Conflict of Laws*, iii (1950), 34; German Supreme Court, 6 Nov. 1928, *IPRspr.* 1929, No. 113; 8 Jan. 1930, *IPRspr.* 1930, No. 48, and in the decisions quoted, p. 286, nn. 90, 91.

[39] See *The Despina R.* (and its companion case), [1979] A.C. 685; *Jean Kraut A.G.* v. *Albany Fabrics Ltd.*, [1977] Q.B. 182.

[40] This is obvious, and Rabel, l.c., expressly agrees.

adoption of a rate of conversion of one billion of marks to one reichsmark, the law of the currency gives the creditor nothing but an infinitesimal fraction of a reichsmark. German law, on the strength of the Revalorization Act or of certain principles of the law of contracts, would revalorize the debt to, say, 2,500 reichsmarks. The question whether these German rules can be applied depends on whether revalorization is governed by the law of the currency or by the law of the obligation.[41] If the law of the currency governs, revalorization rules of that law would apply and apply only where sums expressed in that currency were owed, whatever the law of the obligation might be; if German marks were owed under an English contract, an English court would have to revalorize the debt, although English law as the proper law does not know of such revalorization; and if Russian roubles were owed under a German contract, an English court would have to refuse revalorization as being unknown to the law of Russia, although German law would allow revalorization. On the other hand, if the question is governed by the law of the obligation, revalorization rules of that law would have to be applied, whatever the law of the currency might be: if German marks were owed under an English contract, no revalorization would be possible, because it is unknown to English law; if Russian roubles were owed under a German contract, English courts would have to admit revalorization in accordance with the rules of German law.

This is a typical problem of classification[42] which in view of its inherent nature as explained above should be solved in favour of the law of the obligation.[43] This is indeed the view taken by the majority of writers[44] and also by the courts of Germany,[45] Austria,[46] Switzer-

---

[41] If a legal system denies revalorization, this does not entitle the forum to invoke public policy for the purpose of rejecting the consequences inherent in the foreign law. Although it may fairly be described as the foremost protagonist of the fundamental equities of revalorization, the German Supreme Court so held: 14 Dec. 1927, *RGZ.* 119, 259; 13 Dec. 1929, *IPRspr.* 1930, No. 8; see also 25 June 1926, *RGZ.* 114, 171.

[42] Or, as Dicey and Morris, pp. 31 sqq., say, characterization.

[43] Although the German Supreme Court decided differently (23 Jan. 1927, *RGZ.* 118, 370), it should not be doubted that the stipulation of an option of place does not allow revalorization to be regarded as governed by the law of the place of payment. On the other hand, it would seem that, if there is an 'option de change' coupled with an 'option de place', revalorization might be governed by the law of the place of payment (see above, p. 219): if in 1914 under an Austrian contract 1,000 marks in Berlin or 850 kroners in Vienna were promised, the connection of the Berlin option with German law would seem to be so great that the application of German revalorization rules would appear to be justified.

[44] Dicey and Morris, p. 990; Cheshire and North, p. 245; Wolff, *Private International Law*, 2nd ed. (1950), s. 451; Rabel, *Conflict of Laws*, iii (1950), 34; Melchior, *Grundlagen*, pp. 294 sqq.; Frankenstein, ii. 222; Mayer, *Valutaschuld*, p. 53, with further references; Van Hecke, pp. 149, 150; Vischer, *Internationales Vertragsrecht*, p. 221; Krispis, pp. 249, 250; Kegel, No. 674; Degand, *Rép. dr. intern.* (1934), Supplément *sub* 'Valorization', No. 2; Sulkowski, *Rec.* 29 (1929), 29 sqq.—The view that the question is governed by the law of the currency is held by Nussbaum, *Internationales Privatrecht*, p. 254; *Bilanz der Auf-*

[*See opposite page for n. 44 cont. and nn. 45, 46*]

land[47] and other countries,[48] and it is also the solution adopted by the English courts.

*wertungstheorie* (1929), pp. 34 sqq.; by Neumeyer, pp. 368 sqq., and more recently by Ernst, *Die Bedeutung des Gesetzeszwecks im internationalen Währungs- und Devisenrecht* (1963), pp. 11–42.

[45] See the material collected by Melchior and Mayer, l.c., and see Kahn, 14 (1932), *Journal of Comparative Legislation*, 66, 73 sqq. The law of the obligation is applied in numerous decisions, especially: 14 Dec. 1927, *RGZ*. 119, 259, 264; 27 Jan. 1928, *RGZ*. 120, 70, 76; 27 June 1928, *RGZ*. 121, 337; 20 Sept. 1929, *JW*. 1930, 1587; 22 Oct. 1929, *IPRspr*. 1930, No. 32; 6 Feb. 1930, *IPRspr*. 1930, No. 115; 24 Feb. 1930, *Leipziger Zeitschrift*, 1931, 375; 2 June 1930, *Leipziger Zeitschrift*, 1931, 384; 14 Jan. 1931, *Seufferts Archiv*, 85, No. 57; 16 Dec. 1931, *JW*. 1932, 1049; 28 June 1934, *RGZ*. 145, 51, 55. But there are also some decisions which apply the law of the currency: see, for example, 5 Mar. 1928, *RGZ*. 120, 279; 9 Feb. 1931, *JW*. 1932, 583, and others. Applying the law of the obligation, the Supreme Court revalorized kroner debts under German law (decisions of 27 Jan. 1928; 2 June 1930, 14 Jan. 1931) and refused to revalorize mark debts under a foreign law.

[46] For a refusal to revalorize mark debts under Austrian law see Supreme Court, 11 Sept. 1929, Rechtsprechung, 1929, No. 331, also *JW*. 1929, 3519, and Clunet, 1930, 750; 12 Mar. 1930, Rechtsprechung, 1930, No. 234, also *JW*. 1930, 2480, and Clunet, 1931, 296. Revalorization of mark debts under German law: see, for example, 24 Apr. 1927, *JW*. 1927, 1899. In a number of Supreme Court decisions it was also held that the German revalorization rules, even in so far as they were retrospective, were not against Austrian public policy: 24 Apr. 1927, l.c.; 27 Mar. 1929, *JW*. 1929, 3522; 26 June 1930, *JW*. 1931, 635, and Clunet, 1931, 717; the opposite view was taken by the Supreme Court of *Hungary*: RabelsZ. 1937, 179.

[47] Revalorization of a mark debt under German law: 28 Feb. 1930, *JW*. 1930, 1900; 26 Feb. 1932, *JW*. 1932, 1163, and Clunet, 1932, 1163. In these decisions the Federal Tribunal also held that the German revalorization rules, even if retrospective, were not against Swiss public policy. As to revalorization of mark debts under Swiss law according to principles of the Swiss law of contracts see: 3 June 1925, *BGE*. 61, ii. 303, also *JW*. 1925, 1818, and Clunet, 1926, 1118; 17 Feb. 1927, *BGE*. 53, ii. 76, also *JW*. 1927, 2350; 3 July 1928, *JW*. 1928, 3145; 28 Feb. 1930, *JW*. 1930, 1900; 26 Mar. 1931, Clunet, 1932, 227; 13 Nov. 1931, *JW*. 1932, 2337. See, generally, Pierre Lalive, 'Dépréciation monétaire et contrats en droit international privé', 35 (1971), *Mémoires publiés par la Faculté de Droit de Genève*, p. 32.

[48] French courts were never called upon to decide the question. The decision Cass. Civ. 14 Apr. 1934, S. 1935, 1. 201 (with note by Niboyet) and Clunet, 1935, 372, refuses to recognize the retrospective effect of a foreign *tax* law. Cass. Req., 19 Oct. 1938, S. 1938, 1. 381 rests on the lower court's finding that the parties had intended a final discharge, that therefore the scope of German law was exhausted and that there was no room for revalorization under German law. As to the reconcilability of Polish revalorization legislation with French 'ordre public' see Witenberg, Clunet, 1939, 593. The French doctrine was followed by the Court of Appeal at Trieste, 25 Aug. 1936, *Giur. Comp. D.I.P.* iii. 111. *Holland*: See the material collected in *RabelsZ*. 1932, 856, and Degand, l.c., No. 7; the Hoge Raad refused to revalorize a mark debt under Dutch law: 2 Jan. 1931, Weekblad van het Recht 12259, also in *Blätter für internationales Privatrecht*, 1931, 213. *Sweden*: see Michaeli, *Internationales Privatrecht* (Stockholm, 1948), p. 321. *Denmark*: The German revalorization law is not contrary to Danish public policy; in this sense Supreme Court, 22 May 1940, Clunet, 1954, 495. *Czechoslovakia*: Supreme Court, 11 Nov. 1924, *JW*. 1925, 514; 19 Jan. and 6 Dec. 1934, *RabelsZ*. 1936, 172. As to *Poland* see Rost, 'Das internationale Aufwertungsrecht Polens', *Ostrecht*, iii (1929), 1301. *Egypt*: Reversing a judgment of the Mixed Tribunal at Cairo (17 Feb. 1930, Clunet, 1931, 467), the Court of Appeal of the Mixed Tribunal refused to apply German revalorization legislation, in so far as it has retrospective effects, the reason being that the defendant's 'droits acquis' had to be observed and that the later German legislation was not covered by the parties' submission to German law: 11 Apr. 1935, Clunet, 1935, 1060 (three judgments *re* Adjouri).

This is clearly proved by the case of *Anderson* v. *Equitable Assurance Society of the United States*.[49] In 1887 the plaintiff's husband had taken out an insurance policy with the St. Petersburg sub-agent of the Hamburg branch of the defendants. The policy was denominated in German marks, but it expressly provided that the plaintiff's interest under it was governed by English law. After her husband's death in 1922 the plaintiff claimed the sums due under the policy, and, in order to avoid the inevitable consequence of the nominalistic principle as expressed, for example, in *Re Chesterman's Trusts*,[50] relied on German decisions allowing revalorization. But the Court of Appeal (Bankes, Warrington, and Atkin L.JJ.) held them irrelevant. The *ratio decidendi* was clearly that the German revalorization practice 'did not in any way affect or interfere with the fiscal law which gives what shall be the currency of the country',[51] but that it results from principles of the German law of obligations. This being so, Warrington L.J. arrived at the conclusion that the German decisions were irrelevant, because[52]

this contract which we have to deal with is one which has to be carried out in accordance with English law, and the decision of the Court in Leipzig is not one which affects the performance of this contract which is an English contract to be performed according to English Law.

Similarly Atkin L.J. commented on the German revalorization practice as follows:[53]

It seems to me to be impossible to suppose and I think it is not proved that the law in any way affected the currency value of the mark, or indeed affected what we know as legal tender. It seems to me to be obvious that that is a law not affecting the currency, but affecting the particular contracts that come within the scope of it. . . . In other words, it is the debt that is valorized and not the currency; and if that is so, it is obvious that the German law cannot affect the operation of the rule of English law which is laid down in *Re Chesterman's Trusts*.

These words, it is submitted, very strongly suggest that the non-application of the German revalorization rules resulted from the fact that the contract was governed by English law, which means that the Court of Appeal adopted the theory that the law of the obligation governed; had the view been taken that the question of revalorization was governed by the law of the currency, the result would needs have been different. On the other hand, the decision does not confirm the further consequence of the former theory that, if the contract had

---

[49] (1926) 134 L.T. 557 (C.A.).    [50] [1923] 2 Ch. 466.
[51] At p. 565 *per* Warrington L.J.
[52] At p. 565.    [53] At p. 566.

been governed by German law, the German revalorization rules would have been applied.[54]

This conclusion was, it would appear, in fact drawn in the later case of *In re Schnapper*,[55] though it must be admitted that in that case the reasons for which German revalorization rules were applied were not very clearly stated. In 1911 the testator executed a document in which he promised to pay to his niece on her attaining the age of 25 years the sum of 100,000 marks. The promise was governed by German law, under which it was unenforceable. In 1922, when the testator had become domiciled in England, he made an English will in which after reference to the promise of 1911 he declared: 'Now I hereby confirm such obligation and direct my trustees to fulfil such obligation should I die before it has been fulfilled.' The testator died in the latter part of 1922. The niece attained the age of 25 years in 1934, and the questions which now fell to be decided were whether the agreement of 1911 was valid or void and, if it was void, whether a sum of 100,000 marks became payable by virtue of the will, and, if so, by how many pounds sterling this sum was now represented. Clauson J. had no difficulty in holding that the agreement of 1911 was invalid. He also held that by his will the testator did not give a bequest of 100,000 marks, but 'that the direction given to the executors is to make such payment by way of legacy if necessary—that is to say, if the document of 1911 is not legally enforceable, to make such payment by way of legacy as would give Edith Betty Schnapper a sum which he would have had to give her had it been so'. Evidence was given as to the German revalorization practice, and in view of the figures mentioned by German experts it was held that the niece was entitled to a decree 'as a legatee under the will in respect of a sum of £5000'.

In the absence of any discussion of the question it is difficult to understand how German revalorization law came to be applied. The German contract of 1911 was void. The obligation therefore arose under a domiciled Englishman's will which was governed by English law. As English law under which the obligation arose does not know of any revalorization, it might seem that the application of German revalorization rules was due to the mere fact that German marks were promised, which would mean the adoption of the theory, irreconcilable with *Anderson*'s case, that revalorization is governed by

---

[54] It may be noted that the question whether the German rules were part of the law of the currency or of the law of obligations was answered on the basis of German conceptions. The decision is therefore an example of a classification not proceeding from the conceptions of the *lex fori* which are usually held to determine classification. M. Wolff, *Private International Law*, 2nd ed. (1950), p. 160, agrees.

[55] [1936] 1 All E.R. 322.

the law of the currency. Nevertheless, this is probably not the correct interpretation of the case. For it would seem that in effect the view taken by the learned judge was that the German agreement of 1911, though as such invalid, was confirmed by and incorporated into the English' will of 1922 in such a manner that, at least according to the testator's intentions, the real basis of the niece's rights was to be found in that German agreement and that to that extent German law governed the interpretation of the gift. That this is the true meaning of Clauson J.'s decision[56] is suggested by his statement[57] that on its true construction the will did not give a bequest of 100,000 marks to the niece, but directed the executors 'to make such payment by way of legacy if necessary—that is to say, if the document of 1911 is not legally enforceable, to make such payment by way of a legacy as would give E. B. Schnapper a sum which he would have had to give her had it been so'. Though this explanation is not very satisfactory, it seems to be the only one by which the case can be reconciled with the decision of the Court of Appeal in *Anderson* v. *Equitable Assurance Society of the United States.*[58]

The last case on the subject is *Kornatzki* v. *Oppenheimer,*[59] the material facts of which were as follows. Under a contract made in 1905 to compromise an action brought in the German courts the defendant was bound to pay to the plaintiff during her lifetime an annual allowance of 8,000 marks. The present action concerned the question how this obligation was to be fulfilled after the mark currency had been replaced by the reichsmark currency. Farwell J. decided the question on the basis of German revalorization practice, and after having heard evidence thereon, he arrived at the result that the defendant had to pay an annuity of £500.[60] In this case the application of German law was warranted from the point of view of both the currency and the obligation theory, because marks were the money of account and the contract made in 1905 was, as the parties agreed, governed by German law. The application of German law was, however, not derived from the former, but solely from the latter

---

[56] In the same sense Kahn-Freund, *Annual Survey*, 1936, p. 361.

[57] [1936] 1 All E.R. 322, 326.

[58] (1926) 134 L.T. 557.                                   [59] [1937] 4 All E.R. 133.

[60] The plaintiff apparently did not ask for a declaration that the defendant was under liability to pay sterling, and if she had done so, her claim would have been unjustified, since the defendant was only bound to pay reichsmarks, i.e. the currency which had replaced the mark currency. It is therefore astonishing that the learned judge made a declaration to the effect that the defendant had to pay pounds. The serious consequences of this transformation of the money of account are obvious at a time when, after heavy depreciation, the reichsmark has been replaced by the Deutsche Mark and sterling has also depreciated. The plaintiff will have to suffer from the latter, but escape the consequences of the former development, although both the nominalistic principle and justice would require a converse solution. See also p. 362, n. 8 of the third edition of this book.

fact,[61] and therefore the decision supports the view that revalorization is governed by the proper law of the obligation.

The proper law rather than the *lex monetae* will likewise have to
be applied to the converse problem of 'devalorization',[62] i.e. in the
case in which, as a result of deflation, a foreign system of law provides
for a reduction of the nominal amount of the debt. This, or a very
similar, situation also arises where, on the occasion of the introduction of a new monetary system, legal tender legislation provides for
a fixed rate of conversion or a recurrent link,[63] but where exceptions
are made for specified types of debts the nominal amount of which is
scaled up or down to a greater extent. This occurred in 1948 in
Western Germany: the reichsmark was converted into Deutsche Mark
at the rate of 1:1,[64] but certain debts were by a separate and later
statute scaled down at the rate of 10:1. It is believed that the latter
provisions (which expressly referred to certain well-defined types of
contracts) could be applied by an English court only if the obligation
was subject to German law, but that reichsmark debts governed by
English law were converted into Deutsche Mark debts at the rate of
1:1; the reason is that in this case German law is irrelevant in so far
as it contains 'a law not affecting the currency, but affecting the
particular contracts that come within the scope of it.[65]

---

[61] See p. 137, line G: 'There is no doubt whatever that the experts on both sides agree
and the parties are agreed, that this is a matter wholly of German law, and ought to be
decided according to the law of Germany.' But was the experts' agreement relevant?

[62] In this sense, Dicey and Morris, p. 990.

[63] As defined above, p. 44.

[64] Above, p. 102.

[65] See the language of Atkin L.J. quoted above, p. 278. The view set forth in the text
was developed in greater detail by Mann, 'Die Behandlung von Reichsmarkverbindlichkeiten
bei ausländischem Schuldstatut', in *Festschrift für Fritz Schulz*, ii. 298 sqq. (Weimar, 1951).
In *Germany* the Federal Supreme Court held correctly that a reichsmark debt contracted in
1931 under German law when both parties were Germans in Germany was and remained
governed by (West) German law and was, accordingly, reduced at the rate of 10 to 1, though
in 1948 the creditor was a resident of France and the debtor was a British subject resident in
England: 24 Mar. 1960, *WM*. 1960, 940. For the same reason the District Court at Karlsruhe
held correctly that a reduction was excluded where the debt was not governed by German
law: 21 Jan. 1955, *IPRspr*. 1956-7, No. 28a. When, however, the Federal Supreme Court
was called upon to consider the fate of a zloty debt governed by Polish law (under which it
was in 1950 reduced at the rate of 100 to 3), it fell into grievous error: 18 Feb. 1965,
referred to above, pp. 264, 274. See also Court of Appeal at Frankfurt, 2 Apr. 1963, *IPRspr*.
1962-3, No. 164. While the German revalorization practice after 1923 applied irrespective
of the *lex monetae*, the legislation of 1948 reducing certain debts at the rate of 10 to 1
presupposed that the money of account was expressed in terms of reichsmark: Federal
Supreme Court, 22 May 1958, *IPRspr*. 1958 and 1959, No. 100. The reduction prescribed
was, therefore, subject to two conditions, viz. German currency and German law. In non-
German practice, curiously enough, the point did not arise anywhere except in *Austria*
where it was held that, if a debt was subject to West German law, it was not only converted
into Deutsche Mark, but also reduced in accordance with West German law: Supreme Court,
30 Apr. 1953, *SZ*. xxvi. 320, also Clunet, 1957, 1014. In such cases two and sometimes

### III

The discussion up to this point has established the rule of private international law that, while the law of the currency applies to the definition of the money of account (section I, above), all questions relating to the effect of changes of the purchasing power of foreign money on the obligation and its quantum are governed by the law of the obligation, the *lex causae*, or the proper law (section II, above). We now come to the rules of municipal law which determine whether and how, under a given municipal law, such disarrangements of the intrinsic value and the international estimation of foreign money can influence the fate of foreign money obligations.

We have seen in another connection[66] that, with the exception of certain rather extreme cases, nominalism, in so far as it relates to domestic currency within the sphere of its own law, has been carried into full effect, and that it has nowhere been more strictly adhered to than in this country. We have seen that the rule: pound is pound, dollar is dollar, franc is franc, does not only mean that an obligation can always be discharged pound for pound, dollar for dollar, franc for franc, but also that frequently fluctuations in value of the domestic currency cannot even be taken into account as a mere fact for the purpose of measuring damages, obtaining rescission, and so forth.

The legal rules relating to changes in the value of foreign money are in principle identical.[67] The following observations are devoted to the application of those general rules to the specific case of foreign money obligations.

1. As regards the *quantum of simple debts* expressed in foreign money, there is no rule in English law which enables a party to claim a reduction or an increase of the amounts of foreign money payable on the ground of a rise or fall in the international value of such money. If under an English contract 1,000 French francs are promised, the devaluation of the French currency does not enable the creditor to claim compensation. Even if under an English contract marks or roubles were promised which have become worthless, there is no possibility of helping the creditor by revalorizing the debt.[68]

---

three entirely different questions arise. Firstly, which is the money of account the subject-matter of the obligation? On this point see above, p. 262, and the literature there referred to. Secondly, how is the currency thus owed defined? On this point see above, p. 268. Thirdly, is the amount of the currency *in obligatione* revalorized or reduced? On this point see the text.

[66] Above, pp. 80 sqq.

[67] For the general rules of the law of contracts and torts bearing upon the monetary questions involved see above, pp. 80 sqq.

[68] See *British Bank for Foreign Trade* v. *Russian Commercial and Industrial Bank* (No. 2) (1921), 38 T.L.R. 65. The case is discussed below, p. 289.

A somewhat greater liberality has been shown by the law of some other countries.[69] Thus revalorization of debts expressed in marks was allowed in *Switzerland* even if the contract was not governed by German law (in which case the application of German revalorization rules was a natural consequence of the applicable doctrine of private international law),[70] but by Swiss law. Although Swiss law had not developed any general revalorization doctrine, the fact that a foreign money had become completely worthless induced the courts to invoke certain equitable principles of the Swiss Civil Code in order to compensate the creditor for the loss which a strict application of nominalism would have involved.[71] But apart from such cases of a collapse of a currency no deviation from the leading principle was admitted. In *France* no revalorization in respect of debts of French francs was ever admitted,[72] and although even with regard to the worthless mark and rouble currencies of Germany and Russia the law of the currency was generally followed, two decisions of a rather exceptional character must be noted where the circumstances were such as to make it difficult to abstain from assisting the creditor. In the first case [73] the defendants, a French company, had in 1911 promised to the manager of their Odessa works a pension of 2,400 roubles per annum. The court refused to regard the contract as discharged, but allowed revalorization, inasmuch as it gave judgment against the defendants for the pre-war value of the roubles in terms of francs, i.e. for 6,360 francs per annum, without, however, allowing any compensation in respect of the depreciation of the French franc. The court adopted 'une saine interprétation de la volonté des parties' and thus arrived at the result 'que la disparition du rouble comme monnaie de paiement n'a pu avoir pour conséquence de faire disparaître l'obligation contractée par la Société d'assurer des moyens d'existence à son employé sa vie durant; qu'elle subsiste au contraire entièrement et que, pour déterminer la manière dont elle devra être acquittée, il convient de se référer comme l'ont très justement fait les premiers juges, à la valeur qui a été envisagée au jour de la convention, c'est-à-dire au rapport existant à cette époque entre la valeur du rouble et celle du franc.' The second case[74]

[69] As a matter of interest it may be noted that the *Chinese* Supreme Court in Peking held that the loss caused by the depreciation of the rouble currency was to be equally divided between the creditor and debtor, the result being expressly based on the requirements of equity and justice; 5 May 1924 and 14 Apr. 1926, D.P. 1928, 2. 93 sqq. (Bartashevitch *v.* Banque Russo-asiatique).          [70] Above, p. 277, n. 47.

[71] See the decisions of 3 June 1925; 17 Feb. 1927; 3 July 1928; 28 Feb. 1930; 26 Mar. 1931; 13 Nov. 1931 quoted above, p. 277, n. 47.

[72] Accordingly there does not seem to have been any room for 'revalorizing' a 4 per cent Japanese Government Loan of 450m. French francs, which had been issued in 1910 in Paris. The opinion expressed by Von Steyern as *amiable compositeur* (Int. L.R. 29, 4) is without legal value. In relation to the same loan the United States-Japanese Property Commission was well justified in refusing to act as *amiable compositeur*: *United States, ex rel. Continental Insurance Co.* v. *Japan*, Japanese Journal of International Law, 5 (1961), 51, also Int. L.R. 29, 431.

[73] Cour de Paris, 28 Nov. 1927, Clunet, 1928, 119. Similarly *Yugoslavia*: Cass. Zagreb, 21 June 1929, *Annuaire de l'Association yougoslave de droit international*, 1931, 287. It should be remembered that, as mentioned above, pp. 104 sqq., pension, inheritance and similar agreements are in many countries readily subject to revision. No general rule should be derived from such cases.

[74] Cass. Civ. 19 Nov. 1930, Clunet, 1931, 691. See the case above, p. 224, n. 11.

concerned a legacy of 60,000 marks given by the will of a testator who was domiciled in Strasbourg. As the testator died after 15 December 1918, the rate of conversion of 1.25 francs to 1 mark which the French had introduced after the cession of Alsace-Lorraine did not apply to the legacy, such conversion being restricted by French law to obligations created before that date. The Court of Appeal found on construction of the will that the testator intended to divided his estate in equal shares, and on this ground the legacy of 60,000 marks was re-valorized to such a sum that the legatee received an amount of a value equal to that due to the other beneficiaries.

Similar cases came before *American* courts. The decision of the Court of Appeals in New York in *Matter of Lendle*[75] concerned a case where the testator, who was domiciled in and a citizen of the United States, by his will made in 1920 gave certain 'mark' legacies to various persons in Germany. After the testator's death in 1927 it fell to be decided how these legacies were to be paid. The court considered two alternatives, namely, whether the testator intended to make the legacies payable only in depreciated paper marks, or in whatever passed as German marks at the time of his death. It was held that to the testator's mind 'the normal mark must at all times have been the mark as he knew it before the World War. . . . The legacies are payable in marks, not in dollars, and in marks which pass as such in the market at the time the legacies are paid.' Accordingly the mark legacies were equiparated to reichsmark legacies and the legatees, who were given by the will more than 400,000 'marks', received the corresponding amount of 'reichs' marks, reichsmark for mark, or $113,000 odd.[76] In a later case,[77] where the mark legacy had already been satisfied in February 1924 by the payment of the nominal amount of marks, the court

---

[75] (1929) 250 N.Y. 502, 166 N.E. 182; a translation of the decision in *JW*. 1929, 3526. A decision of the District Court of the Northern District of California, which the present writer has been unable to find in any American report, was also published in Germany, where it attracted much attention and obviously caused much misunderstanding: *JW*. 1928, 2884 and the comments in *JW*. 1929, 469 and 1620. See, further, *In re Wirth's Estate*, 132 N.Y.S. 2d 98 (1954), where a New York testator, by his will made in 1939, gave to a German family servant '5.000 Goldmark'. According to the Surrogate it was the Gold Mark value of the legacy at the date of the will that the testator intended to bequeath.

[76] The decision may perhaps be justified on the ground that in view of the circumstances of the case an intention of the testator to equiparate marks to reichsmarks could be ascertained, though it must be said that the material before the court rather suggested the opposite view. Unless this explanation helps, the decision gives rise to criticism. The case was governed by American law, which has accepted the nominalistic principle (above, p. 269, n. 9). Under this principle, which is based on the presumed intention of the parties (above, p. 84) and which is therefore a direct answer to the two alternatives envisaged by the court and mentioned in the text, German law had to be applied in so far, and only in so far, as the definition of the unit of account was concerned. According to the relevant German law, however, one billion of marks is equal to one reichsmark (above, pp. 45, 101). Revalorization would only have been possible under the law of the obligation, i.e. American law which does not know of any such remedy (above, p. 89, n. 47). Even from the point of view of the doctrine which subjects revalorization to the law of the currency (above, p. 276), the decision would be unjustifiable, since the pertinent legislation of the law of the currency was in fact not applied and since, even if it had been applied, a very different result would have followed.

[77] *Matter of Illfelder* (1931), 136 Misc. 430, 240 N.Y. Supp. 413, aff'd. 249 N.Y. Supp. 903.

declined to reopen the transaction on the basis of *Lendle*'s case, which was distinguished on the ground that there the testator had not died until 1927 and that the legacies had not been paid.[78]

The *German* practice in so far as it relates to the revalorization of foreign money obligations is less remarkable. There existed after 1923 in German law an elaborate body of revalorization rules, and in view of the adoption of the theory that revalorization is governed by the law of the obligation[79] there was nothing unusual in their application to foreign money obligations.[80] The only question, which was often ventilated, related to the conditions under which by German municipal law foreign money could be regarded as so greatly depreciated that revalorization was called for. The Supreme Court established the rule that a 'catastrophic depreciation' was required. On this ground debts expressed in roubles or Austrian kroners were revalorized,[81] but with regard to other currencies which suffered a smaller degree of depreciation the application of the doctrine was refused.[82] In such cases, however, a different principle was developed which, although it did not lead to revalorization in the technical sense, sometimes enabled the creditor to claim payment of an amount exceeding the nominal amount of the debt. The basis of this development is the rule of German law[83] that in case of an unforeseen change of relevant statutory provisions a construction of the contract may not only lead to its discharge, but to its revision in the sense that the party injured by the fundamental change of the basis of the contract is allowed compensation in respect of the disequilibrium between concurrent obligations. The leading case in which this principle was applied to foreign money obligations concerns a contract for the sale of yarn made between a German importer and a German manufacturer in June and July 1931; the purchase price, which was expressed in pounds sterling, was due and paid after England had gone off the gold standard, the buyer paying in reichsmarks calculated at the current rate of the paper pound.[84] As it was held that the stability of the pound sterling was a basic fact inducing the parties to adopt the pound

---

[78] On American views see also Professor Corbin referred to above, p. 103, n. 112 and below, p. 341, n. 31; also Rashba, 'Debts in Collapsed Foreign Currencies', 54 (1944) *Yale L.J.* 1, who propound the view that, if the contract is subject to American law, this provides relief in case of the complete collapse of a foreign currency, and that, if the contract is subject to a foreign legal system which grants inadequate or no revalorization, American courts would invoke public policy or the rules against confiscation respectively. This seems very doubtful.

[79] Above, p. 276, n. 45.

[80] Difficulties arose in connection with the application of certain statutory provisions which were primarily intended to apply to mark debts. See, for example, the decisions mentioned in the following note.

[81] 27 Jan. 1928, *RZG.* 120, 70, 76 (Austrian crowns); 2 June 1930, *Leipziger Zeitschrift*, 1931, 384 (roubles); 16 Dec. 1931, *JW.* 1932, 1048 (Austrian crowns), and numerous other cases.

[82] *French francs*: 6 Apr. 1925, *JW.* 1925, 1986, No. 2; 25 Feb. 1926, *JW.* 1926, 1323; 22 Feb. 1928, *RGZ.* 120, 193, 197. *Dutch florins*: 3 Mar. 1925, Warneyer, Rechtsprechung, 1925, No. 134. *Pound sterling*: 6 May 1933, Warneyer, Rechtsprechung, 1933, No. 112; 21 June 1933, *RGZ.* 141, 212; 28 June 1934, *RGZ.* 145, 51, 55. *U.S.A. dollars*: 13 May 1935, *RGZ.* 147, 377; 15 Mar. 1937, *RGZ.* 154, 187, 192; 20 Apr. 1940, *RGZ.* 163, 324, 333.

[83] See, for example, 15 Jan. 1931, *RGZ.* 131, 158, 177.

[84] Supreme Court, 21 June 1933, *RGZ.* 141, 212.

sterling as the money of account, revision was allowed on the above principle; but the additional amount due to the seller was not simply the difference between the value of the gold pound and that of the paper pound, but depended on an investigation into the facts of the case showing whether and how far the depreciation of the pound sterling meant a loss or a profit to both parties' financial position regarded as a whole. These rules have been considered in a number of later cases arising out of the depreciation of the pound sterling and the dollar,[85] but it should be emphasized that their application requires great care, not only in view of the necessity of reviewing all the facts of the case, but also because of the strong emphasis laid on the pre-requisite of a disturbance of the intended equilibrium between the mutual performances. This principle prevented the application of the rule in case of a loan,[86] or in cases where both parties had already fulfilled their obligations and where the consideration depreciated in the hands of the creditor,[87] or if the parties had in fact envisaged a depreciation of the dollar or pound sterling.[88]

2. If the international value of the foreign money of account depreciates between the date of maturity and the date of payment, the question arises whether the creditor is entitled to claim damages for the loss suffered.

As in *Germany* damages due to the delayed payment of a debt are on principle not limited to interest, and as under German law the creditor of a mark debt, whether he be German or non-German, may in certain circumstances claim damages in respect of the depreciation of the German mark,[89] it was a natural consequence to hold that a German creditor of foreign money may claim damages in respect of the depreciation of the foreign currency concerned;[90] but in the absence of special circumstances it must be strictly proved that the creditor would have avoided the loss, if the debtor had paid at maturity.[91] Similarly in

---

[85] See especially Supreme Court, 2 Apr. 1935, *RGZ*. 147, 286; 28 May 1937, *JW*. 1937, 2823; 28 May 1937, *RGZ*. 155, 133; 20 Apr. 1940, *RGZ*. 163, 324. But see 15 Mar. 1937, *RGZ*. 154, 187; 7 Feb. 1938, *JW*. 1938, 1109. As to the Hungarian practice which apparently rested on similar grounds see above, p. 269, n. 9.

[86] Supreme Court, 28 June 1934, *RGZ*. 145, 51, 56.

[87] Supreme Court, 13 Oct. 1933, *RGZ*. 142, 23, 34, 35.

[88] Supreme Court, 9 July 1935, *RGZ*. 148, 33, 41, 42; Danzig, 27 June 1934, *JW*. 1934, 2074.

[89] Above, p. 108.

[90] Supreme Court, 25 Feb. 1926, *JW*. 1926, 1323 (francs); 22 Feb. 1928, *RGZ*. 120, 193, 197 (francs); 13 May 1935, *RGZ*. 147, 377 (dollars), and many further decisions.

[91] See, especially, the decision of 22 Feb. 1928. If a French creditor of French francs claims damages in respect of the depreciation of the French currency proof of damage must be particularly strict: Supreme Court, 25 Feb. 1926, *JW*. 1926, 1323; 4 Jan. 1938, *JW*. 1938, 946. It is, however, by no means certain whether the formulation in the text is still correct and whether the law has not taken a different turn. The headnote of a decision of the Federal Supreme Court, 18 Feb. 1976, *NJW*. 1976, 848 (the text of which does not seem to be published) indicates that the burden of proof is reversed: where a German seller sells to a German buyer for dollars and, on account of the buyer's failure to accept delivery, sells the goods elsewhere for dollars which depreciate in value, the buyer has to prove that the seller did not suffer any damage by reason of the fact that he applied the dollars to the discharge of old dollar debts.

*Austria*[92] and *Switzerland*[93] it was held that, if the payment of a pound sterling debt was delayed until after the depreciation of sterling in 1931, an Austrian or Swiss creditor was entitled to damages, as his contention that he would have avoided the loss by converting the pounds sterling into Austrian or Swiss currency was accepted. While in *France* and certain countries influenced by the French Civil Code the law seems to be unsettled,[94] it is established practice in *Belgium*[95] that under Belgian law the debtor of foreign currency which depreciates after default has to pay damages to compensate for the loss, while in *Italy* the creditor of non-Italian money is not entitled to damages in respect of the devaluation of the foreign money after the date of maturity.[96]

In this country such damages cannot be usually claimed.[97] Thus Scrutton L.J. said:[98]

It occurred to me it might possibly be that subsequent variation in the exchange could be included in the damages in the nature of interest. I have been unable to find that interest by way of damages has ever been allowed to cover alteration in the exchange, and Counsel have also been unable to find any such

[92] Austrian Supreme Court, 18 Mar. 1932, *JW.* 1932, 2839 and Clunet, 1932, 1082; 28 Nov. 1934, Clunet, 1936, 191.

[93] Federal Tribunal, 10 Oct. 1934, *BGE.* 60, ii. 340, and Clunet, 1935, 1100. It was even held that the German creditor of a Swiss franc debt due from a Swiss debtor could claim damages for the devaluation of the Swiss franc by 30 per cent in 1936: Federal Tribunal, 31 Oct. 1950, *BGE.* 76, ii. 371, also *Jahrbuch für schweizerisches Recht*, 1952, 265 with note by Gutzwiller. The ground was that the creditor would have converted into reichsmark. See, generally, Henggeler and Guisan, *Zeitschrift für schweizerisches Recht*, 56 (1937), 227a sqq., 336a sqq. As to *Greece* see Art. 292, Civil Code.

[94] *France*: see Planiol–Ripert, vii, Nos. 880, 1161. *Egypt*: The Court of Appeal of the Mixed Tribunal (4 Nov. 1936, *Gazette des Tribunaux Mixtes*, 28 (1938), 151) refused to compensate a Belgian creditor for the depreciation of the Belgian currency during the Egyptian debtor's default. The Award in *Société Européenne* v. *Yugoslavis*, Clunet, 1959, 1074, or Int. L.R. 1957, 761 was made by Messrs. Ripert and Panchaud as *amiables compositeurs*, and is therefore without any legal value. The decision to translate 190 m. French francs of the value of 1932 into about 4.439 m. French francs of the value of 1956 was arrived at without reference to any legal rule, partly on the ground that the arbitrators were dealing with an international contract (which is reminiscent of certain French ideas), partly on the ground of 'good faith' (which is a German and, perhaps a Swiss conception), partly by reason of the debtor's default which justified the award of damages for the wrong caused by the delay. The last argument is probably the most persuasive to a lawyer. The enforcement of the award has led to much litigation in Holland and France and is discussed by Klein, *Festschrift für F. A. Mann* (1977), p. 617. The decision by the Cour de Paris there mentioned was reversed by Cass. Civ., 14 June 1977, Clunet, 1977, 864.

[95] Cass., 4 Sept. 1975, *Pasicrisie*, 1976 I 16. In the *Netherlands* a remarkable result was reached as a result of a decision of the Hoge Raad of 8 Dec. 1972, *N.J.* 1973, 1041: although according to Art. 1286 of the Civil Code the defaulting debtor is liable only for interest, this restriction does not apply where the debtor owes to a Dutch creditor foreign currency which depreciates.

[96] Corte de Cassazione, 30 Mar. 1966, *Foro Italiano*, 1966, i. 1539, also Clunet, 1968, 377.

[97] *Di Ferdinando* v. *Simon Smits & Co.*, [1920] 3 K.B. 409, 416 *per* Scrutton L.J.; see *Manners* v. *Pearson*, [1898] 1 Ch. 581; *Société des Hôtels le Touquet* v. *Cummings*, [1922] 1 K.B. 451, 460, 461 *per* Scrutton L.J.; *S.S. Celia* v. *S.S. Volturno*, [1921] 2 A.C. 544, 560 *per* Lord Parmoor, at pp. 567, 568 *per* Lord Carson.

[98] *Di Ferdinando*'s case, *ubi supra*.

case. I think the reason is the one I have already given—namely, that those damages are too remote. The variation of exchange is not sufficiently connected with the breach as to be within the contemplation of the parties.

This language makes it clear, however, that in truth a question of fact is involved. It is, therefore, by no means inconceivable that upon proof of the necessary facts damages for delayed payment of a foreign currency debt will be recoverable in England.[99] More recently such a claim was in fact allowed by Donaldson J. (as he then was) on the ground that the loss was foreseeable,[100] and though the case does not seem to have been argued or reasoned with great elaboration, it has clarified English law in a sense which will no doubt be welcomed by the commercial community.

It should be noted that a different point arises where foreign money is not promised to be paid as money, but is promised to be delivered as the object of a commercial transaction of purchase and sale.[101] If in consideration of a payment of £250 my banker undertakes to deliver to me in New York 1,000 Swiss francs, he fulfils his contract by delivering in New York at the due date whatever are 1,000 Swiss francs; but if he delays delivery until a date when the Swiss franc has depreciated, the general principle applies that damages for late delivery may be claimed, such damages consisting of the difference between the value of the goods at the date fixed for delivery and their value when delivered.[102] This was so held in the interesting New York case of *Richard* v. *American Union Bank*.[103] The plaintiff, a foreign exchange dealer in New York, contracted with the defendants, a New York bank, to establish on 17 November 1919 a credit of 2,000,000 lei in the plaintiff's favour in a bank in Roumania. The plaintiff paid $72,755, but when the credit was established, in August 1921, the market value of the lei had depreciated to $24,440. The plaintiff claimed damages amounting to $48,315. It was held that, as both parties understood the lei to be purchased for resale as a commodity in New York rather than for use as a medium of exchange, the buyer was entitled to damages equivalent to the difference between their market value at the stipulated time of delivery and the actual date of performance.

3. When we come to the determination of the amount of *unliqui-*

---

[99] See above, p. 109, on the similar position in regard to sterling. The alleged rule that interest on the money is the only measure of damages would apply only if it is accepted that a foreign currency debt is a monetary obligation: see above, p. 190.

[100] *Ozalid Group (Export) Ltd.* v. *African Continental Bank Ltd.* (1979), 2 Ll.L.R. 231.

[101] As to this distinction see above, p. 190.

[102] On this principle see Benjamin, *Sale of Goods* (1974), No. 1296; *Wertheim* v. *Chicoutimi*, [1911] A.C. 301 (P.C.); *Elbinger A.G.* v. *Armstrong* (1874), L.R. 8 Q.B. 313.

[103] (1930) 253 N.Y. 166, 170 N.E. 532. See also the French case Cour de Paris, 10 Nov. 1962, S. 1963, 147.

*dated damages* measured in a foreign currency, we find that here too the possibility of taking account of a rise or fall in the international value of the foreign currency concerned depends on the rules of substantive law relating to the measurement of the loss suffered.[104]

No case, in England or abroad, seems to have treated any aspect of the problem as peculiar to foreign money obligations. It is only necessary to mention *Pilkington* v. *Commissioners for Claims on France*[105] where the Privy Council *obiter* expressed the opinion that the confiscation by the French Government of assignats of English claimants was a wrong done by the French Government which must be completely undone, and if the wrongdoer 'has received the assignats at the value of 50*d.*, he does not make compensation by returning an assignat which is only worth 20*d.*; he must make up the difference between the value of the assignats at the different dates'. This observation may have a little value where damages for conversion or detinue arise in terms of foreign currency and the effect of changes in monetary value falls to be considered.

4. The question whether the depreciation of the foreign currency promised to be paid entitles the creditor to treat the contract as frustrated or otherwise rescinded, is, at any rate in England, likely to be answered in the negative. Once again[106] the reason is that 'rarely if ever is it a ground for inferring frustration of an adventure that the contract has turned out to be a loss or even a commercial disaster for somebody'.[107] The result should be different only in cases in which the currency has so completely collapsed as to be worthless, for in such a case it may be said with force that the consideration is destroyed and has ceased to exist altogether.[108]

5. The last question whether within the framework of *equitable remedies* the court may grant relief on account of fluctuations in the international value of foreign money, must be answered in the negative. The authority for this rule is to be found in the decision of Russell J. (as he then was) in *British Bank for Foreign Trade* v.

---

[104] They have been explained above, pp. 116 sqq., where comparative material will be found. A different view from that expressed in the text seems to be taken by Dicey and Morris, pp. 987, 988.

[105] (1821) 2 Knapp, P.C. 7, 20; Sir William Grant based himself on the dicta in *Gilbert* v. *Brett* which have been referred to above, p. 107, n. 129. On *Pilkington*'s case see the somewhat unfortunate remarks of Scrutton L.J. in *Société des Hôtels Le Touquet* v. *Cummings*, [1922] 1 K.B. 451, 460, 461, who treated the maxim *mobilia sequuntur personam* as being in force. It has long been exploded: Dicey and Morris, p. 556.

[106] See above, p. 111.

[107] *Larrinaga & Co. Ltd.* v. *Société Franco-Américaine de Medulla* (1923), 129 L.T. 65, at p. 72, *per* Lord Sumner.

[108] It is possible that the somewhat vague discussion by Corbin, *On Contracts* (above, p. 103, n. 112), contemplates only the type of case referred to in the text.

*Russian Commercial and Industrial Bank.*[109] This was an action for redemption of a loan of 750,000 Russian roubles advanced to the plaintiffs against certain securities. The defendants were held liable to deliver the securities to the plaintiffs against payment of the stipulated amount of Russian roubles which had become valueless. The defendants' argument that the plaintiffs in a redemption action sought equitable relief and must act equitably was rejected. The learned judge said that the plaintiffs were entitled to redeem if they fulfilled their contract and that there was 'no authority and none had been cited that, because the mortgage contract from unexpected causes was alleged to operate harshly on the mortgagee, the Court could refuse redemption or vary the terms on which it would be granted'. The risk of depreciation or the benefit of appreciation was with the lender, and the defendants' request to throw the risk of fluctuation upon the plaintiffs could not be acceded to, as this 'would in effect be changing the loan from a paper rouble to a sterling loan'.

The conclusion to be drawn from these discussions is that in connection with foreign money obligations the implications of nominalism are, in English law, the same as in the case of sterling obligations.

## IV

It thus appears that the adoption of a foreign money of account, though it is very often due to the desire to protect the parties against fluctuations in monetary value, frequently fails to produce the intended guarantee. For the preceding discussions have shown that, whatever justification there may have been at the time when the contract was made for placing confidence in the stability of the chosen foreign money, its international value may suffer changes from which the parties can escape only to a very limited extent even if their contract is governed by a law other than that of the currency.

Hence it is not surprising that, in connection with foreign money obligations no less than in connection with domestic money obligations, methods have been devised which are intended to provide the protection not supplied by the stipulation of mere (domestic or foreign) money obligations. The principal means available for this purpose have already been noted. The stipulation of an option of currency[110] is a particularly valuable method, because the depreciation of one money of account is without any influence on the quantum of money owed under other alternative promises and, unless all the currencies concerned depreciate, the creditor may thus

---

[109] (No. 2) (1921), 38 T.L.R. 65, 67.     [110] On which see above, pp. 207 sqq.

escape from any loss. Another useful method consists in coupling the foreign money with a currency clause: 100 U.S.A. dollars, 1 dollar being equal to 4.20 Swiss francs; here it appears that the amount of dollars owed by the debtor is linked to the Swiss franc, which may mean that the fate of the dollar as such does not necessarily affect the quantum of the debt.[111] For international purposes the only other protective clause which at present is available is a 'basket clause' such as the SDR, but no such clause has as yet come before the courts and for good reasons few have found favour with private investors.[112]

The gold clause[113] which for many decades was the most popular protective clause has completely disappeared from current commercial practice and is unlikely to be revived so long as gold is not reinstated in its former role. Yet the rules of the conflict of laws which were developed in relation to the gold clause,[114] especially its American type (which, as a result of its abrogation by the Joint Resolution of Congress of 5 June 1933, has so often come before the courts) cannot be ignored, for they will give guidance if and when similar problems fall to be considered. Although much of the following

---

[111] See above, pp. 201 sqq.                    [112] On SDR see above, p. 159 and below, p. 507.

[113] Above, pp. 140 sqq.

[114] On the gold clause in English private international law see, in particular, Cheshire and North, pp. 245; Dicey and Morris, Rule 175; M. Wolff, *Private International Law*, pp. 469–71; see also Wortley, *British Year Book of International Law*, 17 (1936), 112 and Lord Wright, *Legal Essays and Addresses* (1939), pp. 147 sqq. In foreign countries the gold clause has led to a flood of litigation and to a very extensive amount of literature. The following discussion in the text will, in general, disregard foreign decisions rendered by courts other than Supreme Courts. Foreign publications of particular value are Nussbaum, pp. 414 sqq. (with many further references); J. Weigert, *The Abrogation of Gold Clauses in International Loans* (1940), being No. 4 of the Series of Contemporary Law Pamphlets (School of Law, New York University); Sauser-Hall, *Rec.* 60 (1937), 658; Hamel, *Nouvelle Revue de droit international privé*, 1937, 499. Duden, *RabelsZ.* 9 (1935), 615, 891; Rabel, *RabelsZ.* 10 (1936), 492; Reiss, *Portée internationale des lois interdisant la clause-or* (Paris, 1936); Bagge, *Revue de droit international et de législation comparée*, 1937, 457 sqq., 786 sqq.; Krispis, pp. 252 sqq.; Van Hecke, pp. 151 sqq. Further material will be found in these publications and in numerous works by Plesch and Domke, though they are now likely to be obsolete; see, for example, Plesch-Domke, *Die österreichische Völkerbundsanleihe* (1936); Domke, *La Clause-or* (1935); Domke, *B.I.J.I.* 34 (1936), 198; Clunet, 1936, 574; *Nouvelle Revue de droit international privé*, 1936, 29; 1937, 3; *Transactions of the Grotius Society*, 1937, 1 sqq.; *Revue de Science et de Législation financière*, 34 (1936), 612; Mr. Plesch has also published two volumes of various judgments on the gold clause: *The Gold Clause*, i (1936); ii (Dec. 1936). The reader must, however, be warned against the belief that these collections convey a complete and reliable picture. It is particularly regrettable that, while there is published in the first volume a judgment of a court of first instance relating to a loan of the city of Antwerp (p. 106), the important judgment of the Brussels Court of Appeal of 4 Feb. 1936, relating to the same loan and published in *Gaz. Pal.* 1936, 1. 513 (14 Mar. 1936) is omitted, and that the Dutch Supreme Court's judgment of 13 Mar. 1936 in the matter of the *Bataafsche* loan which is published in *B.I.J.I.* 34 (1936), 315 is not reported, though it involves an important qualification of the same court's judgment of the same day in the matter of the Royal Dutch Loan published by Plesch, ii. 8 (see below, p. 302, n. 171). See already Duden, *RabelsZ.* 9 (1935), 1001; 11 (1937), 335 and Nussbaum, p. 414, n. 1.

discussion may strike the reader as outmoded, many of the underlying ideas and principles remain instructive.

1. The question whether or no a contract contains a gold clause so obviously concerns the construction of the contract (not of the gold clause) that it must be governed by the proper law. This was indeed so held by the Court of Appeal in *St. Pierre* v. *South American Stores (Gath & Chaves) Ltd.*[115] The contract contained the promise of a rent of '93,500 pesos of 183,057 millionths of a gramme of fine gold monthly which shall be paid at the option of the owner either in Santiago de Chile ... or remitted to Europe according to the instructions which the owner may give'. The question arose whether this provision was a gold clause or whether it merely was a transcription of the relevant article of the Chilean monetary statute. The latter view prevailed, because it was held to be the view taken by Chilean law, which was the proper law of the contract. But the Court of Appeal also expressly held (contrary to the plaintiff's contention) that the exercise of the option to remit the money to Europe could not in any way affect the control of the proper law of the contract, and lead to the application of English law as the law of the place of performance.[116] Greer L.J. said:[117]

I think that, this being a Chilean contract, the obligations of both parties having to be determined by the law of Chile, if the performance takes place in this country, the law to be applied as to the rights and liabilities under the contract is the law of Chile, and not the law of the place of performance, if that happens to be different from the law of Chile.

Slesser L.J. observed:[118]

What is here being debated is the construction of the contract. What has to be ascertained is the amount, be it in gold, in paper, or in other measurement of money, which has to be paid somewhere to the owner. That is a question of construction, and not a question of performance of the contract, the determination of that which has subsequently to be performed. That, by all views, must be taken to be a question of Chilean law, and not one of English law.

2. The question whether a gold clause is to be construed as a gold coin or a gold value clause is also governed by the proper law of the

---

[115] [1937] 3 All E.R. 349; see also *In re Chesterman's Trusts*, [1923] 2 Ch. 466 (C.A.) at pp. 487, 488 *per* Younger L.J.

[116] The plaintiff relied on the dictum of Lord Roche in *The King* v. *International Trustee for the Protection of Bondholders A.G.*, [1937] A.C. 500, 574, on which see above, p. 215, n. 145. The dictum of Lord Wright in *Adelaide Electric Supply Co.* v. *Prudential Assurance Co.*, [1934] A.C. 122, 151, would have been a stronger argument. But in *St. Pierre's* case there was only one place of payment in the proper sense (see above, p. 76), namely Santiago de Chile, and as the proper law of the contract was also Chilean, the whole problem should not have arisen.

[117] At p. 352 C, D.                                            [118] At p. 354 D.

contract. This rule which does not appear to have ever been doubted is confirmed by the decision of the Court of Appeal in *International Trustee for the Protection of Bondholders A.G.* v. *The King*,[119] where it was held that the contract was governed by English law, and where, by applying the rules of construction laid down in *Feist* v. *Société Intercommunale Belge d'Electricité*,[120] the result was reached that a gold value clause was intended. Other decisions are not quite so clear in that they approve of the finding of a gold value clause in application of what has come to be known as the '*Feist* construction' although the proper law was held to be the law of a foreign country such as New York[121] or although the question of the proper law was expressly left undecided.[122] It is submitted that a court should not pass upon the existence of a gold coin or value clause without first having ascertained the proper law.

3. The proper law of the contract also governs the material validity of the contract, in particular the question whether at the time when the contract was made the parties could validly stipulate a gold clause, or whether a gold clause, once validly created, is discharged or invalidated by subsequent legislation.

These and similar questions cannot be subject to the law of the currency to which the gold clause is attached; for although enactments abrogating the gold clause are due to reasons of monetary policy and therefore often described as monetary laws, their effect on the parties' rights and liabilities is purely a matter of contract. In three countries, it is true, statutes were at one time enacted which made all or some gold clauses subject to the law of the currency,[123]

---

[119] [1937] A.C. 505 sqq., at p. 511 *per* Lord Wright.

[120] [1934] A.C. 161.

[121] This applies to *The King* v. *International Trustee for the Protection of Bondholders A.G.*, [1937] A.C. 500, at p. 556 *per* Lord Russell. See Cheshire and North, p. 246, n. 4.

[122] This applies to all the opinions delivered in *New Brunswick Rly.* v. *British and French Trust Corporation*, [1939] A.C. 1: see Lord Maugham at pp. 18, 25; Lord Thankerton at pp. 25, 26; Lord Russell at pp. 26, 29; Lord Wright at pp. 30, 31; and Lord Romer at pp. 39, 46.

[123] *Poland*: Art. 4 of the Statute of 12 June 1934 (see the comments by von Bossowski and von Wendorff and some pertinent decisions of the Polish Supreme Court in *Zeitschrift für osteuropäisches Recht*, i (1935), 499; ii (1936), 410 sqq.). *Austria*: Statute of 4 Apr. 1937, Clunet, 1937, 643, *RabelsZ*. 1937, 267 and *B.I.J.I.* 37 (1937), 108, comments by Koessler, Clunet, 1937, 496. *Germany*: Statute of 26 June 1936, *Reichsgesetzblatt*, 1936, i. 515, and Ordinance of 5 Dec. 1936, *Reichsgesetzblatt*, 1936, i. 1010; see the regulations issued by the Foreign Exchange Board, 27 Dec. 1937, *Reichssteuerblatt*, 1938, 6 and the articles by Hartenstein, *JW*. 1936, 2017; Domke, *B.I.J.I.* 36 (1937), 189; Duden, *RabelsZ*. 1937, 265; von Schelling, *Niemeyers Zeitschrift für Internationales Recht*, 52 (1938), 252. In a decision of 1 Feb. 1938, *BGE*. 64, ii. 88, A.D. 1938–40, No. 57, the Swiss Federal Tribunal held the German Statute to be irreconcilable with Swiss public policy. The German statute, the application of which extended to all cases of devaluation, but was confined to bonds, was a direct consequence of the fact that the German Supreme Court refused to give effect to the Joint Resolution of Congress of 5 June 1933 as being against public policy (see

but they are isolated cases and do not impair the general rule that the proper law of the contract governs—a rule which is firmly established not only in the majority of foreign countries,[124] but also in England.[125]

There remains, however, the problem whether in case the proper law of the contract and the law of the place of payment differ, the general rule of the control of the proper law should be allowed to

below, p. 102, n. 170). These statutes, which cannot be more closely considered here, raise very intricate questions of private international law, especially as they involve the difficulty of a *renvoi*. On the ambit of the law of the currency see, in particular, Gutzwiller, *Der Geltungsbereich der Währungsvorschriften* (1940). It is of course a different matter that, when in a particular case the proper law is to be ascertained, considerable weight should be attached to the parties' choice of the currency, though not so much weight as Weigert (above, p. 291, n. 114) suggests. For a clear statement that the abrogation of the gold clause is not subject to the *lex monetae*, see Swiss Federal Tribunal, 1 Feb. 1938, *BGE.* 64, ii. 88; A.D. 1938–40, No. 57.

[124] *Austria*: Supreme Court, 11 Sept. 1929, Rechtsprechung, No. 332; 8 July 1935, Rechtsprechung, No. 164; but see 12 Mar. 1930, *JW.* 1930, 2480 and below, p. 298, n. 144. *Germany*: Supreme Court, 6 Oct. 1933, *JW.* 1933, 2583; 28 May 1936, *JW.* 1936, 2058, Clunet, 1936, 951 with note by K. Wolff; and Plesch, *Gold Clause*, ii. 30; Federal Supreme Court, 24 Mar. 1960, *WM.* 1960, 217. *Sweden*: Supreme Court, 30 Jan. 1937, *B.I.J.I.* 36 (1937), 327 and *British Year Book of International Law*, 18 (1937), 215. *Norway*: Supreme Court, 8 Dec. 1937, below, p. 303, n. 174; *Denmark*: Supreme Court, 30 Jan. 1939, below, p. 303, n. 175; *Belgium*: Cour de Cassation, 24 Feb. 1938, *B.I.J.I.* 39 (1938), 105. *Holland*: see the decisions quoted below, p. 302, n. 171. *Egypt*: Court of Appeal of the Mixed Tribunal at Alexandria, 18 Feb. 1936, D. 1936, 2. 78 (Crédit Foncier Egyptien) where the notion of a 'contrat international' is exposed as meaningless. *Canada*: *Derwa v. Rio de Janeiro Tramway Light & Power Co.* (1928), 4 D.L.R. 542 (Ontario Supreme Court). In *France* the practice (on which see also below, p. 301, n. 164) has followed a different course. As a result of the peculiar French doctrine to which reference has been made (above, p. 163) a gold clause involving a 'paiement interne' was invariably invalid, but a gold clause involving a 'paiement international' was at one time held to be valid even if it is invalid under the proper law; in the latter case it was thought to be open to the parties 'de convenir, même contrairement aux règles impératives de la loi interne appelée à régir leur convention, une clause valeur-or': Cass. Civ. 21 June 1950, Clunet, 1950, 1196; S. 1951, 1. 1; or *Rev. Crit.* 1950, 609, relating to a Canadian loan issued in 1927 in Canada by Messageries Maritimes. See Lerebours Pigeonnière, Clunet, 1951, 4. It seemed that this remarkable doctrine was extended by a second decision relating to the same loan: Cass. Civ., 24 Jan. 1956, Clunet, 1956, 1012. But the most recent decision, again relating to the same loan, seems to adopt the more traditional course of approving the application of the proper law of the contract, viz. French law under which the gold clause, involving an international payment, was valid: Cass. Com. 29 Oct. 1964, Clunet, 1965, 637 with useful note by Goldman. The Conseil d'Etat also allows the proper law to govern: 28 Nov. 1958, Clunet, 1960, 444. Outside France the distinction between 'paiement international' and 'paiement interne' will have to be applied if French law governs the contract; it would not be permissible to disregard those French rules on the ground that they are derived from considerations of French public policy or that they are part of French private international law, not of French substantive law: see Trieste Court of Appeal, 25 Jan. 1934, *Recueil général de droit international*, 2 (1935), 101 and *RabelsZ.* 10 (1936), 980, but in New York the tendency seems to be that the French rule is one of public policy and therefore inapplicable outside France: *De Sayve v. De la Valdene* (1953), 124 N.Y.S. 2d 143, at p. 153.

[125] *The King v. International Trustee for the Protection of Bondholders A.G.*, [1937] A.C. 500 (see the comments by Nussbaum, p. 425; 46 (1937) *Yale L.J.* 891, the note by Hamel in D. 1937, 2. 73), and Mann, *British Year Book of International Law*, 1959, 42.

prevail or whether preference should be given to the law of the place of payment.

If the former view is adopted, a gold clause contained in an English contract and providing for payment in New York could be enforced, because the Joint Resolution of Congress of 5 June 1933 would not have applied directly, the proper law being English, nor would it have applied indirectly under the head of the doctrine of supervening impossibility of performance as laid down in *Ralli*'s case,[126] the law of the United States not having made it illegal to fulfil the promise.[127] If the latter view was adopted, the gold clause, providing for payment in New York would have been caught by the Joint Resolution and therefore been void, although the proper law was English. But a gold clause contained in a contract governed by the law of the United States and providing for payment in London would have been enforceable.

The judgments of the Permanent Court of International Justice at The Hague in the cases of the *Serbian and Brazilian Loans*[128] are sometimes believed to warrant reliance on the law of the place of payment rather than on the proper law of the contract. The former of these cases[129] concerned bonds issued by the Serbian Government which were denominated in 'francs-or' and made payable in various places (option of place); the holders demanded payment in Paris. The court in the first place proceeded to determine the law governing the obligations at the time they were entered into, and it arrived at the result that 'this law is Serbian law and not French law, at all events in so far as concerns the substance of the debt and the validity of the clause defining it' (p. 42). Under Serbian law, it appeared, 'the validity of the obligations set out in the said bonds is indisputable' (p. 42). The court then continued (p. 44):

But the establishment of the fact that the obligations entered into do not provide for voluntary subjection to French law as regards the substance of the debt, does not prevent the currency in which payment must or may be made in France from being governed by French law. It is indeed a generally accepted principle that a State is entitled to regulate its own currency. The application of the laws of such State involves no difficulty so long as it does not affect the substance of the debt to be paid and does not conflict with the law governing such debt. In the present case this situation need not be envisaged, for the contention of the Serbian Government to the effect that French law prevents the carrying out of the gold stipulation, as construed above, does not appear to be made out.

[126] [1920] 2 K.B. 287 (C.A.).
[127] *International Trustee for the Protection of Bondholders A.G.* v. *The King*, [1936] 3 All E.R. 407 (C.A.).
[128] Collection of Judgments (1928–30), Series A, Nos. 14, 15.
[129] The latter is so similar that a separate discussion is unnecessary.

This statement has been frequently criticized.[130] In particular it has been asserted that the court applied French law because the mode of payment was governed by French law, the place where payment was demanded being in Paris and the money there payable being French.[131] There is, however, no justification for this interpretation and it is submitted that the court's dictum is free from ambiguity. The court did not apply French law at all. It had held that Serbian law applied under which the validity of the contract was indisputable; but as the Serbian Government contended that French law applied and invalidated the gold clause, the court proceeded to show that the application of French law 'need not be envisaged, for the contention of the Serbian Government . . . does not appear to be made out'. Thus, by showing that under French law, if it applied, the result would be the same, the court avoided, but did not solve, the problem under examination.[132]

This problem was, however, dealt with in the decision of the Court of Appeal in *British & French Trust Corporation* v. *New Brunswick Railway Company*.[133] The defendants, a Canadian railway company, in 1884 had issued mortgage bonds of £100 each, the company promising to pay to the bearer '£100 sterling gold coin of Great Britain of the present standard weight and fineness at its agency in London, England, with interest thereon . . . or at the option of the holder at the office of the company in New Brunswick'. The bonds which, it should be emphasized merely provided for an option of place fell due in 1934, when the plaintiffs demanded payment in England on the basis of a gold value clause. Early in 1936 Hilbery J. dismissed the action.[134] In the Court of Appeal and the House of Lords the main question in issue was whether the abrogation of gold clauses by the Canadian Gold Clauses Act, 1937, prevented the plaintiffs from succeeding. In the result the answer was in the negative. In the House of Lords the *ratio decidendi* was limited to a narrow point of statutory interpretation rather than of monetary law: it was held that the Canadian Act of 1937 could not, and did not intend to, encroach upon a claim which existed, and ought to have been upheld by Hilbery J., before the Act came into force. The Court of Appeal, however, proceeded on different lines.[135] Greer L.J.[136] relied on the

---

[130] See, especially, Nussbaum, p. 418.

[131] This is the view held, for example, by the Brussels Court of Appeal, 4 Feb. 1936, *Gaz. Pal.* 1936, 1. 513 and S. 1937, 4. 1, with note by Mestre (Ville d'Anvers); Reiss (quoted p. 291, n. 114) at p. 120.

[132] Rabel, *Conflict of Laws*, iii (1950), 40 agrees with the suggestion in the text.

[133] [1937] 4 All E.R. 516, affirmed (subject to a slight variation) on different grounds, [1939] A.C. 1.                                          [134] [1936] 1 All E.R. 13.

[135] In the House of Lords the views expressed in the Court of Appeal recurred only in the opinion of Lord Romer (at p. 44).                  [136] [1937] 4 All E.R. 516.

dictum of Lord Wright[137] that 'whatever is the proper law of a contract regarded as a whole, the law of the place of performance should be applied in respect of any particular obligation which is performable in a particular country other than the country of the proper law of the contract', and thus he felt 'bound to hold that the measure of payment falls to be determined by the law of the place of performance which in the present case is the law of England'. In Slesser L.J.'s view[138] the Canadian legislation did not 'affect the substantial obligations between the parties which in the present case are clearly governed by Canadian law',[139] but only the 'mode and measure of discharge' which were governed by English law as the *lex loci solutionis*. In Scott L.J.'s judgment, too, the contract was governed by Canadian law, but as to 'the interpretation of the payment clause, and . . . its judicial enforcement in London', he applied the *lex loci solutionis*, i.e. English law.[140]

None of these reasons is convincing. Whether Lord Wright's dictum is right in principle and whether, if it is, its authority stands unimpaired;[141] whether it was right in the case then before the learned Lord and whether it was made *per incuriam*,[142] all this, it is submitted, is somewhat doubtful. On the other hand, to say that the effect of the abrogation of a gold clause upon the obligation is a matter falling under the head of the mode of performance unexpectedly strains the meaning of that conception; one would have thought that the abrogation of a gold clause is a matter which affects, and very materially affects, the substance, namely the quantum, of the debt.[143]

---

[137] In *Adelaide Electric Supply Co.* v. *Prudential Assurance Co.*, [1934] A.C. 122, 151. As to this dictum see above, pp. 216, 237. The limitations placed upon it by Lord Wright when he delivered the judgment on the Privy Council in *Mount Albert Borough Council* v. *Australasian Temperance and General Mutual Life Assurance Society*, [1938] A.C. 224 (see above, p. 217), were held by Greer L.J. to be irreconcilable with the *Adelaide* case.

[138] p. 528.

[139] On this ground the learned Lord Justice distinguished the *Mount Albert Borough Council* case, *ubi supra*.

[140] pp. 540, 541. The reasons which produced this result are not quite clear. He seems to have been misled by the totally different principle that *for the purpose of ascertaining the proper law of a contract* there is a presumption in favour of the *lex loci solutionis*, if there is a conflict between that legal system and the *lex loci contractus* (see above, p. 229). He also relied on the fact that the words of the clause 'the present standard of weight and fineness' pointed to an English statute. The *Mount Albert Borough Council* case, *ubi supra*, was distinguished on the ground that it related to the effect of subsequent legislation of the country where the place of payment is situate, not of the country the law of which was the proper law.

[141] On these points see above, pp. 237 sqq.

[142] See above, pp. 237 sqq., where, *inter alia*, it was suggested that Lord Wright's dictum was due to the failure to appreciate the difference between the rule of private international law relating to the law of the place of payment and the rule of municipal law relating to the money of the place of payment and its determination.

[143] See Lord Wright's warning mentioned above, p. 216, n. 148.

The view expressed by the Court of Appeal, though supported by the practice in some foreign countries,[144] has not, on the whole, met with approval in this country.[145] Neither the fact that a place of payment has been expressly agreed by the parties, nor the fact that the currency of the place of payment is stipulated as the money of account,[146] is sufficient for inferring an intention to submit to the *lex loci solutionis* such matters as relate to the substance of the debt. It is only in those cases in which the parties have provided for an option of currency (coupled with an option of place)[147] that a different construction is permitted,[148] for in that event there exists evidence of the parties' desire to create independent monetary obligations. However, in connection with the abrogation of gold clauses, even this suggestion can only be put forward with diffidence, seeing that it was not ventilated in *The King* v. *International Trustee for the Protection of Bondholders*[149] although it would have considerably facilitated the road to the goal reached by the House of Lords.

4. If, in application of the principles developed in the preceding section, the protective clause is governed by English law, an English court will enforce it, there being no rule of English law rendering it invalid. In particular it would be without relevance that under the law of the debtor's residence or place of business the clause may be invalid or even illegal. If, however, according to the law of the place

---

[144] See Court of Appeal, Zürich, 21 Feb. 1941, *Nouvelle Revue de droit international privé*, 1942, 451 (*re* Royal Dutch Loan), relying on Swiss Federal Tribunal, 23 May 1928, BGE. 54, ii. 257 and Clunet, 1929, 500: where there is one of several places of payment in Switzerland and the money of payment (not the money of account) is Swiss, Swiss law applies 'dans la mesure que l'exécution de ces engagements est demandée en Suisse'. The idea that the *lex loci solutionis* applies to matters of performance in a wide sense was again approved in principle by the Federal Tribunal, 7 July 1942, BGE. 68, ii. 203; Clunet, 1946-9, 208, but held to be displaced by the express submission of the contract to a specific legal system. Austrian Supreme Court, 26 Nov. 1935, *RabelsZ*. 9 (1935), 891, 897, as explained in the decision of 20 May 1936, *RabelsZ*. 10 (1936), 680, and of 10 July 1936, Rechtsprechung, 1936, 194, also in *RabelsZ*. 11 (1937), 269 and Clunet, 1937, 334; see also Austrian Supreme Court, 1 June 1937, B.I.J.I. 37 (1937), 245, where it was said that, if there is a gold coin clause, the law of the place of payment decides whether or not the creditor is entitled to be paid in gold coin. Great care should be taken not to count among the adherents to this doctrine such foreign courts as have adopted the suggestion which will presently be made in the text in regard to the wholly distinct case of the option of currency.

[145] Dicey and Morris, p. 993; Cheshire and North, p. 247; Martin Wolff, *Private International Law*, 2nd ed. (1950), p. 470; but see 'E.', *British Year Book of International Law*, 18 (1937), 220.

[146] If the currency of the place of payment is merely the money of payment, there is still less justification for applying the *lex loci solutionis*. This was overlooked by the Swiss decision referred to above, n. 144.

[147] In the sense discussed above, pp. 207 sqq.

[148] For a general discussion of this suggestion which, in the result, is accepted by Van Hecke, p. 206, see above, p. 219.

[149] [1937] A.C. 500.

of payment the clause is not only invalid, but also illegal, then the implications of the familiar, but far from transparent rule in *Ralli's* case[150] will have to be considered.

In the event of the English protective clause being sought to be enforced in a country the law of which renders it invalid, illegal or contrary to public policy the court, it is submitted, can disregard it only by virtue of the forum State's *ordre public*. In an American court a gold clause attached to a dollar obligation which is subject to English law should between 1933 and 1978 have been enforced, for it is difficult to see that vital interests of the United States demanded the effects of the proper law to be displaced.[151] The problem continues to exist in the Federal Republic of Germany on account of s. 3 of the Currency Act of 1948.[152] German courts are unlikely to treat the section as a matter of *ordre public*, for it does not create any illegality, but leaves room for dispensation by licence.[153]

5. If it appears that the effects of the abrogation of the gold clause are subject to the law of the country[154] which has enacted the abrogation, that law governs all further questions. Thus it determines its own territorial and personal ambit,[155] it decides whether the gold clause has become void or illegal, and so forth.

A number of attempts have, however, been made to defeat the application of, for example, the Joint Resolution of 5 June 1933, even on the basis of United States law being the governing law. These attempts were not considered by the House of Lords in the case of *International Trustee for the Protection of Bondholders A.G. v. The King*,[156] where the finding that American law applied immediately led to the dismissal of the suppliants' claim. But they had not even been put forward in argument, and since they are therefore not expressly disposed of so far as the law of this country is concerned, and also because they have acquired prominence on the Continent, a short investigation cannot be dispensed with, however obvious it may be that *a priori* their importance can only be slight.

(*a*) It has been said that the reference by the parties to United

---

[150] [1920] 2 K.B. 287 on which see above, p. 66 and below, p. 420.

[151] The problem arose, but was avoided by the court in the American case mentioned above, p. 141, n. 25.

[152] See above, p. 170, n. 184.

[153] In this sense Mann, *Zeitschrift für Handelsrecht*, 133 (1969–70), 397.

[154] The matter is of course different if the law of that country is not to be applied as the proper law, but is merely taken into account by another law as a factual incident: see p. 216, n. 149, and text thereto.

[155] See above, p. 169. See also above, p. 197, n. 68 on the applicability of the Joint Resolution in the event of an option currency.

[156] [1937] A.C. 505.

States law must be so construed as to be confined to the law of the United States existing at the time when the contract was made, and that consequently it does not comprise subsequent alterations such as the Joint Resolution, unforeseen and unforeseeable by the parties; it has also been said that the reference to United States law was not intended by the parties to include enactments of such extraordinary character as that resolution. In this connection particular reliance is placed on the frequently occurring clauses by which the debtor waives any rights of relief granted by subsequent legislation.[157]

This contention[158] touches a problem of private international law, which does not arise only in connection with the supervening abrogation of gold clauses.[159] Notwithstanding a decision of Younger J.[160] (as he then was), which causes a difficulty, it must now be considered as settled law that the parties who submit their contract to a foreign legal system, submit to the foreign law 'as it is from time to time'[161] and cannot escape from the consequences of their choice save by making explicit and detailed provisions for the application of an alternative legal system.

(b) Another heresy lies in the contention that, irrespective of the ambit claimed by themselves,[162] laws abrogating the gold clause

---

[157] Such clauses are usually valueless. For if United States law governs the contract, it will not give effect to them. If, on the other hand, United States law is not the governing law, they are superfluous: see Nussbaum, *Internationales Privatrecht*, p. 258; Rabel, quoted below, n. 161.

[158] It was, in connection with the abrogation of the gold clause, expressly rejected by the Belgian Cour de Cassation, 24 Feb. 1938, *B.I.J.I.* 39 (1938), 105; *German* Supreme Court, 28 May 1936, *JW.* 1936, 2058, 2059; Clunet, 1936, 951 with note by K. Wolff; and Plesch, *Gold Clause*, ii. 30, 33; Düsseldorf Court of Appeal, 26 Sept. 1934, *IPRspr.* 1934, 300; Cologne Court of Appeal, 13 Sept. 1935, *JW.* 1936, 203, *Swedish* Supreme Court, 30 Jan. 1937, *B.I.J.I.* 36 (1937), 334 (Kreuger and Toll); *Brussels*, Court of Appeal, 4 Feb. 1936, *Gaz. Pal.* 1936, 1. 513 and S. 1937, 4. 1 with note by Mestre. Cf. *Compañia de Inversiones* v. *Industrial Mortgate Bank of Finland*, 269 N.Y. 22, 198 N.E. 617, *B.I.J.I.* 34 (1936), 84, cert. den. 297 U.S. 705 (1936). If and in so far as the decision of the Federal Supreme Court, 18 Feb. 1965, *BGHZ.* 43, 162 or *JZ.* 1965, 448 with note by Mann, expresses a different view, it is contrary to established principles, ignores the essence of the doctrine of the proper law and is inconsistent with the demands of justice.

[159] It was, for example, used by the Court of Appeal of the Mixed Tribunal at Alexandria in the three *Adjouri* judgments mentioned above, p. 277, n. 48.

[160] *In re Friedrich Krupp Aktiengesellschaft*, [1917] 2 Ch. 188, 193.

[161] *In re Chesterman's Trusts*, [1923] 2 Ch. 466, at p. 478 *per* Lord Sterndale M.R., at p. 484 *per* Warrington L.J. (as he then was), *Kahler* v. *Midland Bank*, [1950] A.C. 24, at p. 56 *per* Lord Radcliffe, and the numerous other cases referred to by Dicey and Morris, pp. 47, 820, also the Supreme Court of India in *Delhi Cloth & General Mills* v. *Harnam Singh*, Supreme Court Reports, 1955, ii. 402. In the same sense, for example, M. Wolff, *Private International Law*, s. 405, or Rabel, *RabelsZ.* 10 (1936), 492, 508 sqq. or Van Hecke, p. 208. For a different Swiss view see Niederer, *Einführung in die Allgemeinen Lehren des Internationalen Privatrechts* (Zürich, 1954), p. 206, but see also Vischer, *Internationales Vertragsrecht* (1962), p. 80.

[162] See above, p. 171.

cannot be recognized as having any extraterritorial effects. In France the dogma has been produced that monetary laws have 'un effet strictement territorial',[163] and some French courts have indeed applied it to the abrogation of gold clauses.[164] Even the Supreme Court of Delaware thought it possible (though no more than that) that the abolition of a silver clause by the law of China in 1935 could be a 'revenue law' without extraterritorial effect.[165]

This doctrine which occurs again and again in French discussions of all aspects of monetary law,[166] is without any theoretical attraction,[167] contrary to the requirements of justice, and certainly far removed from the manner in which English lawyers have dealt with, and tend to approach, monetary problems in general and the international implications of the abrogation of the gold clause in particular.[168] It may suffice, therefore, to mention it in passing.

(c) A similar, but equally unfounded suggestion advocates the non-recognition of the abrogation of gold clauses on the ground of its allegedly confiscatory character. No municipal court seems

[163] See Paris Court of Appeal, 19 Apr. 1928, Clunet, 1928, 695 (Société de Charbonnages de Sosnowice); 26 Oct. 1933, Clunet, 1934, 943 (Travellers Bank); Trib. Civ. de la Seine, 27 Mar. 1935, Clunet, 1936, 590, and B.I.J.I. 33 (1935), 103 (Bethlehem Steel Co.); see also the decisions quoted, p. 267, n. 4 above, and see p. 277, n. 48.

[164] In addition to the cases mentioned above, p. 294, n. 124, see Trib. Civ. de la Seine, 31 May 1933, and Paris Court of Appeal, 3 Apr. 1936, D. 1936, 2. 88 (Crédit Foncier Égyptien; the former decision also in Clunet, 1934, 368): the abrogation of the gold clause is not recognized 'en matière de payement international réclamé hors du territoire égyptien'. Similarly, Trib. Civ. de la Seine, 23 July 1936, S. 1938, 2. 25 with note by Mestre, and Plesch, Gold Clause, ii. 76 (Siemens and Halske). In the same sense Court of Appeal of the Mixed Tribunal at Alexandria, 4 June 1925, Clunet, 1925, 1080 (Suez Canal); 18 Feb. 1936, D. 1936, 2. 78 (Crédit Foncier Égyptien), where it was obiter suggested (p. 83) that the Egyptian statute abrogating the gold clause would have been inapplicable, if 'la monnaie stipulée est une monnaie étrangère échappant de par sa nature à l'autorité strictement territoriale des lois de cours forcé'. But see now Court of Appeal of the Mixed Tribunal, 31 Mar. 1938, B.I.J.I. 39 (1938), 352. The doctrine was expressly rejected by the Brussels Court of Appeal, 4 Feb. 1936, Gaz. Pal. 1936, 1. 513 and S. 1937, 4. 1, and by Düsseldorf Court of Appeal, 26 Sept. 1934, IPRspr. 1934, 300, 301.

[165] Judah v. Delaware Trust Co., 378 A. 2d 624 (1977). Even if the contract had been governed by Chinese law (which the court did not seem to contemplate) the conclusion would have been untenable.

[166] It has been proclaimed in a generalized form by Arminjon, Annuaire de l'Institut de Droit International, 43 (1950), ii. 1, and by Frankenstein, Projet d'un Code Européen de Droit International Privé (Bibliotheca Visseriana, 1950), Art 437.

[167] See Mann, Report of the International Law Association, 45th Conference (Lucerne, 1952), pp. 236, 284, and Van Hecke, p. 207, who rightly disapproves cognate suggestions to the effect that the laws referred to in the text could or should be rejected as being allegedly political, fiscal or public laws: the fact that the abrogation 's'inspire de considérations d'intérêt public n'est pas de nature à lui enlever ce caractère'.

[168] Cf., however, Du Costa v. Cole (1688), Skin. 272 referred to above, p. 270, and below, p. 303, and Lord Maugham's suggestion in New Brunswick Rly. Co. v. British and French Trust Corporation, [1939] A.C. 1, 24 that a Canadian statute abrogating the gold clause 'cannot be held to diminish or destroy the rights of an English creditor, and it may be added without compensation, after he has commenced an action in this country'.

to have accepted such a view which, indeed, is untenable for the reasons given a century ago by the Supreme Court of the United States:[169] the constitutional prohibition of the taking of property without compensation

has always been understood as referring only to a direct appropriation, and not to consequential injuries resulting from the exercise of lawful powers. It has never been supposed to have any bearing upon or to inhibit laws that indirectly work harm and loss to individuals. A new tariff, an embargo, a draft or a war may inevitably bring upon individuals great losses, may indeed render valuable property almost valueless. They may destroy the worth of contracts. . . . But was it ever imagined that this was taking private property without compensation or without due process of law?

(d) Greater weight has been accorded to the view that the encroachment upon the creditor's rights, brought about by the abrogation of the gold clause, is against the public policy of third countries and therefore unenforceable. Subject to far-reaching restrictions, this opinion found favour with the Supreme Courts of Germany[170] and Holland,[171] but it

---

[169] *Knox* v. *Lee* and *Parker* v. *Davis* (1870), 12 Wall. 457, at pp. 551, 552 *per* Mr. Justice Strong on behalf of the court. In the same sense, *Norman* v. *Baltimore & Ohio Railroad Co.* (1935), 294 U.S. 240, at p. 306 *per* Chief Justice Hughes on behalf of the court.

[170] 28 May 1936, *JW.* 1936, 2058; Clunet, 1936, 951, with note by K. Wolff; and Plesch, ii. 30, 35 sqq. (with the qualification that at the time of the promulgation of the Joint Resolution the bonds must have been in German possession). *Contra*: Düsseldorf Court of Appeal, 26 Sept. 1934, *IPRspr.* 1934, 300, 302; Cologne Court of Appeal, 13 Sept. 1935, *JW.* 1936, 203, 204. To an unbiased mind the Supreme Court's reasoning will be wholly unconvincing; it has the characteristics of a political rather than a legal argument. An opinion which was given by Professor Wahl and which apparently exercised a certain influence on the Supreme Court's decision is published in *Niemeyers Zeitschrift für Internationales Recht*, 52 (1938), 277. The decision has attracted much criticism and is unlikely to be followed today as regards public policy.

[171] 13 Mar. 1936, *B.I.J.I.* 34 (1936), 304, A.D. 1935–7, p. 203 and Plesch, ii. 8 (Royal Dutch). The Joint Resolution was, however, applied in a second judgment rendered on the same day in the *Bataafsche* case: 13 Mar. 1936, *B.I.J.I.* 34 (1936), 315. The distinction between the two decisions lies in the fact that in the former case payment was to be made and was demanded in Amsterdam, while in the second case the sphere of Dutch conceptions was in no way touched, 'attendu . . . que la naissance, l'exécution et l'extinction du contrat d'emprunt de l'espèce se passent exclusivement dans les limites du territoire des États-Unis'. In a very similar third case relating to bonds which were subject to American law and provided for payment in New York, the application of Dutch public policy was also denied: Supreme Court, 11 Feb. 1938, A.D. 1919–42, p. 26 and *B.I.J.I.* 38 (1938), 282 (Vereeniging voor den Effectenhandel *v.* Mayor of Rotterdam), affirming the decision of the Court of Appeal at The Hague, 24 Dec. 1936, *B.I.J.I.* 36 (1937), 315. The detailed arguments advanced in the third decision are apt to increase the doubt one entertains in respect of the first decision. In a fourth decision of 28 Apr. 1939, A.D. 1919–42, p. 28, S. 1939, 4. 20 or *Rev. Crit.* 1939, 469 (Messageries Maritimes), however, the Canadian abrogation of the gold clause was held to be against Dutch public policy, because 'les Messageries, ayant en vue la participation du public de ce pays (Pays-Bas), ont assumé l'engagement d'exécuter leurs obligations aussi aux Pays-Bas'.

was expressly rejected in Austria,[172] Sweden, [173] Norway,[174] Denmark,[175] and Belgium.[176]

Although the general problems connected with the concept and scope of public policy in private international law lie outside the range of the present discussion,[177] it can be said with safety that the abrogation of gold clauses does not violate English public policy. The decisive reason is to be found in the fact that legislative measures necessitated by the exigencies of monetary policy have become so general that they cannot nowadays be said to be immoral, however injurious they may be. Whether they amount to devaluation to which this country was driven in 1931, 1949, and 1967, or the 'floating' of sterling, as happened in 1972, or to the abrogation of gold clauses, they are always characterized by the causing of loss to some, though not necessarily to all. Consequently no country is entitled to reject the application of another country's laws merely on this ground, particularly as these laws are likely to be identical with or similar to those enacted by the *lex fori* itself. The doctrine of *Du Costa* v. *Cole*,[178] advanced in 1688, has, as we have seen,[179] long since been exploded. It was, therefore, with complete justification that the Brussels Court of Appeal remarked:[180]

Attendu, d'autre part, que la notion de l'ordre public varie non seulement dans l'espace, mais aussi dans le temps; qu'en Belgique elle a évolué de manière notable sous la pression des évènements; que les nombreuses prescriptions d'une portée analogue, édictées dans le pays depuis la guerre, empêchent le juge belge d'admettre que la prohibition de clause-or, ou de clauses valeur-or, ou l'annulation rétroactive, en tout ou en partie, de conventions qui avaient été légalement formées, sont actuellement en opposition avec cette notion.

[172] Supreme Court, 26 Nov. 1935, *RabelsZ.* 9 (1935), 891, 897; 10 July 1936, *Rechtsprechung*, 1936, p. 114.

[173] Supreme Court, 30 Jan. 1937, *B.I.J.I.* 36 (1937), 327 and *British Year Book of International Law*, 1937, 215, 217. It is to be observed that the question was considered worthy of examination only by reason of the fact that the existence of a certain though insufficient contact with Swedish law was undeniable.

[174] Supreme Court, 8 Dec. 1937, *RabelsZ.* 13 (1942), 850.

[175] Supreme Court, 30 Jan. 1939, Clunet, 1954, 489 or *RabelsZ.* 13 (1942), 825.

[176] Cour de Cassation, 24 Feb. 1938, *B.I.J.I.* 39 (1938), 105 or Clunet, 1939, 413 or *Revue de droit international et de législation comparée*, 19 (1938), 323, affirming Brussels Court of Appeal, 4 Feb. 1936, *Gaz. Pal.* 1936, 1. 513 or S. 1937, 4. 1.

[177] It may, however, be pointed out that the theory that the application of rules of public policy requires a sufficient legal or factual connection of the case with the forum and that the mere institution of proceedings does not provide such a connection, since otherwise the forum would claim to impose a 'world law', is strengthened by the Dutch and Swedish decisions mentioned above, n. 171, and n. 173, and also by the Swiss decision referred to below, p. 304, n. 181, which in many other respects also is a landmark in the development of the law of public policy. The problem is of far-reaching general importance.

[178] Skin. 272.                                        [179] Above, p. 271.

[180] 4 Feb. 1936, *Gaz. Pal.* 1936, 1. 513 or S. 1937, 4. 1 (Ville d'Anvers). In the sense of the text Dicey and Morris, p. 992; Van Hecke, pp. 209 sqq., among many others.

The result may be different if the abrogation of the gold clause is discriminatory in that, for instance, it involves damage to foreign creditors exclusively.[181] But no such intention prevailed in the case of the recent measures taken by many countries and it certainly did not prevail in the case of the Joint Resolution of Congress of 5 June 1933.[182]

[181] See, particularly, the decision of the Swiss Federal Tribunal, 1 Feb. 1938, *BGE.* 64, ii. 88, which on such grounds rejected the application of the German statute referred to above, p. 293, n. 123.

[182] Nussbaum, 44 (1934) *Yale L.J.* 53, 75 sqq., regards the equal treatment of non-American debtors as well as creditors as the decisive reason for the non-application of public policy. But no doubt English public policy may well be violated by an individual measure of a foreign country, although the foreign country's own subjects are also affected thereby. While the unequal treatment of foreigners may demand the application of the public policy rules of the forum, the equal treatment does not necessarily exclude it.

# XI

# The Payment of Foreign Money Obligations

I. The problems to be considered. II. The money of payment: (1) the problem and its solution in foreign laws; (2) the rules of English law; (3) the effective clause; (4) the rule of private international law. III. The discharge of foreign money obligations: (1) in English municipal law: (a) the due payment; (b) payment after repudiation; (2) in English private international law: (a) accord and satisfaction; (b) tender; (c) deposit. IV. Conversion for the purpose of adjustment.

## I

THE preceding chapters have been built upon questions raised by an imaginary case which has served as a guide to a logical and systematic exposition of the law of foreign money obligations. The case of a promise, made in Vancouver by a Montreal business man, to pay to a San Francisco firm '100 dollars' in London necessitated an investigation of the nature of foreign money obligations in general (Chapter VII); it has then to be ascertained whether Canadian or United States of America dollars were the subject-matter of the obligation, and we thus came to a discussion of the problems surrounding the determination of the money of account in general (Chapters VIII and IX); finally, we had to examine the various problems connected with the value of the foreign money of account and the quantum of the obligation (Chapter X). No doubt the abundance of problems led far away from the questions directly raised by the hypothetical case. But it served both as a starting-point and as a sign-post, and when we now return to it, consistency requires us to investigate the rules relating to the performance of the debtor's promise. This involves two distinct matters: we must establish the mode of payment or the money of payment, i.e. the currency in which the promise to pay a certain sum of a foreign money of account is discharged; we must ascertain what it is that constitutes a payment, i.e. the concept of payment.

## II

As regards the former of these matters no difficulties arise if the parties themselves have provided for a conversion into the money of payment and for the rate of exchange to be adopted for effecting it: 100 Canadian dollars payable in pounds sterling in the City of London at the rate of 3 dollars to 1 pound. It seemed expedient to treat this case in another connection.[1]

The problem to be dealt with here is different. It is concerned with the question of how (quomodo) the debtor should discharge his obligation to pay a sum of foreign money which he owes and the identity (quid) and extent (quantum) of which is defined. It can be stated in simple terms: is the San Francisco firm which owes 100 Canadian dollars in the City of London bound to tender 100 Canadian dollars, or is it entitled or even bound to tender the equivalent in sterling? In other, more technical and also more general language, can the *moneta loci solutionis* be substituted as the money of payment for the agreed money of account in case there is a lack of identity between them,[2] so that the mode of payment is different from what appears to be determined by the substance of the obligation?

The problem does not arise frequently, but its reality is undeniable. Just as in the vast majority of cases the duty to pay a sum of domestic money is, with the creditor's express or implied consent, discharged otherwise than in cash, so it is only on few occasions that the law has to consider the method of tender in the case of foreign money obligations. Yet rarity of occurrence does not, and has not anywhere, been allowed to relieve the law of its responsibility. And just as in the case of domestic money obligations litigation is no substitute for a doctrine of tender, so in the case of foreign money obligations the requirements of tender are independent of the affect of legal proceedings.[3]

1. The substance of the debt, i.e. its subject-matter and extent, being fixed, it is clear that the payment must be effected in such a manner as to ensure that the creditor or the debtor does not receive or pay more or less than what he contracted for. The best way to reach this goal is to require payment of the stipulated sum *in natura*. If there is a promise to pay 100 Canadian dollars in London and if it is performed by the payment of 100 Canadian dollars, neither party has any ground of complaint, whatever may be the value of the dollar or the pound at the time of payment. As the discussion

---

[1] Above, p. 201.

[2] It is necessary to stress this point. If the contract provides for payment of French francs in France, a problem of conversion does not arise in England except in connection with the institution of legal proceedings.

[3] There are, indeed, many reasons why the rule of substantive law must be found. Most debtors do not desire to litigate. There may be an 'effective clause'. The rate of exchange to be employed by the debtor may need definition.

on nominalism and its effects has shown, it is irrelevant that since the time when the contract was made or since the debt fell due the dollar has depreciated in terms of sterling, for under English law the creditor must bear the risk of currency depreciation and cannot normally claim damages in respect of the depreciation of the foreign money of account during the debtor's default,[4] and if it is the pound sterling which has depreciated, the justification of the refusal to allow the debtor to benefit therefrom lies in the fact that pounds sterling are entirely outside the substance of the obligation. In both cases it is clear that the mode of payment is in accordance with what is determined by the substance of the debt, because money of account and money of payment are identical.

On the other hand, there are many cases where no prejudice to either creditor or debtor would be involved if, for the purpose of performing the contract, the money of account was converted into a different money of payment. This is so in times of monetary stability and sometimes even when monetary values fluctuate, especially if payment is made at the due date. If the English creditor of 100 Canadian dollars is paid in London, not 100 such dollars (whether in notes or by cheque), which in all probability he would at once convert into sterling, but the proper sterling equivalent, he will normally have no objection at all. But it must always be borne in mind that such a mode of payment cannot be allowed to interfere with the substance of the debt, by compelling creditor or debtor to accept or pay anything else than the exact equivalent of what is *in obligatione*.[5] To achieve this aim it is in the first place necessary to remember that any conversion into the money of payment presupposes the determination of the money of account, fixing the substance of the debt, and thus the amount of the money of payment, and that, if the units of account of two currencies have the same name, great injury may ensue from the failure to differentiate between money of account and money of payment.[6] Secondly, it becomes necessary to ascertain whether and for whose benefit the right of conversion exists; on the basis of what rate of exchange the conversion is to be effected; whether and how the right of conversion can be excluded; and which law, in case of a conflict of laws, governs the question.

The origins of the modern right of conversion lie in the law merchant of the Middle Ages. In connection with bills of exchange

---

[4] Above, p. 187.

[5] See already the dictum of Paulus, *D*. 46. 99: 'Creditorem non esse cogendum in aliam formam numos accipere si ex ea re damnum aliquid passurus sit.'

[6] See also below, p. 317.

it was conceived at any early date[7] that, from the point of view of both parties and the State, it was convenient and advisable to avoid, by paying to the creditor the medium of exchange circulating in his own country, the recurrent remittance of moneys foreign to that of the place of payment. It is, therefore, not surprising that at the present time the right of conversion is everywhere (including the United States of America)[8] most firmly recognized in the law relating to bills of exchange[9] but ultimately it found its way into the general law of almost the whole world.[10]

[7] See Endemann, *Studien in der romanisch-kanonistischen Wirtschafts- und Rechtslehre bis gegen Ende des 17. Jahrhunderts* (Berlin, 1883), ii. 214 sqq., speaking of the fungibility of money.

[8] Section 3-107 of the Uniform Commercial Code which applies throughout the United States reads as follows: 'A promise or order to pay a sum stated in a foreign currency is for a sum certain in money and, unless a different medium of payment is specified in the instrument, may be satisfied by payment of that number of dollars which the stated foreign currency will purchase at the buying sight rate for that currency on the day on which the instrument is payable or, if payable on demand, on the day of demand. If such an instrument specified a foreign currency as the medium of payment the instrument is payable in that currency.'

[9] The text of Art. 41 of the Uniform Law on Bills of Exchange and Notes (*League of Nations, Official Journal*, xi (1930), 993), with which Art. 36 of the Uniform Law on Cheques (*League of Nations, Official Journal*, xii (1931), 802) is almost identical, is as follows:

> When a bill of exchange is drawn payable in a currency which is not that of the place of payment, the sum payable may be paid in the currency of the country, according to its value on the date of maturity. If the debtor is in default, the holder may at his option demand that the amount of the bill be paid in the currency of the country according to the rate of the day of maturity or the day of payment.
>
> The usages of the place of payment determines the value of foreign currency. Nevertheless the drawer may stipulate that the sum payable shall be calculated according to a rate expressed in the bill.
>
> The foregoing rules shall not apply to the case in which the drawer has stipulated that payment must be made in a certain specified currency (stipulation for effective payment in foreign currency).

As to paragraph (4) of the Article, see above, p. 229, n. 37. The Uniform Law on Bills of Exchange and Notes has been adopted in more than thirty countries: see Strupp-Schlochauer, *Wörterbuch des Völkerrechts*, iii. 168, 170.

[10] *South Africa: Barry Colne & Co. (Transvaal) Ltd.* v. *Jackson's Ltd.* (1922), South African L.R., Cape Prov. Div. 372; Wessels, *Law of Contract in South Africa* (2nd ed., 1951), section 2223; *Austria*: see Ehrenzweig, *Recht der Schuldverhältnisse* (1928), p. 24. *France*: see the case mentioned below, pp. 312, nn. 21, 22, 23; p. 313, nn. 25, 26, 27, and Planiol-Ripert, vii, Nos. 1161, 1193; Degand, *Change*, *Rép. dr. int.* iii (1929), Nos. 143 sqq.; Paiement, *Rép. dr. int.* x (1931), Nos. 70 sqq.; Hubrecht, *Variations monétaires*, pp. 317 sqq.; Mater, *Rev. dr. banc.*, 1926, 241; 1937, 298, 337. *Belgium*: De Page, *Traité élémentaire de Droit Civil Belge*, iii (1967), s. 459. *Brazil*: Art. 947 of the Civil Code, discussed by Garland, *American-Brazilian Private International Law* (New York, 1959), p. 67. *Venezuela*: Art. 26 of the Law of Money of 17 Feb. 1954 on which see Lambard, *American-Venezuelan Private International Law* (New York, 1965), p. 86. *Germany*: s. 244, Civil Code. *Greece*: Art. 291, Civile Code. *Hungary*: Art. 326, Commercial Code. *Italy*: Art. 1278 of the Civil Code. *Romania*: Art. 41, Civil Code. *Lithuania*: see the decision of the Supreme Court, 14 June 1935, *Zeitschrift für osteuropäisches Recht*, 3 (1936), 127. *Poland*: Arts. 1 sqq. of the Ordinance of 12 June 1934 (see von Bossowski, *Zeitchrift für osteuropaïsches Recht*, 1 (1935), 499, 501). *Switzerland*: Arts 84, 756 Obligationenrecht.

While there thus exists widespread agreement on the principle, a variety of answers has been given to the questions[11] whether the debtor must or may convert, and on the basis of what rate of exchange the conversion is to be effected in the absence of arrangements by the parties. One cannot help feeling that in both connections a certain influence is to be attributed to the development of the domestic currency and its relations with foreign currencies. If and so long as the creditor's domestic currency is stable and it is the foreign currency which depreciates, the conversion on the basis of the rate of exchange of the day of maturity appears to be more just, for by this method the creditor receives what he ought to receive and does not suffer from any depreciation of the foreign money during the debtor's default. On the other hand, a depreciation of the creditor's domestic currency leads to the adoption of the rate of exchange of the day of payment, because in such circumstances non-payment at the due date does not involve any loss to the creditor or any profit to the debtor. It is, however, obvious that both solutions, though they can be explained by the monetary history of a country, are based on a one-sided view of the problem. The first solution will lead to hardship if the tide turns and the creditor's domestic money depreciates after the day of maturity, because the conversion at the rate of exchange prevailing on the day of maturity puts the risk of further depreciation of the domestic currency on the creditor, not on the defaulting debtor. Conversely, the second solution may injure the creditor if his domestic currency remains stable, but the foreign money of account depreciates, and

*Yugoslavia*: Cass. Zagreb, 28 Dec. 1923 and 3 Aug. 1928, *Annuaire de l'Association Yougoslave de droit international*, 1931, 281. *Egypt*: Court of Appeal of the Mixed Tribuman at Alexandria, 9 Apr. 1930, *Gazette des Tribunaux mixtes*, 21, 360, No. 400. For a general and illuminating comparative survey see Dach, *American Journal of Comparative Law*, 3 (1954), 155; Van Hecke, pp. 169 sqq. In some cases the discussion of the problem referred to in the text overlaps with that of the problem of legal proceedings, to which the following chapter is devoted.

[11] It was for this reason, among others, that the International Law Association took up the subject and in 1956 accepted the 'Dubrovnik Rules' which its Monetary Law Committee had prepared: *Report of the 47th Conference* (1956), p. 294. These Rules which are discussed, for instance, by Evan, Clunet, 1958, 406, and which, probably, withstood his criticism, subsequently were considered, together with much other material, by the Council of Europe. After very thorough and elaborate preparatory work the Council in 1967, opened for signature the European Convention on Foreign Money Liabilities (European Treaty Series No. 60). The text of the Convention and its Annex is printed below, p. 576, and see p. 353. The Convention is not yet in force and it is doubtful whether it will ever come into force, for the law on the Continent is substantially in harmony with the Convention and such relatively small changes as it may require are insufficient to justify putting the legislative process into motion. As a result of developments since 1967 the law of the United Kingdom, as will appear in the text, has become very similar to the law in foreign countries, so that a ratification of the Convention would now be possible, but less urgent.

if there is no claim to damages for delay; in this case it would have been preferable, and would have precluded the debtor from speculating at the creditor's cost, if the conversion could have taken place with reference to the day of maturity.

This Scylla and Charybdis[12] might be less harmful if from the outset the right of election were given to the creditor; but this would be an impracticale solution, since the debtor would often not know in time how he should pay. It follows that no satisfactory solution can be derived from the rigid adoption of either date of conversion. Both are dangerous: if the money of account depreciates, a conversion at the rate of exchange of the day of payment might be unjust; if the money of payment depreciates, the selection of the day of maturity may be improper. In both cases, apart from fluctuations in the money of account or the money of payment, much may depend on the stability of the currency of the creditor's home country in which he usually keeps his accounts and which may be different from both the above. In truth the crux of the matter lies in the fact that the selection of either date cannot replace the absence of a claim for damages in respect of currency depreciation during the debtor's default. Where such damages are allowed[13] the problem is of minor importance, though an unsatisfactory duplication of proceedings may ensue. Where no such damages are allowed, neither of the available solutions is satisfactory or always capable of compensating the creditor for the inadequacies of the law of damages.

In these circumstances the solution adopted by the two modern uniform statutes on Bills of Exchange and Notes, and on Cheques,[14] is a great and real improvement: the debtor may choose to pay in the currency of the place of payment at the rate of exchange of the day of maturity; but if he delays the payment, the creditor may select whether payment is to be made at the rate of that day or at that of the day of payment. Thus the debtor cannot profit from his delay and the creditor always receives the full value promised by the substance of the debt.

But outside the sphere of those laws this happy solution has not always been found.[15] In one group of countries it is an undoubted

---

[12] It is not always appreciated by the advocates of the one or the other solution.

[13] See above, pp. 286 sqq.                                      [14] See p. 308, n. 9.

[15] It was foreshadowed by some *German* decisions (see Berlin Court of Appeal, 26 June 1920, *Rechtsprechung der Oberlandesgerichte*, 40, 307), which were, however, overruled by the decision of the Supreme Court mentioned below, p. 311, n. 16, and in effect it has perhaps also found its way into *French* law, see pp. 311-13. It was formally adopted in *Poland* (see p. 308, n. 10) and by the Vienna Rules passed in 1926 by the International Law Association, where, however, the debtor's right to convert is not recognized except

principle that it is the debtor who may elect whether to pay in the promised currency or in that of the place of payment, and that, if he adopts the latter alternative, the conversion is to be effected at the rate of exchange of the day of payment.[16] In other countries the debtor has the right of option, but the rate of exchange of the day of maturity if decisive.[17]

In *France*[18] a more flexible and subtle solution seems to have been arrived at, which is not very far from the ideal. It treats the question as a problem of construction. In the absence of special circumstances any payment to be made in France must be made in French francs.[19] The conversion is usually to be effected on the basis

where payment in the stipulated foreign money is 'impossible' (see the report on the 34th Conference at p. 718 and the comments by Nussbaum, *Vertraglicher Schutz gegen Schwankungen des Geldwerts* (1928), pp. 65 sqq.).

[16] *South Africa*: p. 308, n. 10. *Austria*: see Ehrenzweig, l.c.; *Germany*: Supreme Court (United Chambers) 24 Jan. 1921, *RGZ*. 101, 312. In *Germany* the Federal Supreme Court repeatedly had occasion to emphasize that the creditor cannot demand payment in German currency, that, therefore judgment has to be given in terms of foreign currency and that it is the debtor's option to decide whether he proposes to pay in foreign or in local currency: 22 May 1958, *WM*. 1958, 822; 30 Sept. 1968, *WM*. 1969, 26; 29 May 1980, *NJW*. 1980, 2017. In the same sense the Italian decisions mentioned in the following note. *Greece*: Art. 291, Civil Code, *Venezuela* and *Lithuania*: see p. 308, n. 10. But in Austria and Germany damages for depreciation during the time of the debtor's default are allowed, see above, p. 286.

[17] Switzerland, Hungary, Italy, Romania, Yugoslavia, see p. 308, n. 10. In Switzerland it is, however, well established that the statutory provision does not relate to the quantum of the payment, but only to the quomodo, and that consequently the Swiss debtor who owes pounds sterling to his Swiss creditor and who may undoubtedly pay in Swiss francs, cannot effect the conversion at the rate of exchange of the day of maturity if the pound sterling has depreciated; though the statute would appear to justify a different result, in such circumstances the rate of exchange at the date of payment is decisive: see von Tuhr-Peter, *Allgemeiner Teil des schweizerischen Obligationenrechts* (3rd ed., 1979), i. 65 with further references, also Henggeler, *Zeitschrift für schweizerisches Recht*, 56 (1937), 228a. As to Hungary see the decision of the Supreme Court, 29 May 1934, *Zeitschrift für osteuropäisches Recht*, 1 (1936), 496. As to Italy compare Cass., 28 June 1924, Clunet, 1925, 485, and Cass., 10 July 1934, Clunet, 1935, 1051. In Italy it is well established that the defaulting debtor has to pay the difference between the rate at maturity and the rate at the date of payment; see the elaborate dicussion by Ascarelli, pp. 366 sqq., in particular p. 391, and the decisions of the Corte di Cassazione, 12 March 1953, No. 580, Giustizia Civile 1953, 830; 27 April 1954, No. 1296, ibid. 1954, 936; 21 June 1955, No. 1912, ibid. 1955, 1823. In Brazil (see Art. 947 of the Civil Code) the option is given to the creditor; he may demand payment in the foreign money or in Brazilian money at the rate of exchange of the day of maturity: Supreme Court, 22 May 1918, Clunet, 1921, 993.                    [18] And probably in Switzerland: see the preceeding note.

[19] See Cass. Req. 17 Feb. 1937, below, p. 312, n. 24. The statement of principle there quoted is identical with that laid down by Cass. Req., 11 July 1917, S. 1918, 1. 215 and also underlies Cass. Com., 30 April 1969, *Bull. Civ.* 1969, iv. No. 149. It is accepted by writers (see, for instance, Dayant, *Jurisclasseur*, Fasc. 552E, Nos. 43 sqq.), but it is difficult to see how in modern conditions French financial institutions and others can operate in practice if all payments in France have to be made in French francs, irrespective of contractual terms. Perhaps the principle, however categorically formulated, is intended to apply only as a matter of last resort, viz. in the event of the enforcement of judgment.

of the rate of exchange of the day of payment. But there may be cases (and, most significantly, they are cases where foreign money of account depreciates in terms of francs) in which the creditor may demand payment in francs at the rate of exchange of the day of maturity. A decision of the Cour de Cassation relating to the latter group seems to be the starting-point of the recent development. The plaintiff, a Reval merchant, had a claim of 10,045 roubles against the defendant, a Paris merchant, which the latter failed to pay, but in respect of which, long after maturity, he tendered to the creditor Russian bank-notes which were refused. Judgment was given for the franc equivalent of the roubles at the day when the writ was issued.[20] The Cour de Cassation said:[21]

> Attendu . . . qu'avec raison la Cour a refusé de valider les offres réelles de Schreter, faites à Paris en monnaie étrangère; que la Cour constate, en effet, *par une interprétation souveraine des conventions*, que le paiement devait être effectué en France; qu'il est de principe que *tout paiement fait en France*, quelle qu'en soit la cause, *doit être effectué en monnaie française* et qu'il n'apparait d'ailleurs en rien des circonstances retenues par les juges du fond que les parties aient entendu déroger à cette règle.[22]

In a second case[23] relating to roubles the conversion at the rate of exchange of the day of maturity was also approved of:

> le prêteur n'a droit au remboursement de ces roubles que d'après leur valeur au jour où il a fait au débiteur sommation de les payer.

More recently the same rule was applied to a case where a French debtor, having failed to pay at the due date the promised sum of dollars to his French creditor, desired to pay in dollars at a time when, it may be guessed, the dollar had depreciated:[24]

---

[20] Though it is recognized that the real choice lies between the day of maturity and the day of payment, this decision and some later ones have given rise to a discussion whether the rate of the 'jour de sommation' or of the 'jour de l'assignation' was, or might also be, considered; see the authors mentioned, p. 308, n. 10. But where the rate of these latter days was taken as a basis, this was done by the plaintiff, and as it was more favourable to the defendant, the courts were content to say that the rate of exchange of the day of payment was not to be adopted as of necessity.

[21] Req. 11 July 1917, S. 1918-19, 1. 215.

[22] Italics ours. Note that it is expressly emphasized that the payment was to be made in France.

[23] Cass. Civ. 25 Feb. 1929, Clunet, 1929, 1306; in the same sense, also relating to roubles, Cour de Douai, 15 Dec. 1927, Clunet, 1928, 675. See also the peculiar decision, Cass. Civ. 12 Apr. 1927, Clunet, 1928, 414, and S. 1927, 1. 293: a German creditor of a sum of marks, payable in 1914, brought an action in 1921 and demanded the franc equivalent at the rate of exchange prevailing in 1914. The defendant was only prepared to pay the depreciated value of 1921. His view was upheld on the ground that the plaintiff had waited too long until he demanded payment.

[24] Cass. Req. 17 Feb. 1937, Clunet, 1937, 766 and D.H. 1937, 234. See also Trib.

Mais attendu qu'après avoir constaté que les paiements devaient avoir lieu entre maisons françaises et sur territoire français, l'arrêt décide à bon droit que le règlement se réalisera par la remise d'un nombre de francs correspondant aux soldes débiteurs exprimés en dollars, ceux-ci étant convertis au cours du change à la date à laquelle le paiement aurait dû être effectué; qu'il est de principe, en effet, que tout paiement fait en France, quelle qu'en soit la cause, doit être effectué en monnaie française et que le solde d'un marché fixé en dollars doit être évalué selon le cours du dollar au jour où le débiteur devait payer.

In a greater number of decisions (in most of them, as far as could be ascertained, it was the franc which had depreciated) the debtor was given the right to pay in francs at the rate of exchange of the day of payment,[25] the Cour de Cassation always emphasizing that the judges of fact were to decide the question of interpretation.[26]

That the *Belgian* practice seems to be very similar to the French[27] is perhaps not so remarkable as the fact that in the *United States* also cognate ideas are discernible, although the position is by no means clear. The question whether the debtor of non-American

comm. du Havre, 21 June 1932, *Gaz. Pal.* 1933, 2. 30, relating to depreciated pounds: Court of Appeal at Réunion, 27 Apr. 1945, *Rev. Crit.* 1948, 91.

[25] Cass. Req. 8 Nov. 1922, Clunet, 1923, 576, and S. 1923, 1. 149; Cass. Civ. 9 Mar. 1925, D.H. 1925, 1329, and S. 1925, 1. 257 (5e espèce); Cass. Req. 16 June 1925, D.H. 1925, 498; Cass. Civ. 5 Dec. 1927, S. 1928, 1. 138; Cass. Req. 19 Mar. 1930, Clunet, 1931, 1082; Cass. Civ. 8 July 1931, Clunet, 1932, 721; Cass. Req. 25 July 1938, Clunet, 1939, 95; 3 May 1946, S. 1951, 1. 33 with note by Plaisant; Cour de Lyon, 8 June 1920, Clunet, 1922, 997; Cour de Paris, 18 Oct. 1922, Clunet, 1924, 119; Cour de Rouen, 26 Nov. 1924, Clunet, 1925, 672; Cour de Paris, 15 July 1925, Clunet, 1926, 658; 3 May 1926, Clunet, 1927, 1087; and, in particular, 20 Oct. 1952, *Rev. Crit.* 1953, 384 with note by Loussouarn. But there are also decisions relating to the pound sterling before its depreciation where the day of maturity was adopted: Cass. Req. 16 July 1929, Clunet, 1931, 646, and D.H. 1929, 161 affirming Cour de Douai, 12 July 1928, Clunet, 1929, 688 and the Conseil d'Etat, 28 Nov. 1958, Clunet 1960, 444. See also Cass. Civ. 10 Nov. 1929, S. 1928, 1. 57. Commenting on the decision of 16 July 1929, Professor Perroud observes: 'Somme toute on choisit la date le moins favorable au débiteur en faute.' See, however, Cour de Bordeaux, 21 Feb. 1938, Clunet, 1938, 58.

[26] See the decisions of 9 Mar. and 16 June 1925, 5 Dec. 1927, 19 Mar. 1930. See also Cass. Req. 10 Mar. 1925, Clunet, 1926, 70: 'qu'il appartenait aux juges du fond de déterminer, à raison des circonstances de la cause, la date à laquelle la dette de marks avait été convertie en dette de francs luxembourgeois'.

[27] See Piret, pp. 81-99, and the decisions there quoted. According to a decision of the Cour de Cassation (4 May 1922, *Bulletin de l'Institut belge de droit comparé*, 1923, 299) a question of construction is involved. Some decisions adopt the rate of exchange of the day of maturity, especially if the foreign money of account (mark, pound sterling) depreciates (Piret, p. 86). The majority, however, adopts that of the day of payment (Piret, pp. 87 sqq.), even in case of bills of exchange for which Art. 33 of the statute of 20 May 1872 provided for conversion 'au cours du change au jour de l'échéance' (Piret, pp. 91 sqq.). It is interesting to note that in Belgium an argument found expression which, in other countries too, was perhaps subconsciously used in favour of the rate of exchange of the day of maturity, namely, that the application of the rate of the day of payment would involve taking cognizance of the depreciation of the *moneta fori*, which would be contrary to an extreme nominalistic principle (see Piret, p. 87).

money who pays at the due date may or must pay in dollars cannot be answered with certainty. It seems, however, that procedural rules have given rise to the idea that all payments are to be made in dollars. Thus in a case where freight expressed in pounds sterling was payable at the place of destination within the United States it was said that payment was to be made 'of course in American money; our courts cannot give judgments in sterling currency'.[28] On the other hand, the effect of the debtor's default on a foreign money obligation has found a more secure solution. It was stated by Mr. Justice Holmes delivering the judgment of the Supreme Court of the United States in the case of *Hicks* v. *Guiness*.[29] On 31 December 1916 a German debtor owed to an American creditor a sum of 1,079·35 marks on an account stated; the creditor brought an action claiming the dollar equivalent at the rate of exchange prevailing on 31 December 1916. Mr. Justice Holmes said:[30]

> We are of opinion that the Courts below were right in holding that the plaintiffs were entitled to recover the value in dollars that the mark had when the account was stated. The debt was due to an American creditor *and was to be paid in the United States.* When the contract was broken by a failure to pay, the American firm had a claim here, *not for the debt, but, at its option, for damages in dollars. It no longer could be compelled to accept marks.* It had a right to say to the debtors, You are too late to perform what you have promised and we want the dollars to which we have a right by the law here in force . . . The event has come to pass upon which your liability becomes absolute as fixed by law. . . .

As was made clear in a later case,[31] these remarks were based on the assumption that the obligation was subject to the law of the United States. The rule laid down by *Hicks* v. *Guiness* is therefore this: if American law applies, if the place of payment is in America, and if the debtor does not pay the outstanding sum of foreign money at the due date, the creditor acquires an optional right to payment in dollars calculated at the rate of exchange prevailing on the day of breach.[32]

2. As regards the law of *England* there is now no statutory

---

[28] *Pennsylvania Railway Co.* v. *Cameron*, 280 Pa. 458, 124 A. 638 (Supreme Court of Pennsylvania, 1924).

[29] (1925) 269 U.S. 71.

[30] p. 80; italics supplied.

[31] *Deutsche Bank Filiale Nürnberg* v. *Humphreys* (1926), 272 U.S. 517 at p. 519 *per* Mr. Justice Holmes delivering the opinion of the majority of the court. *Sutherland* v. *Mayer* (1926), 271 U.S. 272 was also distinguished on the ground that there American law applied.

[32] That the option to demand payment in the foreign money, which would be useful in case of a subsequent depreciation of the dollar, is of no real value, because an action can only be brought for dollars, will be shown below, p. 340 sqq.

provision.[33] In theory three solutions are conceivable: the debtor may be under a duty to tender foreign money only; or he may have to tender sterling only; or he may have the option of tendering foreign money or sterling.[34] All that can be said with a measure of confidence about the English common law is that, in accordance with universal practice, the first solution does not prevail;[35] there is, in fact, no trace of it in any case or work of authority here or elsewhere.[36] The second solution has, as appears,[37] a counterpart in France where all payments must be made in francs, yet it is unattractive, for it is difficult to see why the law should preclude

[33] S. 72 (4) of the Bills of Exchange Act, 1882 (on which see such cases as *Syndic in Bankruptcy* v. *Khayat*, [1943] A.C. 507 or *Barclays International Ltd.* v. *Levin Bros.*, [1977] Q.B. 270, was repealed by s. 4 of the Administration of Justice Act, 1977 (together with certain other provisions). S. 139 of the Merchant Shipping Act, 1894 was repealed by the Merchant Shipping Act, 1970; it dealt with seamen's wages in regard to which the common law was laid down by *The Nonpareil* (1864), 33 L.J. Ad. 201 and *The Annie Sherwood* (1865), 12 L.T. 582.

[34] This discussion, of course, disregards the effects of exchange control which in certain cases, in certain countries, and at certain times may influence the operation of the common law, here as elsewhere, but should not be regarded as a permanent or universal feature.

[35] It would be surprising if it applied and the creditor could reject a tender of sterling, his own currency. The U.S. debtor who has agreed to pay dollars in London would either have to tender notes (which, to put it at its lowest, the law should not encourage) or a dollar cheque or draft which the creditor would have to send to the United States for collection. While, normally, he may be ready to accept a tender otherwise than in cash, such delay and uncertainty are likely to make him prefer cash, particularly, when, under a system of exchange control, he has in any event to surrender the dollars to the Treasury against cash.

[36] It would be wrong to attach any weight to the mere assumption in *Marrache* v. *Ashton*, [1943] A.C. 311, 317 that a debtor who tenders Spanish pesetas in Gibraltar would specifically perform his obligation to deliver a commodity, and that a breach of his duty involves the liability to pay damages. Subject to what may be inferred from this case the theory mentioned in the text was not suggested at any time or place except by banking experts who gave evidence to the Lord Chancellor's Private International Law Committee, when it was considering the International Law Association's 'Dubrovnik Rules' (above, p. 309, n. 11): Cmnd. 1648 (1962). The majority of the Committee reports (para. 5) that the experts made it clear 'that commercial practice is based on the assumption that, as a matter of substantive law, a debtor's obligation is to pay his debt in the currency in which he has undertaken to pay and that, in practice, s. 72 (4) is of very limited application. This view was maintained even though it was recognized that . . . where there is default by the debtor and proceedings are taken by the creditor in this country the court cannot give judgment in any currency other than sterling.' This was the principal reason for which, considering any other solution 'lamentable', the majority of the Committee, 'in entire agreement with the views of the commercial community on this important practical issue', rejected Art. 1 of the 'Dubrovnik Rules' (para. 11), without considering Arts. 2–5 or 9–11. It is possible that the experts directed their attention not so much to payments in England as to the situation in which an English exporter sells to Ruritania for sterling payable there and in which the buyer might pay in (possibly blocked) local currency. Such reasoning would overlook that it is beyond the power of England to control foreign law, that this is in any event likely to be in line with universal practice and that the English exporter who agrees to payment in Ruritania rather than England may not necessarily be worthy of protection.

[37] Above, p. 311.

a debtor from tendering what he has undertaken to tender; and if as a result of some express stipulation there may be a duty to tender foreign currency, the absence of such a term cannot very well have the effect of excluding the mere right to do so.[38] There thus remains only the classical solution which allows the debtor an option of discharging his obligation in either of two ways. This, in fact, is the English rule: 'I think it is clear that when someone is under an obligation to pay another a sum of money expressed in a foreign currency but to pay it in this country, the person under the obligation has an option, if he is to fulfil his obligation at the date when the money is payable, either to produce the appropriate amount in the foreign currency in question or to pay the equivalent in sterling at the rate of exchange prevailing at the due date. This proposition seems to me to be elementary and a matter of common sense.'[39] The earlier authorities do not usually state the law in this way: they imply it, however, by taking it for granted that the debtor would in fact and can in law pay in sterling (or whatever the *moneta loci solutionis* may be);[40] thus Warrington L.J. said on one occasion[41] 'that the payment having to be made in London would be a payment in sterling', while on another occasion[42] Lord Warrington stated 'that monetary obligations are effectually discharged by payment

---

[38] Again it would be wrong to read too much into an observation by Lord Reid in *National Mutual Life Association of Australasia* v. *Attorney-General for New Zealand*, [1956] A.C. 369, 389 that 'all payments which had to be made in Melbourne must be made in Australian currency'. Rigaux, *Droit International Privé Belge* (2nd ed., 1979), No. 1144, suggests that in accordance with a law of 12 April 1957 'pour être libératoire un paiement doit être fait en francs eblges sur le territoire belge.' But does not Art. 3 of the law of 1957 like similar laws simply mean that if Belgian francs have to be paid in Belgium 'les billets de la Banque Nationale de Belgique doivent être reçus comme monnaie légale'?

[39] *Barclays International Ltd.* v. *Levin Bros.* (1977), Q.B. 270, at p. 277 *per* Mocatta J., whose reference to the date of maturity would seem to need revision (see p. 317, n. 45). In the same sense, Dicey and Morris, Rule 177 (2). (It is odd that the Rule is not so formulated as to make it clear that it is only a presumption.) Substantially in the same sense Cheshire and North, p. 248; Graveson, *The Discharge of Foreign Money Obligations in the English Courts* in *The Conflict of Laws and International Contracts* (Michigan, 1951), pp. 116–19; Wolff, *Private International Law*, s. 447; Nussbaum, p. 361; Rabel, *The Conflict of Laws*, iii (1950), pp. 26, 27.

[40] *Ralli Brothers* v. *Compañía Naviera Sota y Aznar*, [1920] 2 K.B. 287, at p. 291 *per* Lord Sterndale M.R., at p. 294 *per* Warrington L.J., at p. 299 *per* Scrutton L.J.; *Rhokana Corporation Ltd.* v. *Inland Revenue Commissioners*, [1937] 1 K.B. 737, at p. 797 *per* Lord Wright (reversed on other grounds, [1938] A.C. 380); *New Brunswick Railway Co.* v. *British & French Trust Corporation*, [1939] A.C. 1, at p. 23.

[41] *Anderson* v. *Equitable Assurance Society of the United States of America* (1926), 134 L.T. 557, at p. 564.

[42] *Adelaide Electric Supply Company Ltd.* v. *Prudential Assurance Company Ltd.*, [1934] A.C. 122, at p. 138. It will be remembered (see above, p. 237) that from the point of view of the majority of the Law Lords, this case is to be treated as one relating to the money of payment rather than the money of account.

of that which is legal tender in the *locus solutionis*'. In a similar vein Bankes L.J. emphasized that a question of construction was involved.[43]

In my experience I have never heard the proposition challenged that in an ordinary commercial contract where a person has entered into a contract which is to be governed by English law and has undertaken an obligation to pay in foreign currency a certain sum in this country the true construction of that contract is that when the time comes for payment the amount having to be paid in this country will be paid in sterling, but at the rate of exchange of the day when payment is due, applicable to the particular currency to which the contract refers.

Accordingly it does not seem unreasonable, in deviation from an old case,[44] to commend the debtor's opion as the appropriate solution, seeing, in particular, that the creditor may contract in terms of sterling if he does not in any event wish to be paid in foreign money.

If and in so far as conversion takes place, the date with reference to which the exchange is to be calculated raises another, no less difficult, yet much more important problem, for though, as has been said, the creditor is usually not interested in the quomodo, a difference in quantum should not be imposed upon him. Fortunately it is now possible to suggest with confidence that the conversion is to be effected at the rate of exchange at the day of payment. 'This is the clear result of the *Miliangos* case.'[45] It is the rate at the date of actual payment, as opposed to the rate at the date when payment ought to be made, that should govern.[46]

There remains the question how legacies given by the will of a testator domiciled in England and expressed in a foreign currency are to be paid. This problem falls into two parts, namely, whether it is necessary or permissible to effect a conversion, and, if so, at what rate of exchange the conversion is to be carried out. The answer to the former question should be in the negative where the legatee lives abroad and is to be paid a specific sum; in such

---

[43] *Anderson*'s case (above, n. 41), at p. 562, followed by the Court of Appeal in *Heisler* v. *Anglo-Dal Ltd.*, [1954] 1 W.L.R. 1273.

[44] *Willshalge* v. *Davidge*, 1 Leon. 41: where a creditor was entitled to 'ducats' and 'portugues', it was 'in his election' to demand payment of his debt either in the proper coin of the contract or in sterling. To confer the option on the creditor and thus to leave the debtor in a state of uncertainty would be impracticable.

[45] *George Veflings Rederi A/S* v. *President of India* (1979), 1 W.L.R. 59, at p. 63 *per* Lord Denning M.R. The full implications of the *Miliangos* case will be considered below p. 347. In the sense of the text Dicey and Morris, p. 1013 who, however, mention a number of cases the authority of which was swept away by the *Miliangos* case, a decision which necessitates rethinking the whole subject.

[46] More on the rate of exchange below, p. 347.

a case[47] the pecuniary legacy is to be discharged as directed. But if the legatee lives in Britain or if special directions are given with a view to retaining the legacy here, then, according to established judicial practice, the amount is to be converted into sterling at the rate prevailing at the end of the 'executor's year'. The case of *Oppenheimer* v. *Public Trustee*[48] dealt with the direction of a testator that his trustees should out of the proceeds of the sale of the estate set apart two sums of marks as legacies, invest them in British securities, and hold them on trust for the German legatees and their issue; the trustees were given a very full power of postponement. The testator died in 1900, but it was not until 1924, when the mark had become valueless, that the trustees, having postponed the sale and conversion of the estate, were in a position to appropriate these legacies. They purported to appropriate them by setting apart a nominal sum of pounds sterling, which at that date represented the value of the two sums of German marks. It was held both by Eve J. and the Court of Appeal that it was with reference to the last day of the 'executor's year' that the quantum of each of these legacies ought to have been ascertained and that it was immaterial that the trustees had a power of postponement. On the assumption that the legacies were, in fact, expressed in German marks, not in pounds sterling,[49] the *ratio decidendi* was derived from the rule that generally an executor need not satisfy a legacy until the expiration of one year after the testator's death.[50] Independently of this decision Eve J. arrived at the same result in the later case of *In re Eighmie, Colbourne v. Wilks*.[51] An American citizen domiciled in England had given a legacy of 25,000 dollars to a British legatee. The petition asked whether it ought to be satisfied by the payment of sums of the equivalent value in sterling calculated at the rate of exchange existing on the death of the testatrix, or at the expiration of one year thereafter, or on the day when the payment was made. Applying the rule that a legacy does not become payable until the expiration of one year after the testator's death, Eve J. decided in favour of

[47] The distinction drawn in the text is suggested by Dicey and Morris, p. 630. It merits approval and should, in particular, attract those who continue to regard foreign money as a commodity. It was for this (unconvincing) reason that the New York Court of Appeals rightly held in *Matter of Lendle* (1929), 250 N.Y. 502, 166 N.E. 182, that 'mark' legacies given by a New York testator to German relatives had to be satisfied 'in kind' and that no question of conversion arose.

[48] Below, p. 567.

[49] To some extent the decision also rested on the ground that the legacies were, in fact, expressed in sterling, in which case, of course, the problem now under discussion could not arise: see above, p. 224.

[50] s. 44, Administration of Estates Act, 1925; Halsbury (Hailsham), xvii No. 1232; Roper, *On Legacies* (4th ed., 1847), p. 863.          [51] [1935] Ch. 524.

the second alternative.[52] It is submitted, however, that the decision is now of doubtful authority. There is no reason why there should have been any conversion at all and if the executor desired to pay sterling he should have converted at the rate of exchange at the date of actual payment. This, again, is implied in the *Miliangos* case.[53]

3. In all legal systems it is clear that the conversion of a foreign money obligation into the money of the place of payment may be excluded by the parties; this is particularly so in the case of bills of exchange.[54] The German Civil Code, for example, requires an 'express' exclusion,[55] while in France it is said that conversion is excluded if the foreign money is regarded as a commodity.[56] This seems to mean that a problem of construction is involved,[57] which is also the English solution.[58] If a different intention appears,[59] the debtor is bound to tender the stipulated foreign currency and is precluded from tendering the *moneta loci solutionis*. Such a different intention may readily be inferred from the terms of the contract and the surrounding circumstances. It would be quite wrong to require definite indications in the contractual terms; it is the intention of the parties that matters. This may be influenced by the incidence of a system of exchange control which may, but does not by any means necessarily, render transferability to the creditor's country dependent upon the existence of a duty to pay

---

[52] The learned judge referred to Roper l.c., p. 862; but this seems to be due to an oversight, for the author there discusses the rule that, where conversion is necessary, the rate, not the par of exchange, must be applied, and the authority for that rule, *Cockerell* v. *Barber* (1810), 16 Ves. 461, on which see below, p. 436.

[53] On which see below, p. 347. Dicey and Morris, p. 630 treat the case as still being good law, but agree that it requires reconsideration.

[54] Since the abolition of s. 72 (4) of the Bills of Exchange Act, 1882, there is no express provision in England. The so-called 'effective clause' is, however, very usual in the law of bills of exchange throughout the world and there is no reason why it could not be added to an English bill. In particular, such a clause would not deprive the promise to pay which a bill of exchange expresses of its unconditional character.

[55] s. 244. There is an extensive line of Supreme Court decisions relating to the definition of the term 'express'; see the collection by Staudinger–Weber, *Kommentar zum Bürgerlichen Gesetzbuch*, s. 244, n. 61.

[56] Planiol–Ripert, vii, No. 1161.

[57] Thus, if an agent, particularly a banker, is instructed to collect a foreign money debt, it will usually be the proper interpretation of the agreement that it is the collected foreign money which must be paid over to the principal and that the agent is not entitled to convert the money into his or the principal's domestic currency: *French* Cass. Req. 9 Mar. 1925, D.H. 1925, 237 (allowing, however, conversion of dollars collected by a London firm on behalf of a French firm into francs at the rate of exchange of the day of payment); *German* Supreme Court, 10 Jan. 1925, *RGZ*. 110, 48; *Belgium*: see Piret, No. 24.

[58] See the statement of Bankes L.J. (above, p. 317). Dicey and Morris, p. 1014 should perhaps more clearly distinguish between English municipal law and the conflict of laws.

[59] This is the phrase used, for instance, in Art. 1 of the Annex to the European Convention on Foreign Money Liabilities: below, p. 578.

actual foreign currency. As Somervell L.J. said,[60] if and so long as the foreign currency in question is not freely obtainable, it may well defeat the intention of the parties 'to construe contracts in those circumstances as giving the payer the option to pay in sterling'. It is probably appropriate to suggest that, whenever the exercise of the debtor's option to pay in the *moneta loci solutionis* affects not only the mode, but also the quantum of the payment, it is likely to be excluded.

4. The problem of determining the money of payment causes particular difficulties in case of a conflict of laws. Suppose under an English contract 'pounds' are promised to be paid in Cairo.[61] English law would decide the question whether English or Egyptian pounds are the money of account.[62] Under English law, as the proper law of the contract, the promise to pay English 'pounds' in Cairo would be discharged by payment of the appropriate number of Egyptian pounds.[63] But should the latter point not be decided by the law of the place of payment? In other words, should the rule of English municipal law that a monetary obligation is discharged by tendering the *money* of the place of payment be extended to a rule of private international law that the determination of the money of payment (not of the money of account) falls to be decided by the *law* of the place of payment? The problem is the same in the simpler case where the two units of account do not bear the same name: if under an English contract pounds are payable in Paris, the problem arises whether it is the proper law of the contract or the law of the place of payment which decides whether pounds or francs are to be tendered in discharge of the debt.

This situation involves two distinct questions: which is the legal system that determines whether there exists a right or a duty to convert the money of account into the (local) money of payment? which is the legal system that governs the mechanics of the conversion (the type of the rate of exchange to be employed, the date and the place with reference to which the rate is to be ascertained)?[64]

---

[60] *Heisler* v. *Anglo-Dal Ltd.*, [1954] 1 W.L.R. 1273, 1278, where, let it be repeated, the Court of Appeal accepted the statement of the rule by Bankes L.J. in *Anderson's* case, above, p. 317, n. 43. Usually the creditor is interested in transferability only and this is almost always determined by the existence of the necessary licence rather than the identity of the money of payment.

[61] Unlike the Australian and New Zealand pound, on which see above, p. 54 sqq., there cannot be much doubt that the Egyptian pound was not at any time identical with the English pound.

[62] See above, p. 233.                                      [63] See above, p. 316.

[64] For an illuminating comparative study of the problem (as well as the questions of municipal law discussed in the preceding paragraphs of the text) see Birk, *AWD* 1973,

As regards the first point it is necessary to repeat that, except in unusual circumstances, the creditor suffers no prejudice from payment in the *moneta loci solutionis*. It is suggested, therefore, that in general, i.e. where no problem of construction arises, the question of the right or duty of conversion may be treated as one relating to the mode of performance and, consequently, subject to the *lex loci solutionis*.[65] The decision on the second point, however, is liable to encroach severely upon the substance of the obligation: whether the creditor who is entitled to be paid 1,000 Spanish pesetas in Gibraltar must accept the pound equivalent calculated at the rate of peseta notes or of cable transfers to Madrid, or calculated with reference to the rate prevailing at the date of maturity or payment, or calculated at the Gibraltar or Madrid rate—these are substantial matters on which the quantum eventually received by the creditor depends, if payment is not made in actual pesetas. These aspects, therefore, cannot be described as relating merely to the mode of performance, but ought to be subject to the proper law of the contract.[66]

### III

When we now come to the examination of the questions relating to the concept of payment, i.e. to what constitutes a payment, we find that the discussion can be confined to a few, selected topics.

1. In so far as the municipal law relating to the discharge of

425. In *France* it is said by writers of authority 'que la loi du lieu de paiement détermine la monnaie de règlement, c'est-à-dire la monnaie en laquelle le débiteur devra ou pourra se libérer': Batiffol-Lagarde No. 613, in the same sense Loussouarn-Borel, *Droit International Privé* (1978), No. 384, who add that 'l'application de la loi du paiement n'est pas considerée comme impérative.' There is, however, no decision laying down such a principle. The rule referred to above, p. 312, n. 24 is applicable to payments in France only. It is possible that these writers have become subject to a confusion between payment at the place of payment and payment under the law of the place of payment.

[65] In the same sense Dicey and Morris, Rule 177, and (probably) Cheshire and North, p. 248. The control of the proper law is favoured by Wolff, *Private International Law*, 2nd ed. (1950), p. 461; Graveson, 'Foreign Monetary Obligations in English Courts', in *The Conflict of Law and International Contracts* (Ann Arbor, 1951), p. 118; Nussbaum, p. 361.

[66] In the same sense, Dicey and Morris, l.c., and Graveson, l.c., who, however, makes the not altogether clear reservation that 'the actual possibility, legality and process of exchange' should be subject to the *lex loci solutionis*. See, generally, Lord Wright's warning, above, p. 216, n. 148. Anton, *Private International Law* (Edinburgh, 1967), p. 230, seems to advocate the application of the rate of exchange at the place of payment. Wolff and Nussbaum do not discuss the question in terms, but would probably agree with the suggestion in the text. For a thorough discussion of the problem mentioned in the text with reference to German private international law see Melchior, *Grundlagen des internationalen Privatrechts*, pp. 285 sqq. and Mayer, *Valutaschuld*, p. 101.

obligations in general and to the discharge by payment in particular is concerned, this forms a substantial part of the law of contracts as a whole. Most of the problems of purely monetary character have been discussed above.[67] There are only two aspects of the conception of payment which, in connection with foreign money obligations, require specific discussion.

(a) How, in principle, is a foreign money obligation to be paid? The answer is: just as a sterling debt must, except with the express or implied consent of the creditor, be discharged by the payment of legal tender, so a foreign money obligation is prima facie payable in legal tender of the *lex monetae*. This is inherent in the nominalistic principle as understood in England. It does not only define the quantum of the obligation, but also the form of payment. Thus it was held that the obligation to repay a loan of pesetas involved the duty 'to pay in whatever at the date of repayment was legal tender and legal currency in the country whose money was lent';[68] and this, of course, is so irrespective of whether the loan was originally made by paying notes to the borrower or by drawing a cheque in his favour or by making a bank transfer to his credit. The debtor, it is true, may be entitled to pay in sterling.[69] Moreover, the creditor may waive this right to the payment in (foreign or domestic) legal tender and accept payment by cheque or bank transfer. Yet, as a matter of contractual duty this is not what the law envisages as the primary forms of discharge. There are probably many business men to whom the legal principle will come as a surprise, and it is undeniable that, in modern conditions and particularly where large sums are involved, it discloses some lack of realism. But such comment loses force if it is remembered that it is equally apposite to the discharge of sterling obligations in regard to which, in the absence of agreement, the necessity for payment in legal tender cannot be doubted.

(b) Does the ability of the debtor of a foreign money obligation to discharge his debt by paying[70] the agreed amount in foreign currency subsist even after breach? The question is by no means wholly academic. Where payment has to be made in this country, the debtor, it is true, will at maturity often be at liberty to discharge his obligation in sterling at the rate of exchange of the day when

---

[67] pp. 70 sqq.

[68] *Pyrmont Ltd.* v. *Schott*, [1939] A.C. 145, at p. 153 *per* Lord Porter; for similar statements see above, p. 271, n. 13.                                    [69] Above, p. 316.

[70] In *re British American Continental Bank Ltd., Lisser & Rosenkranz's Claim*, [1923] 1 Ch. 276, the liquidator tendered a large sum of marks, but it was rejected. Accordingly he did not pay, and mere tender was held to be insufficient.

payment is made;[71] but, as has been explained, this depends on the construction of the contract and there may, therefore, be cases in which the debtor wishes after maturity to tender the foreign money of account. It is also possible that the debtor, having repudiated his obligation to pay, later wishes to discharge his liability to pay damages by paying the amount of foreign currency originally due from him.[72]

The decision of the Court of Appeal in *Société des Hôtels Le Touquet* v. *Cummings*[73] justifies and, indeed, necessitates the conclusion that after repudiation a foreign money obligation remains capable of being discharged by payment rather than accord and satisfaction. In 1914 the defendant had contracted in France an English[74] debt to the plaintiffs of 18,035 francs, which was to be paid before the end of that year. The defendant having failed to pay, the plaintiffs in 1919, when the value of francs had fallen heavily, commenced an action in this country claiming the amount of sterling which would have been the equivalent of the amount of francs at the end of 1914. While the action was pending the defendant went to France and handed 18,035 francs to the manager of the plaintiffs, who knew nothing about the transaction and who therefore signed a receipt 'as for money deposited with him'.[75] The defendant then pleaded satisfaction. Avory J. held[76] that the plaintiffs were entitled to the sum in English money which was equivalent to the sum of French francs on 31 December 1914 less the value of the amount paid calculated at the rate existing on the day of payment, since this amount was not intended by the plaintiffs to be accepted in discharge and satisfaction of their claim. The Court of Appeal reversed the decision.

Bankes L.J. said[77] that, as the manager had authority to receive the money, as he knew the debtor was paying it in discharge of a debt due to the company, and as the creditor knew all the facts and kept the money without protest, the plea of payment was made

---

[71] Above, p. 371 sqq.

[72] In *New Brunswick Rly. Co.* v. *British & French Trust Corporation*, [1939] A.C. 1, although the case relates to the repudiation of a gold clause, Lord Russell of Killowen said that after repudiation the debtor could 'only tender damages' (p. 29). But it is doubtful whether damages are capable of being tendered.

[73] [1922] 1 K.B. 451.

[74] At p. 463 *per* Atkin L.J. For a proper understanding of the *Le Touquet* case it is important to remember that there was no evidence of French law before the court and that, therefore, the Court was bound to proceed on the footing of English law. Scrutton L.J. in *Lloyd Royal Belge* v. *Louis Dreyfus & Co.* (1927), 27 Ll. L.R. 288, 293 and Younger L.J. in *Re Chesterman's Trust*, [1923] 2 Ch. 466, 493 suggested that it was a distinguishing feature of the *Le Touquet* case that the contract was in every sense a French contract. In truth it was treated as an English contract.    [75] See p. 452.

[76] [1921] 3 K.B. 459.    [77] p. 456.

out, it being immaterial to consider whether the person to whom the money was paid knew what the amount of the debt was or whether or not an action had been commenced to recover it, and it being unnecessary to prove accord and satisfaction, since the claim was not one for damages, but for a debt which had been satisfied.

Scrutton L.J. adopted a different line of argument. He asked two questions:[78] (1) Is such a payment, when retained by the plaintiffs, accord and satisfaction, so as to be a defence to the action? (2) Were the plaintiffs, who received in France the amount of their debt in francs in 1920, entitled to claim in addition such a sum of English money as made up their receipts to the value of that number of francs in English money in 1914 when it was due? The learned Lord Justice held that there was here no accord and satisfaction.[79] He proceeded to consider the second question and arrived at the result[80] that 'the plaintiffs who were owned 18,035 francs payable in France, must be content with 18,035 francs paid in France'.

Atkin L.J. (as he then was) also held that there was no accord and satisfaction.[81] He rejected the suggestion that

for the purposes of the English Court once a writ was issued the debt of francs payable in France became a debt of sterling at the rate of exchange of 31 December 1914, payable in England, and that such debt was not paid. . . . If such were the effect of the transaction, it would follow that the defendant on 1 January 1915 incurred obligations to pay the plaintiffs sum in the manifold currencies of the many countries in the world where she might eventually be sued. It appears to me that she was sued here for a French debt, and it you please for nominal damages, and that by paying the debt in France, she discharged the debt.

Later he added:[82]

For the purposes of this action I have not thought it necessary to decide at what date the exchange should be calculated had the plaintiffs succeeded. The same result follows though the exchange should be calculated as at the date when payment became due. But no case that I know of has yet decided what the position is when a foreign creditor, to whom a debt is due in his country in the currency of his country, comes to sue his debtor in the Courts of this country for the foreign debt. Much may be said for the proposition that the debtor's obligation is to pay, say, francs, and so continues until the debt is merged in the judgment which should give him the English equivalent at that

---

[78] p. 459.

[79] p. 460. The misunderstanding of P. O. Lawrence J. in the *Crédit Liégeosis case*, [1922] 2 Ch. 589, 596, was corrected by Scrutton L.J. in *The Baarn* (No. 1), [1933] P. 251, 265.

[80] p. 461.     [81] p. 464.     [82] p. 465.

date of those francs. It is a problem which seems to require very full consideration, and which I personally should desire to reserve.

In effect all three Lord Justices agreed that, accord and satisfaction being unnecessary, a claim for 18,035 French francs was 'paid' and that therefore the action failed.

This decision which, it is submitted with deference, clearly conforms to principle[83] and good sense,[84] still lays down the law of England. In unknown quarters it seems to have aroused criticism.[85] Its implications, it is true, have not been fully recognized and accepted in later cases and to this extent its authority stands somewhat diminished. But the narrow point which it expressly establishes and with which alone the present observations are concerned, cannot, and ought not to be, challenged.[86] Admittedly, the *Le Touquet* case may not apply where the claim is for unliquidated damges,[87] but this is a different case which in the present context does not arise.

2. When we come to private international law relating to payment, it is a well-established principle of English private international law that the question whether a certain payment operates as a discharge of an obligation is governed by the proper law,[88] the only

---

[83] Any other solution would have been wholly inconsistent with the nominalistic principle.

[84] As Atkin L.J. pointed out (above, p. 324, n. 81) it would be absurd to suggest that upon non-payment the defendant became liable to pay 'sums in the manifold currencies of the many countries of the world where she might eventually be sued'. There was never any warrant for Somervell L.J.'s suggestion in *Cummings* v. *London Bullion Co. Ltd.*, [1952] 1 K.B. 327, at p. 335, that, if legal proceedings are instituted, it could 'be said with force that an obligation to pay the sterling equivalent arises on that date'.

[85] See Scrutton L.J. in *Lloyd Royal Belge* v. *Louis Dreyfus & Co.* (1929), 27 Ll. L.R. 288, 293 ('some doubt had been expressed in various quarters'); see also Greer L.J. in *The Baarn* (No. 1), [1933] P. 251, 271 who found it 'not easy to reconcile' the *Le Touquet* case with *The Volturno*, [1921] 2 A.C. 544.

[86] On this point the decision was followed in an interesting New York case: *Transamerica General Corporation* v. *Zunino*, 82 N.Y.S. (2d) 595 (1948).

[87] Where a claim for unliquidated damages arises under English law it is inherent in the English conception of damages that discharge by 'payment' is impossible. For this reason the conception of payment may be confined to debts. In *The Baarn* (No. 1), [1933] P. 215, 271 Greer L.J. said: 'Assuming for the sake of simplicity a claim is made in an English Court for tort or breach of contract happening in France, say to the extent of 1,000 francs, and the damages were incurred when the exchange was 25 francs to the £, judgment in accordance with the decision in *The Volturno* would necessarily be for £20. Proof by the defendant that he had paid to the plaintiff in France 1,000 francs at a time when they were depreciated and were only worth £8 could not be regarded by an English Court as payment in full of the damages proved to have been sustained.' It is assumed that Greer L.J. was speaking of a liability arising under English law. Even if his remarks can be so qualified, they conclusively prove the unsatisfactory results produced by a conceptualist approach. The necessity for accord and satisfaction should be confined to cases in which damages are at large. Where damages are calculable and calculated, they should be capable of being paid.

[88] Dicey and Morris, p. 818; Cheshire and North, p. 241; on p. 712, however, Cheshire

exception concerns the extinction of a debt by way of a set-off, which is likely to be exclusively governed by English law as the *lex fori*.[89] But however clear the principle may be, it has caused difficulties in three groups of cases which require consideration.

(*a*) It follows from the general rule that the question whether *accord and satisfaction* in the technical sense of English law is necessary or not depends on the proper law, and this has been expressly laid down in *Ralli* v. *Dennistoun*.[90] Accordingly, it depends on the proper law of the obligation whether, and with what effects, tender and payment may be made in respect of a claim for unliquidated damages, and it is irrelevant that under English law no payment, but only accord and satisfaction, is possible in respect of such a claim.[91]

This view is not shaken by a dictum of Maugham L.J. (as he then was), who said:[92]

> It is well settled that the procedure in any action brought in this Court must be governed by the *lex fori*, and it is settled, as a reference to Dicey's *Conflict of Laws*, 5the ed., p. 857 will show, that if the defendant tries to set up a set-off which is not allowed by English law, the set-off is not permitted. It is obvious that if the defendant is defending on the ground of accord and satisfaction he must prove accord and satisfaction according to our procedure. . . .

It is fairly clear that Maugham L.J. was there referring only to the manner of proving accord and satisfaction, in which case he was clearly right in emphasizing that that relates to procedure and is governed by English law. The question whether under the proper law accord and satisfaction is necessary and whether certain facts, proved according to English law of procedure, amount to an accord and satisfaction, relates to substantive law and was not touched upon by the Lord Justice.

(*b*) The effect of a plea of *tender* may be twofold. It may mean that under some foreign legal system tender could be made and resulted in the discharge, or at least in an alteration of the structure, of a monetary obligation. In this case the proper law should govern.[93]

and North seem to take a different view with regard to cases where the payment is made after action has been brought in this country. They there state that, as the quantification of the amount payable is governed by the *lex fori*, that legal system must also decide 'whether in its view payment has in effect already been made'. But it is suggested that *The Baarn* (No. 1), [1933] P. 251, which seems to have been responsible for this view, does not necessitate such a conclusion, which would involve an unfortunate extension of the ambit of the *lex fori*: see below, pp. 328, 329.

[89] Cheshire and North, p. 707; but see Dicey and Morris, p. 1194 whose discussion does not do justice to the problem.

[90] (1851) 6 Ex. 483.                                              [91] Above, p. 70.

[92] *The Baarn* (No. 2), [1943] P. 171, 185.

[93] *In re British American Contential Bank Ltd., Lisser & Rosenkranz's Claim*, [1923]

On the other hand, the plea may mean that by offering the amount due to the creditor the debtor has procured for himself the advantages of a plea of tender in the English sense which, if accompanied by a payment into court, merely entitles the debtor to the costs of the action.[94] Such a plea must be considered in the light of English law as the *lex fori*.

The dictum of Maugham L.J. to which reference is made in the preceding paragraph continues: 'The same thing must be true as regards an alleged tender', and in a later case Lord Maugham L.C. (as he had then become) said:[95]

> I am of opinion that the questions that arise as to the validity or form of a tender, or the advantage of making one in a particular forum, are questions of procedure for the *lex fori*. There may well be special rules in different countries.

It was for this reason that Lord Maugham held that a creditor enforcing a gold clause in England could not be defeated by a Canadian statute according to which 'tender of the nominal or face amount of the obligation [governed by Canadian law] in currency which is legal tender for the payment of debts in the country in the money of which the obligation is payable, shall be a legal tender and the debtor shall, on making payment in accordance with such tender, be entitled to a discharge of the obligation'. It is submitted, with respect, that this amounts to a misinterpretation of the word 'tender' in the Canadian statute. The Canadian legislator clearly intended to effect a reduction, or a discharge *pro tanto*, of certain obligations subject to Canadian law. He did not envisage any interference with the conception of tender in the procedural law of England or any other country. There is, therefore, no justification for Lord Maugham's opinion that upon its true construction the Canadian statute must be confined to cases 'where the action to recover the amount due is brought in Canada'. The opinion, it is submitted, rests upon a failure to distinguish between the different meanings of 'tender'.

(*c*) Finally, the proper law of the obligation should also govern the question whether the method of paying a debt by depositing the amount due with a court (*consignation*), which is known to continental countries and their followers, is available in a given case

---

1 Ch. 276, a tender of marks was made at Hamburg. The question whether its effect fell to be considered by English or German law was not discussed.

[94] Chitty, *On Contracts* (24th ed., 1977), No. 1323.

[95] *New Brunswick Rly. Co.* v. *British and French Trust Corporation*, [1939] A.C. 1, at pp. 23, 24.

and whether such deposit amounts to discharge.[96] It is submitted that this is the reasoning on which the two difficult cases of *The Baarn*[97] were decided.

Both cases arose out of a collision which took place, on what English law regards as the high seas,[98] between a Chilean vessel, owned by a company domiciled in Chile, and a Dutch vessel, owned by the defendants, a Dutch firm. The defendants made a formal admission of liability, which under the Rules of Supreme Court had the effect of an order of the court without being equivalent to a judgment.[99] The plaintiffs instituted proceedings before the registrar to ascertain the amount of damages for expenses incurred by them in Chile in Chilean currency for the repair of the Chilean vessel. In the course of these proceedings the defendants deposited the amount of Chilean pesos spent by the plaintiffs with the proper court in Chile according to certain provisions of the Chilean Code. The question therefore arose whether their liability was thereby discharged.

The economic background of the ensuing litigation can only be understood if it is remembered that the Chilean currency was a 'frozen currency', that is to say that money could not be freely transferred from Chilean territory and that therefore the value of blocked accounts held within the territory was quoted abroad at a discount, although the official rate of exchange was unaltered and although, inside the territory, the money had an undiminished purchasing power.[100]

Langton J., after a careful review of the evidence as to Chilean law, which he assumed to be applicable, arrived at the result 'that this payment is good according to Chilean law'.

On appeal his judgment was reversed. Scrutton L.J., having considered the evidence, took the view 'that there is no final decision by the Chilean court that the payment in depreciated pesos is sufficient while proceedings are pending in London'. Greer L.J. said that, though according to Chilean law a payment was made, it was not established that it had the effect of extinguishing the debt; therefore, in his judgment, 'treating what has happened in Chile as a

---

[96] This was expressly so held by the Supreme Court of the United States in *Zimmerman* v. *Sutherland* (1927), 274 U.S. 253. In the same sense Dicey and Morris, pp. 1014, 1015.

[97] (No. 1), [1933] P. 251; (No. 2), [1934] P. 171.

[98] (No. 2), [1934] P. 171, at p. 176 *per* Scrutton L.J.

[99] (No. 1), [1933] P. 251, at pp. 266, 267 *per* Greer L.J.

[100] As far as the nominal plaintiffs were concerned it therefore did not really matter whether they received pounds sterling or pesos. It is noteworthy that counsel for the defendants felt compelled, and permitted, to warn the court that the case 'must not be looked at with any regard to English underwriters': (No. 1), [1933] P. 251, at p. 260.

payment on account, it will be the duty of the registrar to credit that payment by its equivalent value in sterling at the rate of exchange prevailing on the date when the payment was finally approved by the Chilean Judge'. Romer L.J.'s *ratio decidendi* was[101] that what happened in Chile could have the effect of a payment only in such cases 'where the relation of creditor and debtor prevails between the two parties to the transaction according to the law of Chile and could have no application to such a case as the present where no such relation exists or is claimed to exist'; he thought it quite conceivable that the decision would have been different 'had the defendants' liability to pay the plaintiffs' damages according to Chilean law been established'. Thus in the judgment of Scrutton L.J.[102] there was no payment by Chilean law, while in the judgment of Greer L.J. there was a payment by Chilean law which in England was to be treated as a payment on account. In Romer L.J.'s judgment, too, there was no payment, but his decision rests on the refusal to apply Chilean law at all, since the question fell to be decided by English law.

During further proceedings the question arose whether the order as drawn up by the Court of Appeal in *The Baarn* (No. 1)[103] expressed the judgments given, inasmuch as it was contended that the Court of Appeal did not intend to exclude the possibility of taking the Chilean payment into account *pro tanto*, and to order payment in this country. This contention was rejected both by Bateson J. and by the Court of Appeal.[104] Scrutton L.J. adhered to his view that there was no payment (apparently according to Chilean law); Greer L.J. dismissed the defendants' appeal on the ground of estoppel; Maugham L.J. emphasized that he was 'unable to see that Chilean law has anything to do with the matter before the Court'.[105]

In the result the decisions of the Court of Appeal must, it is submitted with respect, certainly meet with approval. As regards the second decision, Greer L.J.'s reasoning appears to be the most convincing. As regards the more important first decision, the decisive factor appears to be that, the collision having occurred on the high seas and the obligation therefore being governed by English law,[106] the question whether and how the ensuing claim could be discharged was also governed by English law.[107] This was the reason,

[101] p. 273.
[102] As explained in *The Baarn* (No. 2), [1934] P. 171, 178.
[103] [1933] P. 251.        [104] *The Baarn* (No. 2), [1934] P. 171.        [105] p. 184.
[106] Above, p. 251, see p. 329, n. 98.
[107] If the view expressed by Lord Sumner in *The Volturno*, [1921] 2 A.C. 544, 553 was accepted, it could also have been said that there was no claim for Chilean pesos at all, but only for pounds sterling. This line of argument seems to have weighed in Romer L.J.'s

in fact, given by Romer and Maugham L.JJ., while Scrutton and Greer L.JJ.'s reference to Chilean law lacks justification.

IV

While in an earlier chapter the problems relating to the determination of the money of account were treated,[108] and while a preceding section of this chapter was devoted to the problems surrounding the money of payment and its determination, we now come to a group of cases where the money of payment as well as the money of account is ascertained, but where for the purpose of discharging the obligation an item, expressed in a foreign currency, has to be converted into the money of payment. If, for instance, under an insurance policy providing for an indemnity in sterling, a claim is made in respect of a loss which has duly been ascertained to be expressed in a foreign currency, it is clear that a conversion into sterling is required, because the policy gives a right to pounds sterling only. Or if an English banker who guaranteed the debt of a French importer towards an American exporter up to a sum of 100,000 French francs is made liable for a sum of U.S.A. dollars, he must translate that sum into French francs in order to recover his outlays. Similarly, if jewels, given as a security for a loan of French francs, are sold by auction in England for pounds sterling, it becomes necessary to reduce the amount due by the price obtained. In these cases, it appears, both the money of account and the money of payment are ascertained, but there is an item which for the purpose of adjusting it to the terms of the existing obligation must be converted into the currency envisaged by it.[109]

In such cases[110] conversion should be effected at the rate of

---

mind: (No. 1), [1933] P. 251, 271, 272. Cheshire and North, p. 712, explain the decision on the ground that the question under discussion related to the quantification of the amount payable and was therefore governed by the *lex fori*.

[108] pp. 223 sqq.

[109] Sometimes the necessity of conversion has been disregarded. Thus the German Supreme Court dealt with a case where the plaintiff, who had insured with the defendants goods sent from Hamburg to Bombay, advanced a sum of £2. 1s. 4d. in respect of surveyor's costs incurred in Bombay in connection with the determination of damage. Although the policy provided for an indemnity in marks, the Supreme Court allowed a claim for the amount of pounds: 17 Mar. 1924, *JW*. 1924, 1590. But see the note thereon by Nussbaum, who rightly criticizes the decision. See also the German Supreme Court, 28 Apr. 1924, *JW*. 1924, 1593.

[110] They are to be distinguished from cases in which the conversion has been carried out and produces a surplus, so that the question arises which of the parties is entitled to it. Such a case was *Yorkshire Insurance Co.* v. *Nisbet Shipping Co.* (1961), 2 All E.R. 487: a ship having become a total loss, the insurers under a sterling policy paid its full value, viz. £72,000. The owners later recoved C$330,000 from the owners of the negligent ship.

exchange of the day on which, according to the contract and the circumstances of the case, there arose the right to payment or the duty to give credit and, consequently, the occasion for conversion.[111] This rule will make it necessary to turn in the first place to the contract to search for an express or implied agreement between the parties. Thus where a charterparty provides for the revision of hire payable in dollars in accordance with the wages paid to the crew in Deutsche Marks, the latter are to be converted into dollars, not at the date when hire is payable or paid, but at the date when the wages are changed.[112] Or it is of the essence of an indemnity policy that the policy holder is entitled to the value at the time and place of the fire;[113] it follows that, if that value is measured in terms of a foreign currency, it will, for purposes of payment under a sterling policy, have to be translated at the rate of exchange of the day of fire. In the case of marine insurance regard will have to be had to the provision of s. 16 of the Marine Insurance Act, 1906. If a ship is insured, the value at the commencement of a risk will have to be ascertained;[114] if this is measured in a foreign currency, payment under a sterling policy presupposes the conversion into sterling according to the rate of the day on which the risk commences.[115] In the case of the insurance of goods the result will be similar, because their value is represented by 'prime costs',[116] and this means the value at or about the date of shipment.[117]

This produced £125,000. Diplock J., relying on the principles of subrogation, held that the excess of £35,000 belonged to the owners rather than the insurers. In *Lucas Ltd.* v. *Export Credits Guarantee Department* (1973), 1 W.L.R. 914 the defendants, having paid 90 per cent of the sales price, became entitled to 90 per cent of 'any sum recovered' by the buyers. This was a sum of dollars which, when converted into sterling produced more than 100 per cent of the sterling amount insured by the defendants. The Court of Appeal held that the defendants were entitled to 90 per cent of the excess. The result was derived from the construction of the contract. No specific rule of monetary law is applicable to such cases.

[111] See, for example, French Cass. Civ. 3 Aug. 1936, Clunet, 1937, 302: real property of a French wife, forming part of the 'communauté des biens', was sold for pesos and piastres. It was held that conversion into francs was to be effected at the rate of exchange of the days when payments were made by the purchasers.

[112] *The Brunsrode* (1976), 1 Ll. L.R. 501.

[113] MacGillivray and Parkington, *Insurance Law* (6th ed., 1975), s. 1760.

[114] s. 16 (1).

[115] See Ivamy, *Marine Insurance* (2nd ed., 1974), p. 101. In *Chartered Trust & Executor Co.* v. *London & Scottish Assurance Corporation* (1923), 16 Ll. L.R. 151 the mortgagee of a ship which was insured for £225,000 and became a total loss was held to be entitled to recover from the insurers in respect of his mortgage of $240,000 and this was converted at the rate of the day when the total loss occurred (pp. 233, 234). But there does not seem to have been any argument on the point nor is it known whether there was any variation in the rate of exchange.

[116] s. 16 (3).

[117] *Williams* v. *Atlantic Assurance Co. Ltd.*, [1933] 1 K.B. 81 (C.A.). In *Thellusson* v. *Bewick* (1793), 1 Esp. 77, goods carried from Le Havre to Ostend were insured at a time

In the case of reinsurance contracts conversion will take place with reference to the rate of exchange of the date when the insurer pays and the reinsurer's liability arises. This point is impressively illustrated by the decision of the Court of Appeal in *Versicherungs & Transport A.G. Daugava* v. *Henderson*.[118] The defendant, an English underwriter, had reinsured the plaintiffs, a Latvian insurance company, against their liability on a fire insurance policy on buildings in Riga. The insurer's liability towards the assured was ascertained by the Latvian courts in lats and the sum due was paid in January 1932, while the fire had occurred in April 1930. The question arose whether, as between insurer and reinsurer, the sum of lats was to be turned into sterling at the rate of exchange of the date of the fire or at that of the date of the settlement of the insurer's liability. Confirming the judgment of Roche J.,[119] the court adopted the latter rate, the reason being that so long as the insurer's liability is not qualified and satisfied, there is no liability of the reinsurer.[120]

On the other hand, the rule is less clearly exemplified by the decision of Rowlatt J. in *Noreuro Traders* v. *Hardy & Co.*[121] A claim for general average contribution arose in 1914, and according to the charterparty the general average was to be adjusted in Antwerp in Belgian francs, where, however, owing to the German occupation during the Great War, the adjustment could not be made. A provisional adjustment was effected in London and a number of payments in pounds sterling were made. In 1919 general average was adjusted in Antwerp in francs. It was held that the sterling payments were to be converted into francs 'at the rate of exchange which is applicable to the whole thing, and that is the rate of exchange at the date of the sacrifice, and all they were doing provisionally was meant to date back to that'. The learned Judge, however, expressly stated that the conversion might have been made at the rate of exchange of the date of payment, but he had no evidence as to what the rate at that moment was. But it might have been a still better solution to convert the payments at the rate of the date when the final adjustment was made, as it was then only that the claim for

---

when the French crown was worth 24*d*. They became a total loss and by the time of payment the crown was worth 7¾*d*. Lord Kenyon said that 'nothing was clearer than that the insurers did not insure against the debasement of the coin. . . . In case the exchange had risen the insured would have had the benefit of the rise and therefore, in case of a fall, should submit to the loss.' This dictum is probably no longer good law: it is inconsistent with the Act of 1906 and, moreover, may rest on the terms of the particular policy which apparently postponed settlement until after the sale of salvaged goods.

[118] (1934) 49 Ll. L.R. 252.        [119] (1934) 48 Ll. L.R. 54.

[120] No decisive importance was attached to the peculiar clause in the contract between the parties: 'to follow the settlements of Daugava Insurance Company'.

[121] (1923) 16 Ll. L.R. 319.

contribution arose.[122] This was in fact so decided in a Canadian case, though in an entirely different context. In the course of a taxation of costs the successful party claimed a sum of Canadian dollars in respect of disbursements made in another currency. It was held that the date of conversion was 'the date of the certificate of the bill of costs', i.e. in England probably the date of the *allocatur*.[123]

A case in which credit has to be given according to the rate of exchange of the day when it comes into existence, arises, for instance, where the victim of a tort or a breach of contract is entitled to damages in terms of sterling, but in minimizing his damages has obtained a sum of dollars for which credit is to be given: these, it is submitted, are to be converted into sterling at the rate of the date of receipt as opposed to the day, when the damage occurred or the wrongdoer makes payment.[124] In *Pape Williams & Co.* v. *Home Insurance Co.*[125] American owners of cotton lying in Barcelona insured it with an American insurance company in terms of dollars subject to the terms: 'Loss if any payable on the basis of the actual market value at time and place of loss, such loss to be payable in New York exchange to bankers.' The goods were confiscated in Barcelona at a time when they had a dollar value of almost $30,000. Subsequently, the Spanish Government paid to the owners compensation in pesetas which produced $18,000. The court upheld the assured's claim to the difference and rejected an argument of the insurance company to the effect that the loss had been made good by payment of the value at the relevant time in terms of pesetas: the compensation paid by the Spanish Government was merely an

---

[122] See German Supreme Court, 4 June 1924, *RGZ.* 108, 304: the plaintiff had paid £3. 11s. as 'deposit on account of general average'. The adjustment showed that the plaintiffs had to pay only 299·41 marks. The Supreme Court held that this sum of marks was to be converted into pounds sterling at the rate according to which the conversion was effected in the adjustment, and was then to be deducted from the sterling amount already paid. See also Brussels Court of Appeal, 19 Oct. 1935, *Revue de droit maritime comparé*, 1936, ii. 160: if a shipbroker receives freight in Belgian francs and is bound to convert it into pounds sterling, he must effect the conversion at the rate of exchange of the day when the account is made up ('c'est en réalité à ce jour que se feront les compensations et jusque-là les dettes et créances subsistent dans la monnaie dans laquelle elles ont été contractées').

[123] *Dillingham Corporation Canada Ltd.* v. *The Ship Shiuy Maru,* 101 D.L.R. 3d 447 (1980).

[124] Cf. the decision of Germany's Federal Administrative Court, 13 Dec. 1973, *RzW.* 1974, 186: where credit has to be given for the 'value' of certain receipts and dollars were received, their value in DM is determined by the rate of exchange at the date of receipt. Contrast the decision of the German Federal Supreme Court, 12 June 1975, *RzW.* 1975, 301: if I am entitled to the repayment of medical expenses incurred in dollars these are to be converted into DM at the rate of the day when the expenses were incurred.

[125] 139 F. 2d 231 (1943) and [1944] A.M.C. 51 (C.C.A., 2d). Cf. Cass Req. 23 Apr. 1928, D.H. 1928, 302 and German Supreme Court, 22 Apr. 1925, *JW.* 1926, 1970, both relating to the liability of the reinsurer.

item which had to be brought into account and for this purpose to be converted into dollars at the rate prevailing at the time of the receipt of the credit.

Another American case illustrates the problem of calculating a credit which is to be given by a beneficiary under a will. An American testator directed his estate to be divided equally between his brothers and sisters. Debts due from them at the time of his death were 'to be applied against' the debtor's share. At the time of the testator's death in October 1938 two brothers owed certain sums of 'goldmarks'. Were they to be converted into dollars at the rate of exchange of October 1938, or at the rate prevailing in 1952, when the estate was wound up? The court decided in the latter sense on the ground that the purpose of the deduction was to achieve equality, and that the application of any other rate of exchange would work injustice.[126]

Next, attention must be drawn to the statutory provisions relating to the calculation of stamp duties in respect of instruments expressed in a foreign currency,[127] and also to the fact that in certain circumstances the case of the S.S. Volturno[128] might have to be considered in this connection. It concerned a claim for damages in respect of a loss of hire caused by a collision in the Mediterranean. The damages, or at least the items of which the damages consisted, were expressed in Italian lire. If certain observations made by Lord Sumner[129] must be understood as meaning that the damage was expressed 'just as naturally in British currency as in Italian currency', and that therefore the sums of Italian lire were only items to be converted into British currency for the purpose of adjusting them to the British money of account, the case would fall under the head of the present section and it could be well understood that conversion into sterling should take place at the rate of exchange of the day when the expenses were incurred. In truth, however, it is believed that the case had nothing to do with sterling, that the plaintiffs

---

[126] *In re Heck's Estate*, 116 N.Y.S. 2d 255 (1952).

[127] s. 6, Stamp Act, 1891 (relating to the Bills of Exchange and Notes); s. 12, Finance Act 1899 (relating to other instruments).

[128] [1921] 2 A.C. 544.

[129] In *The Volturno*, [1921] 2 A.C. 544, 553, which concerned a claim for damages expressed in Italian lire and caused by the loss of hire owing to a collision in the Mediterranean, he said: 'That compensation was not recoverable in any particular currency, and although for convenience of proof it would be severable into divers heads and items, it would be one gross sum, recoverable once for all. . . . The essential thing to remember, which the appellants somewhat ignored, is that the sum in question here is only an item in a general claim dor damages for a wrong done at sea which was the subject of compensation just as naturally in British as in Italian currency.' This apparently means that a distinction must be made between the 'damages' and the 'items' of which the damages consist.

were entitled to a sum of lire, that there was no room for any conversion and that, as a consequence of *Milliangos*,[130] the case should no longer be treated as good law.

A final example of some interest is supplied by a decision of Vinelott J.[131] In October 1967 a British taxpayer became entitled to German property worth DM 132,000. She sold in July 1973 for DM 152,000. The question was whether the taxable gain was DM 20,000 converted into sterling at the rate for July 1973 or whether it was the excess of the sterling value of DM 152,000 in July 1973 over the sterling value of DM 132,000 in October 1967. The learned Judge decided in the latter sense, so that the taxpayer largely paid tax 'on a gain resulting from the devaluation of the pound in November 1967'. It is submitted that the former solution would have been the correct one. The necessity or, indeed, the occasion of converting anything into sterling arose in July 1973. The mere acquisition of property valued in terms of DM in October 1967 was, for purposes of capital gains tax, an irrelevant fact. It was the sale that was material for ascertaining the gain.

---

[130] Below, p. 349.
[131] *Bentley* v. *Pike*, Simon's Tax Cases 1981, 360.

# XII

# The Institution of Legal Proceedings and its Effect upon Foreign Money Obligations

I. The problem stated. II. Participation in a fund. III. The institution of legal proceedings and its effects in foreign laws. IV. The institution of legal proceedings and its effects in English law. V. A retrospect.

## I

PURSUING the rough scheme which has been adopted for the logical development of the law of foreign money obligations, we find that after determining the money of account, i.e. the substance of the obligation, the quantum of the obligation, and the money of payment (fixing the mode of payment), there must now follow a discussion of the question whether and how, if payment must be enforced by action, legal proceedings affect the structure of foreign money obligations.[1]

At first sight it is tempting to answer that the institution of legal proceedings should have no effect whatsoever on foreign money obligations. Indeed, it cannot be controverted that the object of legal proceedings is neither to create nor to nullify, but to enforce rights existing under the applicable substantive law. Consequently, the law of procedure should not in any way alter the legal character of foreign money obligations as produced by the rules of private international and substantive law, which were explained in the preceding chapters.

Where a claim for the payment of foreign money is made, English law, fortunately, has achieved a solution conforming to these requirements. Such a case, however, has to be distinguished from that in which a share in or a proportion of a fund is in issue. It will be

[1] On this problem see, in particular, McNair, 37 (1921) *L.Q.R.* 387; Negus, 40 (1924) *L.Q.R.* 149. See also Keeton, 19 (1934) *Iowa L.J.* 218; Gottschalk, *Journal of Comparative Legislation*, 17 (1935), 47; Levontin, *Israel L.R.* i (1966), 250. As to America, see below, p. 341, n. 31. Most of this literature is obsolete. More recent contributions are by Morris, *Law and Contemporary Problems*, 41 (1977), 44; Libling, 93 (1977) *L.Q.R.* 212; Knott, 43 (1980) M.L.R. 18; Nygh, 22 (1980) Malaya L.R. 1.

convenient to turn in the first place to this set of facts (below, section II) and thereafter to consider the law relating to proceedings for the payment of foreign money in the principal foreign countries (below, section III) and in Britain (below, section IV). A short review of the developments resulting in the present state of English law will conclude the chapter (below, section V).

II

Where a number of claimants are entitled to share in a fund, this will have to be constituted so as to ensure equality and uniformity of treatment and to avoid considerations of individual equity, chance, or opportunism. For this purpose all assets have to be turned into cash and all liabilities have to be expressed in terms of the *moneta fori* at a uniform rate, that is to say, without regard to the date, when in a given case payment is due. According to what one may describe as a general rule[2] such conversion, at least notionally, takes place at the date, when the constitution of the fund becomes effective.

In the case of the bankruptcy of an individual or the winding-up of a company the relevant date is the day when the receiving order is made or the winding-up of the company becomes effective. This is laid down by the legislation of at least five States[3] and is elsewhere sanctioned by judicial practice.[4] In England the rule was established by what one may respectfully describe as a courageous, but unquestionably correct decision by Oliver J. (as he then was)[5] whom the

---

[2] Both branches of the rule were the subject matter of much discussion in the *Case of Barcelona Traction, Light & Power Ltd.* (*Belgium* v. *Spain*) in the International Court of Justice, but the court refrained from making any pronouncement upon it. It is noteworthy that Belgium asserted the existence of the rule, while Spain described it as 'a pure invention' (Pleadings).

[3] *Austria*: Art. 14 (1) of the Bankruptcy Law of 1914; *Germany*: s. 69 of the Bankruptcy Law, and see the comments by Jaeger, *Konkursordnung* (8th ed., 1958), s. 69, n. 8; *France*: Art. 475 of the Code de Commerce as amended in 1955 (on which see Nadelmann, *American Journal of Comparative Law*, 1955, 582); *Italy*: Art. 59 of the Bankruptcy Law (on which see Ascarelli, p. 419); *Brazil*: Art. 213 of the Bankruptcy Law (on which see Garland, *American–Brazilian Private International Law* (New York, 1959), pp. 67, 68).

[4] See, in particular, Dölle, *Rechtsvergleichendes Handwörterbuch*, v. (1933), 114, with references. As to *Belgium* see Piret, p. 119 with references, or Trochu, *Conflits de lois et de juridictions en matière de faillite* (Paris, 1967), p. 139; as to the *Argentine* see Court of Appeal Buenos Aires, 14 Apr. 1969, Clunet, 1969, 947 with interesting discussion; *Netherlands*: Hoge Raad, 4 Feb. 1977, N.J. 1978, 66. But in the *United States of America* it was held by the Court of Appeals, 6th Cir., that in bankruptcy the rate of exchange to be applied was that prevailing on the day of the order allowing the creditor's claim: *Wyse* v. *Pioneer Cafeteria Feeds Ltd.*, 340 F. 2d 719 (1965), at p. 725; no reason was given apart from a reference to *Deutsche Bank* v. *Humphreys*, 272 U.S. 517 (1926) which is not in point, but is discussed below, p. 342. On the problem in general see Hanisch, *Annuaire Suisse de Droit International*, 1980, 127.

[5] *In re Dynamics Corporation of America* (1976), 1 W.L.R. 757, where all the earlier authorities are reviewed. Most of them were obsolete on account of the decision in *Miliangos*

Supreme Court of Israel, by a majority of three to two, regrettably refused to follow.[6] Similarly, where an order for the administration of the estate of a deceased person is made, conversion takes place at the date of the order.[7] Or where a limitation fund is constituted, Art. 8 of the Convention in Schedule 4 of the Merchant Shipping Act 1979 provides for conversion at the rate of exchange at the date of the fund's constitution.[8]

A striking illustration of the same basic principle is the decision in *Re Chesterman's Trust.*[9] The question was how much of a fund in Court, representing the mortgaged property, was to be paid to mortgagees who were entitled to a sum of German marks and to whom one of those entitled to share in the fund had mortgaged his interest. It was made clear both by Russell J. (as he then was), and by the majority of the Court of Appeal, that the court was not dealing with an action on the covenant in the mortgage to recover the money, but was 'dividing the funds' and for this purpose had to ascertain what sums were payable to the mortgagees.[10] It was held that the proper date for the conversion was the date of the Master's certificate in the inquiry. This decision was followed in Canada in a case in which a trustee for bondholders claimed an account for the purpose of ascertaining the principal and interest due to the bondholders out of the proceeds of sale of the mortgaged property. The date of the Master's report was ordered to be taken as the date of conversion.[11] This was

on which see below, p. 347. On cases in which the money is due after the date of the receiving order or the winding-up order, see s. 30 (4) of the Bankruptcy Act, 1914 and s. 316 of the Companies Act, 1948, respectively, and the decisions in *Re Russian Commercial and Industrial Bank* (1955), Ch. 145 and *Re Parana Plantations Ltd.* (1946), 2 All E.R. 214 (C.A.).

[6] *In re Israel–British Bank Ltd.* (*Wallace Brothers Commodities Ltd.* v. *Milo*), decision of 16 Jan. 1979. The author was supplied with an English translation.

[7] *In re Hawkins* (1972), 3 W.L.R. 255. The decision preceded the case of *Miliangos*, but by a different route reached a satisfactory result.

[8] The Merchant Shipping (Liability of Shipowners and Others) Act, 1958, giving effect to the International Convention relating to the Limitation of the Liability of Owners of Sea-going Ships signed in Brussels on 10 Oct. 1957 (Cmnd. 353), provided for the limitation of liability in terms of francs defined as a unit consisting of $65\frac{1}{2}$ milligrams of gold of millesimal fineness 900. S.I. 1958, No. 1287 of 1 Aug. 1958 specified £23. 13s. $9\frac{27}{32}d.$ as the sterling equivalent of 1,000 francs. After the devaluation of 18 Nov. 1967, S.I. 1967, No. 1725 substituted the sum of £27. 12s. $9\frac{1}{2}d.$ This was held to apply in all cases in which the limitation decree was made after Nov. 1967, irrespective of the date when the damage occurred: *The Abadesa*, [1968] P. 656; *The Mecca*, [1968] P. 665. The incident is interesting, because, as a result of an international agreement, the British legislator remedied what was the likely result based on earlier judicial practice in England, but opposed to practice abroad as well as to common sense and justice.          [9] [1923] 2 Ch. 466.

[10] At p. 474 *per* Russel J., at p. 479 *per* Lord Sterndale M.R. at p. 485 *per* Warrington L.J. (as he then was). It is noteworthy that the amounts payable to the mortgagees were due and payable by the mortgagors long before the date of the Master's certificate.

[11] *Montreal Trust Co.* v. *Abitibi Power & Paper Co. Ltd.* (1944), Ontario Reports 515, at pp. 523–5.

(rightly) so decided, although the bonds and coupons[12] had fallen due for payment many years before, namely in August 1932.[13]

## III

In 1898 Lord Lindley said[14] that

'if the defendants were within the jurisdiction of any other civilized State and were sued there, as they might be, the courts of that State would have to deal with precisely the same problem, and to express in the currency of that State the amount payable by the defendants instead of expressing it in Mexican dollars'.

But, at least at the present time, the idea that the issue of a writ renders it necessary to convert the sum of foreign currency claimed by the plaintiff into the *moneta fori* is by no means so general as to warrant that statement.

In the following countries, among others, it is established that writ as well as judgment may be for a sum of money foreign to the forum: Austria,[15] Brazil,[16] Denmark,[17] Egypt,[18] Germany,[19] Italy,[20] Norway,[21] Switzerland.[22] In some of these countries it is emphasized that the creditor of a foreign money obligation cannot sue otherwise than by demanding the foreign money of account, that an

---

[12] Although the point is outside the scope of the present work, it may interest some readers that, following two earlier Canadian decisions, the learned Judge held at p. 523 that presentation of the coupons would have been an 'idle gesture', and that therefore the want of it was not a valid objection. In England the Court of Appeal decided in the opposite sense: *U.G.S. Finance Co. Ltd.* v. *National Bank of Greece* (1964), 1 Ll. L.R. 446.

[13] Cf. *Re United Railways of Havana and Regla Warehouses Ltd.*, [1961] A.C. 1007, a decision which in *Rossano* v. *Manufacturers Life Insurance Co.*, [1963] 2 Q.B. 352, at p. 360, McNair J. described as 'a case of immense complexity'. The difficulty largely arises from the fact that in the view of the majority it was decisive that the claimant-trustee was proving rentals which had fallen due long before the order for the company's winding-up and were, therefore, subject to the 'breach-date rule'. Yet it was also accepted that the trustee was only entitled to such amounts of rent as were required to discharge outstanding certificates; his claim, therefore, was not and could not be ascertained or crystallized before those amounts had been ascertained, i.e. at the earliest on 4 Dec. 1956 when Roxburgh J. held that only 331 certificates had to be provided for. The Court of Appeal, accordingly, had applied the principle underlying *In re Chesterman's Trusts, ubi supra.* The House of Lords does not mention this decision at all, yet does not overrule it. The difficulty arises from the absence of an explanation as to why *In re Chesterman's Trusts* (where, as mentioned at p. 338, n. 10 above, the money due to the mortgagees had been payable since long before the proceedings) was either inapplicable or wrongly decided. Fortunately the decision of the House of Lords of 1961 has since been overruled and in this as in many other respects is now only a curiosity.

[14] *Manners* v. *Pearson*, [1898] 1 Ch. 581, 587.

[15] Austrian Supreme Court, *Rechtsprechung*, 1934, No. 267 and *RabelsZ.* 10 (1936), 777; 30 Apr. 1953, *Juristische Blätter*, 1954, 199.

[16] Garland, *American–Brazilian Private International Law* (New York, 1959), p. 68.

[17] Alan Philip, *American–Danish Private International Law* (New York, 1957), p. 51.

[18] Court of Appeal of the Mixed Tribunal, 13 Apr. 1932, *Gazette des Tribunaux Mixtes*, 23, 281, No. 288; 7 June 1934, ibid. 24, 347, No. 410; 23 Apr. 1936, ibid. 28, 150.

[19] See below, nn. 23, 24.          [20] See Ascarelli, pp. 187, 375.

[21] Frederiksen, *34th Report of the International Law Association* (1926), p. 559.

[22] See below, n. 26.

action in which a sum of *moneta fori* is claimed may even be dismissed, and that it is within the discretion of the defendant to decide whether or not he wishes the judgment, if it is given against him, to provide for an option to pay the equivalent in the *moneta fori* at the rate of exchange of the day of payment.[23] The question how execution is to be issued on a judgment which does not provide for such an option is a matter of some difficulty in Germany;[24] but in Egypt it has been held that the judgment debtor may pay in Egyptian money at the rate of exchange of the day of payment,[25] and in Switzerland the point is settled by statute.[26]

In some countries, such as France,[27] Belgium,[28] and the Argentine,[29] the judgment may or perhaps must be for such a sum of francs as is equivalent to the sum of foreign money at the rate of exchange of the day of payment. In effect this amounts to a judgment providing for a sum of foreign money.

In the United States it was enacted as early as 1792 that 'all proceedings in

---

[23] This is so in Austria (above, n. 15), Italy (above, n. 20), and Germany: Supreme Court, 4th June 1919, *RGZ*. 96, 121, 123; 29 Sept. 1919, *RGZ*. 96, 270; see also 24 Oct. 1923, *JW*. 1924, 1518 and Staudinger–Weber, *Kommentar zum Bürgerlichen Gesetzbuch*, s. 244, n. 81. If the plaintiff first obtains a judgment for a sum of marks which does not suffice to satisfy the claim for a sum of foreign money, he may demand the balance in a second action, there being no estoppel: Supreme Court, *JW*. 1921, 22; as to the reasoning of the decision see above, p. 192, n. 47.

[24] See Supreme Court, 16 Dec. 1922, *RGZ*. 106, 76 and Staudinger–Weber, s. 244, n. 82. But it seems that even if the judgment does not provide for the option mentioned in the text, the judgment debtor may pay in German money at the rate of exchange of the day of payment: Supreme Court, 15 Dec. 1924, *JW*. 1925, 467 at p. 469.

[25] See the decision quoted, p. 339, n. 18.

[26] See Art. 67, Schuldbeitreibungsgesetz of 11 Apr. 1889, and the decisions of the Federal Tribunal of 12 Oct. 1917, *BGE*. 43, iii. 270; 1 Dec. 1920, *BGE*. 46, ii. 406; 10 June 1925, *BGE*. 51, iii. 180.

[27] Whether writ and judgment could be for a sum of foreign money only is doubtful; a negative answer is given by the Cour de Paris, 26 Jan. 1929, Clunet, 1930, 380, and *Revue de droit maritime comparé, Supplément*, 7 (1929), 157. The usual method is to sue for a sum of foreign money 'ou la contrevaleur en francs français au cours du jour de paiement'. See Cass. Req. 8 Nov. 1922, S. 1923, 1. 149, and Clunet, 1923, 576; 9 Mar. 1925, 1. 257 (5ᵉ espèce), and Clunet, 1926, 103; 19 Mar. 1930, Clunet, 1931, 1082; Cass. Civ. 8 July 1931, Clunet, 1932, 721; Cass. Req. 27 Oct. 1943, *Rev. Crit.* 1946, 254; Cass., 18 Nov. 1952, Bull. Civ. 1952, iii, No. 355; 22 July 1957, Bull. Civ. 1957, iii, No. 239; 25 Oct. 1961, Bull. Civ. 1961, ii, No. 488; 15 Jan. 1962, Bull. Civ. 1962, i, No. 28 (with a particularly clear statement). As the note by Lévy points out, the Criminal Chamber rendered a wholly isolated decision when it decided that conversion had to take place at the date of judgment rather than payment: Cass. Crim. 7 July 1966, Clunet, 1968, 79.

[28] Art. 3 of a statute of 30 Dec. 1885 prevents a judge from giving judgment for a sum of foreign money; see Brussels Court of Appeal, 23 Dec. 1922, *Revue de droit bancaire*, 1 (1923), 534; Liège Court of Appeal, 10 Feb. 1939, *B.I.J.I.* 40 (1939), 283, and Piret, No. 28. But a judge may order a defendant to pay 'la somme nécessaire pour reconstituer à l'appelant au jour du payement l'équivalent de £1487': Cass. 17 Jan. 1929, *Revue de droit maritime comparé*, 21 (1930), 164 and 23 (1931), 91, and see Rigaux, *Droit International Privé*, ii (1979), No. 1217 or Piret, Nos. 29 sqq., who enumerates a number of decisions applying the rate of exchange of the day of breach; or H. De Page, *Traité élémentaire du Droit Civil Belge*, iii (1967), p. 457.

[29] Court of Appeal Buenos Aires, 26 Mar. 1957, Clunet, 1957, 180. In *Poland* courts cannot as a rule give judgment otherwise than in Polish currency: Supreme Court, 27 June 1969, Clunet, 1977, 144.

the courts shall be kept and had' in dollars.[30] But the question of the method of converting a sum of foreign money into dollars for the purpose of legal proceedings was not definitely answered until comparatively recent times.[31]

The modern practice of the Federal courts which was anticipated in two decisions of Judge Augustus N. Hand,[32] and developed in some decisions of the Supreme Court of the United States, rests upon the following distinction. Where the breach or wrong occurred in a foreign country (especially by non-payment of money due there), the damages are measured in the currency of that country and the dollar equivalent calculated at the rate of exchange obtaining at the date of judgment can be recovered; where the breach or wrong occurred in the United States (especially by non-payment of foreign money due there), the damages, being measured in dollars, are to be converted at the rate of exchange of the day of breach or wrong.

The latter part of this statement is supported by *Hicks* v. *Guiness*,[33] which related to a debt of 1,079 odd marks owed by a German debtor to an American creditor on 31 December 1916, and where Mr. Justice Holmes delivered the

---

[30] See above, p. 198, where a similar Canadian enactment is mentioned.

[31] The question is discussed by Gluck, 22 (1922) *Col. L.R.* 217; Drake 23 (1925) *Mich. L.R.* 696; 25 (1927) *Mich. L.R.* 860; 28 (1930) *Mich. L.R.* 229; Rifkind, 26 (1926) *Col. L.R.* 559; Maw (whose authorship is disclosed by Professor Beale, *Conflict of Laws*, s. 424), 40 (1927) *Harv. L.R.* 619; Fraenkel, 35 (1935) *Col. L.R.* 360; C. T. McCormick, *Handbook on the Law of Damages* (1935), pp. 190 sqq.; Mitchell, *Texas L.R.* 34 (1956), 457; note in 65 (1965) *Col. L.R.* 490; Becker, *American Journal of Comparative Law*, 25 (1977), 152; and many of the usual textbooks, in particular see the two standard works on Contracts by Williston, s. 1410A and Corbin, v (1964), s. 1005. Both authors discuss many matters not strictly relating to procedural conversion and do not always clearly distinguish between the numerous distinct aspects of monetary law. Professor Corbin advocates 'a broad variety of remedies and flexibility in their application' so as to achieve whatever result may in a given case be just. The answer is that everything depends on the meaning of 'justice'. It is the present writer's submission that the function of 'remedies' is to enforce substantive rights; that the latter are, and should be, determined, not by procedural rules (such as the Anglo-American practice of conversion discussed in the present chapter), but by the law of contracts, torts, and so forth, i.e. by the proper law; that its identity should be defined by the conflict of laws rather than the law of procedure; that to the forum the justice of the results sanctioned by the proper law should be immaterial, except where public policy intervenes; that if the proper law denies the recovery of substantial damages flowing from the debtor's default, it is neither unjust to give effect to the proper law nor permissible to substitute a procedural remedy for the defective substantive law. On many points of detail Professor Corbin's argument is lacking in persuasiveness. Thus his approval (in note 73) of *Sternberg* v. *West Coast Life Insurance Co.*, 196 Cal. App. 2d 519 (1961) and his disapproval (pp. 62, 63) of *Anderson* v. *Equitable Life Assurance Society* (1926), 134 L.T. 557 seems inconsistent. On these cases see above, pp. 278, 269, n. 9, where it is made clear that, contrary to Professor Corbin's assumption, German courts would have decided the case in the same way as the English courts. The idea that *Fibrosa* v. *Fairbairn*, [1943] A.C. 32 should have any bearing upon the point is far off the mark.

[32] Sitting in the District Court, Southern District of New York. In *The Verdi* (1920), 268 Fed. 908, he held that where owing to a collision of ships in New York harbour a claim for damages arose, the damages being measured in sterling, the rate of exchange of the day of wrong was to be applied, since the tort was committed in the United States. In *The Hurona* (1920), 268 Fed. 911, he held that an advance of 119,000 French francs made and repayable in Marseilles was recoverable at the rate of exchange of the day of judgment. See also *The Saigon Maru* (1920), 267 Fed. 881, District Court, District of Oregon.

[33] (1925) 269 U.S. 71.

opinion of a unanimous court. The opinion rests on the ground that according to American substantive law, which was held to be applicable to the contract, the plaintiff, upon the defendant's default, had acquired an optional right to be paid in dollars; the decision therefore merely applies a rule of American substantive law which was discussed in another connection[34] and which prevents it from falling under the head of the problem now under examination.

The authority for the former part of the above statement is *Deutsche Bank Filiale Nürnberg* v. *Humphreys.*[35] The plaintiff, an American citizen, had deposited with the defendants in Germany a sum of marks payment of which he unsuccessfully demanded on 12 June 1915. The courts below held that the marks were to be translated into dollars at the rate of exchange of the day when the demand was made, i.e. the day of breach. A sharply divided Supreme Court reversed the judgments, Mr. Justice Holmes delivering the opinion of the majority.[36]

'In this case unlike *Hicks'* v. *Guiness* at the date of the demand the German bank owed no duty to the plaintiff under our law. It was not subject to our jurisdiction and the only liability that it incurred by its failure to pay was that which the German law might impose. It has incurred no additional or other one since. A suit in this country is based upon an obligation existing under the foreign law at the time when the suit is brought, and the obligation is not enlarged by the fact that the creditor happens to be able to catch his debtor here. We may assume that when the bank failed to pay on demand, its liability was fixed at a certain number of marks both by the terms of the contracts and by the German law— but we may also assume that it was fixed in marks only, not at the extrinsic value that those marks then had in commodities or in the currency of another country. On the contrary, we repeat, it was and continued to be a liability in marks alone and was open to satisfaction by the payment of that number of marks, at any time, with whatever interest might have accrued, however much the mark might have fallen in value as compared with other things. See *Société des Hôtels Le Touquet* v. *Cummings*, [1922] 1 K.B. 451. An obligation in terms of the currency of a country takes the risk of currency fluctuations and whether creditor or debtor profits by the change the law takes no account of it. Obvi-

---

[34]  Above, p. 314.

[35]  (1926) 272 U.S. 517. Sir Frederick Pollock agreed with the decision: see Holmes–Pollock Correspondence, ii. 190. Later the plaintiff received compensation from the American-German Mixed Claims Commission which adopted the rate at the date of demand: Hackworth, *Digest*, v. 735. The decision had been preceded by *The Vaughan and Telegraph*, 14 Wall. 258 (1872). A cargo of barley shipped from Canada and valued at the time and place of shipment at Can$2,436, was lost owing to a collision in the river Hudson. Since the U.S. and the Canadian dollar were at the time of equal value, the District Court's judgment in favour of the plaintiffs was for U.S.$2436 and interest. When the case came before the Circuit Court of Appeals, the U.S. currency had so depreciated that 100 U.S. dollars in gold were worth 201 dollars in notes. Consequently, in Mar. 1870 the Circuit Court of Appeals converted the Canadian dollars at that rate into American dollars and gave judgment for U.S.$4,896.36 dollars and interest. Thereafter the U.S. dollar greatly appreciated in value, so that U.S.$4,896.36 would produce much more than Can.$2,436. By a majority the Supreme Court affirmed the decision on the ground that the judgment was correct when it was rendered and that any hardship to the defendants was due to their own delay in payment.

[36]  p. 519.

ously in fact a dollar or a mark may have different values at different times, but to the law that establishes it, it is always the same. If the debt had been due here and the value of the dollars had dropped before suit was brought, the plaintiff could recover no more dollars on that account. A foreign debtor should be no worse off.'

And later he added:[37] 'Here we are lending our courts to enforce an obligation (as we should put it, to pay damages) arising from German law alone and ought to enforce no greater obligation than exists by that law at the moment when suit is brought.' It is generally held that the concluding three words of Mr. Justice Holmes are due to an obvious error and that he meant to and did apply the rate of exchange prevailing at the date of judgment.[38] The distinction between *Hicks* v. *Guiness*, where the debt was held to be payable in New York and subject to American law, and *Deutsche Bank Filiale Nürnberg* v. *Humphreys*, where it was payable in and subject to the law of a foreign country, was again stressed by Mr. Justice Holmes in *Zimmerman* v. *Sutherland.*[39]

Though the doctrine thus propounded by the Supreme Court of the United States has since been followed in the Federal courts,[40] some details are not yet clearly established. In *Hicks* v. *Guiness* the obligation was both subject to American law and payable in America; in *Deutsche Bank Filiale Nürnberg* v.

---

[37] (1926) 272 U.S. 517, 520.

[38] *Thornton* v. *National City Bank* (1930), 45 F. (2d) 127, 130; *Tillmann* v. *Russo-Asiatic Bank* (1931), 51 F. (2d) 1023, 1025; *Royal Insurance Co.* v. *Compañia Transatlántica Española* (1932), 57 F. (2d) 288, 292; *The Integritas*, [1933] A.M.C. 165 (District Court, District of Maryland, 1933); *The Macdonough*, [1934] A.M.C. 234 (District Court of New York); *Indian Refinery Co.* v. *Valvoline Oil Co.*, 75 F. 2d 797 (Court of Appeals, 7th Cir.); *The West Arrow*, [1936] A.M.C. 165 (U.S. Circuit Court of Appeal, 2d, 1936), and other cases referred to and followed in *Reissner* v. *Rogers*, 276 F. 2d 506 (1960), where the Court of Appeals, District of Columbia Circuit, said (at p. 511): 'The view urged here that *Deutsche Bank* has been misread and that it really establishes as the conversion date the date on which the claim was filed has been considered and rejected in several of the cases cited above. We think that question is now to be regarded as settled and that we are bound to apply the judgment date rule in cases like the present.' The most recent cases seem to be *The Island Territory of Curaçao* v. *Solitron Devices Inc.*, 356 F. Supp. 1 (1973), at p. 14 and *Gutor International A.G.* v. *Raymond Packer Co.*, 493 F. 2d 938 (1974), at p. 943 (Court of Appeals, First Circuit). It would not have been necessary to quote this passage at length had not the House of Lords *In re United Railways of Havana and Regla Warehouses Ltd.*, [1961] A.C. 1007, rejected the argument of Mr. Wilberforce Q.C. (as he then was), which was based on the present footnote, and stated that it was the conclusion of the majority in the *Deutsche Bank* case 'that the date when the suit is brought, not the date when the debt is payable nor the date of judgment, is the date at which the rate of exchange must be fixed': at p. 1048 *per* Viscount Simonds; at p. 1052 *per* Lord Reid. It is plain that Holmes J. did not mention the rate at the date of judgment. But he was so understood by Mr. Justice Sutherland speaking for the minority, and by many later judges and commentators. Even if he was misunderstood at the time, continuous practice during a period of more than fifty years has produced what must be considered the true interpretation. See H.L. Jones, *The International Lawyer*, iii. (1969), 277. The point was put right by Lord Wilberforce in *Miliangos' Case*, [1976] A.C. 443, at p. 469.

[39] (1927) 274 U.S. 253, at pp. 255, 257; see also *Sutherland* v. *Mayer* (1926), 271 U.S. 272.

[40] See above, n. 38. For a recent example see *Paris* v. *Central Chiclera S. d. R.L.*, 193 F. (2d) 950 (C.C.A., 5th, 1952) with note in 61 (1952) *Yale L.J.* 758 and the interesting case of *The Tamaroa*, 189 F. (2d) 952 (C.C.A., 2d, 1951), also [1951] A.M.C. 1273: In

*Humphreys* it was both subject to German law and payable in Germany. The questions how the conversion is to be effected if the place of payment is in another country than that to whose laws the contract is subject, which law governs the determination of the situs of the place of payment, and how the money of account is to be ascertained, have not yet received a satisfactory answer; in the last connection it is apparently assumed that, if an obligation 'arises' in a certain country, it is subject to the laws and payable in the money of that country.[41,42] On the other hand, it appears that no distinction is made between a claim for damages and a claim for payment of a debt.[43] The most serious outstanding question, however, is whether the judgment-date rule applies only 'in Admiralty and other fields of purely federal statutory cognizance' or extends to 'diversity cases' in which federal courts have to apply the law of the State in which they are sitting. The United States Court of Appeals for the Ninth Circuit answered in the former sense, and held that, where an Argentinian seller claimed damages from a Californian buyer who had bought for pesos, 'the

---

1944 a collision occurred in English territorial waters between a British and a U.S. ship. The British ship was repaired in the United States at a cost of $118,000 odd which sum was paid to the repairers on behalf of the British Government and debited by it to the owners at the sterling equivalent of £29,000 odd. In 1951, after the devaluation of sterling, the owners were awarded $82,000 odd, i.e. the then dollar equivalent of £29,000, the court (Chase and Frank Ct. JJ., Swan Ct. J. dissenting) applying the judgment-date rule. It is respectfully submitted that the decision is open to much doubt, for it is uncertain whether there arose any problem of conversion: see above, pp. 247, 248. Perhaps the owners were entitled to the damage of $118,000. The case, which is also known as *Shaw, Savill, Albion & Co.* v. *The Fredericksburg*, is discussed by Brandon, *International & Comparative L.Q.* 1953, 313. Another recent example is *Conte* v. *Flota Mercante del Estado*, 277 F. 2d 664 (1960, C.C.A., 2d), where the court applied Argentine law both to questions of liability and quantum and stated very succinctly (p. 761): 'Conversion is made at the rate prevailing at the date of judgment, but we determine the amount to be converted as would the foreign court.' See, on the other hand, *The Gylfe* v. *The Trujillo*, 209 F. 2d 386 (1954, C.C.A., 2nd), where it was held that, where repairs were paid in foreign currency, the rate at the date when the expenditure was made, rather than the rate at the date of judgment applied.

[41] Such a view becomes plausible if it is remembered that Professor Beale's territorial theory always exercised great influence on Mr. Justice Holmes's mind: see, for example, his opinion in *Slater* v. *Mexican National Railway Co.* (1904), 194 U.S. 120.

[42] In *The Verdi, ubi supra*, it was apparently believed that the mere fact that the tort was committed in New York meant that the damages were payable there. In *The West Arrow, ubi supra*, the court seems to have assumed that, as the breach was in Holland and the ensuing obligation was expressed in Dutch guilders, it was performable in Holland. In *Det Forenede Dampskibs Selskab* v. *Insurance Company of North America*, 28 F. (2d) 449 (Southern District of New York 1928) aff'd 31 F. (2d) 658, cert. den. (1929), 280 U.S. 571, it was held that the right to contribution in general average 'crystallized upon the termination of the voyage, and since the voyage ended in an American port the owner became then and there entitled to receive contribution in dollars. This indebtedness arose in the United States, was payable in its currency and subject to its laws'. Therefore, the rate of exchange prevailing on the date of the termination of the voyage was applied. See also *Nevillon* v. *Demmer* (1920), 114 Misc. 1, 185 N.Y. Supp, 443, where francs which were promised in a note and were payable in Paris were converted into dollars at the rate of exchange prevailing at the commencement of the action, because the notes 'became payable in dollars (*sic*) upon plaintiff's demanding of defendant their payment in this state. The commencement of the action was equivalent to such a demand.'

[43] *The Integritas, ubi supra*.

Californian courts today would, in the domain of contract law, follow the so-called New York doctrine' rather than the federal rule.[44] Yet the First Circuit[45] and a New York District Court[46] did not hesitate to apply the judgment-date rule in a diversity suit.

The doctrine of the Supreme Court of the United States was not unequivocally followed by the New York courts, although it is put forward as a general proposition by the Restatement (Second) of the Conflict of Laws.[47] Already before that doctrine was formulated the New York courts had enunciated the principle that in the absence of special circumstances showing such rule to be inappropriate, a foreign money obligation the subject-matter of an action in New York must be converted into dollars at the rate of exchange prevailing on the date of breach or wrong.[48] It is not an exceptional circumstance within the meaning of this rule that the action is for a debt, not for damages,[49] or that the fluctuations of exchange went against the (American) plaintiff,[50] or that the obligation is subject to the laws of and payable in a foreign country.[51] The judgment-date, or rather the trial-date rule was, however, applied in *Sirie* v. *Godfrey*,[52] which related to a claim for 10,450 French francs made by a Paris ladies' dressmaker under a French contract in respect of goods sold to the defendant in 1914 in Paris. The plaintiff was not allowed to recover at the rate of exchange prevailing in 1914:

'This was a French contract for the sale in France of French goods for which the purchaser agreed to pay in French francs at Paris, France. At any time before

---

[44] *Compañia Engraw Commercial E. Industrial S.A.* v. *Schenley*, 181 F. 2d 876 (1950). For a similar result see the Court of Appeals for the District of Columbia in *Dante* v. *Miniggio*, 298 F. 845 (1924), 33 A.L.R. 1278, though it was decided before the *Deutsche Bank* case.

[45] *Gutor International A.G.* v. *Raymond Packer Co.*, 493 F. 2d 938 (1974) at p. 943.

[46] *The Island Territory of Curaçao* v. *Solitron Devices Inc.*, 356 F. Supp. 1 (1973), at p. 14.

[47] §144.

[48] *Gross* v. *Mendel* (1918), 225 N.Y. 633, 121 N.E. 871; *Hoppe* v. *Russo-Asiatic Bank* (1923), 200 App. Div. 400, 193 N.Y. Supp. 250, aff'd 253 N.Y. 37, 138 N.E. 497; *Kantor* v. *Aristo Hosiery Co.* (1928), 222 App. Div. 502, 226 N.Y. Supp. 582, aff'd 248 N.Y. 630, 162 N.E. 553; *Sokoloff* v. *National City Bank* (1928), 250 N.Y. 69, 164 N.E. 745; *Richard* v. *National City Bank of New York* (1931), 231 App. Div. 559, 248 N.Y. Supp. 113, see 31 (1931) *Col. L.R.* 882; *Parker* v. *Hoppe* (1931), 257 N.Y. 333, 178 N.E. 550, see 45 (1932) *Harv. L.R.* 1119; *Sulka* v. *Brandt* (1935), 154 Misc. 534, 277 N.Y. Supp. 421: the rule was applied to the detriment of the American plaintiff, who had sold goods to France for French francs and who had to suffer loss owing to the depreciation of the dollar. The New York rule (which has been held to prevail in California: *Compañia Engraw* v. *Schenley Distillers Corporation* (1950), 181 F. (2d) 876) was more recently applied in *Hughes Tool Co.* v. *United Artists Corporation*, 110 N.Y.S. 2d 383, 279 App. Div. 417 (1952), affirmed 304 N.Y. 942, 110 N.E. 2d 884 (1953); *De Sayve* v. *De la Valdene*, 124 N.Y.S. 2d 143 (1953), at p. 154, affirmed 130 N.Y.S. 2d 865; 131 N.Y.S. 881 and 307 N.Y. 861, 122 N.E. 2d 747. See also *Marburg* v. *Marburg* (1866), 26 Md. 8; *Nickerson* v. *Soesman* (1867), 98 Mass. 364.

[49] *Kantor* v. *Aristo Hosiery Co., ubi supra.*     [50] *Sulka* v. *Brandt, ubi supra.*

[51] *Gross* v. *Mendel, Hoppe* v. *Russo-Asiatic Bank, Kantor* v. *Aristo Hosiery Co., ubi supra; Taubenfeld* v. *Taubenfeld*, 198 Misc. 108, 97 N.Y.S. (2d) 158 (1950). Therefore the breach-date rule is applied even where according to *Deutsche Bank Filiale Nürnberg* v. *Humphreys, ubi supra*, the judgment-date rule would apply.

[52] (1921) 196 App. Div. 529, 188 N.Y. Supp. 52.

suit was brought the defendant could have tendered the plaintiff at Paris, France, the 10,450 francs in full payment of her claim, and plaintiff would have been compelled to accept same. . . . The purchase price of the goods in question was not payable in American dollars, nor was it payable in German marks. It was payable in French francs, and by merely bringing action in this jurisdiction the plaintiff, I apprehend, acquired no right to a more favourable judgment than she could have obtained had action been brought in France.'

On very similar facts this decision was followed in *Metcalf* v. *Mayer*,[53] and in *Buxhoeden* v. *Estonian State Bank*,[54] but it was distinguished in the startling case of *Orlik* v. *Wiener Bankverein*,[55] where the facts were practically on all fours with *Deutsche Bank Filiale Nürnberg* v. *Humphreys*.[56] The plaintiff had 60,000 kroners on deposit with the defendants in Vienna for which in July 1919 he had paid $2,190. In September 1919 he demanded payment in Vienna, which was refused. On the authority of *Sirie* v. *Godfrey*[57] the defendants contended that the only obligation was to pay 60,000 kroners which at the time of trial had a value of $19.50. The court discussed the English cases of *Di Ferdinando* v. *Simon Smits & Co.*[58] and of *Société des Hôtels Le Touquet* v. *Cummings*[59] and, relying on Scrutton L.J.'s remarks[60] about *Pilkington* v. *Commissioners for Claims on France*[61] and about the rule that 'personal property follows the domicil', it arrived at this conclusion:

'In the case at bar, however, the plaintiff is not a resident of Austria. The delivery promised was to a foreigner, an American resident, of 60,000 kronen on demand. This contract was broken on 2nd September 1919, and within the authorities above cited plaintiff was entitled to the exchange value of such kronen at the time of breach.'

The picture becomes even more confused by the fact that, while two relatively recent cases seem to adopt the federal rule,[62] the latest decision reverts to the breach-date rule.[63] French francs were due to the French seller from the New York buyer at a date well before the devaluation of the French franc on 8 August 1968. After referring to a few of the conflicting precedents the New York Supreme Court applied the breach-date rule on the ground that 'the equities favor' it, for if it were not applied 'the defendant would be rewarded for defaulting in his obligation'.

This observation may well be indicative of the tendency which may come to prevail in New York: the courts may apply such rate as in a given case 'the equities favor'. The true equity and the real reason should be that it is not the function of legal proceedings to interfere with substantive rights. It is their function to enforce rights. The idea that default or breach creates entitlement to a

---

[53] (1925) 213 App. Div. 607, 211 N.Y. Supp. 53.
[54] (1951) 106 N.Y.S. (2d) 287.
[55] (1923) 204 App. Div. 432, 198 N.Y. Supp. 413.
[56] (1926) 272 U.S. 517.                                        [57] Above, n. 52.
[58] [1920] 2 K.B. 704.                                           [59] [1922] 1 K.B. 451.
[60] At pp. 460, 461; they are discussed above, p. 271, n. 13, and p. 323.
[61] (1821) 2 Knapp P.C. 7.
[62] *Application of United Shellac Corporation*, 97 N.Y. Supp. 2d 817 (1950); *Bonell* v. *Schultz*, 95 N.Y. Supp. 2d 617 (1950).
[63] *Librairie Hachette* v. *Paris Book Center Inc.*, 309 N.Y. Supp. 2d 701 (1970).

currency which previously was not the money of account, whether actual or potential, lacks both justification and attraction.

## IV

In England the law had a long development which began in the early seventeenth century and in modern times led to many problems and difficulties and serious criticism on a national and international level. But the history became uninteresting and worthless and the accumulated case law[64] was rendered obsolete, when in 1975 the law was radically changed by a remarkable piece of judicial legislation. It has resulted in a pattern which allows the law to be stated in a few simple sentences and produces throughout wholly satisfactory solutions so as to leave no room for academic discussion.

It is now clear that English law does not require any foreign money obligation to be converted into sterling for the purpose of instituting proceedings or of the judgment; on the contrary, where the plaintiff claims a sum of foreign money, he is both entitled and bound to apply for judgment in terms of such foreign money[65] and it is only at the stage of payment or enforcement that conversion into sterling at the rate of exchange then prevailing takes place.[66] This is so whether the claim is for payment of a specific sum contractually due[67] or for damages for breach of contract[68] or tort[69] or for a just sum due in respect of unjustified enrichment,[70] or for restitution.[71] Nor does it matter whether the contract sued upon is governed by English[72] or by foreign[73] law. Nor is it necessary to ask for specific performance rather than payment:[74] in either case the defendant will

---

[64] It was collected and discussed in detail in the third edition of this book.

[65] *Miliangos* v. *George Frank (Textiles) Ltd.*, [1976] A.C. 443.

[66] *Miliangos'* case, *ubi supra*, at pp. 463, 468 and 469 *per* Lord Wilberforce, 497–8 *per* Lord Cross of Chelsea, at p. 501 *per* Lord Edmund-Davies approving Lord Denning's formula in *Schorsch Meier G.m.b.H.* v. *Hennin*, [1975] Q.B. 416, at p. 427.

[67] As in *Miliangos'* case itself.

[68] *Services Europe Atlantique Sud* v. *Stockholm Rederi Aktiebolag Sven*, [1979] A.C. 699; approving *Jean Kraut A.G.* v. *Albany Fabrics Ltd.*, [1977] Q.B. 182.

[69] *The Despina R.* (1979), A.C. 685 on which see Knott, 43 (1980) M.L.R. 18.

[70] *B.P. Exploration Co. (Libya) Ltd.* v. *Hunt* (1979), 1 W.L.R. 783, 840–1 *per* Robert Goff, J., affirmed [1981] 1 W.L.R. 232, at p. 245.

[71] See *Re Dawson* (1966), 2 N.S.W.R. 211: a defaulting trustee who in 1939 wrongfully took £4,700 New Zealand currency was in 1966 liable to restore the then value in terms of Australian currency, i.e. £A 5,829. Lord Wilberforce in *Miliangos'* case, *ubi supra*, at p. 468 approves the decision.

[72] *Federal Commerce and Navigation Co. Ltd.* v. *Tradax Export S.A.*, [1977] Q.B. 324 reversed on other grounds by the House of Lords [1978] A.C. 1.

[73] As in *Miliangos'* case itself.

[74] It had before 1961 been held that specific performance could not be claimed: *Lloyd Royal Belge* v. *Louis Dreyfus & Co.* (1927), 27 Ll.L.R. 2888, at p. 293 *per* Romer J.; *In re United Railways of Havana and Regla Warehouses Ltd.*, [1961] A.C. 1007, at p. 1052 *per*

be ordered to pay foreign money. Moreover an award in an English arbitration may be expressed and enforced in foreign currency[75] and a foreign award or judgment so expressed may be enforced like the English award or judgment.[76] Certain statutory provisions are designed to ensure similar results in the fields of law covered by them.[77] In short, in the realm of legal proceedings foreign money is being treated in almost exactly the same way as sterling.[78]

This means that the incidence and effect of nominalism, a rule of substantive law, is allowed to operate without any influence of the purely procedural implications of a law suit. Law has been victorious over procedure and there is in this context no longer room for Plucknett's dictum which in previous editions used to introduce the present chapter: 'One of the most significant themes in the study of legal history is the growth of the power to think of law apart from its procedure.'

If the foreign currency depreciates in terms of sterling the law as it now stands allows the creditor to recover the amount of foreign currency he is entitled to and does not attempt to compensate him for the loss which he suffers as a result of the debtor's default in discharging his obligations. The consequences of that default have to be decided upon, not by the law of procedure which is concerned with the enforcement rather than the creation of rights, but by the proper law of the contract or the substantive law governing the particular obligation under consideration. Where the applicable law is English it is, therefore, most important in the interest of justice and in accordance with suggestions made earlier in this book[79] to develop a sound rule permitting the recovery of damages for the loss caused by the depreciation of foreign money—a rule such as many foreign countries have evolved and which, it is submitted, is or ought to be concomitant to the modern English law.[80] Such a rule is particularly

Lord Reid. But, as Lord Wilberforce recognized in *Miliangos'* case, at p. 467, it was difficult to maintain this in the face of *Beswick* v. *Beswick*, [1968] A.C. 58.

[75] *Jugoslavenska Oceanska Plovidba* v. *Castle Investment Co. Inc.*, [1974] Q.B. 292.

[76] See s. 4 (2) (b) of the Administration of Justice Act 1977.

[77] As to Carriage by Air see Art. 22 (3) of the Convention in Schedule 1 to the Carriage by Air and Road Act 1979; as to carriage of passengers and their luggage see Art. 9 of the Convention in Part II of Schedule 3 to the Merchant Shipping Act 1979; see also the Carriage of Goods by Road Act 1965, Art. 27 (2) of the Convention in the Schedule.

[78] There was and is no rational ground for restraining the Admiralty Marshall from selling a ship for dollars and retaining them pending distribution of the proceeds: *The Halcyon the Great* (1975), 1 W.L.R. 515.

[79] See above, pp. 108, 287.

[80] Dicey and Morris, p. 1017 suggest that in the case under discussion 'no doubt the creditor cannot for that reason (i.e. the depreciation of the foreign currency) claim more in foreign currency than the agreed amount of the debt'. This cannot be a rule of the conflict of laws and in so far as the learned authors intend to discuss municipal law their statement needs much qualification. See above, p. 287.

necessary in cases in which the contract provides for conversion into sterling at the rate of a certain date: the courts will give effect to the parties' agreement and leave it to the law of damages to decide whether the creditor is entitled to compensation for any loss resulting from delayed payment.

If, on the other hand, sterling depreciates in terms of foreign currency, the creditor of a foreign money obligation who brings proceedings in England is no longer penalised by doing so: he will recover judgment for what he is entitled to without being prejudiced by a quirk of English procedural law.

The present English law was readily adopted in Scotland[81] and by the High Court of Ontario[82] and will, it is hoped, also find favour elsewhere in the British Commonwealth of Nations where the old English law was unfortunately far too uncritically followed.[83]

## V

The present interest of the pre-1975 law and of the evolution which resulted in the law summarized in the preceding section lies in the lessons taught to the student of jurisprudence rather than monetary law. What occurred in 1975 was 'a revolutionary change'[84] accomplished by the judiciary in circumstances which merit a few comments.

From a purely legal point of view the basic error consisted of the remarkably narrow interpretation which the courts placed upon their powers by asserting that they could only give judgment in terms of sterling.[85] Even if one accepts the principle (which, as has been shown, is by no means unknown elsewhere), there was, one should have thought, nothing to prevent a court from giving judgment for such sum of sterling as at the date of payment represents the equivalent of the due sum of foreign money. Yet immediately after the first

[81] *Commerzbank A.G.* v. *Large*, 1977 S.L.T. 219 (First Division of the Inner House).

[82] *Batavia Times Publishing Co.* v. *Davis*, 88 (1979) D.L.R. 3d 144 (Carruthers J. sitting in the Ontario High Court), though he adopts the rate at the date of judgment rather than payment, since Canadian judgments must be expressed in terms of Canadian dollars. See also above, p. 198.

[83] Sykes and Pryles, *Australian Private International Law* (1979), p. 372, suggest that 'there are sound reasons why *Miliangos* should be followed in Australia'.

[84] *Miliangos* v. *George Frank (Textiles) Ltd.*, [1976] A.C. 443, at p. 482 *per* Lord Simon of Glaisdale.

[85] This was stated in terms by Sir Nathaniel Lindley M.R. in *Manners* v. *Pearson*, [1898] 1 Ch. 581, 587, and subsequently taken for granted and sometimes repeated: *Di Ferdinando* v. *Simon Smits & Co.*, [1920] 3 K.B. 409, 415 *per* Scrutton L.J.; *The Volturno*, [1921] 2 A.C. 544, 560 *per* Lord Parmoor; *In re Chesterman's Trust*, [1923] 2 Ch. 466, 490 *per* Younger L.J.; *Re United Railways of Havana and Regla Warehouses Ltd.*, [1961] A.C. 1007, at p. 1043 *per* Viscount Simonds, at p. 1052 *per* Lord Reid, at p. 1069 *per* Lord Denning.

world war the courts propounded the breach-date rule by insisting upon judgment being given for a sum of sterling calculated by converting the foreign money at the rate of exchange of the date of breach or wrong[86]—a rule for which previously there was hardly any authority, although in 1961 Viscount Simonds thought[87] that the form of action employed in 1626 was 'extremely enlightening if not decisive'.

In the 1920s sterling was strong and the foreign currencies which fell to be considered tended to depreciate. The application of the breach-date rule, therefore, had the effect of allowing the creditor liquidated damages for the debtor's default:[88] it protected the creditor of sterling against the depreciation of other currencies and could, in justice, be supported on such grounds. In fact, however, the reasoning was quite different: it was purely conceptualist and based on the alleged character of the foreign money obligation as an obligation to deliver a commodity and of its breach as giving rise to a claim for damages. As a matter of logic and truly legal appreciation and reasoning the theory was untenable, irrespective of the absurd result in the converse case, possibly not envisaged, yet never remote, of a depreciation of sterling.

Indeed, from 1931 onwards the value of sterling in relation to many foreign currencies began to fall and, though at first this did not become apparent in judicial practice,[89] after the second world war the economic consequences of the breach-date rule, originally intended to benefit the creditor of non-sterling currency, were liable to be highly prejudicial to him and might well be described as amounting to a penalty.

---

[86] As to debts expressed in foreign currency see *In re British American Continental Bank Ltd., Credit General Liegeois Claim*, [1922] 2 Ch. 589; *Uliendahl v. Pankhurst Wright & Co.* (1923), 39 T.L.R. 628; *Peyrae v. Wilkinson*, [1924] 2 K.B. 166; *Lloyd Royal Belge v. Louis Dreyfus & Co.* (1927), 27 Ll. L.R. 288 (C.A.); *Société des Hôtels Le Touquet v. Cummings*, [1922] 1 K.B. 451, 465 *per* Atkin L.J.; *Cummings v. London Bullion Co. Ltd.*, [1952] 1 K.B. 327, and, finally, the decision of the House of Lords *In re United Railways of Havana and Regla Warehouses Ltd.*, [1961] A.C. 1007. As to damages for breach of contract see *Ottoman Bank v. Chakarian* (No. 1), [1930] A.C. 277; *Di Ferdinando v. Simon Smits & Co.*, [1920] 2 K.B. 704; *Bain v. Field* (1920), 5 Ll. L.R. 16; *In re British American Continental Bank Ltd., Goldzieher & Penso's Claim*, [1922] 2 Ch. 575; *Lisser & Rosencranz's Claim*, [1923] 1 Ch. 276, among other cases and dicta. As to damages for tort see *The Volturno*, [1921] 2 A.C. 544. There were numerous other cases in related fields and the rule was accepted in Scotland, Australia, and Canada. For details see the previous editions of this book.

[87] *In re United Railways of Havana and Regla Warehouses Ltd., ubi supra*, at p. 1043.

[88] This was frankly admitted by the New York Supreme Court, when it said in *Librairie Hachette S.A. v. Paris Book Center Inc.*, 309 N.Y. Supp. 2d 701, 705 (1970): 'In this case the equities favor application of the "breach day rule". If it were not applied, the defendant would be rewarded for defaulting in his obligation to pay for the merchandise.'

[89] *Madeleine Vionnet & Cie v. Wills*, [1940] 1 K.B. 72.

The first edition of this book had strongly criticized the rule and all its aspects and implications. In 1952 the Monetary Law Committee of the International Law Association took up the subject and in 1956 produced the 'Dubrovnik' Rules[90] adoption of which would have led to the conversion at the date of payment. In the following year the Lord Chancellor referred the Dubrovnik Rules to the Private International Law Committee. It considered the matter for not much less than six years. At the end of 1961 the majority of the Committee which included its Chairman, Mr. Justice Cross, and Mr. Justice Wilberforce (as they then were), refrained from recommending any change of the law mainly on the ground that there were 'wide differences of view' within the Committee and that any change would give rise to 'extremely difficult questions of practice and procedure' which would 'fall far outside the proper scope and purview of the Committee'.[91]

The next step was that, in the absence of the United Kingdom, but with the present writer acting as Special Consultant, the problem was taken up by the Council of Europe. A large international Committee produced the European Convention on Foreign Money Liabilities which in December 1967 was opened for signature.[92] It did not become effective, because most countries did not need it and Britain stood aloof until the events of 1975 made it there largely superfluous.

These events were due to a reconsideration of the legal issues by a House of Lords presided over by Lord Wilberforce (who had represented the unsuccessful respondents in 1961 in *Re United Railways of Havana and Regla Warehouses Ltd.*),[93] and including Lord Cross of Chelsea, but it must not be overlooked that there were also other and perhaps more potent reasons for a change of the law. In the first place under the leadership of Lord Denning M.R., who in 1961 had been a consenting party to the decision of the House of Lords just referred to, but who by 1970 found the common law on the subject 'most unsatisfactory',[94] the Court of Appeal (Lord Denning M.R., Lawton L.J., and Foster J.) revolted in 1975[95] and refused to follow the breach-date rule on grounds which in strict law were far from convincing, but produced the result that in justice could only be described as compelling. It is no exaggeration to say that the House, when shortly afterwards it was confronted with a different

---

[90] *Report of the 47th Conference* (Dubrovnik, 1956), p. 294.

[91] Cmnd. 1648, paragraph 14.

[92] For the text see below, p. 576. The Convention was signed by Austria, France, Germany, and Luxembourg.

[93] [1961] A.C. 1007.          [94] *The Teh Hu*, [1970] P. 106, at p. 124.

[95] *Schorsch Meier G.m.b.H.* v. *Hennin*, [1975] Q.B. 416.

case involving the same legal problem, could not have disapproved of the Court of Appeal's decision without doing a great disservice to the English and international commercial community.

There was, however, also a strong commercial force at work. In 1974 the Court of Appeal, with the unmistakable support of the City of London, had held that an English award could be made and enforced in terms of foreign currency.[96] This was a most important development which had been advocated in the third edition of the present work and was necessary to prevent London's death as a centre of international arbitration. Once this step, dictated by the demands of economic self-protection, had been taken, it would have been paradoxical for the House of Lords, as it expressly recognized, to maintain the old rule for purposes of litigation.

Finally, it is illuminating to observe how the 'extremely difficult questions of practice and procedure' which had oppressed the majority of the Private International Law Committee were disposed of by a few words of Lord Denning's which the House of Lords approved. He held that judgment could be given for the amount of foreign money claimed 'or the sterling equivalent thereof at the date when the court authorises enforcement of the judgment in terms of sterling'.[97] In view of foreign examples this was an obvious solution which the minority of 1961 had suggested, but it required a Lord Denning to blow away the cobweb of allegedly unsurmountable technicalities.

The legal developments and the movement for reform during the half-century from about the end of the first world war to 1975 are now only history which is liable to be forgotten quickly. Yet they are also an instructive illustration of the vicissitudes of legal reform in a field which is free from any political connotation, but, on the contrary, involves merely technical legal considerations of an almost elementary character.[98]

---

[96] *Jugoslavenska Oceanska Plovidba* v. *Castle Investment Co. Inc.*, [1974] Q.B. 292.

[97] *Miliangos'* case, *ubi supra*, at pp. 468, 469 *per* Lord Wilberforce. The technicalities relating to execution founded upon a judgment for the payment of foreign money are outside the scope of this book. They are dealt with in *Practice Directions* which are published, for instance, in (1976) 1 W.L.R. 83 and in the *Annual Practice*, but are without statutory force. No practical problem of any consequence has become known. It is perhaps appropriate to submit that in many respects a judgment debt is not different from an ordinary debt. Accordingly, (1) an English judgment for a sum of foreign money may, at the debtor's option, at any time be discharged by payment in sterling, England necessarily being the place of payment (see above pp. 76, n. 70, 316); it would be absurd if sterling could only be paid after commencement of execution. (2) if there occurs a depreciation of the foreign currency the subject-matter of the English judgment in relation to sterling between its date and actual payment, the judgment creditor should be entitled to damages: see above p. 348. No question of *res judicata* arises. A judgment debt should in this respect not be treated otherwise than any other debt.    [98] For an additional note on this, see p. 580.

# PART III

# EXCHANGE CONTROL
# AND VALUATION OF
# FOREIGN CURRENCIES

# INTRODUCTION

I T will be recalled that it was the primary object of the first part of this book to consider a domestic (English) currency within the setting of its own domestic (English) law, and that the second part dealt with foreign (for example, French) currency within the sphere of domestic (English) law. The relationship between a given domestic currency, on the one hand, and a foreign currency, on the other hand, could not be entirely ignored; thus reference had to be made to certain problems of conversion,[1] particularly to the question of the date with reference to which conversion has to take place.[2] However, notwithstanding some overlapping and some unavoidable inelegancies, the main problem of the exchange of one currency for another remains to be treated separately in the following, third part of this book. The *homo oeconomicus* of the twentieth century knows that exchange, and the balance of payments, has become its conundrum and one of its principal diseases. The effect on the law has been profound. It justifies and requires a more extensive and careful treatment of exchange control and of the rate of exchange, these being the two headings which convey to the lawyer the relationship and interconnection between the domestic and the foreign currency.

Accordingly, the following chapters will be devoted to exchange control in the United Kingdom (Chapter XIII), to the special rules developed by the International Monetary Fund (Chapter XIV), to the effect of other countries' exchange control in England, i.e. the private international law of exchange control (Chapter XV), and to the valuation of currencies (Chapter XVI).

The fact that, in so far as the substantive law of exchange control is concerned, the discussion will be confined to the law of the United Kingdom, will not cause any surprise. A comparative treatment of

---

[1] Above, pp. 306, 330, 339 sqq.
[2] Above, pp. 309, 330 sqq.

these matters is neither necessary nor possible. In their kernel the exchange control regulations of the world are identical, though they may differ in detail; moreover to a large extent they are liable to undergo rapid changes; they are, in general, not intended as permanent measure, however long the temporary control may last.[3] A comparative treatment would also have involved a departure from the basic objects of this book which is a treatise on the law of money rather than a monograph on the law of exchange control.

Within the context of municipal legislation the definition of exchange control or exchange restrictions did not in the past and is unlikely in the future to cause any difficulty. Hence it is unnecessary at this stage to deal with such problems of definition as there may be,[4] nor is it usual for exchange control legislation to include references to convertibility or inconvertibility,—terms peculiar to public international law.[5] It must suffice to point out that exchange control in the ordinary sense of the term and as understood by most is concerned with the limitation of outward movements of payments or transfers. In recent years there have been countries which imposed restrictions upon the inward payment of money. Thus the Federal Republic of Germany had for a time a system of cash deposit requirements[6] or Switzerland adopted limitations on interest payments to, and on purchases of Swiss securities by, foreigners as well as certain charges in the nature of special taxes to restrain capital inflows from abroad.[7] No such restrictions have been introduced in Britain, although there have been times, when, for instance, the importation of foreign goods gave rise to an import deposit repayable after 180 days.[8] If and when legislation of this type should come into force in England, its interpretation and application will be subject to established principles and does not at present require separate discussion.

---

[3] There exist some comparative works on exchange control, but in the nature of things they are bound to become rapidly obsolete. The book by Lemkin, *La Réglementation des Paiements Internationaux* (Paris, 1939), is now of little value. For more recent and, therefore, more useful surveys see Liebich, *Elemente des Devisenrechts* (Basel, 1955), or *Le Contrôle des Changes* (edited by the Institut de Droit Comparé, Paris, 1955). On the French law in 1960 see Jeantet, 'Exchange Control Regulations in France' in Stein and Nicolson, *American Enterprise in the European Common Market*, i (1960), 189 sqq. An introductory survey of the legal position in member States is to be found in the International Monetary Fund's Annual Reports on Exchange Restrictions.

[4] See below, p. 518.                                    [5] See below, p. 519.

[6] Hahn, 'Bardepot und Währungsrecht', in *Verwaltung im Dienste von Wirtschaft und Gesellschaft (Festschrift für Ludwig Fröhler*, 1980), p. 413.

[7] See the Annual Reports of the International Monetary Fund on Exchange Restrictions.

[8] Customs (Import Deposits) Act 1968.

# XIII

# Exchange Control in the United Kingdom

## I

THE regulation of payments made from this country to foreign countries has a long history which by no means justifies the popular belief that recent legislative events constitute a new development. It was at the beginning of the fourteenth century that laws against the export of gold and silver 'became a really important part of the commercial regulations of England'.[1] From then onwards through the centuries numerous enactments were passed which made the export of the precious metals illegal without the King's licence. A particularly ambitious scheme of control was set up in the year 1576. Its effects have been summed up by R. H. Tawney in words which so aptly fit the modern problem into its historical frame that they should be quoted.[2]

Attempts at stabilisation, the pegging of exchanges, a public change department or Devisencentrale, the prohibition of business except on a certificate showing bona fide commercial transactions[3]—such expedients are no longer to-day the unfamiliar heresies which they would have appeared in the Arcadia of economic harmony whose funeral oration has been rehearsed so often since 1914 by the mournful admiration of economists. In the sixteenth century, which was the victim of a similar attack of that disease of distorted currencies which poisons the twentieth, the suspension of private exchange transactions was . . . part of the traditional policy for raising the value of sterling, and there was nothing surprising in the Government of Elizabeth reverting to it.

[1] Feavearyear, p. 3.

[2] Introduction, pp. 134–54, at p. 151 to his edition (1925) of Dr. Thomas Wilson, *A Discourse upon Usury* (1572). On the history of French export and import restrictions of money see Dareste de la Chavanne, *Histoire de l'Administration en France*, ii (1848), 157; at p. 159 the interesting fact is stated that 'on regardait l'argent exporté comme perdu, parce qu'on ne tenait pas compte de ce qu'on recevait en retour'.

[3] Today we would speak of current transactions.

The whole matter was again dealt with by two Acts of 1663[4] and 1696[5] which remained in force until, at the end of the Bank Restriction period, Parliament repealed[6] the long list of statutes prohibiting the export of precious metals and, after more than 500 years, finally established complete freedom of trade.[7] During the war of 1914–18 there was no specific prohibition of the export of gold (nor exchange control in general), but by purely administrative measures the Government succeeded in preventing any such export;[8] in 1919 an Order-in-Council prohibiting export was made,[9] and in 1920[10] the power given by this Order was extended until the end of 1925. Complete freedom of trade was restored in 1925[11] and remained intact until the outbreak of the Second World War.

The first Order-in-Council, made in pursuance of s. 1 of the Emergency Powers (Defence) Act, 1939, and containing the Defence (Finance) Regulations, 1939, in their original form, was dated 25 August 1939.[12] However, for many years the Defence (Finance) Regulations Amendment Order of 23 November 1939[13] was the basis of exchange control in the United Kingdom. It was frequently amended, but the last remnants disappeared only in 1964.[14] Today exchange control is mainly founded upon the Exchange Control Act, 1947, which came into force on 1 October 1947.[15] It has been supplemented by numerous Statutory Instruments and so-called Notices to Banks by which the Exchange Control Authorities explain their policy and inform the banking world of the cases in which they will or will not give a permission.[16]

Whether the continuation of exchange control after the end of the

---

[4] 15 Chas. II, ch. 7, s. 12.   [5] 7 & 8 Will. III, ch. 19.

[6] 59 Geo. III, ch. 49, ss. 10–12; 1 & 2 Geo. IV, ch. 26, s. 4.

[7] On this development see Feavearyear, pp. 3, 4, 221.

[8] Ibid., p. 307 of the 1st edition. The passage is omitted from the second edition.

[9] Under the power given by s. 8 of the Customs and Inland Revenue Act, 1879, and by the Customs (Exportation Prohibition) Act, 1914. The Order in Council was published in the *London Gazette* of 1 Apr. 1919.

[10] Gold and Silver (Export Control, &c.) Act, 1920.

[11] See Feavearyear, p. 359.   [12] S.R. & O. 1939, No. 950.

[13] Ibid., No. 1620; for a survey see Mann, 'Exchange Restrictions in England', 3 (1939–40) *Mod. L.R.* 202.

[14] As a result of s. 22 and Schedule 2 of the Emergency Laws (Re-enactments and Repeals) Act, 1964. Earlier repeals had been effected by s. 2 of the Emergency Laws (Repeal) Act, 1959, and by the Exchange Control (Transitional Provisions) Order 1947, S.R. & O. 1947, No. 2052 and by S.I. 1953, No. 1207.

[15] S.R. & O. 1947, No. 2035; for a survey see Mann, 'The Exchange Control Act, 1947', 10 (1947) *Mod. L.R.* 411. The book by F. C. Howard, *Exchange and Borrowing Control* (1948), with Supplement (1950), is now obsolete. The book by Anthony Parker, *Exchange Control* (3rd ed., 1978), is purely descriptive and makes no attempt at scholarly analysis. Ss. 21, 22, and 42 were slightly amended by s. 55 of the Finance Act, 1968.

[16] These Notices do not have the force of law.

Second World War resulted from economic reasons or political aims, whether in fact it was necessary or avoidable, whether, as a matter of policy, it must be deemed a sound or an unwise measure, these are questions which a lawyer cannot answer and is not even required to raise. But there is no doubt that that decision constituted a most fateful step which determined the course of British economic development and the consequences of which will be felt for long. That at any rate up to 1959 the Bank of England considered it 'most detestable' comes as no surprise, but, in the interest of history, deserves to be recorded.[17]

At last, after a few days more than 32 years, on 19 October 1979 the Treasury made nine Orders granting general exemption from all prohibitions and consents to all transactions and thus deprived the Act of practical effect.[18] As from 13 December 1979 these Orders were replaced by another Order[19] which in substance provided that 'no obligation or prohibition imposed by or under the Exchange Control Act 1947 shall bind or apply to any person in or resident in the United Kingdom or the Channel Islands or apply in relation to any transaction, and, in so far as the permission of the Treasury for any transaction is required by or under the said Act, such permission is hereby given.'[20] The Act, however, was not repealed and its operation is, therefore, liable to be reinstated. Hence it is unfortunately impossible to suppress the present Chapter. It can only be hoped that economic difficulties or political doctrinairism will

---

[17] On 31 Aug. 1959 *The Times* published a letter from Mr. H. A. Siepmann, a former director of the Bank of England, who stated that for some fifteen years he had been responsible for exchange control and that his successors, though they 'may not feel free to reply', probably would not repudiate him as their unofficial spokesman. The letter continued: 'Exchange control is the most pervasive and intrusive of all controls. It directly affects not only professional dealers or business men, but every citizen, irrespective of his status or activities. Not only that, it touches the individual in his most personal and private concerns: his family relationships, his secret benefactions, and what he regards as his moral obligations. Considering how few of us are fitted to be judges in our own cause, exchange control ought to be the most hated, as it is the most destestable, form of Government interference. In a phrase which I claim to have originated, it was dubbed "futile and mischievous" by the Brussels Financial Conference of 1920. It has not proved to be that; but it might well have proved to be much worse than that. Yet in this country how has it turned out? Experience entitles me to say that the public as a whole has been amazingly docile. The control which, of all controls, could be expected to provoke the most resentment, has been the least resented. I assert this as a fact. And the reason for this astonishing result? . . . It is that exchange control has, from the first, been administered by the Bank of England with two things constantly in mind: First, that it is by its very nature hateful; and, secondly, that although like any other administration it has to be governed by general rules and categories, justice requires that every particular case should be regarded and treated as circumstantially unique.' It is possible that things have changed a little since then.

[18] S.I. 1979, Nos. 1331 to 1339.

[19] S.I. 1979, No. 1660.

[20] Articles 2 and 4.

never become such as to confer renewed relevance upon it. In order to mark the present position the remainder of this Chapter is being printed in smaller type. On the other hand it did not seem possible to substitute the past for the present tense; the latter is probably less liable to mislead than the former, particularly in so far as secondary legislation is concerned.

## II

The general scheme of the Exchange Control Act[21] 'follows the "streamlined" pattern, that is to say, it takes powers for controlling and prohibiting far more than it could conceivably be desirable to control and prohibit in practice'.[22] Hence it establishes a system of considerable complication, though it would appear that it works with greater efficiency and flexibility than those of most other countries; to some extent this is no doubt due to the fact that the Treasury which, by the Act, is entrusted with exchange control, has delegated its powers to the Bank of England which in turn has sub-delegated many of its powers to the leading banks.[23] The powers conferred by the Exchange Control Act, 1947, are very substantially enlarged by the far too little-known provision of s. 2 of the Emergency Laws (Re-enactments and Repeals) Act, 1964: 'where the Treasury are satisfied that action to the detriment of the economic position of the United Kingdom is being, or is likely to be, taken by the government of, or persons resident in', any country, the Treasury may give directions blocking such government's or person's money, gold, and securities in the United Kingdom. No case has become known in which these almost extravagant powers have been exercised in peace-time; if any such case should ever occur, it may attract the international responsibility of the United Kingdom.

It cannot be the purpose of the following pages to aim at something like a commentary on English exchange regulations or a description of English exchange control practice. Such an attempt would not be in line with the general character of this book and, moreover, would meet with almost unsurmountable practical difficulties. It must suffice to draw attention to the most important legal characteristics of the English exchange control system; even these continue to be largely unexplored, chiefly because since 1939 only a few relevant decisions have been reported in the books.[24]

The Act is divided into six Parts: gold and foreign currency; payments; securities; import and export; miscellaneous; and supplemental provisions.

---

[21] On its background and implications in international law see below, p. 522.

[22] *The Times*, 14 Nov. 1946, p. 5, where the Bill is also described as a 'Draconian measure'.

[23] The Treasury, however, in practice has retained some sort of an appellate jurisdiction. The exercise of exchange control is an act done *jure imperii* and in respect of any such act any bank and, in particular the central bank is in a foreign court entitled to immunity: *Pan American Tankers* v. *Republic of Viet-Nam*, 296 F. Supp. 361 (1969); Cass. Civ. 19 May 1976, *Rev. Crit.* 1977, 359.

[24] This must be noted as a very remarkable fact.

In addition there are six schedules. Many provisions of the Act are not concerned with money in the narrow sense of the term, but with monetary resources. Thus, Part III relates exclusively to securities, their issue, transfer, and deposit, while s. 30 deals with the restrictions which may be imposed upon foreign companies by reason of the fact that those controlling them are resident in this country.

Most of the provisions of the Act contain prohibitions. They are not usually absolute in character, but are relative in the sense that they are predicated upon the absence of the Treasury's permission, consent, or authority. This may be general or special, absolute or conditional, limited in point of time or unlimited, it may also be revoked,[25] but cannot be given with retrospective effect,[26] but it is doubtful whether it must be in writing and whether it may be implied.[27] Failure to observe the prohibitions contained in the Act usually, but not always,[28] makes the transaction illegal and void,[29] and also involves the criminal liability of 'any person in or resident in the United Kingdom' and of 'any such person who conspires or attempts, or aids, abets, counsels or procures any other person' to contravene the restrictions imposed by the Act.[30] The question to what extent *mens rea* is required is an open one. It is, however, clear that, apart from the special case of s. 37 (3), mere ignorance of the provisions of the Act or error of

---

[25] s. 37.

[26] The question whether an administrative permission may have retrospective effect is one of construction: *Howell* v. *Falmouth Boat Construction Co. Ltd.*, [1951] A.C. 837. In the case of the Exchange Control Act, it will have to be answered in the negative, because by expressly providing for retroactivity in certain cases (ss. 18 (2), 28 (2) and 29 (2)) the Act would seem to deny it for other cases. In *Mortarana* v. *Morley* (1958), 108 Law Journal 204, Judge Cohen, sitting in the Marylebone County Court, held (probably rightly) that an Italian plaintiff who had lent to the British defendant 130,000 lire when the latter fell ill in Sicily and had exhausted his travel allowance could not, in view of s. 1 of the Act, recover from the defendant notwithstanding the grant of permission by the Treasury shortly before the trial. The case illustrates the shocking injustice which the Act is likely to cause. See on this point also below, p. 366.

[27] This is again a question of statutory interpretation of great difficulty: see *Howell*'s case (preceding note) or *Jackson Stansfield & Sons* v. *Butterworth* (1948), 64 T.L.R. 481.

[28] See, for example, s. 29 (2).

[29] Consequently, where the payment or transfer is illegal, it cannot be recovered by means of an action for money had and received: *Boissevain* v. *Weil*, [1950] A.C. 327, at p. 341 *per* Lord Radcliffe. This is different only if the plaintiff, in ignorance of the law and as a result of the defendant's fraud, made a payment contrary to the provisions of the Act: *Shelley* v. *Paddock* (1980), 2 W.L.R. 647. In *Swiss Bank Corporation* v. *Lloyds Bank Ltd.* (1980), 2 All E.R. 419, at p. 431, the Court of Appeal, speaking through Buckley L.J., said that contraventions of the Act attracted criminal sanctions, they were 'clearly *mala prohibita*, not *mala in se*' and, therefore, they were 'not acts the validity of which the law refuses to countenance for any purpose. As such they are not devoid of any effect: they merely expose the culprit to the penalties prescribed by the Act.' It is possible that this dictum was intended to be limited to violations of s. 16 (2) of the Act with which the case was primarily concerned and is justified within its context. If the Court of Appeal intended to lay down a general rule applicable to the Exchange Control Act 1947 as a whole, it would be necessary most respectfully to express grave doubts about its correctness. More than 150 years ago Best J. said in *Bensley* v. *Bignold* (1822), 5 B. and Al. 335, at p. 341: 'the old-fashioned distinction between *mala prohibita* and *male in se* is long since exploded.'

[30] Clause 1 of the Fifth Schedule, Part II.

law is no defence. Moreover, the Act will be strictly enforced, for, as Lord Goddard C.J. has said,[31] it

> was passed to protect sterling in the serious financial situation which exists in this country at the present time, and it is of the utmost importance that its provisions should be observed by all citizens.

On the other hand Lord Goddard has also said that 'the Act does not provide a moratorium for debtors but only controls the immediate destination of the payments they make'.[32]

It is one of the outstanding features of the Exchange Control Act, 1947, that a sharp distinction is drawn between authorized dealers and other persons. The former, in effect, are bankers in the United Kingdom as listed from time to time in orders made by the Treasury under s. 42. They are entitled to buy and sell, borrow and lend gold and foreign currency, and to retain specified currency (ss. 1 and 2). It has thus been possible for British banks almost without hindrance to carry on foreign business in gold and foreign currency with other British banks or with non-residents. As a consequence the City of London has been able to preserve and even to develop much of its traditional role by putting into operation an almost complete dichotomy between internal and external business.

## III

The Exchange Control Act applies to all persons, irrespective of whether or no they are in the United Kingdom or are British subjects,[33] but this does not mean more than that absence from the United Kingdom or foreign nationality does not of necessity exempt a person from the obligations and prohibitions imposed by the Act. In a positive sense those persons are subject to the requirements of the Act who (i) are and act in the United Kingdom, even if they are domiciled or resident in or nationals of a foreign country, or (ii) are and act outside the United Kingdom, provided they are residents of the United Kingdom. The test, therefore, is a combination of presence and residence: persons in the United Kingdom are subject to certain obligations while in the United Kingdom; persons resident in the United Kingdom are subject to those obligations wherever they may be. This, at any rate, is the rule,[34] but certain provisions apply only to residents,[35] while others apply only to persons 'in the United Kingdom',[36] and in a fourth group of cases they apply to all persons who act in the United Kingdom, even if they are not here.[37]

The implications of those provisions which apply to all persons in the United

---

[31] *Pickett v. Fesq*, [1949] 2 All E.R. 705, at p. 707.
[32] *Contract & Trading Co. (Southern) Ltd. v. Barbey*, [1960] A.C. 244, at p. 254.
[33] s. 42 (5).
[34] ss. 1, 2, 7, 10, and others.
[35] See, for example, ss. 6, 24, 28, 29, 30.
[36] See, for example, s. 3.
[37] See, for example, s. 5: 'no person shall do any of the following things in the United Kingdom'.

Kingdom are far-reaching and may, in certain contexts, exceed the jurisdiction which international law allows a State to exercise. A resident of New York who spends a night in a London hotel is not allowed to borrow even the smallest sum of dollars from another resident of the United States whom he meets in the hotel, and commits a criminal offence if he does so.[38] The same probably applies if he borrows a sum of dollars standing to his fellow guest's credit in a New York bank. Furthermore, 'any person in . . . the United Kingdom' is liable to furnish to the Treasury 'any information in his possession or control which the Treasury . . . may require for the purpose of securing compliance with or detecting evasion of this Act'.[39, 40]

Those provisions which apply to residents only involve the difficulty that residence is an elusive conception. The Act, it is true, gives the Treasury power to determine the residence of a (physical or legal) person[41] and to treat an emigrant as a resident,[42] and the personal representative is treated as resident in the country of the deceased's residence.[43] Moreover, an English branch of a foreign business is treated as a resident, but otherwise a branch or head office of a business is treated as if it were a body corporate resident where the branch or head office is situate.[44] Yet there remain many cases in which the decision must be very doubtful.

It should be noted that nationality is not wholly irrelevant: it is the practice of the Treasury to grant certain exemptions to a foreign national resident in the United Kingdom, particularly by dispensing him from the duty to surrender currency of his own country[45] and by allowing him, on emigration, to take his property with him.[46]

## IV

The effect of exchange control upon contractual obligations is a matter of

---

[38] s. 1, on which see below, p. 365. According to Art. 2 (a) of the Exchange Control (Payments) Order 1967, S.I. 1967, No. 1189, the American who pays in dollars (or, incidentally, English legal tender legally imported into this country) is exempted from the provisions of s. 5 of the Act, that is to say he can make the payment for any purpose other than that of lending or selling foreign currency (which is dealt with in s. 1).

[39] Clause 1 (1) of the Fifth Schedule, Part I. But this does not apply to counsel or solicitors.

[40] The Exchange Control (Temporary Visitors' Exemption) Order 1947, S.R. & O. 1947, No. 2049, however, exempts a person in the United Kingdom who is resident outside the United Kingdom from the provisions of s. 2 which imposes an obligation to surrender gold and foreign currency.

[41] s. 41 (2). It is doubtful whether this section gives the Treasury power to declare a person as resident in this country, if such person in fact never has been so resident. It is submitted that the Treasury has no absolute discretion in this connection.

[42] Such a direction may even be made after the emigrant has left this country: s. 40.

[43] s. 41 (1).

[44] Exchange Control (Branches & Residence) Directions, 1951, S.I. 1951, No. 962. This revokes S.R. & O. 1947, No. 2054, under which *Marcus* v. *Director of Public Prosecutions*, [1950] W.N. 279 was decided.

[45] See para. 8 of the Chancellor of the Exchequer's Memorandum, Cmd. 6954.

[46] In this way the United Kingdom discharges what may be an international duty. British emigrants are at present subject to severe restrictions.

some difficulty. The Act itself deals with the problem in s. 33[47] of which one can only say with Lord Radcliffe that 'it is not plain . . . exactly why s. 33 (1) was thought to be needed in this context, nor does it explain itself'.[48] Nor have the implications of a decision of the House of Lords[49] been finally worked out.

It is, however, suggested that, as the law stands at present, it is necessary to distinguish between executory contracts, executed contracts, and debts. In each of these cases regard will have to be had to English law; if the proper law of the contract should be foreign, s. 33 cannot be applicable and English law will be relevant only in so far as a public policy so demands.[50] Where the contract is between residents and non-residents, it will, in addition, be necessary to consider Art. VIII (2) (b) of the Bretton Woods Agreement.

1. *Executory contracts* are in no way prohibited by the Act. Thus, a person is not precluded from agreeing to lend foreign currency, although, in the absence of permission, s. 1 prohibits the lending itself. The Act may affect executory contracts in four different ways.

(a) The parties make their contract subject to the express condition that such permission as may be required will be given.

Such a condition does not negative the existence of a contract, but merely means 'that there is being introduced into the contract a condition that a licence must be obtained and neither party will be liable to perform the duties under the contract unless the licence is obtained'.[51] At the same time, however, the party who has to do something requiring permission must 'use reasonable

---

[47] The first subsection reads as follows:

> It shall be an implied condition in any contract that, where, by virtue of this Act, the permission or consent of the Treasury is at the time of the contract required for the performance of any term thereof, that term shall not be performed except in so far as the permission or consent is given or not required: Provided that this subsection shall not apply in so far as it is shown to be inconsistent with the intention of the parties that it should apply, whether by reason of their having contemplated the performance of that term in despite of the provisions of this Act or for any other reason.

[48] *Contract and Trading Co. (Southern) Ltd.* v. *Barbey*, [1960] A.C. 244, at p. 255.

[49] See preceding note, and below, p. 366.

[50] It is clear that no English court will enforce an obligation to do something forbidden by English law: see Dicey and Morris, p. 794, and in particular *Boissevain* v. *Weil*, [1950] A.C. 327 decided under the Defence (Finance) Regulations. It is comforting to think that such a decision as this is now most unlikely to occur, because, as has been pointed out, according to s. 3 (1) of the Emergency Powers (Defence) Act, 1939, the test was largely based on nationality, while under the Exchange Control Act it is normally residence that matters. *Boissevain* v. *Weil* was a case in which a loan of French francs made during the war by a Dutch subject resident in Monaco to a British subject resident there was held to be illegal and irrecoverable. Admittedly it would have required great judicial strength to arrive at a different result. Unfortunately it was lacking. Lord Radcliffe indicated (at p. 342) 'that the escaping prisoner of war can be left out of consideration. His would have been a wholly exceptional case and would have been so treated.' But Lord Radcliffe does not indicate the distinguishing feature. It is submitted that there is no legally relevant distinction between the escaping prisoner and the British resident of Monaco who was compelled either to borrow money or to allow her son to be sent to death. The decision is open to much doubt: Mann, *Rec.* 111 (1964, i), 124.

[51] *Windschuegl Ltd.* v. *Alexander Pickering Ltd.* (1950), 84 Ll. L.R. 89, at p. 92 *per* Devlin J.

endeavours to obtain a licence and unless he can show that he has used such endeavours, he cannot take advantage of the condition so inserted'.[52] Consequently both parties are bound to allow a reasonable time for the permission to be obtained. If it is given, the contract is to be performed; if it is refused, performance is excused. If there is a failure to use diligence in obtaining a permission, a claim to damages for breach of contract would arise under the general law.

(b) The contract does not contain an express condition, but the parties contemplate performance in a legal manner.

Under English law s. 33 of the Act applies and the contract is deemed to contain an implied condition that performance shall not be made except in so far as permission is given or not required. Consequently, the legal position is the same as in the case discussed in section (a) above.

(c) The parties contemplate performance in a legal manner, but their contract does not permit the implication of any condition, for example, because it contains a clause in terms excluding all express or implied conditions. Probably, even in this case, the statutory implication prescribed by s. 33 will be possible.

(d) The parties contemplate performance in a manner inconsistent with the provisions of the Exchange Control Act. Irrespective of the proper law, the contract is invalid under the general law.[53]

2. As to *executed contracts*, s. 1, in particular, prohibits the buying[54] and selling and the borrowing and lending of gold[55] and foreign currency.[56] These words will have to be construed strictly: although it is well settled that, for example, the word 'sell' is not necessarily 'to be construed with reference to the niceties of the law of contract of sale or to the distinction between

---

[52] Ibid. at p. 93. This is settled law: see, in particular, *Brauer & Co. (Great Britain) Ltd.* v. *James Clark (Brush Materials) Ltd.*, [1952] 2 All E.R. 497. Whether there is an express condition may sometimes be doubtful: see *Peter Cassidy Seed Co. Ltd.* v. *Osuustuk-kupauppa I.L.*, [1957] 1 W.L.R. 263. The question which of the parties has to apply for permission is one of construction, but usually it will be the party who is subject to the prohibition and has the information required to obtain the permission: *Pound & Co Ltd.* v. *Hardy & Co. Inc.*, [1956] A.C. 588.

[53] *Waugh* v. *Morris* (1873), 8 Q.B. 202 and many other cases.

[54] In regard to a similar term occurring in the exchange control regulations of South Africa it was held that the provision 'hits at the entering into' of an agreement to buy and that the purchase of dollar travellers' cheques constituted a purchase of foreign currency, although travellers' cheques were not foreign currency: *S.* v. *Katsikaris*, 1980 (3) A.D. 580, —a very doubtful case in so far as the interpretation of the expression 'buy' is concerned.

[55] Under s. 42 this means gold coin and gold bullion. The former term means coins issued by authority, i.e. money, whether English or foreign. The latter means a lump of gold. Both terms exclude imitation coins. In this sense *Freed* v. *Director of Public Prosecutions*, [1969] 2 Q.B. 115.

[56] As defined by subsection 3. In the South African case referred to in n. 54 above it was further held that travellers cheques were not 'currency': 'in order to constitute currency such promissory documents must also be in general circulation or use . . . in the sense that they are, without more, freely transferable from hand to hand like the coins or banknote' (at p. 592). In England too travellers' cheques would not come within the definition of 'foreign currency' in s. 1 (3) (a), but are specifically dealt with in ss. 4 and 22 (1) (e) (iv).

a sale and an agreement to sell or to the question whether the property in the goods has passed', but may be understood in a popular sense,[57] this cannot be so in the present connection, because agreements to sell, buy, borrow, or lend are covered by other provisions.[58] According to a decision of Plowman J., where the plaintiff has paid money at the defendant's request, the latter has not 'borrowed' money and is therefore liable to repay[59] even in the absence of Treasury consent. Whether a sale of gold or foreign currency can be said to include an exchange or barter is a much more doubtful question; the answer will probably have to be in the negative, since in view of the criminal sanction a strict interpretation is required. Those words certainly do not cover a gift or a bailment. However, in so far as foreign currency as opposed to gold is concerned, such transactions will frequently be caught by Part II of the Act which prohibits a large variety of payments.[60]

It should be noted that s. 1 applies to any foreign currency (which term includes bank accounts), while the duty to surrender and the bailee's duty to notify imposed by ss. 2 and 3 of the Act extend only to gold and such foreign currency (which term does not include blocked accounts) as is specified currency.[61]

3. *Debts* (which term probably includes all monetary oblligations)[62] are in a special category. If they arise from valid contracts, they include an implied condition under s. 33, and if the performance of any term requires permission that term will not have to be performed without permission; the same, no doubt, applies to an express condition. Under established principles[63] one of the parties, probably the debtor, will have to apply for consent, but in the event of its refusal he cannot and need not pay. This position radically changes when the creditor brings proceedings: neither s. 5 nor s. 33 provides a defence, but the creditor will obtain judgment which will have to be satisfied by payment into court. The transformation is due to the provision according to which 'a claim for the recovery of any debt shall not be defeated by reason only of the debt not being payable without the permission of the Treasury and of that permission not having been given or having been revoked'.[64] This remarkable result follows from a decision of the House of Lords:[65] Lombard Odier & Cie., Geneva, were the holders in due course of a bill of exchange drawn by a French firm and accepted by the defendants. The permission of the Treasury for payment by the defendant as required by s. 5 was not given. Nonetheless the plaintiffs recovered judgment on the ground that, whatever s. 33 might say, there was

---

[57] *Lambert* v. *Rowe*, [1914] 1 K.B. 38.

[58] s. 33 and Art. VIII (2) (*b*).

[59] *In re H.P.C. Productions Ltd.*, [1962] Ch. 466, discussed by Mann, 25 (1962) *Mod. L.R.* 236, where considerable doubt about the decision was expressed.

[60] Below, pp. 369 sqq.

[61] But since 1967 all foreign currencies are specified: S.I. 1967, No. 556.

[62] *Contract and Trading Co. (Southern) Ltd.* v. *Barbey*, [1960] A.C. 244, at p. 252, *per* Lord Simonds.

[63] See above, pp. 364, 365.

[64] Exchange Control Act, 1947, Fourth Schedule, para. 4.

[65] *Contract and Trading Co. (Southern) Ltd.* v. *Barbey*, *ubi supra*. Nothing is known about the underlying facts.

'a debt but it must not be paid without permission. It does not for that reason cease to be a debt'.[66]

The principle thus established would seem to cover a large variety of cases arising, in particular, under ss. 5, 6, and 7,[67] but it does not extend, so it is submitted, to cases in which there never was a valid monetary obligation. Thus in the case of a borrowing contrary to s. 1 the lender has no valid debt and his proceedings should be dismissed.[68] If gold is bought contrary to s. 1 the buyer who has paid the price cannot recover the gold, and the seller who has delivered the gold cannot recover the price. Nor has para. 4 of the Fourth Schedule any bearing upon the question whether a debtor who, particularly as a result of an application having been made but refused, on the due date is not in possession of the requisite permission is in default within the meaning of a statutory or contractual provision which may, for instance, impose a duty to pay interest; probably the answer should be in the negative.[69]

# V

When one comes to transfers of property, one finds that the Act contains surprisingly few prohibitions and imposes even fewer duties.

1. Apart from very detailed provisions relating to the issue and transfer of securities,[70] the Act deals only with three types of transfer. S. 28 makes it illegal for a resident of the United Kingdom to transfer to or for the account of a person resident outside the scheduled territories any policy of assurance.

[66] Viscount Simonds, at p. 252.

[67] It is by no means easy to understand why the principle stated in the text did not lead to a different result in the curious case of Shaw v. Shaw, [1965] 1 All E.R. 638. This was an action to recover a payment made in association with the purchase of a property in Spain. The Court of Appeal struck the pleading out on the ground that the plaintiff based himself on nothing but the illegal payment. Lord Denning would have allowed the plaintiff to say 'that the money has been paid over on a consideration which had wholly failed, but he does not attempt to do that' (p. 639). Yet this is what the plaintiff did: p. 639 at C. The effect of the Fourth Schedule was not discussed.

[68] This provision has resulted in shocking injustice and is badly in need of being re-modelled. See the cases referred to above, p. 361, n. 26, and p. 364, n. 50. The Israeli Supreme Court had to deal with a case in which an Israeli resident, while in Bulgaria, lent to a Bulgarian friend a sum of Bulgarian currency to enable him to escape and go to Israel. The friend succeeded in doing so. In view of the provision of Israeli law corresponding to s. 1 of the English Act the action for the recovery of the loan failed: Moshcovitz-Varkoni v. Papo, Jerusalem Post, 13 Mar. 1956. In England the result would be the same and equally unacceptable.

[69] The point has provoked debtate in Germany. The Federal Supreme Court affirmed the existence of default in the latest of a series of decisions: 12 July 1963, NJW. 1964, 100. But see Staudinger–Werner, s. 284, n. 2 and now Loewisch in 12th ed. (1979) n. 3.

[70] Part III of the Act comprising ss. 8 to 20. According to ss. 8 (1) and 18 (1) the purported issue of a security in a manner prohibited by the Act renders the issue wholly void: In re Transatlantic Life Assurance Co. Ltd., [1979] 3 All E.R. 352. But where in breach of s. 16 (2) scrip is handed over to the holder of a charge registered in accordance with s. 95 of the Companies Act 1948, this does not preclude the scrip from being included in the charge, and notwithstanding s. 17 (2) the absence of permission does not invalidate the charge in respect of the scrip: Swiss Bank Corporation v. Lloyds Bank Ltd., [1981] 2 W.L.R. 893 on which see above, p. 361.

The owner of 'a right (whether present or future and whether vested or contingent) to receive any specified currency or to receive from a person resident outside the scheduled territories a payment in sterling' may not cause the receipt of that currency or payment to be delayed or to cease.[71] According to s. 29 no resident in the United Kingdom 'shall settle any property, otherwise than by will, so as to confer an interest[72] in the property' on a person resident outside the scheduled territories.

It thus appears that there is nothing in the Act that would prohibit the conveyance of land wherever situate by a resident to a non-resident, whether it be made by way of sale or by way of gift. Nor is there anything that would prohibit the transfer of movables, at any rate if they are not exported.[73] As mentioned above, without permission it is not possible to 'settle' property. Hence it is an odd result that a resident is not allowed to transfer property to a resident trustee to hold it upon trust for a non-resident, but that the same resident can convey or transfer property to a non-resident direct. But in view of the technical meaning of the word 'settle' and in view of the terms of s. 29[74] this astonishing result is hardly open to doubt.

Patents, trademarks, and copyrights are nowhere mentioned in the Act and can, therefore, be freely transferred.

The assignment of a debt due from a resident debtor to a resident assignor does not require permission, even if the assignee resides outside the scheduled territories;[75] the debtor, it is true, cannot make payment to the non-resident assignee[76] except by way of a payment into court,[77] but the assignment may make a set-off possible. Assignments of debts due from a resident debtor may freely be made by the non-resident creditor in favour of a resident or non-resident assignee.

The position is much more obscure in regard to shares in a partnership, undivided shares in joint property, interests in trust funds, and interests in foreign corporations in respect of which a certificate of title has not been issued. Such interests do not come within the definition of securities.[78] They are affected by the Act only if and in so far as they confer at least a future or contingent right to receive specified currency or to receive sterling from a person resident outside the scheduled territories; in that event s. 24 applies and they are treated in the same way as debts. Whether such interests in fact involve the right to specified currency or sterling payable by a non-resident must be decided in each case.[79]

---

[71] s. 24.

[72] It would seem that the appointment of foreign trustees does come within these words.

[73] For restrictions on export see ss. 22 and 23. Bills of exchange accepted by English debtors and sent to French creditors in breach of s. 22 (1) (c) (iii) are enforceable in England notwithstanding the 'illegal incident in the formation of the contract': *Crédit Lyonnais* v. *P.T. Barnard & Associates Ltd.* (1976), 1 Ll. L.R. 557.

[74] See, in particular, subsection 4 (a), from which it appears that there is no settlement within the meaning of the section, unless 'the property becomes subject to a trust'.

[75] s. 24 deals only with sterling debts due 'from a person resident outside the scheduled territories'.

[76] s. 5.          [77] Fourth Schedule, paras. 2 and 4.          [78] s. 42 (1).

[79] It should be remembered that a transfer or assignment may involve a payment. In that event ss. 5, 6, and 7 would apply. They will presently be discussed in the text.

2. Among the duties which the Act imposes the most important is, probably, the duty to offer gold and specified currency for sale to an authorized dealer at a price not exceeding that authorized by the Treasury.[80] Certain types of specified currency such as capital sums as defined from time to time by the Bank of England could for many years be sold to others than the Treasury at a premium which at certain periods stood at more than 100 per cent. Until the early part of 1979, i.e. until shortly before the abolition of this market, a quarter of the capital sums available had to be sold to the Treasury at the 'official' rate, i.e. without the premium. The owner or his purchaser could invest the 75 per cent in the purchase of securities denominated in specified currency. There thus developed a separate market of premium funds and premium securities.[81]

By ss. 2 (5) and 27 the Treasury is given power in certain cases to vest in itself gold, specified currency, rights, goods, and other property as defined in the Act. The only case in which the exercise of this power has become publicly known is a vesting order made in respect of a dollar account in a New York bank owned by a British resident and subject. As a result of such order the United Kingdom started proceedings against the bank in New York.[82] The outcome is not recorded, but the action was bound to fail, because the powers of vesting conferred by the Act must be treated as limited to property in Britain,[83] and in any event the United Kingdom could not enforce in New York rights of a plainly prerogative character.[84]

# VI

Part II of the Act, comprising ss. 5, 6, and 7, deals with those transactions which, from a practical point of view, are of greater importance than any others, viz. payments.

The Act prohibits the making of 'any payment' to (or for the credit of) certain persons without anywhere defining the term 'payment'. In view of the mischief at which the Act aims it would seem clear that, where the means of payment is money in the legal sense, i.e. coin or notes, a payment is involved irrespective of its purpose: the handing over of money is caught by the Act not only if the intention is to discharge a debt, but also if the transaction

---

[80] s. 2. The statutory duty is to 'offer for sale'; the Act does not state how long the offer will have to be open for acceptance. The duty is imposed upon a person 'entitled to sell'. It is submitted that this phrase does not include an agent or trustee who under the terms of his contract or trust has no right to sell to an authorized dealer as provided in s. 2. A different view was taken by a majority of the Supreme Court of Israel in A.G. v. Zenter (in relation to a provision corresponding to the former Defence (Finance) Regulations in England): International Lawyers Convention in Israel (Jerusalem, 1959), p. 302.

[81] On the legal characteristics of this market as explained by the Judicial Committee of the Privy Council see below p. 436.

[82] Solicitor for the Affairs of H.M. Treasury v. Bankers Trust, 107 N.E. 2d 448 (1952). The decision itself deals with a procedural point without interest.

[83] For the reason given by Maxwell, Interpretation of Statutes (12th ed., 1969), pp. 169 sqq., and developed by Mann, Rec. 111 (1964, i), 65, or Studies in International Law, p. 54.

[84] See below, p. 428.

constitutes a loan, a deposit, a bailment, or a gift of money. The conception of payment raises much more difficult questions when it is not money that passes, but a chattel (such as a picture or jewellery), land, or an intangible right such as a patent. The transfer of such property, as has been shown, is not usually illegal; is it to be regarded as a 'payment' and therefore illegal, if it is made in satisfaction of a debt? Does the purpose matter where a medium other than money is involved? It is submitted that the answer ought to be in the affirmative, although an *argumentum e contrario* might be drawn from the fact that the legislator has thought it necessary to deal specifically with one form of 'payment' by means other than money, viz. the placing of a sum to the credit of a person.[85]

The Act envisages three types of payment.

1. S. 5 is of the greatest significance in practice. Its effect may be summarized by the formula that no person may in the United Kingdom make a payment (*a*) to or for the credit of a person resident outside the scheduled territories, or (*b*) to or for the credit of a person resident in the scheduled territories by order or on behalf of a person resident outside these territories.[86] The range of transactions so caught is enormous.

If *A* is a resident in the United Kingdom and *B* and *C* are residents of New York temporarily staying at a London hotel, neither *A* nor *B* can pay *C*'s bill incurred with the hotel, although, if *A* has made the contract with the hotel, he can pay the bill rendered to him by the hotel for the room occupied by *C*.[87] Again, as Lord Goddard C.J. has remarked,[88]

> it has been pointed out by high authority that, if a person plays a game of cards in this country with a person who does not live in one of the scheduled territories—as, for instance, in America—and at the end of the game he hands him 5*s*. which he has lost to him, he is really committing an offence.

And it is also obvious that no bank in the United Kingdom could credit the account of its American client, whether the payment is made on behalf of another American client or a resident of the United Kingdom or the scheduled territories, nor could the bank credit the account of its resident client, if this is done on behalf of an American client.

The examples need not be multiplied to show that these provisions, if they were not subject to qualifications, would in practice make international intercourse almost impossible. In fact important exceptions have been grafted upon the rules laid down by the Act.

(*a*) In the first place certain payments *in cash* may be made in the United Kingdom to persons resident outside the scheduled territories. Such persons may be paid by a resident of the scheduled territories up to £10 in value; by

---

[85] s. 5 (*c*).

[86] In addition s. 5 (*c*) prohibits the placing of any sum to the credit of any person resident outside the scheduled territories.

[87] In this case no payment for the credit or on behalf of a non-resident within the meaning of s. 5 (*a*) and (*b*) is made. *A*, a resident, pays to another resident, the proprietor of the hotel, on his own behalf an amount due from him.

[88] *Pickett* v. *Fesq*, [1949] 2 All E.R. 705, at p. 707.

an English banker unlimited amounts out of moneys standing to the recipient's credit with that banker; by a person resident outside the scheduled territories unlimited amounts, if such payment is made with money legally imported into this country or withdrawn from the payer's account with an English bank.[89]

(b) Payments by *bank transfer* used to be dealt with by a system of considerable complexity, but, at the same time, of considerable flexibility. For more than ten years, however, the rules have been very simple. A transfer by a resident to the sterling account of a non-resident is, of course, subject to permission. But amounts standing to the credit of the sterling account of a person resident outside the scheduled territories with a United Kingdom bank may be freely transferred to the sterling account of any person with a United Kingdom Bank.[90] The residence of the transferee does not matter. Nor is the reason for or the purpose of the transfer in any way relevant. Sterling, once credited to the bank account[91] of a non-resident, is freely 'convertible'.

2. S. 6 relates only to residents of the United Kingdom and makes it illegal for them to make any payment outside the United Kingdom to a person resident outside the scheduled territories. The effect of this provision would again be very far-reaching were it not for subsection (2), according to which it does not apply to foreign currency obtained or retained in accordance with the Act.

3. S. 7 relates to compensation deals and prohibits a payment to a resident of the scheduled territories if it is made in consideration for or in association with the receipt of a payment or the acquisition of property outside the scheduled territories.[92] Thus a resident of the United Kingdom cannot pay the bill incurred by an American visitor with a London hotel if the American visitor promises to repay in the United States. The terms of the section are so wide that not even another American who happens to be but is not resident in the United Kingdom can pay his friend's hotel bill if the latter makes or promises to make repayment in New York.

---

[89] See Art. 2 of the Exchange Control (Payments) Order, 1967, S.I. 1967, No. 1189.
[90] Art. 1 of the Order mentioned in the preceding note.
[91] This does not include money paid into court.
[92] The section was considered in *Shaw* v. *Shaw*, above, p. 367, n. 67.

# XIV

# Exchange Control under the International Monetary Fund Agreement

I. Introduction. II. The legal character of Art. VIII (2) (*b*). III. Public policy under the Agreement. IV. The scope of Art. VIII (2) (*b*): (1) initially enforceable contracts; (2) initially unenforceable contracts; (3) invalidity outside Art. VIII (2) (*b*); (4) effects outside the realm of contracts; (5) no general recognition of foreign exchange control; (6) no exclusion of capital transactions; (7) application to all member States. V. The interpretation of Art. VIII (2) (*b*): (1) exchange contracts; (2) which involve the currency; (3) of any member; (4) and are contrary to the exchange control regulations; (5) of that member; (6) maintained or imposed consistently with this Agreement; (7) shall be unenforceable.

## I

AS between the 141 members or so of the International Monetary Fund the law of exchange control differs from the general rules applicable to exchange control. In all member States the rule of positive law laid down in Art. VIII (2) (*b*) of the Articles of Agreement of the International Monetary Fund[1] applies:

Exchange contracts which involve the currency of any member and which are contrary to the exchange control regulations of that member maintained or imposed consistently with this Agreement shall be unenforceable in the territories of any member.

This provision constitutes a new departure. Although its interpretation obviously raises many points of difficulty which will have to be considered,[2] and although the courts have shown a marked astuteness

---

[1] The steps necessary to incorporate the provision into municipal law are everywhere determined by constitutional law. In this country it was the Bretton Woods Agreements Order 1946 (S.R. & O. 1946, No. 36) which made the provision part of English law. It may be assumed that it applies in all member states because, according to Art. XX (1) of the Agreement, each member has deposited 'with the Government of the United States of America an instrument setting forth that it has accepted this Agreement in accordance with its law and has taken all steps necessary to enable it to carry out all of its obligations under this Agreement'.

[2] See section V, below. The literature on the interpretation of the Article has become vast. Much of it contains some very special pleading. The most valuable and thoughtful contributions come from the pen of Sir Joseph Gold, the General Counsel and Director of the Legal Department of the Fund. His essays which appeared up to 1976 and many of which were translated into German and other languages were collected in two volumes, *The Fund Agreement in the Courts* (Washington, D.C., 1962 and 1976). Since then the series was continued by articles in the *International Monetary Fund's Staff Papers*, 1977,

in neutralizing its effects,[3] there is no justification for the suggestion that it is unlikely to 'assume any major importance'.[4] On the contrary it is the duty of lawyers to support and render effective a measure that results from international legislation on so grand a scale.[5]

## II

The first question to which Art. VIII (2) (b) gives rise relates to 193; 1978, 343; 1979, 583; 1980, 601. Other contributions appeared in the International Monetary Fund's pamphlet series; see, in particular, *The International Monetary Fund and Private Business Transactions* (1965) and *The Cuban Insurance Cases and the Articles of the Fund* (1966). The principal other publications are the following: Alexandrovicz, *World Economic Agencies* (1962), p. 189; Anselme–Rabinovitch, *Revue de la Banque*, 1955, 317; Banque, 1965, Nos. 228-9; Aufricht, *Oesterreichische Zeitschrift für öffentliches Recht*, vi (1955), 529; P.O.R. Böse, *Der Einfluss des zwingenden Rechts auf Internationale Anleihen* (1963), pp. 109 sqq.; Cabot, 99 (1950) *University of Pennsylvania L.R.* 476; Van Campenhout, ii (1953) *American Journal of Comparative Law* 391; Carreau, pp. 457 sqq.; Coing, *Wertpapiermitteilungen* 1972, iv 838; Conforti, *L'esecuzione delle obbligazioni nel diritto internazionale privato* (1962), p. 296; Delaume, pp. 290 sqq. and Clunet, 1954, 332; Dicey and Morris, p. 898; Drakidis, *Rev. Crit.* 1970, 363; Förger, *NJW.* 1971, 309; Gianviti, *Rev. Crit.* 1973, 471, 629; Kägi, *Der Einfluss des Devisenrechts auf schuldrechtliche Verträge* (1961), p. 94; Kern, *Der Internationale Währungsfonds und die Berücksichtigung ausländischen Devisenrechts* (1968); Krispis, p. 286; Lachmann, *Nederlands Tijdschrift voor Internationaal Recht*, ii (1955), 148; Lazar, *Transnational Economic and Monetary Law*, volumes ii and iii; Madsen–Mygdal, *Nordisk Tidsskrift for international Ret* 25 (1955), 63; Meyer, *Yale L.J.* 62 (1953), 867; Nussbaum, p. 539; Paradise, *University of Florida L.R.* 18 (1965), 29; Schnitzer, *Report of the 47th Conference of the International Law Association* (1956), 299; Seidl-Hohenveldern, *Oesterreichische Zeitschrift für öffentliches Recht*, viii (1957), 82; Tullio Treves, *Il controllo dei cambi nel diritto internazionale privato* (1967), p. 210; Williams, *Virginia Journal of International Law*, 15 (1975), 319.

[3] This tendency appears most clearly from the decision Cass. Civ. 16 Oct. 1967, *Rev. Crit.* 1968, 661, also 48 Int. L.R. 229: Janda, a Czechoslovakian, entrusted in Mar. 1948 in Prague $30,000 to Kosek, a naturalized U.S. citizen who was about to leave Czechoslovakia, to transfer it to the United States. Janda followed later and in July 1951 obtained an acknowledgement of debt from Kosek. The latter's defence based on Art. VIII (2) (b) failed, because the Court of Appeal found that Czechoslovakia had not become a member of the International Monetary Fund, and the Cour de Cassation felt unable to interfere with this finding of fact. In truth Czechoslovakia was a member of the Fund and was compelled to withdraw only in 1955. This is, of course, a matter of public record, and can be ascertained from the Fund's Annual Reports or other documents. The legal aspects of the withdrawal have frequently been described; see, for instance, Mann, *British Year Book of International Law*, 1968-9, p. 7, with further references. But the French case was one of a class which has often been noted in this book and in which no court could be expected to allow the defendant to succeed. Another example is the New York decision of *Barton v. National Life Assurance Company of Canada*, 398 N.Y. Supp. 2d 941 (1977), where, without considering anyone of the numerous other questions arising for decision, the judge held that payments under a life insurance policy issued in Jamaica had to be made in New York on the ground that Art. II of the Treaty between Britain and the United States of 1899 guaranteed to U.S. citizens the right to take possession and dispose of personal property. Although the attitude of the United States is uncertain, the I.M.F. Articles of Agreement in all probability suspended, as concerns exchange control, the operation of the 1899 Treaty. The point on which see below p. 523, n. 54, in any case required careful investigation, but was ignored by the court.        [4] Nussbaum, p. 545.

[5] On the method of approach to the provision see Mann, *Report on the International Law Association's 45th Conference* (Lucerne, 1952), pp. 236 sqq., 284 sqq.

the legal nature of the provision. The general view, accepted and propounded unquestioningly in the earlier editions of this book, is that the provision belongs to the conflict of laws and super-imposes a special rule upon the general body of a member State's private international law.[6]

If one looks at the wording as it stands such a conclusion cannot readily be drawn, for the text does not, as a conflict rule would do, provide for the applicability of a particular system of law, but prescribes a rule of substantive law: in certain circumstances certain types of contract shall be unenforceable. This is not the language of private international law nor the method of laying down a conflict rule. The text seems to establish a rule of uniform substantive law of the kind known to the lawyer from such treaties as the Conventions on Carriage by Air or the protection of copyright.

Yet it is not difficult by an alteration of the wording to turn the provision into a conflict rule: the enforceability in the territories of any member of exchange contracts which involve the currency of any member shall be determined by the exchange control regulations of that member maintained or imposed consistently with this Agreement.

The difference between the two versions is considerable. If the provision is a conflict rule it will have to be understood as a rule, and to be construed in the light of the *lex fori*, due regard being had to foreign experiences as resulting from comparative law. If the provision is a rule of (uniform) substantive law it is applicable in the sense attributed to it by the proper law of the contract governing the exchange contract as a whole. In the former case in proceedings in England a contract, even if subject to French law, would for the purposes of Art. VIII (2) (*b*) be subject to English conceptions, for instance, on the nature of exchange contracts, on the meaning of unenforceability and so forth. In the latter case the French interpretation of Art. VIII (2) (*b*), if properly pleaded and proved, would be applicable in England to a contract governed by French law.[7]

So important a distinction should not turn on terminology only, though the text cannot be entirely overlooked. The decision must be found in reason and justice. From this point of view it is submitted

---

[6] *Sharif* v. *Azad*, [1967] 1 Q.B. 605, at pp. 617, 618 *per* Diplock L.J. (as he then was).

[7] See *Rustenberg Platinum Mines Ltd.* v. *South African Airways* (1979), 1 Ll. L.R. 19, particularly *per* Eveleigh L.J., as discussed by Mann, 95 (1979), *L.Q.R.* 346. And see the important decision of the Hamburg Court of Appeal, 30 Nov. 1978, *IPRspr.* 1978, No. 36a which holds s. 662 of the German Commercial Code incorporating the Hague Rules applicable only where the bill of lading is subject to German law; in other words, it is not 'overriding', as Dicey and Morris, p. 22, assert.

that it is unattractive and contrary to common sense to allow a foreign contract and its interpretation in one specific respect to be governed by the *lex fori* rather than the proper law. There is no need for so unusual a procedure nor can the *lex fori* claim that its interpretation of Art. VIII (2) (*b*), if there is a difference, is necessarily superior to that of the proper law.

Accordingly it is submitted that in an appropriate case and subject to the appropriate conditions Art. VIII (2) (*b*) should be treated as a rule of substantive law in the incarnation of the proper law of the contract. The following pages intend to state the English law in the light of a comparative survey.

The preceding suggestions imply the rejection of the view which treats Art. VIII (2) (*b*) as a rule of the conflict of laws and also of the peculiar theory of the Federal Supreme Court of Germany which in a long line of decisions, described as 'firmly established practice',[8] has held that an infringement of the exchange control regulations of a member State, which according to Art. VIII (2) (*b*) affects the enforceability of exchange contracts, constitutes a procedural obstacle. This unique doctrine will have to be considered in another context.[9]

III

Whatever the relationship between exchange control and public policy may be in general, it is impossible to suggest that any member State or its judicial or administrative organs are entitled to treat as contrary to *ordre public* such exchange control regulations as operate in conformity with the Agreement.[10] This is to be inferred not only from Art. VIII (2) (*b*), which, within certain limits, enjoins recognition of the exchange control regulations of member States and also overrides any different rule of municipal laws,[11] but

---

[8] 8 March 1979, *NJW.* 1980, 520.

[9] Below, p. 398.

[10] In this sense *Perutz* v. *Bohemian Discount Bank*, 304 N.Y. 533 (1953); also Int. L.R. 1955, 715. In the context of Art. VIII (2) (*b*) the only relevance of this much overworked case is that it establishes the point made in the text. Similarly *Banco Frances e Brasileiro S.A.* v. *John Doe No. 1*, 36 N.Y. 2d 592, 331 N.E. 2d 502 (1975), where the Court said: 'United States membership of the IMF makes it impossible to conclude that the currency control laws of other member States are offensive to this State's policy so as to preclude suit in tort by a private party.'

[11] This is probably the only, though obvious, point effectively made in the interpretation of the meaning and effect of Art. VIII (2) (*b*), which the Fund's Executive Directors issued in June 1949 and which has frequently been published (see, for instance, *Selected Decisions of the Executive Directors* (Third Issue, Jan. 1965), p. 73, or *Annual Report*, 1949, 82, or *British Year Book of International Law*, 1968-9, 8). The interpretation does not seem to establish any other legal point of substance, and it certainly fails to clarify any of the

also underlies other provisions of the Agreement. Member States cannot by a solemn treaty concede to each other the unconditional right to 'exercise such controls as are necessary to regulate international capital movements'[12] or the conditional[13] right to 'impose restrictions on the making of payments and transfers for current international payments',[14] yet claim the liberty to reject as contrary to public policy that which they have allowed each other to do. Rather it is possible to suggest that in certain contingencies public policy may within the framework of the International Monetary Fund require respect for other members' exchange control regulations, even outside the precise limits of Art. VIII (2) (b). Thus, where, in accordance with the permission given by the Agreement, members agree to 'cooperate in measures for the purpose of making the exchange control regulations of either member more effective',[15] and with this object in view enter into a bilateral treaty, compliance with its provisions may have to be treated by a judge as a matter of public policy, even though they are not incorporated into the municipal system.[16]

Yet it would seem that, although exchange control regulations as a whole may be maintained consistently with the Fund Agreement, certain of their specific effects may be such as to require or permit the refusal to apply them in a given case on the ground of public policy.[17] This may occur when their application would be discriminatory or penal in character or otherwise obnoxious. There is nothing in the Fund Agreement that would compel the courts in a given case to reach decisions which are offensive to their sense of justice; they are precluded only from ignoring a member State's exchange control regulations as a matter of principle or of *a priori* reasoning. It is likely that such is the rationale underlying an important, but not altogether clear, decision of the Dutch Hoge Raad, which rejected Indonesian exchange control regulations.[18]

---

numerous points which give rise to doubt and will be discussed in the text. In *Wilson Smithett & Cope Ltd.* v. *Terruzzi*, [1976] 1 Q.B. 683, at p. 693 Kerr J. (as he then was) rightly said that the interpretation was 'little more than a re-statement of the provisions of the article in slightly different language.'

[12] Art. VI (3).              [13] The conditions are referred to below, p. 518.

[14] Art. VIII (2) (a).         [15] Art. VIII (2) (b), second sentence.

[16] On the very delicate problem referred to in the text see Mann, *Transactions of the Grotius Society*, 44 (1958-9), pp. 43 sqq. The less diffident suggestions made in the second edition of this book and in the publications there referred to cannot be maintained.

[17] In this sense, in particular, Seidl–Hohenveldern, p. 94; Treves, pp. 284 sqq.

[18] 17 Apr. 1964, *Nederlands Tijdschrift voor Internationaal Recht*, 13 (1966), 69 or Int. L.R. 40 (1970) 7, where the court said that Art. VIII (2) (b) was no obstacle to an assignment in contravention of Indonesian regulations, because Bretton Woods is 'intended solely for the regular financial relations between States'. For earlier Dutch decisions, see District Court Maastricht and District Court Arnhem, summarized in *RabelsZ.* 1966, 716.

Public policy ought to have been and perhaps was one of the reasons why the New York Court of Appeals in *J. Zeevi & Sons Ltd.* v. *Grindlays Bank (Uganda) Ltd.*[19] disregarded Ugandan exchange control restrictions: 'As typified by strong anti-Israel and anti-semitic suggestions made by Uganda's President to the Secretary General of the United Nations', the Bank of Uganda purported to cancel all payments to Israel companies such as the plaintiffs and the defendant relied on these cancellations, described by the Court as 'confiscatory and discriminatory acts of the Ugandan Government', to avoid liability under an irrevocable letter of credit validly opened before the date of the directive; this surely was contrary to *ordre public* and could not afford a defence.

## IV

The scope of Art. VIII (2) (*b*) is limited, for it only renders certain contracts unenforceable; it is very far from requiring the universal recognition and enforcement of exchange control legislation among members. The principal limits of the provisions's field of application are as follows:

1. Art. VIII (2) (*b*) is concerned with the effectiveness of contracts, that is to say, with their initial 'validity' rather than the legality or possibility of their performance. Accordingly, a contract which at the time of its conclusion is fully effective, for instance because a licence was given or not required, does not become unenforceable in the event of a licence necessary for its performance being withdrawn or withheld. Thus a contract made between two residents of France and lacking any international aspects can be enforced in England if, for example, one of the parties establishes his residence here, even though such enforcement is contrary to French exchange control regulations, for the contract was not an exchange contract when made and does not become an exchange contract by the change of a party's (or, indeed, of both parties') residence. Similarly, an exchange contract validly made between a resident of France and a resident of Belgium is enforceable in England, even though, for example, as the result of the revocation of a licence without retrospective effect, its performance has become contrary to French or Belgian law; this is another reason which supports the result reached by the New York Court of Appeals in *J. Zeevi & Sons Ltd.* v. *Grindlays Bank (Uganda) Ltd.,*[20] where the authorities purported to revoke a licence that had been granted. In short, Art. VIII (2) (*b*)

---

[19] 37 N.Y. 2d 220, 333 N.E. 2d 168 (1975).          [20] Above, n. 19.

gives international recognition to the original ineffectiveness of an exchange contract, but does not touch a contract which during its life bcomes an exchange contract contrary to regulations.

The result is that only in so far as questions of the initial validity of an exchange contract are concerned the general rules are amplified by Art. VIII (2) (*b*).

The preceding submission[21] finds some support in the legislative history. An early draft referred to 'exchange transactions . . . which evade or avoid the exchange regulations prescribed'. Evasion and avoidance, by an exchange contract, is possible only at the time of the conclusion of the contract. There is no evidence that on this point the international legislators' intentions changed.[22] A stronger argument is derived from the text of the provision that speaks of 'contracts which . . . are contrary' to certain regulations. Contracts which at the date of their conclusion are consistent with, but during their lives become contrary to the regulations cannot be caught by such a text. The wording is even less apt to comprise contracts which at no time are contrary to regulations, but the performance of which merely becomes impossible on account of a licence being withheld or withdrawn. Again, the suggested interpretation is in line with the purpose of the provision as defined by the heading of s. 2. It covers the '*avoidance* of restrictions on current payments'.[23] Next it must be remembered that international payments are dealt with

---

[21] It was accepted by the Federal Supreme Court of Germany (21 Dec. 1976, *WM*. 1977, 332 or *IPRspr*. 1976, No. 118) which formulates as follows: 'Art. VIII (2) (*b*) concerns the effectiveness of exchange contracts, i.e. not the permissibility of their performance, but their validity, whether initial . . . or subsequently procured as a result of a licence . . .'.

[22] Such material as exists is to be found in vol. i of *Proceedings and Documents of United Nations Monetary and Financial Conference* (Washington, 1948). The Report of Committee 1 of Commission I of 13 July 1944 lists three proposals, the first being the Drafting Committee's proposal dealing only with transactions 'outside the prescribed variations', the second relating to contracts which 'evade or avoid', the third making such transactions an offence. All three suggestions were referred to Commission I (p. 576). The latter considered them on the same day and referred them to a new Special Committee (p. 599). On the following day this asked the Drafting Committee 'to reconcile the differences between' the language of the first and that of the second proposal (p. 605). Also on 14 July 1944 the Special Committee's Report was considered, not by the Drafting Committee, but by Commission I itself (p. 604) and Art. VIII 'was adopted as presented by the Drafting Committee, with the inclusion of Section 2 . . . as reworded' (p. 628). Finally, the Second Report of the Drafting Committee of Commission I stated (p. 808): 'All the material contained in this report has been approved in principle by the Commission at previous sessions. The present report contains, however, a new formulation of certain provisions.' There follows the final text of Art. VIII (2) (*b*). Although there is an important distinction between the first and the second proposal and although the final text differs from both proposals, it is clear that the members of the Conference thought that the differences related to wording and formulation. There is no evidence that they had any object other than that of the prevention of evasion and avoidance in mind.

[23] On capital payments see below, p. 382.

separately in Arts. VI, s. 3, and VIII, s. 2 (*a*); therefore questions relating to the performance of a valid or enforceable contract, whether by payment or otherwise, are unlikely to come within the scope of Art. VIII, s. 2 (*b*). Finally, restrictions would be intensified rather than avoided if assistance was given to a State's policy to defeat the performance of contracts validly concluded, for such a policy lends itself to abuse. International commerce would be gravely prejudiced if, irrespective of the proper law, States had to recognize so serious an inroad on contractual duties as the subsequent imposition of unenforceability,—an imposition which may even have been preceded by part performance.

2. The fact that Art. VIII (2) (*b*) is concerned with the enforceability of the exchange contract at the time of its conclusion rather than its performance and that, therefore, an enforceable exchange contract cannot, after its conclusion, become unenforceable, does not mean that an initially unenforceable contract cannot become enforceable. A licence granted by the time of performance would render the contract enforceable *ab initio*.[24] The lifting of exchange control or emigration is in fact and in law tantamount to the grant of a licence,—at any rate for the purposes of Art. VIII (2) (*b*), for there will then be no longer any need or legislative rationale for construing the provision so as to maintain a consequence not required by the law of the member State concerned. In short, when Art. VIII (2) (*b*) speaks of contracts which 'are contrary' to the member State's exchange control regulations, it should be understood as meaning 'are and remain' so contrary.[25]

3. Art. VIII (2) (*b*) supplements the law of the member States. Where there is no room for its application, the contract is not necessarily valid and enforceable. On the contrary, it may well be unenforceable, for instance because it forms part of a wider scheme involving the commission of illegal acts.[26] It is by no means unusual that a broad principle of law, derived from public policy, has greater scope and is more effective than the narrow text of a statutory provision. Moreover, Art. VIII (2) (*b*) does not exhaustively define the scope within which effect may have to be given to foreign exchange control regulations. If, for instance, the proper law of the contract is that of a country which invalidates the contract in

---

[24] This should be derived from a construction of Art. VIII (2) (*b*), but the German Federal Supreme Court, 11 March 1970, *JZ*. 1970, 727 renders the point subject to the proper law of the contract.

[25] The views put forward in the text (which differ from the previous edition) are in the result supported by the German Federal Supreme Court: 17 Feb. 1971, *BGHZ*. 55, 335; 21 Dec. 1976, *WM*. 1977, 332 or *IPRspr*. 1976, No. 118; 8 March 1979, *NJW*. 1980, 520.

[26] See *Regazzoni* v. *K. C. Sethia (1944) Ltd.*, [1958] A.C. 301.

circumstances in which Art. VIII (2) (*b*) does not apply effect will have to be given to the foreign law by the forum in accordance with general rules.[27]

4. Art. VIII (2) (*b*) is conerned with the enforceability of certain contracts (or its absence). In other respects there is no room for the application of the provision. Actions *in rem*, actions in tort,[28] quasi-contracts, actions for the enforcement of obligations arising *ex lege* or of a judgment[29] are exclusively governed by the general rules.

Some support for these submissions may be derived from the decision of the New York Court of Appeals in *Banco de Brasil* v. *Israel Commodity Co. Inc.,*[30] though it is far from easy to appreciate the relevance of Art. VIII (2) (*b*) to the case. The plaintiff, an instrumentality of the Government of Brazil, claimed damages for conspiracy alleged to have been committed by the defendant and a Brazilian exporter of coffee with a view to depriving the plaintiff of American dollars to which, under Brazilian foreign exchange regulations, it was entitled. The plaintiff argued that the defendant's participation in the violation of Brazilian exchange control laws afforded a ground of recovery, not, as one would perhaps have

---

[27] The text differs from dicta which, probably obiter, were made by the Court of Appeal in *United City Merchants (Investments) Ltd.* v. *Royal Bank of Canada* (1981), 1 W.L.R. 242, where it was said that Art. VIII (2) (*b*) displaced the common law principle laid down by *Regazzoni*'s case, *ubi supra*. This was derived from a dictum by Diplock L.J. (as he then was) in *Sharif* v. *Azad*, [1967] 1 Q.B. 605, at p. 617F. It is, however, submitted with respect, that Art. VIII (2) (*b*) lays down a rule of English law relating to the validity of an exchange contract, but does not override a great principle of public policy, which condemns wilful violations of foreign mandatory law by acts done in the foreign country. The Federal Supreme Court of Germany also said that the legal consequences of the violation of a member State's exchange control regulations were 'conclusively regulated by Art. VIII (2) (*b*)': 17 Feb. 1971, *BGHZ*. 55, 334, 339. It is believed, however, that the Court's remark should be understood in the same limited sense as Diplock L.J.'s dictum.

[28] For a different view see District Court Hamburg, 24 Feb. 1978, *IPRspr.* 1978, No. 126: under an unenforceable exchange contract the defendant had received a large sum of money for the plaintiff's account. The court declined to treat the refusal to pay as an embezzlement giving rise to tortious liability on the ground that this would amount to the indirect enforcement of an unenforcable exchange contract. So shocking a result ought to and could have been avoided by confining Art. VIII (2) (*b*), as the wording demands, to contractual claims. For a decision on similar facts see Court of Appeal Berlin, 8 July 1974, *IPRspr.* 1974, No. 138.

[29] This was clearly so held by the German Federal Supreme Court, 11 Oct. 1956, *BGHZ*. 22, 24, at p. 31.

[30] 12 N.Y. 2d 371 (1963), also Int. L.R. 32 (1966), 371. And see *J. Zeevi & Sons Ltd.* v. *Grindlays Bank (Uganda) Ltd.*, (above, p. 377, n. 19) which, notwithstanding certain wide formulations, merely (and rightly) decides that if a private tort was committed in connection with the fraudulent operation of foreign currency control laws this does not render the action inadmissible by virtue of the rule against the enforcement of foreign 'revenue' laws or, to put it more precisely, of foreign prerogative rights. The court regrettably described this as 'an old chestnut'. In truth, it is a principle of great strength and wisdom. See Mann, *Rec.* 132 (1971, i), 166; *Studies in International Law* (1973), p. 492.

expected, on account of rules of general law, but 'because of' Art. VIII (2) (*b*). The argument was bound to fail, for, as the Court said, the unenforceability of an agreement 'is far from implying that one who so agrees commits a tort in New York'.[31]

Similarly, Art. VIII (2) (*b*), it is submitted, has no bearing upon the type of situation with which the House of Lords was faced in two cases.[32] Where the owner of securities, a resident of Czechoslovakia, enters into a contract of bailment with a Czechoslovakian bank whereby the latter undertakes to hold the securities with a sub-bailee in England, Art. VIII (2) (*b*) does not preclude the owner from claiming the securities from the sub-bailee by bringing an action in detinue against him. Although in the lower courts reference was made to the provision, it is not surprising that in the House of Lords the sub-bailees admitted their inability to rely upon it.[33]

Finally, Art. VIII (2) (*b*) does not preclude liability for what certain Continental legal systems describe as *culpa in contrahendo* or 'faute quasi-délictuelle', i.e. liability for a party's failure to apply for such consent as may be necessary or to inform the other party of its absence so as to cause the latter to believe in the validity of the contract and to act accordingly.[34] In English law the Misrepresentation Act, 1967, or the doctrine of estoppel or the tort of negligence or fraud may, in certain cases, justify a similar result without hindrance by Art. VIII (2) (*b*).

5. While, as has been shown, Bretton Woods does not, as a rule, permit the disregard *a priori* of a member State's exchange control legislation on the ground of its inconsistency with public policy, it does not require respect for and the application of such legislation except to the extent prescribed by Art. VIII (2) (*b*).

It is impossible, therefore, to support a formula used (as opposed, perhaps, to a decision rendered) by Germany's Federal Supreme Court.[35] A German claimed commission from an Austrian firm. The defence was that the defendant lacked the consent of the Austrian exchange control authorities. It was not clear whether consent would have been required to the conclusion of the contract

---

[31] p. 376.

[32] *Kahler* v. *Midland Bank*, [1950] A.C. 24, and *Zivnostenska Bank* v. *Frankman*, [1950] A.C. 57. Nor does the provision apply where the facts are similar to those in *Ellinger* v. *Guinness, Mahon & Co.*, [1939] 4 All E.R. 16.

[33] *Kahler* v. *Midland Bank, ubi supra*, at p. 43 *per* Lord MacDermott.

[34] In this sense see an interesting and persuasive decision of the Cour d'Appel in Paris, 14 May 1970, *Rev. Crit.* 1974, 486, affirmed by Cass. Com., 7 March 1972, ibid. p. 491 with note by Eck.

[35] 19 Apr. 1962, *IPRspr.* 1962 and 1963, No. 163.

(in which event Art. VIII (2) (*b*) would have been applicable) or to its performance. The court stated that even though German law applied,[36] as a result of Bretton Woods member States were 'contractually bound mutually to have regard to their exchange control legislation'. If this observation was meant to cover the case of illegality or impossibility of performance or, indeed, any question other than that of the enforceability of certain contracts it would be without foundation.

6. It has been suggested in Germany[36a] that Art. VIII (2) (*b*) does not relate to capital transactions. It is true that the heading of Art. VIII (2) mentions 'current payments'; that Art. XXX (*d*) so defines them as to exclude almost all capital payments; and that the control of capital transactions is permitted by Art. VI (3) and, therefore, clearly distinguished from current transactions. These are points of some strength, but they would lead to the exclusion from the ambit of Art. VIII (2) (*b*) of such transactions as gifts, loans or purchases of foreign assets, which from the point of view of a State's financial resources are particularly undesirable and more dangerous than contracts for the supply of goods and services, where usually adequate consideration is being furnished. Such results cannot have been intended by the legislator. They are inconsistent with the clear purpose of the provision. They rest on arguments of a formal character, which would be appropriate to the interpretation of a domestic statute, but ought not to prevail in the case of a treaty such as the Bretton Woods Agreement which, as will appear, was drafted in peculiar circumstances and is by no means free from verbal discrepancies.

7. Finally, Art. VIII (2) (*b*) is now likely to apply for and against all member States, irrespective of whether or no they have invoked the privilege of the transitional period (Art. XIV) or accepted the obligations under Art. VIII, ss. 1, 2, and 3. As a matter of construction, as opposed to substance and merit, the point is a very doubtful one and there are weighty reasons supporting a decision in the opposite sense. On the other hand in July 1949 the Fund's Executive Directors rendered an interpretative decision under Art. XVIII to the effect that the rule 'applied to all members, whether or not they have availed themselves of the transitional arrangements of Art. XIV, section 2'.[37] Nowhere has there been any dissent from

[36] On this point see above, p. 178, n. 21.

[36a] By Professor Coing (above, p. 172, n. 2). The Federal Supreme Court of Germany described his view as 'doubtful': above n. 21. It is, however, inconsistent with *Sharif* v. *Azad*, [1967] 1 Q.B. 605 and the decisions of the Court of Appeal in Paris, 20 June 1961, Clunet 1962, 718, and 4 May 1970, *Rev. Crit.* 1974, 486, at p. 489.

[37] *Selected Decisions of the Executive Directors* (3rd ed., 1965), p. 75.

this decision. Nowhere, indeed, does the point seem to have been taken, discussed or even appreciated. It is now probably foreclosed.[38]

## V

The interpretation of Art. VIII (2) (*b*) unfortunately raises many doubts which, perhaps, could have been avoided if the lawyers had been allowed a larger share in drafting the Agreement of Bretton Woods.[39] The text is so unsatisfactory[40] that it would certainly have been desirable if, in exercise of the powers under Art. XVII and Art. XVIII, the Fund had amended or interpreted it. But so long as this has not been done, it is both the right and the duty of the courts to construe the provision and, with respect, there is no justification for the opinion that 'in view of Art. XVIII of the Agreement it is undesirable for the Court to express a view'.[41] Art. VIII (2) (*b*) has become part of English law and is applicable as between any two parties; Art. XVIII applies in case any question arises between member States and does not, therefore, permit a municipal

[38] On the effect of an interpretation see *British Year Book of International Law*, 1968-9, 1, at p. 18 or *Studies in International Law* (1973), 591.

[39] In *Wilson Smithett & Cope Ltd.* v. *Terruzzi*, [1976] 1 Q.B. 683, at p. 712, Lord Denning M.R. suggested that the comment in the text was unjustifiable and that lawyers did play a large part. The *travaux préparatoires* which are available in print would seem to support the text. The Articles of Agreement as a whole are so full of discrepancies and drafting obscurities that no other conclusion is possible. The *Collected Works of John Maynard Keynes*, Vol. xxvi (1980), published for the Royal Economic Society explain the circumstances: The Conference of 44 nations and about 200 Delegates was an unusually rushed and confused affair. It started on 3 July and ended on 22 July 1944, after 'three extra days needed to reduce strain on the Delegates' (p. 96) and 'unbelievable pressure' (p. 106),. It was 'as though, in the course of three or four weeks, one had to accomplish the preliminary work of many interdepartmental and Cabinet committees, the job of the Parliamentary draftsmen, and the passage through several Houses of Parliament of two intricate legislative measures of major dimensions . . .' (pp. 10, 107). No wonder that by the end of the first week 'everyone was beginning to show signs of wear and tear' (p. 83). The Delegates believed they had covered 'a field of great intellectual and technical difficulty' (p. 101), which many, it seems, later confessed not to have understood. No wonder that the Conference was 'hardly over before questions began to arise' (p. 113). There were altogether nine lawyers, among them W. E. Beckett (as he then was), who was as it seems the only English lawyer. Although Lord Keynes paid a handsome tribute to the lawyers and others (p. 102), they hardly had a chance to do their work properly or to make themselves fully familiar with a strange subject.

[40] In *Terruzzi*'s case (see preceding note) Kerr J. at p. 691 called it a 'curiously truncated piece of legislation'.

[41] *Kahler* v. *Midland Bank*, [1948] 1 All E.R. 811, 819 *per* Evershed L.J. (as he then was); for similar reluctance see *Cermak* v. *Bata Akciova Spolecnost*, 80 N.Y.S. (2d) 782, 785 (1948). In more recent years no court has displayed any hesitation to interpret the provision. As regards England, in particular, see *Sharif* v. *Azad*, [1967] 1 Q.B. 605 (C.A.) or *Terruzzi*'s case (see note 39 above). An interpretation made by the Fund by virtue of Art. XVIII would not in any case be binding upon courts: see Mann, *British Year Book of International Law*, 1968-9, 1, at p. 13 or *Studies in International Law* (1973), p. 606.

court to shirk the task of giving effect to and, for that purpose, construing Art. VIII (2) (*b*).

In discharging that task the courts, it is submitted, should to a large extent be guided by the paramount purpose of the International Monetary Fund, which is 'to promote international monetary co-operation'.[42] The text should not be construed as if it was merely a piece of English legislation, but as a multilateral treaty which, according to well-established principles of 'general acceptation', are subject to the canons of liberal interpretation developed by public international law.[43]

1. It is to be regretted that the term *exchange contracts*, which is of particular importance in that it defines the scope of the provision, is wholly obscure.

In so far as reference is made to 'contracts', no difficulty of interpretation, it is true, ought to arise. The governing principles to which reference has been made above render it inappropriate to attribute a strictly technical meaning to the word 'contracts', but put it on the same level as 'transactions' so that it becomes capable of comprising a conveyance, a transfer or assignment,[44] as well as a settlement or a declaration of trust.[45] The creation of or participation in a foreign partnership or the subscription of shares in a foreign limited company should be treated as included in the term. On the other hand a bailment is unlikely ever to be an exchange contract.

However, it is the term 'exchange' that characterizes and at the same time narrows the class contemplated by the legislators. What are 'exchange contracts'?

Two different answers have, in the course of the last thirty-five years or so, achieved a measure of support. Nussbaum suggested that the Section contemplated contracts to exchange the currency of one country for that of another as well as contracts which are 'monetary transactions in disguise'.[46] This definition conforms to the

---

[42] Art. I (i).

[43] In favour of a liberal construction see *Sharif* v. *Azad*, [1967] 1 Q.B. 605, at p. 618 *per* Diplock L.J. The principles which should govern the interpretation of 'uniform statutes' have been authoritatively laid down in *Fothergill* v. *Monarch Airlines Ltd.*, [1981] A.C. 251.

[44] The Paris Court of Appeal, 20 June 1961, Clunet; 962, 718, also Int. L.R. 47, 46 held that the assignment of shares in a 'société à responsibilité limitée' created under French law was an exchange contract.

[45] In this sense Mann, *British Year Book of International Law*, 1949, 279. The suggestion in the text is rejected by Dicey and Morris, p. 1029, but the idea that the term 'unenforceable' cannot be applied to a transfer or conveyance is unacceptable. Why should a Land Registry or the Registrar of a company not be entitled and obliged to refuse the transfer of land or shares on the ground of its 'unenforceability'? Why should a court be bound to recognize an assignee? Why should a court be bound to enforce a declaration of trust transferring a person's property to a foreign beneficiary?

[46] Pp. 542, 543 and see already 49 (1949) *Yale L.J.* 426.

ordinary meaning of the words[47] and has the great advantage that it confines a singularly unattractive provision to the narrowest possible limits, for exchange contracts in Nussbaum's sense hardly ever occur in ordinary life, but on the whole are the privilege of bankers who, as authorized dealers,[48] are in many countries independent of individual exchange control licences. Nonetheless the definition which would blur the distinction between exchange contracts and 'exchange transactions between [a member's] currency and the currency of other members' in Articles IV (3) and IV (4) (b) was adopted both by Kerr J. and the Court of Appeal (Lord Denning M.R., Ormrod and Shaw L.JJ.) in Terruzzi's case[49] in 1976, where, in circumstances not appearing from the reports, the Italian defendant's case was so unmeritorious that a different decision would have strained the judicial conscience. It is perhaps not surprising that the Court of Appeal's interpretation has remained unique and that the Italian courts have refused to recognize and enforce the English judgment.[50]

According to another suggestion,[51] formerly accepted by Lord Denning,[52] 'exchange contracts' are contracts which in any way affect a country's exchange resources so as to be liable to reduce them. This would appear to be in better harmony with the purpose of the Agreement and the true intentions of its authors to be gathered from it, but admittedly makes the word 'exchange' redundant: in order to express the idea, the provision could have referred simply to 'contracts which involve the currency of any member'. So to disregard an important word may run counter to established principles of interpretation. Yet it is submitted that this objection, grave though it may be, is outweighed by the fact that no

---

[47] See, for instance, Lord Radcliffe in a wholly different context and entirely obiter in *Re United Railways of Havana and Regla Warehouses Ltd.*, [1961] A.C. 1007, at p. 1059.

[48] See, e.g., s. 1 of the Exchange Control Act 1947.

[49] *Wilson, Smithett & Cope Ltd.* v. *Terruzzi*, [1976] 1 Q.B. 683. See critical comment by Lipstein, *Cambridge L.J.* 1976, 203.

[50] Court of Appeal at Milan, 10 June 1977, *Rivista di diritto internazionale privato e processuale* 1979, 271. affirmed by Corte di Cassazione, 13 April 1981, ibid. 1981.

[51] Originally made by Mann (above, p. 184, n. 45) and maintained in the two preceding editions of this book, including its German translation. An earlier suggestion at 10 (1947) M.L.R. 418 was to the effect that exchange contracts are contracts providing for consideration in the form of exchange, i.e. currency, was clearly untenable, because it was both too wide and too narrow. Gold, *The Fund Agreement in the Courts* in *IMF Staff Papers* xxiv (1977) 219 suggests that the Section envisages 'contracts requiring international payments or transfers in foreign or domestic currency'. This is very much in line with what is being put forward in the text except for the word 'international' which introduces much uncertainty. The gift or loan by a resident to a non-resident who happens to be in England was forbidden by the Exchange Control Act 1947 (as by most exchange control laws), but can hardly be described as an international payment or transfer.

[52] *Sharif* v. *Azad*, [1967] 1 Q.B. 605, at pp. 613, 614.

other interpretation would achieve the overriding purposes of the Agreement.

The last-mentioned solution was adopted by the French and German courts. Thus the Court of Appeal in Paris refused to enforce a contract whereby in contravention of Dutch exchange control a Dutch resident sold to a German shares in a French company for French francs[53] or a contract between a Japanese company and a Frenchman who was appointed the former's European representative at a fixed monthly remuneration and certain commissions payable in respect of films imported into Japan;[54] this decision which was affirmed by the Cour de Cassation[55] declares it to be sufficient 'qu'il s'agisse de contrats mettant en cause la monnaie d'un Etat membre, c'est-à-dire de contrats dont l'éxecution affecte les ressources en devises de cet Etat, selon la définition qui en est le plus généralement donnée et qui a déja été accueillie dans la jurisprudence.' The German Federal Supreme Court treated as an exchange contract a guarantee given by a Dutch company to a German seller to secure payment of a purchase price due from a Germany buyer;[56] a DM bill of exchange accepted by the defendant Dutch company to secure a credit granted to a German debtor;[57] an agreement between a French buyer, the plaintiff, and a German seller, the defendant, whereby the former was entitled, but failed, to deduct 4 per cent of the purchase price claimed in the action;[58] an agreement between a German and a French firm, under which as a result of a compromise agreement a certain rebate was claimed by the former;[59] an agreement between the plaintiff, a German, and Austrian manufacturers who had appointed him their German sales agent and were alleged to owe him commission.[60] At an early stage

[53] 20 June 1961, Clunet 1962, 718 with note by Gold and Lachman, ibid. p. 666, also Int. L.R. 47, 46. The essential passage reads (p. 724): 'Mais considérant que les accords de Bretton Woods ont pour but principal, selon les termes mêmes de leur article premier, "d'encourager une collaboration monétaire internationale"; qu'il convient par suite, pour assurer le maximum d'efficacité à cette collaboration de rechercher si le contrat dont il s'agit peut avoir un effet préjudiciable sur la situation financière de l'Etat membre, si, en d'autres termes, il peut affecter, de quelque manière que ce soit, les resources de change de ce pays.'

[54] 14 May 1970, *Rev. Crit.* 1974, 486.

[55] 7 March 1972, *Rev. Crit.* 1974, 486, 491 with note by Eck.

[56] 11 March 1970, *JZ.* 1970, 727.

[57] 27 April 1970, *JZ.* 1970, 728. The Court said of bills of exchange that 'these very obligations may have particular effect upon the balance of payments so that without their inclusion an effective limitation of exchange transactions would hardly be possible'.

[58] 24 June 1970, *IPRspr.* 1970, No. 102.

[59] 17 Feb. 1971, *BGHZ.* 55, 334. The Court is guided by the purpose of Art. VIII (2) (*b*) which is 'the international protection of the currency resources of a member State to the extent to which such member State itself claims protection by exchange control regulations.' (p. 337).

[60] 19 April 1962, *IPRspr.* 1962 & 1963, No. 163.

the Court of Appeal at Schleswig treated a loan of U.S. $1,000 given by one Austrian resident to another as an exchange contract;[61] twenty years later the Court of Appeal in Berlin treated as an exchange contract the right granted by the plaintiff, a resident of Israel, to the defendant's predecessor-in-title to collect and keep for the plaintiff certain DM income arising in Berlin.[62] And the Court of Appeal at Bamberg treated a licence agreement relating to a patent as an exchange contract, stating expressly that the term comprised all contractual obligations, including those arising from trade in goods and services, which are calculated to have effect upon the member State's balance of payments.[63] All German courts made from time to time statements to the effect that in construing the term 'exchange contract' it was necessary to have regard to the purpose of the provision which was 'to safeguard the currency resources of the member State'[64] or to prevent 'prejudicial effect upon the member State's balance of payments.'[65] Or, as the Court of Appeal in Berlin put it,[66] 'the notion of an exchange contract is not confined to currency exchange transactions in the narrow sense. Only a wide interpretation takes account of the economic purpose of the treaty. Currency interests are always affected where the currency reserves of a country are involved.'

These views which in the Court of Appeal in England were described as arising from 'a tortuous and erroneous construction', as being inconsistent with 'ordinary intelligence', as involving 'obfuscation', as constituting 'not interpretation, but mutilation' and as representing 'intemperate logic'[67] should, it is submitted with great respect, continue to be preferred to those expressed in *Terruzzi*'s case. The judgments rendered in that case put much emphasis on the fact that according to Article I of the IMF Articles

[61] 1 April 1954, *IPRspr.* 1954, No. 163 or *Jahrbuch für Internationales Recht*, v (1955), 113 with note by Bulck, also Int. L.R. 1955, 727. Similarly the District Court Hamburg held that a sale by a Hamburg merchant to a Belgian firm for dollars was an exchange contract: 28 Dec. 1954, *IPRspr.* 1954 & 1955, No. 164 or Int. L.R. 22, 730. The Tribunal Luxembourg said obiter that there existed an exchange contract where a French firm sells goods to a resident of Luxembourg and a third party, in violation of French exchange control regulations, makes an (invalid) payment to the seller; the actual decision was that a French judgment ordering the defendant to pay could not, among members of the Bretton Agreement, be contrary to *ordre public*: 9 May 1953, Int. L.R. 22, 722.

[62] 8 July 1974, *IPRspr.* 1974, No. 138.

[63] 5 July 1978, *IPRspr.* 1978, No. 127.

[64] See, for instance, n. 59 above.

[65] See n. 62 above, where it is rightly pointed out that currency movements outside the restricting State reduce its resources. In a decision of 21 Dec. 1976 the Court describes it as doubtful whether movements of capital outside the restricting State are covered by Art. VIII (2) (*b*): WM. 1977, 332. See above n. 36a.

[66] Above, n. 62.

[67] [1976] 1 Q.B. 683, at pp. 719, 722, 724, 725 *per* Shaw L.J.

of Agreement the purposes are not only 'to promote international monetary co-operation', but also 'to facilitate the expansion and balanced growth of international trade' among other purposes which include the promotion of exchange stability, the establishment of a multilateral system of payments and the elimination of exchange restrictions. Lord Denning, in particular, said 'that it is in the interest of international trade that there should be no restriction on contracts for the sale and purchase of merchandise and commodities and that they should be enforceable in the territories of the members.'[68] But Lord Denning also said that the defendant was 'a gambler in differences. He speculates on the rise or fall of the price of zinc, copper and so forth. He speculated in 1973 on the London Metal Exchange.'[69] It is legitimate for a State and, indeed, the international community, to prevent, and unjustifiable for individuals or tribunals to support in defiance of official policies, such or similar activities. The promotion of trade does not mean that it is not for State policies to determine the type of trade, whether in essentials or luxuries, in commodities or securities, in raw materials or manufactured articles, and the terms of such trade that it wishes to promote. This can be done by customs duties or financial charges or by exchange control;[70] for many years the United Kingdom itself has pursued such policies both by physical and by exchange control, as the Exchange Control Act 1947, among other statutes, proves. The aim of Art. VIII (2) (b) plainly is, not to promote trade without qualification, but to ensure a measure of respect for a member State's financial control. Furthermore there exists a vast number of transactions which do not come within the Court of Appeal's definition of exchange contracts and which, on account of their danger to the economy, a legislator is justified not only in prohibiting, but also in expecting to be shunned. This applies to trade in securities with non-residents, to the. transfer of valuables or to loans to non-residents, particularly while they happen to be within the country. Perhaps in some of these cases the Court of Appeal would speak of exchange contracts in disguise, but such a definition only obscures realities and creates uncertainty. In short, respect for a member State's currency resources and balance of payments is by no means alien to the letter or the spirit of the IMF Articles of Agrement: respect only for the prohibition openly

---

[68] At p. 713.                                              [69] At p. 709.

[70] This obvious truth was elegantly put by French authors: 'Commerce et monnaie sont indissociables . . . Les restrictions commerciales quantitatives ont des effets analogues aux restrictions de change même si elles relèvent de techniques différentes.' (Carreau, Juillard et Flory, *Droit International Economique*, (2nd ed., 1980, p. 129). The whole passage is worth reading.

or in disguise to exchange the currency of one country for that of another disregards so wide a range of potentially dangerous trans-actions, such legitimate policies of member States and such clearly available and frequently practised methods of implementing them that no international legislator can be expected to have confined himself to it.[71]

Although doubts on the construction here suggested have been expressed by the New York Court of Appeals which inclined to the view that a wide construction of Art. VIII (2) (b) was 'doing con-siderable violence to the text',[72] the majority of learned writers would seem to support it on the ground of its conformity with the legislative purpose.[73]

It is inherent in the submissions on the scope of Art. VIII (2) (b)[74] that the question whether or not a contract is an exchange contract must be decided with reference to the time when it is made.

Moreover, the test must be complied with by the specific con-tract in issue, so that the existence of an exchange contract cannot be inferred from a variety of different contracts, taken as a whole,

[71] Numerous incidental points were made in *Terruzzi*'s case the more important of which must shortly be mentioned. (1) The word 'exchange' is indeed often used in the Articles of Agreement to refer to currency, but the Agreement is throughout characterized by inconsistency and sloppiness of language. (2) The term 'exchange contract' as under-stood here is very wide indeed, but so are, for instance, sections 1 to 7 of the Exchange Control Act 1947, which, to take an example given by Kerr J., make it impossible without permission to engage and pay a foreign lawyer, though the free use of allocated exchange for hotel accommodation or taxis is, of course, permitted. (3) As regards the avoidance of restrictions on current transactions referred to in Art. VIII (2) (a) this is subject to Art. XIV and in any event raises the different question of interpreting the words 'maintained or imposed consistently with this Agreement', on which see below, p. 395. Moreover, the words 'avoidance of restrictions' have a technical meaning: they do not contemplate the abolition of exchange control regulations, but the appropriate application of such regula-tions or a method of control which avoids restrictions in fact, though not in law: see below, p. 518. The Articles of Agreement are a treaty which binds member States. Only Art. VIII (2) (b) binds individuals. To interpret this provision by references to the Agreement requires the techniques of the public international lawyer. (4) Other points that have been made are best answered by reference to the Exchange Control Act 1947 which would lead to the same result and require the same international recognition as Italian regulations were it not for the fact that in so far as debts are concerned payment into court is permitted and may be enforced: see above, p. 366; this is a concession which no country is legally bound to make.

[72] *Banco de Brasil v. Israel Commodity Co. Inc.* (1963), 12 N.Y. 2d 371, at pp. 375, 376; 190 N.E. 2d 235; Int. L.R. 30, 371. In *J. Zeevi & Sons Ltd. v. Grindlays Bank (Uganda) Ltd.*, 37 N.Y. 2d 220, 333 N.E. 2d 168 (1975), the same court stated that it had 'frowned on an interpretation . . . which sweeps in all contracts affecting any member's exchange resources.' Against this dictum Williams, 9 *Cornell International L.J.* 239, at p. 246.

[73] In particular Sir Joseph Gold in the course of earlier writings: see, for instance, *The International Monetary Fund and Private Business Transactions* (1965), p. 25.

[74] Above, pp. 377–9.

none or only some of which, regarded separately, come within the definition. In other words, it is necessary to consider each contract separately rather than the totality of a scheme or an arrangement. In effect the Court of Appeals in New York so decided as early as 1959:[75] a debt of dollars due from a New York bank to a New York corporation is not an exchange contract, even though the dollars held by the bank as well as the assignment to the corporation of the title to the debt were derived from a transaction between other parties involving Italian lire and contrary to Italian law. Similarly the English Court of Appeal held[76] that a sterling cheque drawn on an English bank by a resident of England in favour of another resident of England was not an exchange contract, although it was drawn as a result of and in connection with a transaction involving the currency and infringing the law of Pakistan.[77] On grounds which were far from convincing this case (which clearly established a sound principle) was distinguished by the Court of Appeal (Stephenson, Ackner and Griffiths L.JJ.) in a later case: X in England sold goods to Y in Peru at a price which at the latter's request, but in breach of Peruvian exchange control regulations was doubled, one moiety to be repaid by the sellers to an associated company of the buyers in the United States. The total price was payable by way of an irrevocable and transferable letter of credit which was issued by a Peruvian bank, confirmed by the defendants and assigned to the plaintiffs (who were presumably unaware of the scheme violating Peruvian law). It was held that the letter of credit could not be regarded in isolation from the contract of sale (which in the circumstances was an unenforceable exchange contract within the meaning of the English rule), that, while international trade required the enforcement of the letter of credit, international comity required the enforcement of the Bretton Woods Agreement and that the latter requirement should prevail,[78] although only to the extent

---

[75] Southwestern Shipping Corporation v. National City Bank, 6 N.Y. 2d 454, 160 N.E. 2d 836 (1959), also International L.R. 28 (1963), 539.

[76] Sharif v. Azad, [1967] 1 Q.B. 605, on which see Mann, International and Comparative Law Quarterly 1967, 539.

[77] For the reason stated in the text a guarantee is not an exchange contract merely by reason of the fact that the debt it secures is an exchange contract. A guarantee is a separate and independent contract which is an exchange contract if it comes itself within the definition. On close analysis the obscure decision of the Federal Supreme Court of Germany of 21 May 1964, Wertpapiermitteilungen 1964, 768, is unlikely to express a different view. In the sense of the present submission now the Federal Supreme Court of Germany, 11 Mar. 1970, NJW. 1970, 1002.

[78] United City Merchants (Investments) Ltd. v. Royal Bank of Canada (1981), 1 W.L.R. 242. The underlying sales contract was held to be an exchange contract in disguise. There plainly was a conspiracy between buyers and sellers and the contract of sale was void for the reason given above, p. 379.

of the moiety the payment of which Peruvian law considered unlawful.[79] It is submitted that there is nothing in the text of the
Bretton Woods Agreement which permits treating a contract as an
exchange contract if in the light of its own terms it cannot be so
characterized; consequently there is no justification for interfering
to an intolerable extent with the requirements of international
trade which demands the complete independence or autonomy of
a letter of credit (and of a bill of exchange). It is to be hoped that
if the House of Lords has the opportunity of considering the point
it will prefer the views of the New York Court of Appeals:[80] Where
an Israeli corporation sold local currency to the defendants, a bank
in Uganda which in accordance with instructions opened an
irrevocable dollar letter of credit in favour of the plaintiffs, 'an
Israeli partnership', the New York Court of Appeals denied that the
letter of credit (which, rightly, it considered in isolation) was an
exchange contract. No clear reason was given, and on the facts the
Court's somewhat abrupt treatment of the question of definition
is not free from doubt,[81] yet the conclusion is greatly to be preferred
to that reached by the Court of Appeal in England.[82]

2. The phrase *which involve the currency* contemplates, it is
submitted, not the denomination in a particular currency, but the
financial area within which the transaction has economic effects.
'Currency' should be construed in the broad sense of economics
rather than in a strictly legal sense. The term may include gold,
securities of whatever denomination, even land, movables or
intangibles; the transfer of such property may 'involve the currency'
of a member State. A significant example is supplied by the decision
of the Court of Appeal in Paris:[83] a resident of Holland sold participations in a French company for French francs to a resident of
Germany. This was an exchange contract involving the currency of
Holland, because it affected Dutch financial resources, although
neither the participations nor the price were expressed in terms of
Dutch currency. A less satisfactory result was reached by the
Austrian Supreme Court:[84] the plaintiff, then resident in Yugoslavia,

[79] On this point see below, pp. 397, 398.
[80] *J. Zeevi & Sons Ltd.* v. *Grindlays Bank (Uganda) Ltd.*, 37 N.Y. 2d 220, 333 N.E. 2d
168 (1975).
[81] The result was plainly correct: see above, p. 377, n. 19; p. 380, n. 30.
[82] Where bills of exchange or letters of credit are exchange contracts, but reach the
hands of purchasers for value without notice, the contract should be held to be enforceable
and free from the defect created by Art. VIII (2) (*b*). If this were not so the autonomy
or abstractness of negotiable instruments would be prejudiced to an intolerable extent.
[83] Above, p. 386, n. 53.
[84] 2 July 1958, *Juristische Blätter*, 1959, 73, on which see Schwind, ibid., p. 65, also
*International L.R.* 26 (1958, ii), 232.

paid a sum of Yugoslavian currency to his Zagreb bank which remitted it to a Vienna Bank for the purpose of opening a letter of credit in favour of the plaintiff's suppliers. The credit was not taken up. The plaintiff emigrated to Vienna, where the Austrian bank held the money on a blocked account for its Zagreb principals. The action against the latter succeeded, because according to the Supreme Court the blocked account was without any relevant connection with Yugoslavia's currency resources.

The question whether the currency of a member is 'involved' is independent of the adequacy of the consideration; or, to put it differently, the question whether an exchange contract is prejudicial or advantageous to the member's currency is immaterial, and in particular, cannot be decided upon by the parties or a judge. This has been doubted and it has been held that normal trading transactions such as the sale of goods are not caught by Art. VIII (2) (b).[85] Such a view must be rejected, because it would lead to the conclusion that contracts which are clearly contrary to regulations are valid merely on account of what appears to be their 'normal' character, and that the administrative authorities called upon to supervise such contracts would be deprived of their functions.

The involvement of the currency must, however, be due to the particular exchange contract in issue. Thus, if an English firm buys timber from a Swedish firm it is prima facie immaterial that the latter obtains its supplies from Poland and that its contract with the Polish seller is contrary to Polish exchange control regulations. But if the English buyer's contract specifies timber of Polish origin, then it may well be regarded as an exchange contract, affecting Polish financial resources, and therefore involving Polish currency.

3. The words *of any member* have been held to mean that the State whose currency is involved in the exchange contract must be a member of the Fund at the date of judgment; hence, if at that date the State has ceased to be a member the provision does not apply.[86] Similarly, if at that date the State in question is a member,

---

[85] Court of Appeal at Hamburg, 7 July 1959, *IzRspr.* 1958-9, No. 135a.

[86] This was decided in *Stephen* v. *Zivnostenska Banka*, 140 N.Y.S. 2d 323 (1955), also *International L.R.* 1955, 719, and was the primary reason for which in the Cuban insurance cases (referred to below, p. 415, n. 65), Art. VIII (2) (b), was held to be inapplicable after the withdrawal of Cuba from the Fund in 1964: *Pan-American Life Insurance Co.* v. *Blanco*, 362 F. 2d 167 (Circuit Court of Appeals, Fifth Circuit, 1966); *Confederation Life Association* v. *Vega y Arminan* (1968), 207 So. 2d 33 (District Court of Appeal of Florida), affirmed (1968) 211 So. 2d 169 (Supreme Court of Florida). Before Cuba's withdrawal Art. VIII (2) (b) was held to be applicable by the Supreme Court of Florida: *Confederation Life Association* v. *Ugalde*, 164 So. 2d 1 (1964), also *International L.R.* 38, 138. In truth the provision was at no time applicable, for (a) at the relevant date, viz. the date of their conclusion, the insurance contracts were not exchange contracts (see above, p. 377); (b)

but at the date of the contract the State was not a member the provision does not apply either. In the former case the result may be said to be founded upon the rule of construction expressed by the adage *cessante ratione cessat lex*. The result in the latter case is supported by the fact that Art. VIII (2) (*b*) looks to the date of the conclusion of the contract.[87]

4. The next phrase, *'and which are contrary to the exchange control regulations'* refers to enactments that control the movement of the currency, property, or services for the purpose of protecting the financial resources of a country.[88] Tariffs, trade restrictions, price control or trading with the enemy regulations[89] are outside the scope of the provision. Although the problem of definition will not always be free from doubt, it ought to be clear that, for example, the American system of foreign funds control cannot be described as an exchange control regulation, for its purpose is not the protection of the dollar currency.[90] Nor is the statutory prohibition to enter into contracts providing for payment

in the event of the date of payment being material, payment in the United States cannot have been contrary to Cuban laws (see below, p. 416). See, generally, Sir Joseph Gold's pamphlet mentioned below, n. 92.

[87] See above, p. 377. The point was discussed by van Rooij in his comments on the decision of the Hoge Raad, 12 Jan. 1979, *Rev. Crit.* 1980, 68, at p. 72. Although, as appears from these comments, Art. VIII (2) (*b*) was relied upon before the Hoge Raad, the decision does not mention it and must therefore be assumed impliedly to accept the view expressed in the text.

[88] This definition, first put forward in the second edition of this book, is not fundamentally different from Upjohn J.'s (probably much too narrow) definition of a foreign exchange law which he described as 'a law passed with the genuine intention of protecting its (*sic*) economy . . . and for that purpose regulating . . . the rights of foreign creditors': *In re Helbert Wagg & Co. Ltd.*, [1956] Ch. 323, at p. 351. On the other hand the International Monetary Fund goes much too far when it describes it as the guiding test whether a measure 'involves a direct governmental limitation on the availability or use of exchange as such': Decision No. 1034 of 1 June 1970, *Selected Decisions* (1976), p. 139. On the problem of definition see Shuster, *The Public International Law of Money* (1973), pp. 31, 73, 229.

[89] Such as American 'freezing orders': Nussbaum, pp. 455, 456.

[90] Such freezing or blocking orders used to be made (for instance, in the case of Cuba) under s. 5 (*b*) of the Trading with the Enemy Act which enables the President to control foreign assets during any 'period of national emergency'. Cf. *Nielsen* v. *Secretary of Treasury*, 424 F. 2d 833 (1970). They are now authorized by s. 203 (*a*) (1) of the International Emergency Economic Powers Act. Their function is different from the control of United States exchange resources. President Carter's Executive Order of 14 Nov. 1979 blocking Iranian assets in response to the taking of U.S. citizens as hostages in Iran was described as 'a rough form of exchange control' requiring other States to give effect to it by virtue of Art. VIII (2) (*b*): Gianviti, *Rev. Crit.* 1980, 279, at p. 294. The argument is unconvincing, for Art VIII (2) (*b*) is concerned with the unenforceability of contracts rather than the blocking of property, it contemplates the protection of exchange resources rather than defensive measures against a foreign country and in any event deals only with the effectiveness of contracts at the date of their conclusion rather than exchange control subsequently introduced (see above, p. 377).

in terms of foreign currency an exchange control regulation.[91] That legal tender legislation in the accepted sense of the term cannot be described as exchange control regulation hardly requires emphasis.[92]

In accordance with earlier submissions the reconciliability of the exchange contract with the exchange control regulations must, in principle, be judged as at the date of the contract. That the contract or its performance becomes illegal may be a material point under the general law, but is not caught by Art. VIII (2) (b). If, therefore, the plaintiff legally buys a dollar cheque in Cuba (and thus clearly concludes an enforceable exchange contract), smuggles it out of Cuba and sues upon it in New York, thus acting contrary to Cuban law, Art. VIII (2) (b) does not bar the action.[93]

Conversely, if at the date of its conclusion the exchange contract is contrary to the exchange control regulations, then, as has been shown,[94] their repeal or the subsequent grant of a licence or emigration or the assignment of the debt to a resident[95] removes the rationale underlying Art. VIII (2) (b) and renders the contract enforceable.

The contract that has to be contrary to exchange control regulations is the particular exchange contract that is under consideration. In *United City Merchants (Investments) Ltd.* v. *Royal Bank of Canada*[96] the Court of Appeal rightly held that a letter of credit issued by the Royal Bank of Canada was an exchange contract, but it also held it unenforceable on the ground that the underlying sales contract violated Peruvian exchange control regulations. This, it is submitted, should not be allowed to matter: whatever the legal validity of the sales contract may have been, the letter of credit was established through a Peruvian bank and, considered by itself, was in no way contrary to Peruvian regulations.

Is a contract contrary to exchange control regulations even if, according to its express or implied terms, it is to take effect only upon the repeal of the provision which creates the illegality? The answer, it is submitted, depends on the terms of the exchange control regulations against which the contract offends. The legal system to which these belong may provide guidance to their interpretation, but it does not, in the technical sense, govern the question,

---

[91] In this sense Court of Appeal Karlsruhe, 15 Dec. 1965, *IPRspr.* 1964 and 1965, No. 194.

[92] Suggestions to the opposite effect which were made in the United States were rightly rejected by Gold, *The Cuban Insurance Cases and the Articles of the Fund* (1966), p. 36.

[93] But see *Brill* v. *Chase Manhattan Bank*, 220 N.Y.S. 2d 903 (1961), on which see below, p. 409, n. 44.                                [94] Above, p. 379.

[95] German Federal Supreme Court, 8 March 1979, *NJW.* 1980, 520.

[96] [1981] 1 W.L.R. 242; see above, p. 390.

nor can the *lex monetae* or the proper law of the contract fill the gap.[97]

5. The meaning of the words, '*of that member*', is, in substance, determined by the earlier phrase 'which involve currency of any member'. If, as has been submitted, the provision contemplates, not the currency in the legal sense, but the member's economic resources which are affected by the exchange contract, then the exchange control regulations contravened by the exchange contract are those of the country whose resources are so affected. In other words, one looks, not to the *lex monetae*, but to what one may call the *lex patrimonii*.[98]

The resources which are involved and the regulations which are contravened must belong to the same country.

Yet, although the provision refers to a member in the singular, it may well be that the resources of more than one country are affected and that, therefore, the exchange control regulations of more than one member will have to be considered. Thus the supply of and payment for goods may involve two currencies and contravene both currency systems' exchange control regulations.

6. The next phrase, '*maintained or imposed consistently with this Agreement*' gives rise to many difficulties.

The word 'maintained' refers to exchange control regulations which were in force when the Articles of Agreement took effect, i.e. 27 December 1945.[99] In this sense the provision had retrospective effect.

It is not each single provision that has to be consistent with the Agreement. It is the existence of the regulations and their character as a whole that must meet the Agreement's express or implied requirements. It is conformity with the Agreement that matters and that any court is entitled and bound to investigate independently; the view of the Fund may provide a guide to construction, but cannot be a substitute for the Agreement itself and its interpretation. On the other hand, in order to be consistent with the Agreement the regulations must have certain features which are plainly regarded as fundamental.

Thus effect must have been given in the foreign country to Art. VIII (2) (*b*).[100] This follows from the specific, though perhaps unnecessary, reference in Art. VIII (1) to a measure of reciprocity.

[97] According to a decision of the Court of Appeal at Frankfurt, 27 Feb. 1969, *Aussenwirtschaftsdienst des Betriebsberaters*, 1969, 509, the proper law of the contract would be applicable.
[98] The expression was suggested in 1952: *Report of the 45th Conference of the International Law Association* (Lucerne), p. 242.
[99] See Gold, *The Fund Agreement in the Courts*, p. 65.
[100] Nussbaum, p. 545.

Moreover, in so far as member States no longer rely on the transitional provision of Art. XIV, but have accepted the obligations of Art. VIII, ss. 2, 3, and 4, (at present 48), exchange control regulations cannot ordinarily be consistent with the Agreement if they are imposed so as to restrict payments and transfers for current international transactions. There thus exists the likelihood that a municipal judge will have to decide the extremely difficult question what meaning is to be attached to the word 'restrictions'[101] and to the conception of 'current transactions' which is only very inadequately defined by Art. XIX (i). It must suffice to point, by way of example, to the great difficulties raised by the question whether, and to what extent, the various types of payments made in respect of life insurance contracts can be classified as current rather than capital transactions.[102]

There remain certain cases in which it can be suggested that exchange control regulations would be so unreasonable, or perhaps even so plainly contrary to public international law, that they are inconsistent with the Agreement. Suppose that a life insurance contract is validly concluded between a resident of Cuba and a United States insurance company; that the policy-holder emigrates to the United States where he demands payment; that both the United States and Cuba are members of the Fund; that the insurance company invokes Art. VIII (2) (b) and that, contrary to the above submission, this relieves the debtor of the duty to perform a validly concluded contract. In such a case Cuba could not have the right under international law to control payments of dollars to be made by one resident of the United States to another resident of the United States out of United States resources.[103] This is probably what the Supreme Court of Louisiana had in mind, when it said not only that 'a contract payable in the state of Louisiana in United States currency is not a foreign exchange contract', but also that Cuban exchange control regulations cannot 'have any force and effect over the persons of these litigants who are not only without Cuba, but, as refugees, are not subject to its in personam jurisdiction'.[104]

7. The last words requiring explanation are 'shall be unenforceable'.

---

[101] On this point see below, p. 518.

[102] On this example see Gold (above p. 394, n. 92), pp. 37 sqq.

[103] Cf. Gold (above, p. 394, n. 92), p. 28.

[104] *Theye y Ajuria* v. *Pan-American Life Insurance Co..*, 161 So. 2d 70 (1964), at p. 74, also *Int. L.R.* 38, 456. Cf. *Rodriguez* v. *Pan-American Life Insurance Co.*, 311 F. 2d 429 (1962). The argument suggested in the text is likely to be at the root of the decision in *Re Silk's Estate*, 129 N.Y.S. 2d 134, also *Int. L.R.* 1955, 721. On the facts assumed in the text it would be unreasonable to expect any court to deny recovery.

In many countries the word 'unenforceable' or its equivalent has a technical meaning. It refers to agreements which are valid, but in respect of which it is open to a party to plead that the contract is not binding upon it. Although some writers have understood the word in this sense,[105] its correct meaning must be different, because it would be contrary to the legislative purpose to leave it to one of the parties to decide whether it wishes to plead the exchange control regulations, and to preclude courts and administrative authorties from treating the contract as unenforceable on their own initiative. This is now the view of English law. In *Batra* v. *Ebrabim*[106] the plaintiff paid to the defendant a sum of pounds sterling in consideration of the latter's undertaking to pay in India a sum of rupees greatly in excess of the amount corresponding to the official rate of exchange. The contract was governed by and valid under English law, but contrary to Indian exchange control regulations. The plaintiff claimed damages for non-performance and succeeded in the lower court where Art. VIII (2) (*b*) was not relied upon. It, was, however, raised in the Court of Appeal. Lord Denning M.R., with whom Lawton and Bridge L.JJ. agreed said:

This makes it necessary for us to consider the exact impact of Art. VIII (2) (*b*). What does it mean when it says that such an exchange contract shall be unenforceable? . . . If the word 'unenforceable' were used in the strict sense in which an English lawyer uses that word, the courts would leave it to the parties to decide whether or not to raise the point, just as they did in the Statute of Frauds. If the defendant did not raise Art. VIII (2) (*b*) in his defence, the court would take no notice of it. I cannot think that would be right. We should construe this Article in the same way as we construe other international agreements. We should adopt such a construction as will promote the general legislative purpose: see *Buchanan* v. *Babco*, 2 W.L.R. 112–113. On this basis it seems to me that if it appears to the court that a party is suing on a contract which is made unenforceable by Art. VIII (2) (*b*), then the court must itself take the point and decline to enforce the contract. It is its duty to do so.

What is ineffective, invalid or void is the exchange contract as a whole. In *United City Merchants (Investments) Ltd.* v. *Royal Bank of Canada*[106a] the Court of Appeal stated, possibly obiter, that where

---

[105] Particularly Dicey and Morris, p. 1029.

[106] Unreported except in *The Times* of 3 May 1977, but available at the Bar Library. The decision is dated 2nd May 1977.

[106a] On the facts of the case see above, p. 390. It is not easy to reconcile the attitude of the Court of Appeal referred to in the text with the observations mentioned in n. 27 above. Among the English authorities relied on by the Court of Appeal is *Ralli Bros.* v. *Compania Naviera Sota y Aznar*, [1920] 2 K.B. 287, which should always be read together with the decision of Bailhache J. in [1920] 1 K.B. 614, where the Case Stated by the umpire is reproduced. *Ralli's* case does not support the Court of Appeal's interpretation, because

there was an unenforceable exchange contract the plaintiff could yet recover so much as would be consistent with the member State's exchange control regulations, i.e. in the instant case one moiety of the amount due under the letter of credit. This result was derived from certain English authorities relating to the effect of severance. It is submitted that the point exclusively depends on the interpretation of Art. VIII (2) (b). This does not permit the splitting contemplated by the Court of Appeal, for it renders the exchange contract as a whole unenforceable.

On the other hand, it has not been suggested anywhere that the word intends to express the other extreme, namely illegality.[107] Hence there does not necessarily exist any bar to the restitution of moneys paid or transfers made in pursuance of the unenforceable contract.

Another view, adopted only by the German Federal Supreme Court from about 1970 onwards,[108] is to the effect that Art. VIII (2) (b) imposes a procedural requirement the absence of which, like immunity or lack of jurisdiction, the court is bound to notice *ex officio,* but which does not affect the validity of the contract.[109] No reason has ever been given for this theory which, it is suggested, is unacceptable. In the first place it applies only within the realm of proceedings with the result that administrative authorities, land registrars or similar officers in charge of non-contentious business could not have regard to the provision even if an interested party relied upon it. Secondly, where the principal debt is unenforceable according to Art. VIII (2) (b), but a guarantee given in respect of it is not caught by it, the guarantor could not invoke the provision, for it is not a defence; he would have to pay the creditor, yet could not recover from the principal debtor. Or if in breach of French exchange control regulations a Frenchman sells shares to a German who resells them to another German the Frenchman could not recover the shares from the latter and the object of the provision (which is to protect the French economy) would be stultified. Thirdly and perhaps most importantly, a party would be precluded from suing upon the contract and, at the same time, from recovering payments made under the (valid) contract, as the German Federal Supreme Court in fact decided on more than one

---

one half of the freight had been paid at the agreed rate of £50 at the time of loading and the only question was whether payment of the balance had become impossible by Spanish law.

[107] In *Sharif* v. *Azad*, [1967] 1 Q.B. 605, at p. 618 Diplick L.J. in fact rejected the idea of illegality. Lord Denning in *Batra* v. *Ebrahim, ubi supra,* expressed agreement.

[108] 27 April 1970, *NJW.* 1970, 1507 or *JZ.* 1970, 728; 17 Feb. 1971, *BGHZ.* 55, 334; 21 Dec. 1976, *WM.* 1977, 332; 8 March 1979, *NJW.* 1980, 520.

[109] See on the German practice above, pp. 375, 380 and *passim.*

occasion.[110] These results are unjust and in every respect contrary to and, indeed, partly exceeding, partly narrowing the purpose and rationale of Art. VIII (2) (*b*). This provision renders certain contracts unenforceable, but does not touch claims arising from unenforceable contracts.

Such results are avoided and the legislative purpose can be achieved if unenforceability is understood as meaning ineffectiveness, invalidity or voidness. This is the view which underlies the decision of the Court of Appeal in *Batra* v. *Ebrahim*,[111] where Lord Denning M.R. said: 'If money has been paid under it—and the consideration has failed—then the money can probably be recovered back . . . In this respect it may be different from a contract which is illegal by English law.' This was also the view of the Court of Appeal in Paris in 1961[112] and 1970:[113] of the latter decision the Cour de Cassation said that it proclaimed 'l'inefficacité' of the contract.[114] The same view clearly inspired a decision of the Cour de Cassation of 1969 which allowed repayment of a sum paid in contravention of Art. VIII (2) (*b*).[115] No theory denying so fair a result merits support, for it would attach the severe consequences of illegality to what the legislator described as mere unenforceability.[116]

Irrespective of whether the peculiar theory of the Federal Supreme Court is right or wrong, it should be clear that, in so far as the conditions of Art. VIII (2) (*b*) are not fulfilled, the contract is governed by its proper law. Suppose a contract offends against the exchange control law of Utopia which, during its currency, ceased to

---

[110] Most clearly in the decision of 21 Dec. 1976, *WM.* 1977, 332, but the same conclusion is implied by other decisions which proclaim in terms that Art. VIII (2) (*b*) 'leaves the validity of the contract unaffected': 8 March 1979, *NJW.* 1980, 520 and other cases mentioned in note 108 above.

[111] Above, p. 397, n. 106. It is quite different from a violation of the English Exchange Control Act 1947: see above, p. 361, n. 29.

[112] 20 June 1961, Clunet 1962, 718, at p. 726.

[113] 14 May 1970, *Rev. Crit.* 1974, 486.

[114] 7 March 1972, ibid., p. 491.

[115] 18 June 1969, *Rev. Crit.* 1970, 465 or *Int. L.R.* 52, 10.

[116] Gold has on many occasions criticized the view expressed in the text on the ground that it may involve a more severe sanction than the foreign State's exchange control regulations prescribe. But if they provide for something less than invalidity, the contract is unlikely to be 'contrary' to their terms. It is difficult to understand what Gold's solution is. He seems to confine himself to the statement that 'the judicial or administrative authorities of another member will not give a party assistance, for example, by decreeing performance or by awarding damages for non-performance of his contract' (*The International Monetary Fund and Private Business Transactions*, 1965, p. 23), and a similar formula occurs in the Fund's interpretation of 1949 (*Annual Report*, 1949, p. 82). Is a contract which is subject to the consequences outlined by Gold not invalid? Or is it Gold's intention to deny the right to restitution? This would be most unjust. It is submitted that the law does not recognize any other categories of unenforceability than those discussed in the text. For a recent and comprehensive discussion of the problem see Treves, pp. 248 sqq.

be a member of the International Monetary Fund, so that, in accordance with earlier submissions, Art. VIII (2) (*b*) no longer applies. If the proper law of the contract is English its validity would not be open to question. If, however, the proper law is Utopian then, independently of Art. VIII (2) (*b*), the contract may well be invalid. It is, therefore, not possible to suggest that, among member States of the International Monetary Fund, the consequences of a violation of exchange control regulations are exclusively and conclusively regulated by Art. VIII (2) (*b*).[117]

Finally, the undertaking to indemnify a party against the risk of a contract being inconsistent with the exchange control regulations of a foreign country and, therefore, unenforceable according to Art. VIII (2) (*b*) may be contrary to the public policy of the forum, but is not contrary to the Bretton Woods Agreement, unless it fulfils itself the statutory conditions or constitutes an integral part of the principal contract.

[117] But see above, p. 380, n. 27. In *White* v. *Roberts*, Annual Digest 1949, 27, the Supreme Court of Hong Kong had to deal with a claim to the repayment of a sum of money paid in China under a contract governed by, but illegal under, the law of China. The Chinese law denied the claim and, therefore, the action in Hong Kong was bound to fail.

# XV

# The Private International Law
# of Exchange Control

I. Introduction. II. The question of principle: public policy or control by the proper law?
III. The effect of foreign exchange control on the validity of contracts (1) governed by
the law of the restricting State; (2) governed by English law. IV. The effect of foreign
exchange control upon the performance of contracts (1) governed by the law of the
restricting State; (2) governed by the law of England; (3) the effect of foreign exchange
control upon the manner of payment (the problem of bank notes). V. The effect of foreign
exchange control upon rights of property. VI. Foreign exchange control as an unenforceable
prerogative right.

## I

THE private international law of exchange control, i.e. that part of the
conflict of laws which deals with the reaction of English law to foreign
exchange control regulations,[1] is undoubtedly one of the most important aspects of modern monetary law. Unfortunately, it is in a state
of evolution which renders its treatment a matter of difficulty.

The Bretton Woods Agreements, at present binding upon more
than 140 nations,[2] not only express a definite legal policy, but also
contain formal rules of law.[3] Both that policy and those rules differ
from traditional practice and theory. Moreover, Bretton Woods
does not lay down a complete code: it leaves many gaps which will
have to be filled by resorting to general principles.

On one point the two systems overlap: public policy, a much
overworked and misunderstood doctrine in relation to exchange
control, is bound to be influenced by Bretton Woods even where
non-members are concerned, for an attitude of mind to which
almost 140 nations subscribe cannot leave the other members of the
family of nations indifferent. Yet even without Bretton Woods
public policy is, here as elsewhere, a bad guide to legal decision.

## II

It has frequently been said that the private international law of

---

[1] As to the relationship between English exchange control regulations and foreign law
see above, p. 364.      [2] See the International Monetary Fund's *Annual Report*, 1980, p. 83.
[3] They are discussed below, pp. 513 sqq.

exchange control[4] is, or ought to be, dominated by the principle that exchange control regulations are incapable of international recognition. Although other alleged doctrines such as the public law character[5] or the 'territorialité' of monetary law[6] have been invoked in support of this solution, primarily and in essence it is public policy[7] that is said to require it.

Such is (or was[8]) the attitude adopted by the highest tribunal of *Switzerland.*[9] Thus, in one of the many cases which came before it, the Swiss Federal Tribunal had to deal with an action for the recovery of a debt due by a German to a Swiss firm which had

[4] The literature is immense and to a large extent obsolete. For recent discussion see Nussbaum, pp. 446 sqq.; M. Wolff, *Private International Law*, pp. 472–6; Dicey and Morris, p. 1023; Friedmann, 26 (1951), *St John's L.R.* 97; Cabot, 99 (1951), *U. of Pa. L.R.* 476; Freutel, 'Exchange Control, Freezing Orders and the Conflict of Laws', 56 (1942), *Harv. L.R.* 30. Among modern foreign contributions the following are outstanding: Hjerner, *Främmende Valutalag och Internationell Privaträtt* (Stockholm, 1956–7) with an insuffiently detailed summary in English, which fails to do justice to what is believed to be a work of considerable significance; Benedetto Conforti, *L'Esecuzione delle Obbligazioni nel Diritto Internazionale Privato* (1962); Van Hecke, pp. 213–53; Tullio Treves, *Il Controllo dei Cambi nel Diritto Internazionale Privato* (Padova, 1967); Krispis, pp. 277 sqq. The most helpful discussion of the position reached by the beginning of 1938 is to be found in R. Neumann, *Devisennotrecht und Internationales Privatrecht* (Bern–Leipzig, 1941). See also Bergmann, *B.I.J.I.* 35 (1936), 29; Cohn, 52 (1936) *L.Q.R.* 474; 55 (1939) *L.Q.R.* 23, 552; Domke, *Revue de Science et de Législation financière* 34 (1936), 612; 35 (1937), 217; Clunet, 1937, 226, 990; *Journal of Comparative Legislation*, xxi (1939), 54; *Trading with the Enemy in World War II* (1943), ch. 20, with Supplement (1947); Mezger, *Nouvelle Revue de droit international privé*, 1937, 527; Anonymous, 47 (1938), *Yale L.J.* 451; Weiden, *Foreign Exchange Restrictions*, New York University School of Law Pamphlets No. 11 (1939); Lemkin, *La Réglementation des paiements internationaux* (Paris, 1939) and, most recently, Gianviti, *Rev. Crit.* 1980, 479 and 659.

[5] For references see Neumann, l.c., p. 3. This unacceptable doctrine is particularly fashionable in Switzerland, where, however, wiser views are coming to the fore: Pierre Lalive, 'Droit public étranger et Ordre Public Suisse', in *Mélanges Maridakis* (1964), iii. 190. See, generally, Heiz, *Das fremde öffentliche Recht im Internationalen Kollisionsrecht* (Zürich, 1959).

[6] This familiar doctrine, thoroughly refuted by Neumann, l.c., pp. 17 sqq., raises its head mainly in France. See, for example, the decision of 30 June 1933, referred to below, n. 12. See also the German cases below, n. 15.

[7] In this sense in particular Nussbaum, pp. 461 sqq.; Neumann, l.c., pp. 35 sqq.; Rashba 41 (1943), *Mich. L.R.* 777, 1089; Rabel, *Conflict of Laws*, iii. (1950), 49.

[8] This qualification is necessary because it is not always certain whether earlier decisions will be followed in the changed circumstances prevailing since the end of the Second World War.

[9] 18 Sept. 1934, *BGE.* 60, ii. 294, also *JW.* 1935, 239; 8 Oct. 1935, *BGE.* 61, ii. 242, also *B.I.J.I.* 34 (1936), 110 or *JW.* 1935, 3503 or Plesch, *Gold Clause,* ii. 98: 19 Feb. 1936, *BGE.* 62, ii. 108, also Clunet, 1937, 963; 2 Mar. 1937, *BGE.* 63, ii. 42, also Clunet, 1937, 965 or *Nouvelle Revue de droit international privé*, 1937, 624; 28 Sept. 1937, Clunet, 1937, 192 where the conclusion was drawn that, as foreign exchange restrictions are against Swiss *ordre public*, 'leur inobservation par les parties ne heurte pas les bonnes mœurs', see below, p. 410, n. 51; 1 Feb. 1938, *Nouvelle Revue de droit international privé*, 1938, 893; 4 Feb. 1969, *BGE.* 95, ii. 109, 114. On the Swiss practice see, generally, Schnitzer, *Handbuch des Internationalen Privatrechts* (4th ed., 1958), ii. 782; Oberson, *L'Ordre public en matière monétaire* (1956).

assigned it to the plaintiff. The debtor contended that under German law the assignment, made without the Foreign Exchange Board's consent, was invalid and that performance otherwise than by payment into a blocked account with a German bank was impossible. Although German law governed both the assignment and the contract, the court refused to give effect to German currency regulations, because it held them to be irreconcilable with Swiss public order, as they violated the vested rights of the creditor and constituted a 'spoliatory encroachment' upon them.[10] Similarly, with reference to the exchange control laws of Czechoslovakia, the Cour de Cassation of *France* said in the course of a most remarkable decision[11] 'que les effets de la réglementation des changes de cet État ne pouvaient être reconnus en France'. This follows an earlier line of decisions,[12] when, for instance the Cour de Paris held it to be irrelevant that a contract made between Russians in Russia violated the provisions of a Russian statute setting up exchange control and making the infringment a criminal offence, the reason being[13]

que ces lois, plus spécialement celle du 25 juin 1917 qui prévoit des pénalités diverses suivant les infractions commises, constituent des textes d'une portée politique dont l'application ne peut par suite qu'être territoriale; que n'ayant d'autre objet que de protéger la monnaie nationale, elles demeurent sans effet devant une juridiction française même en cas de contestation entre ressortissants russes.

Similar views have occasionally, though by no means uniformly, been expressed in decisions rendered in Austria,[14] Germany,[15] and Norway,[16] but, as will appear in the course of the further discussion in this chapter, are alien to the judicial practice of most other

[10] Decision of 8 Oct. 1935, referred to above, n. 9.

[11] 16 Oct. 1967, Bull. Civ. 1967, i, No. 296, or *Rev. Crit.* 1968, 661.

[12] Cour de Paris, 30 June 1933, Clunet, 1933, 963; Cour de Colmar, 16 Feb. 1937, Clunet, 1937, 784; Cour de Paris, 26 Mar. 1936, Clunet, 1936, 931, and *Rev. Crit.* 1936, 487; 20 July 1939, *Revue de Science et Législation financière*, 37 (1939), 608; Cour d'Appel Aix-en-Provence, 14 Feb. 1966, Clunet, 1966, 846, also Int. L.R. 47, 157.

[13] Decision of 30 June 1933, referred to in the preceding note.

[14] According to the Supreme Court (30 Apr. 1953, SZ. xxvi, No. 117, *Juristische Blätter*, 1954, 199, and Clunet, 1957, 1014) foreign measures of exchange control will not be given effect in Austria, if they encroach upon the interests of an Austrian creditor. But see 25 Sept. 1934, *Rechtsprechung*, 1934, 206, and Clunet, 1935, 191, and 12 June 1934, *Rechtsprechung*, 1934, No. 377.

[15] Federal Supreme Court, 17 Dec. 1959, BGHZ. 31, 368 on which see below, p. 407, n. 32, p. 430. On other German cases see below, p. 409, nn. 39, 40. The Court of Appeal Hamburg, 7 July 1959, IzRspr. 1958-9, No. 135A states *obiter* that French exchange control regulations must be ignored by the German judge, 'as they are foreign public law'. See Court of Appeal Berlin, 27 Oct. 1932, JW. 1932, 3773; 11 July 1961, IPRspr. 1966-7, No. 190. For the opposite view see Court of Appeal Schleswig, 1 Apr. 1954, *Jahrbuch für Internationales Recht*, v (1955), 113, in part also *International L.R.* 1955, 725.

[16] City Court of Oslo, 10 Feb. 1936, *B.I.J.I.* 34 (1936), 284, No. 9476.

countries, such as Holland,[17] Italy,[18] and the Anglo-American world. In the face of many assertions to the contrary[19] it is particularly necessary to stress that no American court has ever based its decision on the alleged incompatibility of foreign exchange control with American public policy.[20]

It would indeed be impossible to justify so wide a principle especially in those cases in which exchange control is not a super-venient event, but is in force at the time of the contract or in which the domestic party invoking it is a debtor rather than a creditor whose proprietary rights are said to be injured. Exchange control regulations usually originate from an emergency and are applied everywhere for the legitimate purpose of protecting a state's currency resources, just as customs duties are universally enforced

---

[17] See below, p. 406, n. 25.     [18] See below, p. 408, n. 38.

[19] See, for example, Cohn, 55 (1939) L.Q.R. 557; M. Wolff, *Private International Law*, p. 473. The misunderstanding arose from some strong words which, in the pre-war period, American courts justifiably used in regard to the nature and effects of German exchange control. The point made in the text is that such pronouncements did not constitute the *ratio decidendi*.

[20] See the numerous references which will appear below, p. 412, n. 53, p. 415, n. 65, and see the dictum of Clark C.J. in *Egyes* v. *Magyar Nemzeti Bank*, 115 F. 2d 539, 541 (C.C.A., 2d, 1948): 'In view of all that has happened in the world it seems profitless to characterize the currency manœuvres of foreign governments as unconscionable.' See also the numerous ticket cases which came before the Court of New York and in which Jewish immigrants claimed the refund of moneys paid in Germany for a passage on German ships which, on account of the war, failed to sail. In most cases it was held that the contract was governed by German law, that its provisions precluded a refund in the United States, and that this was not against public policy: *Steinfink* v. *North German Lloyd Steamship Co.*, [1941] A.M.C. 773 (New York Supreme Court); *Ornstein* v. *Compagnie Générale Transatlantique*, [1941] A.M.C. 1592, and 31 N.Y.S. (2d) 524, affirmed 32 N.Y.S. (2d) 243 (1942); *Branderbit* v. *Hamburg-American Line*, [1942] A.M.C. 226 (New York Supreme Court); *Loewenhardt* v. *Compagnie Générale Transatlantique*, [1942] A.M.C. 735 (New York Supreme Court); *Schlein* v. *Nederlandsch Amerikaansche Stoomvart*, [1942] A.M.C. 1529 (New York Supreme Court); *Eck* v. *Nederlandsch Amerikaansche Stoomvaart*, [1945] A.M.C. 70, also A.D. 1946, No. 13 (New York Supreme Court, Appellate Division); *Rosenblueth* v. *Nederlandsch Amerikaansche Stoomvart*, 27 N.Y.S. (2d) 922, affirmed 30 N.Y.S. (2d) 843, leave denied 31 N.Y.S. (2d) 666; *Zimmern* v. *Nederlandsch Amerikaansche Stoomvart*, 177 Misc. 91, 28 N.Y.S. (2d) 824 (Supreme Court, App. Div., 1st Dep., 1942). But in *Kassel* v. *Nederlandsch Amerikaansche Stoomvaart*, [1941] A.M.C. 335 (New York Supreme Court) the contract expressly provided for a refund if owing to circumstances beyond his control the traveller was prevented from using the ticket; the court allowed a refund at the official rate. This decision was followed in *Baer* v. *United States Lines*, [1942] A.M.C. 1461 and *Spiegel* v. *United States Lines*, [1942] A.M.C. 1426 (both decisions of a Municipal Court). On these cases see Moore, 27 (1942) *Corn. L.R.* 267. American law is now likely to have become crystallized by the decision of the Court of Appeals of New York in *French* v. *Banco Nacional de Cuba*, 23 N.Y. 2d 46 (1968) where, citing this work, the court held unanimously that exchange control practices are 'recognized as a normal measure of government' (p. 63 *per* Chief Justice Fuld, p. 88 *per* Keating J.); a majority of four held, but a minority of three denied that in the particular case Cuban law could 'not be characterized as so unreasonable or unjust as to outrage current international standards of governmental conduct' (p. 64 *per* Chief Judge Fuld). See below, p. 418.

for the protection of a country's industry. They may, it is true, seriously prejudice a foreign creditor who has relied on a system of free transfer of money, and the Swiss courts were right in equiparating some of the effects of exchange control to spoliation. Yet this does not make those regulations inconsistent with public policy. The reason does not lie so much in the fact that very many States have been compelled from time to time to adopt them and that, consequently, it is not open to the courts to condemn foreign legislation that is not different from the legislation of their own country. The real reason is that exchange control is merely an aspect or a ramification of a system of physical control to which the modern world has become used, which it does not in general abhor, and to which it applies established principles of law. Export and import restriction operating on the side of goods, on the delivery aspect of a transaction, have become almost universal expedients of economic policy and nobody hesitates to give effect to them. The result cannot be different, if control operates on the side of money, on the payment aspect of a contract. If goods are sold from Brazil to France and France introduces import restrictions, judges will examine the effects of any impossibility which thus arises without regard to an alleged principle of public policy; if France introduces exchange control and makes payment of the price impossible, the approach cannot be different.[21] In truth the public-policy theory which, incidentally, its adherents admit to be subject to many exceptions,[22] is a child of the past.[23] It was brought to life in order to combat the effects of exchange control supervening during the term of a contract. It cannot possibly apply where legal relationships arise under an existing system of exchange control.[24] In such circumstances international monetary co-operation would appear to be a better guide or, at any rate, aim.

All this is not intended to convey the idea that public policy cannot in any circumstances be opposed to foreign exchange control.

---

[21] On the close connection between trade restrictions and exchange control see the facts of *Brauer & Co.* v. *James Clark*, [1952] 2 All E.R. 497, and on the close connection between customs duties and exchange control see the Arbitral Decision of 16 Sept. 1950 in *Revue hellénique de droit international*, iv (1951), 373 where it was held that the excess which a Greek buyer of foreign exchange had to pay over and above the sum of drachmas calculated at the official rate of exchange involved a 'réajustement monétaire', not an 'impôt ou taxe d'importation' prohibited by a Concession granted by Greece, See below, p. 516.                                        [22] Nussbaum, pp. 471 sqq.

[23] Outside England this is accepted, for instance, by Van Hecke, pp. 238 sqq., or by Treves, pp. 87 sqq. with many references.

[24] This has frequently been overlooked. The failure to distinguish between two entirely different situations accounts for many of the misconceptions which burden current discussions.

The legislation of foreign countries may be so oppressive or discriminatory in character or application[25] or so inconsistent with treaty obligations[26] or so obviously preparatory or incidental to acts of illegal warfare[27] or of trade warfare or so contrary to the fundamental right of man's personal freedom[28] or otherwise so opposed to the policy of English law that it may have to be denied recognition in this country. In view of the special status which as a result of modern treaties they have come to enjoy, and of the very grave impact flowing from legislative interference with them, payments for current transactions have a peculiar claim to inviolability: their sudden stoppage, to the detriment of unpaid foreign sellers, may well be offensive. But in view of the English courts' well-known reluctance to have resort to public policy even such cases will require very careful consideration.

The point was put admirably by Upjohn J. (as he then was).[29] He accepted that, where under English conflict rules the law of the foreign State is applicable, English courts have to give effect to its undoubted right 'to protect its economy by measures of foreign

[25] Cf. Slade J. in *Re Lord Cable deceased* (1976), 3 All E.R. 417, at p. 435. It is in the nature of things that exchange restriction discriminates between residents and non-residents. What is envisaged in the text is discrimination between non-residents of different nationalities or between residents of different groups. An example of the latter situation occurred in Nazi Germany, when the foreign exchange legislation introduced in 1931 in a wholly unobjectionable manner became, in its application to Jews, an instrument of discrimination and an abuse of governmental power. This was so decided on numerous occasions by the courts concerned with restitution of the property of victims of Nazi oppression. See, for instance, Supreme Restitution Court in Berlin, 7 Nov. 1955, *RzW.* 1956, 15; 5 Jan. 1960, *RzW.* 1960, 157; 29 Dec. 1976, *RzW.* 1977, 87 with references; Supreme Restitution Court in Herford, *RzW.* 1958, 220. In the same sense the important decision of the Federal Supreme Court, 25 Oct. 1961, *RzW.* 1961, 118, and the Supreme Court of Israel in *Deklo* v. *Levi,* 26 (1958, ii) Int. L.R. 56. Similarly the Dutch Hoge Raad, 17 Apr. 1964, No. 16, noted *Nederlands Tijdschrift voor International Recht,* 1966, 58 or Int. L.R. 40 (1970) 7, rejected Indonesian measures directed against Dutch nationals.

[26] Thus if a member of the International Monetary Fund introduces or administers exchange restrictions in disregard of its contractual duties, public policy is likely to assert itself.

[27] Many aspects of German exchange control practice during the years preceding the outbreak of the Second World War were incidental to the German policy of war and extermination and on this ground effect ought to have been refused to them.

[28] For this reason the Federal Constitutional Court of Germany held that the exchange control laws in the German Democratic Republic had to be disregarded so as to render it impossible to enforce in the Federal Republic a criminal judgment based on the infringement of those laws: 24 Jan. 1961, *BVerfGE* 12, 99 or *NJW.* 1961, 653.

[29] *In re Claim by Helbert Wagg & Co. Ltd.,* [1956] Ch. 323, at pp. 351, 352, discussed by Michael Mann, 5 (1956) *I.C.L.Q.* 295, and E. Lauterpacht, ibid., p. 301, and by F. A. Mann, 19 (1956) *Mod. L.R.* 301. In many respects other than those referred to in the text the case is not free from difficulty. In particularly it is difficult to understand how the conception of confiscation could be material (unless it was employed in a very loose sense). Moreover, in view of clause 12 of the contract the discussion about the proper law was perhaps otiose. The case is further discussed below, p. 414.

exchange control and by altering the value of its currency'. None the less

this court is entitled to be satisfied that the foreign law is a genuine foreign exchange law, that is, a law passed with the genuine intention of protecting its economy in times of national stress and for that purpose regulating (*inter alia*) the rights of foreign creditors, and it is not a law passed ostensibly with that object, but in reality with some object not in accordance with the usage of nations.

Moreover, it was recognized that the court was entitled to investigate the often very realistic question whether an exchange control law, passed originally with the genuine object of protecting the State's economy, did not later 'become an instrument of oppression and discrimination'.[30, 31]

In these circumstances neither reason nor justice nor precedent require (or permit) the application of any general principle other than that well-established rule which is the basis of the whole of our conflict of laws: the control of the proper law. This means, in particular, that effect should be given to the proper law of the contract: if the transaction is governed by the foreign law which has set up currency restrictions, the provisions of the proper law must, on the whole, be accepted; if the transaction is governed by a legal system other than that which has set up exchange control, the proper law must again be applied and the exchange control regulations are, in general, immaterial.[32]

---

[30] It should perhaps be added that in England there is now fortunately no room for the doctrine that foreign 'revenue' laws (which could not in any event include exchange control laws) and foreign public laws cannot be applied. See Dicey and Morris, p. 93. That they cannot be enforced in England, remains true, but is an entirely different point. See below, p. 428.

[31] There remains the question whether a foreign judgment rendered in disregard of foreign exchange regulations operating in the country in which it is to be enforced, may or must be rejected by the courts of the latter country as being contrary to *ordre public*. Subject to local regulations the answer would seem to be in the affirmative. In a wholly unconvincing decision the Federal Supreme Court of Germany held that it was open to the court to judge whether in each individual case the transaction the subject-matter of the foreign judgement is likely to prejudice German foreign exchange resources: 11 Oct. 1956, *BGHZ.* 22, 24.

[32] The principle suggested in the text underlies the judicial practice of most of those countries which do not *a priori* refuse to give effect to the implications of foreign exchange control legislation, and is supported, for instance, by Dicey and Morris, p. 1023, or Wolff, pp. 472 sqq. It should be noticed, however, that in selecting the proper law of the contract courts have frequently allowed themselves to be influenced by the not unnatural wish to reach acceptable results. The only country in which the courts may be following a different theory is Germany. According to a decision of the Federal Supreme Court of 19 Apr. 1962, *IPRspr.* 1962 and 1963, No. 163, the applicability of exchange control legislation does not depend on the proper law of the contract, but on the *situs* of the debt or other property the subject-matter of the action, though in the event of there being property in Germany

## III

The suggested principle applies to all questions of the material validity of contracts.

1. If the exchange control regulations of a foreign country the law of which governs the contract render it invalid, then it is invalid in England. This is in harmony with the general rule of the conflict of laws[33] and would not require any comment were it not for a certain type of hard case which occurs wherever and whenever there is persecution and which is liable to produce some bad law. Suppose that in 1917 A and B are Russians in Russia, but wish to leave the country. A has money in England, but none in Russia; B has money in Russia, but none outside. B pays for A's expenses connected with his departure on the understanding that A will pay him an agreed sum of sterling after his arrival in England. Both A and B succeed in leaving Russia, but A refuses to pay and relies on the invalidity of the contract under Russian exchange control regulations. The French Cour de Cassation,[34] and the Swiss Federal Tribunal,[35] enforced B's claim, the latter clearly on the ground of its a priori rejection of foreign exchange laws. The same result was reached by the Austrian Supreme Court[36] on the remarkable ground that, although the parties did not originally intend Austrian law to apply, their subsequent emigration to Austria justified the implication of the intention to let the law of their final destination govern. In New York[37] recovery was likewise allowed on the ground of the proper law being that of the forum.[38] In one case the German Supreme

the law of the *situs* of the debt is, perhaps, immaterial (see also Federal Supreme Court, 17 Dec. 1959, *BGHZ*. 31, 368). The *situs* of property cannot, however, affect contractual relationships.

[33] Dicey and Morris, Rule 149 (p. 789).          [34] Civ., 16 Oct. 1967, above, n. 11.

[35] 28 Feb. 1950, *BGE*. 76, ii. 33, also *Schweizerisches Jahrbuch für Internationales Recht*, 1951, 234 with persuasive note by Gutzwiller. The facts were different from those assumed in the text: see below, p. 410, n. 51. In accordance with this practice the Swiss courts gave judgement for a Romanian refugee against another Romanian to whom he had paid in Romania local currency in consideration of a promise to pay the equivalent in Swiss francs in Switzerland. When the plaintiff tried to enforce the (apparently unreported) Swiss judgment in Italy, the Court of Appeal in Milan on 19 May 1961 rejected the application on the ground that Swiss courts could not hold a contract valid which was void under the *lex loci*: see Treves, *Rivista si diritto internazionale privato e processuale (R.D.I.P.P.)* 1965, 284 and 504. The Corte di Cassazione, 12 June 1964, Foro Italiano 1964 I 1994, reversed on account of the lower court's failure to investigate whether Romanian law or its application was not contrary to *ordre public*. The Court of Appeal in Turin, 1 Dec. 1968, *R.D.I.P.P.* 1968, 411 or Clunet 1976, 178 denied any violation of Italian *ordre public*. As Treves rightly points out, the Italian courts were probably not entitled to reopen the Swiss decision on the merits. They were bound by it, even if they disagreed with it.

[36] 12 Aug. 1953, *SZ*. xxvi, No. 205, also Clunet, 1957, 1020.

[37] *In re Silk's Estate*, 129 N.Y.S. 2d 134 (1954), also Int. L.R. 1955, 721.

[38] In Italy the point has arisen only indirectly: see Treves, pp. 307 sqq.

Court also upheld *B*'s claim, the contract being held to be subject to the law of Germany where the parties intended to settle after their emigration;[39] but in another case the contract was held to be governed by Russian law and the action failed.[40]

In England facts similar to those assumed above fell to be considered by Roxburgh J. who did not see his way to hold the contract to be subject to English law, so that the Russian émigré's claim was dismissed.[41] A similar result was reached by the Ontario Court of Appeal.[42] It will, of course, have to be remembered that a failure of the contractual claim does not mean that an action based on rights of property,[43] trust, tort, or unjustified enrichment would likewise fail; these are questions which demand separate examination in the light of the provisions of the relevant legal system. Nor is an action based on a negotiable instrument such as a cheque or bond tainted with illegality merely by reason of the fact that the instrument was smuggled out of a country.[44] Nor is it certain that, if the contract is subject to English law, an action *ex contractu* would necessarily succeed.

If, on the other hand, a contract is governed by the law of a foreign country which renders it valid, but is to be performed in England where it is contrary to English exchange control regulations, it is (probably) void *ab initio*, for it will be contrary to public policy.[45]

2. The validity of a contract under its proper law will not usually

---

[39] 3 Oct. 1923, *RGZ.* 108, 241. The decision which has been extensively discussed by learned writers (see the material collected by R. Neumann, l.c., p. 128) has frequently been misunderstood, because weight has been attached to certain dicta rather than to the *ratio decidendi*, viz. the fact that the contract was governed by German law. On this premiss the decision was right. Whether the premiss was correct is a matter outside the scope of this book.

[40] 1 July 1930, *IPRspr.* 1930, No. 15; see above, p. 403, n. 15.

[41] *In re Banque des Marchands de Moscou*, [1954] 1 W.L.R. 1108.

[42] *Etler* v. *Kertesz*, 26 D.L.R. 2d 209 (1961) or (1960) Ontario Reports 672.

[43] For example, *A* hands jewellery to *B* who in accordance with his instructions smuggles it out of a foreign country. *A* would seem to be able to recover the jewellery from *B* in England. The Supreme Court of Israel even held that, notwithstanding the illegality of the contract, an action for money had and received, being in the nature of a proprietary claim, could be maintained: *Abaronset* v. *Neuman*, Jerusalem Post of 24 July 1956.

[44] Cf. *Brill* v. *Chase Manhattan Bank*, 220 N.Y.S. 2d 903 (1961), where some of the remarks by the dissenting judges go much too far. A cheque legally obtained in Cuba, but illegally smuggled out of Cuba and sued upon in New York does not, it is submitted, constitute an illegal 'transaction'. But see p. 410, n. 49 below and p. 368, n. 73.

[45] In the case of a contract subject to Swiss law, but providing for payment in Austria where exchange control made this illegal, the Austrian Supreme Court held the contract to be void: 24 June 1959, *Zeitschrift für Rechtsvergleichung*, 1961, 18 with note by Bydlinski. The court seems to have adopted the view that matters relating to performance were in any event subject to the *lex loci solutionis*. Similar reasoning will, perhaps, find favour with English courts. Cf. *Boissevain* v. *Weil*, above, p. 364, n. 50.

be affected by exchange control regulations existing in a foreign country. Thus, where a contract is subject to and valid by English law, it matters not that under the exchange control laws of a foreign country in which the contract is made[46] one of the parties resides or carries on business or of which he is a national the contract is invalid or a criminal offence on account of the absence of a licence or for some other reason.[47]

It may, however, be against English public policy to enforce such a contract, 'if the real object and intention of the parties necessitates them joining in an endeavour to perform in a foreign and friendly country some act which is illegal by the law of such country',[48] or, perhaps, if only the main purpose of the contract is to derive an advantage from the commission of an act which, in a purely objective sense, is contrary to the law of the foreign country.[49] There is no convincing reason which would preclude this rule from operating in regard to smuggling in defiance of foreign exchange control laws.[50] The view taken by English law may be very strict,[51] but its

[46] This particular point was decided by the Court of Appeal at Reims, 25 Oct. 1976, Clunet 1978 with note by Pierre Mayer: if two Frenchmen contract in Algiers according to French law their contract is valid notwithstanding the fact that it involves a violation of Algerian exchange control laws.

[47] In this sense the South African case *Cargo Motor Corporation* v. *Tofalos Transport Ltd.,* 1972 (1) *South African L.R.* 186, 195–197 and the Dutch Hoge Raad, 12 Jan. 1979, *Rev. Crit.* 1980, 68 with illuminating note by van Rooij. The law was stated with particular clarity by Brieant J., sitting in the U.S. District Court, Southern District of New York, in the case of *Irving Trust Company* v. *Mamidakis,* which was decided on 18 October 1978, but is unfortunately unreported. The defendant was a Greek national and resident who, by contracts governed by New York law, had guaranteed debts incurred by companies controlled by him. The defence was that the guarantees were null and void under the exchange control laws of Greece, no licences from the Greek government having been obtained. The court gave summary judgement for the plaintiffs, for it considered Greek law irrelevant. A rule such as that suggested by s. 40 of the *Restatement (Second) of the Foreign Relations Law of the United States* (1965) would probably not be applied in New York and to allow the defendant to avoid his obligations on the ground that he would be exposed to criminal penalties in Greece 'would impede international financial transactions of precisely the sort present here. Traditionally in the absence of treaty provisions to the contrary, our courts have not enforced the foreign exchange controls of other nations, because these controls are contrary to our professed faith in the free enterprise system'. There follows a reference to *J. Zeevi and Sons* v. *Grindlays Bank (Uganda),* 37 N.Y. 2d 220, 226228 (1975).

[48] *Foster* v. *Driscoll,* [1929] 1 K.B. 470, 521 *per* Sankey L.J.

[49] This extension of the rule would seem to be necessitated by *Regazzoni* v. *K. C. Sethia Ltd.,* [1958] A.C. 301, on which see Mann, 21 (1958) *Mod. L.R.* 130. The decision rests on a singularly cursory analysis of the facts and since its promulgation has not gained in persuasiveness.

[50] Dicey and Morris, p. 805. A New York court has applied the doctrine of *Foster* v. *Driscoll, ubi supra,* to a contract made to defy foreign exchange control: *Hesslein* v. *Matzner,* 19 N.Y.S. (2d) 462 (1940). See also *Southwestern Shipping Corporation* v. *National City Bank of New York,* 6 N.Y. 2d 454, 160 N.E. 2d 836 (1959), also *Int. L.R.* 28, 539. So did the Hoge Raad in Holland: 16 Nov. 1956, *N.J.* 1957, No. 1, also *Nederlands Tijdschrift voor International Recht,* 1957, 212, and *RabelsZ.* 1959, 314.

[51] See, generally, Blas, 'Contrebande' in *Rép. dr. int.* (1929), 225 sqq.; Messinesi, *La*

moral foundation is such as to bar every possibility of compromise or qualification except in cases in which the application of the foreign law involves persecution, oppression or discrimination.[52]

## IV

There can be no doubt that the influence of foreign exchange

*Contrebande en droit international privé* (Paris, 1932). The *German* Supreme Court held that contracts the immediate subject-matter of which is smuggling into a friendly country are invalid under s. 138, German Civil Code; but the vendor's mere knowledge of the purchaser's intention to use the goods for the purpose of smuggling does not suffice: 9 Feb. 1926, *JW.* 1926, 2169, and Clunet, 1930, 430; 10 Mar. 1927, *JW.* 1927, 2287, and Clunet, 1928, 1070; 17 Oct. 1930, *JW.* 1931, 928. It also seems that the violation of foreign statutes based on reasons of economic policy, not of sanitary policy (as in case of the prohibition of alcohol), does not invalidate a contract governed by German law: Supreme Court, 24 June 1927, *JW.* 1927, 2288, and Clunet, 1930, 428. This formula, being so much wider than that relating to mere revenue laws, would perhaps save from invalidity a German contract envisaging the smuggling of money out of or into a country. On illegal exports from the United States to Communist countries see Federal Supreme Court, 21 Dec. 1960, *BGHZ.* 34, 169; 24 May 1962, *NJW.* 1962, 1436 (relating to insurance). As to *Austria* see Austrian Supreme Court, 3 Mar. 1931, Clunet, 1931, 1080. The *French* Cour de Cassation held that an insurance policy which to the knowledge of the company was intended to cover the illegal shipment of alcohol into the United States was valid: Cass. Req. 28 Mar. 1928, S. 1928, 1. 305 with note by Niboyet. As to smuggling of foreign currency in particular see Cour de Colmar, 24 June 1932, S. 1934, 2. 73, with note by Niboyet and Clunet, 1933, 337; 16 Jan. 1937, Clunet, 1937, 784; the plaintiff who had undertaken to smuggle the defendant's money out of Germany was found out and convicted in Germany; he successfully claimed compensation from the defendant in respect of the fine paid, the expenses for his defence, and the confiscation of his car; the court held that the German exchange restrictions were 'essentiellement territoriales' and that for this reason the contract was valid. The general problem is discussed by Batiffol-Lagarde, *Traité élémentaire de droit international privé* (1976), s. 598. Similarly the *Swiss* courts treat contracts involving the violation of foreign exchange restrictions as valid: Federal Tribunal, 28 Sept. 1937, Clunet, 1939, 192; 28 Feb. 1950, *BGE.* 76, ii. 33. In the latter case the court enforced a Swiss contract guaranteeing the payments due under a Roumanian contract which involved the transfer of currency from Romania to Switzerland and was illegal under Romanian law. The exchange restrictions were held to be 'mere trade laws' and therefore did not aim at 'the protection of interests of the individual or the human community which according to universal conceptions are of fundamental and vital significance . . . or according to ethical views are more valuable than the freedom of contract under which the transaction would be valid in Switzerland'. See above, n. 35. An even stronger case is the decision of 30 March 1954, *BGE.* 80 II 49 or *Schweizerisches Jahrbuch für Internationales Recht* 1955, 268 with note by Max Gutzwiller, which the present writer has repeatedly ventured to criticize: see, for instance, *Rec.* 132 (1971, i), pp. 195, 196.

[52] Cf. *Regazzoni* v. *K. C. Sethia Ltd.*, [1958] A.C. 301, at p. 320 *per* Viscount Simonds, at p. 325 *per* Lord Reid, at p. 330 *per* Lord Somervell. In the last resort all the questions discussed in the text may become a matter of public policy: if the law of the restricting State applies, the invalidity ordained by it and, if English law applies, the enforcement of the contract may (or may not) be against English public policy. The Israeli courts so proceeded: if during the period of persecution contracts were made between Jews in Poland or Bulgaria to save one of the parties from destruction and such contracts were contrary to the local exchange control legislation, public policy requires any illegality under the local law to be disregarded: *Mazur* v. *Kirschbaum*, Clunet, 1964, 162 or Jerusalem Post, 9 Oct. 1956; *Deklo* v. *Levi*, Int. L.R. 26 (1958, ii), 56.

control upon the performance of obligations falls to be assessed in accordance with the established principle that the discharge of contracts is governed by their proper law.

1. Where, therefore, the law of the restricting state and the proper law are identical, English courts[53] will give effect to such of the restricting State's provisions as relate to payment, to suspension or impossibility of performance, or to similar aspects of exchange control.[54] If the law of the contract is the law of the restricting State, 'that law not merely sustains but because it sustains, may also modify or dissolve the contractual bond. The currency law is not part of the contract, but the rights and obligations under the contract are part of the legal system to which the currency belongs.'[55]

[53] In considering the American cases it must be borne in mind that many of them proceed from a different rule: American courts tend to apply the *lex loci solutionis* to all questions relating to performance. They thus reach the result that the performance of contracts which are clearly subject to the law of the restricting State is not affected by exchange control if the creditor resides outside the restricting State; this explains, for example, *Sabl* v. *Laenderbank*, 30 N.Y.S. (2d) 608 (1941), affirmed without opinion 43 N.Y.S. (2d) 270 (1943), or *David* v. *Veitscher Magnesitwerke*, 348 Pa. 335, 35 A. (2d) 346 (1944), and may possibly explain *Stern* v. *Pesti Magyar Kereskedelmi*, 278 App. Div. 811, 105 N.Y.S. (2d) 352 (1951), affirmed 303 N.Y. 881, 105 N.E. (2d) 106 (1952), though the decision is without value, because both courts refrained from writing opinions. On the other hand, the principle explains *Werfel* v. *Zivnostenska Banka*, 260 App. Div. 747, 23 N.Y.S. (2d) 1001 (1940), reversed on other grounds 287 N.Y. 91, 38 N.E. (2d) 382 (1941), and *Kraus* v. *Zivnostenska Banka*, 64 N.Y.S. (2d) 208 (1946), where recovery was denied, apparently because the place of performance was in Czechoslovakia. *South American Petroleum Corporation* v. *Colombian Petroleum Co.*, 177 Misc. 756, 31 N.Y.S. (2d) 771 (1941) is a case which may rest on the same principle, but in which it was in any event difficult to see how Colombian exchange control could come into the picture. *Cermak* v. *Bata Akciova*, 80 N.Y.S. (2d) 782 (1948), also A.D. 1948, No. 8 or Clunet, 1953, 796 with note by Delaume, is a case which contains many questionable dicta, but rests on special facts. From the English point of view it is necessary to use the utmost care in appreciating, and attributing persuasive weight to, American decisions in this field. The New York rule as to the significance of the place of performance, which in view of the implications of the decision of the Court of Appeals in *Perutz* v. *Bohemian Discount Bank*, 304 N.Y. 533 (1953), may now be of doubtful validity, also prevails in Switzerland and in connection with exchange restrictions was referred to by the Federal Tribunal, 7 July 1942, *BGE*. 68, ii. 203.

[54] The question whether in fact the proper law makes performance impossible or renders a licence necessary or what the effect of the debtor's failure to apply for a licence is must be decided on the basis of expert evidence. The proper appreciation of such evidence will not usually be difficult, but a remarkable misunderstanding occurred to the Appellate Division of the New York Supreme Court, when it decided in *Perutz* v. *Bohemian Discount Bank*, 279 App. Div. 386, 110 N.Y.S. (2d) 446 (1952) that under the law of Czechoslovakia a licence was required, not for a (Czechoslovakian) judgment in favour of a non-resident creditor, but only for payment to him (after judgment), and that therefore it was open to the New York courts to give a judgment (in dollars) for the American creditor. This was, of course, tantamount to the prohibited thing, i.e. payment without licence, and resulted from a failure to appreciate that the New York courts were not concerned with the procedural question whether a Czechoslovakian court could give judgment, but with the question whether the debtor was allowed to pay. Fortunately the decision was reversed: see 304 N.Y. 533 (1953).

[55] *Kahler* v. *Midland Bank*, [1950] A.C. 24, at p. 56 *per* Lord Radcliffe.

If in these circumstances the law of the restricting State provides for the conversion of a sterling debt into a debt expressed in local currency or for the discharge of the debt by payment into a blocked account[56] or if it renders payment illegal or subject to a condition precedent such as a consent, this will be recognized by English courts. Thus in *De Beéche* v. *South American Stores (Gath & Chaves) Limited*[57] the respondents, companies incorporated in England, but doing business in Chile, had promised to pay the rental for premises in Chile leased to them by the appellants' predecessors in title. The leases provided that 'payment shall be effected monthly in advance in Santiago de Chile . . . by first class bills on London'. The respondents alleged that Chilean foreign currency regulations rendered it impossible or illegal to acquire foreign exchange in Chile or to pay the rents by drafts on London, and they deposited in court in Chile the amount of the rents in Chilean pesos at the current rate of exchange, subject to a 20 per cent deduction directed by Chilean law. The appellants did not accept this payment and sued for the agreed sums of pounds sterling. The action failed. If the contract was governed by Chilean law, which would seem to be the better view,[58] Chilean currency regulations made the result inevitable,

[56] This has been expressly decided in New York: *Konstantinidis* v. *Tarsus*, 248 F. Supp. 280, at p. 287 (1965). In the case of a contract governed by Yugoslav law the *Austrian* Supreme Court refused to give effect to Yugoslav exchange control legislation: 2 July 1958, *Juristische Blätter*, 1959, 73 or Clunet, 1959, 868; the reasoning of the decision which is discussed by Schwind, *Juristische Blätter*, 1959, 65, is far from clear. The *German* Federal Supreme Court held that, on account of the alleged territoriality of exchange control legislation, payment by the East German debtor to the East German State Bank under a contract governed by East German law did not discharge, notwithstanding the express provisions of East German legislation: 28 Jan. 1965, *IzRspr.* 1964–5, No. 68.

[57] [1935] A.C. 148.

[58] See the facts of the case: premises in Chile; plaintiff Chilean subject, though resident in Paris; defendants English companies doing business in Chile; leases executed before Chilean Consul at Buenos Aires. By the courtesy of Messrs. Smiles & Co., solicitors, to whom the author's thanks are due, he has been supplied with copies of the judgments in the courts below. It would appear to have been taken for granted throughout the case that the contract was governed by Chilean law, the applicability of which the defendants had pleaded in para. 5 of their defence, and Lawrence L.J. expressly said: 'The leases are couched in the Spanish language and deal with Chilean property. They are Chilean contracts to be performed in Chile and have to be construed and given effect to according to Chilean law.' See also the later case of *St. Pierre* v. *South American Stores (Gath & Chaves) Limited*, [1936] 1 K.B. 382 at p. 390 *per* Greer L.J., at p. 394 *per* Scott L.J. It is submitted that on this basis the decision loses much of its general importance. The view that the proper law of the leases was Chilean and that this explains the decision has been accepted by Dicey and Morris, p. 797, n. 6, and Wolff, p. 474. According to Mac-Kinnon and Du Parcq L.JJ. in *Kleinwort Sons & Co.* v. *Ungarische Baumwolle Industrie*, [1939] 2 K.B. 678, at pp. 693, 694, 697, the decision involves an application of the *Ralli* principle as formulated by Dicey and Morris (p. 794), according to which a contract, lawful by its proper law, is invalid in so far as its performance is unlawful by the *lex loci solutionis*. Cheshire and North, p. 229, n. 1, also seem to think that the House of Lords proceeded on

and the only remarkable point is that no question of a refusal to recognize Chilean legislation on grounds of English public policy was even raised. The second case of *St. Pierre* v. *South American Stores (Gath & Chaves) Limited*[59] is easier to follow, inasmuch as the Court of Appeal expressly proceeded on the basis of Chilean law governing the contract. The defendants had taken a lease of premises in Chile, which lease provided, in so far as material here, that the rent was to be paid 'either in Santiago de Chile at the residence or the office of the latter (owner) . . . or remitted to Europe according to instructions which the owner may give. . . .' The plaintiffs, *inter alia*, claimed a declaration as to the effect of this option and its position under Chilean currency legislation prohibiting the export of money. Branson J. held[60] that

if the plaintiffs exercise validly qua the contract their option to call for such a remittance, they are asking for an impossibility which, as it has supervened by the operation of the law of the place of performance, excuses the defendants from performance. The only alternative is for the plaintiffs to appoint someone in Santiago to receive there the rents which the defendants are ready and willing to pay, and have in fact lodged in Court in default of any such appointment.

The Court of Appeal affirmed the decision, but only Slesser L.J. expressly treated the question under discussion; he said:[61]

when the option is exercised, it must be an option of remission to Europe from Chile, from which it would follow that, if there be laws in Chile excluding the possibility of remission from that country, this contract can have its obligations discharged in Chile, but not elsewhere.

The third case is *Re Helbert Wagg & Co. Ltd.*[62] in which Upjohn J. (as he then was) held a contract between an English bank and a German debtor to be subject to German law; hence payment in German currency to a Conversion Office in Germany in accordance with German exchange control law extinguished the debt, notwithstanding the place of payment being in England and sterling being the money of account. Similar principles were followed when it was held that insurance policies issued in Israel and Egypt respectively by a Canadian insurance company were governed by the law of

the footing of English law. This explanation is open to the comment that the House of Lords did not only give effect to the Chilean law which made payment by first class bills on London unlawful, but also held, by clear implication, that payment into the Chilean court after deduction of 20 per cent operated as a discharge. If English law applied, there could be no question of discharge.

[59] [1937] 3 All E.R. 349.          [60] [1937] 1 All E.R. 206, 215.

[61] At p. 356.

[62] [1956] Ch. 323 on which see above, p. 406, n. 29.

Ontario.[63] The Canadian Supreme Court[64] and, on the whole, American courts[65] adopted similar processes of reasoning, when they

[63] *Pick* v. *Manufacturers Life Insurance Co.* (1958), 2 Ll. L.R. 93; *Rossano* v. *Manufacturers Life Insurance Co.*, [1963] 2 Q.B. 352.

[64] *Imperial Life Assurance Co. of Canada* v. *Colmenares* (1967), 62 D.L.R. 2d 138.

[65] The facts were not always the same, but, broadly, they were as follows: American insurance companies, through their Cuban branches, contracted life insurance policies with Cubans in terms of U.S. dollars; usually the contracts provided for all payments to be made in Cuba. In 1951 Cuban legislation provided for the conversion of dollars into pesos at par. In 1959 the Cuban legislator enacted Law No. 568, whereby, so it was alleged, payment in dollars by American companies in the United States to persons there resident were prohibited. When policy-holders escaped from Cuba and demanded payment in the United States several questions arose none of which was considered with that elaboration and insight that the problems demanded and which, unfortunately, were not always clearly distinguished. (In appreciating the decisions it is necessary to remember that, as a result of appeals, the picture changed from time to time; in this note only decisions of courts of last resort are referred to and the intermediate stages of development are disregarded.) Those questions were the following: (*a*) Was the contract as a whole governed by the law of a state of the Union or by Cuban law? (*b*) If Cuban law applied, were pesos substituted for dollars and, if so, what was the amount, if any, payable in the United States? (*c*) If Cuban law applied and payment was to be made in Cuba only was it open to the assured to enforce any rights in the United States? (*d*) If Cuban law applied to the contract as a whole, was it possible by way of equitable relief to sever the option to call for the surrender value and submit it to the law of a state of the Union? (*e*) Did the Bretton Woods Agreement render the contract unenforceable either before or after 2 Apr. 1964 when Cuba withdrew from the International Monetary Fund? Question (*a*) which one would expect to be decisive was not always clearly faced or decided, but in *Theye y Ajuria* v. *Pan-American Life Insurance*, 161 So. 2d 70 (1964), also Int. L.R. 38, 456, the Supreme Court of Louisiana held the contract to be subject to Louisiana law. In the same sense *Blanco* v. *Pan-American Life Insurance*, 221 F. Supp. 219 (1963), affirmed probably on the same ground by the Court of Appeals, 5th Circ., 362 F. 2d 167 (1966). But in *Confederation Life Association* v. *Ugalde*, 164 So. 2d 1 (1964), also Int. L.R. 38, 138, the Supreme Court of Florida affirmed the holding of the District Court of Appeal at 151 So. 2d 315 (1963) that Cuban law applied. This was followed in *Johansen* v. *Confederation Life Association*, 447 F. 2d 175 (1971) and *Santovenia* v. *Confederation Life Association*, 460 F. 2d 805 (1971), among many other cases. As to question (*b*), see above, p. 256. Where the company undertook to pay dollars, these were invariably awarded, but where the policies provided for payment in pesos, it was held that the current rate of exchange had to be applied: *Pan-American Life Insurance Co.* v. *Blanco*, 362 F. 2d 167 (1966), followed, for instance, in *Oliva* v. *Pan-American Life Insurance Co.*, 448 F. 2d 217 (1971). As to question (*c*) see below n. 71 and above, n. 58. As to question (*d*), this was answered in the affirmative by the Superior Court of Pennsylvania in *Varas* v. *Crown Life Insurance Co.*, 203 A. 2d 505 and by the Supreme Court of Florida in *Confederate Life Association* v. *Vega y Arminan*, 211 So. 2d 169 (1968), affirming District Court of Appeal at 207 So. 2d 33 (1968). This has become firmly established law of Florida, particularly as a result of a further decision of the Supreme Court of Florida in *de Lara* v. *Confederation Life Association*, 257 So. 2d 42 (1971), cert. den. 409 U.S. 225 (1972); see also the District Court of Appeal of Florida in *Confederation Life Association* v. *Alvarez*, 276 So. 2d 95 (1973). But when in *de Lara*'s case the Supreme Court refused to grant *certiorari*, Mr. Justice Brennan and Mr. Justice Douglas wrote a strong and convincing dissent and in a well reasoned decision in *Fernandez* v. *Pan-American Life Insurance*, 281 So. 2d 779 (1973) the Court of Appeal of Louisiana refused to follow the Florida doctrine and dismissed the action on the ground that Cuban law prevailed. The Supreme Court of Canada (above, n. 64) at p. 144 described the Florida doctrine rightly as an 'unprecedented proposition'. Question (*e*) was as a rule answered in the negative; see above, p. 392.

held that Cuban law did not preclude Canadian and American insurance companies from honouring policies held by Cuban refugees.

While the results in these cases clearly follow from principle and are not opposed to the requirements of justice,[66] there remain two further questions of great difficulty.

(a) The first may be defined by asking whether in the case of *In re Helbert Wagg & Co. Ltd.*, the decision would have been the same if the debtor had been resident in England, or whether in *De Beéche*'s case it would have made any difference if the leases, though subject to Chilean law, had provided for payment by and to an English resident in London. Or, to put it generally, is it open to the debtor to invoke the law of the restricting State *qua* proper law as a defence in cases in which both he and the creditor are outside that State and performance or payment is not contractually bound to be made in or from that State only, but may and, perhaps, must be made outside it? The answer depends primarily upon a close investigation of the content of the proper law: it is difficult to believe, and can frequently be disproved, that the exchange control regulations of the proper law purport to apply to the assumed facts.[67] Alternatively, if the proper law does intend to control the type of case in question, it may frequently appear that, in relying upon the exchange control regulations of the proper law, the debtor, in substance and effect, asserts and pursues the prerogative rights of the restricting State to ensure the implementation of the latter's policy outside the limits of its jurisdiction. This the debtor cannot do any more than the restricting State itself.[68]

The point was discussed in the decision of the Court of Appeals, 2nd Cir., in *Menendez v. Saks & Co.*[69] When exporters of Cuban cigars, who had escaped to the United States, sued their buyers for payment of the price expressed in dollars and due under a contract assumed to be subject to Cuban law, the defendants argued that they had to pay in Cuba only where the sellers would receive Cuban pesos. The court rejected the argument 'upon basic policy

[66] The parties must be taken to have assumed the risks involved in the submission to any particular legal system.

[67] In *Rossano* v. *Manufacturers Life Insurance Co.*, [1963] 2 Q.B. 352, at pp. 373, 374 McNair J. held that Egyptian exchange control legislation, had it been applicable by virtue of the proper law being Egyptian, would not by any means have had the effect that 'a payment by the defendants' head office outside Egypt would be illegal'. In the American cases referred to above, p. 415, n. 65, it seems to have been assumed rather than held that Cuban Law No. 568 had such effect. *Sed quaere.*

[68] See below, p. 428, where the principle is further discussed. It is submitted that the point made in the text is the true *ratio decidendi* of the decision of the Dutch Hoge Raad, 26 May 1939, A.D. 1918–42, p. 29.

[69] 485 F. 2d 1355 (1973).

grounds. Currency controls are but a species of revenue laws. . . . As a general rule one nation will not enforce the revenue laws of another.'[70, 71]

(b) The second problem arises if it is assumed that the foreign legislator does not permit any method of payment at all, but provides that, while the debtor cannot pay, the obligation remains in abeyance and that the debtor remains in default.[72] If the debtor pays his creditor in accordance with the proper law, the creditor, as has been shown, cannot normally complain; if the proper law excuses the debtor from paying and the obligation is discharged, the creditor again cannot complain. But if[73] the proper law itself upholds the debtor's obligation yet deprives him of the means for its performance, English courts should not give effect to the proper law. Where under the appropriate substantive law there is a right, the remedy and its enforcement are matters of procedure exclusively governed by English law. The debtor's plea that, although the debt exists, he is prevented or prohibited from paying it would in effect amount to an interference with that principle, because, if accepted, it would make part of the debtor's property exempt from execution, which would be beyond the proper law's power. That a judgment thus given might compel the debtor to do an illegal act would not

[70] At p. 1366. At p. 1367 the court emphasized that the case before it was not one 'in which the debtor's obligation was limited by agreement to payment in foreign currency or in a country where currency control was in effect.' By way of examples the court mentioned *Blanco* v. *Pan-American Life Insurance*, 362 F. 2d 167 (1966) and *In re Claim by Helbert Wagg & Co. Ltd.*, [1950] Ch. 323. Had the obligation been so limited reasons of American constitutional law would have precluded its enlargement as a result of the fact that 'the creditor happens to be able to catch his debtor here.' This would have involved a denial of due process, but did not arise, because the debtor owed dollars. No such point can be made in England. If pesos had been due in Cuba the creditor should be awarded their equivalent in dollars; the problem would be one relating to the rate of exchange; see below, p. 445.

[71] The point ought to have been, but was not taken in certain of the Cuban Insurance cases. Where the insurance contract was held to be subject to Cuban law and provided for payment in Cuba only and where the company offered payment in Cuba, the courts at first held that there was no breach of contract and therefore no claim in the United States: *Confederation Life Association* v. *Ugalde*, 151 So. 2d 315 (1963) and *Santovenia* v. *Confederation Life Association*, 460 F. 2d 805 (1972). But in *Confederation Life Association* v. *Conte*, 254 So. 2d 45 (1971) the District Court of Appeal of Florida had decided in the opposite sense on the ground that the plaintiff was a refugee from Cuba who could not go to Cuba to collect the money due to him and that therefore 'equitable considerations' required the company to make payment in Florida. *Santovenia's* case rests on the fact that there no such inability to collect in Cuba had been alleged by the plaintiff. It may be assumed that after 1972 such inability was invariably asserted by the plaintiff and that for this reason 'equitable considerations' prevailed.

[72] This somewhat unusual situation existed in Germany as a result of the decision of the Supreme Court of 23 May 1936, *RGZ.* 151, 116. It was changed by a statute of 27 May 1937, *Reichsgesetzblatt*, i. 600.

[73] It is necessary to emphasize this condition.

only be an irrelevant but also a wrong argument, because compulsory satisfaction of a claim can never expose the judgment debtor to criminal liability.[74]

The point fell to be considered in a striking manner by the Court of Appeals of New York.[75] In 1957 an American citizen invested a large sum of dollars in Cuba and under Cuban investment laws received a certificate whereby the defendant undertook, on certain conditions, to pay to him a sum of U.S. dollars by cheque on New York, free from any tax on the exportation of money. In 1959 Cuba suspended for the time being the redemption of the certificate. The suspension was continuing in 1968, when the action against the bank was dismissed. The case primarily turned on the peculiarities of the American Act-of-State doctrine. The court sharply disagreed on the further question whether the Cuban law was 'a normal measure of government', or an unlawful taking of a foreigner's property. Four of the seven Judges answered in the former sense. Although the case was an extreme one, neither public policy nor the point of law put forward above was (or, according to the law of the United States, probably could be) discussed.[76] It is to be hoped that in England the result would have been different.

2. If the contract is governed by the law of a country other than the restricting country, no effect can be attributed to the exchange control regulations of the restricting country which interfere with the performance of the contract as contemplated by the parties. In other words, when it comes to the performance of an English contract, the existence of exchange restrictions in a foreign country need not, as a matter of principle, be considered.[77] The existence of such restrictions at the time of the contract, it is true, may

---

[74] A view such as that put forward in the text may have been at the back of the mind of the Appellate Division of the Supreme Court of New York in *Perutz*'s case, on which see above, p. 412, n. 54. The fact that criminal liability in the country of the debtor's residence or nationality is irrelevant and in no sense an excuse for non-performance in the circumstances assumed in the text is established by such cases as *Kleinwort Sons & Co.* v. *Ungarische Baumwolle Industrie* (1937), 2 K.B. 678 or the New York case of *Irving Trust Company* v. *Mamidakis*, above, p. 410, n. 47. And see below, p. 419, n. 80. The suggestion made in the text was expressly rejected by Rabel, *Conflict of Laws*, iii (1950), pp. 48, 49.

[75] *French* v. *Banco Nacional de Cuba*, 23 N.Y. 2d 46 (1968). See below, pp. 474, 475.

[76] The argument was that (a) the Cuban law was an Act of State, (b) the court was required to give effect to it, (c) there was an exception in case of confiscation in violation of international law, (d) currency regulation was a normal measure of government, not confiscatory, and (e) in the particular case there were no special circumstances requiring a different characterization. It was mainly point (d) on which the court disagreed, and which raises the principal difficulty.

[77] Cf. *Seligman Bros.* v. *Brown Shipley & Co.* (1916), 32 T.L.R. 549, where it was held as a matter of construction that when an English contract speaks of 'payment', it means in such manner as to enable the creditor to dispose of the money, and payment into a blocked account will not constitute a discharge.

influence the construction of an English contract or, more particularly, of what the parties intended as due performance. Thus if English and Turkish merchants enter into an English contract, a condition may have to be read into it according to which its operation or performance is subject to the grant of a licence by the Turkish Exchange Control Authorities. Or if I buy from my banker Chilean pesos to be paid to my creditor in Santiago de Chile, it will be an implied term of the contract that the payment will be effected in accordance with the laws of Chile so as to enable the creditor to accept and keep the money.[78] But these are special cases which do not derogate from what must be regarded as an obvious rule.

Its most important application in practice is to be found where under an English contract money is due in *England* and the debtor resides in a restricting State which makes it impossible for him to discharge his obligations. Such consequences of the restricting State's laws are wholly immaterial, because they are extraneous to a contract subject to English law and performable in England. This is now clearly established in this country[79] as well as abroad;[80]

[78] This statement may derive some support from the dictum of Scrutton L.J. in *Ralli* v. *Compañia Naviera Sota y Aznar*, [1920] 2 K.B. 287, 304 quoted below, p. 420. As to the law of *France* see Cour de Paris, 26 Mar. 1936, Clunet, 1936, 931; 8 Dec. 1936, *Chronique Hebdomadaire du Recueil Sirey*, 1937, No. 2; Cour de Colmar, 11 Mar. 1938, Clunet, 1938, 812; 9 Dec. 1938, 41 (1939) *B.I.J.I.* No. 10785, p. 59. In all these cases the defendants had undertaken to make payments on the plaintiffs' behalf in Germany. They caused them to be made in a manner inconsistent with German exchange control. The courts held that in such circumstances the defendants had failed to make effective payments within the meaning of the contracts.

[79] *Kleinwort Sons & Co.* v. *Ungarische Baumwolle Industrie A.G.*, [1939] 2 K.B. 678 and, perhaps even more strikingly, *Toprak Mahsulleri Ofisi* v. *Finagrain Compagnie Commerciale* (1979), 2 *Lloyd's L.R.* Cf. *Kahler* v. *Midland Bank*, [1950] A.C. 24, at p. 51, where Lord Reid rejected the idea that it would be 'a good defence to an action on a contract, the proper law of which is English law, for the defendant to show that his performance of his obligation in England would subject him to penal liability in his own country'. See Dicey and Morris, pp. 797, 1025, 1026 and Kerr J. (as he then was) in *Dalmia* v. *National Bank* (1978), 2 Ll. L.R. 223, at p. 267.

[80] *New York*: the leading cases are *Central Hanover Bank & Trust Co.* v. *Siemens & Halske A.G.*, 15 F. Supp. 927 (1936), also Clunet, 1936, 1129; 35 (1936) *B.I.J.I.* 136 and Plesch, *Gold Clause*, ii. 67; affirmed 84 F. (2d) 993 (C.C.A. 2d, 1936), cert. den. 299 U.S. 585, and *Pan American Securities Corporation* v. *Friedr. Krupp A.G.*, 256 App. Div. 955, 10 N.Y.S. (2d) 205 (1939), but there exist numerous other decisions to the same effect. It must be remembered, however, that all of them are based on the principle mentioned above, p. 412, n. 53, rather than on the proper law of the contract. *Italy*: Corte di Cassazione, 30 July 1937, *Rivista del Diritto Commerciale* 1938, ii. 117, or *Nouvelle Revue de droit international privé*, 1938, 408. *Holland: Hoge Raad*, 12 Jan. 1979, *Rev. Crit.* 1980, 68 with note by van Rooij; *Austria*: Supreme Court, 10 Dec. 1935, *Rechtsprechung*, 1936, 22, 23, also in RabelsZ. 10 (1936), 398 and Clunet, 1937, 333; see also Wahle, *RabelsZ.* 9 (1935), 779 sqq., who discusses the decision of 29 Sept. 1934, Clunet, 1935, 191. *Germany*: Court of Appeal, Berlin, 27 Oct. 1932, *JW.* 1932, 3773; see also District Court, Berlin, 19 Feb. 1932, *JW.* 1932, 2306. *France*: Cour de Paris, 20

indeed, the uniformity of practice is such that it is no longer necessary to discuss the cogent if elementary reasons supporting it.[81]

While normally, therefore, the creditor is not concerned with the means whereby the debtor procures the prerequisites of payment at the agreed place, a refinement may be required in a case in which an essential step leading to payment is, under the contract, to be taken in the restricting country, although its law is not the proper law and although the place of performance is not situate there. Thus if payments of Eurodollar bank deposits are habitually paid and repaid and, indeed, can only be paid through the 'Chips' system in New York,[82] then it may well be an implied term of an English contract of deposit that the impossibility of using that system is a relevant fact which, one would expect,[83] would involve the suspension rather than the discharge of the English bank's obligation to pay in England; but it must be emphasized that this can only be so if the contract includes express or implied terms requiring the exclusive use of a specific method of payment which becomes unavailable.

The law is very much less settled in those cases in which under an English contract money is payable *in the restricting State,* and supervening[84] exchange restrictions of that State make the payment impossible. The starting-point of the discussion must be the decision of the Court of Appeal in *Ralli* v. *Compañia Naviera Sota y Aznar.*[85] A contract which was held to be an English[86] contract provided that freight should be paid in Barcelona where, however, by the time of payment a Spanish statute had made it illegal both[87] to pay and to receive more than a maximum freight of 875 pesetas per ton, i.e. much less than agreed. The action for the recovery of the amount due under the contract was dismissed, the reason being stated by Scrutton L.J. in these words:[88]

Where a contract requires an act to be done in a foreign country, it is in the

---

July 1939, *Nouvelle Revue de droit international privé,* 1940, 120; *South Africa: Cargo Motor Corporation* v. *Tofalos Transport Ltd.,* 1972 (1) *South Africa L.R.* 186, 195–197. *Zambia: Commonwealth Development Corporation* v. *Central African Power Corporation, African L.R. (Commercial Series)* 1968 (3) 416.

[81] They were set forth in the first edition of this book, pp. 274 sqq.; see also Wolff, p. 475; Dicey and Morris, p. 797.

[82] See above, p. 194.

[83] This depends on the effect of *Ralli's* case, on which see, for instance, below, p. 421.

[84] Where exchange restrictions exist at the time of the contract, other considerations may arise: above, p. 418.

[85] [1920] 2 K.B. 287.

[86] At p. 290 *per* Lord Sterndale M.R.; at p. 293 *per* Warrington L.J.

[87] It is necessary to emphasize this point.

[88] p. 304.

absence of very special circumstances an implied term of the continuing validity of such a provision that the act to be done in the foreign country shall not be illegal by the law of that state.

*Ralli*'s case has not only given rise to a large measure of misunderstanding,[89] but is also open to criticism from the point of view of monetary law,[90] for it seems to mean that if under an English contract made between persons resident in England *A* is under a duty to pay *B* a sum of sterling in Chile and the law of Chile makes it impossible to pay in sterling, *A* is discharged from this obligation altogether.[91] *Ralli*'s case may even mean that, if the law of Chile imposes the duty on *A* to pay to *B*'s blocked account in Chile a sum of Chilean pesos rather than sterling, *B* must accept this in discharge.[92] If this were so, the *lex loci solutionis* would have the power not only of discharging, but also of modifying a monetary obligation created by English law, though Scrutton L.J. spoke merely of the effect of the *lex loci solutionis* upon the 'continuing validity' of the obligation.

It is not intended to question the principle of English municipal law that the courts of this country 'will not compel the fulfilment of an obligation whose performance involves the doing in a foreign country of something which the laws of that country make it illegal to do'.[93] The only problem is whether this principle, derived from the construction of the contract, really leads to the consequences attributed to it. It is inherent in the nature of a monetary obligation that its performance does not ever become impossible.[94] The intention in any circumstances to treat the debtor as released otherwise than by payment cannot reasonably be imputed to contracting parties. Suspension of the obligation is likely to be in better harmony with their views. But the soundest interpretation which in many (though not all) cases could be given to the presumed intention of the parties would probably be to the effect that, if the supervenient law of the place of performance makes payment impossible, that place is shifted elsewhere.[95]

[89] It is responsible for much of the confusion underlying some of Lord Wright's dicta: above, pp. 216, 237 sqq.      [90] Above, p. 66, n. 19.

[91] Discharge would be the normal consequence of supervening impossibility, frustration or illegality. The judgments delivered in *Ralli*'s case leave a remarkable gap in that they do not make it clear what the fate of the contract was. They merely decide that the contractual freight was not payable. Was a freight of 875 pesetas paid or payable?

[92] If the case was governed by English law (on which point see above, p. 413, n. 58), this follows from *De Beéche* v. *South American (Gath & Chaves) Stores Limited*, [1935] A.C. 148.

[93] *De Beéche*'s case, at p. 156 *per* Lord Sankey L.C.; *Kahler* v. *Midland Bank*, [1950] A.C. 24, at p. 36 *per* Lord Normand.

[94] See above, p. 273.

[95] For an unsatisfactory finding of fact with which the Cour de Cassation felt unable to

3. The effect of foreign exchange control upon the manner of discharging monetary obligations requires special consideration. This is due to the peculiar problems which exchange control frequently creates in regard to what the law regards as the primary means of payment, namely bank notes. Many systems of exchange control prohibit both the exportation and the importation of domestic bank notes.[96] The greater part of such bank notes as are situate ouside the restricting State has come there in the course of smuggling transactions and cannot be used except for smuggling purposes, though small sums will always be required by travellers. In these circumstances the value of such external notes is often much depreciated.[97]

Yet, from a legal point of view, the essential fact is that, however limited the possibilities of making use of them may be, bank notes issued by but situate outside the restricting State retain the quality of lawful money. If they were to be demonetized, this would require both an express provision of the *lex monetae* governing them and a distinguishing earmark. The restricting State's mere prohibition of the import to or export from its territory does not affect the legal tender quality of the notes. In no case will it be permissible to deduce any counter-argument from the fact that the notes are likely to have been smuggled out of, or to be smuggled back into, the country of their issue or that they have less 'value' than payments made by bank transfer, cheque, bill of exchange, or some similar method. The latter argument is irreconcilable with the principle of nominalism; a creditor of a sum of foreign money must accept whatever is legal tender under the law of the currency; he cannot insist on a method of payment for which he has not contracted and his complaint about loss of 'value' is not more valid in the case of payment by notes than it would be if, for example, notes had been substituted as legal tender for gold coins current at the date of the contract. As to the contention based on the likelihood of smuggling, it overlooks not only that the inference of

interfere see Cass. Civ. 1 Dec. 1954, *Rev. Crit.* 1957, 43 with note by Anselme–Rabinovitch. By a contract made in 1918 in Russia the defendant undertook to pay £600 to the plaintiff at the Westminster Bank, London. On account of French exchange control the defendant could not pay. The plaintiff's action for payment of French francs in France was dismissed, as such payment would involve an inadmissible modification of contractual terms. This is another case in which the significance and function of the place of payment was probably misunderstood and exaggerated.

[96] Under the Exchange Control (Import and Export) Order, 1966 (S.I. 1966, No. 1351), no traveller could export more than £15 from the United Kingdom. The amount was changed from time to time. The importation of sterling notes was not prohibited.

[97] See Ciano, 'The Pre-War "Black" Market for Foreign Bank Notes', 8 (1941) *Economica*, 378. This article answers some of the questions which were treated as unanswerable in *Rex* v. *Haddock*: A. P. Herbert, *Codd's Last Case and other Misleading Cases* (London, 1952), pp. 112 sqq.

smuggling and resmuggling cannot by any means be regarded as inevitable (since the notes may have been lawfully exported), but also that smuggling has no tainting effect except if it is the contractual purpose common to both parties.[98] Such purpose would exist if a contract between two Englishmen necessarily involved the introduction of notes into the country of their issue in contravention of that country's laws.[99] But even if the creditor who is paid in notes did not intend to sell them on the market, but to engage directly in smuggling transactions and if the debtor knew this, the mere payment of the notes would not be a dealing which necessarily involves the joint commission of an illegal act by the parties.[100]

It follows that as a rule the restricting State's bank notes can be used in discharge of all debts which are expressed in its currency and payable outside its boundaries. This is obviously so where the obligation is subject to a legal system other than that of the restricting State, for the only connection with the restricting State's law is to be found in its legal tender legislation which, *ex hypothesi*, is silent on the matter. But even where the law of the restricting State governs the obligation the result is the same, unless that law contains specific provisions prohibiting the payment by bank notes.[101] Whether (undervalued) bank notes are in fact the method of payment envisaged by the parties is a matter of construction in each case;[102] particularly in connection with trading transactions

[98] *Foster* v. *Driscoll*, [1929] 1 K.B. 470 as approved by *Regazzoni* v. *K. C. Sethia (1944) Ltd.*, [1958] A.C. 301.

[99] *Marrache* v. *Ashton*, [1943] A.C. 311, 319 *per* Lord Macmillan.

[100] See the formula of Sankey L.J. (as he then was) in *Foster* v. *Driscoll*, [1929] 1 K.B. 470, 521.

[101] The law as explained in the text is now clearly established by *Marrache* v. *Ashton*, [1943] A.C. 311 which probably renders *Graumann* v. *Treitel*, [1940] 2 All E.R. 188, 200 bad law. For a full discussion of these cases see below, pp. 446 sqq. For a different but untenable view see Cohn, 55 (1939) *L.Q.R.* 552, on whom see Mann, 3 (1940) *Mod. L.R.* 214, n. 55. A different view is also taken by the Swedish Supreme Court, 29 July 1952, *RabelzZ.* 22 (1957), 292, and among writers, by Mayer, *Valutaschuld*, p. 13; Nussbaum, pp. 485 sqq.; Treves, pp. 315 sqq.; Van Hecke, p. 229. For a recent survey see Lothar Hirschberg, *Das Interzonale Währungs- und Devisenrecht der Unterhaltsverbindlichkeiten* (1968). On the whole, however, the practice of foreign courts is in conformity with the English view as stated in the Text. As to *Switzerland*, Commercial Court, Zürich, 10 Oct. 1937, *Nouvelle Revue de droit international privé*, vi (1938), 288 and (1940-1) *B.I.J.I.* No. 10923, affirmed by Swiss Federal Tribunal on 8 Feb. 1938 (unreported). As to *Germany*, see the remarkable decision of the Court of Appeal, Karlsruhe, 26 Sept. 1940, *Deutsches Recht*, 1941, i. 209. As to *France*, see Tribunal Civil de la Seine, 18 July 1938, *Nouvelle Revue de droit international privé*, vi (1938), 171 and 42 (1940) *B.I.J.I.* No. 11028; Trib. Com. de la Seine, 16 Nov. 1938, D.H. 1939, 63 and A.D. 1938-40, No. 190; see generally Silz, Clunet, 1939, 545. See also the decisions of the Berlin District Labour Court, 25 Nov. 1932 and of the Supreme Labour Court, 10 Dec. 1932, *Zeitschrift für Ostrecht*, 1933, 527, 529, with note by Melchior. But see Court of Appeal, Breslau, 18 Mar. 1937, *Höchstrichterliche Rechtsprechung*, 1938, No. 693.

[102] Where the parties expressly provide for payment at the 'free rate', payment cannot,

made after the introduction of exchange control or where large sums are involved it may well be found that the parties did not envisage payment by legal tender, but by bank transfer, cheques, or other means permitting the payee to receive full value in the restricting State.

On the other hand, where payment is to be made within the restricting State, it cannot be made by means which under the local law are illegal. While, therefore, payment can and, indeed, must normally be made by bank notes and while bank notes are readily available within the restricting State, they cannot be imported for the purpose (except under licence) and need not be accepted by a payee knowing that they were illegally imported. This is so even where the contract is subject to a legal system other than that of the restricting State, either on account of the rule that the *lex loci solutionis* governs the mode of performance[103] or because the contract contains an implied term that performance in a foreign country must be in harmony with the requirements of the foreign law.[104]

## V

The effect of exchange control upon rights of property situate in England, whether tangible or intangible, and, in particular, upon the transfer and assignment of property cannot easily be ascertained. The reason does not lie in the peculiarities of exchange control, but in the fact that the pertinent rules of the conflict of laws as a whole are in no sense firmly established. In the circumstances it must suffice to refer to those rules, such as they are, and to say that they determine whether and to what extent the exchange control regulations of a foreign country are capable of having effect upon property situate here. It is not unlikely that by and large such effect will be slight only, for there exists authority for 'the simple rule that generally property in England is subject to English law and to none other'.[105] This rule, firmly established in regard to movables and statutory assignments, will preclude foreign exchange legislation from changing title to, or restraining dispositions of, English property, without rendering it necessary to inquire into

of course, be made on the basis of the rate for banknotes: Austrian Supreme Court, 21 Nov. 1951, *SZ*. xxiv, No. 316, p. 746, or Clunet, 1955, 192.

[103] Dicey and Morris, p. 812.

[104] This is the principle underlying *Ralli* v. *Compañía Naviera Sota y Aznar*, [1920] 2 K.B. 287 and the cases founded upon it.

[105] *Bank voor Handel en Scheepvaart* v. *Slatford*, [1953] 1 Q.B. 248, at p. 260 *per* Devlin J. It should be noted that this decision applies both to tangible property (gold bars) and intangible property (bank debts).

such legislation's confiscatory character. Thus, in the eyes of English law, a foreign legislator exceeds his powers if he decrees[106] that the English property of persons who were once resident within but have emigrated from the restricting State remains subject to control by the latter. Or if a foreign exchange control authority has powers similar to those which under the Exchange Control Act, 1947, enable the Treasury to vest in itself certain property even if situate abroad,[107] an English court should refuse recognition.[108] As regards the voluntary assignment of debts situate in England, but governed by the law of foreign restricting State, English courts are likely to follow such general rules as exist,[109] though in this particular context foreign courts have displayed remarkable determination to avoid the invalidating effects of exchange control legislation.[110]

It would be both logical and desirable to extend that 'simple rule' to questions of possession as opposed to title. However, in view of the leading if disastrous case of *Kahler* v. *Midland Bank*[111] it would seem[112] that to a substantial degree the exchange control regulations of foreign countries have the power to interfere with the right to the possession of English property. That decision apparently countenances the following proposition: *A* and *B*, both resident in London, enter into a contract subject to the law of Czechoslovakia, whereby *A* deposits War Loan in bearer form in *B*'s safe in London. Under the law of Czechoslovakia *B* cannot part with the bonds without the consent of the Czech National Bank, which is refused. Accordingly *A* cannot recover the bonds from *B* and must, presumably, stand by while *B* encashes the coupons.[113]

---

[106] This was the position under s. 55 of the German Foreign Exchange Act, 1938.

[107] ss. 2 (5), 24 (2), 26 (2), 27 (1). It is likely that in their application to foreign countries these provisions involve an excess of international jurisdiction. See also below, p. 439.                                                           [108] See Dicey and Morris, p. 823.

[109] See, for example, Dicey and Morris, p. 573.

[110] Thus the Swiss Federal Tribunal, 8 Oct. 1935, *BGE*. 61 ii. 242, one of the earliest Swiss decisions rejecting the application of foreign exchange control legislation *in toto*; German Federal Supreme Court, 17 Dec. 1959, *BGHZ*. 31, 368, relying on the alleged inapplicability of foreign public law.

[111] [1950] A.C. 24, and see the companion case of *Zivonstenska Banka* v. *Frankman*, [1950] A.C. 57 which involved an action against a bailee, not a sub-bailee; though it was an action in detinue (p. 62), the decision rested on the particular contract made between the parties. It lacks, therefore, general interest, though it supports the example to be given in the text.

[112] While every effort should be made to restrict the decision to its narrowest limits, it is not easy to define them. In *Re Helbert Wagg & Co. Ltd.'s Claim*, [1956] Ch. 323, at p. 352, Upjohn J. (as he then was) suggested that *Kahler*'s case might have been due to 'the difficulties which arose on the pleadings' and was therefore wholly exceptional. The explanation may not be logically convincing, but if it serves to distinguish an unfortunate decision it will be wholly acceptable.

[113] It is a remarkable fact that the fate of the dividends paid in respect of the plaintiff's

In *Kahler's* case the plaintiff, then a resident of Prague, had deposited bearer securities with a Czechoslovakian bank, the Bohemian Bank, which in turn had deposited them with the defendants. The plaintiff, having left Czechoslovakia, brought an action in detinue against the defendants claiming delivery-up of the securities. He succeeded before Macnaghten J., but failed both in the Court of Appeal[114] and in the House of Lords[115] (Lords Simonds, Normand, and Radcliffe, Lords MacDermott and Reid dissenting). The majority of the House of Lords held that (i) in order to succeed the plaintiff had to prove affirmatively that he was entitled to immediate possession; (ii) his right to immediate possession depended on his contract with the Bohemian Bank; (iii) this contract was in existence and binding upon the plaintiff, and (iv) subject to Czechoslovakian law; (v) although under the contract the plaintiff could at any time call for the securities, the law of Czechoslovakia had 'so far modified his right so to recover possession of the shares as to make the consent of the National Bank a condition precedent'[116] and such consent had been refused; (vi) such prohibition was not penal or confiscatory in character.

Propositions (i) and (ii) are matters of the general law of England and cannot now be questioned.[117] Propositions (iii) and (iv) involved questions of fact and must be accepted for present purposes.[118] Propositions (v) and (vi) require comment.

As regards the former, it is clear that the law of Czechoslovakia made it impossible for the Bohemian Bank to perform the contract by redelivery. But, with respect, it does not follow that the plaintiff's right to immediate possession thus came to an end or became suspended or that the plaintiff must be treated 'as having ceded the

securities was not referred to at any stage of the proceedings in *Kahler's* case. Presumably they continued to be paid to the National Bank of Czechoslovakia where, the plaintiff was credited in terms of korunas. However, as will be explained in the text, the House of Lords denied that the Czech law was confiscatory.

[114] [1948] 1 All E.R. 811, discussed by Mann, 11 (1948) *Mod. L.R.* 479.

[115] [1950] A.C. 24, discussed at length by Mann, 'Nazi Spoliation in Czechoslovakia', 13 (1950) *Mod. L.R.* 206. In the present context it is impossible to discuss in detail all aspects of the decision and reference is therefore made to that article. Nussbaum, p. 467, n. 32*a*, says of the decision of the House of Lords that 'common sense would have demanded the opposite decision'. It is perhaps doubtful whether this country can hope to become again an international banking centre so long as this decision stands.

[116] At p. 56 *per* Lord Radcliffe.

[117] It remains to be seen whether it will be held that, if *A* hires *B*'s motor-car for a fixed period and it is stolen from *A*, *B* cannot recover it from the thief.

[118] For the reasons discussed elsewhere proposition (iii) was most doubtful. It should be emphasized that Lord Normand recognized the existence of the contract only 'because the appellant himself has dissociated it from the confiscatory measures of which he was the victim' (p. 36). Proposition (iv) is described by M. Wolff, p. 475, n. 3, as 'not unassailable' and questioned by Cheshire and North, p. 144.

lawful possession of his shares for an existing though indeterminate period'.[119] Impossibility of performance is a purely contractual aspect but does not affect the owner's possessory rights against a sub-bailee in England, which one would expect to be governed by English law.[120] It is perhaps arguable that the majority of the House of Lords did not fully consider this point which may not have been taken by the plaintiff and to which the expert witness did not address his mind.

Proposition (vi) is from the point of view of monetary law the most interesting, for it is clear that the Czechoslovakian National Bank, administering the exchange control regulations of Czechoslovakia, was allowed effectively to block dealings with English property and to prevent its lawful owner from recovering it. None of the learned Law Lords considered this as confiscation. Lord Simonds stated shortly that 'the relevant law relating to foreign exchange . . . is not in my opinion a law of such penal or confiscatory nature that it should be disregarded by the Courts of this country',[121] though in *Frankman*'s case he admitted the 'possibility' that the principle according to which an English court refuses to enforce the penal or confiscatory law of another country might apply 'where it appears that the law, which is sought to be enforced or relied on, is in reality confiscatory though in appearance regulatory of currency'.[122] In Lord Normand's view the defendants' success did 'not involve the enforcement of Czechoslovakian revenue laws or penal laws'.[123] Lord MacDermott did not deal with the point. According to Lord Reid exchange control regulations did 'not come within the category of confiscatory or fiscal legislation of a foreign country which English courts cannot recognise'.[124] Finally, Lord Radcliffe denied that currency regulations 'were no more than the penal or revenue laws of another State the existence of which our courts are traditionally disposed to ignore'.[125] These expressions are perhaps not altogether happy in that penal, confiscatory, fiscal, and revenue laws are all treated indiscriminately, in that regard was had to the character of exchange control laws as such rather than to their consequences in specific directions and their application to particular circumstances, and in that the reference to the English courts' practice not to recognize certain foreign laws at all may be going too far. However, it cannot be denied that in so far as the law of England is concerned it is now almost impossible to assert that foreign

---

[119] At p. 57 *per* Lord Radcliffe.
[120] Dicey and Morris, pp. 837, 838, seem to agree.
[121] p. 27.  [122] p. 72.  [123] p. 36.
[124] pp. 46, 47.  [125] p. 57.

exchange control regulations which interfere with the possession of English property must be disregarded on the ground of their confiscatory nature. This is a result which many may think regrettable, which the courts of New York seem to be strongly disinclined to follow,[126] which was rejected in South Africa[127] as well as in Austria[128] and which, indeed, is tolerable only if it is remembered that the House of Lords, while rejecting the idea of confiscation, did not in turn deal with the 'simple rule' applicable to questions of title. Perhaps it points the way to limiting the scope of *Kahler*'s case.

There is, however, a further ground which, it is believed has considerable force, was not advanced in *Kahler*'s case and thus greatly reduces the scope and persuasiveness of the decision. It is provided by the principle to be developed in the following section.

VI

Exchange control is a field which has frequently tempted States to assert extraterritorially their statutory rights of controlling, collecting or retrieving private property or other rights vested in them or their instrumentalities. Such efforts are bound to fail, for by virtue of a firmly established and universally accepted principle of public international law no State is entitled directly or indirectly to enforce outside its own territory its prerogative rights or public laws.[129]

---

[126] *In re Liebl's Estate*, 106 N.Y.S. (2d) 705 and 715 (1951). Earlier cases to the same effect are *Loeb* v. *Bank of Manhattan*, 18 N.Y.S. (2d) 497 (1939); *Bercholz* v. *Guaranty Trust Company of New York*, 44 N.Y.S. (2d) (1943); *Marcu* v. *Fisher*, 65 N.Y.S. (2d) 892 (1946); cf. *Feuchtwanger* v. *Central Hanover Bank & Trust Co.*, 27 N.Y.S. (2d) 518 (1941), affirmed 263 App. Div. 711, 31 N.Y.S. (2d) 671, affirmed 288 N.Y. 342, 43 N.E. 434 (1942). Cf., however, *In re Muller's Estate*, 104 N.Y.S. (2d) 133 (1951) where it was held, in effect, that the New York courts had to recognize German exchange control laws which allegedly precluded a resident of Germany from disclaiming a legacy arising under the will of a domiciled American; this decision was followed in *Re Meyer*, 238 Pa. 2d 597 (1951) and in *Kent Jewelry Corporation* v. *Kiefer*, 119 N.Y. Supp. 2d 242 (1952), but will be wholly unacceptable to English law, particularly in so far as it relies upon and purports to interpret governmental policies; it also misapplied German law: Supreme Court of Bavaria, 28 Nov. 1952, *NJW*. 1953, 944. In *Callwood* v. *Virgin Islands National Bank*, 221 F. 2d 770, 775 (1955), the Court of Appeals, 3rd Cir., held that a debt situate in the United States could not be effectively assigned in Germany in violation of German exchange control regulations, the reason being the allegedly 'generally accepted common law rule' according to which the effect of an assignment was governed by the law of the place where it was executed. No such rule, it is submitted, exists.

[127] *Standard Bank of South Africa Ltd.* v. *Ocean Commodities Inc.*, 1980 (2) *South Africa L.R.* 175, where the Full Bench of the Transvaal Provincial Division refused to follow *Kahler*'s case on the primary ground that 'the *lex situs* was ignored in' it (p. 184).

[128] Supreme Court, 24 April 1968, *Juristische Blätter* 1969, 339.

[129] See, generally, Mann, 40 (1955), *Transactions of the Grotius Society* 25 or *Studies*

There is one case in which the United Kingdom, in disregard of the principle, tried to enforce by proceedings in New York rights over a British resident's New York bank account which it claimed to have acquired by virtue of a vesting order made under the Exchange Control Act.[130] The action, which is reported only on an interlocutory point of procedure, could not succeed, for the Act does not purport to confer extraterritorial rights upon the Treasury and, even if it did, the law of New York would not recognize them, just as in the converse case the law of England would, it is submitted, refuse to enforce a foreign sovereign's rights. In fact the law of New York has since been reaffirmed by the Court of Appeals.[131] Under the law of Brazil the exporter of coffee to the United States had to surrender the dollar proceeds of sale to the plaintiffs, the Banco do Brasil S.A., an instrumentality of the Government of Brazil, against payment at 90 cruzeiros to the U.S. dollar. The exporter and the defendants were alleged by the plaintiff to have conspired so as to enable the exporter to obtain the free market rate of 220 cruzeiros per dollar. As a result of the alleged conspiracy the plaintiff suffered a loss. The action for its recovery failed, because *inter alia*, the plaintiff was held to be trying to enforce a 'revenue law' and since the days of Lord Mansfield 'one State does not enforce the revenue laws of another'.[132] The fact that the claim was clothed in the form of an action for damages for conspiracy under the law of New York did not render the court oblivious of the substance of the matter, viz. the assertion of an injury to the plaintiff's prerogative rights.[133] More recently the New York Court of Appeals made some less fortunate pronouncements in the case of *Banco Frances e Brasilerio* v. *John Doe*,[134] though it may in part have arrived at a correct result. The plaintiff, a private bank in

in *International Law* (1973), pp. 492 sqq. and pp. 124 sqq.; also *Rec.* 132 (1971, i), pp. 166 sqq.; *Rec.* 111 (1964, i), 141 sqq.; Dicey and Morris, Rule 3. The prominent example to which the doctrine applies is taxation.

[130] *Solicitor for the Affairs of H.M. Treasury v. Bankers Trust*, 107 N.E. 2d 448 (1952).

[131] *Banco do Brasil S.A. v. Israel Commodity Co. Inc.*, 12 N.Y. 2d 371, 190 N.E. 2d 235 (1963) or Int. L.R. 30, 371, discussed by Gold, *I.M.F. Staff Papers* 1964, 468; Trickey, 62 (1964) *Mich. L.R.* 1232; Baker, 16 (1963) *Stanford L.R.* 202 (a valuable contribution); Anon., 63 (1963) *Col. L.R.* 1334.

[132] In truth, of course, exchange control laws cannot be described as revenue laws at all. (See, in this sense, *Regazzoni v. K.C. Sethia Ltd.*, [1958] A.C. 301, at p. 324 *per* Lord Reid.) But revenue laws are only one example of a group of laws which are characterized by the fact that they confer prerogative rights upon the State and its instrumentalities. Probably the court did not employ the term in its strict sense. See above, n. 70 and p. 427.

[133] The court discussed at length Art. VIII (2) (*b*) of the Bretton Woods Agreement, but neither this provision nor the Agreement as a whole had any bearing whatever upon the claim made by the plaintiff, which was plainly misconceived. The only surprising feature is that the decision of the Court of Appeals was arrived by a majority of four to three.

[134] 36 N.Y. 2d 592 (1975), decided May 8.

Brazil, claimed damages for fraud and conspiracy 'arising from alleged violations of foreign currency regulations', as Jason J. speaking on behalf of the majority put it. The facts are obscure, but it appears that the defendants improperly obtained from the plaintiffs dollars in exchange for cruzeiros,—as the dissenting judge, Wachtler J., put it, 'no more United States dollars . . . than they would have been entitled to receive at the then currently effective exchange rate.' In these circumstances the plaintiffs cannot have suffered any damage, except perhaps in one respect presently to be mentioned, and quite apart from other considerations the bulk of the claim ought for this reason to have been rejected. But in any event it involved the indirect enforcement of a prerogative right of Brazil and was, therefore, contrary to a great and important principle of international law. The majority spoke in terms of what it chose to describe as 'an old chestnut', viz. the rule, supported by the highest courts in most countries, 'that one State does not enforce the revenue laws of another.' Exchange control laws, it is true, are not revenue laws. But they are a type of those many public laws which confer prerogative rights upon a State and which it cannot extraterritorially assert or enforce. And while 'nothing in the agreement prevents an I.M.F. member from aiding directly or indirectly a fellow member rendering its exchange regulations effective', nothing in the Agreement requires or contemplates so dangerous and unacceptable a decision which a month later the same seven judges failed to follow through[135] and which is contrary to established international practice as well as the practice of United States courts.[136]

Similar cases of the extraterritorial enforcement of exchange control have, in a variety of forms, been brought, in particular, by Indonesia, but none of them succeeded. In a case in which Indonesia claimed rights in respect of the Dutch bank account belonging to

[135] *J. Zeevi and Sons Ltd.* v. *Grindlays Bank (Uganda) Ltd.*, 37 N.Y. 2d 220 (1975), decided June 16, on which see above, pp. 377, 391. The facts and the law were wholly different from the case mentioned in the preceding note, but the case is in point because it adopts a very narrow interpretation of the Bretton Woods Agreement.

[136] In *Her Majesty the Queen in Right of British Columbia* v. *Gilbertson*, 597 F. 2d 1161 (1979), the Court of Appeals, 9th Cir., gave effect to 'the old chestnut' by refusing to enforce a British Columbian judgment for the recovery of taxes and said of it: 'The revenue rule has been with us for centuries and as such has become firmly embedded in the law. There were sound reasons which supported its original adoption, and there remain sound reasons supporting its continued validity' (p. 1166). In *Menendez* v. *Saks & Co.*, 485 F. 2d 1355, at p. 1366 (1973), the Court of Appeals, 2nd Cir., said: 'Currency controls are but a species of revenue law . . . . As a general rule one nation will not enforce the revenue laws of another.' Cuban currency regulations were therefore disregarded. In the case of *Banco Frances e Brasileiro* the court did not notice this statement, though it seems to have been referred to it.

one of its residents the Court of Appeal at Amsterdam held that the plaintiff State could not 'exercise them in the Netherlands or maintain them any more than would be possible with respect to the rights and authority of a foreign Government in the field of military service, taxation, requisition of dwellings or expropriation'.[137] Another highly significant example of the doctrine is supplied by a decision of the Swedish Supreme Court which rejected Bulgaria's attempt to enforce its exchange control legislation in Sweden.[138]

The extraterritorial enforcement of rights of exchange control may take many forms; here as elsewhere it will be necessary to look to the reality and effect of the assertion. Thus it may be made by a private person such as a bank, but for the benefit or perhaps even under the direction of the State. Or it may be made by way of defence rather than attack.[139] This is what, it is submitted, happened in *Kahler* v. *Midland Bank*[140] and ought to have led to the failure of the English bank's defence. By invoking the absence of the Czechoslovakian Government's licence for the delivery-up of the securities in London the bank made itself the tool of that Government. Just as the latter could not, whether directly or indirectly (for instance, through a bank controlled by it) and whether against an English sub-bailee or even the owner himself, enforce its right to possession allegedly arising under exchange control laws and recover possession of the securities, so it could not, by its defence derived from the same laws, block the owner's rights. The foreign Government's well-established inability to recover possession must involve, as a corollary, the owner's right to recover possession without hindrance by the foreign Government's obstruction.[141]

There are, however, exceptional sets of circumstances in which the law may allow a private party to claim an indemnity in respect of payments made to a foreign State by way of fine or for similar reasons.[142] Thus the authorities seem to establish that where an

[137] 9 Apr. 1959, *International L.R.* 30, 25.
[138] 21 Mar. 1961 (*Bulgaria* v. *Takvorian*), summarized Clunet, 1966, 437, and *International L.R.* 47, 40.
[139] See already above, pp. 416, 417.                    [140] [1950] A.C. 24.
[141] See the paper referred to above, p. 428, n. 129. The submission in the text was accepted as a subsidiary ground in the South African case referred to above, p. 428, n. 127. It would appear, however, that the decision of a United States District Court in *N.V. Suikerfabriek Wono-Aseh* v. *Chase National Bank* (1953), 111 F. Supp. 833 is opposed to the suggestions made in the text. On the other hand, the decisions which, notwithstanding the prohibition by exchange control legislation of the proper law, recognize the validity of the assignment of a debt (above, p. 425, n. 110) can, perhaps, be justified by the principle discussed in the text.
[142] The most familiar example occurs where the foreign State claims the repayment of benefits conferred upon or services rendered to the defendant. For details see pp. 173–5 of the paper of 1971 referred to above, p. 428, n. 129.

individual has been compelled to pay[143] taxes or customs duties or a fine or social security contributions he may, under the proper law, be entitled to an indemnity or compensation.[144] In so far as exchange control is concerned such a case may have been the New York case of *Banco Frances e Brasileiro* v. *John Doe*[145] to the extent of the penalty which, as the majority judgment stated,[146] 'was levied by the Central Bank of Brazil and paid by the plaintiff.' If this was a genuine penalty properly imposed upon and actually paid by the plaintiffs[147] then it may well be that Brazilian law which is likely to have been the proper law of the contract allowed them a remedy under general principles of private law. But if, as the dissenting judge put it,[148] penalties were 'to be imposed' then the plaintiffs were no more than an instrument of Brazil to recover a possible fine and the New York courts allowed the indirect enforcement of Brazilian exchange control regulations in the United States. The difference, it is submitted, is significant.[149] In the one case the plaintiffs claimed the repayment of what was, as one must assume, after a proper procedure, adequate submissions by the defence and exhaustion of reasonable remedies, actually paid to the State. In the other case the plaintiffs must have claimed what might in certain, for the time being undefined, circumstances become payable to the State which would no doubt bring its demands into line with the extent of the recovery. For similar reasons there exist grave doubts about the decision of Slade J. in *Re Lord Cable deceased.*[150] The plaintiffs were beneficiaries of a trust which was constituted under Indian law, but had large assets in England. The defendant trustees intended to transfer these assets to India to pay Indian

---

[143] There does not seem to be a continental decision which involved a plaintiff who had not paid but was only liable to pay.

[144] See the cases collected *Rec.* 132 (1971, i), p. 167, n. 5. Add the German Supreme Court's decision 27 Feb. 1924, *JW.* 1925, 1477.

[145] 36 N.Y. 2d 592; on this case see above, p. 429.

[146] P. 599.

[147] It is difficult to believe that if the plaintiffs were innocent parties they could in any civilized country be subject to penalties.

[148] P. 603.

[149] The distinction was clearly made by the British Columbian Court of Appeal in *Re Reid*, 17 D.L.R. 2d 199 (1971), where executors who had paid United Kingdom estate duty were held to be entitled to be indemnified on the ground that in all earlier cases 'success would have enriched the Treasury of the interested State', while 'here the United Kingdom has nothing whatever to do with the respondent's claim to be indemnified' (p. 205). Cf. also the Scottish decision *Scottish & National Orchestra Society* v. *Thomson's Executors*, 1969 S.L.T. 199, where Lord Robertson held that, while normally Scottish executors of a deceased who had died domiciled in Sweden were not entitled to pay money to the Swedish executors to enable them to pay Swedish estate duty, they had to do so where it was necessary to discharge legacies due to Swedish legatees.

[150] (1976), 3 All E.R. 417.

estate duty and to comply with Indian exchange control regulations. The plaintiffs failed to restrain the defendants from doing so. The learned judge, though willing to give full effect to the non-enforceability of foreign prerogative claims, refused to make an order, because, as concerned estate duty, the trustees 'may be exposed to penalties in India of an amount representing double the amount of duty'[151] and, as concerned exchange control, an order against the defendants 'entailed such potentially serious consequences'[152] as fines and possibly imprisonment.[153] Such reasoning includes an element of speculation. Its effect is to enable India to obtain from English sources what she claims to be entitled to under her tax and exchange control legislation; at the same time the beneficiaries have no certainty at all that the net residue if any will be freely transferred and made available to them. This, therefore, is something very different from the defendants' actual liabilities properly incurred and discharged and in law and equity requiring reimbursement. And criminal liability in the country of a person's residence or nationality (if it exists in a case in which a party acts under the compulsion of the order of an English court) is not necessarily an argument for giving effect to a foreign legal system which according to English conflict rules is not applicable.[154] It is to be hoped that *Re Lord Cable deceased* will not be followed by British courts.

[151] P. 436.                                                    [152] P. 434.

[153] It is difficult to believe that the Indian law as set forth by the learned judge on p. 434 could have justified any conviction of defendants who strenuously, but unsuccessfully, defended the English proceedings.

[154] Above, pp. 410, 416, 419 with references to the cases. These relate to facts which involved criminal liability under a law other than the proper law. In the case discussed in the text Indian law was the proper law. Yet by virtue of a great principle of international and English law such Indian law was prima facie unenforceable in England. Therefore the cases referred to are by no means immaterial in the present context.

# XVI

# The Valuation of Foreign Currencies

## I

WHERE there exists an independent monetary system, its relationship with other monetary systems involves not only the problem of making payments to another country, but also that of valuing the one currency in terms of another. The former was dealt with in the preceding three chapters; the latter, or rather some of its aspects, will be discussed in the present chapter.

Monetary systems may be related to each other by two means of measurement, the (nominal) par of exchange and the (real) rate of exchange. The par of exchange is of minor importance in the legal practice of a world in which currencies are 'floating' and will therefore require only a few comments (below section II). On the other hand, the rate of exchange gives rise to many and varied problems which necessitate discussion at some length.

## II

The par of exchange is the equation between two money units each based on a fixed, usually a metallic standard. If it is a gold standard, 'for each of these currencies there is an equation between the value of the money unit and that of a specific quantity, by weight, of gold. From these two equations, each of which has on one side a quantity of gold, a third can be derived which gives the relation between the values of the two money units',[1] namely the par of exchange. A par of exchange can also be found where two currencies are linked to different metals.[2] The par of exchange is sometimes fixed by law; thus the relation of the U.S.A. dollar and the pound sterling had long been fixed

[1] Helfferich, p. 413; Arnauné, *La Monnaie, le crédit et le change* (1922), pp. 123 sqq.
[2] Helfferich, p. 434.

at \$4.44.[3] Under the Bretton Woods system as originally devised and in force from 1946 until about 1971 the par of exchange of most currencies was fixed by treaty, namely the Articles of Agreement of the International Monetary Fund.[4]

The par of exchange is independent of the rates of exchange of the day, and consequently it does not express the current value of a foreign money unit as resulting from general economic principles, especially those of supply and demand. Moreover, if one of the countries or both countries are on a paper standard, the par of exchange is meaningless, unless the rate of the paper money is itself linked to the currency of a gold-standard country. It is therefore not surprising to find that at the present moment the par of exchange is rarely resorted to when two currencies have to be compared for commercial purposes.

The only exception arises in connection with the calculation of a currency's gold content for the purpose of a gold clause[5] and in connection with valuation for customs purposes; it has long been the practice of some countries to take the par of exchange as a basis when ascertaining the value of imported goods within the meaning of the Tariff Acts,[6] and this practice was sanctioned, subject to certain qualifications, by Art. VII (4) (*a*) of the General Agreement on Tariffs and Trade[7] according to which, as a rule, the valuation for customs purposes was based on par values as established under the Bretton Woods agreement.

In continental countries, apparently, the mint par never played any role, but in the United States of America it was long uncertain whether it was the par of the rate of exchange which, in law, indicated the respective value of two monetary units. Story, who discusses the position at length,[8] starts from the principle[9] that it is necessary 'in all cases to allow that sum in the currency of the country where the suit is brought which should approximate most nearly to the amount to which the party is entitled in the country where the debt is payable, calculated by the real par, and not by the nominal par', and consequently he draws a distinction[10] depending on the place of payment: if it is in a country with which there is an established par of exchange the nominal rate applies, in all other cases the real par. Story's discussion shows the divergencies existing in the various American jurisdictions during the earlier part of the nineteenth century, and even in the

---

[3] U.S.A. Revised Statutes, s. 3565, repealed by s. 403 (*d*), Dye and Chemical Control Act, 1921 (67th Congress, ch. 14). See Nussbaum, p. 334. In view of the fact that the weight-for-weight par was \$4.866 (*Encyclopædia Britannica*, 14th ed., vii. 947) the statutory par was bound to become obsolete.

[4] Art. IV; see above, p. 31.  
[5] Above, pp. 151 sqq.  
[6] Nussbaum, p. 337.  
[7] Cmd. 9413.  
[8] ss. 308–13.  
[9] s. 309.  
[10] s. 310.

later part there were decisions to the effect that in an action in one country for debt made payable in another country the plaintiff is entitled to judgment according to the par of exchange.[11] There is, however, no doubt that at the present time the rate of exchange is universally applied in American courts.[12]

In England it was at one time not quite clear that the real par or the the rate of exchange, is the proper indicator of the value of a foreign money unit. In *Cockerell* v. *Barber*[13] the question was whether legacies expressed in sicca rupees were to be paid at the East India Company's rate between India and Great Britain, which was 2*s.* 6*d.* to the rupee, or at the East India Company's rate between Great Britain and India, which was 2*s.* 3*d.* to the rupee, or at the current value of the sicca rupee in England, which was 2*s.* 1*d.* to the rupee. Lord Eldon's declaration adopted the last alternative. But two decades later, in *Scott* v. *Bevan*[14] where an action was brought in England for the value of a given sum of Jamaica currency upon a judgment obtained in that island, it was argued for the plaintiff that no regard should be had to the rate of exchange, while the defendant argued in favour of the real or actual par. Lord Tenterden, while adopting the actual par, said:[15] 'The practice has probably been in favour of the plaintiff, but there is no case that decides the question. Upon the whole we think that the defendant's mode of computation approximates most nearly to a payment in Jamaica in the currency of that island; though, speaking for myself personally, I must say that I still hesitate as to the propriety of this conclusion.'[16] Today, however, it cannot be doubted that the

---

[11] See *Marburg* v. *Marburg* (1866), 26 Maryland 8, a case which was quoted in many of the English decisions preceding the expurgatory case of *Miliangos*, [1976] A.C. 443.

[12] See cases above, pp. 314, 340 sqq.; see especially *Nevillon* v. *Demmer* (1920), 114 Misc. 1, 185 N.Y. Suppl. 443; Sedgwick, *On Damages*, s. 275; Fraenkel, 35 (1935) Col. L.R. 360, 361, 362; Nussbaum, p. 335; but cf. *Frontera Transportation Co.* v. *Abaunza*, 271 F. 199 (C.C.A. 5th, 1921).

[13] (1810) 16 Ves. 461; on this case see Story, s. 313.

[14] (1831) 2 B. & Ad. 78; see also *Delegal* v. *Naylor* (1831), 7 Bing. 460 and *Campbell* v. *Graham* (1830), 1 Russ. & My. 453, 461, affirmed sub nomine *Campbell* v. *Sandford* (1834), 2 Cl & F. 429, 450, where both Sir John Leach and Lord Brougham apparently applied the par of exchange.

[15] At p. 85.

[16] As to this case see Story, s. 308. Story makes it quite clear that these two cases concern the application of the nominal or actual par of exchange; in the same sense Negus, 40 (1924) L.Q.R. 149 sqq. and Rifkind, 26 (1926) Col. L.R. 559, 562. Indeed, this interpretation seems to be so obvious and any reference in these cases to the proper date of the conversion is so clearly *obiter* that it is difficult to understand how it came about that in *The Volturno*, [1921] 2 A.C. 544 and in the other cases connected with the date of conversion (see above, pp. 148 sqq.) they were so strongly relied upon. In *Re United Railways of Havana & Regla Warehouses Ltd.*, [1961] A.C. 1007, at p. 1046, Viscount Simonds firmly, but unconvincingly, rejected the suggestion that the case could relate to a problem other than the date of conversion; see also Lord Denning at p. 1070. But in *Di Ferdinando* v. *Simon Smits & Co. Ltd.*, [1920] 3 K.B. 409 both Bankes L.J. at p. 412 and Scrutton L.J. at

current par or the rate of exchange is almost universally applicable.[17] Perhaps the most interesting proof is supplied by the case of *Atlantic Trading and Shipping Co.* v. *Louis Dreyfus*.[18] The respondents as charterers and agents of a ship owned by the appellants became entitled to the repayment of certain expenses incurred by them in dollars, and to two sums of sterling in respect of dispatch money and commission. In payment they received from the appellants in Buenos Aires 66,727.30 Argentine dollars in paper, any unexpended balance of which was to be repaid by them to the appellants. The respondents converted the sterling amounts due to them at the rate of $5.04 to the pound sterling. There remained a surplus of $3,433 in paper, which the respondents paid to the appellants in sterling after having converted them at the rate of exchange of $3.66 to the pound. The appellants contended that the respondents, when they deducted the sterling sum due to them from the dollar sum received, should have employed the rate of $3.66 to the pound, not that of $5.04. The former rate was the actual rate of exchange of the day, but the latter was fixed in an Argentine law of 1881 by which, for the purpose of stabilizing the relative value of the Argentine currencies, it was decreed that the value of the currency and the units in circulation, being legal tender in the country, as compared with the lawful units established by the Currency Law Act, should be reckoned, *inter alia*, in terms of the English sovereign at the rate of 5.04. By this law, which Lord Sumner[19] held to be 'merely a legal tender law, fixing the parity at which certain gold coins then passing current in the Republic should be made legal tender concurrently with the national currency then recently established', the rate of the Argentine paper money was stabilized in terms of a (nominal) par of exchange with certain gold standard currencies.[20] The House of Lords took the view that the contract was governed by English law and that it provided for payment in English currency and in England;[21] it followed that the contract could not be regarded 'as anything but one to pay the commercial equivalent of the sums, measured in sterling'[22] and that the equivalent had 'to be ascertained not by a permanent legal tender law relating to currency, but by the

p. 415 appear to have adopted the correct view. See also *In re Tillam Boehme & Tickle Pty., Ltd.* (1932), Vict. L.R. 146, 148, where the application of the par of exchange was expressly rejected and where *Scott* v. *Bevan* was understood as an authority for such a view. The point is now of limited historical interest only.

[17] See the cases above, pp. 307, 339 sqq.

[18] (1922), 10 Ll. L.R. 447, 703 (H.L.); followed in *Ellawood* v. *Ford & Co.* (1922), 12 Ll. L.R. 47 and in *Williams & Mordey* v. *Muller & Co.* (1924), 18 Ll. L.R. 50.

[19] p. 704.

[20] See Helfferich, p. 436.

[21] Lord Buckmaster at p. 703; Lord Sumner at p. 705.

[22] Lord Buckmaster at p. 704.

current quotation for the exchange rate of sterling', or by the commercial rate of exchange of the day, while the law of 1881 merely 'regulates the parity of sovereigns with Argentine currency, but does not affect international transactions or obligations under contracts to pay in England'.[23] The House of Lords, therefore, allowed the appeal and reversing the order of the Court of Appeal[24] restored that of Rowlatt J.[25]

A similar case came before Kerr J. (as he then was) in *Lively Ltd.* v. *City of Munich.*[26] The point for decision was how, for purposes of converting a sum of U.S. dollars into sterling on 1 December 1973, Article 13 of the Agreement on German External Debts of 1953 had to be construed. This provides that the rate of exchange is to be 'determined by the par values of the currencies concerned in force on the appropriate date as agreed with the International Monetary Fund', and 'if no such par values are or were in force' the current rate of exchange 'for cable transfers' is to prevail. By 1 December 1973, as we know,[27] the par value system of the International Monetary Fund had collapsed, though, on paper, par values were still in existence and, for certain intergovernmental purposes, were even in use. But for commercial purposes and 'in a commercially realistic sense' they were not 'in force' or, as the learned Judge put it, 'the fact that par values continue to exist does not necessarily mean that they remain in force'.[28] Since *in casu* the rate of exchange was intended to measure the amount payable on the due date in respect of bonds issued by the City of Munich on the London market, the court disregarded the nominally existing par value rate and applied the commercial rate of exchange of the day.

## III

Whenever it is necessary to employ a rate of exchange for the purpose of converting a sum of money from one currency into another, four problems are liable to arise which, at the risk of repetition, must again be stated in a comprehensive manner.

1. In so far as payments are concerned which are contractually to be made in England, it has been suggested[29] that all questions relating to the rate of exchange should, as a rule, be governed by the proper law of the contract. As to payments which under the contract are to be made outside England in a currency other than sterling, the necessity

---

[23] Lord Sumner at p. 705.     [24] (1921), 6 Ll. L.R. 427.
[25] (1920), 5 Ll. L.R. 287; see also (1920), 3 Ll. L.R. 108.
[26] (1976), 1 W.L.R. 1004.     [27] Above, p. 34.
[28] p. 1016.     [28] Above, p. 321.

for conversion into sterling occurs only in connection with the enforcement of judgments in England.[30] In such cases English courts apply English law to all such points as are incidental to the process of conversion. The following observations aim at a summary of English municipal law.

2. As regards the date with reference to which the rate of exchange is to be ascertained, the law is to a large extent settled. In connection with conversion for the purpose of proceedings the payment-date rule is firmly established.[31] Outside proceedings the date depends on the construction of the contract, but there exists a strong tendency to apply the payment-date rule.[32]

3. Rates of exchange frequently differ from place to place. The question of determining the legally material place, if it is not fixed by the parties, has not yet been clarified. It is submitted, however, that the rule formerly contained in s. 72 (4) of the Bills of Exchange Act, 1882, now repealed, is of general import and that, accordingly, the rate of exchange at the place of payment should prevail. This, it is believed, is the place where, according to the express or implied terms of the contract, payment ought to be made, as opposed to the place at which payment is actually made; it is the rate at the latter place which was formerly applied within the ambit of s. 139 of the Merchant Shipping Act, 1894.

The suggested principle is supported by a dictum of Vaughan Williams L.J.[33] the accuracy of which has never been doubted:

The amount of the English judgment or order must be based on the quantity of English sterling which one would have to pay here to obtain in the market the amount of the debt payable in foreign currency delivered *at the appointed place of payment.*

Similarly, it has been held in New York that the rate at the agreed place of payment is decisive.[34] The justification for the rule lies in the fact that the application of another rate would not necessarily secure to the creditor that amount which he is entitled to have at the agreed place of payment rather than elsewhere.[35]

---

[30] Above, p. 347.        [31] Above, p. 347.        [32] Above, p. 317.

[33] *Manners* v. *Pearson*, [1898] 1 Ch. 581, 592. The view expressed in the text is also supported by *Marrache* v. *Ashton*, [1943] A.C. 411.

[34] *Richard* v. *National City Bank of New York*, 231 App. Div. 559, 248 N.Y.S. 113 (1931).

[35] More on these problems below, pp. 445 sqq. Where statutes deal with the right of conversion, they usually refer in terms to the rate of exchange at the place of payment. See, for instance, s. 244 of the German Civil Code, but also s. 661 of the Commercial Code which renders s. 244 applicable to the payment of freight, but provides that the conversion is effected according to the rate of exchange which at the date of the ship's arrival prevails at the place of destination.

4. The most troublesome problem of the rate of exchange is that of defining the type of rate to which resort is to be had for the purpose of effecting a conversion.[36] This is a matter which deserves close investigation.

## IV

1. There does not at present exist on the London market any rate of exchange which can be described as official in the sense of exclusive or conclusive. The London Foreign Exchange Market is unofficial and informal, consisting of independent brokers and dealers, viz. the operators in the foreign exchange departments of financial houses. The dealings which occur from day to day on the market do not produce what can be described as a uniform or generally acceptable or authoritative rate. Many banks have their own rates and their loan agreements often provide for the application of the particular bank's rate at a particular hour. Reuters maintain a computerized monitoring service which provides regular information. Although the differences are invariably very small indeed, every well-drawn agreement should define the applicable rate, even though it may be merely by reference to the rate published in a particular newspaper or as certified by the Bank of England. In case of dispute it is a matter of evidence to prove, not what was the London rate, but what was the most reliable of several rates.

The arrangements of a somewhat informal character prevailing in England, the United States of America, and elsewhere are the consequence of the fact that at present there does not exist any fixed standard and that currencies are 'floating', so that no rate can be 'official'.[37] This was different under the International Monetary Fund's par value system which, in principle, did not allow rates to differ from parity by more than one per cent, and may still be different in certain countries in which rates are determined by the monetary authorities, but in the principal centres which are interconnected by telephone and telex multiplicity and fluidity of rates have become a burdensome fact of commercial life.

2. Within very narrow limits it is still possible to distinguish four principal types of rate of exchange.

(a) The spot rate gives the price of payments or transfers effected

---

[36] This problem was dealt with by Mann, 'Problems of the Rate of Exchange', 8 (1945) *Mod. L.R.* 177 which, subject to not inconsiderable alterations, forms the basis of the following observations.

[37] On the question of what is an official rate of exchange in Germany see German Federal Supreme Court, 23 May 1962, *RzW*. 1962, 509; 13 Feb. 1963, *RzW*. 1963, 449: it is the rate which the competent authorities such as a central bank have calculated or ascertained.

by telex. This method of payment involves no risk of loss, no loss of interest, and no stamp duties. Hence the spot rate is almost invariably used and even what used to be known as the T.T. rate, i.e. the rate for telegraphic or cable transfers has disappeared.[38] The rates charged by a bank to purchasers of telex or telegraphic transfers are dearer than for any other form of remittance, since there is no period of transmission during which the bank could earn interest.

(b) The M.T. (mail transfer) rate is quoted for a payment which the bank instructs its agent to make by letter. It was usually cheaper than the spot rate, since during the period from the dispatch to the receipt of the letter the bank earned interest on the money paid by its customer, but it is now hardly ever in use.[39]

(c) The rate for sight drafts (or cheques) is normally identical with the M.T. rate, since the bank which draws on its agent and hands the document to its customer for transmission has the use of the money during the period of transit.

(d) The rate for coins and notes is based on the spot rate, but is influenced by loss of interest and the cost of packing, postage, and insurance. It is ascertained by the Foreign Money Departments of the big banks and certain other specialists. The amounts involved are usually small and dependent on the incidence of tourist traffic. It is only as the result of exchange control that the market for notes at times became enlivened and led to quotations which were largely independent of the spot rate, but were determined by the laws of supply and demand expressing, in this case, the opportunities of smuggling and resmuggling rather than a measure of valuing the foreign currency as such.

There are certain other rates, such as short, long, and tel quel rates, the intricacies of which are hardly of any interest to the legal practitioner.

3. Another concomitant of exchange control is to be found in the growth of so-called multiple currency rates. These come under the heading of discriminatory currency practices which are forbidden to the members of the International Monetary Fund except in so far as approved by the Fund or engaged in during the transitional period.[40]

Whatever the reasons for the introduction of a system of several effective rates of exchange may be,[41] their effect is nearly always the

[38] Raymond G. F. Coninx, *Foreign Exchange Today* (1978), pp. 82 sqq.; H. E. Evitt, *A Manual of Foreign Exchange* (7th ed., by R. E. Pither, 1971), p. 40, still uses the phrase 'T.T. rate'. For a useful description of the foreign exchange market in London see an anonymous contribution in the Bank of England's *Quarterly Bulletin* 1980, 437.

[39] See Evitt, l.c., p. 41.                                    [40] Art. VIII, s. 3.

[41] See the International Monetary Fund's *Annual Reports* and the *Annual Report on Exchange Restrictions*.

same. A country has established a basic rate of exchange, but it super-imposes special rates at which it purchases foreign currency derived from and at which it sells foreign currency required for special trans-actions. The system which is mainly used in South America means, for instance, that the basic rate of exchange of Bolivia is Bolivianos 60 = U.S. $1, but if a resident of Bolivia exports certain minerals to certain countries, the Central Bank of Bolivia will pay him 130 Boli-vianos for $1 and if he imports certain goods from certain countries, for which he pays dollars, he must buy them from the Central Bank at 130 Bolivianos or even at 190 Bolivianos for $1.[42]

From a legal point of view it is conceivable that in particular circum-stances it may become necessary to take note of and to apply a rate of exchange which, though effective and legitimate, is not the official one. But such cases are bound to be rare and have not as yet occurred in English judicial practice.[43]

4. While multiple currency practices lead to the establishment of a variety of genuine rates of exchange, another aspect of exchange con-trol has produced what can only be described as a pseudo-rate of exchange. It is incidental to exchange control that the accounts or credits or balances of non-residents are blocked in the sense that they cannot be freely dealt with, whether their use be excluded or limited.[44] Outside the restricting country such blocked accounts can frequently be sold at a discount the extent of which depends on their origin, nature, and availability for commercial purposes. Where there is such a market, it does not lead to a rate of exchange in the legal sense of the term. What happens in law is that a price is being paid for the assignment

---

[42] International Monetary Fund, *Third Annual Report on Exchange Restrictions* (1952), p. 49, or for a more recent survey see the Annual Report 1979 on *Exchange Arrangements and Exchange Restrictions*, pp. 17, 18. In Mar. 1952 the Government of Israel introduced multiple rates for dollars, viz. $2.80, $1.80, and $1 to the £1. At the same time the Govern-ment specified the cases in which these rates were respectively to apply both as regards the sale and the purchase of foreign currency. This led to the difficulty of determining the appropriate rate of exchange in cases in which before 1952 a debtor had undertaken to pay Israeli pounds 'at the official rate of exchange for dollars'. The problem and, incidentally, also the meaning of the term 'official rate' was considered in numerous cases. For summaries of three decisions see *Aaronson* v. *Kaplan*, Jerusalem Post, 2 Oct. 1955; *Levin* v. *Esheg Ltd.*, ibid., 24 May 1956; *Tillinger* v. *Jewish Agency*, ibid., 22 Apr. 1958.

[43] An interesting case, however, was decided in Canada: *Djamous* v. *Alepin*, Rapports Judiciaires Officiels de Québec (Cour Supérieure), 1949, 354. The defendant received in Syria Syrian pounds and undertook to pay dollars to the plaintiff. For such transactions to be effected at the official rate the permission of the Syrian Government was necessary, but un-obtainable. There existed, however, a 'marché libre, connu et toléré par les gouvernements intéressés' (p. 357). This 'free' rate was held to be applicable. It is important to note that it was not an illegal market to which it applied. Had there been such illegality the 'free' rate could not be applied.

[44] On blocked accounts under the Exchange Control Act, 1947, see s. 32 and the Third Schedule.

of a debt;[45] such a price is something entirely different from the price at which the unit of account of one currency can be exchanged into a unit of account of another currency. Thus the rate of exchange between the United Kingdom and Brazil is at present about 135 cruzeiros to the pound. But if an Englishman holds what is known as 'blocked cruzeiros' which he can sell in London at a discount, he holds a cruzeiros account with a banker in Brazil. 'Blocked cruzeiros', therefore, is not a currency or unit of account which has a rate of exchange, but a chose in action which is bought and sold at a price.[46]

## V

There does not exist any rule of law determining the type of rate of exchange appropriate in all cases. Certain authorities, it is true, have been empowered by Parliament to prescribe the rate which, in connection with transactions falling within their province, forms the basis for a conversion of foreign currency into sterling[47] and in 1882, when, owing to the state of technical evolution, it was still usual to effect payments by mail and therefore to employ what is now known as the M.T. rate, s. 72 (4) of the Bills of Exchange Act, repealed in 1977, prescribed that the amount of a bill expressed in foreign currency was to be converted into sterling 'according to the rate of exchange for sight drafts'. But these are exceptional cases; they have no bearing upon the question what rate of exchange should be regarded as decisive in the legal sense.

In case of an undisturbed exchange market this problem has more than academic interest only when the law is concerned with a contract involving foreign currency as a commodity.[48] Thus a dispute between a foreign exchange broker and dealer may make it necessary to determine whether a deal was transacted on the basis of the spot or the mail transfer rate. It is in the event of wide divergencies between the

---

[45] This is frequently overlooked by economists, because they regard bank accounts as money. It would appear that even the Federal Reserve Bank fell into error when in 1940 it certified the existence of a 'free' rate for the pound sterling. The error was not seen by the Supreme Court of the United States when it decided *Barr* v. *United States* (1944), 324 U.S. 83: The plaintiff had paid for English goods at the 'free' rate of $3.45 to the pound. Although the Secretary of the Treasury had, for customs purposes, published an 'official' rate of $4.03, it was held that the plaintiff had to pay customs duties on the basis of the 'free' rate. Nussbaum, 45 (1945) *Col. L.R.* 412, 417 and *Money*, p. 484, who strongly criticizes the decision, points out that what was sold at the 'free' rate was so-called 'old sterling', i.e. American sterling credits in English banks which could be assigned. Cf. Bronz, 'Conversion of Foreign Currency in Customs Administration', 34 (1955), *Texas L.R.* 78.

[46] For consequences flowing from this view see below, p. 449.

[47] For example, for the purpose of stamp and customs duties or, within the E.E.C., for the purposes of the Common Agricultural Policy.

[48] In the sense developed above, p. 185.

various rates, such as are brought about by restricted markets, that the definition of the legally relevant rate becomes important to the numerous cases in which foreign currency functions as money and must be converted into sterling.

The solution furnished by the law is, it is believed, that no single type of rate is entitled to pre-eminence, that, while for purely factual reasons the spot rate will have to be applied most frequently, no presumption in its favour exists, but that in each case the appropriate rate is determined by the context in which the necessity for conversion arises: the determination of the rate depends on the construction of the material statutory provision or the interpretation of an agreement or the nature of the transaction.

1. Where under the terms of a contract foreign currency is employed as a measure of liability rather than an instrument of payment and an exchange operation is contemplated as a necessary incident to performance,[49] the parties may be taken to have impliedly agreed upon the application of the spot rate (as opposed, chiefly, to the rate for notes), the reason being that as a matter of fact the spot rate is applied by the commercial community in the vast majority of their transactions and is therefore the most familiar. The spot rate is, in such cases, the 'reasonable' rate which applies in the absence of an express stipulation, in the same way as the law imputes an intention to pay a reasonable price if the price is not fixed in the contract.[50]

Thus, if a contract provides for a payment to be made 'at the current rate of exchange' or 'at the rate of exchange of the day' or 'at the rate of exchange in London', it is a matter of construction to ascertain the rate envisaged by the parties, but in default of special circumstances it will be found to be the commercially usual rate, i.e. the spot rate. The result will be the same where, the money of account and the money of payment being fixed, an 'item' must be converted:[51] for example, if a London underwriter reinsures a foreign insurance company against its liability under a fire insurance policy on buildings abroad, the amount of his sterling liability depends on the sum of foreign currency paid by the insurer to the assured. The parties must be taken to have contemplated the conversion of this 'item' into sterling at the spot rate. Similar cases occur where the price payable by the buyer is fixed with reference to a quotation in a foreign market; thus, if a merchant in London buys grain from a Liverpool importer at 'Buenos Aires quotation plus 10 per cent' or

---

[49] This distinguishes the cases envisaged in the text from the case in which the debtor has undertaken to pay a sum of foreign currency in England and may but need not pay in sterling: below, p. 448.

[50] s. 8 (2) of the Sale of Goods Act, 1979.

[51] In the sense discussed above, p. 330.

if he buys through his stockbroker Argentine shares in the Buenos Aires market 'at 94 per cent', the buyer will normally owe, and pay, such amount of pounds sterling as corresponds to the agreed amount of pesos converted at the spot rate. To apply in such cases any other rate would do violence to the intention of the parties. They contract in sterling, they are not concerned with the delivery of specific foreign money, they merely contemplate an exchange operation to be effected on the basis of the usual commercial rate.

2. In the case of a promise to pay a liquidated sum of foreign currency a conversion into sterling may occur for reasons of either substantive law or the law of procedure.

A contract between two London merchants may provide for the payment of dollars. The construction of the contract may lead to the determination not only of the date with reference to which the conversion is to be effected,[52] but also of the type of rate which is to be employed, and it is not difficult to picture situations in which the application of the spot rate is required.[53] However, construction of the contract will not always help. It is never available where a French contract made in France between Frenchmen provides for the payment of French francs in France and is enforced here, where an English judgment for francs is obtained and conversion is necessary solely for the purpose of enforcing it. It is essential, therefore, to find a rule prima facie applicable to foreign currency debts.

The rate of exchange to be applied in such circumstances is the rate at the place of payment for whatever is legal tender under the law of the currency in which the debt is expressed; usually[54] this will be the rate for bank notes. The reason is that according to well-established principles a promise to pay a given number of units of foreign currency is a promise to pay whatever may be legal tender at the time of payment in the country where such foreign currency circulates,[55] and that the debtor may pay in such legal tender.[56] Since the amount of sterling into which the sum of foreign currency is to be converted should most closely correspond to the value of that which the debtor has promised to pay and which, if paid, would

---

[52] Above, p. 317.

[53] For example, an English manufacturer buys foreign goods from an English importer. They have a market value in England which is obviously based on the spot rate. If the purchase price is expressed in the currency of the country of origin, construction of the contract may well require the conclusion that the buyer must pay the sterling equivalent calculated according to the spot rate. Where payment in banknotes is excluded (above, p. 423), conversion at the rate for notes will also be excluded.

[54] For exceptions see above, p. 424.

[55] Above, p. 271.

[56] Above, p. 316.

discharge the debt, the appropriate rate must be that for legal tender of the country concerned.[57]

The application of the rate for notes was rejected by Atkinson J. in *Graumann* v. *Treitel*.[58] The decision arose out of a contract which was made in Germany between parties then resident in Germany and governed by German law. Under it the defendant was indebted to the plaintiff in the sum of RM. 78,000 odd. The place of performance in respect of the debt was Berlin, but the learned judge apparently held that it had shifted to London when both parties established their residence there.[59] The plaintiff claimed the sterling equivalent of RM. 78,000 at the 'official' rate of exchange of about RM. 12 to the pound. The defendant argued that at the relevant date reichsmark notes could be bought on the foreign exchange market in London at about RM. 36 to the pound and that therefore this rate should be applied. Atkinson J., who felt 'a little puzzled' about that contention, agreed that, if the defendant had chosen to buy the appropriate number of reichsmark notes and to pay them to the plaintiff, this would have been a good discharge.[60] Yet he applied what he described as 'the official rate of exchange' for two reasons. The first was that it had 'never been suggested that, when for the purposes of judgment one comes to convert the amount of the debt into sterling, one can take the rate at which foreign currency could or might have been bought on the foreign exchange market in London'. Secondly, it was pointed out that the 'official' rate did not do any injustice to the

---

[57] This view has now been accepted by Dicey and Morris, p. 1013. It will be readily appreciated that under a free exchange market little emphasis had to be placed upon this rule. It is, however, noteworthy that as early as 1917 Professor Martin Wolff recognized the principle by pointing out that the debtor who had contracted to pay foreign currency in Germany and, exercising his option under s. 244 of the German Civil Code, chooses to pay in German currency 'at the rate of exchange prevailing at the date of payment at the place of payment', must pay according to the rates for foreign legal tender: *Ehrenberg's Handbuch*, iv (1), 641. This view was followed by Staudinger–Weber, *Kommentar zum Bürgerlichen Gesetzbuch*, 11th ed. (1967), s. 244, note 68 and von Maydell in *Münchener Kommentar*, s. 244 n. 52, among others, but rejected without justification by Nussbaum, *Das Geld* (1925), p. 222, and Düringer–Hachenburg–Breit, *Kommentar zum Handelsgesetzbuch* (1932), iv, 757. The latter view is also held in regard to the similar provision of Art. 84, of the Swiss *Obligationenrecht*, by Oser-Schönenberger, *Kommentar* (1929), Art. 84, n. 18.

[58] [1940] 2 All E.R. 188, followed in *Ginsberg* v. *Canadian Pacific Steamship Ltd.* (1940), 66 Ll. L.R. 20.

[59] This is emphasized by Morton L.J. (as he then was) in *Re Paraná Plantations Ltd.*, [1946] 2 All E.R. 214, at p. 219. The reasons which Atkinson J. gave for his conclusion are insufficient and the judgment has repeatedly been criticized on this ground: Kahn-Freund, 4 (1940) *Mod. L.R.* 149; Nussbaum, p. 466, and others. But the conclusion may be justified on the ground stated above, p. 214, and also because there is a long line of German decisions, starting with Supreme Court, 4 Dec. 1923, *JW.* 1924, 1357, No. 3 and reaffirmed in recent cases, according to which the place of payment probably shifted to London.

[60] At p. 200, relying on *Société des Hôtels Le Touquet-Paris Plage* v. *Cummings*, [1922] 1 K.B. 451, discussed above, p. 323.

defendant, since 'in arriving at the marks to be paid out by the defendant at the dissolution of the partnership between the parties the value of the English capital was turned into marks at the same rate'. The latter point might have supported the existence of an implied agreement between the parties and would, therefore, not be of general validity. The former point seems to rest on a misunderstanding of the true nature and function of the 'official' rate and of the character of an obligation to pay a liquidated sum of foreign currency, and also on the absence of authority.

This has now been supplied by the decision of the Privy Council in *Marrache* v. *Ashton*[61] which may be said to supersede, though it does not *stricto sensu* overrule, the decision in *Graumann* v. *Treitel*. The appellant was indebted to the respondents in the sum of 110,000 Spanish pesetas which fell due for repayment on 25 May 1939. All parties were residents of Gibraltar, the law of which governed the contract and where payment was to be made. At the date of the contract gold and silver coins were legal tender in Spain, but as from 20 January 1939, Bank of Spain peseta notes were, apart from gold, the only legal tender in Spain. Under Spanish law it was illegal to export from or import into Spain such peseta notes. Yet there was a market for them in Gibraltar, London, and elsewhere. Their rate was about 132 pesetas to the pound, the 'official' rate, recognized by the Spanish authorities, being 53 pesetas to the pound. The appellant admitted liability for the sterling equivalent of the peseta amount at the rate of 132 and paid it into court after action brought. Reversing the judgment of the Gibraltar court the Privy Council decided that this was sufficient to discharge the debt. Lord Macmillan said:[62]

All that the Court had to do was to ascertain what was legal tender in Spain for so many pesetas and then to inquire whether there was a market in Gibraltar for the sale and purchase of such currency, and if so, what was the market rate. Bank of Spain notes were legal tender in Spain, there was a market for such notes in Gibraltar and the rate there prevailing was 132 pesetas to the pound sterling.

Both in *Marrache* v. *Ashton* and in *Graumann* v. *Treitel* the place of payment determining the rate of exchange[63] was or was held to be outside the money of account's home country, i.e. Spanish pesetas or German reichsmarks were payable in Gibraltar or London respectively.[64] But the legal principle is the same where the place of payment

---

[61] [1943] A.C. 311, discussed 59 (1943) *L.Q.R.* 301; on the two cases discussed in the text see R. Lachs, 93 (1943) *Law Journal*, 299, 307.

[62] p. 319.                                    [63] Above, p. 419.

[64] Is it possible, then, to draw any valid distinction between the two cases? It is submitted that the answer is in the negative. Three points may be made, none of which is material in law. Firstly, in *Marrache* v. *Ashton* the debtor had made a payment into court,

is situate within the boundaries of the money of account's home country, for example, in Madrid or Berlin: the rate for notes at the place of payment applies. The practical difference between the two cases, however, will frequently be considerable,[65] because mainly as a result of exchange control it may be possible to obtain Spanish peseta notes, for instance, more cheaply in London than in Madrid.[66] Such discrepancy as there may be is justified by and inherent in the terms of the contract.[67] There is, moreover, nothing unusual in the result, since it is a not uncommon feature of monetary obligations that decisive consequences are derived from the situation of the place of payment. It must be remembered, however, that the place of payment may shift and that in that event the rate of exchange prevailing

while in *Graumann* v. *Treitel* no payment had been made. This cannot make any difference, because it should be accepted as fundamental that no judgment should order the defendant to pay more than he would have had to pay had he paid voluntarily. Secondly, in *Graumann* v. *Treitel* the *lex monetae* and the *lex causae* were identical, both being German; in *Marrache* v. *Ashton* the contract was subject to the law of Gibraltar, while the *lex monetae* was Spanish. But in both cases it was the *lex fori* which was held to govern the question. Thirdly, in *Graumann* v. *Treitel* it was held that the claim for the sterling equivalent of a reichsmark debt was a claim in debt, while *Marrache* v. *Ashton* proceeds from the premiss that the plaintiff was entitled to damages. The existence of this wholly unrealistic problem of classification cannot be denied (above, p. 214), but the number of cases to the solution of which it is material, should not be extended. It is remarkable, however, that *Graumann* v. *Treitel* was not referred to by Counsel in their argument in *Marrache* v. *Ashton*.

[65] On this point see also *Re Paraná Plantations Ltd.*, [1946] 2 All E.R. 214 which will be discussed below, p. 453. Cf. the decision of a District Court in Florida in *Sun Insurance Office Ltd.* v. *Arauca Fund*, 84 F. Supp. 516 (1948): the plaintiffs were entitled to general average which under the bill of lading was to be adjusted and paid in Germany under German law. In Apr. 1940 the plaintiffs were awarded RM. 21,000 odd. The plaintiffs claimed against a fund in the United States. It was held that they were not required to go to Germany, but were 'entitled to proceed against the shipowner at any place where property of the debtor can be found'. But the reichsmarks had no value in terms of dollars at the date of the judgment so that the plaintiffs recovered nothing.

[66] Under a system of exchange control this is almost inevitable (see above, p. 422), but otherwise divergencies in the rates are unlikely.

[67] It should be recognized as a paramount rule that the parties should neither suffer nor benefit from the conversion. If an Englishman owes pesetas in Madrid and if, therefore, he has to pay peseta notes to his creditor in Madrid, he cannot, under a system of exchange control, buy these notes in London and send them to Madrid, for importation of such notes into Spain is prohibited. His only method of discharging his debt is to buy in London a credit in Madrid (which he can do only on the basis of the rate for cable transfers or sight drafts) and then to instruct the Spanish bank to pay the notes to the creditor. In this way the creditor receives what he is entitled to, and if he is compelled to come to London to enforce payment, he is justified in effecting the conversion at the spot rate which alone will produce such amount of sterling as will give him the contractual amount of pesetas in Madrid. On the other hand, if the pesetas are payable in London, no transfer of currency from one country to another is involved for the purpose, and within the meaning, of the contract; the creditor, it is true, will normally remit the money to his home country, but this is not a contractually relevant intention. In these circumstances, therefore, the debtor discharges his obligation by the payment in London of whatever is legal tender in Spain or by the payment of such sum of sterling as corresponds in London to the required amount of Spanish legal tender.

at the substituted place of payment is decisive; such shifting may occur under the proper law of the contract[68] or may have to be inferred from the circumstances.[69]

In no case is there any room for the application, not of the rate for legal tender at the place of payment, but for the 'rate' for foreign blocked accounts. The latter rate has frequently been advocated for situations which, subject to an important variation, are exemplified by *Graumann* v. *Treitel.*[70] If in the 1930s a resident of Berlin promised to pay reichsmarks in Berlin, and in Berlin only, to another resident of Berlin and proceedings for the recovery of the money are brought in this country where, at the time of the proceedings, both parties have taken up their residence, it is tempting to argue that, had payment been duly made in Berlin, German exchange restrictions would have resulted in the creditor enjoying outside Germany only a fraction of the nominal amount paid by the debtor and that, therefore, the English judgment should give the creditor only such amount as he would have been able to *transfer* from Germany had payment been made there. Why, so it may be asked, should proceedings here have the effect of a windfall for the creditor? The idea of damage and restoration, however, is not germane to the issue. The debtor who has to discharge his promise to pay a fixed sum of money at a certain place is burdened with the debt wherever he resides.[71] His argument that circumstances entirely extraneous to him (in this case the creditor's emigration from Germany) should bring about a reduction of the burden is incompatible with the nature of the bargain and the conception of debt. Consequently it is not possible to subscribe to the theory underlying some New York decisions. Thus, in one of the numerous 'ticket' cases which came before American courts,[72] the plaintiff, then resident in Vienna, had paid to the defendants' Vienna agency RM. 420 to enjoy a credit of that amount on board one of the defendants' ships on which he intended to travel to New York. Since owing to the outbreak of war he could not travel by such ship, he claimed repayment of the 'board money' in dollars at the 'official' rate of exchange. The action was dismissed. After an elaborate discussion of the German currency system the court pointed out that the defendants were liable to refund the board money in Vienna and that, if they had discharged their obligation there, the plaintiff would have received emigrants' blocked marks:

[68] This, it is believed, is the true explanation of the case of *Graumann* v. *Treitel, ubi supra.* The learned judge was right in thinking that the place of payment had shifted to London (above, p. 446, n. 59), but, with respect, he was wrong in rejecting the rate for German legal tender quoted in London.

[69] In the paper 8 (1945) *Mod. L.R.* 177, at p. 190, reference was made to an implied agreement. It should be remembered that (*a*) great care will have to be taken in ascertaining the place of payment, if it is not expressly fixed by the parties (see above, p. 76) and (*b*) that 'place of payment', if it is the connecting factor in a conflict of laws rule, is always interpreted according to English law and (*c*) that a creditor under an English judgment, though residing abroad, has only a right to be paid in England: *In re A Debtor*, [1912] 1 K.B. 53.

[70] [1940] 2 All E.R. 188 where the place of payment was held to be in London.

[71] This, it must be admitted, has sometimes been ignored in English decisions: above, p. 66, n. 19, and below, p. 453, n. 84.

[72] Most of them are listed above, p. 404, n. 20.

Such marks are not dealt in here or elsewhere outside of Germany and were not dealt in on January 26, 1940, the date of breach. They had no market value here on January 26, 1940, and the only way such Reichsmarks could be disposed of for dollars was to offer them for sale to the Deutsche Golddiskontbank in Berlin. That bank occasionally purchased such marks and in January 1940 paid in Berlin for such marks between 1.6 c. and 2 c. per mark. . . . The restricted internal marks in which the excess board money deposit was repayable is without demonstrable foreign exchange value in dollars. The plaintiff cannot, therefore, recover dollars for them here.[73]

This reasoning, though it was followed in other cases,[74] is unacceptable. The price at which blocked accounts of a certain type can be sold and transferred to another country is something entirely different from the rate at which the reichsmark, a unit of account, may be converted into another currency.[75] If the plaintiff had claimed arrears of interest, the defendants would not have been allowed to deduct an amount equal to the income tax which the plaintiff would have had to pay were he still resident in Germany or Austria; in the same way the loss or profit which the plaintiff would have made had the defendants paid at the agreed place of payment is no concern of the defendant.[76] Or, as the Swiss Federal Tribunal put it in a case in which the plaintiffs, residents of England, were entitled to be paid by the German defendants RM. 108,046.47 in Berlin, but claimed payment in Switzerland,[77] the object of conversion is

out of the defendants' Swiss property to make available to the plaintiffs so much monetary value in Swiss currency as is required to enable them to obtain with it RM. 108,046.47 in Berlin. . . . In this connexion only an objective

---

[73] *Halpern* v. *Holland–America Line*, [1942] A.M.C. 786. In the same sense already *Zimmern* v. *Holland–America Line*, [1941] A.M.C. 954.

[74] *Freund* v. *Laenderbank*, 111 N.Y.S. (2d) 178 (1949) affirmed without opinion 277 App. Div. 770, 97 N.Y.S. (2d) 549 (1950), on which see Cohn, 3 (1950) *Int. L.Q.* 99. The theory now rejected in the text was first put forward in the first edition of this book, p. 52, n. 1, but was given up in the article referred to above, p. 449, n. 69.

[75] See above, pp. 462, 463.

[76] The position is, of course, different where the plaintiff claims damages for breach of the defendant's obligation to account for money held in a foreign country on blocked account: *Hughes Tool Co.* v. *United Artists Corporation*, 279 App. Div. 417, 110 N.Y.S. (2d) 383 (Supreme Court, Appellate Division, First Department), affirmed without opinion (1953) 304 N.Y. 942, where, notwithstanding many unfortunate observations, it was correctly stated that 'in evaluating foreign currency the circumstance that it is blocked is a factor of prime importance which makes it impossible to use the official rate as the sole standard'.

[77] 27 June 1946, *BGE.* 72, iii. 100. The court applied the spot rate. No argument in support of the legal tender rate was addressed to the court. The decision is of great general interest. German Restitution Courts repeatedly had to consider the question whether a sum of sterling, for instance, paid in London represented a fair price for real property which was situate in Germany, was sold by a victim of Nazi persecution, and the market value of which necessarily had to be calculated in terms of German currency. The conclusion arrived at by the Supreme Restitution Court seems to have been that the proper rate was not the official rate nor the rate for banknotes nor any rate tainted by persecution, but the rate for such type of blocked mark accounts as could be freely bought outside Germany and used for the purchase of German real property: 13 July 1955, *RzW.* 1955, 328; 11 Apr. 1957, *RzW.* 1957, 226.

standard should be applied. It is, therefore, irrelevant whether it would perhaps have been impossible for the plaintiffs, for special personal reasons (as Jews, foreigners, non-residents) to accept or enforce payment in Berlin or to make use of the sum of Reichsmarks paid to them. . . . There is no question of transferring German property to Switzerland (in which event the plaintiffs would certainly make a loss). . . .

More recently the 'windfall' argument was rejected by the United States Court of Appeals, 2nd Cir., in circumstances which were by no means the same, but involved the same principle. New York debtors owed to the plaintiffs, Cuban emigrants in the United States, dollars which were assumed to be payable in Cuba in accordance with Cuban law. The dollars, when paid in Cuba, would have had to be surrendered to the authorities in exchange for pesos and thus become unavailable to the plaintiffs. But they were held to be entitled to dollars and it was irrelevant that after payment in Cuba the plaintiffs would have been left with inconvertible pesos.[78]

3. To determine the appropriate rate of exchange for the conversion of damages expressed in foreign currency is a matter of considerable difficulty, because their treatment in the law of money is throughout surrounded by many doubts.

The damages may really be a liquidated amount. This is so, for example, where the value of a thing at a certain place is to be restored: the seller fails to deliver goods at a place abroad and is therefore liable to pay damages measured by the market value at that place, or goods are converted by the defendant abroad, or an employee claims damages for wrongful dismissal. Here it seems appropriate to apply the rules developed above in connection with the rate for debts.

Then there are cases where damages are at large, as, for example, in case of a motor accident abroad. An English court will probably assess them in sterling so that a problem of the rate of exchange is unlikely to arise.

Damages expressed in foreign currency may be suffered here. They should be made good at the rate of exchange for sterling at which the plaintiff is in fact compelled to buy the required amount of foreign currency. In *Arcos Ltd.* v. *London & Northern Trading Company*[79] the plaintiffs had sold Russian timber to the defendants who repudiated the contract and became liable for damages; the contract between the parties who were English companies was governed by English law. The plaintiffs alleged, *inter alia*, that they had incurred expenses in storing the goods in Russia, and they claimed a sum of 40,000 roubles which they translated into sterling at the spot rate of 7.42

---

[78] *Menendez* v. *Saks & Co.*, 485 F. 2d 1355 (1973), 1365–1367.
[79] (1935) 53 Ll. L.R. 38.

roubles to the pound. The defendants replied that the rate was wholly fictitious, inasmuch as the real value of the rouble in terms of sterling was infinitely smaller. MacKinnon J. (as he then was) arrived at the conclusion[80] 'that the great bulk of exchange transactions between this country and Russia as between roubles and sterling are carried out at that (i.e. the spot) rate'. He rejected as irrelevant the assertions that at some black markets in Berlin or Switzerland rouble notes, the importation of which was forbidden by Russia, were much cheaper, that the amount claimed by the plaintiffs was much higher than that which would be paid in Finland for similar work, and that inside Russia roubles at the spot rate had greater purchasing power than those used by the populace and the workmen who did the business of storing. The last two contentions surely were irrelevant. As to the first, the decisive question would seem to have been at what rate the plaintiffs in fact purchased or could have purchased the roubles which they spent in Russia. If there was no cheaper method available to the plaintiffs than to buy roubles in London at the spot rate, then the plaintiffs were clearly right. If it should have been possible to buy rouble notes at a discount and to send them to Russia to pay for the storing expenses, then the plaintiffs, being bound to minimize damages and for this purpose to make use of the special facilities which no doubt they enjoyed, could only claim the sterling equivalent of such notes which, it must be assumed, were legal tender,[81] and it did not matter that they could only be bought at a 'black' market. If, finally, the plaintiffs had used funds standing to their credit in Russia, but desired to be indemnified in London, then the London value of a rouble credit in Russia would appear to be the appropriate measure of damages.

4. The principle that the appropriate type of rate of exchange is determined by the context in which the necessity for conversion arises affords a guide to the solution of a number of special cases.

(a) It is clear law that the salved value is the value of the ship at the time when and the place where the services ended. This rule explains the decision of Bucknill J. (as he then was) in *The Eisenach*.[82] In connection with the award of remuneration for salvage services the learned judge had to ascertain the salved value of a German ship towed into Dover harbour. The usual basis for assessing the value of the ship and the salvage services is the market value of the ship. Subsequently to the salvage the *Eisenach* had been sold by the owners for 550,000 reichsmarks, which amount, converted into pounds sterling at the official rate of exchange of the day of 12.20 marks to the

---

[80] p. 47.     [81] Above, p. 422.
[82] [1936] 1 All E.R. 155; (1936), 54 Ll. L.R. 354.

pound, corresponded to £45,000. Bucknill J. refused to accept this sum as the salved value, because the nature of the sale by the owners 'was such that the owners of the *Eisenach* were obliged by law to spend the proceeds of sale on building new tonnage in Germany. They were not allowed by their law to convert the proceeds of sale into sterling—even if they had been able to do so.' The learned judge also found that 'the relative values of the mark and the £ sterling appear to be, on the evidence, in a very fluid and uncertain state so far as transactions like the sale and purchase of a ship are concerned', and he therefore did not believe that there was any reliable standard by which he could convert the sum of 550,000 reichsmarks into sterling. In the circumstances the sale of the ship was not effected in the open market, as it is usually understood, and for the purpose of determining the market value it was therefore justifiable to disregard that sale altogether. The decision is explained by the fact that no problem of conversion in the strict sense was involved, but that in making his award the learned judge was concerned only with the question to what extent the sale of the ship should be taken into account as an element of the assessment.

(*b*) A similar latitude is enjoyed by those who have to estimate the sterling value of a debt which is expressed in foreign currency and is payable in a foreign country at some future date. This is the basis of the difficult and perhaps not too satisfactory decision of the Court of Appeal in *Re Paraná Planatations Ltd.*[83]

Under a contract governed by German law the claimant, then resident in Germany, paid RM. 20,000 odd in Germany to the company which was an English limited company. As a result of the outbreak of war in 1939 the performance of the contract became impossible and the claimant, then resident in England, became accordingly entitled to the refund of the money paid by him. The Court of Appeal held in the first place that prior to the winding-up of the company in 1944 the claimant had no right enforceable in England to the refund of the money at all. The reason was that under the contract the refund was to be made in Berlin, and only in Berlin, and that in consequence of the very fact which gave rise to the liability to refund, viz. the outbreak of war, it was impossible for the company to pay in Berlin. On the footing of this reasoning which, with respect, is far from convincing and ignores the real character of monetary obligations,[84] the further question arose as to how a debt of reichsmarks

---

[83] [1946] 2 All E.R. 214.

[84] The court assumed that a debt was payable at the place of payment, but nowhere else. This is in line with the theory underlying *Ralli Bros.* v. *Compañia Naviera Sota y Aznar*, [1920] 2 K.B. 287 which was criticized above, p. 66, n. 19. Even from the point of view of English law the claimant ought to have been held to be entitled to enforce his claim here;

payable by an English company to a resident of England at some uncertain date in the future in Germany should be valued at the commencement of the winding-up in 1944. The court applied, in effect,
what is now s. 316 of the Companies Act, 1948, and expressed the
view that in making 'a just estimate' of the rate the liquidator would
be acting fairly and reasonably if he adopted the rate of RM. 40 to
the pound at which, when Germany became occupied by the Allies
in 1945, British soldiers could buy German marks from the Field
Cashiers. The claimant thus received approximately £500 and, once
the decision of the Court of Appeal on the first point is accepted as
sound, was treated with great generosity, seeing that under the German Currency Reform of 1948 he would have received only DM.
2,000 or about £165[85] at the then rate of exchange. Again the court
was concerned, not with a real problem of conversion, but with a
just estimate.

(c) For purposes of taxation it is often necessary to express in
terms of sterling the value of foreign property or income. Taxation is
concerned with value in terms of sterling and, therefore, it would
often be misleading if the value of the foreign property or income
were first ascertained in terms of the local currency and then translated into sterling at the spot rate. The real question is: what is the
sterling value of the foreign property or income in the United Kingdom? Thus, in connection with capital transfer tax, the 'value' is the
estimated price which the property would fetch if sold in the open
market at the time of transfer[86] and, one must add, in England. As
regards income tax, a similar rule should apply. The issue has not yet
arisen in this country,[87] but two American decisions must be noted.
In the leading case of *Eder* v. *Commissioner of Internal Revenue*[88]

payment in Berlin was not illegal, while in *Ralli*'s case no payment whatever could be made
at the *locus solutionis*. The fact that the company could not remit money to Berlin and that
the claimant could not accept it there was irrelevant. The only problem in the case was one
of the rate of exchange. However, the court's view that payment was to be made in Berlin
only is also open to grave doubt. Since the writer was professionally engaged in the case, he
is in a position to explain that the argument that the money was payable in Berlin only was
not pressed by the company before the appeal was opened in the Court of Appeal. Consequently, the evidence which was before the court was not directed to this question and the
court was unaware of the German practice (above, p. 66, n. 19) according to which the
place of payment shifted to London. See also above, p. 421.

[85] The second part of the decision is free from criticism. The observations by Cohn, 3
(1950) *International L.Q.* 99, 101, rest on a misunderstanding of the basis of the decision.

[86] s. 38 of the Finance Act, 1975.

[87] See Income and Corporation Taxes Act, 1970, s. 418. *Inland Revenue Commissioners*
v. *Paget*, [1938] 2 K.B. 25 and *Cross* v. *London and Provincial Trust Ltd.*, [1938] 1 K.B.
792 relate to different points. The latter decision is superseded by s. 417 of the Income and
Corporation Taxes Act, 1970.

[88] 138 F. (2d) 27 (1943); see Anonymous, 'Taxation of Foreign Currency Transactions',
61 (1952) *Yale L.J.* 1181.

the taxpayer was under a duty to treat as his own the income of an investment company in Colombia, which was 'blocked'. The commissioner valued the Colombian pesos at the spot rate for dollars. This method was rejected by the Circuit Court of Appeals which suggested that the true test was what 'economic satisfaction' the taxpayer could have received in Colombia, and that it could perhaps be measured by means of price indices. In a later case[89] the same court simply applied the 'commercial' rate, i.e. apparently the rate at which the Brazilian income in question could be disposed of in the United States of America.

(d) There are other cases in which it is necessary, in the interest of justice, to have regard to the purchasing power of money and, for this purpose, to adopt a standard of measurement other than the rate of exchange. Suppose a wife, resident in the United States and enjoying an income of $6,000, claims maintenance in England from the husband who has an income of £6,000. If one converts at the rate of exchange of $2.40 to the £ and assumes that the wife should receive one third of the joint income, she would be awarded $800 or about £333. But statistical investigation may establish that $4 have the purchasing power of £1. This 'rate', it is submitted, would as a matter of law be much more appropriate for purposes of comparison. It would provide the wife with $4,000 or about £1,660. Wherever a person's standard of living has to be ascertained or secured, comparisons of cost of living or purchasing power equivalents rather than the rate of exchange should be used, however difficult it may frequently be to procure the statistical evidence.[90, 91]

[89] *Edmond Weil Inc.* v. *Commissioner of Inland Revenue*, 150 F (2d) 950.

[90] Apart from *Eder*'s case (above, n. 88) the problem does not seem to have arisen anywhere except in the Federal Republic of Germany in connection with claims to maintenance by residents of the Soviet zone against residents of the Federal Republic. Although a vast judicial practice developed, no uniformity seems to have been achieved. Some, though by no means all, courts compared 'shopping baskets', i.e. the purchasing power: see, for example, Staudinger (Weber) ii, Part 1a, pp. 1121 sqq. or Lothar Hirschberg, *Das Interzonale Währungs- und Devisenrecht der Unterhaltsverbindlichkeiten* (1968), p. 32. The Federal Republic's legislation about compensation payable to victims of Nazi persecution provides that in certain cases the victim's non-German income shall be brought into account, not according to the rate of exchange, but on the basis of purchasing power equivalents. The problem thus created for German courts was one of economics and statistics, i.e. of evidence. Economists made significant contributions: see Bernhard Hartmann, *Die Kaufkraftparität von U.S.-Dollar und DM-West* (1959); Keller, RzW. 1959, 529; Hartmann, ibid., p. 534. Numerous decisions of the Federal Supreme Court discussed fundamental aspects of the process of comparison: 28 Oct. 1960, RzW. 1961, 121; 15 Feb. 1961, RzW. 1961, 319; 7 June 1961, RzW. 1961, 549, and others. In many decisions the Federal Supreme Court considered the 'rate' applicable to particular currencies: 7 Dec. 1958, RzW. 1959, 178 for U.S.A.; 24 Jan. 1962, RzW. 1962, 318 for Chile; 27 Apr. 1962 for Brazil; 9 May 1962, RzW. 1962, 510 for South Africa; 10 Oct. 1962, RzW. 1963, 120 for Uruguay; 13 Feb. 1963, RzW. 1963, 449 for Argentina. As to Israel, see the table for the years 1948–66 in RzW. 1966, 541. On the practice of the Federal Social Tribunal see the decisions 27 July 1961, BSGE 15, 5; 10 Feb.

[See p. 456 for n. 90 cont. and n. 91]

(*e*) If *A* has a blocked peseta account in Madrid which can only be used for specific purposes (e.g. the payment of Spanish taxes) and *B* agrees with *A* that he should use his Spanish account to pay taxes due from *B*, *A* cannot claim the sterling equivalent of the pesetas so spent, whether at the spot rate or the rate for legal tender. The transaction, properly analysed, consists in the sale to *B* of a blocked peseta account or part thereof. Hence *B* does not owe *A* a certain amount of pesetas, but a reasonable price for the credit sold to him, so that, as a rule, he will have to pay such price as *A* would have realized had he sold his credit on the London market.

(*f*) What is a specific price or value of an asset is sometimes erroneously described as representing a certain rate of exchange. Under a system of exchange control such as existed in the United Kingdom until 1979 certain foreign capital assets belonging or accruing to a resident of the United Kingdom could be sold to other residents at a 'premium', i.e. at a higher price than that available in the open market. The demand by residents for foreign investments was at times so strong that the premium reached more than 100 per cent and at a time when the rate of exchange was $2.40 to the pound the resident could obtain for $2.400, not £1,000, but more than £2,000. The foreign asset thus had an inherent quality, namely a 'premium value'. But the rate of exchange in the legal sense was the same throughout and, whatever popular language may have been used, it would not have been correct in law to speak of a premium rate. The asset had a higher value in the 'premium market' constituted by resident buyers and sellers. Nor was the premium 'a profit or gain derived from the sale' of the foreign asset, for even before the sale the value of the asset in the resident market included the potentiality of commanding a higher price (the 'premium') than in the general market.[92]

(*g*) Where a person is entitled to a share in or a proportion of a fund which is expressed in or consists of foreign currency, no problem of conversion will normally arise on distribution. The participants are entitled to distribution in specie or to the sterling proceeds of the fund. Sometimes it is not obvious that the claimant is entitled to a share in a fund rather than a fixed sum of money and that, accordingly, a problem of conversion does not arise. Thus, if under a German will *A* is entitled to a legacy of DM. 10,000 payable upon the death

1972, *BSGE* 34, 72; 16 Jan. 1970, *BSCE* 70, 241. The details of the German experience cannot be pursued here, but merit scholarly attention. See also Federal Supreme Court, 23 Apr. 1970, *RzW*. 1970, 405.

[91] The special character, in the eyes of monetary law, of obligations to pay maintenance, pensions, etc., had to be noted more than once: see above, pp. 102 sqq., 283 sqq.

[92] In this sense the decision of the Privy Council in *Holden* v. *Commissioner of Inland Revenue*, [1974] A.C. 868.

of a life tenant and the executor-trustee transfers the estate to England, it may be found that under the proper law, in this case German law, the legatee cannot claim the fixed sum of DM. 10,000 at all, but has a claim to a proportion of the estate, viz. to such sum of sterling as represents DM. 10,000 in the fund: if before the transfer from Germany there were DM. 50,000 available which yielded £1,000, the legatee is entitled to £200.[93]

# VI

The absence of a rate of exchange indicating the relation between two currencies may have a twofold character.

The discontinuance of quotations may be absolute, i.e. dealing in a particular currency may be suspended altogether; this usually occurs in the course of a revolution or a civil war when, at least temporarily, there is nowhere any market for the currency of the country concerned. Here the question will arise whether, in cases in which the date material to the conversion occurred during the period of suspension, the transaction should be liquidated on the basis of the rate prevailing prior to or immediately following upon the suspension. Probably the former should be adopted, because the law always presumes a given state of affairs to continue so long as it is not proved to be changed. Thus in an American case[94] it became necessary to determine the market value of cotton at Barcelona on 6 October 1936 in terms of U.S. dollars. On 21 September the rate was $0.1365 to the peseta. On account of the Spanish Civil War no exchange rates were available from 22 September to 13 November 1936, when the value of the peseta was considerably depreciated. The court held that it must be taken that on 6 October the cotton was worth the same in terms of dollars as on 21 September.[95, 96]

The discontinuance of quotation is relative if there exists a rate of exchange as between a particular currency and some but not all others. Thus in war-time, while the currency of a belligerent is quoted in allied and neutral countries, no rate exists as between the currencies

---

[93] On the nature of a legacy under German law see above, p. 104, n. 115.

[94] *Pape Williams & Co.* v. *Home Insurance Co.*, 139 F. (2d) 131 and [1944] A.M.C. 51.

[95] See also *Melzer* v. *Zimmermann*, 118 Misc. Rep. 407, 194 N.Y.S. 222 (1922), affirmed without opinion 198 N.Y.S. 932 (1923), and *Birge-Forbes Co.* v. *Heye* (1920), 251 U.S. 317, at p. 325.

[96] In the absence of a regular rate of exchange between the Federal Republic of Germany and the Soviet Zone the Federal Supreme Court in one case observed that the conversion had to be effected according to purchasing power equivalents: 10 July 1954, *BGHZ.* 14, 212. But it seems that the large majority of later decisions simply adopted a rate of 1:1. The German material on the point is enormous. See also Federal Supreme Court, 13 Feb. 1963, *RzW.* 1963, 449.

of hostile countries. The difficult problems to which this situation gives rise are of great practical significance, yet in neither of the two last wars have they been authoritatively answered.

If a rate for the conversion of hostile currencies has to be found with reference to a date during war, the value of the enemy currency is sometimes prescribed by law. Thus under Art. 1 (iv) (d) of the Trading with the Enemy (Custodian) Order, 1939, the Treasury could determine the rate appropriate for payments to the Custodian of Enemy Property.[97] Apart from such provisions there are only three possibilities—should the creditor who is entitled to reichsmark in January 1945 in London be paid at the pre-war rate or at the first official post-war rate[98] or should the reichsmark be converted into Swiss francs and the Swiss francs into sterling? The first and second solutions are arbitrary, because they exclude any real valuation at the material date. The rates quoted in neutral countries are probably much fairer. Conversion 'through a neutral country' is supported by the case of *Pollard* v. *Herries*,[99] from which it may be deduced that the court would be inclined to have resort to 'the indirect course of exchange'; by the practice of the Mixed Arbitral Tribunals;[100] and by an analogy to be derived from the law relating to the sale of goods: where for the purpose of assessing damages it is necessary to ascertain the market value of goods at the place of delivery, but there is no market available at that place, the market value at the nearest available place will usually constitute the measure of damages.[101]

In no event, however, should the interposition of a market in a neutral country lead to the indirect recognition of such enemy legislation as a belligerent country would not directly recognize. If, for example, after the invasion of Holland in 1940 the Germans had fixed the Dutch guilder at a certain rate to which the Swiss quotations would give expression, it would be impossible to convert guilders into sterling on the basis of these Swiss rates. In such a case, therefore, an English court would have to apply other standards of

[97] See *Bank Mizrahi Ltd.* v. *The Chief Execution Officer Tel Aviv*, Palestine Law Reports 1943, 364: in the absence of any other rate the rate fixed by the Custodian of Enemy Property was applied for the conversion of a debt expressed in French francs, while France was enemy-occupied territory.

[98] This is the solution favoured by judicial practice in the United States: *Sutherland* v. *Mayer*, 271 U.S. 272 (1926); *International Silk Guild* v. *Rogers*, 262 F. 2d 219 (1958); *Aratani* v. *Kennedy*, 317 F. 2d 161 (1963). These cases only apply where payment is to be in the United States. Cf. Cohn, 50 (1962), *Geo. L.J.* 513.

[99] (1803), 3 B. & P. 335.

[100] Anglo-German Mixed Arbitral Tribunal in M.A.T. iv (1925), 261 (*Catty* v. *German Government*) and vi (1927), 17 (*Strauss* v. *German Government*).

[101] *Rodocanachi* v. *Milburn* (1886), 18 Q.B. 67, 76 *per* Lord Esher; *The Arpad*, [1934] P. 189 (C.A.) and other cases referred to by Halsbury (Simonds), xxxiv. 153. On the problem discussed in the text see Nussbaum, pp. 336, 337.

valuation, such as the rate between sterling and the Dutch Colonial guilder, or the rate prescribed by the Custodian of Enemy Property or the pre-war rate, or the rate usually applied by the British Government in its dealings with the Allied country in question.

# PART IV

# THE PUBLIC INTERNATIONAL LAW OF MONEY

# INTRODUCTION

THE preceding Parts of this book have shown that to some extent the municipal law of money is directly derived from public international law. The connection has been established mainly by the Articles of Agreement of the International Monetary Fund, for they determine the public policy of more than a hundred States in regard to exchange restrictions introduced by member States[1] and they contain a specific provision which deals with the enforceability of certain contracts in member States.[2]

These are certainly important rules which international law has grafted upon the municipal law of money. Yet their scope is relatively limited and modest. It is the whole field of monetary law that is, or ought to be, a matter for international concern. There cannot be any doubt that its claim to treatment on an international level is as strong as and probably stronger than that of the law of the sale of goods or the law of the air or taxation. The reason for the absence of a comprehensive international law of money lies not only in the grave practical difficulties which stem from political and economic causes as well as from the fact that in many respects a common standard is lacking, but is also to be found in the widespread impression that the existing body of international law has failed to develop any rules of conduct in monetary affairs. That impression is wrong, and the more quickly and firmly it is dispelled the nearer will be the day when it will become possible to contemplate a Monetary Convention which will regulate and unify a branch of the law that is in urgent need of and, notwithstanding all differences of approach, readily permits international regulation and unification.

The existence of what may be termed an international law of money has for some time been obvious. Already before the end of the Second World War a number of scholars had given their attention to it.[3] The second edition of this book which, in these matters,

---

[1] Above, p. 375.  [2] Above, p. 372.

[3] Nolde, 'La monnaie en droit international public', *Rec.* 27 (1929), 247; Griziotti, 'L'évolution monétaire dans le monde depuis la guerre de 1914', *Rec.* 49 (1934), 7; Gutzwiller, *Der Geltungsbereich der Währungsvorschriften* (1940), pp. 78–92; Nussbaum, pp. 502 sqq. (based on an illuminating article which appeared in *American Journal of International Law*, 38 (1944), 242).

was in turn based on an article of 1949,[4] and a course of lectures given in 1959 at the Academy of International Law at The Hague,[5] provided opportunities for a systematic review of the peculiarly legal problem which has to be faced and reaches far beyond the purely descriptive treatment that characterizes certain earlier and even some modern writings on the subject. That problem lies in the elucidation and the development of the rules of a substantive international law of money. Since 1959 the discussion has been much enriched not only by contributions to general works on international law,[6] but also by two recent monographs[7] and, in so far as the International Monetary Fund is concerned, by numerous publications which were written by past and present members of its Legal Department, particularly its former General Counsel, Sir Joseph Gold, and to which all students of the subject are indebted.

The following Chapters XVII and XVIII will be devoted to customary international law. They will treat, respectively, the State's rights over its own currency, or, in other words, State sovereignty over money, its scope and limitation, and the State's duties towards the currencies of other States, that is to say, the right of protection which members of the family of nations enjoy in respect of their currency systems under general international law. The next two chapters will discuss monetary international law as derived from treaties. Chapter XIX contains a short review of relevant international structures which create the multilateral and bilateral framework for the substantive law contained in treaties and propounded in Chapter XX. Finally, Chapter XXI is concerned with the numerous and important questions of monetary law which arise from contractual as well as tortious inter-State obligations.

[4] *British Year Book of International Law*, 1949, 259.

[5] *Rec.* 96 (1959, i), 1. Many, but by no means all parts of these lectures have been incorporated into the present edition.

[6] Dahm, *Völkerrecht*, ii (1961), pp. 608 sqq.; O'Connell, *International Law*, ii (1970), pp. 1011 sqq. See also Giuliano, *Rec.* 124 (1968, ii), 557.

[7] D. Carreau, *Souveraineté et Coopération Monétaire Internationale* (Paris, 1970) and M. R. Shuster, *The Public International Law of Money* (1973). See also D. Carreau, *Le Système Monétaire International, Aspects Juridiques* (Paris, 1972), Focsaneanu, 'Droit International Public Monétaire', in *Juris-Classeur Droit International*, Fasc. 136 (1980); Silard, 'Money and Foreign Exchange' in *Encyclopedia of Comparative Law*, Vol. xvii, Chapter 20.

# XVII

# Monetary Sovereignty, its Scope and its Limitation

I. The principle of monetary sovereignty and some of its effects in the event of (1) deprecia-tion; (2) devaluation; (3) failure to revalorize; (4) exchange control. II. Monetary sovereignty and the international character of legal disputes. III. Monetary legislation as confiscation. IV. Monetary legislation in disregard of fair and equitable treatment of aliens.

## I

MONEY is an institution of municipal law. It is the product of the *jus cudendae monetae* belonging to the supreme power in every state.[1]

The State's undeniable sovereignty over its currency is tradition-ally recognized by public international law; to the power granted by municipal law there corresponds an international right to the exercise of which other States cannot, as a rule, object.[2] As the Permanent Court of International Justice has said,[3] 'it is indeed a generally accepted principle that a state is entitled to regulate its own cur-rency'. Money, like tariffs or taxation or the admission of aliens, is one of those matters which prima facie must be considered as falling essentially within the domestic jurisdiction of States (Art. 2 (7) of the Charter of the United Nations).

It follows that, subject to such exceptions as customary inter-national law[4] or treaties[5] have grafted upon the rule, the municipal legislator is free to define the currency of his country, to decide whether or no it should be based on gold, to depreciate or appreciate its value, to permit or abolish gold clauses, to impose exchange control or to take other measures affecting monetary relations. Customary international law does not normally fetter the municipal legislator's discretion in these matters or characterize his measures as an international wrong for which he could be held responsible, just as it leaves him the freedom to decide whether he wishes to

---

[1] Above, p. 14.

[2] This passage was approved by the Foreign Claims Settlement Commission of the United States in *Re Boyle*, Annual Report of the Commission for 1968, p. 81.

[3] *Serbian and Brazilian Loan* case: Publications of the Court, Series A, Nos. 20–1, at p. 44.  [4] See below, p. 472.  [5] See below, p. 510.

introduce a particular type of tax and whether he levies tax at a particular rate. And where international relations arise, customary international law allows each State to devise its own system of private international law and thus to determine the extent to which the monetary laws of foreign States are applicable within its boundaries. Thus the legislator or the judiciary of a particular State may take the view that the question of the revalorization of depreciated debts should be subject to the *lex monetae*, while in another State the same question may be subject to the proper law of the obligation, the *lex causae*. Customary international law contains no rule which would prescribe the application of the one or the other solution.[6]

The principle of monetary sovereignty, it is true, has not always been unquestioned. On many occasions ideas have been expressed which would seem to aim at a qualification of the State's right to determine its monetary policy at its discretion. In 1688 Holt C.J. refused to give effect to the depreciation of the Portuguese currency because 'the King of Portugal may not alter the property of a subject of England'.[7] The same idea is hinted at in the remarkable Note which in 1800 John Marshall, then Secretary of State and shortly afterwards to become Chief Justice of the Supreme Court of the United States, sent to the American Minister to Spain for transmission to the Spanish Government. The United States Government protested against the debasement of the Spanish currency on the ground that 'between discharging a debt by paying one-half of its nominal amount, and the whole of its nominal amount possessing only one-half of its real value, there is no difference'. There was no question of a sovereign nation's absolute right on its own territory. 'But coextensive and coeval with it is the privilege of a foreign friendly nation to complain of, and remonstrate against such acts of sovereignty as are injurious to its citizens or subjects.'[8] Even in

---

[6] Nor was the unique French doctrine of the *paiement international* (on which see above, pp. 163, 196, 294) a rule of international law. It would have been unnecessary to make this obvious point had it not led to some confusion in the arguments of those who represented France in the *Case of Certain Norwegian Loans*, I.C.J. Reports, 1957, 9. Beginning with her *Mémoire* France emphasized the 'caractère international' of the Norwegian loans and relied heavily on the practice developed by French courts: Pleadings i. 29 sqq.; ii. 29 sqq. The underlying misunderstanding was forcibly, repeatedly, and very rightly pointed out by Norway: Pleadings i. 127 sqq., 286 sqq., 430 sqq., particularly at p. 431, 467 sqq. There is no privilege or immunity that international law necessarily grants to loans on the ground of their international character. In fact France had no cause of action arising under public international law: see Mann, *Rec.* 96 (1959, i), pp. 80–2, and Carreau, pp. 95–7, 103.

[7] Above, p. 270.

[8] Moore, *A Digest of International Law* (1906), vi. 754; on another case, the facts of which are not quite clear, see ibid., p. 729.

modern times, in France and the countries influenced by her legal teaching, the curious and in reality almost meaningless statement can be found that 'les lois monétaires sont strictement territoriales'.[9] Usually the consequences which one would expect to flow from such a maxim are not being drawn, but the Supreme Court of Syria went so far as actually to hold that a contract for the payment of a sum of 'francs' made between the Syrian Government and an Egyptian firm was subject to an international rule by which legal tender legislation, enacted after the date of the contract, applied only internally and did not affect contracts with a foreigner.[10]

There cannot be any doubt, however, that such attempts to limit the international recognition of monetary changes must today be considered as obsolete and extravagant, and that the principle as stated above is firmly established by precedent and good sense.

1. As regards the international effects of (internal) monetary depreciation, we know that all monetary obligations, whether they are expressed in domestic or in foreign currency, are subject to nominalism:[11] the promise to pay 10,000 French francs is satisfied by the payment of whatever are declared to be 10,000 French francs by French law. This rule of municipal law is for all practical purposes universally accepted. In order to be consistent with it, public international law must follow suit; if under all relevant municipal systems effect is given to the French law, France cannot be said to violate any international duty by the exercise of her sovereign powers over her currency. It is therefore only natural to find that all available modern authorities proclaim the complete harmony between international and municipal law on this point by recognizing a State's right to allow its currency to depreciate. Thus the American-British Claims Commission, established under the Treaty of 5 May 1871, decided in *Adam*'s case that, where a British subject held bonds issued by an American Railway Company and suffered a loss from the issue of greenbacks and the consequent depreciation of the dollar, 'the matters alleged in the memorial do not constitute the basis of any valid claim'.[12] Similarly, the Upper Silesian Arbitral Tribunal was concerned with the question whether the holder of a German bank note, issued before the First

[9] See above, pp. 267, 273, 300, 402.
[10] Decision of 30 Dec. 1931: *Annual Digest*, 1931–2, Case No. 151. See also Dupuis, *Rec.* 32 (1930, ii) 164, according to whom 'la spoliation des créanciers par une altération du système monétaire est une injustice dont un État ne peut faire porter le poids aux créanciers étrangers sans manquer au respect des droits acquis et donc à l'obligation de respect mutuel des États'.
[11] Above, p. 267.
[12] Moore, *International Arbitrations* (1898), iii. 3066.

World War, had a vested right within the meaning of the Polish-German Convention of 1922[13] to obtain payment in gold; the Tribunal had no difficulty in giving a negative answer.[14] In a case which came before the former Supreme Court of Germany, the Italian plaintiff whose German debtor had repaid a loan in depreciated German marks claimed to be entitled to payment on a gold basis. He alleged the existence of a rule of public international law to the effect that loans made by foreigners were invariably repayable according to their gold value. Referring to the practice in England and other countries the court summarily disposed of so absurd a contention.[15]

2. It is inherent in the preceding observations that, as a rule, a State is within its rights to bring about the (external) devaluation of its currency.

Once again this follows from the universal acceptance of nominalism[16] and was stated with great precision by the Government of Canada:[17]

Un principe bien établi en droit international exhonore les gouvernements de toute responsabilité pour les pertes dues à une dévaluation de leurs devises, pourvu que cette dévaluation s'accomplisse sans discrimination.

The rule seems to have been followed by the European Commission of Human Rights[18] and was repeatedly affirmed by the Foreign Claims Settlement Commission of the United States[19] as well as the French Foreign Claims Commissions.[20] A few treaties[21] and academic

---

[13] Art. 4, para. 2 (3).

[14] *Muller* v. *Germany* (*Recueil des décisions des tribunaux arbitraux mixtes*, 2 (1923), 32). In *Quella* v. *Germany* the Tribunal held that exchange restrictions did not constitute an encroachment upon vested rights within the meaning of Art. 4, para. 2 (3), because by their nature they were only temporary emergency measures (ibid. 6 (1927), 164).

[15] 6 June 1928, *RGZ*. 121, 203, and *Annual Digest*, 1927–8, Case No. 230.

[16] See above, p. 267.

[17] Statement of 7 Dec. 1966, reported by Gottlieb, *Canadian Yearbook of International Law*, 1967, 268.

[18] See Fawcett, *Application of the European Convention on Human Rights* (1969), p. 350. Fawcett, *Rec.* 123 (1968, i) 246 agrees with the text.

[19] *Claim of Tabar*, Int. L.R. 1953, 211. A further fundamental decision is *Claim of Zuk*, Int. L.R. 1958, ii. 284, which emphasizes an exception in case 'a State pursues a deliberate course of injuring or discriminating against foreigners', and which was followed in numerous subsequent cases such as *Claim of Mascotte*, ibid., p. 275; *Claim of Bondareff*, ibid., p. 286; *Claim of Malan*, ibid., p. 290; *Claim of Chobady*, ibid., p. 292; *Claim of Mureson*, ibid., p. 294; *Claim of Endreny*, ibid., p. 278. The decisions are here mentioned in chronological order. See also the 1961 Harvard Draft Convention on International Responsibility, Art. 10, para. 5, on which see Sohn and Baxter, *American Journal of International Law*, 1961, 554, 562.

[20] B. H. Weston, *International Claims: Post-war French Practice* (1971), p. 135.

[21] For an exception see the German-Swiss Mortgage Treaties of 6 Dec. 1920 and 25 Mar. 1923 (*Nouveau Recueil général des traités*, 3rd ser., 15, pp. 812 and 817), on which

writers' opinions[22] to the opposite effect do not prejudice the firmness of the rule or the soundness of its foundation.

3. Next it is within a State's discretion to decide whether or not it should legislate with a view to revalorizing debts which have arisen on the level of private law[23] and which, as a result of the depreciation of the State's currency, have become worthless or at least considerably reduced in intrinsic value.

There is no evidence of any general principle of law recognized by civilized nations, according to which revalorization has to be provided for. The number of countries which have taken care of the effects of the depreciation of currency by providing for revalorization is small.[24] The number of countries which have taken exception to the absence of revalorization in foreign countries whose currencies have depreciated is even smaller; even the German Supreme Court which can fairly be described as the foremost protagonist of the fundamental equities of revalorization refused to apply *ordre public* in favour of a German national who was entitled to the payment of a debt expressed in old mark currency under a contract governed by the law of Czechoslovakia, which did not allow revalorization.[25] And although after the end of the Japanese occupation several States in South East Asia introduced legislation to revalorize debts which had been discharged by worthless Japanese military notes,[26] the Philippines' failure to do so was not, as the Supreme Court of the Philippines rightly held,[27] open to criticism on legal grounds and, contrary to the contentions of Charles Cheney Hyde,[28] did not

see Nussbaum, p. 444. These were concluded in quite unusual circumstances and are of no permanent interest. Nor is the general principle in any way affected by the provisions in the Peace Treaties of 1920, according to which debts due to nationals of victorious nations were payable at the pre-war rate of exchange or in gold (Art. 296 (4) (d) of the Treaty of Versailles; Art. 248 of the Treaty of St. Germain; Art. 176 of the Treaty of Neuilly, and Art. 231 of the Treaty of Trianon). No similar provision is contained in the Paris Peace Treaties of 1947. The Financial Agreement between the United Kingdom and Italy made in Rome on 17 Apr. 1947 in pursuance of Art. 79 of the Treaty of Peace with Italy (Cmd. 7118) provides by Clause 14 that the rate of exchange for the payment of lire debts 'will be that current when the debt became due'.

[22] Borchard, *State Insolvency and Foreign Bondholders*, i (1951), 137, suggests that monetary devaluation arising from 'a deliberate act on the part of the debtor government' may be a ground for international responsibility even in the absence of discrimination against foreign nationals. Though Wortley, *Expropriation in Public International Law* (1959), p. 107, expresses approval, there is no justification for this view.

[23] Debts which arise on the footing of public international law are dealt with below, p. 541.          [24] Above, pp. 102 sqq.

[25] 14 Dec. 1927, *RGZ.* 119, 259; see also 25 June 1926, *RGZ.* 114, 171, a very special case.          [26] Below, p. 491

[27] *Gibbs* v. *Rodriguez*, Int. L.R. 1951, 661, following and developing *Haw Pia* v. *China Banking Corporation*, Int. L.R. 1951, 642 on which see below, p. 488, n. 27.

[28] *Philippine Law Journal*, 24 (1949), 141. In *Dawsons Bank* v. *Ko Sin Sein*, Int. L.R. 36, 497, the Chief Court of Burma held in 1963 that 'it would virtually be a confiscation

by any means constitute 'international illegal conduct upon the part of the Philippine Government which is productive of a solid claim for compensation in behalf of alien nationals or creditors who suffered loss as a direct consequence of such decision'.

It is true that a different result may be required in certain cases which a widespread practice of States treats in a privileged manner. This, as has been seen,[29] occurs in the case of pensions. It is, accordingly, a remarkable and welcome precedent that, when the value of pensions expressed in Argentine pesos and due to British pensioners of Argentine companies was, as a result of the devaluation of the Argentine pesos in 1955, cut by some 60 per cent, the British Government made representations asking for 'an equitable solution' and that the Argentine Government in substance acceded to them.[30] On the other hand, no exception applies to purely financial claims such as were the subject-matter of the correspondence between the British and French Governments in regard to the rights of British holders of *rentes* which the French Government had issued in England between 1915 and 1918.[31] These issues, denominated in terms of francs, resulted in cash subscriptions of approximately £50 m., but owing to the depreciation of the france by 1930 their capital value was in the neighbourhood of £13½ m. only. The British Government pointed to the special circumstances[32] in which the bonds were issued and to the fact that the French Government demanded from the Goverments indebted to it payment in gold francs, and suggested 'an equitable measure of compensation' to the British holders of the *rentes*. As the French reply emphasized, the British Government did not at first try to impugn the legal correctness of the French attitude, but in a subsequent communication the British Government suggested submission of the dispute to an arbitrator 'to decide the equitable and just basis upon which, having regard to all circumstances affecting the case and to international custom' payment should be made. In their final answer the French said that the 'request for an arbitration which aims at increasing, on grounds of equity, the amount which a country is bound to pay in law, constitutes a real innovation'. They added that 'the determination both of the financial policy of a State, so long as that policy is not disputed on grounds of law, and of any measures of equity which it may be considered proper to take in

on the part of the Japanese military authorities to declare as extinguished debts which had been repaid in Japanese military notes which became practically worthless toward the end of their occupation'. But nothing in the decision suggests confiscation by Burma.

[29] Above, p. 456, n. 91.
[30] Hansard, vol. 552, 72 (7 May 1956), also E. Lauterpacht, *I.C.L.Q.* v (1956), 426.
[31] Cmd. 3779.                    [32] See H. Samuel, *The French Default* (1930).

connection with that policy, is entirely a matter for the State in question, i.e. in the present case, for France'. The French Government concluded that their refusal to agree to the British proposal was dictated 'by the legitimate reluctance to call into question, when not obliged by any grounds of law or of equity to do so, a reform which has assured monetary stability in France'. There the matter rested. The significance of the correspondence lies in the fact that the British Government did not rely on any rule of law or equity in support of its case; if an arbitrator had been appointed to decide upon a delictual claim for damages, no such rule, nor any 'international custom', would have guided him; his task would have been an impossible one.[33] The British Government may perhaps be assumed to have accepted this in the end.

4. While it does not seem ever to have been doubted that, in principle, a State is entitled to abrogate gold or similar protective clauses,[34] there is much authority in support of the further right to introduce exchange control with all its incidental ramifications.[35]

The British Government,[36] the Government of Canada,[37] and, since 1932, the Government of the United States[38] have frequently so stated. Thus Canada 'recognizes the right of each country to control its foreign exchange resources, and restrictions of this nature, so long as they are not discriminating against Canadian citizens, cannot give rise to a claim'.[39] The Foreign Claims Settlement Commission of the United States has propounded the same principle on numerous occasions,[40] and so have International Claims Commissions.[41] It also

---

[33] The opinion which was rendered by Mr. Nils von Steyern as *amiable compositeur* on the 4 per cent Japanese Bonds of 1910 and which is referred to above, p. 283, n. 72 (see also *Rec.* 96 (1959, i), p. 87, n. 4) should not in any way be treated as a precedent.

[34] But see Borchard, *State Insolvency and Foreign Bondholders*, i (1951), 138.

[35] In the same sense Giuliano, *La Cooperazione degli Stati e il commercio internazionale* (3rd ed., 1972), 25, 26 who, however, seems to be a little too absolute in that he does not mention exceptions.

[36] See, for instance, Hansard, House of Commons, 14 May 1956, vol. 552, col. 1633, among numerous other statements to the same effect.

[37] See the two statements reproduced by Gottlieb, 'Canadian Practice in International Law' 1964, in *Canadian Yearbook of International Law*, 1965, 328. The second of these statements, presently to be quoted in the text, also condemns the case where the State is guilty of 'arbitrary intervention'.

[38] Hackworth, ii, pp. 68–70; Hyde, *International Law*, i (1945), 690–2. For a more recent statement by the Department of State (1 Mar. 1961) see *American Journal of International Law*, 1965, 165, which emphasizes that 'the right to regulate foreign exchange does not, however, include the right to discriminate against nationals of a particular country, or to deprive an owner of an account of all rights of ownership'. See also the War Claims Commission's Report set forth in Whiteman, viii. 981.          [39] See above n. 37.

[40] The basic decision is *Claim of Tabar*, Int. L.R. 1953, 242. For later decisions see the following footnotes.

[41] *Malamatinis* v. *Turkey*, in Nielsen, *American-Turkish Claims Settlement* (1937), p. 603, at pp. 611, 612; and see the references by Whiteman, viii. 985.

underlies those numerous treaties which, while accepting it, have attempted to alleviate its effects.[42] Accordingly, blocking or 'freezing' measures[43] are no less permitted than provisions requiring the surrender of foreign currency,[44] or export restrictions,[45] or modifications of the contractual terms.[46]

As a result of developments in the field of treaty law it is, however, possible that customary international law now recognizes it as illegal to restrict transfers for current transactions, or transfers of capital in those cases in which capital has been introduced into a State's economy with its approval and on terms providing for the retransfer of the capital, profits, and the compensation if any.[47]


# II

The fact that the regulation of its currency falls within the State's sovereign jurisdiction does not mean that it is withdrawn from any control by international law. Monetary laws are fully capable of giving rise to legal disputes concerning international law within the meaning of Art. 36 (2) of the Statute of the International Court of Justice.

It would not be necessary to state so platitudinous a proposition had the failure to appreciate it not been at the bottom of one of the arguments which Norway presented to the International Court of Justice in the *Case of Certain Norwegian Loans*.[48] Before the First World War both the State of Norway and certain Norwegian undertakings took up loans in various European centres, in respect of which bearer bonds were issued. All these bonds were alleged to contain a gold clause. In 1923 Norway abolished the gold clause.[49] French bondholders denied the international validity of this law and espousing their case France in 1955 instituted proceedings

---

[42] Below, p. 527.

[43] *Claim of Chobady*, Int. L.R. 1958, ii, p. 292; *Claim of Mureson*, ibid., p. 294; *Claim of Evanoff*, ibid., p. 301. In the same sense the practice of the French Foreign Claims Commissions as reported by Weston (above, p. 468, n. 20), p. 131. And see above, p. 468, n. 19.

[44] *Arbitral Commission on Property Rights and Interests in Germany*, Collection of Decisions, iv, p. 173 (*Maeyer v. Federal Republic*).

[45] See the two decisions mentioned by Whiteman, viii. 988, 989.

[46] *Claim of Kuhn*, decided by the American-Mexican Claims Commission (1948) and mentioned by Whiteman, viii. 990. And see in *Re Helbert Wagg & Co. Ltd.*, [1956] Ch. 323 and *Kahler v. Midland Bank*, [1950] A.C. 24.

[47] Below, p. 528. And see *Report of the International Law Association's 54th Conference at The Hague* (1970), p. 550 on the proposed Article 13 and the discussion relating thereto.      [48] I.C.J. Reports, 1957, 9.

[49] I.C.J. Reports, 1957, p. 19 for the text. The Norwegian Supreme Court later considered the statute and its effect in the decision referred to above, p. 141, n. 21.

in the World Court. Norway pleaded to the jurisdiction[50] and in the end the court upheld her argument. One of her preliminary objections was to the effect that the jurisdiction of the court was confined to legal disputes concerning international law, but that the case submitted by France required the court 'de se prononcer sur des questions de droit interne et non de droit international'.[51] Such reasoning was clearly induced by serious gaps in the French argument.[52] Nevertheless there should be no doubt that France was justified in submitting that 'à partir du moment où les deux États ont officiellement discuté l'étendue de l'obligation du débiteur et se sont définitivement opposés, un différend international existait entre eux',[53] for, as Judge Sir Hersch Lauterpacht said in his Separate Opinion,[54] 'national legislation—including currency legislation—may be contrary, in its intention or effects, to the international obligations of the State. The question of conformity of national legislation with international law is a matter of international law. The notion that if a matter is governed by national law it is for that reason at the same time outside the sphere of international law is both novel and, if accepted, subversive of international law'. It is, therefore, now possible to conclude that, although monetary legislation is of necessity domestic legislation, as soon as its international effects are challenged by a foreign State, such State raises a legal dispute concerning international law, so that the jurisdiction of the International Court under Art. 36 (2) cannot be questioned.

## III

What, then, are the causes of action upon which the attack against a State's monetary legislation may be based?

The first cause of action arises from the rule, for present purposes assumed to be established, that it is contrary to international law to confiscate or take the property of an alien without payment of compensation or, perhaps, to deprive an alien of his property.

[50] One cannot help sharing Judge Read's regret (p. 83) that contrary to her traditional adherence to the ideals of justice and the pacific settlement of disputes Norway took more than one 'highly technical argument designed for the sole purpose of preventing justice from being done'. Those who regard it as likely that Norway would have succeeded on the merits will be particularly saddened by the technicalities which were raised and which deprived the court of the opportunity of clarifying an important branch of the law.

[51] Pleadings, i. 129, 286 sqq., 462 sqq. The Norwegian argument could have been supported by a reference to Nussbaum, p. 428.

[52] See Rec. 96 (1959, i) 81, 82. It was at a very late stage that France made some (insufficient) submissions on her cause of action under public international law.

[53] Pleadings, i. 172; similarly, pp. 176 and 384.

[54] p. 37; see also Judge Read at p. 87.

It is submitted, however, that in view of the clear analogy of private law[55] this principle is not normally encroached upon by monetary legislation. A legislator who reduces rates of interest or renders agreements invalid or incapable of being performed, or prohibits exports, or renders performance more expensive by the imposition of taxes or tariffs does not take property. Nor does he take property if he depreciates currency, or prohibits payment in foreign currency, or abrogates gold clauses. Expectations relating to the continuing intrinsic value of a currency, or of contractual terms such as the gold clause are, like favourable business conditions and goodwill, 'transient circumstances, subject to changes',[56] and suffer from the 'congenital infirmity'[57] that they may be changed by the competent legislator. They are not property, their change is not deprivation.[58]

Yet there are certain features of monetary legislation which are so extreme that they come within the conception of confiscation[59] in the traditional sense of the term.[60]

Perhaps the clearest case is a Cuban law of 1961 which, among other unusual provisions, declared all Cuban currency situate outside Cuba to be null and void. The Foreign Claims Settlement Commission of the United States rightly held that the owner had been deprived of his property, and Cuba was enriched by being relieved of a corresponding debt.[61] In another case the Romanian legatee

[55] See, for instance, above, p. 96, n. 75 and *passim*.

[56] *Case of Oscar Chinn*, Permanent Court of International Justice, Series A/B, No. 63 (1934), at p. 88.

[57] *Norman v. Baltimore & Ohio Railroad Company*, 294 U.S. 240 (1934), at p. 308 *per* Chief Justice Hughes.

[58] The passage in the text was approved by the majority of the Court of Appeals of New York in *French* v. *Banco Nacional de Cuba*, 23 N.Y. 2d 46 (1968), at p. 55 *per* Chief Judge Fuld. See also C. C. Hyde, *International Law*, i. 690-2. It should be noted, however, that in *Sardino* v. *Federal Reserve Bank of New York*, 361 F. 2d (1966), at p. 111 the Court of Appeals (Second Circuit) held that United States regulation freezing the New York property of a Cuban resident in Cuba except for certain limited purposes constituted deprivation within the meaning of the due-process clause: 'we find it hard to say there is no deprivation when a man is prevented both from obtaining his property and from realizing any benefit from it for a period of indefinite duration which may outrun his life'. The case does not seem to have been quoted in *French*'s case. In the sense of the text see also the Foreign Claims Commission of the United States in *Re Furst*, Int. L.R. 42, 153, and Carreau, pp. 115-19.

[59] If the international rule condemns deprivation rather than confiscation, then the monetary measures inconsistent with international law may be more numerous.

[60] See Fawcett, *Rec.* 123 (1968, i) 247. It may be that on full analysis international law would appear in truth to recognize a single head of illegality, for the taking of the property of aliens is illegal only if uncompensated, and such a taking may be said to be so excessive a measure as to constitute a misuse of power. The justification of this approach exceeds the scope of the present study which will have to adhere to traditional methods and treat the two causes of action as distinct: see the present section III, and section IV, below, p. 475.                    [61] *Claim of Boyle*, above, p. 465, n. 2.

under a New York will would have received in Romania about 12 lei to the dollar (or about twice the rate for commercial transactions), while in New York the rate was 32 lei to the dollar. The Supreme Court of New York held the rate of 12 lei to be confiscatory.[62] *In re Helbert Wagg & Co. Ltd.*[63] German exchange control laws allowed a German debtor to discharge his sterling debt due to an English creditor by paying the equivalent amount of German currency to a German Government Agency for the creditor's account. Upjohn J. (as he then was) treated this as a confiscation which, however, he did not hold to be contrary to either public international law or English public policy. If the premiss of confiscation is right (which, it is submitted, it is not),[64] then it is very likely that, as a matter of international law, the learned Judge's conclusion cannot easily be supported.[65] An even more difficult case is *French* v. *Banco Nacional de Cuba.*[66] In June 1959, six months after the inception of the Castro regime, the plaintiff acquired certain dollar certificates issued by the defendant and the Cuban Government's Currency Stabilization Fund, and providing for payment by a cheque on New York. In July 1959 the Cuban Government issued a decree suspending redemption of the certificates in order to stop the outflow of foreign currency. In 1968 the majority of the Court of Appeals of New York held that this was a breach of contract, not a taking of property. According to the minority the decree was 'in line with Cuba's consistent quest to acquire the last remnants of foreign private capital in the country': by rescinding the certificate the Cuban Government 'has simply added to its currency resources by this ploy' and added to the 'great number of regulations enforced to implement the Cuban Government's policy of expropriating the property of foreigners'.[67] It is this particular point which may be a distinguishing feature of great weight.

## IV

As appears from the discussion of the principle of monetary

---

[62] *In re Greenberg's Estate*, 260 N.Y.S. 2d 818 (1965), also 38 *International L.R.* 142— a very doubtful case. The question was whether the legatee would have 'the benefit or use or control' of the money. It is difficult to see why the answer was in the negative, seeing that the New York executor could have bought lei at 32 to the dollar and sent a lei cheque for the resulting amount to Romania.

[63] [1956] Ch. 322 on which see above, p. 406 with references.

[64] The German legislation provided for a method of discharge and related to contractual rather than property rights.

[65] If property was taken without compensation, the German legislation clearly offended against the international rule.

[66] 23 N.Y. 2d 46 (1968). See also *Nielsen* v. *Treasury*, 424 F 2d 833 (1970).

[67] pp. 88, 93.

sovereignty and its emanations,[68] there are numerous and varied pronouncements which, while affirming the rule, have also qualified it so as to exclude its application in the event of the monetary legislation discriminating against foreign nationals,[69] or constituting 'arbitrary intervention',[70] or assuming 'an arbitrary or offensive character'.[71] On other occasions the exception has been founded on the theory of denial of justice.[72] Then, again, it has been the doctrine of abuse of rights that has been invoked, viz. the idea of the legislation lacking 'a reasonable relation to a legitimate end', or being operated in a manner or for purposes repugnant to its accepted function.[73] Here as elsewhere the formulation of a comprehensive yet precise principle is a difficult process.[74] Here as elsewhere the descriptions of the international wrong differ. But it is submitted (and for present purposes it is assumed) that, whether one speaks of unjustifiable discrimination, deliberate injury, arbitrariness, denial of justice *lato sensu* or abuse of rights, the essence of the matter is always the same. It is fair and equitable treatment or, as it is sometimes put, good faith that every State is internationally required to display in its conduct towards aliens. It is the lack of fair and equitable treatment, or of good faith, that is the real and fundamental and, at the same time, the most comprehensive cause of action of which all other aspects of State responsibility (except negligence, in itself a doubtful head of liability) are mere illustrations.[75] The difficulties lie in the application rather than the existence of a doctrine the substance of which it is hard to deny. There are few precedents such as judicial decisions, diplomatic incidents or factual events from which the law may be developed and which suggest legal conclusions. In the last resort the matter

---

[68] Above, section I.

[69] See, for example, above, pp. 468, 471, 474, n. 57.

[70] Above, p. 471, n. 37.                                      [71] Nussbaum, p. 476.

[72] *Claim of Zuk*, Int. L.R. 1958, ii. p. 285.

[73] Much useful material on the general status of *abus de droit* in public international law will be found in the submissions of Counsel in the *South West African* case, I.C.J. Reports, 1966, 7, and in the *Barcelona Traction* case, I.C.J. Reports, 1970, 3. The judgments contain nothing on the point, but attention should be drawn to p. 481 of Judge Forster's Dissenting Opinion in the former case and it should perhaps be mentioned that in a Separate Opinion in the latter case, which is surely one of the least persuasive judgments ever rendered, Judge Ammoun described abuse of rights as an international tort enshrined in a general principle of law (paragraph 32 with reference to another opinion by the same Judge). As regards the specific application of the doctrine to monetary matters see the arguments presented in the latter case on behalf of Belgium, *Oral Proceedings*, VIII, 55–109 and X, 46–82, and see Mann, *Rec.* 96 (1959, i), pp. 92–5.

[74] *Metliss* v. *National Bank of Greece*, [1958] A.C. 509, at p. 524 *per* Lord Simonds.

[75] It is impossible within the present context to develop the submission in the text or to attempt a definition of the various heads of responsibility there referred to. The problem far transcends the sphere of monetary law.

will be one of degree: while normally the State is entitled at its discretion to regulate its monetary affairs, there comes a point when the exercise of such discretion so unreasonably or grossly offends against the alien's right to fair and equitable treatment, or so clearly deviates from customary standards of behaviour, that international law will intervene.

The following are examples which throw light upon the principle, and from which a firm and well-delineated rule will perhaps, in due course, be derived.[76]

1. If the monetary legislation or practice of a State pursues the deliberate purpose of injuring foreigners as a whole, this amounts to an international delinquency. Thus, if it were true[77] that during the years 1921 to 1923 the German Government deliberately created or at least aggravated the depreciation of the mark, so that it assumed its well-known astronomical proportions, for the purpose of eliminating Germany's foreign indebtedness, such a policy would stand condemned by international law.[78] The most recent instance of an alleged international impropriety was dealt with by the European Court of Justice in *Pool* v. *E. C. Council*,[79] when by virtue of Art. 215 (2) of the E.E.C. Treaty damages were claimed for determining the conversion rate applicable to the pound sterling under the Common Agricultural Policy so as to overvalue it, with the result that United Kingdom prices were fixed at too low a level and the plaintiff, a British cattle breeder, suffered loss. The Advocate-General asked for a dismissal of the action in this 'extraordinarily complex' case on the ground that the prerequisites of Art. 215 (2) had not been established. The Court, in an almost incomprehensible judgment, dismissed the action on the ground that the plaintiff had not suffered any damage. The fundamental difficulty is that the facts of the case, including in particular the monetary aspects, are left wholly obscure. Irrespective of the question of damage, it is impossible to ascertain the circumstances in which the rate for the pound sterling was determined or what precise effect it had. The lack of factual elucidation and legal reasoning, so typical for the European Court of Justice, tends to hide the monetary implications of the case and deprives it of any value as a precedent or even as a paradigm.

[76] In view of the present grievous state of international litigation the process is likely to be very slow.

[77] The suggestion has been made, for instance, by Rashba, 54 (1944) *Yale L.J.*, at p. 34, n. 137, but there is no evidence to support it.

[78] See also the German-Polish incident referred to above, p. 273, n. 29.

[79] xxix (1980) C.M.L.R. 279. On the E.E.C.'s system of monetary compensation see Gilsdorf, *European L.R.* 1980, 341.

2. Cases in which foreign nationals have become the victims of unreasonable and unfair discrimination are better documented. An interesting case is that of the Tobacco Monopoly Bonds issued by Portugal. They carried an option of currency (*option de change*) in terms of escudos, sterling, Dutch florins, and French francs. In 1924 Portugal withdrew the options for sterling and Dutch florins, but as a result of British protests reinstated the sterling option for British holders. The United States of America protested against a measure which unjustifiably discriminated against American holders, and Portugal extended the reinstatement of the sterling option to American nationals.[80]

It is necessary to emphasize the word 'unjustifiably'. There would be no actionable discrimination if the inequality of treatment were necessitated, for instance, by genuine reasons of exchange control. The fact that the United Kingdom at times made certain payments to creditors resident in the sterling area (or, technically, the scheduled territories), but withheld them from creditors in the United States was, in principle, unobjectionable. It is for this reason that it is so extraordinarily difficult even to understand the nature of the French allegation in the *Case of Certain Norwegian Loans*[81] that Norway had discriminated against French nations by paying Swedish and Danish bondholders in Swedish and Danish currency.[82] The primary French point was that Norway had wrongfully abrogated the gold clause. If Norway had paid Swedish and Danish bondholders on the basis of an existing gold clause, but had set up the abrogation *vis-à-vis* French bondholders, the abusive character of the discrimination could hardly have been in doubt. But although the complaint was in many respects obscure, this is, apparently, not what happened or was alleged. It is much more likely that Swedish and Danish bondholders were paid, though to a reduced extent, for reasons of inter-Scandinavian exchange control regulations.[83]

[80] For details see *Foreign Relations*, 1926, ii. 880; Hackworth, v. 677; Borchard–Wynne, *State Insolvency and Foreign Bondholders*, ii (1951), 383. See also Hackworth, v. 616-18, for an interesting, but not entirely clear case in which the United States objected to an Ecuadorian law fixing a rate of exchange. For not dissimilar facts see the Exchange of Letters which accompanied the Anglo-Egyptian Financial Agrement of 31 Mar. 1949 (Cmd. 7675). The Egyptian Government claimed that Egypt's sterling balances held in London 'should have the benefit of a gold clause identical to that granted to some other countries'. It seems that this refers to gold guarantees given, for instance, to Uruguay (Cmd. 7172), Argentina (Cmd. 7346, Art. IV (*e*) and (*f*), and Cmd. 7735, Arts. 21 and 26), Iran and Portugal (*The Economist*, 157 (1949), 682). As a result of the devaluation of sterling in 1949 these guarantees were estimated to have cost the United Kingdom £68m.: see *The Economist*, loc. cit. In the circumstances the Egyptian demand would appear to have been justified.                                                    [81] I.C.J. Reports, 1957, 9.

[82] For the French allegation which to some extent is dealt with by Judge Read, *Judgment*, pp. 88, 89, see *Pleadings*, i. 33, 178, 179, 400, 401; ii. 66, 67.

[*See opposite page/page 479 for n. 83*].

The wrongful character of discrimination based on reasons of nationality, religion, race, or sex should today not be open to question. After 1918 Poland introduced in her newly acquired western provinces a rate of exchange of 1 mark to 1 zloty for the conversion of mark debts into Polish currency. German courts rightly refused to apply the prescribed rate on the ground that it was specifically intended to injure German subjects.[84] Furthermore, it was clearly abusive, as has frequently been decided, for Nazi Germany to persecute Jews, whether of German or non-German nationality, and to compel them to leave the country, yet to apply to them her stringent exchange control laws.[85] A similar practice, unfortunately, still (or again) prevails in certain countries of the Communist block.

3. Though it did not fall to be dealt with on an international level, a striking case of abuse of monetary powers was held to have occurred when in 1935 the then German legislators enacted a law according to which bonds issued by Germans outside Germany and expressed in non-German currency, whether with or without a gold clause, were redeemable only to the extent of the devalued non-German currency, even if the contract was subject to German law.[86] Thus, where a German debtor had issued dollar bonds in the United States and, under a contract governed by German law, agreed to pay gold value, the gold clause was overridden and the debtor had to pay only the nominal amount in terms of the devalued dollar. The Swiss Federal Tribunal refused to give effect to these provisions.[87] It held that their sole purpose was to protect certain German debtors, mostly German industrial undertakings of vital importance. Moreover, they contemplated only bonds issued outside Germany and, therefore, presumably held by non-German owners. 'Such violent measures, designed to enrich the economy of the legislating State at the expense of foreign States, are irreconcilable with the Swiss sense of justice.' If this interpretation of the German legislation and its purpose was correct (which is not entirely free from doubt),[88] then the Swiss Federal Tribunal was probably

---

[83] The true nature of the point is even more obscured by the Norwegian defence that the treatment of Swedish and Danish bondholders was a matter of 'bonne volonté' and that certain payments were made ex gratia: *Pleadings*, i. 91, 254, 255, 257, 258, 293, 294. This was not a valid defence: see Max Huber in *Affaires des Biens Britanniques au Maroc Espagnol*, Reports of International Arbitral Awards, ii. 652.

[84] Above, p. 273, n. 29.        [85] Above, p. 406, n. 25.

[86] *Reichsgesetzblatt*, 1936, i. 515; for literature see above, p. 293, n. 123.

[87] 1 Feb. 1938, *BGE*. 64, ii. 88, also 39 *Bulletin de l'Institut Juridique International* (1938), 111. The relevant passages are in section 7 of the judgment.

[88] See, among others, Weigert, *The Abrogation of Gold Clauses in International Law* (1940), pp. 6 sqq.

justified in invoking Swiss *ordre public*, and an international tribunal would be equally justified in treating the German law as an international wrong.

4. A clear case of *abus de droit* would arise if, in the event of State succession, the successor State cancelled the rights of holders of the predecessor's currency at the time of succession. It is, on the contrary, the clear duty of the successor State under international law to provide for the continuing validity of such of the predecessor's currency as is to be found in the territory or to make arrangements for its exchange into currency of the successor State at a reasonable rate.[89]

5. While international law does not, as a rule, take exception to exchange control legislation, an international tribunal, like an English court, 'is entitled to be satisfied that the foreign law is a genuine foreign exchange law . . . and is not a law passed ostensibly with that object, but in reality with some object not in accordance with the usage of nations',[90] or, in other words, is not abusive. This condition would not be fulfilled if, for instance, the legislation, in substance, were an instrument of economic warfare or a measure preparatory to war or an instrument of oppression or discrimination. The German Moratorium Law of 30 June 1933 was held in England not to come within this exception class,[91] but as a matter of international law the point is not free from doubt,[92] though now wholly academic.

6. Exchange control legislation is so grave an enchroachment upon private rights and liabilities and may cause such serious prejudice, that good faith requires the restricting State to formulate and operate the law with due regard for the legitimate interests of aliens. The restricting State's failure or refusal to enable a non-resident alien to bring proceedings against a resident debtor for the recovery of a debt would clearly be abusive, though the refusal to permit the transfer of the fruits of the judgment would be unobjectionable. Or suppose A in England is unable to pay his debts, because all his assets are situate in Ruritania which, in implementation of its exchange control legislation, refuses to allow the transfer of any money to A. Unless the contract is subject to the law of Ruritania, the Ruritanian legislation would not provide a defence in England and by English law, no doubt, A could be make bankrupt. Yet Ruritania, it is submitted, acts abusively if it does not protect A

[89] O'Connell, *State Succession*, i (1967), pp. 191, 192 whose observations the text accepts. For cognate duties of a belligerent occupant see below, p. 490.

[90] *In re Helbert Wagg & Co. Ltd.*, [1956] Ch. 323, at pp. 351, 352.

[91] S.C.; and see above, p. 406.

[92] See the Agreement on German External Debts of 27 Feb. 1953 (Cmd. 8781), and the discussion in the note by Mann, above, p. 400, n. 29.

against being jeopardized in Ruritania by the effects of the Ruritanian legislation on his legal position there and if it does not prevent execution against $A$'s property in discharge of debts which its legislation forbids him to pay. Thus, if on the application of a Ruritanian creditor the Ruritanian courts declare $A$ bankrupt, seize all his Ruritanian property and sell it in the course of a forced sale at an undervalue, while the Ruritanian Government deprives $A$ of the possibility of applying his property to the discharge of his debts, this would be an international tort. If Ruritania makes it impossible for $A$ to pay his debts, it and its organs must, in good faith, prevent the exploitation, to the detriment of $A$, of the impossibility created by it.[93] Or, to put it differently, if Ruritania prevents $A$ from paying his debts, then it must prevent Ruritanian creditors and Ruritanian courts from compulsorily enforcing a duty which $A$ cannot perform voluntarily.

7. Since exchange control is designed to protect a State's exchange resources, the mere refusal to allow the transfer of funds abroad can hardly ever be such misuse of discretion as to be unfair and inequitable. Normally, and subject to the qualification implied in the preceding paragraph, it will even be lawful for the restricting State to limit or exclude the internal use of the non-resident alien's internal funds: if $A$ has blocked funds in Ruritania, he has no internationally recognized right to have them released to enable him to travel to Ruritania.

Special circumstances, however, may require a different solution. In the *Case of Barcelona Traction*[94] Belgium alleged an abuse of rights committed by Spain's undenied failure to allow Barcelona Traction's Spanish debtor, Ebro, to apply available peseta sums to the discharge of peseta liabilities due from it to Spanish creditors, although the use of such peseta sums for the payment of interest in respect of the same liabilities was, and had been, invariably permitted. This, so it was alleged, was done in order to deprive a prosperous, but unpopular Belgian-controlled group of its Spanish investments and play them into the hands of a protegé. Such facts, if established, would, it is believed, clearly constitute an international tort.[95]

Similarly an abusive operation of exchange control occurs when

---

[93] The situation indicated in the text was at the bottom of the facts which led to the *Case of Barcelona Traction*, I.C.J. Reports, 1970, 3. For reasons not now material the argument alluded to in the text was not advanced by Belgium. It is nonetheless believed to be valid and supported by the most elementary demands of justice.

[94] I.C.J. Reports, 1970, 3.

[95] As to references to the Belgian argument see above, p. 476, n. 73. The facts alleged by Belgium were infinitely more copious and colourful than the summary in the text suggests.

this is employed for purposes extraneous to it, e.g. in order to inflict punishment upon an alien or to secure tax claims which the tax authorities cannot, or have failed to, secure by such means as may be open to them. Nor must the grant or refusal of consents necessary under exchange control legislation depend upon the alien applicant's answers to questions about matters which are outside the scope of exchange control. Thus the State must not abuse exchange control to obtain information on questions of restrictive practices, commercial policy, patent rights, taxation, or similar matters, unless, exceptionally, they are genuinely material to the application and its fate. Nor must a State so excessively delay its reply to an alien applicant as to cause him an injustice. In short, 'the right to accord or refuse permission is in all the circumstances interpreted not as one of absolute discretion but of controllable discretion, one which must be used reasonably and not capriciously, one which must be exercised in good faith'.[96]

The examples could be multiplied. The fundamental principle governing all cases is always the same. As a legal principle it is clear and simple. Its application to facts involves an appreciation of degrees and is, therefore, difficult.

[96] *Case of Right of Passage* (*Portugal* v. *India*), *I.C.J. Reports* 1960, 107, per Judge Sir Percy Spender.

# XVIII

# The Protection of Foreign Currency Systems

I. The principle. II. The duty to prevent counterfeiting. III. The duties of a belligerent occupant in regard to currency: (1) the three principal methods of currency management and their legality; (2) the problem of responsibility; (3) the duties of the belligerent occupant and the legitimate sovereign in regard to the operation of the currency.

## I

A STATE's duty to protect the monetary systems of other States may arise from treaties or even from informal arrangements such as used to characterize the sterling area; a duty of this type has been laid down by the Articles of Agreement of the International Monetary Fund, particularly by Art. VIII, in so far as certain aspects of exchange control are concerned,[1] and is often created by bilateral treaties.[2]

However, apart from treaties, it would at present not be possible to maintain that customary public international law imposes upon the State the general duty of affording protection to the monetary systems of the other members of the family of nations.[3] The existence of such a duty could be asserted only if the development of international law had progressed so far as to outlaw all activities injurious to a foreign state or even to demand the adoption of positive measures to safeguard a foreign state's interests. This is not the present position.

Yet it is well recognized that in special circumstances an international duty of protection may come into existence. Discussion usually concentrates on revolutionary or terrorist activities, boycott, or the preparation of war;[4] it is in no way inconceivable that financial practices may acquire a character which would justify international law in demanding their suppression. When the Hungarian revolutionary Louis Kossuth had bank notes printed in England with

---

[1] Below, pp. 517 sqq.  [2] Below, p. 527.

[3] Gold, *Special Drawing Rights* (Washington, 1969), p. 2, expresses astonishment about the statement in the text. Yet the learned author fails to indicate why it is open to criticism. In the sense of the text see also Carreau, p. 31.

[4] Oppenheim, *International Law*, i (8th ed. by Lauterpacht, 1955), 292 sqq.

the avowed object of introducing them into Hungary upon his return to that country, and had them inscribed: 'in the name of the nation: Louis Kossuth', the Emperor of Austria instituted proceedings in the English courts claiming an injunction and other relief. From a strictly legal point of view his claim was not free from doubt.[5] He alleged, and the court found, an infringement of his proprietary rights,[6] but it is significant that Lord Campbell felt it necessary also to hint at the broad ground 'that in an English Court of Justice the manufacturing in England of such notes for such a purpose . . . cannot be defended';[7] if it were permitted this would justify diplomatic protests. Moreover, in days of a free money market, concerted speculations designed to undermine the international value of a foreign currency may constitute acts of hostility which could be said to engage the international responsibility of a State. In the nature of things these will be exceptional cases which will have to be judged in the light of the peculiar circumstances surrounding them; their treatment will not be beyond the power of traditional international law. The very absence of a general duty of protection, however, makes it clear that today the purpose of research must lie in ascertaining whether a State is under any specific duties towards foreign monetary systems.

## II

There is certainly one such duty which has become firmly established in public international law: it is the responsibility of every member of the family of nations to prevent and punish the counterfeiting of a foreign State's currency.

This rule, apparently first propounded by Vattel,[8] was recognized by the Supreme Court of the United States in 1887:[9]

> The law of nations requires every national Government to use 'due diligence' to prevent a wrong being done within its own dominion to another nation with which it is at peace or to the people thereof; and because of this, the obligation of the one nation to punish those who, within its own jurisdiction, counterfeit the money of another nation has long been recognized.

At the time the court's view may have been 'hardly sufficiently documented',[10] but it represented a courageous and far-sighted

---

[5] See *Transactions of the Grotius Society* 40 (1955), 25, at p. 37 or *Studies in International Law* (1973), p. 505.

[6] *Emperor of Austria* v. *Day* (1861), 3 De G.F. & J. 217.    [7] Ibid., p. 236.

[8] *The Law of Nations* (translation by Fenwick, 1916), p. 46; cf. the observation by Oresmus, quoted by Johnson, *The De Moneta of Nicholas Oresme and English Mint Documents* (London, 1956), p. 10.

[9] *United States* v. *Arjona* (1887), 120 U.S. 479, at p. 483. See also *United States* v. *Grosh* (1965), 342 F. 2d 141 or Int. L.R. 35, 65.

[10] Nussbaum, p. 322; cf. Lord McNair, *International Law Opinions*, i. 126.

pronouncement the correctness of which is not now open to doubt. The Convention for the Suppression of Counterfeiting Currency, concluded under the auspices of the League of Nations in 1929,[11] has substantially become part of the law of very many countries. It has formalized the broad principles of modern public international law on this point. There may be differences of detail, but they are of small significance so long as the practice of the various States in general conforms to the rules established by the Convention.

This does not, however, affect the question whether it is a legitimate means of warfare to counterfeit the enemy's currency for the purpose of destroying his monetary system and credit. A few cases of such counterfeiting seem to be on record.[12] They have attracted little attention and still less condemnation and cannot, therefore, at present be stigmatized as contrary to international law.

## III

On the other hand, the duties of a belligerent occupant towards the occupied territory's currency[13] have become more clearly defined.

1. There are three courses open to him: he may allow the territory's currency to remain in circulation or he may create a new currency or he may use his own currency in the occupied region, and these methods may be combined. His decision must be determined not by any principle of the law of money, but by the terms and the spirit of the Hague Regulations, particularly Art. 43, according to which he must 're-establish and ensure, as far as possible, public order and safety, while respecting, unless absolutely prevented, the laws in force in the country'.

At first sight this provision speaks in favour of the retention of the occupied region's own currency system. Where this occurs the belligerent occupant may even introduce a new currency system if public order so requires.[14] Yet such retention will frequently be impracticable,

---

[11] Hudson, *International Legislation*, iv. 2692; for literature see Oppenheim, *International Law*, i (8th ed. by Lauterpacht, 1955), 333.

[12] Nussbaum, p. 493. About alleged German attempts at forgery during the Second World War, see Murray Teigh Bloom, *Money of Their Own* (1957), 234 sqq., and Walter Hager, *Unternehmen Bernhard* (1955).

[13] For a learned and comprehensive discussion written in English see Skubiszewski, *Jahrbuch für Internationales Recht*, 9 (1959–60), 161. See also McNair and Watts, *Legal Effects of War* (4th ed., 1966), pp. 391, 392.

[14] Thus the Constitutional Court of the Federal Republic of Germany, 3 Dec. 1969, *BVerfGE* 27, 253, at p. 279, held that the Allies were entitled in 1948 to substitute the DM. currency for the RM. currency, that their measures did not offend against their duty to protect private property, and that the clear cut made between debts existing before and after

for instance when, as happened during the German occupation of Belgium between 1914 and 1918, the printing plates of the occupied territory's central bank as well as the assets covering the circulating notes are removed abroad,[15] or when gold, securities, and other cover of the currency are strictly the property of the occupied State and have lawfully been taken over by the occupant.[16]

In such or similar circumstances the adoption of the second of the above-mentioned solutions, i.e. the introduction of a new currency, cannot be considered as unlawful. No objection can therefore be taken to the mere fact that during the occupation of Belgium in the First World War the Germans entrusted the issue of new Belgian bank-notes to a private bank, the Société Générale, and promulgated a decree attributing the quality of legal tender to them. The real problem in this case is not the legality of the issue, but is one of cover; where should the occupant find cover for the new issue? In the Belgian situation from 1914 to 1918 the Germans secured the notes by opening at the Reichsbank a mark credit in favour of the Société Générale. This deposit, amounting to 1,600 million marks, was subsequently transferred to the Belgian Government, but, as a result of the depreciation of the mark, became worthless. The ensuing controversy between the Belgian and German Governments was settled only by the Convention of 13 July 1929[17] whereby Germany

21 June 1948 was not arbitrary. The decision is of great general importance and clearly right, except that according to the better view the Hague Regulations did not apply to the occupation of Germany between June 1945 and Sept. 1949. See p. 487, n. 21.

[15] Feilchenfeld, *The International Law of Belligerent Occupation* (1942), pp. 70 sqq.; Nolde, pp. 306 sqq.; Neumeyer, *Internationales Verwaltungsrecht*, ii. 245 sqq.; Nussbaum, pp. 159 sqq. All these writers have collected a large bibliography. An illuminating description of the facts is given by Schacht, *The Stabilization of the Mark* (1927), pp. 26–8. The German Supreme Court held that the measures taken by the Germans in Belgium in 1914 were consistent with Art. 43 of the Hague Regulations (22 Apr. 1922, *JW.*, 1922, 1324; 20 Dec. 1924, *RGZ.* 109, 357, 360).

[16] See Art. 53 of the Hague Regulations. It is often difficult to define the conditions in which a country's monetary reserve is the property of the occupied State. For literature see Oppenheim, *International Law*, ii (7th ed., by Lauterpacht, 1952), 399, n. 3. There exists a tendency to attach, in this connection, too much importance to legal forms rather than functions. The interpretation which the Allies placed upon the term 'monetary gold' does not support that tendency: see the decision of Jenkins J. (as he then was) in *Dollfus Mieg & Co.* v. *Bank of England*, [1949] 1 Ch. 369, 392, where it was decided that gold possessed by the Governments of the United Kingdom, the United States of America, and France was held for public purposes within the meaning of the rules of immunity, although it admittedly belonged to the plaintiffs at the time of its seizure by the Germans and may still have belonged to them at the date of the writ. The decision of the House of Lords rests on other grounds: [1952] A.C. 582. See on the problem of 'monetary gold' above, p. 29, n. 3.

[17] *Nouveau Recueil général de traités*, 3rd ser., 24 (1931), 527. The parties concluded the Convention 'tout en maintenant chacun leur point de vue juridique'. From the point of view of international law the Convention is inconclusive also because it relates not to the specific question discussed in the text, but generally to 'les questions encore pendantes entre l'Allemagne et la Belgique et relatives aux dommages économiques spéciaux résultant de

undertook to pay to Belgium certain annuities by way of indemnity. But there is force in Professor Nussbaum's submission that the Treaty of 1929 'can hardly be considered a precedent for the future'.[18] If the issue of notes as such was authorized by the Hague Regulations and if it is admitted that the depreciation of the mark in itself did not afford a ground for relief, the breach of duty could only be found in the selection of a mark deposit as coverage. The alternative, however, would have been to use Belgian assets as cover. It would not necessarily have been a less harmful solution than the use of the occupant's own deposit. Allied practice during the Second World War not only confirms the proposition that the mere introduction of a new currency is not, as a rule, open to criticism, but also indicates a method of providing cover which is not essentially different from that adopted by Germany in Belgium between 1914 and 1918. The Allies issued Allied Military Currency denominated in the currency of the occupied territory[19] (lire,[20] reichsmarks,[21] schillings[22]) and gave it the force of legal tender. At any rate in so far as Allied Military lire were concerned, both the British and the United States Governments caused the equivalent of the lire issued in Italy to be credited, in sterling and dollars respectively, to special accounts to provide for the contingency of the lire in the future becoming a charge against the occupying Powers.[23] On the other hand, during the last war the Germans organized new central banks in most of the occupied countries and, having (probably

l'occupation de celle-ci'. The further history of the Convention appears from Cmd. 8653, p. 23. See also the Romanian-German Agreement of 11 Nov. 1928 (ibid. 21, p. 484) whereby Germany undertook, inter alia, to settle all outstanding financial questions by the payment of RM. 75.5m.

[18] Op. cit., p. 160; these words do not occur in the second edition (1950).

[19] See, generally, Kemmerer, 'Allied Military Currency in Constitutional and International Law', in Money and the Law, Supplement to the New York University Law Quarterly Review (1945), p. 83; Southard, The Finances of European Liberation (1946); Fraleigh, 35 (1949–50) Corn. L.Q. 89, 107 sqq.

[20] See Smith, British Year Book of International Law, 21 (1944), 151, at p. 153, and, in particular, Professor Southard's book (quoted in the preceding note) which is written with special reference to Italy. See also Holborn, American Military Government (1947), who at pp. 114 sqq. prints the Combined Directive on Military Government in Sicily dealing in detail with matters of currency.

[21] Law No. 51, Military Government Gazette, Germany, 21st Army Group Area of Control, p. 16; see also Southard, op. cit., passim. For the text of the Combined Directive for Military Government in Germany see Holborn, op. cit., pp. 135 sqq. In June 1948 the Allies replaced the reichsmark by the Deutsche Mark currency (see above, p. 485, n. 14). They acted as the supreme authority in the Western Zones and according to the better view the Hague Regulations did not fetter their discretion. In Eisner v. United States, 117 F. Supp. 197 (1954), also Int. L.R. 1954, 476 it was expressly held that in the circumstances prevailing in Germany the Allies had 'the power to establish a rational monetary system'.

[22] See Southard, op. cit. For the American Directive on Military Government in Austria see Holborn, op. cit., pp. 177 sqq.

[23] Southard, op. cit., p. 25.

unlawfully)[24] appropriated the existing banks' gold and other reserves, admitted German currency and credits with the Reichsbank as cover, although in Poland they also created a mortgage on all real estate in the territory in favour of the new central bank.[25] In so far as the creation of the new central banks and their equipment with cover in the form of German credits were merely the consequence of the illegal spoliation of the original central banks' assets and an incident of the scheme to enrich the occupant and strip the territory of its resources, Germany clearly committed a breach of her international duties.[26] In the Philippines, in Burma, and in other countries occupied by them, the Japanese issued military currency. Although nothing is known about its cover, there is no reason to doubt the legality of the issue.[27]

The third method, i.e. the use of the occupant's own currency, is a universal and necessary practice, at any rate in the early stages of an occupation, and must be treated as lawful.[28] During the Second World War the Americans used the 'yellow seal' dollar,[29] the German Army was provided with 'Reichskreditkassenscheine' denominated in reichsmarks,[30] but in Jersey regular German reichsmark notes seem to have been introduced.[31] In all these cases the occupant's currency was made legal tender in the occupied territory.

[24] Lemkin, *Axis Rule in Occupied Europe* (1944), pp. 57, 58, who attaches decisive importance to the fact that the central banks concerned were privately owned. But see p. 486, n. 16 above.

[25] See Lemkin, op. cit., pp. 53 sqq., who at pp. 267 sqq. prints the relevant texts.

[26] Ibid., pp. 55, 56. The Supreme Court of Poland held that the introduction of the Polish mark in occupied Poland by Germany during the First World War was not permitted by Art. 43 of the Hague Regulations (28 Aug. 1919, *JW.* 1922, 1689). The opposite view was taken by the German Supreme Court in a decision which contains interesting material on the issue of 'Darlehenskassenscheine' in Poland in 1916 (28 Nov. 1921, *RGZ.* 103, 231). The opposite view was also taken by the Supreme Court of Poland in regard to zloty notes issued by the central bank which had been set up by the Germans: 27 June 1947, Int. L.R. 26, 719. Similarly, the Civil Court of Singapore in *Public Trustee* v. *Chartered Bank*, Int. L.R. 1956, 687, at pp. 694, 696.

[27] As to the Philippines, see Supreme Court of the Philippine Republic in *Haw Pia* v. *China Banking Corporation, The Lawyer's Journal* (Manila), 13 (1948), 173, also Int. L.R. 1951, 642 (a majority decision of seven to three), where Japanese military pesos were held to have been lawfully issued. The decision was followed by the Supreme Court of the Philippines in *Gibbs* v. *Rodriguez*, Int. L.R. 1951, 661 which contains a long discussion of Professor Hyde's criticism referred to below, p. 490, n. 43, and by the Court of Appeals in *Madlambayan* v. *Aquino*, Int. L.R. 1955, 994, and in *Singson* v. *Veloso*, Int. L.R. 1956, 800. In the same sense *Aboitiz & Co.* v. *Price*, 99 F. Supp. 602 (District Court, Utah, 1951); Fraleigh, l.c.; Fitzmaurice, *Rec.* 73 (1948), 342 who also enumerates the conditions for the legality of occupation currency. As to Burma, in *Dooply* v. *Chan Taik*, Int. L.R. 1951, 641, the Supreme Court denied the right of the Japanese to issue military rupees or dollars.

[28] In the same sense Oppenheim, *International Law*, ii (7th ed., 1952, by Lauterpacht, p. 438).

[29] Southard, op. cit.                                    [30] Lemkin, op. cit., p. 51.

[31] See Duret Aubin in *Journal of Comparative Legislation*, 3rd ser., 31 (1949), 8, at p. 10.

2. From the question of the legality of the currency system adopted by the occupant for the occupied territory it is necessary to distinguish clearly the problem of responsibility. Where the occupant introduces his own currency, it would seem clear that he is responsible for it, though in Jersey the Treasury authorized the exchange of reichsmarks for sterling at the rate current at the time of the liberation, viz. 9.36 reichsmarks to the pound;[32] it is for this reason that an occupant will normally discontinue using his own currency as soon as possible.[33] Where, however, the occupant introduces military notes, he does not engage his own credit but that of the occupied country in which he exercises supreme power. This is the view taken by the Allies in regard to the military currency issued by them in the course of the Second World War,[34] but it is remarkable that the Japanese war notes issued as legal tender at par with the peso in the Philippines were guaranteed by the Japanese Government 'which takes full responsibility for their usage having the correct amount to back them up'.[35] From a practical point of view the problem is of very limited significance, because the victorious belligerent will usually obtain an indemnity from, and impose the duty of redemption upon, the defeated enemy, as the Allies did in the Armistice with Italy,[36] in the Treaties of Peace concluded with Italy, Romania, and Hungary in 1947,[37] and in the State Treaty with Austria.[38] The fact, therefore, that after the First World War similar arrangements were made with Germany in regard to her monetary policy in Belgium and Romania does not justify the principle postulated by Baron Nolde that 'la liquidation des mesures relatives au papier-monnaie qui peuvent être introduites par l'État occupant, appartient en droit à ce dernier'.[39]

3. Finally, whichever type of monetary organization is adopted by the occupant and whichever answer is given to the problem of

[32] Duret Aubin, op. cit., p. 10.    [33] Southard, op. cit., p. 23.

[34] Ibid., pp. 49 sqq., with interesting material. According to the same author (pp. 29 sqq., 55, 56), the Italian Government demanded complete reimbursement in a Memorandum of 9 Jan. 1945, which, unfortunately, has not been published, as a matter of right in appropriate foreign currency for all lire spent by Allied forces. The American decision of 10 Oct. 1944 to reimburse Italy in dollars equivalent to the lire personally expended in Italy by American troops ('net troop pay') was obviously due to reasons other than legal ones (see Southard, op. cit., p. 30).

[35] See the decrees mentioned in the decision referred to on p. 412, n. 55.

[36] Clause 23; for the text see Holborn, op. cit., p. 123.

[37] Art. 76 (4) of the Treaty with Italy; Art. 30 (4) of the Treaty with Romania; Art. 32 (4) of the Treaty with Hungary.

[38] Art. 24 (4) in Cmd. 9482. Where British military notes were issued in Allied territory, the Government of the latter usually assumed responsibility: see, for example, the Treaty with Greece of 7 Mar. 1955 (Cmd. 9481), para. 13 (a).

[39] Rec., 27 (1929), 311. In common with others, he seems to confuse the question of cover with that of the responsibility for redemption.

responsibility, there arises the distinct question of defining the occupant's duties in regard to the operation and management of the occupied territory's monetary system. To lawyers it is of a peculiarly elusive character, because it depends upon matters of valuation and quantum about which only economists can speak with authority. Recent experience, however, permits the formulation of a few rules of conduct that would not seem to be open to any serious doubt. Thus it can be stated with confidence that the occupant who introduces a new or his own currency may do so only to such extent as is required to satisfy military needs or to supplement an inadequate amount of circulating local currency.[40] Moreover, where the occupant establishes a rate of conversion as between the military and local currency, he must carry out a process of valuation which requires, but is not always accompanied by, a high degree of disinterestedness. It has been said that by overvaluing the reichsmark and undervaluing the currencies of the occupied territories,[41] the Germans obtained unjustifiable economic advantages; on the other hand, the Allies seem to have overvalued both the lira and the reichsmark[42] and, accordingly, to have undervalued their own currencies. Lastly, the occupant commits a breach of duty if he allows an extraordinary increase of the quantity of circulating money, if he promotes, or at least does not stop, inflation and depreciation of the value of money. Provided that he does not wish to impose responsibility for circumstances beyond the occupying Power's control, Professor Hyde is right, therefore, in suggesting 'a general rule of International Law forbidding the occupant to make it possible for the debtor to rob his creditors by the satisfaction of a debt through a greatly depreciated and practically worthless currency'.[43] In the last resort all these matters depend on facts, on economic conditions which a lawyer cannot judge without evidence bearing on each case. His general conclusion must be that no rule of strict law governing all eventualities can be stated. He must fall back upon the idea pervading the law of belligerent occupation, according to which the occupant, while allowed to make war support war, may not exceed the functions of an 'administrator and usufructuary'[44]

[40] This point appears clearly from Southard, op. cit., particularly p. 15. See the District Court of Luxemburg, 20 June 1951, Int. L.R. 1951, 633.

[41] Lemkin, op. cit., p. 52.

[42] Kemmerer, op. cit., p. 89. The text deals with the early stages of the occupation of Germany when the Hague Regulations undoubtedly applied.

[43] 'Concerning the Haw Pia case', in Philippine Law Journal, 24 (1949), 141, 144. See also Fraleigh in 35 (1949) Corn. L.Q. 89, 107 sqq. who emphasizes (p. 113) that the occupant is not under an absolute duty to prevent depreciation of currency.

[44] See the language of Art. 55 of the Hague Regulations.

who within the limits of military needs acts for the public benefit of the inhabitants.[45]

On the other hand, there does not as yet exist a rule of international law defining the duties of the legitimate Government in regard to the measures which, upon its restoration, it is expected to take in order to deal with the management of the currency by the belligerent occupant. In the absence of retrospective legislation notes issued by the occupant must be recognized as having been legal tender capable of discharging debts, even pre-occupation debts.[46] Although the legitimate Government will usually provide for the conversion of the existing stock of occupation currency into the lawful money of the country, it is a question of private law, as opposed to public international law, to what extent the discharge of pre-occupation debts by the payment of occupation money should be recognized and revalorization of debts repaid in greatly depreciated military currency is necessary or advisable. The possibilities of judicial revalorization are limited.[47] In extreme cases the legislator will no doubt intervene, and after the end of the Second World War he did so in Malaya,[48] Burma,[49] the Netherlands East Indies, Hong Kong, Singapore,[50] and elsewhere in South East Asia. But the liberated State's failure to effect legislative or judicial revalorization will not amount to an international wrong.[51]

---

[45] Oppenheim, *International Law*, ii (7th ed., revised by Lauterpacht, 1952), 437; and see p. 438, where the principle applicable to currency is very clearly stated.

[46] Above, p. 18; in the same sense Nussbaum, p. 500.

[47] Above, pp. 100 sqq.

[48] O'Connor and Buhagiar, *Journal of Comparative Legislation*, 3rd ser., 33 (1951), 5–8.

[49] Maung, op. cit., at p. 15.

[50] Hyde, op. cit., p. 155; Fraleigh, l.c., p. 109. On the legislation in South East Asia see Bergman, *International and Comparative L.Q.*, 1962, 765 sqq. The legislation in Sarawak was considered by the Privy Council in *Chartered Bank of India, Australia and China* v. *Wee Kheng Chiang*, Int. L.R. 1957, 945. Miss Satz, in *Journal of Comparative Legislation*, 31 (1949), 3, reports about Danish law that, although the value of the Danish currency depreciated on account of the abundance of money arising from the German demands for the printing of paper currency, payment of a debt or the redemption of a mortgage during the occupation is valid.

[51] See p. 470.

# XIX

# Patterns of Monetary Organization

I. Monetary Unions. II. Monetary Areas: (1) the Sterling Area; (2) the French Franc Area; (3) the *Case Concerning Rights of Nationals of the United States in Morocco*. III. Monetary Agreements: (1) Political Agreements; (2) Technical Agreements (in particular Clearing and Payments Agreements). IV. Monetary Institutions: (1) in general; (2) the International Monetary Fund.

I

THE unification of the monetary system of several States is a phenomenon of recent origin.

It is true that for long theoretical writers have devoted attention to the possibility of creating a 'world money',[1] though in recent years such ideas have been recognized as illusory. It is also true that history provides many examples of Conventions which, while not contemplating a single or even a uniform monetary system, established a common basis of the participating countries' monetary structure: the independent monetary systems of various States were not merged into a single one, but organized on a common basis. The Latin Monetary Union, formed between France, Belgium, Switzerland, Italy, and Greece, 'pour ce qui regarde le titre, le poids, le diamètre et le cours de leurs espèces monnayées d'or et d'argent', was between 1865 and 1921 the most significant example of efforts which have rightly been described as having a 'standardizing' function.[2] Such attempts are of little, if any, value. Economic experience has shown that the regulation of coinage, or of instruments of payment in general, does not touch the essential problems. Hence the movement towards 'standardizing' the currency is obsolete.

Where, on the other hand, a truly common market exists or is intended to be created and economic integration develops, States will almost be compelled to co-ordinate and, eventually, to unify their currency systems, for money is only an instrument or a mechanism of the market, and a common market needs a common instrument. A real Monetary Union is the West African Monetary Union created on 12 May 1962 between Dahomey, Ivory Coast, Mauritania, Niger, Senegal, Togo, and Upper Volta.[3] In the words of the treaty, the

---

[1] Nussbaum, p. 547.  [2] Nussbaum, p. 502. See above, p. 52.
[3] Text of the treaty in *Jurisclasseur, Outre-Mer*, v. 16. For a helpful description of the

Union 'se caractérise par l'existence d'une même unité monétaire',[4] namely 'le franc de la Communauté financière africaine',[5] generally known as the C.F.A. franc. The exclusive right to issue it is entrusted to a common organization, the Central Bank of the West African States.[6] It has 'pouvoir libératoire' throughout the Union[7] whose members are bound to permit the free circulation of currency and freedom of transfers within the Union,[8] and to adopt uniform rules relating, *inter alia*, to external exchange control.[9]

Both the European Common Market and the East African Common Market, as will appear later,[10] have so far failed to reach a similar degree of unification, but the Partner States of the latter at least undertook to allow, subject to exchange control laws, their respective currency notes to be exchanged without undue delay within their territories at official par value without exchange commission.[11] Yet for the time being it can only be suggested that these treaties bring 'into the realm of realistic planning the matter of a full currency merger among the participating countries'.[12] The machinery for promoting this aim is available under the terms of both treaties.[13]

## II

Monetary Areas are characterized by the fact that restrictions on transfers within the area are abolished, or much reduced; usually there exists in all participating States a similar system of exchange control *vis-à-vis* third States; frequently certain resources such as foreign exchange and, in particular, gold are pooled.

C.F.A. Franc System see Leduc (above, p. 53, n. 135) and *International Monetary Fund Staff Papers*, x (1963), 345 and xvi (1969), 289; Shuster (above, p. 464, n. 7), p. 240; Burdeau in *International Law and Economic Order (Essays in Honour of F. A. Mann)*, p. 657; Carreau, ibid., p. 674 (though to a large extent he treats the law relating to Monetary Zones generally). For a helpful general discussion see Henri Guitton et Gérard Bramoullé, *La Monnaie* (4th ed., 1978), pp. 483–8.

[4] Art. 1.            [5] Art. 5.            [6] Art. 6.            [7] Art. 7.
[8] Art. 4, No. 3.            [9] Art. 10.            [10] Below, p. 503.
[11] Art. 24 of the Treaty for East African Co-operation of 6 June 1967 between Kenya, Tanzania, and Uganda (*International Legal Materials*, 1967, 932). Political events have since rendered the Treaty inoperative.
[12] Triffin, *Europe and the Money Muddle* (1957), p. 288.
[13] See, in particular, Art. 105 of the Treaty establishing the European Economic Community, which provides for the Monetary Committee. The inadequacy of the present arrangements and the need for a unified currency system in a market which is truly common is most vividly illustrated by the facts of a decision of the Finance Court, Hamburg, of 15 Oct. 1980, *RIW/AWD* 1981, 53, whereby the problem was referred to the European Court of Justice. Its decision is not yet known. The broad facts were that goods were imported from Taiwan via Hamburg where, as a result of the rate of conversion fixed by the EEC, customs duties to the extent of some DM 70,000 had to be paid. If the goods had been imported via an Italian port the amount of customs duty would have been less than half. The lack of equality and the distortion of the 'common' market is obvious.

1. The most important monetary area was for many years the sterling area.[14] It comprised the territories which s. 1 (3) of the Exchange Control Act 1947 described as the scheduled territories enumerated in the First Schedule to the Act as amended from time to time and within which payments and transfers could freely be made. For all practical purposes this area ceased to exist in June 1972,[15] but the abolition of exchange control in 1979 restored complete freedom, not only within the former sterling area, but universally. Whether there now exist informal arrangements between central banks is unknown.

The sterling area was not subject to any organization. Its substantive rules were unwritten, unpublished, flexible, and largely without legal force. Most, if not all the countries forming part of the sterling area had their independent currency systems, and parity with sterling was formally maintained through the International Monetary Fund rather than through treaties between the members of the sterling area. Each country had its own exchange control system which, subject to certain exceptions, did not operate in relation to transactions with other parts of the sterling area. Each had, in principle, the right to deal with its reserves as it liked. There were other points which proved the lack of uniform organization. Yet the sterling area existed as a fairly homogeneous unit. It rested largely on informal understandings, on political, historical, commercial, financial, and other facts rather than on law.

It was only on rare occasions that it was possible for the lawyer to have a glimpse of what the sterling area really was. The sterling area's pooling arrangements were at one time supposed to come to an end as a result of the Financial Agreement between the United States of America and the United Kingdom on 6 December 1945.[16] The attempt failed, but a more effective relaxation occurred four years later as a result of an Agreement between the United Kingdom and Ceylon: under the heading of Monetary Co-operation the two Governments recognized 'that Ceylon is at all times free to dispose of her currency savings abroad'; the United Kingdom Government agreed 'that Ceylon may retain from that surplus an independent reserve of gold or dollars' which during the period ended 30 June 1950 should amount to no more than one million dollars; 'subject to this, Ceylon intends to contribute her surplus dollar earnings to the foreign exchange resources of the scheduled territories'.[17]

[14] See, generally, Shuster (above, p. 464, n. 7), p. 238; Bareau, *The Sterling Area* (1948); A. R. Conan, *The Sterling Area* (1952); W. M. Scammell, *International Monetary Policy* (1967), pp. 242 sqq.

[15] As a result of S.I. 1972 No. 930.

[16] Cmd. 6708, Clause 7, provided that 'the sterling receipts from current transactions of all sterling area countries . . . will be freely available for current transactions in any currency area without discrimination with the result that any discrimination arising from the so-called sterling area dollar pool will be entirely removed and that each member of the sterling area will have its current sterling and dollar receipts at its free disposal for current transactions anywhere'. On the problem generally, Richard N. Gardner, *Sterling-Dollar Diplomacy* (Oxford, 1956).

[17] Cmd. 7766, and see Cmd. 8165. For a reference to gold reserves of the sterling area see the Anglo-Egyptian Financial Agreement of 31 Mar. 1949 (Cmd. 7675), Letter No. 1.

An even more significant step towards formality occurred in the autumn of 1968. The problem of the sterling balances, i.e. liabilities of the United Kingdom towards foreign States and their nationals, most of which were incurred during the war to pay for local supplies and services and which in December 1947 amounted to more than £3,600 million, was first broached by the Anglo-American Financial Agreement of 1945.[18] It was subsequently regulated by a large number of treaties which provided for the release of certain parts of the balances over a period of years.[19] The final development came as a result of the devaluation of the pound in November 1967 which 'was, of course, a shock to the sterling system', because the great majority of the 39 countries forming part of the sterling area did not devalue and therefore suffered loss 'not only in terms of dollar purchasing power but . . . in terms of their own currency also'.[20] Twelve States outside the sterling area and including Austria and Germany granted Britain the 'Basle facility' of $2,000 million. At the same time Britain entered into formal treaties with the sterling area countries guaranteeing to maintain the dollar value of 90 per cent of their official sterling reserves, while those countries undertook to maintain an agreed proportion of their total reserves in sterling.[21] Nine-tenths of the sterling area's official sterling reserves were secured by a dollar clause.[22]

2. The French Franc Area[23] or the Operations Account Area, as it is technically, but unattractively called since 1 February 1967,[24] is considerably more closely organized. It comprises the territories of the French Republic, Monaco, the West African Monetary Union, the countries of the Central African Customs and Economic Union,[25] three North African countries, the Malagasy Republic, and Mali, and is given a legal status by such treaties as that between France and the West African Monetary Union of 12 May 1962.[26] The French Republic allowed to the Central Bank of the West African States 'la dotation de 500 millions'[27] and then proceeded to guarantee the free

[18] Cmd. 6708. See, generally, Richard N. Gardner, *Sterling-Dollar Diplomacy* (1956), particularly pp. 204 sqq., 326 sqq.

[19] See, for example, treaties with Ceylon (Cmd. 8165), Pakistan (Cmd. 8380), India (Cmd. 8953), Egypt (Cmd. 7675), Uruguay (Cmd. 7172), Iraq (Cmd. 7201).

[20] Cmnd. 3787; the quotations in the text are taken from para. 7.

[21] Cmnd. 3834, 3835, 4224, 4115. These Sterling Area Agreements were prolonged for a period of two years from 25 September 1971: Cmnd. 4884 and 4885. See also the Agreement with Bangladesh of 6 Nov. 1972, Cmnd. 5325.

[22] The guarantee invariably read that the United Kingdom undertook 'to maintain the sterling value in terms of the United States dollar of the balances'. What would be the effect of a devaluation of the dollar? It is submitted that, notwithstanding the wording of the guarantee, there would be no reduction of the sterling value of the balances. For an analogy see above, pp. 204 sqq.

[23] See, generally, above, p. 53, n. 135.

[24] For details, see the International Monetary Fund's *Annual Report on Exchange Agreements and Exchange Restrictions* (1979), p. 159.

[25] Cameroon, Central African Republic, Chad, Congo (Brazzaville), Gabon.

[26] Clunet, 1963, 868, as amended by a Convention of 21 Feb. 1963, Clunet, 1964, 267.

[27] Art 2. The reference presumably is to French francs.

convertibility of the C.F.A. franc into French francs. For this purpose the French Treasury opened 'un compte d'opérations' in favour of the Central Bank, the terms of which were the subject-matter of a separate Convention.[28] Art. 4 then continues: 'Les États prendront toutes dispositions utiles pour que soient centralisés au compte d'opérations les avoirs extérieurs de l'Union Monétaire.' This important provision in substance creates the legal obligation to pool foreign exchange resources.

3. If, as has been suggested, freedom of internal transfers of currency is one of the characteristics of a monetary area, then it would seem to follow that the exchange, i.e. the importation and exportation, of goods within the same area is necessarily also free. It is the corollary of this situation that the control of transfers outside the monetary area implies of necessity the control of imports into the area.

This submission is contrary to the puzzling decision of the International Court of Justice in the *Case Concerning Rights of Nationals of the United States of America in Morocco*.[29]

On 9 September 1939 the authorities in Morocco promulgated a law[30] whereby, subject to exceptions to be made by regulations, the importation of all goods other than gold was prohibited. On the same day a decree made by virtue of that law provided,[31] *inter alia*, that all goods 'originaires et en provenance de la France et de l'Algérie' were admitted without formality. A further law of 10 September 1939[32] imposed a system of exchange control in Morocco and a decree of the same date,[33] issued by virtue of the Law of 10 September 1939, made specific provision for imports. While exempting imports from France and French possessions from the supervision of the Exchange Control Authorities,[34] it required for the importation of goods the presentation of a licence to the effect that either the supply of the necessary foreign exchange had been authorized or the importation 'ne nécessite aucun règlement en devises étrangères';[35] the latter method, described as 'importation sans paiement' or 'importation sans devises',[36] would be employed where the importer had at his disposal foreign exchange which he was able and willing to use for the payment of the exporter, or where the exporter was prepared to accept the currency of Morocco in satisfaction. After certain other regulations had been temporarily in force, a decree

---

[28] Art. 4.

[29] I.C.J. Reports, 1952, 176. The analysis presented in the text is to a large extent accepted by Carreau, pp. 307–10.

[30] Pleadings, i. 96; in English, i. 328.     [31] Pleadings, i. 97.

[32] Pleadings, i. 92.     [33] Pleadings, i. 94.

[34] Art. 7.     [35] Art. 1.     [36] Pleadings, i. 15.

of 30 December 1948[37] reinstated the full operation and effect of the decree of 9 September 1939 in its original form, so that the importation of goods other than goods of French origin was prohibited.

The United States of America alleged that the decree of 30 December 1948, or rather that of 9 September 1939, infringed its treaty right of 'economic liberty without any inequality' in that it discriminated against the goods of United States nationals by prohibiting the importation of their goods, while allowing the unrestricted importation of French goods. The allegation was resisted by France on numerous and varied grounds of which the following were basic: (1) The Act of Algeciras did not confer upon the United States an unequivocal and enforceable legal right to economic liberty;[38] (2) even if the United States enjoyed a legal right as alleged, the decree of 30 December 1948 was an enactment relating to exchange control; (3) exchange control was permitted. The court decided in favour of the United States on the ground that the second proposition was wrong and that, consequently, there was no necessity for considering the third. The reasons are expressed in four sentences:[39]

The Government of France has submitted various contentions purporting to demonstrate the legality of exchange control. The Court does not consider it necessary to pronounce upon these contentions. Even assuming the legality of exchange control, the fact nevertheless remains that the measures applied by virtue of the decree of December 30, 1948, have involved a discrimination in favour of imports from France and other parts of the French Union. This discrimination cannot be justified by considerations relating to exchange control.

In other words, the court held that the impugned decree related to the control of imports or quantitative restrictions, not to exchange control, and that, therefore, the attempt to justify the latter missed the point.

The 'laconisme' of the court's reasoning has rightly been emphasized and regretted.[40] But there is room for the impression that, as on its face the decree of 9 September 1939 (as reinstated by that of 30 December 1948) concerned exclusively the importation of goods, the court was entitled to state, rather than elaborately justify, its conclusion. This would have been different only if France had not only made an assertion, but also developed a closely reasoned argument to the effect that in truth and in substance the decree was an essential element of a system of exchange control. Yet on this crucial step the French argument could perhaps have been more helpful and

[37] Judgment, p. 183; Pleadings, i. 106.
[38] This point failed, but the reasons are puzzling. See below, p. 512.
[39] Judgment, p. 186.
[40] Laubadère, *Revue Juridique et Politique de l'Union Française*, 6 (1952), 429, 460, among others.

penetrating. Indeed, there are a number of aspects of the arguments of both parties which might have gained from clear and succinct exposition.[41]

It must in the first place be pointed out that neither Party made an attempt to explain the prima facie puzzling relationship between the Laws and Decrees of 9 September 1939 and those of 10 September 1939, or to show that the former were an essential ingredient of the system of exchange control set up by the latter. Throughout the French representatives emphasized that, as they put it in the first sentence of their Mémoire, 'le litige soumis à la Cour met en cause un régime dit des importations sans paiement'.[42] This was a regime contemplated by the decree of 10 September 1939. But the American attack was directed against the decree of 9 September 1939. It may have been the result of this apparent misunderstanding that the French representatives failed to explain the functions of and the connection between the two sets of enactments.[43] The French case would perhaps have been put in a clearer perspective if, in addition to a specific interpretation of the decrees in question, the French representatives had submitted to the court the opinion of an economist setting forth, in such language as lawyers can understand, the thesis that import control and exchange control are inseparable emanations of a single system of planning.[44]

Even assuming, however, that this thesis could not be maintained, there remains the remarkable fact that an entirely different line of argument may have been open to France, but was not put forward at all. It was, of course, common ground between the Parties that, presumably with the consent or acquiescence of the United States, Morocco was at all material times included in the 'zone franc'. Is it not elementary that a monetary area necessarily results in and is, indeed, characterized by the free movement of money and, therefore, of goods within the area? Do not economists exhort us to look through the 'veil of money' to the goods behind it, and to realize that where money moves freely it is in truth the goods which move freely? If such questions required an affirmative answer (which was a matter for expert evidence), then the defence to the American claim would have been that by its consent to the inclusion of Morocco

---

[41] The case involved many and varied issues and imposed a particularly heavy burden on the Parties' representatives.

[42] Pleadings, i. 15.

[43] See, in particular, a passage in the argument of Professor Gros, Pleadings, ii. 150; see also i. 83. The argument of Mr. Fisher on behalf of the United States was no less dogmatic and abstract: Pleadings, ii. 237.

[44] It would have been helpful to point to the interplay between the International Monetary Fund and GATT: see below, p. 509. See also Art. 21 of the Agreement establishing the Caribbean Free Trade Association of 30 Apr. 1968, *International Legal Materials*, 1968, 935.

in the franc area the United States allowed France the privileges inevitably flowing from such inclusion, that accordingly the United States was not, and could not be, entitled to commercial equality with France, but that in the matters relevant to the case the standard of equality was determined by the rights of all those States which, like the United States, were not members of the 'zone franc'. Perhaps an argument on such lines would have avoided a result that may appear as striking. In no event should the decision be accepted as an authority for the general thesis that, either in general or within a monetary zone, import control and exchange control are necessarily and invariably different and unconnected instruments of economic policy.[45]

<h1 style="text-align:center">III</h1>

Monetary Agreements are treaties which, without creating a distinct institution with its own rules, regulate specifically and exclusively monetary matters.[46] Such Agreements frequently have an almost political flavour or, contrariwise, are of a highly technical character.

1. The former type is exemplified by the Declaration establishing the 'gold block' which between 1933 and 1936 was formed by France, Belgium, Italy, the Netherlands, Switzerland, and Poland. These States confirmed 'their intention to maintain the free functioning of the gold standard in their respective countries at the existing gold parities and within the framework of existing monetary laws'. They asked their Central Banks to keep in close touch to give the maximum efficacy to this Declaration.[47] In 1936 a Declaration which was still more frankly political was made by the United States of America, France, and Great Britain, and subsequently adhered to by Belgium, Switzerland, and the Netherlands. These States reaffirmed their intention to continue their monetary policies 'one object of which is to maintain the greatest possible equilibrium in the system of international exchanges and to avoid to the utmost the creation of any disturbance of that system by British (French, etc.) monetary action'. The participating States also extended an invitation to other

[45] The importance of this point far transcends the particular case discussed in the text. See, for instance, *Rec.* 96 (1959, i.), 61. And see below, pp. 509 and 521. W. Kewenig, *Der Grundsatz der Nichtdiskrimierung im Völkerrecht der internationalen Handelsbeziehungen* (1972), pp. 85, 86, appears to agree with the criticism put forward in the text.

[46] On monetary institutions see below, p. 502. On bilateral treaties which, among many other subjects, incidentally also deal with aspects of monetary conduct see below, p. 527.

[47] *Documents on International Affairs*, 1933, p. 45. This Declaration was supplemented by a Protocol of 20 Oct. 1934 (Hudson, *International Legislation*, v., No. 396, where some literature will also be found).

nations 'to realise the policy laid down in the present Declaration'.[48] Such Declarations, it is submitted, do not, nor are they intended to, impose any legal fetters upon the States' sovereignty in monetary matters.

2. Technical Agreements are usually intended, not to make a contribution to the development of an international monetary system, but to establish a temporary expedient or machinery for the purpose of solving a particular problem. As a rule they aim at facilitating the transfer of funds from one country to another so as to maintain the balance of payments in a state of reasonable equilibrium.

Such was the object of the clearing system which was widely resorted to up to the end of the Second World War, particularly by Switzerland,[49] but also, for instance, by the United Kingdom in its dealings with Roumania,[50] Italy,[51] Turkey,[52] and Spain.[53] The clearing system which now seems to have disappeared is characterized by the fact[54] that debtors in each country pay to a Central Clearing Office which applies the amounts so received to the payment of the creditors in the other country who are satisfied according to a variety of principles.[55] The clearing system has, particularly in Switzerland, led to many decisions and much academic discussion.[56] The reason is that the clearing system can operate only if private traders strictly

---

[48] *Documents on International Affairs*, 1936, p. 668.

[49] It has been estimated that in 1949, 13.8 per cent of Switzerland's foreign trade was still subject to clearing: Langen, *Internationale Zahlungsabkommen* (1958), p. 6. The Swiss Federal Tribunal said that Switzerland had entered into the Clearing Agreement with Germany 'in a position of constraint; she had to make an effort to attenuate, through countermeasures and international agreements, the disastrous effects of German exchange control legislation' (Decision of 8 Oct. 1935, *BGE*. 61, ii. 242, at p. 248, translation by Nussbaum, p. 513).

[50] Clearing Office (Roumania) Order 1936, S.R. & O. 1936, No. 427, as amended by S.R. & O. 1936, No. 1306; 1938, Nos. 235 and 908; 1939, No. 750; and 1940, No. 963, in each case with the Agreements in the Schedule. All these Orders were made under the Debts Clearing Office and Import Restrictions Act, 1934.

[51] Clearing Office (Italy) Order 1936, S.R. & O. 1936, No. 696, as amended by S.R. & O. 1936, No. 1193; 1938, No. 234; and 1943, No. 1436, in each case with the Agreements in the Schedule.

[52] Clearing Office (Turkey) Order 1936, S.R. & O. 1936, No. 1251 as amended by S.R. & O. 1938, No. 580; 1940, Nos. 31 and 208; 1945, No. 559, in each case with the Agreements in the Schedule.

[53] Clearing Office (Spain) Order, 1936, S.R. & O. 1936, No. 2, as amended by S.R. & O. 1936, Nos. 557 and 1305; 1940, No. 456; 1941, No. 944; 1942, No. 1419; and 1947, No. 590, again with the Agreements in the Schedule.

[54] See the formulation by Langen (above, n. 49) at p. 11.

[55] For a helpful descriptive statement, see J. E. Meade, *The Balance of Payments* (1951), pp. 390, 391.

[56] The literature is collected by Nussbaum, p. 517 sqq., the best and perhaps the only source of legal information on this topic in the English language, Hug, *Rec.* 79 (1951, ii) 540, or Langen (above, n. 49). On the currency clauses in Clearing Agreements see Krulj, *Rev. Crit.* 1970, 401.

observe the stringent regulations intended to ensure the payment for all goods covered by the treaty to the Clearing Office exclusively, a condition liable to cause much hardship to creditors. Indeed, the main issue in litigation related to the creditor's rights in payments made to the debtor's,[57] or received by the creditor's, Clearing Office.

Since the end of the Second World War[58] bilateral Monetary Agreements have usually[59] taken the form of so-called Payment Agreements of which, at times, there were almost four hundred in force.[60] The first[61] such Agreement was the Anglo-Belgian Monetary Agreement of 1944 which exemplified the normal type of Payment Agreement 'with limited credits'.[62] Such an Agreement does not interfere with the normal course of business. It merely presupposes the observance by traders of their respective local exchange control regulations. But the two central banks sell to each other limited amounts of the respective currencies, so that these can be used for the purposes of

[57] Thus in the only English case in which the clearing system fell to be considered, *Fischler* v. *Administrator of Roumanian Property*, [1960] 3 All E.R. 433, the question was whether a credit balance standing in the books of the Anglo-Roumanian Clearing Office in London was 'property, rights or interests' of the Roumanian exporter or of his Roumanian bank to whose credit the payment had been made. The House of Lords answered in the former sense. Similar issues arose in Sweden.

[58] A Payments Agreement of a special kind was concluded already before the war between Nazi Germany and the United Kingdom, whereby Germany undertook, *inter alia*, to earmark 55 per cent of the value of her exports to the United Kingdom to discharge commercial debts: Anglo-German Payments Agreement of 1 Nov. 1934 (Cmd. 4963) as amended by the Agreement of 1 July 1938 (Cmd. 5787); see also the Anglo-German Transfer Agreements of 4 July 1934 and 1 July 1938 (Cmd. 4640 and 5788).

[59] See, however, the Agreements between the United Kingdom and Indonesia of 1 August 1967 as extended and amended (Cmnd. 3528, 3885, 4045, and 5204) and between the United Kingdom and Chile of 8 November 1972 and 30 October 1974 (Cmnd. 5209 and 5922), which regulated the payment and transfer of certain commercial debts due to British creditors from Indonesian and/or Chilean debtors. There were also numerous Agreements on the commercial debts of Turkey, in particular Cmnd. 7529, 8071, and 8189. The last-mentioned Agreement, for instance, makes payments in Turkish lire an 'official obligation of Turkey' and guarantees the transfer of all payments in accordance with a transfer scheme. For this purpose refinancing loans were simultaneously granted to Turkey: Cmnd. 8209 and 8210.

[60] In 1954 Trued and Mikesell, *Postwar Bilateral Payments Agreements* (Princeton, 1955), p. 10, counted 388. In 1980 there were 123 Agreements in force: International Monetary Fund, *Annual Report on Arrangements and Exchange Restrictions* (1980), p. 19.

[61] According to Trued and Mikesell, loc. cit., p. 35. The Agreement was published as Cmd. 6557. For a long list of other Agreements to which the United Kingdom was a party see the second edition of this book, p. 352, n. 2. The latest Payments Agreement, probably, is that concluded on 10 Oct. 1964 between Sierra Leone and Guinea: *International Legal Materials*, iv (1965), 332; this provides for reciprocal payment facilities up to £500,000 and in Art. IV prescribes certain adjustments in case of a change of the gold parity of the pound sterling.

[62] Meade, loc. cit., p. 393. On the legal questions arising from Payments Agreements see Langen, loc. cit.; Rudolf Erb, *Die bilateralen Zahlungs- und Kreditabkommen, Festgabe für Eugen Grossmann* (Zürich, 1949); Wabnitz, *Der zwischenstaatliche Zahlungsverkehr auf der Grundlage Internationaler Zahlungsabkommen* (1955); Paroutsas, *Interstate Agreements on International Payments* (Athens, 1970).

trade, any excess being due to be paid in gold. Thus the Bank of England would sell to Belgium £5 million for Belgian francs 883,125,000, so that Belgian importers could draw on the sterling fund to pay their British exporters, while the National Bank of Belgium would sell Belgian francs 883,125,000 for £5 million, so that British importers could use the Belgian francs to pay their Belgian exporters. These figures establish the 'swing' up to which any unbalance does not require settlement during the life of the Agreement.

Finally, a Monetary Agreement of a technical character, but with a much extended scope, was the European Payments Union which existed during the ten years ended in December 1958, and constituted an International Clearing Union involving 'the full and automatic off-setting of all bilateral surpluses and deficits incurred by each participating country with all others'.[63] It was succeeded by the European Monetary Agreement[64] which again provided for a multilateral system of settlements, but applied only to settlements outside the freely operating market through which, under the re-established regime of convertibility, the vast majority of settlements were effected.[65]

# IV

Monetary Institutions, in the present context, are international organizations the principal and specific object of which is the initiation and implementation of monetary policies and facilities.

1. Such Institutions, accordingly, do not include financial, particularly banking organizations like the International Bank for Reconstruction and Development or the European Investment Bank, whose functions lie outside the field of monetary policies. Nor do they comprise entities whose manifold and very general purposes of an economic character extend incidentally to monetary ones with the result that on occasion such entities may supplement and reinforce the tasks and responsibilities of monetary Institutions *stricto sensu*. A significant illustration is supplied by the Constitution of the

[63] This definition is used by Triffin, *Europe and the Money Muddle* (New Haven, 1957), pp. 168, 169. On the European Payments Union, now a matter of the past, see Mann, *Rec.* 96 (1959, i), pp. 28–30, and the literature there referred to; W. M. Scammell, *International Monetary Policy* (1967), pp. 288, 311 sqq.

[64] Cmd. 9602. In 1965 it was extended to the end of 1968 and slightly amended: *European Yearbook*, xiii (1965), 321.

[65] For details, see Mann (above, n. 63) at pp. 30, 31, the literature there cited and, in particular, Elkin, *European Yearbook*, vii (1961), 148 and Shuster (above, p. 464, n. 7), p. 260. On European Payments generally, see Dahm, *Völkerrecht* ii (1961), 648 with further references; on economic and financial aspects see Graham L. Rees, *Britain and the Post-War European Payments System* (1963). The European Monetary Agreement came to an end on 31 December 1972: Hahn and Weber (below, p. 503, n. 67, p. 247, who also deal with the subsequent development.

Organization for European Economic Co-operation,[66] or of its successor organization, the *Organization for Economic Co-operation and Development*.[67] The principal aim of the latter is the achievement of 'the highest maintainable economic growth'.[68] In consequence the Member States, which now amount to twenty-four,[69] have entered into a number of undertakings; among them is the duty to 'pursue their efforts to reduce or abolish obstacles to the exchange of goods and services and current payments and maintain and extend the liberalisation of capital movements'.[70] It was as a result of such aims and undertakings that the European Payments Union and, later, the European Monetary Agreement came into being[71] and that a Code of Liberalization[72] was adopted on 18 August 1950 and often revised and enlarged. It was intended to bring about the liberalization of trade by the progressive elimination of restrictions on imports and on what has become known as invisible transactions listed in Annex B to the Code. It is not impossible, therefore, that in a given case a State's duties in the monetary field may be derived from, or at least amplified by, the terms of the Constitution of O.E.C.D.

A similar position arises under the treaty establishing the *European Economic Community*. It is probably fair to say that in the monetary field each member State's overriding duty is to 'pursue the economic policy necessary to ensure the equilibrium of its overall balance of payments and to maintain confidence in its currency, while ensuring a high level of employment and the stability of the level of prices'.[73] The co-ordination required for the purpose of promoting the policy so defined is entrusted to a Monetary Committee with consultative status.[74] There are some provisions dealing with the alteration of rates of exchange, difficulties in maintaining a balance of payment, mutual assistance, and emergency measures.[75]

---

[66] See Cmd. 7388 and, generally, Elkin, *European Yearbook*, iv (1958), 96.

[67] It was established by a treaty of 14 Dec. 1960, Cmnd. 1646. On O.E.C.D. generally, see Dahm, *Völkerrecht*, ii (1961), 641, and in particular, Hahn and Weber, *Die OECD* (1976) with references to literature at pp. 7 and 397.

[68] Art. 1.

[69] I.M.F.'s *Annual Report on Exchange Arrangements and Exchange Restrictions 1979*, p. 7.

[70] Art. 2 (d).                                                    [71] Above, p. 502.

[72] On the effect of the Code on the liberalization of capital movements see Grewlich, *RIW/AWD* 1977, 252.

[73] Art. 104.                                                     [74] Art. 105.

[75] Arts. 107, 108, 109. The only decision of the European Court of Justice seems to be the difficult case of *Compagnie d'Approvisionnement, de Transport et de Crédit S.A. v. Commission of the EEC, European Court of Justice Reports* 1972 I 391 or *C.M.L.R.* 1974, 452, where compensation was claimed for the Commission's alleged failure to order France to pay adequate subsidies for losses resulting from the devaluation of the franc. It was held (p. 406) that Art. 107 leaves it to 'each Member State to decide upon any alteration of the rate of exchange of its currency under the conditions laid down in that provision'. Although

The Treaty thus provides a framework within which it is possible to proceed to a harmonized or common monetary system or, as has recently been suggested, even a Monetary Union. The more specific duties in regard to the movement of capital and current payments[76] which are in force now and, as will be shown later,[77] very largely supplemental in character, would no doubt be absorbed by developments of such far-reaching scope.[78]

The European Economic Community's most important practical achievement in the monetary field is the creation of what is known as the European Monetary System.[79] This was established in consequence of a Resolution of the European Council of 5 December 1978 and came into effect early in 1979. The United Kingdom does not at present participate. The System's operation cannot readily be ascertained and assessed and in any event will have to prove its effectiveness in critical circumstances. It is based on the European Currency Unit, the ECU, which is identical with the European Monetary Unit established in 1975 in the place of the original European Monetary Unit, adopted in 1959 and affirmed in 1973, of 0.88867088 gramme of fine gold (the gold content of a dollar between 1934 and 1972). The ECU is defined 'as the sum of the following amounts of the currency of the Member States, viz. 0.828 German mark, 0.0885 pound sterling, 1.15 French francs, 109 Italian lire, 0.286 Dutch guilder, 3.66 Belgian francs, 0.14 Luxembourg franc, 0.217 Danish krone, 0.00759 Irish pound', and may be revised from time to time, but 'revisions have to be mutually accepted'. The value of the ECU is being calculated daily and published in news-

---

Art. 103 (2) empowers the Council to alleviate the effects of a devaluation or a revaluation, 'it does not follow that the Council must compensate for all those effects in so far as they are adverse' to traders. The Council has 'a wide power of discretion'. And although Art. 40 (3) establishes the principle of non-discrimination in matters of agricultural policy, the Council is under no duty in the case of a devaluation to make provision for French producers of grain to put them on the same level as producers in other Member States.

[76] Arts. 67–73, 106.                                        [77] Below, p. 517.

[78] Similar duties were imposed by the defunct Treaty for East African Co-operation: *International Legal Materials*, vi (1967), 938, Art. 25. It also includes the familiar undertaking 'to pursue an economic policy aimed at ensuring the equilibrium of its overall balance of payments and confidence in the currency' (Art 27). The Partner States affirmed their 'endeavour to harmonize their monetary policies to the extent required for the proper functioning of the Common Market and the fulfilment of the aims of the Community', such consultation, co-operation, and review being entrusted to the Governors of the three Central Banks (Art. 27).

[79] The details (most of which were included in *The European Monetary System*, Cmnd. 7419) appear from an E.E.C. publication entitled *Texts concerning the European Monetary System* (1979). These texts are very confusing, mainly because the System has not been set up by a single and comprehensive document; moreover, as usual in these cases, the terminology cannot easily be understood by a lawyer and suffers from the defect described by Sir Winston Churchill (see the Preface to the third edition of this work).

papers.[80] Each currency has 'an ECU-related central rate.' Adjustments of central rates—no doubt a euphemism for devaluations and revaluations—are 'subject to mutual agreement'—a provision which, if it is observed in fact and if it were capable of enforcement, would constitute a far-reaching limitation of monetary sovereignty and may well have been the cause of the United Kingdom's failure to participate. The central rate is intended to be protected, if necessary, by interventions in participating currencies. Fluctuation margins of ±2.25 and, in the case of presently floating currencies, ±6 per cent, i.e. a spread of 4.50 and/or 12 per cent, are allowed and, 'when the intervention points defined by the fluctuation margins are reached', intervention[81] becomes compulsory; in addition, when the 'threshold of divergence', i.e. 75 per cent of the maximum spread is reached, 'this results in a presumption that the authorities concerned will correct this situation by adequate measures'. Moreover the European Monetary Co-operation Fund which exists since 1973[82] has received from each participating country 20 per cent of its gold holdings[83] as well as of its 'gross dollar reserves' in 'the form of three-month revolving swaps' against ECUs. These may be used as a means of settlement and for transactions between central banks and the Fund.

The purpose of the ECU is to serve as the denominator (numéraire) for the exchange mechanism, as a basis for a divergence indicator, as the denominator for interventions and credit mechanisms, and as a means of settlement between monetary authorities of the E.E.C. It

[80] See the publication in the *Financial Times* of 1 May 1981:

EMS EUROPEAN CURRENCY UNIT RATES

| | ECU central rates | Currency amounts against ECU May 1 | % change from central rate | % change adjusted for divergence | Divergence limit % |
|---|---|---|---|---|---|
| Belgian Franc | 40.7985 | 41.3076 | +1.25 | +1.19 | ±1.5361 |
| Danish Krone | 7.91917 | 8.00607 | +1.10 | +1.04 | ±1.6413 |
| German D-Mark | 2.54502 | 2.53953 | −0.22 | −0.28 | ±1.1386 |
| French Franc | 5.99526 | 6.02220 | +0.45 | +0.39 | ±1.3638 |
| Dutch Guilder | 2.81318 | 2.82333 | +0.36 | +0.30 | ±1.5159 |
| Irish Punt | 0.685145 | 0.693698 | +1.25 | +1.19 | ±1.6688 |
| Italian Lire | 1262.92 | 1264.60 | +0.13 | +0.13 | ±4.1116 |

Changes are for ECU, therefore positive change denotes a weak currency. Adjustment calculated by Financial Times.

See also below, p. 508, n. 101.

[81] By whom?

[82] Council Regulation No. 907/73 of 3 April 1973, *Official Journal* of 5 April 1973 or *International Legal Materials 1973*, 1154. On the Fund see Ehlermann, *Europarecht*, 1973, 193.

[83] Is this a step towards the 'remonetization' of gold?

is a curious fact that no mention is made of any intention to use the ECU as the universal unit of account for purposes of the E.E.C. itself, i.e. in particular for the Community's budget, customs and the agricultural policy. In these and certain other respects the practice prevailing for about two years as well as its history is extraordinarily confusing and complex; the details are devoid of general interest, but were described in contributions of great specificity.[84] Since 1 January 1981, however, the ECU unit of account is in force for all purposes of the Community.

2. Whatever the monetary powers and responsibilities of Institutions primarily devoted to far more comprehensive tasks may be, in the strictly monetary sphere paramount status doubtless attaches to the *International Monetary Fund*,[85] an international organization now comprising member States. Its aims, policies, and functions are probably the source from which smaller entities derive their inspiration.

The Fund,[86] conceived at Bretton Woods in the year 1944, in existence since 27 December 1945 and in operation since 1 March 1947, is intended to fulfil, so it may be suggested, three broad functions. In the first place the Fund 'is established and shall operate' for, and shall in all its policies and decisions be guided by, the purposes of, *inter alia*, promoting 'international monetary cooperation through a permanent institution which provides the machinery for consultation and collaboration on international monetary problems'.[87] This implies, in particular, the expansion of monetary trade, the promotion of exchange stability, and the creation of a multilateral system of payments. Secondly, as a method of carrying out these overriding objects, the Articles of Agreement, as has already been explained,[88] imposed certain specific duties upon

---

[84] Carreau, *Revue du Marché Commun*, 1979, 399; Focsaneanu (above, p. 464, n. 7) Nos. 85 sqq.; Hahn, *Europarecht* XIV (1979), 337 and *Gedächtnisschrift für Sasse* (1981), p. 441; H. J. Timman, *Die europäischen Rechnungseinheiten* (1979); Rainer Hellman, *Das Europäische Währungssystem* (1979). There does not seem to be any survey in the English language nor have many English traders participated in the flood of litigation which has come before the European Court of Justice and relates to (frequently immensely narrow and technical questions of currency. But see now an article in English by Radicati di Brozolo, Riv. di Dir. Internazionale 1980, 330.

[85] Cmd. 6546, as amended in 1969 and 1978. For literature, see above, p. 31, n. 16, and Focsaneanu, Clunet, 1968, 239.

[86] For literature see above, p. 31, n. 16. In his pamphlet *The Rule of Law in the International Monetary Fund* (1980), p. 2, Sir Joseph Gold states that 'before the Articles of Agreement of the Fund came into existence international monetary law, whether customary or conventional, was negligible'. The whole of Part IV of the present work proves the contrary, but the statement is characteristic of Sir Joseph's tendency to overrate the relevance and significance of the Fund and its practice to the law in general and monetary law in particular.

[87] Art. 1.     [88] Above, pp. 31 sqq.

member States by creating a system of par values with a strictly limited 'spread', for which, as from 1 April 1978 the Second Amendment substituted an inherently feeble system of surveillance over exchange arrangements.[89] It leaves the Fund with no more than nominal legal rights and member States with no more than nominal duties in regard to the all-important problem of exchange stability. Thirdly, in order to increase their liquid international reserves, member States are allowed access to the Fund's pool of currencies. Originally this was derived only from the member States' subscriptions. It is available for certain transactions with the Fund, viz. the purchase of another member's currency either for gold[90] or in exchange for the purchasing member's own currency;[91] in addition a member is at certain intervals obliged to repurchase certain holdings of its own currency from the Fund in exchange for gold or convertible currencies.[92] These transactions which give rise to many difficulties of interpretation[93] failed to ensure a fully adequate measure of international liquidity and, therefore, in 1969 the Articles of Agreement were amended so as to provide for a system of Special Drawing Rights,[94] a facility defined in terms of even greater obscurity.

An SDR[95] is simply a book entry, viz. a credit in the books of the International Monetary Fund in favour of participating members, in respect of which the Fund pays interest in terms of SDR at a rate determined by it.[96] The value of a unit of SDRs which originally was 0.888671 gram of fine gold, i.e. equal to the gold value of the 'classical' dollar[97] and was in the summer of 1974 without any change of the Articles of Agreement based on the 'standard basket method of

---

[89] Art. IV as amended. For literature on the Second Amendment see above, p. 34, n. 30.

[90] Art. V, s. 6.

[91] Art. V, s. 3.

[92] Art. V, s. 7.

[93] See, generally, Triffin, *Europe and the Money Muddle* (1957), pp. 111, 128 sqq.; L'Huillier, *Théorie et Pratique de la Coopération Economique Internationale* (1957), pp. 398, 399; Dahm, *Völkerrecht* ii (1961), 612; Gold, *The Reform of the Fund* (1969), pp. 32 sqq.; 12 (1963) *I.C.L.Q.* 1 (on Stand-by Agreements); 16 (1967) *I.C.L.Q.* pp. 320 sqq. (on Borrowing and Stand-by Agreements); J.-D. Kramer, *Die Rechtsnatur der Geschäfte des Internationalen Währungsfonds* (1967).

[94] Now Articles XV to XXV.

[95] For literature see the writings of Sir Joseph Gold, in particular *Special Drawing Rights* (Pamphlet No. 13, 1970); *Floating Currencies, Gold and SDRs* (Pamphlet No. 19, 1976); *Floating Currencies, SDRs and Gold* (Pamphlet No. 22, 1977); *SDRs, Gold and Currencies* (Pamphlet No. 26, 1979, and No. 33, 1980); *IMF Staff Papers* xxiii (1976), 295; Shuster (above, p. 464, n. 7), pp. 198 sqq.; G. Schlaeger, *Die internationale Buchgeldschöpfung* (Frankfurt 1971); Franz R. Walter, *Die Sonderziehungsrechte* (Berlin, 1974).

[96] Art. xx, Sections 1 to 3.

[97] Art. xxi Section 2 of the original version of the Articles of Agreement.

valuation'[98] is since the Second Amendment determined by the Fund.[99] At first it was again the sum of the values of sixteen currencies, but these were changed in July 1978 mainly by the substitution of the Saudi Arabian riyal and the Iranian rial for the Danish krone and the South African rand, in the latter case no doubt for political rather than commercial reasons. Since 1 January 1981 the SDR is the sum of the value of five currencies.[100] The value of the SDR in terms of currencies is published in the daily newspapers and therefore readily ascertainable.[101] SDRs, when allocated by the Fund to

[98] The composition of the basket was as follows:

|  | Weight (in per cent) | Amount (in units of each currency) |
|---|---|---|
| U.S. dollar | 33 | 0.40 |
| Deutsche mark | 12.5 | 0.38 |
| Pound sterling | 9 | 0.045 |
| French franc | 7.5 | 0.44 |
| Japanese yen | 7.5 | 26 |
| Canadian dollar | 6 | 0.071 |
| Italian lira | 6 | 47 |
| Netherlands guilder | 4.5 | 0.14 |
| Belgian franc | 3.5 | 1.60 |
| Swedish krona | 2.5 | 0.13 |
| Australian dollar | 1.5 | 0.012 |
| Danish krone | 1.5 | 0.11 |
| Norwegian krone | 1.5 | 0.099 |
| Spanish peseta | 1.5 | 1.10 |
| Austrian schilling | 1 | 0.22 |
| South African rand | 1 | 0.0082 |
|  | 100 |  |

[99] Art. xv, Section 2.

[100]

|  | Weight (in per cent) | Amount (in units of each currency) |
|---|---|---|
| U.S. dollar | 42 | 0.54 |
| Deutsche mark | 19 | 0.46 |
| French franc | 13 | 0.74 |
| Japanese yen | 13 | 34 |
| Pound sterling | 13 | 0.071 |
|  | 100 |  |

[101] *Financial Times*, 1 May 1981:

| April 29 | Bank rate % | Special Drawing Rights | European Currency Unit |
|---|---|---|---|
| Sterling | 12 | 0.560551 | 0.536194 |
| U.S. $ | 13 | 1.20098 | 1.14987 |
| Canadian $ | 17.40 | 1.43769 | 1.37616 |
| Austria Sch. | 6¾ | 18.7173 | 17.9379 |
| Belgium F | 14 | 43.1993 | 41.3837 |
| Danish K | 11 | 8.33600 | 7.99560 |
| D mark | 7½ | 2.64732 | 2.53833 |

participating members[102] to the extent of (undefined) percentages of (undefined) 'quotas'[103] as determined by the Fund,[104] confer the right upon participants either by agreement with other participants to exchange them for an equivalent amount of currency[105] or in the event of a need being proved[106] 'to obtain an equivalent amount of currency from a participant'[107] who will be designated by the Fund.[108] In both cases participants using their Special Drawing Rights 'shall reconstitute their holdings of them'[109] in accordance with rules which are far from clear,[110] but probably involve the repayment of the currency received. In these circumstances an SDR is a standard of value. It is also a method of obtaining temporarily a foreign currency asset. Those who regard 'bank money' as money[111] in the legal sense will attribute the same quality to SDRs. The point is, however, of no practical significance. The reasons which rendered it necessary and appropriate to exclude the law of banking and credits from the scope of this book require and justify the conclusion that the admittedly peculiar type of credit which the SDR represents should in the present context not be discussed in detail.

A discussion, however summary, of the International Monetary Fund as an Institution of international monetary policy cannot be concluded without a reference to the *General Agreement on Tariffs and Trade*.[112] In order to understand the interrelationship it is necessary to remember that 'trade restrictions and exchange controls are largely interchangeable techniques to achieve the same results'.[113] The Fund's Articles of Agreement excluded trade restrictions from its purview, and thus created 'enormous loopholes'[114] to which the Fund drew attention in its first Annual Report.[115] GATT is intended to fill them. It does so not only by providing for close co-operation with the Fund,[116] but also by laying down the clear duty that 'Contracting Parties shall not, by exchange action, frustrate the intent of the provisions of this Agreement, nor, by trade action, the intent of the provisions of the Articles of Agreement of the International Monetary Fund'.[117]

| | | | |
|---|---|---|---|
| Guilder | 9 | 2.94660 | 2.82177 |
| French Fr. | 9½ | 6.27692 | 6.01495 |
| Lira | 19 | 1318.68 | 1262.84 |
| Yen | 6¼ | (U) | 246.589 |
| Norwgn. Kr. | 9 | 6.64622 | 6.36739 |
| Spanish Pts. | 8 | 106.84 | 102.338 |
| Swedish Kr. | 12 | 5.70922 | 5.46900 |
| Swiss Fr. | 4 | — | 2.31606 |
| Greek Dr'ch. | 20½ | — | 61.7939 |

[102] Art. xv, Section 1.   [103] Art. xviii, Section 2.   [104] Art. xviii.
[105] Art. xix, Section 2 (b).   [106] Art. xix, Section 3.   [107] Art. xix, Section 2 (a).
[108] Art. xix, Section 5.   [109] Art. xix, Section 6.   [110] Schedule G.
[111] Above, p. 6.   [112] Cmd. 9413.
[113] Triffin (above, p. 507, n. 93), p. 124.   [114] Triffin, loc. cit.
[115] p. 38.   [116] Art. XV.   [117] Art. XV (4).

# XX

# Treaty Rules of Monetary Conduct

I. Conventional and customary international law of money. II. The title to enforce treaty rights. III. Treaty law and treaty purposes. IV. The duty of co-operation and consultation in monetary affairs. V. The duty to maintain the stability of currencies. VI. Discriminatory currency arrangements and multiple currency practices. VII. The duty of convertibility for current international transactions: (1) the meaning of 'restrictions' on convertibility and of exchange control under the International Monetary Fund; (2) the general effect of the duty of convertibility; (3) the meaning of current transactions; (4) exchange restrictions and import restrictions. VIII. Bilateral Treaties: (1) the duty of equal treatment in operating exchange control; (2) the duty of fair and equitable treatment in operating exchange control. IX. Bilateral Treaties (continued): the duty (1) to pay for goods and (2) to transfer new investment capital and profits.

I

RULES of monetary conduct, which arise from treaties, in principle apply only as between the contracting Parties. It would be wrong to assume that they express universally binding duties.

In some cases, it is true, treaties merely repeat, perhaps in slightly different language, what in essence is a duty imposed by customary international law; the foremost example is the familiar provision whereby States undertake to 'accord fair and equitable treatment' to each other's nationals,[1] and which in law is unlikely to amount to more than a confirmation of the obligation to act in good faith, or to refrain from abuse or arbitrariness. In other cases the question may be put whether any of the rules of conventional international law have become so universal in application and so intensive in character as to lead to the creation of rules of customary international law. When do the provisions of a treaty cease to constitute the law between the parties and become evidence of the law as between all? The problem is a general one, and will have to be viewed in the light of the principles followed in a recent decision of the International Court of Justice.[2] One cannot help feeling that in the field of monetary law the development, spread over a period of

---

[1] This phrase occurs, for instance, in Art. 1 of all the American Treaties of Friendship, Commerce, and Navigation to which reference will be made below, p. 524.

[2] *North Sea Continental Shelf Cases*, I.C.J. Reports, 1969, 1. Whatever one may think about the decision in the particular case, it is possible that the general approach of some of the dissenting opinions, particularly the opinion of Judge Lachs, is agreeably progressive in character. For a general discussion see Baxter, *Rec.* 129 (1970, i) 31.

thirty-five years, has been so rapid as to demand restraint upon any inclination to deduce rules of customary law from rules of conventional law. Where a very large international organization such as the International Monetary Fund with its almost 140 members has developed a clearly definable rule, the hesitation may be less pronounced. Thus if 141 States grant each other the right 'to regulate international capital movements',[3] it is impossible to suggest that the imposition of such control is necessarily and always contrary to customary international law.

Subject to such highly exceptional cases, however, the distinction between customary and conventional international law should not become blurred.

## II

It follows that the right to enforce treaty obligations is ordinarily vested in the contracting Parties.

Thus the question whether the nationals of a contracting State or a third State may derive benefits from a treaty is governed by the general law. So is the very important question, thrown up by the Articles of Agreement of the International Monetary Fund, whether a duty laid down by these Articles exists only between the member States and the Fund or also as between the member States themselves. Construction of the Articles, to which one would primarily have resort in searching for an answer is hardly likely to lead to an unequivocal result. In particular, the fact that the Articles provide the Fund with certain sanctions against a member in default does not justify the conclusion that innocent members or any one of them is precluded from exercising the remedies which international law normally allows against a contracting party for breach of a treaty. Accordingly, it may be necessary to inquire whether there is room for the submission that in the private law of the representative systems of law the charter of a corporation is considered as a contract both between the corporation and its members and between the members themselves, and that the analogy so discovered ought to supply guidance. The problem[4] transcends the scope of the present work, but should probably be answered in favour of the second and wider solution. It will underlie many of the following observations, and may acquire great practical importance if, for

---

[3] Art. VI, S. 3; see on the point above, p. 375.

[4] It has not been possible to find any material bearing upon the problem. On its position in private law, see s. 20 of the Companies Act, 1948, and Gower, *Modern Company Law* (4th ed., 1979), p. 315 with further references.

instance, a member State, contrary to Art. VIII (2) (*a*) of the Fund Agreement, restricts current payments.

## III

All treaties establishing rules of monetary conduct pursue specific purposes which are frequently defined and of which those mentioned in the first Article of the constitution of the International Monetary Fund are probably representative. They include, in particular, the promotion of international monetary co-operation, the stability of exchanges, the creation of a multilateral system of payments, the elimination of exchange restrictions and of any disequilibrium in the international balance of payments. Such statements provide valuable and frequently indispensable aids in construing the treaty, but they should not be treated as laying down legally binding rights and duties. It would be wrong, therefore, to derive from the very broad terms of Art. I of the International Monetary Fund Agreement specific legal duties which are not reflected in the express terms of the treaty.

This would be a somewhat platitudinous submission were it not for certain pronouncements made by the International Court of Justice in its judgment in the *Case concerning Rights of Nationals of the United States of America in Morocco.*[5] In that case the United States alleged that its citizens were entitled to the benefits of the principle of 'economic liberty without any inequality', and that that principle had been violated by France restricting Moroccan imports from the United States. It is clear that the principle was assured to the United States by a number of treaties made before 1906 either with it direct or with other States, but subject to a most-favoured-nation clause. The court, however, held that the Moroccan decrees 'contravened the rights which the United States has acquired under the Act of Algeciras' of 7 April 1906.[6] Whether that Act in fact conferred any rights which could be said to be put in issue by the Moroccan decrees in question is extraordinarily doubtful. The principle is mentioned in one Article relating to the alienation of public services.[7] It is also mentioned in the Preamble.[8] Such ephemeral references should not be regarded as the source of a firm and general legal duty.[9]

[5] I.C.J. Reports, 1952, 176.
[6] p. 185, and see p. 184.                                    [7] Art. 105.
[8] Pleadings i. 578.
[9] See, generally, *Rec.* 96 (1959, i), pp. 38–40. It is odd that the general literature on the interpretation of treaties has failed to analyse the judgment's aspects which are mentioned in the text.

## IV

Even where a treaty includes the promotion of international monetary co-operation among the express obligations of the contracting States rather than the purposes of the treaty,[10] it may be open to some doubt whether a legally enforceable duty is created. The same applies to the duty of consultation which many treaties of a monetary character introduce.[11] Both duties, it is true, must be discharged in good faith and reasonably. To adapt the language of the International Court of Justice used in relation to the duty to negotiate,[12] the contracting States are under an obligation to co-operate or to consult with a view to arriving at a result, and not merely to go through a formal process of co-operation or consultation. They are under an obligation so to conduct themselves that the collaboration is meaningful.

Yet, in the last resort, such duties leave the sovereignty and discretion of the contracting States almost completely intact. Private law does not provide an analogy for making them more than 'indefinite and elastic',[13] or for denying that they are capable of being fulfilled 'by a somewhat nominal act'.[14] Nor do precedents taken from the sphere of monetary law lead to a different impression, particularly because in monetary matters there often exists a real need for secrecy which is likely to be prejudiced by intensive consultation. It is for this reason that one can perhaps understand, though not forgive, the much-criticized failure of the British Government

[10] See, for instance, Articles of Agreement of the International Monetary Fund, Art. IV, s. 4 (a); General Agreement on Tariffs and Trade, Art. XV; Common Market Treaty, Arts. 105, 107; Convention on the Organization for Economic Co-operation and Developments, Art. 3 (c). See also numerous bilateral Agreements, such as Arts. 6 and 8 of the former Anglo-Belgian Monetary Agreement of 1944 (Cmd. 6557).

[11] The Articles of Agreement of the International Monetary Fund do not introduce a general duty of consultation; by Art. IV, s. 3 (b), and Art. VIII, ss. 3 and 6 they limit it to certain cases. Under the terms of the 'letter of Intent' which borrowing States usually address to the Fund and which the United Kingdom, for instance, wrote on 22 May 1969 (*The Times*, 24 June 1969), the duty of consultation is extended to 'the course of the United Kingdom economy and any further measures affecting the balance of payments that may be appropriate'. See, further, General Agreement for Tariffs and Trade, Arts. XV (2) and XXII; Convention on the Organization for Economic Co-operation and Development, Art. 3 (b); and numerous bilateral Agreements.

[12] *North Sea Continental Shelf Cases*, I.C.J. Reports, 1969, 1, at p. 47; see also Permanent Court of International Justice in the *Case concerning the Railway Traffic between Poland and Lithuania*, Series A/B, No. 32, p. 116. On the other hand in *Greece* v. *Federal Republic of Germany*, Int. L.R. 47, 418, the Arbitral Tribunal for the Agreement on German External Debts would appear to have put the duty imposed by a *pactum de negotiando* much too high.

[13] Lauterpacht, Second Report on the Law of Treaties (International Law Commission, 6th Session) U.N. Document A/CN 4/87, p. 5.

[14] Lauterpacht, First Report on the Law of Treaties (International Law Commission, 5th Session) U.N. Document A/CN 4/63, p. 25.

to comply even in a nominal sense with its duty of consultation with the Fund[15] and other Governments before it devalued sterling in September 1949. What happened in fact has been described as follows:[16]

It is no longer a secret that the British, irked by a previous American-led Fund campaign in favour of sterling devaluation and uneasy about news leaks from the unwieldy Executive Board session, did not propose a new par value for sterling in accordance with the Fund's Articles of Agreement. They merely told the Board one tense Saturday afternoon that the British Chancellor of the Exchequer would broadcast to the world on the following day the Cabinet's decision to devalue the pound from $4·03 to $2·80. The Chancellor would 'appreciate' it if he could announce at the same time the concurrence of the Fund with this 'decision'. . . . The Board agreed, in fact, the very same Saturday afternoon.

The British action may well have been a breach of duty, but international legislators ought not to impose duties of consultation which cannot reasonably be expected to be kept. In practice the intensity of co-operation and consultation must depend on the circumstances of each case.

# V

A clearly defined legal duty to maintain stable currencies does not at present exist.

The members of the Organization of Economic Co-operation and Development have merely undertaken to 'pursue policies designed to achieve . . . internal and external financial stability'.[17] Similarly, the members of the European Economic Community are bound to 'pursue the economic policy necessary to ensure the equilibrium of its overall balance of payments and to maintain confidence in its currency, while ensuring a high level of employment and the stability of the level of prices'.[18] Moreover, a member is bound to 'treat its policy with regard to exchange rates as a matter of common interest'.[19] But a member is free to let its currency float or to alter its exchange rate.[20]

[15] Art. IV, s. 5 (b) and (c) of the original version.

[16] Triffin, *Europe and the Money Muddle* (1957), p. 119. The British Government spoke of one day's notice of its intention to devalue: Hansard, Parliamentary Debates, House of Commons, 27 Sept. 1949, col. 10. See the letter from Mr. John Foster in *The Times*, 3 Oct. 1949; Williams, *World Affairs*, iv (1950), 23, or *The Economist*, 157 (1949), 681. On the devaluations of 1967 and international law see Carreau and others, *Annuaire Français de Droit International*, 1968, 597.

[17] Art. 2 (c).          [18] Art. 104.          [19] Art. 107 (1).

[20] Cf. Art. 107 (2). According to this provision, if a member alters its exchange rate in a manner incompatible with Art. 104, other members may be authorized to take measures

Within the International Monetary Fund, on the other hand, entirely different rules originally applied at any rate to those members who, like the United Kingdom, had established a par value of their currencies. Such members were under the specific duty,[21] firstly, to maintain the par value and, secondly, not to change it except in the conditions envisaged by the Articles of Agreement or to allow their currencies to 'float'. Nor, thirdly, were they ever under a duty to propose a change of the par value.

This system, spelled out by the original version of Art. IV, broke down in 1971 and is now only of historical interest as an experiment in the international management of money, which operated reasonably successfully for about twenty-five years, but was unable to withstand an economic crisis caused by the abrogation of the dollar convertibility into gold.[22] When on 1 April 1978 the new Art. IV came into force all that was left was the members' undertaking 'to collaborate with the Fund and other members to assure orderly exchange arrangements and to promote a stable system of exchange rates.' At the same time the Fund has the duty to 'oversee the international monetary system to ensure its effective operation' and 'the compliance of each member with its obligations' mentioned in the preceding sentence. Although the duties thus laid down are defined in some further detail, in essence they remain as vague as the quoted words suggest.[23] In particular, the par value system has disappeared and can only be introduced if the Fund so determines by an eighty-five per cent majority of the total voting power.

It is obvious, therefore, that there does not at present exist a realistic legal duty to ensure the international stability of currencies.


VI


A definite legal duty is laid down, when Art. VIII (3) provides

of protection or retaliation, but the legality of the alteration would seem to be clear. See the decision referred to above, p. 61, n. 168. As regards a refusal to alter an exchange rate which prejudices the economic policy required by Art. 104, this is sometimes said to constitute a breach of the Treaty: see Hoffmann-Riem, *Betriebsberater*, 1969, 1374, n. 4. The point is open to much doubt.

[21] See above, p. 32 sqq., where the literature is referred to. Hoffmann-Riem, *Betriebsberater*, 1969, 1378 (and, according to him, the German Federal Bank) agrees that the introduction of floating rates, even for a short period, was a clear breach of the treaty and, therefore, contrary to public international law. For the number of members to whom the duties applied, see the Schedule of Par Values, 1970. For the initial determination of par values, see Art. XX, s. 5.

[22] For an argument that this constituted a violation of the I.M.F.'s Articles of Agreement see Zehetner, *Die Suspendierung der Goldkonvertibilität des Dollars* (Vienna, 1973).

[23] Sir Joseph Gold, *Selected Essays* (1980), p. 390, is reading far too much into the duty to collaborate.

that, in the absence of approval by the International Monetary Fund, no member may engage in 'any discriminatory currency arrangements or multiple currency practices'.[24]

The meaning of the former term is far from clear and has led to very little discussion.[25] It could be understood as referring to arrangements in the nature of a treaty, which are directed against a particular currency or currency area and thus discriminate against it. But probably the phrase does not carry so narrow a meaning and is intended to refer to 'practices', as the heading in fact indicates. On the other hand, the nature of multiple currency practices, though hardly anywhere defined by a form of words, can be more readily gleaned from the rich material which accumulated during the last three decades. Such practices involve offering different rates for foreign currency according to the way in which it has been earned, i.e. according to the goods or services which have been sold, and charging different rates for foreign currency according to the way in which it is to be used, i.e. according to the goods and services which it is intended to buy.[26] Infinite variations are possible. The legal difficulty is to distinguish between a currency practice and a quantitative restriction, such as a concealed tariff or an export subsidy.

Thus the exaction of a tax or charge or premium on the occasion of the acquisition of exchange from a Central Bank for the payment of a certain type of goods is rightly regarded as a multiple currency practice. This was so held by an important Award[27] relating to a concession which Greece had granted and which exempted imports 'de toute imposition quelle qu'elle soit . . . sous forme de droits d'importation, d'impôts ou de taxes'. Greek law required the payment of a premium over and above the official rate of exchange for the purchase of sterling from the Bank of Greece for payment of certain imports. The majority of the Arbitrators (M. Paal Berg and Professor Spiropoulos, Me. André Mater dissenting) held that this was a measure of monetary readjustment, and was therefore not prohibited by the concession which contemplates only the payment of import duties and similar charges.

The International Monetary Fund itself refers to surcharges in

[24] Art. VIII, s. 3, which at present applies only to 54 member States, including Britain: I.M.F.'s *Annual Report* for the year ended 30 April 1980, p. 122. Multiple currency practices do not necessarily presuppose a system of exchange control: see W. M. Scammell, *International Monetary Policy*, p. 196.

[25] See, however, Gold, *The International Monetary Fund and Private Business Transactions* (1965), p. 14.

[26] See Scammell, loc. cit., pp. 108, 196. See above, p. 441.

[27] *Société Générale Hellénique S.A.* v. *Greece*, 4 (1951) Revue Hellénique de droit international, 373.

respect of the applicable customs duties, import deposits, exchange taxes, or taxes on travel and seems to suggest that such measures may involve multiple currency practices. Similarly, arrangements to encourage exports, such as tax rebates, cash subsidies, interest rate subsidies, and official export credit insurance, seem capable of coming within the Fund's definition.[28] The test must be whether the restriction or practice affects or is concerned with the currency and its characteristics such as the rate of exchange, i.e. the price of currency rather than the goods, their price or value. Thus this country's Customs (Import Deposits) Act, 1968, created 'a duty of customs', a tariff as opposed to a currency practice;[29] it is a clear example of legislation which cannot come under the heading of exchange restrictions. In view of the remaining provisions of Art. VIII which will presently be discussed it is probably unnecessary to analyse other, much more doubtful cases.

## VII

Those member States of the International Monetary Fund which no longer enjoy the protection of the transitional period under Art. XIV[30] have assumed the duty, laid down by Art. VIII (2) (*a*), not without the Fund's approval to 'impose restrictions on the making of payments and transfers for current transactions'.

The provision is supplemented by Art. VIII (4), according to which a member State shall buy for gold or foreign currency balances of its currency held by another member and resulting from current transactions. It is to be contrasted with its counterpart, namely Art. VI (3), according to which 'members may exercise such controls as are necessary to regulate international capital movements'.[31]

[28] International Monetary Fund's Annual Report on *Exchange Arrangements and Exchange Restrictions* 1979, pp. 8 sqq. and 1980, 17 sqq. or Silard, sections 60 sqq. who reports that, not surprisingly, the International Monetary Fund has found it difficult 'to distinguish clearly' between restrictions, multiple currency practices, and discriminatory currency arrangements.

[29] See Verbit, *Trade Agreements for Developing Countries* (1960), p. 96.

[30] Above, p. 516, n. 24. Here as elsewhere in this book, Art. VII dealing with scarce currencies is being ignored, for 'no currency has as yet ever been declared "scarce" and there are serious doubts as to whether Art. VII as drafted is workable in practice': Radcliffe Report (Cmnd. 827), para. 690.

[31] How is the word 'necessary' to be construed? Objectively necessary? If so, who decides? Or is it the subjective appreciation by the member State concerned that is contemplated? It is submitted that at any rate in those cases in which the restriction is objectively unnecessary, but maintained for purely political reasons, the member State is in breach of its obligations. Another very difficult question of construction is whether Art. VI (3) is so general in scope as to exclude, or is, on the contrary, subject to, Art. VIII (3) which prohibits discriminatory arrangements and multiple currency practices. According to Fawcett, *British Year Book of International Law*, 1964, 46, the Fund takes the former

These are truly fundamental rights and duties which are reinforced by the terms of other treaties,[32] and likely to necessitate an entirely novel approach towards the whole of the international law of exchange control.[33]

1. The Articles of Agreement of the International Monetary Fund aim at 'the elimination of foreign exchange restrictions which hamper the growth of world trade'.[34] They do not anywhere require the abolition of an existing, nor do they condemn the introduction of a new, system of exchange control, i.e. of an administrative machinery regulating international payments or other transfers. They merely demand that such systems of exchange control as exist or are introduced and as are and remain lawful should in fact be so administered and applied that the member State complies with the terms of the Agreement. That this is so is conclusively proved by the coexistence of Art. VIII (2) (a) and Art. VI (3). As the Radcliffe Committee pointed out,[35] control over capital movements, expressly authorized by Art. VI (3), 'requires the exercise of exchange control, however loose, over current transfers as well, since otherwise, as the Bank of England emphasised, it is not possible to identify capital movements and check them'. Consequently, when Art. VIII (2) (a) precludes the imposition of restrictions on current payments, it contemplates measures which in fact prevent or limit payments. It does not deny the legality of such requirements as the filling of forms, the submission of applications, the adducing of evidence and all the other paraphernalia which a bureaucratic system of control

view, but its correctness is far from certain; it must not be forgotten that Art. VIII deals with the 'general' obligations of member States.

[32] See, in particular, Arts. 67 and 106 of the Treaty of Rome; Art. 25 of the Treaty for East African Co-operation (*International Legal Materials* vi (1967), 957); or Art. 42 of the Agreement on Andean Subregional Integration between Bolivia, Colombia, Chile, Ecuador, and Peru, of 26 May 1969 (*International Legal Materials* viii (1969), 910) and the numerous bilateral treaties mentioned below, p. 527. As to the European Common Market see Börner, 'Die fünfte Freiheit des Gemeinsamen Markts: Der freie Zahlunsverkehr', in *Festschrift für Ophüls* (1965), 199, who concludes that in view of Arts. 108 and 109 of the Treaty the alleged free system of payments in the Common Market rests 'on feet of clay'. The ACP–EEC Convention signed in Lomé on 31 Oct. 1979 between 58 African, Caribbean and Pacific and nine European States includes Articles 156–159 relating to current payments and capital movements. They afford a measure of protection, but the escape clauses are so far-reaching that the legal obligation hardly amounts to more than the duty to act in good faith and without discrimination.

[33] It is illuminating to read two prominent participants of the Bretton Woods Conference, Sir Dennis Robertson and Lord Keynes, on their understanding of the interplay of Art. VIII (2) (a) and (4). Their contributions, entitled, respectively, 'An Essay in Rabbinics' and 'An Essay in Metarabbinics', disclose such differences of opinion that fresh doubt is thrown not only upon the intentions of, but also upon the texts produced by the drafters: *The Collected Writings of John Maynard Keynes*, xxvi (1980, ed. by Moggridge), pp. 114–127. See also above, p. 238, n. 39.

[34] Art. I (iv).

[35] Cmnd. 827, para. 727.

unfortunately, yet necessarily involves. The Articles of Agreement, in other words, condemn factual obstacles to current payments rather than a legal machinery which retards and burdens, but does not inevitably restrict payments and which, as appears from Art. VIII (2) (*b*), they call 'exchange control regulations'.

2. Convertibility[36] or transferability in the factual sense just discussed is guaranteed by Art. VIII (2) (*a*) for the benefit of non-residents. If a resident trader is to be paid by another resident for the sale of goods or other property abroad this is not an international transaction within the meaning of the Articles, whatever local exchange control regulations may provide. On the other hand, although the text is silent, the privilege is guaranteed only to member States of the Fund, including, it is believed, such members as have not yet accepted the obligations under Art. VIII (2), (3) and (4). This follows from Art. I (iv) according to which the Fund aims at 'a multilateral system of payments in respect of current transactions *between members*'.

Moreover, Art. VIII (2) (*a*) prohibits even partial restrictions of any kind. Thus convertibility is not accomplished if as a result of multiple currency practices payments are transferable at a discount.[37] Nor is it consonant with the Articles to limit convertibility to transfers to certain countries or in certain currencies. A non-resident creditor can require payments for current transactions to the country of his residence or anywhere else, and it would not be the function of authorities in the transferor country to ensure observance of any restrictions imposed by a foreign country. 'The guiding principle in ascertaining whether a measure is a restriction on payments and transfers for current transactions under Art. VIII (2), is whether it involves a direct governmental limitation on the availability or use of exchange as such.'[38]

Serious problems arise from the possibility of the Fund approving restrictions. Is it consent in a particular case or in a particular class of cases that under the Articles is required? Can the approval be given retrospectively? Can the approval be given for reasons other than the safeguarding of the balance of payments? It is not unnatural that the Fund does not consider itself a suitable forum for the discussion of the political and military considerations leading to restrictions which are solely related to the preservation of national or international security; the Fund is prepared to approve such restrictions at least by

[36] On this term see Sir Joseph Gold, *Rev. Crit.* 1980, and his earlier pamphlet *The Fund's Concept of Convertibility* (1971).

[37] See Art. IV, s. 1 (*b*).

[38] *Selected Decisions of the Executive Directors* (1976), p. 139 (decision No. 1034 of 1 June 1960).

silence and thus treats approval of restrictions based on reasons other than economic ones as *intra vires*.[39]

Art. VIII (2) (*a*) is concerned only with the 'making' of payments and transfers. If exporters are allowed to sell only for certain currencies to the exclusion of others, this is not contrary to the provision, though it may be caught by Art. VIII (3) which in principle prohibits discriminatory arrangements and multiple currency practices.[40] Nor does the provision touch the fate of payments after receipt. Member States are free to impose the duty upon exporters to surrender foreign currency received by them.

3. The definition of 'payments for current transactions' is supplied by Art. XIX. The term

means payments which are not for the purpose of transferring capital and includes, without limitation,

(1) All payments due in connection with foreign trade, other current business, including services, and normal short term banking and credit facilities;

(2) Payments due as interest on loans and as net income from other investments;

(3) Payments of moderate amount for amortization of loans or for depreciation of direct investment;

(4) Moderate remittances for family expenses.

It may be assumed that experience in practice has proved the definition to be somewhat cursory; it is possible that its interpretation and effect will be made clearer by a reference to Annex VII to the Treaty for East African Co-operation[41] which lists no less than twenty-seven different types of current payments.

The definition itself renders the distinction between capital and current transactions dependent upon subjective elements.[42] It is, therefore, impossible to establish a test applicable to all cases. The examples mentioned in Art. XIX introduce a complication by treating as a current transaction what is undoubtedly a capital transfer, namely payments for the amortization of loans; it is equally remarkable that amounts paid in redemption of share capital are not mentioned and payments for depreciation (which is normally only a book entry) are specifically included. If a person resident in London buys in New York a valuable painting or a quantity of copper, is the payment of the price made for the purpose of transferring capital

---

[39] Ibid., pp. 133, 134 (Decision No. 144 of 14 Aug. 1952). The point is perhaps not entirely free from doubt.

[40] See Fawcett, *British Yearbook of International Law*, 1964, 44.

[41] Above, p. 518, n. 32, at p. 1027.

[42] See Mann, *British Year Book of International Law*, 1945, 251.

or in connection with foreign trade? From the point of view of the seller in New York a transaction connected with foreign trade is involved. From the point of view of the English buyer the payment may be made to create and keep a capital asset in New York, but he may also intend sooner or later to resell. This type of problem cannot be satisfactorily solved even by the exercise of the Fund's power to 'determine whether certain specific transactions are to be considered current transactions or capital transactions'.[43]

It follows from Art. VIII (2) (*a*) itself (and, curiously enough, is not repeated in Art. XIX) that the current transaction must always be an international one. The question when a transaction is international is a *quaestio famosissima* in law.[44] Suppose, to revert to the above example, a picture dealer carrying on business in London happens to be in New York and buys there a picture in the shop of a New York art dealer. Is this a current international transaction? The analogy of private law would clearly demand an answer in the negative, but it is far from certain whether the result should be the same in the context of the Fund Agreement. The comparative lawyer will be aware of many other cases of similar difficulty.

4. As a rule, as has been pointed out,[45] import restrictions are clearly distinguishable from exchange restrictions, so that provisions dealing with the former do not extend to the latter and vice versa. Thus when the Treaties of Friendship, Commerce and Navigation concluded by the United States provide[46] that 'neither Party shall impose restrictions or prohibitions on the importation of any product of the other Party . . . unless the importation of the like product . . . of all third countries is similarly restricted or prohibited', exchange restrictions are not thereby forbidden. Where a treaty speaks of 'quantitative restrictions on imports', the result is even clearer. Nor should it be open to doubt that, when a treaty speaks of 'measures having an equivalent effect' to quantitative restrictions on imports, exchange restrictions cannot usually be meant by such 'measures', for they are hardly ever directed against the quantity of goods to be imported: they affect the quantity of the available currency rather than the quantity of goods to be paid for. It follows that, when the numerous treaties which the European Economic

---

[43] Art. XIX (i) in fine.

[44] See, for instance, Art. 1 of the Uniform Law on the International Sale of Goods, and the discussion surrounding it, which is shortly referred to by Graveson and Cohn, *Uniform Law on International Sales Act* (1969), p. 48, who report that Art. 1 is 'the most fundamental and delicate of all the Articles'.

[45] See above, p. 498.

[46] See, for instance, Art. XIV (2) of the Treaty with the Federal Republic of Germany which, together with many other similar Treaties is referred to below, p. 524, n. 57.

Community has concluded with non-member States such as Switzerland, Austria, or Iceland[47] prohibit new measures having effects equivalent to restrictions on imports, exchange restrictions are not caught; in particular, such non-member States are not bound by the interpretation which the European Court of Justice, having jurisdiction within the Community, may have put on similar words appearing in the EEC Treaty. For the purpose of its Art. 30 the European Court has held since 1974[48] that measures having an equivalent effect to quantitative restrictions exist wherever they 'are likely to hinder directly or indirectly, actually or potentially imports between member States.' This definition which fails to take any account of the word 'quantitative' would even within the Community be unacceptable[49] had it not been sanctioned by firmly established judicial practice. It clearly brings exchange restrictions within its net. It is likely, therefore, that, subject to Articles 108 (2) and 109 of the Treaty, a member State which has no system of exchange restrictions is not allowed to introduce one that is capable of rendering imports from member States more burdensome.

Where, on the other hand, treaties prohibit exchange restrictions, as in the case of Art. VIII (2) (*a*), they do not extend to import restrictions, for these do not involve direct governmental limitation on the availability or use of exchange as such.[50]

## VIII

The Articles of Agreement of the International Monetary Fund, as appears from the preceding discussion, leave the member States' sovereign rights in regard to exchange control to a substantial extent intact. The whole field of capital transfers is largely free from contractual restraints.[51] As concerns current transactions, 87 out of 141 member States still maintain restrictions by virtue of Art. XIV and even the remaining 54 members of the Fund may receive approval to fresh restrictions.[52] There is, therefore, room for further

[47] See Article 13 of these three treaties concluded on 22 July 1972, Cmnd. 5159, 5181 and 5182.

[48] *Procureur du Roi* v. *Dassonville* (1974), E.C.R. 837 or (1974) 2 C.M.L.R. 436, and many later cases all of which repeat the same formula and apply it in a manner which can only be described as astonishing and cannot be justified by any purposive method of interpretation. It is a piece of judicial legislation, and as such subject to grave doubts and objections.

[49] For a full, but now largely obsolete, discussion see Mann, *Festschrift für Kurt Ballerstedt* (1975), p. 421.

[50] See the Fund's persuasive definition above, p. 519, n. 38.

[51] Art. VI (3), which, however, also includes a provision protecting against undue delay in the discharge of commitments. See above, p. 517, n. 31.

[52] Art. VIII (2) (*a*). The scarce currency Art. VII is again being disregarded.

international regulation and not only on a multilateral level,[53] but also by way of bilateral Agreements.[54]

The latter do not normally limit the introduction, or require the abolition, of systems of exchange control. Rather they are devoted to the manner in which these are to be operated or administered.

1. The first question is whether a measure of equality or non-discrimination may be derived from a most-favoured nation or, to a lesser extent, from a national-treatment clause.

A broad and general clause which confers on the nationals of the contracting States the right to the benefits and privileges granted by either State to the nationals of a third State or to its own nationals, is unlikely to afford in any meaningful sense protection against the implications of exchange control, for it will probably have to be so construed as to condemn discrimination only on the ground of nationality. The operation of all systems of exchange control is characterized by discrimination between residents and non-residents. The purpose of these systems is the preservation of the currency resources of a country, i.e. a territorial unit.[55] It is residence in, rather than nationality of, the country that indicates the legally definable and relevant connection with a currency area. It is not surprising that economists prefer to speak of discrimination against a currency, such as the dollar, rather than against the nationals or residents of a currency area. A most-favoured-nation clause, however, does not, as a rule, preclude discrimination based on residence.

[53] A 'Code of Fair Exchange Practices' has been advocated by Lord Crowther, *An Outline of Money* (1948), p. 275, and Mikesell, *Foreign Exchange in the Postwar World* (1954), pp. 457 sqq.

[54] So long as exchange restrictions are lawfully maintained under the auspices of the International Monetary Fund it must be assumed that member States have agreed to a suspension *pro tanto* of those clauses in numerous bilateral treaties which guarantee to the Contracting Parties' nationals 'full power to dispose of their personal property within the territories of the other, by testament, donation or otherwise': see, for instance, the Anglo-American Convention of 2 Mar. 1899. In this sense an unpublished letter from the Treasury of 24 Jan. 1951 (ECA 510/247). It is, however, doubtful whether this argument which would appear to be correct would be accepted by the United States. The doubt arises from the submissions which the United States addressed to the International Court of Justice in the *Case concerning Rights of Nationals of the United States of America in Morocco*, I.C.J. Reports, 1952, 176 and which was fully analyzed in *Rec.* 96 (1959, i), 68–70. Those submissions were so plainly wrong that it is, perhaps, unnecessary to repeat their refutation. See *Barton v. National Life Assurance Company of Canada*, 398 N.Y. Supp. 2d 941 (1977) and above, pp. 496, n. 599. As regards municipal law, it should be remembered that even where such treaties are incorporated into municipal law, they are usually superseded by the introduction of exchange control; in this sense the German Supreme Court, 2 Mar. 1933, *RGStr.* 67, 130, also A.D. 1933–4, p. 11.

[55] The Defence (Finance) Regulations which came into force in Britain in 1939 were, according to *Boissevain v. Weil*, [1950] A.C. 327, based to some extent on a different principle. If this case, on which see above, p. 364, n. 50, was rightly decided (which is open to much doubt) Britain was probably guilty of an excess of international jurisdiction: *Rec.* 111 (1964, i), p. 124, or *Studies in International Law*, p. 108.

Normally it protects against discrimination on the ground of nationality[56] and, therefore, has hardly any bearing upon the practice or effects of exchange control.

More difficult questions of construction are likely to arise where the most-favoured-nation clause is expressly concerned with exchange control. No firm rule can be suggested nor has any uniform practice developed. Thus most of the important Treaties of Friendship, Commerce, and Navigation concluded and ratified by the United States of America since the end of the Second World War[57] contain provisions of the following type:[58]

Nationals and companies of either Party shall be accorded national treatment by the other Party with respect to the assumption of undertakings for, and the making of, payments, remittances, and transfers of moneys and financial instruments.

There is no doubt that this provision 'is only designed to preclude discrimination against nationals and companies on a nationality basis in the application of foreign exchange regulations'.[59] Such texts,

[56] See, generally, the *Case of Oscar Chinn*, Series A/B, No. 63 (1934), p. 88, and in particular Nussbaum, p. 475; Metzger, *International Law, Trade and Finance* (1962), pp. 112, 113; Mann, *Rec.* 96 (1959, i), 71. The opposite view has recently been argued with much force by Kewenig, 16 (1966–7), *Buffalo L.R.* 377, at pp. 391–8, who treats membership of a currency area as nationality. Such a construction may in a given case be possible, but, however desirable it may be, it will usually be too hazardous.

[57] See twenty-one Treaties, with Belgium of 21 Feb. 1961, Art. 10 (U.N.T.S. 480, 149); China of 4 Nov. 1946, Art. XIX (U.N.T.S. 25, 69); Denmark of 1 Oct. 1951, Art. XII (U.N.T.S. 421, 105); Ethiopia of 7 Sept. 1951, Art. XI (U.N.T.S. 206, 41); France of 25 Nov. 1959, Art. X (U.N.T.S. 401, 75); Germany of 29 Oct. 1954, Art. XII (U.N.T.S. 273, 3); Greece of 3 Aug. 1951, Art. XV (U.N.T.S. 224, 279); Iran of 15 Aug. 1955, Art. VII (U.N.T.S. 284, 93); Eire (falsely called Ireland) of 21 Jan. 1950, Art. XVII (U.N.T.S. 206, 269); Israel of 23 Aug. 1951, Art. XII (U.N.T.S. 219, 237); Italy of 2 Feb. 1948, Art. XVII (U.N.T.S. 79, 171; 404, 326); Japan of 29 Aug. 1953, Art. XII (U.N.T.S. 206, 143); Korea of 28 Nov. 1956, Art. XII (U.N.T.S. 302, 281); Luxembourg of 23 Feb. 1962, Art. XI (U.N.T.S. 474, 3); Muscat and Oman of 20 Dec. 1958, Art. IX (U.N.T.S. 380, 181); Netherlands of 27 Mar. 1956, Art. XII (U.N.T.S. 285, 231); Nicaragua of 21 Jan. 1956, Art. XII (U.N.T.S. 367, 3); Pakistan of 12 Nov. 1959, Art. XII (U.N.T.S. 404, 259); Thailand of 29 May 1966, Art. VII (652 U.N.T.S. 253); Togolese Republic of 8 Feb. 1966) (680 U.N.T.S. 159); Viet-Nam of 3 Apr. 1961, Art. VII (U.N.T.S. 424, 137). The provisions are by no means always identical. In addition, there are many earlier treaties. Of 510 Commercial Treaties concluded between 1931 and 1939, no less than 79 dealt with the subject: R. C. Snyder, *The Most-Favoured-Nation Clause* (1948), pp. 92, 134, 140. See also Hackworth, ii. 75 sqq.

[58] This is Art. XII, para. 1, of the Treaty with the Federal Republic of Germany of 29 Oct. 1954. For a similar provision see Art. 4 of the Trade Agreement between China and Japan of 4 January 1974, *International L.M.* 1974, 872. In *Kolovrat v. Oregon*, 366 U.S. 187 (1961), also *International L.R.* 32, 203, the United States Supreme Court decided that in a federal State the power to make policy with regard to foreign exchange is a national one, and that, therefore, the Federal Government is alone entitled to say whether a foreign State's laws meet the standards of treaties concluded with it. This is the only point of monetary law which can fairly be treated as having been decided by the Supreme Court in that case.

[59] See para. 14 of the Protocol to the Treaty with Germany referred to in the preceding

accordingly, are unlikely to have greater scope than a most-favoured-nation clause expressed in general terms. On the other hand, according to the Anglo-Greek Treaty of Commerce and Navigation of 16 July 1926[60] the conditions under which, in the event of Greece introducing exchange control, foreign currency was to be made available to pay for imports from Britain 'shall be not less favourable in any respect than the corresponding conditions under which foreign currency may be made available to pay for imports the produce or manufacture of any other foreign country'. In this case an infringement of the clause would seem to occur even if the discrimination is not based on nationality. This would, indeed, be a wholly sensible result, though, as has been shown, it will frequently be a utopian one.

2. If, then, the standard of equality, based on nationality, will almost always fail to provide protection against discrimination in matters of exchange control, the question arises whether the test of fair and equitable treatment is likely to be more effective.

Such a duty, in relation to the allocation of exchange, has been laid down in numerous treaties.[61] In particular it occurs in most of the Treaties of Friendship, Commerce, and Navigation concluded by the United States of America:[62]

3. Neither Party may, with respect to the other Party, in any manner impose exchange restrictions which are unnecessarily detrimental to or arbitrarily discriminate against the claims, investments, transportation, trade or other interests of nationals and companies of such other Party or their competitive position. Should either Party impose exchange restrictions with respect to the other Party, it will remove them as rapidly as it is able to do so considering its economic condition.

4. The two Parties, recognizing that the international movement of investment capital and the returns thereof would be conducive to the full realization

note; in the same sense the Protocols to the Treaties with France, the Netherlands, and Pakistan.

[60] Cmd. 2790, Art. 11. The prohibition of discrinination on a geographical basis rather than on the basis of nationality is by no means unfamiliar: Hyde, International Law (2nd ed., 1945), pp. 1504–6.

[61] For a list of earlier United States Treaties see Kewenig (above, p. 524, n. 56) at p. 400, n. 72. See, further, Exchange of Notes between the Union of South Africa and Czechoslovakia of 27 Jan. 1937, Art. III (L.N.T.S. 189, 97); Trade Agreement between Netherlands and Ecuador of 27 May 1937, Art. VII (ibid. 194, 180); Trade Agreement between Canada and Guatemala of 28 Sept. 1937, Art. V (Cmd. 6240).

[62] This is again taken from the Treaty with the Federal Republic of Germany (above, p. 524, n. 57). The wording of some treaties is different. For the latest version see the Treaty with Thailand, Art. VII. The United States of America also entered into a number of Trade Agreements which provide for payment 'in freely convertible currency': Art. 4 of the Agreement of 18 Oct. 1972 with the Soviet Union, Int. L.M. 1972, 1321; Art. VI of the Agreement of 2 April 1975 with Romania, ibid. 1975, 672; Art. V of the Agreement of 7 July 1979 with China, ibid. 1979, 1046.

of the objectives of the present Treaty, are agreed that such movements shall not be unnecessarily hampered. In accordance with this mutually agreed principle, each Party undertakes to afford to nationals and companies of the other Party reasonable facilities for the withdrawal of funds earned by them as a result of making or maintaining capital investments as well as for the transfer of capital investments. The same principle applies with respect to the compensation referred to in Article V, paragraph 4.[63]

5. The term 'exchange restrictions' as used in the present Article includes all restrictions, regulations, charges, fees, and other requirements imposed by either Party, which burden or interfere with the assumption of undertakings for, or the making of, payments, remittances, or transfers of moneys and financial instruments.

6. All questions arising under the present Treaty concerning foreign exchange restrictions will be governed by the provisions of the present Article.

Thus a network of bilateral treaties[64] proclaims the duty not to apply[65] exchange restrictions[66] so that they are 'unnecessarily detrimental to or arbitrarily discriminate against' the interests and competitive position of the other Party. There is a further duty to afford 'reasonable facilities' for the transfer of capital investments and the income derived from them. It is possible, though in most respects unlikely,[67] that, in order to constitute an infringement, the conduct complained of may have to be based on the ground of nationality. It is also noteworthy that monetary sovereignty is limited to a far greater extent than the Articles of Agreement of the International Monetary Fund envisage; in particular it is much reduced in regard to capital transfers. What is an unnecessary detriment, an arbitrary discrimination, a reasonable facility, or, as other treaties put it,[68] what is a

---

[63] This deals with compensation for expropriated property.

[64] The American example was followed by the Federal Republic of Germany on at least two occasions. Thus the Commercial Treaty with Italy of 21 Nov. 1957 (*Bundesgesetzblatt*, 1959, ii. 949) requires exchange restrictions to be applied 'in as liberal a manner as possible' and 'adequate possibilities for the transfer of invested capital and income and compensation' (Art. 15). The Treaty with the Dominican Republic of 23 Dec. 1957 (*Bundesgesetzblatt*, 1959, ii. 1468) requires the avoidance of 'unnecessary obstacles' and 'unnecessary prejudice' (Art. 15).

[65] As appears from the text, most treaties provide that neither Party may 'impose' certain exchange restrictions. On its true construction the provision refers to the administration rather than the imposition of exchange control. The mistake has been corrected in later treaties: see, for instance, the Treaty with Thailand, Art. VII, para. 1, which uses the word 'apply'.

[66] It is possible that the definition included in most treaties and set forth, for instance, in para. 5 of the Treaty with Germany, is not altogether satisfactory. For details see *Rec.* 96 (1959, i), p. 53.

[67] Only the possibility was referred to at *Rec.* 96 (1959, i), p. 72; it does exist, particularly in so far as arbitrary discrimination is concerned. But Kewenig (above, p. 524, n. 56), at pp. 400, 401 is right in criticizing such a construction. The formulation in the text takes care of his argument.

[68] See, for instance, the Treaty with Japan, Art. XII, para. 2.

restriction 'necessary' to prevent monetary reserves from falling below, or to increase moderately above, 'a very low level'—these are questions of degree which often will give rise to much doubt and difficulty. They can be solved only be experience, by the slow evolution of judicial and diplomatic practice, and by evidence, though for the time being the wholly objective nature of the tests should be noted. From the point of view of Britain which does not appear to have agreed upon any treaty clauses on exchange control similar to those laid down in the great American precedent, the principal value of the latter lies in the corroboration of the rules of customary international law, which it so clearly supplies. It is, indeed, possible that that precedent constitutes merely a (helpful) illustration or reformulation of the overriding principle of 'fair and equitable treatment',[69] which, it must be repeated, in turn is perhaps no more than a (welcome) contractual recognition and affirmation of that principle of customary international law[70] which requires States to act in good faith, reasonably, without abuse, arbitrariness, or discrimination.

## IX

There exists, finally, a network of bilateral treaties which, in wholly unqualified terms, lay down a specific duty to assure the transfer of moneys from one country to another.

1. This is so in the case of the numerous treaties concluded by the European Economic Community with non-member States. The Treaty with Switzerland of 22 July 1972,[71] to take only one of many examples,[72] is representative. It provides in Art. 19 as follows:

Payments relating to trade in goods and the transfer of such payments to the Member State of the Community in which the creditor is resident or to Switzerland shall be free from any restrictions.
The Contracting Parties shall refrain from any exchange or administrative restrictions on the grant repayment or acceptance of short and medium-term credits covering commercial transactions in which a resident participates.

A provision of this type goes a long way towards the development of a duty of customary international law to assure the payment for goods (and services) received before the introduction of exchange

---

[69] It is expressed in Art. I of almost all the American Treaties referred to above, p. 524, n. 57.
[70] Above, p. 476.  [71] Cmnd. 5181.
[72] See, for instance, treaty with Austria of 22 July 1972, Cmnd. 5159; with Iceland of 22 July 1972, Cmnd. 5182; with Israel of 11 May 1975, Cmnd. 6249.

control. While it is clear that the second paragraph of Art. 19 establishes a duty between the Contracting Parties, from which individuals cannot benefit, the first paragraph is likely, under the law of the EEC, to be part of the internal law of the Member States so as to impose rights and duties upon the residents of such States and to be enforceable in judicial proceedings: thus in an English court a Swiss defendant could probably not rely on any relevant restriction imposed by Switzerland, which might otherwise be applicable, for instance in the event of the contract being governed by Swiss law.

2. There are treaties which assure the transfer not only of income from capital investments, but also of capital itself and which, therefore, are far less modest than the Articles of Agreement of the International Monetary Fund. These are treaties for the promotion and protection of new investments such as have been concluded with numerous developing countries since the late 1950s. They invariably apply to investments made since the recipient State became independent and are usually supplemented by municipal investment laws which purport to carry the policy of controlling and protecting new investments into legal effect.[73]

This is not the place to supply a complete list of such Agreements or to analyse their legal character or to assess their effect upon the development of international law in general.[74] For present purposes the significant point is that what in the past may have been an implied duty has become explicit. Thus the Federal Republic of Germany seems to have concluded more than forty such Agreements.[75] The earliest, that with Pakistan of 25 November 1959,[76] covers investments made at any time after 1st September 1954, and like most of the other Agreements provides in Art. 4:

---

[73] In 1977 the International Chamber of Commerce published a booklet concerning Bilateral Conventions about international investments, according to which between 1945 and May 1976, 141 Conventions were concluded. Since then many additional Conventions have been concluded. Some seventeen of such municipal laws are discussed by Aufricht in Starke (ed.), *The Protection and Encouragement of Private Foreign Investment* (1966). Preiswerk, *La Protection des investissements privés dans les traités bilatéraux* (Zürich, 1963) lists (p. 11) sixty-one treaties up to 1963. Krishna, 'Exchange Controls under West German Treaties for the Protection of Private Foreign Investment', in *The Australian Year Book of International Law* 1965, 71, mentions forty-seven States having special legislation regulating and protecting investments.

[74] They conclusively prove the continuing force of the protection which international law affords to private property.

[75] Many of them are listed and discussed by Berger, *Aussenwirtschaftsdienst des Betriebsberaters*, 1965, 1; 1968, 14. The most recent ones are those with Mali (28 June 1977), Syria (2 August 1977), Israel (21 February 1978), Romania (12 October 1979). See, generally, Alenfeld, *Die Investitionsförderungsverträge der Bundesrepublik Deutschland* (1971).                                        [76] *Bundesgesetzblatt*, 1961, ii. 793.

Either Party shall in respect of all investments guarantee to nationals or companies of the other Party the transfer of the invested capital, of the returns and in the event of liquidation the proceeds of such liquidation.

According to Art. 6 transfers under Art. 4 as well as compensation for expropriated property 'shall be made without undue delay and at rates of exchange applicable to current transactions on the date the transfer is made'. The rate of exchange shall be based on par value or, in its absence, shall be such rate as 'is just and reasonable'. Other States have entered into similar Agreements,[77] in particular Denmark,[78] France,[79] Japan,[80] Switzerland,[81] Sweden,[82] and the United Kingdom.[83, 84]

---

[77] Since 1948 the United States has provided for a system of investment guarantee and insurance, which is now based on s. 221 of the International Development Act, 1961. It assures to the private investor protection against, *inter alia*, the inability to convert into U.S. dollars moneys received as earnings from or repayment of the investment or as compensation. By 1964 such guarantees had been given in respect of sixty countries and for more than 1,000 billion dollars. For details see Metzger, 50 (1964) *Va. L.R.* 594, pp. 612 sqq., or Clubb and Vance, 72 (1963) *Yale L.J.* 475.

[78] Treaty with Malawi, 1 August 1966, U.N.T.S. 586, 22.

[79] Treaty with Zaire, 5 Oct. 1972, *Rev. Crit.* 1975, 795; with Egypt, 22 Dec. 1974, *Rev. Crit.* 1976, 171; with Korea, 22 Jan. 1975, Clunet 1975, 630, 632; with Singapore, 8 Sept. 1975, *Rev. Crit.* 1977, 165. See, generally, Juillard, Clunet 1979, 274, who mentions sixteen such treaties.

[80] Treaty with Egypt, 28 Jan. 1977, International L.M. 1979, 44.

[81] See the Treaties with Tunisia, Niger, Guinea, Senegal, Ivory Coast, Congo and Cameroons concluded in 1962 and 1963.

[82] See Art. VIII of the Treaty between Sweden and Malagasy of 2 Apr. 1966, *International Legal Materials*, vi (1967), 48. Metzger (above, n. 77) also mentions treaties concluded by Denmark, Norway and Japan.

[83] Treaty with Egypt, 11 June 1975, Cmnd. 6141; Singapore, 22 July 1975, Cmnd. 6300; Romania, 19 March 1976, Cmnd. 6500; Korea, 4 March 1976, Cmnd. 6510; Indonesia, 27 April 1976, Cmnd. 6858; Thailand, 28 Nov. 1978, Cmnd. 7732; Jordan, 10 Oct. 1979, Cmnd. 7945; Senegal, 7 May 1980, Cmnd. 8079; Bangladesh, 19 June 1980, Cmnd. 8013; Sri Lanka, 13 Feb. 1980, Cmnd. 7984; Philippines, 3 December 1980, Cmnd. 8148; Lesotho, 18 Feb. 1981, Cmnd. 8246; Papua New Guinea, 14 May 1981, Cmnd. 8307; Paraguay, 4 June 1981, Cmnd. 8329. In the British treaties the guarantee of the free transfer of the capital of and the returns from investments is usually subject to the 'right in exceptional financial or economic circumstances to exercise equitably and in good faith powers conferred by its laws'. Such a clause is liable greatly to prejudice the right of free transfer. In the case of the payment of compensation for expropriated property there is usually a further qualification to the effect that 'the Contracting Party concerned may require the transfer thereof to be effected in reasonable instalments.' This provision would not cover the case of damages for an illegal confiscation.

[84] The original Convention concluded between the European Economic Community and eighteen African States at Lomé (Republic of Togo) on 29 July 1969 (*International Legal Materials 1970*, 485) contained similar provisions in Articles 37 to 39. The latest Lomé Convention of 31 Oct. 1979 between 58 African–Caribbean–Pacific States and the European Economic Community (*International Legal Materials 1980*, 327) does not contain any similar provisions, but contemplates bilateral agreements: Art. 64. This would seem to be a retrograde development.

These Agreements[85] may lead to the acceptance of the broad principle[86] of customary law and equity that a Government which has approved the importation of capital is bound to approve its re-exportation, that new capital invested in an economy with Government approval must be returned and profits arising from it must be remitted.[87]

---

[85] See Mann, 'Britain's Treaties for the Promotion and Protection of Investments', *British Year Book of International Law* 1981.

[86] See *Report of the 55th Conference of the International Law Association* (New York, 1972), p. 248.

[87] Under Art. VIII (2) (*a*) the International Monetary Fund has power to approve the imposition of restrictions on the making of payments and transfers for current international transactions. The Treaties of Friendship, Commerce and Navigation concluded by the United States are usually made subject to that power: see, e.g., Art. XII (2) of the Treaty with Germany. The investment treaties mentioned in the text, however, usually constitute *lex specialis*: they are made notwithstanding, rather than subject to, any powers of the Fund. The rule of customary international law suggested in the text is, therefore, not inconsistent with Bretton Woods. Moreover, by its approval under Art. VIII (2) (*a*) the Fund only sanctions a system of restrictions. It is not concerned with the application of the system to specific cases.

# XXI

# The Monetary Law of
# Inter-State Obligations

I. Introduction. II. The determination of the money of account (1) in case of debts and (2) in case of damages and compensation. III. Nominalism as applicable to treaties: (1) the principle; (2) revalorization as a possible remedy; (3) damages for delayed payment; (4) the calculation of damages. IV. Protective clauses: (1) the existence of a gold clause; (2) the effect of the abrogation of gold clauses. V. The payment of inter-State debts: (1) where?; (2) how?; (3) in which currency?; (4) at which rate of exchange?; (5) which type of rate of exchange? VI. The effect of exchange control.

## I

WHEN one comes to monetary obligations arising under public international law, that is to say, normally, obligations arising between international persons, one is concerned with problems which are almost identical with those arising under the municipal legal systems of all countries. The primary task, therefore, is to ascertain the extent to which the solutions evolved by municipal law are acceptable to international law. But two complications must be borne in mind. In the first place, international practice, which must form the background of legal research, has developed over a long period of time, discloses many varieties, and is dispersed over numerous treaties; it is so elusive that caution is required before a rule of customary international law can be deduced from it. Secondly, the international legal order lacks an international currency of its own. It is, consequently, compelled to avail itself of national currencies as its instruments; not even the Special Drawing Right or the European Currency Unit should be described as a standard of international value, because they are derived from and reflect the value of national currencies made up into a basket.[1] The resulting interplay of international and municipal law creates problems which, in this connection, as in so many others, involve peculiar difficulties.

Their impact is eliminated or at least substantially reduced where international law resorts to the device of adopting a unit of account which is independently defined and which actually is, or may soon become, an imaginary one. Thus in the first seven decades of the

[1] See above, pp. 505-9.

present century multilateral treaties have been concluded on the basis of the gold franc of 100 centimes weighing 10/31 of a gramme and of a fineness of 0.900[2] or of the gold franc containing $65\frac{1}{2}$ milligrams of gold of a fineness of 900/1,000[3] or of European Monetary units of account.[4] In these and similar cases[5] the definition is identical

[2] See, for example, Universal Postal Union of 1964 (Cmnd. 3141), Art. 7; Telecommunication Convention of 9 Dec. 1932, Art. 32 (Hudson, vi, No. 316), adopted by the Agreement of 23 Sept. 1944 between the United Kingdom and the U.S.S.R. for the Establishment of a direct Radiotelephone Service between their respective countries (Cmnd. 7028); African Telecommunications Union Agreement of 30 Oct. 1935, Art. 28 (Hudson, vii, No. 431); African Telecommunications Agreement of 1948, Art. 20 (Peaslee, International Government Organizations (1956), i. 43); Convention on the Transport of Goods by Rail, 25 Feb. 1961, Art. 57, Cmnd. 2810; Convention on the Transport of Passengers and Luggage by Rail, 25 Feb. 1961, Art. 57, Cmnd. 2811.

[3] Thus, for instance, Convention for the Unification of certain Rules relating to Damage caused by Aircraft to Third Parties on the Surface, 23 May 1933, Art. 19 (Hudson, op. cit. vi, No. 329) and Convention on Damage by Foreign Aircraft to Third Parties on the Surface, 7 Oct. 1952, Art. 11 (4) (Cmd. 8886); Convention for the Unification of Certain Rules regarding Air Transport, 12 Oct. 1929, Art. 22 (ibid. v. 100), incorporated into the law of England by the Carriage by Air Act, 1932; Art. 11 of the Hague Protocol of 1955 adopted by the Carriage by Air Act, 1961; Art. 3 (6) of the Convention relating to the Limitation of the Liability of Owners of Sea-going Ships of 10 Oct. 1957 (Cmnd. 353) adopted by the Merchant Shipping (Liability of Shipowners and Others) Act, 1958 (by s. 1 (3) of the Act the Minister may define the sterling equivalent of the gold franc and he did so by S.I. 1958, No. 1287 and, after sterling's devaluation, 1967, No. 1725). On the effect of these Orders see *The Abadesa*, [1968] P. 656, and *The Mecca*, [1968] P. 665; International Convention on Oil Pollution Damage of 29 Nov. 1969 (Cmnd. 6183), Art. V; Art. 2 of the Protocol to the International Convention for the unification of certain rules relating to Bills of Lading signed in Brussels on 23 Feb. 1968, Cmnd. 6944; Art. 9 of the Convention relating to the Carriage of Passengers and their Luggage by Sea of 1974 (Int. L.M. 1975, 945 or Cmnd. 6326); Art. V (9), International Convention on Civil Liability for Oil Pollution Damage, *RabelsZ* 1970, 338. The Convention on the Liability of Hotel-Keepers of 17 Dec. 1962 (Cmnd. 3205) provides that liability shall be limited 'to the equivalent of 3,000 gold francs', though the liability in respect of any one article may be limited to 1,500 gold francs as defined in the text above (Art. 1 of the Annex, Art. 2 of the Convention). Although the United Kingdom has ratified the Convention, liability remains limited in accordance with s. 2 of the Hotel Proprietors Act, 1956, viz. in principle to £50 in respect of any one article or £100 in the aggregate. These figures are clearly lower than the internationally agreed limits.

[4] Art. 7 of the Convention on Third Party Liability in the Field of Nuclear Energy of 29 July 1960 as amended by the Protocol of 28 Jan. 1964 (Cmnd. 3755) or Art 1, Protocol No. 7 of the Convention between the EEC and African States, *International Legal Materials* 1970, 485. The definition is to be found in Art. 24 of the European Monetary Agreement of 5 Aug. 1955 (*European Yearbook*, iii. 213), according to which 'accounts of the Fund shall be kept in terms of a unit of account of 0.88867088 grammes of fine gold'. This was up to 1972 the par value in terms of gold of one dollar of the United States of America. It was also the E.E.C.'s unit of account and as late as 30 May 1975 was adopted in Art. V of Annex II of European Convention for the Establishment of a Space Agency (Int. L.M. 1975, 855, 898); the Agreement establishing the African Development Fund of 29 Nov. 1972 (Cmnd. 7551) adopted the gold content of the devalued dollar, 0.81851265 gramme of fine gold, as a unit of account.

[5] The Statutes of the Bank for International Settlements provide that the authorized capital of the Bank shall be 500 m. Swiss gold francs equivalent to 145,161,280.32 grammes fine gold (Art. 5, Cmd. 3766). The case is strictly speaking not on the same level as that discussed in the text, because reference is made to the *Swiss* franc. The Memorandum respecting the International Convention on Financial Assistance, signed at Geneva on 2 Oct.

with that of a national unit of account as constituted at the material time, i.e. the French franc or the U.S. dollar, yet by incorporating the full definition in their text these treaties achieved more than they could have done by a mere reference to the national unit of account or the adoption of a mere gold clause: they created their own monetary system which could not be affected by municipal legislation. As a result of the 'demonetization' of gold and its sometimes twentyfold rise in market price the reference in practically all these cases has been replaced by a reference to Special Drawing Rights[6] or European Currency Units, so that more than ever international practice works with national currencies.

II

1. Contracts made according to private law frequently fail to clarify the money of account with reference to which the parties are contracting: are dollars mentioned in the agreement United States or Canadian dollars? When entering into treaties States will usually take care of questions of this kind, but where an express definition of the money of account is omitted, the real intention of the parties will be deduced from the construction of the terms of the treaty or from the circumstances attending its conclusion. Thus the Convention concerning the Régime of the Straits of 20 July 1936 speaks of 'francs gold'.[7] Although it was entered into at Montreux, the fact that Switzerland did not, but France did, participate in it readily leads to the conclusion that the parties contemplated French francs. The Agreement for the Creation of an International Office for dealing with Contagious Diseases of Animals, signed in Paris on 25 January 1924,[8] provides in Art. 11 of the Organic Statutes for an annual contribution of the members expressed in units which are calculated 'on the basis of 500 francs per unit'. Since the seat was to be in Paris, French francs are no doubt referred to. The Agreement concerning the creation of an International Association for the Protection of

1930 (but never put into force), provided in Art. 26 that for the purposes of the Convention 'the gold franc shall mean a monetary value equivalent to 0.322581 gramme or 4.97818 grains of gold nine-tenths fine' (Cmd. 3906). No truly 'international standard' was established by the Statutes of the International Hydrographic Bureau of 1947 (Peaslee, l.c. ii. 190), Art. 24, according to which the receipts of the Bureau and the salaries of the Director and Secretary General were to be 'calculated on the basis of an international standard which is the gold franc'.

[6] Above, p. 159. For further examples of SDRs being used, see Agreement of 9 April 1975 establishing a Financial Support Fund of the O.E.C.D., Int. L.M. 1975, 979; Convention on limitation of liability for maritime claims, 19 Feb. 1976, Int. L.M. 1976, 600.

[7] Annex I. See Hudson, *International Legislation*, vii, No. 449, at p. 401.

[8] Ibid., ii. 1239; Cmd. 2663.

Children, signed in Brussels on 2 August 1922,[9] provides for an annual contribution of '3000 Frs. or more payable by members (Art. 4). The seat of the Association was to be in Brussels (Art. 1) and Belgian francs were probably meant by the parties. A peculiar case occurred in a Convention between France and the Federal Republic of Germany in 1967,[10] France undertook to pay 'a sum of 163 million French francs (132 million DM)' and Germany undertook to pay '43 million French francs (35 million DM)'. It would seem likely that in both cases the bracketed words were added only *informationis causae* and were without contractual effect. In case of doubt the solution must always be found in the circumstances. The suggestion that prima facie debts arising under public international law are expressed in the currency of the creditor State[11] is without foundation.

As to judicial practice, it was apparently only once that an international tribunal was faced with the problem of determining the money of account, and this occurred in somewhat special circumstances in the arbitration between Greece and the United Kingdom relating to the *Diverted Cargoes*,[12] which led to an Award by Monsieur René Cassin. In April 1941 ships bound for Greece were diverted by British forces to territories outside Greece, where their cargoes, the property of Greek consignees, were discharged and taken over by the British authorities for use in the war against the common enemy. In February 1942 Greece and the United Kingdom agreed by treaty[13] that the Greek Government would prevent the owners of the cargoes from making any claim against the British Government and the latter would credit the Greek Government with 'the f.o.b. cost of such cargoes'. Some of them had been bought in the United States of America for dollars, others had been purchased in the United Kingdom for sterling. The Parties were agreed upon the vital fact that even in respect of goods bought in the United States of America the

---

[9] Hudson, op. cit. ii. 876.

[10] Art. 2 of the Convention printed in Cmnd. 6457. A similar case was dealt with by the European Court of Justice in *S.A. Générale Sucrière* v. *Commission of E.E.C.*, E.C.R. 1977 I 445: the Court had expressed a fine in terms of '80.000 units of account (F.F. 444 235.20)'. This meant that the fine was expressed in French francs the amount of which had been calculated by reference to the unit of account used by the E.E.C. for purposes of the budget.

[11] Neumeyer, *Internationales Verwaltungsrecht*, iii, Part 2 (1930), pp. 121 sqq., 124.

[12] In English: International L.R. 1955, 820; in French: *Rev. Crit.* 1956, 278 or *Reports of International Arbitral Awards*, xii. 53. The case is discussed by Simpson, *International and Comparative L.Q.* 1956, 471; Batiffol, *Rev. Crit.*, l.c.; Mann, *British Year Book of International Law*, 1957, pp. 41 sqq. and, in particular, by Dach, *American Journal of Comparative Law*, 1956, p. 512, who says not without justification that criticism of the award 'should be as vociferous as respect for the prestige and the outstanding learning of the arbitrator permits'.

[13] Printed in Cmd. 9754.

credit was to be given to Greece in terms of sterling.[14] The issue was whether the f.o.b. value of the goods of American origin was to be converted into sterling at the pre-September 1949 rate of $4.03 to £1 (as the British Government contended) or at the post-September 1949 rate of $2.80 to £1 (as the Greek Government contended). This case which could well have arisen in the sphere of municipal law[15] involved the question of construction of which rate of exchange was to be employed; no problem of the identity of the money of account or the money of payment fell to be considered, for both were admittedly sterling. Yet the first of three questions which the Arbitrator thought it right to ask himself was: What was the currency—dollar or sterling—which the Parties chose in 1942 as the money of account, the *monnaie de contrat*, 'for the effective settlement of the claim'?[16] In view of the fact that the f.o.b. cost of goods of British origin was expressed in sterling and that the two constituent elements of a single claim could not be separated the Arbitrator decided that the treaty of 1942 'created a single account in a single currency, and it was a credit in pounds sterling that the British Government undertook to give . . . to the exclusion of any other currency'.[17] This would appear to be a sound result[18] and up to this point, therefore, the Award is authority for, and an example of, the proposition, evident though it may be, that the determination of the money of account is, in public international no less than in private law,[19] a matter of construction.[20]

2. The problem of determining the money of account in which unliquidated damages are expressed is very familiar to international practice.[21] In some cases the Convention creating an international

---

[14] This followed from the Terms of Reference set forth in Cmd. 9754.

[15] See above, pp. 317, 330.

[16] Int. L.R. 1955, 826.                                    [17] Ibid., 829.

[18] At the same time it was probably an irrelevant result, because, if the Arbitrator had reached the opposite conclusion and held dollars to be the money of account, the problem of conversion would have remained precisely the same.

[19] Above, p. 224.

[20] Perhaps it is convenient at this point to mention shortly the second question which the Arbitrator asked: Was the sterling credit to be given to Greece to be 'calculated by reference to the dollar as the unit of value and as the money of account' ('comme étalon de valeur et comme monnaie de compte')? The conclusion was that the treaty of 1942 'retained the dollar . . . as a standard of value, as a currency intended to measure the quantity of pounds' owing by the United Kingdom: Int. L.R. 1955, 829, 830. This point cannot readily be followed. How can the f.o.b. cost of American goods shipped from the United States be calculated otherwise than in dollars? The sterling sum was necessarily determined by an amount of dollars. The answer to the second question, therefore, merely states the obvious and does not have any bearing upon the cardinal problem of conversion or, indeed, upon any problem which will have to be discussed in the text. On the third question see p. 556 below and the literature above, n. 12.

[21] See Nussbaum, pp. 411 sqq.

tribunal has specified the currency to be employed for the assessment of damages.[22] In the absence of express directions tribunals have searched for other indications in the Conventions. In the Mexican arbitrations they have frequently found them in the provision according to which any *balance* due from the one to the other government after the disposal of all claims shall be paid 'in gold coin or its equivalent to the Government of the country in favour of whose citizens the greater amount may have been awarded'.[23] In view of this provision the United States-Mexico General Claims Commission adopted the practice of rendering awards in United States currency,[24]

having in mind the purpose of avoiding future uncertainties with respect to rates of exchange which, it appears, the two Governments also had in mind in framing the first paragraph of Art. IX of the Convention of September 8, 1923 with respect to the payment of the balance therein mentioned in gold or its equivalent.

This somewhat arbitrary method had the grave disadvantage of involving an exchange operation and thus giving rise to many difficulties[25] which also came to light in other connections and which

[22] See the Treaty between the United States of America and Columbia of 17 Aug. 1874 relating to an indemnity in respect of the steamer *Montigo* (Moore, *International Arbitrations* (1898), v. 4698): 'and if indemnity be given, the same shall be expressed in the legal coin of the United States of Colombia' (Art. 4); Treaty between the United States of America and Venezuela of 19 Jan. 1892 (ibid., p. 4818): 'damages shall be expressed in American gold' (Art. V); Treaty between the United States of America and Ecuador of 28 Feb. 1893 for arbitration in respect of Santos' claim (ibid., p. 4713): damages 'shall be specified in the gold coin of the United States of America' (Art. V); Treaty between the United States of America and Venezuela for the establishment of a Mixed Claims Commission, Protocol of 17 Feb. 1903 (Ralston, *Venezuelan Arbitrations of 1903* (1904), at p. 1): 'all awards shall be made payable in United States gold or its equivalent in silver' (Art. I); Agreement for Arbitration between the United States of America and Venezuela of 13 Feb. 1909 relating to the Orinoco Steamship Company (Scott, *The Hague Court Reports* (1916), pp. 239 sqq.): 'all awards shall be made in gold coin of the United States of America or its equivalent in Venezuelan money'; Agreement between the United States of America and Mexico of 22 May 1902 relating to the *Pious Fund* case (ibid., pp. 7 sqq.): 'The findings shall state the amount and the currency in which the same shall be payable' (Art. 10); Agreement between the United States of America and Peru of 21 May 1921 (*Reports of International Arbitral Awards* (United Nations), i. 347): 'The amount granted by the Award . . . shall be made payable in gold coin of the United States' (Art. XII).

[23] United States of America and Mexico General Claims Commission, Convention of 8 Sept. 1923 (Art. IX); United States of America and Mexico, Special Claims Commission, Convention of 10 Sept. 1923 (Art. IX); France and Mexico Claims Commission, Convention of 25 Sept. 1924 (Art. IX); Germany and Mexico Claims Commission, Convention of 16 Mar. 1923 (Art. X); Spain and Mexico Claims Commission, Convention of 25 Nov. 1925 (Art. 9); Great Britain and Mexico Claims Commission, Convention of 19 Nov. 1926 (Art. 9); Italy and Mexico Claims Commission, Convention of 13 Jan. 1927 (Art. 9).

[24] Feller, *The Mexican Claims Commissions 1923-1934* (1935), p. 313; De Beus, *The Jurisprudence of the General Claims Commission United States and Mexico* (1938), p. 272.

[25] De Beus, op. cit., p. 273; see also Ralston, *The Law and Procedure of International Tribunals, Supplement* (1936), p. 183.

public international law has not yet overcome.[26] That method, however, was not followed by the British-Mexican, French-Mexican, German-Mexican, and Spanish-Mexican Claims Commissions,[27] all of which awarded damages in gold pesos.

Where the tribunal cannot find any guidance in the Convention from which it derives its existence, no definite rule of law emerges until[28] the finding by the Permanent Court of International Justice in *The Wimbledon* case that the damages which Germany was ordered to pay to France for her refusal to allow a French ship to pass through the Kiel Canal should be paid in French francs:[29]

This is the currency of the applicant in which his financial operations and accounts are conducted and it may therefore be said that this currency gives the exact measure of the loss to be made good.

This would seem to be a sound principle, for which some authority can be found in private law.[30] It will not, however, be appropriate to all cases and cannot, therefore, be said to be of general validity.[31]

Thus the value of a house which was burnt in the course of a rebellion and for the loss of which the respondent Government has to indemnify the owner can only be assessed in terms of the currency of the country in which it was situate. Similarly, when Greece in 1929 wrongfully took over certain lighthouses operated by a French firm under a prematurely terminated concession, the Arbitration Tribunal

[26] See, for example, *United States of America on behalf of Socony-Vacuum Oil Co. Inc. v. The Republic of Turkey*, in Nielsen, *American-Turkish Claims Settlement* (1932), pp. 369 sqq. The case related to the assessment of the value of property requisitioned without compensation in Turkey. The Tribunal said: 'The claimant in the present case and other claimants have as a general rule converted Turkish money into American money at rates understood to prevail at the time of the taking of the property.' This practice was approved. The discussion is elaborate, but a little confused.

[27] Feller, op. cit., p. 314; Great Britain and Mexico Claims Commission, Award of 19 May 1931, *In re Watson* (*Annual Digest*, 1931–2, Case No. 113).

[28] It must be admitted, however, that the practice is still by no means uniform. For example, it is difficult to understand why pounds sterling were awarded in *Madame Chevreau*'s case (*American Journal of International Law*, 27 (1933), 153).

[29] Publications of the Court, Series A, No. 1, p. 32. See also the *Corfu Channel* case, I.C.J. Reports, 1949, 244, where the International Court of Justice had no difficulty in assessing damages in terms of sterling. In *Lauritzen v. Chile* (Int. L.R. 1956, 708, at p. 753) the Supreme Court of Chile, applying international law, held that Danish shipowners whose ships had been requisitioned by Chile during the war, were entitled to compensation in terms of dollars; one of the reasons was that this had become international practice and that dollars were 'used as an international medium of exchange'.

[30] Above, p. 245.

[31] In *Withall* v. *Administrator of German Property, British Year Book of International Law*, 1934, 180, Maugham J. (as he then was) held that the charge which the Treaty of Versailles imposed upon German assets to secure British nationals in respect of their claims against Turkey for the requisitioning and destruction of their property in Turkey was for sums expressed in Turkish currency to be converted into sterling at the rate of exchange prevailing at the date of the Treaty of Versailles.

was fully justified in determining 'the value of the concession in 1928 . . . by calculating successively the annual receipts of the concessionaire and his corresponding expenses' in terms of drachmae.[32] Again, where property is (lawfully) taken or (wrongfully) confiscated, as a rule its value will initially have to be expressed in terms of the currency of the State where it is situate.[33] But it is important to remember that after the determination of the currency a further operation becomes necessary to assess the value in the currency so determined and that thereafter the amount so calculated may have to be converted into the money of payment.[34]

Nor should it be overlooked that in many cases the claimant Government may, in effect, be claiming its outlays by way of damages (or, possibly, by way of unjustified enrichment) and that in such a case the principles applicable in private law may require the restoration of the claimant Government's currency with which the respondent Government's currency was procured to make the investment.

Although the claimant was an individual, the decision of the European Court of Human Rights in the case of *Ringeisen*[35] may conveniently be mentioned here. Since the applicant was a resident of the Federal Republic of Germany, the Court ordered the Republic of Austria to pay compensation in a sum of Deutsche Mark to him, and

[32] *Lighthouse Arbitration between France and Greece*, Reports of International Arbitral Awards xii. 155, at p. 247. For an English translation see International L.R. 1956, 301. The English translation is complete, but unfortunately not published in consecutive order. The Award by Messrs. Verzijl, Mestre, and Charbouns is very closely reasoned and greatly illuminating on monetary law. Only one part, i.e. that relating to interest is singularly unconvincing and, it is respectfully submitted, wrong.

[33] The law on this point is far from clear and frequently stated in terms which obscure the three different stages of the argument referred to in the text and emphasized again in the following note. The Harvard Draft Convention of 1961 on the International Responsibility of States provides in Art. 39 that damages and compensation should in principle 'be computed and paid in the currency of the State of which the injured alien was a national', except where he is a natural person and had his habitual residence in the territory of the respondent State for an extended period prior to the injury: Sohn and Baxter, *American Journal of International Law*, 1961, 545, at p. 583. See also Bindschedler, *Verstaatlichungsmassnahmen und Entschädigungspflicht nach Völkerrecht* (Zürich, 1950), pp. 55 sqq., and *Rec.* 90 (1956, ii) 269; Foighel, *Nationalization* (1957), pp. 122 sqq.; Friedman, *Expropriation in International Law* (1953), pp. 218, 219; Wortley, *Expropriation in Public International Law* (1959), pp. 133, 134, and many others.

[34] Accordingly, there are three stages: the determination of the currency in which the value of the property damaged or taken is expressed; the date and manner of assessment of such value in terms of the currency so determined; the payment of the amount so assessed and its conversion into another currency such as that of the claimant country (below, p. 555). It is only in the last-mentioned context that the influence of exchange control falls to be considered. In stating that there is no rule of customary international law requiring that any other than the local currency of the taking State, whether it is convertible into foreign exchange or not, be paid for taken property, Metzger, 50 (1964) *Virginia L.R.* 594, at p. 603 may possibly fail to make the necessary distinctions; he thus comes to suggest a result which is not necessarily persuasive.

[35] Int. L.R. 56, 501 (1973).

to do so by paying 'in that currency and in the Federal Republic of Germany'.

## III

1. Treaties providing for the payment of a sum of money have become a matter of almost daily occurrence.[36] Yet international law has so far disregarded the fundamental problem of the law of money, viz. the principle of nominalism, its extent, and its force in inter-State relationships. Is it a rule of international law that a gold clause must be read into all treaty obligations of a monetary character or, in other words, that the debtor State must pay so much 'value' as was agreed at the date when the treaty was made? Or is the debtor State bound and entitled to pay the nominal amount of the agreed currency, irrespective of the 'intrinsic value' in terms of gold, purchasing power, or another currency at the date of payment? And is any extrinsic alteration of the currency effective for the purposes of an obligation subject to international law? By a treaty of 26 June 1803[37] the Duke of Mecklenburg-Schwerin was granted by the King of Sweden the usufruct of Wismar for a period of 100 years against payment of 'une somme totale de 1,250,000 écus (Reichsthaler) de Banque de Hambourg' (Art. VI); it was further agreed that, if at the end of the term the King of Sweden should retake possession, 'alors Sa dite Majesté engage de la manière la plus positive . . . de restituer à Son Altesse Sérénissime la somme hypothécaire primitive' (Art. IV). If the treaty of 20 June 1903[38] had not rescinded the King of Sweden's right to the beneficial possession of Wismar and, accordingly, his obligation to repay the agreed sum of Reichsthaler Hamburg Banco, the question would have arisen of how this was to be paid in 1903. Would the amount of Reichsthaler, in accordance with German legislation of 1871, have been converted into 416,600 marks (which have since become reichsmarks and then, perhaps, Deutsche Marks)? And would the clause 'Hamburg Banco'[39] have been disregarded?

It is submitted that nominalism prevails in public international law.[40] By contracting on the footing of a specific national currency States incorporate into their treaties the monetary legislation of the country concerned and to that extent their treaties contain a *renvoi* to the *lex monetae*. The problem is one of construction: when States

[36] The material collected by Feilchenfeld and Kersten, 'Reparations from Carthage to Versailles', in *World Polity*, i (1957), 29 sqq., proves that for many centuries such clauses have been usual in Treaties of Peace imposing indemnities.

[37] Martens, *Recueil de traités*, 8 (1835), 54.

[38] *Nouveau Recueil général*, 2nd ser., 31, pp. 572, 574.

[39] On this see p. 8, n. 28.          [40] Carreau, pp. 169 sqq., agrees.

resort to the use of an institution which is created by, and cannot be defined otherwise than by reference to, a municipal system of law, they adopt *pro tanto* that legislation. In a contract which is subject to English law and which stipulates for the payment of a sum of foreign money, the law regulating that money 'becomes for this purpose a part of the "proper law" of the contract'.[41] It is for this reason that the definition of what the stipulated unit of account means is referred to the *lex monetae* by a universally followed rule of the conflict of laws. It is for the same reason that monetary obligations under public international law are subject to the *lex monetae* in so far as the definition of the unit of account is concerned.

On this basis, however, the further question arises whether the reference to the *lex monetae* envisages the particular law of the currency as it exists at the time of the conclusion of the treaty, or, generally, such law of the currency as may develop from time to time. In private law nominalism has the latter meaning. The ratio underlying this rule also applies to inter-State obligations. Where parties refrain from introducing a gold clause or a similar protective measure, the intention, if any, to secure a particular 'value' remains unexpressed and is, therefore, legally irrelevant.

In connection with inter-State obligations it is necessary, moreover, to ask whether nominalism as usually understood controls even in those cases in which a State relies on its own monetary legislation to the prejudice of the promisee State. A negative answer must clearly be predicated where the municipal monetary legislation constitutes a breach of international obligations. Thus a devaluation of a debtor State's currency in defiance of the duties imposed upon the debtor by the original version of the Articles of Agreement of the International Monetary Fund would have to be disregarded for the purpose of ascertaining the amount payable under a treaty concluded before the devaluation.[42] But it may be argued that, even in the absence of specific treaty obligations, the promisor State's monetary legislation must be ignored by public international law on account of its inconsistency with the overriding principle of *pacta sunt servanda*; that a waiver of the right to rely on municipal legislation must accordingly be read into the treaty; that, just as the State cannot by its own legislation reduce its indebtedness created under public international law, it cannot circuitously do so by paying 'the whole of [the debt's] nominal amount possessing only one-half of its real value';[43] that

[41] Above, p. 180.

[42] According to the Parties' intentions the *renvoi* to private law is unlikely to comprise such consequences as the primarily applicable public international law, whether customary or conventional, considers unlawful.

[43] See above, p. 466, n. 8.

instead of there being in the undertaking of a State . . . to pay a reservation of a sovereign right to withhold payment, the contract should be regarded as an assurance that such a right will not be exercised. A promise to pay, with a reserved right to deny or change the effect of the promise, is an absurdity.[44]

Although this line of reasoning will perhaps appeal to some, it cannot be accepted as sound. The quality and extent of the protection which public international law affords to a treaty are impaired if and in so far as the treaty incorporates or refers to municipal law. Monetary obligations, in particular, are, and are generally known to be, 'subject to the constitutional power of the government over the currency, whatever that power may be, and the obligation of the parties is therefore assumed with reference to that power'.[45] Consequently, when States contract on the basis of the promisor's money of account and fail to secure the promisee State by special clauses, no material exists which could lead to reading into the treaty a waiver rather than a reservation of the right of alteration.[46]

2. That, in the event of a catastrophic depreciation of a currency, international law would decree the revalorization of inter-State debts does not at present seem unlikely. As a matter of principle there is much to support an international rule of revalorization. The paramount maxim of good faith that pervades the interpretation of treaties may provide the tools. The French doctrine of *imprévision* and the revalorization and price revision practice developed in numerous continental countries after the First World War[47] may be regarded as analogies to which an international tribunal could turn. The fact that the Anglo-American countries, among others, reject the idea of revalorization or adjustment does not mean that an international tribunal should refrain from affording relief even in an extreme case. Nor is the point foreclosed by the fact that there is no rule of public international law that compels a State to enact revalorizing legislation in the event of a catastrophic depreciation of its currency[48]—

---

[44] *Murray* v. *Charleston* (1877), 96 U.S. 432, 445, *per* Mr. Justice Strong; *Hartman* v. *Greenhaw* (1880), 102 U.S. 678; cf. *Perry* v. *United States* (1935), 294 U.S. 330.

[45] *Knox* v. *Lee* and *Parker* v. *Davies* (1870), 79 U.S. 457, 548 *per* Mr. Justice Strong.

[46] It is possible that a different view, wholly unsupported by reasoning, was intended to be expressed by M. Cassin, when in the *Diverted Cargoes* case, Int. L.R. 820, at p. 836, he said: '*A fortiori* the creditor is entitled to reject, in so far as it would affect the substance of his claim, the effect of any action taken by the debtor State itself to devalue its currency.' If the Arbitrator intended to refer to a creditor State (as Wortley, *Expropriation in Public International Law* (1959), p. 109, not unreasonably thinks), then his dictum is relevant to the present discussion, but, for the reasons developed in the text, unacceptable. If the Arbitrator intended to refer to a creditor who is a private person, and has contracted with the debtor State on the footing of private law, then his dictum is wrong as a matter of private law which upholds the principle of nominalism (see above, pp. 84 sqq. and pp. 267 sqq); there is no trace of an exception for State debts.

[47] See above, p. 102 sqq.                                          [48] Above, p. 469

debts created by treaty may well deserve and require a special degree of equitable adjustment if the depreciation is such that, in compliance with the famous test, it would 'shock the conscience and produce an exclamation mark'.[49] In the last resort the question is one of degree.

Accordingly, too much should not be read into the decisions of international tribunals which were concerned with service agreements between international organizations and their employees and which held that the devaluation of the Swiss franc did not entitle a pensioner of the League of Nations to a revalorization of his pension.[50] Similarly, the general principles of law were held not to support a claim to the revalorization of a sum of French francs.[51] In neither case was depreciation catastrophic.[52]

It follows that where the depreciation is not extreme an adjustment of amounts due from one State to another can only be founded upon the express or implied terms of the treaty. After a delay of some thirty years only one express provision seems to have become available. On 27 June 1949 the United Kingdom entered into an Agreement on Trade and Payments with Argentina.[53] This provided, *inter alia*, that during the first year of the Agreement beginning on 1 July 1949 the average price for all types of meat purchased in the Argentine was £97.536 per long ton. The Agreement was accompanied by an unpublished confidential Note of 27 June 1949 addressed by the British Ambassador to the Argentinian Government. This included a paragraph (*d*) which, interestingly enough, dealt with the possible devaluation of sterling at the time so strenuously denied by the British Government:[54]

(*d*)  in the event of a change in the parity of sterling following direct action by the United Kingdom resulting in a depreciation of sterling arising from meat

---

[49] Above, p. 50, n. 124.

[50] *Desplanques* v. *Administrative Board of the Staff Pension Fund of the League of Nations*, A.D. 1941–2, Case No. 132; *Niestlé* v. *International Institute of Intellectual Co-operation*, Int. L.R. 1955, 762, at p. 764. Bindschedler, *Verstaatlichungsmassnahmen und Entschädigungspflicht nach Völkerrecht* (Zürich, 1950), p. 38, n. 103, states correctly that, in general, public international law does not impose the duty of revalorization.

[51] *Rothbarth* v. *International Institute of Intellectual Co-operation*, Int. L.R. 1951, 463, 465, where, however, damages for delay were allowed. And see *Weiss* v. *International Institute of Intellectual Co-operation*, Int. L.R. 1951, 458.

[52] It is necessary once more to emphasize that the text is concerned only with monetary obligations under treaties or other contracts governed by public international law. The different questions whether public international law requires a State to revalorize debts arising under private law or, in the event of the debtor State's default, grants damages for the depreciation which occurred between the date of default and the date of an award to the claimant State espousing its national's cause, are dealt with elsewhere: see, on the one hand, above, p. 468, and, on the other hand, below, p. 543. On the problem discussed in the text see Carreau, pp. 68–73.    [53] Cmd. 7735.

[54] The material is now available at the Public Record Office at Kew under Reference Number FO 371/74362 and 74363.

sales in terms of the peso (applying the provisions of Article 23 of this Agreement) the Argentine Government shall have the right at any time during the first year of currency of this Agreement to require discussions on the price fixed in this Agreement for these meat supplies in respect of which the relative sterling exchange had not been covered forward with the Central Bank of the Argentinian Republic under paragraph C of the letter of guarantee agreed upon between the Bank of England and the Central Bank of the Argentinian Republic.

On 21 September 1949, three days after sterling's devaluation, the Argentinian Government sent a Note to the British Ambassador whereby it invoked this provision and informed him 'that the price for future deliveries of meat . . . will be £140.382 thus counterbalancing the depreciation of 30.52 per cent on the average price of £97.536 per long ton'.[55] It thus came to light that the confidential Note of 27 June contained a remarkable error of translation. While the English text gave Argentina the right 'to require discussions', the Argentinian text speaks of 'el derecho . . . de demander que se ajusten los precios'.[55] On 29 September 1949 the British Ambassador replied by a Note in which he stated that, while the United Kingdom was 'fully prepared to enter upon discussions', there was 'no provision in the Notes of 27 June for automatic and proportionate price adjustments as a result of a change in the sterling-peso exchange rate'.[55] The dispute was settled on 23 April 1951, when the United Kingdom undertook 'to pay . . . the sum of £6.25 million . . . as total and final adjustment of prices for meat shipped against provisional invoices during the first year of the 1949 Agreement and up to the end of the calendar year 1950'.[56]

3. Where depreciation occurs after the date of maturity of an international debt, it would seem that international law is inclined to accept the rule, known to most legal systems on the Continent but not necessarily accepted by English law, according to which the debtor must make good the damage flowing from his *mora*.

The oldest case on the point is probably the decision of the Privy Council in *Pilkington* v. *Commissioners for Claims on France*[57] which may well be considered as an international case. In the course of the Napoleonic war the French Government confiscated money due to the English claimants; subsequently it provided a fund for compensation. The Privy Council held that the wrong done by the French Government must be completely undone and that, if the wrongdoer 'has received the assignats at the value of 50d, he does

---

[55] Reference No. FO 371/74420.
[56] Letter No. 1 annexed to the Protocol of 23 April 1951, Cmd. 8268.
[57] (1821), 92 Knapp 7, 20.

not make compensation by returning an assignat which is only worth 20d; he must make up the difference between the value of the assignats at the different dates'. On 12 January 1863 the Claims Commission between the United States of America and Peru awarded one *Montano*, a citizen of Peru, the sum of $24,151.29 'payable in the current money of the United States'. When Montano in 1864 applied to the United States of America for payment, the sum due to him was worth only $15,000 in gold. The umpire of the commission to whom the matter was referred decided that payment should be made in gold.[58] In *Cerruti*'s case an award made by President Cleveland in 1897 had decided that the claimant, an Italian subject, was entitled to be indemnified in respect of the debts arising out of a business which he had carried on in Colombia, but which had been confiscated. One of the debts was expressed in Colombian money which greatly depreciated, but in 1903 the creditor in question recovered payment under a judgment obtained against the claimant in Italy for some 181,000 lire. The claimant was apparently granted full compensation, for another international tribunal held in 1911 that 'on doit . . . se remettre autant que possible dans l'état existant avant la confiscation des biens du sieur Cerruti survenue aux mois de janvier et février 1885'.[59]

The Greek-Bulgarian Mixed Arbitral Tribunal had to deal with a claim to a sum of 14,000 leva odd which was due to the claimant under a judgment of 1911. The First World War brought about long delays as well as a severe depreciation of Bulgarian currency. 'Jugeant en toute équité' the Tribunal in 1929 awarded 100,000 leva.[60] Three arbitrations between Germany and Romania point in the same direction. In one case the value of an expropriated estate in 1914 was found to be 1,000,000 lei which as a result of a currency reform in 1929 became 32,000,000 lei, but 'vu la dépréciation du leu depuis 1929' the Arbitrators awarded in 1929 64,000,000 lei.[61] In another case a Romanian concern was indebted to a German bank in 1914 in the sum of £16,818 odd; allowing interest at the rate of $5\frac{1}{2}$ per cent the Arbitrators awarded in 1940 a sum of £40,867 'valeur-or' and thus eliminated the effect of the devaluation of

[58] Moore, *Digest of International Law* (1906), vii. 51; *International Arbitrations* (1898), ii. 1638, 1645, 1649.

[59] *Revue générale de droit international public*, 19 (1912), 268, 273.

[60] *Fontana v. Bulgaria, Recueil des Décisions des Tribunaux Arbitraux Mixtes*, ix. 374. It should be made clear that the decisions referred to in the text do not always distinguish clearly between the revalorization of a debt expressed in terms of a catastrophically depreciated currency and damages for delayed payment in the case of a less radical depreciation. It is in harmony with the general approach of public international law to take a broad view of these and similar distinctions derived from municipal law.

[61] *Affaire Junghans*, Reports of International Arbitral Awards, iii. 1885.

sterling.[62] In the third case Romanian buyers had in 1914 paid a sum of marks to Berlin sellers. In 1921 the former received an indemnity representing one-sixth of the sum paid. In 1929 the distinguished sole arbitrator awarded to them compensation for the remaining five-sixths.[63] The problem was elaborately discussed by the Swiss Government in 1961 in relation to a case in which Swiss owners of French property became in 1935 entitled to a sum of French francs. When it was paid in 1951 it represented less than 5 per cent of the gold value of 1935. The Swiss Government expressed the Opinion that France was liable to pay the difference.[64] Perhaps the most important case is the *Lighthouse Arbitration between France and Greece*[65] in which the devaluation of the drachma was held to require 'an adjustment based on good faith'. Admittedly this related to a tariff rather than a liquidated sum, but this does not appear to be a material distinction:

Indeed the principle of good faith in the interpretation of the concession required that, by reason of the devaluation of the drachma and the resulting disturbances of the financial equilibrium of the concession, the successor State should proceed to the necessary measures to ensure the continuation of the concession on equitable terms.

Notwithstanding this substantial body of authority[66] it is not always easy to ascertain the extent to which the amount awarded in cases of default is increased as a result of the debtor Government's *mora*, or as a result of the tribunal interpreting the law of damages so as to assess them at the date of judgment. It would seem that, even in the absence of *mora*, the principle of effectiveness of compensation makes it necessary to indemnify the victim also in respect of monetary depreciation.

[62] *Affaire Deutsche Bank*, ibid., p. 1895.

[63] *Goldenberg*'s case, ibid., ii. 901, at p. 909, where some general remarks will be found; the Award itself rests on the specific provisions of the Treaty of Versailles.

[64] *Annuaire Suisse de Droit International*, 1964, 148 or *Jurisprudence des Autorités Administratives de la Conféderation*, 1961 (fascicule 30), pp. 8 sqq. The Opinion concludes (p. 17) by noting 'une tendance très nette et généralement affirmée à indemniser la victime d'un dommage pour la perte qu'elle subit par suite de la dépréciation de la monnaie entre le moment où l'acte dommageable a été commis et celui du paiement de la réparation'.

[65] Reports of International Arbitral Awards, xii. 155, at pp. 224–8, also Int. L.R. 1956, 342, at pp. 345, 346.

[66] See also Ralston, *The Law and Proceedure of International Tribunals* (1926), p. 51, and *Supplement* (1936), p. 183. Cf. Art. 11 of the Agreement between the Federal Republic of Germany and the State of Israel (published by Van Dam, Die Haager Vertragswerke, p. 26): 'if during the currency of the present Agreement, circumstances change in such a manner as to result in an essential reduction of the substance of the obligation undertaken by the Federal Republic of Germany under the present Agreement, the Contracting Parties shall consult with a view to adjusting to such changed circumstances the annual instalments still payable'. In certain cases relief may be given by allowing rescission of agreement. This remedy does not require separate discussion.

4. When, on account of the respondent State's international responsibility, the claimant State is entitled, not to a liquidated sum, but to compensation for property taken from, or to damages for a wrong done to, itself or its national, the law of nations once again takes a broad view of the monetary implications and approaches them without undue concern for conceptualist refinements or subtle distinctions.[67] The need for treating aliens fairly and equitably and consistently with the demands of good faith precludes results which would allow the respondent State to benefit from delay or jeopardize the principle of the effectiveness of any award. International law has always emphasized that principle and should, therefore, not find it difficult to award such sums of money as will effectively take care of changes in monetary value, from which, in justice, the creditor should not be required to suffer, and, accordingly, to compensate the injured Party for currency depreciations which have occurred since the date of the act complained of.[68]

There are, in the first place, cases in which no harm is done by assessing the value at the date of the taking or the wrong. This is so where no subsequent change in value occurs or where any such change as does occur can be taken care of by an award of damages for delayed payment. Such circumstances were envisaged by the Permanent Court of International Justice in the case of the *Chorzów Factory*.[69] In discussing the problem of the assessment of damages the court pointed out that what it had to deal with was 'not an expropriation to render which lawful only the payment of fair compensation would have been wanting', and continued[70]

It follows that the compensation due to the German Government is not necessarily limited to the value of the undertaking at the moment of dispossession plus interest to the day of payment. This limitation would only be admissible if the Polish Government had had the right to expropriate and if its wrongful act consisted merely in not having paid to the two companies the just price of what was expropriated.

There are, secondly, cases in which changes in monetary values do occur, but it is impossible or inconvenient to effect the valuation as at a date later than that of the taking or the wrong, and the tribunal succeeds in neutralizing those changes by converting the amount of the valuation into a stable currency. Such a procedure was adopted in 1933 by M. Osten Undén as Sole Arbitrator between Greece and

---

[67] See above, n. 60.

[68] The suggestions in the text were expressly approved in the Opinion of the Swiss Government referred to above, n. 64.

[69] Series A, No. 13.

[70] pp. 46, 47.

Bulgaria[71] and, although it was more recently rejected by the Arbitral Commission on Property, Rights, and Interests in Germany,[72] it is sanctioned by the high authority of the Award in the *Lighthouse Arbitration between France and Greece*.[73] Having held that the lighthouse concession was wrongfully revoked in 1929, that the indemnity due to France was to be determined in terms of drachmae, and that the value of the concession had to be assessed as in the year 1929, the tribunal stated that

the injured party has the right to receive the equivalent at the date of the award of the loss suffered as the result of an illegal act and ought not to be prejudiced by the effects of a devaluation which took place between the date at which the wrongful act occurred and the determination of the amounts of compensation. To this end the tribunal must as far as possible use as medium a stable currency, and as such it accepts . . . the United States dollar.

The practical results are unlikely to be different where it is possible or just to apply the third method of valuing the property as at the date of the award—a method which is supported by the analogy of private law and is probably most usual. It was employed, in particular, by the Permanent Court of International Justice in the *Case of the Chorzów Factory*.[74] The Court held that it had to consider the effects of an illegal act and that, therefore, *restitutio in integrum* would normally be the relief granted by the Court:

it involves the obligation to restore the undertaking and, if this is not possible, to pay its value at the time of the indemnification, which value is designed to take the place of restitution which has become impossible.

The same principle was followed by the International Court of Justice in the *Corfu Channel* case.[75] A destroyer built in 1943 at a cost

---

[71] *Affaire des Forêts du Rhodope Central*, International Arbitral Awards, iii. 1391, particularly pp. 1434 sqq.

[72] *Rousseau v. Germany*, Decisions of the Arbitral Commission on Property, Rights, and Interests in Germany, iii. 297, or Int. L.R. 29, 329.

[73] Int. L.R. 1956, 299, at p. 302.

[74] Series A, No. 13, at p. 48; see also p. 50. It was on this point that Lord Finlay dissented. He regarded it as a general principle of international law that 'damages should be assessed upon the basis of the value of the undertaking at the time of the seizure' (p. 71). In truth he was stating what at that time appeared to be a principle of English law, and it is to be welcomed that it was not carried into international law. It has been suggested that if the defendant State has to pay damages for goods destined for resale, their value has to be assessed with reference to the date of loss, while the value of possessions intended to be preserved and utilized as such is to be ascertained with reference to the date of judgment: Salvioli, 'La Responsabilité des États et la Fixation des Dommages', *Rec.* 28 (1929, iii), 235, at p. 239, who adduces no evidence in support of his statement that the practice of the Mixed Arbitral Tribunals was based on this distinction. The assumption underlying and the results produced by it would seem to be arbitrary and unattractive. They were rightly rejected by Sibert, *Traité de Droit International Public*, i (1951), 327.

[75] I.C.J. Reports, 1944, 244. Judge Ecer dissented on the ground that 'the rise or fall in

of £554,678 became a total loss in 1946. Its replacement value at the time of the judgment in 1949, so it was held, had to be ascertained, because it is at that time that the injured State must be put in a position to effect replacement.[76]

## IV

In view of the situation described in the preceding sections it is not surprising that States have frequently resorted to measures designed to protect them against the effect of currency depreciation. An early[77] example of a protective clause is the foreign currency clause contained in the Treaty of 30 April 1803 by which the United States of America acquired Louisiana from France.[78] The purchaser agreed to pay 60 million francs by creating $11,250,000 6 per cent Redeemable Stock. At the same time the parties agreed (Art. III)

that the dollar of the United States specified in the present Convention shall be fixed at five francs $\frac{3333}{10.000}$ or five livres eight sous tournois.

The most modern and elaborate clause that seems to have found its way into a treaty is another foreign currency clause included in the Treaty of 3 March 1935 for the Sale of the Chinese Eastern Railway by the U.S.S.R. to Japan.[79] Japan undertook to pay a sum of 140 million yen in Japanese currency (Art. I). By Art. VIII the parties agreed that

in case the exchange rate of the yen in terms of the Swiss franc should rise or fall by not less than 8 per cent., the amount of any instalment shall be increased or

reduced as the case may be 'so that the value in Swiss francs of the

prices is a factor not depending on the author of the illegal act and, therefore, one for which he cannot be held responsible' (p. 255). The Judge was thus once again using an argument which has frequently been advanced, and refuted, in private law, particularly in France.

[76] Cf. the decision of the international tribunal constituted in 1933 under the chairmanship of M. J. G. Guerrero in order to make arrangements between Hungary, Austria, and Yugoslavia for the exploitation and reorganization of two railway systems which, in consequence of the First World War, extended across the new frontiers. Although in many respects amounts expressed in the old Austrian currency had to be considered in these complicated cases, the tribunal, making 'une équitable évaluation' or 'une juste appréciation des circonstances' based in 1934 its decision throughout upon the gold franc of the Latin Monetary Union: *Affaire du Chemin de Fer de Barcs-Pakrac*, International Arbitral Awards iii. 1571, at pp. 1577 sqq; *Affaire des Chemins de Fer Zeltweg-Wolfsberg et Unterdrauburg-Woellan*, ibid. iii. 1797, at pp. 1806 sqq. It is very remarkable that a judgment was expressed in a currency which never existed as such and which by 1934 certainly had lost all vestiges of existence. It is even more remarkable that the judgment did not provide for conversion into some existing currency.

[77] For still earlier examples see Feilchenfeld and Kersten (above, p. 539, n. 36), at p. 38, n. 3.

[78] Malloy, *Treaties, Conventions, International Acts, Protocols, and Agreements between the U.S.A. and Other Powers (1776–1909)* (1910), i. 511.

[79] *Nouveau Recueil général*, 3rd ser., 30, p. 649.

instalment shall be the same as it is at the date of the coming into force of the present agreement'. The Treaty also contains detailed provisions dealing with any alteration of the gold parity of the Swiss franc and with the suspension of its convertibility into gold. Another carefully devised currency clause was that included in the Convention made on 29 November 1947 between France and Italy[80] whereby the latter country agreed to pay 1,500 million lire in consideration of the release of all Italian property from the charge imposed by Art. 79 of the Treaty of Peace of 1947. Such sum was subject to a dollar clause at a fixed rate so that the amount due was equal to $28,965,117 *monnaie de compte*. Payments to the debit of the lire account are measured on the basis of a dollar clause (Art. 6), the interpretation of which is not free from doubt.[81] There are also cases in which States have agreed upon a currency clause of a type so well known to private law.[82] Thus a Trade Agreement between India and Yugoslavia provided for 'the event of a change in the parity rate of the Indian rupee in terms of the British pound sterling'. Did the clause apply, when, unexpectedly, sterling depreciated in terms of the rupee? As in private law, the correct answer probably was in the negative, for the intention of the clause was to protect against a change in the value or a devaluation of the rupee.[83]

The more usual method, however, was for many years the stipulation of a gold clause.[84] Except in cases of multipartite treaties[85]

[80] *Rev. Crit.* 1949, p. 148.

[81] Ch. 5, Art. 1 (4) of the Convention on the Settlement of Matters arising out of the War and the Occupation between the Western Allies and the Federal Republic of Germany of 26 May 1952 (Cmd. 8571, p. 104) defines 'substantial value' as a value 'of not less than 200,000 French francs at the 1st January 1951 purchasing power'—a highly unsatisfactory terminology. For an exchange guarantee in respect of the French franc see Art. 7 of the Anglo-French Agreement of 11 Apr. 1951 (Cmd. 8224). For a case of a *facultas alternativa* see the Financial Agreements between Canada and Belgium of 25 Oct. 1945 (U.N.T.S. 230, 127, clause 9) and between Canada and the Netherlands of 5 Feb. 1946 (U.N.T.S. 43, 3, clause 9): to 'pay in Canadian dollars or fine gold at the option of the Government' of the debtor State.

[82] Above, p. 205.

[83] When member States undertake to contribute to or share in the resources of a financial institution, they frequently undertake to maintain the value: see, for instance Art. V (11) of the IMF Articles of Agreement or Art. V (3) of the Agreement relating to the Inter-American Development Bank (Cmnd. 6271).

[84] Apart from the examples mentioned in the subsequent notes the following deserve a reference: Art. 262 (2) of the Treaty of Versailles: 'For the purpose of this Article the gold coins mentioned above shall be defined as being of the weight and fineness as enacted by law on 1 January 1914'; Agreement between the United Kingdom, Canada, and the Soviet Union relating to the sale of the nickel mines in the district of Petsamo to the Soviet Union which was to pay United States dollars 'reckoned at the value of 35 dollars to one ounce of gold' (*The Times* newspaper, 20 Oct. 1944, p. 3); according to the Paris Peace Treaties the reparations due to the Soviet Union and to some extent to Greece, Yugoslavia, and Czechoslovakia were expressed in United States dollars 'at its gold parity on 1 July 1946, i.e. $35 for one ounce of gold': Treaty of Peace with Italy, Art. 74 (A); with Romania, Art. 22; with

[See p. 550 for n. 84 cont. and n. 85.]

Great Britain as creditor does not appear to have ever adopted that device, but the United States of America has almost invariably done so up to the time when, in 1933, by the Joint Resolution of Congress the gold clause was declared to be contrary to the public policy of American municipal law. Numerous other countries have inserted a gold clause into their treaties and, if the existence of nominalism in public international law still required proof, it would be supplied by the fact that States have thought it necessary to protect themselves against its effects by agreeing on a gold clause. It is a remarkable fact that as late as 1975 an international corporation[86] was formed with a capital expressed in dollars 'en prenant pour base la valeur de 0.81851276 grammes d'or pur pour un dollar'. This, however, is probably an isolated case and it is likely that in present circumstances international law will have no alternative but to work with Special Drawing Rights or European Currency Units.[87] But the international law which developed around gold clauses cannot be ignored, for, as in private law, it remains relevant at least as a paradigm. It would be inappropriate, therefore, to refrain from a discussion of the rich material relating to the gold clause in the context of public international law.

1. Even in private law it will now have to be regarded as the rule that, wherever the word 'gold' is used in connection with a monetary obligation, a gold clause exists, and that the artificial and sterile

Bulgaria, Art. 21; with Hungary, Art. 23; with Finland, Art. 23. Similarly Art. 22 (6) of the State Treaty with Austria of 15 May 1955 (Cmd. 9482). In Art. VI of the International Wheat Agreement of 6 Mar. 1948 (Cmd. 7382) prices were agreed in dollars of 'Canadian currency at the parity for the Canadian dollar determined for the purposes of the International Monetary Fund as at March 1, 1949'. The Agreement between the U.S.S.R. and the Central People's Government of the Republic of China of 14 Feb. 1950 (*The New York Times* newspaper, 15 Feb. 1950, p. 11) provides for credits 'of 300 m. American dollars calculated on the basis of 35 American dollars to one ounce of fine gold' (Art. I). A similar formula in Art. V of the Vienna Convention on Civil Liability for Nuclear Damage of 21 May 1963 (*International Legal Materials*, ii (1963), 727). A gold clause is in effect incorporated into Art. 997 of the International Labour Code 1951 (embodying Art. 5 of the unratified Wages, Hours of Work and Manning (Sea) Convention (Revised) 1949); it provides that in the event of a change in the par value of pounds or dollars the wages of an able seaman are to be adjusted 'so as to maintain equivalence'. On the conversion of Migrants' pension rights see Art. 743 of the International Labour Code 1951. On gold clauses designed to maintain the value of the capital resources of international institutions see Delaume, pp. 262 sqq. On gold clauses in treaties see Treves, *Italian Yearbook of International Law*, 1975, 132.

[85] Art. 262 (1) of the Treaty of Versailles provided that all sums due from Germany and expressed in gold marks should be paid at the option of the creditors in pounds sterling, gold dollars, gold francs, or gold lire. The gold clause is contained in Germany's promise to pay gold marks as defined by Art. 262 (2); see the preceding note. Nothing was gained, therefore, by adding a gold clause to the moneys of payment, and the omission to use the word 'gold' in connection with sterling is without significance.

[86] Statutes of the Compagnie Maritime Arabe des Transports Pétroliers, Clunet 1975, 969, 975.

[87] Above, pp. 505–9.

distinction between gold coin and gold value clauses has become obsolete.[88] This is certainly the position in public international law: no debtor State will be allowed to say, for instance, that, because it agreed to pay 'in gold coin', this is merely a descriptive *clause de style*, not a gold clause, or merely refers to the mode of payment and ceases to have effect when the circulation of gold coins is discontinued. The use of the words 'in gold' is much more likely to indicate a gold bullion clause, for in the realm of inter-State obligations there is nothing unusual in payments being made by the delivery of bullion.

What public international law does have in common with private law is the requirement that the existence of a gold clause cannot be presumed,[89] but depends upon an agreement between the Parties, which, except in very special circumstances, cannot be implied in a treaty.

The most famous controversy about the existence of a gold clause arose in connection with the 'Boxer Indemnity'. By the Treaty of 29 May 1901[90] China undertook to pay to the Powers an aggregate sum of 450 million Haikwan taels which were to 'constitute a gold debt calculated at the rate of the Haikwan tael to the currency of each country' as indicated in a Schedule according to which a Haikwan tael was equal to 0.742 gold dollar, 3/-sh. of sterling currency, 1.796 Netherlands florin, and so forth. It was also provided that capital and interest should be paid in gold or at the rates of exchange corresponding to the dates at which the different payments fell due. Notwithstanding its elaborate character the clause left room for much doubt. China's payments were made in silver. The dispute which thus arose and led to lengthy diplomatic correspondence[91] was settled by a Protocol of 2 July 1905 whereby China recognized that 'the sum of 450 million taels constitutes a debt in gold; that is to say, for each Haikwan tael due to each of the Powers China must pay in gold the amount which is shown in Art. VI' of the Treaty of 1901, and whereby China undertook to pay a lump sum of 8 million taels in settlement of arrears and to make future payments 'either in silver . . . or in gold bills or in telegraphic transfers at the choice of each

---

[88] Above, p. 151.

[89] In the *Pious Fund* case (Scott, *The Hague Court Reports*, p. 48) Sir Edward Thornton awarded in 1875 a sum of Mexican gold dollars, apparently without any detailed discussion relating to the gold clause. When in 1902 the second *Pious Fund* case came before the Arbitral Tribunal (Reports of International Arbitral Awards ix. 11) the question was considered. It was held 'que le dollar d'argent ayant cours légal au Mexique le paiement en or ne peut être exigé qu'en vertu d'une stipulation *expresse*'. This may go too far. It is interesting to note that the decision of 1875 was not held to constitute *res judicata* on the point. In the sense of the text see also Carreau, p. 172.

[90] Art. VI, see, for example, Malloy, *Treaties*, ii. 2006.

[91] *Foreign Relations of the United States*, 1904, pp. 177 sqq.

Power'.[92] Fresh difficulties arose during and after the First World War when China proposed to pay some of the creditor States in their depreciated currencies.[93] In February 1923 the representatives of England, France, Belgium, the Netherlands, Italy, Spain, Japan, and the United States addressed a Note to China expressing their respective Governments' unanimous opinion that the arrangements of 1901 and 1905 'establish in an absolutely clear and incontestable manner the fact that the indemnity of 1901 should be paid in gold, that is to say, that for every Haikwan tael owed to each Power China should pay the amount in gold indicated in the said Art. VI as the equivalent of a tael'.[94] China replied by a Note of 26 December 1923.[95] Its principal argument was that the words 'in gold' merely meant 'the respective gold currencies of the Signatory Powers in contrast with the Haikwan tael which is a silver standard and in the terms of which the indemnity of 1901 is stipulated. In other words, by "gold" is not meant the gold metal, but simply gold currency.' This reasoning, familiar to the private lawyer,[96] was refuted by a Note addressed to China by the Ministers of Great Britain, France, Belgium, the Netherlands, Italy, Japan, and the United States on 11 February 1924.[97] The dispute was settled in 1925 by the adoption of the U.S.A. dollar instead of the gold franc as a medium of exchange in respect of such parts of the indemnity as had not yet been remitted by the Powers concerned.[98] In the result the controversy is mainly a commentary on the art of drafting (or its absence) in international practice.

On the other hand, the analogy of private law together with the liberal rules of construction, which are applicable to treaties, lead to the submission that almost any reference to gold is sufficient to signify a genuine gold clause.[99] Moreover, although a properly drawn

---

[92] *Foreign Relations of the United States*, 1905, p. 156; the correspondence is set forth at pp. 145 sqq.

[93] Ibid., 1922, i. 809 sqq.; 1923, i. 592 sqq.

[94] Ibid., 1923, i. 593.                                                    [95] Ibid., pp. 600 sqq.

[96] Above, p. 140.                                    [97] *Foreign Relations*, 1924, i. 564.

[98] *Survey of International Affairs*, 1925, ii. 358 sqq., 368–70; for a summary see Hackworth, v. 628, 629.

[99] It is believed that, notwithstanding many difficulties of interpretation which arise from the English translations, a gold clause is most likely to be included in the numerous treaties for the provision of economic and technical assistance which the Soviet Union has entered into. Usually loans of x million 'roubles (one rouble is equivalent to 0.222168 grammes of fine gold)' are granted. In this sense the treaty with Iraq of 16 Mar. 1959 (U.N.T.S. 346, 142), which in Art. 7 contains an obscure provision for repayment; treaties with the United Arab Republic of 27 Aug. 1960, Art. 3 (U.N.T.S. 399, 37) and with Ghana, Art. V (ibid., p. 62); the Treaties with the Somali Republic of 2 June 1961 (U.N.T.S. 475, 274) and with Iran of 13 Jan. 1966 (*International Legal Materials*, v (1966), 419) are similar, though the rouble is said to contain 0.987412 grammes of fine gold. For a loan 'in gold, United States dollars or other currencies . . . to a total amount equivalent to 8,886,720 grammes of fine gold or 40 million roubles on the basis of a rouble fine-gold content of

gold clause requires a definition of the gold's weight and fineness, it is only rarely that States care to clarify this point.[100] Usually the conclusion that the parties were contemplating the conditions existing at the time when the treaty was made is a matter of inference.

2. It is the prevailing tendency in private law to submit the question of the effect of the abrogation of the gold clause to the proper law of the contract rather than the law of the currency. If the classification accepted by public international law were similar, it would follow that the abrogation of the gold clause by national legislation could not in any event affect the debtor State's obligations under a treaty. If public international law regarded the gold clause as belonging to the law of the currency, its abrogation would have validity also within the ambit of treaties. Although the abrogation of the gold clause is a measure of monetary policy and although, it must be admitted, there is something artificial in the submission of a single

0.222168 grammes' see the treaty with Finland of 6 Feb. 1954 (U.N.T.S. 221, 148), and for loans in terms of gold dollars see the treaty with China of 14 Feb. 1950 (U.N.T.S. 226, 25) and the treaty with Cuba of 13 Feb. 1960 (U.N.T.S. 369, 10). A gold clause is probably also included in Art. 156 of the Protocol to the French-Algerian Convention on Hydrocarbon Affairs of 29 July 1965 (*International Legal Materials*, iv (1965), 809, 905), which provides for payments to be made on the basis of International Monetary Fund parities.

[100] See p. 552, n. 5, and p. 536, n. 22; for other examples see: Convention for the Establishment of an International Central American Tribunal, concluded between Guatemala, El Salvador, Honduras, Nicaragua, and Costa Rica (Hudson, op. cit. ii, No. 79): the minimum honorarium of each of the arbitrators shall be 1,000 American dollars gold per month (Art. 23); the Agreement for the establishment of an International Wine Office of 1924–25 (Cmnd. 5475 or 5834) providing in Art. 5 for a 'contribution unit' of '3000 gold francs' without further definition; Regulations for the Execution of the Convention of the Postal Union of the Americas and Spain of 10 Nov. 1931 (ibid. v, No. 297b): the expenses of the International Office may not exceed the annual sum of 13,000 Uruguayan gold pesos; Convention between the United States and Denmark for the cession of the West Indies of 4 Aug. 1916 (*American Journal of International Law*, 11 (1917), *Supplement*, p. 53a): payment of '25 m. dollars in gold coin of the United States'; Treaty between Austria and Turkey relating to Bosnia-Herzegovina of 26 Feb. 1909 (*Nouveau Recueil général*, 3rd ser., 2, p. 661): Austria was to pay for Turkish real property in the ceded territory '2½ millions de livres turques en or' (Art. V); Treaty of Versailles between Germany and France of 26 Feb. 1871 (ibid., 19, p. 652): France undertook to pay 'cinq milliards de francs' (Art. 2) and by Art. 7 of the Treaty of Frankfurt of 10 May 1871 (ibid., p. 688) all payments were to be made 'en métal or ou argent, en billets de la banque d'Angleterre, de Prusse, des Pays-Bas ou de la Belgique'; Treaty between the United States of America and Colombia of 6 Apr. 1914 (ibid. 12, p. 131): for the rights in respect of the Panama Canal Zone the United States of America paid 'the sum of $250 m. gold United States money'; Baltic Geodetic Convention of 31 Dec. 1925 (Hudson, op. cit. iii. 1823): annual contributions fixed in 'gold dollars' (Art. 7); Agreement concerning the liquidation of German property in Switzerland of 25 May 1946 (Cmd. 6884): '250 m. Swiss francs payable on demand in gold in New York' (Clause II. 2); the Carriage of Goods by Sea Act, 1924, based on the International Convention for the Unification of certain Rules relating to Bills of Lading (*League of Nations Treaty Series*, cxx. 155, Art. 9) provides that 'the monetary units mentioned in these Rules are to be taken to be gold value'. See above, p. 142. A very special case is that of the Convention establishing an International Organization of Legal Metrology of 12 Oct. 1955 (Cmnd. 1858); Arts. XXIV and XXVI speak of 'gold francs' which are not defined, but 'parity between the gold franc and the French franc' in which contributions may be paid shall be that quoted by the Banque de France.

clause to different systems of law,[101] it must probably be regarded as decisive that it is the very purpose of the gold clause to protect the parties against the effects of the *lex monetae* and that, therefore, the parties cannot have intended to submit it to that legal system.[102] The parties to a treaty, in particular, cannot be presumed to extend their reference to municipal law, made by the adoption of a national currency, further than the terms of the treaty necessitate. Gold clauses and their abrogation must be subject to public international law.[103] The question became practical, but was not decided, in connection with Art. 14 of the Convention for the construction of the Panama Canal of 18 November 1903[104] whereby the United States undertook to make to Panama an annual payment of $250,000 in gold coin of the United States. When in 1933 the United States enacted legislation invalidating gold clauses, she refused (unjustifiably, it is submitted) to pay more than the nominal amount of the annuity. Panama did not accept the position that the municipal legislation of the United States could prejudice her treaty obligations. The dispute was settled by a Convention of 2 March 1936 by which the United States undertook to pay an annuity of 430,000 balboas, i.e. currency of Panama, the gold content of which was simultaneously reduced.[105]

## V

In international law, as in private law, the money of payment of an inter-State obligation may be different from the money of account which has been determined by the process discussed above[106] and in which the quantum of the obligation is expressed.[107] The principal problems relating to the payment of inter-State obligations are the following:

1. Where, in the absence of express terms, is a sum of money due from an international person to another international person to be paid? It is suggested that strong tendencies prevailing in private law[108] and the requirements of reasonableness and justice

---

[101] This is one of the principal points of Gutzwiller's book, *Der Geltungsbereich der Währungsvorschriften* (1940).

[102] Carreau, pp. 172 sqq. agrees.

[103] In the same sense see Nussbaum, p. 442; Van Hecke, p. 212.

[104] *Nouveau Recueil général*, 2nd ser., 31, p. 599; Malloy, op. cit. ii. 1349.

[105] *American Journal of International Law*, 34 (1940), *Supplement*, p. 139, and the Note on p. 157. On the Convention see Wolsey in *American Journal of International Law*, 31 (1937), 300; Sauser-Hall in *Rec.*, 60 (1937), 653, 751; Hackworth, v. 630.

[106] Above, p. 533.

[107] On the quantum see the preceding sections III and IV.

[108] Above, pp. 76–8.

favour the rule that payment is to be made in the capital of the creditor State.[109]

2. How is an inter-State obligation to be discharged? In private law it is apparently everywhere the rule that tender is to be made in cash or, more precisely, by the payment of that which according to the *lex monetae* constitutes legal tender.[110] In public international law, which will usually be concerned with very large sums, this rule is clearly inappropriate. The proper method of payment will be payment by bank transfer or by drafts drawn by one Central Bank on another Central Bank or, possibly, by drafts drawn on private banks of unquestionable standing.

3. Which is the currency that in public international law is to be employed in discharge of an inter-State debt? Does the debtor State in international law have the option, recognized in private law,[111] of employing the *moneta loci solutionis* as the money of payment, if payment is to be made in a State in which the money of account is not in circulation? If, for instance, Switzerland has undertaken to pay hundreds of millions of Swiss francs to the United States of America in New York,[112] does she pay in Swiss francs or in United States dollars? In the former event the creditor State would have the burden of collecting the draft in Switzerland and arranging for the amount to be remitted to the United States; it would not at the due date obtain payment in the *locus solutionis*. It is suggested, therefore, though with some hesitation, that the option granted to the debtor by private law should also be recognized by international law in favour of the debtor State.'[113]

---

[109] The London Agreement on German External Debts (Cmd. 8781) provided in Annex VII, s. I (2) (*a*), that a privileged Gold mark debt of a 'specific foreign character' exists where the parties have expressly agreed upon a non-German place of payment. The Mixed Arbitral Tribunal, established under the Agreement, held that the 'place of payment' was not defined by German law which governed the contract between private parties, but by international law and meant the place at which the creditor was entitled actually to receive the money due to him: Int. L.R. 25 (1958 i), 33 and 326 or *Zeitschrift für ausländisches öffentliches Recht*, 19 (1958), 761, discussed by Johnson, *British Year Book of International Law*, 1958, 363 or W. Lewald, *NJW.* 1959, p. 1017. The decision was a majority decision of five against four. That part of it which held that a place of payment in Switzerland had been 'expressly' agreed by the parties is very doubtful indeed. See above, p. 214, n. 140.

[110] Above, p. 267.                                    [111] Above, p. 308.

[112] Cf. the treaty between the Allied Governments and Switzerland made in Washington in 1946, whereby Switzerland undertook to pay '250 million Swiss francs payable on demand in gold in New York': Cmd. 6884, Clause II (2). By a treaty of 25 May 1959 Japan undertook to pay U.S.$1,175,000 to Denmark, payment to 'be remitted in United States dollars to the Danish Ministry of Finance, Copenhagen' (*Japanese Annual of International Law*, 1960, 203). One wonders how this was expected to be put into effect.

[113] The problem arises only where there is no express agreement between the Parties about the method of payment. The Agreement establishing the OPEC Fund for International Development of 27 May 1980 recognizes the U.S. dollar as the money of account, but

It is not unlikely, however, that international law has adopted a much broader rule to the effect that, in general, payment is to be made in the currency of the creditor State. This, at any rate, is the solution sanctioned by the Award in the *Lighthouse Arbitration between France and Greece.*[114] Having found that the various amounts to be credited to both Parties were expressed in numerous currencies and that, in particular, one important item had been calculated in terms of dollars,[115] the Arbitrators thought it necessary[116]

> to convert the total amounts to be awarded to the parties into one single currency. To that end, the Tribunal can, in this case, take into consideration two currencies only—the present-day drachma, the currency of Greece, and the present-day French franc. The final resulting balance being in favour of the firm of Collas & Michel, the question arises whether it is the money of the debtor or the creditor which ought to be chosen. The Tribunal is of opinion that it is the present-day French franc which should be adopted as the currency of payment; it is the currency in which the firm undertook all its operations and kept all its accounts.

4. Which is the date with reference to which any conversion under public international law is to be effected?

In the *Lighthouse Arbitration* just referred to the Arbitrators ordered conversion into French francs, the currency of the creditor State, to take place at the rate of exchange of the day on which the definitive award determining the compensation is published.[117] This may have been an adequate solution in a case in which a final sum of French francs, representing the balance resulting from numerous conversions, had to be awarded. In the absence of such special circumstances the rate of exchange of the day of payment would seem to be preferable. The reasons are the same as in private law.[118] In the *Case of Diverted Cargoes*[119] the Arbitrator, M. René Cassin, in fact expressed the view that the payment-date rule was supported by 'so decisive a monument of international case law' that it constituted a general principle of law. This statement, clearly made *obiter*, at the time was an exaggeration and unfounded.[120] Nevertheless it antici-

provides that payments are to be effected 'in freely usable currencies the amount of which shall be equivalent at the time it is received by the Fund to the U.S. dollar amount required for payment'. The term 'freely usable currencies' is carefully defined. See Art. 4.04 as reproduced in Int. L.M. 1980, 880.    [114] For references see above, p. 545, n. 65.

[115] Above, p. 547.    [116] Int. L.R. 1956, 674.    [117] Ibid., 302, 674.

[118] Above, p. 312. There are, however, some cases in which conversion was ordered to take place at the rate of exchange of the day when the claim arose: decisions of the U.S./ Mexican Claims Commission in *Case of George W. Cook* (1927), in Nielsen, *International Law applied to Reclamations*, p. 195; *Case of George W. Cook* (1930), ibid., p. 500; *Case of Moffit* (1929), ibid., p. 404.    [119] Int. L.R. 1955, 836.

[120] See the comments referred to above, p. 534, n. 12 and, particularly, *British Year Book of International Law*, 1957, p. 43.

pated the welcome development which has since then occurred and which renders it possible to suggest that international law should adopt the payment date rule. It is founded on reasons of justice, provided it is understood that damages for default and delay may be awarded.

As in private law there are in international law cases in which the problem of the proper date for conversion is solved by the express or implied intention of the Parties. Thus the real and, probably, the only point of law involved in the *Case of Diverted Cargoes* was one of construction: was the f.o.b. value of goods of American origin convertible into sterling at the dollar rate prevailing at the time of the treaty or at the time when credit was actually given?[121] The Arbitrator answered the question in the latter sense. His reasons are unconvincing, particularly because they fail to take account of an analogy provided by private law:[122] where an item expressed in foreign currency has to be converted into the currency in which both the money of account is expressed and payment is to be made, conversion will as a rule be effected at the rate of exchange of the day on which there arises the right to payment or the duty to give credit.

5. Which is the type of rate of exchange that has to be employed in converting a monetary obligation arising under public international law?

In the large majority of cases it cannot be open to doubt that the official rate of exchange, the rate most closely in line with the requirements of the International Monetary Fund, the rate for cable transfers of a commercial character will be applicable. Yet in certain circumstances the incidence of exchange control leads to much difficulty for the State which espouses a claim originally vested in one of its nationals. It has been shown that, where the national is entitled to damages for the destruction, or to compensation for the taking, of property situate in the territory of the debtor State, his claim is, in general, expressed and measured[123] in terms of the currency of such State except in cases in which there exists something in the nature of an international market for investments of the type in question; no other solution is practicable. The real problem arises only, when one comes to transferability: is the amount due to be converted at all and, if so, at the official rate of exchange or at that rate which would have been available to the private owner had the debtor State paid him, and which may have been lower than the official rate? In regard to compensation for takings it has been suggested that the law should operate so as to put the alien investor in a better position than that

---

[121] For the circumstances in which the question arose see above, p. 534.
[122] Above, p. 330.                                  [123] Above, p. 537.

which he would have occupied if his property had not been taken: 'once he has lost his investment it would be inequitable to require him to keep his funds in the territory of the State that has deprived him of it'.[124] But this argument is not invariably convincing, for it is hard to see why, in the absence of treaty protection,[125] the alien investor should be allowed to derive actual advantage from the respondent State's international wrong. It would seem safer to find the solution in the principle of effectiveness of compensation and payment, which international law clearly recognizes and which has often been laid down.[126] Most, if not all, of the Treaties of Friendship, Commerce, and Navigation concluded by the United States since 1945[127] express it in a form which is likely to correspond to customary public international law: the compensation must be paid promptly and 'in effectively realizable form',[128] and, where there are exchange restrictions, 'reasonable provision for the withdrawal in foreign exchange in the currency of the other Party' must be made, the rate of exchange being that approved by the International Monetary Fund or, alternatively such a rate as 'is just and reasonable'.[129] These rules, it is true, primarily envisage the legal rights of the alien owner himself. But the State espousing his claim is certainly in no worse position. In particular, where there is illegality and a claim to damages, it may well be in a better position, as appears from the following section.

---

[124] Comment on s. 190 of the Foreign Relations Law of the United States (1965). A similar thought underlies the suggestion by Brandon, 'Legal Aspects of Foreign Investment', *Federal Bar Journal*, xviii (1958), 316, according to which 'compensation must be effective in the sense that it should be payable in the currency in which the original capital was imported into the nationalizing State'.

[125] See above, p. 536.

[126] See s. 190 referred to in n. 124 above. It provides that, unless compensation is paid in the currency of the State of which the alien was a national, 'the cash must be convertible into such currency' and withdrawable. See also Art. 39 of the Harvard Draft (*American Journal of International Law*, 1961, p. 583) and Art. 3 of the Draft Convention on the Protection of Foreign Property of 12 Oct. 1967 prepared by the Organization for Economic Co-operation and Development (*International Legal Materials*, vii (1968), 117), according to which compensation representing 'the genuine value of the property' must be 'transferable to the extent necessary to make it effective for the national entitled thereto'.

[127] For a complete list see above, p. 524, n. 57, and see p. 529.

[128] For representative examples see the Treaty with Japan, Art. VI (3); Iran, Art. IV (2); Germany, Art. V (4). In the same sense paragraph (9) of the Exchange of Letters of 1 Aug. 1966 between Denmark and Malawi, U.N.T.S. 586, 20, among many other similar agreements.

[129] See, for instance, Treaty with Japan, Art. XII (3); Iran, Art. VII (2); Netherlands, Art. XII (3). The Treaty with Germany would seem to be to the same effect, but is less clearly expressed.

## VI

Domestic exchange control legislation cannot, as a rule, have any effect upon inter-State monetary obligations governed by public international law.[130] This applies even where the claimant State espouses its national's claim which is almost of necessity derived from municipal law; as a result of the debtor State's wrong and the espousal by the claimant State it becomes an international claim, though, of course, it comprises only the actual damage suffered.[131] The reason for the rule is that a State cannot rely on its or, indeed, on any municipal law to avoid its international obligations, except in so far as this has been adopted by and incorporated into the treaty made between international persons. On the other hand, if a State has a sum of money standing to its credit with a bank in a foreign State, whether it be a private bank or the Central bank, the relationship will in all probability be governed by private law and the local exchange control legislation may be applicable.[132]

There are, however, also intermediate and, therefore, doubtful cases. Thus by a treaty of 25 November 1958[133] the United Kingdom agreed to lend to Turkey a sum of sterling to be paid 'to a transferable account in the United Kingdom to be designated by the Government of the Turkish Republic'. The account so credited would, it is submitted, be subject to English exchange control. Yet, when Turkey has used the credit and comes under a duty to make repayment, it would not be open to her to invoke her own exchange control laws.[134]

[130] Many treaties, particularly those relating to financial institutions provide expressly for freedom from exchange restrictions. Thus the Agreement establishing the Inter-American Development Bank, an international person, of 8 April 1959 (Cmnd. 6271) includes elaborate provisions to exempt the resources of the Bank from such restrictions: Art. V and Art. XI (6); similarly Art. 5 of the Agreement establishing the International Fund for Agricultural Development of 13 June 1976, Cmnd. 6787.

[131] Hence the Harvard Draft of 1961 correctly provides in Art. 39, para. 4 that damages and compensation payable under the Article 'shall be exempt from exchange controls': *American Journal of International Law*, 1961, p. 583.

[132] This is clearly so, where the State or one of its instrumentalities acquires a private law debt by way of assignment or subrogation, as happens frequently under arrangements for export credit guarantees or insurance.

[133] Cmnd. 615.

[134] By another treaty (Cmd. 9120) Turkey agreed to pay a sum of sterling to the United Kingdom by instalments to 'be converted into Turkish liras at the buying rate of exchange . . . and paid into an account' of the United Kingdom at the Turkish Central Bank. It is likely that this account became subject to Turkish municipal law, including exchange control, as seems to follow from the further clause that 'the Turkish liras deriving from the aforementioned annual instalments may be used freely for the purchase of any kind of Turkish products intended for internal consumption in the United Kingdom.'

# APPENDIX I

# Hopkins *v*. Compagnie Internationale Des Wagon-Lits[1]

*(King's Bench Division*—Mr. Justice Swift)

SIR ALBION RICHARDSON K.C. and OSBERT PEAKE for the plaintiff.

F. H. MAUGHAM K.C. and J. B. LINDON for the defendants.

The facts and arguments appear from the Judgment.

26 Jan. 1927. SWIFT J.: In the year 1913 the defendant company, which is a company providing sleeping-coaches for railways, restaurant-carriages, and so on, and whose headquarters are in Belgium, issued bonds for the purpose of raising money to be used in their undertaking, and they issued some 30,000 bonds of 500 francs each. The bonds provided for the repayment of the moneys advanced according to drawings. The plaintiff, Mr. Walter Bernard Hopkins, has become possessed of two of those bonds, which were drawn for redemption on 6 November 1926, and he was entitled to receive £42. 1*s*. 6*d*. in respect of the bonds, provided that the franc was at the same rate of exchange in November 1926 as it was in January 1913. When, however, he came to collect the money which he conceived to be due to him, he was offered only a sum of some £6 odd, and it was contended on behalf of the defendants that, the value of the franc having depreciated, he was not entitled to more. He brings this action claiming a declaration that he is entitled to receive, on the redemption of the two bonds which are in his possession, a sum of money which shall be equivalent to the value of 500 francs in January 1913. Sir Albion Richardson, in support of his contention, suggests that the bond which secures the repayment of 500 francs must be taken to mean that it is to secure the repayment of 500 gold francs, because he says that a number of countries had agreed upon the standard of the gold franc by various treaties from 1865 onwards, and that it must have been in the contemplation of the parties when the bargain which is contained in the bond was made that there should be repayment in that which he has from time to time lapsed into calling the international franc, but which he says he does not really mean to call the international franc. All that it is is a standard which the different countries have agreed upon between themselves which their franc shall attain, and on condition that it attains that standard it shall be freely interchangeable between the treasuries of the various high contracting parties. The substance of Sir Albion Richardson's contention is that the

---

[1] By the courtesy of the defendants it has been possible to report the decision here.

word 'franc' in this bond means a gold franc, that it means something for which he was entitled to have, when his bonds came to be redeemed, a certain quantity of gold. Quite apart from authority, I should have thought that that was wrong. I should have come to the conclusion that all that the bond gave him, being made in Belgium, and having, in my view, to be construed according to the laws of Belgium, was a right to receive 500 francs, or their equivalent in value, whatever their value might be when the date came for redemption, but I think that in this case there is very clear authority that Sir Albion Richardson's contention made on behalf of the plaintiff is wrong. I cannot distinguish this case from the case of *In re Chesterman's Trusts*[2] or from the case of *Anderson* v. *The Equitable Life Assurance Society of the United States.*[3] Those two cases seem to me to bind me. They certainly confirm me in the view which I had taken of this matter before Mr. Maugham called my attention to them. I therefore think that the plaintiff is not entitled to the declaration for which he asks, nor to the payment for which he asks, but on the other hand, the defendants are entitled to judgment, with costs.

*Solicitors:*   Messrs. Parker & Hammond (for the plaintiff).
           Messrs. Ashurst Morris Crisp & Co. (for the defendants).

[2] [1923] 2 Ch. 466.                    [3] (1926) 42 T.L.R. 302.

# APPENDIX II

# Franklin *v.* Westminster Bank[1]

### (*King's Bench Division and Court of Appeal*)

The plaintiff appeared in person.

Sir Patrick Hastings K.C., Eric O'Donnell, and Rodger Winn for the defendants.

The facts appear from the Judgments.

13 May 1931. MacKinnon J.: In this case the plaintiff sues the Westminster Bank on a cheque. I hope I am justified in believing that the plaintiff will not be able to complain that the has not been fully heard here and that I have not listened to everything he desired to advance; but I cannot help, notwithstanding that, expressing my regret that the time of the court should have been wasted for nearly a whole day in regard to a claim that is essentially absurd and ridiculous.

The plaintiff, or to be accurate a company called Webster Brothers Limited, on 27 September 1923 paid £15 to the defendant bank under its then name of the London County and Westminster Bank, and in exchange for that were given a cheque drawn upon the Darmstädter Bank, Berlin, for a sum in marks. At that time the mark in Germany was fantastically depreciated and accordingly the £15 that Messrs. Webster paid bought a cheque in exchange for which Messrs. Webster on presentation at the Darmstädter und Nationalbank, Berlin, at the proper time would have been entitled to receive 9,000,000,000 marks of the then depreciated currency. We have tried this case upon the assumption that for value this cheque was endorsed first to a brother of the plaintiff and then by that brother to himself and that the plaintiff is the holder of it. In point of fact it was not presented in 1923 or until after 11 October 1924. On 11 October 1924 a law was passed in Germany by which the legal currency of the previously existing marks of the description of which this cheque entitled the holder to receive 9,000,000,000 marks was abolished, and a new form of mark was introduced; and it was provided that the new mark should be exchanged for the old marks which were thereby abolished at the rate of one billion of the old marks for one mark of the new currency. The effect of that law was as from 11 October 1924 that on presentation of this cheque dated 23 September 1923, subject to any other objection to its being cashed, the person who presented it would be entitled to receive 9/1000ths of a mark. The cheque was

---

[1] The publication of the judgment, a German translation of which appeared in *JW.* 1931, 3163, is due to the kind assistance rendered by the defendants' solicitors. Short reports were published in *The Times* newspaper of 14 May and 17 July 1931.

presented by Mr. Boehme on behalf of the plaintiff on 15 December 1926. The cashier, as I gather, viewed the document with some disfavour and intimated that he was not going to give anything for it. Mr. Boehme desired his refusal to be intimated in due form, whereupon the cashier wrote the contemptuous word 'wertlos' upon the cheque and stamped it with a stamp upon the back. It came back to the plaintiff. The plaintiff thereupon gave notice to the defendant bank, or I will assume that he gave notice to the defendant bank, that this cheque had been dishonoured, and on 26 September 1929, a date which may accidentally be one day less than six years from the date of the cheque but which may have some relation to another legislative provision of ours, by his writ of that date he claimed damages from the defendant for the dishonour of this cheque. The Statement of Claim alleges that the measure of those damages to which he is entitled is £459,000,000 sterling upon the basis that 9,000,000,000 marks at the rate of exchange on 26 September 1929 were worth that sum in exchange. I will not discuss the matter at any length. I ventured to describe the claim as fantastic and ridiculous, but it is perhaps better to use less colourful epithets. As I have said, the only amount for which the holder of this cheque was entitled to be paid after 11 October 1924 was 9/1000ths of a mark, a sum which it is impossible to pay because there is no coin in the world which is small enough to provide it.

There is another defence open to the defendants which I need only mention and that is this. It is provided by the German cheque law of 1908 that cheques must be presented within a certain period of their being drawn. With regard to foreign cheques, that is cheques drawn abroad on a German bank and payable in Germany, they must be presented within such period as is fixed by the Federal Council, and by a Decree or notice or other appropriate form of 19 March 1908, the Federal Council appointed three weeks as the appropriate period for presentation of a foreign cheque. This cheque, of course, was not presented within the three weeks. It was presented some three years after it was drawn, namely in December 1926. That also seems to me to be a sufficient defence, but the main and obvious defence is that there was no dishonour of this cheque. It was worthless when presented and, therefore, the cashier was quite right in saying he could not honour it because he had no coin small enough with which to pay it.

The result is that there must be judgment in this case for the defendants with costs.

The plaintiff appealed.

16 July 1931. LORD HANWORTH M.R.: This appeal fails, and indeed I am rather reluctant to say more than that the court agrees with the decision reached by Mr. Justice MacKinnon and with the reasoning on which that conclusion has been come to. At the same time, as the plaintiff has appeared in person and has had a full opportunity of presenting his case, it is perhaps courteous to him to show that we have fully appreciated the point that he has put before us and, therefore, to give a somewhat more extended judgment than is really necessary.

The action is brought by the plaintiff, Mr. Leon Franklin, against the Westminster Bank Limited, and it is based upon the ground that the plaintiff claims to be the holder in due course of a bill or note which was issued to Messrs. Webster Brothers Limited, on 27 September 1923. The terms of the note must be carefully noticed: they are a direction to the Darmstädter und Nationalbank in Berlin to pay to Messrs. Webster Brothers Limited 9,000,000,000 marks. It is important to note that these are marks of that currency then existing: they are wholly different from reichsmarks and there must be no confusion between those two units. When this document or bill had been drawn it was apparently issued to a Company called Webster Limited; the Company called Webster Limited paid £15 into the defendant bank, whose name then was the London County and Westminster Bank, and in exchange for that were given a cheque drawn by the Darmstädter Bank in Berlin for these 9,000,000,000 marks. At that time the £15 that Messrs. Webster paid bought a cheque which meant that at the appropriate time the holder would have been entitled to receive these 9,000,000,000 marks of this depreciated currency. Mr. Justice MacKinnon said: 'We have tried this case upon the assumption that for value this cheque was endorsed first to a brother of the plaintiff and then by that brother to himself and that the plaintiff is the holder of it.' I pause there for a moment to note that that assumption is very favourable, perhaps too favourable, to the plaintiff. He tells us that he became the holder and received this bill from his brother, paying to his brother cash for it. No evidence was given of any entry in any book which proved or confirmed that statement, and the plaintiff's own statement to this court was that he paid the money to his brother out of cash in his hands at the time when he was carrying on a business. He says that it was a personal transaction with his brother, but I cannot help noting that on the plaintiff's own statement, there are certain matters which would be all the better for being properly cleared up by some reference to an entry justifying the statement that the cash was the cash of the plaintiff and paid by him to his brother and was not in any way a part of the cash which was in the plaintiff's hands as cash in the business which he carried on.

I turn to section 72, subsection 5, of the Bills of Exchange Act, which says that where a bill is drawn in one country and payable in another the due date thereof is determined according to the law of the place where it is payable. There have been some cases decided upon that arising out of the War. Thus in a case where a bill was drawn in England and payable in Paris three months after the date on which it was drawn, but before it was due, a moratorium law was passed in France in consequence of the War postponing the maturity, the maturity of the bill was for all purposes to be determined by French law. So one has to look at the due date here of this payment to be received at the Darmstädter und Nationalbank by reference to the law of the county where that is to be received.

There was evidence before the learned judge of two relevant laws—foreign law being, of course, a question of fact. First of all, there was a Bank law which made a new constitution of Reichsbank, which is a bank with a standing equivalent to the Bank of England in this country, and it authorized the issue of reichsmarks and notes of reichsmarks—a different currency entirely from the currency in which this note was to be paid. Then there was a Mint law operating as from October 1924, under which the old currency was abolished as from then and the old currency was to remain legal tender only up to 11 October 1924, and no further; then from that date the new currency took its place. That provided also that the old currency should be exchanged on the basis of 1 million million marks—that is a billion marks—of the old denomination for one new mark.

Going back to the facts, this note was presented for payment on 15 December 1926. It will be noted, therefore, that it was presented after both the laws to which I have referred had come into full operation. Some comment is obviously required as to the delay between the date at which the note was drawn for payment and the date of presentation. Having regard to the uncertainty of the currency at the date of its being drawn and the various uncertainties through which the German currency went, one would have thought that this note drawn on 27 September 1923, would have been presented for payment sooner than that, after the lapse of three years and two months. However, let that pass. It is said that notice of dishonour was given on 28 September, but when the note was presented for payment it was marked as 'worthless'—the fact being that under the operation of the two laws to which I have referred the 9,000,000,000 marks of the old currency had become worth 9/1000ths of a reichsmark, 9/1000ths of what was approximately equal to 1s. 0d. 9/1000ths of 12 pence, if you work that out, come to 27/250ths of a penny, something less than 1/10th of a penny. The word 'worthless' seems to be fully justified on that basis.

Mr. Justice MacKinnon in the course of his judgment has pointed out that the law to which I have referred reduced the value of this delayed cheque to this sum, of which the law would take no notice at all on the basis of the maxim which I quoted in argument. There was another difficulty in the way of the plaintiff, because there is a German Cheque law of 1908 under which certain dates can be fixed as the time limits within which cheques ought to be presented for payment. Evidence was given before the learned judge that by a Decree of the Federal Council of 19 March 1908 the Federal Council appointed three weeks as the appropriate period for presentation of a foreign cheque. That limit was not complied with. It was presented, as I have said, rather more than three years after it ought to have been presented; and, more than that, if it was in the hands of an endorsee there was a further limit giving, I think, three months to the endorsee in which to present it if in Europe. That limit was also exceeded. The result is that on the actual day of presenting the cheque the duty of presenting the cheque was not fulfilled according to the tenor of the law of the country where it was to be presented for payment. That also forms a good defence to the action.

What is now suggested is that under the Treaty of Peace or other clauses, which do not in any way deal with the matter that we have to consider, the plaintiff has some rights. We have followed his argument; we have looked at the Treaty of Peace; we have looked at the case which he cited, *In re Chesterman's Trusts*,[2] and, after giving attention to all the points that have been advanced, one comes back to the two defences which are fully dealt with by Mr. Justice

---

[2] [1923] 2 Ch. 466.

MacKinnon and which fully and finally establish that the plaintiff has no right to sue in respect of this cheque. I am of opinion that the defendants were abundantly justified in their defence and that the judgment of the learned judge giving judgment for the defendants with costs was right, and equally that the appeal here must be dismissed with costs.

LAWRENCE L.J.: I agree, and have nothing to add.

ROMER L.J.: I agree.

Appeal dismissed.

*Solicitors:* Messrs. McMillan & Mott (for the defendants).

# APPENDIX III

# Oppenheimer *v.* The Public Trustee[1]

*(Chancery Division and Court of Appeal)*

Counsel for the plaintiffs: MR. C. A. BENNETT K.C., MR. H. B. VAISEY K.C., and MR. WILFRID LEWIS.

Counsel for the defendant: MR. GOVER K.C. and MR. J. H. STAMP.

The facts and arguments are set out in the Judgments.

4 Nov. 1926. EVE J.: I do not think I need trouble you, Mr. Gover.

The question involved in this summons is at what date the quantum of these two settled legacies expressed in German currency and bequeathed by the testator to two of his daughters, their issue and appointees, ought to be ascertained. The legacy is given in language which I will read. It is a direction that the trustees should out of the proceeds of the sale of his real and personal estate set apart sums, one of 240,000 marks and the other of 177,500 marks, and invest in the manner thereinbefore directed for the investment of the residuary estate and stand possessed thereafter, shortly on trust to pay the income of each legacy to one of his daughters with remainder to their children, and in default of children as they shall by will appoint. His will was made in 1892 and he died in 1900. At the date of the testator's death his property was largely represented by freehold and leasehold property and by two large mortgages and for many years after his death the property, or a large portion of the property existing at his death was retained in its then existing state of investment pursuant to a very full power of postponement conferred on the trustees by will, but ultimately in 1924, five years after the death of his widow who enjoyed an annuity of £3,000 a year, the Trustees were in a position to appropriate these legacies and they purported to have appropriated the legacies by a nominal sum which would at that date represent the cost of these two sums in German marks. In consequence of the unfortunate war between this country and Germany and the Peace Treaty which followed, the recipients, at any rate, of these legacies are not now able to receive their income, they are vested in the respondent to this summons, and the question which is raised is as between the trustees to the will, who happen also to be the residuary legatees, and the custodian, the assignee I might say of the interest of these ladies, whether the appropriation of this nominal sum satisfies the obligations of the trustees under the will or whether they must ascertain the value of the legacies at an earlier

[1] The author's thanks are due to Mr. Albert M. Oppenheimer and to Messrs. Cruesemann and Rouse, who supplied transcripts of the judgments of Eve J. and of the Court of Appeal respectively.

date, and the earlier date is the date at which the legacy ought or would properly have been appropriated if the condition of the estate had been such, and the executors in the exercise of their discretion had seen fit to realize the estate during the period which is generally spoken of as 'the executor's year', the twelve months immediately expiring after the testator's death. The respondent to the summons says: On 21 June 1901, at the expiry of that year, the legacy having vested, that was the moment of time at which the quantum of each of the legacies ought to have been ascertained, and I agree with him. I think at that point the fact that the condition of the estate was such that the bona-fide exercise of the trustee's discretion prevented them being able to realize the estate, is no answer to the claim of the legatee whose legacy was vested, and he was entitled to treat it as then set aside, although not appropriated in consequence of the condition of the estate preventing the trustees from making any proper appropriation on that date. That is a mere question of the condition of the estate, a mere election of the trustees, I have no doubt a very wise and prudent election, to leave the estate unconverted to a very much later date, but that cannot possibly, it seems to me, prejudice the right of the legatee to have the legacy ascertained at the date when, if the estate had been perfectly free and there had been no difficulty of administration, the legacies would have been properly set aside and invested. I must answer the questions that are put to me in the negative, and perhaps go on to say that the proper sums to be set aside are the amounts which, on 21 June 1901, would have been required to purchase in one case 240,000 marks, and in the other case 177,500 marks.

The plaintiffs appealed.

24 Feb. 1927. LORD HANWORTH M.R.: This is an appeal from a judgment of Mr. Justice Eve given on 4 November of last year upon a question raised by an Originating Summons as to the true construction to be placed upon the terms of a will which was made by Sir Charles Oppenheimer. The date of the will was 29 November 1892. The testator, Sir Charles Oppenheimer, died on 21 June 1900, and probate in this country was granted on 1 August 1900.

Now it appears that Sir Charles, who had been born in the Duchy of Nassau, afterwards incorporated in the German Empire, had become many years ago, as far back as July 1871, naturalized as a British subject. When he died he was in fact living at Frankfurt, where I believe at the time he held the position of British Consul-General. I only refer to these facts (they do not appear to have any importance in regard to the question which we have to decide) because some question was raised as to whether or not the matter would have to be considered in the light of German law, or possibly by a German court.

The point that we have to determine is what is the effect of the true interpretation of two legacies which were given to two of his daughters who are now Frau von Kornatzki and Frau von Tuercke. Sir Charles had two sons and five daughters, and he was at the time of his death possessed of valuable sites and properties in the city of London; he also had some property, a house in which he lived, at Frankfurt.

By the terms of his will the trustees are to sell and convert both the real and personal estate, and they are to stand possessed of the moneys to arise from the sale and conversion on the terms that after payment of his just debts there is to be an annuity paid to his wife, who is to be given the opportunity of living in the house at Frankfurt, and after the provision of the annuity to his wife there is to be a legacy to Frau Kornatzki and to his other daughters referred to, and particularly to the daughter Frau von Tuercke.

On looking into the terms of the will it appears that in the case of his daughter Emily, who had already been married at the time the will was drawn, he wished to complete his provision for her up to the sum of 240,000 marks which, if one takes the standard value of marks at or about that time, 20 marks to the pound would mean that he had made a provision for that daughter of £12,000. As the will recites, he had already under the contract of marriage made at the time when the wedding took place, made a provision of 62,500 marks. I ought to say that the marriage had taken place with a gentleman who was a captain in the German Army and had taken place in Germany. The provision in the will is that the sum passing to his daughter Emily under the will should be brought up to the full sum of 240,000 marks by providing the 177,500 marks which would be the balance of the 240,000 marks after taking into account the original payment on the marriage of the 62,500 marks.

I need not refer to the provisions or to the terms in which the daughter Helena and the daughter Minnie and the daughter Sascha are referred to, except to take note that in the case of these last two, Minnie and Sascha, their portion is in both cases to be also 240,000 marks. The particular case of the daughter Helena required separate and different treatment for the reasons which he stated in his will. Also he refers to his second son, Albert Martin, to whom he gives a sum of £12,000.

Before one comes actually to the terms of the will, it would seem from the outstanding considerations which appear from the parts of it to which I have referred, that the provision he made for the daughters to whom I have referred, and to the son to whom I have referred, was a sum of £12,000 each, and one cannot overlook the fact that the 240,000 marks would be substantially, if not quite accurately, £12,000. He also gives a power to his trustees in their absolute discretion to postpone the sale of his property. He says this: 'It would be lawful for my trustees or trustee for the time being to postpone the sale and conversion of any part of my real and personal estate so long as they or he shall in their uncontrolled discretion think it expedient so to do.' As a matter of fact, the trustees in their discretion did postpone the sale and conversion of a large portion of the estate, particularly of the properties which the testator owned in the City. It was thus in fact not possible, or perhaps I ought to say not convenient, to pay all these pecuniary legacies at a time close to the testator's death, and the postponement was in the interests of nursing the estate as a whole.

On 11 November 1919 the testator's widow, Lady Oppenheimer, died. As we all know, the war between Germany and this country was declared on 4 August 1914. At that time, and up to that time, the trustees had postponed the sale and conversion of the property in this country. After the war had commenced, no such operation could be undertaken, and so it was not until Lady Oppenheimer had died that the trustees were able to proceed with the sale and conversion, and they say that they were unable to appropriate a sum for the purpose of the payment of the two legacies in question, that is the balance due to Frau von Kornatzki and to Frau von Tuercke, until a date in July 1924. At that time they made an appropriation. We are told by Sir Francis Oppenheimer, in paragraph 6 of his Affidavit which is sworn on 15 October 1924, 'By the said Will it was expressly declared that it should be lawful for the trustees to postpone the sale and conversion of any part of the testator's real or personal estate so long as they in their sole discretion should think it expedient to do so. The said trustees in their discretion set aside or invested on or about 5 July 1924 such sums in sterling in $4\frac{1}{2}$ per cent Conversion Stock and 4 per cent Funding Loan as were the equivalent at the current rate of exchange on the said date to the capital sums of 177,500 marks and 240,000 marks respectively referred to' in the Affidavit, in respect of these two sums. It so happens that at that date the mark was at its lowest point. In the report which has been before us it appears that at or about the date, and perhaps a little earlier or a little later (I am not quite sure) the mark had become of such low value that a billion marks went to a shilling; indeed the mark had become valueless. The result is that if that date, the date of the appropriation in July 1924, is to be taken as the date at which these legacies are to be quantified, the sum in sterling which represents in the first place Frau von Kornatzki's 177,500 marks, and in the second case Frau von Tuercke's 240,000 marks, is negligible. It is said on the part of the respondent to this appeal—that is the Public Trustee, for these sums would be charged under the Treaty of Peace Order—that that date, July 1924, is not the right date, and that the true date at which the value of these legacies is to be ascertained and their amount quantified is to be at the close of what is called the executor's year, namely one year after the death of the testator, which in this case would make the date in question to be 21 June 1901. Mr. Justice Eve has held that that latter contention is right, and for my own part I should be prepared to say that I agree with the judgment of Mr. Justice Eve and the reasoning upon which it is based, except for the fact that the matter is of some importance and that we have had the advantage of the case being fully argued in this court.

The argument of the appellants I think may be said to be this. Although in form there are these two legacies, each of them bringing the value of the legacy up to 240,000 marks, each legacy itself is a legacy of marks, intended to be a legacy of marks, and it is to be measured in marks; and if the trustees have, in accordance with their duty and their absolute discretion, postponed the sale and conversion of the estate, they are not to be held bound by any such rule as taking the legacy as vested and quantified at the close of the executor's year, but that their power to postpone the sale and conversion overrides any other direction, and thus the moment at which the amount of the legacy is to be ascertained is the date at which the trustees, in their uncontrolled discretion, find themselves able to appropriate a sum towards the payment of these marks.

I am unable to accept that view. I think that one must consider what was the intention of the testator. It appears to be clear from the terms of the will that his intention was to make provision for these two daughters just as he did for his sons and for the other daughters, by providing them with an amount of £12,000 sterling.

To pass to the more intricate terms of the will, the duty of the trustees was to provide that sum, in particular the 177,500 marks, in this way: they were to set aside that sum, which was to be invested in the manner thereinbefore directed for the residue of his trust estate, and then to apply the income for the advantage of his daughter. Now, those directions as to the investment that he gave were for investment in British securities, British gilt-edged stock, British premier securities, railways, and the like; they were all British securities. For my part I think there is force in the argument that is presented to us by Mr. Gover, that there is ground for saying that the intention was to complete the legacy by an investment in British securities, and that the only purpose of the measurement given in marks is to give the standard by which you are to read, in the case of the lady already married to a German, the sum which will be equal to a total of £12,000. It appears to me, however, in any event, that the marks are merely the medium by which the provision is to be made for his daughter, and that it would be mistaking the intention of the testator altogether to say that his object and purpose was to provide his daughters with marks as marks, and not for the purpose of such an investment as might be obtained through the medium of those marks.

Now, if that be so, it appears that this legacy is general and not specific, and that there is in fact no definite time fixed for its payment. In the case of *Lord* v. *Lord*,[2] Lord Cairns, then Lord Justice, said this:[3] 'The rule of law is clear, and there can be no controversy with regard to it, that a legacy payable at a future day carries interest only from the time fixed for its payment. On the other hand, where no time for payment is fixed, the legacy is payable at, and therefore bears interest from, the end of a year after the testator's death, even though it be expressly made payable out of a particular fund which is not got in until after a longer interval.' Those words are explicit and definite. More than that, in the House of Lords in a comparatively recent case, the case of *Walford* v. *Walford*,[4] that rule which was laid down by Lord Cairns was accepted and adopted by Lord Haldane, then Lord Chancellor, and by the other Law Lords, including Lord Macnaghten, as the ordinary rule. Lord Haldane quotes those very words, and he says this:[5] 'The question I put to myself is, Is there to be found here a direction that the legacy is not to be paid till the fund falls in, which displaces what would be the ordinary principle of administration?' In the present case I can find no direction which displaces the ordinary principle of administration. The illustration of the applicability of that rule as laid down by Lord Cairns in *Walford* v. *Walford*[6] is a strong one, because there a testator who predeceased his father bequeathed to his sister a sum of £10,000 to be paid out of the estate and effects inherited by him from his mother, but as a matter of fact the testator was entitled in reversion expectant on the death of his father to a fund appointed to him under the will of his mother subject to his father's life interest therein. The result was that at the time of his death he had not, and would not get until his father died, the sum of £10,000 which he had bequeathed to his sister. On the death of the father later, the question was raised from what

<hr />

[2] L.R. 2 Ch. 782.  
[4] [1912] A.C. 658.  
[5] Ibid., p. 665.  
[3] Ibid., p. 789.  
[6] Ibid.

date the legacy of £10,000 carried interest, and it was held that the will contained no direction express or implied that the payment of the legacy was to be postponed until the falling in of the reversionary funds, and consequently that the legacy was payable at, and carried interest from, the expiration of one year from the testator's death. That is a strong case to show that unless you can find some direction in no uncertain terms to displace the ordinary principle of administration, the legacy is payable at and from the close of the executor's year and carried interest therefrom.

In the present case there appears to be no direction which could prevent that rule applying, because there is no time fixed for the payment of the legacy, and no explicit direction which contravenes or militates against the application of the rule. But it is said that that contrary effect is to be found in this will by reason of this fact that there is this power to postpone the sale and conversion to which I have already referred. It does not appear to me that this is effective for the purpose, and indeed the case of *In re Whiteley*[7] appears definitely to decide otherwise. In that case the testator 'gave his residuary real and personal estate to his general trustees upon trust for sale and conversion, with power to postpone such sale and conversion for such a period as they might think proper . . . and he declared that his general trustees should, as soon after his death as circumstances would permit, having regard to the amount of his residuary estate and the possibilities of sale and realization thereof, and having regard also to the directions thereinafter contained with respect to such sale and realization, set apart and appropriate out of the residue of the moneys to arise from such sale and realization a sum or sums . . . not exceeding the sum of £1,000,000 sterling' for a particular purpose. 'Owing to circumstances connected with the realization of the testator's estate, no part of the sum of £1,000,000 had been paid' by the date in question, which was 1909, the testator having died in 1907. It was held that the directions contained in the will in no way interfered with the application of the ordinary rule that a legacy carries interest from the expiration of twelve months after the testator's death. It appears to me, therefore, that upon that decision, a decision of this court, it is impossible to say that the power to postpone has the effect of abrogating the rule laid down by Lord Cairns.

The result in the present case is that the date at which the legacy became vested from which it carried interest is the year from the day of the testator's death, namely 21 June 1901, and that is the date at which it must be estimated what is the sum due to the legatees, having regard to the value of the mark at that date; in other words, that the trustees have not a right to wait until they were minded to make an appropriation in their behalf, and to appropriate a sum which represents an insiginficant value, because numerically it would buy, at that date of appropriation, a sufficient number of marks.

As I say, I should have been content to leave the matter where Mr. Justice Eve had left it, but in deference to the arguments that have been addressed to us I have thought it right to give reasons of my own. For the reasons given by Mr. Justice Eve and those which I have added I think the appeal must be dismissed with costs.

[7] (1909) 101 L.T. 508.

SARGANT L.J.: I am of the same opinion. I can appreciate, and to some extent feel sympathy with the motives wich probably have directed this appeal, because I quite appreciate the hardship which is sought to be cast upon the legatees by virtue of the charge in the Peace Treaty, but we have nothing to do with that; we have to deal with the case precisely as if the appeal were an appeal by the ordinary legatees against the trustees who took the residue, and it is impossible to give any greater or less right to the legatees because of the existence of this charge, which of course in many cases does work very great hardship.

Now, to my mind, the matter is perfectly clear and is absolutely concluded by the authority over and over again. It is concluded directly, I think, by the *Whiteley Homes*[8] case. That case itself followed *Wood* v. *Penoyre*[9] and *Lord* v. *Lord*[10] and there has been the subsequent case in the House of Lords to which the Master of the Rolls has referred, *Walford* v. *Walford.*[11] Indeed, if this appeal were allowed it would upset the ordinary administration of a very very large proportion of estates, because this direction which we find in the present will to convert the real and personal estate and out of the real and personal estate pay legacies, followed by the ultimate discretion to defer the sale and conversion for the convenience of the estate, occurs over and over again in a very large proportion of wills. I should have thought that nobody, apart from this special circumstance and the circumstances as to the marks, would have contended to-day that the power to postpone could have any effect whatever upon the date at which the legacies were to become payable and to carry interest. If that is so (and I will not deal further with the matter except to say that in my opinion it is fully established that it is so), we have this that there is a direction to pay at a year from the death a sum of 177,500 marks in one case, and 240,000 marks in the other case, and to invest the sums so set aside in English securities. Mr. Gover argued very ingeniously that the mention of marks was only a means of indicating pounds sterling, and that really these were gifts of sums in pounds sterling. Without going as far as that, I think it is at least clear that the gift of the marks or the setting aside was to be followed immediately by a process of converting those marks into pounds sterling and of investing the pounds sterling in British securities. That would be the only practical way of giving effect to the directions in the will, and in that state of things we have this: one year after the death of the testator there was to be set aside those sums of marks to be turned into pounds and invested in British securities. That being so, it seems perfectly clear by the cases that have been decided with regard to the debts due in marks, that the sum of marks that has to be paid under a direction of that sort, constituting a debt due, is to be measured at the rate of exchange on the day upon which the sum is due to become payable. Mr. Justice Eve accordingly was in my opinion right in directing that those sums of marks in this case were to be ascertained at the rate on that day. I agree that the appeal should be dismissed with costs.

LAWRENCE L.J.: I agree. In my opinion, on the true construction of the

---

[8] (1909) 101 L.T. 508.      [9] 13 Ves. 325.
[10] L.R. 2 Ch. 782.      [11] [1912] A.C. 658.

will the two legacies in question are in substance and in fact legacies of sterling, whether you arrive at that in the way suggested by Mr. Gover or whether you arrive in the way of a notional purchase and sale. It appears to me that the testator was merely speaking in terms of marks in order to quantify the benefit in sterling which his daughters should take. This I think is made quite plain when he speaks of the legacy in terms of marks long after it has in accordance with his own directions in the will been converted into sterling and been invested.

The will itself, to my mind, gives a clue for that method of disposition, and it is this, that he had already pledged himself in marks to his daughters by convenant, had already paid sums in marks to his daughters or their trustees, and was desirous by his will of equalizing those benefits, and to my mind he could have adopted no better method than to continue to speak of his benefits in terms of marks, meaning that they should be satisfied in pounds sterling.

If that be the true construction, I am of opinion that Mr. Gover's argument that the time for payment or setting aside of these legacies is one year after the testator's death, is right, and that neither the power to postpone the conversion nor the exercise of that power, nor indeed the inability to realize within that period, has the slightest effect upon the well-established rule that in the contemplation of the law the legacy is payable at the expiration of one year from the testator's death. That rule of convenience is a very ancient rule and is past all cavil at the present time. It is clearly laid down by Sir William Grant in the case of *Wood* v. *Penoyre*[12] and it was reasserted in *Lord* v. *Lord*,[13] reaffirmed *In re Whiteley*,[14] and again confirmed in *Walford* v. *Walford*.[15] It seems to me that it is hopeless now to contend the contrary to that rule.

Now, Mr. Bennett, in his forcible argument, has placed great reliance upon the case of *Byrchell* v. *Bradford*.[16] To my mind, that case has no application whatsoever to the facts in this case. In that case a sole trustee had, in gross breach of trust, retained a legacy of a beneficiary in his own hands uninvested, and has represented to her that the legacy had been invested. The direction in the will was to invest in public stocks. The beneficiary brought an action discovering that the sum had not been invested in order to claim from the trustee who had so committed a breach of trust the value of the rise in the stocks which would have accrued to her had the investment been made when it should in effect have been made, that is to say when he distributed the residuary estate. That was the sole claim made against the trustee for a gross breach of trust in that action. Sir John Leach, in giving judgment, says that at that time the practice of the courts was, in administration actions, not to take any notice where there was a public stock legacy, of the price of the public funds at that period or at any other period, but merely to treat it as a cash legacy of the nominal amount of the funds. That rule does not happen to prevail now in our courts. Then he goes on to say that assuming the executor and the trustee were different persons, the executor would have handed over to the trustee when he had realized the estate, and the trustee would then have

---

[12] 13 Ves. 325.  
[14] (1909) 101 L.T. 508.  
[16] (1822) 6 Madd. 235.

[13] L.R. 2 Ch. 782.  
[15] [1912] A.C. 658.

been liable from that time, and only from that time, for non-investment. As a matter of fact, a rise there had taken place between the date when the estate was clear and the date when the action was brought and he applies that analogy in making the trustee make good the loss which the beneficiary has sustained by reason of his non-investment. It seems to me that the facts of that case only need to be stated to show how entirely different they are from the facts which have arisen here. In my opinion that case does not govern and has really no application to the facts of this case. In my judgment Mr. Justice Eve was perfectly right in applying the ordinary well-known rule, and I agree that this appeal ought to be dismissed with costs.

Appeal dismissed.

*Solicitors:*   Mr. Albert M. Oppenheimer (for the plaintiffs).
        Messrs. Coward Chance & Co. (for the defendant).

# European Convention on Foreign Money Liabilities

THE member States of the Council of Europe, signatory hereto,

Whereas the aim of the Council of Europe is to achieve a greater unit between its Members, in particular by the adoption of common rules in the legal field;

Considering that it is advisable to harmonise certain rules relating to foreign money liabilities,

Have agreed as follows:

### ARTICLE 1

1. Each Contracting Party undertakes that within twelve months of the date of entry into force of the present Convention in respect of that Party, its national law shall conform with the rules set forth in the Annex appended hereto.

2. The application of the rules of the Annex shall extend to all liabilities under which a sum of money is due, whether originally expressed in money or not.

3. Each Contracting Party has the right, in specific matters, not to apply the provisions of the Annex or to apply them with the modifications it finds necessary.

### ARTICLE 2

Each Contracting Party shall have the right to substitute the date from which the debtor finds himself in *demeure* for the date of maturity referred to in Article 4 of the Annex.

### ARTICLE 3

Each Contracting Party shall have the right to make its law conform to one only of the alternatives referred to in Article 5 of the Annex.

### ARTICLE 4

This Convention shall not prevent any Contracting Party from maintaining or introducing into its legislation provisions concerning exchange control or prohibiting in certain cases the conclusion of contracts and the payment in foreign money.

### ARTICLE 5

This Convention shall be without prejudice to the provisions of any treaties, conventions or bilateral or multilateral agreements concluded or to be concluded, governing in special fields matters covered by this Convention.

## ARTICLE 6

1. Any Contracting Party may, at the time of the signature or when depositing its instrument of ratification, acceptance or accession, declare that, in regard to non-contractual liabilities, it reserves the right not to apply the provisions of paragraphs 1 and 2 of Article 4 and Article 6 of the Annex or to apply them with the modifications it finds necessary.

2. Any Contracting Party may wholly or partly withdraw a reservation it has made in accordance with the foregoing paragraph by means of a declaration addressed to the Secretary General of the Council of Europe, which shall become effective as from the date of its receipt.

## ARTICLE 7

Each Contracting Party shall transmit to the Secretary General of the Council of Europe the official text of any legislation concerning the matters governed by the Convention. The Secretary General shall transmit copies of the texts to the other Parties.

## ARTICLE 8

1. This Convention shall be open to signature by the member States of the Council of Europe. It shall be subject to ratification or acceptance. Instruments of ratification or acceptance shall be deposited with the Secretary General of the Council of Europe.

2. This Convention shall enter into force three months after the date of the deposit of the third instrument of ratification or acceptance.

3. In respect of a signatory State ratifying or accepting subsequently, the Conversion shall come into force three months after the date of the deposit of its instrument of ratification or acceptance.

## ARTICLE 9

1. After the entry into force of this Convention, the Committee of Ministers of the Council of Europe may invite any non-member State to accede thereto.

2. Such accession shall be effected by depositing with the Secretary General of the Council of Europe an instrument of accession which shall take effect three months after the date of its deposit.

## ARTICLE 10

1. Any Contracting Party may, at the time of signature or when depositing its instrument of ratification, acceptance or accession, specify the territory or territories to which this Convention shall apply.

2. Any Contracting Party may, when depositing its instrument of ratification, acceptance or accession or at any later date, by declaration addressed to the Secretary General of the Council of Europe, extend this Convention to any other territory or territories in the declaration and for whose international relations it is responsible or on whose behalf it is authorised to give undertakings.

3. Any declaration made in pursuance of the preceding paragraph may, in

respect of any territory mentioned in such declaration, be withdrawn according to the procedure laid down in Article 10 of this Convention.

## ARTICLE 11

1. This Convention shall remain in force indefinitely.

2. Any Contracting Party may, in so far as it is concerned, denounce this Convention by means of a notification addressed to the Secretary General of the Council of Europe.

3. Such denunciation shall take effect six months after the date of receipt by the Secretary General of such notification.

## ARTICLE 12

The Secretary General of the Council of Europe shall notify the member States of the Council and any State which has acceded to this Convention of:

(*a*) any signature;

(*b*) any deposit of an instrument of ratification, acceptance or accession;

(*c*) any date of entry into force of this Convention in accordance with Article 8 thereof;

(*d*) any declaration received in pursuance of the provisions of paragraphs 2 and 3 of Article 10;

(*e*) any reservation made in pursuance of the provision of paragraph 1 of Article 6;

(*f*) the withdrawal of any reservation carried out in pursuance of the provisions of paragraph 2 of Article 6;

(*g*) any notification received in pursuance of the provisions of Article 11 and the date on which denunciation takes effect.

In witness whereof the undersigned, being duly authorised thereto, have signed this Convention.

Done at Paris, this 11th day of December 1967, in French and English, both texts being equally authoritative, in a single copy which shall remain deposited in the archives of the Council of Europe. The Secretary General of the Council of Europe shall transmit certified copies to each of the signatory and acceding States.[1]

## ANNEX

### ARTICLE 1

1. Any sum of money due in a currency which is not that of the place of payment may be paid in the currency of the place of payment, unless a different intention of the parties appears, or a different usage is applicable.

2. The debtor may not avail himself of this option if he knows or ought to know that payment in the currency of the place of payment would involve for the creditor a substantial prejudice.

[1] The Convention has so far been signed by Austria, France, the Federal Republic of Germany, and Luxembourg.

## ARTICLE 2

If a sum of money is due in a currency other than that of the place of payment, the creditor may, if the debtor is unable, or alleges his inability, to make settlement in that currency, require payment in the currency of the place of payment.

## ARTICLE 3

If, in accordance with Articles 1 or 2, the debtor pays in the currency of the place of payment, the conversion shall be effected at the rate of exchange at the date of actual payment.

## ARTICLE 4

1. If the debtor does not pay at the date of maturity and if after such date the currency in which the sum of money is due depreciates in relation to the currency of the place of payment, the debtor, whether he pays in the currency due or in the currency of the place of payment as provided in the preceding Articles, shall pay an additional amount equivalent to the difference between the rate of exchange at the date of maturity and the date of actual payment.

2. Nevertheless, the above-mentioned additional amount shall not be payable to the extent that the inability of the debtor is due to default of the creditor, or to *force majeure*, or the creditor has not suffered loss resulting from the depreciation. The debtor bears the burden of proof.

3. The provisions of paragraph 1 do not in any way limit other rights which the creditor may be in a position to claim from the debtor.

## ARTICLE 5

In the event of any proceedings for the recovery of a sum of money expressed in a currency other than that of the forum, the creditor may, at his choice, demand payment in the currency to which he is entitled or the equivalent in the currency of the forum at the rate of exchange at the date of actual payment.

## ARTICLE 6

Article 4 remains applicable even if during proceedings instituted in conformity with Article 5, the currency in which the sum of money is due depreciates in relation to the currency of the place of payment.

## ARTICLE 7

1. If a judgment entitles the creditor either to a sum of money in a currency other than that of the forum or the equivalent of such a sum in the currency of the forum, and a depreciation of the currency other than that of the forum in relation to that of the forum occurs between the date of the judgment and the date of actual payment, the debtor is obliged to pay an additional amount corresponding to the difference between the rate of exchange at the date of the judgment and the date of actual payment.

2. The provisions of paragraphs 2 and 3 of Article 4 shall apply *mutatis mutandis.*

## ARTICLE 8

The place of payment referred to in the preceding Articles shall be the place where payment is due.

## ARTICLE 9

For the application of the preceding Articles the rate of exchange shall be that intended by the parties, or, failing such intention, that which may enable the creditor to procure the sum due without delay. Usages shall be taken into account.

### ADDITIONAL NOTE
*(see p. 352 above)*

See now the Law Commission's Report of July 1981 on the Convention on Foreign Money Liabilities referred to above, p. 351 n. 92 (Cmnd. 8318). This, it is submitted, inadequately deals with the problem mentioned in the text (among others). The Report's principal point seems to be that Articles 4 and 6 of the Annex to the Convention proceed from a 'fundamental philosophy' which is 'in sharp contrast to the present law' (paragraphs 22–5, 37, 41, 53). Contrary to the assertion in paragraph 53 the case of *Miliangos* does not directly or indirectly deal with the question of damage occurring as a result of depreciation of currency during the debtor's default (*mora*). If, as has been submitted in the text and as the Report seems to accept in footnote 35, the creditor is under English law entitled to 'special damage' occurring during default, the point of the Convention's Articles 4 and 6 is that, subject to certain exceptions, the creditor should be entitled to a kind of liquidated damage equal to the depreciation of the foreign currency during default. In other words the Convention contemplates not much more than a reversal of the burden of proof. The Report ignores the true nature of the problem and of its solution. It also ignores comparative law and therefore neglects the advantages of a uniform law in the European countries. It is, unfortunately, impossible to discuss in the present context numerous other aspects of the Report, which are open to criticism.

# INDEX